Nineteenth-Century
Literature Criticism

Guide to Gale Literary Criticism Series

When you need to review criticism of literary works, these are the Gale series to use:

If the author's death date is: **You should turn to:**

After Dec. 31, 1959
(or author is still living)

CONTEMPORARY LITERARY CRITICISM

for example: Jorge Luis Borges, Anthony Burgess,
William Faulkner, Mary Gordon,
Ernest Hemingway, Iris Murdoch

1900 through 1959

TWENTIETH-CENTURY LITERARY CRITICISM

for example: Willa Cather, F. Scott Fitzgerald,
Henry James, Mark Twain, Virginia Woolf

1800 through 1899

NINETEENTH-CENTURY LITERATURE CRITICISM

for example: Fedor Dostoevski, Nathaniel Hawthorne,
George Sand, William Wordsworth

1400 through 1799

LITERATURE CRITICISM FROM 1400 TO 1800
(excluding Shakespeare)

for example: Anne Bradstreet, Daniel Defoe,
Alexander Pope, François Rabelais,
Jonathan Swift, Phillis Wheatley

SHAKESPEAREAN CRITICISM

Shakespeare's plays and poetry

Antiquity through 1399

CLASSICAL AND MEDIEVAL LITERATURE CRITICISM

for example: Dante, Homer, Plato, Sophocles, Vergil,
the Beowulf Poet

Gale also publishes related criticism series:

CHILDREN'S LITERATURE REVIEW

This series covers authors of all eras who have written for the
preschool through high school audience.

SHORT STORY CRITICISM

This series covers the major short fiction writers of all nationalities
and periods of literary history.

ISSN 0732-1864

Volume 23

Nineteenth-Century Literature Criticism

Excerpts from Criticism of the
Works of Novelists, Poets, Playwrights,
Short Story Writers, Philosophers, and Other
Creative Writers Who Died between 1800
and 1899, from the First Published Critical
Appraisals to Current Evaluations

**Janet Mullane
Robert Thomas Wilson**
Editors

Robin DuBlanc
Associate Editor

 *Gale Research Inc.*

DETROIT • NEW YORK • FORT LAUDERDALE • LONDON

STAFF

Janet Mullane, Robert Thomas Wilson, *Editors*

Cherie D. Abbey, Robin DuBlanc, *Associate Editors*

Rachel Carlson, Grace Jeromski, Michael W. Jones, Ronald S. Nixon, *Assistant Editors*

Denise Michlewicz Broderick, Susan Harig, Melissa Reiff Hug, *Contributing Assistant Editors*

Jeanne A. Gough, *Permissions & Production Manager*
Linda M. Pugliese, *Production Supervisor*
Jennifer E. Gale, Suzanne Powers, Maureen A. Puhl, Lee Ann Welsh, *Editorial Associates*
Donna Craft, David G. Oblender, Linda M. Ross, *Editorial Assistants*

Victoria B. Cariappa, *Research Supervisor*
Karen D. Kaus, Eric Priehs, Maureen R. Richards, Mary D. Wise, *Editorial Associates*
Rogene M. Fisher, Filomena Sgambati, *Editorial Assistants*

Sandra C. Davis, *Text Permissions Supervisor*
H. Diane Cooper, Kathy Grell, Josephine M. Keene,
Kimberly F. Smilay, *Permissions Associates*
Maria L. Franklin, Lisa M. Lantz, Camille Robinson, Shalice Shah, Denise M. Singleton,
Permissions Assistants

Patricia A. Seefelt, *Picture Permissions Supervisor*
Margaret A. Chamberlain, *Permissions Associate*
Pamela A. Hayes, Lillian Quickley, *Permissions Assistants*

Mary Beth Trimper, *Production Manager*
Marilyn Jackman, *External Production Assistant*

Arthur Chartow, *Art Director*
C. J. Jonik, *Keyliner*

Laura Bryant, *Production Supervisor*
Louise Gagné, *Internal Production Associate*
Shelly Andrews, *Internal Production Assistant*

Computerized photocomposition by
Western Publishing Co.
O'Fallon, MO

Printed in the United States of America

Contents

Preface   vii

Authors to Be Featured in Upcoming Volumes   xi

Acknowledgments   xiii

Preface

The nineteenth century was a time of tremendous growth in human endeavor: in science, in social history, and particularly in literature. The era saw the development of the novel, witnessed radical changes from classicism to romanticism to realism, and fostered intellectual and artistic ideas that continue to inspire authors of our own century. The importance of the writers of the nineteenth century is twofold, for they provide insight into their own time as well as into the universal nature of human experience.

The literary criticism of an era can also give us insight into the moral and intellectual atmosphere of the past because the criteria by which a work of art is judged reflect current philosophical and social attitudes. Literary criticism takes many forms: the traditional essay, the book or play review, even the parodic poem. Criticism can also be of several types: normative, descriptive, interpretive, textual, appreciative, generic. Collectively, the range of critical response helps us to understand a work of art, an author, an era.

Scope of the Series

Nineteenth-Century Literature Criticism (NCLC) is designed to serve as an introduction for the student of nineteenth-century literature to the authors of that period and to the most significant commentators on these authors. Since the analysis of this literature spans almost two hundred years, a vast amount of critical material confronts the student. For that reason, *NCLC* presents significant passages from published criticism to aid students in the location and selection of commentaries on authors who died between 1800 and 1899. The need for *NCLC* was suggested by the usefulness of the Gale series *Twentieth-Century Literary Criticism (TCLC)* and *Contemporary Literary Criticism (CLC),* which excerpt criticism of creative writing of the twentieth century. For further information about *TCLC, CLC,* and Gale's other criticism series, users should consult the Guide to Gale Literary Criticism Series preceding the title page in this volume.

Each volume of *NCLC* is carefully compiled to include authors who represent a variety of genres and nationalities and who are currently regarded as the most important writers of their era. In addition to major authors who have attained worldwide renown, *NCLC* also presents criticism on lesser-known figures, many from non-English-speaking countries, whose significant contributions to literary history are important to the study of nineteenth-century literature. These authors are important artists in their own right and often enjoy such an immense popularity in their original language that English-speaking readers could benefit from a knowledge of their work.

Author entries in *NCLC* are intended to be definitive overviews. In order to devote more attention to each writer, approximately ten to fifteen authors are included in each 600-page volume, compared with about forty authors in a *CLC* volume of similar size. The length of each author entry is intended to reflect the amount of attention the author has received from critics writing in English and from foreign critics in translation. Articles and books that have not been translated into English are excluded. However, since many of the major foreign studies have been translated into English and are excerpted in *NCLC,* author entries reflect the viewpoints of many nationalities. Each author entry represents a historical overview of critical reaction to the author's work: early criticism is presented to indicate initial responses, later selections represent any rise or decline in the author's literary reputation, and current analyses provide students with a modern perspective. In each entry, we have attempted to identify and include excerpts from all seminal essays of criticism.

An author may appear more than once in the series because of the great quantity of critical material available or because of a resurgence of criticism generated by events such as an author's centennial or anniversary celebration, the republication or posthumous publication of an author's works, or the publication of a newly translated work. Usually, one or more author entries in each volume of *NCLC* are devoted to individual works or groups of works by major authors who have appeared previously in the series. Only those works that have been the subjects of extensive criticism and are widely studied in literature courses are selected for this in-depth treatment. George Eliot's *Daniel Deronda* and Nathaniel Hawthorne's *The Marble Faun; or, The Romance of Monte Beni* are the subjects of such entries in *NCLC,* Volume 23.

Organization of the Book

An author entry consists of the following elements: author heading, biographical and critical introduction, principal works, excerpts of criticism (each preceded by explanatory notes and followed by a bibliographical citation), and an additional bibliography for further reading.

- The *author heading* consists of the author's full name, followed by birth and death dates. The unbracketed portion of the name denotes the form under which the author most commonly wrote. If an author wrote consistently under a pseudonym, the pseudonym will be listed in the author heading and the real name given in parentheses on the first line of the biographical and critical introduction. Also located at the beginning of the introduction are any name variations under which an author wrote, including transliterated forms for authors whose languages use nonroman alphabets. Uncertainty as to a birth or death date is indicated by a question mark.

- A *portrait* of the author is included when available. Many entries also feature illustrations of materials pertinent to an author's career, including manuscript pages, letters, book illustrations, and representations of important people, places, and events in an author's life.

- The *biographical and critical introduction* contains background information that introduces the reader to an author and to the critical debate surrounding his or her work. When applicable, biographical and critical introductions are followed by references to additional entries on the author in other literary reference series published by Gale Research Inc., including *Dictionary of Literary Biography, Children's Literature Review,* and *Something about the Author.*

- The list of *principal works* is chronological by date of first book publication and identifies the genre of each work. In those instances where the first publication was in a language other than English, the title and date of the first English-language edition are given in brackets. Unless otherwise indicated, dramas are dated by the first performance, rather than first publication.

- *Criticism* is arranged chronologically in each author entry to provide a useful perspective on changes in critical evaluation over the years. All titles by the author featured in the critical entry are printed in boldface type to enable the user to ascertain without difficulty the works being discussed. Also for purposes of easier identification, the critic's name and the publication date of the essay are given at the beginning of each piece of criticism. Unsigned criticism is preceded by the title of the journal in which it appeared. When an anonymous essay is later attributed to a critic, the critic's name appears in brackets at the beginning of the excerpt and in the bibliographical citation. Publication information (such as publisher names and book prices) and parenthetical numerical references (such as footnotes or page and line references to specific editions of works) have been deleted at the editor's discretion to provide smoother reading of the text.

- Critical essays are prefaced with *explanatory notes* as an additional aid to students using *NCLC*. The explanatory notes provide several types of useful information, including the reputation of the critic; the importance of a work of criticism; a synopsis of the essay; the specific approach of the critic (biographical, psychoanalytic, structuralist, etc.); and the growth of critical controversy or changes in critical trends regarding an author's work. In some cases, these notes include cross-references to related criticism in the author's entry or in the additional bibliography. Dates in parentheses within the explanatory notes refer to the year of a book publication when they follow a book title and to the date of an excerpt included in the entry when they follow a critic's name.

- A complete *bibliographical citation* designed to facilitate the location of the original essay or book follows each piece of criticism.

- The *additional bibliography* appearing at the end of each author entry suggests further reading on the author. In some cases it includes essays for which the editors could not obtain reprint rights.

The acknowledgments section lists the copyright holders who have granted permission to reprint material in this volume of *NCLC*. It does not, however, list every book or periodical reprinted or consulted for the volume.

Cumulative Indexes

Each volume of *NCLC* includes a cumulative index listing all the authors who have appeared in *Contemporary Literary Criticism, Twentieth-Century Literary Criticism, Nineteenth-Century Literature Criticism, Literature*

Criticism from 1400 to 1800, Classical and Medieval Literature Criticism, and *Short Story Criticism,* along with cross-references to the Gale series *Children's Literature Review, Authors in the News, Contemporary Authors, Contemporary Authors Autobiography Series, Dictionary of Literary Biography, Concise Dictionary of American Literary Biography, Something about the Author, Something about the Author Autobiography Series,* and *Yesterday's Authors of Books for Children.* Readers will welcome this cumulated author index as a useful tool for locating an author within the various series. The index, which lists birth and death dates when available, will be particularly valuable for those authors who are identified with a certain period but whose death dates cause them to be placed in another, or for those authors whose careers span two periods. For example, Fedor Dostoevski is found in *NCLC,* yet Leo Tolstoy, another major nineteenth-century Russian novelist, is found in *TCLC* because he died after 1899.

Each volume of *NCLC* also includes a cumulative nationality index to authors. Authors are listed alphabetically by nationality, followed by the volume numbers in which they appear.

Title Index

An important feature of *NCLC* is a cumulative title index, an alphabetical listing of the literary works discussed in the series since its inception. Each title listing includes the corresponding volume and page numbers where criticism may be located. Foreign language titles may be followed by the titles of English translations of these works or by English-language equivalents of these titles provided by critics. Page numbers following these translation titles refer to all pages on which any form of the title, either foreign language or translation, appears. Titles of novels, dramas, nonfiction books, and poetry, short story, or essay collections are printed in italics, while all individual poems, short stories, and essays are printed in roman type within quotation marks.

Suggestions Are Welcome

In response to various suggestions, several features have been added to *NCLC* since the series began, including: explanatory notes to excerpted criticism that provide important information regarding critics and their work; a cumulative author index listing authors in all Gale literary criticism series; entries devoted to criticism on a single work by a major author; more extensive illustrations; and a cumulative title index listing all the literary works discussed in the series.

Readers who wish to suggest authors to appear in future volumes, or who have other comments and suggestions for expanding the coverage and enhancing the usefulness of the series, are cordially invited to write the editors or call our toll-free number: 1-800-347-GALE.

Authors to Be Featured in Upcoming Volumes

James Beattie (Scottish philosopher, poet, and critic)—A leading figure of the eighteenth-century Scottish Renaissance, Beattie was a versatile writer whose works spanned the transition from Neoclassicism to Romanticism. His best known philosophical work, *An Essay on the Nature and Immutability of Truth,* harshly criticizes the sceptical philosophy of David Hume. *The Minstrel,* a narrative poem written in Spenserian stanzas that depicts in the character Edwin the progress of a "poetic genius," is considered an important example of pre-Romanticism and a major influence on the leading Romantic poets.

Georg (Karl) Büchner (German dramatist)—An exponent of radical socialism who emphasized fatalism and despair in his view of the human condition, Büchner is noted for dramas that anticipate twentieth-century styles and themes, particularly those associated with naturalism. *Danton's Death,* a piercing study of the French Revolution, and his unfinished masterpiece *Woyzeck,* a portrait of the isolated, exploited, helpless Everyman, express with Büchner's celebrated poetic facility his austerely pessimistic vision.

George Crabbe (English poet)—Considered a key figure in the shift in English poetry from the Augustan to the Romantic mode, Crabbe was one of the first English poets to invoke a realistic, unsentimental view of nature. While retaining the eighteenth-century heroic couplet, Crabbe's poetry is considered advanced for its time in its powerful, graphic descriptions and subtle psychological insights into human character. His best known work is *The Village,* a pessimistic observation of the English countryside and its humble inhabitants.

Charles Dickens (English novelist, short story writer, dramatist, poet, and essayist)—One of the greatest and most popular novelists in world literature, Dickens is admired for his comic gifts, deep social concerns, and extraordinary talent for characterization. *Great Expectations,* one of his most successful novels, will be the subject of an entire entry in *NCLC.* Portraying Philip Pirrup's sudden rise to wealth and his subsequent downfall, *Great Expectations* is regarded as a brilliant study of pride and guilt and is ranked as one of Dickens's finest works.

Stephen Collins Foster (American songwriter)—Foster was the composer of such perenially popular folk classics as "My Old Kentucky Home," "Camptown Races," and "Oh! Susanna."

William Hazlitt (English critic and essayist)—Hazlitt was one of the most important and influential commentators during the Romantic age in England. In his literary criticism and miscellaneous prose he combined discerning judgment with strongly stated personal opinion, producing essays noted for their discursive style, evocative descriptions, and urbane wit.

Francis Jeffrey (Scottish journalist, critic, and essayist)—An influential literary critic, Jeffrey was also a founder and editor (1803-1829) of the prestigious *Edinburgh Review.* A liberal Whig, Jeffrey often allowed his political beliefs to color his critical opinions, and his commentary is judged the most characteristic example of "impressionistic" critical thought during the first half of the nineteenth century. Today, he is best remembered for his brutal attacks on the early Romantic poets, exemplified by the first sentence of a review of William Wordsworth's *Excursion:* "This will never do."

Archibald Lampman (Canadian poet, journalist, and essayist)—A central figure in the development of Canadian poetry, Lampman is best remembered for sonnets and lyric poems that sensitively and vividly describe the Canadian landscape. Lampman's verse not only helped provide Canada's nascent literature with a sense of national identity, but it also revealed a technical and thematic complexity that anticipated modern Canadian poetry.

Charles-Marie-René Leconte de Lisle (French poet)—Leconte de Lisle was the leader of the Parnassians, a school of French poets that rejected the tenets of Romanticism in favor of emotional restraint, clarity of expression, and attention to artistic form. Inspired by the civilizations of ancient Greece, Scandinavia, and India, as well as by his love of nature, Leconte de Lisle's poetry has been described as impassive and pessimistic yet sensitive and acutely attuned to beauty.

George Henry Lewes (English philosopher, critic, journalist, novelist, and dramatist)—The longtime lover of novelist George Eliot and a significant influence on the development of her fiction, Lewes was a prolific and versatile man of letters in his own right. He wrote philosophical works, scientific studies, dramatic and literary criticism, plays, and novels, and served as editor of two influential periodicals, the *Leader* and the *Fortnightly Review.*

Herman Melville (American novelist, novella and short story writer, and poet)—A major figure in American literature, Melville is recognized for his exploration of complex metaphysical and moral themes in his novels and short fiction. *NCLC* will devote an entry to his novella *Billy Budd,* a symbolic inquiry into the nature of good and evil, innocence and guilt.

John Henry Newman (English theologian and writer)—An influential theologian, Newman was a key figure in the Oxford movement, whose adherents advocated the independence of the Church of England from the state and sought to establish a doctrinal basis for Anglicanism in the Church's evolution from Catholicism. Newman's subsequent conversion to Roman Catholicism inspired his best-known work, *Apologia pro vita sua,* an eloquent spiritual autobiography tracing the development of his beliefs.

Dmitry Ivanovich Pisarev (Russian critic and essayist)—Pisarev was the most militant of the Russian Civic Critics, an influential group of mid-nineteenth-century literary commentators who evaluated literature primarily on the basis of its social and political content. He is remembered for his controversial assault on the aesthetics and art of Alexander Pushkin as well as for his essays calling for radical social and political reform.

(Joseph) Ernest Renan (French theological writer, historian, and critic)—Renan is considered one of the most important exponents of the progressive, scientific spirit of nineteenth-century critical thought. His works sought to uncover the historical and psychological basis for modern religions through a careful consideration of geography, culture, politics, and other local factors. He is best known as the author of *The Life of Jesus,* an unorthodox work that rejected the divinity of Christ but reaffirmed the literary and humanistic aspects of the Bible. The sentimental yet incisive style of Renan's works is thought to have profoundly influenced the course of French literary criticism, particularly the writings of Anatole France.

Acknowledgments

The editors wish to thank the copyright holders of the excerpted criticism included in this volume, the permissions managers of many book and magazine publishing companies for assisting us in securing reprint rights, and Anthony Bogucki for assistance with copyright research. We are also grateful to the staffs of the Detroit Public Library, the Library of Congress, the University of Detroit Library, the University of Michigan Library, and the Wayne State University Library for making their resources available to us. Following is a list of the copyright holders who have granted us permission to reprint material in this volume of *NCLC*. Every effort has been made to trace copyright, but if omissions have been made, please let us know.

COPYRIGHTED EXCERPTS IN *NCLC*, VOLUME 23, WERE REPRINTED FROM THE FOLLOWING PERIODICALS:

American Literature, v. XXVIII, November, 1956. Copyright © 1956, renewed 1984 by Duke University Press, Durham, NC. Reprinted by permission of the publisher.— *American Transcendental Quarterly,* v. 1, 1969. Copyright 1969 by Kenneth Walter Cameron. Reprinted by permission of the publisher.—*Cahiers Victoriens & Edouardiens,* n. 26, October, 1987. All rights reserved. Reprinted by permission of the publisher.—*The Connecticut Review,* v. 5, April, 1972 for "Joel Barlow's Poetics: 'Advice to a Raven in Russia' " by Robert D. Arner. © Board of Trustees for the Connecticut State Colleges, 1972. Reprinted by permission of the author.— *Early American Literature,* v. VII, Spring, 1972 for "The Smooth and Emblematic Song: Joel Barlow's 'The Hasty Pudding' " by Robert D. Arner; v. X, Winter, 1975-76 for " 'The Columbiad' and 'Greenfield Hill': History, Poetry, and Ideology in the Late Eighteenth Century" by John Griffith; v. XVII, Spring, 1982 for "The Contexts and Themes of 'The Hasty-Pudding' " by J. A. Leo Lernay. Copyrighted, 1972, 1976, 1982, by the University of Massachusetts. All reprinted by permission of the publisher and the respective authors.—*Eighteenth-Century Studies,* v. 11, Fall, 1977. © 1977 by The American Society for Eighteenth-Century Studies. Reprinted by permission of the publisher.— *ELH,* v. 31, September, 1964; v. 37, September, 1970. Both reprinted by permission of the publisher.—*Essays in Literature,* v. 14, Spring, 1987. Copyright 1987 by Western Illinois University. Reprinted by permission of the publisher. —*The Georgia Review,* v. XXIV, Fall, 1970. Copyright, 1970, by the University of Georgia. Reprinted by permission of the publisher.—*Harvard Library Bulletin,* v. XVIII, October, 1970; v. XIX, January, 1971. Copyright 1970, 1971 by the President and Fellows of Harvard College. Both reprinted by permission of the publisher.—*Novel: A Forum on Fiction,* v. 18, Fall, 1984. Copyright © Novel Corp., 1984. Reprinted by permission of the publisher.—*Studies in American Humor,* n.s. v. 1, October, 1982. Copyright © 1982 by Southwest Texas State University. Reprinted by permission of the publisher.—*Studies in Eighteenth-Century Culture,* v. 11, 1982. Copyright © 1982 American Society for Eighteenth-Century Studies. All rights reserved. Reprinted by permission of The University of Wisconsin Press.—*Studies in the Novel,* v. XIX, Fall, 1987. Copyright 1987 by North Texas State University. Reprinted by permission of the publisher.—*Theatre Journal,* v. 31, December, 1979. © 1979, University and College Theatre Association of the American Theatre Association. Reprinted by permission of the publisher.—*Thoth,* v. III, Winter, 1962. Reprinted by permission of the publisher.—*The William and Mary Quarterly,* third series, v. VIII, July, 1951. Copyright, 1951, by the Institute of Early American History and Culture. Reprinted by permission of the Institute.

COPYRIGHTED EXCERPTS IN *NCLC*, VOLUME 23, WERE REPRINTED FROM THE FOLLOWING BOOKS:

Adams, Robert M. From *Stendhal: Notes on a Novelist.* The Noonday Press, 1959. Copyright © 1959, renewed 1987 by Robert M. Adams. Reprinted by permission of Farrar, Straus and Giroux, Inc.—Alter, Robert, with Carol Cosman. From *A Lion for Love: A Critical Biography of Stendhal.* Basic Books, 1979. Copyright © 1979 by Robert Alter. Reprinted by permission of Basic Books, Inc., Publishers.—Auerbach, Erich. From *Mimesis: The Representation of Reality in Western Literature.* Translated by Willard R. Trask. Princeton University Press, 1953. Copyright 1953, renewed 1981 by Princeton University Press. Reprinted with permission of the publisher.—Auty, Susan G. From *The Comic Spirit of Eighteenth-Century Novels.* Kennikat Press, 1975. Copyright © 1975 by Kennikat Press Corp. All rights reserved.—Balzac, Honoré de. From "Stendhal," in *Novelists on Novelists: An Anthology.* Edited by Louis Kronenberger. Doubleday & Company, Inc., 1962. Copyright © 1972 by Louis Kronenberger. All rights reserved. Used by permission of Doubleday, a division of Bantam, Doubleday, Dell Publishing Group, Inc.—Baym, Nina. From *The Shape of Hawthorne's Career.* Cornell University Press, 1976. Copyright © 1976 by Cornell University. All rights reserved. Used by permission of the publisher, Cornell University Press.— Beauvoir, Simone de. From *The Second Sex.* Edited and translated by H. M. Parshley. Knopf, 1953. Copyright 1952, renewed 1980 by Alfred A. Knopf, Inc. Reprinted by permission of the publisher.—Blum, Léon. From "A Theoretical Outline of 'Beylism'," translated by

Joel Barlow

1754-1812

American poet, essayist, and pamphleteer.

Often associated with the Connecticut (or Hartford) Wits, a group of politically conservative early New England poets, Barlow is best known as the author of *The Hasty-Pudding,* a mock-heroic poem on the subject of a favorite American food, and *The Columbiad,* a patriotic epic poem written in celebration of America's past history and future destiny. During the turbulent era between the American and French Revolutions, Barlow also wrote influential political essays articulating revolutionary and republican principles. Although these political essays have attracted little scholarly attention, for his role as pamphleteer and politician, Barlow has been accorded a significant, if minor, place in American history.

Born and raised on a farm in Reading, Connecticut, Barlow was educated locally until the age of nineteen, when he was sent to Moor's Indian School in Hanover, New Hampshire, to prepare for Dartmouth College. Shortly after Barlow entered Dartmouth, however, his father died, leaving him an inheritance that allowed him to enroll at Yale College in New Haven, where he studied from 1774 until 1778. While at Yale, Barlow was exposed to orthodox Puritan theology as well as the prevailing Federalist belief in a strong central government. Barlow's first poems, a satire and a parody mocking collegiate life, were published during his undergraduate years and generated enthusiastic response among students and teachers. The American Revolution, in which Barlow served as a volunteer, interrupted his studies several times, yet he managed to graduate in 1778 as class poet. At the commencement ceremony, he read *The Prospect of Peace,* a poem depicting the glorious future of America after the Revolution. The immediate publication of this poem and the admiration of his peers prompted Barlow to briefly pursue poetry as a vocation, but the financial hardships of a life devoted solely to writing proved overwhelming. In 1780, after having passed a theological examination, Barlow became a chaplain in the Revolutionary army, a position that allowed him time to work on his poetry. After his term in the army ended in 1782, Barlow settled in Hartford, where, in search of some means of support, he founded a weekly newspaper, the *American Mercury,* and decided to study law. It was in Hartford, also, that Barlow was reunited with several of his Yale classmates, including David Humphreys and John Trumbull. Barlow and the others became known as the Connecticut Wits for the similarity of their political views and for their satirical attack on the problems of the new American republic in the strongly Federalist poem, *The Anarchiad,* a collaboration published in the *New Haven Gazette and Connecticut Magazine* in 1786-87. Barlow's lengthy poem *The Vision of Columbus,* which had been in preparation for a number of years, also appeared in 1787 and received much popular and critical acclaim for its patriotic themes.

In 1788, Barlow journeyed to Paris to represent an Ohio land company attempting to sell property to Europeans. Biographers are unanimous in noting the importance of this move, for it was during his extended sojourn in Europe that Barlow's political views underwent significant change. Exposed

to the liberal thinking of such acquaintances as Thomas Jefferson, Thomas Paine, Mary Wollstonecraft, and Joseph Priestley, Barlow gradually shifted to a more democratic viewpoint and became, at the same time, an ardent supporter of the French Revolution. When, in 1790, the British statesman Edmund Burke published his conservative *Reflections on the Revolution in France,* Barlow responded with *Advice to the Privileged Orders.* Though not the most noteworthy of the many replies to Burke's antirevolutionary essay, Barlow's work was influential in its plea for basic human rights and democratic government. Barlow established his reputation as a political pamphleteer with this essay, labelled seditious by the British government, and published other political writings in the course of the next few years. As the result of the publication of *A Letter to the National Convention of France,* in which Barlow argued for French democracy, he was made an honorary citizen of that country. In America, however, Barlow's political reputation suffered from his radical leanings. By the end of the century, he had become alienated from the Connecticut Wits, to whom he seemed a traitor. It was not until 1804, after the establishment of the Jefferson presidency, that he returned to the United States. Barlow's *Columbiad,* a reworking of *The Vision of Columbus,* appeared in 1807, the most elegantly bound and printed book yet produced in America. Popular and critical reaction to the poem was negative, however. In 1811, Barlow again travelled abroad, this time at the request of President James Madison, who wanted Barlow to negotiate a treaty with Napoleon. Sometime in 1812, Barlow wrote his last poem, "Advice to a Raven in Russia," a work that remained unpublished until the twentieth century. Barlow died of pneumonia contracted from exposure to bitter winter weather during Napoleon's retreat from Russia at the end of 1812.

Barlow's prose works have been the least studied of his writings. Of interest to scholars primarily for their delineation of Barlow's radical, humanitarian philosophy, all are infused by his belief in the American system of republican government and its capability to encourage the growth of freedom throughout the world. *Advice to the Privileged Orders,* the most representative and frequently discussed of his prose works, articulates Barlow's position that the state should protect all members of a society, not just those of one class, and that the individual welfare of citizens is a proper matter for public concern. Specifically, Barlow argues that freedom of the press, separation of church and state, and reform of property, tax, and commerce laws would change the nature of government, spreading liberty and peace and eventually eliminating the necessity of funding a large military. As scholars point out, Barlow's theme is the unlimited perfectibility of humankind's lot through the offices of good government; to Barlow, it was possible to create a utopian age of peace and prosperity on earth, a process he felt had been initiated by the American and French Revolutions. Among Barlow's other political writings, *A Letter to the National Convention of France* and *Lettre adressée aux habitans du Piémont (A Letter Addressed to the People of Piedmont),* in particular, support the efficacy of a worldwide republican revolution in producing such an environment. Other prose works, including *Joel Barlow to His Fellow Citizens of the United States of America, Letter II* and the later *Prospectus of a National Institution,* explore the practical ramifications of revolutionary political change, illustrating the beneficial results of religious toleration, universal education, and an improved and expanded transportation system in the building of an American utopia.

Barlow's poetry, like his prose, exhibits humanitarian and utopian themes: human rights, human progress, and the possibility of creating peace and prosperity on earth through science, philosophy, and engineering are basic concerns. In terms of form, the poetry is modelled on the heroic couplets of Alexander Pope; its structure and imagery show the influence of classical epic poetry and such works as John Milton's *Paradise Lost.* Barlow's earliest verse, informed by Christian and Federalist ideology, has for the most part been dismissed, but among these initial poems, *The Vision of Columbus* is of interest to scholars as it represents his first attempt to compose an epic on an American theme. In this work, an angel relates the events of American history to Columbus, the aged hero, eventually revealing a harmonious, progressive future for the country. Geographical and historical descriptions figure prominently as Barlow considers the destiny of both North and South America. On a lesser subject, *The Hasty-Pudding,* Barlow's most well-known and most often anthologized poem, is also the vehicle for a patriotic American theme. A nostalgic tribute to the pleasures of cornmeal mush, the poem is a pastoral evocation of American rural life, mock-epic in form and tone. *The Columbiad,* Barlow's later version of *The Vision of Columbus,* is the work that has been most widely discussed by critics. In this poem, Barlow broad-

ens the content and heightens the language of his earlier poem to underscore the epic qualities of the American experience, the Revolutionary War being highlighted as an event of particular significance. Barlow also revised various elements of the story, including characters and symbols, to accommodate the evolution of his political views.

In the history of Barlow criticism, his prose has received scant literary attention, but those critics who have considered it are in almost unanimous agreement about its superiority to his poetry. These commentators highly praise Barlow's political writings, citing not only his humanitarianism, social responsibility, and well-reasoned ideas on good government, but also his clear, logical, balanced prose. Some commentators believe that Barlow deserves literary recognition on the weight of these merits alone and lament the fact that his prose works are not better known. *Advice to the Privileged Orders,* in particular, has been acclaimed as an essay that should be accorded an important place in the history of ideas along with other, better known political writings.

While Barlow's early *Vision of Columbus* was a popular and critical success and *The Hasty-Pudding* has always been regarded as a poem possessing intrinsic literary value for the harmony of its subject matter, theme, and versification, criticism of Barlow's poetry has centered on *The Columbiad.* Contemporary response was largely unfavorable. Early reviewers disliked it for its lack of dramatic action and unity, want of feeling and imagination, and what they termed its pompous diction. English reviewers, especially, disliked Barlow's innovative spelling and word usage. Throughout the years, scholarly reaction has been similar, with most critics during the middle and late nineteenth century terming the epic a failure. Twentieth-century critics, however, although admitting that the work has serious flaws, have increasingly focused on Barlow's political philosophy and purpose in writing epic poetry, granting the poem importance within the history of the American epic. For this reason, as well as for his expression of American democratic ideals in *The Hasty-Pudding* and his other works, Barlow continues to be regarded as an articulate, influential spokesman of the American Revolutionary War period.

(See also *Dictionary of Literary Biography,* Vol. 37: *American Writers of the Early Republic.*)

PRINCIPAL WORKS

The Prospect of Peace (poetry) 1778
A Poem Spoken at the Public Commencement at Yale College in New-Haven, September 12, 1781 (poetry) 1781
The Vision of Columbus (poetry) 1787; also published in revised and enlarged form as *The Columbiad,* 1807
Advice to the Privileged Orders in the Several States of Europe, Resulting from the Necessity and Propriety of a General Revolution in the Principle of Government. 2 vols. (essay) 1792-93
The Conspiracy of Kings: A Poem Addressed to the Inhabitants of Europe, from Another Quarter of the World (poetry) 1792
A Letter to the National Convention of France on the Defects of the Constitution of 1791, and the Extent of the Amendments Which Ought to Be Applied (open letter) 1792
Lettre adressée aux habitans du Piémont sur les avantages de la révolution française et la nécessité d'en adopter les principes en Italie (open letter) 1793

[*A Letter Addressed to the People of Piedmont on the Advantages of the French Revolution and the Necessity of Adopting Its Principles in Italy*, 1795]

The Hasty-Pudding (poetry) 1796

The Political Writings of Joel Barlow (essay, open letters, and poetry) 1796

Joel Barlow to His Fellow Citizens of the United States of America, Letter I: On the System of Policy Hitherto Pursued by Their Government (open letter) 1799?

Joel Barlow to His Fellow Citizens of the United States of America, Letter II: On Certain Political Measures Proposed to Their Consideration (open letter) 1801; published in *Letters from Paris to the Citizens of the United States of America on the System of Policy Hitherto Pursued by Their Government Relative to Their Commercial Intercourse with England and France, &c.*

Prospectus of a National Institution to Be Established in the United States (treatise) 1806

Letter to Henry Gregoire, Bishop, Senator, Compte of the Empire and Member of the Institute of France, in Reply to His Letter on "The Columbiad" (open letter) 1809

*The Anarchiad: A New England Poem [with David Humphreys, John Trumbull, and Lemuel Hopkins] (poetry) 1861

**"Advice to a Raven in Russia" (poetry) 1938; published in periodical *Huntington Library Quarterly*

The Works of Joel Barlow. 2 vols. (essays, treatise, addresses, open letters, and poetry) 1970

---

*This work was originally published in the periodical *New Haven Gazette and Connecticut Magazine* from 26 October 1786 to 13 September 1787.

**This work was written in 1812.

THE CRITICAL REVIEW, LONDON (essay date 1788)

[*In this excerpt from a review of* The Vision of Columbus, *the critic focuses on the subject matter of the poem.*]

The subject of this poem [*The Vision of Columbus*], in regard to the author's local situation, is well chosen; the design grand and extensive, adapted for the display both of his descriptive and reflecting powers. The attempt is arduous, and, in general, he shews himself not unequal to it. (p. 31)

As an American . . . [Barlow] is partial to his countrymen, and we commend him for it. A certain degree of enthusiasm is laudable both in a patriot and a poet. We find likewise, in this performance, many philosophical disquisitions on the cause of the dissimilarity among nations; on the peopling of America; on the progress of arts and sciences; and the extensive influence which the discoveries of Columbus may have upon the interest and happiness of mankind. That subjects so extensive and arduous should not always be accurately investigated, that several faulty passages might be selected from a poem of such magnitude as the present, cannot be wondered at, and ought not to detract from its general merit. Mr. Barlow thinks with freedom, and expresses himself with spirit. The introduction, which contains the life of Columbus, is written in an agreeable easy manner: the dissertation on the genius and institutions of Manco Capac, in which the Peruvian legislator is compared or contrasted with Moses, Lycur-

gus, Mahomet, and Peter of Russia, from its acuteness and perspicuity, reflects credit on the talents both of the hero and author of the essay. (pp. 34-5)

A review of "The Vision of Columbus: A Poem," in The Critical Review, *London, Vol. LXV, January, 1788, pp. 31-5.*

THE MONTHLY MAGAZINE, AND BRITISH REGISTER (essay date 1798)

[*This anonymous critic praises Barlow's* Vision of Columbus.]

The subject of [*The Vision of Columbus*] was popular; and the active zeal of the friends of the author, secured for it a favourable reception. But its merit, over-rated at first, is now under-valued. The warmth of friendship, and the decision of an American, may be suspected of partiality; but, after every deduction, the *Vision of Columbus* must be considered as a specimen of talents highly honourable to so young a man. The ease, correctness, and even sweetness of the versification, and the philosophical turn of thought, which it displays throughout, are much towards compensating for the inherent defects of plan, and the absence of those bold and original flights of genius, which have been designated as among the indispensible characteristics of the Epopea; and the poem may be repeatedly perused with pleasure, although the reader may not be able to forget that some of its most interesting passages are close copies of correspondent descriptions and relations in the Incas of Marmontel. (pp. 250-51)

"Account of Mr. Joel Barlow, an American Poet," in The Monthly Magazine, and British Register, *Vol. VI, No. XXXVII, October, 1798, pp. 250-51.*

JOEL BARLOW (essay date 1807)

[*In the following excerpt from the preface to* The Columbiad, *first published in 1807, Barlow describes the form, subject matter, and purpose of his epic poem.*]

In preparing this work for publication it seems proper to offer some observations explanatory of its design. The classical reader will perceive the obstacles which necessarily presented themselves in reconciling the nature of the subject with such a manner of treating it as should appear the most poetical, and at the same time the most likely to arrive at that degree of dignity and usefulness to which it ought to aspire.

The Columbiad is a patriotic poem; the subject is national and historical. Thus far it must be interesting to my countrymen. But most of the events were so recent, so important and so well known, as to render them inflexible to the hand of fiction. The poem, therefore, could not with propriety be modelled after that regular epic form which the more splendid works of this kind have taken, and on which their success is supposed in a great measure to depend. The attempt would have been highly injudicious; it must have diminished and debased a series of actions which were really great in themselves and could not be disfigured without losing their interest.

I shall enter into no discussion on the nature of the epopea, nor attempt to prove by any latitude of reasoning that I have written an Epic Poem. The subject indeed is vast; far superior to any of those on which the celebrated poems of this description have been constructed; and I have no doubt but the form I have given to the work is the best that the subject would admit. It may be added, that in no poem are the unities of time, place and action more rigidly observed: the action, in the technical sense of the word, consisting only of what takes place between Columbus and Hesper; which must be supposed to occupy but few hours, and is confined to the prison and the mount of vision.

But these circumstances of classical regularity are of little consideration in estimating the real merit of any work of this nature. Its merit must depend on the importance of the action, the disposition of the parts, the invention and application of incidents, the propriety of the illustrations, the liveliness and chastity of the images, the suitable intervention of machinery, the moral tendency of the manners, the strength and sublimity of the sentiments; the whole being clothed in language whose energy, harmony and elegance shall constitute a style every where suited to the matter they have to treat.

It is impossible for me to determine how far I may have succeeded in any of these particulars. This must be decided by others, the result of whose decision I shall never know. But there is one point of view in which I wish the reader to place the character of my work, before he pronounces on its merit: I mean its political tendency. There are two distinct objects to be kept in view in the conduct of a narrative poem: the *poetical* object and the *moral* object. The poetical is the fictitious design of the action; the moral is the real design of the poem.

In the *Iliad* of Homer the poetical object is to kindle, nourish, sustain and allay the anger of Achilles. This end is constantly kept in view; and the action proper to attain it is conducted with wonderful judgment thro a long series of incidents, which elevate the mind of the reader, and excite not only a veneration for the creative powers of the poet, but an ardent emulation of his heroes, a desire to imitate and rival some of the great actors in the splendid scene; perhaps to endeavor to carry into real life the fictions with which we are so much enchanted.

Such a high degree of interest excited by the first object above mentioned, the fictitious design of the action, would make it extremely important that the second object, the real design of the poem, should be beneficial to society. But the real design in the *Iliad* was directly the reverse. Its obvious tendency was to inflame the minds of young readers with an enthusiastic ardor for military fame; to inculcate the pernicious doctrine of the divine right of kings; to teach both prince and people that military plunder was the most honorable mode of acquiring property; and that conquest, violence and war were the best employment of nations, the most glorious prerogative of bodily strength and of cultivated mind.

How much of the fatal policy of states, and of the miseries and degradations of social man, have been occasioned by the false notions of honor inspired by the works of Homer, it is not easy to ascertain. The probability is, that however astonishing they are as monuments of human intellect, and how long soever they have been the subject of universal praise, they have unhappily done more harm than good. My veneration for his genius is equal to that of his most idolatrous readers; but my reflections on the history of human errors have forced upon me the opinion that his existence has really proved one of the signal misfortunes of mankind. (pp. v-ix)

In the poem here presented to the public the objects, as in other works of the kind, are two: the fictitious object of the action and the real object of the poem. The first of these is to sooth and satisfy the desponding mind of Columbus; to show him that his labors, tho ill rewarded by his contemporaries, had not been performed in vain; that he had opened the way to the most extensive career of civilization and public happiness; and that he would one day be recognised as the author of the greatest benefits to the human race. This object is steadily kept in view; and the actions, images and sentiments are so disposed as probably to attain the end. But the real object of the poem embraces a larger scope: it is to inculcate the love of rational liberty, and to discountenance the deleterious passion for violence and war; to show that on the basis of the republican principle all good morals, as well as good government and hopes of permanent peace, must be founded; and to convince the student in political science that the theoretical question of the future advancement of human society, till states as well as individuals arrive at universal civilization, is held in dispute and still unsettled only because we have had too little experience of organised liberty in the government of nations to have well considered its effects.

I cannot expect that every reader, nor even every republican reader, will join me in opinion with respect to the future progress of society and the civilization of states; but there are two sentiments in which I think all men will agree: that the event is desirable, and that to believe it practicable is one step towards rendering it so. This being the case they ought to pardon a writer, if not applaud him, for endeavoring to inculcate this belief. (pp. xi-xiii)

My object is altogether of a moral and political nature. I wish to encourage and strengthen, in the rising generation, a sense of the importance of republican institutions; as being the great foundation of public and private happiness, the necessary aliment of future and permanent meliorations in the condition of human nature.

This is the moment in America to give such a direction to poetry, painting and the other fine arts, that true and useful ideas of glory may be implanted in the minds of men here, to take place of the false and destructive ones that have degraded the species in other countries; impressions which have become so wrought into their most sacred institutions, that it is there thought impious to detect them and dangerous to root them out, tho acknowledged to be false. Wo be to the republican principle and to all the institutions it supports, when once the pernicious doctrine of the holiness of error shall creep into the creed of our schools and distort the intellect of our citizens.

The Columbiad, in its present form, is such as I shall probably leave it to its fate. Whether it be destined to survive its author, is a question that gives me no other concern than what arises from the most pure and ardent desire of doing good to my country. To my country, therefore, with every sentiment of veneration and affection, I dedicate my labors. (pp. xix-xx)

Joel Barlow, in a preface to his The Columbiad: A Poem, with the Last Corrections of the Author, *Joseph Milligan, 1825, pp. v-xx.*

THE MONTHLY MAGAZINE, LONDON   (essay date 1808-09)

[*In the following excerpt, the critic examines the dramatic unity, subject matter, and characterization of* The Columbiad *as well as Barlow's use of American spelling and vocabulary.*]

Every nation that can boast of an epic poem of sufficient merit to become a classical work, has certainly a good cause for self-complacency. Such a work inspires an additional interest, when built on a national subject; when the author, who is destined to gratify his countrymen by soaring to this highest flight of human genius, can find among their own annals an action capable of supporting a strength of pinion equal to the task. . . .

Mr. Barlow has been particularly happy in respect to [the subject of his epic poem, *The Columbiad*]. The discovery of America is in itself a great action; but its importance is infinitely augmented by the consequences resulting from the discovery. These consequences comprise by far the most interesting portion of modern history; and their interest is strongly concentrated in his country, it being that part of the new world which has first manifested its own importance, by giving birth to a great and civilized nation.

The settlement therefore of the British colonies, the wars and revolutions through which they rose to independent states, that vast frame of federative republican government on which they now stand, and which in the eyes of our enthusiastic bard is to extend itself over the whole of North America, and give an example to the world, composes the principal part of the active scenery of the poem. But other and far more extensive views of human affairs, drawn from other countries, and from ages past, present, and future, are likewise placed beneath our eye, and form no inconsiderable portion of this magnificent work; magnificent it certainly is beyond any thing which modern literature has to boast, except the *Paradise Lost* of Milton. (p. 403)

The author in his preface [see excerpt dated 1807] makes some pertinent remarks on the nature of the subject, and the difficulties it presented as to the best mode of treating it. "*The Columbiad* (says he) is a patriotic poem; the subject is national and historical; thus far it must be interesting to my countrymen. But most of the events were so recent, so important, and so well known, as to render them inflexible to the hand of fiction. The poem therefore could not with propriety be modelled after that regular epic form which the more splendid works of this kind have taken, and on which their success is supposed in a great measure to depend. The attempt would have been highly injudicious; it must have diminished and debased a series of actions, which were really great in themselves, and which could not be disfigured without losing their interest." So far I agree with the poet; who seems to understand the real value of the rules of his art, too well to think himself obliged in all cases to follow them.

He farther observes, "I shall enter into no discussion on the nature of the epopea, nor attempt to prove, by any latitude of reasoning, that I have written an epic poem." Neither will I enter into such a discussion, but I must apply to the present work the sentiment of Addison, with regard to *Paradise Lost.* If it is not an epic poem, it is something better.

Mr. Barlow has dealt freely with mythological and allegorical personages; several of whom take conspicuous parts in the conduct of affairs. Hesper, as the guardian genius of the Western Continent, is made to play a great role; the continent is called after his name, Hesperia; and from the part he acts, he must be considered at least the second character in the poem. He is introduced near the beginning, and continues to the end; and there is no personage but Columbus whose existence seems so incorporated with the body of the work. Atlas,

the guardian of Africa, is the elder brother of Hesper, according to the account of this mythological family which the author gives us in a note. Atlas appears but once in the course of the action; and it is to present us with as sublime a set of images as we have ever met with in poetry, including in his speech a most awful denunciation of vengeance on the people of America, for the slavery of the Africans. These two brothers, with several river-gods, and the demons of War, Cruelty, Inquisition, Frost, Famine, and Pestilence, compose the celestial actors who take charge of the hyperphysical part of the machinery.

The human characters are mostly real and known, some few of them fictitious; they are I believe more numerous than those employed in any other poem, not excepting the *Iliad;* and they are as much varied as the subject requires. (pp. 403-04)

[The fictional design of the poem] is one, it is simple, clear, easy to be perceived, and is finally attained; the action is one, and as simple as the design, being, in fact, no more than what passes between the two principal personages, Columbus and Hesper; all the subordinate events, conducted by other actors, being represented in vision, recounted from history and fable, or predicted by the celestial personages. The time also, and the place are kept each within the limits of strict dramatic unity, as is noticed in the preface; the place not extending beyond the prison and the mount of vision; and the time not exceeding two days.

So far, therefore, as I am to judge by the technical requisites of epic song, the *Columbiad* must be ranked in that class of works; and so far as the real object and intrinsic character of the poem are to guide the decision, the reader indeed must form his own, but mine would assign it a high rank; indeed, in that class it would even incline me to pronounce, that only three poems ought to stand above it, the *Iliad, Eneid,* and *Paradise Lost.*

[As a specimen of the composition of the poem, the] monologue of Columbus in prison, with which the poem opens, has considerable pathos, and some good description, but I think it too long. It is always a delicate business for a hero to complain, it is not a heroic employment; and in no situation will he find it more difficult to keep up his dignity. I am sensible that this case is a singular one; he is alone in a dungeon at midnight, his spirits broken down by a long train of cruel calamities, injustice, and ingratitude. A variety of subjects must crowd upon his feelings, and his feelings demand utterance in a manner too strong to be resisted by a mind which, without ceasing to be great, must be enfeebled by suffering.

These circumstances furnish some apology. Indeed it requires one; and the merit of the lines, though great, would not be deemed a sufficient one for extending such a solo to 74 lines, and that at the beginning of the poem. Other critics on this passage may differ from me in opinion; and I hope they will, as this is the only instance I have noticed in this author of any want of judgment in proportioning the parts to each other, or to the whole. (p. 407)

• • • • •

[Barlow's prose style in his preface and notes to *The Columbiad*] is remarkable for its harmony and eloquence. He has likewise attained a degree of purity, so far superior to any other of his countrymen, whose writings we have seen, that, were it not for the danger of giving offence to him, or them,

I should perhaps ascribe it to his long residence in this country.

I intended, however, when I began this article, to notice a few oddities in his orthography and his neology. He is so sensible of having laid himself open to animadversion in this respect, that he has written a postscript to his notes in justification of the liberties he has taken with our language. But as he has explained himself fully on this subject, I will only add a word of regret at seeing a disposition in American writers for innovating so fast in our common national language, as must in a few generations more produce an irreconcilable dialect. Such a tendency is certainly to be deprecated; and I am sorry to find that so great an example as Mr. B's writings must prove to his countrymen should have given countenance to these innovations. (p. 523)

> *A review of "The Columbiad," in* The Monthly Magazine, *London, Vol. XXVI, Nos. 178 and 179, December 1, 1808 and January 1, 1809, pp. 403-09, 518-23.*

OLIVER OLDSMITH   (essay date 1809)

[*This American critic, while lauding the subject matter of Barlow's* Columbiad, *criticizes the narrative unity, characterization, metrics, and vocabulary of the poem.*]

A quarto epic poem—polished by twenty years labour—issuing in all the pomp of typographical elegance from an American press—the author an American—the theme, the history of our own country! What an era in our literature! What an epoch in the history of our arts! What a subject for the reviewer.

Employed, as the critic in this country has long been, in hunting down party pamphlets and boarding-school novels, fast-day sermons, and "such small deer," it is with proud satisfaction that he at length sees his field enlarged—his subjects rise in dignity and importance. As some young knight of Arthur's court, who, through lack of fair achievement, yet bore his shield unblazoned and his spurs ungilt, after many a tedious hour of journey, at length espied some Paynim castle huge and rude, with "donjon high where captives wail," and every promise of adventure meet for knightly prowess, even so, gentle reader, with such feelings does the critic now gaze on the splendid volume before him. Proudly he turns from the detection of vulgar imposture and the ridicule of wild absurdity to meet his nobler task.

The subject of the **Columbiad** is national and patriotic. It was Mr. Barlow's early ambition to raise the epic song of his nation—to select from her annals the most brilliant portions of American history—to wreath them into one chaplet of immortal verse, and present the splendid offering with filial reverence to the genius of his country. Mr. B. readily perceived that [see excerpt dated 1807] "most of the events of the revolution were so recent, so important, and so well known as to render them inflexible to the hand of fiction."

"The poem, therefore, could not be modelled after that regular epic form which the more splendid works of this kind have taken, and on which their success is supposed in a great measure to depend. The attempt would have been highly injudicious; it must have diminished and debased a series of actions which were really great in themselves, and could not be disfigured without losing their interest."

Hence it became necessary for the poet to look around for some interesting tale of history or fiction which might give unity and effect to the mass of unconnected facts, and thus (to borrow an image of Dr. Darwin) form a festoon of roses connecting together his series of miniature history pieces. (pp. 61-2)

We look, but look in vain, for that unity of fable, that regular succession of incident and vivid exhibition of varied character, which constitute the most powerful charm of a narrative poem. Mr. Barlow's work is a sort of poetical magic lantern; and while ten thousand gaudy figures dance rapidly along the wall of Columbus's dungeon, the Genius of America kindly officiates as a showman, and informs the spectator that here he may "see Quito's plains o'erlook their proud Peru," and there

> —Sage Rittenhouse with ardent eye
> Lift the long tube and pierce the starry sky;

Yonder you may behold Mrs. Wright making wax-work, and a little farther to the other side

> Yon meteor-mantled hill see Franklin tread:
> Heaven's awful thunders rolling o'er his head;

Presently a map of North America flits before us; and then come Washington and Manco Capac, the river Delaware and lord Cornwallis, the genius of Cruelty, and general Greene. They "come like shadows, so depart," leaving the mind bewildered and the memory confused.

From this radical error in the general design and groundwork of the poem, beside the want of interest, other defects almost spontaneously arise. The author has heaped together such an immense, discordant mass of characters, facts, and descriptions—such an *Iliad* of heroes is crammed into a nutshell, that the space allotted to each compartment must of necessity be very small. Hence the poet is almost necessarily compelled to an exuberant use of allegorical delineation. As his characters have no room to develop themselves by action, he is obliged to decorate his personages with emblematic badges, and to embody their passions and motives into allegorical forms. Thus his sages are presented to your view (as you may see portraits in the window of a print-shop) surrounded by air-pumps and telescopes, piles of books and heaps of chymical apparatus. With the same rage for allegorical personification, Cruelty is seated on the deck of the prison-ship, Inquisition stalks over Spain, and War attended by his whole family, his wife Discord, and his twin daughters Famine and Pestilence, strides across the Atlantic, disgorging from his mouth

> Pikes, muskets, mortars, guns and globes of fire,
> And lighted bombs that fusing trails expire.
>
> (pp. 64-5)

Thus much for the general disposition of the whole. Let us now cast a rapid glance on the execution of the parts. The first thing which strikes the cursory reader is a certain wearisome sameness and dull repetition of favourite phrases and perpetually recurring rhymes. For example, when the poet has decked one of his personages with the emblems of his character or his occupation, and placed him in some theatrical attitude, he invariably gives him an "ardent eye," and places a crown of science or of triumph upon his brow. The same barren lack of invention is stamped upon every part of his geographical description; in which, as we above hinted, he indulges himself beyond all bounds, to the great annoyance of the patient reader. After having travelled through many a heavy couplet,

> From sultry Mobile's gulf-indented shore
> To where Ontario hears his Lawrence roar,

when we have seen proud Maragnon and Paraguay's deep channel, broad Delaware and majestic Hudson, gay Piscataway and swift Kennebec, we begin to wish for repose. But alas! it is in vain. Our indefatigable bard continues to whirl us backward and forward, with the rapidity of a postboy, from "Penn's beauteous town," to "imperial Mexic" and "Cusco's shining roofs." At length a total indifference, bordering on disgust, creeps upon us. Even the speeches and conflicts of his river-gods, fail to rouse us from our apathy, and we see,

> New-York ascend o'er Hudson's seaward isles
> And fling the sunbeams from the glittering tiles,
> Albania opening thro the distant wood
> Roll her rich treasures o'er her parent flood,

with much the same feelings with which we read in Dr. Morse's Gazetteer that "Weathersfield is a post-town in Connecticut, five miles south-east from Hartford, adorned with an elegant brick meeting-house, and famous for the beauty of its girls and the savour of its onions."

Next after geography, philosophical declamation seems to be Mr. B.'s favourite employment for his muse. Of the many pages through which he indulges this propensity, some are filled with original and ingenious theories, many with commonplace rant (as Sir Archy M'Sarcasm would say) "varra true and varra novel," and more,—by far the greater part,—with the cant of the Darwinian and Parisian schools. We presume that, at this time of day, few of our readers have much further curiosity on this subject. We will, however, refer them to the disquisition on the causes of the dissimilarity of men in different climates, contained in the beginning of the second book, as exhibiting no unfavourable specimen of our author's powers of reasoning in verse.

Mr. B. appears to have but an imperfect command of the inferior and mechanical arts of poetry. His rhymes are deficient in variety and richness, and often grossly inaccurate; and his versification is sometimes disfigured by the most feeble and prosaic lines, such as these:

> Mark modern Europe with her feudal codes,
> Serfs, villains, vassals, nobles, kings, and gods,
> Wage endless wars; not fighting to be free,
> But *cujum pecus* whose base herd they'll be.

And again,

> Wide over earth his annual freshet strays,
> And highland *drench* with lowland *drains* repays.

Many of his most poetical passages are debased by unlucky vulgarisms, or ludicrous minuteness of description. The fiend Cruelty is introduced with very powerful effect, and the personification is supported with great ability till she displays her "slow poisonous drugs, and loads of putrid meat," while

> Disease hangs drizzling from her slimy locks,
> And hot contagion *issues from her box.*

The simile of the archer Tell is marred by a ludicrous alliteration, the arrow flies from the hand of the patriot father, and "*picks* off the *pippin* from the smiling boy." In another passage, the poet, in the true spirit of the bathos, makes channels to "*tap* the redundant lakes." All this surprises us not a little. In the present state of literature, every writer, if he has matter, is seldom deficient in style; almost every one who rhymes, rhymes with tolerable elegance. That a writer of Mr. Barlow's powers should fail in these minutiae is singular indeed.

There is a strange incongruity in the versification and style of the *Columbiad.* Some portions of it seem to be modelled on the manner of Dryden and the fathers of English song; while the rest glitters with all the trick and prettiness of the school of Darwin. All the verses, however, whether of ancient or modern structure, move along with apparent labour and effort. The sense seems to follow the rhyme, not the rhyme the sense. Every couplet appears to have been separately laboured, and then the whole strung together as conveniently as might be. Hence the sense is often broken and disjointed, and we are even sometimes at a loss for the grammatical construction of the sentence. This, however, although the general, is not the universal character of our poet's verses. He occasionally bursts forth in short but vigorous flights, some of which, had they been found in Absalom and Achitophel, would not have dishonoured Dryden in his noblest efforts. Take for instance the following burst of patriotic indignation in his narrative of the expedition against Quebec, headed by the traitor Arnold:

> Ah! gallant troop! deprived of half the praise,
> That deeds like yours in other times repays;
> Since your prime chief (the favourite erst of fame)
> Hath sunk so deep his hateful hideous name,
> That every honest Muse with horror flings
> The name unsounded from her sacred strings;
> Else what high tones of rapture must have told
> The first great actions of a chief so bold,
> 'Twas his, 'twas yours, to brave unusual storms,
> To tame rude nature in its drearest forms, &c.

We cannot dismiss Mr. Barlow as a poet without first taking him to task for some petty offences against the purity of the English language. The first misdemeanor in this way is of New-England origin; we mean the using neuter verbs as actives, and vice versa. Thus "Nature *broods* the mass," for broods over; Columbus "*sweats* the cold earth," for sweats upon; Egyptian gardens "*grow* the vegetable god," and the "lordling knave *filches* whom he can." With the same latitude nouns are transmuted into verbs, as to bulwark—to base—to scabbard—to bluff. The poet's next offence, doubtless at the instigation of the Devil, against the peace of English scholars and their dignity, is a most violent propensity to the introduction of strange new-fangled words—words from which Lexiphanes himself would have shrunk back in dismay. In place of the honest old English word "*sad*" he astounds us with *trist* and contrised. Then he thunders upon us with his crasse, condependent, cosmogyre, cosmogyral, colon (not in a grammatical or anatomical sense, but in a French idiom, for cultivator, colonist) croupe, role, fluvial, multifluvian, brume, impalm, beamful, fulminents, imbeaded, ludibrious, and many more, which, to pronounce, would require the lungs of Stentor, and the mouth of Garagantua.

We have now, we trust, with much impartiality, delivered our opinion of the poetical merits of the *Columbiad.* We will not elevate our American bard to the rank of the *Dii majorum gentium* of poetry, nor degrade him to the level of the heroes of the *Dunciad.* We place his work "behind the foremost, and before the last," on the same shelf with Wilkie's *Epigoniad,* Hoole's *Arthur,* and Pye's *Alfred;* and perhaps but little below the *Madoc* of Southey, the *Conquest of Canaan* of Dwight, and the *Exodiad* of Cumberland and Burgess. The notes to the ***Columbiad*** are full of strange and curious matter; these may perhaps furnish a subject for some future review. (pp. 67-70)

> *Oliver Oldsmith, in a review of "The Columbiad: A Poem," in* The Port Folio, *n.s. Vol. I, No. 1, January, 1809, pp. 61-70.*

[FRANCIS JEFFREY] (essay date 1809)

[*Widely influential as a writer throughout his lifetime, Jeffrey was a founder and editor of the* Edinburgh Review, *a journal that significantly raised the standards of periodical reviewing in early nineteenth-century England. In the following excerpt, Jeffrey offers a largely negative appraisal of* The Columbiad, *faulting numerous aspects of the poem, including its characterization, style, diction, dramatic unity, and epic pretensions.*]

As epic poetry has often been the earliest, as well as the most precious production of national genius, we ought not, perhaps, to be surprised at [***The Columbiad,***] this goodly firstling of the infant Muse of America. The truth however is, that though the American *government* be new, the *people* is in all respects as old as the people of England; and their want of literature is to be ascribed, not to the immaturity of their progress in civilization, but to the nature of the occupations in which they are generally engaged. These federal republicans, in short, bear no sort of resemblance to the Greeks of the days of Homer, or the Italians of the age of Dante; but are very much such people, we suppose, as the modern traders of Manchester, Liverpool, or Glasgow. They have all a little Latin whipped into them in their youth; and read Shakespeare, Pope and Milton, as well as bad English novels, in their days of courtship and leisure. They are just as likely to write epic poems, therefore, as the inhabitants of our trading towns at home; and are entitled to no more admiration when they succeed, and to no more indulgence when they fail, than would be due, on a similar occasion, to any of those industrious persons.

Be this, however, as it may, Mr Barlow, we are afraid, will not be the Homer of his country; and will never take his place among the enduring poets either of the old or of the new world. The faults which obviously cut him off from this high destiny, may be imputed partly to his country, and partly to his subject—but chiefly to himself. The want of a literary society, to animate, controul and refine, and the intractableness of a subject which extends from the creation to the millennium, and combines the rude mythologies of savages with the treaties and battles of men who are still alive, certainly aggravated the task which he had undertaken with no common difficulties. But the great misfortune undoubtedly is, that Mr Barlow is in no respect qualified to overcome these difficulties. From the prose which he has introduced into this volume, and even from much of what is given as poetry, it is easy to see that he is a man of a plain, strong, and resolute understanding,—a very good republican, and a considerable despiser of all sorts of prejudices and illusions; but without any play or vivacity of fancy,—any gift of simplicity or pathos,—any loftiness of genius, or delicacy of taste. Though not deficient in literature, therefore, nor unread in poetry, he has evidently none of the higher elements of a poet in his composition; and has accordingly made a most injudicious choice and

unfortunate application of the models which lay before him. Like other persons of a cold and coarse imagination, he is caught only by what is glaring and exaggerated; and seems to have no perception of the finer and less obtrusive graces which constitute all the lasting and deep-felt charms of poetry. In his cumbrous and inflated style, he is constantly mistaking hyperbole for grandeur, and supplying the place of simplicity with huge patches of mere tameness and vulgarity. This curious intermixture, indeed, of extreme homeliness and flatness, with a sort of turbulent and bombastic elevation, is the great characteristic of the work before us. Instead of aspiring to emulate the sublime composure of Milton, or the natural eloquence and flowing nervousness of Dryden, Mr Barlow has bethought him of transferring to epic poetry the light, sparkling, and tawdry diction of [Erasmus Darwin, 1731-1802], and of narrating great events, and delivering lofty precepts in an unhappy imitation of that picturesque, puerile, and pedantic style, which alternately charms and disgusts us in the pages of our poetical physiologist, infinitely more verbose and less spirited than Darwin however, he reminds us of him only by his characteristic defects; and, after all, is most tolerable in those passages in which he reminds us most of him.

Such is the general character of this transatlantic Epic as to style and taste in composition. As for the more substantial requisites of such a work, it is unfortunately still more deficient. Though crowded with names, and confused with incidents, it cannot properly be said to have either characters or action. In sketching the history of America from the days of Manco Capac down to the present day, and a few thousand years lower, the author, of course, cannot spare time to make us acquainted with any one individual. The most important personages, therefore, appear but once upon the scene, and then pass away and are forgotten. Mr Barlow's exhibition accordingly partakes more of the nature of a procession, than of a drama. River gods, sachems, majors of militia, all enter at one side of his stage, and go off at the other, never to return. Rocha and Oella take up as much room as Greene and Washington; and the rivers Potowmak and Delaware, those fluent and venerable personages, both act and talk a great deal more than Jefferson or Franklin.

It is plain, that in a poem constructed upon such a plan, there can be no development of character,—no unity, or even connexion of action,—and consequently no interest, and scarcely any coherence or contrivance in the story. Of a work of this magnitude and curiosity, however, it is proper that our readers should be enabled in some measure to judge for themselves; and therefore, we shall proceed to lay before them a short abstract of the plan. . . . (pp. 24-6)

Columbus, it is well known, was repaid for his great discovery with signal ingratitude; and was at one time loaded with chains, and imprisoned on the instigation of an envious rival. The poem opens with a view of his dungeon, and a long querulous soliloquy addressed to its walls. All on a sudden the gloom is illuminated by the advent of a celestial personage; and the Guardian Angel of America is introduced by the name of Hesper, who consoles and soothes the heroic prisoner, by leading him up to a shadowy mount, from which he entertains him with a full prospect of the vast continent he had discovered, and sets before him in a long vision which lasts till the end of the poem, all the events which had happened, and were to happen, in that region, or in any other connected with it.

Thus, the whole history, past, present, and future, of America, and inclusively of the whole world, is delivered in the clumsy and revoking form of a miraculous vision; and thus truth is not only blended with falsehood and fancy, but is presented to the mind under the mask of the grossest and most palpable fiction. Mr Barlow, of course, judges differently of his plan; and maintains, not only that it gives great interest and dignity to the story, but that it has enabled him 'to observe the unities of time, place, and action, more rigidly than any other poet,—the whole action consisting in what takes place between Columbus and Hesper, which must be supposed to occupy but a few hours.' There never was so cheap and ingenious a method of satisfying the unities as this. Here is a poem of some seven or eight thousand verses, containing a sketch of universal history, from the deluge to the final conflagration, with particular notices of all the battles, factions, worthies, and improvements in America, for the last half century; and when we complain of the enormous extent and confusion of this metrical chronicle, we are referred to some fifty forgotten lines at the outset, from which, it appears, that Columbus came to the knowledge of all these fine things by seeing them rehearsed before him one dark night on the top of a mountain in Spain. If this apology is to be received, Mr Scott might hold out his beautiful *outlaw,* the *Lay of the Last Minstrel,* as a perfect pattern of the unities,—since the whole story is told in one afternoon in the dressing-room of the Dutchess of Buccleugh. The antient poets, in like manner, had nothing more to do than to prefix a notice, that the whole piece was dictated to them by a muse in any given grotto or bower. Nay, even a degenerate modern, it would seem, might, upon the same principle, securely evade this most rigorous law of the unities, by merely notifying in verse, that his rambling Epic was all composed by him in the course of one term, and within the precincts of one garret. Is it possible that self-partiality should have so far blinded a man of Mr Barlow's acuteness, as to make it necessary to remind him, that the unity which the reader requires in a long poem, must be in the subject, and not in the manner of introducing it; and that the miscellaneous history of four thousand years does not become one story, by being represented in one vision, any more than by being bound up in one volume? It is time, however, to give a short sketch of this visionary legend.

The first part of it belongs rather to geography than to civil history; and contains a long description of the American hills, lakes, rivers, and vegetable productions. The next chapter goes on to the animal kingdom; and is chiefly occupied with the physiology of its human natives, and a theory about its population. Two whole books are then devoted to the fabulous exploits of Manco Capac and Oella, the Osiris and Isis of the Peruvian mythology,—their institutions civil and religious, and their conquest and conversion of the more ferocious savages around them. After this, there is a very short sketch of the Spanish oppressions, followed out by a speculation upon the Popish superstition, the Jesuits, and the Inquisition. The voyages of Sir Walter Raleigh, and the colonisation of Virginia, are then commemorated: and the next book contains the history of the Canadian war 1757, with the defeat of Braddock and the death of Wolfe; and then begins the story of the colonial war, which is given with considerable detail in the course of the two following books. This ends the historical, and introduces the prophetic part of Mr Barlow's poem. The eighth book is dedicated to a survey of the prog-

ress which America is destined to make in art, virtue and happiness; and the ninth and tenth, which close the work, to a view of the general happiness of mankind, when all the nations of the earth shall have been taught, by the example of America, to renounce war and violence, to unite in one great federal republic, and to hold a grand annual congress of sages in Egypt, for the purpose of renouncing all prejudices, and consulting for the general happiness. With this beatific vision Hesper closes his splendid exhibition; and leaves Columbus quite comforted and satisfied in his dungeon. (pp. 26-8)

[This] American bard frequently writes in a language utterly unknown to the prose or verse of this country. We have often heard it reported, that our transatlantic brethren were beginning to take it amiss that their language should still be called English; and truly we must say, that Mr Barlow has gone far to take away that ground of reproach. The groundwork of his speech, perhaps, may be English, as that of the Italian is Latin; but the variations amount already to more than a change of dialect; and really make a glossary necessary for most untravelled readers. As this is the first specimen which has come to our hands of any considerable work composed in the American tongue, it may be gratifying to our philological readers, if we make a few remarks upon it.

It is distinguished from the original English, in the first place, by a great multitude of words which are radically and entirely new, and as utterly foreign as if they had been adopted from the Hebrew or Chinese; in the second place, by a variety of new compounds and combinations of words, or roots of words, which are still known in the parent tongue; and, thirdly, by the perversion of a still greater number of original English words from their proper use or signification, by employing nouns substantive for verbs, for instance, and adjectives for substantives, &c. We shall set down a few examples of each.

In the first class, we may reckon the words *multifluvian— cosmogyral—crass—role—gride—conglaciate—colon* and *coloniarch—trist* and *contristed—thirl—gerb—ludibrious— croupe—scow—emban—lowe—brume—brumal,* &c. &c.

The second class is still more extensive, and, to our ears, still more discordant. In it we may comprehend such verbs as, to *utilise,* to *vagrate,* to *oversheet,* to *empalm,* to *inhumanise,* to *transboard,* to *reseek,* to *bestorm,* to *smeed,* &c. &c.; such adjectives as *bivaulted, imbeaded, unkeeled, laxed, forestered, homicidious, millennial, portless, undungeoned, lustred,* &c.—*conflicting fulminents;* and a variety of substantives formed upon the same plan of distortion.

The third or last class of American improvements, consists mainly in the violent transformation of an incredible number of English nouns into verbs. Thus we have, 'to *spade* the soil'—'to *sledge* the corn'—and 'to *keel* the water.' We have also the verbs, to *breeze,* to *rainbow,* to *hill,* to *scope,* to *lot,* to *lamp,* to *road,* and to *reroad,* to *fang,* to *fray,* to *bluff,* to *tone,* to *forester,* to *gyve,* to *besom,* and fifty more. Nor is it merely as verbs that our poor nouns are compelled to serve in this new republican dictionary; they are forced, upon a pinch, to do the duty of adjectives also; and, accordingly, we have science distinguished into moral science and *physic* science; and *things* discussed with a view to their *physic* forms and their final ends.

The innovations in prosody are not less bold and meritorious. We have *galaxy* and *platina* with the middle syllable long.

New constellations, new *galaxies* rise.
The pale *platina* and the burning gold.

Contents, allied, bombard, and *expanse,* are accented on the first syllable.

Each thro' the adverse ports their *contents* pour,
&c.

And *empyrean* is made short in the penult; as in that fine line,

Empalms the *empyrean,* or dissects a gaz.

The rhimes are equally original;—*plain* rhimes to *man*—*blood* to *God,* and *share* to *war,* in three successive couplets.

Before closing these hasty and imperfect notices of the characteristics of this new language, it seems proper to observe, that if Mr Barlow's authority is to be relied on, it may also be known from all other tongues by an utter disregard of all distinction between what we should call lofty and elegant, and low and vulgar expressions. These republican literati seem to make it a point of conscience to have no aristocratical distinctions—even in their vocabulary. They think one word just as good as another, provided its meaning be as clear; and will know no difference, but that of force and perspicuity. Thus, we hear of rivers that *tap* the upland lakes and are told, that, in North America, there are 'hills by hundreds,' of such a height, that, if set beside them,

Taurus would shrink, Hemodia *strut* no more.

In the same taste, in an elaborate description of the celebrated feat of William Tell, our attention is particularly directed to the stretching of his *knuckles* as he draws the cord, and to the skill with which *'he picked the pippin'* off his boy's head. Niagara, we are afterward informed, *'bluffs high his head,'*

And Chili *bluffs,* and Plata *thats* the coast.

And, in a pompous description of a storm, we see the crew *'spring to quarters,'* *'haul their wind,'* and get their shrouds *afoul;* and learn, after all, that

Crew *and cargo* glut the watery grave.

The great river Plata, too, appears with extraordinary magnificence—

And highland drains with *lowland drench* repays.

Inland navigation is justly extolled for the saving which it occasions in the *carrier's* toil. Contagion is said to be promoted by 'heaps of putrid *meat;'* and steams are represented as arising from her *'box.'* With an equal regard to dignity, the flames in a great conflagration are represented as *'sucking up the cinders.'* Some of the republican forces are said to be *'hard pusht;'* and others are obliged to *'climb hard'* up a hill, to get out of the reach of the enemy. The tripod of the Delphic priestess, moreover, is elegantly called her *'stool;'* and the watchword of the night sentinels is pleasantly termed *'sly.'*

From the view which we have now given of the diction of this American Epic, it might perhaps be concluded, that the whole must be equally unintelligible and intolerable to an English reader; and that we could not be serious in saying, that Mr Barlow had stolen the style of Darwin, who versifies, in general, with great elegance, and seldom mixes any thing with his English but terms of science or of art. The truth is, however, that the greater part of Mr Barlow may be understood by a careful reader, even in this country; that his versifi-

cation is generally both soft and sonorous; and that, notwithstanding the occasional lowness and constant want of purity of his diction, there are many passages of rich and vigorous description, and some that might lay claim even to the praise of magnificence. The fatal want of simplicity, passion and character, unfortunately leave no room to doubt of his destiny as an Epic poet; but there is a power, now and then, both in his descriptive and didactic passages, that, under stricter management, might turn to some account in another department of poetry. (pp. 28-30)

As a great national poem, [*The Columbiad*] has enormous—inexpiable—and, in some respects, intolerable faults. But the author's talents are evidently respectable: and, severely as we have been obliged to speak of his taste and his diction in a great part of the volume, we have no hesitation in saying, that we consider him as a giant, in comparison with many of the puling and paltry rhymsters, who disgrace our English literature by their occasional success. As an Epic poet, we do think his case is desperate; but, as a philosophical and moral poet, we think he has talents of no ordinary value; and, if he would pay some attention to purity of style, and simplicity of composition, and cherish in himself a certain fastidiousness of taste,—which is not yet to be found, we are afraid, even among the better educated of the Americans,—we have no doubt that he might produce something which English poets would envy, and English critics applaud. In the mean time, we think it quite certain, that his present work will have no success in this country. Its faults are far too many, and too glaring, to give its merits any chance of being distinguished; and indeed no long poem was ever redeemed by the beauty of particular passages—especially if its faults were owing to affectation, and its beauties addressed rather to the judgment than to the heart or the imagination. (pp. 39-40)

There is one thing, however, which may give the original edition of Mr Barlow's poem some chance of selling among us,—and that is, the extraordinary beauty of the paper, printing and embellishments. We do not know that we have ever seen a handsomer book issue from the press of England; and if this be really and truly the production of American artists, we must say, that the infant republic has already attained to the very summit of perfection in the mechanical part of bookmaking. If her home sale can defray the expense of such a publication as the present, it is a sign that a taste for literature is spreading very widely among her inhabitants; and whenever this taste is created, we have no doubt that her authors will improve and multiply to a degree that will make all our exertions necessary to keep the start we now have of them. (p. 40)

[Francis Jeffrey], in a review of "The Columbiad: A Poem," in The Edinburgh Review, *Vol. XV, No. XXIX, October, 1809, pp. 24-40.*

THE LONDON REVIEW   (essay date 1809)

[*Using Barlow's preface to* The Columbiad *(see excerpt dated 1807) as a guide for evaluating the poem, this anonymous critic censures the organization, language, imagery, rhyme, and various other facets of the work.*]

Mr. Barlow informs us, in his preface [to *The Columbiad*], that he "will not attempt to prove, by any latitude of reasoning, that he has written an epic poem;" and that "circumstances of classical regularity are of little consideration, in estimating the real merit of any work of this nature."

Its merit (he says) must depend on the importance of the action; the disposition of the parts; the invention and application of incidents; the propriety of the illustrations; the liveliness and chastity of the images; the suitable intervention of machinery; the moral tendency of the manners; the strength and sublimity of the sentiments: the whole being clothed in language, whose energy, harmony, and elegance, shall constitute a style every where suited to the matter they have to treat.

(p. 306)

Judging . . . of Mr. Barlow's design and execution [in *The Columbiad*] by the criteria which he has himself selected, we are by no means inclined to congratulate him on his success. In our opinion, "the action" is unimportant; the "disposition of the parts" inartificial; "the application of incidents" unhappy; the "moral tendency of the manners" pernicious; and the "intervention of machinery" inappropriate. . . . [We now] enquire how far these defects are counterbalanced by the propriety of the illustrations, the liveliness of the images, or the purity and elegance of the language.

His comparisons have neither the beauty of a simile, nor the clearness of an illustration. As Achilles fought with Hector, so does an American hero with an English bully; as the sands of the Scamander glided beneath the steps of the nimble-footed Grecian, so do the sands of the western ocean beneath the march of the British infantry; and as the Nile descends from his parent heaven, so descends the roaring Napo from the misty sky. It is evident that these comparisons do not ennoble; and it is still more evident that they cannot illustrate. When we are told, that the Rhine "rolls on its course majestic" like the Danube, the comparison is not intelligible to those who have seen neither of those rivers: and the language of poetry ought to be universal.

His personifications are generally incorrect, and his metaphors confused. In the first of the following lines, sire Ocean is a venerable personage, and in the second, he seeks in vain the shore; but when he is described as moving up his bed, and "surging strong with high and hoary tide," he loses at once his metaphorical identity.

> Sire Ocean hears his proud Maragnon roar,
> Moves up his bed, and seeks in vain the shore;
> Then surging strong with high and hoary tide,
> Whelms back the stream, and checks his rolling
>   pride:
> The stream ungovernable foams with ire,
> Climbs, combs tempestuous, and attacks the sire.

His attempts at philosophy are not distinguished by precision or ingenuity: he enunciates the most hacknied truisms with all the pomposity of an original discoverer, and degrades the most simple and important truths by the redundant inflation of his diction: the correctness of his positions is not, however, always in proportion to their vulgarity. He is a perfect master of the jargon of democracy; and his most shining passages are mere versifications of the senseless rhapsodies of the early Jacobins. (pp. 311-12)

It now . . . remains for us to inquire how far he deserves the praise of having "cloathed his sentiments in language whose energy, harmony, and elegance shall constitute a style every where suited to the subject he had to treat;" and as this is a point on which he seems to be secure of critical approbation, we shall examine it with particular minuteness.

The chief fault of Mr. Barlow's style is a cloudy indistinctness of expression, through the medium of which the images that he endeavours to convey to the imagination, are dimly and inaccurately definable. We can only collect a few faint traces of his meaning, as the traveller recognizes the outlines of a well known landscape, through the haziness of a fog, by previous acquaintance with the scenery before him. (p. 313)

He is totally deficient in that intuitive perception of the lighter shades of synonomic gradation, which enables a poet to embody the untangible emanations of thought, and to give force and distinctness to the evanescent graces of metaphysical association. From many words agreeing in one general proximity of meaning, but distinguished from each other by those minuter shades of difference, on which depends all felicity of expression; he seems to have no other principle of selection, than such as was dictated by the cadence of his verse. For example, in the ensuing quotation, he wishes to describe the grief of Columbus at beholding the deplorable consequences that result from his discoveries—*compassionate* would probably have been the proper epithet; but, compassionate would not glide into verse, and Mr. Barlow remembering that the tender were generally compassionate; either concludes, or finds it convenient to conclude, that the converse must be true. He therefore applies to the brave, the noble, and the generous Columbus, an epithet which an English writer would only have conferred on the love-sick heroine of a novel;—

> While sorrows thus his patriarch pride control,
> Hesper reproving, soothes his *tender* soul.

Again—

> Her locks loose rolling mantle deep her breast,
> And wave luxuriant round her *tender* waist.

(pp. 313-14)

The next great characteristic of his style, is an eternal and invincible monotony. This defect is principally occasioned by a perverse propensity towards the balancing of his epithets. The noun that is governed, is always accommodated with an attendant adjective to proclaim its equality with the noun that governs. If the one be splendid, orient, and divine, the other must be glorious, occidental, and sublime. If the first two feet of a verse be big with the roar of "sounding waves," the fourth and fifth must glitter with the brilliance of "resplendent zones." From the first half of the line we can easily anticipate its conclusion; and the reader who is once accustomed to the dull uniformity of sing-song modulation, occasioned by this peculiarity of structure, proceeds to the continuation of his task in hopeless listlessness: neither exhilarated by the variation, nor captivated by the sweetness of his harmony. (pp. 314-15)

The languid insipidity of his verse is considerably aggravated by the *uniformity and incorrectness* of his rhymes. [It] happens, indeed, that those which recur most frequently, [are] the most inaccurate. Nothing can be more discreditable to a poet, or more fatiguing to the reader, than the continual repetition of couplets, in which the second line may be guessed from the ending of the first. It shews at once frigidity of thought, and barrenness of language, and deprives a writer of all claim to the vigour of genius, or the grace of art. (pp. 315-16)

That there are some passages [in *The Columbiad*] which prove Mr. Barlow not to be deficient in learning, or ability, we are willing to confess: but his happiest efforts neither please by their felicity, nor astonish by their brilliance. The stream of his verse is always muddy, or interrupted; it never glides along in tranquil clearness; nor "rushes impetuous down" in a torrent of unpremeditated melody. His lighter productions are without the simplicity of nature, or the elegance of art; and his loftier flights rather resemble the tiptoe flutterings of the ostrich, than the towering and adventurous soarings of the Maeonian eagle. If a correct ear and an intimate acquaintance with English literature, animated by an anxious desire for literary fame, and an enthusiastic attachment to the political institutions of his country, could atone for the higher qualities of taste and genius; Mr. Barlow might claim preeminence over all the poets who have preceded him. But deficient in their higher, and necessary qualities, the talents that he really possesses have been warped, and degraded by political prejudices and the disadvantages of local situation. Instead of filling a nich by the side of those great masters of heroic poetry, whose excellencies he has vainly essayed to emulate, he now only stands distinguished as a melancholy monument of talents misapplied; and as a friendly beacon to those whom vanity, or ignorance might seduce to enter the irremeable paths of poetical ambition. (pp. 318-19)

A review of "The Columbiad: A Poem," in The London Review, *No. IV, November, 1809, pp. 294-323.*

THE ANALECTIC MAGAZINE   (essay date 1814)

[*In the following excerpt, the critic assesses the merit of Barlow's prose and poetry, focusing on his use of language and imagery in* The Columbiad.]

All of Barlow's prose writings bear the stamp of an active, acute, and powerful mind, confident in its own strength, and accustomed to great intrepidity of opinion. His political and moral speculations are often original, always ingenious, but deficient in those comprehensive views and that ripeness of judgment, which are required by the complex nature of the subjects he examines. He surveys accurately what is before him, but rarely casts his eye over the wide surface of society to trace the mutual bearing and relation of its several parts. He has no reverence for authority, and little fear of ridicule; hence he sometimes wanders into wild extravagance of theory.

In those confident anticipations of the future improvement of society, and the progress of the human race towards virtue and happiness, which pervade all his writings, he undoubtedly attributes by far too much to political, and too little to moral causes. But the principle itself is a generous one, and I trust well founded. It has been disgraced and exposed to shallow ridicule, by being connected with the unholy dreams of Godwin. But better, far better, are the wildest absurdities founded on this hope, than that cold-blooded scepticism, which would teach us to look with heartless indifference upon the future prospects of our kind. Let us rather hold, with Dugald Stewart, that, "as in ancient Rome, it was regarded as the mark of a good citizen never to despair of the fortunes of the republic; so the good citizen of the world, whatever may be the political aspect of his own times, will never despair of the fortunes of the human race; but will act upon the conviction, that prejudice, slavery, and corruption, must gradually give way to truth, liberty, and virtue."

Throughout all Barlow's speculations, as soon as the first fer-

vour of French democracy had gone over, he rested his hopes chiefly upon the extension of the federal system, united with representative democracy, a frame of government which he justly terms "a magnificent stranger upon earth." It is the first and most vigorous offspring of the genius of our own country. It is now the hope of the world, and may hereafter become its example.

Barlow's prose style is perspicuous and forcible, without native grace, and with little elaborate elegance; much better fitted for didactic composition than for popular effect. But it was on his poetry that Barlow rested his chief claim to literary reputation. *The Columbiad* was the work of half his life, conceived and planned in the ardour of youth, and corrected, polished, and enlarged after his mind had been aroused and invigorated by an extended acquaintance with various forms of nature, with books, and with men. This poem has a radical defect of plan, which it would have been difficult for any degree of poetical genius to have completely overcome. It is the narrative of a vision and a dialogue, continued through ten cantos, and nearly 7,000 lines. Its time of action extends from a remote period of antiquity to distant futurity, and the scene shifts, with the rapidity of a pantomime, from one part of the globe to another. It has no regularly connected narrative, or series of action, by which characters might be developed, interest excited, and the attention kept alive.

Besides, the constant mixture of real and familiar history with allegory and fiction, is a combination utterly destructive of that temporary illusion by which we are led to interest ourselves in the adventures of an epic hero. Thus the effect of this poem upon the mind is like that of a bird's-eye view of an extensive prospect upon the eye; it is half map and half picture; a thousand objects are seen, but nothing vividly; every single part is too unimportant to fix the attention, yet there is no point of union to connect them together.

Even were these defects removed, Barlow could not be ranked in the first class of poets. His conceptions were vivid, and his mind was stored with knowledge; but he had no luxuriance of fancy, no grace of expression, nor delicacy of taste, and, above all, he was deficient in that indescribable power of touching the feelings, and exciting the imagination of the reader, without which all poetry, however elegant or sonorous, is but *as sounding brass, or a tinkling cymbal.* His verses bear no signs of poetical inspiration; it is evident that they have all been worked out by dint of resolute labour. All the offspring of his imagination have something gross and material about them; and in straining after sublimity he works himself up into a cold-blooded extravagance, which fills his pages with noise and tumult, with frigid personifications and gigantic hyperboles, and all those false and inflated figures. . . . The threatening harangue of Atlas, the combat of the "flouncing godhead of the river Delaware," aided by "almighty Frost," against Washington's army, and another between the Amazon and his sire, old Ocean, are all curious specimens of this corrupted taste.

He is most happy in philosophical discussion and moral declamation, in which his elevation of sentiment successfully supplies the place of spirit and animation; and in some of his descriptions, where, by an elaborate assemblage of images, he produces an air of magnificence, which is yet rather gorgeous than grand.

Barlow's taste, in style and versification, was originally formed upon the poetry of Pope and Goldsmith, and his *Vi-*

sion of Columbus is a pretty successful imitation of their manner; but he was afterwards strongly smitten with the gaudy ornaments, the flaunting finery, and all the harlotry of the muse of Darwin.

His description of southern scenery may be selected as a pleasing specimen of his first and best manner.

> Beneath tall trees in livelier verdure gay,
> Long level walks a humble garb display;
> The infant corn, unconscious of its worth,
> Points the green spire, and bends the foliage forth;
> Sweetened on flowery banks, the passing air
> Breathes all the untasted fragrance of the year;
> Unbidden harvests o'er the regions rise,
> And blooming life repays the genial skies.
> Where circling shores around the gulf extend,
> The bounteous groves with richer burdens bend;
> Spontaneous fruits the uplifted palms unfold,
> The beauteous orange waves a load of gold;
> The untaught vine, the wildly wanton cane,
> Bloom on the waste, and clothe the enarbour'd
>   plain;
> The rich pimento scents the neighbouring skies,
> And woolly clusters o'er the cotton rise.
> Here, in one view, the same glad branches bring
> The fruits of autumn, and the flowers of spring;
> No wintry blasts the unchanging year deform,
> Nor beasts unsheltered fear the pinching storm;
> But vernal breezes o'er the blossoms rove,
> And breathe the ripen'd juices through the grove.
> Beneath the crystal wave's inconstant light,
> Pearls undistinguished sparkle on the sight, &c.

It is difficult to conceive how a poet, who had once written thus, should have afterwards so vitiated his taste as to delight in language and imagery like those of the following lines, which are chosen, at random, from among many passages in the same taste.

> So the contristed Lawrence lays him low,
> And hills of sleet, and continents of snow
> Rise on his crystal breast, his heaving sides
> Crash with the weight, and pour their gushing tides
> Asouth, whence all his hundred branches bend,
> Relenting airs with boreal blasts contend;
> Far in his vast extremes, he swells and thaws,
> And seas foam wide between his ice-bound jaws.
> Indignant Frost, to hold his captive, plies
> His hosted fiends, that vex the polar skies,
> Unlocks his magazines of nitric stores,
> Azotic charms and muriatic powers;
> Hail with its glassy globes, and brume congeal'd,
> Rime's fleecy flakes, and storm that heaps the field,
> Strike through the sullen stream with numbing
>   force,
> Obstruct his sluices, and impede his course.
> He calls his hoary sire; old Ocean roars
> Responsive echo, through the Shetland shores,
> He comes the father! from his bleak domains
> To break with liquid arms the sounding chains
> Clothed in white majesty, &c. &c.

This "hoar fiend" of Frost, who "robes in muriat flakes his nitrous form," is a favorite personage with our poet. I do not know whether he produces the same effect on others, but, in my mind, he is always associated with the idea of that goblin fiend of the nursery, little Jack Frost, with whose exploits we are all made familiar in our childhood. The poet who deals much in these bold allegories, should be extremely careful to avoid the danger of such ludicrous associations.

In some couplets the peculiarities of the Darwinian manner are carried to still greater extravagance: for instance—

> Prometheus came, and from the floods of day,
> Sunn'd his clear soul with heaven's internal ray;
> Th' expanding spark divine that round him springs,
> And leads, and lights him through the immense of
>   things,
> Probes the dense earth, explores the soundless
>   main,
> Remoulds their mass through all their threefold
>   reign,
> O'er great, o'er small, extends his physic laws,
> Empalms the empyrean, or dissects a gaz,
> Weighs the vast orbs of heaven, bestrides the sky,
> Walks on the windows of an insect's eye—

His language is debased by the two opposite faults of gross colloquial vulgarism and of pedantic innovation, both rendered more remarkable by their contrast with many passages of great purity and elegance. His new words are not necessary, and very uncouth, such as *cosmogyre, cosmogyral, fluvial, ludibrious, croupe, brume, gerb, colon, coloniarch, numen, emban, contristed, asouth,* and many more.

Faults numerous and offensive as those which I have noticed, would have at once sunk the work of any inferior mind into utter contempt; but Barlow has great power of thought and amplitude of knowledge, and on certain topics displays a grave and philosophical enthusiasm, which for a time makes us forget the want of poetical fire. He is certainly entitled to rank above the greater number of the writers who fill up the huge collections of the British Poets. Though his poem can never rise to extensive popularity it will not sink into oblivion; his verses will not live in the memory, but they may long keep a respectable station in our libraries.

> A mortal born, he meets the general doom,
> But leaves, like Egypt's kings, a lasting tomb.

It is, I think, much to be regretted that, by some unaccountable blindness to the character of his own genius, he thus turned the powers of his vigorous mind into a direction so unfortunate for his literary reputation. There is scarcely any species of intellectual exertion in which he would not have been, beyond comparison, more successful than in that to which so great a part of his life was devoted. Had he applied the same labour to his contemplated history of America, there can be little doubt but that he would have produced one of the most valuable histories of modern times. Or, had he applied himself with the same ardour and indefatigable industry to some course of investigation in legislation or political economy, though he might have been led astray from sober truth by the love of system or of novelty, yet he would have opened so many new views, he would have struck out so many original thoughts that his name could not have failed to go down to posterity in honourable association with those of Bentham, of Malthus, and of Brougham.

Even considering his works as they are, and not as they might have been, he must be considered as a man of whom his country has reason to be proud. He was not, indeed, our Homer; nor am I at all inclined to risk our whole literary reputation on his ***Columbiad.*** His genius was not a luminary which could singly fill our hemisphere with its radiance; but happy the nation which can boast of many such minds. They are given to bless and to cheer—each one singly may shine with fitful and uncertain lustre, but where they are clustered in constellations, they pour a broad stream of light and glory over the land. (pp. 152-58)

*"Sketch of the Life and Writings of Joel Barlow,"
in* The Analectic Magazine, *Vol. 4, August, 1814,
pp. 130-58.*

SAMUEL KETTELL   (essay date 1829)

[*An American author and editor, Kettell is chiefly remembered
for his* Specimens of American Poetry, with Critical and Biographical Notices *(1829), compiled in answer to the question
"Who reads an American book?" In the following excerpt from
this work, he provides a survey of Barlow's poetry, concentrating on the subject matter, versification, and language of* The
Columbiad.]

Barlow, as a poet, can by no means be allowed the highest
rank among his countrymen, even those of his own day; yet
he has drawn upon himself by the publicity of his career, and
the efforts he made for that purpose, a greater degree of notice, than any other of our native bards. To the European
world, Barlow was the only transatlantic poet. The witlings
of the British periodical press pointed their gibes at our literature in the person of this single writer, and regarded the *Columbiad* as the sum total of American genius in the shape of
verse. A better standard of taste has now lowered the estimation of his powers among us, and it is no longer fashionable
to consider the literary reputation of the country as resting
upon his attempt at epic poetry. Still, the talents which he has
unquestionably displayed in his writings, entitle him to no
small share of our attention.

The Conspiracy of Kings is a vehement invective against the
potentates of Europe, and the enemies of the French revolution. In this piece, he expatiates upon the common topics of
the writers in the same cause, with great warmth and spirit.
It is a good specimen of animated, vigorous declamation.

The Hasty Pudding will probably retain a greater share of
popularity than any other portion of his works. This poem
is executed in a lively and entertaining manner, and affords
in the familiar and homely nature of the subject, and the gaiety with which it is treated, an agreeable contrast to the gravity and stateliness of the author's general style.

The *Columbiad* has met with small favor from the critics, and
its faults, both in plan and execution, were severely commented upon at its first appearance. The absurdity of attempting
to give an epic unity and interest through the medium of a
vision, to a series of actions so unconnected in date and subject: and the strange and awkward neologisms by which the
language of the poem is disfigured, called forth the reprehensions of the reviewers in every quarter. It had no popularity
among us, and is now fallen quite into neglect,—a fate which
the reader may ascribe to the improved taste and understanding in literary matters, of the present day, but which was in
part occasioned by the higher character which the poem assumed over the work as it stood in its original state. *The Vision of Columbus,* while no one claimed for it any very exalted rank, continued to be spoken of in terms of respect. But
in its new shape it came out with the high pretensions of an
epic, and having been pronounced a failure, nobody reads it.

In his preface he avows the object of the *Columbiad* to be altogether of a moral and political nature. Most epic poems are
regarded as having some similar aim. They were designed to
leave some more important and durable impression than

what arises from contemplating the interest of the story or
the beauty of the language. We are led to conclude, however,
from Barlow's explanation of his plan, that he considered
more the philosophy than the poetry of his work; that he was
less solicitous for the classical regularity and interest of the
fable, than for the general sentiments and moral effect of the
performance, forgetting that without a proper degree of skill
in arranging the narrative which was to be the vehicle of the
sentiments, they must fail of accomplishing their object. It is
surprising that Barlow's judgment should have allowed him
to imagine that to render his poem perfectly national in character, it was necessary that it should embrace the history and
topography, as it were, of the whole American continent; or
that he could have hoped to excite interest by a story which
extended through hundreds of years; which treated of Manco
Capac and Washington, described the conquest of Mexico,
and the battle of Bunker Hill; and contained long philosophical speculations upon almost every subject—political, moral,
and scientific. How utterly he has failed in this particular we
need waste no criticism in showing. His notions of what was
requisite to give the epic dignity to his performance seem to
have embraced the most objectionable part of the old doctrines upon the subject with ideas of his own altogether novel.
The machinery which he deemed it necessary to introduce,
accomplishes hardly anything of its destined purpose in controlling the main events, or bringing about the catastrophe of
the story; and the topics which he had occasion to handle offered such a temptation to speculate, descant, and moralize,
that the quantity of matter in a digressory strain which he has
embodied in the work, gives it the character in some parts of
a philosophical instead of a narrative poem, a defect of plan
which the highest graces of composition could hardly redeem.

The versification in this poem is elaborated with great care,
but it is not flowing nor graceful. The language is often tumid,
and extravagant, and disfigured with ornaments which de-
note a vitiated taste. There is throughout a want of imagination, fire, and the marks of that inbred faculty of the soul, that
refined intellectual feeling which pours out its energies with
a fervor that reaches the heart. Barlow was a poet by dint of
study and labor; but in the creations which his fancy has bodied forth, we seek in vain for the breathings of that spirit of
unearthly tone, which act like a spell upon the senses, whose
visitings thrill the bosom in its deepest and most hallowed recesses, stir our sympathies with a magic potency, and stamp
the memory with a deep and abiding impression.

His powers were inadequate to the accomplishment of the undertaking which he meditated in the *Columbiad.* The poem
cannot be commended as a whole, but there are portions of
it which exhibit the author's talent in a very favorable manner. It has many passages of spirited, rich, and splendid description: and in expatiating in a moral and philosophical
strain, he displays a loftiness of sentiment, and an enthusiasm, which inspire noble thoughts and kindle some of our
most exalted emotions. The moral scope of the work, in spite
of its miscarriage as an epic, will recommend it to our regard
as the earnest endeavor of a sincere philanthropist to further
the progress of the human race in their advances to political
and moral perfection. (pp. 10-13)

Samuel Kettell, "Joel Barlow," in his Specimens of
American Poetry, with Critical and Biographical
Notices, *Vol. II, S. G. Goodrich and Co., 1829, pp.
1-13.*

REV. CHARLES W. EVEREST   (essay date 1843)

[*In his brief assessment of* The Columbiad, *Everest outlines the work's literary shortcomings while praising its patriotic sentiments.*]

While every praise is due to the author for the patriotic spirit which his poem displays, and while it abounds with many passages of beauty and eloquence, and is generally faultless in harmonious versification, yet *The Columbiad,* as an epic, has been generally deemed a failure. The author himself seems aware of the chief difficulty attendant upon his design. He states in his preface that "most of the events were so recent, so important, and so well known, as to render them inflexible to the hand of fiction; and that therefore the poem could not with propriety be modelled after that regular epic form which the more splendid works of this kind have taken, and on which their success is supposed in a great measure to depend." Thus *The Columbiad* possesses no unity of fable—but its story, if such it may be called, is a mere narration of facts extending through a long period of years, and embracing the history of the whole continent. In a word, the poem is but a poetical history.

The Columbiad was noticed by the leading journals of the day, both in this country and in Europe; but generally with little praise. While its want of unity was strikingly apparent, it was also justly deemed to be rather a work of laborious art than of imaginative power, and to be sometimes extravagant in its language. The execution fell below the conception; but to have conceived such a work, and attempted it, not wholly without success, is an honor beyond the reach of many far more popular writers. Barlow possessed the mind of a sage, and the ear of an accomplished versifier, but not the eye of a poet. All his descriptions are general, and his imagery falls into a kind of habitual mould, which is quite too vague and abstract. But the merit of large views and noble sentiments belongs eminently to his Muse; and, although too much of the Frenchman of that day had found its way into his speculations, yet they cannot be read without leaving the impression of a certain patriotic grandeur of idea, worthy of the first days of our republic. (pp. 79-80)

> *Rev. Charles W. Everest, "Joel Barlow," in* The Poets of Connecticut; with Biographical Sketches, *edited by Rev. Charles W. Everest, 1843. Reprint by Barnes & Burr, Publishers, 1864, pp. 73-81.*

THE ATLANTIC MONTHLY   (essay date 1886)

[*In this excerpt from a review of the first full-length biography of Barlow by Charles Burr Todd (see Additional Bibliography), the critic evaluates Barlow's works and his place in American literature.*]

Barlow's public life, although very creditable, was neither long continued nor important in results. He is chiefly interesting to-day as a rather striking figure in the society of the time and in our literary history. His contributions to literature have in themselves no particular merit. He wrote some vigorous controversial papers, and was master of a pleasant prose style, but his pamphlets have retired to the store-houses of history, and are read only by students. It was to verse, however, not to prose, that he looked for fame and remembrance. He regarded himself as a great poet, and as such wished to be held in recollection; but his poetry is unread and forgotten. It is not surprising that he felt as he did, for he had a lofty idea of his own importance, and indeed of his greatness in all respects, which crops out in his letters with a most amusing frankness. With such a disposition, it was a matter of course that he should place a high value on his performances, which were extolled both at home and abroad, in a way which it is difficult now to understand. Mr. Todd says that the *Vision of Columbus* met with high favor at the hands of the "Parisian *raconteurs,*" which is no doubt true, although we cannot conjecture how their opinion was obtained, or why they should be selected by Mr. Todd as the literary arbiters of the day. It is at all events certain that Barlow's poems were widely read and extravagantly praised on both sides of the water. This arose, in the one case, probably, because we then had nothing that could be called either literature or poetry; and in the other, because Europe regarded an American poet as Swift did the parrot: "The bird does not talk well; the wonder is that he talks at all."

Barlow was not a poet. He wrote graceful verses with much facility, but they have neither imagination nor originality. *The Columbiad,* which belongs to the school of Pope in its extreme decadence, is a dreary, didactic poem, written according to a set plan previously drawn up, like a lawyer's brief. An early poem, written to celebrate Burgoyne's defeat, is a pale reflection of Dryden. His *Hasty Pudding,* the best of his more ambitious poems, is a mock heroic of Pope's school also, and is not without merit. But all alike are echoes, more or less distinct, of the work of other men acting on a quick and impressionable mind. Some short, occasional poems are really the best things Barlow ever wrote, and have both ease and grace. The chief value of his work, and of that of the little literary coterie at Hartford to which he belonged, lies in the fact that it forms a starting-point in the development of our national literature. The historian and the collector will read the *Columbiad,*—the former in the way of business, and the latter because he loves handsome folios; but no one else will wade through those heavy lines.

In this way, as an early figure in our literary history, Barlow has a claim upon us; but he has a much stronger claim as a witty and cultivated man of the world, an agreeable letter-writer, and a successful and bold diplomatist during the brief time that he held office. . . . [His] life well deserved writing, and after all deductions are made a very real debt of gratitude is due to Mr. Todd for a spirited biography, and for well-chosen selections from the interesting material at his disposal. (pp. 278-79)

> *"Joel Barlow," in* The Atlantic Monthly, *Vol. LVIII, No. CCCXLVI, August, 1886, pp. 275-79.*

MOSES COIT TYLER   (essay date 1895)

[*An American teacher, minister, and literary historian, Tyler was one of the first critics to adopt a scholarly approach to the study of American literature. His* History of American Literature during the Colonial Time: 1607-1765 *(1878) and* The Literary History of the American Revolution: 1763-1783 *(1897) are examples of his methodical research, authoritative style, and keen insight. In the following excerpt, Tyler compares* The Columbiad *with* The Vision of Columbus, *detailing the strengths and weaknesses of the two versions of the poem.*]

However great may be the faults to be found with the execution of [*The Columbiad*], it is hardly possible to deny that its idea, at any rate, is both poetic and noble; it is to connect, in a work of high imaginative literature, all that is beneficent and soul-stirring in the aggregate contribution made by America to the general stock of the world's welfare, with all that is heroic and pathetic in the career of him, the undismayed idealist, the saint, the admiral of boundless faith and sorrow, who made America known to the rest of the world.

Barlow's earlier and less ambitious project for his poem, as seen in his draft written in 1779, was the wiser one: "The poem will be rather of the philosophic than epic kind" [see Charles Burr Todd, *Life and Letters of Joel Barlow,* in Additional Bibliography]. Even eight years afterward, at the time of its first publication, he still saw that, as the stupendous consequences of the discovery of America could be represented to Columbus only in vision, so such representation would be likely to produce, not a real story, but merely a succession of scenes painted on the air, too impalpable and flitting, as well as too disconnected, for the purposes of an epic. No title for the poem, therefore, could have been better than its first title, *The Vision of Columbus;* because, being perfectly accurate, it was also quite unpretentious, and involved no hazards by a challenge which might result in discomfiture and derision. Unfortunately, in his final reconstruction of the poem, this sane thought seems to have yielded to the cravings of an inordinate literary ambition; and by the new title which he gave to his work, and by its new prelude, and by its new supernatural machinery of river gods and other clumsy and incongruous imitations of Homer and Virgil, he claimed for his poem the awful honors of an epic, and thereby invoked upon it literary comparisons and critical tests which it could not endure. Nay, it may perhaps be said, that the very pomp and opulence of typographical costume which attended its re-entrance into the world, its grandiose and too prosperous equipment, even its physical magnitude—its arrogant and preposterous bigness, as a mere book,—all had the effect of averting sympathy and of inviting scorn, as though it were an attempt by mere bulk and bravado and good clothes to overawe the sentinels who guard the approaches to Parnassus.

Better would it have been, both for the poem and for the poet, if, in his later revision of the work, he had attempted no change in its essential character. A philosophical poem exhibiting, under the device of a vision seen by the discoverer of America, the vast and benign function assigned to the New World in the development of mankind, might have deserved and received in our literature the homage at least of serious consideration. Of course, never upon any plan could the poem have taken rank as a work of genius, or have escaped the penalties of the author's great literary defects. Under any character, it would have had no tender or delicate qualities, no lightness of touch, no flashes of beauty, not a ripple of humor, no quiet and dainty charm; a surfeit, rather, of vehemence and proclamation,—sonorous, metallic, rhetorical; forced description, manufactured sentiment, sublimity generated of pasteboard and starch; an ever-rolling tattoo of declamation, invective, eulogy; big, gaudy flowers of poetry which are also flowers of wax. Moreover, not even genius could have saved this poem from the literary disaster involved in its adoption of that conventional poetic diction and of that worn-out metrical form from which, after a whole century of favor, English literature was just then turning away in a recoil of weariness and disgust.

And yet, with all his limitations as a poet, the author of *The Columbiad* is entitled to the praise due to a sturdy and effective ethical teacher in verse. In didactic expression, the poem is often epigrammatic, trenchant, and strong; nay, in strenuous moral exposition and enforcement, it is at times even noble and impressive. Everywhere is the author faithful to the great object of his poem, namely, "to inculcate the love of rational liberty, and to discountenance the deleterious passion for violence and war; to show that on the basis of the republican principle all good morals, as well as good government and hopes of permanent peace, must be founded; and to convince the student in political science that the theoretical question of the future advancement of human society . . . is held in dispute and still unsettled only because we have had too little experience of organized liberty in the government of nations, to have well considered its effects" [see excerpt dated 1807]. Everywhere in the poem one finds an invincible hope for human liberty, for the victories of reason, for the ultimate conquest of moral evil in the world. It represents, too, the manifold intellectual aspirations of the time in which he lived, its scientific progress, its mechanical ingenuity and daring, its wish to reject all degrading forms of faith, the unquenchable confidence of human nature in the final and happy solution of all those problems that then pained the earth with their unutterable menace. Finally, there breathes through the poem the most genuine love of country. In the eyes of this writer America is, by favor of Heaven, the superior land of all the earth. His love for America is something more than a clannish instinct, something better than the mere greed of provincialism; and this huge political and philosophical essay in verse, the writing of which formed the one real business of Barlow's life, may be accepted by us, whether we are proud of the fact or not, as an involuntary expression, for that period, of the American national consciousness and even of the American national character itself, as sincere, and as unflinching as were, in their different ways, the renowned state-paper of Jefferson, the constitution of 1789, and Washington's farewell address. (pp. 165-70)

> *Moses Coit Tyler, "The Literary Strivings of Mr. Joel Barlow," in his* Three Men of Letters, *G. P. Putnam's Sons, 1895, pp. 131-80.*

VERNON LOUIS PARRINGTON   (essay date 1927)

[*An American historian, biographer, and critic, Parrington is best known for his unfinished literary history of the United States,* Main Currents in American Thought *(1927-30). Written from the point of view of a Jeffersonian liberal, Parrington's work is considered a significant first attempt at fashioning an intellectual history of America based on a broad interpretive thesis. In the following excerpt from* Main Currents, *Parrington investigates Barlow's political ideology as expressed in his prose and poetry.*]

That he should have long associated with the Hartford Wits and collaborated with them in defense of Connecticut Federalism must have seemed to Joel Barlow in after years the choicest bit of comedy in his varied career. His subsequent adventures led him far from the strait path of Yale orthodoxy. In those ripe later years life had pretty well emptied him of all dogmatisms and taught him the virtue of catholic sympathies. He had become acquainted with diverse philosophies and had observed the ways of alien societies, and from such contacts the horizons of his mind had broadened and his character mellowed. It was a long road that he traveled from New Haven to his Washington salon. Born a Connecticut Yankee, he accepted in his youth all the Connecticut conventions, and graduated from Yale with as complete a stock of

THE

COLUMBIAD.

A Poem,

WITH

THE LAST CORRECTIONS OF THE AUTHOR.

BY JOEL BARLOW.

Tu spiegherai, Colombo, a un novo polo
Lontane si le fortunate antenne,
Ch'a pena seguira con gli occhi il volo
La Fama, ch' ha mille occhi e mille penne.
Canti ella Alcide, e Bacco; e di te solo
Basti a i posteri tuoi, ch' alquanto accennet
Che quel poco dara lunga memoria
Di poema degnissima, e d'istoria.

GREUOI. Lib. Can. xv.

WASHINGTON CITY:
PUBLISHED BY JOSEPH MILLIGAN, GEORGETOWN.
JUNE 1, 1825.

Title page from the American revised edition of The Columbiad.

respectable opinions as his classmate Noah Webster. An energetic capable fellow, he wanted to get on in life. He wanted to be rich and famous, and he tried many roads that promised to lead to that desirable goal—law, politics, journalism, poetry, psalmody, speculation. Needing a job he volunteered soon after graduation as chaplain in the army. He had not prepared for the ministry and while preaching somewhat indifferently to ragged soldiers he dreamed of poetic fame, and devoted more time to his couplets than to pious meditation. His abilities discovering no more profitable field for exercise than writing verse, he was pretty much at a stand till chance sent him abroad as agent for one of the speculative land-companies that were springing up like mushrooms in post-war America. There he found his opportunity. In France, where he established his headquarters, he entered a world of thought vastly different from that of prim little Hartford. It was an extraordinarily stimulating experience into which he threw himself with zest. Seventeen years, from 1788 to 1805, he spent abroad on that first visit, and those years changed the provincial Yankee into one of the most cosmopolitan Americans of his generation. From a member of the Hartford Wits, ardent in defense of the traditional Connecticut order, he had become a citizen of the world, outspoken in defense of the rights of man.

It was this later Barlow, completely new-outfitted by French

romantic tailors, that after years remember and that early friends could not forgive. In adopting the Jacobin mode and setting himself to the serious business of political thinking, he invited the caustic criticism of his former associates; yet nothing in his life was more creditable or marks him more definitely as an openminded, intelligent man. He was as receptive to new ideas as Timothy Dwight was impervious. He plunged boldly into the maelstrom of speculation then boiling in Europe. He moved in the society of the intellectuals, inquired into the latest political and social theories, turned humanitarian, reëxamined his Calvinistic theology in the light of current deism, and became one of the free democratic thinkers swarming in every European capital. He was equally at home in London and Paris, passing long periods of time in both cities. An active member of the Constitutional Society of London, he was intimate with Joseph Priestley, Horne Tooke, and Tom Paine, sympathized with every liberal movement, and offered his pen to the cause of a freer England. His *Advice to the Privileged Orders* was eulogized by Fox on the floor of Commons, and the Pitt ministry was moved to suppress the work and proscribe the author. Thereupon Barlow went into hiding. There seems to have been considerable provocation for the government's action. "It is safe to say," remarks his biographer, "that no political work of the day created so wide an interest or was so extensively read." With Paine and Barlow both loose in England there was need of the government looking to its fences. (pp. 387-89)

The later reputation of Barlow has been far less than his services warranted or his solid merits deserved. His admirable prose writings have been forgotten and the *Columbiad* returns always to plague him. The common detraction of all Jacobins and democrats fell heavily on so conspicuous a head. "It is simply impossible," says his biographer, "for the historian of Federal proclivities and environment to do justice to the great leaders of Republicanism in America." Barlow was forced to pay a heavy price for his intellectual independence. Detraction was always lying in wait for him. John Adams, who had suffered many a sharp thrust from him, wrote to Washington, "Tom Paine is not a more worthless fellow." Of the Yale dislike Barlow was well aware, for he once confessed that he would have presented the school with some needed chemical apparatus but he "supposed that, coming from him, the college authorities would make a bonfire of them in the college yard." Yet it is hard for a later generation to discover wherein lay the viciousness of his life or principles. A warmhearted humanitarian, he was concerned always for the common well-being. The two major passions of his life were freedom and education. During the last years at Washington he was ardently promoting a plan for a great national university at the seat of government, and had he lived ten years longer his wide influence would probably have accomplished it. His sins would seem to have been no other than an open break with the Calvinism and Federalism of the Connecticut oligarchy—somewhat slender grounds on which to pillory him as an infidel and a scalawag.

The social foundation of Barlow's political philosophy is lucidly presented in the *Advice to the Privileged Orders,* a work that deserves a place beside Paine's *Rights of Man* as a great document of the times. It does too much credit to American letters to be suffered to lie buried with a dead partisanship. It is warm with the humanitarian enthusiasm that had come down as a rich heritage from the Physiocratic school of social thinkers. Two suggestive ideas lie at the base of his speculations: the doctrine of the *res publica,* and the doctrine of social responsibility for individual well-being. The former, given wide currency by the *Rights of Man,* resulted from the imposition of social conscience on abstract political theory, out of which was derived a new conception of the duties and functions of the political state—the conception that the state must be the responsible agent of society as a whole rather than the tool of a class, and that its true concern is the *public thing,* safeguarding the social heritage as a common asset held in trust for succeeding generations; the latter resulted from the inquiry into the relations of the political state to the individual citizen—its responsibility as the social agent, for the social waste of wrecked lives and thwarted happiness, a waste that a rational social order would greatly lessen if not eradicate. Barlow flatly denied that the primary function of the state is the protection of property interests; its true end lies in securing justice. But justice without equal opportunity is a mockery; and equal opportunity is impossible unless the individual citizen shall be equipped to live on equal terms with his fellows. Hence the fine flower of political justice is discovered in education; in that generous provision for the young and the weak that shall equip them to become free members of the commonwealth. Like Paine's *Agrarian Justice,* the **Advice to the Privileged Orders** is an extraordinarily modern work, far more comprehensible today than when it was written. That the "State has no right to punish a man, to whom it has given no previous instruction," and that "She ought not only to instruct him in the artificial laws by which property is secured, but in the artificial industry by which it is obtained," are doctrines that seem far less preposterous to us than they seemed to Timothy Dwight. The president of Yale College was greatly troubled over Calvinistic sin; Joel Barlow was greatly troubled over social injustice; in that difference is measured the distance the latter had traveled in company with the French Jacobins.

The root of his political thinking is the doctrine of equalitarianism. "Only admit," he says, "the original, unalterable truth, *that all men are equal in their rights, and the foundation of everything is laid.*" Accepting the romantic doctrine that human nature is excellent in its plastic state, and capable of infinite development, he is untroubled by the fact of human selfishness. He sees no bogey in democracy to frighten timid souls, no specter of anarchy in the rule of the people.

> They say mankind are wicked and rapacious, and "it must be that offences will come." This reason applies to individuals; but not to nations deliberately speaking a national voice. I hope I shall not be understood to mean, that the nature of man is totally changed by living in a free republic. I allow that it is still *interested* men and *passionate* men, that direct the affairs of the world. But in national assemblies, passion is lost in deliberation, and interest balances interest; till the good of the whole community combines the general will.
>
> If government be founded on the vices of mankind, its business is to restrain those vices in all, rather than to foster them in a few.

It was his sensitive social conscience that brought him to revolt against all class government. He had seen the naked sordidness of such governments in Europe, and he watched with concern the beginnings of like government in America. The significance of the Hamiltonian program could not escape so shrewd an observer as Barlow; he was too much a realist to take political professions at face value. "I see," he wrote, "immense fortunes made by our funding legislators out of the

public funds which they funded for themselves." Politics for profit was a sorry spectacle to him, and he occupied his mind much with the problem of erecting the machinery of an adequate democratic state that should be faithful to its stewardship as agent of the whole.

It was this difficult problem with which he dealt in his **Letter to the National Convention of France.** In this suggestive work two ideas determined his thinking: the doctrine of the sovereignty of the majority will, and the doctrine of government as a social agent. In both he returned to the position of Roger Williams a hundred and fifty years before. The sovereignty of the majority will he conceives to be continuous and immediately effective; it cannot be held in check by a rigid constitutionalism, for as Paine had pointed out, such constitutionalism is no other than government from the grave. He proposed therefore, that the fundamental law be amendable by legislative enactment, one legislative body proposing and the next determining, under full publicity. As a guarantee that such action should express the popular will, that love of power on the part of the agent should not defeat the purpose of society, he held that there must be annual elections. Representatives should be periodically excluded from candidacy, and other representatives fresh from the people sent up, for "power always was and always must be a dangerous thing." The principle of recall he regarded as indispensable in a democratic government, for it "will tend to maintain a proper relation between the representatives and the people, and a due dependence of the former upon the latter. Besides, when a man has lost the confidence of his fellow citizens . . . he is no longer their representative; and when he ceases to be their's, he cannot in any sense be the representative of the nation." The fundamental principle of state-craft Barlow states thus: "Every individual ought to be rendered as independent of every other individual as possible; and at the same time as dependent as possible on the whole community." The familiar romantic doctrine of the diminished state is implicit in all his reasoning. Like Paine he would do away utterly with the old mystery of government under which ambitious men cloak their will to power; "for whatever there is in the art of government, whether legislative or executive, above the capacities of the ordinary class of what are called well-informed men, is superfluous and destructive and ought to be laid aside."

A thoroughgoing radical in economics and politics, Barlow was no innovator in polite literature. He had pulled himself out of many a Connecticut provincialism, but he stuck fast in the bog of provincial poetry. It has long been the fashion to make merry over **The Columbiad,** and there is only too patent a reason for it. To criticize it is a work of supererogation. The appeal of "the grand style" seems to have been too much for him. Some explanation doubtless is to be found in the fact that he was working over an earlier poem done in the days of an ebullient patriotism. It was a mistake to return to it, for the heroic note in the vein of a political pamphleteer must play havoc with it. What he now attempted, in the light of his long European experience, was to embody in the narrative suitable political ideas, transforming **The Vision of Columbus** into an epic glorifying the great republican experiment. His purpose is set forth in the preface [see excerpt dated 1807].

> [The] real object of the poem is to inculcate the love of national liberty, and to discountenance the deleterious passion for violence and war; to show that on the basis of republican principle all good morals, as well as good government and hopes of permanent peace, must be founded; and to convince the

student in political science, that the theoretical question of the future advancement of human society, till states as well as individuals arrive at universal civilization, is held in dispute and still unsettled only because we have had too little experience of organized liberty in the government of nations, to have well considered its effects.

The humanitarian note is strong. War, slavery, monarchy, injustice, the tyranny resulting from political inequality, and a host of other evils, social and political, are assailed in vigorous declamation. It may not be good poetry but the sentiments are those of an enlightened and generous man. The conclusion rises to a vision of a golden age of international commerce and universal peace, when "earth, garden'd all, a tenfold burden brings," and the sundered nations shall draw together, and—

> . . . cloth'd majestic in the robes of state,
> Moved by one voice, in general congress meet
> The legates of all empires.

In that future time science will have learned "with her own glance to ken the total God," and philosophy will "expand the selfish to the social flame." Of the political ideas incorporated in the massive work some suggestion may be got from the following lines:

> Ah, would you not be slaves, with lords and kings,
> Then be not Masters; there the danger springs.
> The whole crude system that torments this earth,
> Of rank, privation, privilege of birth,
> False honor, fraud, corruption, civil jars,
> The rage of conquest and the curse of wars,
> Pandora's total shower, all ills combined
> That erst o'erwhelmed and still distress mankind,
> Boxt up secure in your deliberate hand,
> Wait your behest to fix or fly this land.
>
> Equality of right is nature's plan;
> And following nature is the march of man.
> Whene'er he deviates in the least degree,
> When, free himself, he would be more than free,
> The baseless column, rear'd to bear his trust,
> Falls as he mounts and whelms him in the
>   dust. . . .
>
> Too much of Europe, here transplanted o'er,
> Nursed feudal feelings on your tented shore,
> Brought sable sires from Afric, call'd it gain,
> And urged your sires to forge the fatal chain. . . .
> Restore their souls to men, give earth repose,
> And save your sons from slavery, wars and woes.
>
> Based on its rock of right your empire lies,
> On walls of wisdom let the fabric rise;
> Preserve your principles, their force unfold,
> Let nations prove them and let kings behold.
> EQUALITY, your first firm-grounded stand;
> Then FREE ELECTION; then your FEDERAL BAND:
> This holy Triad should forever shine
> The great compendium of all rights divine,
> Creed of all schools, whence youths by millions
>   draw
> Their themes of right, their decalogues of law;
> Till men shall wonder (in these codes inured)
> How wars were made, how tyrants were endured.

Diverse politics incline to diverse literary judgments, and the critics are not yet done with Joel Barlow. If he was not a great poet or a great political thinker, he was at least capable, open-minded, generous, with a sensitive social conscience—

certainly the most stimulating and original of the literary group that foregathered in Hartford. Injustice has long been done him by overlooking his picturesque career, and his services to America, and restricting his introduction to posterity to a few lines from *Hasty Pudding.* To make a mush of so honest a thinker, to ignore his very considerable contributions to the cause of democracy, is to impose too heavy a penalty for his defection from Connecticut respectability. He suffered quite enough in his lifetime. In the thick of his revolutionary struggles abroad his wife begged him "to go home and be respectable"; but it was not in the ardent nature of Joel Barlow to listen to such counsel of timidity. He was in too deep to go back, and so while Timothy Dwight was gathering laurels from every bush in Connecticut, this apostle of humanitarianism, this apostate from Calvinistic Federalism, was content to remain a byword and a shaking of the head in the villages of his native commonwealth. For all which, perhaps, the Washington salon and the intimate association with Jefferson may have served as recompense. Better society could not be found even in Hartford. (pp. 389-95)

Vernon Louis Parrington, "The War of Belles Lettres," in his Main Currents in American Thought, an Interpretation of American Literature from the Beginning to 1920: The Colonial Mind, 1620-1800, *Vol. I, Harcourt Brace Jovanovich, 1927, pp. 364-400.*

CHAUNCEY BREWSTER TINKER   (essay date 1948)

[A distinguished American educator, Tinker was instrumental in acquiring for Yale University the world's largest collection of writings on James Boswell and Samuel Johnson. As an editor and writer, Tinker is particularly remembered for his Letters of James Boswell *(1924) and for his popular biography* Young Boswell *(1922). In the following excerpt, Tinker admires* The Vision of Columbus *for its patriotism and American subject matter, also praising Barlow for his confidence in the worth of American poetry.]*

Connecticut, I am confident, is the only state in the union that ever produced two epic poets at once. They were Timothy Dwight and Joel Barlow, young men who had lived through the American Revolution and had come out of college filled with ambition for the newborn nation. Why should not America like Greece and Rome have an epic poem? The former of these young aspirants therefore wrote a long poem about Moses, Joshua, and the entry of the Israelites into the Promised Land, and called it *The Conquest of Canaan;* and the other, Barlow, wrote a long reflective poem, *The Vision of Columbus,* printed at Hartford in 1787, the title of which was, many years later, altered to the *Columbiad,* by which name it is known today to the few who remember poems more remarkable for their noble plan and admirable intention than for their successful execution. Neither of our epic aspirants was a poet in any but the loosest sense; yet both of them served the muse and their country in a very definite and perhaps not unworthy way.

Barlow's epic which, in its first form was in nine books, may well have been begun or at least projected, while its author was an undergraduate in Yale College during the Revolutionary War. We know from his own testimony that the whole poem, save a portion of the seventh book, was composed before the termination of that war. But even if we had no such information about it, we should easily identify the poem as a work of the author's early years, for nothing ever glowed more ardently with the emotions and illusions of youth. The juvenile poet is consumed with pride in America and in her destiny among the nations. There is no doubt in his confident young heart that the political future of the nation will be as splendid as the mountain chains and expansive lakes that lend majesty to her landscape. He believes that, under the leadership of America, the human race will move on from glory to glory. Commerce is destined to bring about the brotherhood of man and the equal distribution of the world's wealth. All nations, kindreds, and tribes will be molded into one great family, with a universal language and a universal conviction that the needs and aims of the component nations may all be reconciled by a central parliament, meeting apparently in Asia Minor, and in a vast palace where are to deliberate the federated peoples of the world. (Barlow, thou shouldst be living at this hour.) He has, or rather Columbus has, a vision of the place, and it is the crowning and final blessing bestowed upon him:

> Clothed majestic in the robes of state,
> Moved by one voice, in general council meet
> The fathers of all empires: 'twas the place
> Near the first footsteps of the human race . . .
> In this mid region, this delightful clime,
> Rear'd by whole realms, to brave the wrecks of
>   time,
> A spacious structure rose, sublimely great,
> The last resort, the unchanging scene of state . . .
> Hither the delegated sires ascend,
> And all the cares of every clime attend.

But there are earlier visions revealed to Columbus. He is shown the whole panorama of American history (with excursions into Chile and Peru). He is shown General Washington in his early and in his later career as a soldier. He is present at the battle of Bunker Hill and sees in vast epic procession—for is there not always room for such matters in epic narrative?—the great leaders of America. Much of this recalls the lists of ships and peoples in the *Iliad* and the Mount of Vision at the close of *Paradise Lost.* It is pleasant to be able to record in passing that when the poem was announced for publication, General Washington put his name down for twenty copies, and the Marquis de Lafayette for ten. With their fine generosity and interest in the arts to be practiced in the New World, there may have mingled a very natural desire to see what role would be assigned to them in the American epic.

There are two defects in *The Vision of Columbus* which, to mention no others, must forever prevent it from being reckoned a poem. In the first place, the author's style is quite without passion or distinction of any kind. So far as epigram or beauty is concerned, the following couplet is about as good as any that Barlow can write, and, indeed, quite above his average:

> But who can tell the dewdrops of the morn
> Or count the rays that in the diamond burn?

In the second place his epic is without a hero—"an uncommon want," as Byron asserted—since Columbus has nothing whatever to do. He only gazes upon visions called up before him; and as these extend over centuries and over whole continents (seen in bird's-eye) the epic is inevitably without any unity of subject.

It is well to admit all this, for nothing is gained by claiming for a poet qualities that he cannot be shown to possess. But there are features of *The Vision of Columbus* on which we may dwell with pleasure. In 1807, nearly a quarter of a centu-

ry after its composition in its original form, the poem was revised, expanded, and (rashly, I think) renamed *The Columbiad.* At that time Barlow announced that it was to be regarded as a political poem, designed to encourage republican principles and pride of country. He, perhaps wisely, suppressed the original dedication to King Louis XVI. Such action is judicious and middle-aged, but it lacks something of the boyish spontaneity of *The Vision.* I may smile at the lines,

> The epic Muse sublime
> Hails her new empire on the western clime,

but I like their enthusiasm. I grow somewhat weary of sophisticated young men who have laid aside patriotism with their marbles and their hoops. I am pleased with a young man who felt in all sincerity that his country should and could become eminent in the arts as well as in commerce. I can even be pleased with a young man who believed that our feet were set in a blessed path, a path leading through material progress to a goal and a celestial city. The young Barlow actually believed that the world of 1787 was nearer to the millennium than it had ever been before, and that it was the peculiar privilege of America to lead mankind toward that consummation. A great poet once entitled a volume of verse dealing with poems of a political stripe, *Songs before Sunrise.* Barlow's *Vision* might well have been entitled the *Epic of the Dawning Day;* for in the eighth book the poet concerns himself with the progress of civilization and the poem becomes a kind of *Essay on Man,* his nature and his destiny, now and in future.

There are passages in the epic which startle one by the familiar things or scenes which they mention, even while they make us smile at the incongruous part assigned to them among the nation's young glories. Our colleges, for example. The "seats of science" exist to "nurse the arts and point the paths of fame." So far, so good. But what is this?

> Great without pomp the modest mansions rise:
> Harvard and Yale and Princeton greet the skies.

And then there is Philadelphia, whose walls and pavements sparkle to the sun, and where "the crossing streets in fair proportion run." Independence Hall does not pass unnoticed and neither Penn nor Franklin is forgotten. Indeed, Franklin's lightning rod is, perhaps for the only time, made the subject of descriptive verse. Franklin has taught the children of Columbus to ward off the "bolts of Fate":

> The pointed steel o'ertops the ascending spire,
> And leads o'er trembling walls the harmless fire.
> In his glad fame while distant worlds rejoice,
> Far as the lightnings shine or thunders raise their
>   voice.

In one respect Barlow's judgment was quite right. He spoke with pride of the American painters, Benjamin West, Copley, Stuart, and John Trumbull, who, for genius, may fairly be associated with their European contemporaries. It is not strange that he thought his friends Dwight and Trumbull destined similarly to excel in the poetic art. In this he happened to be wrong, but the very illusion has something splendid about it, and again I am pleased with a young man who wishes his country to excel in such ways.

In certain very important respects Barlow's sentiments were not only admirable but everlastingly right. He could see no reason why a poet should not flourish in America and find material for poetry all about him. He thought that American poetry should be American and not a feeble reflection of classical or English models. He could see no reason why recent events and familiar scenes should not be used by poets. He speaks freely of the cotton plant and the cornfield.

> The rich pimento scents the neighboring skies,
> And woolly clusters o'er the cotton rise.

Even

> Tobago's plant its leaf expanding yields.

It was not his lot, by his own example, to make these familiar things and familiar scenes glorious in poetry; but he was right in thinking that it might be done. Why should not the Housatonic and the Connecticut rivers be as instinct with poetry as the Tiber and the Thames?

In the ardor of his passionate youth, Joel Barlow believed that the nation which he had just seen come to glorious birth was no less grateful to the poetic aspirant than Greece or Rome; and in such verse as he was capable of producing he set forth this view. The attempt, if not the result, endears him to us. If we as a people have failed to realize the high destiny that he foresaw for us, the fault is ours, not Barlow's, whose conception of the function of poetry was as sound as it was noble. (pp. 37-42)

> *Chauncey Brewster Tinker, "Joel Barlow's 'Vision of Columbus','" in his* Essays in Retrospect: Collected Articles and Addresses, *Yale University Press, 1948, pp. 37-42.*

ROBERT F. DURDEN　(essay date 1951)

[*Durden analyzes Barlow's ideas on the relationship between government, religion, economics, and liberty in* Advice to the Privileged Orders.]

Barlow's thoughts on the "propriety" of an all-European revolution were clearly nurtured by the circumstances in which he found himself [in France in 1791-92]. Observation of social abuses in England and on the continent aroused warm humanitarian impulses in him; the middle-class America he had known seemed far different. He was especially disgusted by the cynicism and venality which he detected in an English election. In *Reflections on the Revolution in France,* Burke attacked Dr. Price, one of Barlow's earliest English friends. Barlow was as indignant as were Mary Wollstonecraft and Thomas Paine, both of whom had already issued blasts answering the great "apostate" to reform. In this atmosphere Barlow wrote his longest and most important prose work, *Advice to the Privileged Orders in the Several States of Europe, Resulting from the Necessity and Propriety of a General Revolution in the Principles of Government.*

Barlow was no great philosophic originator or systematizer. Those who trace his ideas do so, it seems, at the risk of appearing slightly ridiculous. Who would not expect Paine and Barlow to share ideas concerning perfectibility, progress, the importance of education, and a dozen other commonplaces of late eighteenth-century liberalism? Traces of Cicero, Blackstone, Locke, Montesquieu, Burlamaqui, Rousseau, Beccaria, Holbach, Volney, Price, Priestley, and Paine, among others, may be found in the work. But the important thing is that Barlow stamped the book with his own individuality, expressed himself in a clear and vigorous style, and apparently reached a wide audience. He considered the European revolution "irresistible" in view of the French example

and the existing conditions in the rest of Europe; he therefore offered to indicate to all classes of society what they stood to gain or lose from the impending changes. Then they would be able "to buy in or sell out" of the revolution like "prudent stock-jobbers."

Barlow divided the *Advice to the Privileged Orders* into five sections on the feudal system, the church, the military, the administration of justice, and revenue and public expenditure. The evils resulting from the feudal system, an ancient edifice whose foundations had been worn away by the current of events, Barlow blamed on "habits of thinking" based on the "mysticism of inequality." Banish this mysticism of inequality, he proclaimed, and you banish "almost all the evils attendant on human nature." Specifically, he confidently expected the abolition of the laws of entailment and primogeniture, when coupled with freedom of the press, to insure the continuance of liberty wherever it might be established. The church, as an essential component of the feudal system, rested primarily on the credulity of human nature while having no aim other than "to play upon and extinguish the light of reason." Barlow qualified his attack here by explaining that liberty was incompatible with religion only where there existed an established or national church. In America where there was no church in the "corporate" sense he perceived much religion without any heresy, apostasy, or schism. The military system, with honor as its basis, served only as an expedient to kings who had to make slaughter honorable. Abolition of the war-breeding military system by itself would be ineffective; rather, the principle of government had to be changed. Only then would there be "such a total renovation of society, as to banish standing armies, overturn the military system, and exclude the possibility of war." Barlow excused the French for preserving the monarchy and adding priests to the state payroll, but he warned that their enormous military force would be "totally and directly subversive of the end they had in view." He could not recognize as justifiable any such arguments for a large standing army as defense of frontiers or tranquillity of the state.

In his treatment of the administration of justice, Barlow lapsed completely into a Godwinian view of government and its role in shaping human nature. "If it be in the power of a bad government to render men worse than nature has made them," he asked, "why should we say it is not in the power of a good one to render them better? and if the latter be capable of producing this effect in any perceivable degree, where shall we limit the progress of human wisdom, and the force of its institutions, in ameliorating, not only the social condition, but the controlling principles of man?" Society, therefore, was obligated to furnish the means whereby men could obtain subsistence, for society had usurped part of every man's "birth-right." Mankind's "common stock," however, included only knowledge and the contributions (taxes) necessary from each individual; private property was in no way involved.

Barlow's economic ideas are best expressed in the portion of his essay which deals with revenue and public expenditure; here the guiding premise is that human liberty depends in large part on liberty of commerce. What Barlow panegyrizes as "the spirit of commerce" would make nations mutually advantageous to each other and thereby eliminate war. Barlow particularly assailed the two features of existing financial arrangements which he considered the greatest evils, the funding system and indirect taxation. Like all his Physiocratic friends in England and in France, he argued that taxes should be derived from the productive element, land. Barlow's ideas concerning the importance of free trade, direct taxation on land, and the wonder-working "spirit of commerce" take on added significance in connection with the business career he later followed. In the meantime, the **Advice to the Privileged Orders** made Barlow an important man and brought him to the fore of the English reform agitation. (pp. 335-37)

> Robert F. Durden, "Joel Barlow in the French Revolution," in The William and Mary Quarterly, *third series, Vol. VIII, No. 3, July, 1951, pp. 327-54.*

ROY HARVEY PEARCE (essay date 1961)

[*In the following excerpt, Pearce focuses on the development of the American epic poem, outlining* The Columbiad's *influence on the evolution of the genre.*]

When, in 1807, Joel Barlow published his **Columbiad,** he was confident that it was proof of the very progress which it so amply narrated. This was a modern epic, freed, as only something made in America could be, of the fetters and forms of tradition. In **The Columbiad** Barlow much enlarged and revised his earlier **Vision of Columbus,** bringing to the later poem the results of the liberalism for which he fought throughout the last quarter of his life. He who had seen revolutionary France at first hand, had been friend to Tom Paine and Mary Wollstonecraft, and had declared himself unwaveringly on the side of the new democratic order—he most certainly could sense the need for an epic which would at once celebrate the establishment of that order, inculcate its ideals in those who participated in it, and project its glorious possibilities into the future. In the epic, he wrote in his Preface [see excerpt dated 1807], "there are two distinct objects to be kept in view . . . : the *poetical* object and the *moral* object. The poetical is the fictitious design of the action; the moral is the real design of the poem." Achievement and worth could in the end be measured only in terms of the "real design." Barlow condemned the *Iliad,* for example, because of its "pernicious [i.e., anti-democratic] doctrine." Unlike some of his contemporaries, he could not subscribe to the flourishing historical relativism which was a means to prove that the *Iliad* was right for its age and could be therefore said to be great for his. The epic too was caught up in the idea of progress. Barlow wanted a poem like the traditional epic—memorializing the history of a society, chiefly in the heroic person of one of its members, thereby strengthening and guiding it. Yet he would have in this poem none of the archaic trappings of the societies out of which had come the great epics and epic heroes of tradition:

> My object is altogether of a moral and political nature. I wish to encourage and strengthen, in the rising generation, a sense of the importance of republican institutions; as being the great foundation of public and private happiness, the necessary aliment of future and permanent ameliorations in the condition of human nature.
>
> This is the moment in America to give such a direction to poetry, painting and the other fine arts, that true and useful ideas of glory may be implanted in the minds of men here, to take [the] place of the false and destructive ones that have degraded the species in other countries. . . .

(pp. 59-60)

Barlow was too much a man of his time to manage that fusion of "the *poetical* object and the *moral* object" which he knew was the essential criterion for a genuinely "new" epic. Hence he was, as is well enough known, no poet; his **Columbiad** is dull and lifeless, its figurative language merely clogs and clots its attempt to attain a moral and political object. Such life as it has is the half-life of the essay at poetry which somehow expresses the aspirations and commitments of the culture out of which it comes—indeed, which in its very inadequacy seems to make inevitable such larger, imaginatively self-sustaining work as comes after it. It is, in the light of what Barlow hoped for it and of what followed, a premonitory analogue: a prime exemplar of the first stage in the history of the American poet's attempt to create that strange, amorphous, anomalous, self-contradictory thing, the American epic.

He set himself an impossible task—writing an epic without the sort of linear, form-endowing narrative argument which takes its substance and its very life from the hero, the suprahuman being, at its center. "The major theme of all epic poetry," as has been recently said, "is heroism itself, heroism as the perilous mythification of man. . . ." Such mythification was impossible for Barlow; yet he could envision a time and a condition of the imaginative use of language when mythification, or something like it, would be altogether possible. The history of the American epic is the history of attempts to realize that possibility. Four poems, and their makers' hopes for them, count most here: *Song of Myself,* the *Cantos, The Bridge,* and *Paterson.* These are plotless epics in which poetical and moral objects are fused; poems in which the working of imaginative language itself is managed in such a way that the fictitious and the real design of the poem have become one. They are poems centripetal to their culture; like that culture, like Barlow's culture, they have no proper hero. This is the form and substance, the basic style, of the American epic; its strategy is to make a poem which will create rather than celebrate a hero and which will make rather than recall the history that surrounds him. In the American epic what is mythified is the total milieu and ambiance, what the poet takes to be the informing spirit of his times and his world. As milieu and ambiance project not a plot but a series of events, so these poems exist above all as events. The poet intends to overpower his readers, so that their discovery of themselves as new men in a new world will be entirely bound up in their new-found sense of the event. These are meant to be poems not of a new order, but rather of a new ordering. Pound's words for the process are accurate: Make it new, he says; achieve a new Paideuma (his word, borrowed from Frobenius, "for the tangle or complex of the unrooted ideas of any period"). It is an impossible task, an outsider can say, if only because it is a task whose movement is at most barely dialectical, not plotted, and always by definition unfinished. Yet it has gone on and likely will continue to do so, so long as poets like Barlow, Whitman, Pound, Crane, and Williams feel the need to contain the whole of their culture—or all they think is worthwhile in it—in one poem; so long as such poets are driven to make of poetry an institution whereby that total culture is given form, substance, and meaning. Herein a basic style is deliberately sought after and cultivated. The poet must cut straight through to its very source—in Pound's words to the "centre," the "general root."

The poet who aspired toward making an American epic bore the heavy burden of his Puritan heritage, however transmuted. As poet, he was constitutionally the one in whom the latent antinomianism of his culture was most likely to erupt. Then how could he find the means—the source in some *numen,* some absolutely authoritative power—to discover and describe that culture hero required to make a proper epic? In what could the poet believe except in his power to believe? In whom could he believe except himself? For Barlow and his contemporaries, the answer was quite simple: The poet was endowed, they knew, with such an abundance of reason, common sense, and moral sensibility—with such "sympathy" for his fellows—that he could discover the potentiality for heroism in them, see how that potentiality had been realized in the past, and hope with great good cheer for its realization in the future. In a poet like Barlow (whose intellectual horizons were neatly defined by his training in the Scottish common-sense philosophy which dominated American intellectual life in his time) the implications of antinomianism were minimized; for when the poet looked within himself and wrote, he found there only that which made him like others and others like him, not that which inevitably made his relations to others (as Emerson was to say in "Experience") "casual and oblique." *The Columbiad* reflects an era of good, if shallow, feelings; of life lived in public, not in private; of a new nation so busy in establishing its outward existence that it had no need to worry about its inward existence. But yet, being a poem, it will not obey its master's injunctions completely. Thus, at least distantly, it anticipates *Song of Myself.* It marks a halfway point between poems like Tompson's *New Englands Crisis* (and also historical work like Mather's *Magnalia*) and *Song of Myself.* (pp. 60-2)

[Barlow's *Columbiad*] was a tale signifying almost everything relevant to that rise toward freedom which it was the destiny of his country to manifest. The manifestation was *a priori* good, true, and beautiful.

The Columbiad begins thus:

> I sing the Mariner who first unfurl'd
> An eastern banner o'er the western world
> And taught mankind where future empires
> lay. . . .

However, it is not Columbus' actions which are sung, but rather the inexorable progress of free institutions in the Americas as he envisions them. The life of *The Columbiad,* and also such life as is in its protagonists, derives entirely from the idea of progress which it manifests. To Columbus despairing in prison comes Hesper, the guardian Genius of the western continent, who takes him to a mount of vision. The poem unfolds in a series of visions in which Columbus cannot, of course, be made to take part. He cannot be a hero. He is from the outset utterly passive; he observes, is troubled, hopes for the best, and is reassured regularly by Hesper. He cannot *do* anything. He is, in fact, the ideal type of *reader* of the American epic as it was to develop. He looks on and, now comprehending the history he envisions, is somehow changed; or at least his exacerbations are assuaged. The vision is meant to do its work on him, as in *Song of Myself,* the *Cantos, The Bridge,* and *Paterson,* the vision, the lived-through quality of the poetic experience itself, is meant to do its work on us. But Barlow is not poet enough to give his poetic rendering of Columbus' vision even the least power to work in this way. What is unfolded in the twelve books are dreary, insistent, intemperate, and homogenized descriptions of places, people, and events—all of value only as they aspire (even the places, as Barlow's enlightened environmentalism

takes over, somehow aspire) toward the reason and freedom and joy of a new society in a new world.

With Columbus, we see America topographically, its natives anthropologically (Barlow's science is firmly founded in learned treatises of his own time); we are told of their future and are given a whole Book which details the heroic lives of the Inca Capac and his people. But the Incas were to be destroyed; for progress meant a sacrifice of a lower to a higher good (here too Barlow is in accord with the social science of his time), and the good of European civilization had to come. As Barlow puts it in his summarizing note, the great period came with the "Rise and progress of more liberal principles." The last six books of *The Columbiad* are given to an exposition of that rise and progress: of the American colonies; of the Revolutionary War, battle by battle, hero by hero; of Peace in a new America; of the arts there; of the American Federal System when it should extend "over the whole earth." The final vision, the final Book, is charged with an unabashed utopianism—a vision of the brave new world, at last unified through a universal language, so that all is caught up in one grand political harmony.

Acceleration of progress toward this utopia begins when Columbus sees America and is enraptured. Hesper comments:

> Here springs indeed the day, since time began,
> The brightest, broadest, happiest morn of man.
> In these prime settlements thy raptures trace
> The germ, the genius of a sapient race,
> Predestined here to methodise and mould
> New codes of empire to reform the old.

The achievements of the race and the quality of its sapience are outlined in detail: "freeborn sons" shall find their "genius unconfined"—

> Here social man a second birth shall find,
> And a new range of reason lift his mind,
> Feed his strong intellect with purer light,
> A nobler sense of duty and of right,
> The sense of liberty . . .

The American, finding "FREEDOM" to be "his new Prometheus," will lead the way to utopia:

> . . . one confederate, condependent sway
> Spread with the sun and bound the walks of day,
> One centred system, one all ruling soul
> Live thro the parts and regulate the whole.

Or rather, the spirit of progress, as it suffuses his culture, will lead him to lead the way. Columbus' vision is intended to be a projection of this spirit into a series of epic actions; the actions, as he sees them, quiet his despair and make him joyfully accept his part in them. Sharing in that vision, Barlow's readers too were to be newly created; for they could see the trajectory of their destiny. The spirit of *The Columbiad* would be their spirit and would make them heroic too.

Barlow's actual hero is what he and his contemporaries liked to call the "republican institution," toward which all history, natural and human, progressed. No strictly private human motivation can interest the poet, for all motivation is a product of men being caught up in the spirit of the times. To a degree, as Barlow claims in his Preface, Columbus' prison despair, turning to hope in the light of his vision, makes for motivation and thus for the design of the poem. Nonetheless, that motivation does not derive from anything that Columbus, as a man, as a hero, does. His passion is that of a voyeur, since he does not participate in the vision, as the protagonists of dream-vision poems had traditionally done. For this is not a dream-vision. It is real. It is earnest. It is history. And so are Columbus, Barlow's readers, and his subject. They do not make history; they are made by it. The poem, indeed, would have us see how history literally creates its protagonists—or what is the same thing, creates the values which gives its protagonists their worth.

Surely Barlow did not consciously mean his poem to have such an effect. What is involved here are those, as it were, subliminal implications of Barlow's theory and practice in the epic which point it away from its traditional mode and function. For try as hard as he will, Barlow cannot hold to the epic tradition; subordinating fictional to real, moral design, he perforce creates a poem which works neither as would the traditional epic, in which fictional and moral design are fused and so move to a higher level of reality, nor as would the essentially propaedeutic poem which, subliminally, he seems to have wanted. Barlow could not write a traditional poem. But he was not artist enough—here we must take this fact as a given, although recent scholarship will let us make informed guesses as to the reason why—to conceive and work out the pattern of the new kind of poem which he wanted: a specifically American epic which would do the kind of task he wanted his poem to do—achieve an "altogether . . . moral and political" object. The trappings of *The Columbiad* are traditional: for example, the opening "I sing . . ."; the concentration on superhuman actions; the elaborate cataloguing and passing-in-review; the focussing on the "sublime"; the couplets which Pope and others had institutionalized as a proper vehicle for the epic in English. As a close student of Pope's efforts to achieve the epic manner has written, "The chief function of a heroic style is to convey . . . [a] feeling of urgency, of constant pressure and constant significance." In the epic of tradition, such urgency, pressure, and significance were imminent in the substance of the poem itself; the poet's task, and that of his imitators and translators, was to invent a style which would derive the feeling from the substance. Dismissing the substance as immoral, Barlow would yet hold on to the style and use it to derive the feeling from a totally new substance, in which heroes are made by their culture—not, as in the traditional epic, with and through their culture. He made an inferior poem at best. He might have made a new kind of poem.

Some of his contemporaries, to be sure, objected to his poem, not on the grounds that it might have been something new but that it failed to be something old. Here are the words of one of them, summing up opinion of *The Columbiad* in the 1820's [see excerpt dated 1829]: "The absurdity of attempting to give an epic unity and interest through the medium of a vision, to a series of actions so unconnected in date and subject: and the strange and awkward neologisms by which the language of the poem is disfigured, called forth the reprehensions of the reviewers in every quarter." Yet it is not the neologisms *in* the poem but those whose possibility it projects which in the end catch our interest.

For Barlow seems to have had a curiously vague sense of one of the preconditions to a new kind of epic poem; or perhaps the very logic of his attempt to Americanize the epic forced him into a sense of this precondition. The precondition was a new poetics, deriving from a new use of imaginative language, this deriving in turn from a new language itself. Barlow's conception is two or three times removed from that of a poetics which would make the new epic possible; but it is nonetheless there, however vaguely. It occurs as part of the utopian vision of Book x:

> At this blest period, when the total race
> Shall speak one language and all truths embrace,
> Instruction clear a speedier course shall find,
> And open earlier on the infant mind.
> No foreign terms shall crowd with barbarous rules
> The dull unmeaning pageantry of schools;
> Nor dark authorities nor names unknown
> Fill the learnt head with ignorance not its own;
> But wisdom's eye with beams unclouded shine,
> And simplest rules her native charms define;
> One living language, one unborrow'd dress
> Her boldest flights with fullest force express;
> Triumphant virtue, in the garb of truth,
> Win a pure passage to the heart of youth,
> Pervade all climes where suns or oceans roll,
> And warm the world with one great moral soul,
> To see, facilitate, attain the scope
> Of all their labor and of all their hope.

This is perhaps just a plea for a universal language as rationalized as Esperanto and as unclouded as Basic English. It is utterly simplistic, tending (except perhaps in the eighth line) to reduce the complexities of existence to a spiritless least common denominator. Yet, coming as it does in the midst of Barlow's vision of a utopia totally expressive of his altogether moral and political object, it is something more. It is a description of the necessary and sufficient qualities of a poetic language which would both project a vision like Columbus' and work on its reader as that vision is said to have worked on him: so as to have given him at once a sense of certitude and of authenticity, of being fully and creatively at one with his culture. At the very end of *The Columbiad,* Hesper says to Columbus:

> Then let thy stedfast soul no more complain
> Of dangers braved and griefs endured in vain,
> Of courts insidious, envy's poison'd stings,
> The loss of empire and the frown of kings;
> While these broad views thy better thoughts compose
> To spurn the malice of insulting foes;
> And all the joys descending ages gain. . . .

Certainly this is a conventionally utopian rationale. It could be said to imply the withering away of the imaginative use of language and of poetry itself; or, perhaps, the leveling up of all language until it had attained the status of poetry. In any case, it implies that language will be used, if not differently, at least more intensely and exactly: a language such as to "win a pure passage to the heart of youth"—to the sensibilities of its auditors and readers. A new language: a new soul: a new world.

To say all this is to push the implications of Barlow's poetizing to their farthest limits, in order to interpret his work as a foreshadowing of the American epics which come after it. For in literary history such implications constitute an order of fact. Barlow was not alone in his time in wanting an American epic. But he is the only poet (or would-be poet) before Whitman who had enough conviction and ability to run the risks involved in striving to use traditional means and forms to break away from tradition itself. If his vision failed him, it was not because he lacked the courage to be visionary, but rather because he lacked the talent (not to say the genius) to substantiate it. Failing in *The Columbiad,* he nonetheless established, or stumbled upon, the necessary conditions for the achievement of an authentic American epic. What *The Co-lumbiad* might have been and what it might have done—this is its meaning for the history of the literary imagination in America. (pp. 63-9)

Roy Harvey Pearce, "The Long View: An American Epic," in his The Continuity of American Poetry, Princeton University Press, 1961, pp. 59-136.

HYATT H. WAGGONER (essay date 1968)

[*Suggesting that* The Columbiad *is a more impressive achievement than critics usually acknowledge, Waggoner contrasts Barlow's deistic philosophy in the poem with the tenets of Puritanism as exhibited in the works of Edward Taylor, a seventeenth-century American metaphysical poet. Waggoner's remarks were first published in 1968.*]

In the seventy-eight years between the death of Edward Taylor and the publication of Joel Barlow's *The Columbiad,* the Puritan faith that had shaped [American] poetry of the first hundred years was destroyed. To the conservatives of the time, fearful that the softening influence of rationalism would destroy the faith entirely, it seemed that the death of the old way was the work of freethinking infidels and Jacobins inspired by the Devil and the French Revolution.

But it might with at least equal justice be said that Puritanism had committed suicide. The very rigor of its self-defense exposed its inner contradictions. As it fought off doubts within and doubters without, it came to seem to many what it had always seemed to Anglicans and others, a superstitious set of beliefs designed chiefly to absolutize the interests of those who held them by destroying those of everyone else. By Barlow's time what seemed to the religious conservatives a battle between orthodoxy and infidelity, seemed to the religious liberals a struggle not only between superstition and enlightened knowledge but between the right of the few and the right of all men to have hope.

Barlow wastes no time in *The Columbiad* attacking Puritanism. He simply ignores it as irrelevant. Assuming the natural goodness of man as the Puritans had assumed his natural depravity, he placed his hope in Reason, Science, and free institutions. In sprightly, often deft, heroic couplets he redefined the work of the Christian pilgrim: It was now to build the City of God on earth. Reason and freedom would be his tools, but tools used in the service of an unchanged end—universal love. Men find it difficult to accept the guidance of Reason at first; its radiance comes as a shock, but eventually

> All nations catch it, all their tongues combine
> To hail the human morn and speak the day divine.

With a rare hexameter Barlow emphasizes his point: a "human" morn, not a dawn conceived in terms of what Taylor called "nothing Man." But the human morn expresses the immanence of the Divine by the very quality of its humanity: it initiates "the day divine." If Barlow's liberalism looks forward to Emerson and Whitman, there is also a sense, less obvious but not unimportant, in which it may be seen as inverting Puritanism in order to salvage what could be saved from the wreck, a sense of man's high destiny, particularly in America, where the old corruptions and inequities of Europe no longer prevailed.

> Here social man a second birth shall find,

> And a new range of reason lift his mind,
> Feed his strong intellect with purer light,
> A nobler sense of duty and of right,
> The sense of liberty; whose holy fire
> His life shall temper and his laws inspire,
> Purge from all shades the world-embracing scope
> That prompts his genius and expands his hope.

It would be easy to see Barlow as reversing everything Taylor stood for and asserting its opposite. Reading his rational, often witty, and smoothly polished lines, so lacking in the sense of tension and difficulty that marks, and sometimes mars, Taylor's best work, we may come to this conclusion. But it would be only partially justified. On hope, for instance. Barlow is a very hopeful poet; but so, in a different way, is Taylor. The locus of Barlow's hope is in the future, in a Utopian society to be achieved when man has had time to use his reason freely, as he would have in the past if he had not been prevented by evil institutions. Taylor's hope rests on his faith in God; its locus is beyond time. Both are hopeful poets, hoping for different things.

So with other contrasts. If Barlow and other men of the Enlightenment located the Celestial City on earth, in the future, still they took seriously its "celestial" character: it was for them an ideal of a juster, freer, happier society in which man could realize his full potential as a creature made in the image of God. Their conception of it was "secular" compared with Taylor's, but it would be better to speak of a shift of emphasis than of a reversal of ideals. Whether the Kingdom would come in time or out of it has always been a moot question for Christian orthodoxy. Barlow might have claimed—as Jefferson, whose thought was very similar, did claim—that the end result of his revisions in inherited doctrine was to recover the true essence of the faith.

At any rate he was convinced that what was needed was not faith and prayer but for man to use his God-given powers to their limit. He had no doubt that in this new Eden of the West, where no Fall had occurred, man *would:*

> But when he steps on these regenerate shores,
> His mind unfolding for superior powers,
> FREEDOM, his new Prometheus, here shall
>   rise . . .

And with freedom would come that natural, indeed inevitable, unfolding of man's natural powers that kings and churches had hitherto prevented. "Progressive are the paths we go": The dialectic of history is certain; the very geography of America will inevitably produce a new and finer type. Barlow takes the determinism implicit in the Puritan notion of the Predestination of the Elect and the Damned and gives it first a biological, then a social and racial, emphasis, but his version retains its character as Providential. As he explains in the Argument to Book II, modern knowledge shows

> That the human body is composed of a due proportion of the elements suited to the place of its first formation; that these elements . . . produce all the changes of health, sickness, growth, and decay; and may likewise produce any other changes which occasion the diversity of men; that these elemental proportions are varied, not more by climate than temperature and other local circumstances; that the mind is likewise in a state of change, and will take its physical character from the body and from external objects . . .

The new land, in short, will produce the new Adam, unfallen

and in no need of divine redemption through a vicarious atonement. We think of Whitman, who exulted that he was "formed from this soil," and of Stevens' Crispin in "The Comedian as the Letter C": "Nota: his soil is man's intelligence . . . Crispin . . . planned a colony."

Man's religion in the past has been the product, Barlow tells us in the poem, of his fear—

> He bows to every force he can't control . . .
> Hence rose his gods, that mystic monstrous lore
> Of blood-stained altars and of priestly power,
> Hence blind credulity on all dark things,
> False morals hence, and hence the yoke of kings.

This false religion has made man "despise the earth" which produces him. In the new land, though, free of the yoke of kings and priests, he will "reject all mystery" and become at last mature:

> Man is an infant still; and slow and late
> Must form and fix his adolescent state,
> Mature his manhood and at last behold
> His reason ripen and his force unfold.

Only when this has happened will he realize his true potential—

> Soaring with science then he learns to string
> Her highest harp, and brace her broadest wing,
> With her own force to fray the paths untrod,
> With her own glance to ken the total God,

and so to celebrate adequately at last the "harmony divine" immanent in the world. Again we think of Emerson and Whitman and their continued expression of Barlow's Enlightened vision. But as we do so, we are aware of a depth of meaning in their re-expression of it that is quite lacking in Barlow. Or we think of Warren's *Brother to Dragons* and of what Jefferson had to learn in that poem. Barlow's rationalism, though it rests on and promotes noble sentiments and generous ideals, comes at last to seem too easy, even naive. Evil is surely not so easily disposed of.

But *The Columbiad* is more interesting and significant than noting the limitations of Barlow's rationalism would imply. Many readers are likely to find it the first really *readable* long poem in American literature. Barlow handles the heroic couplet with ease and skill. If he uses it imitatively, so, in a sense, did everyone who used it after Pope, who would seem to have completed the exploration of all its possibilities. It serves Barlow well for humor, of which he has a good deal, and exhibits nicely the strength of his thought, which lies in its clarity and coherence. If it is sometimes facile, it moves in a sprightly way. If it lacks depth of suggestiveness, it is urbane and reasonable. Barlow is our closest equivalent in poetry to Jefferson in prose. Though he had a more limited imagination than Jefferson, and closed himself to new ideas sooner, his growth from Calvinistic Federalism, as we see it in *The Vision of Columbus,* to Deistic, physiocratic progressivism in the later version of the same poem, *The Columbiad,* is impressive. Here was a man who, up to a point at least, could learn from experience. His ideas often strike us as crude, when we paraphrase them, but his way of holding—and expressing—them entitles him to be called a genuine poet.

> *Hyatt H. Waggoner, "Puritans and Deists," in his*
> American Poets: From the Puritans to the Present,

· revised edition, Louisiana State University Press, 1984, pp. 5-32.

ARTHUR L. FORD   (essay date 1971)

[*Ford surveys Barlow's major prose works, discussing their themes, style, and political significance. The critic argues that Barlow's prose, rather than his poetry, represents his greatest contribution to American literature.*]

In an age of poor poetry, most of Barlow's was mediocre; in an age of great prose, Barlow's was among the best. Only in prose did Barlow consistently practice that moderation and rationality that he called for in everything he wrote. Although the best prose of the national period is noted for the logic of its argument and balance of its construction as men discussed and debated the course their country should take in domestic and foreign policy, much of it consisted of bitter name-calling tirades against persons with different political and religious ideas. Although Barlow was constantly attacked by his political enemies as an anarchist, an atheist, and a traitor, it must be said to his credit that rarely did he write against a particular individual, and then he emphasized the ideas the man held rather than his personality or his private affairs.

Throughout all of Barlow's prose one finds a number of ideas that reveal his unified and consistent view of man, of society, and of the role given to government. Barlow was always giving advice to anyone who would listen, partly because he thought he had something important to say and partly because he had a firm faith in the ability of people to respond correctly when they understood the choice they have. At the basis of all his advice is a belief that America had almost miraculously discovered a unique combination of political concepts that would produce greatness on the North American continent and spread inevitably throughout the Western world. The republican principles adopted by the framers of the Constitution insure liberty to all citizens, and the federation of the states insures security for the nation. Other countries had utilized one concept or the other, but only the United States had combined them.

Two of Barlow's other recurring themes describe courses of action necessary to insure both a republican and a federalized country. First, all men need to be educated so that they can determine wisely how their republic shall be run; they are the rulers, and they must understand the choices confronting them. Second, the citizens of the country must develop a feeling that they are part of one total political and social unit and not isolated from the main portion of the nation. To insure this unity, transportation must be facilitated throughout the country; waterways, bridges, and roads must be constructed and maintained. In short, attention must be given to internal improvements which will become even more vital as the country expands westward and northward, an expansion which Barlow believed was inevitable.

In order to obtain the funds necessary for these projects which would insure a federalized democracy, Barlow urged continually that the United States reduce and finally eliminate its national debt by instituting economic pressures for a standing army and a large navy and by discontinuing the practice of funding. Barlow also believed that the country could prosper by insisting on complete freedom of the seas, thereby increasing greatly its own commerce and, again, reducing the need for a large navy. Practices such as these would, he thought, provide more than enough funds for the internal-improvement projects he suggested.

Finally, the humanitarian strain in all of Barlow's thinking, his deep concern for the results of both the French and the American revolutions, and his belief in the sovereignty of the individual within the limits of social responsibility produced two themes again manifest in most of his prose. One of the sources of greatest sorrow for Barlow during his last twenty-five years was the almost constant friction between his native and his adopted countries. He believed that if the two could understand each other, they could lead Europe into a republic resembling that established in North America. Consequently, he spent a great deal of effort trying to persuade America that France was her friend; and he suffered many personal attacks in the effort. But, perhaps the most serious attacks came as a result of his religious beliefs. Because of his support of the "atheistic" French and because of his comments on established religion in both his poetry and his prose, he was regarded by the proper New Englanders as a lost soul. Occasionally, Barlow paused to point out that the basis for his religious belief had broadened but not crumbled and that a toleration of religious views would be desirable; but, generally, his prose was concerned almost completely with political issues.

Beginning with a firm belief in the importance of the individual and the individual nation, Barlow advised several governments and two generations in several specific courses of action. An examination of his prose reveals a deeply concerned and consistently logical humanitarian as well as a skilled writer.

Barlow's best-known, most highly praised prose work is *Advice to the Privileged Orders.* One of the many replies to Edmund Burke's *Reflections on the Revolution in France,* Barlow's has always remained in the shadow of Thomas Paine's *The Rights of Man,* although at least one student of Barlow insists that, "as literature, it far surpasses *The Rights of Man*" [see entry by Victor Clyde Miller in Additional Bibliography]. *Advice to the Privileged Orders* was published in February, 1792, at a time when Barlow's faith in the French Revolution was at its highest. He was convinced that the revolution would sweep western Europe, crushing all forms of authoritarianism before it; and his advice to the privileged orders was that they should recognize the inevitability of this movement for their own good. At the conclusion of the Introduction, he states his purpose: "Taking it for granted, therefore, that a general revolution is at hand, whose progress is irresistible, my object is to contemplate its probable effects, and to comfort those who are afflicted at the prospect."

Behind all Barlow's thinking are two basic principles: *"all men are equal in rights,* and . . . the *government is their own."* He believed that governments had traditionally worked against these two ideas; some men were given rights others did not have, and the mass always worked solely for the small minority who had these privileges. Barlow felt strongly that these false notions were vestiges of feudal society and that they could be changed by appealing to the reasoning power of the people. When they understood, these remnants of feudalism would be eliminated as they had been for the most part in America and in France. (pp. 107-10)

Barlow's *Advice to the Privileged Orders* is a response to Burke's contention that societal change is unwise because it disturbs the status quo. Disturbance, Barlow maintained, is just what the status quo needs and will receive. The people, if only made knowledgeable, will demand equality and a government which will serve them. In *The Conspiracy of Kings* Barlow took a dull hatchet and chopped away at Burke and the monarchists. In this work, he cut with surgeonlike deftness into the heart of society and suggested a cure.

In his poetry Barlow felt a need to use a style which seems overly conventionalized and too contrived to a later age. His prose, however, remains just as vital and effective today as it was when it was written. *Advice to the Privileged Orders* is effective primarily because of Barlow's use of rationality and the logical progression of his thought. His faith in the reasonable nature of man is seen vividly in the style he chose to adopt. For instance, the development of his argument for a militia, instead of a standing army, is presented step by step, beginning with the basic principle that all men are equal:

> Only admit the original, unalterable truth, that *all men are equal in their rights,* and the foundation of everything is laid; to build the superstructure requires no effort but that of natural deduction. The first necessary deduction will be, that the people will form an equal representative government; in which it will be impossible for *orders* or *privileges* to exist for a moment; and consequently the first materials for standing armies will be converted into peaceable members of the state. Another deduction follows, That the people will be universally armed: they will assume those weapons for security, which the art of war has invented for destruction. You will then have removed the *necessity* of a standing army by the organization of the legislature, and the *possibility* of it by the arrangement of the militia; for it is as impossible for an armed soldiery to exist in an armed nation, as for a nobility to exist under an equal government.

The logical structure of his argument is additionally strengthened by the balance and parallelism of his sentences. At the end of Chapter One, Barlow describes France now that it has shed its feudal shackles:

> But in France their hands are at last untied; the charm is broken, and the feudal system, with all its infamous idolatries, has fallen to the ground. Honor is restored to the heart of man, instead of being suspended from his button-hole; and useful industry gives a title to respect. The men that were formerly dukes and marquisses are now exalted to farmers, manufacturers and merchants; the rising generation among all classes of people are forming their maxims on a just estimate of things; and society is extracting the poisoned dagger which conquest had planted in her vitals.

Advice to the Privileged Orders reflects in content and in style a reasonable man speaking confidently to other reasonable men.

The year 1792 saw two other important pamphlets published by Barlow, both of which are related to France's attempts to revise its 1791 constitution. In October, 1792, Barlow's friend, Thomas Paine, delivered before the National Convention Barlow's *A Letter to the National Convention of France On the Defects in the Constitution of 1791, and the extent of the amendments to be applied,* in which he reaffirmed his faith in republican principles and presented a list of thirteen suggestions for the new constitution. Near the end of that year Barlow wrote *A Letter Addressed to the People of Pied-*

mont On the advantages of the French Revolution, and the necessity of adopting its principles in Italy, an appeal to the people of Piedmont which bordered the French province of Savoy to welcome the French army which promised to liberate them in the spring. This pamphlet restated the principles of the French Revolution and its inevitable spread throughout Europe.

Speaking of *Letter to the National Convention,* Vernon Louis Parrington made the following observation: "Two ideas determined his thinking: the doctrine of the sovereignty of the majority will, and the doctrine of government as a social agent" [see excerpt dated 1927]. Barlow attempted in the first part of his letter to show *"that kings can do no good,"* that a state church is evil, and that the people can best judge what is best for themselves. In the second part, he listed his thirteen proposals—specific suggestions which would insure the right of the majority to rule themselves.

After attacking a monarchy, even a limited one such as France still had, because of its expense and inevitable corruption and because the king, through flattery and the security of an inherited title, would probably be either weak or wicked, he asserts his faith in majority will: "A republic of beavers or of monkies, I believe, could not be benefited by receiving their laws from men, any more than men could be in being governed by them." And more directly: "The sure and only characteristic of a good law is, *that it be the perfect expression of the will of the nation.*"

Barlow's thirteen proposals show how he could translate political and social theory into practical suggestions. It is impossible to determine how influential Barlow's advice was in the framing of the 1793 Constitution, although it did incorporate several of the ideas Barlow described. It is equally impossible to determine how much of an impact the United States Constitution had on Barlow's thinking. It is certain, however, that *Letter to the National Convention* provides a link between these two republican statements. (pp. 112-14)

A Letter Addressed to the People of Piedmont arose from Barlow's belief that the French Revolution would sweep Europe. Piedmont lay next to Savoy, separated by the Alps. During December, 1792, it was reasonable to assume that the French army would be in Italy by the spring of 1793; therefore, Barlow hoped to prevent bloodshed by convincing the Italians that the French were their friends and that they would be much better off under new rule. Once again, Barlow demonstrated his belief that a rational appeal to rational people is sufficient to spread truth. When speaking of the French Revolution as a movement to be emulated, he said: "If the example were bad, your good sense would teach you to shun it; it would need only to be known, to be despised, and it ought to be explained to all people, that they might learn to avoid such a dangerous innovation. If it be good, it ought to be taught by your teachers, and imitated by all the world. But be assured that the very caution they use to prevent your coming to the knowledge of the fact, is a proof that such a revolution would be an advantage to you and a disadvantage to them."

His letter also gave him an opportunity to reply to some of the common accusations made against the revolution. In answer to the charge of atheism, he said that revolution had rid France of the state church, in this case Roman Catholicism, but that it also guaranteed freedom of worship to all religions. He answered the charge that private property was not al-lowed by saying that sinecures were paid for when seized and that church property always did belong to the people. Finally, he admitted that the charge of cruelty and murder was unfortunately true to some extent but that these actions were the result of habits instilled in the people by the former government.

After an implied ultimatum to the people of Piedmont to join the revolution peacefully or have thousands slaughtered by the invincible French army, Barlow closed with a definition of France's role in the renovation of Europe. The forces of right and reason are combining to allow man to reconstruct society so that the masses instead of a few fortunate ones will benefit, and France is demonstrating that this reconstruction is not only possible but imminent:

> France has been forced into the field, to encounter this infamous combination of robbers, this war of all crimes against the principles of all virtue. She has undertaken the defense of human nature. She has assumed a new kind of tactique unknown to the art of war, and irresistible to the armies of kings. She has armed herself in the panoply of reason; her manifesto is the rights of man, her sword the pledge of peace. In this species of warfare we need not be astonished at her success. What people can resist the hand that comes to break their chains? The armies of liberty are every where triumphant, while their standards are scarcely stained with blood. Victory completes her work, before they arrive to celebrate the conquest; and the entrance of the French troops into the conquered country is regarded by the people rather as the procession of a civic feast than as the dreaded violence of war. Their general, instead of punishing the new recovered citizens with confiscation, imprisonment, and death, meets them in their Jacobine societies, and invites them to form their primary assemblies. The forts and garrisons which he erects to secure his conquests, are printing presses and reading clubs.

Unfortunately for Barlow and the revolution, forces threatening France from without and violence from within made the spring invasion of Italy impractical. Barlow's words, however, remain a passionate defense of the principles of the French Revolution. (pp. 115-16)

The *Letters from Paris* were completed in Paris on March 4, 1799, and December 20, 1799, and were probably printed in 1800. The first letter, *On the System of Policy Hitherto Pursued by Their Government,* was written in response to a letter which Barlow had sent to Washington and which was mangled by editors when it was published without his permission; the second letter, *On Certain Political Measures Proposed to Their Consideration,* was concerned with Barlow's plan for a world society based on freedom of the seas. Barlow's advice to his fellow Americans was somewhat different from the advice he had been passing out in Europe earlier in the decade. Earlier he had seen France sowing peaceful revolutions throughout Europe; now he was urging the United States to avoid conflict, especially with France, and to work instead on the internal affairs of the country.

In both letters he suggested several ways in which the country could avoid a war which, after all, would divert funds needed elsewhere and simply increase the power of the federal government and in particular the executive branch. Barlow believed that the United States could avoid foreign entanglements by insisting on complete freedom of the seas for itself and for all nations. Since both public and private sources owed money to those countries who were plundering the seas, Barlow suggested a sequestering of these debts in proportion to the damage done to American shipping. This method, he felt, was an honorable and practical substitute for war. Barlow also believed that this principle of economic coercion could lead to a "United States of Europe." In fact, in the second letter, Barlow proposed a Maritime Convention made up of various countries which would insure freedom of the seas under penalty of a Ban of Commerce, consisting of prohibition of trade with the offending country and a penalty to be paid by that country. Cooperation of this sort could easily lead to more encompassing political cooperation.

Barlow opposed war, standing armies, and navies on moral grounds; but he also opposed them because they were expensive, thereby draining off money needed elsewhere, and because they led to other questionable and equally expensive practices. One of these questionable practices which war necessitates is the funding system or the building up of a large public debt. In Chapter Five of *Advice to the Privileged Orders,* Barlow argued at length against passing one generation's debts on to later generations; and he is again saying the same thing. Furthermore, he believed that a national debt would bind the United States to nations that were inferior and, therefore, restrict the progress that a young, vigorous country should make. "Your physicians have gone to a decrepid [*sic*] intemperate old man, and borrowed his strong cordials, his bandages, and gouty velvet shoes, to administer them with cruel empiricism to a sturdy plowboy."

In the second letter, Barlow's advice becomes most specific when he explains how America can insure freedom for the people within its borders. Barlow, as well as others, was concerned at this time with the future of those lands west and north of the United States; in fact, he expressed some concern for the Western states which he felt were being isolated from the government located in the East. The United States cannot rely upon European means of insuring unity, a state religion, or a threat from neighboring countries; therefore, it should develop its own means of insuring unity. As Barlow expressed elsewhere and was to express later, he believed that improved means of transportation and the construction of a national system of republican education—physical and mental contact—would insure a stable country. He urged that the national debt be eliminated as soon as possible so that this money could be used for the construction of a system of roads and canals "to harmonize the interests of the states, and to strengthen their present union." And in his discussion of the need for education, he stated with his usual clarity the vital connection between education and a representative democracy:

> A universal attention to the education of youth, and a republican direction given to the elementary articles of public instruction, are among the most essential means of preserving liberty in any country where it is once enjoyed; especially in the United States. The representative system must necessarily degenerate, and become an instrument of tyranny, rather than of liberty, where there is an extraordinary disparity of information between the generality of the citizens and those who aspire to be their chiefs. And as to the federal ties between the different states, how shall they be maintained but by extending the views and enlightening the minds of those whose votes are frequently to be consulted,

and whose actions are always irresistible by their numbers, and the direction which they take.

Within a year of writing these letters to his fellow citizens, the crisis with France had eased and Barlow's friend and political ally, Thomas Jefferson, was elected president. Those ideals which Barlow had argued for and suffered slander for now showed signs of being realized. (pp. 117-19)

Joel Barlow's great period of prose was the last decade of the eighteenth century. In a series of public documents he propounded a political and social theory together with practical suggestions for its implementation. His advice, though not original, is important because it so clearly and forcefully presents a view of man and society that is both consistent and visionary. As in his poetry, Barlow saw in his prose the possibility of a better, even a perfect, world; but, unlike his poetry, which gives generalized glimpses of this future utopia, his prose explains carefully how this utopia might be realized in the near future. This prose presentation and not *The Columbiad* was his greatest gift to America. (p. 125)

> *Arthur L. Ford, in his* Joel Barlow, *Twayne Publishers, Inc., 1971, 144 p.*

ROBERT D. ARNER   (essay date 1972)

[*Arner demonstrates how meter, alliteration, metaphor, and symbol complement subject matter and theme in "Advice to a Raven in Russia." For further commentary by Arner, see excerpt below.*]

[The poem **"Advice to a Raven in Russia"**] is generally considered to be one of the best—if not the best—that Barlow wrote. It is the work of a mature poet who has served a long apprenticeship with the heroic couplet, not only in writing *The Hasty Pudding* but also in transforming *The Vision of Columbus* (1787) into the epic *Columbiad* (1807). The hard work at last paid off, for almost instinctively, it seems, Barlow exploits the potential of the couplet form to underscore and advance his central themes: Napoleon's insatiable lust for war and his betrayal of the French people, whom he leads into death and slaughter. He structures the poem around a set of poetic figures which gives dramatic vividness to his charges against Napoleon and which effectively presents the horror of war in a series of grotesque images. Inspiration and art appear to have fused, and Barlow produced a work that ranks among the best written during the early years of the American republic.

Throughout the satire, Barlow judges Napoleon's deeds against an ideal of order represented by the heroic couplet itself. He contrasts its balanced precision with the chaotic excesses of warfare, its rationality with the mad passion for conquest that drives Napoleon from one war to another, ceaselessly. He presents the consequences of Napoleon's love of carnage, his thirst for blood, and his indifference to human suffering in a predominantly monosyllabic vocabulary, so that the force of internal stresses works to subvert the stability of the couplet unit, just as Napoleon subverts world harmony and order. Barlow employs this stylistic contrast effectively in many passages in the poem, but nowhere with greater success and impact than in the concluding ten lines:

> War after war his hungry soul requires,
> State after State shall sink beneath his fires,
> Yet other Spains in victim smoke shall rise

And other Moskows suffocate the skies,
Each land lie reeking with its people's slain
And not a stream run bloodless to the main.
Till men resume their souls, and dare to shed
Earth's total vengeance on the monster's head,
Hurl from his blood-built throne this king of woes,
Dash him to dust, and let the world repose.

After the passion of this passage and its apocalyptical visions of destruction, the reader arrives with a sense of relief at "repose," a word which, by virtue of its position in the poem and its syllabic structure, enforces the action which it describes. As the only polysyllabic word of the final nineteen, and with its combination of two long vowels, it compels us to come to a halt. Musically, it resolves the various "r" and "o" tones of "hurl," "from," "throne," "woes," and "world." Its long vowels, counterpointing the brusque, emphatic consonants of "blood-built," "dash," and "dust," insist, even as Barlow concludes his poem, that harmony may yet be possible once Napoleon has been disposed of, though hope for the preservation of peace rests, paradoxically, upon success in war.

Alliteration lends additional force to Barlow's monosyllables and, in so doing, renders the stability of his couplet units still more precarious. Yet alliterative consonants also function to bind subject to verb, object to action, or similar actions to each other, often without regard to clearly defined syntactical and grammatical relationships. In line 18, for instance, the reiterated "s" sound of the first and final words—"Sweep over Europe, hurry back to Spain"—has the effect of emphasizing the precipitousness of the raven's flight and, by association, the rapid progress of Napoleon's armies. The sound compresses the meaning of the sentence by linking the action with the country where it concludes, as if all Europe could not detain Napoleon in his haste to return to Spain. Less subtle but still effective are the sibilants of the first seven lines of the ten-line passage previously quoted, where Napoleon's hungry soul is alliteratively associated with what it takes to appease that hunger, "State after State," which "*shall sink*" to feed his appetite. A more specific elaboration of the idea follows, as Barlow identifies "Yet other Spains" whose "victim *smoke shall* rise" to "suffocate the *skies;*" lands shall lie reeking with "*slain*" in countries where "not a *stream*" runs "bloodle*ss* to the main." This insistent repetition of the same sound ultimately contributes to the emotional intensity of Barlow's castigation of Napoleon, for we are compelled to speak of the French Emperor's deeds through clenched teeth. The language of the satire is heavily incantational and always verges on crossing the line between satire and curse.

Of course, alliteration may be the simplest of rhetorical devices, and not all of Barlow's uses of it function as effectively or as complexly as the ones already discussed. But he seldom employs it for the sake of sound alone. His heavy reliance on the device to add nuances of meaning to his lines calls to mind the technique of Old English oral-formulaic poets, whose works are similarly dependent upon consonantal repetition to bind images and ideas together. Thus in his opening four lines—

Black fool, why winter here? These frozen skies,
Worn by your wings and deafen'd by your cries,
Should warn you hence, where milder suns invite,
And day alternates with his mother night—

the repeated "w's" and "w-r" combinations, by creating an onomatopoetic image of the sound of wind sweeping over a barren landscape, reinforce the theme of desolation and es-

tablish a mood at the outset of the poem which is sustained and intensified throughout.

These first four lines also introduce three of the central metaphors or emblems of death around which Barlow structures his poem. The most important and obvious of these is the "black fool," the raven to whom the entire poem is addressed in an extended personification. Ravens have long been associated with death and sorrow in folklore, and in Old English poetry the bird is one of three "beasts of battle"—the eagle and the wolf are the other two—which presages impending conflict and carnage. Another literary precedent for Barlow's use of the raven as a death symbol is the anonymous folk ballad, "The Twa Corbies," which takes its title from two ravens who have witnessed the murder of a "new slain knight" and are planning to make a feast of his unburied body. The murder was arranged by the knight's unfaithful lover, an element not present in **"Advice to a Raven,"** but both the anonymous balladeer (or balladeers) and Barlow know how to use personification and gory naturalistic details to emphasize the crime of betrayal on the one hand and, on the other, Napoleon's betrayal of the French nation and the horror of his criminal lust for blood. Both of these analogues, the "beasts of battle" motif and the ballad, point in the direction of oracular literature and the folk imagination. They suggest one reason for the effectiveness of Barlow's central symbol of death: it calls forth responses from the dark recesses of the mind and probes thoughts and feelings that lie (as Theodore Roethke charted the terrain in "Night Crow") "deep in the brain, far back."

The temporal setting of the poem, winter, blends history and metaphor so well that we are likely to overlook the metaphorical suggestions of death and think only in terms of the actual historical scene. Though death also reigns in the southern countries mentioned in the poem, it wears a particularly grotesque aspect in the frozen north. Here even the surviving troops are more dead than alive, walking zombies merely. Their bodies are "marbled thro with frost"; here there is an obvious but effective irony in "marbled." When the men die, their corpses change to crystal,

Mere trunks of ice, tho limb'd like human frames
And lately warm'd with life's endearing flames,
They cannot taint the air, the world impest,
Nor can you [the raven] tear one fiber from their
    breast.
No! from their visual sockets, as they lie,
With beak and claw you cannot pluck an eye.
The frozen orb, preserving still its form,
Defies your talons as it braves the storm,
But stands and stares to God, as if to know
In what curst hands he leaves the world below.

Like the raven and winter, night, the third metaphor of death, is a folkloristic and archetypal one. In his introduction of the image in line four, "And day alternates with his mother night," Barlow alludes to Goethe's *Faust,* the first part of which was published in 1808, to give additional meaning to the idea of darkness. The struggle between day and night, order and chaos, is the subject of one of Mephistopheles' earliest speeches to Faust; and to the extent that Barlow's poem, as a satire, concerns a similar cosmic opposition between harmony and discord, peace and war, reason and unreason, his allusion seems intended to recall not only Mephistopheles' remarks but also Faust's reply:

MEPHISTOPHELES:
   . . . I am a part of the Part which gave birth to
     light,
   To that haughty light which is struggling now to
     usurp
   The ancient rank and realm of its mother Night,
   And yet has no success, try as it will . . . .

FAUST:
   Ah, now I know your honorable profession!
   You cannot destroy on a large scale,
   So you are trying it on a small.

The allusion, then, identifies Russia as a land under control
of the Prince of Darkness through one of his deputies, Napoleon. The relationship between Satan and the French leader
is also implied in the Miltonic, "Hurl from his blood-built
throne this king of woes," which recalls Satan's expulsion
from a position of power and authority in heaven in *Paradise
Lost.* Both Napoleon and Satan are spirits of negation, opposed to life and order, and both share a similar destructive
energy and force. Barlow specifically contrasts Napoleon's
will to God's in lines where the frozen eyes of the dead stare
"to God, as if to know / In what curst hands he leaves the
world below." Likewise, the portrait of Napoleon "clothed
in his thunders, all his flags unfurl'd. / Raging and storming
o'er the prostrate world" emphasizes his blasphemous assumption of the weapons of God (thunders), which he turns
to demonic ends in his attempt to destroy God's created universe.

The raven furthers the association between Napoleon and
Satan, for the bird is the ensign of both. It functions as the
embodiment of Napoleon's lust for war, the Emperor's alter
ego, as it were. The bird's gluttonous appetite for human flesh
is shared by Napoleon, whose "hungry soul" requires "war
after war." Napoleon's legions "please best their master"
when they toil for the raven, spreading death to others and
bringing it upon themselves, so that the wishes of the man
and the bird are identical. The identification between the two
becomes final and explicit in the epithet, "Imperial Scaven-
ger." Thus through his metaphoric identity with the raven,
as well as through his actions and his associations with the
Devil, the Commander-in-Chief of the Grand Army becomes
a fourth figure of death in the poem.

As the Emperor of France, Napoleon breeds death not only
through his acts of overt violence and hostility, but also
through his legislative decrees. Two of his proclamations, the
order of conscription, which insures a supply of bodies for his
armies, and the ban against importing goods from England
provide the occasions for introducing two final images of
death into **"Advice to a Raven."** Conscription Barlow portrays in the traditional iconography of the borders of New
England elegies and gravestones, the Grim Reaper who
wields "her annual faulchion o'er the human field" in an ironic parody of the harvest. The ban is represented by Cerberus,
the three-headed hound of Hell, a monster bred in classical
mythology and familiar to readers of Dante and Milton as a
symbol of the Underworld. The three heads of the ban suggest the Decrees of Berlin, Fontainebleau, and Milan, designed by Napoleon to provide opportunities for the advancement of French industry and agriculture and, incidentally, to
reduce the trade of England. Though both these figures are
conventional and though Barlow does not develop them to
any extent, they contribute to the satiric attack on Napoleon
by giving objective form to the consequences of Napoleon's
legislation, functioning as metonymies that join cause to ef-

Robert Fulton's portrait of Barlow.

fect, and by underlining Napoleon's associations with death
and darkness.

"Advice to a Raven in Russia" is, then, a rich and well-
wrought poem, drawing part of its power from the intensity
of passion which Barlow brings to it and part from the artistic
ability he had cultivated over a long career of couplet writing.
By containing Napoleon's campaigns within a sequence of
heroic couplets, Barlow simultaneously judges the Frenchman's disordered and chaotic nature and implies that rationality will prevail after all, though at the moment madness
seems in the ascendency. The tactic of addressing the work
to a raven underlines Napoleon's fall from rationality, for it
suggests that the animal possesses greater powers of reason
than does the French general; otherwise, the poet would have
addressed him directly. As a folkloristic symbol of death
backed by a long tradition in English literature, the raven also
calls forth strong emotional responses, as do other archetypal
images of death woven into the poem. Altogether, **"Advice
to a Raven"** blends form, style, subject matter, theme, and
image to achieve a unity of effect of which Edgar Allan Poe
might have been proud and which no poet need be hesitant
to acknowledge as his own. (pp. 39-43)

> *Robert D. Arner, "Joel Barlow's Poetics: 'Advice to
> a Raven in Russia',"* in The Connecticut Review,
> *Vol. 5, No. 2, April, 1972, pp. 38-43.*

ROBERT D. ARNER (essay date 1972)

[*In the following excerpt, Arner explores Barlow's use of rheto-*

ric, rhyme, and imagery in The Hasty-Pudding. *For further commentary by Arner, see excerpt above.*]

The reputation of Joel Barlow as the best poet among the Connecticut Wits seems as secure in our century as it was throughout most of the last, although, curiously, the grounds of it are seldom examined. What we seem to be saying when we give Barlow this distinction, in fact, is not so much that he was an accomplished writer as that the others—Trumbull, Dwight, and the rest—were relatively uninspired amateurs. Barlow's poetry is not often discussed as poetry, but rather as political doctrine. To be sure, *The Vision of Columbus* (later revised, enlarged, and otherwise metamorphosed as *The Columbiad*) invites this kind of treatment, but Barlow's best-known work, *The Hasty Pudding,* is long overdue for a consideration of its intrinsic poetic merits. In its skillful use of rhetoric, inventiveness and energy of rhyme, and deployment of images, as I hope to demonstrate, it is one of the best examples of American neoclassic poetry, well deserving of the wide circulation it has received by virtue of many reprintings in American literature anthologies.

Barlow's familiarity with the devices of formal, classical rhetoric is documented indirectly by Leon Howard [see Additional Bibliography], who calls attention to the popularity enjoyed by John Ward's *System of Oratory* among students at Yale. Ward's book, which was typical of rhetoric texts of the time, was useful both as a means of training for the bar and as a composition text. The majority of the chapters dealt with stylistic matters. Their content was derived mostly from the theories of Aristotle, Cicero, and Quintillian, with supplemental illustrations from other Greek and Roman writers and from Milton and Addison. Ward discussed the low, sublime, and middle styles, the sixteen internal and three external means of organizing a discourse, and the topics of "elegance" (the purity and clearness of language) and "composition" (the turn and harmony of periods). Ten lectures were devoted to "dignity," an explanation of the figures and tropes employed in the sublime and middle styles. In all, Ward mentioned four primary tropes, eight secondary tropes, and thirty-seven different figures. Though we cannot be certain that Barlow knew this particular rhetoric text, Howard's discussion of the book establishes the importance of rhetoric in both the formal and the informal academic preparation of the Yale student. Given Barlow's interest in literature and his intention to pursue a law career, it is not to be supposed that he would have neglected a close study of the rules of composition and oratory.

Exactly how seriously Barlow applied himself to the learning of rhetoric may be inferred from the opening lines of *The Hasty Pudding:*

> Ye Alps audacious, thro' the Heavens that rise,
> To cramp the day and hide me from the skies;
> Ye Gallic flags, that o'er their heights unfurl'd,
> Bear death to kings, and freedom to the world,
> I sing not you. A softer theme I chuse,
> A virgin theme, unconscious of the Muse,
> But fruitful, rich, well suited to inspire
> The purest frenzy of poetic fire.

Merely to catalogue and to identify specific rhetorical devices are not [my intentions], yet some mention should be made of Barlow's use of apostrophe, anaphora, synecdoche, antithesis, and zeugma ("Bear death to kings, and freedom to the world.") The first four and one-half lines might also be regarded as a type of *occupatio,* since Barlow's claim that he

will not sing of Alps or Gallic flags is to some extent contradicted by the fact that he has already sung of them, though briefly. Metrically, "I sing not you" is built entirely of spondees, and the repeated stresses bring the flowing iambs of the first four lines to an abrupt halt, just as the sense of the words collides against the expectations established in the initial lines and announces a countermotion that begins immediately after the end punctuation. The full stop caesura reinforces the reversal of motion and meaning. The shift in diction from the elevated and noble "Ye" to the common and familiar "you" prepares us stylistically for the change from sublime scenery and noble deeds to a simple topic, and this change is emphasized in the next two half-lines, which feature a pun on "softer" and a version of anadiplosis in the repetition of the word "theme"; by repeating the word, Barlow helps to restore the rhythmic flow and smoothness which had been interrupted by the spondaic half-line. The adjective "virgin" functions to announce the theme of innocence, which is one of Barlow's main concerns throughout the poem. Finally, of course—and this is true of the entire work—since these rhetorical figures are properly the province of the middle or the sublime style, they serve as a constant source of ironic tension, exploiting the disproportion between a common subject and an elevated diction.

Rhetoric is for Barlow, then, not merely a means of attaining felicity and elegance of expression but also a device of compression, a way of indicating subtle shifts in tone, theme, and intention upon which his humor and his full meanings depend. When Barlow finally gets around to announcing the true subject of his song after deferring his readers' expectations for seventeen lines, for instance, he constructs the introduction with great care:

> I sing the sweets I know, the charms I feel,
> My morning incense, and my evening meal,
> The sweets of Hasty-Pudding. Come, dear bowl,
> Glide o'er my palate, and inspire my soul.

The reader who remembers that Barlow's first end-stopped half-line was his disclaimer of intention to sing of Alps or Gallic flags may find it more than a coincidence that his next use of the same pattern should come in the line that announces what *is* going to sing about. The structure not only gives emphasis to the announcement but also recalls the earlier line and is therefore a device of unity. Whether this is intentional on Barlow's part is difficult to say; what is almost certainly intentional is his pun on "meal" in "evening meal." The same phrase also is part of a suspended chiasmus in which "incense" stands in relation to "inspire" and "soul" as "meal" stands to "glide" and "palate." The antithetical structure of each separate line involved in the chiasmus syntactically insists upon the equality of body and soul, while the total figure functions to separate the two again. The ironic tension here established between food for the soul and food for the body is maintained throughout the poem and lies behind the claim in line 186 that hasty pudding can "shield the morals while it mends the size." So, too, Barlow calls upon the language of religion and of religious experience to supply one dimension of the sublime style as he simultaneously elevates the commonplace to the highest level of experience and reduces the grand to the usual and familiar. Thus when he writes, "Fear not to slaver; 'tis no deadly sin," he achieves an almost Popean catechresis, the juxtaposition of a breach of good manners to the Christian concept of a vice punishable by an eternity in Hell. The point is very nearly the same as the one underlying Pope's *The Rape of the Lock:* that in a society which mistakes form for intrinsic value, breaches of decorum *are* breaches of morality. The irony is only superficially directed at the rudeness of the American's eating habits; at a deeper level, the thrust is against European society, which is so preoccupied with artificial rules for the sake of preserving appearances that its members have no appreciation of the essential and the natural.

As the rude gusto of the Yankee collides against the formality of the etiquette of fashionable society and gives rise to a new set of rules suitable for eating and enjoying hasty pudding, so Barlow's catechretical line phonetically performs the violation of decorum that it counsels. Much of the effect of the line depends upon the contrast between the smoothness of Barlow's basic poetic vocabulary and the cacophonous key verb, "slaver," which strikes the ear with a sound as unrefined and uncultured as the action it describes. The verb is an element of the low rather than of the sublime or middle styles, and its presence in the poem demonstrates Barlow's willingness to exploit the rules of decorum to achieve humorous ends.

A good deal of Barlow's wit, in fact, depends upon arranged collisions among elements of the low, sublime, and middle styles. For instance, his account of how the yellow flour

> Swell[s] in the flood and thickens to a paste,
> Then puffs and wallops, rises to the brim,
> Drinks the dry knobs that on the surface
>   swim

is delightful principally because the elevated diction of the first half-line is gradually diminished through the second phrase, where grammatical parallelism emphasizes the difference in levels of diction between "swells" (a verb appropriate to the dilation of Satan by pride in *Paradise Lost*) and "thickens," "flood" (an example of comic exaggeration) and "paste"; in the next half-line grammatical structure is altered to speed the descent through "puffs" until what began as the sublime style ends abruptly at the onomatopoetic colloquialism "wallops." Style ascends again slowly in the next half-line. This type of regular and rhythmic rise and fall of levels of diction is characteristic of the entire poem and is surely a chief source of the pleasure we take in reading Barlow's lines.

Barlow achieves perhaps his most successful combination of things commonplace with things refined and sophisticated in the passage in which the speaker's father explains the etymology of the term "Hasty Pudding":

> "In *haste* the boiling cauldron o'er the blaze,
> Receives and cooks the ready-powder'd maize;
> In *haste* 'tis serv'd, and then in equal *haste*,
> With cooling milk, we make the sweet repast.
> No carving to be done, no knife to grate
> The tender ear, and wound the stony plate;
> But the smooth spoon, just fitted to the lip,
> And taught with art the yielding mass to dip,
> By frequent journeys to the bowl well stor'd,
> Performs the hasty honors of the board."

Rhetorically, this sort of excessive elaboration of a point is termed *periergia* by Quintillian. The passage parodies several epic conventions simultaneously, including the convention of the old hero's grave speech to the young warrior and the convention of the naming of a hero by reference to deeds done in his youth. There are in it traces of folk etymology as well. Mock heroic circumlocution mixes well with native American tall tale techniques, for we have only to imagine Barlow's lines written in dialect to become aware of their folksy quality

and their connections with such well-known pieces of American humor as A. B. Longstreet's "Georgia Theatrics" or Twain's "Celebrated Jumping Frog." (pp. 76-80)

Barlow's artistry is evident not only in his skillful use of rhetorical devices, but also in his use of rhyme to pace his verse and to suggest additional gradations of thought. The delight of rhyme lies in its being a discovery of phonetic similarity where no similarities of any kind were thought to exist. The couplet presents the poet with a special challenge, for in its metrical regularity and rigidity of rhyme scheme it invites monotony and boredom. But Barlow's metrics easily avoid monotony, as we have seen in his earlier use of spondees . . . and this is true of his rhyme also. Characteristically, he rhymes verbs with nouns (see the opening eight lines, for instance) or adjectives with adverbs, and thus sets his phonetic relationships against grammatical differences. He gains variety by rhyming polysyllables with monosyllables, or he joins "freight" to "dilate" and plays our ear against our eye. He links foreign words or words of foreign origin to English ones—"*Levant-Polante*" or "beaux-rows"—and proper nouns to common—"joy-Savoy"—to add other surprises to his verse; we discover that dissimilar languages have something in common, or that a city which has geographical uniqueness shares its sound with an ordinary noun. Occasionally, his rhymes suggest a judgment, as when he yokes "prigs" to "pigs" and thereby implies that the one has many things in common with the other. So, too, the rhyme of "chaste" with "taste" condenses the essential thought of the couplet into two words. Considered as an integral part of the work, the rhymes of *The Hasty Pudding* lend verbal energy and, on occasion, subtle implications to the poem.

Yet another dimension of *The Hasty Pudding* is provided by Barlow's apparent parody of James Thomson's *The Seasons,* a work which enjoyed great vogue in England for several decades after its publication in London in March, 1726. (pp. 80-1)

[Reminiscent] of Thomson's verses is Barlow's address to the cow, in which the use of anaphora and exclamation points are keys to the ironic exaggeration Barlow intends:

> How oft thy teats these pious hands have prest!
> How oft thy bounties prove my only feast!
> How oft I've fed thee with my fav'rite grain!
> And roar'd, like thee, to find thy children
>   slain!

As the speaker gradually grows more and more rapturous in his praise of the cow and in his identification with her until, finally, he shares her grief, her food, her voice, and presumably, her intellect, Barlow's criticism of the excessive sentimentality of Thomson and his followers becomes clear. Barlow's readers would doubtless have remembered the idea if not the exact phrasing of the rustic's lament from their reading of Thomson:

> But you, ye flocks,
> What have ye done? ye peaceful people, what,
> To merit death? you, who have given us milk
> In luscious streams, and lent us your own coat
> Against the Winter's cold? And the plain ox,
> That harmless, honest, guileless animal,
> In what has he offended? he, whose toil,
> Patient and ever ready, clothes the land
> With all the pomp of harvest; shall he bleed,
> And struggling groan beneath the cruel hands

Even of the clowns he feeds . . . ?

If Barlow allows himself this one laugh at the expense of both Thomson and, more generally, the excessive sentimentality associated with popular pastoralism, however, he more than compensates for it by treating rural ideals seriously throughout most of *The Hasty Pudding.* Thus the poem belongs to a tradition that begins with Virgil's *Georgics* and extends through Barlow's English predecessors John Philips (*Cyder*), John Dyer (*The Fleece*), John Gay (*The Shepherd's Week*), and Christopher Smart (*The Hop-Garden*), among others. Of the basic characteristics and conventions of the georgic—didacticism, moral and ethical reflection, information about nature, description, genre sketches, panegyric, introductory and transitional devices (theme statement, dedication, invocation, recapitulation, and so on), narrative episode, country-city opposition, and the pageant of the seasons—Barlow makes significant use of all except narrative episode. He expands the conventional country-city comparison to include a contrast between America and Europe and in this way adds an international dimension to his pastoral that prefigures later American fictional treatments of the international theme. Similarly, he employs the panegyric in praise of the anonymous Indian maiden who first discovered how to grind corn into flour for hasty pudding. In general, he tends to Americanize classical conventions of the georgic mode, in keeping with his effort to Americanize the tastes of Europe and to champion the superiority of simple fare over elegant dishes.

But Barlow does not rely entirely upon pastoral conventions or upon his modifications of them to determine the content and direction of his poem. As an attempt to affirm American innocence and virtue and to portray the native American's unique and personal relationship to the land that sustains him, *The Hasty Pudding* is structured around a complex of closely related images and metaphors: the sun, the growing maize, the hasty pudding itself, and the fire on the hearth. These are linked figuratively as actually in mutual interdependence. The sun grows the corn, which in its color reflects the hue of the sun; the corn is ground into meal, from which the hasty pudding is made, and the pudding, golden like the sun, is heated over a fire that not only is sun-colored but also possesses some of the sun's light, warmth, and life-giving power. Thus the total image grouping suggests in a general way life, creativity, and abounding cosmic energy. More specifically, the hearth stands for family unity in much the same way that the fireside in Whittier's *Snow-Bound* serves as the focal point of family activity, as well as for peace, plenty, and contentment. The planting and growing of the corn, the harvesting of the matured crop, the husking and grinding of the grain, and finally the preparation and eating of the pudding constitute a kind of ritual (hence another reason for the abundance of religious terminology in the poem) simultaneously affirming faith in the continuity of rural human experience and participation in the undying life of the natural world. The cycle of the seasons, endlessly repeating itself year after year, generation after generation, is reassuring symbolic evidence that the old verities of life will not give way or change. The hasty pudding itself is the key image, linking the outdoor world of sunny abundance to its domestic reflection, the indoor world of human creative endeavor. Directly or indirectly, through the processes that are necessary to produce it or to consume it, hasty pudding unites man to nature, to his

family, his rural community, his region, his nation, and to his fellow men throughout history.

Almost from the outset of the poem, Barlow makes it clear that man is happy insofar as he conforms the order of his life to the harmony of nature. The entire second section moves forward according to the movement of the seasons, from spring to summer to autumn and winter; man's activities are regulated by this same seasonal cycle, so that man's identity depends in large measure upon his attuning his life to the alterations of the seasons. He is now sower, now reaper, now celebrant of the harvest home, but each only in accord with nature's time cycle. The close relationship between man and his crops is established when the tall-standing stalks provide a shelter for lovers and thus insure the continuance of love, marriage, and children.

> Now the strong foliage bears the standards high,
> And shoots the tall top-gallants to the sky;
> The suckling ears their silky fringes bend,
> And pregnant grown, their swelling coats distend;
> The loaded stalk, while still the burden grows,
> O'erhangs the space that runs between the rows;
> High as a hop-field waves the silent grove,
> A safe retreat for little thefts of love,
> When the pledg'd roasting-ears invite the maid;
> To meet her swain beneath the new-form'd shade;
> His generous hand unloads the cumbrous hill,
> And the green spoils her ready basket fill;
> Small compensation for the two-fold bliss,
> The promis'd wedding and the present kiss.

The cycle of the seasons which controls the development of the second section of *The Hasty Pudding* is extended into the third section, where the kinship between the corn and the sun is stated in terms of the heat and energy which both parts of nature provide for man. The corn is the sun's surrogate. Barlow describes the hasty pudding as

> A wholesome dish, and well-deserving praise,
> A great resource in those bleak wintry days,
> When the chill'd earth lies buried deep in snow,
> And raging Boreas drives the shivering cow.

The sun is the controlling circle; it inspires and determines the progress of the seasons and, by insuring the growth of the corn, insures the survival of man.

The hasty pudding which is made from the corn has the power to bestow the blessings of domestic felicity and harmony; it unifies the family in appreciation of its excellent flavor and healthful virtues, as is suggested in the scene described in the prose note at the end of the poem. There Barlow stresses the love and affection members of the family feel toward each other, attitudes which hasty pudding seems somehow to aid in generating. He writes: "A prudent mother will cool it [the hasty pudding] for her child with her own sweet breath. The husband, seeing this, pretends his own wants blowing too from the same lips. A sly deceit of love. She knows the cheat, but feigning ignorance, lends her pouting lips and gives a gentle blast, which warms her husband's heart more than it cools his pudding."

In the poem itself, similar idealized moments of happiness and love are also associated with the eating of the hasty pudding. Characteristically the family's portrait is painted by Barlow as parents and children are either grouped around the hearth or seated in a circle around a heavily laden table; thus the fire and the table become important secondary images in the poem. But he who eats hasty pudding shares more with his family than the simple joys of the moment. He takes part in an act which provides a touchstone for individual and family identity in the past as well as in the present. "So taught our sires," says the speaker of the poem, referring to the rules which govern the eating of hasty pudding, "and what they taught is true." As in the world of nature, which preserves through repetition its essential identity even though season follows season and year follows year, the family sustains its identity from one generation to the next through reverence for family wisdom and accumulated traditions. More than nostalgia or the simple comedy of exaggeration is involved in such passages of soaring praise for hasty pudding as the following:

> My father lov'd thee through his length of days:
> For thee his fields were shaded o'er with maize;
> From thee what health, what vigor he possest,
> Ten sturdy freemen sprung from him attest;
> Thy constellation rul'd my natal morn,
> And all my bones were made of Indian corn.

Here the speaker traces his line of descent equally to its human and its vegetative sources, affirming that he is both the son of his father and a child of the corn; he boasts a lineage for himself that may remind some readers of Walt Whitman's later proclamation:

> My tongue, every atom of my blood, form'd from
>   this soil, this air,
> Born here of parents born here from parents the
>   same, and their parents the same. . . .

The speaker's sense of his personal identity is reinforced by hasty pudding not only because it symbolizes his participation in an integrated and harmonious family unit with well-established and well-revered traditions, but also because the pudding—or, rather, the corn from which the pudding is made—provides the opportunity for his participation in a still larger communal unit: the rural community. By celebrating the harvest of the corn and by joining in husking bees, two autumnal festivals which suggest remote analogues in vegetative rituals of pagan antiquity, the speaker shares in both the blessings of the soil and the friendship of his neighbors. As in the portraits of family felicity, so in the scenes depicting the rustic swains and maidens at the husking bee, emphasis falls on laughter and love. Courtship becomes indistinguishable from rural folkways having to do with corn, and the "laws of husking" are also the laws of love:

> For each red ear a general kiss he gains,
> With each smut ear she smuts the luckless swains;
> But when to some sweet maid a prize is cast,
> Red as her lips, and taper as her waist,
> She walks the round, and culls one favored beau,
> Who leaps, the luscious tribute to bestow.
> Various the sport, as are the wits and brains
> Of well pleas'd lasses and contending swains:
> Till the vast mound of corn is swept away,
> And he that gets the last ear, wins the day.

The same images that implied unity and harmony in the scenes of domestic bliss—light, fire, and the groaning board—are once more employed as the husking bee ends, fittingly, with a feast of hasty pudding which suggests, among other things, a kind of communion. In the eating, each member of the rural community partakes in some measure of the cheerful good fellowship and affection that seem to be inspired by the corn itself. The meal confirms the identity of the speaker within a group which is, as the images make clear, as closely knit as a family unit.

If local folkways and folk festivals reinforce the speaker's security by helping to define and simultaneously reaffirm his rural identity, folk speech helps him to keep his ties to his native soil intact whenever he travels. When he wanders to other American regions, he finds good food and entertainment, but given the choice he always selects hasty pudding in preference to other American dishes, hoecake and Johnny-cake included. Sometimes, as he discovers, it is difficult to choose his favorite food because hasty pudding bears other names in different locales:

> E'en in thy native regions, how I blush
> To hear the Pennsylvanians call thee *Mush*!
> On Hudson's banks, while men of Belgic spawn
> Insult and eat thee by the name *suppawn*.
> All spurious appellations, void of truth:
> I've better known thee from my earliest youth,
> Thy name is *Hasty-Pudding*! thus our sires
> Were wont to greet thee fuming from their fires.

The Yankee traveler in Europe quickly learns to expect little hasty pudding there. It is pure accident, as the speaker feels, that he has found some in Savoy. Climates without the sun cannot grow corn, child of the sun, and cities and nations where tastes have become corrupted cannot hope to offer a food which is an emblem of rural simplicity and pastoral innocence. Memories of hasty pudding, then, serve as the American's contact with his homeland and his innocence, and they preserve his "heart and palate chaste" and "pure hereditary taste" amidst the corruption and decadence of Europe. The pudding is a touchstone not only of family, local, and regional identity, but of the national American identity as well. Barlow juxtaposes the image of the sun and the ideas of pastoral bliss and innocence to the following description of various European nations:

> For thee thro' Paris, that corrupted town,
> How long in vain I wandered up and down,
> Where shameless Bacchus, with his drenching
>   hoard
> Cold from his cave usurps the morning board.
> London is lost in smoke and steep'd in tea;
> No Yankee there can lisp the name of thee:
> The uncouth word, a libel on the town,
> Would call a proclamation from the crown.
> For climes oblique, that fear the sun's full rays,
> Chill'd in their fogs, exclude the generous maize;
> A grain whose rich luxuriant growth requires
> Short gentle showers, and bright etherial fires.
>   But here, tho' distant from our native shore,
> With mutual glee we meet and laugh once more,
> The same! I know thee by that yellow face,
> That strong complexion of true Indian race,
> Which time can never change, nor soil impair,
> Nor Alpine snows, nor Turkey's morbid air;
> For endless years, thro' every mild domain,
> Where grows the maize, there thou art sure
>   to reign.

America is, then, the country of the sun, in contrast to the nations of gloomy fog in Europe; it is the land of Ceres, not of Bacchus. The American Ceres is, appropriately, an Indian maiden. Her claim to reverence and immortality is that she first learned the secret of grinding corn to make the flour for hasty pudding. In lines faintly anticipatory of Archibald MacLeish's "Landscape as a Nude," Barlow voyages back into an American mythic past which establishes the Indian maiden as a fertility goddess. He discovers as well an American historical past, the red past, in which the American can ground his idealism, patriotism, nationalism, and sense of himself as a citizen of the New World. Again the passage is built around solar imagery and related ideas: heat, light, color, dryness, and life. The Indian maiden's tawny complexion reflects the hue of the sun, as does also the color of the corn, so that by means of color imagery Barlow hints at what he later says explicitly: like the corn, the Indian girl is "Sol's sweet daughter." As we have previously seen, he makes the same figurative claim of solar parentage for the rural white American. Thus he seems to be suggesting that an important element helping to form the American identity is consciousness of the aboriginal past of the continent and of its primitive inhabitants, who were here long before the discovery of the New World by Columbus. Although the effect produced by seeing an Indian maiden treated in elegant and classically regular couplets is somewhat similar to our reaction to the anonymous seventeenth-century portrait of Pocahontas sitting awkwardly and stiffly in white woman's clothing, Barlow seems to be in earnest in locating American history in the red man's past. The Indian maiden, a familiar symbol of America in the late eighteenth and early nineteenth centuries, acquires a new dignity and new dimensions of significance in the context of Barlow's poem.

But Barlow treats more than American uniqueness in his description of the "tawny Ceres." Perhaps unintentionally, he has incorporated into his portrait of the Indian maiden an insight into the total cultural situation of eighteenth-century America. In her role as fertility goddess in a land which had not heard of Greek culture before the landing of Columbus and the later influx of colonists, the anonymous Indian girl strengthens the bond among all men. American foods and the American climate may be different from those of the Old World, but the New World shares the same Greek and Roman heritage that has shaped all of Western civilization. Though the Indians did not call their earth goddess Ceres, the principle of reverence for the soil is universal. This covert theme of American similarity in singularity is enforced by other mythological allusions planted in the poem, allusions which define America in terms of an Old World heritage. For instance, reference to the dried maize as it is shaken through a sieve as a "golden shower" and again as "powder'd gold" suggests the visitation of Danaë by Zeus and the begetting of the hero Perseus, a myth which ties in with other allusions, direct and indirect, to solar parentage and solar heroes. The old myths of the origins of heroes, Barlow's buried allusions imply, have a new applicability and a new relevance in a New World where a race tied closely to the soil is being bred. (pp. 82-8)

Though Barlow was well aware that "the muse but poorly shines / In cones, and cubes, and geometric lines," perhaps we may be permitted to borrow the figure of a series of concentric circles to illustrate the interlocking and expanding image structure of *The Hasty Pudding.* Circles of identity surround the speaker: the family and its ancestors, the rural neighborhood, the New England region, the American nation. America is contained within and at least partly defined by European modes of artistic expression, which in turn depend upon Greek and Roman models. In a way which is almost mystical, when the American eats hasty pudding, he renews his awareness of these parts of his total identity. Most important, however, eating the humble dish becomes a kind

of communion with nature, which forms the outermost circle in Barlow's scheme of interlocking circles of identity.

In light of this internal evidence of careful craftsmanship, it is difficult to accept without reservation Leon Howard's claim that *The Hasty Pudding* is a wholly spontaneous product; the art, as Barlow well knew, is to conceal the art, and the sprightly verses of his mock heroic poem form effective disguises. Nor is it possible to agree with Howard's opinion that the controlling idea of *The Hasty Pudding* is sentimental nostalgia for the days of Barlow's Connecticut boyhood. In spite of the lighthearted tone which Barlow adopts, his subject is far from trivial and unimportant. It is nothing less than his concept of the American identity as the product of "the very physics and chemistry of . . .[America's] soil and climate," a theme which he states prosaically in the Argument to Book II of *The Columbiad.* But in *The Hasty Pudding,* that vision is embodied in images and metaphors and comes across not as political prophecy or nationalistic propaganda, but as poetry of a high order. (pp. 89-90)

> *Robert D. Arner, "The Smooth and Emblematic Song: Joel Barlow's 'The Hasty Pudding',"* in Early American Literature, *Vol. VII, No. 1, Spring, 1972, pp. 76-91.*

JOHN GRIFFITH (essay date 1975-76)

[Griffith shows how Barlow's belief in an eighteenth-century progressive interpretation of history is manifested in the theme, characterization, language, and imagery of The Columbiad.*]*

In the New England states in the decades just following the Revolutionary War, part of the general outburst of activity on several fronts was the flaring up of an especially fervent interest in the study of history. To New England readers of the period, writes H. Trevor Colbourn, a student of early American libraries, "history was the main field of interest." It was universal, not just American, history that drew their attention; translations of the classical historians were especially popular as New Englanders tried to comprehend the whole of man's recorded past. "Their history reading was purposeful," Colbourn writes, "part of their quest for a usable past as a guide to the present and the future." Like many of their European contemporaries, they had questions to put to history—questions of statecraft, economics, military strategy, religion, morality—and they valued its study for the practical use to which it could be put.

But if they agreed that history had lessons to teach, they often disagreed about exactly what those lessons were. Two dominant schools of historical interpretation emerged in this era: (1) the secular millenialism of men like Thomas Paine and Philip Freneau, who believed history was a single upward curve that, through the progressive tendencies of political democracy, free trade, religious toleration, and scientific discovery, would lead to a temporal paradise, created and controlled by self-reliant men; and (2) the cyclicalism of men such as John Adams and Charles Chauncy, who believed history to be a long series of cycles in which nations and societies rise and fall in apparently endless sequence, their rises depending on their adherence to moral law, their falls the result of departing from it.

Each historical theory was linked with a specific social scheme or ideology. The progressives found in virtually every development of modern times—"the cumulative nature of technology, the liberating power of science, the kindling of feelings of social right"—a limitless possibility for good. Hence the appropriate ideology was one of encouraging change, of giving humanity its head, that it might gallop toward its instinctive and inevitable goal, Utopian democracy. The cyclical theorists, on the other hand, were social and political conservatives. To them, human aspiration for unlimited progress was vain and presumptuous; the lesson they took from history was that man must conserve the social virtues as long as he can, for the years of every society's life are numbered. A flourishing society depended on a sound relationship with God. Man's best access to God's unchanging moral principles was his common sense; and common sense, they believed, taught the solid social virtues—industriousness, sobriety, patience, meekness, neighborliness. Men should accept the legitimate authority of church and state—not exactly in the old feudal way, but with a sensible respect for learning and experienced wisdom.

These strong political and ideological implications are of course eminently characteristic of American culture of the time. The climate of opinion in New England of the 1780s and 1790s had in it an element of urgent social-political-moral didacticism (the three categories seldom being really separated) that affected not only the few formal histories written then, but almost every other form of literature: campaign speeches and pamphlets, sermons, essays in the burgeoning periodicals, and imaginative literature as well. This element might be called the age's ideological preoccupation, its sense of a persistent need to translate the large axioms of Puritanism and rationalism into concrete, practical rules to live by. The preoccupation constitutes a fundamental intellectual bent in the country's consideration of the past, and contributes greatly to the characteristic flavor of its public literature. It is more than a theme or subject: it frequently becomes almost a mode of perception, a radical habit of thought and understanding that pervasively affects an author's work. (pp. 235-37)

Barlow's poem [*The Columbiad*] wholeheartedly represents the progressive interpretation of history, with all its liberal corollaries. . . . [In this poem], we can witness the complex interaction between a man's conception of history, his social and religious and political values, and the imaginative forms in which he expresses himself.

When Barlow set out to write his American epic, he recognized that his ideological evangelism was not really part of the traditional epic; but he was confident that he and his own age had discovered what poets and historians of the past had failed to understand: that the ultimate purpose of all good writing was the betterment of society. Poets and historians "from Homer down to Gibbon," Barlow wrote, have had their merits; but they have "led astray the moral sense of man" as they celebrated mayhem and tyranny in their stories of kings and soldiers. Homer would have done better if, "instead of the Iliad, he had given us a work of equal splendor founded on an opposite principle; whose object should have been to celebrate the useful arts of agriculture and navigation; to build the immortal fame of his heroes and occupy his whole hierarchy of gods, on actions that contribute to the real advancement of society, instead of striking away every foundation on which society ought to be established or can be greatly advanced."

To Barlow, the historian's responsibility is essentially the same as the poet's. The poet, of course, may invent his own fable, and the historian must relate the facts of the past as they really happened. But the historians "should likewise develop the political and moral tendency of the transactions he details." Barlow himself is under no illusions about his ideological purpose: the "real object" of his poem, as he sees it, "is to inculcate the love of rational liberty, and to discountenance the deleterious passion for violence and war; to show that on the basis of the republican principle all good morals, as well as good government and hopes of permanent peace, must be founded; and to convince the student in political science that the theoretical question of the future advancement of human society, till states as well as individuals arrive at universal civilization, is held in dispute and still unsettled only because we have had too little experience of organized liberty in the government of nations to have well considered its effects."

To this frankly propagandistic end, he chooses a subject that is "national and historical"; for he believes it is in the skillful recounting of history, arranged so as to emphasize the progressive tendencies leading to the establishment of the United States of America, that the value of the republican principle is most clearly to be seen. To give his poem a framework, he appropriates the image of the great Columbus, thrown in prison and languishing there in the sad delusion that he has failed to further the general progress of mankind. A supernatural visitor appears to him (in the poem's original version, *The Vision of Columbus* the visitor is an angel; in the consistently secularized *Columbiad* he has become Hesper, Genius of the Western World) and comforts him with visions of the immense advances resulting from his discovery. Thus, as Barlow points out, the "fictitious" or "poetical object" of the poem is to "soothe and satisfy the desponding mind of Columbus; to show him that his labors, tho ill rewarded by his cotemporaries [sic], had not been performed in vain; that he had opened the way to the most extensive career of civilization and public happiness." In fact, Barlow is urging the American people (just as Hesper urges Columbus) to take heart and to view the future optimistically, as a republican inspiration. With this object in view, the poem presents the entire history of the world, shaped toward the forming of the American Republic: in Books IX and X, Hesper recounts the world's career from beginning to end, from the time Nature begins to shape galaxies and planets from "the black breast of Chaos," until man has appeared, grown up, traversed a long history of trial and error, and finally achieved a perfect, harmonious mastery of the earth, symbolized in a great Assembly of Mankind resting on American soil and American principles.

In this extremely long historical view, individual men are very nearly invisible. Copernicus, whose astronomy is one of three essential advances on which modernity is said to be built, receives three couplets; Francis Bacon, six; the printing press, seven. The advancement of society here is seen (in Hesper's metaphor) as a mighty river that

> Bands half the globe and drinks the golden sun,
> Sweeps onward still the still expanding plain,
> And moves majestic to the boundless main.

If individual faces and particular historical events are scarcely visible, the central principle is obvious—the progressive principle of the free exercise of the human reason and its power to overcome all barriers on its way to perfect republicanism.

The Columbiad has no single hero, on the order of Homer's Odysseus or Virgil's Aeneas, upon whose adventures the poet can focus (Columbus does not *do* anything in Barlow's poem; he just watches.) But the poem nonetheless concerns itself with a heroic spirit, which is embodied in a dozen figures populating the poem from its introduction to the concluding prose notes. One might call this admittedly rather abstract spirit Man as *philosophe,* Man the Enlightened. As he is the hero of Barlow's conception of history, so is he the hero of Barlow's poem. He has many names: he is Columbus, a civilized humanitarian who carries out a great exploration in the interest of human advancement. He is Manco Capac, the lawgiver of the Incas, founder of a benevolent and durable social structure among savage tribes. He is Copernicus, Galileo, Martin Luther, Francis Bacon, the "gallic sages" who convinced Louis XVI to aid the Americans in their revolution; he is Jefferson, Hancock, John and Samuel Adams, and Washington. In all these incarnations, Barlow's hero is identifiable by two qualities: the ability to reason clearly, and a position in history which sets him over against superstition and oppression. His is the universal situation in which Barlow and his fellows of the Enlightenment found themselves—heirs to the intellectual courage of pioneers like Galileo and Newton and Hume; and heirs also to a world unhappily fettered by the remnants of feudalism: monarchies, established churches, standing armies, superstitions of all kinds. To Barlow, history had advanced through an indeterminate number of confrontations between liberal heroes and feudal reactionaries, every liberated intellect adding its mite of truth to a growing sum.

The poem's most fully developed image of the Barlow hero is in the account of Manco Capac, founder of the Incan dynasty in Peru, to whose adventures are devoted more than eleven hundred lines in Books II, III, and IV. At the beginning of that passage, Capac, scion of a ruling family in one of the many savage Peruvian tribes, awakes to manhood in a culture immersed in superstition and social disorder. His people inhabit a rich and fertile land, but they waste their lives in wandering and fighting. Capac, simply by being reasonable, understands the vast social possibilities open to them. Though his world has always known only war, Capac sees how "to conquer nations on a different plan, / And build his greatness on the good of man." His device depends on religious deception; he and his queen appear to the people dressed in radiant white clothes, claiming to be children of the sun, possessed of divine authority over the tribes. The deception works; Capac's "institutes" are benevolent and just, even though their practical foundation is the people's religious gullibility. Capac's lie, as Barlow tells us in a prose note, later proved to be the system's fatal flaw; for when the people came to doubt Capac's absolute supernatural sanction they grew rebellious and their civilization crumbled. But while Capac's order lasted, it was a prodigious social benefit.

A large part of the Capac episode is taken up with describing the mission of Manco's son Rocha to civilize the fierce peoples who threaten the growing Incan civilization. Barlow included much of this description probably because he liked the epic action and Gothic horror it provided (the enemy tribes eat their slain enemies, offer up children as blood sacrifices, and wear clothing made to resemble the hides of the vultures, tigers, and wolves they worship). Whatever Barlow's immediate motives, his description in fact makes a very suitable dramatization of the poem's basic conflict—the young Capac, clad in white and preaching worship of the sun, op-

posing the dark subhuman figures of the priest-ridden savages in their animal costumes. Barlow's depiction of the final battle between the dark-toned savages and the light-toned civilized people rather vividly presents the conflict between a liberated ideology and a superstitious one.

Barlow's reason for dwelling so much on the image of the liberal hero in his poem is the traditional one of the didactic poet: his hero is proposed as the reader's model, a "mythification" of the qualities the poet wants to teach—rationality, social concern, a scientific or empirical attitude. But the poem has other means, as well, for advancing its author's thesis. One of the most ingenious of these is the way it incorporates the idea that progress is inevitable.

It is Hesper, the immortal Titan, who proclaims the inevitability of progress. In Book IX of the poem, the worried Columbus, although witnessing the *apparent* advance of human fortunes, asks for some assurance that mankind will not even yet regress; and Hesper gives him that assurance. Progress, he says, is a principle of the very universe.

> Nature herself (whose grasp of time and place
> Deals out duration and impalms all space)
> Moves in progressive march.

Any human doubt of this principle is due to the finite range of man's knowledge, which cannot encompass the full pattern. It takes a superhuman intelligence (such as Hesper's) to perceive the entire plan.

But this, to use terms Barlow uses elsewhere, is merely the "fictitious" or "poetical" explanation of progress—Hesper is not *really* an emissary from God giving to man superhuman assurance of universal progress; he is a fiction. The real reason for accepting the belief in progress is given in Barlow's prose note:

> One of the most operative means of bringing forward our improvements and of making mankind wiser and better than they are, is to convince them that they are capable of becoming so. Without this conviction they may indeed improve slowly, unsteadily and almost imperceptibly, as they have done within the period in which our histories are able to trace them. But this conviction, impressed on the minds of the chiefs and teachers of nations, and inculcated in their schools, would greatly expedite our advancement in public happiness and virtue. Perhaps it would in great measure insure the world against any future shocks and retrograde steps, such as heretofore it has often experienced.

The argument for inevitable progress, in other words, has the same purpose as does the entire poem—to inspire the "rising generation" to a belief in the success of the American scheme. To an ideologist like Barlow, there are many "speculative" areas (such as questions of the universal tendency of history) in which absolute truth is not so important as what men believe to be the truth. "Absurdities in speculative opinion" can be dangerous, says Barlow. "They get wrought into our intellectual existence and govern our modes of acting as well as thinking." It is a primary duty of the teacher-historian-poet to root out harmful habits of thinking and to cultivate beneficial ones; for "the public mind, as well as the individual mind, receives its propensities; it is equally the creature of habit. Nations are educated, like a single child. They only require a longer time and a greater number of teachers.

It is with this thought in mind that Barlow produced other

poetic oddities in *The Columbiad.* He was trying to work on his audience's "habits of thinking," trying to educate his readers along lines that he believed appropriate to the enlightened intellect of a republican—lines of scientific objectivity, cosmopolitanism, and lofty abstraction, the conventional hallmarks of the Enlightenment. The peculiarities of his diction, for example, clearly show this intention. He uses a new simplified spelling, writing "thro" and "tho" and "mixt" and "markt," because it is more efficient. He appropriates interesting scientific terms like "azotic" and "embryon," and French words like "colon" (for "colonist") and "trist" (for "sad"), as well as introducing some coinages of his own in his effort to expand and refine his readers' vocabularies. To the student of Barlow, "rivers" do not "freeze," but rather "waves conglaciate instant," and frost dresses "his nitrous form" in "muriat flakes."

There is something of the conventional Augustan love of periphrasis in Barlow, of course. But it is clear that he is intent on doing more than merely avoiding vulgar usage, and that he knowingly goes beyond established poetic practice in his attempt to educate. The text in rhetoric Barlow studied at Yale—Lord Kames's *Elements of Criticism*—insisted that the most successful poetic image is precisely and consistently made, so that the reader can picture its "ideal presence" in his mind. To mix one's metaphors is, in Kames's scheme, a cardinal sin, for it prevents the reader's forming a clear picture in his imagination. Yet despite Kames's preaching, Barlow makes free with "pictures" like this:

> Proud Mississippi, tamed and taught his road,
> Flings forth irriguous from this generous flood
> Ten thousand watery glades; that, round him
> curl'd,
> Vein the broad bosom of the Western world.

The comparison is badly mixed: the Mississippi is first a tamed creature, then the possessor of a "generous flood" that we can only suppose to be the river itself, from which he can fling "watery glades"—which, in turn, become veins in the world's bosom. Being mixed, the image cannot be visualized; no one can form in his mind the image of a river as a man walking a road and owning a river from which he throws glades that are veins. What Barlow provides is not an image of what one would *see* as he looked at the Mississippi River, but something of what he might *know* about the river from studying a map. And this of course is Barlow's point; he has more immediate educational goals in mind than merely providing his readers with a striking naturalistic image. Readers should take from the poem some abstract knowledge about the geographical nature of America's greatest river. The poet is at work on cultivating or improving his readers' habits of thinking, not just playing on them.

The Columbiad is filled with such miniature lectures on divers subjects. The Arctic, according to Barlow, is where "Earth's lessening circles shrink beyond the day," an allusion to theoretical lines of latitude, about which every literate man should know. The animals of the north are "the beasts all whitening there"—whitening, Barlow explains in a note, "partly from the food they eat thro successive generations and partly from the objects with which they are usually surrounded." In the midst of an epic-allegorical battle between Hesper and Frost over the issue of whether Washington shall cross the Delaware, Barlow inserts a note on soil conservation. Hesper is said to have

> seized a lofty pine, whose roots of yore
> Struck deep in earth, to guard the sandy shore
> From hostile ravages of the mining tide,
> That rakes with spoils of earth its crumbling side.

The same concern for his readers' "habits of thinking" can be seen even in the poem's monotonous prosody, its endlessly marching heroic couplets. Barlow always wrote heroic couplets; they were a reliable convention, a comparatively effortless way of putting things in order. He had no use for poetry of erratic, inspired vision or raw and powerful physical or emotional adventures. He wanted his poem to give a sense of order—the order of logic, the order of reason, the order of progress—for order is the principle on which his ideology was to rest. For this purpose the heroic couplet was ideal.

Certainly the meter of *The Columbiad* is of a piece with its other qualities. All experience in the poem is pervaded with a cold, knowing intellectuality that affects the diction, the imagery, the sense of character, as well as the meter; it is a poem "sicklied o'er with the pale cast of thought." Barlow's thought is not profound nor even very original, perhaps; but it is a conscious ratiocination that sets *The Columbiad* significantly apart from poetry that appeals primarily to the senses or to the emotions, and ties it unmistakably to the habits of rational, abstract thought that Barlow believed the necessary condition for an acceptance of his liberal ideology. (pp. 237-43)

> *John Griffith, " 'The Columbiad' and 'Greenfield Hill': History, Poetry, and Ideology in the Late Eighteenth Century," in* Early American Literature, *Vol. X, No. 3, Winter, 1975-76, pp. 235-50.*

J. A. LEO LEMAY   (essay date 1982)

[*In the following excerpt, Lemay examines the themes of* The Hasty-Pudding *and illustrates how contemporary cultural and political trends influenced the subject matter of Barlow's poem.*]

Although Joel Barlow's *The Hasty-Pudding* has been a standard anthology piece since it appeared in the *New York Magazine* in January 1796, only once has it been the subject of critical analysis. Robert D. Arner wrote an excellent examination of its intrinsic literary merit [see excerpt dated Spring, 1972], but as I said in reviewing Arner's article in *American Literary Scholarship* in 1972, I did not think he did entire justice to the political and religious implications of the poem. A patronizing attitude toward *The Hasty-Pudding* still exists in the criticism and anthologies. The current best-selling anthology of American literature concludes its prefatory notice with these words: "Later ages now remember him best as a poet of simple pleasures whose only masterpiece was an eulogy to a lowly pudding." Although "a poet of simple pleasures" is less condescending than the characterizations ("the poet of cornmeal mush") by earlier editors, Barlow is still generally regarded as a poet devoid of complexity and his *The Hasty-Pudding* as a simple poem. I intend to show that Joel Barlow's *Hasty-Pudding* reflects late eighteenth-century avant-garde, radical thought; that politics, language, religion, and myth are philosophical subjects of the poem; that it concerns the nature of men and the bases of culture; and that the primary thesis of *The Hasty-Pudding* parallels the fundamental thinking of Johann Gottfried von Herder, a basic theorist for nineteenth-century Western culture.

A mock-heroic poem, *The Hasty-Pudding* amusingly burlesques epic conventions, and repeatedly undercuts inflated diction with humorous low words. Barlow's description of hasty pudding's preparation typifies his humorous tone:

> In boiling water stir the yellow flour:
> The yellow flour, bestrew'd and stir'd with haste,
> Swells in the flood and thickens to a paste,
> Then puffs and wallops, rises to the brim,
> Drinks the dry knobs that on the surface swim;

The low connotations of "thickens to a paste" undercut the high rhetoric of "Swells in the flood"; and on one level, the successive antithetic qualities within the phrase "puffs and wallops" microcosmically mirror the poem's repeated rhetorical pattern. But on even a cursory reading, several passages clash with the humorous tone and homesick celebration of family and rural pleasures. Is the second couplet in the poem merely present for the sake of an ironic contrast with hasty pudding?

> Ye Gallic flags, that o'er their heights unfurl'd
> Bear death to kings and freedom to the world.

While Barlow was composing the poem in January 1793, this reference to the deposal and execution of Louis XVI (tried on January 19, sentenced to death on January 20, and beheaded on January 21) was hardly a subject for humor. The revolutionary political note recurs in Canto II, with the addition of anti-Catholic sentiment:

> A frightful image, such as school-boys bring
> When met to burn the pope or hang the king.

Indeed, on close inspection we find the poem filled with radical allusions.

The persona of *The Hasty-Pudding* is extraordinarily cosmopolitan. Not only does the speaker reveal his knowledge of the epic traditions in classical literatures, but he also echoes major English poems of the seventeenth and eighteenth centuries, including Pope's masterpiece in the mock-epic genre, "The Rape of the Lock." Further, the speaker of *The Hasty-Pudding* reveals a knowledge of present and past religions and mythologies of Near Eastern and Western cultures, as well as American Indian mythologies. The speaker is an experienced European traveler, alluding not only to such cities as London and Paris, but to a variety of rural areas in Europe and America. Both the chronological progress piece (wherein the poet chronicles the origin and rise of hasty pudding) and the brief geographical progress piece (wherein the poet traces the names of hasty pudding in various parts of the world) emphasize the speaker's posture as a sophisticated cosmopolitan.

But at the poem's opening, the speaker is cursed. He is an archetypal Wandering Jew "Doom'd o'er the world through devious paths to roam, / Each clime my country, and each house my home." The curse is lifted only when the speaker finds hasty pudding. On the literal level, the curse is a joke—merely a gross exaggeration of the speaker's homesickness. But thematically, the curse is real and nicely ties in with the poem's religious, mythical, and democratic themes. In his epic *The Vision of Columbus,* Barlow had demonstrated his interest in comparative religion and his knowledge of solar deities and fertility cults. He continued those same interests in *The Hasty-Pudding.* Early in the poem, he defines hasty pudding as the gift of "Sol's sweet daughter," i.e., as a gift of a solar deity. And throughout the poem, corn will also stand as a symbol of the sun—as, indeed, "corn" (i.e., grain) was

in Egyptian mythology. Like Osiris or Manco Capec, the speaker is a vegetation spirit doomed to wander "up and down" in the "cold" world of the dead until he finds the sun—which will restore life to the race of man. The speaker, then, is a version of Osiris in the underworld, searching for the sun. The descriptions of the chill and fogs, characterizing those lands where the speaker has been wandering, reinforce his identification as a solar deity who will not only bring back the sun and life to mankind but will also . . . reinstitute true civilization. Of course the speaker, an American, is also like Osiris and Manco Capec because his true home is in the West where the sun sets.

But the speaker's characterizations as cosmopolitan, as Wandering Jew, and as a sun god are all relatively submerged. The persona loudly proclaims he is a hick, a provincial Yankee, the celebrant of hasty pudding, the poet of cornmeal mush. The speaker as hick is part of the tradition of Yankee (and American) humor, as it existed in such works as the great American folk song "Yankee Doodle," or such newspaper pieces as John Adams's "Humphrey Ploughjogger" essays, or such native characters in early American comedies as Jonathan in Royall Tyler's *The Contrast,* or in such tall tales as those by the colonial Pennsylvania frontiersman Benjamin Sutton. The real joke is that the supposedly sophisticated audience will accept this persona at face value and think of the speaker as a hick. So Barlow, the avant-garde radical of London and Paris, an intellectual peer of William Godwin, Thomas Jefferson, and Thomas Burke, repeatedly calls himself a "Yankee" and invites the reader to regard him as a foolish "poet of cornmeal mush."

The reader who takes this obvious aspect of the speaker seriously thereby reveals his own ignorance. Further, the condescending reader is completely undercut by being identified with the "gaudy prigs" of corrupted taste who are the opposition within the poem's fictive world. The "gaudy prigs" are identified with excessive luxury and conspicuous consumption. They are the enemy in the eighteenth-century world of values, especially in American democratic and French radical thought. On the other hand, Barlow's persona is identified with rural virtues and plain wholesome food. Nearly thirty years before Barlow wrote *The Hasty-Pudding,* Benjamin Franklin replied to anti-American condescension to corn. In a London newspaper, Franklin adopted an American persona who, like Barlow's, identified America with superior virtue because of its purity and simplicity. Using the splendid pseudonym "Homespun," Franklin wrote: "Pray let me, an American, inform the gentleman, who seems quite ignorant of the matter, that Indian corn, take it for *all in all,* is one of the most agreeable and wholesome grains in the world; that its green ears roasted are a delicacy beyond expression; that *samp, Hominy, succatash,* and *nokehock,* made of it, are so many pleasing varieties; and that a *johny* or *hoecake,* hot from the fire, is better than a Yorkshire muffin." Like Franklin, Barlow deliberately emphasizes the Americanness and provincialism of Indian corn, using a variety of local names for hasty pudding (*mush, suppawn*) and for other corn dishes (*succotash, hoe-cake, johnny-cake,* and *charlotte*).

And just as Franklin's "Homespun" scorns the true ignorance of his supposedly superior opponent, so Barlow's Yankee undercuts his opponents by labeling them "gaudy prigs." Barlow says that "gaudy prigs / Compare" the man who is brought up on corn to "pigs," because corn is used to feed swine. We all recall Johnson's slur on Scotland and oats in his *Dictionary,* where the Great Sham defined oats as "a grain, which in England is generally given to horses, but in Scotland supports the people." Some anti-American English writers may have castigated corn and America in this way. But I believe that Barlow has in mind Edmund Burke's reference to the "swinish multitude" in his *Reflections on the Revolution in France* (1790). The phrase quickly became famous, and opponents of Burke used the pseudonym "Swinish Multitude." In his *Reflections on the Revolution in France,* Burke attacked Barlow's friend, the Rev. Richard Price. Thomas Paine (Barlow's close friend) wrote the most famous reply to Burke, *The Rights of Man.* Barlow composed *The Hasty-Pudding* in 1793, after writing the first of two parts of his own reply to Burke, *Advice to the Privileged Orders, in the Several States of Europe, Resulting from the Necessity and Propriety of a General Revolution in the Principle of Government*. . . . Barlow's formal prose reply to Burke deals with several of the same subjects as *The Hasty-Pudding*.

Advice to the Privileged Orders asserts that the state is the responsible agent of *all men* rather than of the privileged class; that all are equal in their rights; and that the state should preserve and enhance the social heritage of all its citizens, present and future. Barlow celebrates the common man throughout his *Advice.* In concluding the introduction, Barlow writes: "It depends not on me, or Mr. Burke, or any other writer, or description of writers, to determine the question, whether a change of government will take place and extend through Europe. It depends on a much more important class of men, the class that cannot write; and in a great measure, on those who cannot read. It is to be decided by men who reason better without books, than we do with all the books in the world."

The radical democracy that Barlow expressed in *Advice to the Privileged Orders* pervades *The Hasty-Pudding.* The "gaudy prigs" associated with the pope and kings in the poem's fictive world are Burke and his fellow conservatives. Barlow cleverly undercuts the "gaudy prigs" even as he tells of their insults:

> There are, who strive to stamp with disrepute
> The lucious food, because it feeds the brute;
> In tropes of high-strained wit, while gaudy prigs
> Compare thy nursling, man, to pampered pigs.

Literally, Barlow recounts that some writers who use "high-strained" tropes have stamped corn with disrepute because it feeds animals and that gaudy prigs have compared man to pigs. But notice how "pampered pigs" balances "gaudy prigs," implying that the "prigs" are the "pigs." Again, "thy nursling, man" is singular in number, making the plural "pigs" seem to complement the plural "prigs." Barlow's syntax too, which reverses the normal position of the adjective phrase ("In tropes of high-strained wit"), putting it before "while gaudy prigs," also makes it seem as if "prigs" and "pigs" complement one another, an impression reinforced by the dominant rhyme coupling the two words. Besides introducing the opposition within the poem's fictive world, this passage also directly questions the nature of man. How does he differ from the beasts? The speaker's attitude is ironic and self-mocking:

> What though the generous cow gives me to quaff
> The milk nutritious; am I then a calf;
> Or can the genius of the noisy swine,

> Tho' nursed on pudding, thence lay claim to mine?
> Sure the sweet song, I fashion to thy praise,
> Runs more melodious than the notes they raise.

In undercutting both himself and his poem, Barlow also attacks man's pride. He questions man's superiority to animals and reminds us that all men, even the "gaudy prigs" mentioned earlier in this verse paragraph, share bodily functions and cyclic processes with the animals. Eating and drinking, here named, are merely the first of numerous identifications of men with animals. Barlow implies that man is an animal, albeit distinguished by reason. (pp. 3-7)

Near the end of Canto II, Barlow cites the "one advantage" wherein man is clearly superior to animals:

> We've one advantage where they take no part,—
> With all their wiles they ne'er have found the art
> To boil the Hasty-Pudding; here we shine
> Superior far to tenants of the pine;
> This envy'd boon to man shall still belong,
> Unshar'd by them in substance or in song.

Like most of the poem, this passage seems at first merely humorous; but then one realizes that Barlow is saying that man's superiority is manifested by fire. Making squirrels and raccoons "envy" man the "boon" of fire recalls the gods' supposed wrath because of Prometheus's theft. The Promethean allusion reinforces the poem's religious and mythical themes and especially Barlow's repeated identification of the sun as the all-important source both of life and . . . of the gods.

The speaker's underlying attitude toward his subject is serious. The tone is obviously humorous, with the high, epic style repeatedly undercut by low diction and by the traditionally low subject matter. But Barlow has learned his lesson well from Pope. The underlying themes in *The Hasty-Pudding,* like those in "The Rape of the Lock," concern the nature of man and his relation to the fundamental institutions of civilization. In *The Hasty-Pudding,* Barlow celebrates the superiority of simple rural foods to a rich, heavy diet, the superiority of the democratic to aristocratic traditions, and of Protestantism to Catholicism. He sets forth a theory of the *origin* of culture's basic institutions and advances a program whereby a valid, wholesome civilization may replace his present, degenerating one.

The Hasty-Pudding contains an early, sustained use and praise of folklore and folk customs in highbrow American poetry. Barlow reflects the late eighteenth-century concern with folklore and folk poetry, with native mythology and ancient customs, and with the new theories about the origins of cultures. The context of Barlow's use of American folk materials is provided by James Macpherson's Ossianic poems, Thomas Percy's *Reliques of Ancient English Poetry,* Thomas Chatterton's Rowley poems; selected poems of Thomas Gray, James Beatty, and William Collins, such as Collins's "Ode on the Popular Superstitions of the Highlands"; the works of late eighteenth-century students of folklore or "popular antiquities," such as Joseph Strutt's book on English sports and games; the studies of nonclassical mythology; and especially the published theories of Herder. I cannot say for certain which of these works Barlow knew—but it would be surprising if he did not know at least all of those I've just mentioned, and more.

In *The Hasty-Pudding,* Barlow echoes two New England folk songs. "Yankee Doodle" and "New England's Annoyances." One group of Yankee Doodle stanzas concerns the activities at a husking, where, of course, "Yankee Doodle" would have been one of the tunes that the rural farmers of Barlow's boyhood played on their fiddles and fifes, that they sang and danced to. Barlow must have himself sung the common eighteenth-century refrain:

> Corn stalks twist your hair off,
> Cart-wheel frolic round you,
> Old firey dragon carry you off,
> And mortar pessel pound you.

In this Yankee Doodle chorus, the corn spirit is speaking, describing its own death and its transformation which will subsequently bring life to man. These verses are eighteenth-century versions of ancient harvest festival celebrations of the fertility god, remnants of which appear in Shakespeare, as the masque in Act IV of *The Tempest* proves. And common folksongs such as "Sir John Barleycorn" carry down the ancient traditions until the present day. The Yankee Doodle harvest celebration stanzas, like the folk song "Sir John Barleycorn," uneasily combine burlesque with the sacred and ceremonious.

So too does *The Hasty-Pudding.*

The other New England folk song Barlow evidently knew is "New England's Annoyances." It probably dates from about 1643, and turns up in two printed versions, both recorded from oral tradition, in the middle and latter part of the eighteenth century. Two stanzas in "New England's Annoyances" describe the planting and cultivation of corn:

> But when the spring opens, we then take the hoe
> And make the ground ready to plant and to sow;
> Our corn being planted and seed being sown,
> The worms destroy much before it is grown.
>   And while it is growing some spoil there is made
>   By birds and by squirrels that pluck up the blade.
>   And when it is come to full corn in the ear,
>   It is often destroyed by racoon and by deer.

Canto II of *The Hasty-Pudding* similarly describes planting and cultivating corn, and the farmer's attempts to protect it:

> But when the tender germ begins to shoot,
> And the green spire declares the sprouting root,
> Then guard your nursling from each greedy foe,
> The insidious worm, the all-devouring crow.
>   . . . but now the moon
> Calls from his hollow tree the sly raccoon;
> And while by night he bears his prize away,
> The bolder squirrel labors through the day.

Although some scholars may reasonably doubt that Barlow actually echoes either "Yankee Doodle" or "New England's Annoyances" (for Barlow's diction is different), yet the fact that two early American folk songs contain subjects similar to *The Hasty-Pudding* proves that Barlow's descriptions of agricultural practices and husking rituals reflect a dynamic aspect of American folk culture. Further, the folkways described in these folk songs and especially in *The Hasty-Pudding* are intimately allied with ritual, religion, and mythology.

Religious diction appears throughout the poem and dominates several verse paragraphs. Barlow is clearly a euhemerist, believing that the gods of mythology were originally human beings whose extraordinary deeds caused them to be celebrated and finally deified. Thus Barlow says that "Some tawny Ceres, goddess of her days, / First learn'd with stones to crack the well-dried maize." And, referring to Book 2 of his epic *The Vision of Columbus,* Barlow claims "If 'twas Oella, whom I sang before, / I here ascribe to her one great virtue more." Oella, then, Manco Capec's wife in Inca mythology, is tentatively credited with discovering how to prepare and preserve corn. The reference to *The Vision of Columbus* (which Barlow was revising for its 1793 reprinting in Paris) is especially significant, for the 1787 epic proves Barlow's fascination with comparative religion and mythology years before he wrote *The Hasty-Pudding.* Indeed, *The Vision of Columbus* marks the first important use of American Indian mythology in poetry. In his "Dissertation on the Genius and Institutions of Manco Capec," which Barlow inserted between Books 2 and 3 of *The Vision,* the poet reveals the influence of Voltaire's *Philosophical Dictionary,* of William Robertson's *History of America,* and of Garcilaso de la Vega's *The Royal Commentaries of Peru.* Like Voltaire, Robertson, and other Enlightenment intellectuals, Barlow examined the origin and development of culture's institutions, including religion, in order to explain their present state. Although critics differ about the degree of Christian and deistic elements in *The Vision of Columbus,* Barlow attacks "superstitious lore" in the poem, and finds that various false religions have been created by "local creeds." Even in 1787, his opinions clearly tended toward a cosmopolitanism and comparativism that characterize deistic and anti-Christian thought.

In *The Hasty-Pudding,* Barlow sketches out an implied history of religion and mythology. The contexts in which Barlow refers to "mother earth" and to "the parent sun" imply that this "mother" and "father" spawned the various gods of primitive agricultural societies. . . . Barlow not only celebrated the sun as a god throughout *The Hasty-Pudding,* he also refers to the zodiac in a way that implies that all religions descend from its symbols. (pp. 8-11)

The zodiac references, in conjunction with the pervasive allusions to solar deities, to the corn as a solar deity, to the speaker as a version of the Wandering Jew, and to agricultural and fertility rituals, all suggest that Barlow is tracing the origin and development of religion from sun worship to star symbolism, to ever increasing complex forms. (p. 12)

Mythological allusions pervade *The Hasty-Pudding* but they are not so common as allusions either to the sun as a god or to the corn as a surrogate solar deity. Manco Capec and his wife, Oella, were sun gods. Barlow may have directly known the American Indian myths on corn's supernatural origins, and he must have known Benjamin Franklin's famous bagatelle, "Remarks Concerning the Savages of North America," which retells one of those fables. Further, when Barlow describes dried corn being shaken through a sieve as a "golden shower" and when he concludes Canto II with the new life-giving "powder'd gold" exterminating the old, he seems both to allude directly to the solar mythology and to suggest it indirectly by allusions to classical mythology. As Robert D. Arner points out, these two images recall the "visitation of Danae by Zeus and the begetting of the hero Perseus, a myth which ties in with other allusions . . . to solar parentage and solar heroes." Further, as I suggested above, the references to man's control of fire seem to allude to the Prometheus myth. And the speaker himself is a version of Manco Capec, a solar deity.

A major purpose of the solar myth allusions is to affirm that the normal rituals of life are, or should be, sacred. In the 1787 edition of *The Vision of Columbus,* Barlow celebrated the

Inca Indians for their sacred attitudes toward agriculture: "The cultivation of the soil, which in most other countries is considered as one of the lowest employments, was here regarded as a divine art. Having had no idea of it before, and being taught it by the children [Capec and Oella] of their God [the sun], the people viewed it as a sacred privilege, and considered it as an honour, to imitate and assist the Sun in opening the bosom of the earth and producing vegetation." So *The Hasty-Pudding*'s Canto II is a mock-georgic, describing the rituals of planting, cultivating, and harvesting. But first, the poet portrays the typical New England morning meal in a scene that deliberately understates its celebration of familial love, democratic institutions, and daily rituals:

> Not so the Yankey—his abundant feast,
> With simples furnish'd, and with plainness drest,
> A numerous offspring gathers round the board,
> And cheers alike the servant and the lord;
> Whose well-brought hunger prompts the joyous taste,
> And health attends them from the short repast.
>   While the full pail rewards the milk-maid's toil,
> The mother sees the morning cauldron boil;
> To stir the pudding next demands their care,
> To spread the table and the bowls prepare;
> To feed the children, as their portions cool,
> And comb their heads, and send them off to school.

In Barlow's fictive world, labor is not a curse attending man because of his fall from Eden, but is instead necessary to health and a primary satisfaction of life. Idleness is the true curse. In *Advice to the Privileged Orders,* Barlow anticipates DeTocqueville's celebrated thoughts on the influence of aristocracy and democracy on attitudes toward work. Barlow claims that "noble birth has entailed . . . a singular curse; it has interdicted" the nobility of "every kind of business or occupation." Barlow points out that in an aristocracy, "Agriculture, commerce, every method of augmenting the means of subsistence and raising men from the savage state, must be held ignoble." In the new order of the state that Barlow believes will emerge as a result of the French Revolution, "The men that were formerly dukes and marquisses are now exalted to farmers, manufacturers and merchants." In labor, man finds health and satisfaction:

> But since, O man! thy life and health demand
> Not food alone, but labour from thy hand,
> First in the field, beneath the sun's strong rays,
> Ask of thy mother earth the needful maize;
> She loves the race that courts her yielding soil,
> And gives her bounties to the sons of toil.

Barlow celebrates the growing corn as a fertility god, and, in an anticipation of Emerson, implies that the arts are based upon man's imitations of natural forms:

> Then start the juices, then the roots expand;
> Then, like a column of Corinthian mould,
> The stalk struts upward, and the leaves unfold;
> The bushy branches all the ridges fill,
> Entwine their arms, and kiss from hill to hill.

As the corn matures and reproduces, so too do the young adults who are in harmony with nature. The courting scene closes with a portrait of the rich crop and full harvest, implying the farmer's identification with the natural cycles of life. And the canto's final lines strongly convey the ritualistic death of the old and birth of the new:

> The lab'ring mill beneath the burthen groans,
> And show'rs the future pudding from the stones;
> Till the glad house-wife greets the powder'd gold,
> And the new crop exterminates the old.

The ritualistic elements are even more dominant in Canto III, where Barlow emphasizes the social ceremonies of rural life, rather than agrarian labor: "A frolic scene, where work, and mirth and play, / Unite their charms, to chase the hours away." Barlow describes a husking frolic, emphasizing the "laws" of husking and the "rules" for preparing and eating hasty pudding. The "laws" and "rules" recall eighteenth-century literary theory, especially decorum, genre criticism, and the theory of the unities. Indeed, the diction of literary criticism pervades the poem, second only in importance to religious diction. Such repeated words as *significant, clear, chaste, pure, heart, rules, laws,* and especially *art* and *taste* suggest that Barlow is praising a kind of poetry as well as a particular food. In Canto I, after giving a mock derivation of "Hasty-Pudding," the speaker says:

> Such is thy name, significant and clear,
> A name, a sound to every Yankee dear,
> But most to me, whose heart and palate chaste
> Preserve my pure hereditary taste.

Although Barlow is obviously celebrating the qualities of the name "hasty-pudding," he does so in terms that recall seventeenth- and eighteenth-century language theory. Since at least the time of the founding of the Royal Society in London in 1660, English linguists had been writing about the relation between the idea/thing and its sign. Early linguists deplored the fact that the sign was increasingly divorced from its referent in "higher" civilizations. They believed that the relationship between the symbol and its referent was especially close in primitive societies. Barlow had studied such theorists while a student at Yale. When he claimed, in Part Two of his *Advice to the Privileged Orders,* that "the order of nature is inverted," he found the certain indication of the inversion was that "names are substituted for things." Like his American successors in language theory, Emerson and Thoreau, Barlow celebrates rural New England life partially because he believes that the relationship between sign and symbol is clearer if one is living in communion with nature. So modern "gaudy prigs" (like Burke) write "In tropes of high-strained wit," while the writer should endeavour to imitate the simple "melodious" sounds of animals and nature, even though Barlow ironically compares his own "sweet song" to the noises of pigs.

Canto II opens with two echoes of Pope. Barlow tells us that "vicious rules of art" have killed the stomach and sunk the heart, that cookbooks have spoiled cooking, and that children raised on fancy food have lost their playfulness, been given medicines, and died. Barlow's lines, as Theodore Grieder has pointed out, closely parallel the opening of Pope's prologue to Addison's *Cato.* At the same time, Barlow's subject echoes a passage in Pope's "The Second Satire of the Second Book of Horace Paraphrased":

> Now hear what blessings Temperance can bring:
> (Thus said our Friend, and what he said I sing.)
> First Health: The stomach (cram'd from ev'ry dish,
> A Tomb of boil'd, and roast, and flesh, and fish,
> Where Bile, and wind, and phlegm, and acid jar,
> And all the Man is one intestine war)
> Remembers oft the School-boy's simple fare,
> The temp'rate sleeps, and spirits light as air!

Although Barlow's only verbal echo is "Cram o'er each dish," the similarity of subjects and themes in both poems makes the allusions certain. Pope's satire praises "old Simplicity" and "the middle state." Pope locates the oppositions in "Coxcombs" and "Coxcomb-pyes." Pope also praises working up an appetite and the traditions of "our Fathers."

Like Pope, Barlow celebrates simplicity and plain wholesome food; and like Pope, he uses the imagery of taste and eating, in conjunction with the diction of literary criticism, to talk about literature. Barlow constantly implies that the primitive, simple language is the best poetic language. The Age of Poetry existed in mankind's youth. This common eighteenth-century critical position was advanced by John Husbands in 1731, echoed by Thomas Blackwell in *Inquiry into the Life and Writings of Homer* (1735), and adopted by the Scottish philosophers whom Barlow studied at Yale. Barlow reflected these theories in the 1787 *Vision of Columbus* where he opined that in "those arts which depend on the imagination, such as Architecture, Statuary, Painting, Eloquence and Poetry," ancient civilizations had made the greatest progress. "In several, and perhaps all of these, ancients remain unrivaled." But Barlow, following Pope, believes that "some rules" are valuable in literature, "For nature scorns not all the aids of art." Besides "skill" and "care," "experience"— by which Barlow means both the inherited traditions (past examples of great literary works) and the individual's own experience—contributes to the creation of the "rules." The third canto's penultimate verse paragraph adds the final touch to Barlow's implied theory of literary criticism and echoes Pope's *Essay on Criticism.*

> There is a choice in spoons. Tho' small appear
> The nice distinction, yet to me 'tis clear.
> . . . The shape, the size,
> A secret rests unknown to vulgar eyes.
> Experienc'd feeders can alone impart
> A rule so much above the lore of art.

The ultimate requirement in an artistic work is genius. Although the artist should exercise "choice" and "nice distinction," and although the "laws" and "rules" can be a guide, the last, "secret" necessity is the *je ne sais quoi,* which Pope so splendidly expressed as "a Grace beyond the Reach of Art," and which Barlow identifies as traditions "so much above the lore of art." Indeed, with the context of Pope's lines in mind, we can see that Barlow's "Experienc'd feeders" are, in a punning way, those of the most exquisite *taste,* or, in Pope's language "Master-Hands."

> Some Beauties yet, no Precepts can declare,
> For there's a *Happiness* as well as *Care.*
> *Musick* resembles *Poetry,* in each
> Are *nameless Graces* which no Methods teach,
> And which a *Master-Hand* alone can reach.
>   . . .
> Great Wits sometimes may *gloriously offend,*
> And *rise* to *Faults* true Criticks *dare not mend;*
> From *vulgar Bounds* with *brave Disorder* part,
> And *snatch* a *Grace* beyond the Reach of Art,
> Which, without passing thro' the Judgment, gains
> The *Heart,* and all its Ends *at once* attains.

Barlow's *Hasty-Pudding* concerns literature, mythology, politics, and culture. In literature, Barlow primitivistically finds that the rural farmers—the illiterate "folk"—preserve ancient traditions which are keys to the Age of Poetry. In this belief he differs from Pope and is close to Herder. The folk, then, keep intact the purest literary traditions, as they do the greatest religious traditions. Of course it is ironic that Barlow should embody a primitivistic message in such an ultra-sophisticated genre as a mock-heroic, but by doing so, he appeals (as the numerous reprints of *The Hasty-Pudding* prove) to his primary audience—educated Americans. Further, conflicting elements within the persona (an ultrasophisticated European traveler who asserts his provincial Yankee identity) complement Barlow's strategy in his implied theory of literary criticism, for he celebrates the "rules" and "laws" of criticism while basing the rules on so-called primitive literature—and then says that true genius can ignore the rules.

It does, indeed, seem entirely fitting that Barlow's *The Hasty-Pudding,* should conclude with echoes of Pope's *Essay on Criticism.* For the "pamper'd prigs" who object to corn are in Pope's poem the "vulgar eyes" who do not know the simple pleasures of the art of life. Barlow claims that aristocrats and critics like Burke and Johnson—both defenders of the Old Order, of aristocracy, and of feudalism—follow perverted institutions. Like second-rate literary critics, they apply false rules where nature, all around, points out the true unerring path, which is enshrined in the seasons and the folk culture of agrarian societies. Folkways reveal the true bases for language, religion, law, and politics. And as long as man is both in direct contact with these customs and not blinded by the false beliefs of the "pamper'd prigs," he knows the true basis of society and culture, and can enjoy a sacred awareness of life.

Just as the speaker of *The Hasty-Pudding* is an extraordinary cosmopolitan who, like Franklin, pretends to be a "Homespun" hick, so *The Hasty-Pudding* is an intellectual and deeply religious poem, despite its seemingly anti-intellectual celebration of common man, despite its satire of Catholicism, and despite its implied satire of Christianity and other institutional religions. Like Jefferson, Barlow believes that the mass of mankind, rather than just the wealthy and the aristocracy, are the best hope for man's future progress. With education, a natural *aristoi* will continually rise from Burke's "swinish multitude." In the late eighteenth century, Barlow's belief was still radical doctrine. Like Herder, Barlow believed that culture was originally based upon folkways. The simplest customs, founded on familial love and the natural cyclic processes of life, are the bases for the dominant institutions of society, and these customs are, and should be, regarded as artful, ritualistic expressions of man's true religious nature. In *The Hasty-Pudding,* Barlow attempted to fulfill the role that he had, in his 1787 "Dissertation on the Genius and Institutions of Manco Capec" ascribed to the Inca sun-king Manco Capec, for Barlow (like Emerson and Thoreau) advocated a truer and greater civilization, although one solidly founded upon avant-garde theories concerning the origin and development of mankind's institutions, especially religion and language.

Beside reflecting a variety of avant-garde late eighteenth-century intellectual forces, *The Hasty-Pudding* also anticipates later American subjects and themes. Barlow's celebration of the common man and of commonplace folk themes and folk culture prefigures the poetry of Whittier and Whitman and the prose of William Dean Howells and the American realists. More surprising, his poetic use of the gods, mythology, and the archetypes of rural experience looks ahead to the Romantic writings of Poe, Emerson, Thoreau, Hawthorne, and Melville. But perhaps the writer closest to the spirit and attitudes of Barlow in *The Hasty-Pudding* is the

Ernest Hemingway of *In Our Time,* especially in those stories where Hemingway, looking back across the gulf of his European war experiences, finds permanent, affirmative values in simple, ritualistic reenactments of his innocent boyhood initiations. (pp. 13-19)

> *J. A. Leo Lemay, "The Contexts and Themes of 'The Hasty-Pudding'," in* Early American Literature, *Vol. XVII, No. 1, Spring, 1982, pp. 3-23.*

ADDITIONAL BIBLIOGRAPHY

Arner, Robert D. "The Connecticut Wits." In *American Literature, 1764-1789: The Revolutionary Years,* edited by Everett Emerson, pp. 233-52. Madison: University of Wisconsin Press, 1977.
Includes a survey of Barlow's poetic works that treats their patriotic purpose and such topics as their imagery and themes.

Blau, Joseph L. "Joel Barlow, Enlightened Religionist." *Journal of the History of Ideas* X, No. 3 (June 1949): 430-44.
Examines liberal religious ideas in Barlow's prose works and in *The Columbiad.*

Bottorff, William K., and Ford, Arthur L. Introduction to *The Works of Joel Barlow.* Vol. I, *Prose,* pp. vii-xviii. Gainesville, Fla.: Scholars' Facsimiles & Reprints, 1970.
A biographical and critical introduction to Barlow's works.

Boynton, Percy H. "Joel Barlow Advises the Privileged Orders." *The New England Quarterly* XII, No. 3 (September 1939): 477-99.
Traces the political influences on Barlow's *Advice to the Privileged Orders* and describes the growth of his liberal thought.

Brooks, Van Wyck. "New England." In his *The World of Washington Irving,* pp. 44-65. New York: E. P. Dutton & Co., 1944.
A discussion of early New England literature that contains a short survey of Barlow's major works. Brooks emphasizes Barlow's divergence from the political ideology of the Connecticut Wits.

Christensen, Merton A. "Deism in Joel Barlow's Early Work: Heterodox Passages in *The Vision of Columbus.*" *American Literature* XXVII, No. 4 (January 1956): 509-20.
Investigates unorthodox religious views in Barlow's *The Vision of Columbus.*

Davis, David B. Prefatory Note to *Advice to the Privileged Orders in the Several States of Europe Resulting from the Necessity and Propriety of a General Revolution in the Principle of Government,* by Joel Barlow, pp. v-viii. Ithaca, N.Y.: Cornell University Press, Great Seal Books, 1956.
An overview of the historical background and political philosophy of Barlow's *Advice to the Privileged Orders.*

Dos Passos, John. "Citizen Barlow of the Republic of the World." In his *The Ground We Stand On: Some Examples from the History of a Political Creed,* pp. 256-380. New York: Harcourt, Brace and Co., 1941.
An account of Barlow's life that details the evolution of his political career.

Grieder, Theodore. "Joel Barlow's *The Hasty Pudding:* A Study in American Neoclassicism." *Bulletin of the British Association for American Studies* n.s. No. 11 (December 1965): 35-42.
Describes the influence of English neoclassical literature on the form, genre, and tone of *The Hasty-Pudding.*

Howard, Leon. *The Vision of Joel Barlow.* Los Angeles: Grey Bow Press, 1937, 31 p.
Compares the themes of *The Vision of Columbus* and *The Columbiad,* highlighting Barlow's emphasis on human perfectibility in the later poem.

——. "Joel Barlow and Napoleon." *The Huntington Library Quarterly* II, No. 1 (October 1938): 37-51.
A history of Barlow's trip to France in 1811 and the events preceding it. The article also contains the first publication of the text of "Advice to a Raven in Russia."

——. *The Connecticut Wits.* Chicago: University of Chicago Press, 1943, 453 p.
A highly regarded study of the literary works of John Trumbull, Timothy Dwight, David Humphreys, and Joel Barlow that includes chapters on Barlow's life in Connecticut and Europe.

Kretzoi, Charlotte. "Puzzled Americans: Attempts at an American National Epic Poem." In *The Origins and Originality of American Culture,* edited by Tibor Frank, pp. 139-48. Budapest: Akadémiai Kiadó, 1984.
Compares Barlow's political views in *The Vision of Columbus* and *The Columbiad* and assesses the literary value of the later poem.

Leary, Lewis. "Joel Barlow: The Man of Letters as Citizen." In *The Humanist as Citizen,* edited by John Agresto and Peter Riesenberg, pp. 37-56. Chapel Hill, N.C.: National Humanities Center, 1981, 267 p.
Evaluates Barlow's contribution to the literature of his age, focusing on his articulation of his political and social ideals in *The Vision of Columbus* and *The Columbiad.*

Loschky, Helen. "The 'Columbiad' Tradition: Joel Barlow and Others." *Books at Brown* XXI (1966): 197-206.
A study of the relationship between Barlow's alterations to *The Vision of Columbus* and two contemporary epic poems treating similar subject matter.

Miller, Victor Clyde. *Joel Barlow: Revolutionist, London, 1791-92.* Britannica, edited by Emil Wolff, vol. 6. Hamburg: Friederichsen, de Gruyter & Co., 1932, 99 p.
An account of Barlow's revolutionary activities during 1791-92, providing information on both his life and his political writings.

Parrington, Vernon Louis. Introduction to *The Connecticut Wits,* edited by Vernon Louis Parrington, pp. ix-xlviii. New York: Harcourt, Brace and Co., 1926.
An essay on the historical, philosophical, religious, and literary background of the Connecticut Wits. Parrington discusses Barlow's relationship to the Wits and his political ideology as expressed in his prose and poetry.

Pearce, Roy Harvey. "Toward an American Epic." *The Hudson Review* XII, No. 3 (Autumn 1959): 362-77.
Postulates a theory of the American epic and examines the poetics of three examples: *The Columbiad,* Walt Whitman's *Song of Myself* (1855), and Ezra Pound's *Cantos* (1919-59).

Richardson, Robert D., Jr. "The Enlightenment View of Myth and Joel Barlow's *Vision of Columbus.*" *Early American Literature* XIII, No. 1 (Spring 1978): 34-44.
Analyzes the mythic structure of Barlow's *Vision of Columbus* against the background of eighteenth-century theories concerning myth.

Sutton, Walter. "Apocalyptic History and the American Epic: Cotton Mather and Joel Barlow." In *Toward a New American Literary History: Essays in Honor of Arlin Turner,* edited by L. J. Budd, E. H. Cady, and C. L. Anderson, pp. 69-83. Durham, N. C.: Duke University Press, 1980.
Discusses Mather's *Magnalia Christi Americana* (1702) and Barlow's *Columbiad.* Sutton demonstrates that these works, al-

though flawed, present distinctive views of history and anticipate the themes of later American epics.

Tichi, Cecelia. "Joel Barlow and the Engineered Millennium." In
her *New World, New Earth: Environmental Reform in American Literature from the Puritans through Whitman,* pp. 114-50. New
Haven: Yale University Press, 1979.
   Explores Barlow's belief in promoting American material progress through the development of nature, focusing on the manifestation of this theme in *The Columbiad.*

Todd, Charles Burr. *Life and Letters of Joel Barlow, LL.D.: Poet,
Statesman, Philosopher.* 2 vols. New York: G. P. Putnam's Sons,
Knickerbocker Press, 1886.
   The earliest full-length biography of Barlow. Scholars note that
   Todd's editing of Barlow's letters is not always trustworthy.

Woodress, James. *A Yankee's Odyssey: The Life of Joel Barlow.* Philadelphia: J. B. Lippincott Co., 1958, 347 p.
   Highlights Barlow's versatility as poet, politician, businessman,
   pamphleteer, and diplomat through an exploration of such subjects as his early connection with the Connecticut Wits, his long
   sojourn in Europe, and his appointment late in life as minister
   to France.

Zunder, Theodore Albert. *The Early Days of Joel Barlow, a Connecticut Wit.* New Haven: Yale University Press, 1934, 320 p.
   A biography of Barlow that treats in detail the events of his life
   between 1754 and 1787, concentrating on the history of his
   early poetic works.

George Eliot

1819-1880

(Pseudonym of Mary Ann (or Marian) Evans) English novelist, essayist, poet, editor, short story writer, and translator.

The following entry presents criticism of Eliot's novel *Daniel Deronda* (1876). For criticism focusing on her novel *Middlemarch: A Study of Provincial Life* (1871-72), see *NCLC,* Vol. 13. For further information on her life and works, see *NCLC,* Vol. 4.

Daniel Deronda, Eliot's last novel, is regarded as her most ambitious yet perhaps her least successful work. In it she examines a broad spectrum of nineteenth-century European society—from the titled upper classes, whose leisure time is spent at continental resorts, to the shopkeepers and merchants of London's East End—and addresses such themes as spiritual growth, human potential for good and evil, and the idea of vocational calling. Composed of two distinct yet related narratives, the integration of which has usually been considered severely flawed, the novel is unusual in Victorian fiction in its positive portrayal of Jewish characters, culture, and nationalistic aspirations in the section of the work chronicling the history of Daniel Deronda. However, critical praise usually centers on the heroine of the other portion of the work, Gwendolen Harleth. Eliot's subtle and insightful analysis of Gwendolen's character and motivations is judged by some critics the pinnacle of her achievement. On the whole, scholars generally deem *Daniel Deronda* a commendable but not entirely successful artistic experiment, yet it is one that has been the subject of extensive study, standing as an important and controversial work in Eliot's oeuvre.

Eliot's father, Robert Evans, was an estate manager and farmer, her mother, Christiana Pearson Evans, the daughter of a farmer. Eliot, the youngest of their children, demonstrated a keen intelligence at an early age and was sent away to school in Attleborough in 1824. During her school years she absorbed a wide range of knowledge and established an important friendship with one of her teachers, Maria Lewis, a devout Evangelical whose religious convictions shaped Eliot's early thought. Even after she left school and assumed the duties of housekeeper for her widowed father, Eliot continued to read avidly in addition to studying Latin, Greek, Italian, and German. In 1841, influenced by her friendship with the freethinking skeptical philosophers Charles Bray and Charles Hennell, Eliot experienced a "deconversion" from the piously Evangelical outlook of her upbringing to a rational humanist stance.

Eliot's writing career began in the early 1850s when, after the death of her father, she set out to support herself as a regular contributor to London's *Westminster Review.* As a member of its editorial staff from 1851 to 1854, she played an instrumental role in the periodical's success. In London's literary circles Eliot came into contact with many of the leading English writers of her day—most importantly, the journalist and drama critic, George Henry Lewes. A close, supportive relationship grew between them, and, although Lewes was married and unable to obtain a legal divorce, Eliot consented in 1854 to live with him, defying Victorian mores and alienat-

ing her family. With Lewes's encouragement and assistance, Eliot published her first work of fiction, *Scenes of Clerical Life,* in 1858 under the pseudonym George Eliot. In the next few years she produced a succession of well-received novels that drew on her memories of her early life in rural England—*Adam Bede, The Mill on the Floss,* and *Silas Marner.* In her later novels, *Romola, Felix Holt,* and *Middlemarch,* she portrayed a wider range of characters and settings, incorporating historical and political issues into her fiction. Her popularity was at its peak following the publication of *Middlemarch* in 1871 and 1872; fueled by the positive response to this lengthy and complex novel, Eliot began research for *Daniel Deronda* in 1873, reading Jewish history and viewing firsthand Jewish communities and synagogues in Frankfurt, Germany, and elsewhere in Europe. She was occupied in the actual composition of the novel from 1874 to 1876. Although she suffered from intermittent periods of self-doubt and ill-health, Eliot persevered in writing what she called her "big book," bolstered by much-needed support and encouragement from Lewes and her publisher, John Blackwood. *Daniel Deronda* eventually appeared in eight monthly parts from February to September 1876.

Daniel Deronda opens *in medias res,* with a scene set in a European casino. A beautiful, vivacious young woman, Gwendolen Harleth, is absorbed in a winning streak of gambling until she becomes aware of the scrutiny of a handsome stranger, Daniel Deronda. Sensing his disapproval, she loses her concentration and all her winnings. Gwendolen pawns an heirloom necklace to raise money for further gambling, but when Deronda redeems it and returns it to her, Gwendolen is chastened and recognizes him as her moral superior. From this initial incident, the novel divides into two related but discrete plots. In one, Eliot chronicles Gwendolen's courtship and disastrous marriage. When her family faces financial ruin, Gwendolen consents to marry Henleigh Mallinger Grandcourt, heir to Sir Hugo Mallinger's extensive estates, thus breaking her earlier promise to Lydia Glasher, Grandcourt's mistress and the mother of his four children. While Gwendolen's marriage appears happy, she is broken in spirit, suffering both from Grandcourt's sadistic treatment of her and from the knowledge that her actions have wronged Mrs. Glasher and her children. She finds herself increasingly drawn to Deronda, whom she encounters occasionally at social events, and despite his evident disapproval of her and his reluctance to serve as her confessor, expresses some of her moral distress to him. When Grandcourt drowns in a boating accident, Gwendolen turns to Deronda for counsel and to alleviate her guilt in having failed to save her husband. He advises her to alter her selfish lifestyle and cultivate moral and spiritual growth.

The other plot centers on Deronda, a well-educated, sensitive young man raised in ignorance of his parentage as the ward of Sir Hugo Mallinger. Though talented and conscientious, he is undecided as to what to do with his life. After saving a young Jewish woman, Mirah, from suicide and embarking on a search for her lost family, he becomes increasingly involved with the European Jewish community, finding himself attracted to its people, history, religion, and culture. His growing attachment to Mirah, who through his efforts is happily reunited with her brother Mordecai, culminates in their marriage, for when Deronda finally meets his mother, he learns that he too is of Jewish origin. He then recognizes his vocational calling, resolving to devote his life to the realization of Mordecai's vision of a Zionist homeland, and the novel ends with his departure with Mirah for Palestine.

Eliot wrote in a letter that she "meant everything in the book to be related to everything else there." However, critics, from the earliest reviewers to modern scholars, have consistently faulted the novel's disjointed structure and Eliot's attempts to integrate disparate plots and themes. Early reviewers generally praised the first segments of the novel, giving particular emphasis to Eliot's vivid characterization of Gwendolen and her penetrating insight into Gwendolen's moral development. However, with the publication of the later portions of the novel, which deal more extensively with Jewish characters and the concerns of the Jewish people, enthusiasm for the work abated. Some critics, objecting particularly to Eliot's lengthy historical digressions and Mordecai's Zionist speeches, found the depiction of Jewish culture "alien" and therefore irrelevant to English readers. Moreover, many faulted Eliot's idealistic characterization of Deronda, her didacticism, and her scholarly tone. Nonetheless, as the work of an author recognized as a master of the English novel, *Daniel Deronda* was the subject of detailed critical analysis. Henry James, in his 1876 "*Daniel Deronda:* A Conversation," set the tone for much later study of the work with his guarded praise of some aspects of the novel and suggestion that the portions dealing with Daniel, Mirah, and Mordecai are artis-

tically inferior to the portrait of Gwendolen. While Eliot was disappointed by her audience's failure to accept the work as an organic whole, she was gratified by the praise lavished on her work by Jewish readers; in fact, portions of the novel, including Mordecai's eloquent affirmations of Zionist ideals and Eliot's warm tributes to Jewish culture, were widely known among Eastern European Jews in translation.

Daniel Deronda shared in the general decline of Eliot's critical reputation in the late nineteenth and early twentieth century, when her novels were dismissed as heavy, didactic, and overly scholarly. Little attention was given to her works until the 1940s, when F. R. Leavis wrote a number of influential essays reaffirming the greatness of Eliot's achievement. In a 1945-46 essay devoted to *Daniel Deronda,* Leavis elaborated on James's judgments, praising parts of the work, but rejecting wholesale the portions dealing with Jewish characters. He advocated that the "bad parts" be deleted completely, leaving only the history of Gwendolen Harleth, which, in his opinion, constituted Eliot's finest artistic achievement. Leavis's essay sparked dissenting and concurring criticism, and much subsequent discussion of *Daniel Deronda* has been devoted to considerations of the novel's complex structure. Various critics have supported Eliot's claims that the work is an organic whole by studying the stylistic parallels, symbols, allusions, thematic issues, and plot developments with which she intended to unify the two narratives. Most, however, contend that the novel is structurally flawed by Eliot's inadequate integration of her two narrative lines. Critics argue that Eliot's complex manipulation of chronology and interweaving of her two narratives fail because those narratives describe settings at odds with one another, are written in varying tones, and employ different diction and style. For example, commentators point out that the realistic, slightly satirical mode of Eliot's portrayal of English gentry is at variance with the portions of the work dealing with Jews, which have been variously described as allegorical, mythic, visionary, and symbolic.

Scholars have also studied the novel in terms of the central characters, and this approach, too, highlights the disparity of the two narratives. For most critics, Gwendolen dominates the book, standing as one of Eliot's most successful, memorable, and realistic creations—a complex, selfish, yet appealing and potentially tragic character. Eliot's focus on Gwendolen's thought and motivations has led some critics to identify the novel as a *Bildungsroman,* or novel of psychological development, charting the growth of Gwendolen's moral conscience. The novel's other principal personage, Deronda, is widely considered a failure. An idealized, romantic figure in his role as both a personal and national redeemer, he is judged a stilted and unconvincing moral paragon and a vehicle for Eliot's didactic message rather than a fully developed individual. The secondary characters of *Daniel Deronda* have also been the focus of consideration. Grandcourt has been viewed as a profound study of human potential for evil and as a chillingly effective portrayal of a moral sadist. Mordecai, a portrait of a dedicated visionary, is of interest to scholars as one of the most sympathetic treatments of a Jewish character in Victorian literature. Finally, Eliot's depictions of female characters in the novel, including her negative characterization of Deronda's mother and her idealized treatment of Mirah, have been examined as indications of Eliot's ambivalent attitudes toward feminism and woman's role in society.

Although *Daniel Deronda* is generally considered an uneven work and, in the final analysis, an artistic failure, it has been the subject of a diverse and rich body of criticism. Critics agree in recognizing Gwendolen Harleth as one of Eliot's most complex, brilliant creations. Moreover, they generally applaud Eliot's artistic aims and extended scope in *Daniel Deronda,* praising her attempt to transcend the limits of her earlier fiction through her treatment of allegorical and ultimately universal themes. As Barbara Hardy stated, "As an experimental novel, *Daniel Deronda* is a work of peculiar excitements and certain difficulties. It pushes beyond the achievement of its predecessors, and the very nature of its push makes it less easy and less entertaining than these predecessors. . . . It is one of those works of art whose greatness is inextricably bound up with imperfection."

(See also *Dictionary of Literary Biography,* Vol. 21: *Victorian Poets before 1885;* Vol. 35: *Victorian Poets after 1850;* and Vol. 55: *Victorian Prose Writers before 1867.*)

[R. H. HUTTON] (essay date 1876)

[*Hutton was an English theologian and critic and the editor of several prominent nineteenth-century magazines. These included the influential Unitarian journal* National Review, *whose editorship he shared with Walter Bagehot from 1855 to 1862, and the* Spectator, *a liberal weekly newsmagazine where Hutton served as joint-proprietor and editor for thirty-five years. Under the editorship of Hutton and his partner Meredith Townsend, the* Spectator *continued its traditional advocacy of human freedom and support for such unpopular causes as workers' rights, colonial independence, and the emancipation of West Indian slaves. In contrast to its liberal political stance, the magazine espoused conservative views on art and literature, generally reflecting the opinions of its upper-middle-class Victorian readership. Hutton's own literary perspective was strongly influenced by his religious beliefs, and his critiques often emphasize the moral value of a work of art. At the same time, Hutton is praised by commentators as a sympathetic and fair-minded critic whose aesthetic judgments remained distinct from his moral views. Hutton reviewed several of the monthly segments of* Daniel Deronda *in the* Spectator. *In this excerpt from his mixed appraisal of the completed novel, Hutton focuses on Eliot's style, characterization, and treatment of religious and moral concerns.*]

There are both blemishes and beauties in *Daniel Deronda* which belong exclusively to this work of its great author. No book of hers before this has ever appeared so laboured, and sometimes even so forced and feeble, in its incidental remarks. No book of hers before this has ever had so many original mottoes prefixed to the chapters which, instead of increasing our admiration for the book, rather overweight and perplex it. No book of hers before this ever contained so little humour. And no doubt the reader feels the difference in all these respects between *Daniel Deronda* and *Middlemarch.* On the other hand, no book of hers before this, unless, perhaps, we except *Adam Bede,* ever contained so fine a plot, so admirably worked out. No book of hers before this was ever conceived on ideal lines so noble, the whole effect of which, when we look back to the beginning from the end, seems to have been so powerfully given. No book of hers before this has contained so many fine characters, and betrayed so subtle an insight into the modes of growth of a better moral life within the shrivelling buds and blossoms of the selfish life which has been put off and condemned. And last of all, no book of hers before this has breathed so distinctly religious

a tone, so much faith in the power which overrules men's destinies for purposes infinitely raised above the motives which actually animate them, and which uses the rebellion, and the self-will, and the petty craft of human unworthiness, only to perfect the execution of His higher ends, and to hasten His day of deliverance. It is true that so far as this book conveys the author's religious creed, it is a purified Judaism,—in other words, a devout Theism, purged of Jewish narrowness, while retaining the intense patriotism which pervades Judaism; and that the hero,—who is intended for an ideal of goodness as perfect as any to which man can reach at present,— evidently sees nothing in the teaching of Christ which raises Christianity above the purified Judaism of Mordecai's vision. But however much we may differ from her here, it is not on such a difference that our estimate of the power or art of this fine tale can turn. So far as its art is concerned, there neither is nor can be any issue of a dogmatic nature embodied in it. But it would be as idle to say that there is no conception of Providence or of supernatural guidance involved in the story, as to say the same of the Œdipean trilogy of Sophocles. The art of this story is essentially religious.

The struggle between evil and good for Gwendolen, her fear of the loneliness and vastness of the universe over which she can exert no influence, and the selfish plunge which she makes, against all her instincts of right and purity, into a marriage in which she fancies she can get her own way, only to find that she has riveted on herself the grasp of an evil nature which she cannot influence at all, though every day makes her fear and hate that nature more; the counteracting influence for good which Deronda gains with her by venturing,—as a mere stranger,—to warn her and help her against her gambling caprice, and thus identifying himself in her mind with those agencies of the universe beyond the control of her will which "make for righteousness," to use Mr. Arnold's phrase; and lastly, that disposal of events which always brings her within reach of Deronda's influence when she most needs it, till good has gained the victory in her, and that influence, too, is withdrawn, to make room for a more spiritual guidance,—all this is told with a power and a confidence in the overshadowing of human lives by a higher control which is of the essence of the art of the story, and essentially religious. And still more essentially religious is that part of the tale which affects Deronda himself. His mother's attempt to separate him in infancy from the Jewish people, whose narrowness, though a Jewess herself, she detested, and to get him the footing of an English gentleman; the effect which this parentless and ambiguous condition of life has in so training Deronda's natural sensitiveness as to make him study the habits, and wants, and feelings of others even before his own; the controlling power which brings him into special relations with his own people, though he does not know them to be his own people; the victory of conscience over his mother when a fatal disease strikes her, and she fulfils her father's wishes, in spite of her own repulsion to them, by revealing to her son to what race he belongs, and what dreams of his future his Jewish grandfather had indulged; and most of all, the effect which human rebelliousness and self-will had in aiding rather than foiling those higher purposes against which they tried to make war,—all this is told with a force that at times resembles that of the Hebrew prophet's belief in the Eternal purposes, and at times that of the Greek tragedian's mysterious trackings of that inscrutable power which now seems to mock us with its irony, and now again to smile on us in compassion. Whatever the blemishes of the story, no one who can appreciate Art of the higher kind will deny that the history of Gwendolen's moral collapse and regeneration, and of Deronda's mother, and her eventual submission to that higher spirit of her father which, by its want of breadth and sympathy with her own individual genius, had utterly alienated her, in the brilliancy of her youth, till she strove with all her might to ignore what was noble and even grand in it, is traced with a sort of power of which George Eliot has never before given us any specimen.

At the same time, it cannot be denied that while there is more which reaches true grandeur in this story than in perhaps any other of the same writer's, there is much less equality of execution and richness of conception. The hero himself is laboured. And though in some of the closing scenes, especially those with his mother and with Gwendolen, we are compelled to admit that the picture is a noble one, so much pain has been expended on *studying* rather than on *painting* him, that throughout (say) three-quarters of the story, we are rather being prepared to make acquaintance with Deronda than actually making acquaintance with him. Again, we are not satisfied with the Jewish heroine, Mirah. After the first scene in which she appears, where in her misery she is contemplating suicide, and, with a minute forethought characteristic of times of excitement, takes care to dip her long woollen cloak in the river, in order that she may sink the more easily when she puts it on,—after this scene, we say, Mirah does not gain upon us, but rather irritates us against her by her intolerable habit of crossing her hands on her breast, in sign, we suppose, of the meekness and patience of her disposition,—a sign, however, which excites arrogance and impatience in the mind of the readers, and sends a nerve-current through their hands which would be likely to show itself in a sort of action very different from that of Mirah's. The vagueness of the picture of the hero till within a few fine scenes of the end, and this ostentatious humility of the heroine's, seem to us real blots on the higher art of the book.

Then, again, as we have said, the incidental thoughts of the book are in general greatly laboured, and often not only laboured, but feeble. For example, "A certain aloofness must be allowed to the representative of an old family; you would not expect him to be on intimate terms even with abstractions." That is forcible-feeble. Or take this, which is still worse—*à propos* of the poverty of the Jewish reformer, Mordecai:— "Such is the irony of earthly mixtures, that the heroes have not always had carpets and teacups of their own; and seen through the open window by the mackerel-vendor, may have been invited with some hopefulness to pay three hundred per cent. in the form of fourpence." When one realises that all which this laborious sentence means, is that the heroes of the world have often been poor enough to seem fit subjects to be made the prey of grasping costermongers, one is almost bewildered that one of our greatest writers could say anything of so little worth with so elaborate an emphasis. Yet like instances of at once laborious and insignificant remarks are very numerous in *Daniel Deronda.* A similar criticism applies to the original headings prefixed to many of the chapters. Some of them are, as they always used to be, both original and beautiful. But others, again, though even in this book they are certainly the exceptions, are artificial, and even tiresome. . . . Add to this that the small pedantries, like talking of "emotive memory" and a "dynamic" glance, are more numerous than ever, and that perhaps the only sketch of really great humour in the story, is the picture of the composer and pianist Klesmer, and we have shown some reason, we think,

for the opinion which is so widely expressed, that at least in some respects *Daniel Deronda* falls far below the level of *Middlemarch.* On the other hand, the cynicism of the incidental irony is certainly much less, and the whole spirit of the book is wider and higher.

But what makes it, after all, uncertain whether, in spite of the much greater inequality of execution and style, *Daniel Deronda* may not rank in the estimate of the critics of the future as a greater work altogether than any which George Eliot has previously written, is the powerful construction of the plot,— almost a new feature in her stories,—and the occasional grandeur of the conceptions which she successfully works out. The whole of the seventh part and the explanation between Gwendolen and Deronda in the last, seem to us to contain perhaps the highest work George Eliot has ever given us. The scene in which Deronda's mother describes the invisible force which is upon her in her pain and weakness to make her,— involuntarily almost,—revoke her own deliberately executed and apparently successfully executed purpose,—the magnificence of the picture of the woman, half-queen, half-actress, and yet wholly real, as she discloses her unmaternal character to the son whom she admires, but neither loves nor cares to have loving her,—the shrinking and yet imploring tenderness which she awakens in her son,—the constraint and yet the passion of their mutual upbraidings, and their efforts to suppress them,—all produce an almost magical effect on the imagination, such as cannot be paralleled, we think, in any former work of this writer's. There is in this interview something of the high scenic imagination of Sir Walter Scott, blended with the greater knowledge of the individual heart possessed by George Eliot. Not so magical in its force,—we might almost say splendour,—but quite as delicate and much more subtly tender, are the later scenes between Gwendolen and Deronda, after the former has lost her husband in the manner which makes her almost accuse herself of his death. It would be hardly possible to exceed the pathos of the parting interview, where Gwendolen suddenly becomes aware that Deronda is not only engaged to another woman, but preparing to leave for the East, to absorb himself in a life in which she has no interest or concern. There is a subtlety in the relations of the two,—relations which have never in any way been those of passion,—and a delicacy in the painting both of her forlorn sinking of the heart and of his natural tenderness for her, which seem to us among the most original conceptions of modern literature. (pp. 1131-32)

We have avoided criticising the no doubt very prominent and important character of Mordecai, the Jewish prophet, simply because we find it very difficult to make up our mind about him. The picture in some respects is a singularly fine one. But the *ideas* and creed of the man, on which, in a case like this, so very much turns, are too indefinitely and vaguely sketched to support the character. Before such a being as Mordecai could seriously have proposed to restore nationality to the Jews, in order that they might resume their proper mission of mediating, as religious teachers at least, between East and West, he must have had a much more defined belief than any which the author chooses to communicate to us. And the result is to make us feel that he is rather a fine torso than a perfectly conceived and sculptured figure. We admire him, we revere him, we are touched by him, but we are puzzled by him. He would remind us now and then of Mr. Disraeli and the 'great Asiatic mystery,' if his moral nature were not so much more noble and definite than anything of which Mr. Disraeli ever caught a glimpse. On the whole, Mordecai's influence on Deronda is only half-justified. We cannot dismiss Deronda on his journey to the East without feeling uncomfortably that he is gone on a wild-goose chase,—to preach ideas which have only been hinted, and which must rest on a creed that has hardly been hinted at all. *Daniel Deronda* thus seems to us much more unequal than *Middlemarch.* But it rises at certain points definitely above that great book. Its summits are higher, but its average level of power is very much lower. (p. 1133)

[*R. H. Hutton*], *in a review of "Daniel Deronda," in* The Spectator, *Vol. 49, No. 2515, September 9, 1876, pp. 1131-33.*

THE SATURDAY REVIEW, LONDON   (essay date 1876)

[*In this excerpt, the anonymous reviewer finds Eliot's depiction of Jewish characters and Zionist themes alien and comments on the intensity of her idealized portrait of Deronda.*]

The reader, in closing the last book of *Daniel Deronda,* can hardly be certain to what cause is due the impression that the present work is a falling off from *Adam Bede,* and *Middlemarch,* and a whole train of favourites. He knows very distinctly what his feeling in the matter is, but he has to ask himself whether the conviction that the author has fallen below her usual height is owing to any failure of power in herself, or to the utter want of sympathy which exists between her and her readers in the motive and leading idea of her story. This is a question which can hardly be settled. Some resolute admirers may indeed endeavour to adjust their sympathies to this supreme effort, but there can be no class of sympathizers. Jew and Christian must feel equally at fault; and those who are neither one nor the other are very unlikely to throw themselves with any fervour into the mazes of Mordecai's mystic utterances. Yet we recognize George Eliot's distinctive excellences all through; we never detect a flat or trivial mood of mind; if anything, the style is more weighty and pregnant than ever, we may even say loaded with thought. Nobody can resort to the time-honoured criticism that the work would have been better for more pains, for labour and care are conspicuous throughout, and labour and care which always produce suitable fruit; but the fact is that the reader never—or so rarely as not to affect his general posture of mind—feels at home. The author is ever driving at something foreign to his habits of thought. The leading persons—those with whom her sympathies lie—are guided by interests and motives with which he has never come in contact, and seem to his perception to belong to the stage once tersely described as peopled by "such characters as were never seen, conversing in a language which was never heard, upon topics which will never arise in the commerce of mankind."

And not only are these personages outside our interests, but the author seems to go out with them into a world completely foreign to us. What can be the design of this ostentatious separation from the universal instinct of Christendom, this subsidence into Jewish hopes and aims? We are perpetually called away from the action of the persons of the drama to investigate the motive for such a choice of theme. It might be explained if it were the work of a convert, but *Daniel Deronda* may be defined as a religious novel without a religion, and might have been composed in the state of mind attributed to the hero when "he felt like one who has renounced one creed before embracing another." We are at sea throughout. Nobody seems to believe in anything in particular. Nobody

has any prejudices. If it were not for the last page, we should be utterly at a loss to know what is the hero's aim in life, to what purpose he is going to devote it. Nobody expects a novel to contain a religious confession, and the reader of strictest personal faith may pass over latitude in this matter in an author whose legitimate work of delineating human nature is well executed; but when a young man of English training and Eton and University education, and, up to manhood, of assumed English birth, so obliging also as to entertain Christian sympathies, finishes off with his wedding in a Jewish synagogue, on the discovery that his father was a Jew, the most confiding reader leaves off with a sense of bewilderment and affront—so much does definite action affect the imagination, and we will add the temper, more than any implication or expression of mere opinion. It is impossible to ignore differences which lead to such a conclusion. It is true that everything has its turn, and it may perhaps be regarded as significant that the turn of Judaism has come at last; that almost simultaneously with the last book of *Daniel Deronda* there has appeared the first of a series of papers "On the Liturgy of the Jews, by a Jew," in a popular contemporary, where, to the uninitiated, the subject seems most curiously incongruous. We gather from it that party spirit runs high between Hebrew Conservatives and Liberals, or the writer would not have exposed to the ridicule of the Gentile world certain portions of the "Liturgy" recited in the synagogues every Sabbath from the Piyutim; and hence that there may be Jews willing to accept the aid of auxiliaries who regard them, not on the side of their faith, but of their race, which we need not say is the point of sympathy and attraction with the present author.

Force of imagination this writer certainly possesses; but a fertile imagination is not one of her distinctive gifts. To one class of her admirers the stores of her exact memory, treasured by the keenest observation, and set off by a humour especially rare in women, and a power of analysis rare in all writers, have supplied one main charm of her novels. The scenes and persons which strike them as a sort of glorified, harmonized, poetized reproduction come most readily to their recollection in recalling her masterpieces; but such stores must necessarily come to an end. No experience holds inexhaustible examples of mother wit and wisdom, of quaint rustic ignorance and cunning, of strong prejudice which has never felt the breath of cultivated opinion. Each work hitherto has been enriched by some lifelike portrait drawn from this source, but with sign of more and more effort. At first these resuscitations from a vivid past mix themselves with the body of the story, act in it, and assist its development. We cannot think of *Adam Bede* without Mrs. Poyser, or of the *Mill on the Floss* without Mrs. Tulliver and the wonderful group of aunts and their husbands, or of *Silas Marner* without Dolly Winthrop and the company so ensnaring to her husband at the "Rainbow." But this transfusion of the characters derived from memory into the very heart and substance of the story, so that they have entered into the first plan and conception of it, necessarily gives place in time to another use of these diminished stores, when they are brought in for the purpose of enlivening a narrative to which they are not essential; as we see in *Felix Holt,* where the hero's mother says strange things to show herself off and amuse the reader, not to advance the plot, outside of which she stands. The same may be said of the group of "waiters for death" in *Middlemarch.* The present story has no representatives of this class. We recognize no figure as certainly a portrait drawn out of the past. The Jew pawnbroker and his family fill the place of these recollections, but they are clearly a study of more recent date; a study, the reader suspects, made with a purpose, and not from the simple early instinct of observation to which we have assumed the others to be due. The failure of one source of supply must necessarily induce more labour. To reproduce, to revivify a cherished memory is a more loving and congenial task than to educe from inner consciousness the personages fitted to illustrate certain views and theories. We feel that the writer's earlier works must have flowed more easily from her pen and been a more invigorating effort than to personify an idea in the person of Mordecai; because, for one reason, the labour of composition, never slight in work of so high a standard as hers, must have been cheered by confidence in the sympathy of her readers, by notes of approval sounding in her ears; but what security of that kind, what echo of wide sympathy, can have encouraged the unwinding of Mordecai's mazy, husky sentences, with their false air of prophecy without foretelling anything? She must know her public too well to have allowed herself any delusion here, and must have been fully aware that Mordecai would be caviare to the multitude, an unintelligible idea to all but an inner circle. The mystery lies, not so much in himself, for this readers would not care to unravel, but in the question as to what reason the author can have had for thrusting him on their unwilling attention. The ordinary reader indeed ignores these mystic persons, and in family circles Gwendolen has been as much the heroine—if we may so term the central and most prominent female figure—as if there were no Mirah.

Of course in the design of **Daniel Deronda** we are reminded of the part played by Fedalma in the **Spanish Gipsy**. Fidelity to race stands with this author as the first of duties and of virtues, nor does it seem material what the character of the race is. Fedalma feels her gipsy blood, as soon as she is made aware of her origin, to be as strong and imperious a chain as his Jewish descent is with Deronda. In each, race, as linking past and future together, is the idea of an earthly perpetuity. In obedience to this sentiment, the one throws over faith and lover and takes ship with her people; the other, except that he is lucky in a Mirah, follows the same course, throws over every previous association, and takes ship to the vague East.

It is not often that the poet or novelist sets himself to draw a perfect man. The effort is commendable, for it is mostly its own reward. . . . Deronda is so far successful as a portrait that we believe no other writer of our day, inspired by the same intention, could have imparted the degree of amiability, life, and reality which our author has infused into her ideal. It has evidently been a labour of love to apply her special talents to the embodiment of cherished ideas in an external form; to dramatize them, as it were, and make them speak for themselves, through the person and action of her hero; and no one is more successful in helping her readers to realize, not through elaborate and ineffective description, but by conveying an image through its effect on others. Deronda does nothing, but he has a curious influence. Thus "there was a calm intensity of life and richness of tint in Deronda's face, that on a sudden gaze from him was rather startling, and often made him seem to have spoken; so that servants and officials asked him automatically 'What did you say, sir?' when he had been quite silent." And, again, his eyes "had a peculiarity which has often drawn men into trouble; they were of a dark but mild intensity, which seemed to express a special interest in every one on whom he fixed them, and might easily help to bring on him those claims which ardently sympathetic people are often creating in the minds of those who need help." And the qualities of his mind are indicated with the

same characteristic art. We are left to assume his intellectual elevation, but his moral nature is the thing to be described, as inevitably resulting in a certain view of life. His youth suffers under the pain and social disadvantage of not knowing his birth, "such as easily turns a self-centred unloving nature into an Ishmaelite. But in the rarer sort the inexorable sorrow takes the form of fellowship, and makes the imagination tender," "raising a strong array of reasons why he should shrink from getting into that routine of the world which makes men apologize for its wrong doings." Persons attracted him in proportion to the possibility of his defending them. He had to resist an inclination to withdraw coldly from the fortunate. "What I have been most trying to do," he says, "for fifteen years is to have some understanding of those who differ from myself." His imagination had so wrought itself to the habit of seeing things as they probably appeared to others, that a strong partisanship, unless it were against an immediate oppression, had become an insincerity to him." Hence there was, as his mind ripened, a tolerance towards error. Few men were able to keep "themselves clearer of vices than he; yet he hated vices mildly, being used to think of them less in the abstract than as a part of mixed human natures, having an individual history which it was the bent of his mind to trace with understanding and pity." In all these things Deronda acknowledges no teacher. No state of mind can be described more incompatible with strong dogmatic convictions.

But what is wanting in himself Deronda yet seems to supply to others. The author invests him with many spiritual functions, not scrupling to add certain adjuncts impressive to the imagination, as where it is noted, in Gwendolen's confession in the library, that a joint fragrance of Russian leather and burning wood gave the idea of incense, "of a chapel in which censers have been swinging." Not only is he Gwendolen's preacher, confessor, and director, but he is her conscience, and in this capacity she calls his eye dreadful. There are occasions even when he arrives at an elevation higher than this; when he suggests the idea of a Providence, when he is a Being with a capital B, and is foretold by his grandfather as Deliverer with a capital D, and finally he represents to Mordecai, whose inward need of a prolonged self had been dwelt on, something beyond even this. The dying Jew commits his soul into his charge. "Where thou goest, Daniel, I shall go. Is it not begun? Have I not breathed my soul into you? We shall live together." It is not easy to reconcile these qualities, functions, or attributes—whatever we may call them—with the costume of the day, whether evening full dress, which he sets off so well, or that morning drab suit which sets off him. The task which the author has set herself to accomplish in these volumes is to bring together past and present; to modify, by certain explanatory analogies, ancient beliefs into modern doubt, and in her own case to show how the keenest insight into the world's doings may work side by side with a vein of speculation far removed and alien from ordinary sympathies. (pp. 356-58)

A review of "Daniel Deronda," in The Saturday Review, *London, Vol. 42, No. 1090, September 16, 1876, pp. 356-58.*

R. E. FRANCILLON   (essay date 1876)

[*Francillon, a novelist and journalist, considers* Daniel Deronda *fundamentally different from Eliot's other novels, identifying it as a romance in both matter and form.*]

When a great artist, whose very name has become a sure note of excellence, produces a work that the great fame-giving majority refuses to accept on the sole ground that it is his, or hers, there is a matter for dull congratulation. Such an event shows that past triumphs have been neither decreed blindly on the one hand, nor on the other accepted as a dispensation from the duty of making every new work a new and original title to future laurels. And such an event is the production of *Daniel Deronda.*

The author herself can have looked for no immediate fortune but that of battle. The very merits of the book are precisely the reverse of those to which the wide part of her fame is due. Not a few critics have already said that *Daniel Deronda* is not likely to extend George Eliot's reputation. That is unquestionably true—the sympathies to which it appeals are not, as in the case of *Adam Bede,* the common sympathies of all the world. But whether *Daniel Deronda* is not likely to *heighten* her reputation is an entirely different question, and will, I firmly believe, meet with a very different answer when certain natural and perhaps inevitable feelings of disappointment have passed away, and her two generations of admirers have reconciled themselves to seeing in her not only the natural historian of real life, whom we know and have known for twenty years, but also a great adept in the larger and fuller truth of romance, whom as yet we have only just begun to know.

Daniel Deronda is essentially, both in conception and in form, a Romance: and George Eliot has not only never written a romance before, but is herself, by the uncompromising realism of her former works, a main cause for the disesteem into which romantic fiction has fallen—a disesteem that has even turned the tea-cup into a heroine and the tea-spoon into a hero. George Eliot should be the last to complain that the inimitable realism of *Middlemarch* has thrown a cold shade over the truth and wisdom that borrow the form of less probable fiction in *Daniel Deronda.* She is in the position of every great artist who having achieved glory in one field sets out to conquer another. The world is not prone to believe in many-sided genius: one supremacy is enough for one man.

In short, I cannot help thinking that George Eliot's new novel has caused some passing disappointment because it is not another *Adam Bede* or *Middlemarch,* and not because it is *Daniel Deronda.* The first criticism of a book is sure to be founded on a comparison with others. Fortunately, *Daniel Deronda* lies so far outside George Eliot's other works in every important respect as to make direct comparison impossible. It cannot be classed as first, or second, or third, or last—that favourite but feeble make-shift for criticism, as if any book, or picture, or song could be called worse in itself because another is better, or better because another is worse. I believe that *Daniel Deronda* is absolutely good—and the whole language of criticism contains no stronger form of literary creed. Not only so, but I believe that it promises to secure for its author a more slowly growing, perhaps less universal, but deeper and higher fame than the works with which it does not enter into rivalry. In any case it marks an era in the career of the greatest English novelist of our time. It is as much a first novel, from a fresh hand and mind, as if no scene of clerical life had ever been penned. And, as such, it calls for more special criticism even than *Middlemarch*—the crown and climax of the series that began with the sad fortunes of the Reverend Amos Barton. It is not even to be compared with *Romola*—that was no romance in the sense that

the term must be applied to *Daniel Deronda* as the key to its place and nature. (pp. 411-12)

Daniel Deronda is very broadly distinguishable from all its predecessors by not dealing with types—with the ordinary people who make up the actual world, and with the circumstances, events, characteristics, and passions that are common to us all. We have all been so accustomed to see ourselves and all our relations and friends mirrored and dissected that we naturally expected to find the same familiar looking-glass or microscope in *Daniel Deronda.* It is small consolation to a plain man, who looks forward to the ever-new pleasure of examining his own photograph, to be presented with the portrait of a stranger, though the stranger may be handsomer and less common than he. Nevertheless it may well be that he will prize the picture most when he is in the mood to remember that the world does not consist wholly of types, and that the artist who ignores the existence of even improbable exceptions gives a very inadequate, nay, a very false representation of the *comédie humaine.* If George Eliot can be said to have shown any serious fault as an artist, it is that she has hitherto almost timidly kept to the safe ground of probability. Of course the law on this subject is well understood, and has been clearly laid down a hundred times. Fiction is bound by certain rules of probability; fact by none. But this is only sound law where what is called realistic fiction—the novel of types and manners—is concerned. Applied to the Romance, it is not sound law. Romance is the form of fiction which grapples with fact upon its whole ground, and deals with the higher and wider truths—the more occult wisdom—that is not to be picked up by the side of the highway. "This, too, is probable, according to that saying of Agathon: 'it is a part of probability that many improbable things will happen,'" says George Eliot herself, quoting from Aristotle. "It is easier to know mankind than to know a man," she quotes from Rochefoucauld. And, as she herself says, "Many well-proved facts are dark to the average man, even concerning the action of his own heart and the structure of his own retina." But this is not the line upon which she has hitherto proceeded. Her practice is best described in her own words—"Perhaps poetry and romance are as plentiful as ever in the world except for those phlegmatic natures who I suspect would in any age have regarded them as a dull form of erroneous thinking. They exist very easily in the same room with the microscope and even in railway carriages: what banishes them is the vacuum in gentlemen and lady passengers." That vacuum she has hitherto done her best to supply and has supplied it so far as such a thing is possible. We have learned—and we are apt to forget how ill we knew the lesson before *Adam Bede* made its mark upon the literature of the century—that poetry and romance are among the chippings of a carpenter's workshop, are even hovering about the whist-tables of a Middlemarch drawing-room, and are not strangers to the shops of Holborn pawnbrokers. But are poetry and romance, any more than wit and wisdom, to be looked for only in studies and railway trains? We shall find plenty of all by taking the train for St. Oggs, or Treby Magna, or paying a visit to Mrs. Poyser of Dale Farm, or, for that matter, by staying at home among our own relations and friends. But we may travel far before we make the acquaintance of a complete Gwendolen Harleth or an entire Henleigh Mallinger Grandcourt in the flesh, though we may come here and there upon scraps and fragments of them—farther still before meeting a Hebrew prophet in a second-hand book-stall, or hearing from a Frankfort banker the legacies of wisdom bequeathed by a Daniel Charisi. And why should we not, for once in a way, travel away from ourselves? By risking the immediate disappointment of a large number of her most ardent admirers, George Eliot has paid us a higher compliment than if she had given us another Silas Marner. She has practically refused to believe the common libel, upon us who read fiction, that we only care to look at our own photographs and to be told what we already know.

Gwendolen Harleth is as much a romance heroine as Undine. When we are first introduced to her across the green table at Leubrunn we are not, like Deronda himself, puzzled by the question whether the good or the evil genius was dominant in her eyes. . . . In Gwendolen we see at once not a soul, but only the possibility of a soul—not an actual, but only possible battle-field for the good genius and the evil. The faun in broadcloth, in Hawthorne's *Transformation,* is more than matched by this nymph with the *ensemble du serpent* in sea-green and silver. Of course thus far Gwendolen Harleth is obviously typical: just as there are many Maggie Tullivers with grand ready-made souls all at sea among mean, narrow, and vulgar surroundings, so, by way of contrast, are there many Rosamond Vincys and Gwendolen Harleths. The bitter tragedy of Rosamond and Lydgate tells how one of these soulless creatures can act as the basil plant to which the Middlemarch surgeon likened his wife in after times—"a flower that flourished wonderfully on a murdered man's brains." That story demands for its development nothing but the plainest and simplest realism and the closest and most exclusive connection with every-day things—the smaller and commoner the better. But, suppose it had been part of George Eliot's plan to endow Rosamond Vincy or Hetty Sorrel with a soul—the realistic, every-day machinery of **Adam Bede** and **Middlemarch** must have ignominiously broken down. It would have been as adequate to endow Aunt Pullet herself with one. The seeming transformation of which we may fairly and without fear of being misunderstood—at least by any reader of **Daniel Deronda**—speak as the birth of a human soul is a possible thing in every case, but, in any given case, absolutely unlikely. It must depend upon outward circumstances, and the circumstances must necessarily be of an exceptional kind—either unlikely in themselves, or so intensified as to seem unlikely. That is to say, it demands the unbounded, open air of Romance for its representation, where Nature may be seen at work in her rarer aspects: where things are not as we all see them every day, but as some few people may see them once in a lifetime, and thus become exceptionally wise themselves, and, if they impart their rare experience, make others wiser. Gwendolen in St. Oggs, Gwendolen in Treby, Gwendolen in Middlemarch, *must* have lived and died "with her gunpowder hidden," as Sir Hugo Mullinger would say: with her goodness always at that stage of harvest when "it lies all underground, with an indeterminate future . . . and may have the healthy life choked out of it by a particular action of the foul land which rears or neighbours it." To make the original situation more striking, the difficulties of transformation more insuperable, the creator of Gwendolen Harleth has shown remorseless cruelty in depriving the possible, invisible harvest of every chance of showing a single blade. She is not only "the spoiled child," but is narrowed and grooved by spoiling. "To be protected and petted, and to have her susceptibilities consulted in every detail, had gone along with her food and clothing as matters of course in her life." She was not high enough placed to dream of playing a part in the great world, or low enough to have a share in the battles of the wide one. She had no exceptional powers or affections or passions or ambitions. Her only talents were an eccentric sort of beauty that was not likely to prove marketable, and a cold sharp tongue, pointed by a scornful wit of the sort that frightens men and repels women. She is only a bright ripple upon a dead background. Not one of her surroundings can possibly, except in a negative way, have the smallest influence upon her for good or evil. When by accident she comes in contact with great things, as in the person of Herr Klesmer, her thin nature shrivels up: she is nothing, and nowhere. The lively impertinences with which she amused herself at the expense of Tasso and Mrs. Arrowpoint, Jennings and young Clintock, turn into mere shafts of ill-temper when let fly in a broader horizon. She is a real woman: and her blank horizon is more hopelessly, even more tragically, real than the indefinite tragedy which opens in prospect when she is made to faint, with a presentiment of conscience, at a sudden sight of the picture behind the panel at Offendene. It is more pathetic even than the gross and vulgar surroundings of Maggie Tulliver. She could not have found openings and revelations in chance looks and chance words like the miller's daughter. Poor Maggie's soul was above circumstance: circumstance stood to poorer Gwendolen in the place of a soul. George Eliot, who is never weary of dwelling upon the all-importance of early associations in developing character, and of showing how "what we have been makes us what we are," has carefully and explicitly denied her even the remembrance of a fixed dwelling. "Pity," she says, "that Offendene was not the home of Miss Harleth's childhood, or endeared to her by family memories! A human life, I think, should be well rooted in some spot of a native land . . . a spot where the definiteness of early memories may be inwrought with affection. . . . At five years old mortals are not prepared to be citizens of the world, to be stimulated by abstract nouns, to soar above preference into impartiality. . . . The best introduction to astronomy is to think of the nightly heavens as a little lot of stars belonging to one's own homestead." Gwendolen knew but of one star: and that was Gwendolen.

The whole of the first book is devoted to this portrait of Gwendolen—it is a masterly picture, and, in spite of the careful and even exaggerated extraction from her life of all positive circumstance, in spite of the extraordinary difficulty of giving life to a character with no more tangible consistency than a moonbeam, we soon grow to know her as well as her familiar contrast, Maggie Tulliver. I feel tempted to say as well as we know the blacksmith's boy who set Rex Gascoigne's shoulder, for the sake of dwelling upon the marvellous skill with which George Eliot has more than once compressed a whole character, which suggests a whole history apart from events, into a sentence or two. He comes and goes, and we feel as if he had set our shoulder, instead of Rex Gascoigne's. But even before we can guess at the nature of the story, beyond a suspicion that exceptional sin, or exceptional sorrow, beyond common experience, is needed to transform the young lady of Offendene into a woman, the shadow of Grandcourt appears. The manner of his entry is striking and artistic. He, also, at first sight, resembles one of Gwendolen's surrounding *vacua*—the addition of a cypher to a line of cyphers. It is only by degrees that he assumes the rank of the integer before them that gives them value. And, as he develops, he also develops the significance of Deronda. Passages from George Eliot's works could easily be multiplied to show how intensely she regards our active personal influence upon one another from without, the blows, so to speak, given and taken in the battle of life, rather than self-consciousness or self-culture, as the machinery for growth and change. She believes in the mesmeric effect of personality. Nearly every one of her novels contains an influencing character, in a greater or less degree—Dinah Morris, Edgar Tryan, Felix Holt, Dorothea Brooke, Savonarola are only more strongly marked instances. Naturally, in novels of types and manners, such personal influence mostly takes a large religious or social form. But to bring Gwendolen Harleth into relation with such men and women as these—the experiment would be absurd. That "utterly frustrated look, as if some confusing potion were creeping through her system," still repeats itself, I am sure, though she is married to Rex and corresponds with Deronda, whenever she feels herself standing on the edge of an idea—though she has no doubt given up the childish experiment of trying to read learned books in order to make herself wise. Her experiences were bound to be special and peculiarly her own: "Souls," said Dorothea Brooke to her sister, "have complexions too: what will suit one will not suit another." And so happened to her what is utterly unlikely, and therefore utterly inadmissible in representations of typical life and character such as all George Eliot's former works have been: perfectly necessary for the complete study of Gwendolen's transformation, and therefore perfectly legitimate in Romance, which studies human nature in its seeming exceptions, and not in its rules. The end is exceptional: the machinery must be exceptional also. And so the life of Gwendolen Harleth became bound up with that of Henleigh Grandcourt on the one hand and with that of Daniel Deronda on the other.

No doubt the main interest attaching to Deronda and Grandcourt is their relation to Gwendolen. Taken apart from her, and from the romance of her destiny, their intensity would savour of exaggeration. But nobody would dream of talking about exaggeration in connection with the fiend and the angel who, in the well-known picture, are playing at chess for a human soul. There are many men more or less like Grandcourt, or rather like parts of Grandcourt: but he, taken as a whole, is a cunning combination of all the qualities, positive and negative, fit—to refer again to the harvest simile—to choke out the germ "by damage brought from foulness afar," just as her earlier life represented the evil action of the rearing and neighbouring land. George Eliot has shown the force of her genius by turning this necessary *dysdaemon* into an actual man, and by bringing him into relation with Gwendolen in a simple and natural way, that serves to illustrate both his character—apart from his intended use—and hers. His original conception seems to belong to a speech of Mrs. Transome in *Felix Holt,* "A woman's love is always freezing into fear. She wants everything, she is secure of nothing. This girl has a fine spirit—plenty of fire and pride and wit. Men like such captives, as they like horses that champ the bit and paw the ground: they feel more triumph in their mastery. What is the use of a woman's will?—if she tries, she doesn't get it, and she ceases to be loved. God was cruel when he made women." This one-sided, poetical outburst is translated for Gwendolen into plain and bitter prose. She required to be crushed out of her very small self before she could expand into a self that was larger: and as such a preliminary process was a labour of Hercules we have a Grandcourt to fulfil the labour. One of the many passages to which I have already referred as illustrating George Eliot's stress upon personal influence is quite as applicable to her relations with her husband as to her feelings about Deronda: "It is one of the secrets in that change of mental poise which has been fitly named conversion that to many among us neither heaven nor earth has any revelation till some personality touches theirs with a peculiar influence, subduing them into receptiveness. It had been Gwendolen's

habit to think of the persons around her as stale books, too familiar to be interesting." Had she been left to Grandcourt alone, only half the process of transformation could have been possible: she would have undergone all the grinding sorrow, all the heart-breaking self-contempt, and all the longing to destroy life so that she might destroy her bonds; but she would have escaped from all this in time—her soul would have been strangled in its birth: she would have ended by becoming assimilated more and more to her tyrant, and would have been worse than at first because, instead of having no soul at all, she would have had the soul of a slave. That would not have been transformation, but degradation. It is at this point we see the full force of the title-page motto,

Let thy chief terror be of thine own soul

For the soulless nymph is growing a soul now, and it is a soul to be feared. When she saw Mrs. Glasher riding in the park, unrecognised by Grandcourt, "What possible release could there be for her from this hated vantage-ground, which yet she dared not quit, any more than if fire had been raining outside it? What release, but death? Not her own death. Gwendolen was not a woman who could easily think of her own death as a near reality, or front for herself the dark entrance on the untried and invisible. It seemed more possible that Grandcourt should die: and yet not likely. The power of tyranny in him seemed a power of living in the presence of any wish that he should die. The thought that his death was the only possible deliverance for her was one with the thought that deliverance would never come; the double deliverance from the injury with which other beings might reproach her, and from the yoke she had brought on her own neck. No! She foresaw him always living, and her own life dominated by him; the 'always' of her young experience not stretching beyond the few immediate years that seemed immeasurably long with her passionate weariness. The thought of his dying would not subsist: it turned as with a dream-change into the terror that she should die with his throttling fingers on her neck avenging that thought. Fantasies moved within her like ghosts, *making no break in her more acknowledged consciousness and finding no obstruction in it: dark rays doing their work invisibly in the broad light.*" I have emphasised these last words because they express directly, and not merely suggest, the part that Grandcourt is intended to play in what promises to be her soul's tragedy.

Of course Deronda's part, if we remember the depth and subtlety of the drama that is being played, is obvious. It was necessary that we should perceive the action of the good as distinctly and intensely as that of the evil. And in incarnating the good influence, so to speak, I do not think that George Eliot has altogether succeeded so completely in enlisting our sympathies as usual. It is true the difficulties of the task were almost insurmountable. We know what men in general are apt to call men in particular who talk with never failing wisdom, and in whose armour of virtue there is no flaw. We know also what women for the most part think of such men, and therefore we know what novel readers in general will say and think of Gwendolen's good angel. I must own to a feeling of relief when Deronda was conscious of a wish to horsewhip Grandcourt; it was a touch of good warm-blooded sympathetic humanity. However, the sneer is a very cheap and not very effective form of criticism. Nobody dreams of sneering at the Red Cross Knight, in another romance, or at Bayard, *sans peur et sans reproche,* in romantic history. Nobody has ever suggested that ideal beauty of soul differs from ideal beauty of face in not being worth painting. It is one of the highest privileges of the romance to idealise: to show what, under intensely favouring circumstances of nature or culture, may be the best goodness as well as the worst wickedness of a man. If it is true that we needs must love the highest when we see it, it is well that we should have an opportunity of seeing the highest from time to time. In relation to Gwendolen, it is not so much with Deronda himself as with the wisdom and the goodness of Deronda that we are concerned. But he justly gives his name to the novel in so far as he, if not the principal actor in any drama, is a moving influence in three dramas which are only very subtly and indirectly connected—the stories of Gwendolen, of Mirah, and Mordecai.

Deronda is certainly not one of those who find nothing but barrenness from Dan to Beersheba. There are persons in real life who cannot walk from Charing Cross to Temple Bar and not meet with an adventure for every flag-stone: and he is one of these people. If Gwendolen is a nineteenth century nymph, he is a nineteenth century knight errant, and a fortunate one. . . . [The] remarkable circumstances of his birth and bringing up, his harmonious nature, his unbounded and all-sided sympathies, and by no means least, his wonderful talent for finding adventures at every turning, from his cradle to his marriage, qualify him to serve as the conductor whom we need to lead us, by natural steps, into the wide air of romance which Gwendolen must breathe if she is not to die. Through his eyes, which do not look upon common things commonly, we see that romance, the natural history of exceptions and intensities, is as true as reality, and more true than much that seems real. It is very remarkable that, in dealing with him, George Eliot has not only adopted the spirit of romance but its forms—nay, often its common and conventional forms, and that with deliberate preference and intention. Many of her novels contain a romantic incident, and some introduce many, but that is a different thing. Here we have the romantic framework made up of separate incidents not very unlikely in themselves, but which when added or rather multiplied together make up a very unlikely whole. What is the "plot" of Daniel Deronda's history, if it is condensed after the manner of hurried reviewers? A foreign Jewish singer wishes that her only child may be spared what she considers the miseries of his race and become an English gentleman. He is brought up in luxury and kindness, but in ignorance of his race and parentage, by a baronet who is his mother's rejected lover. He saves from suicide a beautiful young girl—herself a Jewess, which is a rather strong coincidence—whom he afterwards marries. He—another strong coincidence—meets with the most untypical of all untypical Jews, a poor workman in London with the brain of a scholar, the heart of a poet, and the soul of a prophet, who by sheer force of enthusiasm inspires, and naturally inspires, the young man of thought and culture with a Quixotic purpose that is to absorb all his years and powers. Meanwhile he has been recognised at Frankfort, a little mysteriously, by a Jew banker as the grandson of his bosom friend, Daniel Charisi; and Deronda's mother, from some motive that I will not call insufficient only because I cannot understand it, sends for him, tells him his family history, and then passes out from his life again for ever. Thus set out like a pile of dry bones, and covering mysteries and family puzzles to which it is not George Eliot's ordinary habit to give more importance than they are worth, which is at best very little, the events of Deronda's life look like the skeleton of a pre-arranged dream. The effect is even carefully enhanced by such a coincidence as that between Mordecai's second-sighted vision of the manner in which his completer soul

was to appear to him, "distantly approaching or turning his back towards him, darkly painted against a golden sky . . . mentally seen darkened by the excess of light on the aërial background," and the way in which Deronda actually approached him along the river, dark in face and dress, and as "from the golden background" of a glorious sunset. But let us at once put all these things, these wonders let us call them, in sharp, immediate contrast with the story of Gwendolen. The contrast is extreme—all the better. It is not more extreme, in truth, than the contrast between life's limits and conditions as dimly guessed by Gwendolen and its unconditioned boundlessness through Art as felt by Klesmer. We need to feel strongly all the difference between her original soullessness and the largeness of an idealised world. It is a strange sensation to go straight from Gwendolen, who needs a revelation to learn that the world is larger than one of her whims, to Mordecai, the prophet to Jacob—not the less a prophet because Jacob is only little Jacob Cohen, the pawnbroker's son. I think one is not obliged to take any profound interest in the Hebrew politics of the future to appreciate Mordecai, so far as we are capable of extending our sympathies in an upward direction. In any case he amply fulfils a sufficient mission by keeping well before our eyes the existence of an ideal world, where all things, though but in dreams and visions, may seem possible, while we are watching Gwendolen's attempts to see beyond the edge of her gown. The Cohens are a foil to him that he may be the more forcible contrast to her, just as the picture of a Dutch kitchen is the most telling preparation for the study of a picture of saints and angels, and that, in its turn, for sympathy with one of human life or history.

There is no reason to fear that the adoption of the common forms of the romance shows poverty or carelessness in invention, or indeed that it shows anything at all except that there is a limit to the permissible length of a novel which the most popular of writers must not exceed. In the novel of types and manners situations are not more important than the way we arrive at them. In the romance—still using the word in its special and contrasted sense—the effects and situations are all-important, and the artist will not spoil his climax by elaborating preliminary details that are, except in their result, of no importance at all. It is not inartistic to use the romance-framework that comes readiest to hand, just as a musician would be very ill-advised who wasted power in inventing a new form for every new sonata. He would set people thinking about his forms too much, and about his effects too little. The direct, uncompromising adaptation of the spirit and form of the romance to a novel of our own time by the author of *Middlemarch* is in itself a striking and daring, perhaps hazardous, experiment in the art of fiction, and certainly the experiment is the more complete, and its effect the stronger, by using forms which held the same good wine of romance that was drunk by our less exigent fathers. If they are but a ready machinery for saving time that can be used for better purpose, they serve their turn. The mere story of **Daniel Deronda** may not be a particularly good one; but then few people have ever read a novel by George Eliot, unless it was **Silas Marner,** merely, if at all, for the sake of the story. It is more important to note whether she displays the qualities—apart from the close realism she does not affect—for which they are read like the lives of old friends that are always new. And in this respect one striking feature of **Daniel Deronda** is that it is not only George Eliot's first romance, but the first novel in which she has either taken our own day for her date, or the class of whom novel readers in general have most personal experience—excluding prophets and pawnbrokers—for her *dramatis personae.*

In the very first page of the very first of her published works the authoress of "**The Sad Fortunes of the Reverend Amos Barton**" affects to complain that "Mine, I fear, is not a well-regulated mind: it has an occasional tenderness for old abuses; it lingers with a certain fondness over the days of nasal clerks and top-booted parsons, and has a sigh for the departed shades of vulgar errors." And these words were written when a great many things were in full force and vigour that have since joined those departed shades. If *Adam Bede* and *The Mill on the Floss* were old world pictures when they were published, what are they now? They have almost fallen back into idylls, so far as that indefinite word implies any idea of obsolete antiquity. They already illustrate history, and—as somebody once suggested in the case of Dickens—will soon require an archaeological museum for their illustration, including, for example, a parish clerk, a parson's top-boots, and Master Marner's loom. . . . [George Eliot] has the air at times of looking upon the present only as a link between the past that we love and regret and the future that we love and hope for. And, in so far as she is thus historical, the outward, circumstantial aspects of her novels must inevitably lose some amount of living interest as time goes on. . . . For our own immediate selves, there is all the difference between *Daniel Deronda* and *The Mill on the Floss* that lies between Now and Once upon a Time. But there is a greater difference still. Each and all her works may be very easily separated into its accidents of period and circumstance and its essentials of what is true and human always, under all circumstances, and everywhere. I will say nothing about Shakespeare, but she certainly has a share in the genius and therefore probably in the fortunes of Chaucer, who is as great as he is obsolete in small things, as enduring as he is great in large. It is precisely in the detailed elaboration of the little, characteristic, everyday things which procure universal acceptation for a book at once that we are most conscious of an unusual want in *Daniel Deronda.* In this respect also it is distinctively of the nature of the Romance, which tends to bring universal and essential things into prominence, and to leave accidental and transitory things on one side. It will never require a department in the museum, at least until the peculiarities of Jews are merged in the yet greater oddities of Gentiles, and that time looks too far off to be worth considering. Its drawing-room atmosphere is only a roughly washed-in background: and then the atmosphere of the drawing-room is not likely to be changed, any more than that of the studio. Whatever of truth, wisdom, and human nature it contains is *absolutely* independent of circumstances and backgrounds. So far as Deronda and Mordecai are unlikely now, they will always be unlikely: but their creation will always be of equal value, because they are not men of this time in particular, but bring out into idealised prominence the history of the birth of Gwendolen's soul, which is a woman's soul. It would be surprising indeed if *Daniel Deronda* achieved at once the public triumph of *Adam Bede*—it is a novel professedly treating of our own day, and of the novel-reading class, and yet does not base its interest upon the afternoon tea-table. But it is one of the few books that can afford to wait for a long and quiet triumph with patient security. That also is one of the privileges of Romance: and of all books that recognise and reveal the truth that lies in the well of dreams. (pp. 412-24)

[The] comparative method of criticism, unsatisfactory always, is extraordinarily inapplicable to *Daniel Deronda.* It cannot be said to differ from *Adam Bede,* or *The Mill on the Floss,* or *Silas Marner,* or *Middlemarch,* or *Felix Holt,* or even from *Romola* in degree, because it differs from them all in kind—in conception, scope, circumstance, and form. They deal with men and women in the aggregate, as they are or have been: this with individual men and women as they may be or can be. They treat prominently of manners: this leaves manners out of the question. They have to do with the broad passions and emotions common to us all; this with exceptional moods and passions, brought out by exceptional circumstances, special to individuals. They develop the study of healthy anatomy: this of pathology. They exclude, this includes, the unlikely. They reflect, this magnifies. They teach us to know ourselves, this helps us to guess at others. They appeal straight to the heart, this takes the road of the mind. They combine facts, this expands them into fancies. In a word, *Daniel Deronda* differs from them in being a Romance—and that of the highest kind—and moves upon different though converging lines according to different laws. Thus considered, it is practically a first book by a new author, and must be judged accordingly. We are not justified in saying whether we prefer this to any other novel or any other to this: we can go no farther than preferring one kind of novel to another. So far as truth to human nature is concerned, both forms are of equal virtue, and indeed supply each other's deficiencies. It would be a "poor tale," as George Eliot's midland farmers say, if any form or feature or guess at truth of any kind were to be left hidden because some kind of machinery for extracting them is forbidden by critical laws. A certain kind of fiction, which simply reflects faithfully, must of course be bound to accurate, typical fidelity by the strictest laws. But fiction at large, which has as much to do with unlikely things as Nature herself, has only one law, and that is the complete attainment of its end by any means, by the sacrifice of anything but possibility—and what is not possible, where human nature is concerned, is proverbially hard to say. If the machinery of the Arabian Nights were necessary for extracting an additional scrap of human nature worth having out of the mine, then let it be used by all means, and gratefully. Fortunately we need not fear being driven to any such desperate resource when we see how powerful the ordinary forms of the Romance are in the hands of a great artist for depicting what surely cannot be shown by painting everyday types and everyday manners: the invisible transformation of a germ into a soul. No mere naturalist, who only knows what he sees, could describe the birth of the moth from the worm. "Deronda laughed, but defended the myth. 'It is like a passionate word,' he said; 'the exaggeration is a flash of fervour. It is an extreme image of what is happening every day.'" Such is not the mere apology for the romance—it is its more than sufficient reason for being.

It is, of course, idle to speculate whether *Daniel Deronda* marks the beginning of a new manner, as musical biographers say, on the part of its author. In its romance aspect it may be simply a parenthesis, a brilliant display of strength in a foreign field. But it would be pleasant to regard it as the forerunner of a line of fiction that will immediately concern ourselves and our children who live in the England of to-day. We cannot help envying the England of yesterday the painter it has found. As she says of Deronda, "To glory in a prophetic vision . . . is an easier exercise of believing imagination than to see its beginning in newspaper placards, staring at you from a bridge beyond the corn fields: and it might well happen to most of us dainty people that we were in the thick of the battle of Armageddon without being aware of anything more than the annoyance of a little explosive smoke and struggling on the ground immediately about us." George Eliot has hitherto too much neglected the newspaper placards upon the railway bridges and thought—I dare not add the words "too much"—of the cornfields. She has abandoned the houses, not of St. Oggs or Middlemarch, but of London, too freely to those who try to copy the close realism that she herself popularised among us without "the force of imagination that pierces or exalts the solid fact, instead of floating among cloud-pictures." After all, there is something better than pleasure and vanity in our wishing to see our own selves as we are, and we have a right to complain that we have been neglected—until to-day. Our afternoon tea-tables have been photographed *ad nauseam:* it is time for the cover to be removed, that we may see underneath them. We welcome *Daniel Deronda,* not only as a grand romance of a woman's soul, in the highest sense of the word, but also the first novel that gives us the hope of studying ourselves in the same spirit with which we have been able to study mankind at large as typified by our fathers. There are incomplete Grandcourts and imperfect Derondas who will repay study as fully as the more picturesque class of country-town people and Loamshire farmers, and no less for their own sakes than as means to an end. Gwendolen Harleth alone is enough to show how closely and deeply she can study our drawing-room Undines, if such there be. And *Daniel Deronda* alone (the book, not the man) is proof enough that its author has the courage to enter upon the surest road to the highest kind of popularity—that which apparently leads above it. There is not a sentence, scarcely a character, in *Daniel Deronda* that reads or looks as if she were thinking of her critics before her readers at large, or of her readers at large before the best she could give them. She has often marred a stronger and more telling effect for the sake of a truer and deeper—and this belongs to a kind of courage which most artists will be inclined to envy her. But her processes of construction open another question, too long to speak of in a few words. Apart from all considerations of such processes in detail, *Daniel Deronda* is a probably unique example of the application of the forms of romance to a rare and difficult problem in human nature, by first stating the problem—(the transformation of Gwendolen)—in its extremest form, and then, with something like scientific precision as well as philosophic insight, arranging circumstance so as to throw upon it the fullest light possible. From this point of view even the objects of Mordecai's enthusiasm have their place in the drama as supplying the strongest contrast to common lives and thoughts obtainable in these days, and Deronda's perfection as affording the ideal we must keep in our minds in order to study whatever falls short of it. Less even in its intrinsic merits, with all their greatness, than in the promise it gives of doing tardy justice to the profounder poetry of our own immediate day, lies the highest value of this true Romance of Gwendolen Harleth and Daniel Deronda. (pp. 425-27)

> R. E. Francillon, "George Eliot's First Romance," in The Gentleman's Magazine, n.s. Vol. XVII, October, 1876, pp. 411-27.

GEORGE ELIOT   (letter date 1876)

[*In the following excerpt from a letter to a close friend, the landscape artist Barbara Leigh Smith Bodichon, Eliot reports briefly on responses to* Daniel Deronda. *For additional commentary by Eliot, see letters dated 1876 and 1877.*]

I have had some very interesting letters both from Jews and from Christians about *Deronda.* Part of the scene at the club is translated into Hebrew in a German-Jewish newspaper. On the other hand a Christian (highly accomplished) thanks me for embodying the principles by which Christ wrought and will conquer. This is better than the laudation of readers who cut the book into scraps and talk of nothing in it but Gwendolen. I meant everything in the book to be related to everything else there.

> George Eliot, in a letter to Mme. Eugène Bodichon on October 2, 1876, in her The George Eliot Letters: 1874-1877, Vol. VI, edited by Gordon S. Haight, Yale University Press, 1955, p. 290.

GEORGE ELIOT   (letter date 1876)

[*In this letter to Harriet Beecher Stowe, the noted American author of the antislavery novel* Uncle Tom's Cabin *(1852), Eliot discusses some of the issues that concerned her in writing on Jewish themes. For further commentary by Eliot, see letters dated 1876 and 1877.*]

As to the Jewish element in *Deronda,* I expected from first to last in writing it, that it would create much stronger resistance and even repulsion than it has actually met with. But precisely because I felt that the usual attitude of Christians towards Jews is—I hardly know whether to say more impious or more stupid when viewed in the light of their professed principles, I therefore felt urged to treat Jews with such sympathy and understanding as my nature and knowledge could attain to. Moreover, not only towards the Jews, but towards all oriental peoples with whom we English come in contact, a spirit of arrogance and contemptuous dictatorialness is observable which has become a national disgrace to us. There is nothing I should care more to do, if it were possible, than to rouse the imagination of men and women to a vision of human claims in those races of their fellow-men who most differ from them in customs and beliefs. But towards the Hebrews we western people who have been reared in Christianity, have a peculiar debt and, whether we acknowledge it or not, a peculiar thoroughness of fellowship in religious and moral sentiment. Can anything be more disgusting than to hear people called "educated" making small jokes about eating ham, and showing themselves empty of any real knowledge as to the relation of their own social and religious life to the history of the people they think themselves witty in insulting? They hardly know that Christ was a Jew. And I find men educated at Rugby supposing that Christ spoke Greek. To my feeling, this deadness to the history which has prepared half our world for us, this inability to find interest in any form of life that is not clad in the same coat-tails and flounces as our own lies very close to the worst kind of irreligion. The best that can be said of it is, that it is a sign of the intellectual narrowness—in plain English, the stupidity, which is still the average mark of our culture.

Yes, I expected more aversion than I have found. But I was happily independent in material things and felt no temptation to accommodate my writing to any standard except that of trying to do my best in what seemed to me most needful to be done, and I sum up with the writer of the Book of Maccabees—'if I have done well, and as befits the subject, it is what I desired, but if I have done ill, it is what I could attain unto.' (pp. 301-02)

> George Eliot, in a letter to Harriet Beecher Stowe on

October 29, 1876, in her The George Eliot Letters: 1874-1877, *Vol. VI, edited by Gordon S. Haight, Yale University Press, 1955, pp. 301-02.*

HENRY JAMES, JR. (essay date 1876)

[*James was an American-born English novelist, short story writer, critic, and essayist of the late nineteenth and early twentieth centuries. He is regarded as one of the greatest novelists of the English language and his works are widely praised for the psychological acuity and complex sense of artistic form evident in them. James defined the novel as "a direct impression of life." The quality of this impression—the degree of moral and intellectual development—and the author's ability to communicate this impression in an effective and artistic manner were the two principal criteria by which he estimated the worth of a literary work. As a young man James traveled extensively throughout Great Britain and Europe and benefited from the friendship and influence of many of the leading figures of nineteenth-century art and literature: in England, he met John Ruskin, Dante Gabriel Rossetti, William Morris, and Leslie Stephen; in France, where he lived for several years, he was part of the literary circle that included Gustave Flaubert, Émile Zola, Edmond de Goncourt, Guy de Maupassant, and Ivan Turgenev. His criticism, praised for its lucidity and insight, is thus informed by his sensitivity to European culture, particularly English and French literature of the late nineteenth century. James was a frequent contributor to several prominent American periodicals, including the* North American Review, *the* Nation, *and the* Atlantic Monthly. *In his review of* Daniel Deronda *for the* Atlantic Monthly, *James offered his critical appraisal in the form of an imaginary conversation between Theodora, a sympathetic reader, Pulcheria, an impatient and disapproving reader, and Constantius, whose mixed praise and faultfinding are believed to mirror James's response to the novel.*]

Theodora, one day early in the autumn, sat on her piazza with a piece of embroidery, the design of which she invented as she proceeded, being careful, however, to have a Japanese screen before her, to keep her inspiration at the proper altitude. Pulcheria, who was paying her a visit, sat near her with a closed book, in a paper cover, in her lap. Pulcheria was playing with the little dog, rather idly, but Theodora was stitching, steadily and meditatively. "Well," said Theodora, at last, "I wonder what he accomplished in the East." Pulcheria took the little dog into her lap and made him sit on the book. "Oh," she replied, "they had tea-parties at Jerusalem,—exclusively of ladies,—and he sat in the midst and stirred his tea and made high-toned remarks. And then Mirah sang a little, just a little, on account of her voice being so weak. Sit still, Fido," she continued, addressing the little dog, "and keep your nose out of my face. But it's a nice little nose, all the same," she pursued, "a nice little short snub nose, and not a horrid big Jewish nose. Oh, my dear, when I think what a collection of noses there must have been at that wedding!" At this moment Constantius steps out upon the piazza from the long parlor window, hat and stick in hand and his shoes a trifle dusty. He has some steps to take before he reaches the end of the piazza where the ladies are sitting, and this gives Pulcheria time to murmur, "Talk of snub noses!" Constantius is presented by Theodora to Pulcheria, and he sits down and exclaims upon the admirable blueness of the sea, which lies in a straight band across the green of the little lawn; comments too upon the pleasure of having one side of one's piazza in the shade. Soon Fido, the little dog, still restless, jumps off Pulcheria's lap and reveals the book, which lies title upward. "Oh," says Constantius, "you have been finishing *Daniel Deronda?*" Then follows a conversation which it will be more convenient to present in another form.

Theodora. Yes, Pulcheria has been reading aloud the last chapters to me. They are wonderfully beautiful.

Constantius (after a moment's hesitation). Yes, they are very beautiful. I am sure you read well, Pulcheria, to give the fine passages their full value.

Theodora. She reads well when she chooses, but I am sorry to say that in some of the fine passages of this last book she took quite a false tone. I could n't have read them aloud, myself; I should have broken down. But Pulcheria,—would you really believe it?—when she could n't go on, it was not for tears, but for—the contrary.

Constantius. For smiles? Did you really find it comical? One of my objections to **Daniel Deronda** is the absence of those delightfully humorous passages which enlivened the author's former works.

Pulcheria. Oh, I think there are some places as amusing as anything in **Adam Bede** or **The Mill on the Floss:** for instance, where, at the last, Deronda wipes Gwendolen's tears and Gwendolen wipes his.

Constantius. Yes, I know what you mean. I can understand that situation presenting a slightly ridiculous image; that is, if the current of the story does not swiftly carry you past that idea.

Pulcheria. What do you mean by the current of the story? I never read a story with less current. It is not a river; it is a series of lakes. I once read of a group of little uneven ponds resembling, from a bird's-eye view, a looking-glass which had fallen upon the floor and broken, and was lying in fragments. That is what **Daniel Deronda** would look like, on a bird's-eye view.

Theodora. Pulcheria found that comparison in a French novel. She is always reading French novels.

Constantius. Ah, there are some very good ones.

Pulcheria (perversely). I don't know; I think there are some very poor ones.

Constantius. The comparison is not bad, at any rate. I know what you mean by **Daniel Deronda** lacking current. It has almost as little as **Romola.**

Pulcheria. Oh, **Romola** is unpardonably slow; it absolutely stagnates.

Constantius. Yes, I know what you mean by that. But I am afraid you are not friendly to our great novelist.

Theodora. She likes Balzac and George Sand and other impure writers.

Constantius. Well, I must say I understand that.

Pulcheria. My favorite novelist is Thackeray, and I am extremely fond of Miss Austen.

Constantius. I understand that, too. You read over *The Newcomes* and *Pride and Prejudice.*

Pulcheria. No, I don't read them over, now; I think them over. I have been making visits for a long time past to a series of friends, and I have spent the last six months in reading

Daniel Deronda aloud. Fortune would have it that I should always arrive by the same train as the new number. I am considered a frivolous, idle creature; I am not a disciple in the new school of embroidery, like Theodora; so I was immediately pushed into a chair and the book thrust into my hand, that I might lift up my voice and make peace between all the impatiences that were snatching at it. So I may claim at least that I have read every word of the work. I never skipped.

Theodora. I should hope not, indeed!

Constantius. And do you mean that you really did n't enjoy it?

Pulcheria. I found it protracted, pretentious, pedantic.

Constantius. I see; I can understand that.

Theodora. Oh, you understand too much! Here is the twentieth time you have used that formula.

Constantius. What will you have? You know I must try to understand, it's my trade.

Theodora. He means he writes reviews. Trying *not* to understand is what I call that trade!

Constantius. Say, then, I take it the wrong way; that is why it has never made my fortune. But I do try to understand; it is my—my—(He pauses.)

Theodora. I know what you want to say. Your strong side.

Pulcheria. And what is his weak side?

Theodora. He writes novels.

Constantius. I have written *one*. You can't call that a side.

Pulcheria. I should like to read it,—not aloud!

Constantius. You can't read it softly enough. But you, Theodora, you did n't find our book too "protracted"?

Theodora. I should have liked it to continue indefinitely, to keep coming out always, to be one of the regular things of life.

Pulcheria. Oh, come here, little dog! To think that *Daniel Deronda* might be perpetual when you, little short-nosed darling, can't last at the most more than eight or nine years!

Theodora. A book like *Daniel Deronda* becomes part of one's life; one lives in it or alongside of it. I don't hesitate to say that I have been living in this one for the last eight months. It is such a complete world George Eliot builds up; it is so vast, so much-embracing! It has such a firm earth and such an ethereal sky. You can turn into it and lose yourself in it.

Pulcheria. Oh, easily, and die of cold and starvation!

Theodora. I have been very near to poor Gwendolen and very near to dear little Mirah. And the dear little Meyricks, also; I know them intimately well.

Pulcheria. The Meyricks, I grant you, are the best thing in the book.

Theodora. They are a delicious family; I wish they lived in Boston. I consider Herr Klesmer almost Shakespearian, and his wife is almost as good. I have been near to poor, grand Mordecai—

Pulcheria. Oh, reflect, my dear; not too near.

Theodora. And as for Deronda himself, I freely confess that I am consumed with a hopeless passion for him. He is the most irresistible man in the literature of fiction.

Pulcheria. He is not a man at all!

Theodora. I remember nothing more beautiful than the description of his childhood, and that picture of his lying on the grass in the abbey cloister, a beautiful seraph-faced boy, with a lovely voice, reading history and asking his Scotch tutor why the Popes had so many nephews. He must have been delightfully handsome.

Pulcheria. Never, my dear, with that nose! I am sure he had a nose, and I hold that the author has shown great pusillanimity in her treatment of it. She has quite shirked it. The picture you speak of is very pretty, but a picture is not a person. And why is he always grasping his coat-collar, as if he wished to hang himself up? The author had an uncomfortable feeling that she must make him do something real, something visible and sensible, and she hit upon that awkward device. I don't see what you mean by saying you have been *near* those people; that is just what one is not. They produce no illusion. They are described and analyzed to death, but we don't see them or hear them or touch them. Deronda clutches his coat-collar, Mirah crosses her feet, and Mordecai talks like the Bible; but that does n't make real figures of them. They have no existence outside of the author's study.

Theodora. If you mean that they are nobly imaginative, I quite agree with you; and if they say nothing to your own imagination, the fault is yours, not theirs.

Pulcheria. Pray don't say they are Shakespearian again. Shakespeare went to work another way.

Constantius. I think you are both in a measure right; there is a distinction to be drawn. There are in *Daniel Deronda* the figures based upon observation and the figures based upon invention. This distinction, I know, is rather a rough one. There are no figures in any novel that are pure observation and none that are pure invention. But either element may preponderate, and in those cases in which invention has preponderated George Eliot seems to me to have achieved at the best but so many brilliant failures.

Theodora. And are *you* turning severe? I thought you admired her so much.

Constantius. I defy any one to admire her more, but one must discriminate. Speaking brutally, I consider *Daniel Deronda* the weakest of her books. It strikes me as very sensibly inferior to *Middlemarch.* I have an immense opinion of *Middlemarch.*

Pulcheria. Not having been obliged by circumstances to read *Middlemarch* to other people, I did n't read it at all. I could n't read it to myself. I tried, but I broke down. I appreciated Rosamond, but I could n't believe in Dorothea.

Theodora (very gravely). So much the worse for you, Pulcheria. I have enjoyed *Daniel Deronda because* I had enjoyed *Middlemarch.* Why should you throw *Middlemarch* up against her? It seems to me that if a book is fine it is fine. I have enjoyed *Deronda* deeply, from beginning to end.

Constantius. I assure you, so have I. I can read nothing of George Eliot's without enjoyment. I even enjoy her poetry, though I don't approve of it. In whatever she writes I enjoy her mind—her large, luminous, airy mind. The intellectual brilliancy of **Daniel Deronda** strikes me as very great, in excess of anything the author had done. In the first couple of numbers of the book this ravished me. I delighted in its tone, its deep, rich English tone, in which so many notes seemed melted together.

Pulcheria. The tone is not English, it is German.

Constantius. I understand that—if Theodora will allow me to say so. Little by little I began to feel that I cared less for certain notes than for others. I say it under my breath—I began to feel an occasional temptation to skip. Roughly speaking, all the Jewish burden of the story tended to weary me; it is this part that produces the small illusion which I agree with Pulcheria in finding. Gwendolen and Grandcourt are admirable. Gwendolen is a masterpiece. She is known, felt, and presented, psychologically, altogether in the grand manner. Beside her and beside her husband—a consummate picture of English brutality refined and distilled (for Grandcourt is before all things brutal)—Deronda, Mordecai, and Mirah are hardly more than shadows. They and their fortunes are all improvisation. I don't say anything against improvisation. When it succeeds it has a surpassing charm. But it must succeed. With George Eliot it seems to me to succeed only partially, less than one would expect of her talent. The story of Deronda's life, his mother's story, Mirah's story, are quite the sort of thing one finds in George Sand. But they are really not so good as they would be in George Sand. George Sand would have carried it off with a lighter hand.

Theodora. Oh, Constantius, how can you compare George Eliot's novels to that woman's? It is sunlight and moonshine.

Pulcheria. I really think the two writers are very much alike. They are both very voluble, both addicted to moralizing and philosophizing *à tout bout de champ*, both inartistic!

Constantius. I see what you mean. But George Eliot is solid and George Sand is liquid. When occasionally George Eliot liquefies,—as in the history of Deronda's birth, and in that of Mirah,—it is not to as crystalline a clearness as the author of Consuelo and André. Take Mirah's long narrative of her adventures, when she unfolds them to Mrs. Meyrick. It is arranged, it is artificial, old-fashioned, quite in the George Sand manner. But George Sand would have done it better. The false tone would have remained, but it would have been more persuasive. It would have been a fib, but the fib would have been neater.

Theodora. I don't think fibbing neatly a merit; and I don't see what is to be gained by such comparisons. George Eliot is pure and George Sand is impure; how can you compare them? As for the Jewish element in **Deronda,** I think it a very fine idea; it's a noble subject. Wilkie Collins and Miss Braddon would not have thought of it, but that does not condemn it. It shows a large conception of what one may do in a novel. I heard you say, the other day, that most novels were so trivial—that they had no general ideas. Here is a general idea, the idea interpreted by **Deronda.** I have never disliked the Jews, as some people do; I am not like Pulcheria, who sees a Jew in every bush. I wish there were one; I would cultivate shrubbery! I have known too many clever and charming Jews; I have known none that were not clever.

Pulcheria. Clever, but not charming!

Constantius. I quite agree with you as to Deronda's going in for the Jews and turning out a Jew himself being a fine sub-

ject, and this quite apart from the fact of whether such a thing as a Jewish revival is at all a possibility. If it is a possibility, so much the better—so much the better for the subject, I mean.

Pulcheria. A la bonne heure!

Constantius. I rather suspect it is not a possibility; that the Jews in general take themselves much less seriously than that. They have other fish to fry! George Eliot takes them as a person outside of Judaism—picturesquely. I don't believe that is the way they take themselves.

Pulcheria. They have the less excuse, then, for keeping themselves so dirty.

Theodora. George Eliot must have known some delightful Jews!

Constantius. Very likely; but I should n't wonder if the most delightful of them had smiled a trifle, here and there, over her book. But that makes nothing, as Herr Klesmer would say. The subject is a noble one. The idea of depicting a nature able to feel and worthy to feel the sort of inspiration that takes possession of Deronda, of depicting it sympathetically, minutely, and intimately—such an idea has great elevation. There is something very fascinating in the mission that Deronda takes upon himself. I don't quite know what it means, I don't understand more than half of Mordecai's rhapsodies, and I don't perceive exactly what practical steps could be taken. Deronda could go about and talk with clever Jews—not an unpleasant life.

Pulcheria. All that seems to me so unreal that when at the end the author finds herself confronted with the necessity of making him start for the East by the train, and announces that Sir Hugo and Lady Mallinger have given his wife "a complete Eastern outfit," I descend to the ground with a ludicrous jump.

Constantius. Unreal if you please; that is no objection to it; it greatly tickles my imagination. I like extremely the idea of Mordecai believing, without ground of belief, that if he only waits, a young man on whom nature and society have centred all their gifts will come to him and receive from his hands the precious vessel of his hopes. It is romantic, but it is not vulgar romance; it is finely romantic. And there is something very fine in the author's own feeling about Deronda. He is a very generous creation. He is, I think, a failure—a brilliant failure; if he had been a success I would call him a splendid creation. The author meant to do things very handsomely for him; she meant, apparently, to make a faultless human being.

Pulcheria. She made a dreadful prig.

Constantius. He *is* rather priggish, and one wonders that so clever a woman as George Eliot should n't see it.

Pulcheria. He has no blood in his body. His attitude at moments absolutely trenches on the farcical.

Theodora. Pulcheria likes the little gentlemen in the French novels who take good care of their attitudes, which are always the same attitude, the attitude of "conquest," and of a conquest that tickles their vanity. Deronda has a contour that cuts straight through the middle of all that. He is made of a stuff that is n't dreamt of in their philosophy.

Pulcheria. Pulcheria likes very much a novel which she read three or four years ago, but which she has not forgotten. It was by Ivan Tourguéneff, and it was called *On the Eve*. Theodora has read it, I know, because she admires Tourguéneff, and Constantius has read it, I suppose, because he has read everything.

Constantius. If I had no reason but that for my reading, it would be small. But Tourguéneff is my man.

Pulcheria. You were just now praising George Eliot's general ideas. The tale of which I speak contains in the portrait of the hero very much such a general idea as you find in the portrait of Deronda. Don't you remember the young Bulgarian student, Inssaroff, who gives himself the mission of rescuing his country from its subjection to the Turks? Poor man, if he had foreseen the horrible summer of 1876! His character is the picture of a race-passion, of patriotic hopes and dreams. But what a difference in the vividness of the two figures. Inssaroff is a man; he stands up on his feet; we see him, hear him, and touch him. And it has taken the author but a couple of hundred pages—not eight volumes—to do it!

Theodora. I don't remember Inssaroff at all, but I perfectly remember the heroine, Elena. She is certainly most remarkable, but, remarkable as she is, I should never dream of calling her so wonderful as Gwendolen.

Constantius. Tourguéneff is a magician, which I don't think I should call George Eliot. One is a poet, the other is a philosopher. One cares for the reason of things and the other cares for the aspect of things. George Eliot, in embarking with Deronda, took aboard, as it were, a far heavier cargo than Tourguéneff with his Inssaroff. She proposed, consciously, to strike more notes.

Pulcheria. Oh, consciously, yes!

Constantius. George Eliot wished to show the possible picturesqueness—the romance, as it were—of a high moral tone. Deronda is a moralist; a moralist with a rich complexion.

Theodora. It is a most beautiful nature. I don't know anywhere a more complete, a more deeply analyzed portrait of a great nature. We praise novelists for wandering and creeping so into the small corners of the mind. That is what we praise Balzac for when he gets down upon all fours to crawl through the Père Goriot or the Parents Pauvres. But I must say I think it a finer thing to unlock with as firm a hand as George Eliot some of the greater chambers of human character. Deronda is in a manner an ideal character, if you will, but he seems to me triumphantly married to reality. There are some admirable things said about him; nothing can be finer than those pages of description of his moral temperament in the fourth book—his elevated way of looking at things, his impartiality, his universal sympathy, and at the same time his fear of their turning into mere irresponsible indifference. I remember some of it verbally: "He was ceasing to care for knowledge—he had no ambition for practice—unless they could be gathered up into one current with his emotions."

Pulcheria. Oh, there is plenty about his emotions. Everything about him is "emotive." That bad word occurs on every fifth page.

Theodora. I don't see that it is a bad word.

Pulcheria. It may be good German, but it is poor English.

Theodora. It is not German at all; it is Latin. So, my dear!

Pulcheria. As I say, then, it is not English.

Theodora. This is the first time I ever heard that George Eliot's style was bad!

Constantius. It is admirable; it has the most delightful and the most intellectually comfortable suggestions. But it is occasionally a little too long-sleeved, as I may say. It is sometimes too loose a fit for the thought, a little baggy.

Theodora. And the advice he gives Gwendolen, the things he says to her, they are the very essence of wisdom, of warm human wisdom, knowing life and feeling it. "Keep your fear as a safeguard, it may make consequences passionately present to you." What can be better than that?

Pulcheria. Nothing, perhaps. But what can be drearier than a novel in which the function of the hero—young, handsome, and brilliant—is to give didactic advice, in a proverbial form, to the young, beautiful, and brilliant heroine?

Constantius. That is not putting it quite fairly. The function of Deronda is to have Gwendolen fall in love with him, to say nothing of falling in love himself with Mirah.

Pulcheria. Yes, the less said about that the better. All we know about Mirah is that she has delicate rings of hair, sits with her feet crossed, and talks like a book.

Constantius. Deronda's function of adviser to Gwendolen does not strike me as so ridiculous. He is not nearly so ridiculous as if he were lovesick. It is a very interesting situation—that of a man with whom a beautiful woman in trouble falls in love, and yet whose affections are so preoccupied that the most he can do for her in return is to enter kindly and sympathetically into her position, pity her, and talk to her. George Eliot always gives us something that is strikingly and ironically characteristic of human life; and what savors more of the essential crookedness of human fortune than the sad cross-purposes of these two young people? Poor Gwendolen's falling in love with Deronda is part of her own luckless history, not of his.

Theodora. I do think he takes it to himself rather too little. No man had ever so little vanity.

Pulcheria. It is very inconsistent, therefore, as well as being extremely impertinent and ill-mannered, his buying back and sending to her her necklace at Leubronn.

Constantius. Oh, you must concede that; without it there would have been no story. A man writing of him, however, would certainly have made him more peccable. As George Eliot lets herself go about him she becomes delightfully, almost touchingly feminine. It is like her making Romola go to housekeeping with Tessa, after Tito Melema's death; like her making Dorothea marry Will Ladislaw. If Dorothea had married any one after her misadventure with Casaubon, she would have married a hussar!

Theodora. Perhaps some day Gwendolen will marry Rex.

Pulcheria. Pray, who is Rex?

Theodora. Why, Pulcheria, how can you forget?

Pulcheria. Nay, how can I remember? But I recall such a name in the dim antiquity of the first or second book. Yes, and then he is pushed to the front again at the last, just in time not to miss the falling of the curtain. Gwendolen will certainly not have the audacity to marry any one we know so little about.

Constantius. I have been wanting to say that there seems to me to be two very distinct elements in George Eliot—a spontaneous one and an artificial one. There is what she is by inspiration, and what she is because it is expected of her. These two heads have been very perceptible in her recent writings; they are much less noticeable in her early ones.

Theodora. You mean that she is too scientific? So long as she remains the great literary genius that she is, how can she be too scientific? She is simply permeated with the highest culture of the age.

Pulcheria. She talks too much about the "dynamic quality" of people's eyes. When she uses such a phrase as that in the first sentence in her book she is not a great literary genius, because she shows a want of tact. There can't be a worse limitation.

Constantius (laughing). The "dynamic quality" of Gwendolen's glance has made the tour of the world.

Theodora. It shows a very low level of culture on the world's part to be agitated by a term perfectly familiar to all decently-educated people.

Pulcheria. I don't pretend to be decently educated; pray tell me what it means.

Constantius (promptly). I think Pulcheria has hit it in speaking of a want of tact. In the manner of **Daniel Deronda,** throughout, there is something that one may call a want of tact. The epigraphs in verse are a want of tact; they are sometimes, I think, a trifle more pretentious than really pregnant; the importunity of the moral reflections is a want of tact; the very diffuseness of the book is a want of tact. But it comes back to what I said just now about one's sense of the author writing under a sort of external pressure. I began to notice it in **Felix Holt;** I don't think I had before. She strikes me as a person who certainly has naturally a taste for general considerations, but who has fallen upon an age and a circle which have compelled her to give them an exaggerated attention. She does not strike me as naturally a critic, less still as naturally a skeptic; her spontaneous part is to observe life and to feel it, to feel it with admirable depth. Contemplation, sympathy, and faith,—something like that, I should say, would have been her natural scale. If she had fallen upon an age of enthusiastic assent to old articles of faith, it seems to me possible that she would have had a more perfect, a more consistent and graceful development, than she has actually had. If she had cast herself into such a current,—her genius being equal,—it might have carried her to splendid distances. But she has chosen to go into criticism, and to the critics she addresses her work; I mean the critics of the universe. Instead of feeling life itself, it is "views" upon life that she tries to feel.

Pulcheria. Pray, how can you feel a "view"?

Constantius. I don't think you can; you had better give up trying.

Pulcheria. She is the victim of a first-class education. I am so glad!

Constantius. Thanks to her admirable intellect she philosophizes very sufficiently; but meanwhile she has given a chill to her genius. She has come near spoiling an artist.

Pulcheria. She has quite spoiled one. Or rather I should n't say that, because there was no artist to spoil. I maintain that she is not an artist. An artist could never have put a story together so monstrously ill. She has no sense of form.

Theodora. Pray, what could be more artistic than the way that Deronda's paternity is concealed till almost the end, and the way we are made to suppose Sir Hugo is his father?

Pulcheria. And Mirah his sister. How does that fit together? I was as little made to suppose he was not a Jew as I cared when I found out he was. And his mother popping up through a trap-door and popping down again, at the last, in that scrambling fashion! His mother is very bad.

Constantius. I think Deronda's mother is one of the unvivified characters; she belongs to the cold half of the book. All the Jewish part is at bottom cold; that is my only objection. I have enjoyed it because my fancy often warms cold things; but beside Gwendolen's history it is like the full half of the lunar disk beside the empty one. It is admirably studied, it is imagined, it is understood; but it is not realized. One feels this strongly in just those scenes between Deronda and his mother; one feels that one has been appealed to on rather an artificial ground of interest. To make Deronda's reversion to his native faith more dramatic and profound, the author has given him a mother who on very arbitrary grounds, apparently, has separated herself from this same faith, and who has been kept waiting in the wing, as it were, for many acts, to come on and make her speech and say so. This moral situation of hers we are invited retrospectively to appreciate. But we hardly care to do so.

Pulcheria. I don't *see* the princess, in spite of her flame-colored robe. Why should an actress and prima-donna care so much about religious matters?

Theodora. It was not only that; it was the Jewish race she hated, Jewish manners and looks. You, my dear, ought to understand that.

Pulcheria. I do, but I am not a Jewish actress of genius; I am not what Rachel was. If I were, I should have other things to think about.

Constantius. Think now a little about poor Gwendolen.

Pulcheria. I don't care to think about her. She was a second-rate English girl who spoke of her mother as "my mamma," and got into a flutter about a lord.

Theodora. I don't see that she is worse than if she were a first-rate American girl, who should speak of her female parent as "mother," and get into exactly the same flutter.

Pulcheria. It would n't be the same flutter, at all; it would n't be any flutter. She would n't be afraid of the lord.

Theodora. I am sure I don't perceive whom Gwendolen was afraid of. She was afraid of her misdeed,—her broken promise,—after she had committed it, and through that fear she was afraid of her husband. Well she might be! I can imagine nothing more vivid than the sense we get of his absolutely *clammy* selfishness.

Pulcheria. She was not afraid of Deronda when, immediately after her marriage, and without any but the most casual acquaintance with him, she begins to hover about him at the

Mallingers', and to drop little confidences about her conjugal woes. That seems to me very indelicate; ask any woman.

Constantius. The very purpose of the author is to give us an idea of the sort of confidence that Deronda inspired—its irresistible potency!

Pulcheria. A lay father-confessor. Dreadful!

Constantius. And to give us an idea also of the acuteness of Gwendolen's depression, of her haunting sense of impending trouble.

Theodora. It must be remembered that Gwendolen was in love with Deronda from the first, long before she knew it. She did n't know it, poor girl, but that was it.

Pulcheria. That makes the matter worse. It is very disagreeable to have her rustling about a man who is indifferent to her, in that fashion.

Theodora. He was not indifferent to her, since he sent her back her necklace.

Pulcheria. Of all the delicate attention to a charming girl that I ever heard of, that little pecuniary transaction is the most felicitous.

Constantius. You must remember that he had been *en rapport* with her at the gaming table. She had been playing in defiance of his observation, and he, continuing to observe her, had been in a measure responsible for her loss. There was a tacit consciousness of this between them. You may contest the possibility of tacit consciousness going so far, but that is not a serious objection. You may point out two or three weak spots in detail; the fact remains that Gwendolen's whole history is superbly told. And see how the girl is known, inside out, how thoroughly she is felt and understood! It is the most *intelligent* thing in all George Eliot's writing, and that is saying much. It is so deep, so true, so complete, it holds such a wealth of psychological detail, it is more than masterly.

Theodora. I don't know where the perception of character has sailed closer to the wind.

Pulcheria. The portrait may be admirable, but it has one little fault. You don't care a straw for the original. Gwendolen is not an interesting girl, and when the author tries to invest her with a deep tragic interest she does so at the expense of consistency. She has made her at the outset too light, too flimsy; tragedy has no hold on such a girl.

Theodora. You are hard to satisfy. You said this morning that Dorothea was too heavy, and now you find Gwendolen too light. George Eliot wished to give us the perfect counterpart of Dorothea. Having made one portrait she was worthy to make the other.

Pulcheria. She has committed the fatal error of making Gwendolen vulgarly, pettily, dryly selfish. She was *personally* selfish.

Theodora. I know nothing more personal than selfishness.

Pulcheria. I am selfish, but I don't go about with my chin out like that; at least I hope I don't. She was an odious young woman, and one can't care what becomes of her. When her marriage turned out ill she would have become still more hard and positive; to make her soft and appealing is very bad logic. The second Gwendolen does n't belong to the first.

Constantius. She is perhaps at the first a little childish for the weight of interest she has to carry, a little too much after the pattern of the unconscientious young ladies of Miss Yonge and Miss Sewell.

Theodora. Since when is it forbidden to make one's heroine young? Gwendolen is a perfect picture of youthfulness—its eagerness, its presumption, its preoccupation with itself, its vanity and silliness, its sense of its own absoluteness. But she is extremely intelligent and clever, and therefore tragedy *can* have a hold upon her. Her conscience does n't make the tragedy; that is an old story, and, I think, a secondary form of suffering. It is the tragedy that makes her conscience, which then reacts upon it; and I can think of nothing more powerful than the way in which the growth of her conscience is traced, nothing more touching than the picture of its helpless maturity.

Constantius. That is perfectly true. Gwendolen's history is admirably typical—as most things are with George Eliot; it is the very stuff that human life is made of. What is it made of but the discovery by each of us that we are at the best but a rather ridiculous fifth wheel to the coach, after we have sat cracking our whip and believing that we are at least the coachman in person? We think we are the main hoop to the barrel, and we turn out to be but a very incidental splinter in one of the staves. The universe, forcing itself with a slow, inexorable pressure into a narrow, complacent, and yet after all extremely sensitive mind, and making it ache with the pain of the process—that is Gwendolen's story. And it becomes completely characteristic in that her supreme perception of the fact that the world is whirling past her is in the disappointment not of a base, but of an exalted passion. The very chance to embrace what the author is so fond of calling a "larger life" seems refused to her. She is punished for being narrow and she is not allowed a chance to expand. Her finding Deronda preëngaged to go to the East and stir up the race-feeling of the Jews strikes one as a wonderfully happy invention. The irony of the situation, for poor Gwendolen, is almost grotesque, and it makes one wonder whether the whole heavy structure of the Jewish question in the story was not built up by the author for the express purpose of giving its proper force to this particular stroke.

Theodora. George Eliot's intentions are extremely complex. The mass is for each detail and each detail is for the mass.

Pulcheria. She is very fond of deaths by drowning. Maggie Tulliver and her brother are drowned, Tito Melema is drowned, Mr. Grandcourt is drowned. It is extremely unlikely that Grandcourt should not have known how to swim.

Constantius. He did, of course, but he had a cramp. It served him right. I can't imagine a more consummate representation of the most detestable kind of Englishman—the Englishman who thinks it low to articulate. And in Grandcourt the type and the individual are so happily met: the type with its sense of the proprieties, and the individual with his absence of all sense. He is the apotheosis of dryness, a human expression of the simple idea of the perpendicular.

Theodora. Mr. Casaubon in **Middlemarch** was very dry, too; and yet what a genius it is that can give us two disagreeable husbands who are so utterly different.

Pulcheria. You must count the two disagreeable wives, too—Rosamond Vincy and Gwendolen. They are very much alike. I know the author did n't mean it; it proves how common a type the worldly, *pincée*, illiberal young Englishwoman is. They are both disagreeable; you can't get over that.

Constantius. There is something in that, perhaps. I think, at any rate, that the secondary people here are less delightful than in **Middlemarch;** there is nothing so good as Mary Garth and her father, or the little old lady who steals sugar, or the parson who is in love with Mary, or the country relatives of old Mr. Featherstone. Rex Gascoigne is not so good as Fred Vincy.

Theodora. Mr. Gascoigne is admirable, and Mrs. Davilow is charming.

Pulcheria. And you must not forget that you think Herr Klesmer "Shakespearian." Would n't "Wagnerian" be high enough praise?

Constantius. Yes, one must make an exception with regard to the Klesmers and the Meyricks. They are delightful, and as for Klesmer himself, and Hans Meyrick, Theodora may maintain her epithet. Shakespearian characters are characters that are born out of the *overflow* of observation, characters that make the drama seem multitudinous, like life. Klesmer comes in with a sort of Shakespearian "value," as a painter would say, and so, in a different tone, does Hans Meyrick. They spring from a much-peopled mind.

Theodora. I think Gwendolen's confrontation with Klesmer one of the finest things in the book.

Constantius. It is like everything in George Eliot, it will bear thinking of.

Pulcheria. All that is very fine, but you cannot persuade me that **Deronda** is not a very awkward and ill-made story. It has nothing that one can call a subject. A silly young girl and a heavy, overwise young man who *don't* fall in love with her! That is the *donnée* of eight monthly volumes. I call it very flat. Is that what the exquisite art of Thackeray and Miss Austen and Hawthorne has come to? I would as soon read a German novel outright.

Theodora. There is something higher than form—there is spirit.

Constantius. I am afraid Pulcheria is sadly aesthetic. She had better confine herself to Mérimée.

Pulcheria. I shall certainly to-day read over the *Double Méprise.*

Theodora. Oh, my dear, don't!

Constantius. Yes, I think there is little art in **Deronda,** but I think there is a vast amount of life. In life without art you can find your account; but art without life is a poor affair. The book is full of the world.

Theodora. It is full of beauty and sagacity, and there is quite art enough for me.

Pulcheria (to the little dog). We are silenced, darling, but we are not convinced, are we? (The dog begins to bark.) No, we are not even silenced. It's a young woman with two bandboxes.

Theodora. Oh, it must be our muslins.

Constantius (rising to go). I see what you mean! (pp. 684-94)

Henry James, Jr., " 'Daniel Deronda': A Conversa-

tion," in The Atlantic Monthly, *Vol. XXXVIII, No. CCXXX, December, 1876, pp. 684-94.*

R. R. BOWKER (essay date 1877)

[*An American critic, publisher, and biographer, Bowker identifies the conflict between character and circumstance as a theme in all of Eliot's novels and as a fundamental issue in the two narrative lines of* Daniel Deronda. *Bowker interprets Eliot's emphasis on moral character and the possibility of self-determination as evidence of her increasingly positive and hopeful view of humanity.*]

A new work by George Eliot commands reverence. It is something to be a contemporary with such genius—strong in the strength of both sexes and, easily first among living writers, challenging place among the greatest of all time. This is also a disadvantage: we are at the foot of Mont Blanc, or under the looming front of St. Peter's, and the greatness before us outreaches vision. We can not get the perspective.

Therefore is reverence, always a first duty of catholic criticism, here peculiarly becoming. It is easy to splutter over the preachments of **Daniel Deronda**—easier indeed than to appreciate rightly this magnificent work of magnificent genius. But the critics who shrugged their shoulders over the violation of the unities, when Shakespeare and his fellows were writing drama, are not thought well of by posterity, which is in fact rather inclined to shrug its shoulders at them. In the presence of a great work, criticism may be asked to question itself first. It may be open for consideration whether those writers of modern fiction, among whom George Eliot is first, have not been giving to that triumph of England's creative genius, the novel, a new meaning. While we are judging a great work by a current standard, the work itself may be creating a new standard by which posterity will judge us. Provided always that it do not violate art truth, a novel "with a purpose," and that a great purpose, may be greater as a novel because of that purpose; and possibly also in asking of the novel the self-unconsciousness of drama, we are asking of it something which does not belong to it. Certainly if a great work in literature is to represent its age, our form of literature, the novel, may properly present that analyzing self-consciousness which, it may be for good as well as for ill, marks our age.

The comparison of George Eliot with Shakespeare is often essayed, but it must be of degree and not of kind. Of **Daniel Deronda** it may be roughly said that Shakespeare "would not an he could, and could not an he would." The two writers represent the essential *differentia* between the drama and the novel: with equal truth they set forth the "what" of being and doing, but it is left to the novelist, the analyst, the psychologist, to divine the "why" which in its deep interplay of elusive motive is not evident even to the actor himself. The world has been querying for centuries whether Hamlet be mad or not: perhaps Shakespeare didn't know. It may be questioned whether human nature is greatly different now from then, whether the modern complexity of life has proportionally increased the complexity of human motive. But psychology is a new science: perhaps it is not too much to say that **Daniel Deronda** could not have been written except Herbert Spencer had first lived, or by any other than a disciple of that Columbus of psychology. We are most of us as ignorant of the hidden sources of our action as of the courses of the vital fluid through our bodies, and the discoveries of human emotion which this book reveals could no more have been made without the Spencerian analysis than the discoveries of modern physical science could have been made without the microscope. Unknown to the men and women themselves, these clues can only be given by the *ego* of the novel, which indeed appeared as chorus in the early drama, to be banished thence to its growing importance in the novel when the *differentia* of the two became clear. That it is only more prominent and not new, in George Eliot's writings, the reader of Fielding can testify, and Thackeray, whom we call the artist, stood always visible at the edge of his stage and rang up and down the curtain himself.

Considering then that a novel with a purpose and with a personality may still be recognized as a novel and as a work of art, we may take it as a chief element of George Eliot's greatness that her books are so persistently occupied with the greatest of problems—the problem, old as humanity, that must forever be set before each man as his question of life or death. As unreligious in the personality of her novels as Shakespeare the dramatist, George Eliot is always dealing with the most profound of practical religious questions. That truceless conflict which the Persians deified into alternating gods of Light and of Darkness; which Protestantism has philosophized into the problem of free-will *vs.* predestination; which is presented in history by the sustaining faith of the Jew on the one hand and the disintegrating fatalism of the Turk on the other; which in the experience of the individual is figured by the immortal parable of St. Anthony's strugglings between the spirit and the flesh—this clashing of the universe, one through its many phases, fought out now with the world for its battle-field, but oftenest in the inmost recesses of the human heart, presents itself to the rationalistic mind of George Eliot as the conflict between character and circumstance. Through all the full harmony of her writings is heard this theme.

Daniel Deronda not only treats of this question; it is built up upon it. The novel has two centres, Gwendolen and Mordecai, between whose circles the author's hero is the connecting link. The evident difference of opinion between the author and her readers, as to which is the leading person of the story, grows out of the conditions of this pervasive problem. She concentrates her attention upon Deronda because he represents character, force—originative in its relations to Gwendolen, transmissive in its relations with Mordecai. The reader looks upon him more as a force than as a person. On the other hand, the reader's attention is concentrated upon Gwendolen, this throbbing, bleeding heart, torn by the thwarting circumstance we all know to our pain, herself the product of circumstance and the battle-field of opposing character—because this is human and near to us. On either hand are the angel and the demon—not above, shadowy in the clouds, but called Deronda and Grandcourt. The one is indeed . . . the messenger of life, the quickener; the other, the mocking spirit of negation which Goethe pictures as truly devil. Both of these men are evidently intended to represent "character" in Emerson's sense. "This is that which we call Character," says this seer, "a reserved force which acts directly by presence and without means." Tito Melema, the antipodes of Deronda, we know through his deeds, but neither Deronda nor Grandcourt *do* any thing. George Eliot has thus set to herself the most difficult task before creative art. There is more in these men than can be told of them, even in real life, and in endeavoring to give to the reader her own impression of Deronda she has returned again and again to the picture, only to find that, with all her pains, the reader must take some-

thing for granted. The reader who will take nothing for granted—in the heavens or under them, who, in a word, has no sense of spiritual force—finds Deronda a nonentity and Grandcourt an impossibility. Gwendolen knew, and we know, that this is not true; these men are those who are able to successfully oppose circumstance, and get the better of events. Perhaps if George Eliot had been content just to give us her word for Deronda, to elaborate him less, she would have accomplished more. We might then have seen him through the eyes of Gwendolen.

There are other readers who pronounce Grandcourt a living realization, but Deronda an unreal and objectionable prig. But Deronda is neither unreal nor a prig. There may be some to whom George Eliot has not made him evident, partly because literary art fails her to paint the real being she knows; partly because they could not, by their nature, know this real being in actual life. We can not make a photograph of a sunbeam, because it is the sunbeam which makes the photograph; we can not make any photograph evident to the blind. But some of us have known these Messianic men—we speak reverently—of whom Deronda is a type: strong with man's strength, tender with the tenderness of woman, touching no life that they did not lighten and inspire. Yet what could we tell of them that should make our friends know them as we know them? It is Deronda's literary misfortune that he is placed in conditions which in many minds attribute to him effeminacy: it doesn't look very manly to treat a woman as if she were in love with you. It is provoking also to poor humanity to gaze long upon too near an approach to unstained goodness, nor do men take kindly to that unpartisan catholicity which, seeing good on both sides as well as ill on both, seems to each party a defender of the other. Thus Deronda arouses manifold prejudices, but they are prejudices and not judgments. His character is justified as the book reaches its real climax and conclusion in that touching sentence of Gwendolen, the noblest testimony a noble soul can have: "It is better—it shall be better with me—because I have known you."

To most readers it goes without saying that this problem of character and circumstance is the mainspring of the Gwendolen side of Daniel Deronda's double history; it will be seen also that what is commonly known as "the Jewish business" no less grows out of it, while even in a side personage like Klesmer we are shown the triumph of character over social circumstance. The history of the Jews appealed powerfully to the imagination of George Eliot, because it presented at once the most remarkable proof of the abidingness of character, in its broader relations, and the most striking illustration of that contact of ideal character and every-day circumstance which, as in the frequent suggestion that Deronda has a modern tailor, she is so fond of pointing out. The Jewish is so far the one race in history that can lay claim to immortality—because the earlier Ezras founded its national life upon a Rock. It was these Prophets of Judea, strong in faith, and defying circumstance, who, with that fire of soul that blazed into the most splendid and fervent oratory the world has known, gave to their petty state that principle of life which could never be quenched by the whole power of the magnificent empires that one after another fell to pieces around it. And it is this people, the chosen of God, who time and time again have turned aside, betrayed by the lusts of the flesh, into the entanglement of circumstance—who, to-day, leave the ancient and splendid ritual of their synagogues, to cheat Jehovah and the Gentiles on the street. "Seest thou," says Mordecai, in one of the great passages of the book, "our lot is the lot of Israel. The grief and the glory are mingled as the smoke and the flame." The very name of Mordecai and his contrasting fellow-Cohens itself tells the story. Associated in our minds with a common order of people, Cohen is . . . the Hebrew word for priest. Always, as in ***The Spanish Gypsy,*** emphasizing the idea of race, the thought of Judaism came also personally home to George Eliot, not so much in the influence of her husband, as has been suggested, as in that of her friend Emmanuel Deutsch, whose *Literary Remains* have shown to the world one whose kindling enthusiasm, thwarted aspirations, and gentle, pathetic life bring to mind both Deronda and Mordecai. For the latter, the direct suggestion came of course from that Cohen who was the leader of the philosophical club described in Lewes's *Fortnightly* article on "Spinoza," but it is doubtless the life of Deutsch that has given life to Mordecai. In his influence upon George Eliot, as in that of Mordecai upon Deronda, is seen that transmissive inspiration and "apostolic succession" of character that is a chief factor and proof of greatness. It is perhaps his enthusiasm for the East, also, that unfortunately started off Deronda upon a mission, of the geographical reunion of the Jews, which, in the light of modern relations, seems useless and absurd, as well as chimerical, and runs counter not least to the usual philosophy of George Eliot herself. (pp. 68-72)

Having asserted that a novel may properly, by reason of its difference from the drama, have purpose and personality, and having endeavored to discover the *motif* and purpose of George Eliot's work, it is now time to ask whether in ***Daniel Deronda*** she has fulfilled, not the rigid canons of a too narrow criticism, but the conditions she has set for herself. It can not be denied that as a writer, as well as artist, she has seriously lapsed. Some indications of this have already been pointed out. The plan of the book is not as diffusive as that of ***Middlemarch,*** and to many readers the interest is more concentrated and continuous, but it oscillates between two plots, neither of which can be considered a sub-plot. This lapse of continuity is not lessened by the frequency with which the chorus occupies so large a portion of the stage, or by the literary fault in which George Eliot unfortunately indorses Browning's worst tendencies. An author may fairly be called upon to give good reason for distracting the reader from his continuity of thought and feeling by sending him to the dictionary for the meaning of a word not generally known, or by calling his attention to a word or phrase so novel or peculiar as to stand out from the text. We don't go to George Eliot as to Sir Thomas Browne, and she herself plans for a wider circle of readers. That the words she uses are pregnant with meaning is not enough; dictionaries of science and of positivism ought not to be the necessary vestibule to a book meant for general reading. Nor is it healthful for a writer to depart far from the usual speech of his day and generation: he is instantly in danger of being led away into affectations which separate him from a wide sympathy with the heart and life of the people. This has wrecked many poets and, despite Miss Evans, some novelists.

There are many who impugn George Eliot for such provoking lack of good taste as the introduction of the little Cohens at Deronda's wedding. But this is connected with a virtue—the perfection of her truth. These contrasts of every-day life are always present to her—as to most of us—and thrust themselves into the picture. The introduction of Mrs. Glasher is resented as an affront not only to good taste, but to good morals. This opens two of the most perplexing problems be-

An 1849 portrait of Eliot by François D'Albert-Durade.

fore a writer: within what limits it is wise to present truth, and the distinction between truth absolute and relative. In dealing with this subject, George Eliot has a special purpose. It has been noted that while certain relations of life, such as that between mother and daughter, are noticeably absent from George Eliot's books, others, brother and sister among them, are returned to again and again. Among these latter also is peculiarly the relation existing between Arthur and Hetty, Tito and Tessa, Grandcourt and Mrs. Glasher, and imputed by false gossip to Maggie Tulliver and Stephen Guest, and even to Deronda. Why does she so build up plots about this subject? Because here again is her one theme, in the shape in which it comes within the possibilities of every human being in whom the angel and the animal, the fortifyings of the spirit and the temptations of the flesh, wage the warfare of character and circumstance. . . . Much as we may regret it, it is perhaps necessary to accept the fact, and insist that the subject shall be rightly treated, for it is here that sentimentalism is dangerous. George Eliot, in contrast with her usual method, treats Mrs. Glasher not as a social problem, but as an individual. The chorus has nothing to say about her. In so doing, she presents a picture of absolute—that is, of individual—truth, if relative truth is little considered. The danger is in considering a person who is not even a type as representing a class, and it may be alleged that in Mrs. Glasher George Eliot is unjust to society. But if we look again—as, unfortunately, most readers may not look—Mrs. Glasher's Nemesis is to be discerned.

In fact, the only possible impeachment of George Eliot's truth seems to be that, except in such distinctively religious persons as Dinah, Savonarola, and Mordecai, she scarcely permits to her characters the usual sense and recognition of a divine existence. In all the strophes and epistrophes of the chorus, there is little clue to the personal religious opinions of this *ego,* any more than in the dramas of Shakespeare. . . .

Not irreligious, but unreligious, her keen analysis and avidity for truth makes her nevertheless a great moralist. "The truth is," says one of her early critics, "we are all moralists when we see the facts in their right light." But there is more than this: in basing her work on this problem which so possesses her, George Eliot, we repeat, deals with the most profound of practical religious questions. Yet she does not treat it religiously, but morally. The Christian lays hold on the outstretched hand of his Redeemer: she sends her reader only to his own conscience and the choice that comes of it. Character is the one thing, and there is an "inexorable law of human souls, that we prepare ourselves for sudden deeds by the reiterated choice of good or evil that gradually determines character." The Christian accepts this, but looks to higher help. Under the limitations of her own creed, the question of George Eliot's moral effectiveness is in good part the question whether she stands with the optimists or pessimists, for faith or fatalism; whether we are to learn from her that men—that is, character—have a fair chance of getting the better of circumstances, or that circumstances for the most part get the better of men. Of course there are facts on both sides, and George Eliot presents them as men and women. But the influence of a great intellect is set one way or the other according as it inspires by the triumph of character or dampens with its defeats by circumstances through the examples it selects. Some of her books are hardly assuring. "Our deeds," she says in **Adam Bede,** "determine us as much as we determine our deeds." And **Middlemarch** is a record of disappointments. But **Daniel Deronda** is positive and an inspiration, and this is the best thing about it. It marks an advance in faith, if not in art. This is the great suggestion of **Daniel Deronda,** that there are men not

> tangled in the fold
> Of dire Necessity,

but able to control circumstance, who "stand for a fact" and are a superior part of law. It is comfortable, therefore, to find in the kindling enthusiasms and character-triumphs of this latest book a contrast with the pitiable demoralization of **Romola**'s Tito, and the thwarted aspirations of **Middlemarch.** It is as though George Eliot had got out into the free air and found hope in life after all.

But George Eliot is too great for the judgment of any less a critic than posterity. It will read her books in a broader light than we, in the light also of the personal history of her life and of the literary material which has gone to the making of her books. In the absence of any thing authentic about Shakespeare, the legendary deer-stealing became an event in English history. There is no writer who has had a more remarkable personal history than Mrs. Lewes, though she is known to the biographical dictionaries only by the dates of publication of her books, or a history that has had more marked influence on the direction of literary activity. It is with all this in view that the verdict of posterity will be given, and that will decide, as we can not, whether **Daniel Deronda** marks for George Eliot a decadence in art or a more hopeful and wholesome outreach in her psychology. (pp. 73-6)

R. R. Bowker, " 'Daniel Deronda', " in The International Review, *Vol. IV, January, 1877, pp. 68-76.*

DAVID KAUFMANN (essay date 1877)

[*A German-Jewish scholar, Kaufmann wholeheartedly praises*

Eliot's portrayal of Jewish history, culture, and life in Daniel Deronda. *Eliot wrote a letter to Kaufmann thanking him for his sympathetic insight into her novel (see letter below).*]

[The] most celebrated authoress of the day, and the pride of English letters—George Eliot—has chosen Judaism and its future as the theme of her latest imaginative creation, with a depth of comprehension hitherto unreached, and with unexampled grandeur and independence of judgment. In the Valhalla of the Jewish people, among the tokens of homage which the genius of centuries has offered and laid down, **Daniel Deronda** will take its place as the proudest testimony of English recognition.

It may be boldly maintained without fear of exaggeration that no great work of any modern literature not written by a Jew has taken Judaism so specially for its subject as this latest creation of the English authoress; and if it were not that every mental product is by nature unfettered and essentially opposed to restriction within narrow limits, I would not hesitate to propose as the formula of this work, expressing its entire significance, and all its tendencies, *the Future of Judaism, and its influence upon its adherents. . . .* It was not to be expected . . . from a genius such as George Eliot, that she would present us, in her work, with a text-book of Judaism, with an exposition of her own preferences, or with a critical comparison between it and other religious systems. She does not introduce us to ideas, but to men and women of flesh and blood in whom these ideas work and act consciously and unconsciously; we are shown not a creed, but its professors— not a faith, but those who have been nurtured in it. None but a poetess cunning to transform *convictions into motives, and thoughts into actions,* would have ventured to animate her work with a sentiment so strange and even unintelligible to the majority of the cultivated as the longing of the Jews for the re-establishment of their kingdom. In contemplating a work of art, it is not a matter of *primary* inquiry whether an idea be true or false, whether a sentiment be authorised or not; we have only to consider whether or not the work has succeeded in adequately representing the power of that idea or the dominion of that sentiment. George Eliot has taken care to draw her figures true; and no sympathetic reader can gainsay her there, that even this much-ridiculed longing after Palestine is well fitted to inform a human life with rapturous and noble impulses. This ardent desire for a national future on the part of the Israelites forms the intellectual centre and heart of her book. (pp. 23-7)

[The] authoress has succeeded in bringing before us, in all its inward, compelling power, and in all its fiery, action-craving impetuosity, no common passion of mankind, well known and easy to understand, but a special sentiment shared by few, strange, and therefore incomprehensible to the many. We have here another confirmation of the saying that the poet is *"von allem Dasein, das Wesen selbst"* of what he represents, and another proof that he has, to use an expression of George Eliot's own, like the hundred-gated Thebes, manifold openings to his soul by which events and phenomena of life, unseen and unheard by his dull fellow-creatures, gain access to him. That this book presents Judaism as the seed of fire and as a motive power, be it among a mere handful on the earth, constitutes not only its poetical truth and beauty, but also its poetical justice; and herein, too, lies the peculiarity which distinguishes George Eliot's treatment of the Jews from the traditional misusage to which other authors have been wont to subject them. . . . Led by cordial and loving inclination to the profound study of Jewish national and family life, she has set herself to create *Jewish Characters,* and to recognise and give presentment to the influences which Jewish education is wont to exercise—to prove by TYPES that Judaism is an intellectual and spiritual force, still misapprehended and readily overlooked, but not the less an effective power, for the future of which it is a good assurance that it possesses in the body of its adherents a noble, susceptible, and pliant material which only awaits its final casting to appear in a glorious form.

An examination of that part of **Daniel Deronda** which relates specially to the Jews and Judaism is inseparable from an aesthetic estimate of it as a whole. At a first superficial glance it falls apart into two entirely unconnected narratives. . . . Deronda is the centre, however, of both narratives, for he is the magnet towards which Gwendolen is mysteriously drawn and fixed. But this circumstance would, of itself, scarcely be a sufficient and satisfactory apology for the amalgamation by the author of things irrelevant. Two lines which cut one another at a common point of intersection make a mathematical figure, it is true; but they cannot form the subject of a work of art, the unity of which must be preserved in accordance with fundamental axioms. For a writer of fiction to couple narratives which have no essential connection does not lower his work—it sentences it to death outright; and it is solely because contemporary criticism has shut its eyes to the relation of the two stories which run through **Daniel Deronda** that its value as a work of art and its real significance as a book have not yet received full and true expression. (pp. 40-8)

[The] two narratives which run side by side in **Daniel Deronda** are to be regarded as pendants mutually illustrating and explaining one another. But it need scarcely be said that the authoress has not fallen into the error of expressly indicating this relation, by crudely holding the two pictures up opposite each other. Her creation belongs to that more earnest kind of art which opens its treasures only to attentive observation, and which rewards us in proportion to the depth of our insight. The contrast afforded by these two narratives is, in truth, an inexhaustible spring of fruitful remark and gratifying perception for the reflective reader. In perusing a work of genius we need not fear that we shall see and find more meaning than it really holds, for it is certain to contain all and more than all that the author was clearly conscious of, while composing it; and it is a light accusation to have read between the lines, for genius has always *"hineingeheimnisst"* more into her creations than appears upon their surface. What was of old said of Holy Writ, holds true of all great imaginative productions—there is a secret as well as an open meaning in them. And in this spirit it is admissible even to give an allegorical interpretation to a work of art.

It would be an exaggeration to say that light and shade have been thrown upon the two sets of circumstances which environ Deronda and Gwendolen, in such a manner that all the light falls upon the former, and all the shade upon the latter; but it cannot be denied that the morality of Deronda's surroundings is greater than that of Gwendolen's, and their vital purport *deeper* and more hearty. Sharper contrasts than Mirah and Gwendolen cannot be conceived. While the one, the Jewess, follows her path in safety through the rudest storms, led as it were by an *innate moral instinct,* in spite of all the cajolements of her wretched father, and in the tender purity of her nature carries an unblemished conscience to meet her coming happiness; the other, groping blindly around and wholly dependent upon aid and assistance from

without, staggers and stumbles, and finally lies before us shattered and torn by remorse at the very time when freedom and happiness seem within her reach. . . . Then compare Henleigh Grandcourt and Daniel Deronda. In the one we see emptiness and blunted perception, the disgust which is born of satiety, polish and fascinating adroitness combined with absolute want of feeling, and perfect worldly wisdom hiding heartless barbarity; in the other, a full and rich mental life, an open sense for all that is great and beautiful, a moral fibre of the utmost toughness and yet of the utmost delicacy, and the readiest and most willing disinterestedness and self-sacrifice. The one, in a word, is selfishness incarnate—the other, the archetype of self-negation. What splendid misery this of Gwendolen's married life! Her husband she cannot but despise—this man who has already seduced and betrayed one woman, and by whom she too, after she becomes his wife, is maltreated as though she were his dog, and who regards her as the savage may regard the jewel which decks his person. And all this misery must be veiled in the mantle of social observance, and the proprieties must be rigidly adhered to. Everything remains fair outwardly, while beneath the glitter of the tinsel there is naught but hollowness and decay, and while hidden beneath this beauteous envelope the heart is lying broken. Contrast the marriage of Deronda and Mirah, how happy it is! what a joyous radiance illumines it! Must we not look upon Ezra Cohen's humble family even as thrice blessed in comparison with the empty prosperity of Sir Hugo Mallinger, who regards his presumptive heir Grandcourt as a veritable thorn in the flesh, and vainly seeks to quiet his own inward discontent by a thousand idle distractions? The characters seem sometimes to take voices to themselves, and cry, Compare your superficial splendour, your frivolous pleasures, your poor, futile amusements, your gnawing passions, and your absorbing vices, with the deep contentedness, the all-satisfying delights, and the moral purity of the higher Jewish life, and see if these Jews are, after all, so much more contemptible than yourselves! What is Gascoigne's son? A victim of unrequited love, at variance with himself. In Hans Meyrick, even, there is nothing but the light temperament of the artist, for he turns round bitter and hostile upon Deronda, his best friend and well-wisher, when the latter's interests come into collision with his own. How shallow, how unsatisfactory, almost mask-like these characters appear, wanting as they are in deep purpose and high yearning, beside Mordecai, that noble flower springing from the dust, that humble Jewish hero! What a people must that be which can produce from its very lowest ranks so pure and lofty a religious genius as Mordecai; and what a system must that be in which a mother's ideal presence is sufficient to keep a daughter modest and dutiful in the very slough of temptation! I am far from imagining that a thinker and poetess of George Eliot's calibre would ever have attempted to represent Judaism as the only source of high-mindedness, and the Jews as the sole and hereditary possessors of all morality. . . . The specifically Jewish virtues may go along with the specifically Jewish vices, concerning which hatred has invented so many fables. The contrast of the two sets of circumstances is not meant to lead us to one-sidedness and injustice. On the contrary, we ought to learn from it, above all, that Judaism is no obsolete petrifaction, but a force beating and pulsating in the hearts and minds of men—no indifferent shadow unworthy of our attention, but a fact of incalculable significance—no object to be neglected and despised, but a profound mystery, and a vital challenge to reflection. Men may think and say, as they will, that Judaism is the religion of the past, a piece of road long left behind; but it still possesses the power of producing a Mordecai—it has a *future*. (pp. 49-56)

If, in drawing Deronda, George Eliot has omitted to bring him near to us as a human being, and has preserved him in a certain stately inaccessibility, on the other hand she has effected a miracle in setting before us a prophet, and in bringing a scarcely intelligible and wholly ethereal nature closely home to us. The life which runs in Mordecai's veins is indestructible, and akin to the spirit with which genius has animated a Hamlet, a Wallenstein, and a Faust. If Deronda is the Fulfiller, Mordecai is the Forerunner; if the one is the Accomplisher, the other is his John the Baptist; if the former is the hero, the latter is the soul of the creation. . . . Mordecai is carved of the wood from which prophets are made, and so far as the supersensuous can be rendered intelligible, it may even be said that in studying him we are introduced into a studio or workshop of the prophetic mind. He is one of the most difficult as well as one of the most successful essays in psychological analysis ever attempted by an author; and in his wonderful portrait, which must be closely studied, and not epitomised or reproduced in extracts, we see glowing enthusiasm united to cabbalistic profundity, and the most morbid tension of the intellectual powers united to clear and well-defined hopes. How has the authoress succeeded in making Mordecai so human and so true to nature? By mixing the gold with an alloy of commoner metal, and by giving the angelic likeness features which are familiar to us all. (pp. 65-8)

The marvellous versatility of our authoress, whose brush paints with equal readiness the miniature life of childhood and the most stormy and eventful pictures of passion, is further revealed by her presenting us with the modest and fragrant floweret Mirah, between two such striking growths as Deronda and Mordecai; and the affection which the pair bear for her amid all their imperious longings and stirring ideas affects us as a soft, soothing note heard among resounding chords. Only a master-hand could have succeeded in sketching and finishing her figure on the canvas. The account which she gives her protectress, Mrs Meyrick, in plain, affecting language which reminds us of the Bible, of the wandering life she led with her weak degraded father, of the moral power of her mother's memory, and of the irresistible strength with which her love for race and faith kept ever growing in her heart, is of itself valuable testimony to the frequently unconscious influence which Judaism still exercises upon the feelings and sentiments of its professors. Before the pregnant brevity and depth of feeling with which the winning Jewish maiden tells her tale, prejudices are scattered like the clouds; and proselytism must be silent when it sees with what gentle fervour she cherishes and clings to Judaism in her heart of hearts. (pp. 71-2)

But the colours in *Daniel Deronda* have not been laid on with one-sided preference or blind partiality; and the meaning and truth of the authoress's types become all the clearer when we notice the justice with which shadows both deep and light are brought out in this picture of the Jewish people. The little incidental strokes, for instance, by means of which she gives us an insight into the narrowness of the circumstances of Ezra Cohen and his family, and their calculating, business-like mode of expressing kind feeling, are of inimitable grace. George Eliot's satire has none of the bitterness of hatred, but springs, like all true humour, from love; and for this reason the pictures which she has drawn of the Jews are of far greater force than the caricaturing misrepresentations which an

active hatred hawks about the world. He has been at all times the true poet who could find the rift of blue mirrored in the ditch, and see a trace of the Divine in the most abject of mankind. Thus in placing Mordecai in the family of the pawnbroker Cohen, for whom she certainly has no great affection or esteem, the authoress has paid a gracious tribute of recognition to the Jewish race. (pp. 73-5)

Poetical justice in *Daniel Deronda* finds its account in the care which the authoress takes to blend a degree of shade with the light which streams forth like a halo from Deronda and Mordecai. It is always painful to hear fair lips pronouncing ugly words, and we are wounded and annoyed by the hard and rugged language of Deronda's mother, the daughter of the Genoese physician, Daniel Charisi. . . . Her life as we see it is a broken existence—a picture of apostasy punished, and of treachery betrayed. If any further evidence were wanting to clear the authoress from the imputation of a blind partiality for the Jews, we should find it in her sketch of old Lapidoth, who is a rascal fit to grace any museum of human depravity, and who is drawn with such truth and reality that we forget in looking at him that he is a mere creation of the fancy. But no Jew will find it unnatural that this wretched creature can call Mordecai and Mirah his children, for it is notorious that in Jewish families it is generally owing to the mother that children are prevented from following in the footsteps of their fathers. Thus even the very lowest and most degraded persons in the work we are considering are stamped with a peculiar Jewish impress, and the circumstance that they are Jews is not without significance for their destinies and characters.

Leader of the present so-called realistic school, our authoress keeps up in this work the reputation she has won of possessing the most minute knowledge of the subjects she handles, by the manner in which she has described the Jews—the Great Unknown of humanity. She has penetrated into their history and literature affectionately and thoroughly; and her knowledge in a field where ignorance is still venial if not expressly authorised, has astonished even experts. In her selection of almost always unfamiliar quotations, she shows a taste and a facility of reference really amazing. When shall we see a German writer exhibiting the courteous kindliness of George Eliot, who makes Deronda study Zunz's *Synagogale Poesie,* and places the monumental words which open his chapter entitled "*Leiden*" at the head of the passage in which she introduces us to Ezra Cohen's family, and to the Club-meeting at which Mordecai gives utterance to his ideas concerning the future of Israel? She is as familiar with the views of Jehuda-ha-Levi as with the dreams and longings of the Cabbalists, and as conversant with the splendid names of our Hispano-Arabian epoch as with the moral aphorisms of the Talmud and the subtle meaning contained in Jewish legends. . . . It is by the piety and tenderness with which she treats Jewish customs that the authoress shows how supreme her cultivation and refinement are; and the small number of mistakes which can be detected in her descriptions of Jewish life and ritual may put to the blush even writers who belong to that race. What a loving insight into the spirit of Judaism is expressed by this reflection evoked by the confession of unity in the Shemah:

> The divine unity embraced as its consequence the ultimate unity of mankind. The nation which has been scoffed at for its separateness, has given a binding theory to the human race.

There is no delusion on George Eliot's part that the ideas and characters which she has given to the world in this work will be received with unanimity in Christian circles, or with pleasure by all Jews. She knows as well as any one the objections which may be urged against her leading idea; and Mordecai has to endure some very hard hits at his holy enthusiasm in the Philosopher's Club at the "Hand and Banner." . . . Others will say that the establishment of a national State is not the aim of Jewish history at all. . . . [But the] objections do not touch the value of *Daniel Deronda* as a work of art; and, strictly speaking, not even the ideas of which it is the mouthpiece. For the establishment of a Jewish national centre will not prevent the race from disseminating itself among the other nations of the globe. On the contrary, the influence of the Jews who remain scattered will be strengthened and supported by the consciousness which they will then possess that they are members of a united and recognised community. George Eliot is one of those who believe that Judaism is not only a religion, but a nationality also, and that this has a voice which cries out even in those who have apparently, separated themselves from their people of their own free will, and in those who have been stolen from their race by their parents. (pp. 78-88)

[In whatever way these ideological] questions may be decided, the book remains untouched as a work of art. In judging an imaginative work, it is not the critic's business to determine whether or not its ideas be true, but solely to examine whether these ideas have permeated the flesh and blood of the characters, and made them lifelike, and able to captivate and carry us along with them. And it is not till we have taken up this point of view that the conclusion will force itself upon us that *Daniel Deronda* is a Jewish book not only in the sense that it treats of Jews, but also in the sense that it is pre-eminently fitted for being understood and appreciated by Jews; indeed, they only are qualified to embrace and enjoy its full significance. For what is it that binds us to the poet? What else than his power of expressing the words which rise to all our lips and yet remain unuttered, of giving voice to the feelings of each of us, of weeping with one and making merry with another, and of having something to offer to every human heart which may often have been sighed for, but which has never been realised and grasped so securely hitherto. Naturally it is a Jewish heart alone that can feel the entire magic of a creation woven from the highest hopes of that nation's soul. The book will win friends among the Jews, not only through the feeling of pride which may well arise in the breast of every honest man who sees his people honoured, but also, and chiefly, through the profound satisfaction which it will afford the thinker to find his individuality recognised and explained by a stranger. The one will rejoice heartily at finding what he long ago implicitly discerned, here so definitely expressed; and the eyes of the other will grow dim with tears when he beholds the dear, regretted features of a well-known face greeting him from the framework of the tale. (pp. 89-91)

The majority of readers regard the world to which they are introduced in *Daniel Deronda* as one foreign, strange, and repulsive. Our authoress—whom it has hitherto been the custom to extol to the skies, and to whom the critics have, up to this time, been related more as partisans than as judges—has been abandoned on this occasion by almost the entire body, not one of whom has been able to make up his mind to do homage to a genius which has lost its way in the lowly walks of Jewish life. Indignation and perplexity will doubtless some day vanish, however, and give place to joy, when it is recognised that the literature of the world has been enriched by a work worthy to be crowned and garlanded as a public defence of the right of private judgment against the attacks of prejudice and falsehood.

George Eliot has not thrown herself away upon an unworthy object. It is a beautiful characteristic of Judaism that it cherishes the memory of its alien benefactors in imperishable remembrance and everlasting honour. (pp. 92-3)

David Kaufmann, in his George Eliot and Judaism: An Attempt to Appreciate "Daniel Deronda," *translated by J. W. Ferrier, 1877. Reprint by Haskell House Publishers Ltd., 1970, 95 p.*

M. E. LEWES [GEORGE ELIOT]　(letter date 1877)

[*In this excerpt from a letter written to David Kaufmann, Eliot responds to his praise of her treatment of Jewish themes in* Daniel Deronda *(see excerpt above). For additional commentary by Eliot, see letters dated 1876.*]

Hardly, since I became an author, have I had a deeper satisfaction, I may say a more heartfelt joy, than you have given me in your estimate of *Daniel Deronda.*

I must tell you that it is my rule, very strictly observed, not to read the criticisms on my writings. For years I have found this abstinence necessary to preserve me from that discouragement as an artist which ill-judged praise, no less than ill-judged blame, tends to produce in me. For far worse than any verdict as to the proportion of good and evil in our work, is the painful impression that we write for a public which has no discernment of good and evil.

My husband reads any notices of me that come before him, and reports to me (or else refrains from reporting) the general character of the notice or something in particular which strikes him as showing either an exceptional insight or an obtuseness that is gross enough to be amusing. Very rarely, when he has read a critique of me, he has handed it to me, saying. "*You* must read this." And your estimate of *Daniel Deronda* made one of these rare instances.

Certainly, if I had been asked to choose *what* should be written about my book and *who* should write it, I should have sketched—well, not anything so good as what you have written, but an article which must be written by a Jew who showed not merely sympathy with the best aspirations of his race, but a remarkable insight into the nature of art and the processes of the artistic mind. Believe me, I should not have cared to devour even ardent praise if it had not come from one who showed the discriminating sensibility, the perfect response to the artist's intention, which must make the fullest, rarest joy to one who works from inward conviction and not in compliance with current fashions. Such a response holds for an author not only what is best in "the life that now is," but the promise of "that which is to come." I mean that the usual approximative, narrow perception of what one has been intending and professedly feeling in one's work, impresses one with the sense that it must be poor perishable stuff without roots to take any lasting hold in the minds of men; while any instance of complete comprehension encourages one to hope that the creative prompting has foreshadowed, and will continue to satisfy, a need in other minds.

Excuse me that I write but imperfectly, and perhaps dimly, what I have felt in reading your article. It has affected me deeply, and though the prejudice and ignorant obtuseness which has met my effort to contribute something to the ennobling of Judaism in the conception of the Christian community and in the consciousness of the Jewish community, has never for a moment made me repent my choice, but rather has been added proof to me that the effort was needed—yet I confess that I had an unsatisfied hunger for certain signs of sympathetic discernment, which you only have given. (p. 703)

> *M. E. Lewes [George Eliot], in a letter to D. Kaufmann on May 31, 1877, in* The Athenaeum, *No. 2822, November 26, 1881, pp. 703-04.*

LESLIE STEPHEN   (essay date 1902)

[*Stephen is considered one of the most important English literary critics of the late Victorian and early Edwardian eras. In his criticism, which is often moralistic, Stephen argues that all literature is nothing more than an imaginative rendering, in concrete terms, of a writer's philosophy or beliefs. It is the role of criticism, he contends, to translate into intellectual terms what the writer has told the reader through character, symbol, and plot. Stephens's analyses often include biographical judgments of the writer. As he once observed: "The whole art of criticism consists in learning to know the human being who is partially revealed to us in his spoken or written words." In the following excerpt from a 1902 essay, Stephen discusses* Daniel Deronda *primarily in terms of the principles embodied in the main characters, Gwendolen Harleth and Daniel Deronda.*]

[*Daniel Deronda*] is really two stories put side by side and intersecting at intervals. Each gives a life embodying a principle, and each illustrates its opposite by the contrast. Gwendolen Harleth, a young lady with aspirations in a latent state, is misled into a worldly marriage, and though ultimately saved, is saved "as by fire." Daniel Deronda is throughout true to his higher nature, and is, in George Eliot's works, what Sir Charles Grandison is in Richardson's—the type of human perfection. The story of Gwendolen's marriage shows undiminished power. Here and there, perhaps, we have a little too much psychological analysis; but, after all, the reader who objects to psychology can avoid it by skipping a paragraph or two. It is another version of the old tragic motive: the paralysing influence of unmitigated and concentrated selfishness. . . . Grandcourt, to whom Gwendolen sacrifices herself, is compared to a crab or a boa-constrictor slowly pinching its victim to death: to appeal to him for mercy would be as idle as to appeal to "a dangerous serpent ornamentally coiled on her arm." He is a Tito in a further stage of development—with all better feelings atrophied, and enabled, by his fortune, to gratify his spite without exerting himself in intrigues. . . . [Grandcourt] suggests, to me at least, rather the cruel woman than the male autocrat. Some critic remarked, to George Eliot's annoyance, that the scenes between him and his parasite Lush showed the "imperious feminine, not the masculine character." She comforted herself by the statement that Bernal Osborne—a thorough man of the world—had commended these scenes as specially lifelike. I can, indeed, accept both views, for the distinction is rather too delicate for definite application. One feels, I think, that Grandcourt was drawn by a woman; but a sort of voluptuous enjoyment of malignant tyranny is unfortunately not confined to either sex. Anyhow, Gwendolen's ordeal is pathetic, and she excites more sympathy than any of George Eliot's victims. Perhaps she excites a little too much. At least, when she comes very near homicide . . . , and withholds her

hand from her drowning husband, one is strongly tempted to give the verdict, "Served him right." She, however, feels some remorse; and Daniel Deronda, who becomes her confessor, is much too admirable a being to give any sanction to this immoral source of consolation. She is so charming in her way that we feel more interest in the criminal than in the confessor. "I have no sympathy," she says on one occasion, "with women who are always doing right." Perhaps that is the reason why we cannot quite bow the knee before Daniel Deronda.

That young gentleman is a model from the first. He has a "seraphic face." There is "hardly a delicacy of feeling" of which he is not capable—even when he is at Eton. He is so ethereal a being that we are a little shocked when he is mentioned in connection with *entrées*. One can't fancy an angel at a London dinner table. That is, indeed, the impression which he makes upon his friend. A family is created expressly to pay homage to him. They are supposed to have a sense of humour to make their worship more impressive; but they certainly keep it in the background when speaking of him. People, says one of the young ladies, must be content to take our brothers for husbands, because they can't get Deronda. "No woman ought to want to marry him," replies her sister . . . "fancy finding out that he had a tailor's bill and used boothooks, like our brother." Angels don't employ tailors. They compare him to his face to Buddha, who gave himself to a famishing tigress to save her and her cubs from starvation. To Gwendolen this peerless person naturally becomes an "outer conscience"; and when he exhorts her to use her past sorrow as a preparation for life, instead of letting it spoil her life, the words are to her "like the touch of a miraculous hand." She begins "a new existence," but it seems "inseparable from Deronda," and she longs that his presence may be permanent. Happily she does not dare to love him, and hopes only to be bound to him by a "spiritual tie." That is just as well, because by a fortunate accident he has picked a perfect young Jewess out of the Thames, into which she had thrown herself, like Mary Wollstonecraft. Moreover, by another providential accident—Providence interferes rather to excess—he has walked into the city and stumbled upon a virtuous Jewish pawnbroker; and at the pawnbroker's has met the Jewess's long-lost brother Mordecai, who turns out to be as perfect as Deronda himself.

It must be admitted that the Jewish circle into which Deronda is admitted does not strike one as drawn from the life. That is only natural, as Mordecai is the incarnated pursuit of an ideal. Mordecai is devoted to the restoration of the Jewish nationality—a scheme which to the vulgar mind seems only one degree less chimerical than Zarca's plan for a gypsy nationality in Africa. It gives a chance to Deronda, however. For a perfect young man in a time of "social questions," he has hitherto been rather oddly at a loss for an end to which he can devote his powers. This is explained by a lengthy dissertation on his character. He is too good. "His plenteous flexible sympathy had ended by falling into one current with that reflective analysis which tends to neutralise sympathy." He is not vicious, but he "takes even vices mildly"; he is "fervidly democratic" from sympathy with the people, and yet "intensely conservative" from imagination and affection. He likes to be on the losing side in order to have the pleasure of martyrdom; but he is afraid that too much martyrdom will make him bitter. The solution comes by the discovery, strangely delayed by a combination of circumstances, that he was a genuine Jew by birth. Now he can accept Mordecai for his prophet and take "heredity" for his guide. "You," he says to that inspired person, "have given shape to what, I believe, was an inherited yearning—the effect of brooding passionate thoughts in many ancestors—thoughts that seem to have been intensely present with my grandfather." He has always longed for an 'ideal task'—some "captainship, which should come to him as a duty and not be striven for as a personal prize." The "idea that I am possessed with," as he afterward explains, is "that of restoring a political existence to my people, making them a nation again, giving them a national centre such as the English, though they too are scattered over the face of the globe." It seems from her volume of essays (***Theophrastus Such***) that George Eliot considered this to be a reasonable investment of human energy. As we cannot all discover that we belong to the chosen people, and some of us might, even then, doubt the wisdom of the enterprise, one feels that Deronda's mode of solving his problem is not generally applicable. George Eliot's sympathy for the Jews, her aversion to Anti-Semitism, was thoroughly generous, and naturally welcomed by its objects. But taken as the motive of a hero it strikes one as showing a defective sense of humour. "One may understand jokes without liking them," says the musician Klesmer; and adds, "I am very sensible to wit and humour." There can be no doubt that George Eliot was very sensible to those qualities, and yet she refuses to perceive that Daniel Deronda is an amiable monomaniac and occasionally a very prosy moralist. (pp. 185-89)

George Eliot was intensely feminine, though more philosophical than most women. She shows it to the best purpose in the subtlety and the charm of her portraits of women, unrivalled in some ways by any writer of either sex; and shows it also, as I think, in a true perception of the more feminine aspects of her male characters. Still, she sometimes illustrates the weakness of the feminine view. Daniel Deronda is not merely a feminine but, one is inclined to say, a schoolgirl's hero. He is so sensitive and scrupulously delicate that he will not soil his hands by joining in the rough play of ordinary political and social reformers. He will not compromise, and yet he shares the dislike of his creator for fanatics and the devotees of "fads." The monomaniac type is certainly disagreeable, though it may be useful. Deronda contrives to avoid its more offensive peculiarities, but at the price of devoting himself to an unreal and dreamy object. Probably, one fancies, he became disgusted in later life by finding that, after Mordecai's death, the people with whom he had to work had not the charm of that half-inspired visionary. He is, in any case, an idealist, who can only be provided with a task by a kind of providential interposition. The discovery that one can be carrying out one's grandfather's ideas is not generally a very powerful source of inspiration. "Heredity" represents an important factor in life, but can hardly be made into a religion. So far, therefore, as Deronda is an aesthetic embodiment of an ethical revelation—a judicious hint to a young man in search of an ideal—he represents an untenable theory. From the point of view of the simple novel reader he fails from unreality. George Eliot, in later years, came to know several representatives in the younger generation of the class to which Deronda belonged. She speaks, for example, with great warmth of Henry Sidgwick. His friends, she remarks, by their own account, always "expected him to act according to a higher standard" than they would attribute to any one else or adopt for themselves. She sent Deronda to Cambridge soon after she had written this, and took great care to give an accurate account of the incidents of Cambridge life. I have always fancied—though without any evidence—that some

touches in Deronda were drawn from one of her friends, Edmund Gurney, a man of remarkable charm of character, and as good-looking as Deronda. In the Cambridge atmosphere of Deronda's days there was, I think, a certain element of rough commonsense which might have knocked some of her hero's nonsense out of him. But, in any case, one is sensible that George Eliot, if she is thinking of real life at all, has come to see through a romantic haze which deprives the portrait of reality. The imaginative sense is declining, and the characters are becoming emblems or symbols of principle, and composed of more moonshine than solid flesh and blood. The Gwendolen story taken by itself is a masterly piece of social satire; but in spite of the approval of learned Jews, it is impossible to feel any enthusiastic regard for Deronda in his surroundings. (pp. 190-91)

Leslie Stephen, in his George Eliot, *Macmillan and Co., Limited, 1926, 213 p.*

F. R. LEAVIS   (essay date 1945-46)

[*An influential English critic, Leavis articulated his views in his lectures, in his many critical works, and in* Scrutiny, *a quarterly that he cofounded and edited from 1932 to 1953. His methodology combines close textual analysis with an emphasis on moral and social concerns and the development of "the individual sensibility." Leavis believed that the artist should strive to eliminate "ego-centered distortion and all impure motives" in order to be able to explore the proper place of persons in society. Although Leavis's advocacy of a cultural elite and the occasional vagueness of his moral assumptions were sometimes criticized, his writings remain an important, if controversial, force in literary criticism. Leavis wrote a number of highly influential critical evaluations of Eliot's works for* Scrutiny *in which he sought to identify her strengths and weaknesses as a novelist. In the following excerpt, first published in 1945-46, Leavis asserts that* Daniel Deronda *is divided into two distinctly disparate stories. He finds that the "bad parts" of the work—those dealing with Deronda and Zionist themes—are marred by subtle insincerity, self-indulgence, and confusion, while the "good parts," or* Gwendolen Harleth, *as Leavis titles the portion of the novel devoted to Gwendolen's moral struggles, are Eliot's most mature and brilliant writing and demonstrate the depth of her insight into human nature. D. R. Carroll rejects aspects of Leavis's argument in the excerpt dated 1959, claiming that the novel's two narratives are well integrated.*]

In no other of [George Eliot's] works is the association of the strength with the weakness so remarkable or so unfortunate as in ***Daniel Deronda.*** It is so peculiarly unfortunate, not because the weakness spoils the strength—the two stand apart, on a large scale, in fairly neatly separable masses—but because the mass of fervid and wordy unreality seems to have absorbed most of the attention the book has ever had, and to be all that is remembered of it. That this should be so shows, I think, how little George Eliot's acceptance has rested upon a critical recognition of her real strength and distinction, and how unfair to her, in effect, is the conventional overvaluing of her early work. For if the nature of her real strength had been appreciated for what it is, so magnificent an achievement as the good half of ***Daniel Deronda*** could not have failed to compel an admiration that would have established it, not the less for the astonishing badness of the bad half, among the great things in fiction.

It will be best to get the bad half out of the way first. This can be quickly done, since the weakness doesn't require any sustained attention. . . . It is represented by Deronda himself, and by what may be called in general the Zionist inspiration. (pp. 79-80)

[George Eliot] didn't need to reconstruct Anti-Semitism or its opposite: the Jews were there in the contemporary world of fact, and represented real, active and poignant issues. All her generous moral fervour was quite naturally and spontaneously engaged on their behalf, and, on the other hand, her religious bent and her piety, as well as her intellectual energies and interests, found a congenial field in Jewish culture, history and tradition. Advantages which, once felt, were irresistible temptations. Henry James in his "Conversation" on **Daniel Deronda** [see essay dated 1876] speaks (through Constantius) of the difference between the strong and the weak in George Eliot as one between 'what she is by inspiration and what she is because it is expected of her'. But it is the reverse of a 'sense of the author writing under a sort of external pressure' (Constantius) that I myself have in reading the bad part of **Daniel Deronda.** Here, if anywhere, we have the marks of 'inspiration': George Eliot clearly feels herself swept along on a warm emotional flow. If there is anything at all to be said for the proposition (*via* Constantius again) that 'all the Jewish part is at bottom cold', it must be that it can be made to point to a certain quality in that part which relates it to the novel in which D. H. Lawrence tries, in imaginative creation, to believe that the pre-Christian Mexican religion might be revived—*The Plumed Serpent,* the one book in which Lawrence falls into insincerity. The insincerity, of the kind he was so good at diagnosing and defining, lies, of course, in the quality that leads one to say 'tries'—though it is flow rather than effort one is conscious of. And there is certainly something of that quality in **Daniel Deronda**—something to provoke the judgment that so intelligent a writer couldn't, at that level, have been so self-convinced of inspiration without some inner connivance or complicity: there is an element of the tacitly *voulu.*

But this is not to say that George Eliot's intellect here prevails over the spontaneities, or that there isn't a determining drive from within, a triumphant pressure of emotion; there is, and that is the trouble. The Victorian intellectual certainly has a large part in her Zionist inspirations, but that doesn't make these the less fervidly emotional; the part is one of happy subordinate alliance with her immaturity. . . . [This] alliance comes very naturally (for the relation between the Victorian intellectual and the very feminine woman in her is not the simple antithesis her critics seem commonly to suppose); it comes very naturally and insidiously, establishing the conditions in which her mature intelligence lapses and ceases to inhibit her flights—flights not deriving their impulsion from any external pressure. A distinguished mind and a noble nature are unquestionably present in the bad part of **Daniel Deronda,** but it *is* bad; and the nobility, generosity, and moral idealism are at the same time modes of self-indulgence.

The kind of satisfaction she finds in imagining her hero, Deronda (if he can be said to be imagined), doesn't need analysis. He, decidedly, is a woman's creation:

> Persons attracted him . . . in proportion to the possibility of his defending them, rescuing them, telling upon their lives with some sort of redeeming influence; and he had to resist an inclination to withdraw coldly from the fortunate. (Chapter XXVIII.)

He has all the personal advantages imagined by Mordecai,

the consumptive prophet, for the fulfiller of his dream, the new Moses:

> he must be a Jew, intellectually cultured, morally fervid—in all this a nature ready to be plenished from Mordecai's; but his face and frame must be beautiful and strong, he must have been used to all the refinements of social life, his life must flow with a full and easy current, his circumstances must be free from sordid need: he must glorify the possibilities of the Jew. . . . (Chapter XXXVIII.)

We feel, in fact, that Deronda was conceived in terms of general specifications, George Eliot's relation to him being pretty much that shown here as Mordecai's, whose own show of dramatic existence is merely a licence for the author to abound copiously in such exaltations and fervours as the Dorothea in her craves.

Her own misgivings about the degree of concrete presence she has succeeded in bestowing upon Deronda is betrayed, as Henry James points out, in the way she reminds us again and again of the otherwise non-significant trick she attributes to him—the trick of holding the lapels of his coat as he talks. And when he talks, this is his style:

> 'Turn your fear into a safeguard. Keep your dread fixed on the idea of increasing that remorse which is so bitter to you. Fixed meditation may do a great deal towards defining our longing or dread. We are not always in a state of strong emotion, and when we are calm we can use our memories and gradually change the bias of our fear, as we do our tastes. Take your fear as a safeguard. It is like quickness of hearing. It may make consequences passionately present to you. Try to take hold of your sensibility, and use it as if it were a faculty, like vision'. (Chapter XXXVI.)

It is true that he is here speaking as lay-confessor to Gwendolen Harleth ('her feeling had turned this man into a priest'), but that, in George Eliot's conception, is for him the most natural and self-expressive of rôles. And the style of talk sorts happily (if that is the word) with the style in general of the weak half of the book—though one would hardly guess from this specimen of Deronda's speech alone how diffusely ponderous and abstract George Eliot can be, and for pages on end (pages among her most embarrassingly fervid, for the wordiness and the emotionality go together). A juxtaposition of specimens of the worst dialogue with specimens of the best (of which there is great abundance in the book) would offer some astonishing contrasts. But it would take up more room than can be spared, and an interested reader will very easily choose representative specimens for himself.

The kind of satisfaction George Eliot finds in Deronda's Zionism is plain. ' "The refuge you are needing from personal trouble is the higher, the religious life, which holds an enthusiasm for something more than our own appetites and vanities".' But since poor Gwendolen is not in a position to discover herself a Jewess, and so to find her salvation in Deronda's way, she might in time—when Deronda has gone off to Palestine with Mirah—come to reflect critically upon the depth and general validity of his wisdom. We, at any rate, are obliged to be critical of the George Eliot who can so unreservedly endorse the account of the 'higher, the religious life' represented by Deronda. A paragon of virtue, generosity, intelligence and disinterestedness, he has no 'troubles' he needs a refuge from; what he feels he needs, and what he yearns after, is an 'enthusiasm'—an enthusiasm which shall be at the same time a 'duty'. Whether or not such a desire is necessarily one to have it both ways needn't be discussed; but it is quite plain that the 'duty' that Deronda embraces—' "I considered it my duty—it is the impulse of my feeling—to identify myself . . . with my hereditary people" '—combines moral enthusiasm and the feeling of emotional intensity with essential relaxation in such a way that, for any 'higher life' promoted, we may fairly find an analogy in the exalting effects of alcohol. The element of self-indulgence is patent. And so are the confusions. There is no equivalent of Zionism for Gwendolen, and even if there were—: the religion of heredity or race is not, as a generalizable solution of the problem, one that George Eliot herself, directly challenged, could have stood by. In these inspirations her intelligence and real moral insight are not engaged. But she is otherwise wholly engaged—how wholly and how significantly being brought further home to us when we note that Deronda's racial mission finds itself identified with his love for Mirah, so that he is eventually justified in the 'sweet irresistible hopefulness that the best of human possibilities might befall him—the blending of a complete personal love in one current with a larger duty. . . .'

All in the book that issues from this inspiration is unreal and impotently wordy . . .—*Middlemarch* can show nothing to match the wastes of biblicality and fervid idealism ('Revelations') devoted to Mordecai, or the copious and drearily comic impossibility of the working-men's club (Chapter CXLII), or the utterly routing Shakespearean sprightliness of Hans Meyrick's letter in Chapter LII. The Meyricks who, while not being direct products of the prophetic afflatus, are subordinate ministers to it, are among those elements in George Eliot that seem to come from Dickens rather than from life, and so is the pawnbroker's family: the humour and tenderness are painfully trying, with that quality they have, that obviousness of intention, which relates them so intimately to the presiding solemnity they subserve.

No more need be said about the weak and bad side of **Daniel Deronda.** By way of laying due stress upon the astonishingly contrasting strength and fineness of the large remainder, the way in which George Eliot transcends in it not only her weakness, but what are commonly thought to be her limitations, I will make an assertion of fact and a critical comparison: Henry James wouldn't have written *The Portrait of a Lady* if he hadn't read *Gwendolen Harleth* (as I shall call the good part of **Daniel Deronda**), and, of the pair of closely comparable works, George Eliot's has not only the distinction of having come first; it is decidedly the greater. The fact, once asserted, can hardly be questioned. Henry James wrote his "Conversation" on **Daniel Deronda** in 1876, and he began *The Portrait of a Lady* 'in the spring of 1879'. No one who considers both the intense appreciative interest he shows in *Gwendolen Harleth* and the extraordinary resemblance of his own theme to George Eliot's (so that *The Portrait of a Lady* might fairly be called a variation) is likely to suggest that this resemblance is accidental and non-significant. (pp. 81-6)

As for the bad part of **Daniel Deronda,** there *is* nothing to do but cut it away—in spite of what James, as Constantius, finds to say for it:

> The universe forcing itself with a slow, inexorable
> pressure into a narrow, complacent, and yet after
> all extremely sensitive mind—that is Gwendolen's

story. And it becomes completely characteristic in that her supreme perception of the fact that the world is whirling past her is in the disappointment not of a base but of an exalted passion. The very chance to embrace what the author is so fond of calling a "larger life" seems refused to her. She is punished for being "narrow", and she is not allowed a chance to expand. Her finding Deronda pre-engaged to go to the East and stir up the race-feeling of the Jews strikes me as wonderfully happy invention. The irony of the situation, for poor Gwendolen, is almost grotesque, and it makes one wonder whether the whole heavy structure of the Jewish question in the story was not built up by the author for the express purpose of giving its proper force to this particular stroke.

If it was (which we certainly can't accept as a complete account of it) built up by the author for this purpose, then it is too disastrously null to have any of the intended force to give. If, having entertained such a purpose, George Eliot had justified it, **Daniel Deronda** would have been a very great novel indeed. As things are, there is, lost under that damning title, an actual great novel to be extricated. And to extricate it for separate publication as *Gwendolen Harleth* seems to me the most likely way of getting recognition for it. *Gwendolen Harleth* would have some rough edges, but it would be a self-sufficient and very substantial whole (it would by modern standards be a decidedly long novel). Deronda would be confined to what was necessary for his rôle of lay-confessor to Gwendolen, and the final cut would come after the death by drowning, leaving us with a vision of Gwendolen as she painfully emerges from her hallucinated worst conviction of guilt and confronts the daylight fact about Deronda's intentions. (p. 122)

George Eliot's greatness is of a different kind from that she has been generally credited with. And by way of concluding on this emphasis I will adduce once again her most intelligently appreciative critic, Henry James:

> She does not strike me as naturally a critic, less still
> as naturally a sceptic; her spontaneous part is to ob-
> serve life and to feel it, to feel it with admirable
> depth. Contemplation, sympathy and faith—
> something like that, I should say, would have been
> her natural scale. If she had fallen upon an age of
> enthusiastic assent to old articles of faith, it seems
> to me possible that she would have had a more per-
> fect, a more consistent and graceful development
> than she actually had.

There is, I think, a complete misconception here. George Eliot's development may not have been 'perfect' or 'graceful', and 'consistent' is not precisely the adjective one would choose for it; yet she went on developing to the end, as few writers do, and achieved the most remarkable expression of her distinctive genius in her last work: her art in *Gwendolen Harleth* is at its maturest. And her profound insight into the moral nature of man is essentially that of one whose critical intelligence has been turned intensively on her faiths. A sceptic by nature or culture—indeed no; but that is not because her intelligence, a very powerful one, doesn't freely illuminate all her interests and convictions. That she should be thought depressing (as, for instance, Leslie Stephen thinks her) always surprises me. She exhibits a traditional moral sensibility expressing itself, not within a frame of 'old articles of faith' (as James obviously intends the phrase), but nevertheless with perfect sureness, in judgments that involve confident positive standards, and yet affect us as simply the report of luminous intelligence. She deals in the weakness and ordinariness of human nature, but doesn't find it contemptible, or show either animus or self-deceiving indulgence towards it; and, distinguished and noble as she is, we have in reading her the feeling that she is in and of the humanity she presents with so clear and disinterested a vision. For us in these days, it seems to me, she is a peculiarly fortifying and wholesome author, and a suggestive one: she might well be pondered by those who tend to prescribe simple recourses—to suppose, say, that what Charlotte Yonge has to offer may be helpfully relevant—in face of the demoralizations and discouragements of an age that isn't one of 'enthusiastic assent to old articles of faith'.

As for her rank among novelists, I take the challenge from a representative purveyor of currency, Oliver Elton: what he says we may confidently assume that thousands of the cultivated think it reasonable to say, and thousands of students in 'Arts' courses are learning to say, either in direct study of him, or in the lecture-room. He says, then, in discussing the 'check to George Eliot's reputation' given by the coming 'into fuller view' of 'two other masters of fiction'—Meredith and Hardy: 'Each of these novelists saw the world of men and women more freely than George Eliot had done; and they brought into relief one of her greatest deficiencies, namely, that while exhaustively describing life, she is apt to miss the spirit of life itself.' I can only say that this, for anyone whose critical education has begun, should be breath-taking in its absurdity, and affirm my conviction that, by the side of George Eliot—and the comparison shouldn't be necessary— Meredith appears as a shallow exhibitionist (his famous 'intelligence' a laboured and vulgar brilliance) and Hardy, decent as he is, as a provincial manufacturer of gauche and heavy fictions that sometimes have corresponding virtues. For a positive indication of her place and quality I think of a Russian; not Turgènev, but a far greater, Tolstoy—who, we all know, is pre-eminent in getting 'the spirit of life itself'. George Eliot, of course, is not as transcendently great as Tolstoy, but she *is* great, and great in the same way. The extraordinary reality of *Anna Karenina* (his supreme masterpiece, I think) comes of an intense moral interest in human nature that provides the light and courage for a profound psychological analysis. This analysis is rendered in art (and *Anna Karenina, pace* Matthew Arnold, is wonderfully closely worked) by means that are like those used by George Eliot in *Gwendolen Harleth*. . . . Of George Eliot it can in turn be said that her best work has a Tolstoyan depth and reality. (pp. 123-25)

> *F. R. Leavis, "George Eliot," in his* The Great Tradition: George Eliot, Henry James, Joseph Conrad, *Chatto & Windus, 1948, pp. 79-125.*

D. R. CARROLL (essay date 1959)

[*Countering Leavis's assessment of* Daniel Deronda, *(see excerpt dated 1945-46), Carroll seeks to demonstrate the intrinsic interrelationships between the two parts of the novel and argues that to divide the work as Leavis suggests would significantly lessen its meaning.*]

In a letter to Mme Eugène Bodichon, written a month after the publication of the last book of *Daniel Deronda,* George Eliot comments upon some complimentary letters she has received concerning her characterisation of Deronda: 'This is better than the laudation of readers who cut the book into scraps and talk of nothing in it but Gwendolen. I meant everything in the book to be related to everything else there' [see letter dated 2 October 1876]. Yet in his pungent revaluation of George Eliot's novels in *The Great Tradition,* Dr. Leavis can say:

> As for the bad part of **Daniel Deronda,** there *is* nothing to do but cut it away. . . . As things are, there is, lost under that damning title, an actual great novel to be extricated. And to extricate it for separate publication as *Gwendolen Harleth* seems to me the most likely way of getting recognition for it. *Gwendolen Harleth* would have some rough edges, but it would be a self-sufficient and very substantial whole. . . . Deronda would be confined to what was necessary for his rôle of lay-confessor to Gwendolen, and the final cut would come after the death by drowning. . . .

No one has seriously challenged this diagnosis; largely one feels because of the power and the gusto with which Dr. Leavis has displayed the 'good half' of the novel. But before submitting to his drastic treatment, we ought to appreciate a little more fully how rough the 'rough edges' and how 'self-sufficient' the 'whole' of this new novel would be. George Eliot's claim for the organic unity of her novel is not as unfounded as it may at first appear. (p. 369)

In **Daniel Deronda** the visions of Gwendolen and Mordecai, the one of fear and the other of hope, crystallise the essential function of each of the separate halves of the novel in the education of the titular hero. A single quotation will indicate the fundamental relationship of these two visions, and their connection with Deronda, the main character in the novel. Speaking of Deronda's desire for a confidant, George Eliot ends chapter thirty-seven with: 'But he had no expectation of meeting the friend he imagined. Deronda's was not one of those quiveringly-poised natures that lend themselves to second sight.' The next chapter begins:

> 'Second-sight' is a flag over disputed ground. But it is matter of knowledge that there are persons whose yearnings, conceptions—nay, travelled conclusions—continually take the form of images which have a fore-shadowing power: the deed they would do starts up before them in complete shape, making a coercive type; the event they hunger for or dread rises into vision with a seed-like growth, feeding itself fast on unnumbered impressions.

The event which Mordecai 'hungers for', and the event which Gwendolen 'dreads' are linked in this generalisation for the first time; whilst the juxtaposition with the comment on Deronda implies the double rôle he is going to play in relation to these visions—that of fulfiller and that of redeemer.

The event Gwendolen dreads 'rises into vision' most disturbingly and effectively in the charade from *The Winter's Tale* where the intrusion of the painting of the drowning man and fleeing woman just before Gwendolen, as Hermione, is to be recalled to life suggests that before she can emerge from her living death of remorse she has to submit to the full horror of her dreaded vision. It is this incident which introduces us to 'that liability of hers to fits of spiritual dread', which results from her thwarted egoism:

> Solitude in any wide scene impressed her with an undefined feeling of immeasurable existence aloof

from her, in the midst of which she was helplessly incapable of asserting herself.

The horrific picture is a prefiguration of the act she will be forced into as a final gesture of assertion and from which only Deronda will be able to 'resurrect' her.

The event Mordecai 'hungers for' is the arrival of his 'executive self' who will come to fulfil his plan for creating an organic centre for the Jews: 'Revive the organic centre: let the unity of Israel which has made the growth and form of its religion to be an outward reality.' In contrast to Gwendolen's visions which are 'like furies preparing the deed that they would straightaway avenge', Mordecai's are used by him for his own creative purposes. For example, when he describes his past life to Deronda: 'They said, "He feeds himself on visions", and I denied not; for visions are the creators and feeders of the world. I see, I measure the world as it is, which the vision will create anew'. And after Deronda has made his prophesied appearance at Blackfriars Bridge, Mordecai is no longer in doubt that his 'executive self' has arrived. It is worth noticing, even at this stage, the reciprocal nature of the relationship between these two themes. By his participation in each world Deronda is prepared for his rôle in the other. It is thanks to his experience in Gwendolen's genteel world and polite society in general that he comes up to Mordecai's requirements of being an 'accomplished Egyptian' as well as a good Jew; whilst it is only by suddenly introducing Gwendolen to the knowledge of his Jewish activities, 'the larger destinies of mankind', that Deronda is able finally to bring her to a realisation of her own insignificance.

The novel becomes an organic whole by the way in which George Eliot traces the effect of these two people, who represent the two halves of the novel, upon Deronda. The presence of both is required for the education of the titular hero. Early in the novel, immediately before his rescue of Mirah, we come upon Deronda practising experimental empathy:

> He was forgetting everything else in a half-speculative, half-involuntary identification of himself with the objects he was looking at, thinking how far it might be possible habitually to shift his centre till his own personality would be no less outside him than the landscape. . . .

The tendency eventually develops into a fault of character which vitiates any practical aims he might have; he comes to project himself too easily and readily into too many points of views:

> His imagination had so wrought itself to the habit of seeing things as they probably appeared to others, that a strong partisanship, unless it were against an immediate oppression, had become an insincerity for him.

Only his double relationship with Gwendolen and Mordecai can rescue him from this disease of sympathy.

For most of the novel the two claims imposed upon him by the two visions seem completely opposed:

> There was a foreshadowing of some painful collision: on the one side the grasp of Mordecai's dying hand on him, with all the ideals and prospects it aroused; on the other this fair creature in silk and gems, with her hidden wound and her self-dread,

making a trustful effort to lean and find herself sustained.

There is, of course, a connection between Deronda's two rôles: Mordecai requires him to be a national messiah, whilst Gwendolen wants him as her personal saviour. But the 'painful collision' is only resolved at the end of the novel. George Eliot uses one set of symbols to enforce this double pressure upon Deronda, and it is only by insisting upon the unity of the novel that we can appreciate the ambivalent value of these symbols. A simple example will illustrate the point. At the house-party at the Abbey, 'a picturesque architectural outgrowth from an abbey, which had still remnants of the old monastic trunk', we witness Gwendolen suffering an agony of remorse after her unsuccessful marriage gamble and requiring aid of Deronda. During singing in the drawing-room, Deronda 'observed that Gwendolen had left her seat, and had come to this end of the room, as if to listen more fully, but was now standing with her back to everyone, apparently contemplating a fine cowled head carved in ivory which hung over a small table'. He approaches the table, and 'they looked at each other—she seeming to take the deep rest of confession, he with an answering depth of sympathy that neutralised other feelings'. Then standing beneath the ivory head, they converse and Gwendolen makes an oblique attempt at confession. This head when linked with the 'monastic trunk' of the Abbey can clearly be seen as an objectification of Gwendolen's desire to escape from her vision of dread by confessing to Deronda, by turning him in fact into her priest. And at the end of this same chapter the process has developed so far in her mind that George Eliot can define explicitly Gwendolen's dependence: 'without the aid of sacred ceremony or costume, her feelings had turned this man, only a few years older than herself, into a priest'. And with the final sentence of the chapter George Eliot underlines the function of her symbol and also gives a suggestion of the reciprocal nature of this relationship: 'And perhaps in that ideal consecration of Gwendolen's, some education was being prepared for Deronda'. The head is a proleptic symbol of Gwendolen's later, more clearly defined need.

For Deronda, however, the carved head has quite a different significance. In the previous chapter he had first met Mordecai, who is described as 'A man in threadbare clothing, whose age was difficult to guess—from the dead yellowish flatness of the flesh, something like an old ivory carving. . . .' Reminding Deronda of Mordecai, the ivory head at the Abbey is another 'foreshadowing of some painful collision' between the claims of the Jews and the growing dependence upon him of Gwendolen.

In the rest of this same chapter we can see the ambivalent symbolism being used extensively. In the tour of the Abbey we have a prefiguring of Gwendolen's process of regeneration in miniature—in the movement from the purgatorial kitchen with its 'huge glowing fire' ('I wondered how long you meant to stay in that damned place,' comments Grandcourt) to the forestaste of her *paradiso* in the derelict chapel where Deronda, 'who oddly enough had taken off his hat', is cast in the rôle of absolving priest. But these scenes have a different meaning when viewed from the angle of Deronda's relationship with Mordecai. Then the chapel and its occupants becomes a symbol of the modern Jews, ignorant of their inheritance:

> Each finely-arched chapel was turned into a stall, where in the dusty glazing of the windows there

still gleamed patches of crimson, orange, blue, and palest violet; for the rest, the choir had been gutted, the floor levelled, paved, and drained according to the most approved fashion, and a line of loose-boxes erected in the middle: a soft light fell from the upper windows on the sleek brown or gray flanks and haunches; on mild equine faces . . . on the hay hanging from racks where the saints once looked down from the altar-pieces, and on the pale golden straw scattered or in heaps; on a little white-and-liver-coloured spaniel making his bed on the back of an elderly hackney, and on four ancient angels, still showing signs of devotion like mutilated martyrs. . . .

This 'solidity of specification' becomes significant when it is compared with the imagery of the Hebrew verses Mordecai attempts to teach young Jacob Cohen:

> Solitude is on the sides of Mount Nebo,
> In its heart a tomb:
> There the buried ark and golden cherubim
> Make hidden light:
> There the solemn faces gaze unchanged,
> The wings are spread unbroken:
> Shut beneath in silent awful speech
> The law lies graven.
> Solitude and darkness are my covering,
> And my heart a tomb;
> Smite and shatter it, O Gabriel!
> Shatter it as the clay of the founder
> Around the golden image.

The chapel symbolises the decadent state of the Jewish nation deprived of its 'organic centre', and this interpretation casts Deronda in the rôle of Gabriel. Owing to a certain detailed matter-of-factness in George Eliot's use of her symbols, one is even tempted to see the 'liver-coloured spaniel' as the ignored prophet Mordecai, 'a frail incorporation of the national consciousness, breathing with difficult breath—nested in the self-gratulating ignorant prosperity of the Cohens . . .', the Cohens who Mordecai describes as having 'the heart of the Israelite within them, though they are as the horse and the mule without understanding beyond the narrow path they trod'. Thus the ambivalent symbolism again defines the two rôles Deronda is being forced into by the demands of the two visions which form the nodal points of the separate halves of the novel. The ambivalence reflects the conflict in Deronda's mind where the question is, which interpretation of the symbolism will ultimately prevail?

The doubt remains up to the very climax of the novel which is reached in Deronda's sojourn in Genoa, where he goes to meet his mother. Within the space of two days both visions are fulfilled—Deronda learns of his ancestry and realises he is well fitted to act as Mordecai's 'executive self', and on the next day Gwendolen's vision of dread is enacted in Grandcourt's death by drowning and Deronda comes upon her in her *inferno* looking upon him for redemption: 'pale as one of the sheeted dead, shivering, with her hair streaming, a wild amazed consciousness in her eyes, as if she had waked up in a world where some judgment was impending, and the beings she saw around her were coming to seize her'. Both visions are fulfilled, but as yet Deronda is committed completely to neither of the two rôles the visions are trying to force him into. His mother fulfils a dual function at this point. She tells him of his ancestry, fortifying him in his desire to help the Jews by the narration of her life and by handing on to him his grandfather's writings. Her second function is very simi-

lar to Mrs. Transome's at the climax of *Felix Holt.* She appears as a warning to Deronda of what Gwendolen might easily become, thus emphasising the need for his assistance. Both his mother and Gwendolen have attempted to deprive someone of their rightful inheritance, and unless Gwendolen is rescued from her *inferno* of remorse she will come to resemble his mother who 'looked like a dreamed visitant from some region of departed mortals'.

At this penultimate stage of the novel, Deronda is in full sympathy with both his visionaries, but wholly committed to neither. Their claims upon him appear contradictory. In his first meeting with Gwendolen after Grandcourt's death, he rejects the rôle she is trying to thrust upon him: 'He was not a priest. He dreaded the weight of this woman's soul flung upon his own with imploring dependence'. And although he has told his mother, 'I consider it my duty—it is the impulse of my feeling—to identify myself, as far as possible, with my hereditary people . . .', he has not yet accepted a definite line of action with regard to his public rôle. The conflict is resolved and the design of the novel completed at the climax of his visit to Gwendolen when his full realisation of her despair forces him into his acceptance of both rôles:

> . . . it seemed that the lot of this young creature, whose swift travel from her bright rash girlhood into this agony of remorse he had had to behold in helplessness, pierced him the deeper because it came close upon another [his mother's] sad revelation of spiritual conflict: he was in one of those moments when the very anguish of passionate pity makes us ready to choose that he will know pleasure no more, and live only for the stricken and afflicted.

Through his contact with the particular 'lot of this young creature' he has come to embrace instinctively the rôle of messiah to the Jews. So that, when he is accosted by Kalonymos he is able to state with conviction: 'I hold that my first duty is to my own people, and if there is anything to be done towards restoring or perfecting their common life, I shall make that my vocation'. His intense emotional involvement with Gwendolen has acted as the catalyst which has precipitated him into his public rôle. He is cured of his disease of sympathy: ' . . . his judgment no longer wandering in the mazes of impartial sympathy, but choosing with that noble partiality which is man's best strength, the close fellowship that makes sympathy practical'.

In addition, the completion of the main design of the novel has . . . a reciprocal effect upon one of the themes in that design. Paradoxically, Deronda's acceptance of his public rôle is the factor which finally brings Gwendolen to a real self-knowledge. It is the implosion of Deronda's 'wide-stretching purposes in which she felt herself reduced to a mere speck' into her narrow egoistic existence which finally brings her salvation. This sudden expansion of Gwendolen's horizon upon her realisation of the extent of the other half of Deronda's life—of the other half of the novel—is very powerful, so powerful indeed that Henry James thought the Jewish half of the novel justified if only for this one effect:

> Her finding Deronda pre-engaged to go to the East and stir up the race-feeling of the Jews strikes me as a wonderfully happy invention. The irony of the situation, for poor Gwendolen, is almost grotesque, and it makes one wonder whether the whole heavy structure of the Jewish question in the story was not built up by the author for the express purpose

of giving its proper force to this particular stroke [see essay dated 1876].

But this is to forget the reciprocal effect of the Gwendolen half of the novel upon Deronda's messiahship, to forget this it is her despair which thrusts him into the acceptance of his wider task.

This is clearly not the factitious unity implied by Dr. Leavis's 'few rough edges'. It is not a unity obtained by placing the titular hero at an arbitrary point of junction between the two halves of the novel. The organic unity of the novel springs from Deronda's psychological condition: his disease of sympathy is the reason why he finds himself in relationship with Gwendolen and Mordecai, and the reciprocal movement consists in their demands curing him of his disease. Each half of the novel must be viewed against the background of the other half or else it will be lacking in a significant dimension, and only by this means will the final definition of meaning, which George Eliot tentatively approaches at the end of the novel, be intelligible.

This definition is couched in the political and religious terms of the Jewish nation. It is first approached in the discussion at the philosophical working-men's club where we have expressed the two antithetical hopes for the future of the Jews. Gideon, 'a rational Jew', says: 'But I am for getting rid of all our superstitions and exclusiveness. There's no reason now why we shouldn't melt gradually into the populations we live among.' . . . Mordecai replies with the contrary view: 'Revive the organic centre: let the unity of Israel which has made the growth and form of its religion be an outward reality'. At the end of the novel, when Deronda is questioned by Kalonymos as to his future actions, he reconciles these two extreme views: 'I shall call myself a Jew . . .' But I will not say that I shall profess to believe exactly as my fathers have believed. Our fathers themselves changed the horizon of their belief and learned of other races. But I think I can maintain my grandfather's notion of separateness, with communication'. And later in the novel, in one of his less fanatical moments, Mordecai expresses the same idea in transcendental terms:

> 'the *Shemah,* wherein we briefly confess the divine Unity, is the chief devotional exercise of the Hebrew; and this made our religion the fundamental religion for the whole world; for the divine Unity embraced as its consequence the ultimate unity of mankind. See, then—the nation which has been scoffed at for its separateness, has given a binding theory to the human race. Now, in complete unity a part possesses the whole as the whole possesses every part: and in this way human life is tending toward the image of the Supreme Unity . . .'.

When this idea of the balance of 'separateness with communication' is transcribed into terms of personal relationships, we can see its relevance to Gwendolen's attitude to Deronda. Just before Gwendolen's final awakening to self-knowledge, we find her over-emphasising her own claims upon Deronda, exaggerating the element of 'communication' in their relationship:

> . . . she did not imagine him otherwise than always within her reach, her supreme need of him blinding her to the separateness of his life, the whole scene of which she filled with his relation to her. . . .

This 'passionate egoism of imagination' is very similar to Dorothea Brooke's attitude to Casaubon, although she awakens more quickly to the separateness of the individual:

> We are all of us born in moral stupidity, taking the world as an udder to feed our supreme selves; Dorothea had early begun to emerge from that stupidity, but yet it had been easier to her to imagine how she would devote herself to Mr. Casaubon, and become wise and strong in his strength and wisdom, than to conceive with that distinctness which is no longer reflection but feeling—an idea wrought back to the directness of sense, like the solidity of objects—that he had an equivalent centre of self, whence the lights and shadows must always fall with a certain difference.

The discussions on the Jewish state and its religion are a definition on a national level of the meaning of the personal relations in the other half of the novel: only when she has been shaken out of her inability to recognise another person's 'equivalent centre of self' will Gwendolen achieve moral faith and be in a position to communicate helpfully with others. As Lionel Trilling says, commenting on Freud's ability to project himself systematically into the centres of self of his patients:

> And certainly the willing suspension of disbelief constitutes moral faith—the essence of the moral life would seem to consist in doing that most difficult thing in the world, making a willing suspension of disbelief in the selfhood of someone else (*Freud and the Crisis of our Culture*).

But, according to George Eliot, a balance must be held between this quality of self-projection, of full 'communication', and the quality of 'separateness'. If the 'communication' becomes over-emphasised, the resultant condition is Deronda's disease of sympathy, which it has been the task of the novel to cure.

Any amputation of the Jewish half of the novel would obviously necessitate a drastic curtailment of significance for *Gwendolen Harleth,* and deprive the reader of what is perhaps George Eliot's most explicit attempt at a definition of the meaning of her novels. It is definition by means of the thematic structure of the whole novel; and if a theme were to be removed the definition would be invalidated, for, using Mordecai's terms, we can say that 'in complete unity a part possesses the whole as the whole possesses every part', and apply them without exaggeration to the unity of *Daniel Deronda.* (pp. 370-80)

> *D. R. Carroll, "The Unity of 'Daniel Deronda'," in Essays in Criticism, Vol. IX, No. 4, October, 1959, pp. 369-80.*

JEROME THALE (essay date 1959)

[*In this excerpt from his full-length study of Eliot's novels, Thale discusses her increasingly dark view of humanity's potential for evil, focusing on the themes of will, power, and suffering in the portion of* Daniel Deronda *dealing with Gwendolen Harleth.*]

Daniel Deronda fails to cohere, to add up to something—and it might have been something very great—because, even though one half is splendidly done, the other is wretched. The Deronda story provides almost a catalogue of the vices of the nineteenth-century novel. Though the execution is in some ways not bad and in spots very good, the character of Deronda is nearly a flat failure, for his character rests on a fatal assumption. Deronda is the well-bred (and very nice) English gentleman as Alyosha. George Eliot assumes that the simplicity and insight of the one are compatible with the ordinary acquired virtues of the other, and she does not see that Deronda's debility of will can be a defect. The minor characters in the Deronda plot are forced, vaporous, or sweetly sentimental. Finally, even if the character of Daniel were satisfactory, nothing could make us take Mordecai or the novel's version of Zionism. George Eliot had to give Daniel a goal, but the goal she selected is not rendered credible; her knowledge of Zionism was as external as it was uncritical. (pp. 122-23)

Though the two plots are of unequal value, the use of the double plot points to a continuity with George Eliot's previous novels. *Deronda* continues the line of large and complex works, brought to its fullest development in *Middlemarch.* The book also works with some of the things that George Eliot had been interested in earlier—the heroine who learns through a disastrous marriage (Janet Dempster of *Scenes of Clerical Life,* Romola, Dorothea); and the nice young man who stands through the book as a kind of disengaged confessor and is or ought to be a suitor (Mr. Tryan of the *Scenes,* Philip Wakem, Felix Holt, and Ladislaw). In this respect *Deronda* is a very close reworking of the problems of *Felix Holt,* with the brute more brutal and the nice young man nicer; and the superiority of Gwendolen to Esther Lyon shows an immense development in art. Gwendolen's moral development also recalls Hetty's in *Adam Bede,* where the process is equally naturalistic and every bit as terrifying. Although the tone of *Daniel Deronda* is so different from the earlier works that we may not recognize the similarities, it remains true that almost every aspect, good and bad, of George Eliot's art seems to culminate in *Daniel Deronda.*

Before we go on to discuss the new element in *Daniel Deronda,* we must make some reservation about Gwendolen, whom Dr. Leavis sees as George Eliot's highest achievement [see excerpt dated 1945-46]. Though in a way Gwendolen's is the justest and most accurate portrayal in George Eliot's work, there is something wanting in her. She is less interesting and, one feels, less of an imaginative triumph than Dorothea, or than Isabel Archer, who Dr. Leavis says is both like and inferior to Gwendolen. For George Eliot—and very nearly for English fiction—Gwendolen Harleth is a new type, the bitch taken seriously. And in the nineteenth century even more than in our own time it was extremely difficult for the artist to formulate and render a satisfactory set of attitudes toward such a character. In *Middlemarch* George Eliot was learning how to triumph over her affection for her characters; she succeeded most fully in Lydgate, for with Dorothea there is a certain amount of sympathy that the art has not digested. She was learning also in *Middlemarch* how to triumph over aversion, and she did so in the portraits of Rosamond and Bulstrode. Certainly the presentation of Gwendolen has nothing of the harsh and actinic quality of Hetty's in *Adam Bede.* But a fully successful portrait demands that the author do more than see his character neutrally (rare as that is); he must feel some love, at least some compassion, for his character, and we cannot help thinking that George Eliot shows more justice than charity towards Gwendolen.

This limitation in the characterization of Gwendolen needs simply to be noted. I do not think that Gwendolen is quite the highest point in George Eliot's fiction, but there can be no doubt that she is a high point, not only in George Eliot's art but in English fiction. Whatever Gwendolen's place, our admiration of the rightness of her treatment and our dismay at the feebleness of the Deronda plot may keep us from noticing that with *Daniel Deronda* a radically new tone comes into George Eliot's fiction: a concern with the sinister and malign. It is not just a darkening of the world—which had been somber enough even in *Adam Bede*—but a new and direct confrontation of certain kinds of evil, of perversity, hitherto unacknowledged.

Perhaps this kind of awareness of evil seems so commonplace to us today that we forget that in the nineteenth century it cost a terrible moral effort to attain such a vision, and, given the going conventions of the novel and the status of public morality, raised the most serious artistic problems. The writer's breakthrough often came only late in his career, when he had worked through his own deepest problems and developed the artistic resources for dealing with them. But for these reasons his vision of evil has greater authenticity, gives a greater sense of being hard won, than that of our own time when the omnipresence of evil is a cliché and receives widespread and facile treatment. What the nineteenth-century writer had to discover we can see by comparing the treatment of evil in *David Copperfield* and *Our Mutual Friend,* in *The Warden* and *The Way We Live Now.* We can measure the same distance in George Eliot's own works. In *Silas Marner,* evil is muted by a fairy story; in *Romola* it is external and melodramatic. In *Middlemarch* we begin to feel it as personal and immediate. But, well realized and honest as it is, the evil in *Middlemarch* is that of ordinary life, seen sensitively but in more or less conventional terms.

If it were not for the pun we might speak of *Daniel Deronda* as George Eliot's terrible novel. Ignoring (there is nothing else we can do with it) the Deronda half of the novel, and thinking only of the story of Gwendolen Harleth, we are struck by the darkness of the moral vision as much as by the assurance and maturity of the art. Unpleasant characters have become central in *Daniel Deronda;* Gwendolen, Grandcourt, Lush can, in one sense of the word, be described only as perverse. And their evil has the added horror of insidiousness, for it is perfectly civilized, in no way expressed through direct action. Tito Melema in *Romola* was simply a Renaissance villain, mechanically conceived. Grandcourt is not only a more credible and more oppressive presence; he cannot be described in the ordinary categories of vice, and he is beyond the bounds of sympathy, perhaps even of hate. Though Gwendolen does not go quite beyond the range of sympathy—it would be a sadistic moralist who could be neutral before so painful an account—she is dispassionately presented as morally sinister.

The moral horizon, too, is very different from that of George Eliot's earlier novels. It hardly needs to be said that the vision in both cases is wholly secular, for even Daniel's mission with the Jews is a matter of piety, feeling for race, and not of theology. And I think that the disparity in tone between the Deronda and Gwendolen stories can be related to the perplexities that faced naturalism in George Eliot's time. For secular ethic, drifting out of the orbit of Christian tradition, tended in the mid-nineteenth century towards extreme optimism, that of Comte, for example, and later on towards extreme pessimism, as in Hardy, or towards a terrifying secular confrontation of the fact of original sin, as in Céline. Daniel, the Meyricks, Mordecai, come from the flabby optimistic idealism which also produced *Romola;* Gwendolen and Grand-court represent the other side of the process.

The most striking manifestation of the new development in *Daniel Deronda* is the figure of Henleigh Mallinger Grand-court. The imagery used to describe him is insistent. He is a "lizard," an "alligator," a "boa constrictor" (how apt to de-scribe the slow and powerful movement of his cruelty as it crushes Gwendolen). His perversity—and perhaps it is neces-sary to say that it is a moral perversity, a perversity of the will rather than perversity in the Krafft-Ebing sense—is large, in-tense, and disturbing. (pp. 123-27)

There is a kind of atmosphere of cruelty—and even some-thing beyond simple cruelty—about Grandcourt, and we see it very specially in his relationship to Gwendolen. But al-though Grandcourt as husband is a large presence in the novel, sexuality is with him one aspect of a more general im-pulse to assert and dominate, as we can see in his courtship. When Grandcourt makes his offer, Gwendolen is silent. "The evident hesitation of this destitute girl to take his splendid offer stung him into a keenness of interest such as he had not known for years. None the less because he attributed her hesi-tation entirely to her knowledge about Mrs Glasher." Grand-court's reaction to Gwendolen's acceptance of him is de-scribed in a passage which is surely remarkable.

> She had been brought to accept him in spite of ev-erything—brought to kneel down like a horse under training for the arena though she might have an objection to it all the while. On the whole, Grandcourt got more pleasure out of this notion than he could have done out of winning a girl of whom he was sure that she had a strong inclination for him personally. . . . In any case she would have to submit; and he enjoyed thinking of her as his future wife, whose pride and spirit were suited to command every one but himself. . . . He meant to be master of a woman who would have liked to master him, and who perhaps would have been ca-pable of mastering another man.

In everything Grandcourt seeks power. Not power as the or-dinary ambitious man conceives it, but power conceived ab-stractly and free of the coarseness of personal aims. That is, power considered in relation to his will rather than to the ob-jects or persons involved. For the sheer sake of asserting his will, and even when it is not to his interest, he enjoys doing the opposite of what people expect him to do. He will not take notice of what interests everyone else, finding that " 'It's a bore.' " And he has special pleasure in not speaking, consid-ering most persons and subjects beneath his notice; even his courtesy is of that odious kind whose chief function is to indi-cate contempt.

Gwendolen, though in a less striking way, shows the same new and sinister quality. The imagery of the Gwendolen story suggests in a subtle and muted fashion the dark side of George Eliot's vision. Our first sight of Gwendolen is at the gaming table of a continental spa. She is described as a "prob-lematic sylph" and a "Nereid." And there is a rich cluster of similar images in the comments of the onlookers: " 'She has got herself up as a sort of serpent now, all green and silver, and winds her neck about a little more than usual. . . . A man might risk hanging for her—I mean, a fool might,' " he continues playfully. " 'Woman was tempted by a serpent: why not man?' " " 'It is a sort of Lamia beauty she has.' "

The imagery here announces Gwendolen with the directness characteristic of the art of *Daniel Deronda.* Lamia, the ser-pent, and the other metaphors suggest—what is confirmed later—Gwendolen as attractive, feminine, and at the same time man-devouring and, in a way, sexually morbid. "With all her imaginative delight in being adored, there was a cer-tain fierceness of maidenhood in her." Rex Gascoigne, her first suitor, thinks of her as "instinct with all feeling, and not only readier to respond to a worshipful love, but able to love better than other girls." But as he soon finds out, the sylph becomes something else when she is made love to. She is "pas-sionately averse" and objects "with a sort of physical repul-sion, to being directly made love to." She dislikes being touched and will have no one near her but her mother. And we see the same thing in her relation to Grandcourt; she tol-erates him as a lover because she does not fear that he is going to kiss her.

When she discovers that Grandcourt has kept a mistress for nine years, her revulsion is intensified. " 'I don't care if I never marry any one. There is nothing worth caring for. I be-lieve all men are bad, and I hate them.' " And she suddenly accepts her cousins' offer of a trip to Germany. Her reaction is not a conventional disillusionment about the character of her suitor; rather it springs from her "fierce maidenhood," from the idea of Grandcourt as sexually menacing, something more than the well-bred lover who gives only restrained com-pliments and silence.

For Gwendolen, as for Grandcourt, there is a parallelism be-tween sexuality and will; or, to put it more exactly, sex is with both of them a metonymy for will. Gwendolen's "fierce maid-enhood" comes from her feeling that lovemaking is not so much an overture to the person as a kind of aggression against the will, which offers something that the will cannot handle. She seeks a kind of virginity of the will, in which the will is as inviolable as the body. Her fear of love is the most striking manifestation of such a feeling about the will (yet, in her portionless situation, Gwendolen must more than most come to terms with love and marriage). But her fear of death (she becomes faint when she sees a picture of a corpse), her fear of being alone, and of course her powerful desire for inde-pendence are also a recoil from things which the will cannot handle, which offer a challenge to its sufficiency. Though Gwendolen does not see the connection between fear of sexu-ality and her general desire for dominance, the two are close-ly related, and we feel at last that will is at the bottom of Gwendolen's difficulties.

Gwendolen's perversity of will is less extreme than Grand-court's, but it is essentially the same in its movement and structure. Indeed Grandcourt's conquest of Gwendolen is made more poignant because the two are so similar. Gwen-dolen anticipates the delicious pleasure of refusing Grand-court, and, even to the last, thinks that she will do so. Her triumph is to be heightened by the fact that, as the world and Grandcourt see it, the match is an excellent one and that she does have every reason to accept. And more generally, both her nature and her position lead her to assert her will through a kind of proud independence. Hence her humiliation when Deronda returns the necklace, hence her abhorrence of the idea of being a governess.

Her will is so intense that obstacles, in the beginning at least, only serve to strengthen it. When Klesmer tells her that she cannot succeed as an actress, she redoubles her effort of will: " 'It is useless to cry and waste our strength over what can't be altered. You will live at Sawyer's Cottage, and I am going to the bishop's daughters. . . . We must not give way. I dread giving way.' " Her final acceptance of Grandcourt shows the same kind of resistance before opposition; first she hopes to dominate and then resolves that no one shall know her humiliation, that she will not give way to disappointment or resentment.

The book opens with the image of Gwendolen at the gaming table, and it was from such a scene that the germ of the novel came to George Eliot. The scene prophesies Gwendolen's course—the transactions with Grandcourt where she at first wins, then loses, and then resolves to lose strikingly. It also describes the quality of will which is to bring these things about. Gambling points to the intense and self-destructive powers of pure will asserting itself without reference to circumstance, and Gwendolen's response to gambling is emblematic of her attitudes throughout the novel. When she starts to lose at roulette, her companion urges her to leave.

> For reply Gwendolen put ten louis on the same spot: she was in that mood of defiance in which the mind loses sight of any end beyond the satisfaction of enraged resistance; and with the puerile stupidity of a dominant impulse includes luck among its objects of defiance. Since she was not winning strikingly, the next best thing was to lose strikingly.

From another point of view Gwendolen's progress is concerned not with the will but with the world outside her; it is an initiation into evil. But the very force and quality of her will work to keep her ignorant, innocent. For her will constructs an account of reality in which obstacles to the will do not seriously exist. In fact the most serious obstacle to the will—or to Gwendolen's will—is the evil actions of others. Her scheme of reality—the game that she plays—demands that others do not do evil, that they act according to the rules, if the opportunism which is her assertion of her will is to succeed. Evil is something that pure will cannot deal with. Gwendolen discovers that evil exists in the real world (as it does not in her will) and that she is compelled to act in the face of it. And since the real world does not give way, is harder and tougher than the will, Gwendolen is gradually coerced to an acknowledgment of the insufficiency of the will.

At the beginning of the novel, Gwendolen is knowledgeable enough; she does not have, or manages not to display, the inexperience of the girl of twenty. If she exaggerates her own knowledge and competence, she is quick enough to keep from being caught. But her notions of evil in the world and others are imperfect—at once sophisticated and girlish. Least of all can she see evil in herself, or even see herself in the wrong. As she goes through much of the world, she finds that it scarcely squares with a clever and high-spirited young girl's idea of it. But her obduracy and resilience are so great that her real knowledge of evil comes only through her closest personal relationships. Though Gwendolen is shrewd about people, her egoism blinds and cramps her imagination; thus she can manipulate others but she cannot understand their natures or predict what they will do. Mrs. Glasher opens some new possibilities to Gwendolen. But her principal discovery comes through Grandcourt. For his perversity—though the novel does not force the point upon us—is an extension and exaggeration of her own tendencies. She has thrust upon her a series of experiences which show her the terrible cruelty beneath Grandcourt's correctness and at last

suggest to her—what she could scarcely have guessed—the possibility of her own corruption.

Sex is a kind of focus for Gwendolen's discovery of evil. The fierce maiden, the Diana, finds not an Endymion but Grandcourt. And, as we have seen, sex is for Gwendolen ugly and fearful in itself, and it is as much a violation of the purity of the will as of the body. At one point Gwendolen sees before her two choices: a career in the theater or marriage with Grandcourt; both options are sexually fearful, as Klesmer and Mrs. Glasher make clear to Gwendolen. But one of the two she must choose. (Mirah is in a similar predicament, but her situation is as conventional and melodramatic as Gwendolen's is real and frightening.)

Gwendolen's confrontation with sexuality is simultaneous with and contributes to a more central process, her discovery of the inadequacy of pure assertion of the will. The movement of the novel is a contrapuntal one. It proceeds on the one hand through a series of assertions of Gwendolen's will: gambling, the coquettish acquaintance with Grandcourt, the flight to the continent, the rejection of the position as governess, the proud acceptance of Grandcourt, and finally the determination to make the best of the marriage and not to resist openly. On the other hand it moves as a series of checks to her will: Daniel's disapprobation of her gambling and her discovery that she cannot ignore his disapproval; the humiliating return of the necklace; the loss of the family fortune. These reverses, except for the first, are more or less external

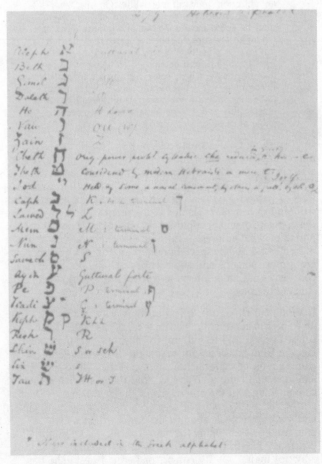

A page from Eliot's notebook on which she recorded the Hebrew alphabet.

and can be dealt with by a stiffening of the will, but they are followed by a series of catastrophes which the will cannot successfully counter. Gwendolen is shocked by Klesmer's discouraging verdict about her talent and by his account of the hard work and time involved in a theatrical career. Then there is Mrs. Glasher's revelation—something Gwendolen's will cannot deal with adequately because she has never recognized such situations as possible in her experience. And the last check—the one that renders Gwendolen's will incapable of asserting itself—is the marriage to Grandcourt. Gwendolen's disillusion and frustration are the greater because she has not expected much and thinks she has no illusions, anticipating that if she cannot dominate Grandcourt, she will at least have greater freedom and will put up with him in a dignified way. But what Gwendolen gets is beyond her previous power of imagining. Even acceptance is impossible under Grandcourt's pressure to master, and Gwendolen's will is completely checkmated.

It is checkmated because more and more it has become involved in concrete circumstances. In a void the will constructs or reconstructs the outer world and allows neither evil nor obstacles. But in the real world both exist, choice is limited, exclusive. At the beginning, with no ties and enough money, Gwendolen can have the illusion of the sufficiency of the will, but as she moves from pure assertion of will to action in the face of people and events, the will is stopped and turns back upon itself in paralysis and self-accusation.

Gwendolen's will resists the checks at first, but as the reverses become so large that they cannot be resisted they begin to render her more receptive to the idea of the limitation of will and the intractability of circumstances. Like Raskolnikov, she undergoes a process the issue of which is remorse and acknowledgment of guilt. But the process is not so much a coercion to remorse as it is a development of the moral sense to a point where it can admit good and evil, guilt and innocence; only when the dry ground of the ego has been broken is moral judgment possible. As James says, "Her conscience doesn't make the tragedy; that is an old story and, I think, a secondary form of suffering. It is the tragedy that makes her conscience, which then reacts upon it; and I can think of nothing more powerful than the way in which the growth of her conscience is traced, nothing more touching than the picture of its helpless maturity" [see essay dated 1876].

Earlier in her career George Eliot had asserted that "the highest 'calling and election' is to *do without opium* and live through all our pain with conscious, clear-eyed endurance," and there is no reason to think that she abandoned the idea. But only in *Deronda* has the fullness of her disenchantment worked itself out in the fullness of her art. Gwendolen's conversion shows us how much deeper and darker a meaning the sentence has in *Daniel Deronda.*

By George Eliot's time the notion that human beings act for self-interested motives and that they are to be understood in terms of naturally explicable causes had been thoroughly domesticated. But a person more sensitive and imaginative than the nineteenth-century economists or political theorists may find in that idea something terrible and perverse. He may discover that the world contains not only the open and somewhat commonplace selfishness of Sir Hugo Mallinger, but the subtle, involuted, and purely destructive egotism of Henleigh Mallinger Grandcourt. He may see not only moral natures, but moral processes, differently and more starkly.

Gwendolen's suffering does not ennoble, it makes the sufferer more miserable, increases self-hatred, and like a fever must get worse before it can get better. And with what a terrible and uncompromising naturalism the process is imagined. From the moment when Deronda looks at her, Gwendolen feels self-reproach, and this is the agent of her regeneration. Deronda is not, as has often been said, her confessor; he is a lay analyst, and a poor one; he conducts her through the dark night of the superego, urging her to self-reproach, to fear of self and of consequences. He feels her regeneration is nearly complete when she accuses herself of murdering Grandcourt, seeing in this a "sacred aversion to her worst self." (pp. 127-36)

Jerome Thale, in his The Novels of George Eliot, *Columbia University Press, 1959, 175 p.*

CAROLE ROBINSON   (essay date 1964)

[*Robinson closely examines the character of Daniel Deronda, finding that Eliot's intent to contrast Deronda's emotive nature and altruistic moral superiority with Gwendolen Harleth's shallow egocentricity is refuted by the aesthetics of the novel: ultimately Gwendolen emerges as the more interesting and appealing character.*]

THEODORA. And as for Deronda himself I freely confess that I am consumed with a hopeless passion for him. He is the most irresistible man in the literature of fiction.

PULCHERIA. He is not a man at all. ("*Daniel Deronda:* A Conversation." By Henry James [see essay dated 1876].)

The political burden of George Eliot's last novel demanded a man in the title role. It had taken a real-life Victorian lady, Florence Nightingale, almost a decade of frustration before she was released to fulfill her eastward mission: George Eliot could not hamper her Zionist missionary in the same way. Otherwise Deronda should have been a woman, as, indeed, are all his counterparts in George Eliot's earlier works. As a child Daniel shows "the same blending of child's ignorance with surprising knowledge which is oftener seen in bright girls": i.e., Maggie Tulliver. He has Maggie's "ardent clinging nature": he is "moved by an affectionateness such as we are apt to call feminine." When he meets his mother Daniel feels himself "changing color like a girl"; "all the woman lacking in her was present in him." Later Daniel pities his mother with "perhaps more than a woman's acuteness of compassion."

This initial fallacy, the faulty construction of a masculine Deronda, is, in a characterization which is finally hopelessly fallacious, scarcely insignificant. George Eliot laboured to render Daniel masculine as she laboured to render him living; the effort resulted in a peculiarly rigid portrait. Deronda's speech, for example, has a chilly circumspection which was intended to convey a restraint both manly and refined. Its effect, however, is to make him sound like his supposed opposite, Henleigh Mallinger Grandcourt. There is little to choose in tone between Grandcourt's proposal to Gwendolen, and Daniel's to Mordecai:

"You will tell me now, I hope, that Mrs. Davilow's loss of fortune will not trouble you further. You will trust me to prevent it from weighing upon her. You will give me the claim to provide against that."

"It seems to me right now—is it not?—that you should live with your sister; and I have prepared a home to take you to in the neighborhood of her friends, that she may join you there. Pray grant me this wish."

The similarity is paradoxical; it obliterates the contrast George Eliot intended between Grandcourt and Deronda, the "Moroni" *versus* the "Titian," the cold man *versus* the apostle of sympathy.

The uncertainty regarding Deronda's masculinity is reflected in the abortive romance with Gwendolen. George Eliot takes pains to explain why Daniel does not fall in love, but her analysis, since it concerns the originally fallacious construct of the masculine Deronda, seems just slightly askew. Daniel is, as Pulcheria complains, "described and analyzed to death" precisely because to a conscientious mind like George Eliot's a faulty concept required perpetual explanation and justification. We may consider two examples of the sort of analysis George Eliot attempted:

With the same innate balance he was fervidly democratic in his feeling for the multitude, and yet, through his affections and imagination, intensely conservative; voracious of speculations on government and religion, yet loath to part with long-sanctioned forms which, for him, were quick with memories and sentiments that no argument could lay dead.

Like many Victorian intellectuals then, Daniel is disposed to disprove that plausible observation, that "every boy and every girl that's born into this world alive, is either a little liberal, or else a little conservative": he inclines to embrace both philosophies, and to reconcile the opposing claims of progress and permanence. He is not a character: he is the embodiment of a compromise. But the nuance which renders the passage truly dubious is George Eliot's effort to attribute these carefully neutral formulations to Daniel as *emotions* rather than ideas. The adverbs give away the show: Daniel is at once "fervidly" democratic and "intensely" conservative; and there is an equally revealing cluster of anxious references to Daniel's emotional involvement: "affections and imagination," "feeling," "voracious," "quick with memories and sentiments." In attempting to invest an intellectual stance with the force of emotion, George Eliot perhaps reflects a Victorian preoccupation with the loss of vivid emotional conviction. Basil Willey has noted [in his "George Eliot," an essay printed in Richard Stang's *Discussions of George Eliot* (1960), the author's] "passion for impartiality," "the instinct—which was deeply imbedded in the consciousness of the century as a whole—to see both sides of any question: to tolerate the ordinary while admiring the ideal, to cling to the old while accepting the new. . . ." Can we doubt, however, that this comprehensive tolerance, carefully cultivated in the face of intellectual diversity, ended for George Eliot by becoming indistinguishable from the "oppressive scepticism" to which Deronda is victim; that the "passion for impartiality" ended by almost extinguishing passion? Deronda feels "no preponderance of desire"; he is "dissatisfied with his neutral life." These are the symptoms which George Eliot sought to cure by offering Daniel the restorative of social dedication.

"The Christian sympathies in which my mind was reared can never die out of me," said Deronda, with increasing tenacity of tone. "But I consider it my duty—it is the impulse of my feeling—to identify myself, as far as possible, with my hereditary people, and if I can see any work to be done for them that I can give my soul and hand to, I shall choose to do it."

With backward homage to the religion of his past Deronda commits himself to the faith of the future; and with qualified ardor, emending "I consider it my duty" to "it is the impulse of my feeling," he embraces "as far as possible" the social task.

Another passage discloses similar ambiguities:

He lay with his hands behind his head propped on a level with the boat's edge, so that he could see all around him, but could not be seen. . . . He was forgetting everything else in a half-speculative, half-involuntary identification of himself with the objects he was looking at, thinking how far it might be possible habitually to shift his centre till his own personality would be no less outside him than the landscape. . . .

The function of this passage is immediately apparent. It is a contrivance intended to "place" Daniel in the novel's moral spectrum, an ethical hierarchy which ascends from personal egotism (Gwendolen) to social sympathy (Daniel). It is meant to indicate how far Daniel is disposed to transcend the limits of egocentricity; (somewhat later in the book he experiences "as was wont with him, a quick change of mental light, shifting his point of view" to that of another). In this passage, however, George Eliot has not defined Deronda's attitude. Is he indeed in a self-forgetful state, or is he rather merely thinking of being in one; is he a mystic, or is he a Victorian intellectual posing as a mystic? George Eliot has straddled the contradiction by calling his mood "half-speculative, half-involuntary," thus again seeking to modulate from the realm of ideas into that of the emotions. As James observed (through Constantius) of George Eliot that "instead of feeling life itself, it is 'views' upon life that she tries to feel," so we may summarize the effect of George Eliot's analyses of her hero by saying they are an effort to persuade us that he "feels" certain "views upon life" which are intimately related to the Victorian intellectual predicament.

It is as a man of feeling above all that George Eliot is concerned to present Deronda. Pulcheria's protest (in James's "Conversation") is clearly just: "Oh, there is plenty about his emotions. Everything about him is 'emotive.' That bad word occurs on every page." Within the space of only two paragraphs George Eliot manages to tell us that her hero regards his home "with affection," has an "ardent clinging nature," a disposition formed for "affections," an "ardently affectionate nature," and finally "an inborn lovingness." Elsewhere Daniel is said to have a "subdued fervor of sympathy," a "mastering affectionateness," "an affectionateness such as we are apt to call feminine." He is of "quick responsive fibre," and "compassionate nature," and his "more exquisite quality" is a "keenly perceptive sympathetic emotiveness." One does not need this last deeply laboured phrase to demonstrate that Deronda's characterization is, from this point of view, exceedingly strained.

Yet George Eliot fails to validate her claims for her hero's sensibilities. For example, she was clearly at pains to emphasize the extent of Deronda's affection for Sir Hugo, his foster father: his "deep-rooted filial" feeling, his "early inwrought affection," "an affection for you which has made a large part of all the life I remember," etc. Filial piety is for George Eliot a primary and symbolically significant form of human obligation. For her, as for Comte, it connoted that reverence for the past which alone assured continuity of tradition and mitigated the turbulence of historical transitions. (At the close of *Daniel Deronda,* in a sort of unpleasant *post script* to the novel, the claims of the past appear in the almost symbolical figure of Lapidoth, the unreverend father whom Mordecai and Mirah do not repudiate.) Yet what George Eliot succeeds in showing of Deronda's attitude toward Sir Hugo, in scene after scene, is hardly filial affection, but filial forbearance of the stuffiest variety, a thin-skinned petulance perpetually held in check. Occasionally indeed, he responds to his foster-father "coldly," or "with angry decision," or with "repressed anger"; but his "resentful impulses" have supposedly been "checked by a mastering affectionateness."

Daniel's fleeting association with his real mother ("popping up through a trap-door and popping down again, at the last, in that scrambling fashion" [as Pulcheria remarks in James's "Conversation"]), provides another test of his "strong bent . . . towards a reverential tenderness." Typically, the letter which brings his mother "nearer as a living reality" throws her "into more remoteness for his affections"; he finds that "his affections had shrunk into a state of comparative neutrality towards her." When they meet Deronda feels "a painful sense of aloofness" and wonders "at his own lack of emotion." Her disclosures arouse "a mixed anger which no reflection could come soon enough to check"; he is "fired with an intolerance which seemed foreign to him." It is hardly surprising that a maternal nature as rigorous as that of the Princess Halm-Eberstein should excite hostile feelings; but the affectionate Deronda proves irrepressible:

> As he felt the smaller hand holding his . . . the strong bent of his nature towards a reverential tenderness asserted itself above every other impression, and in his most fervent tone he said— "Mother! take us all into your heart—the living and the dead. Forgive everything that hurts you in the past. Take my affection."

> Deronda's soul was absorbed in the anguish of compassion. . . . His pity made a flood of forgiveness within him. His single impulse was to kneel by her and take her hand gently between his palms, while he said in that exquisite voice of soothing which expresses oneness with the sufferer— "Mother, take comfort!"

> It seemed that all the woman lacking in her was present in him as he said with some tremor in his voice—"Then are we to part, and I never be anything to you?"

> Deronda's feeling was wrought to a pitch of acuteness in which he was no longer quite master of himself. He gave an audible sob.

V. S. Pritchett says of the George Eliot of *Adam Bede* that "she cannot admit natural passions in a virtuous character." Perhaps we may amend this, regarding Deronda, to read "she cannot admit antipathy in a virtuous character." The insistence upon Daniel's emotion for his mother once again strikes a false note. The parting of mother and son is treated with all the mechanical solemnity of the summary of a schoolroom composition: "Deronda did not know how he got out of the room. He felt an older man. All his boyish

yearnings . . . had vanished. He had gone through a tragic experience which must for ever solemnise his life, and deepen the significance of the acts by which he bound himself to others."

Towards others, Gwendolen, Hans, Mordecai, the old Jew at Frankfort whose touch arouses "a strongly resistant feeling," Deronda's attitude is typified by the repeated adverb, "coldly": "The full face looks too massive . . ." said Deronda, more coldly than was usual with him"; "he managed to slip it away and said coldly, 'I am an Englishman' "; " 'No,' said Deronda, looking at her coolly. . . ." Like the hero of Hans's tragedy Daniel is "a fellow who signed himself over to be good, and was uncomfortable ever after." (pp. 278-84)

The emotion to which Daniel inadvertently confesses is the difficulty of sympathy, rather than sympathy itself. It is for this reason that he strikes us as spurious. He comes before us as an acolyte of the religion of fellow-feeling, the reflection in fiction of the pressures of an unremittingly conscientious agnosticism determined to humanize religion, and to repress antipathetic emotion as one would formerly have put down a heresy. Daniel's "sympathetic emotiveness" was fired in intellectual kilns. For George Eliot, as for Comte and Feuerbach, sympathy and altruism were conditions propitious to the flowering of the new religion of humanity. With moderated optimism George Eliot drew upon the old religious terminology to advocate "worshipping the goodness and the great endeavors that are at least a *partial* salvation, a *partial* redemption of the world." She had translated Feuerbach's notion that human feeling is the true equivalent of theological grace: "the moments which are forsaken by divine grace are the moments destitute of emotion and inspiration." Feuerbach's "grace" is a social, rather than a solitary, endowment:

> Only in the act of imparting do I experience that happiness of beneficence, the joy of generosity, of liberality. But is this joy apart from the joy of the recipient? No; I rejoice because he rejoices. I feel the wretchedness of another, I suffer with him; in alleviating his wretchedness, I alleviate my own;— sympathy with suffering is itself suffering. . . . Just as the feeling of human misery is human, so the feeling of divine compassion is human.

Reiterating her faith in this idea, George Eliot wrote to Charles Bray in 1867 of her "conviction that our moral progress may be measured by the degree in which we sympathize with individual suffering and individual joy." Gradually the idea assumes the place of a religion: despite her sympathy towards the faiths of the past, she writes to D'Albert-Durade in 1859, she finds that "the immediate object and the proper sphere of all our highest emotions are our struggling fellow men and this earthly existence." In 1869 she explained to Harriet Beecher Stowe that "religion too has to be modified . . . and that a religion more perfect than any yet prevalent, must express less care for personal consolation, and a more deeply-awing sense of responsibility to man . . ."; and G. H. Lewes agreed that "righteousness is salvation— and is not to be sought in metaphysical refinements about a 'personal God' but is to be found in our idealization of human relations and human needs."

George Eliot's letter to Mrs. Ponsonby, which is an extended testament of faith in these formulations, was written while *Daniel Deronda* was in progress. In it George Eliot assured Mrs. Ponsonby, who had apparently confided that loss of faith in God had destroyed her sympathy for man, that she herself has been drawn to the opposite conclusion (a repetition of Feuerbachian theology):

> namely, that the fellowship between man and man which has been the principle of development, social and moral, is not dependent on conceptions of what is not man; and that the idea of God, so far as it has been a high spiritual influence, is the ideal of a goodness entirely human (i.e., an exaltation of the human.)

Nor can she accept Mrs. Ponsonby's claim that she has "ceased to pity your suffering fellow-men, because you can no longer think of them, as individualities of immortal duration, in some other state of existence. . . ." She doubts that Mrs. Ponsonby has therefore lost "all belief that your conduct . . . can have any difference of effect on the wellbeing of those immediately about you (and therefore of those afar off), whether you carelessly follow your selfish moods or encourage that vision of others' needs which is the source of justice, tenderness, sympathy in the fullest sense."

Whatever our ultimate evaluation may be of these ideas (and we may note that the sense of personal responsibility which they imply is awesome), in *Daniel Deronda* their effect seems clearly pernicious. Daniel is to be understood and judged as a Feuerbachian hero, a proof of the belief that "the feeling of divine compassion" is indeed a fully human attribute. He is an agnostic's resuscitation of the benevolent gentleman, and in the interim benevolence has taken on a new intensity. Deronda is George Eliot's demonstration that "the idea of God . . . is the ideal of a goodness entirely human (i.e., an exaltation of the human)." The moral contrast which George Eliot intended between Daniel and Gwendolen is exactly that outlined in the letter to Mrs. Ponsonby: the contrast between encouraging the "vision of others's needs" and following one's "selfish moods." Daniel and Gwendolen are repeatedly compared from this point of view: if Daniel thinks about 'shifting his center,' Gwendolen's habitual gesture is to look for her image in the glass; (but the gestures of egotism, if petty, have a concreteness which Daniel's pseudo-speculations quite lack). George Eliot is as concerned to belittle Gwendolen as she is to ennoble Deronda:

> their two lots had come in contact, hers narrowly personal, his charged with far-reaching sensibilities, perhaps with durable purposes, which were hardly more present to her than the reasons why men migrate are present to the birds that come as usual for the crumbs and find them no more.

> And Gwendolen? She was thinking of Deronda much more than he was thinking of her—often wondering what were his ideas "about things," and how his life was occupied. But a lap-dog would be necessarily at a loss in framing to itself the motives and adventures of doghood at large; and it was as far from Gwendolen's conception that Deronda's life could be determined by the historical destiny of the Jews as that he could rise into the air on a brazen horse, and so vanish from her horizon in the form of a twinkling star.

If the dilemma which George Eliot invented for Gwendolen Harleth is a measure of the magnanimity of her genius, the moral lesson which she insisted upon extracting from this true dilemma falsifies the complexity of her vision. George Eliot interprets Gwendolen's final acceptance of Grandcourt and her betrayal of her promise to Mrs. Glasher as a sort of social sin, a victory of the "selfish" over the "unselfish" in-

stincts. It is Deronda's function to rescue Gwendolen from egotism: " 'Look on other lives besides your own. See what their troubles are, and how they are borne. Try to care about something in this vast world besides the gratification of small selfish desires . . .' "; " 'It is the curse of your life—forgive me—of so many lives, that all passion is spent in that narrow round, for want of ideas and sympathies. . . . The refuge you are needing from personal trouble is the higher, the religious life, which holds an enthusiasm for something more than our own appetites or vanities'." These speeches, given the inadequacies in the presentation of Deronda, have the hollow ring of a new cant; and the diction becomes even emptier whenever George Eliot seeks to imply Daniel's harmony, in contrast to Gwendolen, with "the great movements, the larger destinies of mankind," "the fermenting political and social leaven which was making a difference in the history of the world," "the larger march of human destinies." It is to Gwendolen's discredit on the other hand that she is preoccupied with the desire for personal happiness at "a time . . . when ideas were with fresh vigour making armies of themselves, and the universal kinship was declaring itself fiercely." (It is illuminating to find these phrases wielded ironically by Henry James in *The Bostonians,* where Olive Chancellor's opinion of her sister Mrs. Luna is a satirized reflection of George Eliot's and Daniel's judgment upon Gwendolen: Mrs. Luna is "given up to a merely personal, egotistical, instinctive life, and as unconscious of the tendencies of the age, the revenges of the future, the new truths and the great social questions, as if she had been a mere bundle of dress trimmings, which she very nearly was." Unlike James, George Eliot never scrutinizes the element of cant and inadequacy in Daniel's evaluation of Gwendolen.)

The reason that the novel as a whole presents itself provokingly as curiously distorted is that its moral judgment is contradicted by its aesthetic judgment. The disparity between the splendid Gwendolen and the spurious Daniel as literary creatures causes the ethical distinction between them to appear an absurdity. But the truth is that Gwendolen is not only superior to Daniel as a fictional invention, a brilliant Satan to his innocent archangel: she is his moral superior as well. Gwendolen is a protagonist: Daniel is not. Gwendolen is fully engaged in a dilemma: Daniel's only dilemmas are abstractions, the fruits of the novelist's self-doubts. Daniel is represented as totally free—the Jewish fantasy requires this—while Gwendolen confronts the pressures, social, economic, familial, of an actual environment. Gwendolen may not be an enthusiast (she is in James's comment on Isabel Archer, a mixture of "vivacity and indifference"), but she at least is capable as Daniel is not of love and hate, despair and elation. The growing dependence of this real Gwendolen upon this straw Daniel, which is the moral theme of the novel as a whole, thus presents itself as a major fallacy in the book's vision and structure.

To consider the question of what went wrong with *Daniel Deronda* one must explore closely George Eliot's intentions with regard to this central relationship between Daniel and Gwendolen, a germ of which may be discovered in Dinah Morris's sermon on the Hayslope green:

> Saviour of sinners! When a poor woman, laden with sins, went out to the well to draw water, she found Thee sitting at the well. She knew Thee not; she had not sought Thee; her mind was dark; her life was unholy. But Thou didst speak to her. Thou didst teach her, Thou didst show her that her life lay

open before thee, and yet Thou wast ready to give her that blessing which she had never sought. Jesus! Thou art in the midst of us, and Thou knowest all men: if there is any here like that poor woman—if their minds are dark, their lives unholy—if they have come out not seeking Thee, not desiring to be taught; deal with them according to the free mercy which Thou didst show to her. Speak to them, Lord; open their ears to my message; bring their sins to their minds, and make them thirst for that salvation which Thou art ready to give.

[*Adam Bede*]

As a secular transformation of this Christian message, ***Daniel Deronda*** gives us Gwendolen as the unholy woman whose mind is dark, and Daniel as the teacher who makes her thirst for salvation. Unlike Dinah Morris, Daniel is not the representative of the old faith but the embodiment of a new. Pulcheria's comment—"A lay father-confessor—horrid!"—begins to define Daniel's role toward Gwendolen. It is neither sexual nor (since Daniel is here a man) sisterly; it is pseudo-religious.

Daniel is said to be attracted to people "in proportion to the possibility of his defending them, rescuing them, telling upon their lives with some sort of redeeming influence." He redeems Gwendolen's necklace at Leubronn—(according to Pulcheria an "extremely impertinent and ill-mannered gesture"); and later brings a ring to the Jewish pawnbroker, in redeeming which he rescues Mordecai from amongst the Cohens: "Mordecai knew that the nameless stranger was to come and redeem his ring." Thus Daniel's first encounters with Gwendolen and Mordecai embody the same unconscious pun upon the hero as redeemer.

"If you despair of me," Gwendolen warns Daniel (the sinner praying for grace), "I shall despair":

> If you say you wish you had not meddled,—that means, you despair of me and forsake me. And then you will decide for me that I shall not be good. It is you who will decide; because you might have made me different by keeping as near me as you could, and believing in me.

Later she justifies his influence: " 'You have saved me from worse,' said Gwendolen, in a sobbing voice. 'I should have been worse, if it had not been for you. If you had not been good, I should have been more wicked than I am.' " Nor does Daniel dispute her faith, offering this modest parable of their relationship: "You have had a vision of injurious, selfish action—a vision of possible degradation; think that a severe angel, seeing you along the road of error, grasped you by the wrist, and showed you the horror of the life you must avoid." These words are to Gwendolen "like the touch of a miraculous hand." Both George Eliot and Gwendolen devoutly accept the superiority of the "severe angel": "Devoted as these words were, they widened his spiritual distance from her . . . she had a vague need of getting nearer to that compassion which seemed to be regarding her from a halo of superiority. . . ." "He rose as he spoke, and she gave him her hand submissively. . . . The distance between them was too great. She was a banished soul—beholding a possible life which she had sinned herself away from." In their last interview Daniel himself gently but firmly reminds Gwendolen of the disparity in their moral natures: "If we had been much together before, we should have felt our differences more, and seemed to get farther apart. Now we can perhaps never see

each other again. But our minds may get nearer." It is, to say the least, an interesting species of consolation.

The deification of Deronda is most clearly seen in Gwendolen's crisis of faith when Grandcourt insinuates that Daniel is Mirah's lover. She reflects "how very slight were the grounds of her faith in Deronda." She feels a moment's reassurance which comes almost like a divine omen:

> All this went on in her with the rapidity of a sick dream; and her start into resistance was very much like a waking. Suddenly from out the grey sombre morning there came a stream of sunshine, wrapping her in warmth and light where she sat in stony stillness. She moved gently and looked round her—there was a world outside this bad dream, and the dream proved nothing; she rose, stretching her arms upward and clasping her hands with her habitual attitude when she was seeking relief from oppressive feeling, and walked about the room in this flood of sunbeams.

This momentary relief "was not her faith come back again; it was only the desperate cry of faith. . . ." She goes to question Mirah: " 'Tell me—tell me the truth. You are sure he is quite good. You know no evil of him." Mirah's fervour is equal to her own: " 'Who are the people who say evil of him? I would not believe any evil of him, if an angel came to tell it me'." This is spiritual refreshment to Gwendolen, who feels "like one parched with thirst, drinking the fresh water that spreads through the frame as a sufficient bliss." Later when Grandcourt mocks Mirah's testimony, "Gwendolen did not, for all this, part with her recovered faith;—rather she kept it with a more anxious tenacity, as a Protestant of old kept his Bible hidden or a Catholic his crucifix. . . ." (pp. 284-91)

In the relationship of Daniel and Gwendolen George Eliot seeks to substantiate Feuerbach's belief that man is a God to man:

> My fellow man is my objective conscience; he makes my failings a reproach to me; even when he does not expressly mention them, he is my personified feeling of shame. The consciousness of the moral law, of right, of propriety, of truth itself, is indissolubly united with my consciousness of another than myself.

Gwendolen's "divine hope of moral recovery"—the agnostic form of salvation—comes about through Daniel's agency: "So potent in us is the infused action of another soul, before which we bow in complete love." To state this credo George Eliot borrows the grandiose and suspect diction of Mordecai:

> In this way our brother may be in the stead of God to us, and his opinion which has pierced even to the joints and marrow, may be our virtue in the making. That mission of Daniel to Gwendolen had begun with what she had felt to be his judgment of her at the gaming-table. He might easily have spoiled it. . . . Deronda had not spoiled his mission.

Does Daniel, then "save" Gwendolen? The philosophical intentions involved in the novel demanded an affirmative answer. Yet a group of metaphors depicting Daniel as a helpless "saviour" provide a melancholy counterpoint to the official affirmations of the text:

It was as if he saw her drowning while his limbs were bound.

It was as if he had a vision of himself besought with outstretched arms and cries, while he was caught by the waves and compelled to mount the vessel bound for a far-off coast.

The feeling Deronda endured in these moments he afterwards called horrible. Words seemed to have no more rescue in them than if he had been beholding a vessel in peril of wreck—the poor ship with its many-lived anguish beaten by the inescapable storm.

Gwendolen's trust seems to Daniel like "the retreating cry of a creature snatched and carried out of his reach by swift horsemen or swifter waves, while his own strength was only a stronger sense of weakness." He sees her "as if she had been stretching her arms towards him from a forsaken shore." In terms of these metaphors we may interpret Daniel's saving of Mirah when she is about to drown herself: in the world of fantasy which George Eliot builds in the "Jewish" half of the novel, pessimism may be suspended and human saviours may really save.

Daniel rises to his obligations as savior with typical reluctance: "he was not a priest. He dreaded the weight of this woman's soul flung upon his own." He is "worn in spirit by the perpetual strain" of an interview with Gwendolen; and afterward feels "a painful quivering at the very imagination of having again and again to meet the appeal of her eyes and words." Knowing that he is to marry Mirah and leave England Daniel is indeed awkwardly placed regarding Gwendolen, but his discomfort is not so much embarrassment as the trials of one too much under obligation: "Deronda felt a pang, which showed itself in his face. He looked miserable as he said, 'I will certainly come'." And yet George Eliot can allow herself to describe Daniel's feelings toward Gwendolen as "the enthusiasm of self-martyring pity . . . ," resorting to rhetoric to convey the pity or enthusiasm lacking in her hero's demeanor. If we remember Daniel at all, it is perhaps as an embodiment of the discomfort of the importuned ego: "He felt as if he were putting his name to a blank paper which might be filled up terribly."

But George Eliot cannot go into this aspect of her hero's psychology. No more than Gwendolen can she lose faith in her secular redeemer. When sympathy is regarded with reverence, and fellow-feeling may save, then a failure of sympathy is as serious a sin as any breach of a former faith. By taking "egotism" and "altruism" as her alternatives, George Eliot undertook a fatal simplification of the psychological issues of the novel. The dilemma of human responsibility is approached in Daniel Deronda—"We are all of us denying or fulfilling prayers—and men in their careless deeds walk amidst invisible outstretched arms and pleadings made in vain"—but it is treated as a problem to be resolved. George Eliot was a Victorian; she insisted upon providing an answer. She invents Deronda, and defines him wholly in relation to his responsibilities: to Mirah, Mordecai, Gwendolen, and finally to his people. Yet this secular man of sorrows, the most exasperating and least convincing hero in Victorian fiction, is himself in search of rescue. He seeks a cure for spiritual neutrality and failing emotion. He verifies Martin Luther's claim that a Savior cannot be merely human, but must be in part divine: "When I believe that the human nature alone has suffered for me, Christ would be a poor Savior to me: in that case, he needs a Savior himself." Gwendolen looks toward Daniel, while, like a Christ wholly human, Daniel is looking toward Mordecai.

Thus the structure of **Daniel Deronda** presents itself as a chain of discipleships, with Gwendolen at the feet of Daniel, and Daniel at those of Mordecai. If Daniel's association with Gwendolen is inconclusive, he beautifully succeeds with Mordecai. If there is an element not wholly genuine in the relationship with Gwendolen, that with Mordecai is a clear contrivance. George Eliot has mated Daniel and Mordecai with a shameless lack of subtlety: the former seeking an avenue of committment, a "social captainship," a task to be imposed as an irrefutable duty; the latter a dying visionary requiring a Jewish disciple. Daniel returns from Genoa, where he learns of his ancestry, with something "better than freedom—with a duteous bond." In one dramatic stroke he has been transferred from a dubious place on the social periphery to the very center of a communal endeavor. The neutral has become the standard bearer. The crucial Victorian problems of identity and direction have been marvelously resolved. No amount of analysis can supply the sense of emotional conviction which is missing from this grandest of Deronda's self-bestowals. Indeed, Mordecai inspires in Daniel his characteristic reluctance. Mordecai himself has a somewhat repellent aspect: in George Eliot's later work the claims of history and race reach out with a gnarled and ugly hand, like that of the old Jew who clutches Deronda in Frankfort. Daniel feels "the grasp of Mordecai's dying hand upon him. . . ." Like Savonarola in **Romola** or Zarca in **The Spanish Gypsy**, Mordecai is a paternal-spiritual counsellor, offering an avenue of social dedication and vicarious conviction to a wavering disciple: George Eliot saw about him "a radiation . . . nullifying his outward poverty and lifting him into authority." Yet she herself could not dissemble or avoid conveying a certain repugnance to Mordecai, as well as to his earlier analogues. G. H. Lewes had to rebuke John Blackwood for hinting at what the reader must feel: "I was very sorry to find from your last that you did not take cordially to Mordecai—sorry because I think it on the whole one of the greatest of her creations. . . . " "I have been near to poor, grand Mordecai," says Theodora in James's "Conversation"; but Pulcheria responds, with the common reader, "Oh, reflect, my dear; not too near!"

Mordecai's pursuit of Deronda is intense: indeed, their relationship has more of the aspect of a love affair than that of Daniel and Gwendolen:

> In ten minutes the two men, with as intense a consciousness as if they had been two undeclared lovers, felt themselves alone in the small gas-lit bookshop and turned face to face, each baring his head from an instinctive feeling that they wished to see each other fully.
>
> "I will be faithful," said Deronda—he could not have left those words unuttered. "I will come the first evening I can after seven: on Saturday or Monday, if possible. Trust me."
>
> With exquisite instinct, Deronda, before he opened his lips, placed his palm gently on Mordecai's straining hand. . . .

Once again however Daniel plays the part of the reluctant lover, besieged and guilty at the inadequacy of his response. The compassionate Deronda conquers the hesitant one— "the peculiar appeal to his tenderness overcame the repulsion, etc."—but his interviews with Mordecai create an "emotional strain"; he feels "Mordecai's words of reliance like so many cords binding him painfully." He is "not without relief in the prospect of an interval before he went through the strain of his next private conversation with Mordecai." Deronda reflects upon "the grasp of Mordecai's dying hand and upon him, with all the ideals and prospects it aroused": the sentence graphically demonstrates the suppressed ambivalence characteristic of the "emotive" hero. The repugnance implied by the first phrase is recanted in the hollow enthusiasm of the second. (pp. 292-95)

The foregoing pages have largely dealt with the unpleasant portion of *Daniel Deronda,* that dreary terrain through which the reader must pass after the marriage of Gwendolen and Grandcourt. At that point the psychological and social masterpiece ends, and the uncertain tract, preaching salvation through sympathy and sympathy's expansion into social dedication, begins in earnest. These concerns, the ideology of sympathy and the contrast between "social" and "selfish" interests, are the rocks upon which the novel founders. Henry James in his "Conversation" has Constantius remark on "one's sense of the author's writing under a sort of external pressure":

> She strikes me as a person who certainly has naturally a taste for general considerations, but who has fallen upon an age and a circle which have compelled her to give them an exaggerated attention. . . . If she had fallen upon an age of enthusiastic assent to old articles of faith, it seems to me possible that she would have had a more perfect, a more consistent and graceful development than she has actually had. . . .But she has chosen to go into criticism, and to the critics she addresses her work; I mean the critics of the universe. Instead of feeling life itself, it is 'views' upon life that she tries to feel.

Constantius points to the presence in the novel of an ideology, the nature of which has already perhaps been sufficiently identified. By "an age of criticism" Constantius indicates something akin to Comte's "metaphysical" age, falling between the theological and the positivist stages of civilization. In this stage dominated by destructive ideas, the "person who certainly has naturally a taste for general considerations" must make a particularly determined effort to advance new moral values: "Still, I see clearly that we ought, each of us, not to sit down and wail, but to be heroic and constructive, if possible, like the strong souls who lived before, as in other cases [eras?] of religious decay."

The values which George Eliot sought constructively to demonstrate through *Daniel Deronda* may be traced in part to Comte, who regretted that "the social affections are so overborne by the personal, as rarely to command conduct"; who expected the positivist morality to derive its power from "a clear understanding of the influence that the actions and the tendencies of every one of us must exercise on human life"; and who warned that without "a lofty morality" even "the best developed genius must degenerate into a secondary instrument of narrow personal satisfaction, instead of pursuing that large social destination which can alone offer it a field and sustenance worthy of its nature." Each of these ideas will be familiar to the reader of *Daniel Deronda.*

Nevertheless, as we have seen, George Eliot somehow failed to realize the ideology in the novel. (Whether this was the fault of the novelist, or of the ideology itself, must remain a

A drawing of George Henry Lewes.

matter of opinion.) Daniel fails to rise to the demands of his role, while Gwendolen escapes from the confines of George Eliot's moral scheme and surprises the novelist into a magnificent impartiality. In her veracity, Gwendolen transcends the category in which George Eliot proposed to contain her. Perhaps she comes to embody not "egotism," but the stubborn sense of self, the personal *élan,* which we acknowledge as a form of experience more primary than that which Daniel is meant to represent. Her acute antipathies, which George Eliot regards as anti-social, and thus a moral failing, are after all only the expression of what Daniel himself—"his resentful impulses had been early checked by an overmastering affectionateness"—consistently suppresses: "Deronda coloured, and repressed a retort." If Gwendolen seems as effortless as Daniel is laboured, it is perhaps because she necessitated no evasions, releasing George Eliot from the inhibitions Deronda imposed. The portrait of Gwendolen is, as James wrote, "the most intelligent thing in all George Eliot's writing. . . . It is so deep, so true, so complete; it holds such a wealth of psychological detail, it is more than masterly." Daniel embarks on his odyssey of social dedication, the secular immortality of the positivist; but it is to Gwendolen that the true vitality, and thus the literary immortality, belong. (pp. 298-300)

Carole Robinson, "The Severe Angel: A Study of

'Daniel Deronda'," in ELH, Vol. 31, No. 3, September, 1964, pp. 278-300.

JEAN SUDRANN   (essay date 1970)

[Sudrann discusses the theme of alienation in Daniel Deronda, focusing primarily on Gwendolen's search for self and establishment of personal identity.]

In January 1876, while she was struggling to complete **Daniel Deronda,** George Eliot defined her need of "some human figure and individual experience" through which that "set of experiments in life"—her novels—might fulfill her "endeavour to see what our thought and belief may be capable of." This emphasis on experiment and the indivisibility of idea from lived experience coupled with her later assertion that she "meant everything in the book to be related to everything else there" [see letter dated 2 October 1876] is central to any understanding of the structure of George Eliot's last novel. For in **Daniel Deronda,** she does "experiment" to give expression to that "individual" and major "experience" which had been tested on the very pulses of her own life: her complex and long continued isolation from society.

For modern readers to "cut the book into scraps and talk of nothing in it but Gwendolen" reflects a failure to recognize that which should be most recognizable: the way in which the double plot creates for the novel its central definition of isolation in terms which make its relationship to twentieth century treatments of alienation most vivid. I would like to suggest that George Eliot felt her own alienation in terms more "modern" than Victorian, that she sought to define that experience by making it the central subject of her last novel, the only one to have a contemporary setting, and that she then had to bend to new uses the conventional forms of the novel to express the new subject matter.

Attempts to describe the personal experience begin as early as 1848 when Mary Ann Evans addresses an extraordinary outcry to Sara Sophia Hennell:

> Alas for the fate of poor mortals which condemns them to wake up some fine morning and find all the poetry in which their world was bathed only the evening before utterly gone—the hard angular world of chairs and tables and looking glasses staring at them in all its naked prose. It is so in all the stages of life—the poetry of girlhood goes—the poetry of love and marriage—the poetry of maternity—and at last the very poetry of duty forsakes us for a season and we see ourselves and all about us as nothing more than miserable agglomerations of atoms—poor tentative efforts of the Natur Princip to mould a personality. This is the state of prostration. . . .
>
> I feel a sort of madness growing upon me—just the opposite of the delirium which makes people fancy that their bodies are filling the room. It seems to me as if I were shrinking into that mathematical abstraction, a point—so entirely am I destitute of contact that I am unconscious of length or breadth. . . .

Sufficient background for this outburst can be seen in the very physical circumstances of Mary Ann Evans's life during this summer of her twenty-ninth year. She was laboring, with increasing distaste, over the translation of Strauss' *Leben Jesu* at the same time that she was serving as housekeeper, nurse

and companion for her ailing father. But neither the demands of the translation nor of the invalid—or not just those demands alone—account for the paradoxically passionate description of non-being.

The story of Mary Ann Evan's wholly characteristic Victorian revolt needs no rehearsal. The price she paid for her intellectual and emotional honesty—the loss of the communities of family and church and society—created an experience of utter isolation for the author of **Daniel Deronda.** Her letter to Sara Hennell suggests something of the meaning of that experience in its earliest stages, for it begins to define biographically the profound consequences to the sense of self. Full artistic formulation had to wait until the pattern of isolation was broken by an almost complete measure of social acceptance. By 1874, George Eliot was sufficiently able to understand the "sort of madness" she endured in 1848; then she could use that experience of alienation as the effective center of action for her new novel, **Daniel Deronda.**

To do this, she created from her earlier vision of the "naked prose" of a world in which the self is undefinable, a landscape more familiar to the twentieth than to the nineteenth century. The modern reader who comes back to a re-reading of **Daniel Deronda** after he has read, for example, *La Nausée,* can hardly escape noting the extent to which the Eliot novel explores the human condition in terms that would not be wholly foreign to Sartre. Gwendolen Harleth's "world-nausea" and her creator's personal vision of reality reduced to a "miserable agglomeration of atoms" suggest areas of similarity. But Iris Murdoch's description of the determining bias that makes Sartre's Roquentin, the protagonist of *La Nausée,* an "existentialist doubter" reveals the fundamental link between the two worlds. Miss Murdoch asserts that Roquentin is seized by "an old and familiar" metaphysical doubt which he treats in a contemporary fashion because

> . . . he himself is in the picture: what most distresses him is that his own individual being is invaded by the senseless flux; what most interests him is his aspiration to *be* in a different way.

It is possible to define the mode of **Daniel Deronda** as "descriptive brooding upon the doubt situation," springing from the same metaphysical problem Sartre's Roquentin encounters. Unlike so characteristic a Victorian figure of alienation as Carlyle's Herr Teufelsdröckh, George Eliot's characters cannot solve the crisis of separation simply by pitting the everlasting Yea of their own heart beats against the barren mechanism of a clock-work universe. It is precisely their own heart beats which are in question. Gwendolen Harleth's "own individual being is invaded by the senseless flux; what most interests [her] is [her] aspiration to *be* in a different way." Iris Murdoch's description of Roquentin fits George Eliot's heroine as well.

To make the subject of her novel the self's awareness of the self's dissolution and its subsequent struggle to re-form an identity was truly for George Eliot to embark on a major experiment. The formal implementation of that experiment is worked out largely through the double plot and the series of melodramatic episodes which so startlingly disturb the novel's realistic texture. These are the major technical devices definitive of the novel's scope and complexity; through these, the central relevance of its treatment of illusion and will, of terror, self and the world against an echoing background of legend is made apparent.

Early in **Daniel Deronda,** George Eliot offers to the reader a general comment which, while it helps initially to define the curve of the action, nevertheless resounds throughout the novel with an increasingly ironic ring.

> A human life, I think, should be well rooted in some spot of a native land, where it may get the love of tender kinship for the face of earth, for the labours men go forth to, for the sounds and accents that haunt it, for whatever will give that early home a familiar unmistakable difference amidst the future widening of knowledge: a spot where the definiteness of early memories may be inwrought with affection, and kindly acquaintance with all neighbors, even to the dogs and donkeys, may spread not by sentimental effort and reflection, but as a sweet habit of the blood. . . . The best introduction to astronomy is to think of the nightly heavens as a little lot of stars belonging to one's own homestead.

To a striking degree, **Daniel Deronda** is a novel of rootless human lives, lives lacking "homestead," "native land," and a family relation to the heavens. Yet to read this passage as the promise of a story of the exile's return can lead only to the familiar critical lament over the novel's fragmented conclusion; for this glimpse of the poetry of a universe where all things are at home and where each is bound to each is a genuine point of departure, not a prophecy of arrival. Deliberately reminiscent of Romantic expressions of the dynamic relatedness of all aspects of the various universe, the passage serves as the measure of what it means "to wake up some fine morning and find all the poetry in which [the] world was bathed only the evening before utterly gone." It evokes the poetry of loss so that the "naked prose" of the novel itself may more adequately deal with the landscape of exile which is the real stage of **Daniel Deronda.**

The complex irony of the title of the first book, "The Spoiled Child," is characteristic of George Eliot's method in creating that stage for her novel. Is the pampered and wilful Gwendolen "spoiled" because the rod has been spared, or does the adjective suggest other, darker abuses deriving from the failure to establish the "sweet habit of the blood" which creates "the poetry of existence"? The ironic emphasis of the title emerges largely through the treatment in the early chapters of Gwendolen's uncle, the Reverend Mr. Gascoigne, as well as from the reader's introduction to Gwendolen herself. The clerical uncle's generous ease and shrewd benevolence operate so smoothly that his very tone makes the "world in general seem a very manageable place of residence." Yet as the light of George Eliot's irony, affectionate and tolerant though it be, colors this portrait, the reader becomes slowly aware of the extent to which he has been lulled into sharing the Rector's comfortable illusions. These illusions manifest themselves dramatically in his manoeuvres to catch a good husband for his lively young niece, but they are based on vast and wide assumptions. The "world in general" is a comfortable home for the Rector just because he has never lost his early confidence in "the nightly heavens as a little lot of stars belonging to one's own homestead." Gwendolen is "a girl likely to make a brilliant marriage" and the match with Grandcourt is "a sort of public affair . . . which . . . might even strengthen the Establishment"; it is "to be accepted on broad general grounds national and ecclesiastical." Gascoigne's linking of the particulars of Gwendolen and Grandcourt to the astronomy of the Establishment is a beautiful example of his easy assurance of the validity of his knowledge of that world in which he is so thoroughly and so successfully at home. He takes pride in his "daylight" religion and his lack of "mischievous impracticableness." The daylight practicality of those beliefs is epitomized by his attitude toward Grandcourt: "He held it futile, even if it had been becoming, to show any curiosity as to the past of a young man whose birth, wealth, and consequent leisure made many habits venial which under other circumstances would have been inexcusable." The first phrase of the sentence defines Gascoigne's daylight practicality as a full acknowledgment of the necessary limitations of a middle class clergyman who wishes to maintain his illusions. Actions which would, in any case, be unavailing are unbecoming. The wholly appropriate style for a successful clergyman is to further the *possible* action with the proper decorum.

That style, as well as the assumptions on which it is based, is thoroughly exposed in the interview in which Mr. Gascoigne undertakes to point out to Gwendolen that both her duty and her pleasure lie in her acceptance of a marriage with Grandcourt. With clerical and avuncular heartiness and goodwill, he instructs his niece in the follies of coquetry and the advantages of the match. Gwendolen's response is all obedience: " 'I know that I must be married some time—before it is too late. And I don't see how I could do better than marry Mr. Grandcourt. I mean to accept him, if possible.' " Yet the Rector is "a little startled by so bare a version of his own meaning from those young lips. . . . He wished his niece parks, carriages, a title—everything that would make this world a pleasant abode; but he wished her not to be cynical—to be, on the contrary, religiously dutiful, and have warm domestic affections." Nothing could make clearer what Sartre would call the "bad faith" of the Rector's advice. Gwendolen's response, while it promises the effective action, lacks the operative illusion. Because she hopes to do the right thing for the wrong reason, Gwendolen casts—perhaps even momentarily for the Rector himself—a darkening shadow over his daylight vision of the world as a manageable place of residence. As the bourgeoisie of Roquentin's world are sustained by their illusion of morality, so Gascoigne is sustained by a rectitude easily shown to be simply a private illusion.

A different but equally illusory concept governs Gwendolen in the early stages of the novel. She is not, as her uncle so mistakenly judges, cynical about "parks, carriages, a title"; Gwendolen has a healthy respect for these appurtenances nor does it seem unlikely to her that they form the basis of "warm domestic affections." After all, from the opening pages of the novel, she sees herself as "a princess in exile" whose life should abound in those perquisites essential for residence in the world by "so exceptional a person as herself." Yet that is not at all what George Eliot means by "exile"; and Gwendolen, who is "not without romantic conjectures," must undergo a transformation from the fairy-tale princess to the less easily romantic "lost sheep" before her exile is truly accomplished. From the beginning, then, the novel's ironies match the illusory homeland of the Rector with the equally illusory exile of his niece as prologue to the unillusioned and terrible drama of alienation.

Central to the dispelling of these romantic and sentimental illusions of Gwendolen and her uncle is George Eliot's decision to entangle the silly young English girl's life with those of the Jewish characters, archetypal aliens. Not only do these figures elevate and define Gwendolen's dilemma but they create the novels' ultimate import by giving the widest possible significance to the nature of Gwendolen Harleth's life crisis. Alone, at the novel's end, Gwendolen is poised in a solitude quite other than that which surrounds her at the novel's beginning. For at the end, she is aware that she is alone; through that awareness she has been transformed into a true "princess in exile." The novel, then, is concerned not so much with the wanderer's return as it is with the harsh exigencies of how "to be" in exile.

The great variety of "aliens" peopling the world of **Daniel Deronda** define the outer conditions of exile and create the texture essential to establish the work's focus. In addition to the more central figures of Deronda and Mirah, the musician Klesmer, the consumptive prophet Mordecai, and the prima-donna Princess Halm-Eberstein help to establish the nature of the fact as well as the variety of human response to its existence. For each of these aliens, the simple social truth that they are all Jews in a Gentile world marks only the beginning and not the extent of their separateness. Klesmer and the Princess are also artists among Philistines; Mordecai, a seer among the blind—a dying man in the midst of the living. The separateness of Gwendolen is also clear from the beginning of the novel. The only child of the twice-widowed Mrs. Davilow's first marriage, she has been robbed of the rightful heritage of all children: a spot of native land. Moreover, the financial uncertainties of her mother's second marriage have deprived her of the easy means of maintaining the place in society to which her birth entitles her. Acutely conscious of her family's existence in "a border territory of rank," she is deeply anxious that "so exceptional a person as herself" be appropriately situated. Coupled with the family disintegration is her own lack of sympathy with them which confirms her alienation from even that heritage of birth. She has deliberately, we are told, cut herself off from any knowledge of her father, and one of her first actions in the novel is to pawn the necklace made from a chain which had once been his to cover her losses at roulette.

While Deronda must live in ignorance of his family, and Mirah Cohen has forcibly been separated from hers, Gwendolen, like the Princess Halm-Eberstein, chooses to reject her heritage. These are the given facts of external exile with which the story begins. And Deronda's first action in relation to Gwendolen, the restoration to her of the pawned necklace, immediately links the two characters to the novel's central issue by creating a dramatic metaphor of the subsequent story: the attempted restoration of a proper heritage.

That Gwendolen's family has lost its money and status is, like the Judaism of the other characters, simply the social fact to mark the beginning and not the meaning of her exile. It is the pressure of this outer fact on Gwendolen's sense of her self which is crucial. Again, the supporting cast throws into vivid relief the importance of Gwendolen's reaction. There are many ways "to be" in exile, and each of the postures assumed helps to define the dilemma. Klesmer, who calls himself "the wandering Jew" and values himself as musician to be "on level benches with legislators," knows precisely who he is. Mordecai, recognizing that he is "exiled in the rarity of [his] own mind," longs for a more effective identity to implement his lonely dream: "hence it was that his imagination had constructed another man . . . to help out the insufficient first. . . . And as the more beautiful, the stronger, the more executive self took shape in his mind, he loved it beforehand

with an affection half identifying, half contemplative and grateful." The Princess attempts, with a terrible energy of will, simply to reject any identity that will interfere with her desires to appear to the world first as the great singer Alcharisi and then as the Russian aristocrat. In each case it is clear not only that the self must be named but also that the creation of that name is ultimately dependent on some established relationship between self and world.

By exploring Gwendolen's need for this established relationship, George Eliot first exposes the pitiful narrowness of the girl's egoism and then defines the dissolution of her "personality" as she shrinks to "that mathematical abstraction, a point . . . entirely destitute of contact." From the beginning, it is clear that the whole pressure of Gwendolen's will is "to do what is pleasant to herself in a striking manner." Yet her knowledge of that pleasure has no other gauge than the reactions of the world. Pleasure for her, then, becomes "whatever she could do so as to strike others with admiration and get in that reflected way a more ardent sense of living." Thus the very world itself becomes a mirror to create pleasure as it reflects the desired image. This relationship with the world suggests that Gwendolen, like her uncle Gascoigne, begins by finding herself in easy command of that which lies outside the self and creates yet another link between the matching illusions of uncle and niece. What Gwendolen sees in that mirror is the vision of herself as "the princess in exile, who in time of famine was to have her breakfast-roll made of the finest-bolted flour from the seven thin ears of wheat, and in a general decampment was to have her silver fork kept out of the baggage." Only as Gwendolen slowly becomes aware of the implications of Mrs. Davilow's complete financial ruin is that self-image shattered.

The sheer amount of space George Eliot devotes to the description of the destruction of the image is sufficient measure of the importance she attaches to the process itself. Of chief interest is the artistry by which the destruction of what Gwendolen believes to be the world and the destruction of her idea of self are shown to be not two separate actions but a single stroke. The news of the loss of her mother's fortune comes in a letter appealing for her return home which Gwendolen receives after an evening of ill-fortune at a continental roulette table. The night is spent getting ready to meet that summons, and just before dawn, Gwendolen turns to look at herself:

> She had a *naive* delight in her fortunate self, which any but the harshest saintliness will have some indulgence for in a girl who had every day seen a pleasant reflection of that self in her friends' flattery as well as in the looking-glass. And even in this beginning of her troubles, while . . . she sat gazing at her image in the growing light, her face gathered a complacency gradual as the cheerfulness of the morning. . . . till at last she took off her hat, leaned forward and kissed the cold glass which had looked so warm.

The mirror of the world as well as the mirror on the wall testify to the justice of Gwendolen's claim that her "silver fork" be "kept out of the baggage." The caress she bestows on her own reflected image is a proper measure of the harmony of Gwendolen's solipistic world as the novel opens. In subsequent references to this moment, as well as in an elaborate sequence of mirror scenes, George Eliot continues the story of the annihilation of the image of self.

At its simplest, Gwendolen's response to the immediate crisis of financial and social deprivation can be described as her conscious knowledge of the loss of her superiority in the mirror of the world, the giving-up of the sense that the world must necessarily value her as she values herself. Nor is it surprising that her next step is to accept the world's valuation and reject herself: "the self-delight with which she had kissed her image in the glass had faded before the sense of futility in being anything whatever—charming, clever, resolute—what was the good of it all?" All desire to create an image for the mirror is leaving her; how useless it is "to be" any identity at all.

The brilliant scene in which Gwendolen confronts Klesmer with her vulgar artistic ambitions as an avenue to the restoration of the family fortunes through the world's applause is bracketed by two further mirror views. Before Klesmer's arrival, Gwendolen, buoyant with expectancy, watches herself in the drawing room mirror: "seeing her image slowly advancing, she thought, 'I *am* beautiful'—not exultingly, but with grave decision." Klesmer's full and sure knowledge of his own identity as an artist is added to Gwendolen's self-exposure in this scene to evoke the sense of shame with which she meets Klesmer's final judgment: "'you will hardly achieve more than mediocrity'." Yet the full effect of that interview on Gwendolen is not clear until Klesmer leaves. The noonday light at Offendene then brings "into more dreary clearness the absence of interest from her life. All memories, all objects, the pieces of music displayed, the open piano—the very reflection of herself in the glass—seemed no better than the packed-up shows of a departing fair." Explicitly, at this point, the ruin of the relation between self and the world is linked to the disintegration of that self: the image in the mirror is simply disappearing along with the very chairs and tables of the drawing room.

Only once again in the novel does Gwendolen look at herself in the mirror with any pleasure. Just before Grandcourt comes to make his marriage proposal, both Gwendolen and her mother admire "the reflection in the glass" before which the girl is seated and Mrs. Davilow thinks her daughter "is quite herself again." After her marriage, Gwendolen no longer feels "inclined to kiss her fortunate image in the glass." As the new mistress of Ryelands, she is surrounded by images of herself but is either unable to "see the reflections of herself" or, seeing them, "not recognizing herself in the glass panels." The last time in the novel that she looks at herself is while she waits for Deronda to call before the Grandcourts leave on their yachting expedition. This time, she is conscious of her own beauty but it is profoundly disturbing to her, and she seeks to disguise her image by throwing a black lace shawl over her head and neck.

Now that Gwendolen can once again see an image in the glass, her impulse is toward an activity that will alter that image. The novelist's record of the gesture signals not only the return of some sensation of self but also a reviving will toward self-determination. For if George Eliot links self-recognition to the self's relation to the world, she is equally certain of the dependence of the sense of self on the operation of will. Early in the novel she makes that dependency clear when she describes Gwendolen's "usual world" as one "in which her will was of some avail." The "world nausea" and "sick motivelessness" Gwendolen suffers as the Davilows attempt to readjust to narrowed lives is defined as that paralysis of will which marks one aspect of Gwendolen's crisis. Indeed,

her experience of alienation is completed only with that utter subjugation of her "peremptory will" which results from her marriage to Grandcourt. The collapse of Gwendolen's "belief in her own power of dominating" comes as the climax of the vivid drama of conflicting wills which is the courtship and marriage. By the destruction of his wife's will, Grandcourt has completed the dissolution of Gwendolen's sense of self, leaving her in a waste space, a "vastness . . . in which she seemed an exile."

The importance of this clash of wills and the skill with which George Eliot handles it can perhaps best be illustrated by her easy movement from episode to metaphor in the use of horses and riding scenes as she dramatizes Gwendolen's movement from mastery to servitude. The sequence begins quietly enough with Gwendolen's teasing to be permitted to have her own horse in the days when the family fortune, though small, seems secure. Her uncle's indulgence of this desire is a further measure of the "daylight practicality" of his match-making for his niece. In Gwendolen's triumph at the Wessex Hunt, matched by her cousin Rex's fiasco, the image becomes a vehicle for the conclusion of that romance even while it is being reinvested with all of its metaphoric sexual power as a prelude to the courtship of Gwendolen and Grandcourt most of which takes place on horseback or, at least, with Gwendolen dressed in her riding habit while a pair of horses is being walked by the groom someplace in the background.

With the firm establishment of the metaphoric richness of the image, George Eliot is able to move it out of the literal narrative into the mental landscape of the novel. Gwendolen has her vision of marriage as a chariot she will mount "and drive the plunging horses herself, with a spouse by her side who would fold his arms and give her his countenance without looking ridiculous." Grandcourt, too, has his vision of their marriage: "she had been brought to accept him in spite of everything—brought to kneel down like a horse under training for the arena." Even before the marriage takes place, Gwendolen's image has to be adjusted: she begins to feel "as if she had consented to mount a chariot where another held the reins" and where "the horses in the chariot she had mounted were going at full speed." On the wedding day, her image coalesces with Grandcourt's vision: "The cord which united her with this lover and which she had hitherto held by the hand was now being flung over her neck." After that, the image belongs to Grandcourt, who notes how "she answered to the rein," while Gwendolen endures "submission to a yoke drawn on her by an action she was ashamed of." In that last exercise of Grandcourt's will, the ensuring that Gwendolen accompany him in the boat, he acts out of his perfect satisfaction "that he held his wife with bit and bridle."

Although necessarily reductive of the full richness of *Daniel Deronda,* the preceding sketch of the mirror and riding sequences, which function to establish the dramatic development of Gwendolen's crisis, does suggest the importance of the language of metaphor in the organization of the novel. Even more central to the novel's theme is the strand of legendary allusion which permeates the diction to support the parallel in story and motive which George Eliot continually draws between the Jewish figures and the characters from English society. By creating a relationship even closer than that of parallel situation and interacting plot, George Eliot seeks to establish the world of *Daniel Deronda* as one world, its figures all actors in the same fundamental human drama, all joined in a common destiny. As she herself says, it is only "fellowship with human travail, both near and afar," that will keep man from "scanning any deep experience lightly." This fellowship with human travail—this link between the "near" Davilows and the Cohens "afar"—is surely what lies behind her insistence that "everything in the book" is "related to everything else there."

The legend which joins these characters into a single world is after all, as Deronda says, "a very ancient story, that of the lost sheep"—and a story of complex motive and infinite ramification, for it speaks not only of the sheep lost in the wilderness but also of the squandered birthright, the exile in a foreign land, and the exultant return home. Recognition of how variously the story may be told helps in the achievement of the "fellowship with human travail." Whether it is Deronda's likeness to the "youthful heroes going to seek the hidden tokens of their birth and its inheritance of tasks," or Mordecai's resemblance to the Ancient Mariner "on the lookout for the man who must hear" the tale of his dark voyage, or the story of Grandcourt as "a new kind of Jason" caught "between two fiery women" which naturally arouses Deronda's sympathies for "the Hagars and Ishmaels" disinherited and sent into the desert, the language of the novel keeps reminding us that all of the characters are indeed re-enacting the "very ancient story" of the cast-off and the exiled. No wonder, then, that when Deronda returns to London with full knowledge of his name and in full possession of that "precious chest" which is the token of his family and racial heritage, George Eliot describes him as in a "classical, romantic, world-historic position . . . bringing as it were from its hiding place his hereditary armour." Gwendolen, in the climactic stages of her own journey in search of these "hidden tokens" is possessed by a hatred so intense that it can only be described as issuing in "something like the hidden rites of vengeance with which the persecuted have made a dark vent for their rage." "The persecuted" and their "rites of vengeance" link through language the inner turmoil of the English girl to other legends of loss and of "great recognitions" as of "the offspring of Agamemnon," that archetypal prelude to vengeance and the letting loose of the Furies. Gwendolen Harleth's story, then, is equally as resonant with the authority of racial experience as is Deronda's outward quest for visible tokens of identity.

As Deronda moves to reveal the just discovered "hereditary armour," George Eliot reluctantly acknowledges that "it has to be admitted that . . . he wore . . . the summer costume of his contemporaries." This rueful admission points toward a major difficulty: how to convey through these "summer costumes" of the 1860's, through the furnishings of a Victorian world, that "great deal of unmapped country within us which [has] to be taken into account" if the novel is to be a fresh embodiment of those old legends. For George Eliot knows that however she moves her nineteenth century protagonists—from London to Genoa, or simply from Park Lane to Brompton—their real journey is the descent into the self, the dark groping through the "unmapped country within." Her problem is to find an adequate form through which the stages of this journey can be marked so that the Victorian summer costume can be seen as armour indeed. E.S. Gombrich has pointed out that "even the greatest artist—and he more than others—needs an idiom to work in. Only tradition, such as he finds it, can provide him with the raw material of imagery which he needs to represent an event or a 'fragment of nature.'" This need for an idiom and its dependency on the tradition available to the artist at a given moment of time is as real for the writer as it is for the visual artist of whom Gom-

brich speaks. Twentieth century psychologists have given twentieth century novelists their own vocabulary by which to describe the descent into the self. George Eliot uses the idiom available to her, the idiom of melodrama.

Discussions of *Daniel Deronda* tend to overlook how often the story erupts into such melodramatic episode as the attempted suicide and rescue of Mirah, the recognition scene between Mordecai and Deronda at Blackfriars Bridge, the curse laid on the Grandcourt diamonds, and the panel which slides back to reveal the dead face and the fleeing figure. Yet each such episode is directly pointed toward the unfolding of the inner adventures of the characters. In the meeting of Mordecai and Deronda at Blackfriars Bridge, George Eliot makes this abundantly clear. The episode is not, in terms of the novel's dramatic movement, particularly successful. But in its very failure, the novelist's intention is laid bare. The scene is set in a glory of sunset light. Deronda, enfolded in an Inverness cape, drifts down the Thames out of that western sky to be greeted by Mordecai as "the prefigured friend [who] had come from the golden background, and had signalled to him." He tells Deronda, "I expected you to come down the river. I have been waiting for you these five years." For Mordecai, the Bridge is "a meeting place for the spiritual messengers" and Deronda, coming out of the sunset sky, comes as Mordecai's "new life—my new self." He comes as that other man, constructed by Mordecai's imagination from the exile of his own mind. Deronda's sympathetic response issues from a nature "too large, too ready to conceive regions beyond his own experience, to rest at once in the easy explanation, 'madness.'" He is capable of recognizing the possibility that in Mordecai there may be "that preternatural guide seen in the universal legend, who suddenly drops his mean disguise and stands a manifest Power." The relation of the episode to the legendary quest needs no comment. What should also be clear is that George Eliot is telling us quite explicitly here that she has used the melodramatic props of the cloaked figure in the sunset and the raised white hand of greeting to express the regions beyond those of practical daylight experience, regions that belong to "the unmapped country within."

Melodrama functions in *Daniel Deronda* not only as a means of giving outward shape to inner drama but also as a way of evoking horror and dread, essential responses to the necessary terror of the descent into the self, the only avenue to the hiding place of the name and the heritage. George Eliot makes explicit the initial connection between fear and the sense of exile in her analysis of another of these moments, one in the finely conceived and richly used sequence of episodes which concern "the picture of an upturned dead face, from which an obscure figure seemed to be fleeing with outstretched arms." The locked panel in the Offendene drawing room inexplicably springs open to reveal the picture at the climax of Gwendolen's success with her home charades. She has been showing herself off as Shakespeare's Hermione but is startled by the incident out of her role into a primitive display of terror. The narrator explains Gwendolen's excessive response by describing it as:

> that liability of hers to fits of spiritual dread, though this fountain of awe within her had not found its way into connection with the religion taught her or with any human relations. She was ashamed and frightened, as at what might happen again, in remembering her tremor on suddenly feeling herself alone, when, for example, she was walking without companionship and there came some

rapid change in the light. Solitude in any wide scene impressed her with an undefined feeling of immeasurable existence aloof from her, in the midst of which she was helplessly incapable of asserting herself. The little astronomy taught her at school used sometimes to set her imagination at work in a way that made her tremble: but always when some one joined her she recovered her indifference to the vastness in which she seemed an exile: she found again her usual world in which her will was of some avail. . . .

The explicit naming of Gwendolen's state as that of "exile" and the recurrence of the astronomical image makes the passage a counterpart of the earlier definition of the home in the universe which is the inheritance of all who are rooted in a native land. This tremor of fear which comes with a knowledge of the self lost in an uncharted immensity is interwoven through the novel with the sense of alienation, the urgency of the quest. Mirah's "terror of the world," which drives her into the attempted Thames suicide, springs from the same source as the terrible fear which drives the Princess Halm-Eberstein to summon her son to Genoa. Even though Deronda's receptivity to enlarged horizons is set in deliberate contrast to Gwendolen's terror of a widened vista, he is by no means without fear: "It was the habit of his mind to connect dread with unknown parentage." In each case dramatized into melodramatic episode, this fear both creates the action (as in Mirah's suicide attempt) and the response to the action (as in Gwendolen's terror of the dead face and the fleeing figure). The dual function suggests the underlying paradox George Eliot explores in her full depiction of Gwendolen's journey where the negative emotion of fear becomes the positive—and only—means of achieving the necessary courage. Fear can paralyze but it can also release. Thus, the novel's evocation of terrors through melodramatic episode enables the novelist to define the emotional fabric of the experience of alienation and to dramatize the inner activity by which the exile learns the terms on which some new relationship between self and world can be established.

As Grandcourt's courtship of Gwendolen proceeds, George Eliot builds up a rich texture of fears for the young girl. In part, the terror is a terror of self; more accurately, a terror at the failure of knowledge in the face of a newly released self. Just after Gwendolen uses her riding whip to evade once more Grandcourt's proposal, George Eliot tells us that Gwendolen herself does not know what—once the proposal is actually made—her response will be.

> This subjection to a possible self, a self not to be absolutely predicted about, caused her some astonishment and terror: her favorite key of life—doing as she liked—seemed to fail her, and she could not foresee what at a given moment she might like to do.

The fears mounts as the pressures on that unknown self become more complex: the interview with Lydia Glasher, Grandcourt's mistress and mother of his children; Grandcourt's return as her suitor unaffected by the reversal of her family fortunes. With the renewal of the courtship, Gwendolen is strangely poised between triumph and terror; she exults in the renewal of the power of choice and is terror-stricken by the problem of the use of that power.

> Here came the terror. Quick, quick, like pictures in a book beaten open with a sense of hurry, came

back vividly, yet in fragments, all that she had gone through in relation to Grandcourt. . . .

This terror of self and the world, released by the beginnings of her new knowledge of both, can neither be controlled nor used. It can only be repressed, shoved underneath, made to merge back into the darkness of self and world from which it has sprung. From this moment until the moment three months later, when Grandcourt brings his bride in her carriage through the park gates of Ryelands, Gwendolen's whole energy seems to be an energy of repression which reaches its climax on her wedding day when the "mingling of dimly understood facts with vague but deep impressions, and with images half real, half fantastic, [which] had been disturbing her during the weeks of her engagement" is "surmounted and thrust down with a sort of exulting defiance." Yet everything that has been thrust down, mounts to the surface to add its note to the hysterical shrieks with which Gwendolen greets her husband after the message which accompanies Lydia Glasher's restoration of the Grandcourt diamonds has spread its venom: a poison of remembrance.

A subject in "her husband's empire of fear," Gwendolen is momentarily held captive by the fear that paralyzes. Yet at the same time the fear of herself—ignored not conquered during the feverish activities of engagement and marriage—burgeons in the inner darkness. Not until that terror is recognized and, finally, objectified will Gwendolen be released into an understanding of her true heritage. At first she cannot distinguish between her growing fear of the cold force of her husband's will and the equally potent terror of her self's response. She describes the very vagueness of her dread to Deronda: " 'I am frightened at everything. I am frightened at myself. When my blood is fired I can do daring things—take any leap; but that makes me frightened at myself.' " His advice, to make use of this fear, to employ this sensibility " 'as if it were a faculty, like vision' " defines a means of restoration through the reawakened will. By suggesting that Gwendolen direct her fears toward " 'the idea of increasing that remorse which is so bitter to you,' " Deronda does sound rather a prig. Yet the nightmare of her fear spreads to him in terms that violently couple his past rescue of Mirah with her future failure to save Grandcourt: "It was as if he saw her drowning while his limbs were bound." And his advice rings, not in the words of the conventional preacher who exhorts the better self to triumph over the worse, but rather with a full sense of the terrible energy of being: let the evil itself bring to birth the good.

The swift ending of Gwendolen's story concentrates on the manner in which her fear is made to function for her release. The contrasting account of Daniel Deronda's mother, who wills herself to a rejection of her fears and a subsequent return to her chosen exile, expands and intensifies the novel's exploration of the inherent dangers of the terror misunderstood and misused. As Jew, the Princess has rejected her Judaism so that she may be free " 'from the pelting contempt that pursues Jewish separateness' "; as artist, she has rejected her son, so that she may " 'live out the life that was in [her], and not . . . be hampered with other lives.' " The same energy of will makes possible the ultimate resignation of her life as the great singer Alcharisi when she is poised at the very height of her career: " 'I made believe that I preferred being the wife of a Russian noble to being the greatest lyric actress of Europe; I made believe—I acted that part. It was because I felt my greatness sinking away from me. . . .' " The Princess Halm-Eberstein is truly a "princess in exile" in contrast to Gwendolen's childish day-dream of dispossessed royalty. A terrible figure of loss, Deronda's mother is filled with "a great horror" which in itself motivates her summons to her son and her bitter acknowledgement that, instead of mastering the circumstances of alienation by her self-willed rejection of name and family and race, she has made herself forever an exile.

> " . . . it is as if all the life I have chosen to live, all thoughts, all will, forsook me and left me alone in spots of memory, and I can't get away. . . . My childhood—my girlhood—the day of my marriage—the day of my father's death—there seems to be nothing since. Then a great horror comes over me: what do I know of life or death? and what my father called 'right' may be a power that is laying hold of me. . . . Often when I am at ease it all fades away; my whole self comes quite back; but I know it will sink away again, and the other will come—the poor, solitary forsaken remains of self, that can resist nothing. It was my nature to resist, and say, 'I have a right to resist.' Well, I say so still when I have any strength in me. . . . [But] it is beginning to make ghosts upon the daylight."

This passage, closely linked to the analysis of Gwendolen's "fits of spiritual dread," also explores the conditions of self-knowledge and contrasts the certainties of a "life well rooted in some spot of native land" with the blankness of a life cut off from kinship. The "spots of memory," with its echo of Wordsworthian "spots of time," are an ironic reminder of a pastoral unity of being which the Princess herself utterly rejects. For her, the self which in its terror resurrects the family concept of "right" is only an ill and fragmented self. Yet the whole novel points precisely toward that self as the only even potentially valid one. The Princess should, as Deronda points out to Gwendolen, have made full use of the resurrection through terror. Even the partial use she has made of it, the summoning of her son, has had its positive value for it has provided the son with the necessary "native land."

Even while the Princess is making this confession, Gwendolen is undergoing her ultimate crisis of fear as she sails with Grandcourt under the blue Mediterranean sky. Through the very melodrama of this climactic episode, George Eliot magnificently manifests her full control over the immensely varied materials from which she has wrought the account of Gwendolen's perilous journey. The description of "the model couple in high life" at home on the "elegant toy" served by a "picturesque crew" as they sail "southward . . . where one may float between blue and blue in an open-eyed dream that the world has done with sorrow," completes the image of exile. Grandcourt's satisfaction in this excursion, which "gave their life on a small scale a royal representation and publicity" is matched by Gwendolen's knowledge that she is separated from the world by the whole sea, isolated "on the tiny plank-island of a yacht," and fully aware of her own helplessness, her inability to assert herself. Her fancy no longer creates for herself the role of princess-in-exile, however royal the progress in Grandcourt's vision. Gwendolen acknowledges the outer adventure as an ironic metaphor:

> "It came over me that when I was a child I used to fancy sailing away into a world where people were not forced to live with anyone they did not like. . . . And now, I thought, just the opposite had come to me. I had slept into a boat, and my life was a sailing and sailing away—gliding on and no

help—always into solitude with *him,* away from deliverance."

But for George Eliot fully to express the meaning of this journey requires something other than the conventional technique of making the outer action an image of the inner experience. Somehow the terrors of that inner experience must be objectified into outer reality for the reader to see, even as he has earlier seen—in an unforgettable image—Mrs. Grandcourt magnificently decked in the family diamonds while "the words of the bad dream crawled about the diamonds still." The carefully constructed, superbly paced action which climaxes in Grandcourt's drowning is the novelist's solution to the problem: a lurid and complex objectification of Gwendolen's nightmare life which does also, and necessarily, work beautifully as story.

The simple events are these: Grandcourt takes Gwendolen out sailing in a small boat from the Genoa port. As he puts about, a sudden gust of wind fills the sail; Grandcourt goes overboard. Gwendolen hesitates to throw out to him the life rope. Grandcourt drowns. In Gwendolen's description of the events to Deronda, the only description the reader is given, the entire action becomes simply the final vision of her long sustained desire for Grandcourt's death. Yet Grandcourt is *really* dead. The inner activity has not only taken shape as outer action, but there has been a coalescence of the reality that is the story with the reality that is Gwendolen's inner life. Here, if no place else in the novel, George Eliot has successfully used the idiom available to her, the idiom of melodrama, as the form through which to present an event which must be made to express both the inner and outer lives of her characters, both the events and the meaning of the events.

As the last manifestation of the haunting image of the dead face and the fleeing figure, the episode turns what has been Gothic decoration, used to display the heroine's fine sensibilities, into an anguish of lived terror. More important, it makes the final revelation of the function of that terror. When the Davilows first arrived at Offendene and the youngest of the "inconvenient sisters" unlocked the panel to reveal the picture, Gwendolen's whole energy was concentrated on locking the picture up again and retreating to her room to look at herself in the mirror. The decisiveness of this action prefigures the same febrile energy of repression with which she will thrust down, out of sight and thought, the rising fears which assail her during Grandcourt's wooing and the early days of her marriage. In Genoa, Gwendolen's energies are directed not toward repression but confession; and although she cannot explain the sequence of events, she can identify the image: " 'I don't know how it was—he was turning the sail—there was a gust—he was struck—I know nothing—I only know that I saw my wish outside me'." In its own way, this identification of the painting marks the completion of Gwendolen's journey: it demonstrates a self-knowledge based on understanding and acceptance of desire and its consequences.

After this coalescence of inner and outer life, image and action, into the climactic dramatic moment, the novelist makes of the final chapters a new sounding of the old themes to sketch the outlines of her heroine's new identity. Gwendolen's early flight to the continent is matched by her journey home from Genoa. Just as Daniel Deronda parts from his mother knowing that "he beheld the world changed for him by the certitude of ties . . . as if under cover of the night he had joined the wrong band of wanderers, and found with the rise of morning that the tents of his kindred were grouped far off," so Gwendolen goes from Genoa with her mother and uncle on a journey that is no longer a "sailing out" but a return home, a new vision of

> Offendene and Pennicote under their cooler lights. She saw the grey shoulders of the downs, the cattle-specked fields, the shadowy plantations with rutted lanes where the barked timber lay for a wayside seat, the neatly-clipped hedges on the road from the parsonage to Offendene, the avenue where she was gradually discerned from the windows, the hall-door opening, and her mother or one of the troublesome sisters coming out to meet her. All that brief experience of a quiet home which had once seemed a dulness to be fled from, now came back to her as a restful escape, a station where she found the breath of morning and the unreproaching voice of birds, after following a lure through a long Satanic masquerade, which she had entered on with an intoxicated belief in its disguises, and had seen the end of in shrieking fear lest she herself had become one of the evil spirits who were dropping their human mummery and hissing around her with serpent tongues.

In that final sentence, the Gothic vocabulary of the inner journey is matched by the Wordsworthian poetry of the harmonious domesticated universe to suggest that the new knowledge, born of Gwendolen's terror, is a knowledge of the necessity of "some spot of a native land." In Genoa, on the railway journey, at Park Lane, what remains of Gwendolen's energy is directed toward the re-establishment of the earlier home. Yet Deronda's final lesson to her demonstrates the vanity of that desire and the necessity of continuing the inner journey.

The revelation Deronda makes of his own past heritage and future plans testifies to the impossibility of the sentimental return and reminds the reader that the function of the homestead is simply as a defining focus for "the future widening of knowledge." Gwendolen's horizon is no longer "that of the genteel romance." Instead, she is now "for the first time feeling the pressure of a vast mysterious movement, for the first time being dislodged from her supremacy in her own world, and getting a sense that her horizon was but a dipping onward of an existence with which her own was revolving." Solitary, certainly, and aware of "immeasurable existence aloof from her," Gwendolen can no longer be indifferent "to the vastness." Her kindly parting from Deronda, releasing him from responsibility, shows a new—if feeble—action of will in "asserting herself" in the immensity. And Gwendolen's story stops with all the "naked prose" of a morning world. After a day and half a night of hysterical shrieking, "after all, she slept." And when she wakens, she knows: "'I shall live. I shall be better'." Stripped of the support of "parks, carriages, a title," in full awareness that she is not "so exceptional a person" who must be accorded what is pleasant to her, and knowing that "the new existence" which "seemed inseparable from Deronda" must be her own responsibility, Gwendolen Harleth has learned "how to be" in exile. Like her creator, she has passed through a crisis of alienation so that she may possess her self. More than a quarter of a century after her confession to Sara Hennell, George Eliot made the terrors of her own crisis the subject of her final novel. In November of 1876, two months after the completed publication of that novel, George Eliot writes again to Sara Hennell:

> It is remarkable to me that I have entirely lost my *personal* melancholy. I often, of course, have mel-

ancholy thoughts about the destinies of my fellow-creatures, but I am never in that *mood* of sadness which used to be my frequent visitant even in the midst of external happiness. And this, notwithstanding a very vivid sense that life is declining and death close at hand.

By her own full acceptance of all the "naked prose," George Eliot has created the "poetry" of *Daniel Deronda.*

(pp. 433-55)

Jean Sudrann, "'Daniel Deronda' and the Landscape of Exile," in ELH, Vol. 37, No. 3, September, 1970, pp. 433-55.

XAVIER PONS (essay date 1987)

[*Judging* Daniel Deronda *"a great novel—but only in parts," Pons investigates the reasons for the work's ultimate artistic failure.*]

Since it is George Eliot's last novel, ***Daniel Deronda*** might be expected to be the crowning achievement of a distinguished novelist's career, the product of a considerable talent brought to full maturity after nearly two decades of novelistic practice. And yet, although it is a work of no mean power, ***Daniel Deronda*** falls somewhat short of its author's ambition. As most critics have noted, it is an interesting and even challenging novel, but a flawed one too. The flaw, it has been repeatedly pointed out, lies in the Jewish part of the story, which is for the most part wooden and even clumsy, artistically unconvincing, and which does not coalesce very well with the English part. Although George Eliot "meant everything in the novel to be related to everything else", as she wrote to her friend Barbara Bodichon [see letter dated 2 October 1876], apparently she could not make it happen. Even though some critics have argued the case for the essential unity of the novel, the majority remain unconvinced, emphasizing that the parallels between the English and the Jewish parts of the novel are abstract, if not downright contrived and artificial, and that in any case the Jewish part fails to engage the reader's imagination. As Jerome Thale put it, "The Deronda story provides almost a catalogue of the vices of the nineteenth century novel" [see excerpt dated 1959].

This critical consensus highlights the problem, but does not really solve it. Granted that Mirah and Mordecai are unconvincing characters whose language is stilted and stereotyped, that Daniel's missionary zeal is just "vaporous idealism"— granted, in short, that the Jewish half of ***Daniel Deronda*** falls clearly below the other half—the question remains: why is it so? What is it that prevented George Eliot from giving the full measure of her talent in this particular book?

One might incriminate the relatively unfamiliar nature of the material from which she was drawing, and also the unusually didactic purpose of the novel, as she described it to Harriet Beecher Stowe: "precisely because I felt that the usual attitude of Christians towards Jews is—I hardly know whether to say more impious or more stupid when viewed in the light of their professed principles, I therefore felt urged to treat Jews with such sympathy and understanding as my nature and knowledge could attain to" [see letter dated 29 October 1876].

This knowledge was of astonishing range and depth. . . . George Eliot had done her homework well: her grasp of the

Jewish material was entirely adequate, and if she made a few minor errors in her depiction of Jewish customs this can hardly explain why that part of the novel remains artistically unsatisfactory.

Other factors need to be taken into account in trying to explain the shortcomings of *Daniel Deronda,* and not least the fact that these shortcomings are not to be found exclusively in the Jewish half of the novel. To chart our path in the course of this inquiry there is probably no better guide than George Eliot herself, who had a very lucid perception of the requirements of the novelist's craft and consequently a very keen critical mind.

Some twenty years before completing *Daniel Deronda,* she wrote a bitingly sarcastic review of various feminine novels, entitled **"Silly Novels by Lady Novelists"**, in which she mercilessly exposed all that was wrong with most feminine novels published in those days. It would seem, however, that when she was working on *Daniel Deronda* she forgot her own recommendations and fell into some of the traps which she had denounced with such verve in her review.

Among the failings which characterized the weaker sort of feminine novel, George Eliot mentions the use of stock characters, a plot based on convenient coincidences, the absence of a credible social background—replaced by a profusion of clergymen, peers and other members of the upper classes—and, lastly, absurd intellectual ambitions expressed in pretentious diction.

She points out that the heroine of the "mind and millinery" novels, as she dubs them, is almost invariably a beautiful and accomplished young woman, usually an heiress, although it may happen that "rank and wealth are the only things in which she is deficient; but she infallibly gets into high society" and "she has the triumph of refusing many matches and securing the best". To a certain extent, the cap fits Gwendolen Harleth, even though it would be unfair to put her on the same level as the insipid heroines stigmatized by George Eliot. The critical consensus is that the portrait of Gwendolen is one of the novelist's major achievements in *Daniel Deronda*—that it is done with a subtlety and an insight second to none, even to exploring dark areas of the psyche that were ignored or unrecognized by Victorian fiction—that unmapped country within us which would have to be taken into account in an explanation of our gusts and storms". Indeed, George Eliot's *tour de force* is all the more remarkable since the outline of Gwendolen's character, her social background and her brilliance might have caused a lesser novelist to stumble into clichés. Gwendolen's portrait is certainly a very successful one, but it is not hard to see how easily she might have degenerated into the typical heroine of a "mind and millinery" novel.

Among the stock characters in this type of novel, George Eliot mentions "a vicious baronet, an amiable duke, and an irresistible younger son of a marquis as lovers in the foreground". How could this list fail to bring to mind, in a reader of *Daniel Deronda,* the vicious Grandcourt, the amiable Sir Hugo and the irresistible Daniel himself? As for the clergyman and the poet listed next by Eliot, they obviously suggest—*mutatis mutandis*—Gascoigne and Hans Meyrick. Here again, George Eliot's characters are perilously close to the caricature drawn by the novelist herself. That they are more skilfully drawn than their corresponding stereotypes

does not mean that their dramatic function is not to some extent stereotyped.

Silly novels by lady novelists, George Eliot wrote in her review, "rarely introduce us into any other than very lofty and fashionable society". And of course much of *Daniel Deronda* describes precisely that kind of society—a departure from the middle-class background which characterizes George Eliot's other novels. . . . In other novelists, George Eliot associated this upper-class background with a lack of interest in social realities, with a sort of social escapism: their works gave little or no idea of the real world in which men and women have other than futile social activities. In these novels, she said, "The men play a very subordinate part by (the) side (of the heroine). You are consoled now and then by a hint that they have affairs, which keeps you in mind that the working day business of the world is somehow being carried on, but ostensibly the final cause of their existence is that they may accompany the heroine on her 'starring' expedition through life. They see her at a ball and are dazzled; at a flower show and they are fascinated; on a riding excursion, and they are witched by her noble horsemanship".

Here again, this is reminiscent of Gwendolen riding with the hounds, or winning the archery competition, or dancing at Topping Abbey under the admiring eyes of the male guests, who do not appear to be very much preoccupied with the "working day business of the world". True, there are in *Daniel Deronda* a few characters, like the Cohens, who have to work to make a living—but this only makes them objectionable to George Eliot's refined hero, to whom they would seem to be like some entomological species, exotic but somewhat repulsive, of which he had heard but which he had never seen before at such close quarters. As for Gwendolen, she would certainly be appalled by the Cohens if she knew them—to such an extent is gentility the order of the day in *Daniel Deronda,* and in spite of the fact that the hero turns out to be a Jew: Daniel is no shopkeeper or pawnbroker's son—he is a member of the aristocracy of his people. . . . It is all very well for lower-class characters such as the Cohens to care openly about money, but a Grandcourt or a Sir Hugo appears to be above such vulgar considerations. Among people of genteel background, one simply has an income—which may be lost because of the carelessness or dishonesty of one's money managers, but the processes of gain or loss are not very closely examined. This of course reflects the self-righteous attitude of the characters themselves, exemplified in Gwendolen's disdainful attitude: "She had no notion how her maternal grandfather got the fortune inherited by his two daughters; but he had been a West Indian—which seemed to exclude further question". But one might wish the novelist had been a little less allusive in her account of the character's economic preoccupations. As it is, and except for a few insights into those processes, such as the Arrowpoints' economic tropism towards the aristocracy, the characters' financial situation appears to result from some game of roulette rather than from understandable processes: there are winners and losers, but it is all rather random, depending on luck and circumstances rather than work and foresight. As for the more genteel characters, Sir Hugo or Lord Brackenshaw for instance, they seem to have excluded economic concerns from their field of vision. Their wealth is taken for granted, and no explanation is considered necessary beyond the fact that they are landowners—it is as if there had been no economic development since the days of the eighteenth century squire.

Daniel Deronda, then, is not entirely devoid of a social and an economic background, and does raise quite a few social problems such as that of the condition of women in Victorian society, the economic function of marriage, etc. However, as Joan Bennett noted [see Additional Bibliography], this background is "imperfectly focussed", and the underpinning of the novel is moral rather than social or economic.

In this sense *Daniel Deronda* is not unlike that dreaded variety of "silly novels by lady novelists" which George Eliot called the "*oracular* species" and which she defined as "novels intended to expound the writer's religious, philosophical or moral theories". The difference, naturally, is that George Eliot was no intellectual lightweight, and that her opinions on ethical problems are well worth listening to, even though she has a tendency to belabour her points. All the same, *Daniel Deronda* is undeniably something of a didactic novel, and it sometimes threatens to collapse under the sheer weight of ethical meaning it is made to carry. This is especially apparent in the Jewish part of the book, with its artificiality and heavy-handed idealism. George Eliot might have known that to treat such an exotic subject as the Jews was fraught with danger for an English novelist, no matter how truly learned. In her review she had mercilessly criticized those lady novelists who presumed to write about other cultures—usually those of ancient times—than their own. She was especially critical of a novel entitled *Adonijah* which dealt with the Jewish dispersion. She made fun of the closing words of its preface, which announced that "To those who feel interested in the dispersed of Israel and Judea, these pages may afford, perhaps, information on an important subject, as well as amusement". She found this an exceedingly pretentious claim in view of the "heavy imbecility" of the book. Of course *Daniel Deronda* is a very well informed, and therefore instructive novel as far as Jewish questions are concerned, but there is something pedantic about it, especially in the references to Jewish philosophers and poets. It sounds like name-dropping at times—incontrovertible proof that George Eliot was well-read for those who might be impertinent enough to doubt it. But for the average reader, who may not necessarily have a biographical dictionary at his elbow, the going proves rather heavy.

The typical feminine novel, George Eliot argued, has a very trite and improbable plot, based on felicitous coincidences. "The vicious baronet", she said, "is sure to be killed in a duel". One cannot help observing that Grandcourt dies at a very convenient moment too, though not in a duel. His death illustrates the fact that most of the plot of *Daniel Deronda* is in fact based on a series of coincidences, which after a while stretches the reader's credulity a little too much. No one is likely to take offense at the first coincidence of them all—the meeting, at Leubronn, between Gwendolen and a relative of the man she is running away from. This is, after all, the stuff of everyday life. But from then on coincidences are piled thick on top of one another. Thus Gwendolen goes to the pawnshop very early in the morning—before breakfast time—when it is unlikely that anyone will be about to observe her. True, since she has to pass in front of Deronda's hotel—what a coincidence!—there is a small chance that she might be seen by him, but it is really a minuscule one. But of course Deronda stood there watching at precisely the right moment. Furthermore, he must have guessed her purpose at once. . . . Deronda's most salient characteristic is indeed his knack for being always at the right place at the right moment: he was rowing down the Thames when Mirah was about to

drown herself, and yet again when Mordecai was waiting for him on the bridge, and his whole destiny, as a man and as a Jew, depends on these chance encounters. Speaking of Mordecai, how could one help being astonished that Deronda should unerringly find the abode of Mirah's brother almost at first try? All he had to go on was the name Ezra Cohen. After some rambling in London's East End, he came upon a shop with 'Ezra Cohen' written over the window. George Eliot here pauses to observe that "There might be a hundred Ezra Cohens lettered above shop windows"—but Daniel had naturally found the right one. Still another twist is added to the coincidence by the fact that the Ezra who owns the shop is *not* a relative of Mirah's, but nonetheless Mirah's brother does live under his roof! It was a very long shot on the part of Deronda but his accuracy, no doubt because it is of a moral order, is far greater than that of Gwendolen with bow and arrow. Then Mordecai, for no intelligible reason, assures him that he must be Jewish—and lo! he turns out to be Jewish indeed. He also happens to be in Genoa at the very moment when Gwendolen and her husband were there—a moment when she was going to be in very great need of his comforting presence. One could mention a good many other coincidences, such as Deronda's first meeting with Kalonymos in Frankfurt, before he knew of his true parentage, or again Grandcourt's evil genius for anticipating his wife's plans in order to frustrate them. All this would seem to imply, in the characters, the "miraculous foreknowledge" which Grandcourt briefly suspects in his wife, so puzzled he is to meet Deronda in Genoa. This train of coincidental events is a little too pat to be convincing.

George Eliot blamed lady novelists, especially those of the "oracular" type, for using an inflated language which generally resulted in bathos. Here again *Daniel Deronda* shows that she was not always above this kind of error, and that at times she was apt to debase high seriousness into mere portentousness. A number of contemporary reviewers objected in particular to her pompous use of mottoes at the head of each chapter. Thus A. V. Dicey asserted that "any one who doubts that the long-winded reflections taken from the commonplace-book or the unpublished works of George Eliot afford examples of the way in which a statement that has meaning may be overloaded by the conceits in which it is expressed, should examine carefully the motto to the first chapter, and consider honestly whether a rather commonplace sentiment is not beaten out into an inordinate number of words". A similar ponderosity is to be found in the novel itself at times, particularly in the utterances of Mordecai, as when he is vaticinating on "a new unfolding of life whereof the seed is more perfect, more charged with the elements that are pregnant with diviner form". Even Jewish critics were dismayed by Mordecai's "empty verbiage", to use A. A. Naman's words [in *The Jew in the Victorian Novel* (1980)]. Nor is George Eliot in her function as narrator exempt from this defect, as witness the passage when she says that Gwendolen's dependence on Deronda tended to rouse in him "the enthusiasm of self-martyring pity rather than of personal love, and his less constrained tenderness flowed with the fuller stream towards an indwelling image in all things unlike Gwendolen". All this to say that though he felt compassion for Gwendolen, it was Mirah he loved.

Another example of the portentous as a substitute for high seriousness is to be found in Klesmer's lofty pronouncements on the important social function of creative artists: "We help to rule the nations and make the age as much as any other public men. We count ourselves on level benches with legislators", he declares. However, there is little or nothing in the novel to support this conception, since neither Klesmer himself nor the painter Hans Meyrick help in any sense to rule the nation. In fact, as Deirdre David observed [in *Fictions of Resolution in Three Victorian Novels* (1981)], Klesmer "is 'ruled' by ruling class patronage, and he inhabits an age 'made' by commerce". In spite of their impressiveness, his words must therefore remain empty.

George Eliot was also in the tradition of the "silly novels" when she abandoned herself to an excess of sentimentality—a failing all the more surprising when one considers that **Daniel Deronda** was sometimes censured for its dry philosophizing and its abstraction. Nonetheless, the novel—which some critics took to be in fact a romance—includes characters who are much too sweet to ring true and whose mignardise soon becomes cloying. The foremost of these is of course Mirah, this gentle, self-effacing and unselfish girl who is often likened to a fawn or to some other cuddly, appealing animals, and who is George Eliot's Bambi. There is also an excess of affected sweetness and pathos in the Meyrick household, and even in the Cohen household, whose description owes more to the influence of Dickens than to first-hand observation of reality.

Does all this mean that **Daniel Deronda** can be dismissed as another silly novel by a lady novelist? This, obviously, would be throwing the baby out with the bath water.

Daniel Deronda is a great novel—but only in parts. As I have tried to show, somewhat irreverently, it suffers from a good many flaws which seriously mar what might have been a splendid book. Yet this is not to say that the novel is a rough diamond, that with more care and labour George Eliot might not have eliminated the tares from the wheat. On the contrary, it appears that the more labour she expended on her last novel, the more visible the flaws grew. This is the price she had to pay for being innovative and daring. **Daniel Deronda** is a novelistic experiment which went wrong. Had she simply written *Gwendolen Harleth,* as F. R. Leavis called the part of the book he liked [see excerpt dated 1945-46], she would certainly have received greater critical acclaim—and perhaps produced a better novel. However, she had the merit to attempt something new, which is perhaps unusual in a successful writer's last novel, and she did not succeed in gaining adequate artistic—as opposed to intellectual—control of her material. She made a conscious effort to familiarize herself with Jewish customs and beliefs, and from an intellectual point of view she succeeded. Nevertheless Jews and Judaism never became, and could not become, as familiar to her imagination as middle-class provincial life. She felt for the Jews with her brain, not with her guts. They did not provide her with any genuine artistic sustenance, so that her very intellectual seriousness made her fall into some of the very traps she had denounced as characteristic of silly novels by lady novelists.

The various flaws I have pointed out might all be gathered under the single heading "artificiality". There are elements of artificiality in the characters, in the plot, in the themes and in the language. Except in parts, the novel gives little sense of being an organic whole with a necessity of its own. There is too much in it that is, and feels, merely contrived, and therefore uninspired.

It is said that too far east is west: by trying to achieve more it would seem that George Eliot actually achieved less, from an artistic point of view, than in her previous novels. But the attempt was a brave one, and her failure a fairly honourable one. At any rate, and unlike the attempts of a number of lady novelists, it was in no way inspired by a conception of authorship as "a vocation which is understood to turn foolish thinking into funds", as she put it ironically.

(pp. 101-08)

Xavier Pons, " 'Daniel Deronda': A 'Silly Novel by a Lady Novelist'?" in Cahiers Victoriens & Edouardiens, *No. 26, October, 1987, pp. 101-09.*

ADDITIONAL BIBLIOGRAPHY

Alley, Henry. "New Year's at the Abbey: Point of View in the Pivotal Chapters of *Daniel Deronda.*" *The Journal of Narrative Technique* 9, No. 3 (Fall 1979): 147-59.
    Examines the shift in theme, focus, and technique that occurs in chapters 35 and 36, the novel's climactic center.

Amalric, Jean-Claude. "The Opening of *Daniel Deronda.*" *Cahiers Victoriens & Edouardiens,* No. 26 (October 1987): 111-19.
    Studies the novel's first paragraphs for important clues to Eliot's narrative system, characters, and themes.

Baker, William. "George Eliot's Readings in Nineteenth-Century Jewish Historians: A Note on the Background of *Daniel Deronda.*" *Victorian Studies* XV, No. 4 (June 1972): 463-73.
    Traces the influence of Eliot's readings in Hebrew history on her depiction of the Jewish characters and Zionist themes in *Daniel Deronda.*

Bates, Richard. "Gwendolen Harleth—Character Creation or Character Analysis?" *The Cambridge Quarterly* 16, No. 1 (1987): 30-52.
    Argues that Eliot's portrayal of Gwendolen is severely flawed by her tendency to overanalyze the character.

Beebe, Maurice. " 'Visions Are Creators': The Unity of *Daniel Deronda.*" *Boston University Studies in English* I, No. 3 (Autumn 1955): 166-77.
    Identifies parallel ideological issues in the novel's two narratives as a unifying structure.

Beeton, D. R. "George Eliot's Greatest and Poorest Novel: An Appraisal of *Daniel Deronda.*" *English Studies in Africa* 9, No. 1 (March 1966): 8-27.
    Calls the novel "a prime example of how power and ineptness can exist side by side in an indisputably great mind." Beeton claims that the narrative dealing with Deronda represents Eliot at her worst, while Gwendolen's story showcases her greatest powers.

Belkin, Roslyn. "What George Eliot Knew: Women and Power in *Daniel Deronda.*" *International Journal of Women's Studies* 4, No. 5 (November-December 1981): 472-83.
    Explores power and gender issues in Eliot's writing, focusing on her treatment of Gwendolen Harleth.

Bennett, Joan. *"Daniel Deronda."* In her *George Eliot: Her Mind and Her Art,* pp. 181-96. Cambridge: Cambridge University Press, 1962.
    Suggests that Eliot's overly intellectual approach to writing the novel resulted in structural flaws and the reader's occasional awareness of "a rift between the thinker and the artist."

Caron, James. "The Rhetoric of Magic in *Daniel Deronda*." *Studies in the Novel* 15, No. 1 (Spring 1983): 1-9.
  Examines the elements of legend, romance, and folklore incorporated in the novel.

Carpenter, Mary Wilson. "The Apocalypse of the Old Testament: *Daniel Deronda* and the Interpretation of Interpretation." *PMLA* 99, No. 1 (January 1984): 56-71.
  Advocates a reading of the novel with reference to Eliot's study of theology and the biblical book of Daniel.

Carroll, David R. "*Mansfield Park, Daniel Deronda,* and Ordination." *Modern Philology* LXII, No. 3 (February 1965): 217-26.
  Draws parallels between the worldviews set forth in Jane Austen's 1814 novel and *Daniel Deronda.*

————, ed. *George Eliot: The Critical Heritage.* The Critical Heritage Series, edited by B. C. Southam. New York: Barnes and Noble, 1971, 511 p.
  A collection of excerpted contemporary commentary on Eliot's works. Carroll provides an overview of Eliot criticism in his introduction.

Chase, Cynthia. "The Decomposition of the Elephants: Double Reading *Daniel Deronda.*" *PMLA* 93, No. 2 (March 1978): 215-27.
  Identifies "causality" as a central issue in the novel, using Hans Meyrick's letter to Deronda as a key to a deconstructive reading of the text.

Cirillo, Albert R. "Salvation in *Daniel Deronda:* The Fortunate Overthrow of Gwendolen Harleth." In *Literary Monographs,* Vol. I, edited by Eric Rothstein and Thomas K. Dunseath, pp. 201-43. Madison: University of Wisconsin Press, 1967.
  A study of the novel's themes. Cirillo's remarks on the importance of music in *Daniel Deronda* have been praised for their insight.

Dale, Peter. "Symbolic Representation and the Means of Revolution in *Daniel Deronda.*" *The Victorian Newsletter,* No. 59 (Spring 1981): 25-30.
  Considers Eliot's approach to symbolism in philosophical terms.

Fast, Robin Riley. "Getting to the Ends of *Daniel Deronda.*" *The Journal of Narrative Technique* 7, No. 3 (Fall 1977): 200-17.
  Examines how the differing styles of the novel's two narratives create opposite expectations on the part of the reader.

Fisch, Harold. "*Daniel Deronda* or *Gwendolen Harleth?*" *Nineteenth Century Fiction* 19, No. 4 (March 1965): 345-56.
  Defends the novel against the criticism raised by F. R. Leavis (see excerpt dated 1945-46) and others that the two storylines are disjointed, citing Eliot's own claims that the work was conceived as a unified entity.

Fleishman, Avrom. " 'Daniel Charisi': An Assessment of *Daniel Deronda* in the History of Ideas." In his *Fiction and the Ways of Knowing: Essays on British Novels,* pp. 86-109. Austin: University of Texas Press, 1978.
  An examination of Eliot's blend of social criticism and visionary utopianism in the narrative centered on Deronda and Jewish issues.

Forster, Jean-Paul. "Beyond Reticence: The Power Politics Relationship in George Eliot." *Etudes de lettres,* No. 1 (January-March 1983): 13-29.
  Assesses Eliot's narrative technique through an examination of her use of dialogue and related authorial commentary.

Fricke, Douglas C. "Art and Artists in *Daniel Deronda.*" *Studies in the Novel* 5, No. 2 (Summer 1973): 220-28.
  A study of Eliot's definition of true art and her representation of the role of the artist in society.

Gottfried, Leon. "Structure and Genre in *Daniel Deronda.*" In *The English Novel in the Nineteenth Century: Essays on the Literary Mediation of Human Values,* edited by George Goodin, pp. 164-75. Illinois Studies in Language and Literature, no. 63. Urbana: University of Illinois Press, 1972.
  Attributes the novel's incohesiveness to the fact that one of Eliot's plots is "pre-eminently novelistic" while the other is "radically romantic."

Haight, Gordon S. *George Eliot: A Biography.* New York: Oxford University Press, 1968, 616 p.
  The definitive biography.

Handley, Graham, ed. *Daniel Deronda,* by George Eliot. The Clarendon Edition of the Novels of George Eliot, edited by Gordon S. Haight. Oxford: Clarendon Press, 1984, 755 p.
  An authoritative edition of the novel that includes an introduction detailing the circumstances of the work's composition, manuscript and publication information, and textual variants.

Hardy, Barbara, ed. Introduction to *Daniel Deronda,* by George Eliot, edited by Barbara Hardy, pp. 7-30. Harmondsworth, Middlesex: Penguin Books, 1967.
  An acclaimed introduction to the novel. Hardy describes *Daniel Deronda* as "experimental," exploring the complex interrelationships of its structure, characterizations, psychology, and themes.

Heller, Deborah. "George Eliot's Jewish Feminist." *Atlantis* 8, No. 2 (Spring 1983): 37-43.
  Focuses on Eliot's depiction of Princess Halm-Eberstein.

Hester, Erwin. "George Eliot's Use of Historical Events in *Daniel Deronda.*" *English Language Notes* IV, No. 2 (December 1966): 115-18.
  Demonstrates the way in which Eliot uses references to historical events as symbolic images in the novel.

Johnstone, Peggy Ruth Fitzhugh. "The Pattern of the Myth of Narcissus in *Daniel Deronda.*" *University of Hartford* 19, Nos. 2-3 (1987): 45-60.
  Applies the myth of Narcissus and psychoanalytic theories regarding narcissism to Eliot's characterization of Gwendolen Harleth.

Kearney, John P. "Time and Beauty in *Daniel Deronda:* 'Was she beautiful or not beautiful?' " *Nineteenth-Century Fiction* 26, No. 3 (December 1971): 286-306.
  Considers Eliot's complex time structures in the novel important as both a narrative technique and a thematic element.

Kelly, Mary Ann. "*Daniel Deronda* and Carlyle's Clothes Philosophy." *Journal of English and Germanic Philology* 86, No. 4 (October 1987): 515-30.
  Traces the influence of Thomas Carlyle's *Sartor Resartus* (1836) on the novel.

Knoepflmacher, U. C. *Religious Humanism and the Victorian Novel: George Eliot, Walter Pater, and Samuel Butler.* Princeton: Princeton University Press, 1965, 315 p.
  Analyzes the works of the three novelists as expressions of the Victorian attempt to reconcile religious longings with a belief in the evolutionary theories of Charles Darwin and T. H. Huxley. Knoepflmacher considers *Daniel Deronda* with regard to its concerns with theology, Hebraism, and nationalism.

Kubitschek, Missy Dehn. "Eliot as Activist: Marriage and Politics in *Daniel Deronda.*" *CLA Journal* XXVIII, No. 2 (December 1984): 176-89.
  Examines Eliot's themes of power and identity in both interpersonal and political contexts.

Lerner, Laurence. "The Education of Gwendolen Harleth." *The Critical Quarterly* 7, No. 4 (Winter 1965): 355-64.

Chronicles the heroine's conversion from egocentricity to a transcendence of self.

Levenson, Shirley Frank. "The Use of Music in *Daniel Deronda*." *Nineteenth-Century Fiction* 24, No. 3 (December 1969): 317-34.
    A study of the role music plays in the novel.

Levine, Herbert J. "The Marriage of Allegory and Realism in *Daniel Deronda*." *Genre (University of Oklahoma)* XV, No. 4 (Winter 1982): 421-45.
    Discusses Eliot's combination of realistic and allegorical modes in the novel.

Lund, Mary Graham. "George Eliot and the Jewish Question." *Discourse* XIII, No. 3 (Summer 1970): 390-97.
    Examines Eliot's works, including her correspondence and journal, for insight into her sympathetic beliefs concerning Judaism.

McCarron, Robert. "Evil and Eliot's Religion of Humanity: Grandcourt in *Daniel Deronda*." *Ariel* 11, No. 1 (January 1980): 71-88.
    A study of Henleigh Grandcourt exploring Eliot's ambivalent views regarding humanity's potential for evil.

McCobb, E. A. "The Morality of Musical Genius: Schopenhauerian Views in *Daniel Deronda*." *Forum for Modern Language Studies* XIX, No. 4 (October 1983): 321-30.
    Draws parallels between the role Eliot attributes to music in *Deronda* and Arthur Schopenhauer's writings on the subject.

——. "*Daniel Deronda* as Will and Representation: George Eliot and Schopenhauer." *The Modern Language Review* 80, Part 3 (July 1985): 533-49.
    Relates Eliot's readings of the German philosopher to the evident shift in outlook between her earlier novels and *Daniel Deronda*.

Mintz, Alan. "*Daniel Deronda* and the Messianic Calling." In his *George Eliot and the Novel of Vocation*, pp. 151-65. Cambridge: Harvard University Press, 1978.
    Identifies the contrast between "good ambition," seen in Deronda's calling, and "bad ambition," typified by Gwendolen's social aspirations, as a central concern of the novel.

Modder, Montagu Frank. "The End of an Era." In his *The Jew in the Literature of England: To the End of the Nineteenth Century*, pp. 267-309. 1937. Reprint. New York: Meridian Books, 1960.
    Includes a comparison of Eliot's Jewish characters with those of her contemporary, the novelist Benjamin Disraeli.

Moldstad, David. "The Dantean Purgatorial Metaphor in *Daniel Deronda*." *Papers on Language and Literature* 19, No. 2 (Spring 1983): 183-98.
    Stresses the importance of recognizing Eliot's use of Dantean allusions to a complete understanding of the novel. Moldstad views Gwendolen's married life as an extended metaphor for purgatory.

Newton, K. M. "*Daniel Deronda* and Circumcision." *Essays in Criticism* XXXI, No. 4 (October 1981): 313-27.
    A discussion of Eliot's apparent failure to account for Deronda's probable circumcision in her otherwise realistic and detailed narrative. Newton concludes that Eliot addresses the issue indirectly and offers supporting evidence.

——. "*Daniel Deronda*." In his *George Eliot: Romantic Humanist, a Study of the Philosophic Structure of Her Novels*, pp. 168-200. Totowa, N. J.: Harper & Row, Barnes & Noble Books, 1981.
    A detailed analysis of Romantic concerns in the novel.

Novy, Marianne. "*Daniel Deronda* and George Eliot's Female (Re)Vision of Shakespeare." *Studies in English Literature 1500-1900* 28, No. 4 (Autumn 1988): 671-92.
    Relates Eliot's readings of Shakespeare to gender issues in the novel, particularly as they apply to Deronda and Gwendolen Harleth.

Nystul, Nancy. "*Daniel Deronda*: A Family Romance." *Enclitic* VII, No. 1 (Spring 1983): 45-53.
    A reading of the novel focused on its symbolic elements. Nystul sets out to "chart the twin trajectories of the hero/heroine, and demonstrate the ways in which Gwendolen's struggles for selfhood as well as Deronda's embracing Zionism figure the insistence of an archaic organization in the patterns of later mental and social life."

Paris, Bernard J. *Experiments in Life: George Eliot's Quest for Values*. Detroit: Wayne State University Press, 1965, 281 p.
    Contends that for Eliot the creative process was a conscious attempt to discover a system of moral values that would enoble human life in a godless universe. Paris examines the evolution of Eliot's moral beliefs in the first half of his book. In the second half, which includes chapters dealing with *Daniel Deronda*, he analyzes the moral development of her central characters.

Pell, Nancy. "The Fathers' Daughters in *Daniel Deronda*." *Nineteenth-Century Fiction* 36, No. 4 (March 1982): 424-51.
    Views the novel as "an exploration of the difficulties of the daughter in achieving social and cultural legitimacy within an unresponsive, if not actually menacing, patriarchal society."

Poole, Adrian. " 'Hidden Affinities' in *Daniel Deronda*." *Essays in Criticism* XXXIII, No. 4 (October 1983): 294-311.
    A study of Eliot's rich use of allusion in *Daniel Deronda*.

Preyer, Robert. "Beyond the Liberal Imagination: Vision and Unreality in *Daniel Deronda*." *Victorian Studies* IV, No. 1 (September 1960): 33-54.
    A consideration of the way in which Eliot's themes of personal ethics and salvation contributed to her ineffective narrative form.

Putzell-Korab, Sara M. "The Role of the Prophet: The Rationality of Daniel Deronda's Idealist Mission." *Nineteenth-Century Fiction* 37, No. 2 (September 1982): 170-87.
    Examines the rational idealism that informs the Jewish half of the novel, particularly in the characterizations of Deronda and Mordecai.

——. "The Importance of Being Gwendolen: Contexts for George Eliot's *Daniel Deronda*." *Studies in the Novel* 19, No. 1 (Spring 1987): 31-45.
    Discusses the conventions of the melodramatic sensation novel as Eliot adapted them to the history of Gwendolen Harleth and cites sources that may have inspired her characterization.

Pykett, Lyn. "Typology and the End(s) of History in *Daniel Deronda*." *Literature and History* 9, No. 1 (Spring 1983): 62-73.
    A consideration of the ways in which the novel moves beyond realism and history toward symbolism and mythology.

Raider, Ruth. " 'The Flash of Fervor': *Daniel Deronda*." In *Reading the Victorian Novel: Detail into Form*, edited by Ian Gregor, pp. 253-73. New York: Harper & Row, Barnes & Noble Books, 1980.
    A mixed assessment of the novel praising Eliot's aims and philosophy, but ultimately judging the work a failure.

Raina, Badri. "*Daniel Deronda*: A View of Grandcourt." *Studies in the Novel* 17, No. 4 (Winter 1985): 371-82.
    Studies Henleigh Grandcourt's dramatic and thematic functions in the novel.

Roberts, Neil. "*Daniel Deronda*." In his *George Eliot: Her Beliefs and Her Art*, pp. 183-219. Pittsburgh: University of Pittsburgh Press, 1975.
    Identifies the novel as a "striking illustration of the differing relations between George Eliot's beliefs and her art."

Rosenberg, Edgar. "The Jew as Hero and Isaiah Reborn: Eliot." In his *From Shylock to Svengali: Jewish Stereotypes in English Fiction,* pp. 161-84. Stanford: Stanford University Press, 1960.

Deems Eliot's Jewish characters in *Daniel Deronda* "talking puppets" and faults her overly didactic presentation of the Zionist theme.

Saint Victor, Carol de. "Acting and Action: Sexual Distinctions in *Daniel Deronda.*" *Cahiers Victoriens & Edouardiens,* No. 26 (October 1987): 77-88.

Examines gender roles in the "dramatic configuration of performer and observer" as an important element in *Daniel Deronda.*

Shalvi, Alice, ed. *Daniel Deronda: A Centenary Symposium.* Jerusalem, Israel: Jerusalem Academic Press, 1976, 156 p.

A collection of essays including Shmuel Werses's "The Jewish Reception of *Daniel Deronda,*" H. M. Daleski's "Owning and Disowning: The Unity of *Daniel Deronda,*" Laurence Lerner's "*Daniel Deronda:* George Eliot's Struggle with Realism," and Baruch Hochman's "*Daniel Deronda:* The Zionist Plot and the Problematic of George Eliot's Art."

Shuttleworth, Sally A. "The Language of Science and Psychology in George Eliot's *Daniel Deronda.*" In *Victorian Science and Victorian Values: Literary Perspectives,* edited by James Paradis and Thomas Postlewait, pp. 269-98. New Brunswick, N. J.: Rutgers University Press, 1985.

Contends that "contemporary scientific ideas and theories of method provided a basis not only for the psychological theory, but also for the social and moral vision, and narrative methodology of *Daniel Deronda.*"

Still, Judith. "Rousseau in *Daniel Deronda.*" *Revue de littérature comparée* LVI, No. 1 (January-March 1982): 62-77.

Studies a subject examined by both Jean-Jacques Rousseau and Eliot—the psychological processes of offering and receiving counsel.

Swann, Brian. "Eyes in the Mirror: Imagery and Symbolism in *Daniel Deronda.*" *Nineteenth-Century Fiction* 23, No. 4 (March 1969): 434-45.

Examines the symbolic imagery of eyes and mirrors in the novel.

————. "George Eliot and the Play: Symbol and Metaphor of the Drama in *Daniel Deronda.*" *Dalhousie Review* 52, No. 2 (Summer 1972): 191-202.

A study of theatrical metaphor and symbolism in *Daniel Deronda.*

Thale, Jerome. "River Imagery in *Daniel Deronda.*" *Nineteenth-Century Fiction* VIII, No. 4 (March 1954): 300-06.

Contrasts the images of "drifting" with the ideal of purposeful action in the novel.

Wiesenfarth, Joseph. "The Medea in *Daniel Deronda.*" *Die Neuren Sprachen* 22, No. 2 (February 1973): 103-08.

Applies the Medea myth to Eliot's history of Lydia Glasher, Henleigh Grandcourt, and Gwendolen Harleth.

————. "Exile and Kingdom from *The Spanish Gypsy* to *Daniel Deronda.*" In his *George Eliot's Mythmaking,* pp. 210-30. Heidelberg: Carl Winter Universitatsverlag, 1977.

Examines Eliot's use of mythic elements in her predominantly realistic novel.

Witemeyer, Hugh. *George Eliot and the Visual Arts.* New Haven: Yale University Press, 1979, 238 p.

Relates Eliot's pictorial descriptions of characters in *Daniel Deronda* to the novel's themes.

Wolfe, Thomas P. "The Inward Vocation: An Essay on George Eliot's *Daniel Deronda.*" In *Literary Monographs.* Vol. 8, *Mid-Nineteenth Century Writers: Eliot, De Quincey, Emerson,* edited by Eric Rothstein and Joseph Anthony Wittreich, Jr., pp. 1-46. Madison: University of Wisconsin Press, 1976.

A laudatory examination of the novel focusing on Eliot's themes of love, power, egotism, and altruism.

Zim, Rivkah. "Awakened Perceptions in *Daniel Deronda.*" *Essays in Criticism* XXXVI, No. 3 (July 1986): 210-34.

A reading of the novel centering on the character and role of Mirah.

Zimmerman, Bonnie. "George Eliot and Feminism: The Case of *Daniel Deronda.*" In *Nineteenth-Century Women Writers of the English-Speaking World,* edited by Rhoda B. Nathan, pp. 231-37. Contributions in Women's Studies, no. 69. New York: Greenwood Press, 1986.

Suggests that Eliot expresses her personal ambivalence toward feminism in the novel.

(Conte) Carlo Gozzi

1720-1806

Italian dramatist, poet, and autobiographer.

An eighteenth-century Italian aristocrat devoted to upholding the political and cultural traditions of his native Venice, Gozzi is best known for his ten *fiabe teatrali,* or dramatic fables. Written in an attempt to revitalize the commedia dell'arte, a form of improvised comedy established in Italy in the sixteenth century that had stagnated in Gozzi's day, the *fiabe* regaled contemporary audiences with fantastic plots, spectacular stage effects, and the comic talents of extempore actors. While primarily meant to entertain, these plays, the most famous of which are *L'amore delle tre melarance (The Love of the Three Oranges), L'augellino bel verde (The Green Bird),* and *Turandot,* were also satiric and didactic, attacking both the dramatic reformer Carlo Goldoni, who had attempted to replace the commedia dell'arte with realistic comedies of character, and Enlightenment culture, which Gozzi believed was corrupting Venetian society. Although many critics have questioned Gozzi's abilities as a dramatist, they still value his *fiabe* for their assimilation of different dramatic styles, their influence on later writers, and the insights they provide into eighteenth-century Venetian thought.

The sixth of eleven children, Gozzi was born into a family from the Italian nobility whose fortune was steadily declining. He began his education at home under private tutors and then entered a small academy run by two priests. When his family's financial situation barred further schooling, he continued his education on his own, concentrating on literature and writing. Gozzi's brothers and sisters shared his interest in literature and together they staged plays in a small theater on the family estate for their parents, neighbors, and passersby; Gozzi and his older brother, Gasparo, who himself became a well-known man of letters, also competed at improvising verses. In 1738, Gasparo married a woman who subsequently attempted to organize the family finances, but she only aggravated their monetary problems. Home life grew intolerable to Gozzi, and, in 1741, he went to Dalmatia, where he served for three years in a Venetian cavalry unit stationed there. Upon his return home in 1744, he found that his family's financial situation had deteriorated even further. Soon after his father's death the following year, Gozzi initiated legal proceedings to have the remainder of the estate divided between him and his brothers, a process that took Venetian law courts nearly eighteen years.

In 1747, Gozzi allied himself with the Granelleschi, a literary group that sought to preserve Tuscan literature and language from modern influences, primarily Enlightenment philosophy, which glorified reason and realism and which, through its emphasis on bourgeois values, threatened to destroy the aristocratic way of life. The recent dramatic successes of Goldoni, who accepted these new ideas, incensed Gozzi and the Granelleschi. Goldoni wished to substitute written comedies of character focusing on the middle classes for the flexible scenario of the commedia dell'arte, which utilized a cast of stock actors, known as masks, who improvised dialogue and incidental action. Although once creative and spontaneous, by Gozzi's day the commedia dell'arte had degenerated into

a formula of hackneyed routines and inane buffoonery. Considering Goldoni's realism vulgar and believing that the commedia dell'arte merely needed renovating rather than replacing, Gozzi attacked Goldoni's theatrical innovations and exalted the glories of the commedia dell'arte in several works, including *Il teatro comico all'osteria del Pellegrino,* a dramatic parody that was published in 1750, and, more importantly, the poem *La Tartana degl'influssi per l'anno bisestile, 1756,* which was published in 1757. The latter work inspired a literary quarrel between Gozzi and Goldoni, who began viciously attacking one another until Goldoni simply pointed to the popularity of his plays as justification of their literary merit. Gozzi, in turn, argued that crowds were no proof of artistic worth. Accepting a challenge to write a comedy from Pietro Chiari, another successful Venetian dramatist who sided with Goldoni, he wrote his first *fiaba, The Love of the Three Oranges,* to prove that he could draw equal crowds by adapting what he termed "an old wives' fairy-story" to the stage. Assisted by the talents of the Sacchi company, one of the best commedia dell'arte acting troupes in Venice, Gozzi produced the play in 1761. A resounding success, *The Love of the Three Oranges* ended the rivalry between Gozzi and his two antagonists, both of whom soon retired from Venice. During the next four years, Gozzi wrote nine more *fiabe,* almost all of which were greeted enthusiastically by audiences. Recognizing that the novelty of his *fiabe* would be short-lived and that the Venetian public would soon tire of them, Gozzi produced his last *fiaba, Zeim, re dei genii,* in 1765. Afterwards, he turned to writing conventional comedies, most of which were based upon plays by Spanish dramatists, including Pedro Calderón de la Barca and Miguel de Cervantes.

The last important episode in Gozzi's life began in 1771, when a new actress, Teodora Ricci, joined the Sacchi company. Gozzi became the mentor and possibly the lover of Ricci, coaching her in the leading roles of plays he wrote expressly for her. Four years later, Ricci had an affair with Pietro Antonio Gratarol, a Paduan nobleman who was a secretary to the Venetian Senate and who had a promising political career ahead of him. In 1776, Gozzi wrote *Le droghe d'amore,* a play parodying his rival in the character of Don Adonis. Produced in 1777, the play caused a scandal, ruining Gratarol's career in politics. He fled Venice in disgrace to Sweden, where he published *Narrazione apologetica,* which defended his conduct in the affair and vehemently attacked Gozzi and others who were responsible for making it public. Circulated in Venice in 1779, this persuasive work cast a negative light upon Gozzi, who, in 1780, hurriedly attempted to reply to Gratarol's comments with *Memorie inutili della vita di Carlo Gozzi scritte da lui medesimo e pubblicate per umiltà (The Memoirs of Count Carlo Gozzi);* however, Venetian censors would not let him publish the work, wishing to quell a scandal that had already embarrassed other important Venetians besides those directly involved.

Gozzi continued writing plays until 1782, when Antonio Sacchi, the leader of the acting troupe bearing his name, left the stage. However, Gozzi continued writing, updating and expanding his memoirs, which he was at liberty to publish after the Venetian Republic collapsed in 1797. Arrogant in tone and exaggerating Gozzi's own literary importance, the *Memoirs* are nevertheless valued by scholars not only for the insights they provide into Venetian thought and manners, but also for what they reveal about Gozzi's conservatism, his conflicts with Goldoni and Gratarol, and his ideas on the function of art. Gozzi spent his last years in comparative solitude. He died in 1806.

Gozzi wrote thirty-two plays in his lifetime, but of these, only his ten *fiabe* are considered significant contributions to Italian literature. Based upon popular fairy tales and fables derived primarily from Giambattista Basile's *Pentamerone* and from *The Arabian Nights,* the *fiabe* were a new dramatic genre; part verse and part prose, the plays blended fantasy, comedy, tragedy, and satire. Although written in the spirit of the commedia dell'arte and intended to restore the tradition to its former glory, only the first *fiaba, The Love of the Three Oranges,* features the conventional method of allowing the masks—among them, Truffaldino, Pantalone, Tartaglia, and Brighella—to improvise most of the dialogue and incidental action. Nothing of this play remains today except an outline of the plot, which heavily satirizes Goldoni and Chiari, the latter of whom Gozzi depicts as a sorceress who uses insipid verse to cast a fatal spell of boredom and melancholy upon the main character, Prince Tartaglia, a representation of the Venetian public. The spell is eventually broken when the prince is made to laugh at the commedia dell'arte antics of Truffaldino. Because of the controversy that inspired their creation, such satire pervades Gozzi's plays. However, in his later *fiabe,* Gozzi moved away from the buffoonery and burlesque of *The Love of the Three Oranges,* hoping to create

plays that were more artistically polished. While he continued to use dazzling stage effects, colorful costumes, and such supernatural elements as sorcerers, fairies, and talking statues, he reduced the roles of the masks by scripting most of their dialogue—especially if it was satiric in intent—and wrote out all of the principal parts in Tuscan verse. His highly esteemed ninth *fiaba, The Green Bird,* presents the most explicit example of Gozzi's penchant for satire. Recounting the misery caused by the selfishness of two children whose values are nurtured on tracts by the French *philosophes,* champions of the Enlightenment who preached that reason should govern human conduct, the play ends happily when the two children renounce their beliefs and adopt a doctrine of self-sacrifice and kindness to others. While many critics consider *The Green Bird* Gozzi's greatest work because it best reveals his ability to coordinate the various elements of the *fiaba,* other commentators favor his fourth play, *Turandot.* Written in response to criticism that the *fiabe* relied too heavily on mechanical devices to create such magical stage effects as the transformation of a man into a deer in *Il re cervo (The King Stag),* *Turandot* contains almost no supernatural elements, although its setting is both grotesque and exotic. Critics praise this play for its focus on the human aspects of the drama, particularly the development of the title character from a cruel Princess, who poses three riddles to her suitors under the penalty of death if they answer incorrectly, to the loving wife of Prince Calaf, the first to successfully solve her puzzles.

Despite the tremendous success of the *fiabe,* they failed to revive the commedia dell'arte, in part because, as some critics point out, the tide of realism in Italian literature was too overwhelming for Gozzi's fanciful plays to be popular for long. In early nineteenth-century Germany, however, Gozzi's *fiabe* were lauded by the Romantics, who esteemed their imaginative and grotesque qualities. His works influenced several German writers, notably Johann Wolfgang von Goethe, E. T. A. Hoffmann, and Friedrich Schiller, the latter of whom translated *Turandot* into German. These writers viewed Gozzi as an early Romantic poet possessed of genius and intent on championing an artistic ideal. The British critic John Addington Symonds attempted to dispel this notion with his translation of *The Memoirs of Count Carlo Gozzi* in 1890; in his introduction to this work, Symonds insisted that Gozzi was not a literary innovator but rather a keen-witted aristocrat whose primary object was to oppose dramatic and social reforms that defied the traditions of the Venetian Republic.

While acknowledging their historical significance and influence on the German Romantic movement, some nineteenth- and early twentieth-century English-language commentators pointed out that the *fiabe* were incomplete when read and required too much of the reader's imagination to fill in the parts that were once realized by the extempore actors and stage machinery. In addition, critics censured the *fiabe* for their lack of artistic refinement. They found Gozzi's style coarse, his language diffuse and often grammatically incorrect; furthermore, they noted that he frequently lapsed into the Venetian idiom while trying to write in Tuscan. Many of these critics also argued that the plays' diverse elements of tragedy, comedy, fantasy, and satire did not blend harmoniously. This objection was also voiced by the renowned Italian critic Francesco de Sanctis, who attributed Gozzi's failure to achieve greater fame to his contradictory aims; as de Sanctis remarked, Gozzi "wanted to support the masks; he wanted to parody his opponents; he wanted to restore Pulci and Ariosto and the fantastic; he wanted to Tuscanize and at the same time to be modern and popular: he wanted in fact to take his place as a modern while reconstructing the old." However, some recent commentators, recognizing the complexity of the *fiabe,* have praised their combination of these contrasting elements. As David Nicholson writes of *Turandot,* "We have the final impression of incongruous, contradictory elements maintaining an uneasy union in a brilliantly entertaining but unnatural whole. . . . The virtuosity of the playwright's art astonishes us." In addition, the *fiabe* are known for furnishing libretti to such distinguished composers as Giacomo Puccini and Sergei Prokofiev and for influencing the works of several other composers, including Richard Wagner and Wolfgang Amadeus Mozart. Thus, although Gozzi failed to obtain his goal of reestablishing the commedia dell'arte in Italy, he is still remembered for his minor but significant contribution to the progress of world literature.

PRINCIPAL WORKS

Il teatro comico all'osteria del Pellegrino (drama) 1750

La Tartana degl'influssi per l'anno bisestile, 1756 (poetry) 1757

*L'amore delle tre melarance (drama) 1761
  [*A Reflective Analysis of the Fable Entitled "The Love of the Three Oranges": A Dramatic Representation Divided into Three Acts* published in *The Memoirs of Count Carlo Gozzi,* 1890]

*Il corvo (drama) 1761

*La donna serpente (drama) 1762

*Il re cervo (drama) 1762
  [*The King Stag* published in *The Classic Theatre,* 1958]

*Turandot (drama) 1762
  [*Turandot, Princess of China,* 1913; also published as *Turandot* in *The Genius of the Italian Theatre,* 1964]

*La Zobeide (drama) 1763

*Il mostro turchino (drama) 1764
  [*The Blue Monster: A Fairy Tale in Five Acts,* 1951]

*I pitocchi fortunati (drama) 1764

*L'augellino bel verde (drama) 1765
  [*The Green Bird: A Commedia dell'Arte Play in Three Acts,* 1985]

*Zeim, re dei genii (drama) 1765

La marfisa bizzarra (poetry) 1772

Opere. 8 vols. (dramas and poetry) 1772-74

Le droghe d'amore (drama) 1777

Memorie inutili della vita di Carlo Gozzi scritte da lui medesimo e pubblicate per umiltà (autobiography) 1797
  [*The Memoirs of Count Carlo Gozzi,* 1890; also published as *Useless Memoirs of Carlo Gozzi* (abridged and revised edition), 1962]

Opere edite ed inedite. 14 vols. (dramas and poetry) 1801-03

Le fiabe di Carlo Gozzi. 2 vols. (dramas) 1884

*These works are known as Gozzi's *fiabe teatrali.*

CARLO GOZZI (essay date 1797)

[*In this excerpt from his* Memoirs (*1797*), *Gozzi offers his opinion of his dramatic rivals, Carlo Goldoni and Pietro Chiari, and then describes his purposes in writing the* fiabe.]

As regards literature, in the middle of this century, and under the rising sun of Signor Bettinelli, we were condemned to behold a decided change for the worse. All that had been done to restore purity and simplicity, after the decadence of seventeenth-century taste, was swept away by a new and monstrous fit of fashion. The Granelleschi cried out in vain for sound principles and cultivated taste; contended in vain that, Italy being a nation which could boast a mother-language, with its literary usage, its vulgar usage, and its several dialects, reason bade us hold fast by the Della Cruscan vocabulary, and seek to enrich that, instead of disputing its authority. We cried to the winds, and were obliged to look on while the world was deluged with fanatical, obscure, bombastic lucubrations—laboured sophisms, rounded periods with nothing in them, the flimsy dreams of sick folk, sentiments inverted and distorted—and the whole of this farrago indited in a language mixed of all the vernacular dialects, with interlarded bits of the Greek tongue, but above all with so many French words and phrases that our own Italian dictionaries and grammars seemed to have become superfluous. (pp. 108-09)

This new fashion of unlicensed freedom and of sheer enthusiasm made rapid strides, because it was convenient and comfortable. Intellects, misled and muddled, lost the sense of what is good and bad in writing. They applauded the worst and the best without distinction. Little by little, commonplace and transparent stupidities on the one hand—stupidities sonorous and oracular upon the other, were adopted in the practice of literature. Pure, cultivated, judicious, and natural style took on the aspect of debilitated languor and despicable affectation.

The contagion spread so rapidly and so widely, that even men like Doctor Carlo Goldoni and the Abbé Pietro Chiari were universally hailed and eulogized as first-rate Italian authors. Their original and incomparable achievements were lauded to the skies. To them we owed a fit of fashion, which lasted some few lustres, and which helped to overthrow the principles of sound and chaste expression. (pp. 109-10)

A whirlwind of comedies, tragi-comedies, and tragedies, composts of imperfections, occupied the public stage; the one genius of inculture vying with the other in the quantity he could produce. A diarrhoea of dramatic works, romances, critical epistles, poems, cantatas, and apologies by both the Vandals poured from the press and deluged Venice. All the youth were stunned, distracted, and diverted from good sense by din and tumult. Only the Granelleschi kept themselves untainted by this Goldonio-Chiaristic epidemic. (p. 110)

I ought to render a candid account here of the impression made upon me by those two deluges of ink, Goldoni and Chiari. To begin with Goldoni. I recognised in him an abundance of comic motives, truth, and naturalness. Yet I detected a poverty and meanness of intrigue; nature copied from the fact, not imitated; virtues and vices ill-adjusted, vice too frequently triumphant; plebeian phrases of low double meaning, particularly in his Venetian plays; surcharged characters; scraps and tags of erudition, stolen Heaven knows where, and clumsily brought in to impose upon the crowd of ignoramusses. Finally, as a writer of Italian—except in the Venetian dialect, of which he showed himself a master—he seemed to me not unworthy to be placed among the dullest, basest, and least correct authors who have used our idiom. (pp. 111-12)

Proceeding next to Abbé Chiari. In him I found a brain inflamed, disordered, bold to rashness, and pedantic; plots dark as astrological predictions; leaps and jumps demanding seven-league boots; scenes isolated, disconnected from the action, foisted in for the display of philosophical sententious verbiage; some good theatrical surprises, some descriptions felicitous in their blunt *naiveté;* pernicious ethics; and, as for the writer, I found him one of the most turgid, most inflated, nay, the most turgid, the most inflated, of this century. (pp. 113-14)

Both Goldoni and Chiari professed themselves the champions of theatrical reform; and part of their programme was to cut the throat of the innocent *Commedia dell' Arte,* which had been so well supported in Venice by four principal and deservedly popular masks: Sacchi, Fiorilli, Zannoni, and Derbes. It seemed to me that I could not castigate the arrogance of these self-styled Menanders better than by taking our old friends Truffaldino, Tartaglia, Brighella, Pantalone, and Smeraldina under my protection. Accordingly, I opened fire with a dithyrambic poem, praising the extempore comedians in question, and comparing their gay farces favourably with the dull and heavy pieces of the reformers. Chiari and Goldoni replied to my attacks and those of my associates by challenging us to produce a comedy. Goldoni, in particular, called me a verbose wordmonger, and kept asserting that the enormous crowds which flocked together to enjoy his plays constituted a convincing proof of their essential merit. It is one thing, he said, to write subtle verbal criticisms, another thing to compose dramas which shall fill the public theatres with enthusiastic audiences. Spurred by this continual appeal to popularity and vogue, I uttered the deliberate opinion that crowded theatres proved nothing with regard to the goodness or the badness of the plays which people came to see; and I further staked my reputation on drawing more folk together than he could do with all his scenic tricks, by simply putting the old wives' fairy-story of the *Love of the Three Oranges* upon the boards.

Shouts of incredulous and mocking laughter, not unnaturally, greeted this Quixotic challenge. They stung my sense of honour, and made me gird up my loins for the perilous adventure. When I had composed the scheme of my strange drama, and had read it to the Granelleschi, I could see, by the laughter it excited, that there was stuff and bottom in the business. Yet my friends dissuaded me from producing such a piece of child's-play before the public; it would certainly be hissed, they said, and compromise the dignity of our Academy.

I replied that the whole public had to be attacked in front upon the theatre, in order to create a sensation, and to divert attention from our adversaries. I meant to give, and not to sell this play, which I hoped would vindicate the honour and revenge the insults of our Academy. Finally, I humbly submitted that men of culture and learning were not always profoundly acquainted with human nature and the foibles of their neighbours.

Well, I made a present of **L'Amore delle Tre Melarancie** to Sacchi's company of comic players, and the extravaganza was produced in the theatre of San Samuele at Venice during the Carnival of 1761. Its novelty and unexpectedness,—the surprise created by a fairy-tale adapted to the drama, seasoned with trenchant parodies of both Chiari's and Goldoni's plays, and not withal devoid of moral allegory—created such a sudden and noisy revolution of taste that these poets saw in it the sentence of their doom.

Who could have imagined that this twinkling spark of a child's fable on the stage should have outshone the admired and universally applauded illumination of two famous talents, condemning them to obscurity, while my own dramatised fairy-tales throve and enthralled the public for a period of many years? So wags the world! (pp. 128-30)

L'Amore delle Tre Melarancie made a good beginning. My adversaries were driven mad by the revolt it caused among play-goers, by its parodies and hidden meanings, which the newspapers industriously explained, describing many things which I had never put there. They attempted to hoot it down by clumsy abuse, affecting at the same time disgust and contempt for its literary triviality. Forgetting that it had been appreciated and enjoyed by people of good birth and culture, they called it a mere buffoonery to catch the vulgar. Its popularity they attributed to the co-operation of the four talented masks, whom they had sought to extirpate, and to the effect of the transformation scenes which it contained, ignoring the real spirit and intention of this comic sketch in a new style.

Laughing at their empty malice, I publicly maintained that art in the construction of a piece, well-managed conduct of its action, propriety of rhetoric and harmony of diction, were sufficient to invest a puerile fantastic motive, if taken seriously, with the illusion of reality, and to arrest the attention of the whole human race—excepting perhaps some thirty confirmed enemies, who would be sure, when my contention had been proved before their eyes and ears, to accuse a hundred thousand men of ignorance, and to renounce their sex rather than admit the truth.

This proposition was met with new gibes; and I found myself committed to make good my bold assertion. The fable of *Il Corvo,* extracted from a Neapolitan story-book, *Cunto delle cunte, trattenemiento pe le piccierelle,* and treated by me in the tone of lofty tragedy, wrought the miracle. I must add that I assigned some humorous passages to the four masks, whom I wished to keep upon the stage for the benefit of hypochondriacs, and in contempt of misunderstood and falsely applied rules from Aristotle.

The success of **Il Corvo** was complete. The public wept and laughed at my bidding. Multitudes flocked to hear this old wives' tale, as though it had been solemn history. The play had a long run; and the two poets were seriously damaged in their interests, while the newspapers applauded and extolled the allegory as a splendid example of fraternal affection.

I wished to strike while the iron was hot. Accordingly, my third fable, the **Rè Cervo,** appeared with similar results of popularity and sympathetic criticism. A thousand beauties were discovered, which I, who wrote it, had not seen. Folk regarded its allegory as a mirror for those monarchs who allow themselves to be blinded by their confidence in Ministers, and are in consequence transformed into the semblance of monsters. Meanwhile, my opponents persisted in ascribing the great success of these three pieces to stage decorations and the marvellous effect of magic metamorphoses, neglecting the writer's art and science, the charm of his verse, and his adroit employment of rhetoric, morality, and allegory. This impelled me to produce two more fables, **Turandotte** and **I Pitocchi Fortunati,** in which magic marvels were conspicuous by their absence, while the literary art and science remained the same. A like success clinched my argument, without, however, disarming my antagonists.

I had formed the habit of conversing with my family of players in our hours of leisure; and very racy did I find the recreation of their society. In a short space of time I learned to understand and see into the characters and talents of my soldiers, with insight so perfect that all the parts I wrote for them and fitted, so to speak, upon their mental frames, were represented on the stage as though they issued naturally from their hearts and tempers. This added hugely to the attraction of the spectacle. The gift of writing for particular actors, which does not seem to be possessed or put in use by every dramatist, is almost indispensable while dealing with the comic troupes of Italy. The moderate payments which are customary in our theatres prevent these people from engaging so large a number of actors and actresses as to be able to select the proper representatives of all the varied characters in nature. To the accident of my possessing this gift, and the ability with which I exercised it, must be ascribed a large part of my success. Goldoni alone devoted himself with patience to the study of the players who put his premeditated pieces on the boards; but I defy Goldoni and all the writers for our stage to compose, as I did, parts differing in character, containing jokes, witticisms, drolleries, moral satire, and discourses in soliloquy or dialogue, adapted to the native genius of my Truffaldini, Tartaglia, Brighella, Pantaloni, and Servette, without lapsing into languor and frigidity, and with the same result of reiterated applause.

Other playwrights, who attempted to put written words into the mouth of extempore actors, only made them unnatural; and obtained, as the reward of their endeavours, the abuse and hisses of the public at the third representation of their insipid pieces. It is possibly on this account that they revenged themselves by assuming comic airs of grave and serious criticism, treating our miracles of native fun and humour as contemptible buffoons, all Italy as drunken and besotted, myself as the bolsterer up of theatrical ineptitudes, and my prolusions in a new dramatic style as crumbling relics of the old *Commedia dell' Arte.* So far as the last accusation goes, everybody will allow that the Masks which I supported as a *tour de force* of art and for the recreation of the public who rejoiced in them, play the least part in my scenic compositions; my works, in fact, depend for their existence and survival on the sound morality and manly passion, which formed their real substratum, and which found expression on the lips of serious actors.

For the rest, the players whom I had taken under my wing looked up to me as their tutelary genius. Whenever I appeared, they broke into exclamations of delight, and let the whole world know that I was the propitious planet of their resurrection. They professed themselves indebted to me for benefits which could not be repaid, except by an eternal gratitude. (pp. 133-37)

It became a necessity, a sort of customary law dictated by my friendship, to present these actors every year or two with pieces from my pen. The ability with which they had interpreted my fancies deserved gratitude; and the sympathy of the Venetians, who had so warmly welcomed them, called for recognition. Accordingly, I added the **Donna Serpente,** the **Zobeide,** and the **Mostro Turchino** to those dramatic fables which I have already mentioned. (pp. 156-57)

The new *genre* which I had brought into fashion, and which,

by being confined to Sacchi's company, inflicted vast damage on their professional rivals, inspired other so-called poets with the wish to imitate me. They relied on splendid decorations, transformation scenes, and frigid buffooneries. They did not comprehend the allegorical meanings, nor the polite satire upon manners, nor the art of construction, nor the conduct of the plot, nor the real intrinsic force of the species I had handled. I say they did not comprehend the value of these things, because I do not want to say that they were deficient in power to command and use them. The result was that their pieces met with the condemnation which their contempt for me and for the public who appreciated me richly deserved.

You cannot fabricate a drama worthy to impress the public mind for any length of time by heaping up absurdities, marvels, scurrilities, prolixities, puerilities, insipidities, and nonsense. The neglect into which the imitations of my manner speedily fell proves this. Much the same may be said about those other species—romantic or domestic, intended to move tears or laughter—those cultured and realistic kinds of drama, as people called them, though they were generally devoid of culture and of realism, and were invariably as like each other as two peas, which occupied our stage for thirty years at least. All the good and bad that has been written and printed about my fables; the fact that they still hold the stage in Italy and other countries where they are translated in spite of their comparative antiquity; the stupid criticisms which are still being vented against them by starving journalists and envious bores, who join the cry and follow these blind leaders of the blind—criticisms only based upon the titles and arguments I chose to draw from old wives' tales and stories of the nursery—all this proves that there is real stuff in the fabulous, poetical, allegorical *genre* which I created. I say this without any presumptuous partiality for the children of my fancy; nor do I resent the attacks which have been made upon them, for I am humane enough to pity the hungry and the passion-blinded.

Goldoni, who was then at Paris, vainly striving to revive the Italian theatre in that metropolis, heard of the noise my fables were making in Italy, and abased himself so far as to send a fabulous composition of his own fabrication back to Venice. It was called *Il Genio buono e il Genio cattivo,* and appeared at the theatre of S. Giov. Grisostomo, enjoying a long run. The cause of its success lay in the fact that his piece displayed dramatic art, agreeable characters, moral reflection, and some philosophy. I conclude, therefore, that allegorical fables on the stage are not so wholly contemptible.

At the same time, just as there are differences between the different kinds of dogs, fishes, birds, snakes, and so forth, though they all belong to the species of dogs, fishes, &c., so are there notable differences between Goldoni's *Genio buono e cattivo* and my ten *Fiabe,* though all are grouped under the one species of dramatic fable. Goldoni, who has deserved renown for his domestic comedies, had not the gifts necessary for producing poetic fables of this kind; nor could I ever understand why my ridiculous censors cast the ephemeral success of his two *Genj* in my teeth, with the hope of mortifying a pride I did not feel.

The dramatic fable, if written to engage the interest of the public and to keep its hold upon the theatre, is more difficult than any other species. Unless it contains a grandeur which imposes, some impressive secret which enchants, novelty sufficient to arrest attention, eloquence to enthral, sententious maxims of philosophy, witty and attractive criticisms, dialogues prompted by the heart, and, above all, the great magic of seduction whereby impossibilities are made to seem real and evident to the mind and senses of the audience—unless it contains all these elements, I repeat, it will never produce a firm and distinctive impression, nor will it repay the pains and perseverance of our poor actors by its permanent pecuniary value. It may be that my fables possess none of these qualities. Yet the fact remains that they contrived to produce the effects I have described. (pp. 157-60)

> *Carlo Gozzi, in his* The Memoirs of Count Carlo Gozzi, *Vol. II, translated by John Addington Symonds, Scribner & Welford, 1890, 379 p.*

AUGUSTUS WILHELM SCHLEGEL (lecture date 1808)

[*Schlegel was a German critic, translator, and poet. With his younger brother, Friedrich, he founded the periodical* Das Athenäum (*1798-1800*), *which served as a manifesto for the German Romantic movement. He is perhaps best known for his translation of Shakespeare's works into German and for his* Über dramatische Kunst und Literatur (*1809-11;* A Course of Lectures on Dramatic Art and Literature). *In the following excerpt from one of these lectures, which were originally given in Vienna in the spring of 1808, Schlegel praises Gozzi's dramatic fables over his later plays based on Spanish models and also discusses the character of his irony.*]

The excessive admiration of Goldoni, and the injury sustained thereby by the masked comedy, for which the company of Sacchi in Venice possessed the highest talents, gave rise to the dramas of Gozzi. They are fairy tales in a dramatic form, in which, however, along side of the wonderful, versified, and more serious part, he employed the whole of the masks, and allowed them full and unrestrained development of their peculiarities. They, if ever any were, are pieces for effect, of great boldness of plot, still more fantastic than romantic; even though Gozzi was the first among the comic poets of Italy to show any true feeling for honour and love. The execution does not betoken either care or skill, but is sketchily dashed off. With all his whimsical boldness he is still quite a popular writer; the principal motives are detailed with the most unambiguous perspicuity, all the touches are coarse and vigorous: he says, he knows well that his countrymen are fond of *robust* situations. After his imagination had revelled to satiety among Oriental tales, he took to re-modelling Spanish plays, and particularly those of Calderon; but here he is, in my opinion, less deserving of praise. By him the ethereal and delicately-tinted poetry of the Spaniard is uniformly vulgarised, and deepened with the most glaring colours; while the weight of his masks draws the aërial tissue to the ground, for the humorous introduction of the *gracioso* in the Spanish is of far finer texture. On the other hand, the wonderful extravagance of the masked parts serves as an admirable contrast to the wild marvels of fairy tale. Thus the character of these pieces was, in the serious part, as well as in the accompanying drollery, equally removed from natural truth. Here Gozzi had fallen almost accidentally on a fund of whose value he was not, perhaps, fully aware: his prosaical, and for the most part improvisatory, masks, forming altogether of themselves the irony on the poetical part. . . . [This irony] is a sort of confession interwoven into the representation itself, and more or less distinctly expressed, of its overcharged one-sidedness in matters of fancy and feeling, and by means of which the equipoise is again restored. The Italians were not, however, conscious of this, and Gozzi did not find any follow-

ers to carry his rude sketches to a higher degree of perfection. Instead of combining like him, only with greater refinement, the charms of wonderful poetry with exhilarating mirth; instead of comparing Gozzi with the foreign masters of the romantic drama, whom he resembles notwithstanding his great disparity, and from the unconscious affinity between them in spirit and plan, drawing the conclusion that the principle common to both was founded in nature; the Italians contented themselves with considering the pieces of Gozzi as the wild offspring of an extravagant imagination, and with banishing them from the stage. The comedy with masks is held in contempt by all who pretend to any degree of refinement, as if they were too wise for it, and is abandoned to the vulgar, in the Sunday representions at the theatres and in the puppet-shows. Although this contempt must have had an injurious influence on the masks, preventing, as it does, any actor of talent from devoting himself to them, so that there are no examples now of the spirit and wit with which they were formerly filled up, still the *Commedia dell' Arte* is the only one in Italy where we can meet with original and truly theatrical entertainment. (pp. 226-28)

> *Augustus Wilhelm Schlegel, "Lecture XVI," in his* A Course of Lectures on Dramatic Art and Literature, *edited by Rev. A. J. W. Morrison, translated by John Black, revised edition, 1846. Reprint by AMS Press, Inc., 1973, pp. 213-31.*

FRANCESCO DE SANCTIS (essay date 1870)

[*De Sanctis is regarded as a critical innovator whose work provided the basis for modern Italian literary criticism. De Sanctis fused the existing critical criterion of "form" with the additional criterion of "idea," creating an aesthetic approach to literature in which the critic considers a work of art in and of itself, rather than in terms of how it relates to such factors as biography and history. It has been suggested that de Sanctis's work* Storia della letteratura italiana (*1870;* History of Italian Literature), *in its attempt to provide a historical perspective of Italian literature, insolubly conflicts with the author's critical method. Nonetheless, it remains an influential, very highly regarded work of criticism. In the following excerpt from this history, de Sanctis discusses the reasons for Gozzi's failure to have a greater influence on the course of Italian literature.*]

It was . . . in the comedies of Goldoni that the new [Italian] literature appeared for the first time, announcing a restoration of the true and the natural in art. The old literature had sought its effects in the extraordinary and the marvellous in content and in form, and in the avoidance of reality. The new literature on the contrary looked for its basis in the real—in man and Nature studied from life. (p. 873)

Now to Carlo Gozzi that cult of the true and natural was nothing less than the utter ruin, the tomb, of poetry. Though Goldoni's success forced Gozzi in the end to respect him, he never could manage to look on his reform as desirable. In Gozzi's eyes the marvellous and fantastic were an intrinsic part of poetry, were its indispensable elements; to copy from life seemed to him vulgar. And the many and various attacks on the comedy *a soggetto* grieved him to the heart; he saw the improvised comedy as one of the glories of Italy. It was accused of being old and exhausted, of being stale in its repertory, of being nothing now but an outworn mechanism, of being a school of immorality and scurrility, of being "awkward buffoonery and indecent foulness in an enlightened century." Undoubtedly the charges were exaggerated, but all the same there was truth in them. The Italian improvised comedy, the comedy of art or *a soggetto,* had ceased to be fertile, together with the old literature in general. Except for slight variations, those *lazzi* that the public so delighted in were ancient stuff that had been handed down through the centuries. The theatre was feeding on the past; the new actors copied the old ones; the improvised part in the comedies was no more new and no more improvised than the written part was new or improvised. The reason that the comedy *a soggetto* was preferred to the literary comedy was the fact that it was nearer to the people, was more in touch with them. But the Bolognese doctor and Truffaldino had at last begun to be wearisome, like a master who goes on repeating the same old lesson year after year. The champions of the regular comedy, the literati in general, quoted this tedium as an argument for abolishing the masks altogether, and demanded that a sweep be made of that whole type of comedy as "indecent in an enlightened century."

Carlo Gozzi, who objected very much to those "luminaries," and was hostile and suspicious of the novelties that were pouring into Italy from the Continent, dared to defy those enlightened critics and to leap into the arena in defence of the improvised comedy, with example and precept, writing, under the name of *fiabe,* comedies that included masks and therefore an improvised part. These *fiabe* of Gozzi, which today are almost forgotten, had considerable success in their time. Gozzi to his contemporaries seemed the reactionary and Goldoni the reformer; but we of today could wish that the reformer had had a little of the revolutionary ardour that burned in the reactionary, for he would have prosecuted his reforms with more vigour. The "taciturn, solitary Gozzi," as he was called, since he was a man of intelligence was penetrated by contemporary life without knowing it—was influenced by the very ideas that enraged him. In working to restore the old he ended as an innovator and a reformer: in running after the comedy *a soggetto* he met with the comedy of the people, and set it firm on its foundation. But Gozzi's mind was confused, as we see from his **Ragionamenti.** This was the reason for his weakness. Goldoni, on the contrary, knew what he wanted, was perfectly clear as to end and as to means, and went straight and surely to his goal. This was the reason for the very great influence he wielded. Gozzi was confused as to his aim, wanted one thing and did another, and went forward by sudden jerks, pulled this way and that by the different currents. He wanted to support the masks; he wanted to parody his opponents; he wanted to restore Pulci and Ariosto and the fantastic; he wanted to Tuscanize and at the same time to be modern and popular: he wanted in fact to take his place as a modern while reconstructing the old. These aims of Gozzi's were transitory. They were no doubt interesting to his contemporaries, and useful for polemics and for helping him to success in the theatre, but today they are the dead part of his work. They penetrate into the whole of his composition as disturbing elements, not harmonized with the rest. The part of his work that is alive is his conception of popular comedy as opposed to bourgeois comedy. The masks, or in other words, the typical characters or caricatures of the people, like Tartaglia, Pantalone, Truffaldino, Brighella, Smeraldina, exist in his composition as obligatory, conventional elements, superimposed on the content and often grotesque or insipid when compared with it. The content itself is the world of poetry as conceived by the people, avid as always for the marvellous and mysterious, impressionable, emotional—laughing as easily as weeping. It is based on the supernatural, on miracles, witchcraft, and

magic. It is the world, in fact, of the imagination, and the less it is intellectual and the less it is developed mentally, the more it is alive. It is the natural basis of popular poetry under its different forms of tales, novels, romances, comedies, and farces. The old literature had annexed these things, not to destroy them, but to cast on them the little ironical smile of a cultured bourgeoisie.

What Gozzi aimed at was different: he wanted to revive this world in its first ingenuity, dramatizing the *fiaba* and the *fola:* it was there that he sought for the new blood that was to bring back life to the comedy *a soggetto.* And he attempted it in the face of a cultured bourgeoisie, in the century of "luminaries," the century of "great minds" and "fine spirits." That he did succeed in interesting the public proves once more that the world of the imagination possesses an absolute value and responds to certain chords that, handled by an artist, can be counted on to ring in the soul, for every man or woman has a touch somewhere of the child and of the people. At the same time the public continued to be interested in the comedies of Goldoni, so the critics might reasonably have concluded—if a reasonable conclusion had been possible at that time—that both these types of comedy were in keeping with truth, Goldoni's representative of the bourgeois society with its mediocre culture, and Gozzi's of the lower classes with their credulity and their power of amazement. Both types were reforms of comedy: both were the new literature appearing on the scene. But what Gozzi did was not what he thought he was doing. He fell into his reform from pique and from the exigencies of the moment, despising the public that applauded him and not taking his own work seriously. Goldoni imitated the real, so Gozzi threw in his lot with the romantic and the fantastic. Now art, as we know, is something more than individual caprice; art, like religion and philosophy, like political and administrative institutions, is an intrinsic part of society, a natural result of culture and of national life. While Gozzi was trying to revive the world of the imagination, he was pointing to its dissolution in his own **Marfisa.** And he attempted to revive that world when the whole of the cultured and intelligent part of the nation was moving not towards it, but away from it, and when the people, inert and sunk in their poverty, had not the slightest glimmer of a literary life. Now if Gozzi had gone to the people for his inspiration and had mixed with them personally, his work would have been alive. But he was naturally aristocratic, and had the greatest objection to anything that smelt too strongly of democracy, so he passed his life entirely among the members of the Granelleschi, in a circle that was purely literary. Moreover nothing literary could ever have arisen in that day from the people, sunk as they were in a hopeless stagnation. The literary movement in Italy arose from the bourgeoisie, and the national life developed in every direction according to bourgeois tendencies. When the whole mission of the age was to fight imagination in the name of science and philosophy, Gozzi's attempt to revive that world of the imagination was a retrogression. He was born too soon: the time was to come when the bourgeoisie, alarmed by these very exaggerations which disgusted him, were to turn once more to the world of the marvellous as to a rock of salvation. It was then that Gozzi should have lived. (pp. 873-77)

Gozzi in his own day was a warring element, therefore he arrived at nothing definite. His idea, which in the abstract was highly aesthetic, in practice was literary and artificial. He hated novelty, yet all the time he was carrying it within him. He treated imagination as the lawyer Goldoni treated bourgeois society; his works are wanting in chiaroscuro, and in the atmosphere and the feeling of the supernatural. His whole effort is to show the supernatural as though it were real and natural, an ordinary fact accepted by every one, as Goldoni did. So his style is monotonous, his colouring opaque, and his tints are imperfectly fused. By dint of being natural he often falls into the insipid and the ordinary. He did not see that when the world of the imagination is in question naturalness depends on ingenuity—on curiosity, marvelling, suspense, terror, anger, tears, and laughter—as in the stories of primitive peoples. In Gozzi ingenuity has been lost, so naturalness sinks into carelessness and ordinariness. To the author himself those apparitions were a game and a pastime. But nevertheless, though abortive and valueless in themselves, with the help of the scenery and the *lazzi* they still contrive to be effective on the stage, and are pleasant to read, though they leave no trace on the mind. Baretti proclaimed Gozzi as a new Shakespeare, and when he failed to come up to expectations attacked him furiously, as though Gozzi had betrayed him. He ought instead to have been furious with himself for having predicted a Shakespeare in the eighteenth century. Popular comedy relapsed into its quagmire, with its masks, its indecencies, and its vulgarity. Of Gozzi there remained a fine idea, soon to be forgotten. Society took the other road; it followed Goldoni. (pp. 877-78)

Francesco de Sanctis, "The New Literature," in his History of Italian Literature, Vol. 2, *translated by Joan Redfern, Harcourt Brace Jovanovich, 1931, pp. 833-948.*

VERNON LEE [PSEUDONYM OF **VIOLET PAGET**] (essay date 1880)

[*An English novelist, travel writer, and critic who spent most of her life in Italy, Lee wrote widely on art and aesthetics, earning particular praise for her* Studies of the Eighteenth Century in Italy (1880). *Her philosophy of art held that music and the visual arts should be appreciated for their form alone and not be made to serve any intellectual or didactic function, a role she reserved for literature. In this excerpt from the above-mentioned work, Lee attributes Gozzi's early success to the genius of the Sacchi company rather than to his talents as a dramatist.*]

Carlo Gozzi was whimsical, sentimental, metaphysical; in short, a humorist of the temper of Sterne and of Jean Paul: he believed in the superior wisdom of childishness, in the philosophy of old nurses' tales, in the venerableness of clowns; why, he knew not. So he scolded against the prosaic Goldoni, who was driving romance and buffoonery off the stage; sighed at the world growing daily more dull, more obtuse, more philosophical; and cherished the cast-off mummeries of the *Commedia dell' Arte* as if sunshine and youth were lurking in their tatters; objectless and heedless, until one day it flashed across him to build a temple in which the dear and venerable relics would be enshrined and worshipped. (p. 416)

Carlo Gozzi . . . took up and artistically manipulated just those elements of the old *Commedia dell' Arte* which Goldoni had rejected—the masks, the buffoonery, the supernatural, and the tragic. . . . He did not like realities like Goldoni; an aristocrat and a dreamer, he did not sympathise with the people; he would accept their poetry, their fairy tales and quaint sayings, but he would not endure their prose. His matter-of-fact century, philosophic and pedantic, drove him back upon himself, and made him brood over his fancies and whimsies

Tartaglia, one of the commedia dell'arte masks.

more than is healthy for an artist. He found little sympathy without, and he had not enough in himself to suffice for himself. The world surrounding him was prosaic and dull and could not satisfy him, and he had not the power to create a world for himself which should be satisfactory. Every great poet and great humorist creates a sphere into which he can rise and in which dwell in happiness, be it among clouds and rainbows like Shelley, among moss and leafage like Keats, or among Uncle Tobys like Sterne, or advocates of the poor like Jean Paul; Carlo Gozzi could not do this; both as a poet and as a humorist he could rise out of reality only for a few minutes, and then drop back into it wearied and bruised; he was full of aspiration and suggestion: wondrous dreams, beautiful and grotesque, flitted before him without his being able to seize them, like that fiddler trying for a lifetime to reproduce the exquisite sonata heard in sleep from the fiend; here! here it comes, the weird melody—quick! the bow across the strings—alas!—that was not the piece. Carlo Gozzi, like every imaginative mind, saw in everything much more than it contains; but, unlike the great artist, he could not extract that something and make it his own. In his plays he seems for ever pointing to some suggestion of poetry, of pathos, and of humour, calling upon us to understand what he would do but cannot; saying almost piteously, "Do you not see, do you not feel? Does not that situation, that word, appeal to your fancy? Do you not see dimly those fairy princesses, too beautiful to be seized, . . . there, do you not hear the music? Do you not feel that a world of wonder is half visible to you?" Always suggestive, and sometimes successful in working out the suggestion; such must be the final verdict on Carlo Gozzi's plays; and it explains why they have been so warmly admired by individuals and so completely forgotten by the public. Give the world of suggestion contained in *The Stag King,* in *Turandot,* in *The Raven,* to such readers as Goethe and Madame de Staël, as Schiller and Hoffmann, and it will suffice; they will see what poor Carlo Gozzi can only point to. They can sympathise, imagine, and complete. But humanity at large cannot: it can see only what is absolutely shown it; mediocre Mr. A, B, or C, must have complete realization, absolute perfection; he must have Homer, Shakespeare, Raphael, the finished statue with every inch properly chiselled, the finished picture with every line in its place and every colour well laid on; the block of stone with the mysterious figure still veiled in its rough mass, the sketch with its vague faces and forms rising shadowlike out of the confusion of blurs; the indistinct voice in the wind, the hazy shapes in the moonlight, all this is incomprehensible to him; he wants *art,* and he is right; but below art, below the clear, the realised, the complete, is a limbo of fair unborn ghosts, shadowy and vague, of distantly heard melodies, of vaguely felt emotions of pathos and joy. Let us not despise that limbo, that chaos; out of it emerges every masterpiece, and in it lies hidden many a charming or sublime shape which those who know the secret spell can evoke out of the mist of ever-changing forms which surround it.

To this limbo belong the fairy plays of Carlo Gozzi; they are things which in order to be thoroughly enjoyable must be completed; in our days they can be thus completed only by the fancy of the reader; in his own time they were completed by the scenic realisation of the excellent comic company directed by Sacchi. The machinery, improvisations, acting, and dresses of the Teatro San Samuele filled up the gaps left by the insufficient talents of the writer. . . . With the Sacchi company at his command, Carlo Gozzi appeared a genius; as soon as the Sacchi company broke up he was forgotten; and if another such company could be formed, if we could have another Truffaldino-Sacchi, another Brighella-Zannoni, another Pantalone-Darbes, another Fiorilli-Tartaglia, another Teodora Ricci, if we could resuscitate those admirable last buffoons of the *Commedia dell' Arte,* the *fiabesque* comedies of Carlo Gozzi would once more be as popular as a hundred years ago; and Carlo Gozzi would seem as great an author to those compilers of histories of Italian literature in which his very name is omitted, as he seemed to Hoffmann, to Schiller, and to Schlegel.

There is, however, one of Carlo Gozzi's plays which, by some fortunate accident, is almost perfect, which might be read and enjoyed even after *Vathek* or *Chapelmaster Kreisler,* or Alfred de Musset's *Fantasio;* and that is the philosophic fairy play *l'Augellino Bel Verde,* or, if we may translate the untranslatable—*The Little Bird Fair Green;* for in it Gozzi has almost shown us the masks, almost let us hear the improvisations, and has given all the quaint charm of the old nursery tale, originally told by some ancient Hindoo poet to the Persians, moulded into shape by some beautiful Sheherazade, written out in grotesque Neapolitan dialect by Basile in the sixteenth century, re-written in dainty and stately French by Perrault, the architect of Versailles, wandering from country to country, changing now into *Princesse Belle Etoile,* now into *Peau d'Ane,* and still repeated, as the *Uccello Biverde,* in

thick-mouthed Roman or lisping Venetian, by many an illiterate granny beside the blazing ruddy mouth of the bread-baking oven, or in the cool gloom of the farmyard beneath the spreading fig-tree, to the sound of the sawing cicala and the splashing fountain. In this comedy Carlo Gozzi has woven together with wonderful art the prose buffoonery of the Comedy of Masks with the stateliest tragic verse and the sharpest moralising of a satire; his love of the droll Venetian dialect, of the supernatural, of the grotesque, and his moral indignation against the philosophic sophisms of his day, have balanced each other, and united to form a little masterpiece, in which for the only time perhaps in his life Carlo Gozzi has succeeded in making us see and feel completely and satisfactorily all that he wants us to see and to feel. . . . [The] comedy of the *Little Bird Fair Green,* which, with its buffooneries, its transformations, its tragic passion, its philosophising, its moralising antique statue, its apple singing opera songs, accompanied by the dancing water as orchestra, its whimpering comic king, its mephistophelian pork-selling harlequin, its clown poet-seer Brighella (who restores his prophetic vein at the tavern), its hero Renzo madly enamoured of a woman of stone, its bird in love with a mortal, its fantastic, semi-philosophic suggestiveness, has altogether a strange analogy with the second part of *Faust;* an enigmatic work, we know not whether too loftily meaningful or too childishly meaningless for full comprehension; amusing, tickling, pleasing; above all filling the mind with a queer and delightful medley of thoughts. The *fiabesque* comedy of Carlo Gozzi was, in its mixture of humour and pathos, of the grotesque, the fanciful, and the supernatural, the apotheosis of the Comedy of Masks, its highest triumph given it by its most fervent votary; but the apotheosis is a funeral rite, and shows that the old *Commedia dell' Arte* had expired. Little by little discord began to arise in the once united company directed by Sacchi. Teodora Ricci, Gozzi's pupil and goddess, behaved scandalously and went off to France. Sacchi, old and worn out, became cantankerous and headstrong. Darbes died or retired; the other actors, one by one, took other engagements or entirely left the stage; the finances of San Samuele got into disorder, furniture and stage properties were seized; lawsuits began among the various actors; the owner of the theatre ejected the manager; the magnificent Sacchi company, the last company of mask actors in all Italy, was dissolved. (pp. 423-33)

The *Commedia dell' Arte* was dead. Carlo Gozzi relapsed into obscurity. (p. 434)

Vernon Lee [pseudonym of Violet Paget], "Carlo Gozzi and the Venetian Fairy Comedy," in her Studies of the Eighteenth Century in Italy, *second edition, A. C. McClurg & Co., 1908, pp. 413-36.*

LINDA VILLARI (essay date 1886)

[*Villari values the* fiabe *for providing insights into eighteenth-century Italian thought, concluding that they are chiefly of historical interest.*]

The fame of Count Carlo Gozzi, the successful eighteenth century playwright and opponent of Goldoni, has undergone almost as many transformations as the heroes and heroines of his fantastic fairy dramas. From 1761 to almost 1790, his compositions were the delight of the Venetian public, and it was their success that mainly drove Goldoni to settle in France. But the latter's name lives, his representations of every-day human life are true to all time; while Gozzi and his extravaganzas have been almost entirely forgotten even in his own land. For, since the original edition of 1797—now extremely scarce—none of his works had been thought worthy of reprint. Only in the present year a selection of his ten best plays [*Le Fiabe di Carlo Gozzi*] has appeared, carefully edited by Signor Ernesto Masi. . . . (p. 67)

It was part of [Gozzi's] old-fashioned conservatism to detest all attempts at dramatic reform; he was increasingly piqued by the triumphs of the new realistic comedy, and disgusted that his fellow-citizens should applaud the brawls of fish-wives, the prosy lives and sorrows of lawyers and shopkeepers. His most stinging satires missed their mark so long as the public thronged to St. Angelo to clap all that vulgar trash! So, recognizing the need of a fresh weapon, he resolved to fight the enemy on his own ground. And not, according to Baretti's old tale, because directly challenged by Goldoni to produce better plays than his, but simply to prove that popularity was no test of literary merit, and that he, Gozzi, could draw still bigger houses with the tritest nursery tale, "such as was told to babes by serving-maids beside the kitchen fire." And further, as the champion of old forms, he determined to adhere to the lines of the *Commedia dell' Arte.* Luckily for him, the Sacchi troupe, a renowned company, including the best representatives of the four traditional Italian masks, had just returned from Vienna, and was now disengaged. So for this company he wrote his first *Fiaba,* and, to prove that his sole object was the interests of art, refused, both then and afterwards, to accept any payment for his work.

Accordingly, in January 1761, Gozzi's *L'Amor delle Tre Melarance* (*The Love of the Three Oranges*) was produced at the San Samuele Theatre, and achieved a signal success. The Venetians were taken by storm. Here was a familiar nursery tale they had known from their cradles, one, too, common to all countries, and derived from an Eastern source, served up to them in a surprising new dress and spiced with piquant personal spites! The novelty of its stage effects and transformation scenes delighted their eyes, the sharpness of its satire equally delighted their ears. And it was performed by their old favourites, the excellent Sacchi troupe, who still preserved the best traditions of the Comedy of Art, and knew how to improvise brisk dialogue on the lines of a skeleton play. In this case nearly everything depended on the actors, for, excepting scraps of verse caricaturing the respective styles of Chiari and Goldoni, Gozzi's *Love of the Three Oranges* was little more than an outline. (p. 70)

No expense had been spared in scenery and decorations, and Venice delightedly welcomed the traditional masks, Pantalone, Tartaglia, Brighella, and Truffaldino, fantastically attired as a suit of playing-cards, and in novel situations fitted to the display of their usual characteristics. It was easy to read the allegory conveyed by the plot. Prince Tartaglia (or the Venetian public) is dying of an indigestion of Martellian verse; Truffaldino (or the Comedy of Art) alone can effect his cure by making him laugh. The Magician, his protector, and the Sorceress, his persecutor, parody the Goldoni and Chiari wars by quarrelling fiercely over him in legal diction and stilted Pindaric verse.

Thus the laughable extravaganza carried on the battle already fought with pen and ink. Gozzi had turned the simple fable into a battering-ram, and the glitter of stage-tinsel and stage-effect increased the force of his blows. The three oranges concealed in the castle of Creonta, the Sorceress, repre-

sented Tragedy, Comedy, and the Comedy of Art, bound in the fetters of Ignorance. The two oranges rashly opened by Truffaldino before reaching the fountain that is to revive the enchanted maidens inside them, typify the fate of Tragedy and Comedy. The third maiden, released by Tartaglia, and revived by the water brought to her in an iron shoe, personifies the Comedy of Art nourished by the sock (or shoe) of extemporaneous acting.

The published form of this play is very curious reading. It consists of a rhymed prologue and a narrative, or, as Gozzi styles it, a "reflective analysis" of the plot, divided into three acts, and interspersed with stage directions and quaint remarks on the manner in which the actors rendered his ideas, and how these were received by the public. (pp. 70-1)

The play itself was, as we have shown, a medley of criticism, parody, and fantastic improbability, but its fun was the chief cause of its success. This, however, Gozzi would not admit and he never understood that the comic and the fantastic are not altogether a happy combination, and that the introduction of too many elements deprived his work of unity. (p. 71)

Much elated by his wonderful success, Gozzi now propounded a fresh theory. No longer content with proving that any old fable can fill a theatre, he now argued that scenic device, invention and style could give dignity to any theme. This theory had more truth in it than the first, and brought Gozzi nearer to the purpose that was slowly taking shape in his mind, of resuscitating the old stage traditions, which, having dwindled to empty mannerisms, had lost their hold on the public.

But Gozzi's teeming intellect was too full of contradictory ideas to be truly artistic, and, in the effort to reach too many aims, to be at once a keen satirist, dramatist, and philosopher, he betrayed his real dramatic instinct, and forgot to be a poet. He thought himself one, of course, had the intensest belief in his own powers, in the loftiness of his moral mission, and accepted the triumphs won by his farce as a just tribute to his poetic worth. . . .

His second play, *Il Corvo* (*The Raven*), is full of dramatic pathos. Like the *Three Oranges,* it was taken from Basile's Neapolitan collection, *Il Cunto de li Cunte,* and with little alteration, save in the *dénouement.* (p. 72)

Throughout this play the central interest is well sustained, there is pathos in the war of emotions, and the comic scenes of the masks relieve without interfering with the serious business of the piece. And, both in style and versification, the *Raven* is so markedly superior to the other *Fiabe,* that Signor Masi is inclined to think that Gasparo Gozzi must have had a hand in it.

During the next four or five years Gozzi treated the Venetians to eight more spectacular plays. Two of these—*Turandot* and *L'Augellino Bel Verde*—demand special mention. . . . (p. 74)

All [of Gozzi's] plays, with the sole exception of *I Pitocchi Fortunati* (*The Lucky Beggars*), were received with enthusiastic applause. Gozzi had struck a golden vein by his daring medleys of sense and nonsense, supernatural agencies and modern thought, Eastern scenes and ceremonial, hits at passing events and plenty of coarse farce that every gondolier and fisherman could appreciate. The prologue to the *Stag King,* for instance, was delivered by an actor got up to imitate ragged Cigolotti, the well-known street-poet and story-teller. The freedom of Gozzi's anachronisms has a certain analogy with the fantastic license of his painter contemporary, Messer Tiepolo, who in a grave scene of martyrdom introduced a Roman soldier with a pipe in his mouth. And the real feeling, strong dramatic situations, and witty aphorisms, combined by Gozzi with the craziest burlesque and fantasmagoria, responded to the confusion of new ideas and old institutions marking the close of the Venetian Republic.

All the *Fiabe* are pleasant reading. **L'Amor delle Tre Melarance** and **L'Augellino Bel Verde** have more true comedy than the rest, and the latter is in every way the jewel of the set. Founded on the Arabian tale of the *Three Sisters,* and twisted into a sequel of the **Three Oranges,** the **Little Green Bird** is an exquisite medley of fancy and satire. And notwithstanding his championship of romantic idealism, Gozzi was at his best in satire. Like most incomplete intellects, he needed the stimulus of personal motive and antagonism, and this "philosophical fable," as he calls it, affords good scope for his powers. Ingeniously interwoven with its poetic framework are pungent caricatures of the new French philosophy that was so abhorred by the conservative Count. He intended it to be the last of his fairy plays, and accordingly filled it with every delirious device for exciting the public laughter; but in no other work is he so near to being a poet. It is a masterpiece of the short-lived school of which he was the inventor, and that—in his own land at least—has had no disciples. (pp. 74-5)

In **L'Augellino Bel Verde** the author gives utterance to his presentiments of the approaching fall of the Republic. Gozzi was a keen-eyed, if impassioned patriot, and, detecting signs of age in the failing State, sought to shield it from every shock of novelty. The removal of a single stone might, he deemed, precipitate the crash of the tottering edifice.

Yet, with all his hatred of innovation and bitter dislike to theatrical reform, he was careful not to strain the popular favour by harping too long on one string. He ceased writing *Fiabe* while their success was still undiminished, preferring, as he says, to leave the public unsatisfied rather than satiated, and once more turned his attention to Spanish themes. (p. 78)

It is now time to speak of **Turandot,** . . . for though inferior to several of the others, it had, as will presently be seen, very important consequences for the author's fame.

Turandot contains no supernatural element, no fairies, no witchcraft, and was written to confute certain critics who had sneered at the **Stag King,** and asserted that Gozzi's success solely depended on scene-shifting and stage tricks. It is the story of a Chinese Princess, who abhors the idea of marriage. Forced by the laws of the empire to choose a husband, she promises her hand to the first prince able to guess the three riddles she will put to him, and willing to forfeit his life in case of failure. (pp. 78-9)

The framework of this drama is really poetic; it contains scenes of passion and tenderness and well-contrived conflicts of human motives. The comic element is, of course, supplied by the masks. Pantalone is the very bewildered Minister of the Chinese despot; Tartaglia, Brighella, and Truffaldino are officers of the Court, and their strictly European point of view is in droll contrast with their surroundings. But though there is no magic in the play, its events are apparently ruled by a mysterious supernatural force, and this, as a survival of the old Italian tragic masks, was a point specially lauded by Goethe.

The introduction of the masks was a powerful factor of Gozzi's success, particularly in Venice, where it flattered the local pride and lent a piquant flavour of daily life to the most impossible situations. For Pantalone, the Venetian mask, is by no means the senile dotard known to the English stage. He represents national, *i.e.* Venetian, virtue as opposed to the lawlessness and crime of the fantastic world around him. He is an elderly man, often a heavy father, but not too old for important posts. He is sometimes High Admiral, sometimes Prime Minister, sometimes a rich merchant. He is very warm-hearted, very expansive, and his sympathies—expressed in the broadest Venetian—are always on the side of goodness and justice. The Neapolitan mask, Tartaglia, is always a selfish knave, and stammers in his own dialect. He is sometimes sly and foolish, sometimes sly and keen witted, but he generally overreaches himself in the long run. We may note that in the **Three Oranges** the mask Leandro, usually a walking gentleman, has all the characteristics of Tartaglia, save the stammer, but this was an exception to the rule. Truffaldino and Brighella, the Bergamo masks, are generally knaves and clowns, selfish and servile and funny. They are variations of the Clown and Harlequin of the older plays. Smeraldina, the female mask, has little resemblance to the Columbine of English pantomime, but, like the latter, is always the companion, sometimes the lover, of Harlequin Truffaldino or Brighella. She is sometimes ugly and ridiculous, and often a negress.

When we remember that in Gozzi's plays all these characters were represented by first-rate actors, standing favourites of the Venetians, we see that the author had special advantages in his native city. Elsewhere in Italy his reputation was small. His romantic daring jarred on the philosophic spirit of the eighteenth century; his fantastic plots, and outrage of the unities, were despised by those who sought dramatic perfection on the broad highways of classical history and tradition. What did they care for the misty by-paths of fairy lore? Eighteenth century Italy was weary too of the *Commedia dell' Arte* so dear to the Venetian playwright; she had outgrown it, was rather ashamed of it—just as big boys and girls are suddenly ashamed of the toys and games prized before their last birthday. The operatic stage and classic tragedy were diversions better suited to their "grown up" dignity.

So, excepting from anglicized Baretti—who lauded Gozzi as the equal of Shakespeare, and talked of translating the *Fiabe* and offering them to his friend Mr. Garrick—the Venetian writer encountered more blame than praise from Italian critics. (pp. 79-80)

But in Germany he met with a very different fate. There all his plays roused the keenest admiration. . . . The Schlegels, Goethe, Schiller, Hoffman, and Tieck raised their voices in Gozzi's praise; the two latter paid him the compliment of imitation, and Schiller translated **Turandot** for the Weimar stage. (p. 80)

In fact, Gozzi was as much over-praised in Germany as he was under-rated in Italy. German critics gravely ranked him with Aristophanes and Shakespeare at the time when the majority of his countrymen denied him all merit, and declared that his sole title to mention in literature was owed to his noisy strife with Goldoni.

The cause of these contradictory judgments is easily analyzed. Italians have never had a genuine love for the fantastic, have only accepted it when strictly subordinate to clear-cut and definite aims. Germans, on the other hand, having a natural bent for it, prized that element in Gozzi, and found him eminently suggestive to their own richer imaginations. His *Fiabe* appeared during the Neo-Romantic period preceding the true Romanticism of Goethe and Schiller, and harmonized with the tendency that, at this moment, mistook poetic license for poetic truth, and wild extravagance for righteous revolt against the shackles of classic drama. So, seeing in Gozzi only that which they wished to see, they were blind to his lack of melody and defects of style and form. (p. 81)

What verdict, then, must be passed on the *Fiabe?* To us their interest seems mainly historical. With all his championship of the past, Gozzi had touch of his time, and his satires throw keen flashes of light on Italian eighteenth-century thought. His plays are full of ideas, but ideas incompletely worked out. His misty visions make heavy claims on the imagination of his readers; hence the neglect of the general public and the enthusiastic admiration of a few great minds who unconsciously filled in his vague suggestions from their own stores. Naturally, too, his foreign students were less sensitive than his countrymen to defects of style and diction.

Perhaps, of all his critics, Goethe came nearest to deciding Gozzi's place in literature by grounding his chief praise on the intimate relation he discerned between the Venetian's tragico-burlesques and the character of the Venetian people. Seen from an English point of view the *Fiabe* show many points of resemblance with the witty extravaganzas by the late Mr. Planché, that were the delight of the town some twenty-five years ago. Like them they are founded on nursery tales, their personages preserve modern feelings and attributes in the midst of preternatural events; strokes of satire on the actualities of the day are woven into the dialogue of genii, fairies, and magicians, and in place of the popular songs and catch-words utilized by the English playwright we have the drolleries of the masks to relieve the vicissitudes of much-tried heroes and heroines. But the Venetian Count had loftier aims than the genial Englishman, who only wrote to amuse, and these we would not appear to slight. Signor Masi holds that, although it was perhaps natural for Gozzi's *Fiabe* to be forgotten during the mighty changes in literature at the beginning of this century, they deserve resuscitation now. "For," he adds, "in the history of the Italian stage they represent the past as opposed to the modern realism of Goldonian comedy, and as the last form of the ancient *Commedia dell' Arte* and the old popular plays. Also, because in the heat of the philosophical movement that, with the arrogance of intellectual pride, sought to demolish the entire social framework of old Europe, the *fiabe* formed a fantastic literary episode, and their popularity was, for some years, so great as almost to cast doubts on the causes and effects of the Goldonian reform." (pp. 81-2)

Linda Villari, "A Venetian Playwright," in The National Review, *London, Vol. VII, No. 37, March, 1886, pp. 67-82.*

JOHN ADDINGTON SYMONDS   (essay date 1888)

[*An English historian, poet, and critic, Symonds is perhaps best known for his seven-volume history,* Renaissance in Italy *(1875-85). He has also made several highly praised translations of Greek poetry and Italian literature, including* The Memoirs of Count Carlo Gozzi. *In the following excerpt from the introduction to this work, Symonds comments on the style of Gozzi's memoirs and assesses their value. He then presents an overview of the* fiabe, *focusing on their genesis, their artistic unity, and the characteristics of the masks. Symonds's remarks were written in 1888.*]

In the year 1797 there appeared at Venice a book entitled *Memorie inutili della vita di Carlo Gozzi, scritte da lui medesimo e pubblicate per umiltà, Useless Memoirs of the Life of Carlo Gozzi, written by himself and published from motives of humility.* (p. 1)

In the year 1797 [Gozzi] was seventy-seven; and although he had been a man of some mark in his early days, the public had lost sight of him for the last seventeen years. His reputation depended upon a large number of dramatic pieces, satirical poems, and prose compositions, mostly of a controversial kind. Two main episodes in his literary life conferred a slightly dubious notoriety upon his name. The first of these was the long and bitter war he waged against the two playwrights, Chiari and Goldoni, between the years 1756 and 1762. The other was an unfortunate series of events which brought him into collision with a certain Pier Antonio Gratarol in 1777. (p. 2)

This autobiography is distinctly an apologetical work, a portrait drawn by Gozzi in self-defence, and intended to vindicate himself from the aspersions cast by Gratarol upon his character. Its main object is to set forth in the fairest light his own conduct during the unlucky collision to which I have alluded. Yet though so limited in aim, the interest which it possesses for us at the present time, is far wider than belongs to that unhappy squabble, long since buried in oblivion. Gozzi's conception of an *Apologia pro vita sua* was a comprehensive one. He resolved to reveal his character under all its aspects, from his childhood until the date 1777, dealing now with matters of general importance, now with the private affairs of his home, touching upon the literature of his age, discussing fashions, criticising philosophy, entering into minute particulars regarding theatres and actors, describing his love-affairs with a frankness worthy of Rousseau, and painting a series of lively portraits in which a large variety of individuals from all classes are presented to our notice. The result is that his autobiography, although in the strictest sense of that term an occasional production, forms one of the most valuable documents we possess for a study of Venetian society during the decadence of the Republic. Gozzi was gifted with a penetrative and observant mind, strong sense of humour, and a power of brilliant description. On the faults of his style and the defects of his character, I shall speak hereafter. At present it is enough to indicate the importance of the Memoirs as furnishing a vivid picture of Venetian life in the eighteenth century. Venice, at that period, was fortunate in autobiographers. She possessed Goldoni and Casanova as well as Gozzi, not to mention smaller folk like Da Ponte, the poet of Mozart's *Don Giovanni.* But when we compare the three life-records of Goldoni, Casanova, and Gozzi, by far the deepest historical interest, in my opinion, belongs to the last. Casanova's Memoirs are almost excluded from general use by the nature of their predominant pre-occupation. Moreover, they deal but partially with Venice, and only with limited aspects of its social life. Goldoni's, though more humane, and in all that concerns tone impeccable, turn too exclusively upon the history of his dramatic works to be of great importance as an historical document. Moreover, the scene is laid in several provinces of Italy and transferred before its close to France.

Gozzi, on the contrary, never quits the soil of Venice. Except when he served as a soldier for three years in the Venetian province of Dalmatia, he does not appear to have travelled further than to Pordenone on one side and to Padua on the other. Of strong aristocratic instincts, but condemned to comparative poverty by the reckless expenditure of his parents and grandparents, Gozzi enjoyed opportunities of studying the society of Venice from several points of view. His enthusiasm for literature and partiality for professional actors brought him acquainted with the scholars and the Bohemians of that epoch. His management of the encumbered estates of his family introduced him to advocates, solicitors, brokers, Jews, tenants, and all manner of strange people. His birth made him the companion of patricians. His military service involved him in the wild pleasures and perils of scapegrace lads upon a foreign soil. Consequently, the records of a life so varied in experience, while strictly confined within the narrow circuit of Venetian society, could not fail to be rich in details for the student. It may be regretted that Gozzi chose to write in a didactic spirit. We could willingly have exchanged his long-winded excursions into the sphere of moral philosophy for a few more graphic sketches in the style of his Dalmatian adventures. (pp. 3-6)

As a literary performance, this autobiography is remarkably unequal, a thing of rags and patches, some of which are of fine silk or velvet, others of rough sackcloth. Their main defect as regards composition is prolixity. Gozzi does not know when to stop, and he uses three phrases where one would have sufficed. He is also very incoherent, spinning interminable periodic sentences, which sometimes do not hang together grammatically or logically. While insisting so magisterially upon the purity of Italian diction, he indulges in uncouth Lombardisms, and slips at times into Venetian dialect. We must remember that he grew up practically without education. He acquired his knowledge, cultivated his taste, and formed his style by reading without discrimination and by writing without fixed purpose. This accounts for the digressive, irregular, improvisatory manner of his prose. It has its own merits, however, of vehemence, a copious vocabulary, dramatic vigour in narration, and occasionally graphic descriptions.

It may be asked why he called his Memoirs "useless." Partly no doubt out of an ironical self-consciousness, which marked his peculiar species of humour; but partly also as a slap in the face to his readers. He tells them candidly in one of his prefaces that he considers the moral reflections with which the book is filled to be both sound and valuable, but that the false science of the age is certain to render them of no effect. In like manner, when he asserts that the Memoirs were published out of humility, this is partly true and partly false. Gozzi piqued himself on being what I may call a Stoic-Democritean philosopher. It was his pride to bear everything with endurance and to laugh at everything, himself and his own concerns included, with contemptuous indulgence. Yet he deserved the stinging epigram which Goldoni uttered on his character: "A smile upon his lips and venom in his heart." His light-heartedness and risibility were often assumed to hide bitter resentment or boiling indignation. No man had less of genuine humility than Gozzi, or more of the "pride which apes humility." *Umiltà* upon his title-page has much the same effect as *Umiltà* in huge Gothic letters beneath the coronets and crests of the Borromeo family above their haughty palace-portals. As a single instance, I might select the supercilious condescension with which he invariably

treats his friends the actors. They are *canaille,* to be consorted with by a gentleman merely for amusement. His repeated boast that he gave his literary work away, and his sneers at his brother Gasparo for making money, do not savour of a really humble spirit. At the bottom of all he says about his foolhardiness in Dalmatia there lurks a proud self-satisfaction.

To what extent was he truthful? That is a difficult question to answer. I believe that in the main he tried to be, and was, veracious throughout the Memoirs; but that he considered a certain economy of statement, a certain evasion of direct facts, and a certain forensic chicanery to be permissible in openly controversial composition. This renders his account of the Gratarol episode somewhat suspicious. . . . It is clear that he wished to conceal his real age, that he falsified the date of his departure for Dalmatia, and that he somewhat misstated the nature of his intimacy with Mme. Tron. In each of these cases it was his object to put himself in as favourable a light as possible face to face with Gratarol, first by making it appear that he was ten years or so younger than his actual age when he began the liaison with Mme. Ricci, and secondly by slurring over the fact of a partial collusion with Gratarol's deadly enemy. (pp. 19-22)

On the whole, Gozzi strikes me as rather inclined to the vices of too open speech and cynicism than to those of dissimulation and hypocrisy. He can hardly have been a lovable man. His language about his mother proves that. She treated him ill, it is true, and gave him but a scanty share of her maternal kindness. Yet this does not justify the freezing sarcasms with which he refers to her. They are no doubt humorous, but their humour is of a savage kind. (p. 22)

We must divest our minds of the false conception of Gozzi's character with which Paul de Musset hoaxed the French critics and Vernon Lee [see excerpt by Lee dated 1880]. He was no dramatic dreamer and abstract visionary, but a keen hard-headed man of business, caustic in speech and stubborn in act, adhering tenaciously to his opinions and his rights, acidly and sardonically humorous, eccentric, but fully aware of his eccentricities, and apt to use them as the material of burlesque humour. Nobody would have laughed more loudly at De Musset's fancy picture of his fairy-haunted palace than Gozzi would have done, or have more keenly relished the joke of turning his practical self into a sprite-tormented idealist. (pp. 23-4)

· · · · ·

[The] facts about the genesis of Gozzi's *Fiabe* need to be insisted on, since French and German critics have distorted the truth. They regard Gozzi as a romantic playwright, gifted with innate genius for a peculiar species of dramatic art. According to this theory, the *Fiabe* were produced in order to manifest an ideal existing in their author's brain. Minute attention to Gozzi's Memoirs, his explanatory Essays, and the preface appended to each *Fiaba,* shows, on the contrary, that he began to write the *Fiabe* with the simple object of answering a certain challenge in the most humorous way he could devise. He continued them with a didactic purpose. His keen sagacity and profound knowledge of the Venetian public led him possibly to anticipate success. Yet he knew that the attempt was perilous; and he made it, without obeying preconceived principles, without yielding to any imperative instinct, but solely with the view of giving Chiari and Goldoni a sound thrashing. (p. 108)

It is mistaken to suppose that Gozzi was animated by the enthusiasm of a literary innovator. The *Fiabe,* in spite of their fantastic form, were the work of an aristocratical Conservative, bent on striking a shrewd blow for the *Commedia dell' Arte,* which he considered to be the special glory of the Italian race. (pp. 109-10)

The public had been invited to sit as umpires in the controversy between him and their two favourite playwrights. They had been requested to suspend their judgment before finally pronouncing sentence against the *Commedia dell' Arte.* The result of the experiment was a decided triumph for the author of the **Three Oranges,** for Sacchi's company, and for the Granelleschi. But, what was more important, Gozzi, at the commencement of his forty-first year, now discovered himself to be possessed of dramatic ability in no common degree, and of a peculiar kind. The success of the **Three Oranges** suggested the notion that use might be made of fairy tales, not only for maintaining the impromptu style of Italian Comedy, and amusing the public with piquant novelties, but also for conveying moral lessons under the form of allegory, and mingling tragic pathos with the humours of the masks. Accordingly Gozzi composed a succession of similar pieces, gradually suppressing the burlesque elements, enlarging the sphere of didactic satire, pathos, and dramatic action, relying less upon the mechanical attractions of transformation scenes and *lazzi,* writing the principal parts in full, and versifying a considerable portion of the dialogue. (pp. 147-48)

The occasional origin of the *Fiabe,* on which I have already insisted, accounts for their want of plastic unity, their jumble of oddly contrasted ingredients. They were not the spontaneous outgrowth of artistic genius seeking to fuse the real and the fantastic in an ideal world of the imagination; but monsters begotten by an accident, which the creative originality of a highly-gifted intellect turned to excellent account. Gozzi's predilection for burlesque, his satirical propensity and fondness for moralising on the foibles of his age, found easy vent in the peculiar form he had discovered by a lucky chance. But these motives were not subordinated to the higher coherence of imaginative poetry. His fancy, command of dramatic situations, intuition into character, rhetorical eloquence, and inexhaustible inventiveness expatiated in the region of caprice and wonder. Yet we do not feel that he has succeeded in harmonising these divers elements with the spiritual instinct of an Aristophanes or a Shakespeare. Probably he did not seek to do so. The numerous reflections on the *Fiabe,* which are scattered up and down his works, prove that art for art's sake was far from being the leading consideration in their production. They remained with him pastimes, which had partly a practical, partly a didactic purpose—convenient vehicles for indulging his literary bias and airing his ethical opinions—serviceable ammunition in the battle against men whom he regarded as impostors and pretenders—excellent means of putting money into the purses of his protegés, the actors, and of keeping himself in favour with his friends, the actresses. To the last they retained something of the *punctilio,* which, as he says, inspired him at the outset.

In all his *Fiabe* Gozzi employed the four Masks and the Servetta, Smeraldina. He not unfrequently wrote the whole part of a mask, so that nothing remained for impromptu acting but "gag" and *lazzi.* Truffaldino's rôle, however, was invariably left to improvisation; perhaps in compliment to Sacchi's

Pantalone, another character from the commedia dell'arte.

talents and his prominent position. The other masks were dealt with as Gozzi thought best. When the dialogue acquired dramatic or satirical importance, he wrote it out for them. On ordinary occasions he intrusted the whole or a considerable portion of each scene to their extempore ability, only indicating the movement of the plot in a *scenario.* The parts of the masks were treated in dialect and prose. The serious actors, who had to sustain the scheme of the fable, as lovers, magicians, queens, fairies, good and evil spirits, spoke in Tuscan blank verse, occasionally heightened by the use of Martellian rhymed couplets at thrilling moments of the action. Thus it will be seen that the text of Gozzi's plays offers every condition of dramatic utterance, from mere stage-directions, through carefully dictated prose, up to rhetorical soliloquies and dialogues in verse of several descriptions. His dexterity as a playwright is shown in the tact with which he employed these various resources.

The handling of the five fixed characters is masterly throughout. Whether Gozzi writes their lines or only indicates a theme for their impromptu declamation, he shows himself in perfect sympathy with an intelligent and practised group of actors. The humour of the man comes out to best advantage in this department. His language is most idiomatic and spontaneous here. Here too we find his raciest characters. Powerfully conceived and boldly projected, each comic personage breathes and moves with vivid realism. Study of the Masks, as Gozzi treated them, makes us feel what a wonderful thing of plastic beauty the *Commedia dell' Arte* must have been. Here, in a work of carefully considered literary art, we have its long tradition and its manifold capacities preserved for us. Reading a *Fiaba* is like opening a bottle of rare old wine. The bouquet of the fragrant vintage exhales into the chamber, and we taste the bloom of bygone summers. But the very conditions under which Gozzi exhibited this side of his dramatic mastery render translation impossible. In a translation the colours of the dialects are lost. The gradations of style, passing from a laconically worded *scenario* through half-dialogue into elaborated scenes, are bound to disappear. Tuned to a foreign language, our inward eye and ear fail to reconstruct the *lazzi,* which rendered this part of the drama humorous. That is why Schiller's *Turandot* is inferior to Gozzi's; and yet, when Schiller selected this piece for the German stage, he showed a right artistic instinct. It is the one in which the fable predominates, and can best be separated from the humours of the Masks.

I dare not enlarge here upon the variety of shades and complexions given to the five fixed types of character, according as the plot demanded more or less of serious action from the several personages. This inquiry would be interesting, since it reveals their singular elasticity beneath a master's touch. It must, however, be left to amateurs of curiosities in art. The development of the subject in detail implies previous acquaintance with the ten *Fiabe,* and would involve a lengthy dissertation. Some general points may, nevertheless, be indicated.

Pantalone retains marked psychological outlines under all his transformations. He is the good-humoured, honourable, simple-hearted Venetian of the middle class, advanced in years, Polonius-like, with stores of worldly wisdom, strong natural affections, and healthy moral impulses. Gozzi has drawn the character in a favourable light, purging away those baser associations which gathered round it during two centuries of the *Commedia dell' Arte.* His Pantalone recalls the Cortesani, described in a chapter of the Memoirs; but a touch of senility has been added, which lends comic weakness to the type.

Tartaglia stammers, and preserves something of the knave in his composition, burnished with Neapolitan abandonment to appetite and brazen disregard for moral rectitude. This general conception of the character explains the transformation of Tartaglia, in the **Three Oranges,** into the Tartaglia of the **Augellino Belverde.**

Brighella is an intriguing, self-interested individuality, trying to turn the world round his fingers, and not succeeding, or succeeding only by some lucky accident. He frequently assumes the form of a simpleton befooled by his short-sighted cunning.

Truffaldino blossoms before us as an ubiquitous and chameleon-like creature of caprice and humour; the liberal, carnal, careless boon-companion; the genial rogue and witty fool; bred in the kitchen; uttering words of wisdom from his belly rather than his brains; pliable, fit for all occasions; a prodigious coward; trusty in his own degree; taking the mould of fate and circumstance, adapting himself to external conditions; understanding nothing of the higher sentiments and awful destinies which rule the drama; but turning up at its conclusion with a rogue's own luck in the place he started from, and on which his heart is set, the larder. He runs like

an inexpressibly comic thread of staring scarlet through the warp and woof of Gozzi's many-coloured loom. The most serious use made of him is when, in the **Augellino Belverde,** for purposes of pungent parody, Gozzi invests him with the vizard of a Machiavellian egotist. At the close of that supremely caustic scene, Truffaldino drops his disguise, and willingly assumes the rôle of a domestic buffoon. Our author's trenchant irony, that "smile on the lips with venom in the heart," of which Goldoni wrote so lucidly, that touch of bitterness which renders him akin to Swift, was displayed by a stroke of genius here. Truffaldino, the whelp whose antics dispelled melancholy, becomes for once in Gozzi's hands a stick wherewith to beat the dog of modern science.

Smeraldina, under her numerous manifestations, maintains the lineaments of vulgar womanhood. Sometimes a good mother or nurse, sometimes a shifty waiting-woman, sometimes a blustering amazon, sometimes a bad wife or would-be virgin, she never soars into the regions of ideality, and mates eventually with Truffaldino, if she escapes from being burned for blundering atrocities upon the road to commonplace felicity.

With these fixed characters, which form the most delightful ingredients of the *Fiabe,* Gozzi interweaves a fairy-tale, abounding in magic, flights of capricious fancy, marvels, transformations, perilous adventures. There is always a conflict of beneficent and malignant supernatural powers, ending in the triumph of good over evil, the reward of innocence, and the punishment of crime. There is a fate to which the heroes and heroines are subject, and which can only be overcome by protracted trials, by patience through dark years, by sustained endurance, terrible struggles, and faith in supernatural protectors. Thus the texture of the *Fiabe* is similar to that of our pantomimes, except that in the former the fairy-tale and the harlequinade are interwoven instead of being disconnected.

The fairy-tale is always treated in a serious spirit. The didactic allegory, on which the author set such store, and which he regarded as the main purpose of his art, finds expression here. The fairy-tale is romantic, pathetic, heroic, sometimes acutely tragic. Gozzi interests himself in the creatures of fantastic fiction, and forces them to utter tones which vibrate in our entrails. Some scenes, written under the high pressure of dramatic oestrum, stir tears by their poignancy, by the accents of grief and anguish on the lips of *fantoccini.* It is a singular species of art, soaring by spasms and short gasps to dramatic sublimity, casting flashes of electric light on human nature in the garb of puppets, then passing away by abrupt transitions into mechanical improbabilities and burlesque absurdities—an art for marionettes rather than living actors, yet withal so vivid that able representation on the stage might translate it to our senses as an allegory of the masquerade world in which man lives:—

> We are such stuff
> As dreams are made of, and our little life
> Is rounded with a sleep.

The Masks take part in the action, generally as subordinate personages, sometimes as persons of the first rank, never as mere accessories to move laughter, nor as a stationary chorus. In this way the comic element is ingeniously connected with the tragic and didactic. This sounds like a contradiction of what I have said above, about the want of plastic unity in Gozzi's work. Yet the two apparently contradictory statements are true together. Gozzi interweaves the wires of humour and romance with remarkable skill. But he does not fuse them into one poetic substance. He fails to create an ideal world in which both tragedy and comedy are necessary to the spiritual order, as are the systole and diastole of the heart to an organised being. Though interlaced, they stand apart, each upon its own clearly defined basis. You pass from the one sphere to the other, and have sudden shocks communicated to your sensibility. There is a lack of atmosphere in the wonderfully brilliant and exciting picture, an absence of spontaneous transition from this mood to that, a suggestion that the playwright's sympathies have been touched to diverse issues by divers portions of his task. Very probably, the atmosphere, which I have indicated as wanting in the *Fiabe,* may have been communicated by the interaction of the members of Sacchi's troupe upon the stage at Venice. But this is only tantamount to admitting that Gozzi understood the theatre. It does not prove that he was a dramatic poet in the highest sense of that term. Had he been this, we should have submitted to his magic wand while reading him. That is precisely what we wish to do, and cannot always actually do. His *Fiabe* remain stupendous sketches in a style of audacious and suggestive originality. They are not the inevitable products of creative genius, fusing and informing—the children of imagination, "dead things with inbreathed sense able to pierce."

Had Gozzi been a great spontaneous poet, or a consummate artist, this invention of the dramatised *Fiaba* might have become one of the rarest triumphs of artistic fancy. It is difficult to state precisely what his work misses for the achievement of complete success. Perhaps we shall arrive at a conclusion best by inquiry into points of style and details of execution.

By singular irony of accident, the author of the *Fiabe,* though he dealt so much in the fantastic, the marvellous, and the pathetic, was far more a humorist and satirist than a poet in the truer sense. Of sublime imagery, lyrical sweetness or intensity, verbal melody and felicity of phrase, there is next to nothing in his plays. The style, except in the parts written for the Masks, is coarse and slovenly, the versification hasty, the language diffuse, commonplace, and often incorrect. Yet we everywhere discern a lively sense of poetical situations and the power of rendering them dramatically. The resources of Gozzi's inventive faculty seem inexhaustible; and our imagination is excited by the energy with which he forces the creations of his capricious fancy on our intelligence. The passionate volcanic talent of the man almost compensates for his lack of the finer qualities of genius.

What he wants is not the power of poetical conception, but the power of poetical projection; and the defects of his work seem due to the partly contemptuous, partly didactic, mood in which he undertook them. It would be difficult to surpass the pathos of Jennaro's devotion to his brother in *Il Corvo,* or the dramatic intensity of Armilla's self-sacrifice at the conclusion of that play. *Turandot* is conceived throughout poetically. The melancholy high-strung passion of Prince Calaf passes through it like a thread of silver. In the *Rè Cervo,* Angela has equal beauty. Her love of the man in the king, and her discernment of her real husband under his transformation into the person of a decrepit beggar, are humanly and allegorically touching. Cherestani, the Persian fairy, who loves a mortal in spite of the doom attending her devotion, is admirably presented at the opening of *La Donna Serpente.* The subterranean labyrinth of lost women, degraded to monstrous shapes by their tyrannical seducer, in *Zobeide,* merits

comparison with one of the *bolge* in Dante's Hell. Its horror is almost appalling. The love of Barbarina for her brother in *L'Augellino Belverde,* which melts the stony hardness of the girl's heart, and changes her from a vain worldling to a woman capable of facing any danger, is no less romantic than Jennaro's love in *Il Corvo.* The picture of Pantalone and his daughter Sarchè, in *Zeim Rè de' Genj,* passing their quiet life aloof from cities on the borders of an enchanted forest, touches our imagination with something of the charm we find in *Cymbeline. Il Mostro Turchino* is romantically passionate and highly-wrought. It seems to call for music, such music as Mozart invented for the *Zauberflöte.* Or, since Gozzi had little in common with the gracious spirit of Mozart, we might wish that this wild fable had fallen into the hands of Verdi. The composer of *Aïda* would have given it the wings of immortality. Gulindì, by the way, in this last fable, is a terrible portrait of the Messalina-Potiphar's-wife.

In selecting these passages for emphatic praise, I wish to call attention to the power and beauty of Gozzi's conception. Not as finished literature, but as the raw material of dramatic presentation, are they admirable. They need the life of action, the adjuncts of scenery, the illusion of the stage. (pp. 148-59)

The satire, which forms so prominent a feature in the *Fiabe,* impairs their artistic harmony. So far as this is literary (in the *Tre Melarancie, Il Corvo,* and elsewhere), it has lost its interest at the present day. So far as it is philosophical and didactic (as in *L'Augellino Belverde* and *Zeim*), it tends to break the unity of effect by the author's over-earnestness. So far as it is purely ethical, as in *Zobeide,* Gozzi loads his palette with colours too sinister and sombre. Perhaps, the political touches of satire in *I Pitocchi Fortunati* are the lightest and most genially used. Gozzi . . . was a confirmed conservative. An optimist as regarded the institutions, religion, and social manners of the past, he was a bitter pessimist in all that concerned the changes going on around him. The new literature, the new philosophy, the new luxury, the new libertinism, which seemed to be flooding Italy from France, were the objects of his hatred and abhorrence. Calmon, in the *Augellino Belverde,* expresses Gozzi's personal convictions and beliefs in their fullest extent. (p. 160)

Gozzi drew the subjects of his *Fiabe* from divers sources. The chief of these was a book of Neapolitan fairy-tales called *Il Pentamerone del Cavalier Giovan Battista Basile, ovvero lo Cunto de li Cunti.* This collection enjoyed great vogue in Italy during the seventeenth and eighteenth centuries, and is still worthy of attentive study by lovers of comparative folklore. Some of the motives of the *Fiabe* have been traced to the *Posilipeata di Massillo Repone,* the *Biblioteca dei Genj,* the *Gabinetto delle Fate,* the *Arabian Nights,* and those Persian and Chinese stories which were fashionable a hundred and fifty years ago. It was Gozzi's habit to interweave several tales in one action; and this renders researches into the texture of his dramatic fables difficult. But the inquiry is not one of great importance, and may well be dismissed until the star of Gozzi shall reascend the heavens, if time's whirligig should ever bring about this revenge.

L'Amore delle Tre Melarancie is both the simplest in construction and also the most artistically perfect of the ten *Fiabe.* In it alone the fairy-tale and the Masks are brought into complete harmony. No serious note breaks the burlesque style of the piece, while a sustained parody of Chiari's and Goldoni's mannerisms lends it the interest of satire. As he advanced, Gozzi gradually changed the form of his original invention. That fusion of fairy-tale and impromptu comedy in subordination to literary satire, which distinguishes the **Tre Melarancie,** was never repeated in his subsequent performances. The fable, with its romance, pathos, passion, adventure, magic marvels, and fantastic transformations, began to detach itself against the comedy. Both formed essential factors in Gozzi's later work; but the links between them became more and more mechanical. Satire, in like manner, did not disappear; but this was either used occasionally and by accident, or else it absorbed the whole allegory. The three ingredients, which had been so genially combined in the first piece, were now disengaged and treated separately. The sunny light of sportive humour, which bathed that wonder-world of fabulous absurdity, darkened as the clouds of didactic purpose gathered. The fairy-tale acquired an inappropriate gravity. Becoming aware of his dramatic talent, Gozzi assumed the tone of tragedy. He treated the loves and hatreds, the trials and triumphs, the vices and virtues, the heroism and the baseness, of his puppets seriously. Nevertheless, he preserved the preposterous accidents of the fable. On those enchantments, whimsical oracles of fate, metamorphoses, talking statues, monsters, good and wicked genii, he was of course unable to bestow the same reality as on his human characters. Yet, having carried the latter out of the sphere of burlesque, he had to maintain a tone of realism with the former. But he could not wield the Prospero's wand of imaginative insight which brings the supernatural and the incredible within the range of actualities. Thus the marvellous elements of the fable remained stiff and artificial beside the natural pathos and passion of humanity. (pp. 162-64)

> *John Addington Symonds, in an introduction to* The Memoirs of Count Carlo Gozzi, Vol. I, *translated by John Addington Symonds, John C. Nimmo, 1890, pp. 1-183.*

JOSEPH SPENCER KENNARD   (essay date 1932)

[*Focusing on Gozzi's faults as a dramatist, Kennard denounces his unfair treatment of Goldoni and censures, among other things, his extravagance and his incorrect Italian.*]

Sometimes an artist endeavors to make his work a finished picture; sometimes he aims at suggestion, trusting the onlookers' imagination to fill in the detail. In his great poem, Dante minutely describes the shapes and phantoms, and their environment. Milton merely suggests the vague greatness of Satan, the dazzling beauty of Gabriel. He relies on the imagination of his readers to complete the image. Each interpreted the inclinations and capacity of his own people. The Italian spirit is Greek and Roman. Classical training, communion with the masterpieces of antiquity, have made Italians artists and critics; but they are not an imaginative people. Gozzi failed to understand this. He secured the attention of his audience; but he could not rouse the sympathetic interest of his readers.

Italian critics scarcely afford him condescending benevolence; though in Germany, his *fiabe* were translated and welcomed as a splendid reaction from French pseudo-classicism. Hoffmann and Goethe imitated them; Schiller translated **La Turandot.** To Northern critics his extravaganzas indicated genius, and Gozzi is the harbinger of Romanticism. As such he was praised by Madame de Staël, and by Paul de Musset. The English also have applauded Gozzi. From Baretti to Sy-

monds, they all approve of his un-Italian aesthetics. (pp. 105-06)

Gozzi's flights of imagination were the product of his surfeited memory—a formless mixture of such nursery tales as *Le Cunto delli Cunti* by the Neapolitan Basile, or the many Italian translations and imitations of Eastern stories. These early recollections passed from Gozzi's pen unassimilated. In the first of his *Capricci scenici* or *fiabe,* the **Love of the Three Oranges,** he accumulated traditional childish nonsense in order that he might parody Goldoni's and Chiari's plays. Chiari's bombast was easily parodied; and Goldoni's style was sometimes slovenly. But Gozzi's style was not more correct. They all wrote incorrect Italian. They all used dialect and the Italian colloquialisms caused by political and geographical divisions and centuries of foreign oppression.

Though Gozzi and Goldoni championed purism, neither exemplified it. The Venetian dialect was a national tongue; and the study of Tuscan Italian, like the study of Greek and Latin, was a scholastic exercise. When Gozzi and Goldoni wrote Tuscan Italian, it was almost like translating into a foreign language. Hence the incorrectness of their Italian style. Gozzi corrected Goldoni; Baretti scolded them both.

Goldoni used some characteristic Venetian masks of the ancient *Commedia dell' Arte.* He adopted Pantalone, Arlecchino, Brighella, Il Dottore, Truffaldino; he accepted the traditional Leandro and Rosaura; he transformed them and gave them personality. His Pantalone was the typical *paterfamilias,* the honest merchant, the sensible citizen. He represented a whole class of Venetians. He was a living personality and no puppet. Brighella, the country lout from the north, became a devoted servant, a redresser of wrongs, a friend to his rakish young master. Sometimes he rose to the dignity of an innkeeper.

Arlecchino's irreducible pranks were confined to the background; and Rosaura assumed a matronly dignity unknown to Goldoni's predecessors. Even the *Servetta* grew into those delightful creatures *La Serva Amorosa,* that rival the best feminine characters in any theatre. Proud of this achievement, Goldoni was happy to see his fellow citizens adopting his ideas, and applauding his reform. Now Gozzi hated Goldoni; and he loved all the antiquated forms of Venetian government and art. Jealous and vindictive, he attacked Goldoni's reform. The babble, the practical jokes, the vulgar *lazzi* which Goldoni had minimized or omitted, Gozzi recalled to the stage.

This revival of the *Commedia dell' Arte* appealed to Gozzi's Venetian audience. Things that have but lately fallen from public favour are sure to find partisans. These masks, which had come from the antique Roman mimes, had lived across the darkest ages, had impersonated Italian regions and races, had amused so many generations, impersonated so many waves of ideas, should continue to live on the Italian stage.

On the 25th of January, 1761, Gozzi's first *fiaba,* **L'Amore delle tre Melarance,** was performed by the Sacchi troupe with enormous success. Goldoni heard the echo of this applause; and it confirmed his purpose of leaving Venice "To seek in new lands, and new experiences of manners, some better fruit. . . . Some day coming back to my beloved people, who perchance are now tired of me. . . . I may be then less old-fashioned and less unpleasant. . . ."

Such a gentle answer to Gozzi's rude attack! Such humility

in an author of world-wide fame contrasts finely with the pompous prologue of the *fiabe* that sounds like the flourish of trumpets heralding the puppet-show of the mountebank. Here was no *cammino* or *calle,* no modest room with its balcony looking out on the quiet *canale* such as Goldoni preferred, and such as all immediately recognized as familiar and real. Gozzi opened wide the doors of wonderland. (pp. 106-08)

The fickle Venetians were glad to see Goldoni and Chiari parodied. The representation of childhood stories, and the sumptuous staging, together with the extraordinary ability of Sacchi's Truffaldino and Darbes' Pantalone, won their applause; and the people asked for a second and third performance.

Carlo Gozzi knew that such puerile pageantry was shortlived. His aim was obtained by Goldoni's departure. With a theory of his art that was new in Italy, and partly original, he composed the second of his *fiabe, Il Corvo,* wherein an aesthetic thesis replaced the farcical parody. Here the *lazzi* and pranks of his beloved masks were reduced to the secondary rôle; and their parts were partly written by the author. He wished to show that Sacchi, Darbes, and the other actors were essential to Goldoni's success; but he proved that Sacchi, Darbes, and the other actors were essential to Carlo Gozzi.

In *Il Corvo* a magician is made the *deus ex machina* of extravagant, fantastic complications. This magical force, which torments and transforms, does not triumph to the end. Another magical power, a superior sort of justice, interferes with the cruel magician. This double current of mysterious forces originated in those Eastern tales which Gozzi imitated from the Neapolitan Basile. Gozzi reduced the Zoroastrian conception of the struggle between the spirits of light and darkness to this puerile antagonism of sorcerers and magicians.

Gozzi multiplies his personages, accumulates adventures, fills the scene with spectacular pageantry and with incredible apparitions. To Goldoni, painter of reality, chary of adornments, Gozzi opposed this revelry of colours, this swarming of figures and shapes, this mixture of comedy, tragedy, and farce. Gozzi is a harbinger of romanticism. In his *fiabe,* Gozzi gave his beloved comedians full opportunity for displaying their ability. Whether—like Goldoni—he could have persuaded his actors to drop their clownish pranks for a more restrained manner of recitation is questionable.

Within the circle of dreamland, his Venetian masks make vulgar caricatures of real people. Truffaldino and Brighella are transported to the courts of phantom kings, and clothed with gorgeous oriental garments; but their characters are not altered nor their speech or their morals corrected. They speak, play the traditional quips and pranks, and make the same grimaces as those used in plays that imitate the manners of their own people. The contrast was startling; it roused attention and provided matter of discussion.

The *Corvo* (*Raven*) contained all the discordant elements and perplexing aesthetic notions that we have indicated, but it also contained two valuable motives: the idea of punishment for needless cruelty, and strong brotherly affection. Both of these are powerfully expressed. As Millo, King of Frattaombrosa, reclined on his couch, Truffaldino informed the public how the King happened one day to kill a raven beloved by the wicked magician; how this magician sentenced the murderer to suffer until he should find a woman "with hair and eyebrows as black as the feathers of the fatal raven; and

cheeks as red as was his blood, and skin as white as was the marble on which the bird fell and died."

In order to release the King, Millo's brother Jennaro has enticed Princess Armilla of Damascus on board his ship. She is as black-haired and as red and white as the oracle demands Millo's deliverer to be. Jennaro tells his brother's story and entreats Armilla to consent to marry him. The Princess replies that her father, Norando, is a magician who can "stop the sun, upset mountains, turn men into plants." Two doves are sent by the "Power-of-light," mysterious Ormuzd, to counteract the evils that wicked Arismane is preparing for Jennaro. These doves warn Jennaro that when Millo receives the hawk, it will pluck out his eyes. Woe to Jennaro if he warns Millo; he will be turned at once into a statue. The horse that Jennaro brings as a gift will kill Millo as soon as he touches the saddle. Woe to Jennaro if he betrays this secret; he will be turned at once into a statue. There is a third malediction with the same threat. A dragon will attack Millo on the night of his marriage with the Princess. Five long acts develop all this sorcery of witchcraft, of transformations, and of the battle between the powers of Good and of Evil. On the same plan of spectacular staging and superfluous farce are constructed the other *fiabe:* the **Blue Monster,** the **Woman Snake,** and that jewel of the collection, the **Pretty Green Bird.**

In this last play, the buffoonery of Venetian masks, the stateliness of heroic verse, the unassimilated principles of a new philosophy, are mingled with something that is almost genial. Certainly Gozzi was unprepared to dispute the new philosophy. Yet his satire has a ring of bitter sincerity; and the broad humour, local allusions, traditions and proverbs, combine to make up an interesting play. (pp. 109-12)

Gozzi's *fiabe* amused the puerile and decadent Venetians. But the absurdities and impossibilities would surely weary us moderns. The acceptance by those Venetians of the misconstruction and misinterpretation of French philosophy which is found in these *fiabe,* gives pause for thought.

Though he had ridiculed versified plays and abused Goldoni's character studies, Gozzi now produced *I Pitocchi Fortunati* (*The Lucky Beggars*) and *Turandot.* "Fiabe tragicomiche," he called them, though they are merely ordinary comedies written partly in heroic verse, and partly in prose. *Turandot* has been praised by foreign critics.

The heroine, Turandot, daughter of Turan, is borrowed from an Eastern legend that was popular during the Middle Ages. Shakespeare did not ignore her when he traced the delicate picture of Portia and her three caskets. But Gozzi's heroine lacks the sweet Shakespearean maiden's charm. Turandot is a story-book character; her wicked pride requires that the successful suitor must solve three riddles of her invention or else lose his head. As a foil to her pride, her companion, Adelma, is sweetly loving. To this magnificently oriental court comes Prince Calaf, a "Prince Charmant" indeed, though disguised. Prince Calaf loves Turandot, faces the judges, and solves the three riddles.

The merit of the play is in the evolution of Turandot's character. When Calaf has won the prize, Turandot cries out that she hates him and will die rather than marry him. Chivalrous hero that he is, Calaf answers that he will give the Princess another chance. If she solves his riddle, his life will be forfeited. The riddle is to guess his own name. Adelma is in love with Calaf; and, in her eagerness to prevent the marriage, discovers the name and tells it to Turandot. Calaf, having lost, lifts his dagger to pay the penalty. Turandot's love conquers her pride. She entreats Calaf to take her for his wife and obedient slave.

Turandot has preserved the elaborate staging of the other *fiabe,* the display of oriental splendour, in the arrangement of scenes, the grouping of gaily dressed personages. There is also farcical byplay. Truffaldino, Brighella, and Pantalone do not change their manners although they are members of the "Divan." Sometimes they speak Venetian dialect, sometimes in verse, which, avoiding the cadence of the Martelliano line, has lost the harmonious flow of other Italian dramatists. *Turandot,* though the best of Gozzi's plays, is forgotten by Italians. Its length, the pretentious language, the turgid speeches, the puerile characters and situations, and the mixture of prosaic farce and heroic verse are in discord with Italian aesthetics.

Although Gozzi was a real poet, and his creative faculty equalled that of more famous writers, he failed to produce a true work of art. His unbridled nature and his jealousy of Goldoni's success prompted him to extravagant invention, to glaring contrasts. On and on, he urges his imagination; and is persuaded that there can never be too much of a good thing. He accumulates all possible material from ancient and foreign sources, and adds everything that his own imagination suggests. If Gozzi had curbed this indiscriminate appropriation of literary material, if he had made a scholarly study of modern Italian based on a solid knowledge of the classics, if he had not been intent on ruining a fellow worker, he might have been a foremost Italian poet.

Gozzi's failure resulted from the circumstances of his private life and the unwholesome atmosphere that then deadened intellectual activity in Venice. How terrible must have been the agony of the Venetians when they realized that around them was crumbling everything which they had been taught to consider most solid! Other Italian States hailed the French conquerors as liberators from foreign masters, as intellectual light-bearers; but Venice, after centuries of unequalled prosperity and undisputed freedom, now agonized with fear of bearing a yoke.

But sadder for Venetians than the loss of political power was the destruction of their faith in a social order that had proved itself so strong, that was reputed so just. It was not the invasion of soldiers, but the invasion of ideas which distressed and distorted Gozzi's mental balance. As a protest against impending evils, he conjured a fantastic world in which his ideals might shine brighter than reality: a puerile attempt, a pathetic instance of that suffering which attends all intellectual and social progress that is not willingly accepted. (pp. 113-15)

Thus Carlo Gozzi, tall and gaunt, stolid and prejudiced, a knight-errant fighting windmills, presumed to oppose the onward march of new ideas. Deeming Goldoni's realism vulgarity, he opposed to it the meaner vulgarity of masks uncurbed by any rule. When Truffaldino, Brighella, and others still more vulgar were let loose on the stage to improvise their *lazzi,* and were allowed to tickle the audience by their equivocations and vulgar pranks, they were certain to exceed the limit which Goldoni had traced for them.

Carlo Gozzi ridiculed Chiari's romances and plays for their superabundant episodes, adventures, and extravagances. Yet his own plays, stuffed with wonders and transformations,

were worse examples of a decadent literature wandering in search of new aims. (pp. 115-16)

Moreover, Gozzi's plays lacked style. Assuming to stand out as a *Granellescho,* a champion of classical *Trecentism,* he uses absolute terms, faulty phrase-construction, and wanders from all approved form. Like Goldoni, like Alfieri and Manzoni in their younger days, he was handicapped by his use of dialect. But, unlike these really conscientious writers, he does not try to correct himself. Believing that the Venetian dialect ranked with national languages, even as the comedy of masks ranked with the more regular forms of the theatrical art, he supported the traditional masks and their questionable amenities, and did not banish the idioms or constructions that belong to dialect. The harshness and inharmoniousness of Gozzi's verse will explain the severity of the Italian critics and the forgetfulness of the Italian public. (p. 117)

Joseph Spencer Kennard, "The Plays of Carlo Gozzi," in his The Italian Theatre: From the Close of the Seventeenth Century, *William Edwin Rudge, 1932, pp. 105-24.*

ALLARDYCE NICOLL   (essay date 1949)

[*Called "one of the masters of dramatic research," Nicoll is remembered as a theater historian whose works have proven invaluable to students and educators. His* World Drama from Aeschylus to Anouilh, *from which the following excerpt is drawn, is considered one of his most important works. Nicoll here describes the* fiabe, *using summaries of* The Love of the Three Oranges *and* The King Stag *to illustrate Gozzi's style and technique.*]

Gozzi's most representative writings are his so-called *fiabe*—fairy-tales with a purpose—grotesque, absurd, full of theatrical wonder, and, at the same time, closely in contact with the real, humorously ironic in concept, interfused with literary satire. Of his first important composition, *L'amore delle tre melarance (The Love of the Three Oranges),* nothing remains save a 'reflective analysis' (*analisi riflessiva*) presenting the outline of the plot, but even this meagre record is sufficient to indicate its quality, and has proved capable of inspiring later theatrical effort of noteworthy quality. The story tells of a melancholic prince, Tartaglia, who, under the curse of Fata Morgana (in league with the traitors Leandro and Clarice), is doomed to die unless he can be made to smile. The faithful Pantalone persuades King Silvio to introduce the laughter-moving Truffaldino to Court in the hope of curing the young invalid, but his utmost efforts fail until Fata Morgana, an old woman, is knocked head over heels by the acrobatic Truffaldino. At this the prince roars with merriment, and the whole Court is rejoiced. His troubles, however, are only beginning. Enraged, Morgana puts a fresh curse upon him: he is doomed to pine for the Three Oranges. These are kept in an enchanted castle many leagues away, and the prince, attended by Truffaldino, sets forth on the perilous journey. Fortunately aided by the magician Celio—Morgana's rival—he obtains the Oranges, gives them to Truffaldino to carry, and is separated from his companion. Although he knows that the Oranges must not be cut open unless a fountain of water is near by, the foolish Truffaldino, consumed with thirst, opens one. A young girl appears from it, piteously pleading for a draught of water. In terror, Truffaldino cuts open the second Orange, intending to give her the juice, and another young girl comes from this, too: both die of thirst. Just as he is about to cut the third Tartaglia enters, angrily takes it from him, opens it and, when a beautiful maiden appears, gets water from a lake, revives her, and learns that she is a princess, the daughter of Concul, King of the Antipodes. The Prince promises to marry her, but, while he goes off to arrange for the wedding, the wicked Smeraldina, a Moorish girl, causes the Princess Ninetta to be turned into a dove and herself takes her place. It seems as though Tartaglia, bound by his promise, must espouse this dark-skinned girl, when Truffaldino succeeds in bringing Ninetta back to her human form, and the play ends happily.

On the surface this is simply a child's fairy-tale, the theme for a sentimental pantomime. It must, however, be remembered that Tartaglia, Truffaldino, Pantalone, and others are characters of the *commedia dell' arte*, performed by actors to whose personal skill was added a rich inheritance from tradition. To them Gozzi makes magnanimous praise-offering. Describing the scene in which Tartaglia finds Truffaldino with the lifeless bodies of the two young girls who have issued from the Oranges, he declares that no words can adequately convey the effect created by the performers. "The witty actors of the *commedia*," he comments, "in scenes like these improvise such graciously pleasing dialogue and action as may not be expressed in written terms and could not be emulated by any dramatic author."

To appreciate *L'amore delle tre melarance,* therefore, we must use every effort of our imagination to reconstruct for ourselves the original conditions of performance. We must also realize that into this framework Gozzi has infused a kind of philosophic content. His chief aim is to entertain, to offer the comic actors a vehicle of wonder for the exercise of their talents, but throughout the action sly satire plays its part. Fata Morgana and the magician Celio are creators of marvels in this fairy-tale: they are also caricatures of those two contemporary playwrights whom Gozzi most detested—Carlo Goldoni and Pietro Chiari. He disliked their sentimental moralizings, he thought they were murdering the theatre of laughter, and, accordingly, in this guise he held them up to ridicule. He held up to ridicule too the dull, bombastic, tragic style of the age, thus making his entire piece, to use his own words, a "fantastic parody."

The same qualities animate all his later *fiabe* (although in these he provided more written dialogue than he had allowed himself in his earliest effort). *Il corvo* (*The Crow*) followed in 1761, and in 1762 came *Il re cervo* (*The King Stag*), *Turandot,* and *La donna serpente* (*The Woman Serpent*). In *La Zobeide* tragi-comedy ceded to grotesque tragic scenes. This was followed by *I pitocchi fortunati* (*The Fortunate Beggars*), *Il mostro turchino* (*The Turkish Wonder*), and *L'augellin belverde* (*The Magic Bird*), the last characteristically described as a "philosophic *fiaba*," and introducing a poverty-stricken couple, Renzo and Barbarina, who breathe the most moral sentiments of the new French philosophy until they become rich, when all their noble professions of faith vanish in pride, ingratitude, and deliberate evil.

In all of these plays some scenes are left for the improvisation of the actors, but most of the action is fully prepared, with dialogue in prose and verse, by the author. Contrast of every kind is eagerly sought—contrast between the fairy-tale atmosphere and reality, between serious scenes and hilarious, between the imaginative and the satiric, between colloquial prose and delicate verse, between the standard Tuscan tongue and the dialects of Venice or Naples—above all, between

scenes apparently designed solely for entertainment and scenes clearly based on philosophic reflection.

These qualities are excellently revealed in *Il re cervo.* The plot tells of a King Deramo who has been given two wonder-making marvels by the magician Durandarte. The first of these is a statue which makes signs to its master when he is being told an untruth. Vainly the monarch has been seeking for a bride: every princess and noble lady brought to his chamber has had her duplicity revealed by the statue's movements, and now at last the King has decided to interview anyone, no matter how poorly born, who may care to seek an interview. Among these candidates he includes one who has sought to escape the ordeal—Pantalone's faithful daughter, Angela. She alone passes the test, and, to her joy (for she is secretly devoted to her lord), is chosen to be the bride. This action, however, enrages Tartaglia, who, besides himself loving Angela, had hoped his daughter, Clarice, would have been the queen. Through his machinations the King is transformed, by means of the second marvel, into a deer; he is nearly slain, would, indeed, have perished had the magician Durandarte, in the likeness of a Parrot, not opportunely given him his aid.

All means are taken to enchant the audience. The prologue is spoken by Durandarte's servant, Cigolotti, who hints at the wonders to come; the scenes, constantly changing, present a rich and beautiful variety; Pantalone's homely Venetian dialect breaks in upon Tartaglia's Machiavellian Florentinity; and Angela's devotion is revealed sharply against the duplicities of her companions. Although German romanticists sadly erred in praising Gozzi as a supreme genius (sometimes placing him even above Shakespeare), they were right in recognizing that, in the midst of an increasingly lachrymose age, this author's keen wit and sense of wonder possessed a virtue well worthy of attention and of praise. (pp. 379-82)

Allardyce Nicoll, "The Growth of Bourgeois Comedy," in his World Drama from Aeschylus to Anouilh, *George G. Harrap & Company Ltd., 1949, pp. 371-97.*

GRETCHEN MARTIN   (essay date 1957)

[*While acknowledging their historical importance and influence on later writers, Martin emphasizes the* fiabe's *grotesque and sinister elements, arguing that they give the plays additional depth and significance.*]

Had [Gozzi] never written a play, his delightful memoirs—which he chose to call *Memorie inutili*—might have kept some fame for him; but he would scarcely have been a noted figure save for his plays and that quarrel with Goldoni and Chiari which preserves a paragraph for him in literary histories. Chiari is now forgotten; but he and Goldoni were actively writing in a new way—and Venice was flocking to the playhouse to applaud, so Gozzi felt, false sentiment and vulgar modernity. Daily life in the 1760's was bad enough—now one could actually see plays about beautiful innkeepers and merchant fathers with middle-class daughters indulging in middle-class love affairs. Goldoni was lovingly representing Venice, but it was not Gozzi's Venice. Gozzi wanted the enchanted city of palaces and doges, decked out in all the fancy of Byzantium and the Orient; Goldoni did not understand this exotic scene of masks and mysteries; Gozzi's Venice was a city for grand tragedy, or for the traditional comedy of art,

An etching of Gozzi and Sacchi listening as Ricci recites.

masked and improvised—not for the representation of tradesmen and serving maids! (pp. 30-1)

Gozzi thought poorly of the public taste; there was nothing superior, he considered, about Goldoni's pieces; he, Gozzi, could pack a playhouse just as successfully, and do it with a nursery tale for children—so much for Goldoni and his serious innovations! The volatile Venetians wanted only to be startled and amused; above all, they wanted to be amused by their adored, their native Italian, Masks—by Truffaldino and Brighella and Smeraldina from Bergamo, by the stuttering Tartaglia from Naples, by the beloved Pantalone of Venice itself; they wanted their dialects, their buffooneries, their topical quips, their pantomime; any fairy tale would do for the skeleton of a scenario on which one of the most talented companies of the day—Sacchi's troupe, just fled back from Lisbon where the earthquake had cut short their triumphs—might improvise a whole series of actions and sparkling dialogues.

From that happy mint of fairy tales, the *Pentamerone*, Gozzi took the absurd story of *L'amore delle tre melarancie (The Love of Three Oranges)*. He added all sorts of bits of satire on the plays and poetic styles of Goldoni and Chiari (for example, melancholy and monotonous verses in the manner of these writers are used to kill one of the characters by deadly boredom) which the audience of that day, of course, fully appreciated. The poet tossed off three acts replete with marvels

of stage machinery and astonishing devices—oranges that opened to reveal enchanted princesses, flowing fountains, tournaments, devils, processions, music, slapstick comedy, and all provided by those gifted masked mimes and character actors who represented for Gozzi the old, the true, the Venetian spirit of comedy. (pp. 31-2)

It was an overwhelming success: he could not stop here! Gozzi had, apparently, meant only to answer his opponents' challenge and satirize their dramatic theory; he had not planned a great innovation, nor had he perhaps really intended to sit down at the age of forty and make himself a dramatist. But his *jeu d'esprit,* conceived however half-seriously, however half-contemptuously, so enchanted the city—and the actors—that he was importuned to write more in the same vein. Thus *L'amore delle tre melarancie* was the first of the ten fairy pieces on which Gozzi's fame rests. His complete theatre includes thirty-two plays. Twenty-two of these are ordinary enough; they are dramas or comedies, most of them modelled on Spanish originals by Calderón, Tirso de Molina, and others. They had a varying success, but today they rest in that limbo where only the literary historian likes to browse. The work which keeps Gozzi's name alive, the work which contributed to the continuing stream of fantasy, was that of the ten plays written in rapid succession between 1761 and 1765—the *fiabe teatrali,* the fantasy plays. They were really a new genre. *L'amore delle tre melarancie,* although in time it might become an opera, was only a happy burlesque with fun, fantasy, and satire gaily intermingled; the costumes and stage effects were probably as much appreciated by the audience as the attack on Goldoni, which only the literary few would understand and enjoy. But Gozzi was too gifted a poet to continue in such a sterile campaign; he *would* continue to justify his claim that the Masks and their improvised comedy must be retained in the theatre; but he would do it now with art, not with buffoonery. One thing he did reflect upon—the audience adored the element of marvel, of wonder, of the supernatural. He considered that their tastes were coarser, their sensibilities more blunted than his; too few of them were aristocratic either in fact or in spirit; but they too, though already becoming corrupted by the spirit of the age, might be weary of the growing materialism of the rising middle class, of the chill rationalism which had begun to drift from more northerly lands, and might cling longingly to the old values of high honor, of pure love without false sentiment, of beauty unpolluted by the commonplace—in short, they too must long for an ideal, as opposed to a realistic, world. How much of this did Gozzi meditate when he planned his charming plays? This, at least, must have been what he *felt*.

The nine remaining *fiabe* are in verse, save for the dialogue of the Masks (where it is written out), which is in prose. His favorites of the Commedia dell'Arte occur in all—stuttering Tartaglia, whom he seems to have created from a slight original; Pantalone, whom he loves as a faithful representative, humorous and kindhearted, of the true popular Venice; Brighella the Bergomask, whom he makes a character of his own; Truffaldino, another Bergomask (a character, that is, originally from Bergamo in northern Italy); and what we should call the comedienne, the lively Smeraldina. This core of comic players may turn up in Chinese dress, or may be cast as king's ministers or sausage makers in a mythical city, but they retain their names, their dialect, and their tricks. Nevertheless, these nine plays are not really Commedia dell'Arte pieces; indeed, one or two are not what we should now call comedies at all save in the old technical sense of having a happy ending. They are stories of fantastic and intricate plot structure involving magic devices, the machinations of wicked enchanters, disguises and transformations, imprisoned princesses, and all the paraphernalia of the classic fairy tale or the *Thousand and One Nights*. The sources are generally Persian or Arabic, and here of course Gozzi is in the tradition of the Oriental tale and the taste for Oriental décor so widespread in his day. His settings are Eastern—sometimes particularized, as in *Turandot,* which takes place at the Manchu court in Pekin, or in *Il mostro turchino (The Blue Monster),* which is at Nankin; sometimes in that same unlocalized region where Musset, Maeterlinck, Dunsany, and Firbank have placed fictions which they chose to be out of time and place, the better to engage our poetic attention without the distractions of the too near and too well-known. The tone of the plays varies from the high comedy of *L'augellin belverde (The Little Bird of Fair Green)*—Gozzi calls it a "philosophical" *fiaba,* and it is perhaps his masterpiece—to the serious and psychological drama of *Turandot* (which he calls tragicomic)—to the "tragedy" of *Zobeide,* which includes powerful elements of terror and horror. Two of these plays depart from the type in that they do not use the supernatural at all—*Turandot* and *I pitocchi fortunati (The Fortunate Beggars),* but they are sufficiently extravagant to deserve the name "*fiabe*".

Gozzi uses three types of characters: the Masks; the non-supernatural persons such as the hero and heroine, the old king, the falsely imprisoned queen, and so on; and the personages possessed of magic arts or such "characters" as jinns, hydras, speaking statues, and the like. The "straight" characters are of high degree, or, as for instance in the case of Pantalone's daughter in *Il re cervo (The Stag King)* of surpassing virtue and beauty. The Masks may turn up in positions of rank, but this rise in the world merely adds to their absurdity, and they refer wistfully to their old homes in Bergamo or Venice, before they landed (we don't quite know how) in the courts of Samarkand or Cathay.

Now these plays may be read merely for their delightful fancy and humor; their imaginative evocations charmed many of the romantic writers, particularly in Germany, where among others Hoffmann, Tieck, Schiller, and Goethe admired them extravagantly. Schiller translated *Turandot;* this and *L'amore delle tre melarancie* have been transmuted into well-known operas; *La donna serpente (The Serpent Woman)* inspired one of Wagner's early pieces, *Die Feen;* there are echoes of *Il mostro turchino* in *The Magic Flute.* It is difficult to trace Gozzi's "influence," but there is no doubt that it played a part, if only indirectly through the German Romantic movement, in the future course of fantasy, dramatic and fictional.

Is there any deeper significance in the *fiabe* than their surface reflection of a lost epoch or their imaginative play of wonder and sentiment? One can scarcely assert that Gozzi wrote "hermetically," or that he gave profound analysis to the scenes that flowed so casually from his pen; nevertheless, for a few years he chose a certain genre which was quite his own creation, dealt lovingly with certain settings and characters and events, and then, as though he had said all there was to be said of this private world, turned from the land of faery and wrote like other people for the rest of his life. It is possible for a writer to apprehend and transmit poetic truths of which he is himself but dimly aware; it is a commonplace that Shakespeare affords a thousand truths which might astonish him, but which are none the less there, embedded in the rich

layer upon layer of thought and feeling and expression. Gozzi was not a great artist, but he had a subtle mind, he was a man of wit (in the old sense), of great sensibility, a man whose intuitions of another meaning to the sensible world could go so far as to be almost mania (he began to fancy that the evil spirits of his own dramas were come to life and plagued him vengefully; this might be madness, but it is the madness of one who thinks in more than one dimension).

It may be suggested that in the *fiabe* the Masks represent, for Gozzi, the *real* world—the world of everyday experience in which we must live, however crude and materialistic it may be. These characters are not used simply as comic relief—in the way Elizabethan playwrights, for instance, sometimes introduce clownish action in a tragedy—nor as a mere chorus for picturesque effect; they are important in the development of the complicated plots, sometimes to be sure merely as minor but necessary adjuncts, but also as leading protagonists—for instance in *Il re cervo,* where the Bergomask Brighella becomes more villainous than comic and turns his master into a stag, precipitating much of the action of the play.

The other non-marvellous characters, the heroes and heroines for example, represent the *ideal* world of chivalry, honor, love and devotion—the world of all those high virtues so poetically present in the epics and romances, in Ariosto and Tasso, in that absolute realm of ideal aristocracy to which Gozzi clung, although already the men were born who would chop down one tree for the guillotine and plant another in the name of plebeian liberty. These characters, however unrealistic in their perfection, are not completely stylized; there is tender feeling in the brotherly love of Jennaro in *Il corvo (The Crow);* there is warmth in the devotion between brother and sister in *L'augellin belverde*—it is indeed her love for her brother that cures Barbarina of the corroding philosophy of self-interest which she had derived from the doctrines of French *philosophes,* doctrines which Gozzi abhorred; amid all its Arabian Nights marvels, the love of Taer and Dardané glows with purity and sweetness in the tale of *Il mostro turchino;* the character of Zobeide, in the play of her name, has been justly praised for its lofty conception of womanly love and fidelity. Gozzi, in fact, always draws his women with sensitivity and warmth. Such beings, of course, can rarely be found in everyday Venice; although surrounded by ordinary persona—by the Masks—they are rendered more believable by their habitation in far lands where, we may for the illusion of five acts suppose, such pure ideals are still to be found.

There is a third set of characters in the *fiabe,* a third element in the narrative, in the whole poetic conception; these are the enchanters, the jinns, the sorceresses, the creatures who possess more than mortal powers; they are allied with forces of mystery of which we know only the effects, not the capricious and inscrutable causes; they represent that element of the *grotesque* which in itself is one of the strangest and most tenacious phases of art, existent before Gozzi, existent today, most easily detected perhaps in painting and sculpture—there are hints in his Venetian contemporary Longhi—but leaving its lamia trace, bright or very faint, through the Gothic, through the German romantics, through the schools of horror, through Poe and Dickens and Dostoevsky, Maeterlinck and Rimbaud, Hardy and Kafka. The enchanters who lay portentous tasks upon a chance-met prince in order to free themselves from still more mysterious dooms reflect that element of the perverse, the bizarre, which pervades a world where we find ourselves beset by the whim of fate, condemned without a cause, snared into complexities which we are too simple to understand yet which must be unravelled or we perish. The classic transformations of fairy tales have, no doubt, more than one psychological meaning in the racial inheritance of myth and archetype; but among other things we still can often feel that we are living lives not ours, that our spirits are forced into strange bodies compact of fear and pain, given names not rightly ours. These ancient racial tales, so full of symbol, remind us of man's terrible inability to communicate with his fellows: the king (in *Il re cervo*) longs for the love of his wife, but he is metamorphosed into a wretched old man; Taer's heart breaks at the sight of his beloved (in *Il mostro turchino*), but she sees only a repulsive monster. In the grotesque vision of life we are required to do the impossible, or are punished for sins we do not understand; the universe is a place of complete absurdity; the goddess Reason, as some enthusiasts suppose, does *not* reign; water may sing and graven images speak, a parakeet may be a wizard in disguise, a serpent be a fairy princess who longs for mortal love and life; a thoughtless word, a moment of forgetfulness, may destroy any fancied order in life, and the lightest coincidence—as a greater writer, Hardy, so well understood—appear to bring ruin and disaster, not because such careless acts of chance are in *themselves* causes of tragedy, but because they may be used as instruments to bring about dire events necessitated by far other, far more mysterious and incalculable forces.

This quality of strangeness in Gozzi is more than a mere penchant for the marvels of the Oriental story or the European folk tale. He was not, as the romantics probably regarded him, a mere defender of fantasy in an age of reason, nor one who wished simply to preserve the play of fancy, the spirit of harlequinade and comic opera illusions; the fairy tale element is always treated seriously—never with irony or condescension. One might wonder, in fact, how so dark-spirited a man could have written so many comic fantasies if they were, indeed, no more than comic and fantastic. Two of these plays contain no magic at all. *I pitocchi fortunati* is based on the old story of the caliph who disguises himself that he may go about his realm and see the condition of his people for himself; here the strangeness is that of the fortuitous accidents by which men in high estate are hurled to the abyss of misery and poverty—it is the old theme of Fortune's wheel, alike out of the Middle Ages and Baghdad. In *Turandot* (named for the cruel princess who is the leading character) the strangeness has a touch of sinister. In short, even in these two plays there is a brooding shadow upon the extraordinary action, different in quality from the mere pathos of untoward events. This tinge of the sinister becomes a dark glare over the whole drama of *Zobeide,* which Gozzi himself called a tragedy because of its pity and horror; and the scene where the innocent but hideously transfigured wives of the wizard-king appear in the dungeon, is a masterpiece of the macabre.

Only the symbols of magic can free us from the inscrutable dooms and frightful ordeals which strike upon us from the grotesque world in which we are at such disadvantage with powers outside ourselves—we would say today with the forces of Nature; the makers of myth and folk tale would say with greater than mortal forces. Gozzi does use the conventional apparatus of magic swords and incantations, but more importantly it is an inner quality of love and devotion, raised to almost mystic exaltation, which conquers the dark magic of the perverse, the bizarre, the sinister. This spiritual quality gives sweetness and delicacy to his love stories, and allows

identification with his characters and scenes which, if they were all marvel and extravagance, would be only frigid and decorative.

It is this element of the grotesque and the sinister that gives depth and importance to a handful of plays otherwise valuable chiefly for their period interest and the influence of their genre. (pp. 32-9)

Gozzi's fairy plays are an epitome of an idea of fantasy, of an idea pervasive in the period; they transcend that period in so far as that idea is, in itself, inextricably mingled in the literature and culture of succeeding places and times. (p. 39)

Gretchen Martin, "Goldoni's Antagonist: Carlo Gozzi, Venetian Fantasist," in Italian Quarterly, Vol. 1, No. 3, Fall, 1957, pp. 30-9.

DAVID NICHOLSON   (essay date 1979)

[*Nicholson highlights the dramatic techniques that raise Gozzi's* Turandot *to the sophisticated level of a tragicomedy.*]

The ten Fiabe of Carlo Gozzi, written between 1760 and 1765, demonstrate in several ways how the defining characteristics of classical tragicomedy overlap with those of the fairy tale. The folk fairy tale, consisting of serious actions which end happily, is inherently tragicomic in that it offers the literary artist a set of generic possibilities out of which something more precisely defined can be realized. In reinterpreting the tales, a dramatist may choose to bring out the tragedy by darkening the tone and emphasizing the seriousness of the action, inverting or aborting the happy ending; or he may bring out the comedy by brightening the tone and highlighting the movement toward the final transcendence. The third possibility, that of maintaining a tension or balance between the tragic and comic elements, results in tragicomedy, a sophisticated literary product that stands in relation to the naive folktale more or less as the town mouse to his country cousin.

In addition to the heroic quest with its happy ending, classical tragicomedy and the fairy tale have two general features in common. First, in both the action takes place in a special world, removed from that of everyday reality, in which special laws apply. Events which would be unlikely or impossible according to the rules of realistic probability occur naturally here, inviting responses of astonishment, awe, and wonder. This is a world to which marvels, magical creatures, and the grotesque have easy admittance. Second, formal elements are emphasized in both. Folk tales structure themselves according to certain familiar patterns, as we see in the tendency of their elements to repeat in threes. The fairy tale has a special fondness for talismanic artificial objects—slippers, rings, golden balls, etc.—which condense the meanings of the stories and help to give them their abstract, almost schematic quality. Tragicomedy, as if aware of its hybrid nature, typically calls attention to itself and its own problematic status as a literary mode. Its interest in artificiality, revealed in such things as euphuistic language and decorative plotting, carries it in the opposite direction from the simplicity of the folk tale, ending, as in Gozzi's *Turandot,* in the kind of self-conscious theatricality in which the characters seem to wink at the audience, showing that they too are aware of what kind of play they are performing in. Here the similarities between fairy tales and tragicomedy begin to remind us of differences—e.g., simplicity/complexity, naivety/sophistication, clarity/ambiguity—but obviously the two forms have certain affinities that a dramatist of tragicomic bent could recognize and use in adapting fairy tales for the stage. (pp. 467-68)

[Each] of the ten Fiabe is a more or less organic synthesis of three elements: (a) the fable, often a tale from the *Pentamerone* of Basile or the *Arabian Nights,* performed by (b) the commedia masks or by characters associated with them, this whole exotic fabric threaded through by (c) moral allegory or satirical attacks on literary enemies [see excerpt by Symonds dated 1888]. At times, as in **Turandot,** the satire is almost totally absent, so that the essential elements may be reduced to two. This makes a structure that is tragicomic almost by definition: the serious action from the fable is potentially tragic, and the commedia masks guarantee comic effects. In the first of the Fiabe, **The Love for Three Oranges,** these elements are integrated; Tartaglia himself is the prince who goes in quest of the enchanted oranges. In the later plays the fable and the masks are kept separate and the romantic characters play the fairy-tale parts, though here too, as we shall see, the comic element always qualifies and comments on the serious action.

Turandot, the most famous of the Fiabe, is the least typical. It contains no marvels and, according to Symonds, "is the one in which fable predominates, and can best be separated from the humours of the masks." Its romantic story, drawn from the *Arabian Nights,* is based on the familiar fairy-tale motif of the riddle-ordeal, in which the hero wins a bride through the giving and/or solving of a riddle, a theme folklorists have traced all the way back to Greek romance. It belongs to a set of similar tales concerned with tests of cleverness, in all of which the element of the supernatural is subordinate or absent. The play is elegantly constructed around the two ordeals. Acts 1 and 2 describe the arrival in Pekin of an unknown prince (named Calaf) and his successful answers to the riddles of the beautiful but proud Turandot, after which the chagrined princess demands a second test, this time a riddle which she must solve. Acts 3-5 describe her efforts to discover the unknown prince's name by trickery and her growing realization that she loves him, and the play ends with her triumph followed immediately by her giving herself to him in marriage.

Prince Calaf's quest has tragic implications because the penalty for guessing incorrectly is death. The walls of the city are decorated with human heads mounted on spikes (another folk-tale element with an ancient history), and as we watch, the head of Turandot's latest victim is affixed to the wall by "a hideous executioner, his arms naked and bloody." Calaf is warned several times of the dangers, once by Turandot herself. Nevertheless, he must persist: some "occult, irresistible force" compels him. After his success in act 2 Calaf experiences despair when he thinks he will be killed by Turandot's soldiers at dawn. At the end, confronted with Turandot's vindictiveness, he says it would have been better if he had failed the day before, "for this augmented pain is insupportable"; then he pulls out a dagger and tries to kill himself.

Thus the play falls in the category of "averted tragedy," called the most effective kind of tragic plot by Aristotle. The discovery that averts the tragic *dénouement* is Turandot's realization that she loves Calaf; acting on this insight, she stops him from stabbing himself and offers her hand. As a whole the quest has the shape of a tragedy and could have been treated as such if Gozzi had not been interested in other effects. His chief means of qualifying the seriousness of the ac-

tion, besides the happy ending, are three: the conventional romantic treatment, the presence of the commedia masks, and the high theatricality of his form. He aims not at the catharsis of pity and terror, but at a pleasurable climax of suspense and excitement in the adventure, amusement at the skillful play of wit, and a sense of satisfaction in the final submission of Princess Turandot. The result is a hybrid, something much more exotic and vivid, and therefore more interesting, than the conventional tragedy he might have written.

Let us consider first the romantic treatment. Like most fairy tales, **Turandot** is a romance and is constructed according to certain conventional rules. One such rule is that every hero is destined for his own special adventure, and conversely that every adventure awaits its chosen hero. In the Grimms' version of "Sleeping Beauty" the hedge of hawthorn surrounding the enchanted palace closes tightly on all the princes who want to awaken the princess before the appointed time, holding them in the thorns until they die miserable deaths. But when the right prince comes along, the hawthorns blossom out and open wide to receive him. Gozzi takes care to make us feel that Calaf is a similar kind of hero. He has come to Pekin seeking his fortune; and according to fairy-tale convention (we are reminded by the heads on the wall), he who seeks will find the fortune of which he is worthy—or, rather, it will find him. Turandot's portrait is thrown to the ground at Calaf's feet; he picks it up, glances at it, and is immediately caught up in his fate. The aura of the chosen hero goes with him into the court: Altoum says to the princess, "Finally a prince worthy of you has presented himself," and Turandot is moved for the first time.

In romance that is not ironic a hero undergoes suffering, even doubt, but always achieves his goal. Calaf's goal, marriage with the princess, has two aspects, both of which follow from the paradox of Turandot's character. First, as in "Sleeping Beauty" and many other fairy tales, he awakens the princess to love, making it possible for her to give herself to a husband (Bettelheim calls this one of the primary psychological functions of fairy tales). Second, like the typical dragon-slayer, he rids the world of a terrible scourge (Turandot is compared to Medusa and described as "diabolical," "infernal," and "implacable"). That this man-eating monster and the beloved princess are one and the same is no doubt what gives this tale its special fascination. Along with the princess, naturally, goes the throne, that of the Empire as well as of Calaf's own lost kingdom.

Every work of fiction offers a universe with laws of probability that may or may not correspond to those of the natural world. Kitto points out, apropos of Euripidean tragicomedy, that in romance we accept things that we could not accept in tragedy. Romance operates by conventional rather than natural laws: as soon as we recognize the genre, we suspend disbelief and begin to expect certain familiar kinds of characters and events.

Our first glimpse of the scene, dominated by several heads mounted above the city gate, takes us into the romantic world of "Pekin in the distant past," the perilous realm of Calaf's adventure. In romance an image like this, nightmarish and dreadful, prepares us for a compensating image of success and supreme happiness. At the end the prince thanks the gods for his good fortune: "For the gods can transform us in an instant against all human probability. I ask their pardon for my past complaints and lamentations. Their ways are truly unknowable. All we poor mortals can do is live, and pray, and await the just evolution of our destiny." The presence of benevolent gods rules out tragedy by definition if even "human probability" is subject to their control. Though *Turandot* contains none of Gozzi's usual magic, it is full of coincidences and other unlikely developments. The convergence of the hero with his fated adventure, already mentioned, is one example. Another is the obligatory happy ending, unmistakably pointed out ahead of time: Gozzi has a courier arrive during Calaf's night of despair with the totally unprepared-for news that his former subjects have thrown off the invaders and invited him to return. . . . Thus the unlikely events in *Turandot* contribute to the daydream-like qualities required in fairy-tale romance, in which the reader or audience is invited to identify with the hero and participate in his success against all realistic odds.

The suspension of disbelief also subverts the moral response that would be demanded in tragedy or realism. It allows us to accept the idea that Altoum, a sympathetic character, would let his daughter send all the neighboring princes to the block merely because they could not think as fast as she. Why would he proclaim such a cruel, whimsical law, and why, having proclaimed it, would he continue to enforce it? He even wages war on surrounding kingdoms in order to protect the right of their princes to commit suicide by proposing to Turandot. To head off such objections, irrelevant in the context of romance, Gozzi appeals to ritual: the solemn kissing of the book, the reading aloud of the proclamation, and the language of the riddles invest the law with authority of religion. This "tragic cycle" is a pattern which must play itself out, something beyond Altoum's power to change: "We would gladly give our empire to change the law, but we cannot. For we have sworn, with the most solemn oaths of our religion, to execute the cursed edict in each fierce particular. Now new victims present themselves with each fresh wind; and Turandot is implacable." In tragedy, when such absolutes are proclaimed, they remain absolute and take on the nature of fate (e.g., Oedipus's cursing of himself). Later Altoum finds it convenient to change his mind about this law, thus proving that its purpose was to charge the riddle ordeal with the spurious significance of a divinely ordained event. It allows Altoum to escape our censure, and it gives Turandot her demonic aspect.

At the heart of this curiously powerful tale with its contradictory effects is the paradox of Turandot herself. Beautiful but coldly proud, like the stepmother-queen in the Grimms' "Snow-White," she stands in a long tradition of witches and dangerous beauties reaching back to Circe in *The Odyssey*. Her demonic aspect is manifested in the power of her attractiveness to compel princes to offer themselves for her deadly ordeal. This is a kind of enchantment (Calaf calls it an "occult, irresistible force"), but her dangerousness, as we have seen, derives from Altoum's proclamation rather than from supernatural means. Turandot's bloodthirsty hatred of men makes her witch-like, but at the same time it is interpreted in familiar human terms of fear and distrust: "I know too well how treacherous men are; all men without exception. I know that they are false despite their protestations, changeable despite their promises, and shallow. They dissimulate to trap us; and when they have vanquished us, they love us no longer. Then they lightly break the vows they once swore to." It is as a human being, not a supernatural creature, that Turandot is touched by Calaf's love and accepts him as worthy of her trust. We can take her need to win in the end, fierce and im-

placable as it is, as an understandable human desire not to lose face.

But the key to the problem of Turandot's character lies in the nature of the genre: in romance, Northrop Frye reminds us, we are interested in the story itself, not so much in its meanings. The more bizarre the turn, the more amazed we are, and the more curious to see what will come next. For the sake of the story we are asked to take seriously the idea that love could transform Turandot overnight from the maneating monster whose emblems are displayed on the city walls to a submissive wife who will henceforth "love and revere the whole sweet race of men." In accordance with Eric Bentley's formulation, the play is an averted tragedy in which the urge to punish is transcended through forgiveness, as in *The Tempest,* but with one important difference: here we are asked not so much to forgive as to forget what Turandot has done. Such an appeal could be successful only in romance, in which the strong pull of the conventional pattern overpowers moral niceties. But the tension between her dual roles as "scourge" and as "sleeping princess" cannot be fully resolved, even here. It may not occur to Calaf that he is marrying a murderess, but we cannot easily dismiss those severed heads from our minds. This tension—no doubt sought deliberately by the playwright—gives the final scene an ambiguous, dissonant quality, to which we must respond by restraining a wholehearted assent to the joyful conclusion. It is a tone we recognize as the authentic mark of the tragicomic ending.

Thus Gozzi invites us to enjoy the play in terms of expectations set up by the structures of romance, to which he refers us all the way through. In a tale of heroic adventure we are caught up by suspense and reversal in the excitement of the hero's quest. Answering only the needs of the story, the characterization is simple and strongly marked: one is either for the quest or against it. Calaf's steadfastness and his love for Turandot define him as a worthy hero; Barach, the hero's helper, is simply loyal; Adelma's intentions serve the purposes of the intrigue; white-haired Timur provides the pathos; and so on. Turandot, the only complex and changing character, is both for and against the quest, as we have seen; this is, however, a complication based on a very simple principle, and moreover one required by the basic idea of the play. Finally, the setting defines the world of the quest as an exotic, dangerous realm with its own laws of probability and ethics, ruled by divinities who wish the hero well and will see him through to a happy ending.

The romantic treatment came with the tale direct from the *Arabian Nights;* Gozzi's contribution to it consisted essentially in finding dramatic means to replace the narration. But he then altered the meaning of the story by what he added to it— that is, the commedia masks. Their presence in the play further qualifies the seriousness of the action, not only because we know that nothing tragic could occur in a world which they inhabit, but also because they parody and comment satirically on the events so as to render them less weighty. A good example of this parody comes just before the final scene. Having been told by Adelma that he will be killed at dawn, Calaf greets Brighella as his executioner: "So it is to be you, Brighella. Come. Carry out your orders. Take my life. I no longer have any use for it. . . . See that I can face death calmly and without any defense." Brighella is naturally puzzled by this and has to find an explanation: "Poor boy. Obviously went crazy during the night. All those ladies, in and out; declaiming, posturing, beating their breasts, tearing their hair. Finally they drove him crazy. Ah, well. He's not the first lunatic in a high place, and I daresay he won't be the last."

Calaf and the other serious characters seem impervious to this parody effect, as if unaware that the commedia characters are in any way incongruous or out of place in their fabulous world. Where we see Truffaldino and Brighella, familiar rascals to the original audience, the characters in the fable seem to see a perfectly ordinary Chief Eunuch and Master of the Pages; where we see Pantalone and Tartaglia, they seem to see the Chief Minister and Keeper of the Seal. The mask characters, however, know they are not where they are supposed to be. In the midst of the pomp and ceremony of the court, Pantalone says to the Emperor, "You may not have noticed it, but I am not, myself, of Chinese descent." Before his metamorphosis he had never even heard of China, except in the sense of crockery. Then he launches into a long, amusing speech about how different things are back in Venice: "I tell you, if I mentioned any of this back home, they'd clap me in the asylum and lose the key. They'd tie me up in a straitjacket and feed me gruel with a wooden spoon. But here they all act as if it was perfectly natural and normal. No. I give up. I really do. Hard as I try, I'll never understand the oriental mind." According to the stage directions, Pantalone speaks these lines directly to the audience; we imagine the other characters holding a long pause behind him, then, when he steps back into the play, the scene proceeds as if there had been no interruption.

Thus the commedia characters present a comic view of the action, subordinate to but parallel with the serious view at every point. The parody goes right to the heart of the fable. . . . The disjunction of the serious content and the comic manner creates that odd third effect that we call tragicomedy.

Since we are always several steps ahead of the hero, we know, as he does not, that the path is safe and that his bride waits at the end of it. By the time Calaf enters the dreaded palace, for example, we have already seen Truffaldino and Brighella having a comic quarrel about marriage as they set up for the court scene (Truffaldino's role as Chief Eunuch provides good comic material). Or the defusing effect may occur simultaneously with the serious action. At the most tense moment of the riddle-ordeal, as Calaf, dazzled by Turandot's beauty, tries to regain control of himself in order to think of an answer, Tartaglia interjects: "If it weren't for the s-s-s-solemnity of the occasion, I'd run to the kitchen and take a drink." The seriousness affects the comedy in turn, giving it a tense, nervous quality, as we see here. Another example: the third of the four spies who come to Calaf in the middle of the night is Truffaldino, who imagines he can get Calaf to reveal his name if he slips a mandrake root under his pillow and recites a ridiculous spell over him. This sort of thing provides a running comic commentary on the action, draining off its seriousness by means of simultaneous parody.

Let us turn now to the theatrical qualities of the play. The presence of commedia masks in a fairy tale implies an interest on the part of the writer in self-consciously theatricalist effects. Part of our pleasure comes from the witty and ingenious manner in which Gozzi balances incongruous elements so that they qualify but do not negate each other. In other words, we enjoy the virtuosity of the playwright's art as much as that of the players. Naturally this moves us even further from tragedy, since in tragedy any hint that we are being ma-

nipulated, however brilliantly, will destroy the sense of inevitability and therefore the tragic effect. (pp. 468-75)

There are several . . . references to the play itself. When Calaf first hears about Turandot, for example, he does not believe the story because it seems so strange; he calls it one of those "fantastic stories" which the common people tell, which no intelligent person would take seriously. Barach answers, "Sire, this story is true; and it is deadly serious." They discuss the story at length, in part as exposition, but also quite deliberately to bring the audience into the fable: as Calaf is convinced, so are we. But the effect is paradoxical, because the hero's skepticism seems to question the very premises of romance. He holds himself aloof until the moment he looks upon Turandot's image, at which point he is converted and assumes his role as hero.

Later Calaf shows a degree of self-awareness by describing himself in his riddle: "There is a certain prince from a high and noble line who was reduced to begging bread and carrying vile burdens to maintain himself; who, having unexpectedly attained the height of human happiness, was then cast down lower than he had been before." But here the effect is to intensify, rather than to qualify, our belief in the fable, since he refers to himself not as doubter but as hero. In the context of the other riddles, the answers to which are "the sun," "the year," and "life," this riddle universalizes Calaf and assimilates him and his quest with the world of romance. Moreover, it illustrates the folk tale principle that the riddle tends to evolve from the action of the tale itself. Calaf's riddle and his moments of skepticism together show the common interest of fairy tale and tragicomedy in highlighting formal elements, the former by abstracting and universalizing, the latter by self-consciously calling attention to itself.

There are two more such instances in the play, both of which remind us of Gozzi's other Fiabe and of fairy-tale plays in general. In his memoirs Gozzi tells us that he wrote ***Turandot*** without the customary marvels and transformations in order to disarm critics who suggested that the success of his plays depended on spectacular effects [see excerpt dated 1797]. He chose, as we have seen, a fable in which the contest of wits takes the place of magic. When one of her ladies-in-waiting suggests that a wizard might help them discover Calaf's name, Turandot replies, "No, Zelima. Those charlatans, who prey on the ignorance of the vulgar, are beneath my notice." We detect a similar sardonic glint in the author's eyes when Tartaglia describes the mysterious courier from Calaf's kingdom: "A secret messenger . . . some kind of spirit, or demon, or something. I tell you frankly, Prime Minister, when that thing arrived—whoosh—in a billow of black smoke, clutching a scroll in its paw; well, to tell you the honest truth, I left in something of a hurry." Here Gozzi is not only twitting his critics and patronizing the "ignorant vulgar" in the audience, represented by Tartaglia, who might be impressed by such a cheap trick, but is also making good-humored fun of his own plays. The arrival of the courier just in time for Altoum to learn Calaf's name is indeed an improbable coincidence, one that might as well have been accomplished by the author's usual supernatural means. There is in ***Turandot*** little of the literary and social satire that gives Gozzi's ***Love for Three Oranges*** the feeling of allegory; but moments like these, when the author steps from behind his characters and allows us a glimpse of his rhetorical purposes, have a similar effect.

Needless to say, they also increase the sense of self-consciousness in the play.

To conclude, let us consider the sense in which the play is theatrical as well as theatricalist. We have already placed it in the category of romance, or heroic adventure, in part because it appeals first to our interest in an exciting story well told. Having foresworn transformations and magic, Gozzi relies mainly on surprise and suspense. Turandot, who has theatricalized her fear of marriage and hatred of men in the ordeal of the riddles, is naturally the source of these effects. In act 2, for example, when it looks as if Calaf is going to succeed in solving the third riddle, she removes her veil to dazzle and confuse him with her beauty. Turandot's action emphasizes the paradox of her character, but, more important, it delays Calaf's triumph and increases its impact by making it look for a moment as if he might not win after all. An even clearer example occurs in the final scene, which opens with the news, buzzed about by the commedia characters, that Turandot has given in and consented to become Calaf's wife. The princess and her train appear dressed in mourning, as if to signal admission of defeat. But when Altoum invites the prince to lead Turandot to the altar, she throws off her air of sadness and triumphantly announces his name, saying, "I could have had no better vengeance than this; to seem defeated, to all but yield, and then to dash the prince once again to the depths of misery." This deliberately arranged reversal creates consternation in the court and excitement in the audience, especially when followed immediately by a second reversal even more sensational than the first, Turandot's willing submission. When we consider that the second reversal merely negates the first and brings us back to the situation as originally understood (though with the key difference that Turandot, not Calaf, is victorious), we begin to appreciate the sheer artifice of Gozzi's methods and intentions. Altoum's "Can it be possible?" says it for all of us.

The theatricality of the play—that is, the elaboration of its formal elements for the sake of effectiveness in performance—is rooted in the tendency of the folk fairy tale to externalize meanings in concrete objects, figures, and events. Turandot's black dress in the final scene might have come right out of a folk tale; the series of reverses that it introduces is obviously the product of a clever literary mind. This scene illustrates Gozzi's use of the fable in the play as a whole: he highlights the naive romantic aspects of the story and then overlays them with sophisticated meanings through the commentary and parody of the commedia masks and the various self-conscious theatrical effects. We have the final impression of incongruous, contradictory elements maintaining an uneasy union in a brilliantly entertaining but unnatural whole. Within a few moments Calaf passes from happiness to misery and back to an even greater happiness; comedy becomes trag-edy and then comedy again in the blink of an eye. The virtuosity of the playwright's art astonishes us. Turandot's getting married in a black dress of mourning, no doubt herself amused by the incongruity of effects, somehow sums up our feelings as we applaud. (pp. 475-78)

David Nicholson, "Gozzi's 'Turandot': A Tragicomic Fairy Tale," in Theatre Journal, *Vol. 31, No. 4, December, 1979, pp. 467-78.*

ADDITIONAL BIBLIOGRAPHY

Acton, Harold. Introduction to *Useless Memoirs of Carlo Gozzi,* by Carlo Gozzi, edited by Philip Horne, translated by John Addington Symonds, pp. ix-xxii. London: Oxford University Press, 1962.

A summary of Gozzi's confrontations with Pietro Antonio Gratarol.

Dent, Edward J. "Carlo Gozzi and His Fairy Plays." In *The Blue Monster (Il mostro turchino): A Fairy Play in Five Acts,* by Carlo Gozzi, translated by Edward J. Dent, pp. v-xxii. Cambridge: University Press, 1951.

A brief history of the commedia dell'arte, the masks, and Gozzi's *fiabe,* concluding with a plot summary of *The Blue Monster* and comments on how the play should be produced.

Emery, Ted A. "Autobiographer as Critic: The Structure and 'Utility' of Gozzi's *Useless Memoirs." Italian Quarterly* XXIV, No. 94 (Fall 1983): 35-49.

Asserts that Gozzi's autobiography, besides being a polemic against the accusations of Pietro Antonio Gratarol, is an attack on Enlightenment culture.

Rusack, Hedwig Hoffmann. *Gozzi in Germany: A Survey of the Rise and Decline of the Gozzi Vogue in Germany and Austria, with Especial Reference to the German Romanticists.* New York: Columbia University Press, 1930, 195 p.

Traces Gozzi's influence on German and Austrian literature of the eighteenth and nineteenth centuries, examining the works of such writers as Johann Wolfgang von Goethe, Ludwig Tieck, and E. T. A. Hoffmann.

Sanguineti, Edoardo. "*The Snake-Woman* as a Fairy-Tale." *Russian Literature* XII, No. 1 (1 July 1982): 71-9.

Summarizes *La donna serpente* (The Snake-Woman) and praises Gozzi's skill in dramatizing the fairy tale.

Wilkins, Ernest Hatch. "Goldoni and Carlo Gozzi." In his *A History of Italian Literature,* edited by Thomas G. Bergin, pp. 342-54. Cambridge: Harvard University Press, 1974.

A brief survey of Gozzi's life and works.

George Washington Harris

1814-1869

(Also wrote under pseudonyms Mr. Free and Sugartail) American short story writer.

A notable American humorist of the Old Southwest, Harris is remembered for his stories featuring Sut Lovingood, a backwoodsman from the mountains of Eastern Tennessee and a self-described "nat'ral born durn'd fool." Sut satirizes himself and those around him in a series of stories of Southern life that typically include exuberant action, practical jokes, violence, and elements of the tall tale. While tremendously popular among contemporary readers, Harris's writings earned little critical attention; today, the Sut Lovingood stories, although not widely read, garner praise for their mastery of comic effect and for their vivid recreation of Southern customs and vernacular.

Little is known about Harris's life. He was born in Allegheny City, Pennsylvania, and at the age of five, moved with his half-brother, Samuel Bell, to Knoxville, Tennessee, where he later received perhaps eighteen months of formal schooling before becoming an apprentice metalworker in Bell's shop. From his teens onward, Harris earned his living in a wide variety of occupations; he was a steamboat captain, farmer, politician, postmaster, railroad employee, and the supervisor of first a glass works and later a coppermine. He was married twice: first to Mary Emeline Nance, from 1835 until her death in 1867; and then to Jane E. Pride, for a very brief time until his death in 1869. Harris first began writing around 1840, when he composed several political sketches for the Knoxville *Argus and Commercial Herald.* From 1843 to 1847 he published a series of letters and stories that primarily depict the local customs of Eastern Tennessee. He then wrote little until 1854, when he published the story that introduced what is considered his greatest comic creation, "Sut Lovingood's Daddy 'Acting Horse'." (Harris originally spelled the character's name Lovengood, but later changed it to the form given here.) From 1854 to 1861 Harris featured Sut in numerous humorous stories, many of which were political satires. The Civil War years found Harris and his family moving from place to place throughout the South to escape the fighting. Harris resumed writing in 1866, composing both humorous tales and political satires and revising some of his earlier stories for inclusion in his only book published during his lifetime, *Sut Lovingood: Yarns Spun by a "Nat'ral Born Durn'd Fool."* In 1869, while traveling, Harris died suddenly, apparently carrying an unpublished manuscript that has never been found.

Of Harris's works, only the stories depicting Sut Lovingood have received serious critical attention; his earlier pieces are generally examined for the light they shed on his artistic development. Among his earliest writings are four sporting stories written in the form of letters, which were published in 1843 under the pseudonym Mr. Free in the *Spirit of the Times,* a New York weekly magazine renowned for its humor and patterned after contemporary English sporting journals. Unlike his later tales, these letters are written in conventional English from the perspective of a gentleman, who describes

the activities of backwoodsmen. The appearance two years later of "The Knob Dance, A Tennessee Frolic," also in *Spirit of the Times* but under the pseudonym Sugartail, represented an important change for Harris: after an introductory paragraph by the gentleman Sugartail in standard English, the story is narrated by Dick Harlan, a participant at a local dance. Although in subsequent writings through 1847 Harris again relied primarily on a gentleman narrator and conventional English, "The Knob Dance" marks his first use of a backwoods character who describes folk customs from his own point of view and in the Southern vernacular, a technique that he repeated in the Sut Lovingood stories. Harris's last group of works, those featuring Sut Lovingood, includes both political and humorous stories written in the years leading up to and just after the Civil War. In his political satires, Harris frequently uses Sut as a mouthpiece to express not only his enthusiastic support for the South, the Confederacy, and Secessionism but also his vitriolic scorn for Yankees, Republicans, Reconstruction, and Abraham Lincoln. To accomplish this, Harris employed a range of techniques, including dream allegory, caricature, irony, and imagery. Critics have noted that Harris's artistic control often gives way to invective and abuse, especially in the post-Civil War pieces, and consider his political satires less effective than his strictly humorous stories.

Harris's Sut Lovingood stories are frequently linked with those of the Southwestern humorists, a group of American writers active primarily during the mid-nineteenth century. Their work, much of which originated in oral storytelling, generally shares several characteristics: the exaggeration, action, and adventure typical of the era's tall tales; vivid portraits of local customs; depictions of the harsh realities of frontier life; a framework or box-like narrative structure that focuses directly on the storyteller before and after the tale; and robust and exuberant humor. Harris's humorous stories vividly evoke the texture of frontier life. Most rely on a variation of the popular framework structure: the gentleman narrator, George, introduces the story, and Sut Lovingood then takes over, telling the tale in his backwoods dialect. The tales themselves generally describe a "skeer"—a complicated and violent practical joke designed to entrap and humiliate either a hypocrite or a fool. While Sut himself is sometimes the butt of the joke, he is often the perpetrator, choosing as his victims preachers, sheriffs, Yankees, women, and blacks. In the first of the tales, "Sut Lovingood's Daddy 'Acting Horse'," the gentleman narrator begins by describing Sut sitting outside a saloon spinning a yarn for a group of mountaineers. As Sut tells the crowd, his family's only horse had died, so his father harnassed himself to the plow but soon crashed into a hornet's nest. Sut takes great delight in describing his father's anguish as he ripped off his clothes and jumped into a river to escape the hornets. "Sut Lovingood Blown Up," also published as "Blown Up with Soda," is the first in a series of tales depicting Sut's relations with Sicily Burns, a voluptuous mountain girl whom he hopes to seduce. She offers him a "love potion," really soda powder, and the new sensation she had promised Sut turns out to be a mouthful of foam. In another well-known tale, "Sut Lovingood's Lizards," also published as "Parson John Bullen's Lizards," Harris first used a backwoods preacher as the victim of a practical joke. After the parson catches him with a girl and beats him, Sut retaliates by letting a bag of lizards loose into his pants as he delivers a sermon. The preacher, thoroughly discredited, strips off all his clothes and runs naked through the congregation.

During his lifetime, Harris's stories were widely popular: they were frequently reprinted in various newspapers and avidly read, but they were largely ignored by reviewers. Although selections of his work were anthologized during the late nineteenth and early twentieth centuries, they were rarely commented upon: scholars objected to the "coarseness" of the tales and their earthy and ribald humor. In the 1930s, the growing recognition of Southwestern humorists sparked a resurgence of interest in Harris, and respected critics began to comment on his work. Franklin J. Meine, for example, praised the stories' robust humor and celebrated Sut as a "genuine naïve roughneck mountaineer riotously bent on raising hell." This view, which prevailed through the mid-twentieth century, characterized Sut and the stories as somewhat crude but entertaining, lively, and Rabelaisian. Brom Weber, in the introduction to his 1954 edition of *Sut Lovingood*, went further in praise of Harris's stories, claiming for them a moral purpose, as Sut's practical jokes are perpetrated against people representing hypocrisy and injustice. Weber's conclusions contributed to the development of a controversy regarding Sut Lovingood's character and, by extension, the nature of Harris's humor. In an effort to make Harris's work more accessible to modern readers, Weber, like others before him, had standardized much of Harris's spelling and paragraphing and had changed obsolete words, thereby altering his rendering of dialect and, according to some, "cleaning

up" the depiction of Sut's character. Prompted in part by Weber's edition, Edmund Wilson challenged not only this editorial practice but also the common critical view that largely ignored Sut Lovingood's dark side; Wilson, instead, called the stories repellent and described the protagonist as sadistic, malevolent, vituperative, and "a peasant squatting in his own filth." Sut's character still inspires diverse interpretations, as critics have addressed his relation to earlier narrators in Southwest frontier humor, his views on political and social issues, his role as a fool, and the nature of his personality. Some see Sut as a natural hero who battles the forces of hypocrisy, rejects stifling authority, and celebrates life. Others credit Sut with a distinct and sophisticated point of view, which they attribute to Harris's effective use of the framework structure and to his imaginative command of language. For these commentators, much of the stories' humor derives from his handling of language, which is often considered his finest achievement. Scholars have also praised Harris's imagery, use of folklore elements, descriptions of folk customs, treatment of humor and political satire, and gift for transferring tall tales to print. In the words of M. Thomas Inge, "Highly effective characterization, a sharp eye for descriptive detail in action and surroundings and a brilliantly complex command of the Southern vernacular and its potential for meaningful imagery—these are the hallmarks of [Harris's] artistic superiority"—and, according to most modern scholars, the qualities that have made the Sut Lovingood stories minor classics of American humor.

(See also *Dictionary of Literary Biography*, Vol. 3: *Antebellum Writers in New York and the South,* and Vol. 11: *American Humorists, 1800-1950.*)

*PRINCIPAL WORKS

Sut Lovingood: Yarns Spun by a "Nat'ral Born Durn'd Fool" (short stories) 1867
Sut Lovingood Travels with Old Abe Lincoln (short stories) 1937
Sut Lovingood's Yarns (short stories) 1966
High Times and Hard Times (short stories and letters) 1967

*Most of Harris's writings were originally published in periodicals.

GEORGE WASHINGTON HARRIS (essay date 1867)

[*In the preface to the first edition of* Sut Lovingood's Yarns, *"Sut" introduces his book, addressing readers and critics.*]

"You must have a preface, Sut; your book will then be ready. What shall I write?"

"Well, ef I must, I must; fur I s'pose the perducktion cud no more show hitsef in publick wifout hit, than a coffin-maker cud wif out black clothes, an' yet what's the use ove either ove em, in pint ove good sense? Smells tu me sorter like a durned humbug, the hole ove hit—a little like cuttin ove the Ten Cummandmints intu the rine ove a water-million; hits jist slashed open an' the inside et outen hit, the rine an' the cummandmints broke all tu pieces an' flung tu the hogs, an' never tho't ove onst—them, nur the 'tarnil fool what cut em thar. But ef a orthur *mus'* take off his shoes afore he goes intu the publick's parlor, I reckon I kin du hit wifout durtyin my feet, fur I hes socks on.

"Sumtimes, George, I wished I cud read an' write, jis' a littil; but then hits bes' es hit am, fur ove all the fools the world hes tu contend wif, the edicated wuns am the worst; they breeds ni ontu all the devilmint a-gwine on. But I wer a-thinkin, ef I cud write myself, hit wud then *raley* been my book. I jis' tell yu now, I don't like the idear ove yu writin a perduckshun, an' me a-findin the brains. 'Taint the fust case tho' on record by a durned site. Usin uther men's brains is es lawful es usin thar plunder, an' jis' es common, so I don't keer much nohow. I dusn't 'speck this yere perduckshun will sit purfeckly quiet ontu the stumicks ove sum pussons—them hu hes a holesum fear ove the devil, an' orter hev hit, by ge-miney. Now, fur thar speshul well-bein herearter, I hes jis' this tu say: Ef yu ain't fond ove the smell ove cracklins, stay outen the kitchin; ef yu is fear'd ove smut, yu needn't climb the chimbley; an' ef the moon hurts yer eyes, don't yu ever look at a Dutch cheese. That's jis' all ove hit.

"Then thar's sum hu haint much faith in thar repertashun standin much ove a strain; they'll be powerful keerful how an' whar they reads my words. Now, tu them I haint wun word tu say: they hes been preached to, an' prayed fur, now ni ontu two thousand years an' I won't dart weeds whar thuty-two poun shot bounces back.

"Then thar's the book-butchers, orful on killin an' cuttin up, but cud no more perjuce a book, than a bull-butcher cud per-juce a bull. S'pose they takes a noshun tu stick, skin, an' cut up this yere one. Ef they is fond ove sicknin skeers, I advises em tu take holt tu onst; but fust I begs tu refer em respectively tu the fate ove three misfortinit pussons menshun'd inside yere—Passun Bullin, Dock Fabin, an Sheriff Dolton. Read keerfully what happened tu them afore yu takes eny ove my flesh ontu yer claws, ur my blood ontu yer bills, an' that I now is a durnder fool then I wer in them days, fur I now considers myself a orthur. I hes tuck my stan amung the nashuns ove the yeath, fur I, too, hes made me a book, so ef enybody wants dish rags, I thinks hit wud be more healthy fur em not tu tar em ofen my flag.

"Mos' book-weavers seem tu be skeery folks, fur giner'lly they cums up tu the slaughter pen, whinin an' waggin thar tails, a-sayin they 'knows they is imparfeck'—that 'yu'd scace 'speck one ove my age,' an' so forth, so on, so along. Now ef I *is* a-rowin in that boat, I ain't awar ove hit, I ain't, fur I knows the tremenjus gif I hes fur breedin skeers amung durned fools, an' then I hes a trustin reliance ontu the fidelity, injurance, an' speed ove these yere laigs ove mine to tote me an' my sins away beyant all human ritribushuns ur revenge. Now, 'zamin yer hans, ole ferrits an' weazels, an' ef yu don't hole *bof* bowers an' the ace, yu jis' 'pass' hit.

"Ef eny poor misfortinit devil hu's heart is onder a millstone, hu's raggid children am hungry, an' no bread in the dresser, hu is down in the mud, an' the lucky ones a-trippin him every time he struggils tu his all fours, hu hes fed the famishin an' is now hungry hissef, hu misfortins foller fas' an' foller faster, hu is so foot-sore an' weak that he wishes he wer at the ferry—ef sich a one kin fine a laugh, jis' one, sich a laugh as is remembered wif his keerless boyhood, atwixt these yere kivers—then, I'll thank God that I *hes* made a book, an' feel that I hev got my pay in full.

"Make me a Notey Beney, George. I wants tu put sumwhar

atween the eyebrows ove our book, in big winnin-lookin let-ters, the sarchin, meanin words, what sum pusson writ ontu a 'oman's garter onst, long ago—"

"Evil be to him that evil thinks."

"Them's em, by jingo! Hed em clost apas' yu, didn't yu? I want em fur a gineral skeer—speshully fur the wimen.

"Now, George, grease hit good, an' let hit slide down the hill hits own way." (pp. 25-7)

George Washington Harris, in a preface to his Sut Lovingood's Yarns, *edited by M. Thomas Inge, Col-lege & University Press, Publishers, 1966, pp. 25-7.*

MARK TWAIN   (essay date 1867)

[*Considered the father of modern American literature, Twain broke with the genteel traditions of the nineteenth century by endowing his characters and narratives with the natural speech patterns of the common person, and by writing of subjects hith-erto deemed beneath the consideration of serious art. Twain is often regarded as a humorist and children's writer, though very serious subjects are treated in such perennially popular books as* The Adventures of Huckleberry Finn *(1884),* The Adven-tures of Tom Sawyer *(1876), and* A Connecticut Yankee in King Arthur's Court *(1889). Initially a clowning humorist, Twain matured into the role of the seemingly naive Wise Fool whose caustic sense of humor forced his audience to recognize humanity's foolishness and society's myriad injustices. Noting similarities between Twain's work and that of Harris, particu-larly in the two authors' use of regional humor and dialect, many critics posit that Twain was to some degree influenced by Harris. In the following excerpt from an 1867 letter to the San Francisco newspaper the* Alta California, *Twain briefly comments on Harris's humor and his audience.*]

It was reported, years ago, that this writer was dead—accidentally shot in a Tennessee doggery before the war; but he has turned up again, and is a conductor on a railway train that travels somewhere between Charleston, S.C., and Mem-phis. His real name is George Harris. I have before me his book [*Sut Lovingood's Yarns*], just forwarded by Dick & Fitzgerald, the publishers, New York. It contains all his early sketches, that used to be so popular in the West, such as his story of his father "actin' hoss," the lizards in the camp-meeting, etc., together with many new ones. The book abounds in humor, and is said to represent the Tennessee dia-lect correctly. It will sell well in the West, but the Eastern people will call it coarse and possibly taboo it.

Mark Twain, " 'Sut Lovingood',' in Mark Twain's Travels with Mr. Brown, *edited by Franklin Walk-er & G. Ezra Dane, Alfred A. Knopf, 1940, p. 221.*

J. THOMPSON BROWN, JR.   (essay date 1908)

[*Brown briefly assesses the elements that make up the stories' quintessentially American humor.*]

Humor takes its source in the ludicrous or the absurdly in-congruous, and grows both from the subject-matter and from the method of handling. It must be guilt-free of sting, it must laugh *with* and not *at;* past bounds of friendly give-and-take it breaks into horse-play or takes on the acerbity of wit. True humor must bear the stamp of humanity; the flash of wit strikes quick and scorching; the genial glow of humor warms from the heart out. But who shall judge as to what composes the ludicrous? That, perhaps, shall have to remain unanswered. Each nation has its own school, each class its own tenets, each man his own sense, and each mood its own demands.

In estimating the value of Sut Lovingood's humor, we must employ American standards, and bear in mind that our American school has alike the virtues and the sins of unchastised youth. It is bubbling and irrepressible, and not infrequently lacking in dignity. Worse, perhaps, than aught else, three hundred years has not been a sufficient revolutionary cycle to induce an American to place courteous sympathy before his fun. In brief, American humor is boyish, crude, and boisterous, striking heedlessly, regardless of feelings, propriety, and often even of decency. Our country is large and free, our humor broad and unrestrained; there are none so high as to be immune from its slings. Within bounds these characteristics might be tolerated, but how easy it is for the truant school-boy to transgress the limits of noisy though innocent fun-making and become an untiring nuisance.

Not a few of our authors have invoked dialect, perverted spelling, and *patois;* but if they have succeeded, often it has been the triumph of art over artifice. Sut Lovingood has his own dialect, and along with it his homespun attire and unquenchable thirst for "moonshine," likewise his pride in uncivility. Good John Knox two hundred years ago invented the term, "a sinful carcuse." Sut would have thanked him for that word and laid it by for himself had he once got it. And still Sut is not without glory, nor has his day yet fully gone. The original was Harris's assistant, a long, lank, drawling East Tennessee mountaineer, a type worthy of preservation. His picture, though distorted and exaggerated, is none the less the record of a class, so he holds his place in the make-up of our composite nationality. Miss Murfree is far and away the better artist among these folk, but Sut has touches that in realism exceed the ordinary, so let him stand; but pity it is he is not fraught with a single virtue. Miss Murfree has clothed her characters in something of the nobility inherent in a race close to the rock-ribbed mountains, but Sut is *unclothed,* in perfect *unloveliness.* Unique, unrivaled, without a peer he stands alone, though unabashed, in the field of letters.

No recipe for American humor can omit the ingredient of exaggeration, but Sut too often makes exaggeration the lump, leaven, and all. The dough rises, and rightly it should, but it over-pushes all bounds and becomes unfit for either humorous or intellectual diet. Sicily Burns gives him two love powders dissolved in separate glasses of water. That the love prescription was made up of the white and the blue of a seidlitz powder would have been delightful and even refined humor had Sut and the swallowed potions been left to the suggestion of the reader. In truth Sut's silence here would have placed him among the immortals. The details following the internal explosion are, however, over-much in the telling, and our hero loses the wreath within his easy grasp. But after all he may not have wanted it.

Again, to show where he just missed success. He "an' a few uther durn'd fools" were one day lounging around "ole man Rogers's" spring. Hen Bailey rushes madly on the scene. In haste to get a good stolen pull at the ever-abundant, free-flowing corn-whiskey he had snatched up the turpentine bottle and gulped down a large dose. Though horrible agony should the next minute take off the victim, what American is there with sympathies so over civilized as not to appreciate the delicate and delightful fitness of things and record in rib-bursting hilarity the writhings of his exquisitely tickled senses? The long-handled gourd, the frantic dip into the spring, the feverish haste with which Hen throws back his head and opens wide his mouth, the awakening of the lizard who was resting in the handle, the scurry for safety to the nearest haven of retreat, and that retreat Hen Bailey's throat—these are details no true artist could possibly have survived and recorded; but Sut—yes, he lived to spoil the story with the most minute and disgusting details of the recovery of his friend and of the *lizard.*

But sometimes the author forgets himself and gives a really good bit of description. This same Sicily Burns who played Sut such a sorry trick is painted with vigorous and artistic touches, though with probably too much realism. (pp. 2100-02)

J. Thompson Brown, Jr., "George Washington Harris," in Library of Southern Literature, Vol. V., *Edwin Anderson Alderman, Joel Chandler Harris, Charles William Kent, eds., The Martin & Hoyt Company, 1908, pp. 2099-102.*

NAPIER WILT   (essay date 1929)

[*Wilt praises Sut's humor and earthiness, defending the tales against the common charge of coarseness.*]

According to popular legend the character of Sut Lovingood was suggested to Harris by one of his assistants, a tall, uncouth mountaineer who was constantly telling Harris all sorts of tall tales. Certainly Sut seems to depend very little on other literary creations. . . . Sut is the natural, uneducated tough boy. He loves two things: corn whiskey and a joke. And he can appreciate a joke on himself as well as anyone else. He plays all manner of rough pranks, some of which are in the worst possible taste. The language in which he tells of his adventures is exactly what one would expect from such a fellow. Unfortunately, he has always been in bad repute with the critics of American humor. They all apologize for him and wish he were not so coarse. . . . This whole attitude is curious. Certainly Sut is not bad; he is never mean or self-seeking. Compared with Simon Suggs he is goodness itself. And one should notice that there is always a rough sort of justice in his pranks. His special enemies are the hypocritical and the self-righteous. Sut's humor is possibly the nearest thing to the undiluted oral humor of the Middle West that has found its way into print. Probably the unprintable tales which legend attributes to Lincoln were not very different from Sut's. Some of the Huck Finn and Tom Sawyer adventures are but parlor versions of Sut's pranks. The exaggeration, the emphasis on physical catastrophes, the general crudeness of the tales are easily seen. These need no explanation other than that they belong to the life Sut exemplifies. Had the yarns been more refined, had the language been toned down, the effect would have been less artistic. As they stand the tales are perfect examples of natural unrestrained humor of one of the most interesting, if not the most cultured, periods of American life. (pp. 129-30)

Napier Wilt, "George Washington Harris (Sut Lovingood)," in his Some American Humorists, *1929. Reprint 1970 Johnson Reprint Corporation, pp. 129-31.*

FRANKLIN J. MEINE   (essay date 1930)

[*In this excerpt from the introduction to his collection of mid-nineteenth-century Southern and Southwestern tall tales, Meine portrays the humor of the Sut Lovingood stories as "robust and hearty" and "sheer fun," a view that has been contested by later critics. As one of the first to write on Harris in this century, Meine is among those who are generally credited with reviving interest in his works.*]

Sut Lovingood is a unique and original character in American humor. He is a rough, lanky, uncouth mountaineer of the Great Smokies, whose sole ambition in life is to raise "pertickler" hell. As he says of himself:

> Every critter what has ever seed me, ef he has sence enuff to hide from a cummin kalamity, ur run from a muskit, jis' knows five great facks in my case es well es they knows the road to their moufs. *Fustly,* that I haint got nara a soul, nuffin but a whisky proof gizzard, sorter like the wus half ove a ole par ove saddil bags, *Seconly,* that I'se too durn'd a fool to cum even onder millertary lor. *Thudly,* that I hes the longes' par ove laigs ever hung to eny cackus, 'sceptin' only ove a grandaddy spider, an' kin beat *him* a usen ove em jis' es bad es a skeer'd dog kin beat a crippled mud turkil. *Foufly,* that I kin chamber more cork-screw kill-devil whisky, an' stay on aind, than enything 'sceptin' only a broad bottum'd chun. *Fivety,* an' las'ly, kin git intu more durn'd misfortnit skeery scrapes, than enybody, an' then run outen them faster, by golly, nor enybody.

Sut relished the prospect of driving a mad bull into a wedding party, or poking out a hornets' nest into a negro camp-meeting, or stuffing a bag of lizards up the "passun's britches-laig when he were a-ravin' ontu his tip-toes, an a-poundin' the pulpit wif his fis'." Such were Sut's pranks, with his constant companion, his whisky flask, slung at his side.

Sut's humor is always robust and hearty; sometimes rough, possibly coarse, yet he is vastly funny; and the ***Yarns*** are full of comic situation, plot and phrase. Sut reveals the author's spirit in his keen delight for Hallowe'en *fun,*—there is no ulterior motive (except occasionally Sut's desire to "get even"), no rascality, no gambling, no sharping as in *Simon Suggs* or the *Flush Times.* Sut is simply the genuine naïve roughneck mountaineer riotously bent on raising hell.

Harris makes no pretense of literary style. He tells his story in his own way directly and swiftly. Although writers of his time generally tacked morals to most of their stories, Harris was satisfied to tell a story which tickled men's funny-bones and consigned morals to "suckit" riders. The ***Yarns*** are fresh, racy and packed with action. Harris rises above the level of merely objective description of humorous characters or incidents, and concocts with "owdacious" flights of fancy all sorts of grotesque schemes to display Sut's peculiar talents. For vivid imagination, comic plot, Rabelaisian touch, and sheer *fun,* the ***Sut Lovingood Yarns*** surpass anything else in American humor. (pp. xxiii-xxiv)

> *Franklin J. Meine, in an introduction to* Tall Tales of the Southwest: An Anthology of Southern and Southwestern Humor, 1830-1860, *edited by Franklin J. Meine, Alfred A. Knopf, 1930, pp. xv-xxxii.*

WALTER BLAIR   (essay date 1937)

[*Blair details the elements that comprise Harris's storytelling*

artistry, including incisive description of regional customs, humorous characterization, and imaginative language. Blair's commentary on Harris follows his discussion of the "box-like" narrative framework commonly employed by short story writers of the American Southwest.]

[The] author who most consistently uses the framework narrative method to portray his chief character is George W. Harris. His book, ***Sut Lovingood,*** the product of a man who himself was an adept at oral story-telling—a book which is typical of Southwestern humor because it is full of local color, exuberant, masculine, "the nearest thing to the undiluted oral humor of the Middle West that has found its way into print" [see excerpt dated 1929]—has never had the widespread appreciation it deserves, partly, perhaps, because its artistry has never been sufficiently appreciated, partly because its faults have been overemphasized by over-squeamish critics. [Blair elaborates in a footnote: "The book has three faults: (1) Sut employs a dialect which some readers think too hard to translate. (2) Sometimes the details about the plights of the victims or details incidental to the tales are coarse, in bad taste, and unfunny. (3) The repetition in his tales of the motif of physical discomfort is so frequent that it becomes monotonous. None of these faults, in my opinion, should damn the book. Sut's dialect is mastered after a little effort. Harris suggested that those who were troubled by the second fault would be those who had a wholesome fear of the devil, and ought to, and those who hadn't a great deal of faith that their reputation would stand much of a strain; and 'fur a gineral skeer—speshully for the wimen,' quoted the words, 'Evil to him that evil thinks' [see essay dated 1867]. The point is well taken: the stories are no coarser than highly admired stories by some of the greatest writers. And the richness of the detail may well atone for the monotonous resemblances between situations"]. Nevertheless, this volume which, in a sense, may be thought of as a picaresque novel in the form of anecdotes within a framework, represents a highly artistic use of the formula employed by Thorpe in his masterpiece ["The Big Bear of Arkansas"].

Harris's tales have all the qualities made possible by this technique. So artless do they seem that even such a discerning critic as Watterson takes for granted that any reader will observe that in Sut's yarns there is "little attempt at technical literary finish, either in description or proportion . . . ; the author is seemingly satisfied to aim merely at his point, and, this reached, to be satisfied to leave it work out its own moral and effect." Yet a careful study will reveal that there is sufficient artistry splendidly to reveal Sut's character and to underline various incongruities. In the framework, Sut is revealed by direct description—a "queer looking, long legged, short bodied, small headed, white haired, hog eyed" youth, who comes into view at the beginning or the conclusion of various sketches—reining up his bownecked sorrel in front of Pat Nash's grocery or Capehart's Doggery to tell a yarn to a crowd of loafing mountaineers, weaving along the street after a big drunk or a big fight, or stretching his skinny body at full length by a cool spring at noon. Indirectly, too, by showing the reactions of those who listen to Sut's tales, Harris reveals his hero's character. A rat-faced youth who is conquered by Sut's badinage, "George" (Harris), who claims that a part of a tale is not true, or who tolerantly encourages Sut's yarns, even when he is awakened to hear them, the book agent who is insulted and frightened by Sut's onslaught, others affected in various ways by Sut's talk, help us to understand the manner of person he is.

Sut's character is also revealed, moreover, by the tales he tells about himself, tales which display "his keen delight for Hallowe'en *fun,*—there is no ulterior motive (except occasionally Sut's desire to 'get even'), no rascality, no gambling, no sharping as in *Simon Suggs*. . . . Sut is simply the genuine naïve roughneck mountaineer riotously bent on raising hell" [see excerpt by Franklin J. Meine dated 1930]. They indicate his chief passions—telling stories, eating good food, drinking "corkscrew kill-devil whisky," hugging pretty girls, and "breeding scares among darned fools" by playing pranks. Just as revealing are his dislikes: Yankee peddlers, Yankee lawyers, Yankee scissor-grinders—any kind of Yankees, sheriffs, most preachers, learned men who use big words or flowery language, tavern keepers who serve bad food, and reformers. His idea of what is funny shows us what kind of person he is: a comic situation, according to this son of the soil, is usually one in which a character of the sort he hates, or preferably a large number of characters, get into highly uncomfortable circumstances. Comic to him, too, are the procreative and bodily functions, the animal qualities in humans and the human qualities in animals.

The language he employs in his monologues helps reveal his character—a language polished little by book larnin', Rabelaisian, close to the soil, but withal poetic in an almost Elizabethan fashion. The very figures of speech he employs have more than comedy to recommend them. They are conceits, comic because they are startlingly appropriate and inappropriate at the same time, devices for characterization because they arise with poetic directness from the life Sut knows. Consider these passages, redolent of Sut's knowledge of nature and of liquor groceries:

> Bake dwelt long on the *crop* of dimes to be *gathered from that field;* [saying] that he'd make *more than there were spots on forty fawns in July,* not to speak of the *big gobs* of reputation he'd bear away, *shining* all over his clothes, *like lightning bugs on a dog fennil top.*

> . . . her skin was as *white as the inside of a frogstool,* and her *cheeks and lips as rosy as a perch's gills in dogwood blossom time*—and such a smile! why, when it struck you fair and square it felt just *like a big horn of unrectified old Monangahaley, after you'd been sober for a month, attending a ten horse prayer meeting twice a day, and most of the nights.*

> Wirt had changed his *grocery range,* and the spirits at the new *log-lick* had more *scrimmage seed* and *raise-devil* into it than the old *boiled drink* he was used to, and three horns *hoisted his tail,* and *set his bristles about as stiff* as eight of the other *doggery juice* would. So when court sat at nine, Wirt was about as far ahead as *cleaving,* or *half past that.* The *hollering stage of the disease* now struck him, and he roared one good *ear-quivering roar.* . . .

> [Of a man howling in fear and pain:] The noise he made sounded *like a two-horse mowing-machine, driven by chain-lightning, cutting through a dry cane brake on a big bet.*

Recited in Sut's drawl, with far more touches of dialect than are here revealed, in fact, in "the wildest of East Tennessee jargon," these passages and others in Sut's stories contrast

amusingly with the rhetorical framework language. Harris seemed to realize the possibilities of ludicrous antitheses in language, for he liked to put Sut's talk alongside of flowery passages or of learned language in which big words predominated. Humorous, too, is the contrast between the circumstances under which Sut tells his tale and the harrowing scenes he describes. Incidentally, most of the happenings about which Sut tells never could be amusing unless they were removed by several steps from reality.

But the great incongruity in the tales, only partly exploited by Harris, is that between the realistically depicted world of the framework and the fantastically comic world created by Sut in the highly colored, highly imaginative enclosed narrative. His is a world in which the religious life of the Smoky Mountains is grotesquely warped until all its comedy is emphasized, a cosmos wherein the squalor in which the Lovingoods live—squalor without alleviation, without shame—somehow becomes very jolly. It is a world in which the crowds at a camp meeting, a frolic, or a quarter race are revealed in postures and garbs as amusing as those of the earthy and lively figures that throng a canvas by Peter Breughel. Startlingly, it is a world in which scent, sound, form, color, and motion are not only vividly lifelike but also hilariously comic. Here is a mare in that strange country, whose rider has just shouted "Get up!":

> Well she did "get up," right then and there, and staid up long enough to light twenty feet further away, in a broad trembling squat, her tail hid between her thighs, and her ears dancing past each other, like scissors cutting. The jolt of the lighting set the clock [which her rider was carrying and which prodded her unmercifully] to striking. Bang-zee-bang-zee-whang-zee. She listened powerful attentive to the three first licks, and they seemed to go through her as quicksilver would through a sifter. She waited for no more, but just gave her whole soul to the one job of running from under that infernal Yankee, and his hive of bumble bees, rattle snakes, and other awful hurting things, as she took it to be.

Here is a bull on a rampage in the public market:

> . . . just a-tearing, a thirteen hundred pound black and white bull, with his tail as straight up in the air as a telegraph pole, and a chestnut fence rail tied across his horns with hickory withes. He was a-toting his head low, and every lick he made . . . he'd blow whoff, outen his snout . . . He'd say whoff! and a hundred and sixty pound nigger would fly up in the air like unto a grasshopper, and come back spread like a frog . . . Whoff! again, and a boy would turn ten somersaults towards the river. Whoff! and an Amherst woman lit a-straddle of an old fat fellow's neck, with a jolt that jumped his tobacco out of his mouth and scrunched *him,* while she went on down hill on all fours in a fox trot . . . A little bald-headed man, dressed in gold specks and a gold-headed walking stick, was a-passing . . . he looked like he was a-ciphering out a sum . . . in his head . . . Whoff! and the specks lit on the roof of the market house, and the stick, gold end first, sat in a milk can sixty feet off. As to bald head himself, I lost sight of him, while the specks were in the air; he just disappeared from mortal vision somehow, sort of like the breath from a looking-glass.

In such passages as these, in passages which use conceits even more grotesque than those quoted above, in passages of imaginative exaggeration, of strangely linked entities, the world of Sut's stories, tremendously different from the world where Sut's whisky flask flashes in the sun, takes its queer shape to delight the reader. And from the passages about Sut, and from his imaginative tales, emerges a character, coarser and earthier, perhaps, than any other in our literature during the nineteenth century, but at the same time, understandably true to life, an ingratiating mischief-maker, America's Till Eulenspiegel, in his own right a poet and a great creator of comedy.

In *Sut Lovingood,* the antebellum humor of the South reaches its highest level of achievement before Mark Twain. The author of this book, like his contemporaries, was a man of the world who became an author almost by accident. Like them, he wrote tales full of authentic local color, zestful yarns which blossomed from the rich subsoil of oral humor. Encouraged by the *Spirit of the Times* and other publications, he learned to employ the best method for telling a story developed by members of a highly artistic group, making the most of the framework technique for setting forth a mock oral tale, making the most, too, of the mock oral tale itself, with its colloquial richness, its disarming directness, its vivid comic detail. If his writings were better than the rest, they were better because he had more sense of incongruities, more exuberance, more imagination, and because he had greater genius than his contemporaries for transferring the unique artistry of the oral narrative to the printed page. (pp. 96-101)

Walter Blair, "Humor of the Old Southwest (1830-1867)," in his Native American Humor: 1800-1900, *American Book Company, 1937, pp. 62-101.*

EDD WINFIELD PARKS (essay date 1937)

[*In the following excerpt from an essay first published in 1937, Parks highlights the comic artistry of the Sut Lovingood stories.*]

Sut was not, by nature, a political commentator. He was a Hallowe'en prankster who pulled his crude and often cruel practical jokes on every possible occasion, and who told of these exploits with a tremendous Rabelaisian humor, a fine regard for the effect of his story, and a callous disregard of the physical pain to his victims. Until 1861, Harris kept Sut close to home, in the Tennessee mountain region between Virginia and Georgia; not until Lincoln's inaugural journey did he allow Sut to roam into any other section.

The sketches on Lincoln, published in *Sut Lovingood Travels with Old Abe Lincoln,* follow closely the pattern evolved by Harris. They are oral stories, related by a man who can neither read nor write, and the style approximates speech. Harris frequently encloses a yarn within a slight framework, where, in contrast to Sut's crude and vivid speech, he talks with precise correctness. Here, Sut delivers a monologue, but he allows Mr. Lincoln a larger conversational part than he usually permits to other characters. Also, Sut talks more, and does less, than is customary. The wild prank of dressing Lincoln as a cross-barred man is in Sut's best manner, and the teller works up to this; but he depends more on anecdote and verbal wit than he did in the collected [*Sut Lovingood's Yarns*].

Sut lives in a fantastic world of his own creation. His world is at once fore-shortened, and highly magnified. By this treatment, the most ordinary social event becomes unique and peculiar: a dance leads, inevitably, to some trick which cripples half the dancers; a quilting leads Sut to make a horse run away, and kill the lady who gave the quilting; a sermon provides an opportunity for testing the effects of lizards placed in a preacher's pants leg. Fun is largely physical, and the greatest amount of fun is secured by causing a maximum amount of physical discomfiture to a victim—preferably dignified or conceited. Pain hardly exists, save as something humorous; it has no reality.

And conscience has no part in Sut's life: although he has made elaborate preparations to frighten a horse into running away, he says, "tarin down that lim' wer the beginin ove all the troubil, an' the hoss did hit hissef; my conshuns felt clar as a mountin spring." And Sut can answer, as to the cause of Mrs. Yardley's death: "Nuffin, only her heart stop't beatin 'bout losin a nine dimunt quilt. True, she got a skeer'd hoss tu run over her, but she'd a-got over that ef a quilt hadn't been mix'd up in the catastrophy." Harris deals with homely and localized events, but he has exaggerated his characters and incidents until they are far removed from a normal focus. Abraham Lincoln, in the sketches about his journey to the capital, is less a person than an animated clothes-horse, made to serve as the butt of Sut's jokes; he is consistent in the fictitious world, but the character has only the vaguest points of reference with the real person. To appreciate the art of George W. Harris requires a fairly complete and willing suspension of disbelief.

For Harris, on a small scale and within strait limits, was an artist. This is best revealed in his language. He followed the customary practice in misspelling words for comic effect, even when there is no point to the error; but his humor is not dependent on these mistakes. His superiority over his fellow-humorists can best be illustrated through his comparisons. They are apt, concrete, and homely; they spring immediately from the life of the mountaineer; they have poetic exactness combined with a far-fetched yet appropriate descriptiveness. Lincoln's legs go in "at each aidge sorter like the prongs goes intu a pitch fork"; "fools break out like measils"; and, from the *Yarns,* "yu might jis' es well say Woa tu a locomotum or suke cow tu a gal"; "sich a buzzim! Jis' think ove two snow balls with a strawberry stuck but-ainded intu bof of em." (pp. 215-17)

Harris was unsurpassed at the knack of telling a good yarn, and he permitted nothing to get in the way of his story. He pointed no moral; he did not attempt to present realistic or representative scenes and characters; he was not squeamish in his language, which was vividly racy, or in his attitude about sex. These qualities have in the past been held to Harris's discredit, and his work denounced as coarse. It may be, but it is also lively and full of life, and it is superbly humorous. (p. 218)

George W. Harris is remembered today because of Sut Lovingood. The "skeery," long-legged, whisky-drinking and yarn-spinning mountaineer is a slight but authentic creation, who is not likely to be forgotten as long as men like a salty character and a highly-seasoned humorous tale. (p. 222)

Edd Winfield Parks, "Sut Lovingood," in his Segments of Southern Thought, *The University of Georgia Press, 1938, pp. 215-22.*

F. O. MATTHIESSEN (essay date 1941)

[*A respected American literary scholar, Matthiessen is best known for* American Renaissance: Art and Expression in the Age of Emerson and Whitman, *a comprehensive study of the emergence of a uniquely American literature. In the following excerpt from this work, he examines Harris as a humorous writer in the American tradition.*]

[In the stories in *Sut Lovingood*], Harris took the by then traditional framework for the tall tale, and, because he possessed a keen eye and ear, could use it as a means to portray the frontier life with both realism and fantastic extravagance—the union of incongruities most natural to American humor. Sut, who tells all the stories to Harris, is not yet twenty but has a definite philosophy of life: 'Men were made a-purpus jus' to eat, drink, an' fur stayin' awake in the early part of the nites: an wimen were made to cook the vittles, mix the spirits, an' help the men do the stayin' awake. That's all, an' nothin' more, unless it's fur the wimen to raise the devil atwix meals, an' knit socks atwix drams, an' the men to play short cards, swap hosses with fools, an fite fur exercise, at odd spells.' The world that is refracted through Sut's hard and knowing eyes is that of the practical joker who enjoys violence and cruelty, and often ends his situations in complete social disruption. He delights to put lizards in a parson's pants, or to turn loose a hornet's nest at a prayer meeting; and he strews unconscious bodies around the scene of a fight with as much gusto as Fielding. He is specially pleased with the result when the victims are the sheriff or the circuit-rider, who, with Yankee peddlers or anyone from Massachusetts, are the chief objects of Sut's lawless distaste. He can see no sense in preaching: 'Oh, it's jus' no use in their talkin', an' groanin', an' sweatin' theirselves about it; they must jus' upset nature ontu her head, an' keep her thar, or shut up. Lets taste this here whisky.' What Sut enjoys most are social gatherings, quilting parties and dances, and horse races, even though what he contributes to make a lively time livelier generally turns the occasion, as in the case of Sicily Burns' wedding, into the most 'misfortunate' one 'since ole Adam married that heifer what were so fond of talkin' to snakes.'

Sut's life at home with his folks was of a squalor unalleviated and unashamed, but he could admire a hero when he saw one, particularly Wirt Staples, the blacksmith's cousin. Even at the top of Wirt's boast of what he would do to the 'ole false apostil' of the law, you couldn't think for the life of you that he had overbragged a single word:

> His britches were buttoned tite round his loins, an' stuffed 'bout half intu his boots, his shirt bagg'd out abuv, an' were as white as milk, his sleeves were rolled up to his arm-pits, an' his collar were as wide open as a gate, the mussils on his arms moved about like rabbits under the skin, an' ontu his hips an' thighs they play'd like the swell on the river, his skin were clear red an' white, an' his eyes a deep, sparklin', wickid blue, while a smile fluttered like a hummin' bird round his mouth all the while. When the State-fair offers a premium fur *men* like they now does fur jackasses, I means to enter Wirt Staples, an' I'll git it, if there's five thousand entrys.

There is 'the central man' of the Smoky Mountains to stand beside Emerson's. He is a blood brother to Bulkington, whose appearance so struck Ishmael at the Spouter Inn. That mariner 'stood full six feet in height, with noble shoulders, and a chest like a coffer-dam. I have seldom seen such brawn in a man. His face was deeply brown and burnt, making his white

teeth dazzling by the contrast; while in the deep shadows of his eyes floated some reminiscences that did not seem to give him much joy. His voice at once announced that he was a Southerner, and from his fine stature, I thought he must be one of those tall mountaineers from the Alleghenian Ridge in Virginia.' When the *Pequod* sets sail, Melville dwells on the fact that Bulkington is at the helm. Though he had just landed in midwinter from a four years' dangerous voyage, he has unrestingly pushed off again. 'Know ye, now, Bulkington?' Melville symbolizes in him the natural seeker for 'the open independence' of truth's sea, and his last words to him are: 'Bear thee grimly, demigod! Up from the spray of thy ocean-perishing—straight up, leaps thy apotheosis!'

Wirt Staples was troubled with no such tragic thoughts. His temper could be described in Rabelais' words: 'a certain jollity of mind pickled in a scorn of fortune.' Wirt is the common man in his full stature, but he is not quite what Jefferson had foreseen. Still less is he the representative of the race that Noah Webster had hoped to educate by his spelling book, a sober, dignified and well-trained folk, neither peasants on the one hand, nor corrupt aristocrats on the other, but developing the refinements of a wise culture. Wirt roars like a bull, or—in a shift of the animal imagery of which Harris was so fond since it brought man close to nature—when Wirt has had about eight drinks, he hoists his tail and sets his bristles ready for the sheriff, whom he presently knocks out with a leg of venison. The language Harris put in his mouth makes an epitome of what Mencken has found recorded in the American's speech: 'his bold and somewhat grotesque imagination, his contempt for dignified authority, his lack of aesthetic sensitiveness, his extravagant humor.'

Harris' gifts go beyond the difficult one of being able to translate to the printed page such tales as he had heard. Sut may say, 'I ladles out my words at random,' and he may repeat over and again the same comic-strip situations for his exploits; but his inventiveness is astonishing, particularly in the kind of similes that, irrelevant to his narrative, hand you gratis a compressed scene or character-sketch: 'He watched fur openins to work off some kind of devilment, just as close as a ole woman what were wunst unsanctified herself watches her daughters when a circus or a camp meetin' am in heat.' Harris possesses on the comic level something of what Melville does on the tragic, the rare kind of dramatic imagination that can get movement directly into words. This brings a wonderfully kinetic quality to whole situations, to Bart Davis' dance or to the ructions caused in Lynchburg market by an escaped bull. The ability to use every possible verbal gesture of action alone could create this whirlwind description of a preacher attacked by hornets: 'I seed him fotch hisself a lick . . . with both hans ontu the place where they brands Freemasons an' mustangs, an' he shot his belly forwards an' his shoulders back'ards, like ontu a woman shuttin' the nex' to the top drawer of a beauro; an' he come outen that pulpit back'ards a-tarin', his hans a-flyin' round his hed like a pair of windin' blades.'

The panorama of life that flashes by in Sut's yarns may well remind you of Josh Billings' definition of our humor: 'Americans love caustick things: they would prefer turpentine to colone-water, if they had tew drink either. So with their relish of humor; they must have it on the half-shell with cayenne.' But in many casual passages, without consciously intending it, Sut catches more surely the quality of homely existence. In his picture of Wirt's woman he completes his version of

An illustration for the story "Sut Lovingood's Daddy 'Acting Horse'."

the heroic myth, as he celebrates the abundance he has glimpsed and so knows to be possible: 'She ain't one of your she-cat wimmin, always spittin' an' groanin', an' swellin' their tails 'bout their virtue. She never talks a word about it, no more nor if she didn't have any; an' she has as true a heart as ever beat agin a shift hem, or a husband's shirt. But she am full of fun, an' I mout add as purty as a hen canary, an' I swear I don't b'leve the woman knows it.' This makes the prelude to his description of her cooking, for Sut understands the connection between good food and a husband's love, and gives his own kind of hymn to fertility:

> Wirt's wife got early supper, a real circuit-rider's supper, where the woman of the house were a rich b'lever. There were chickens cut up, an' fried in butter, brown, white, flakey, light, hot biskit, made with cream, scrambled eggs, yaller butter, fried ham in slices as big as your hand, pickled beets, an' cowcumbers, roastin' ears, shaved down an' fried, sweet taters, baked, a stack of buckwheat cakes, as full of holes as a sifter, an' a bowl of strained honey, to fill the holes. . . . I gets dog hungry every time I see Wirt's wife, or even her side-saddle, or her frocks a-hangin' on the clothesline.

(pp. 642-45)

F. O. Matthiessen, "Man in the Open Air," in his American Renaissance: Art and Expression in the

Age of Emerson and Whitman, *Oxford University Press, 1941, pp. 626-56.*

DONALD DAY (essay date 1943)

[*Day analyzes character, setting, action, language, and satirical commentary in Harris's humorous stories.*]

Critics have noticed that **Sut Lovingood's Yarns** by George W. Harris is typical in many ways of the humor of the ante-bellum Southwest. Yet Mr. Franklin J. Meine, comparing Harris's work with that of the other humorists, has stated that it is "strikingly different." The purpose of this paper is to see how Harris resembles other humorists of the time and how he differs from them. The study therefore may be enlightening as a detailed consideration of the claim that "in **Sut Lovingood** the ante-bellum humor of the South reaches its highest level of achievement before Mark Twain" [see excerpt by Walter Blair dated 1937]. (p. 391)

Characters appear in Harris's yarns on two levels: first, those who are in the framework; and, secondly, those who are in the yarn told by Sut. The connection between the two groups is maintained by Sut; George (Harris) never enters the world of fantasy as a character (except in **"Eaves-dropping a Lodge of Free Masons"**).

The framework characters help Sut get the yarn under way, relieve the monotony of the monologue, underline the incongruity, and then help bring the setting back from the world of fantasy to the world of realism. George, in particular, helps make this queer looking, long-legged, short-bodied, small-headed, white-haired, hog-eyed, funny sort of a genius," appropriate for the strange tales he is going to relate. Here is how George qualifies Sut to tell his famous shirt story:

> "Why, Sut, what's wrong now? You look sick."
>
> "Heaps wrong, durn my skin—no my haslets—ef I hain't mos' ded, an' my looks don't lie when they hints that I'se sick. I is sick—I'se skin'd."
>
> "Who skinned you—old Bullen?"
>
> "No, hoss, a durnder fool nor Bullen did hit; I jis skin'd myself."
>
> "What in the name of common sense did you do it for?"
>
> "Didn't du hit in the name ove common sense; did hit in the name, an' wif the sperit ove plum natral born durn fool."

When the yarn is under way Sut operates in situations on three levels, each of which demands a different type of character: first, in situations dealing with his Dad's world of "fooldom" (from which Sut stems) in which Sut helps his Dad to merited punishment; secondly, situations in which Sut gets out of his "nat'ral born fool" occupation and thereby comes to grief; and, third, situations in which "Sut's nat'ral born durn'd fool" endowments are pitted against supposedly respectable and intelligent members of society who are in reality hypocrites and whose intelligence cannot save them from his devastating punishment.

"Sut Lovingood's Daddy 'Acting Horse,'" as it appeared in the [*Spirit of the Times*], November 4, 1854, the first of the

Sut yarns, deals with Dad's world of "fooldom" and gives to Sut the following significant kinship:

> Well, thar we was—Dad an' me (counting on his fingers)—Dad, and me, and Sall, an' Jake (Fool Jake we called him fur short), an' Jonass, an' Phineass, and me, and Callime Jane, and Sharlotteean, an' Simeon Saul, an' Cashus Henry Clay, an' Noah Dan Webster, an' me, and the twin gals, an' Cathrine the Second, and Cleopatry Antony, an' Jane Lind, and Tom Bullion, an' the baby, an' the prospect, an' mam herself. . . .

Obviously, this kinship, presided over by Dad, the "king fool" of them all, is tremendously important in the characterization of Sut. Significantly, Harris places this sketch first in the **Yarns** and then ends the book with another story of the same sort, **"Dad's Dog School,"** in which Sut insists that it

> happen'd ur ruther tuck place apupus, in our famerly; hit cudn't a-been did by eny urther peopil on this yeath but us, fur hit am plum clarified dam fool, frum aind tu aind. Dad plan'd hit; an' him, an' mam, an' Sall, an' Bent, an' me—oh, yas! an' the pup.

Sut describes his first effort to leave his proper sphere in **"Sut's New-Fangled Shirt."** He errs by following the advice of Betts Carr, who is "the cussedes' oman" he ever saw "fur jaw, breedin, an' pride." She persuades Sut to put on a "pasted" shirt and in getting out of it, after he has perspired and the shirt has dried, Sut loses a goodly portion of his skin. He swears "never again," but in **"Blown up with Soda"** George says:

> Sut's hide is healed—the wounds received in his sudden separation from his new shirt have ceased to pain, and, true to his instincts, or rather "a famerly dispersion," as he calls it, he "pitches in," and gets awfully blown up by a wild mountain girl.

Obviously, the supporting characters in the first two types of yarns are those suitable for bringing about a merited punishment for Sut's Dad or for Sut. In the third type the chief character (always a hypocrite) is to be punished and is given characteristics which merit that punishment. These characters are usually introduced by Sut in thumbnail descriptions such as that in which Parson Bullen is designated a "durnd infunel, hiperkritikal, pot-bellied, scaley-hided, whisky-wastin, stinkin ole groun'-hog." . . . Mrs. Yardley is put "ahine a par ove *shiney* specks," and Sut warns that such a woman "am dang'rus in the extreme" because she is "a great noticer ove littil things, that nobody else ever seed" such as "that yaller slut ove a hen, a-flinging straw over her shoulder" of which she promises:

> I'll disapint *her* see ef I don't; I'll put a punkin in her nes', an' a feather in her nose. . . . An' sakes alive, jis' look at that ole sow; she's a-gwine in a fas' trot, wif her emty bag a-floppin agin her sides. . . . what a long yearnis grunt she gin; hit cum from way back ove her kidneys. . . . sich kerryin on means no good.

As a usual thing Sut works alone in his punitive endeavors. However, at times, he has assistants. Bake Boyd is a good helper because "thar wur durn'd little weevil in his wheat, mity small chance ove warter in his whisky, and not a drap ove streakid blood in his veins." But it is Wirt Staples, direct-

ly out of the rip-roaring frontier tradition, who is the best. Wirt brags:

> I's jis' a mossel ove the bes' man what ever laid a shadder ontu this dirt. Hit wilts grass, my breff pizens skeeters, my yell breaks winders, an' my tromp gits yeathquakes. . . . An *I kin spit a blister ontu a washpot ontil the flies blow hit.*

And Wirt is just about that good. Sut says that if the state fair will begin to give prizes for men, as it does for jackasses, he will enter Wirt and win the prize every time.

In Sut's fantastic world animals assume human characteristics. Squire Haney's horse

> wer ove a pius turn ove mine, ur ole Haney wudn't a keep him a day. Nobody ever see him kick, gallop, jump a fence, smell uther hosses, ur chaw a bridil. He wer never hearn squeal, belch, ur make eny on sightly soun.

(pp. 397-400)

These few examples give a hint as to the dazzling array of characters found in Harris's yarns. . . . [They] operate in two worlds, one quiet and peaceful and the other teeming with action. Certainly, Harris faces a difficult problem in making the peaceful setting of the framework blend with one for his fantastic world so that his stories will not bog down in descriptions. He does this with such consummate artistry that his settings hardly seem to exist.

The necessary accompaniments for Sut's telling a story consist of a flask well filled with whiskey, a place to lie flat in the shade, of a log to sit on. The framework setting, then, may be "among a crowd of mountaineers" at "Pat Nash's grocery" or "beside a cool spring." Often the story is told to a group gathered around a campfire or while George is waiting for his "fool chain kerriers."

The setting for Sut's oral tale is seldom more complicated. Harris's criterion seems to have been to keep the setting down to an absolute minimum. With his uncanny facility for noting details, he could have described elaborate and minute settings, and in some of his stories (particularly **"Bill Ainsworth's Quarter Race"**) he does so. He seems to have operated on a formula: the more fantastic the tale, the simpler the setting. For example, here is the setting for **"Mrs. Yardley's Quilting"**:

> The morning cum, still, saft, sunshiney; cocks crowin, hens singin, birds chirpin, tuckeys gobblin—jis' the day tu sun quilts, kick, kiss, squeal, an' make love.

> All the plow-lines, an' clothes-lines war straiched tu every post an' tree. Quilts purvailed. Durn my gizzard ef two acres roun that ar house warn't jis' one solid quilt, all a-sunnin, an' tu be seed. They dazzled the eyes, skeered the hosses, gin wimin the heart-burn, an perdominated. . . .

Note how little of this passage is actual setting and how much of it performs other functions. It is particularly important to note that these quilts are to be combined later with action to create a situation around which the story is built. Sut, operating behind them as a screen, prepares for a general "momoxing" of things by fixing a horse so he can break loose, then he

> tore off a palin frum the fence, an' tuck hit in bof

hans, an' arter raisin hit 'way up yander. . . . fotch hit down. . . . an' hit acksidentally happen'd tu hit Wall-eye, 'bout nine inches ahead ove the root of his tail.

The resulting situation must be read about to be appreciated. (pp. 401-02)

[It] is situation, rather than setting, which enlivens Sut's world of fantasy.

With a representative picture of character, setting, and situation, both in the framework and in Sut's world, in mind, the reader can see what an enormous responsibility and load language must carry, if these are adequately translated to the reader. In addition, his language must make up for gestures and vocal intonation with which the oral tale was enlivened.

Harris is a master of vivid metaphors. Lizards running up Old Bullen's legs make a noise "like squirrels a-climbing a shell bark hickory"; Sut's mam gets hostile and soaks "hickory ile intu" his back "ontil hit" greases his "shut buzzum"; and cursing runs out of an old Dutchman "in a solid sluice as thick es a hoe handil." The metaphors are reinforced by a vigorous use of verbs. When mam tangles with Mis' Simmons, they "fit, an' they fout, they scratch'd, an' they claw'd, they grab'd, and they snatch'd, they knock'd, an' they hit, they grunted, an' they groaned. . . ."

As important as the vivid metaphors is the painstaking use of detail. When Sut describes a situation, he makes the whole come to life by a few details. See how this very complex situation unfolds its tremendous activity in a few words:

A monstrous cloud ove dust, like a harykane hed cum along, hid all the hosses; an away abuv hit yu cud see hosses tails an ends ove fence rales a flyin about, an now and then a par ove brite hind shoes wud flash in the sun like two sparks, an away a head wur the baskit [in Old Burns's hand on top of a runaway bull], circklin roun' an about at random. A heap of brayin, sum nickerin, the bellerin ove the bull, clatterin ove runnin hoofs, an a monstrous rushin soun made up the nize.

Sut also uses details to bring out more subtle points. When he wants to picture his unrest in the presence of Sicily Burns he says:

My toes felt like I wer in a warm krick wif minners a-nibblin at em; a cole streak wer a racin up an' down my back like a lizzard wif a tucky hen arter 'im; my hans tuck the ager, an' my hart felt hot an onsatisfied like. . . .

Thus language is used by Harris to fuse the other elements into a whole and bring them to life, and is itself made exactly appropriate to the character or situation, whether it be in the framework or in Sut's world of fantasy. Harris literally seems to breathe life and gestures and intonations and experience into cold words so that they blend with character and situation—so that they become men in action. But he is not content to stop there. After his matter is deftly spun into yarn, then wound into a ball of the correct size for as Sut says, "I ain't like ole Glabbergab; when I'se spoke off what I knows, I stops talking"), he then sews it into a more compact and durable sphere by his satires on the foibles of mankind.

In his earlier writings Harris is content to amuse. The gauge for **"The Knob Dance"** is "fun" which is appropriate to "a regular bilt frolick in the Nobs of 'Old Knox.' " Although amusement continues to be the primary purpose in his yarns, beginning with **"Sut Lovingood's Daddy 'Acting Horse,' "** he adds lusty licks at the foibles of mankind. In order to do this without freighting his stories with moral preachment, he gives to Sut's reasoning processes this characteristic:

Well, I thinks peopil's brains what hev souls, am like ontu a chain made outen gristil, forkid at wun aind; wun fork goes tu the eyes, an' tuther tu the years, an' tuther aind am welded tu the marrer in the backbone, an' hit works sorter so. Thar stans a hoss. Well, the eyes ketches his shape, jis' a shape, an' gins that idear tu the fust link ove the chain. He nickers, an' the years gins that tu tother fork ove the chain, a soun, nuffin but a soun. Well, the two ruff idears start along the chain, an' every link is smarter nur the wun ahine hit, an' dergests em sorter like a paunch dus co'n, ur mash'd feed, an' by the time they gits tu the back-bone, hit am a hoss an' yu *knows* hit. Now, in my case, there's a hook in the chain, an hits mos' ove the time onhook'd, an' then my idears stop thar half made. Rite thar's whar dad failed in his 'speriments; puttin in that durn'd fool hook's what made me a natral born fool. The breed wer bad to, on dad's side; they all run tu durn'd fools an' laigs powerful strong.

This is not a very abstruse explanation for a psychologist, but is a highly appropriate way to have Sut characterize himself. With this random kind of "hooking" provided for, Harris can "hook" that chain in Sut only when it makes the satire of a desired sort possible. Furthermore, it provides for a strange or unusual moral kind of "hooking." A "morril an' sensibil way" of running a quilting for Sut—one that is "good fur free drinking, good fur free eating, good fur free hugging, good fur free dancing, good fur free fiting, an' goodest uv all fur poperlating a country fas' "—differs from the ideas of "the ole mammys."

Whiskey plays an important part in Sut's world. This "barlm of life" is a sort of gateway, an approach, to the good things in life and it is itself the best thing in life: it is not to be enjoyed by those who damn other amusements. With this as a criterion for hypocrisy, the "Hardshell" in **"Bard Davis's Dance"** who lets his "shovel-shaped onder lip" drop outward "like ontu the fallin door ove a stone coal stove" and upsets a gourd of whiskey "inside ove his teef" so that the liquid goes down his throat "like a snake travelin thru a wet sassige gut," is welcome. But when he puritanically tries to interfere with the "innercent mucement" of dancing which follows, he is appropriately punished. This indicates Harris's chief hatred: hypocrites.

His satires, made effective by Sut's punishment, fall on many classes: women, circuit riders, lawyers, sheriffs, dandies, politicians, temperance workers, tavern "perpryiters," professors, pedigree hunters, and many other odious specimens of humanity. But it is at women and circuit riders—two groups which he particularly feels should not be hypocrites—that he aims his most frequent and best directed satires. A few examples of satires at these two groups will indicate his method.

Deceitful women are satirized in the person of Sicily Burns. Delicacy is not the proper attribute of a woman, for as Sut snorts: "There never was a durnder humbug on earth than it is, except the delicates themselves, an' their appurtinances. Oh! its jist so. But a strong-minded woman is worse. If such a woman gets after a man, Sut advises:

. . . jist you fight her like she wore whiskers or run like hell, ef you dont, ef she dont turn you inter a kidney worm'd hog what cant raise bristiles in less nor a month, you are more or less ove a man than I takes you to be. Ove all the varmints I ever seed I's feardest of them.

Old Bullen is Sut's particular hate among the many circuit riders whom he meets. The chief "pint" of this worthy is "durn'd fust rate, three bladed, dubbil barril'd, warter-proof, hypockracy, an' a never tirein appertite fur bald-face." He not only drinks whiskey, which he shouldn't, but also makes and sells whiskey, of which Sut says:

> . . . he puts in tan ooze . . . an' when that aint handy, he uses the red warter outen a pon' jis' below his barn; makes a pow'ful natral color, but don't help the taste much. Then he correcks that wif red pepper; hits an orful mixtry, that whisky ole Bullen makes. . . .

Balanced against this odious group in Sut's fantastic world is a group of "right folks." For instance, Sut has a definite use for women. He thinks that "men folks wur made jist to drink, eat, and stay awake in the early part of the night," and that the women are made "tu cook the vittils, mix the liquor, and help the men tu du the staying awake." Here is his selection for a "helper":

> But then, George, gals an' ole maids haint the things tu fool time away on. Hits widders, by golly, what am the rale sensibil, steady-going, never-skeering, never-kicking, willin, sperrited, smoof pacers. . . . They hes all ben tu Jamakey an' larnt how sugar's made, an' knows how tu sweeten wif hit; an', by golly, they is always ready tu use hit. . . . Nex tu good sperrits, an' my laigs, I like a twenty-five year ole widder, wif roun ankils, an' bright eyes, honestly an' squarly lookin intu yurn, an' saying . . . I hes been thar; yu know hit ef yu hes eny sense, an' thar's no use in eny humbug, ole feller—cum ahead!

> Widders am a speshul means, George, fur ripening green men, killin off weak ones, an' making 'ternal-ly happy the soun ones.

In the final analysis, then, Harris writes humor which is "strikingly different" and which reaches "the higest level of achievement before Mark Twain" simply because he is able to take the same material and the same forms and to do more with them than the other humorists of the Old Southwest. After the war, when life which he has satirized becomes life which he hates and blasts, in one nostalgic effort he writes a sketch about the "good old days" with only the subtlest ironies replacing his usual satire. This sketch, **"Bill Ainsworth's Quarter Race,"** gathers together the excellences of Harris, both in his selection of material and use of technique, mellows and softens his robustness without the loss of any of his strength, and, perhaps, rests at a peak of attainment in American humor. (pp. 402-06)

> *Donald Day, "The Humorous Works of George W. Harris," in* American Literature, *Vol. 14, No. 4, January, 1943, pp. 391-406.*

BROM WEBER (essay date 1954)

[*As editor of a collection of Harris's Sut Lovingood stories, Weber standardized and modernized the original spelling,* *punctuation, and paragraphing and deleted "three lines of an extremely offensive nature." In the following excerpt from his introduction to this collection, he appraises the qualities that make up the humor of the stories, noting especially their relation to the frontier tradition. In addition, Weber sounds a new note in Harris criticism in asserting that through Sut Harris championed "numerous traditional and wholesome values." Edmund Wilson takes exception both to Weber's editorial policies and to his critical conclusions in the excerpt dated 1962; for Weber's response to Wilson see the entry for* The Lovingood Papers *in the Additional Bibliography.*]

Commenting on George Washington Harris in his anthology of Southwestern frontier humor, Franklin J. Meine wrote: "For vivid imagination, comic plot, Rabelaisian touch, and sheer *fun*, the **Sut Lovingood Yarns** surpass anything else in American humor" [see excerpt dated 1930]. The judgment is not mere hyperbole, for the combination of virtues found in Harris's writing is genuinely unique. Nonetheless, this is the first full-length collection of his work to appear in almost a century.

The reasons for neglecting the monologues of Sut, the Southern mountain youth, might virtually be descriptions of their valuable qualities. Permeating the stories throughout is an unadulterated determination to evoke laughter and to reveal the delight of animality. This is achieved by picturing the doings of Great Smoky Mountain folk with racy details and generous sympathy, in a language more faithful to the vernacular and its poetry than most American literature written since has contained. Furthermore, Harris loved to tell a good story and did so with an extraordinary narrative zest. (pp. ix-x)

[The small scope of Harris's world] fostered a lyric intensity which reflects itself in his prodigious outpouring of poetic similes and metaphors. Characters and situations may at times be repetitive in outline, but they are vivified and transcended by imagery which practically never repeats itself. Details flash by at breathless speed; their insight into motive, their re-creation of the sensuous texture of life plunge the reader deep into the heart of Sut's strange world. Working intensively within a limited scope, Harris veritably embraced almost every aspect of his chosen reality and, as will be discussed later, seems to have gone beyond it too. There is not elsewhere in American literature, certainly not in the Nineteenth Century and not even in Twain's masterpiece, *Huckleberry Finn,* a similar portrait of primitive, insular man in all his bestiality, glory, and humor. Nor, for that matter, has anyone equalled the concentrated richness of his style.

A writer's appropriateness for subsequent ages may be measured by the extent to which his fundamental elements have reappeared discernibly. By this test, Harris surely belongs to us. The influence of Twain is undoubtedly responsible in part. In greater part, however, those major artists who resemble Harris—Thomas Wolfe, Erskine Caldwell, and William Faulkner, Southerners all—do so because the American frontier tradition is ineradicable. The continuity may be seen at once in the basically-identical plot structure of Harris's uncollected **"Well! Dad's Dead"** and Faulkner's *As I Lay Dying.* It is more subtly comprehended in Wolfe's largeness, Faulkner's violence, and Caldwell's antic peasantry, though this curt catalog by no means exhausts the similarities. To a limited extent, all three modern writers have composed humor in various forms—grotesque and ironic in Faulkner, grandiose in Wolfe, nostalgic and eccentric in Caldwell—and they have all written in the common tongue. But their humor is pallid, generally without the joyousness of Harris. Their language, which may be brilliant as in Faulkner's "Spotted Horses," is frequently marred by banal and pompous rhetoric in both Wolfe and Faulkner, has been stripped of poetry in Caldwell. There is no intention of suggesting that these men be replaced by Harris, merely a reminder that his refreshing mirth offers relief from their grimness and so merits our gaze. (pp. xiii-xiv)

An understanding of why the Sut Lovingood stories possess the character they do is facilitated by a brief glance at the frontier tradition to which Harris was subjected. The phrase "a new country" is one key to the frontier, and it occurs in Harris's writing as well as in those of other frontier humorists. It found a place in Harris because the spirit of the frontier kept washing back upon relatively-settled lands like East Tennessee and kept their frontier heritage alive. Most significantly for Harris, it returned in the form of written versions of oral anecdotes. These rough transcriptions gradually became more artful and, like his own work, took on the lineaments of a mature literature. (pp. xxi-xxii)

The frontiersman had made light of the new country's hardships by enveloping his misfortunes in a mocking humor. A stubborn pride had encouraged him to glory in adversity, to perversely seize upon difficulty as the cause of heroic action, to grossly and sardonically exaggerate qualities which enabled a man to triumph over circumstances: coarseness, endurance, decision, brutality, shrewdness, trickiness, speed, strength. Weakness, sentimentality, stupidity, regret, thoughtfulness, and respectability were handicaps for survival in a new country, therefore characteristics of the ludicrously inept and worthy only of contempt and ridicule. Yet behind the bravado of the frontier lay a profound fear of the supernatural and the mysterious.

Frontier life influenced the form of its humor as well as its nature. The storyteller could be certain of his audience's attention if he concerned himself with the realities of daily life. Since delayed reactions lessened his entertainment value, he specialized in physical action rather than psychological subtleties, generally developing character by means of objective behavior and descriptive details rather than analysis. The pace of the tale was kept rapid so as to accord with the tempo of existence, though digressions might occur for purposes of emphasis and ironic effect. It was related in the common tongue, where figures of speech which compressed, heightened, and toyed with experience were frequent since life was exuberant and varied. Finally, to underscore the proximity of the homely and the heroic, the extravagant was cloaked in understatement testifying to the narrator's lack of surprise at what he assumed his audience knew was only natural and to be expected.

The events and interests of Harris's life also left their impress on the Lovingood yarns. Primarily, Harris aimed to present imaginary characters in invented situations with all the humor and genius at his command. On the other hand, Sut obviously functions as a device to carry forward a satirical discussion of political and economic affairs, as well as Harris's thoughts about such matters as religion, temperance, women, and sentimentality. These wide-ranging intentions of Harris's overlapped, inevitably so because he was unable to devote himself exclusively to either fiction or journalism. The result was a mixing of themes and emphases which at first

sight appears to negate some of the humor, but actually roots it so firmly that the comic prevails at every level.

The integrated artistry of Sut can be illustrated in his scathing treatment of the circuit-riding preachers whom Sut despises with ceaseless virulence. A member of the Presbyterian church, Harris found it desirable in his satire proper to use "Methodistic" as a term of opprobrium. As it happened, the Methodists (and Baptists, too) dispatched the greatest number of circuit riders into the country and the mountains. These men were not always distinguished for their intelligence, education, or personal behavior. Harris may thus have had sober grounds for his displeasure with them. When Sut undertakes to tangle with them, however, the sobriety of Harris is imbedded in shrewd and homely details which are appropriate for a rebellious character like Sut. The prayerful, supplicating gesture introducing Clapshaw in **"Blown Up with Soda"** is the man ignobly concealing his fright in a ritual motion, but the hypocrisy implicit in the act and under attack has been made laughable because of the ridiculous incongruity of Sut's condensed description.

There are indications that, consciously and unconsciously, Harris intended Sut and his world to be that fusion of the mundane and the cosmic of which an American comic mythology was constructed in the first half of the Nineteenth Century. The geography of mountains, rivers, and states is scrambled together so that Sut bestrides the Appalachians from Virginia down through North Carolina and Tennessee into Georgia, and is everywhere at once. The physical background is vague, though Sut is fully capable of precise description. Recurrent figures and relationships offer the ingredients of a social pattern to some extent, but the resultant society is depicted far too mistily and only the peregrinations and predicaments of Sut bring it into even temporary focus. Sut, like his fellows, has his skirmishes with oppressive forces such as law and religion, but is unhampered by any occupation or home which would call forth definitively-drawn relationships. The very origin of Sut is shrouded in an ambiguity going beyond the needs of simple comic effect; it is likely that Sut is indeed the offspring, not of his "king fool" father, but of the sandhill crane who pursued Mrs. Lovingood and cornered her under the bed one day.

Into that swirling mythological backdrop, with its admixture of the fantastic and the whiskey flowing through Sut's body, Harris wove the particularity of detail and largeness of substance which rescue Sut from the charge that he is merely a poor-white degenerate. With sure comic insight, Harris created a character who boasts of his scariness, his tendency to flee from the very whiff of trouble, his "natural born durned fool" spirit, his petty trickiness, and his conscienceless infliction of pain and discomfiture. Yet out of the seeming chaos and meanness of Sut's personality and actions there gradually arises a superstructure revealing that a morality and a philosophy have been in existence always; that they contain, ironically enough, numerous traditional and wholesome values.

In practically every story, except those in which he is at the receiving-end of the joke, Sut functions as a catalytic agent. The chain of events which he sets in motion is prankish and hilarious, speeded up by Sut's appearance at opportune moments as concealed devil or heavenly messenger with keen knowledge of the secret lives of his fellows. Though sketched with incisive detail, these characters are usually broad portraits of a human trait or a social institution, sometimes both. Characters standing for authority and religion, or such failings as hypocrisy and injustice, usually become Sut's victims and are meted out the retribution which he believes they deserve. In contrast to the objects of Sut's vengeance, there are also characters who embody attributes wholly admirable: Wirt Staples, for example, is the embodiment of American physical grandeur and ready to roar challenges against the law; his wife typifies the woman who is both lover and housewife, simple in bearing, fun-loving, in tune with her husband's appetites. Scattered through the work, furthermore, are observations by Sut expounding his ideas about the cannibalism of society, the fraud of sentimentality, and the like.

It should be kept in mind that the characters, though broad in import, are not always visible as such at first glance because of their individuality as people. Furthermore, the work is kept from the dry realm of allegory by the fact that the plot events are exciting, the interaction of the characters absurd and amusing, and Sut's presence a stimulus to complications. Ultimately, however, the mythic universalities such as heroism, fertility, masculinity, and femininity emerge over a bedrock of elemental human values which Sut has carved out in the course of his adventures, values such as love, joy, truth, justice, etc. These are only some of the positive concepts which Sut has admired and championed, and it is no small feat that they emerge from behind a protagonist who has ironically been deprecated by his creator. This is humor on a grand scale. (pp. xxii-xxvii)

> *Brom Weber, in an introduction to* Sut Lovingood *by George Washington Harris, edited by Brom Weber, Grove Press, 1954, pp. ix-xxix.*

WILLIAM FAULKNER (INTERVIEW WITH JEAN STEIN VANDEN HEUVEL) (interview date 1956)

[*An American novelist and short story writer, Faulkner is one of the preeminent figures in modern American literature. His most renowned works, such as* The Sound and the Fury *(1929),* Light in August *(1932), and* Absalom! Absalom! *(1936), reflect the distinct heritage of the American rural South, yet display radical stylistic innovations as well as psychological and moral depth that lend them universality and have led critics to rank Faulkner among the major figures of world literature. The following excerpt is taken from an interview that first appeared in the* Paris Review, *Spring, 1956. In response to a question about his favorite literary characters, Faulkner cited such classic figures as Falstaff, Don Quixote, Sancho Panza, Lady Macbeth, and Huckleberry Finn. Here, he adds Sut Lovingood to his list.*]

And then I like Sut Lovingood from a book written by George Harris about 1840 or '50 in the Tennessee mountains. He had no illusions about himself, did the best he could; at certain times he was a coward and knew it and wasn't ashamed; he never blamed his misfortunes on anyone and never cursed God for them. (p. 251)

> *William Faulkner, in an interview with Jean Stein Vanden Heuvel, in* Lion in the Garden: Interviews with William Faulkner, 1926-1962, *edited by James B. Meriwether and Michael Millgate, Random House, 1968, pp. 237-56.*

EDMUND WILSON (essay date 1962)

[*Wilson is generally considered twentieth-century America's foremost man of letters. A prolific reviewer, creative writer, and social and literary critic, he exercised his greatest literary influ-ence as the author of* Axel's Castle *(1931), a seminal study of literary symbolism, and as the author of widely read reviews and essays in which he introduced the best works of modern literature to the reading public. The following excerpt is from his review of Brom Weber's collection of Sut Lovingood's stories (see excerpt dated 1954). Here, Wilson attacks Weber's editorial policies and strongly disagrees with the view—held by Weber and others—of Sut as a harmless prankster, arguing that the character is actually sadistic, malevolent, and brutal. For Weber's response to Wilson, see the entry for* The Lovingood Papers *in the Additional Bibliography. Wilson's comments were first published in the* New Yorker *in 1955 and were later revised and included in his 1962 book* Patriotic Gore.]

In attempting to clean up Sut Lovingood and make him attractive to the ordinary reader—an ambition probably hopeless—Mr. Weber has produced something that is not of much value to the student of literature. He is correct in pointing out that Harris, in trying to render Sut's illiterate speech, has inconsistently mixed written misspelling, intended to look funny on the printed page—though Sut has never learned to write—with a phonetic transcription of the way he talks; but the writing does have a coarse texture as well as a rank flavor, and to turn it, as the editor has done, into something that is closer to conventional English, and to dilute it with paragraphs and strings of dots, is to deprive it of a good deal of this. By the time Mr. Weber gets done with him, Sut Lovingood hardly even sounds like a Southerner; it is fatal to the poor-white dialect to turn "naik" and "hit" into "neck" and "it." What is worst, from the scholarly point of view, is to comb out "words [that] are obsolete and others [that] are probably meaningless to all but a handful of contemporary readers." If the book was to be reprinted, the text should have been given intact, and the unfamiliar words as well as the topical allusions explained. (pp. 508-09)

One is also rather surprised at the editor's idea of deleting "three lines of an extremely offensive nature." One of the most striking things about **Sut Lovingood** is that it is all as offensive as possible. It takes a pretty strong stomach nowadays—when so much of the disgusting in our fiction is not rural but urban or suburban—to get through it in any version. I should say that, as far as my experience goes, it is by far the most repellent book of any real literary merit in American literature. This kind of crude and brutal humor was something of an American institution all through the nineteenth century. The tradition of the crippling practical joke was carried on almost to the end of the century with *Peck's Bad Boy*, and that of the nasty schoolboy by certain of the writings of Eugene Field, a professional sentimentalist, who, however, when working for the Denver *Tribune*, betrayed a compulsive fondness for puerile and disgusting jokes: cockroaches and boarding-house hash and collywobbles from eating green peaches. But the deadpan murders and corpses of Mark Twain's early Far Western sketches are given an impressive grimness by the imperviousness to horror their tone implies, and the nihilistic butcheries of Ambrose Bierce derive a certain tragic accent from his background of the Civil War. The boorish or macabre joke, as exploited by these Western writers, does perform a kind of purgative function in rendering simply comic stark hardships and disastrous adventures. The exploits of Sut Lovingood, however, have not even this kind of dignity. He is neither a soldier nor a pioneer enduring a cruel ordeal; he is a peasant squatting in his own filth. He is not making a jest of his trials; he is avenging his inferiority by tormenting other people. His impulse is avowedly sadistic. The keynote is struck in the following passage (I give it in the original Tennessean):

> I hates ole Onsightly Peter [so called because he was selling encyclopedias], jis' caze he didn't seem tu like tu hear me narrate las' night; that's human nater the yeath over, an' yeres more univarsal onregenerit human nater: ef ever yu dus enything tu eny body wifout cause, yu hates em allers arterwards, an' sorter wants tu hurt em agin. An' yere's anuther human nater: ef enything happens sum feller, I don't keer ef he's yure bes' frien, an' I don't keer how sorry yu is fur him, thars a streak ove satisfackshun 'bout like a sowin thread a-runnin all thru yer sorrer. Yu may be shamed ove hit, but durn me ef hit ain't thar. Hit will show like the white cottin chain in mean cassinett; brushin hit onder only hides hit. An' yere's a littil more; no odds how good yu is tu yung things, ur how kine yu is in treatin em, when yu sees a littil long laiged lamb a-shakin hits tail, an' a dancin staggerinly onder hits mam a-huntin fur the tit, ontu hits knees, yer fingers *will* itch to seize that ar tail, an' fling the littil ankshus son ove a mutton over the fence amung the blackberry briars, not tu hurt hit, but jis' tu disapint hit. Ur say, a littil calf, a-buttin fus' under the cow's fore-laigs, an' then the hine, wif the pint ove hits tung stuck out, makin suckin moshuns, not yet old enuf tu know the bag aind ove hits mam frum the hookin aind, don't yu want tu kick hit on the snout, hard enough tu send hit backwards, say fifteen foot, jis' tu show hit that buttin won't allers fetch milk? Ur a baby even rubbin hits heels apas' each uther, a-rootin an' a-snifflin arter the breas', an' the mam duin her bes' tu git hit out, over the hem ove her clothes, don't yu feel hungry tu gin hit jis' one 'cussion cap slap, rite ontu the place what sum day'll fit a saddil, ur a sowin cheer, tu show hit what's atwixt hit an' the grave; that hit stans a pow'ful chance not tu be fed every time hits hungry, ur in a hurry?

In view of this, the comments on Sut Lovingood by our recent academic critics are among the curiosities of American scholarship. We find Mr. J. Franklin Meine, in *Tall Tales of the Southwest,* speaking of this hero's "keen delight for Hallowee'n *fun* [italics the author's]—there is no ulterior motive (except occasionally Sut's desire to 'get even'), no rascality, no gambling, no sharpening. . . . Sut is simply the genuine naïve roughneck mountaineer, riotously bent on raising hell," and again, "For vivid imagination, comic plot, Rabelaisian touch and sheer *fun,* the **Sut Lovingood Yarns** surpass anything else in American humor" [see excerpt dated 1930]. "Ultimately," asserts Mr. Weber, "the mythic universalities such as heroism, fertility, masculinity, and femininity emerge over a bedrock of elemental human values which Sut has carved out in the course of his adventures, values such as love, joy, truth, justice, etc. These are only some of the positive concepts which Sut has admired and championed, and it is no small feat that they emerge from behind a protagonist who has ironically been deprecated by his creator. This is humor on a grand scale."

Now, Sut Lovingood can be called "Rabelaisian" only in the sense that he is often indecent by nineteenth-century standards and that he runs to extravagant language and monstrously distorted descriptions. Unlike Rabelais, he is always malevolent and always excessively sordid. (pp. 509-12)

As for the "fun" of Sut Lovingood, it is true that Harris ex-

plained his aim as merely to revive for the reader "sich a laugh as is remembered wif his keerless boyhood" [see essay dated 1867], and that he liked to express his nostalgia for the dances and quiltings of his youth; but even in one of Harris's pre-Lovingood sketches that deal with one of these, the fun seems mainly to consist of everybody's getting beaten to a pulp, and in the Lovingood stories themselves, the fun entirely consists of Sut's spoiling everybody else's fun. He loves to break up such affairs. One of his milder devices is setting bees and hornets on people. In this way, he ruins the wedding of a girl who has refused his advances and dismissed him with an unpleasant practical joke, and puts to rout a Negro revivalist rally—for he runs true to poor-white tradition in despising and persecuting the Negroes. He rejoices when his father, naked, is set upon by "a ball ho'nets nes' ni ontu es big es a hoss's hed" and driven to jump into the water. Sut gloats over "dad's bald hed fur all the yeath like a peeled inyin, a bobbin up an' down an' aroun, an' the ho'nets sailin roun tuckey buzzard fashun, an' every onst in a while one, an' sum times ten, wud take a dip at dad's bald hed." This leaves the old man "a pow'ful curious, vishus, skeery lookin cuss. . . . His hed am as big es a wash pot, an' he hasent the fust durned sign ove an eye—jist two black slits." Sut, who supposes himself to be his mother's only legitimate child, has nothing but contempt for his father as an even greater fool than himself, who has bequeathed to him only misery, ignorance and degradation. Most of all, however, his hatred is directed against anybody who shows any signs of gentility, idealism or education. On such people, under the influence of bad whisky, to which he refers as "kill-devil" or "bald face," he revenges himself by methods that range from humiliation to mayhem. His habit of denouncing his victims as hypocrites, adulterers or pedants is evidently what has convinced Mr. Weber that Sut Lovingood cherishes "values such as love, joy, truth, justice, etc." But he is equally vicious with anyone who happens for any other reason to irritate him. In the case of an old lady who loves to make quilts, he rides into her quilting party with a horse he has driven frantic, ripping up all the quilts and trampling the hostess to death. This is Sut's only recorded human murder, but animals he has more at his mercy, and he loves to kill dogs, cats and frogs. It is not in the least true, as another of Sut's encomiasts has said [see excerpt dated 1937 by Edd Winfield Parks], that pain does not exist in Sut Lovingood's world. On the contrary, the sufferings of his victims are described with considerable realism, and the furtively snickering Sut enjoys every moment of them. It is good to be reminded by Mr. Meine that his hero is never shown as addicted to gambling or sharping.

Nor is it possible to imagine that Harris is aiming at Swiftian satire. It is plain that he identifies himself with Sut, and his contemporaries referred to him as Sut, just as Anatole France in his day was referred to as M. Bergeret. . . . He is evidently speaking of himself, in his preface to **Sut Lovingood,** when he makes his hero explain that he will "feel he has got his pay in full" if he can rouse to a laugh "jis' one, eny poor misfortinit devil hu's heart is onder a mill-stone, hu's raggid children are hungry, an' no bread in the dresser, hu is down in the mud, an' the lucky ones a-trippin him every time he struggils tu his all fours, hu has fed the famishin an' is now hungry hisself, hu misfortins foller fas' an' foller faster, hu is so footsore an' weak that he wishes he wer at the ferry." (pp. 513-16)

[George Harris] represented the . . . [stratum] of the white "non-planter" who had got himself some education. We know nothing of Harris's early life except that he had once been a jeweller's apprentice; but his origins seem to have been humble—it is not known what his father did or what became of his parents—and he shared with what were called the "poor white trash" something of their consciousness of limitation and of their bitterness against those who did not want them to escape from it.

In Unionist eastern Tennessee, George Harris never wavered from his original allegiance to the Democratic party, which in the South represented the artisans and farmers as against the industrializing Whigs. But he failed in an attempt at farming as well as at his several industrial projects—his sawmill, his glass manufactory, his metal working shop—and it is plain that a sense of frustration—"flustratin'" is one of Sut's favorite words—is at the root of the ferocious fantasies in which, in the character of Sut, he likes to indulge himself. Yet he also uses Sut as a spokesman for his own sometimes shrewd observations, and this rather throws the character out as a credible and coherent creation, since he is made to see the world from a level which in reality would be beyond him. The effect of it is more disconcerting than if Sut were simply a comic monster, for it makes one feel that Sut's monstrous doings really express, like his comments on the local life, George Harris's own mentality. It is embarrassing to find Caliban, at moments, thinking like a human being.

But the book is not without its power, the language is often imaginative, and Sut is a Southern type, the envious and mutinous underling, which it is well no doubt to have recorded. . . . Mr. Weber says truly that Harris has something in common with Caldwell and Faulkner. He is thinking of the tradition of "folk humor"; but what is more fundamental is that these writers are all attempting to portray various species of the Southern poor white. Sut Lovingood is unmistakably an ancestor of Faulkner's Snopses, that frightening low-class family (some of them stuck at Sut's level, others on their way up), who, whether in success or in crime or both, are all the more difficult to deal with because they have their own kind of pride—who are prepared, as Mr. Weber points out in connection with their predecessor, to "take on the whole world." All that was lowest in the lowest of the South found expression in Harris's book, and *Sut Lovingood,* like A. B. Longstreet's *Georgia Scenes,* with its grotesqueries of ear-chewing, eye-gouging fights and yokelish hunts and balls, is needed, perhaps, to counterbalance those idyls of the old regime by Kennedy, Caruthers and Cooke and the chivalrous idealism of Sidney Lanier.

The dreamy nobility of a man like Lanier and the murderous clowning of Harris are products of the same society, and the two men have something in common. George Harris . . . was all in favor of secession. . . . From the moment of Lincoln's nomination, George Harris turned Sut Lovingood loose on the Unionists. Here is a passage from one of his libels on Lincoln—to call them satires would be to give them too much dignity—of which still another infatuated editor, Mr. Edd Winfield Parks, has said that "though good-humored, they reveal his [Harris's] feelings," and of which Mr. Weber, who includes them in his volume, has said that Lincoln "might not have enjoyed [them] as much as a secessionist would" but that "he would have laughed at the exaggeration of ugliness so customary in frontier humor." Sut Lovingood is supposed to be accompanying Lincoln on the latter's incognito journey through Baltimore on his way to the inauguration, and Lin-

Sut Lovingood and Sicily Burns.

coln is supposed to be terrified by the threats of the Maryland secessionists:

> I kotch a ole bull frog once an druv a nail through his lips inter a post, tied two rocks ta his hine toes an stuck a durnin needil inter his tail tu let out the misture, and lef him there tu dry. I seed him two weeks arter wurds, and when I seed ole Abe I thot hit were an orful retribution cum outa me; an that hit were the same frog, only strutched a little longer, an had tuck tu warin ove close ta keep me from knowin him, an ketchin him an nailin him up agin; an natural born durn'd fool es I is, I swar I seed the same watry skery look in the eyes, and the same sorter knots on the backbone. I'm feared, George, sumthin's tu cum ove my nailin up that ar frog. I swar I am ever since I seed ole Abe, same shape same color, same feel (cold as ice) an I'm d———ef hit ain't the same smell.

Sut's tirades after the defeat of the South are vituperative on a level that almost makes the passage above seem the work of a sensitive artist. A new rancor, a new crushing handicap have been added to his previous ones. He can only spew abuse at the Yankees. The election of Grant seems a death-blow. According to Professor Donald Day, the principal authority on Harris, one of the last of the Lovingood stories, called **"Well! Dad's Dead,"** which appeared in a Tennessee paper on November 19, 1868, was inspired by this event. I am not sure that I can accept Professor Day's idea that Sut Lovingood's moronic father has here come to stand for the Old South. He passes, in any case, without lament:

> Nara durn'd one ove 'em [the neighbors] come a nigh the old cuss, to fool 'im into believin' that he stood a chance to live, or even that they wanted him to stay a minit longer than he were obleeged to. . . . That night [after they had buried him], when we were hunker'd round the hearth, sayin' nothin' an' waitin for the taters to roast, mam, she spoke up—"oughtent we to a scratch'd in a little dirt, say?" "No need, mam," sed Sall, "hits loose yearth, an' will soon cave in enuff."

Sut has always claimed that his father sired him as "a nat'ral born durn'd fool," and his habitual falling back on this as an excuse for both his oafish inadequacies and his sly calculated crimes strikes the only touching note in these farces. (pp. 516-19)

> *Edmund Wilson, "The Myth of the Old South; Sidney Lanier; The Poetry of the Civil War; 'Sut Lovingood'," in his* Patriotic Gore: Studies in the Literature of the American Civil War, *Oxford University Press, 1962, pp. 438-528.*

MILTON RICKELS   (essay date 1966)

[Rickels is the author of the first full-length biographical and critical study of Harris. In the following excerpt, he examines Harris's language, focusing on his use of dialect and imagery.]

Since the mid-1930's critics have recognized Harris' language as his finest artistic achievement. His revisions for the **Yarns** show he etched Sut's language with painstaking care. Several times Harris presents Sut as speculating about the limitations of words. Of breaking up the Negro camp meeting, Sut says, "Well, when I larns tu spell an' pernounce the flavor ove a ded hoss, play the shape ove a yeathen war-jug [earthenware jug] ontu a fiddil, ur paint the swifness ove these yere laigs ontu a clapboard, then I'll 'scribe the nise ove that meetin. . . ." The analogies with music and painting reveal in what artistic terms Harris was considering his problem. Other instances occur in the **Yarns** where Harris, from behind the mask of comedy, calls his language to the attention of his audience. Two aspects of Harris' language present the most problems to the reader: his dialect and his imagery.

The dialect is the first quality of language to strike the reader—and often also the last; for many readers give up trying to penetrate the maze of rustic idiom complicated by phonetic spelling of dialectal pronunciations and by "comical" misspellings of no linguistic significance.

Like the other Southwestern humorists, Harris intended his dialect partly to be realistic and partly to be humorous. These humorists were attempting to re-create an oral tradition in writing; and storytellers like Jim Doggett, Simon Suggs, and Sut had to be presented as speaking a believable vernacular. The original function of the frame stories, as they appeared in Porter's *Spirit of the Times,* was to distinguish the folk tellers from the gentleman listeners by their speech habits.

Longstreet, Thorpe, and Hooper used the framework to imply the superior education and social status of the gentleman. Harris expanded the technique to reveal contrasts in character and even, tentatively, in moral vision. George speaks standard English of a stilted, traditional, and formal variety; Sut speaks a lively, vigorous vernacular. The dialect accentuates a basic irony: the illiterate yokel is revealed by his speech as considerably more speculative and articulate than his educated friend, who has achieved stability and accuracy in his language at the expense of its vitality. Pascal Covici has noted that Harris anticipated Twain in turning the ridicule implied in dialect outward against the sophisticated audience rather than against the backwoodsmen [see Additional Bibliography]. From the Mr. Free epistles and **"The Knob Dance"** of the 1840's to the Lovingood tales of the 1850's Harris' interest shifted from focus on customs and speech as picturesque curiosities for an assumedly superior audience to an interest in dialect for its own qualities and for its possibilities for humor and meaning.

To the formally educated reader there is something incongruous and therefore often comic about dialect. The term itself implies deviation from some norm of propriety. The incongruity and therefore the comedy are intensified when dialect speech is put into writing—when an attempt is made to write what is not a written language. Talk like Sut's, readers feel, should be heard, not seen; and to recognize its form is to feel superior in one's own form. Natives of Tennessee who heard such a dialect all their lives could, and obviously did, find it comical when used as a literary vehicle. (pp. 107-08)

Harris wrote Sut's dialect with remarkable consistency. There is seldom a word, a grammatical form, or a pronunciation which does not ring true; and some of the apparent inconsistencies may well be typographical errors—Harris' spelling is admittedly a typesetter's nightmare. Most of the unorthodox spellings are not used in the spirit of the literary comedians, but indicate characteristic details of pronunciation which make an important and cumulative difference in the total effect. There is, for example, a real difference between a Northern *chicken* and a Southern *chickin* to the sensitive ear.

Harris wrote his dialect with increasing respect; and, by the time he finished the **Yarns,** he was using it without condescension and with a "true ear," as Robert Penn Warren has noted. Eventually the vernacular became an object of esthetic delight for him. . . . Harris came to concern himself with the items of dialect as objects of esthetic contemplation and pleasure for their own sake.

The young Mark Twain's interest in Harris' dialect, as well as his re-reading of the **Yarns** during the composition of *Huckleberry Finn,* implies a significant evaluation of Harris. No other American artist could have suggested so much to Mark Twain about the creation of an American literary prose based on the vernacular.

As carefully worked out as the dialect, and of even greater power to create meaning and tone, is Harris' imagery. By artful selection from the vernacular, by original invention, by mining earlier sketches, and by painstaking revision Harris created an imagery through which he projects indirectly Sut's vision of the American backwoods—the people, animals, cabins, doggeries, and clearings of Frog Mountain, Rattlesnake Spring, and Lost Creek. A subtly perceptive, often dark vision is projected through a varied, complex, and tonally consistent body of images. This body is capable, like Harris' few best fables, of bearing the double occasions of laughter; and it shows an even greater capacity to carry incompatible emotions. In his imagery Harris' art is shown at its best, masterful and ingenious in evoking the dark atmosphere of life, somberly fleshly at times, graphic and gestural, to use Erich Auerbach's phrase.

The numerous imagery studies of modern critics have demonstrated that symbolism is not simply a phase of rhetoric. Imagery at its best is not only technique, but also revelation of the author's conscious and less conscious intentions and preoccupations. Harris' imagery embodies his philosophy, his humor, his assessment of reality—in short, his moral vision. His work provides an opportunity to observe the function imagery serves in providing a counterpoint to surface meanings. Notably in the *Yarns,* what his images communicate is not always the same thing that his plots and characters communicate. The coarse and impish, sometimes cruel surface of the tales celebrates the joy of physical movement; delight in food, drink, sexual experience; the excitement of wild confusion; and freedom from all restraint. The tone of the imagery is equally turbulent but darker, more pervasively magical and sensory in its elements of the ugly, the broken, the erotic.

From the first Harris warns his readers that the vision of the world he communicates will not "sit purfeckly quiet ontu the stumicks ove sum pussons" [see essay dated 1867]. The sense of the difficulty of writing and of its absurdity, of the yearning for some permanent esthetic achievement, the sense of a burden of message is heavy in Harris' Preface to the *Yarns.* It is the language, and primarily the imagery, that carries the greatest weight of the vision Harris would communicate.

Most apparent in Harris' images is the frequency with which he uses epithets and complexly developed metaphors and similes. The similes are often extended by elaborate addition and qualification of detail. Almost every line of the *Yarns* contains some kind of imagery. The detail used is concrete, closely packed, and graphic.

The first effect of this frequency is speed and intensity. The reader is whirled into the illusion of ebullient delight in motion and wild action. Racy colloquialisms, nonce words, corruptions of names and of bookish terms, compression of detail, astonishing expansion of connotation, and controlled changes in the tensions of the action and of the language, shifting from litotes to the wildest hyperbole, create an illusion of speed, movement, freedom. Images are expanded by piling detail upon detail until the reader is bewildered in a complexity of emotions and ideas.

The subject matter of the imagery reveals that Harris' world of reference was limited, doubtless with the conscious intent to achieve a close and intense focus. From this world the great body of his metaphors and similes can be classified into a few broad categories that all point to the sharp center of the focus.

The largest group, constituting well over one-third of all images employed, is made up of animal images—mammals, birds, fish, and insects. (pp. 111-13)

At times the image refers to no specific animal but merely to general animal characteristics. In a sexual image, a joker watches for opportunities "jist es clost es a ole 'oman what wer wunst onsanctified hersef, watches her darters when a suckus ur a camp meetin am in heat." Sut says of a Yankee whom he hates: "He wer hatched in a crack." And Sut's starched shirt, with bits of his skin clinging to it, "looked adzactly like the skin ove sum wile beas' tore off alive."

The total effect of Harris' animal imagery is disturbing. It implies speed, wild action, grotesque appearance, suffering, decay and death. Bloody flesh, meat, skin, and bones are everywhere in a welter of disorder.

Next to animals, the second largest category, accounting for one-fifth of Harris' similes and metaphors, is that of machinery and implements: steam engines, locomotives (a pair of angry bulls clash "like two drunk locomotives"), threshing machines, pumps, steamboats, sawmills, grist mills, cotton gins, whiskey stills, corn shellers, welding torches, knives, axes, and the like. The feelings they generate are reactions to sharpness, hardness, threat, motion—frequently of powerful, fearsome, and mindless action.

The third most frequent group of images has to do with the human being in his actions, trades, and professions. An action may be "quick es an 'oman kin hide a strange hat," or one may be "pow'ful b'lever, not a sarcumsised b'lever, but a lie b'lever," or mam, to insult the neighbor woman with whom she is pulling hair over dad, calls her a "merlatter lookin strumpit." Animal characteristics and human trades may be combined: Sut says he may "turn buzzard, an' eat ded hosses fur a livin." Sut once says of George that "eavesdrappin am a durn'd mean sorter way tu make a livin." Of a dog fight, Sut says, "When the ballunce ove the dorgs cum up, (human like,) they all pitched into the poor helpless devil." Thus Harris' characters are compared to types or to typical actions of churchgoers, circuit riders, congressmen, soldiers, rough-and-tumble fighters, drunks, auctioneers, farmers, butchers, tailors, coffinmakers, and other classes, trades, racial groups of the backcountry. (pp. 114-15)

Several generalizations are possible after Harris' imagery is abstracted from the total work and examined as a separate element. First, it rarely suggests beauty or any of the softer emotions. It reinforces the impression Sut creates that the benevolent or good-natured man does not exist. The effect of images of flayed and butchered animals, of diseases and verminous insects, of fatness and thinness, of occasionally seductive women fills the *Yarns* with a sense of the ever-present flesh. The dark chaos of flesh emphasizes Sut's solitary isolation. There is no meaning to discover or to recover in this dark atmosphere but the feeling of the flesh. At the broadest, the human condition is isolated, ugly, dying, without transcendental meaning.

However, it is equally apparent that the effect is not merely ugly. Harris' imagery is formally varied and complex. Usually it is concrete and graphic, but at times it conveys no picture at all. It becomes cryptic and intellectual, communicates ideas and judgments. One example of such sunken imagery is mam's invitation to ole Squire Hanley to leave her home: "We's got no notes tu shave nur gals ole enuf tu convart." Harris' image implies that the squire is interested in cheating and in girls, and that the interest in girls is sexual rather than spiritual. The image comprehends too much for simple visualization. It approaches abstraction. Specifically, it compares the present child with the nubile adolescent to be, and then, shifting the object of the comparison, suggests that a deacon can have no concern for little children. Such sunken imagery exists for its content of ideas. Its generalization is expansive. Recurring images of circuit riders fathering illegitimate children, seducing young girls, fleeing irate husbands, continue an ancient folk tradition of humor and communicate an impression of the hill-country preacher as ignorant, immoral, and as baldly hypocritical as Chaucer's Pardoner or Boccaccio's Friar Onion. Behind the comic fantasy of Harris' practical jokes plays the counterpoint of the imagery, sounding the deeper discords of the American Eden.

Next, the imagery reveals that Harris' imagination ranged from the keen and incisive to the expansive, myth-making visions, and functioned with natural ease and telling effect in symbols and allegories. For example, the imagery associated with Sut's birth moves him in the direction of the heroes of legend. "No," Sut once answers a reporter, "But we kep a sand-hill crane, and Mam and him had a difficulty, and he chased her under the bod." The excesses of the imagery, wild, vigorous, and compelling, match the vaultings of a large and strange imagination—an imagination at times irrational and compulsive but bodying forth from a microcosm of homely images a macrocosm of emotions and ideas.

Finally, the imagery is one of the most enduring elements of comedy in Harris. The most common humorous tendency of the language is to expose foolish or knavish characters to ridicule. The satiric and reductive elements in the imagery are balanced by its frequency and vividness to communicate a sense of the vigor and joy of life. A clerk-like newspaper reporter is "a little, mild, husband-lookin feller in gold specks and a pencil." Among the many tendencies of the satire here, one of them is something near to affection for human variety.

Much of Harris' imagery is witty in the vernacular tradition. One of his techniques is to begin with a common English expression which he then qualifies in some way to cancel its cliché meaning and thus surprise the reader. Two bloody-headed men are dismissed with "Jis' a fis' fight, with sticks: that's all." Recalling an early episode of his poverty-stricken life, Sut remembers mam feeding the "brats ontu mush an' milk, wifout the milk." Sometimes Sut plays on dead images: "wimen went head-fust intu the houses, doors slam'd, sash[es] fell, cats' tails swell'd es they treed onder stabils."

Another kind of verbal humor turns not on imagery but on logic. This type is best exemplified by Rabelais' report of Pope Alexander, who took "the advice of a Jew, his physician, and . . . lived till his dying day in despite of his enemies," or by Mark Twain's telegram which complained that the report of his death was greatly exaggerated. Parson Bullen, excusing his nakedness after Sut loosed lizards up his trousers, took as his text the following Sunday: "Nakid I cum intu the world, an' nakid I'm a gwine outen hit, ef I'm spard ontil then." When Sut expresses sympathy, it is often in an ambiguous form, as when he tells George of a poor, "misfortinit devil [who] happen'd tu steal a hoss by accident."

Harris is fond of vernacular images which both break categories and offer satiric comment, as when old Simon Jerrold chases his wife "wif a drawn corn hoe." A man trying to kill his wife is scandalous enough, but the image of the drawn sword applied to the hoe calls attention to the indignity and impropriety of both the act and the method. The class bias is clear here; Harris' assumption is that the more cultured elements of the community would never use hoes.

The element of fantasy in Harris' imagery is at its best both comic and functional, unlike that of the literary comedians; and it may be conceit-like in the logic of its applications. In **"Sut Lovingood in New York,"** an angry woman is described as "a standin' with all her laigs so clost together that a buckit hoop w'u'd a went roun' all ove em." The comic impropriety

of the "all" disappears, almost, as Harris presents the image of a cat in the next line.

As the reader examines the imagery associated with Sicily Burns or her father, with Sut, with Sut's father, and with other characters, it becomes apparent that it is coherent, that it expands their meanings, and that it objectifies the ancient comic ambivalence of hatred and joy. Sicily is all flesh, power, beauty—as tempting as naked Eve; and the smell of the devil is about her. Old man Lovingood is ugly and cruel authority, and floats before the mind's eye in the harness of a horse, or naked, or dressed in the skin of a bull and lying, at the end of the **Yarns,** bloody-faced on the ground, a poleaxed sacrifice. Connotations of powerful sexuality and of Sut's jealousy cling to the old man. The fool Sut is imaged in his long legs, in his heroic, mythic birth, sired like a Greek hero by a wild bird on a wild hill-country woman. He follows in the succession of his father: dark, fierce, inhuman, squalid, but magical and commanding, ritualistically driving out scapegoats. His life is hatred and revel, attack and flight; and the imagery associated with him is that of isolation, of escape, and of freedom.

Our argument has been that Harris' imagery will bear close scrutiny; it is art of no mean order. It is art as a means to rigorous and austere pursuit of reality. Sut appears to seek sheer fun, but the imagery associated with him, like the fables at their best, enlarges his stature to a figure ambiguously comic and mythy, perceiving an awful reality, and desiring and ritualistically asserting an impossible freedom. He pursues intensity of experience in the flesh, and an abandonment to the obsessive and the irrational. Beneath the plain practical jokes swirl the dark currents of the imagery which bodies Sut's world as occasionally satisfying, but more often ugly, harsh, deceitful, transitory, and meaningless. (pp. 116-19)

Milton Rickels, in his George Washington Harris, *Twayne Publishers, Inc., 1966, 159 p.*

M. THOMAS INGE (essay date 1967)

[*Inge has written extensively on Harris. His edition of Harris's writings includes brief introductory essays to the sporting epistles, early sketches and tales, humorous Sut Lovingood stories, and satires. In this analysis of Harris's political satires, Inge claims that they demonstrate the author's awareness of satiric literary techniques even though he often loses control and descends into invective and indecency.*]

[Harris's satirical sketches reveal] that he remained all his life a faithful member of the Democratic party, a conservative defender of the ante-bellum South as a superior civilization, a militant foe of the encroachment of modern "progress" and materialism on Southern society, and an unreconstructed Southern patriot. Whenever political or social events on the national scene appeared to threaten the safety and influence of what Harris believed in; he was moved to pick up his pen and produce some of the most vigorous and imaginative satires of his day.

Although Harris's achievement as a satirical artist is not comparable with that of such masters as Jonathan Swift or Alexander Pope, an examination of his satiric technique reveals that he was aware of and used the three major rhetorical divisions of satire: invective, burlesque, and irony. Historically, there have been two types of satire: formal verse satire and Menippean satire. All of Harris's work belongs in the latter category, which, according to Alvin Kernan, "originally referred to those satires which were written in a mixture of verse and prose, but . . . has gradually come to include any satiric work obviously written in the third person or, to put it another way, where the attack is managed under cover of a fable." It is interesting to note that in the second part of **"The Early Life of Sut Lovingood, Written by His Dad."** Harris does include some burlesque poetry, true to the Menippean mode in its original form.

When Harris discovered the convenience of Sut as an effective, artistically controllable outlet for his humorous impulses, he also realized that Sut could be manipulated as a mouthpiece for satirical attacks. Thus, the second Sut story Harris wrote, **"Playing Old Sledge for the Presidency,"** was prompted by the desire of Harris to make a satirical comment on the 1856 presidential election in which James Buchanan, Millard Fillmore, and John C. Frémont participated. The story is structured as a dream allegory. Sut recounts to George his dream in which he found himself in Washington, the nation's capital, at a big tavern where a card game of old sledge, or seven-up, was in progress between the three presidential candidates, whose names are slightly altered by misspelling. Allegorically, the plays and strategy of the card players equal the political maneuvering which will be necessary on the part of the candidates to cop the prize. Naturally, the Democratic candidate Buchanan, whom Harris was supporting, out-maneuvers the others and wins, and the fact that such proved to be the outcome makes this story seem prophetic, especially since Harris correctly forecasted victory by a very slim margin. But Harris would have written it this way regardless of the outcome, obviously, and his estimate of the voting margin is simply the result of an interested politician with his eye objectively fixed on current opinion. The accuracy of Harris, however, brought the sketch a wide reprinting after the election and must have given him something of a minor reputation as a political prognosticator.

In the lengthy, four-part political satire called **"Sut Lovingood's Love Feast ove Varmints,"** Harris uses the ancient literary form of the animal fable or allegory. The adoption of this form was suggested by the circumstances in Tennessee in 1859 when the powerful Democratic party was being opposed not by one party but a variety of splinter groups—Whigs, Native-Americans or Know-Nothings, and turncoat Democrats. When these groups tried to get together for a convention in Nashville and unite their forces in an opposition party to break the Democratic stronghold on the state level, Harris viewed the mixed composition of the group with distaste and was inspired to equate them with a gathering of animals banded together for self-preservation. "Ez a general thing," Harris has Sut, who once again serves as the narrator, say, "afore this, humuns hev hed but wun kind ove varmints tu fite et a time. . . . But things am changed now. The whole dam list ove the inimies tu the humans what am in varmint shape am cum tugether in love feas, an ef they kin do half they wunt tu the coon will be squire, the groun-hog constable, an the wolf preacher, an humans mus dig roots fur a livin and the he's howl on the cliff when they wants the company ove the she's." By thus denigrating the political enemies of the Democrats to the position of animals, their motives also become selfish and animal-like. The only thing the various political elements have in common, Harris indicates, is the desire for power of office and the spoils that come with it; thus, says a wild boar, within the allegorical framework, "Thar aint anuther pint on yeath that we ever kin agree on, an so

we wont speak on them, but jist set oursefs on VITTILS. . . . *The fac is we hasent et ontil we hes los all ideas ove size, shape, smell ur taste, an thars but wun thing afore us an that is* 'VITTILS OR DEATH.' "

Harris does not have Sut recount the story of the gathering of the varmints as a dream, but as a whimsical and incredible example of the tall tale. Much of the satiric point and humor is now lost because many of the animals were intended to be caricatures of actual people, and the series closely followed the actual events in Nashville they were meant to ridicule. Although some of the topical references are now impossible to identify, Harris's imaginative skill is evident in the way he could seize upon an actual event, as when a storm nearly tore the roof off the building where one of the convention sessions was held, and use it within the allegory to denigrate the victims satirically: the smell of the varmints in the room, says Sut, "by this time wer must overpowerin tu me, an torrectly I seed the ruff ove the house begin tu rise, an the glass bustin outen the winders. Hit were nuffin on yeath but the cummulated pressure ove the smell." Also, we see Harris use in these pieces a rhetorical device made famous by Rabelais, the "abusive catalogue," as when he describes the convention as composed of "pole cats, coons, groun-hogs, minks, house-cats, hoss-cats, hell-cats, weazels, mus-rats, wharf-rats, bull-bats, owls, buzzards, water-dogs, wild boars, bell weathers, possums, moles, grub-worms and tumble-bugs. . . ." This is a device, of course, he used frequently within the nonpolitical stories told by Sut, as well as in the other satires.

Harris not only aimed his satiric cannon at local politicians, but when Abraham Lincoln, a Republican (the party which eventually emerged from the conglomeration of political elements satirized in the pieces discussed above), was elected President in 1861, he castigated the leader with severity and viciousness. Once again Harris seized on an actual event, the mysterious night ride of Lincoln through Baltimore to avoid a hypothetical threat to his life, an action which neither Lincoln nor many of his friends approved of because of the cowardly appearance it made. Lincoln's enemies naturally exploited it for this reason, and opposition press cartoonists caricatured the event. Harris projects Sut into the situation by first placing him in Baltimore to witness preparation for the supposed assassination, and then sending him across country to join Lincoln at Harrisburg, Pennsylvania, to see him safely through to Washington. A series of three satires were written by Harris describing the journey.

It may be assumed that Harris was not portraying Sut as a Southern turncoat, a deserter to the enemy. Walter Blair has written that the formula Harris used here was "to set up a numb-headed and rather vicious character, show how he traitorously sympathized with the wrong side, have him, in an irritating fashion, give his rascally aid to the enemy, and then have him tell his story" [see Additional Bibliography entry dated 1942]. But Blair's description is inaccurate. Sut is not motivated by a sympathy for the Republican or Union cause but rather by a condescending sympathy for a creature who is even uglier, more cowardly, and a bigger fool than he is himself. Says Sut, "I felt that I wer a standin fur the fust time afore a man I warnt feared ove, an hu I knowd wer scaser ove sense than I wer, an I wer glad I had found him, fur you know George that I thot I wer the king fool ove the world, an allers felt shamed an onder cow about hit." Surely, Harris disliked having a Republican president, but his dislike would not have driven him to approve of an assassination plot as the solution to a political problem; thus Sut is only doing what any humane man, Southerner or not, might have done in protecting a human life, inferior though it might seem.

Also, the entire attitude of the satires is one of harsh criticism and denigration, all of it coming from Sut's mouth. Sut is anything but traitorously sympathetic with the new President. Lincoln is described as a coward, who exclaims at the news of the plot against his life, "I hain't perpared tu die, Sutty, my Sun," and sighs trembling with fear, "The party can't spare me now; besides I ain't fit tu die, an my wiskers hev jus' begin tu grow and I want tu try the vittils in Washintun City. . . ." He is dirty and infested with fleas, and when he asks Sut whether people have trouble with fleas down South, Sut replies that only the dogs do occasionally, "an we allers kicks em out when they scratches." Thus Lincoln is brought down to the animal level of a flea-ridden dog. But Sut draws an even more deadly analogy at another point, often quoted for its vivid but distastefully cruel detail:

> I kotch a ole bull frog once an druv a nail thru his lips inter a post, tied two rocks tu his hine toes and stuck a darnin' needil inter his tail tu let out the misture, an lef him there tu dry. I seed him two weeks arter words, an when I seed ole ABE I thot hit wer an orful retribution cum ontu me, an that hit were the same frog, only stretched a little longer, . . . same shape, same color, same feel (cold as ice) an I'm d——d ef hit aint the same smell.

As Pascal Covici, Jr., has suggested [see Additional Bibliography], Harris is here and throughout the series using the satirical device of *meiosis,* that is "belittling" or "diminition"—"the use of any 'ugly or homely images' which are intended to diminish the dignity of an object." The effect is calculated: Lincoln is not worth taking seriously, and "his ugliness is inhuman enough to suggest that he can be disposed of as easily as any other harmless amphibious reptile."

Naturally, the outcome of the Civil War was to alter radically the temperate balance of humane scorn and invective in Harris's work. In his first postwar satire, **"Sut Lovingood Come to Life,"** Harris tried to control his anger by constructing a fictional framework in which irony could operate, but the invective wins out and overwhelms artistic control. A correspondent of the Wisconsin *State Journal* had traveled briefly through the South and reported that a spark of rebellion still existed there and should forcefully be stamped out, as if Reconstruction were not harsh enough. Harris has Sut appointed by President Johnson as "Fool killer Gineril," and in an "ORFISHUL DOKEYMINT," Sut informs the journalist that his attention has been called to his case as an urgent one.

By requesting the victim to write out a statement in reply to a series of questions, Harris ironically implies what every answer is to be. For example, inferring that the Yankee writer himself shirked military duty, Sut writes, "State fus . . . how meney muskits yu wore plum out a shootin? How meney, you made onsarvisabil, a 'clubbin' em over rebil skulls?" The charge of stealing is laid to the writer when Sut notes: "sit down how meney yu may hev 'lifted' ove the follerin artikils, which am deklared to be contribran ove war: Quilts, frocks, shifts, baby's huckabuck britchis, finger rings, dogratypes ove pepil's dead kin, spoons, love letters. . . ." The catalogue continues with other "personal" items of this sort, in the midst of which appears one item calculated by Harris to arouse a mixture of sentimentality and ire: "the dead baby's shoes." As the mock epistle progresses, the extremity of the

charges is intensified in requiring the Yankee to state the number of females he has ruined, "an' class em intu three shades ove culler, jet black—ash black, an' saddil shirt yaller." But Harris does not stop with the charge of miscegenation. Sut also requires him to state the number of legs the females had "ef over two." Thus the irony forces the reader to permit the victim only two types of sexual relations: with Negroes or with animals. As if the charge of animal sodomy were not sufficient, Harris returns to the charge of miscegenation with a vengeance, incorporating as well a reference to the myth of racial odors:

> Stait if ever yu happend by acksident tu git intu the rong bed, an' be foun' thar by an insashiate Sambo; ef so, what wer yer stratergy? Did yu call 'im "a man an' a bruther," ur did yu jis' 'mizzil?' Ef the las' were yer stratergy, hu fotch yer close tu yu? An' how did yu smell thararter, fur say ten days?

Obviously, if Harris must resort to such bare and brutal invective, he has lost control of the artistry. After nine paragraphs, towards the last, Harris in fact completely drops the thin veil of irony Sut has affected in his question technique and makes a frontal attack on the correspondent as a "suckaig sneak, hu hides ahine the pettecoats at home a suckin the hart's blud ove his country, an' *a fattenin hissef on hit,* while she am strugglin for very life. . . ." Irony and control are replaced by direct, intense abuse. The entire piece is not worked out according to any systematic or logical pattern. It is an exercise in pure invective and insult, and it is to be admired as one would admire the sailor who can curse a blue streak, or in the way that Shakespeare's Hotspur admired a woman who could swear "a good mouth-filling oath." Near the end there is one striking image based upon a sordid aspect of life which would not become acceptable in American literature until the advent of naturalism:

> Hit would breathe new life intu the dead blush on the stoney cheek ove a street walker, jis' tu ax her ef he [the Yankee writer] warnt her secun cuzzin's dorg, an' she'd straitway hang hersef fur shame.

"The Rome Egg Affair" is only a brief declamation of two paragraphs directed against General William Tecumseh Sherman and the newly organized Union political party. It seems that Sut has been accused of sucking six dozen raw eggs at a sitting. Sut says this is impossible since he hasn't "ownd six dozen eggs, since Sherman come yere, an' biled the hens. . . ." Once again, charges of dishonesty are leveled against the radical reconstruction Northerners, and Sut decides that the man who ate the eggs must have been a Southerner willing to betray himself and his country by joining forces with the Union party, "a Georgia delicate to the poor white trash convenshun."

The next satire by Harris continues to reflect his vitriolic contempt for the Northerner. No attempt is even made at any kind of fable or fictional framework in **"Sut Lovingood, On the Puritan Yankee."** Sut is simply allowed to deliver, with the slightest touches of irony, a dissertation against the archetypal Yankee character, distinguished by inventiveness, reforming zeal, hypocritical erudition, and especially commercial genius: "As the dorg vomits, as the mink sucks blood, as the snail shines, as the possum sham's death, so dus the Yankee cheat, *for every varmint hes hits gif*." Not only does Harris direct his invective against the present generation of their "powerful ornary stock," but he goes back to the very first ancestors who arrived in New England on the "Mayflower":

> What cud our Maker be thinkin about, that he forgot to lay his finger on her rotten old snout, an' turn her down in the middil ove the soft sea, wif her pestiferous load of cantin cheats an' moril diseases.

The Indians, Sut says, should have "carcumsized the head ove the las' durn'd one, burnt thar clos, pack'd thar carkuses heads-an-tails, herrin fashun, in thar old ship, sot the sails, an' pinted her snout the way WARD'S ducks went. . . ." The Indians, then, would leave "a savory smell in my snout, in spite ove thar grubwurm oder."

By 1867, Harris's anger still ran high, but he at last subordinated it by returning once more to the dream as a framework device for his satire. Sut relates a dream in which he finds himself in hell, sent there for "votin the Radikil ticket." Not long after his arrival, all the famous radical politicians of Harris's day arrive: Thad Stevens, Charles Sumner, Benjamin Wade, Ben Butler, Wendell Phillips, and John Forney. Rather than disguise them in any fashion, Harris borrows the technique of Dante in his *Divine Comedy,* that of placing them in hell in their own persons, under their actual names. But their presence proves to be such a disruptive force in the operation of hell that the Devil has to expel them. When Phillips tries to persuade the Devil to run hell backwards, the suggestion is too much for him. He fears that "they'd raise a rebellion sure an' destroy the institution, an' then what would the world do, *particularly New England!*" So one by one, they are placed in a big "bomb mortor," and shot out of hell, but not before Harris has had a chance to indulge in pointedly personal caricatures, in which he especially takes advantage of such physical deformities as Butler's defective vision and Stevens' club foot.

Perhaps the most elaborate and artistic of Harris's satires are those in the four-part series **"The Early Life of Sut Lovingood, Written by His Dad."** Ulysses S. Grant was at the moment running for president, and the New York *Ledger* had commissioned Grant's father, Jesse Root Grant, to assist in the preparation of a series for that journal called "The Early Life of Gen. Grant, By His Father." It was Harris's purpose to burlesque the supposed efforts of Grant's father, although because of Jesse Grant's foolish character they turned out to be unintentionally farcical. By directly imitating these pieces, and continually drawing parallels between Sut and Ulysses as prime examples of the genus fool, Harris diminishes and degrades his victim, U. S. Grant, and the literary efforts of his father; hence, Harris's series would most properly be designated a travesty.

In the introductory piece, Harris uses the satiric persona of an "Agent," who proudly announces that Hoss Lovingood has agreed to write the series on his distinguished son Sut. With the purest irony of inversion, he proclaims, "The triumphant close of this important negotiation, should be a cause of gratulation among your personal friends, and will be hailed with joy by the admirers of genius throughout the world." Besides the imaginative way in which Harris has comically imitated the original Grant material, he develops an interesting complexity at one point in the third installment by transforming an incident in the elder Grant's narrative (about the time young Grant broke a wild pony no one else could ride at the circus) into an elaborate, capsule allegory of the entire Civil War in which Lincoln is the ring master, the unmanage-

able pony represents Robert E. Lee, and the rider who finally breaks the pony is Grant (metamorphosed into Sut).

Once the series has made its point and thoroughly lambasted the purported efforts of the pretentious old Jesse Root Grant, Harris does not continue the travesty on all of the original material. He brings back the Agent to report that the elder Lovingood has received too much unfriendly criticism and that he refused to continue: "really he has been very cavalierly treated, simply for thinking his very black crow [Sut] was a very white one; and, no one else volunteering, he blew his own cracked horn to that note, not dreaming that he would become the laughing stock of the continent."

Harris's last satire, **"Sut Lovingood's Allegory,"** is exactly what its title implies. Resorting to an allegorical story about a billy goat, Harris takes a solid swipe at the advent of "progress, an' higher law" in the South. Harris has George clearly designate the object of attack in an overt statement while Sut reminisces with him over "the good old days":

> I was just thinking boys, while Sut was speaking, whether we are the gainer by the discoveries—inventions—innovations, and prayers, of the last forty years. Whether the railway—telegraph—chloroform—moral reform, and other advancements, as they are termed, have really advanced us any, in the right direction or—

Sut interrupts at this point with a brief parable which indicates Harris's regard for the past and tradition:

> Some ove you minds the boy that started to school one sleety mornin', an' slipp'd two steps backward for one forrid. He only got thar, you mine, by turnin' roun', an' gwine tother way. Well! that's the world's fix today. . . .

A retreat to the standards and mores of the past is the only hope for the world's salvation, says Harris.

Within the allegory Sut relates, all that Harris disliked in modern society is embodied in a "progressive . . . meterfistickal, free will, billy goat . . . forty years ahead ove *his* day." His Dutch master, Old Brakebill, personifies the good, solid virtues of the past, a man who does not believe in "outsmarting" anybody and believes in trading only on the principle of value given for value received. The sassy billy goat, "a regular, walkin insult to man, an' beast," who closely resembles the contemporary "business man" ("they am all the go now, you know"), begins to practice some strange experiments in the farmyard, and "like mos' ove these yere human progress humbugs, he jis' played h—l with hissef." Brakebill begins to notice that the recent offspring of the sheep, pigs, dogs, geese, and donkeys all mysteriously show characteristics of the sassy billy goat. This unnatural cross fertilization eventually produces a "curious, little cuss, lookin' like a cross atwixt the devel an' a cookin' stove," and the Dutchman decides that it's time to act. Brakebill whets his knife and performs an operation so that the goat can never *"raise any more family."* Thus, taking again that extreme step he so often did in his satires, Harris suggests that the best method of straightening things out for "this an' the nex generashun" is to emasculate the present and return to a now-lost traditional pattern of life.

Although Harris was at his best in his nonsatiric writings, he at least seems to have tried to channel his indignation into artistic methods of expression. His contempt and spleen too often gain the upper hand and obliterate all artistry and control. When control is lost, his invective reaches fantastic limits and often approaches indecency. Although Harris's artistry is more clearly in evidence elsewhere, the satires do tell us much about the temperament and personality of the man. (pp. 222-31)

M. Thomas Inge, "Satires," in High Times and Hard Times *by George Washington Harris, edited by M. Thomas Inge, Vanderbilt University Press, 1967, pp. 222-31.*

ELMO HOWELL   (essay date 1970)

[*Howell examines Harris's satirical targets, uncovering the moral vision of his character Sut.*]

To what extent are the Lovingood sketches worthy of [extensive critical] attention? At best they are a frail body on which to establish a reputation. Like other works in this vein, they reflect a casual manner which at worst devolves into slipshod writing, and in subject matter they are tirelessly reiterative. The Harris formula is simple: some pompous ass needs to be brought down a buttonhole, the stage is set, and when Sut lifts the curtain all hell breaks loose. A Lovingood sketch is like the last few minutes of an old-time Western movie, when everyone joins in a chase. Harris does this sort of thing with great verve and with a ready command of word and image. One thinks immediately not so much of his contemporaries in the Southwest tradition as of the Elizabethan pamphleteers or eighteenth-century malcontents like Swift and Smollett. He is like Smollett in his salty prose and love of crude joke, but he has the trenchancy of the dark mind of Swift, who said his purpose was to vex the world rather than to divert it. Born into a period of political dissension and always partisan in his devotion to the cause of the South, Harris at best manages to rise above the topical. More than the "fanatical exponent of secession," as Kenneth S. Lynn calls him [see Additional Bibliography], he is an idealist voicing his frustrations in a few spasmodic outpourings to the local papers. Sut Lovingood's tomfooleries pall after a time, but his view of life, which is the rustic version of Harris's own view, reflects an original mind that has something to say about the general human condition.

Sut Lovingood is an illiterate hill-country fellow of East Tennessee who, in spite of his calling himself a fool, has culled enough wisdom from experience to make him discriminate in his choice of men. He particularly enjoys a joke at the expense of Yankees, sheriffs, and ministers, and is not above having a little fun with Negroes, women of a certain kind, and even members of his own family. But in spite of his disaffection, he is basically an amiable fellow in that he is also able to laugh at himself. He says with typical exaggeration that he has no soul, only a "whiskey proof gizzard," and that he is "too durn'd a fool tu cum even onder millertary lor." He gets into "more durn'd misfortnit skeery scrapes than enybody," and escapes only by virtue of his long "laigs," which are his special pride.

Sut's self-appraisal has been taken at face value by some readers who conclude that he is morally degenerate. Edmund Wilson says that he represents all that is "worst in the worst of the South," concluding that he is the ancestor of William Faulkner's Snopeses [see excerpt dated 1962]. "I orter bust my head open agin a bluff ove rocks, an' jis' wud du hit, ef I warnt a cussed coward. All my yeathly 'pendence is in these yere laigs." But on more than one occasion Sut proves that

he is not a coward. His joke about the good use he makes of his long legs means only that to Sut—and to people of his kind in the South—self-depreciation is a form of good manners. If anything can be charged against him, it is an aggressiveness towards those who do not measure up to his ideals of behavior—the bullying sheriff, the meddling parson, the know-it-all Yankee, the snob, the hypocrite, and even a stranger who appears at the doggery and looks down at Sut across his drink, "like I mout smell bad." Sut is a humble fellow himself, and nothing moves him to wrath, and sometimes to violence, faster than a false notion of self-esteem.

The lines of his character were well developed in sketches Harris published on the eve of the Civil War. He first appeared in 1954, in one of his liveliest episodes—Mark Twain recalled it years later [see excerpt dated 1867] **"Sut Lovingood's Daddy Acting Horse."** In order to make the crop and provide for the family after the horse dies, the elder Lovingood has himself put into harness to pull the plow. His main purpose, however, is to cut the fool and have some fun. "While mam wer a-tyin the belly ban', a-strainin hit pow'rful tite, he drapt ontu his hans, sed 'Whay-a-a' like a mad hoss wud, an' slung his hine laigs at mam's hed." Her dour observation is that he "plays hoss" better than he does husband. But the real fun comes when he plows through a sassafras bush and stirs up a nest of ball hornets. This tale at the expense of his father seems unconscionable on the part of Sut unless one remembers that the old man deserves what he gets. "He allers wer a mos' complikated durned ole fool," Sut says, "an' mam sed so when he warnt about."

Three years later in 1857, Sut reappears, this time in a love adventure, **"Blown Up With Soda."** He has fallen in love with a mountain girl, Sicily Burns, who leads him on and then plays a prank on him by feeding him soda powder—new to Sut, who thinks he is poisoned. In this sketch Harris introduces two important characters that indicate the direction his satire will take, the parson and the Yankee. Sut later turns the tables on Sicily and her circuit-riding husband, and in the same year he plays one of his liveliest jokes on another parson, old Bullen, who has meddled in one of Sut's love engagements. Pretending conversion, Sut goes to the service with a sack full of lizards and releases them, at a moment of eloquence, up the parson's breeches.

It was a Yankee peddler that sold the soda powder, supposedly a love potion, to Sicily Burns; and as the war drew on, the Yankee became a favorite target, most often as a salesman in the South, although Sut makes a few improbable trips to the North to observe him on home ground. In 1858, he goes to New York City, and again in 1861 at the outbreak of the war he goes North for a personal encounter with "ole Abe Link-Horn." Sut tells Lincoln that in Tennessee he is called a natural born durned fool, but as for the North, "I think I ken averidge in these parts purty well." After the war Harris continues the attack with greater virulence. In **"The Puritan Yankee,"** in 1866, Sut in effect gives way to Harris himself in the indictment of a civilization.

The Yankee appears most often in Harris as some sort of peddler, whose inventions and gadgets and ingenuity in making money have a dazzling effect on the simple Southern countryman, but which in retrospect strike Sut as an outrage to manhood. He is a deceitful fellow, oily and slippery, who could hold his own in "a pond full ove eels." In New York, Sut is amazed at the commercial activity of the natives, with little men chasing in every direction with papers in their bands, "like pissants afore a rain." "When two ove 'em bumps together, they teches noses, jist like onto the ants, an' then they swops two ur three ove the papers, an' each pot-bellied, trottin', bacon-faced son ove a gun ove 'em is redy tu swar that he's made money by the swap. There's no natral sence, ur corn, ur meat, ur honesty in the whole fixin'." Their manners are offensive. In New York, "they gin you sass enough tu make you fite"—that is, in Tennessee, but not among a people who refuse to take offense. Old Stilyards, the Yankee lawyer who "cum tu this country, onst, a cussed sneakin lookin reptile," tries to bribe Sut with a gill of whisky, generous by New England standards but not by Sut's. "Hit 'sulted me. Now, whu the devil ever hearn tell ove a gill ove whisky in these parts afore? Why hit soundid sorter like a inch of cordwood ur a ounce ove cornshucks." The Yankee is an arrogant fellow who knows all the answers, like the encyclopedia salesman, "ole Onsightly Peter," who stops Sut's narration to correct him in detail. "Yu go to hell, mistofer; yu bothers me." But above all, he is deficient in what Sut considers a man ought to be. North Carolina is noted for pole cats, Georgia for groundhogs, and Tennessee for coons; but New York is noted "in the same line fur dandys," who are neither men nor women since they "can't talk good nor fight like wun, or kiss ur scratch feelin'ly like t'uther."

Kenneth S. Lynn finds in Sut (whose name, he says, is "an ugly contraction of South") the "worst aspects of the slavocracy." But Harris's antipathy to the North goes beyond the political and social issues of the Civil War. Long before Sut appeared, other Southern writers had questioned the New Englander's concept of character, which they found radically different from their own. (pp. 312-15)

At the end of 1866, Harris published his sketch of the puritan Yankee, which allowing for the extravagance of Sut's rhetoric, is a fair appraisal of sectional differences, as viewed by a Southerner after the Civil War. The puritan sings hymns and says long prayers; but his religion does not affect his personal relationships, where his sole aim is to strike a bargain and make money. He has "a winder in his breast" where his heart ought to be. To him a man's word is nothing, unless he has his note of hand also. Harris was particularly sensitive to the intellectual turmoil of New England in the nineteenth century with the breakup of the puritan orthodoxy and the advent of esoteric religions and deviations in manners and morals represented by characters like Joseph Smith, Brigham Young, William Miller, Margaret Fox, and Amelia Bloomers. What a pity, says Sut, that the Mayflower ever landed with "her pestiferus load of cantin cheats an' moril diseases." Or if the Indians had only done their job and "carcumsized the head ove the las' durn'd one" as soon as they landed. "Oh! My grashus, hits too good to think about. Durn them leather injuns; they let the bes' chance slip ever Injuns had to give everlastin comfort to a continent and to set hell back at leas' five hundred year. . . . George, pass the jug; the subjick is overpowerin me."

Harris was a violent partisan in politics, but the indignation that sweeps through his pages is fed by something more fundamental than political difference. After the victory of the North on the battlefield, Sut could do little but amuse himself with futile speculations about the Mayflower and the Indians. But before the war the type of manhood espoused by Harris . . . was the pattern for half a nation, although from the beginning it was apparent that the Yankees, released from the old orthodoxy and obsessed by humanitarian dreams,

were bent on reducing all manners, in the words of Joseph Glover Baldwin, to "the standards of New England insular habitudes." And after the war, they were to follow up their victory on the field, says W. J. Cash, "with the satisfaction of the instinctive urge of men in the mass to put down whatever differs from themselves," by making over the South in their own image.

Thus the attack on the Yankee is only Harris's most dramatic—most topically effective—way of getting at those qualities in human nature which he most dislikes. Too much has been made of the grotesqueries of Sut Lovingood, which are the distinguishing marks of region and class. In spite of his angularities, Sut is a fair approximation of Harris's ideal. His dislike for ministers and his knack for breaking up church meetings, says Milton Rickels, represent "an attack on institutionalized Christianity." The Lovingood yarns, he says, are an escape from the discipline of love as well as the discipline of authority. But Sut's wrath is directed against perversions of Christian morality, not the thing itself. George Washington Harris was a devout Presbyterian, serving for a time as elder in the First Presbyterian Church in Knoxville, and noted throughout his life for his Sabbatarianism and "blue" orthodoxy. Sut would not like the formality of Harris's church, but he does not, as Rickels says, "exist outside Christianity." For all their violence and cantankerous ways, the country people of Sut's class are deeply pious and profoundly orthodox in their religious views—a fact which sets them apart from the New Englanders whom Sut attacks. In his long description of the invalid wife of Sheriff Doltin, Sut makes clear his own convictions. The dying woman bears her suffering and the long neglect of her husband with "a sweet smile" that goes to his heart.

> I 'speck that smile will go back up wif her when she starts home, whar hit mus' a-cum frum. She must onst been mons'us temptin tu men tu look at, an' now she's loved by the angils, fur the seal ove thar king is stamp'd in gold on her forrid. . . . As I look fus' at him, an' then at her, I'd swore tu a herearter. Yes, *two* herearters, by golly: one way up behint that ar black cloud wif the white bindin fur sich as her; the tuther herearter needs no wings nor laigs ither tu reach. When you soaks yerself in sin till yer gits heavy enuf, yu jes' draps in.

Sut is not a rebel against institutions. Rather, he is a conservative, like his creator, lamenting the falling off from the standards of the past. When George, his gentleman friend, thinks back on the Knoxville of his youth, Sut reprimands him for his sentiment. But Sut in his turn is also sentimental.

> That's what makes you compar the days ove the fiddle, loom an' cradle with the peaner, ball-room an' wetnurse, ove these days. In comparin' 'em, you may take one person, a family, or a county, at a time, an' you'll find that we haint gain'd a step on the right road, an' if the fog would clear up we'd find heaven behine us, an' not strength enuff left to reach hit alone, if we were to turn back. No, boys, we aint as *good* as we wer forty years ago.

These rare pensive moments are the obverse side of Sut's wrath. Like Gulliver among the Houyhnhnms, he is inspired by the principle of right reason in human conduct and can never be satisfied again among the Yahoo kind. Though inevitably associated with the altercation of the Civil War period, and with the boisterous mountaineer of his creation, George Washington Harris was the exponent of an ideal which lifts his sketches above the surface excitement of Sut's world and makes them unique among the writings of the Old Southwest. (pp. 316-19)

Elmo Howell, "Timon in Tennessee: The Moral Fervor of George Washington Harris," in The Georgia Review, *Vol. XXIV, No. 3, Fall, 1970, pp. 311-19.*

JAMES M. COX   (essay date 1973)

[*In this excerpt from a survey of the Southwestern humorists, Cox briefly discusses Harris's apparently simplistic and illiterate but actually sophisticated language.*]

Harris drove himself deeper into frontier vernacular than any of his predecessors—so deep that his speaker, Sut Lovingood, embodies in their extremity all the amorality, savagery, meanness, and drunkenness of his progenitors in Southwest humor. But Sut is new. His dialect is practically a new language, for it is a deviation so remarkable that a reader must literally reconstruct his own language as well as Sut's if he is to understand it. Once the process of reconstruction begins, rich and wonderful possibilities of humor literally explode upon the page. Through it all, the figure of Sut Lovingood comes more and more to stand out as a new man himself. All but amoral, Sut seems to be the very principle of life and pleasure and chaos, all concentrated into his deviant language. He is, by his own definition, a "Nat'ral Born Durn'd Fool," and, aggressive though he is, his language reverberates with retaliation against centuries of repression. His very name, Lovingood, signifies the profundity of his relation to the world of sexual love. There is no better illustration of his potentiality as Sexual Lord of Misrule than his performance at **"Sicily Burns's Wedding."** There, he takes vengeance on the bride who has tricked him in an earlier sketch (Harris's whole rich world vibrates along lines of practical jokes as displacement for vengeance) by tormenting a bull with hornets ("insex" Sut calls them). The chaos which that bull visits upon the wedding party speaks worlds about the whole sexual principle so fragilely held in check by social institutions.

I could go on and on about Sut, but it is best to define Harris's master joke, which is, I take it, the pursuit of illiteracy with a language so sophisticated that only the most urbane audience could read it. That joke is, as all great humor must be, on Harris as well as on the reader. For if the reader has to be extraordinarily sensitive to the uttermost reaches of language to read the voice of the illiterate Sut, Harris himself was beginning to imagine for himself not a broad public for his jokes but an elite readership that would probably have surprised even him. Either that, or a large trained audience which he had somehow educated.

Whatever the case, the Civil War came and the humor of the Old Southwest disappeared. . . . (pp. 111-12)

James M. Cox, "Humor of the Old Southwest," in The Comic Imagination in American Literature, *edited by Louis D. Rubin, Jr., Rutgers University Press, 1973, pp. 101-12.*

ALAN HENRY ROSE   (essay date 1976)

[*Rose examines several stories in which Harris uses Sut's pranks as a means of portraying blacks as demons.*]

The two poles of Harris's artistic personality, special concern

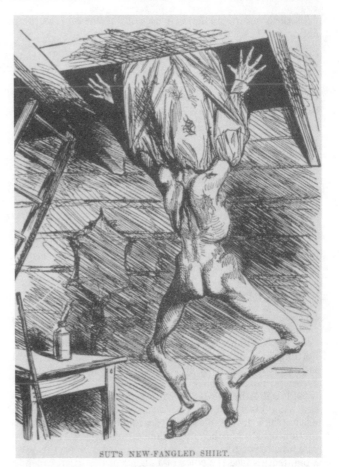

SUT'S NEW-FANGLED SHIRT.

An illustration for the story "Sut's New-Fangled Shirt."

with aesthetic form coupled with quintessentially disordered content, brought about a highly complex situation in regard to racial expression. Harris's impulse toward disorder led inevitably to an involvement with figures of blackness. Sut, setting out to evoke chaos in the tales, sometimes makes use of animals with traditionally violent attributes—wild bulls or horses, for example—but in those tales which move furthest toward the depiction of irrationality this uniquely Southern prankster is drawn to tap the deep font of disordered racial associations in the Southern imagination. The process occurs in a way which reflects the sophistication of Harris's aesthetic capacity. Sut does not simply encounter grotesque Negroes, as does Henry Clay Lewis's narrator; he creates them with paints and brushes, using the tools of the artist in a macabre metaphor of the process of demonic expression in Southern fiction. It is a grim inversion of the intent of the minstrel show. Practicing with his black paint upon the faces of living bodies (and sometimes dead ones) of indiscriminate color, Sut produces not the coveted image of total black benevolence but the feared one of transcendent black diabolism. Similarly, Harris's stylistic accomplishment lends special definition to the repressive counter impulse incurred by the disorder. In a sense Harris shares his fellow humorists' reluctance about depicting the Negro. For in his creation of these black figures he is neither treating the black man realistically nor stereotypically. Rather, in a manner anticipating the fiction of Mark Twain and William Faulkner, Harris presents the first exploration of the metaphoric uses of blackness in Southern fiction.

One of the tales in which Sut plays prankster, **"Old Skissim's Middle Boy,"** dramatically illustrates the process. The story begins as usual for Harris's writings: a minor character irritates Sut, and upon this hapless person Sut focuses the full force of his disordering impulse. It is understandable in this case, for the subject is "a dreadful fat, mean, lazy boy" who "could beat a hog and a hungry dog eatin." But what arouses Sut most about the boy is his continual sleeping: "They waked him to eat, and then had to wake him agin to make him quit eatin; waked him to go to the spring, and waked him to start back agin; waked him to say his prayers, and waked him to stop sayin them. In fact, they were allers a-wakin him, and he were allers a-goin to sleep agin." No wonder this sleeping figure obsesses Sut, leading him to "lay wake of nights for a week, fixin the way to" make the boy the subject of his prank. He is the perfect subject for the trickster. In his formless sleep Sut sees a virtually limitless piece of unconsciousness upon which to work. The boy is a figure with an irresistible potential for irrationality.

Sut identifies his prank in a manner which anticipates a full realization of the sleeper's potential for disorder. Coming upon the boy alone in his family's kitchen "sittin onto a split-bottom chair, plumb asleep all over, even to his ole hat," Sut indicates that the trick he is about to play is indeed one to evoke primordial chaos; that it is "a plan what I thought would wake the Devil." Carrying it out, Sut employs his brush and black paint to transform the sleeping boy into a figure not yet a devil, but a step closer to it in the Southern imagination because of the associations of blackness: "I had him safe now to practice on, and I set in to doin it, sorta this way. I painted his face the color of a nigger coal-burner, except a white ring round his eyes. From the corners of his mouth, sorta downwards, slouch-wise, I left a white strip. It made his mouth look sorta like onto a hoss track and nigh onto as big." At this point the figure is hardly distinguishable from a minstrel darky, yet Sut is out for chaos, and the direction the creation will take is implicit in his point of view. He sees it as "a fine picture to study if your mind were fond of scary things"a fine picture to study if your mind were fond of scary things"; it gives him "dreams of the Devil."

Accordingly, Sut goes on to fill in on this black canvas the forms inherent to the Southerner's "picture" "of the Devil." . . . [Fundamentally] they involve fire. Sut gives his creation the potential for hell-fire, tying "a basket full of firecrackers to the chair back, to his hair, and to his wrists." Furthermore, he magnifies the figure's capacity to objectify the destruction integral to the demonic vision; Sut "screwed onto each of that boy's ears a pair of iron hand-vices. . . . They hung down like over-growed earrings. I tied a gridiron to one ankle and a pair of firetongs to t'other." There is no mistaking the malevolence underlying the image now: Sut has created a vision of the Southern racial nightmare, and its destructive energies tremble on the verge of eruption: "He looked savage as a set steel trap baited with arsenic, and were just fit for treason, stratagem, and to spoil things."

Even so, the evidence of the depth of this figure's unconscious associations is stunning. When Sut activates his black-faced devil, turning "loose a pint of June bugs . . . into his bosom and . . . a big, grey-whiskered, aggravated ole rat . . . into the slack of that boy's britches," the force that flows into it seems overwhelmingly primordial: he began to wake "sorta

gradually—a little faster nor light bread rises and a little slower than a earthquake wakes weasels." The image is surely a likely one, for combining the inexorable quality of bread rising with the sense of the earthquake's limitless subterranean power, the figure seems destined irresistibly to grow to transcendent proportions. With his firecrackers lighted, he does become a fiery black being of supernatural energies: "He fought by the light of ten million sparks; he were as active as a smut-machine in full blast and every grain of wheat a spark," crying "Gloree," causing an "unearthly riot."

Expressing what has now become a content of primal disorder places inordinate strain on Harris's formidable capacity for aesthetic form. To depict it he is driven to the sort of surreal imagery we have come to associate with movie cartoon violence: arms extending and multiplying with greater and greater rapidity, the frenzied figure "grabbed the fire shovel and bounced . . . all over that kitchen, a-striken overhanded, under-handed, up-handed, down-handed, and left-handed at every 'spicious shadow he seed." Still the content of disorder grows: "He made more fuss, hit more licks at more things, were in more places and in more shapes in a shorter time than any mortal auctioneer could tell if he had as many tongues as a basket full of buckles." Beyond even the capacity of an auctioneer to articulate: the figure's level of irrationality must indeed be high. But the homely vernacular language should not distract from the sophisticated concept Harris delineates. By indicating that a virtual infinity of expressive organs is still inadequate to portray the "shapes," to pin down the "places" of the activity, Harris is in effect acknowledging that the demonic black figure has passed beyond the author's limits of aesthetic form. Carrying his expression of the demonic vision to its ultimate extreme, Harris is faced with the dilemma of having evoked an imaginative quality which now seems to defy the control implicit in the process of aesthetic form.

A sense of helplessness now sweeps the narrative. Continuing to grow, the violence becomes seen as "unquenchable," in its infinity of energy seeming "perpetual-motion." Harris finally employs the framework technique by means of concluding the tale and reestablishing narrative perspective, a ploy which Walter Blair has suggested is essential for the continuation of the *Yarn*'s humorous intent [see excerpt dated 1937]. Yet even within this stylistic security, there is a grimness which is absent from Harris's nonracial fiction. The disruption in the tale has extended beyond the kitchen; old man Skissim has been frightened off, and the rest of the family wounded in various ways. Even a final attempt at distance, Sut's resumé of the action, speaks of mass murders and of Sut's jarringly malign impulse to eliminate the figure with "a musket and sixteen buckshot at just about ten steps." The boy's frenzy finally subsides on its own, but instead of a catharized tranquility, the tale ends with a continuing tension which reflects the unresolved narrative issues.

Sut's evocation of black demonism occurs on a markedly broader scale in another prankster story, **"Frustrating a Funeral."** Again Sut employs passive figures upon which to create images of the devil, in this case a drunkard and a corpse. The initial step in the process is unnecessary here; both of the subjects are Negroes. The creation follows the now recognizable pattern: upon the stupored black Sut "set in and painted red and white stripes, time about, runnin out from under his eyes like onto the spokes of a wheel . . . and cross-barred his upper lip with white, until it looked like boars' tushes; and I fastened a couple of yearling's horns onto his head, and plaited a dead blacksnake round the roots of 'em." Turning to the Negro corpse, Sut

> got 'bout a tin cupful of lightnin bugs and cut off the lantern of the last durned one. I smeared 'em all over his face, hair, and ears, and onto the prongs of a pitchfork. I set him up in the corner on end and give him the fork, prong-end up, in his crossed arms. I then pried open his mouth and let his teeth shut onto the back of a live bullfrog; and I smeared its paws and belly with some of my bug-mixture; and pinned a little, live garter-snake by its middle crosswise in Ceaze's mouth, smeared like the frog plumb to the point of his tail. The pin kept the snake pow'ful busy makin circles and other crooked shapes in the air.

In one sweep, Sut has created two vividly diabolical black images, both sharing the basic relationship with hell-fire. The one is "the awful corpse with its face and hair all afire"; the other displays "eyes and their stripes like buggy wheels with red lamps in the hubs."

Sut uses each of these figures in the manner of the trickster, to introduce disorder into the community. The tale is made up of a series of episodes in which the trickster exposes a number of pivotal figures in the town to the devilish blacks, reducing each of them to hysteria. In each episode Sut takes part in the prank, imitating the devil's voice, using his knowledge of town scandal to focus the terror being dealt out. With a preacher, Sut "moaned out in a awful doleful voice: 'Hypocrite, come to hell'." With an adulterer, "in the same doleful sounds . . . [he] said: 'Hunicutt, you'se fell from grace. I'll take you down home *now,* lest you might git good *and die afore you fell agin*'." With a grave-robbing doctor he calls: "You wants some bones to boil, does you? . . . I'se in that business myself—follered it nigh onto thirty thousand years. . . . Let's go. My boilin house is warm . . . you'se cold . . . come, sonny." He plays on the guilt of the sheriff, who had just hanged a Negro: "Rise, Sheriff. He's a-reachin for you with his rope, *and its got a running noose*." At one point involving the devilish black corpse, Sut lends motion to the image, pulling at one victim, pretending to be the devil, dynamically displaying his disordering impulse: "Right then and there, I reached out and grabbed his shirt—a saving hold with both hands—set my cold, sandy foot agin his bare back and leaned into pullin pow'ful strong."

The technique achieves its goal; the phenomenon of the black demon loose in white society induces an almost total destruction, objectifying the Southerner's racial fantasies of social upheaval: "*Hunicutt* gone; . . . *doctor* gone; *parson* gone; *sheriff* gone; and, to cap the stack of vexatious things, the *doggery keeper* gone. Why, the county's ruinated, . . . you kin buy land there for a dime a acre, on tick at that." And beyond such concrete disruption there is the shadow of the depth of the forces which have been released by invoking the black demon. Sut indicates that the destruction has a profound subjective racial source; that it is "the awful consequences of bein scary when a nigger dies." Touched by the surreal associations of the dark figure; the land is "haunted yet with all sorts of awful haunts." Surely the trickster has been drawn to the most effective means of introducing disorder into Southern society.

Yet irrationality in this tale never goes beyond the hint of the surreal. There is of course an eerie quality to the image's

movement: "There were a 'luminated snake a-wavin round; there were the shiny frog movin his legs and paws like he were a-swimmin, . . . there were the [waving] pitchfork with its hot prongs." At no point, however, does the black demon's motion approach the limits of form as in **"Old Skissim's Middle Boy."** It is as if in this tale, unlike the other, there is a pervasive narrative guardedness, an inhibiting reluctance to give full reign to the possibilities for disorder inherent in the demonic expression. This is reflected in the unusual presence of a shadowy self-controlled gentleman narrator, a figure whom, as Lynn points out, reveals the "vestiges of the traditional forms" of controlling narrative techniques in Southwestern humor [see Additional Bibliography]. Occasionally in the other tales this sophisticated character introduces Sut's account, and retreats, to reappear in the concluding framework. In this story he becomes a sort of interlocutor, continually feeding questions to Sut in remote jarringly conventional language such as: "What in the name of the Prophet is 'millsick,' Sut?" Elsewhere, Sut displays exasperation with this repressive figure, crying "now durn your littil santerfied face." In this instance his stilted, self-conscious interruptions form a counterpoint to Sut's diabolical fantasy, fragmenting it, inhibiting its scope.

At the same time the tendency toward restraint in this sketch takes another, significantly new, shape. While Sut is creating one of the figures, he steps back to admire his work, and puts it in a unique perspective: "And durn my legs if I didn't come nigh onto takin a runnin scare myself, for he were a perfect daguerreotype of the Devil, took while he were smokin mad." The image emphasizes distance, for it removes the demon one step from the foreground, viewing it as a picture within the narrative. But more important, it makes use of the qualities of the photograph which stand in direct opposition to the frenzied irrational associations of demonic vision. The theoretical accuracy of this relatively new scientific instrument to record data leads it to serve as a metaphor for form rendered with definitive control. Sut's daguerreotype fixes the disordered black devil in a totally abstract temporal and spatial form, momentarily capturing it in the conclusive stasis of the photographic image. Occurring again and again in subsequent racial fiction, the photograph objectifies the repressive impulse to control demonic expression.

Harris displays the racial variation on Sut's trickster theme in still another of the *Yarns.* In **"Sut Lovingood's Dog,"** Sut ignites two pounds of gunpowder in a character's pocket, and the prank transforms the unfortunate figure into one whose "face wur as black as a pot, sept a white ring roun his eyes, an' the smoke wur still risin frum amung the stumps ove his burnt har. His hed . . . wus the ugliest, scuriest, an' savidgest site I ever seed or spec tu see in *this* wurld, eny how." Once black, Sut labels the figure a murderer: "He's kill'd an 'oman an' nine children, an' I speck a dog, an' like tu whipped anuther plum tu *deth*." Here the black devil is countered by a less sophisticated strategy; he is simply driven away, leaving a trail which "in sum places the fences wer sot afire." But even in this relatively limited instance Harris's vivid aesthetic capacity gives succinct form to . . . the expression of demonic vision in Southern fiction. (pp. 64-71)

Alan Henry Rose, " 'A Plan to Wake the Devil': Race and Aesthetics in the Tales of George Washington Harris," in his Demonic Vision: Racial Fantasy and Southern Fiction, *Archon Books, 1976, pp. 63-71.*

ROBERT MICKLUS (essay date 1982)

[*Micklus explores the repetitive nature of Harris's plots, outlining a series of recurring motifs and explaining how they contribute to the stories' humorous effect.*]

Agreeing with Mark Twain that the humorous American story depends more upon the *manner* of the telling than the *matter,* Neil Schmitz has recently argued that the humorists of the Old Southwest "stress the mode of the tall tale, tall talk, not the *mythos,* the subject of the tall tale." Inadvertently, perhaps, Schmitz is also voicing the approach that most scholars of the Old Southwest have been using for years in discussing tall tales, particularly the tall tales of George Washington Harris. For years, we have been told that the humor in Harris's tales depends more upon Sut's manner of telling them than upon their repetitive plots. Harris's humor, we know, relies heavily upon his use of language. . . . Perhaps Brom Weber puts it best when he writes that no one has "equalled the concentrated richess of [Harris's] style" [see excerpt dated 1954]. The distinctiveness of Harris's humor, Weber suggests, lies in his "lyric intensity" and "prodigious outpouring of poetic similes and metaphors. Characters and situations may at times be repetitive in outline, but they are vivified and transcended by imagery which practically never repeats itself."

Weber and others who have centered the distinctiveness of Harris's humor in Sut's manner of telling the tales are, of course, right. However unwittingly, though, they have fostered the notion that the humor of the Lovingood tales rests almost wholly upon the comic language and imagery with which Sut bombards the reader, and that the plots themselves—the matter of the tales—are, at best, monotonous. Almost any discussion of the Lovingood tales merely notes that their plots generally rely upon the box-like, framework structure typical of many tall tales, and that they normally revolve around [according to Edd Winfield Parks] "an elaborate practical joke . . . a method of pricking certain balloons that the writer thought both obnoxious and dangerous." Elmo Howell eloquently states the common complaint against Harris's plots: "In subject matter they are tirelessly reiterative. The Harris formula is simple: some pompous ass needs to be brought down a buttonhole, the stage is set, and when Sut lifts the curtain all hell breaks loose" [see excerpt dated 1970].

Tirelessly reiterative, yes; tiresomely, no. The force of Harris's humor derives not only from Sut's manner of telling the tales, but also from the plain fact that the plots of the tales are, indeed, so repetitive—a good deal more repetitive than anyone thus far has bothered to point out. Harris conditions the reader to anticipate certain plot motifs that invariably await the poor, unsuspecting victims Sut menaces, and that sometimes await poor, unsuspecting Sut himself. Without these repetitions all the vivid language and imagery in the world cannot save some of Harris's stories from falling flat, and without these repetitions we might not have the slightest idea what makes Sut such a "nat'ral born durn'd fool."

The average Sut Lovingood story is more than just a joke in a box. Because most of the Lovingood tales are so obviously episodic and digressive, it would be foolhardy to pretend that even the best of them are elaborately contrived. Still, the most humorous ones, particularly in the 1867 edition, include many, if not all, of the following plot motifs: (1) as a prelude to the "skeer," Sut or someone who will participate in the

skeer somehow changes his identity, pretending to be someone or something he is not; (2) some sucker (normally Sut or some particularly obnoxious hypocrite or ignorant blockhead) becomes physically or psychologically trapped. In the first type of entrapment, the dupe becomes physically confined in a choice of harnesses, ropes, or other annoying attire; in the second type, which often accompanies the first, the dupe becomes mentally ensnared by some kind of lie, concealment, or disguise; (3) the skeer begins and chaos erupts, replete with ludicrous skirmishes and chase scenes, while the comically discomforted dupe is tormented or imagines himself tormented by some kind of varmint, human or otherwise; (4) as the skeer runs its course, the dupe finds himself behaving like an animal, then (5) being stripped of his clothes; (6) the dupe seeks relief by running for cover—usually the nearest water source—and (7) in cases where he is not the victim, Sut does his best to salt the poor, misfortunit devil's wounds, then runs away before getting his butt kicked. Although this is hardly the kind of plot Tolstoy would envy, it is the pattern Harris conditions us to expect in the Lovingood stories, and generally the most humorous tales are those that satisfy our expectations.

Harris establishes the shape of things to come in the first two Sut stories, **"Sut Lovingood's Daddy, Acting Horse"** and **"Sut's New-Fangled Shirt."** In the first story, Dad sets out to be something he is not—a horse—and finds himself physically confined in a harness. "Mam an' me made geers fur dad," Sut reports, and when they "got the bridil fix'd ontu dad, don't yu bleve he sot in tu chompin hit jis like a rale hoss." Dad impersonates a horse so well that he stupidly blunders into a hornet's nest. Then the skeer is on, the chase begins, and chaos erupts as Dad madly gallops about, trying to rid himself of those ornery varmints. Dad throws off his shirt, then the rest of his clothes, and eventually ends up with "nuffin on the green yeath in the way ove close about im, but the bridil." Seeking cover, Dad heads for the creek, and "tu keep up his karacter es a hoss, plum thru, when he got tu the bluff he loped off, ur rather jis' kep on a runnin. Kerslunge intu the krick he went." Finally, after taunting him about the "hoss-flies" hovering about his head, Sut decides he had better get a head start on Dad while the hornets have him preoccupied.

In the second story, Sut gets a new-fangled shirt in what will shortly become an old-fangled plot. Again, the story begins with a mock change of identity. In this case, Betts Carr decides to deck Sut out in a starched shirt, lawyer-like, and Sut goes along with the idea, hoping to stand "es much pussonal discumfurt as [the lawyer] cud, jis tu git tu sampil arter sumbody human." Physically confined after putting on that "infunel, new fangled sheet iron cuss ove a shut," Sut nonetheless manages to build an ashhopper for Betts, "an' work'd pow'ful hard, sweat like a hoss." After seeking comfort in a jug of bumble bee whisky, Sut falls asleep and dreams that "the judge ove the supreme cort had [him] sowed up in a raw hide." He awakens in a frenzy and decides to rid himself of that varminty contraption, which, he has told us, makes him feel like he is "crowded intu a ole bee-gum, an' hit all full ove pissants." First, he strips himself of his pants, then tears a plank from the loft, nails down his shirt, and jumps through the hole to safety thirteen feet below (approximately half the distance of Dad's twenty-five foot leap into the creek; later, having established himself as Dad's rival for King Fool by the time he narrates **"Taurus in Lynchburg Market,"** Sut also takes a twenty-five foot plunge).

It would be tedious to rehash the plots of all the remaining stories in *Sut Lovingood's Yarns,* not because only Sut's manner of telling them makes them funny, but also because their plots are familiar to most people who would bother to read this essay. The most humorous of these eighteen stories— **"The Widow McCloud's Mare," "Parson John Bullen's Lizards," "A Razor-Grinder in a Thunder-Storm," "Old Skissim's Middle Boy," "Sicily Burns's Wedding"** and **"Old Burns's Bull-Ride"** (read as one selection), **"Sut Lovingood's Chest Story," "Sut Lovingood's Dog," "Sut at a Negro Night-Meeting,"** and **"Hen Baily's Reformation"**—include most of the plot motifs characteristic of Sut's tales. Only two of the stories lacking a majority of these motifs—**"Blown Up With Soda"** and **"The Snake-Bit Irishman"**—remain funny because of the sheer force of the skeer; only one of them— **"Mrs. Yardley's Quilting"**—remains funny almost entirely because of Sut's manner of telling it; but despite Sut's humorous manner of relating them, the others—especially **"Taurus in Lynchburg Market," "Sut Lovingood's Sermon," "Bart Davis's Dance,"** and **"Tripetown: Twenty Minutes for Breakfast"**—all fall flat because they contain so few of the plot motifs prevalent in Sut's best.

By the time we arrive at the last five stories in the *Yarns,* then, we have come to expect certain plot motifs from Harris, and these last tales—**"Frustrating a Funeral," "Rare Ripe Garden-Seed," "Contempt of Court—Almost," "Trapping a Sheriff,"** and **"Dad's Dog School"**—are humorous largely because he does not disappoint us. **"Frustrating a Funeral"** remains among the most humorous Lovingood tales not because we continue to enjoy the spectacle of the black man running around with his eyes bugging out, but because, perhaps more than any other story in the *Yarns,* it employs and repeats all the plot motifs we have come to expect. It begins with the ultimate change of identity as Sut makes a dead man of Major and a talking spirit of Seize by swapping them. Leaving Major physically confined in Seize's coffin, Sut transforms Seize into his "dolefulest skeer makin mersheen" ever, complete with frog and firebugs. When they encounter the devil's varminty emissary, Simon and Hunicutt are scared out of their shirts, the first figuratively and the second literally, flying "outen [his] shut like a dorg outen a badger-barril." Turning then to the havoc Major creates, Sut recalls how, trapped in Seize's coffin, Major pounds on the lid, frightening Seize's wife, Suckey, and the other women who had "swarmed ontu the waggin" when the funeral procession began. Suckey strikes out "a cow gallop fur home," and Major strikes out for the doggery to drown his fears. After seeing his own face in the mirror, however, he strikes out for the river, meeting Sheriff Dozier on his way. Dozier catches the contagion, and "durn ef he didn't sheer outen the road like a skeer'd hoss, an' went ofen the bluff . . . into the river." Hot on Dozier's trail, Major plays "skeered hoss better nur Dozier did, fur he lit furder in the river." And with his customary good grace, Sut concludes his narrative by taunting them both.

Read as one story, **"Rare Ripe Garden-Seed," "Contempt of Court—Almost,"** and **"Trapping a Sheriff"** offer yet another variation of the same structural pattern. **"Rare-Ripe Garden-Seed"** begins this time with a shift in identity as Mary McKildrin marries Wat Mastin and assumes his name. Having psychologically ensnared Wat by concealing her pregnancy and

pretending to love him, Mary continues to meet Sheriff Doltin on the sly even as "Rare Ripe" blossoms in her belly. But after discovering the trick, Wat returns the favor by feigning ignorance and baiting Doltin; then, following a long digression introducing us to Wirt Staples, Sut resumes his narrative in **"Trapping a Sheriff."** The tables turned, Wat, Wirt, and, of course, Sut now ensnare Doltin by again using Mary as bait—or at least what Doltin assumes is Mary. Caught in a cheat, the cheater discovers that he has been braying not to Mary Mastin, but to Wirt's wife, Susan, who has disguised herself as Mary. For beating around the wrong bush, Wirt and the boys strip Doltin of everything but his shirt (eventually that comes off, too) and threaten to hang him. After they slip a noose over his head, Doltin takes a terrible skeer, running away while two tom-cats tear up and down his back, pulling "agin each uther like ontu two wile steers in a yaller-jackids nes'. . . . Jis' think ove two agravated, onsantified he cats at yearnis' war, makin yer bar-back thar battil groun," Sut muses. The thought of those two varmints ripping Doltin's back to shreds is almost too delightful for Sut and— having long expected some kind of varmint to light into Doltin—for us to bear. Doltin heads for Mary's house, hurling curses at her as he passes by, and she takes the skeer too, "jis' bust[ing] thru the standin corn like a runaway hoss." Completely debased, Doltin heads for water: he "shot down the bank, run thru the ferryboat an' plouted off the fur aind head fust intu the river." But even as he swims away, "every now an' then he'd snort like a hoss, an' look back over his shoulder." To make the story complete, all we need now is for Sut to rub it in, but Doltin's wife does that for him, vexing him with questions about how he ever managed to get into such a fix even as she "wer ilin ove his torn hide."

Sut's last story in the *Yarns,* **"Dad's Dog School,"** fittingly concludes the volume not only by returning to Dad's antics, but by again providing nearly all of the plot motifs contained in the most humorous Sut stories. The story begins with the expected change of identity—this time Dad wants to "play ho'ned cattil"—after which Dad becomes physically confined in Suggins's hide. Again, Dad performs admirably as an animal, "a bellerin jis' the bes' sampil ove a yearlin's nise yu ever hearn," and continues his cow impersonation even after that miserable varmint, Sugar, lands "a steel-trap holt ontu the pint ove his snout." Dad's nakedness—"he'd tuck off every durn'd stich ove his close"—further contributes to his discomfort, for while Mam beats him with her repeating beanpole and he "squall[s] low onder hit, like a sore-back hoss," the salted hide begins to salt his wounds. Meanwhile, Squire Hanley pokes his nose into the "famerly 'musement," and for his efforts gets to complete Dad's skeer by taking a plunge with his burr-arsed horse into the creek. For once, though, instead of running off to embark upon yet another skeer, Sut closes his story by taking the rest he always craves and wishing his listeners sweet dreams.

But many of the stories collected in *High Times and Hard Times* are less than sweet and far from amusing. The satires make especially tedious reading today because, as others have pointed out, they are bitter, vindictive, and dated. But more than that, they are tedious because they so infrequently provide the plot motifs we came to relish in the *Yarns.* With the exception, perhaps, of **"Sut Lovingood Lands Old Abe Safe at Last,"** in which Sut alters Abe's identity by packing him in an "elephant" suit and Abe performs a remarkable horse routine during his skeer, the satires are especially humorless not only because they are dated remnants of Harris's bile, but also because, to anyone who has read the *Yarns,* they are disappointingly plotless. Indeed, despite Sut's lively manner of telling them, many of the remaining stories in *High Times and Hard Times* share the same disability as the satires, and only a few—**"Sut Lovingood's Adventures in New York," "Sut Lovingood's Hog Ride," "Sut Lovingood's Big Dinner Story," "Sut Lovingood's Big Music Box Story," "Sut Lovingood, A Chapter from His Autobiography,"** and **"Well! Dad's Dead"**—remain humorous because they combine Sut's comic language and imagery with the plot motifs characteristic of Harris's best stories.

Thus, the most humorous Sut stories are also the most predictable. We look forward to someone being physically ensnared, being scared shutless, being assaulted by some kind of varmint, being reduced to nakedness, and being compelled to seek cover, preferably in the nearest river or creek. By the time Major heads for the doggery in **"Frustrating a Funeral,"** we are just waiting for him to kick up his heels and head for the river. Once Dad puts on Suggins's hide in **"Dad's Dog School"** we look forward to Sugar pestering the hell out of him. We look forward, in other words, to the misfortunes that await Sut or his victims because we know what they are in for long before they do. In no small way, that is what makes the best Lovingood stories so funny.

The repetitive plot motifs therefore cause us to look forward to many of the incidents that reputedly make Sut such a callous brute. Sut, we have been told [by Stephen M. Ross (see Additional Bibliography)], possesses "genuine malice," "real hatred," and a "malicious desire to hurt others." According to Richard Boyd Hauck, "Sut becomes, of course, a sadistic monster," so that "ultimately . . . the reader tends to hate Sut. . . . Sut's laughter at his own vicious antics," Hauck concludes, "is grotesque. We do not laugh at them at all, unless we laugh in derision of Sut himself" [see Additional Bibliography]. I am not ashamed to admit that I laugh plenty at all the poor suckers Sut traps. To be sure, if we isolate particular incidents Sut seems cruel and heartless. He does leave poor Dad fending off the hornets for himself, he does cause poor old Mrs. Yardley to croak, and he does blow up poor Rack Back Davy's backside. But the more Lovingood tales we read, the more we become aware not of Sut the character in the tales who performs these monstrosities, but of Sut the narrator—Sut the conscious artificer of plots designed to make his listeners laugh. We cannot be sure that Sut has actually committed any of the atrocities he relates. In fact, if he is half the coward he tells us he is, we have good reason to suspect that he never committed any of them, and that the tales he relates are simply his way of achieving a kind of bravado he does not possess in real life. What we can be certain of, however, is that Sut is constantly aware of the effect his tales are having upon his audience, and that in his most humorous tales he consciously includes all the ingredients he knows are sure to elicit a grin. (pp. 89-95)

Robert Micklus, "Sut's Travels with Dad," in Studies in American Humor, *n.s. Vol. 1, No. 2, October, 1982, pp. 89-102.*

CAROLYN S. BROWN   (essay date 1987)

[*Brown emphasizes the fictional qualities of the Sut Lovingood stories, arguing that they function as tall tales rather than as depictions of actual experience.*]

Ef yu ain't fond ove the smell ove
cracklins, stay outen the kitchin.

                                    —Sut Lovingood

Certainly they warned us—Sut, the narrator, and George Washington Harris, the author—that the Lovingood *Yarns* would, like much folk humor, be too strong to please every taste [see essay dated 1867]. Indeed, it has been called "the most repellent book of any merit in American literature" [see excerpt by Edmund Wilson dated 1962]. And yet another critic has claimed that "for vivid imagination, comic plot, Rabelaisian touch, and sheer *fun,* the *Sut Lovingood Yarns* surpass anything else in American humor" [see excerpt by Franklin J. Meine dated 1930]. While almost any literary work lends itself to a variety of interpretations, criticism of the *Yarns* is peculiarly split between hilarity and disgust. The main disagreement seems to be over whether Sut's actions are so morally reprehensible as to be ineligible for humor, or whether the sensitive modern reader for some reason can, in good conscience, laugh at the discomfort, pain, and degradation that Sut describes with such relish. It may be that the nineteenth-century male readers these tales were written for, having narrower sympathies and toughened by their own hardships, laughed at pain more easily than most of us do now. Certainly some of the incidents in Harris' stories are tasteless, others grotesque, by the standards of many modern readers. I contend, however, that the radical disagreement over the value of the best of the Lovingood yarns is due more to differing perceptions of the stories' relation to the real world than to our greater squeamishness. To be fully appreciated, the *Yarns* must be understood as written versions of the tall tale.

Our ability to laugh freely at discomfort generally depends upon the degree of discomfort depicted, the level of our identification with the victim, and the perceived distance between the unpleasant event and our own real world. Nearly anyone can enjoy Mark Twain's story of how William Wheeler was caught in a carpet machine and turned into fourteen yards of the best three-ply carpet. But what about Mrs. Yardley being trampled by a horse? The story of Wheeler and his widow, as part of Jim Blaine's absurd monologue in *Roughing It,* is clearly a fiction and a joke. The problem with Sut's yarns is that they are not, at first glance, clearly told as fictions. Modern readers tend to consider Sut's stories to be personal narratives (which, in folk culture, call for belief), and think of him more as a practical joker than a storyteller. Yet when Harris collected the stories, which had originally been published separately in periodicals, he called the book not *The Adventures of Sut Lovingood* but *Sut Lovingood. Yarns Spun by a "Nat'ral Born Durn'd Fool."* Sut is a storyteller, not simply a hell raiser who enthusiastically reports his escapades. Most of the yarns belong among the improbable tall tales: they are realistic enough to be possible, but wild enough and filled with enough ridiculous detail that the initiated listener knows not to take them as factual accounts of the narrator's experiences. Harris intends for us to understand that Sut has played some kind of a joke or gotten into a scrape; but, as with most fiction, we should concern ourselves more with the manner of the telling than with the suffering of fictional victims. The double distance established in fictional tales told by the fictional character Sut allows the reader to concentrate on the craft and the implied or symbolic meanings of the stories.

Beyond the title, our first clue to the fictionality of Sut's tales is in the non-dialect sections that frame the narratives. Each of Sut's tales is introduced by a brief non-dialect passage in which George, the frame narrator, indicates how he happened to hear Sut's yarn. Where many Southwest humorists used the framework device to provide balance, control, and assurance of a morally superior guiding intelligence, Harris uses the frame to establish that Sut's wit and verbal vitality are superior to those around him, and to indicate his position in society as a popular joker and storyteller. In **"Sut Lovingood's Daddy, Acting Horse,"** listeners who presume to challenge his preeminence are quickly quieted by Sut's comebacks: "the rat-faced youth shut up his knife and subsided" and "The tomato-nosed man in ragged overcoat . . . went into the doggery" amidst the laughter of the crowd. Throughout the book, Sut draws to himself the center of attention as groups of men gather inside or in front of the doggery, in camp, or beside a spring.

Sut's apparent popularity and the freedom with which he roams among groups of loafers and hunters seem to belie his frequent claims of outlawry. In **"Sicily Burns's Wedding,"** for example, Sut ends with the claim that "they is huntin' me tu kill me, I is feared." The severity of this statement, however, is undercut not only by Sut's own description of later encounters with wedding guests but also by the incidents in earlier stories. In **"Parson John Bullen's Lizards,"** Parson Bullen's reward poster serves only as a vehicle and inspiration for Sut's wit—not as an inspiration for righteous bounty hunters. Finding copies of the poster "stuck up on every blacksmith shop, doggery, and store door in the Frog Mountain Range," George takes one down for preservation.

AIT ($8) Dullars REW-ARD
TENSHUN BELEVERS AND KONSTABLES!
KETCH 'IM! KETCH 'IM!

This kash wil be pade in korn, ur uther projuce, tu be kolected at ur about nex camp-meetin, *ur thararter* by eny wun that ketches him, fur the karkus ove a sartin wun SUT LOVINGOOD, dead ur alive, ur ailin, an' safely giv over tu the purtectin care ove Parson John Bullen, ur lef' well tied, at Squire Mackjunkins, fur the raisin ove the devil pussonely, an' permiskusly discumfurtin the wimen very powerful, an' skeerin ove folks generly a heap, an' bustin up a promisin, big warm meetin, an' a making the wickid larf, an' wus, an' wus, insultin ove the passun orful.
    Test, Jehu Wethero
       Sined by me,
          John Bullen, the passun.

. . . In a few days I found Sut in a good crowd in front of Capehart's Doggery, and as he seemed to be about in good tune, I read it to him.

"Yas, George, that ar dockymint am in dead yearnist sartin. Them hard shells over thar dus want me the wus kine, powerful bad. *But,* I spect ait dullers won't fetch me, nither wud ait hundred, bekase thar's nun ove 'em fas' enuf tu ketch me, nither is thar hosses by the livin jingo! Say, George, much talk 'bout this fuss up whar yu're been?" For the sake of a joke I said yes, a great deal.

Sut's claims of physical danger are clearly a part of his joke and in fact belong to a popular folk genre. In her studies of tall tales and other modes of "talking trash" in the Okefenokee Swamp Rim, Kay Cothran found that, while rough practical jokes ("nonverbal lies," she calls them) really are played by country men, "much of the fun is in the later narration of

the victim's plight or of the biter's being bit." She also notes that the practical joke story typically ends with a statement that the victim carries a lasting grudge. Most of Sut's stories end with such a claim, and he frequently explains that he escapes from revenge only through the exercise of his long legs. From the glimpses of Sut's life provided in the framing passages we can see that these tales must be taller than life and that they are told for the fun of the telling rather than for their mimetic value.

The frames of the stories also briefly demonstrate how this tale-telling game of Sut's is to be played. In folk culture, the tall tale challenges the listener to prove himself clever or dull, in or out of the group to which the tale belongs, through his ability to recognize and appreciate the fiction. Harris' frame narrator, George, the well-educated, city-bred outsider, has become a temporary insider through his responses to Sut's tales. We get from George nothing but straight-faced reactions, no matter how outrageous the tale. He never moralizes, he never laughs, and he seldom interrupts. Other outsiders—a stranger, a schoolmaster, an encyclopedia salesman—ask stupid or impertinent questions and seem confused or offended by the moral atmosphere of Sut's tales. These listeners evoke insults and threats from Sut and are ostracized from the group, while George's solemn appreciation is rewarded by further yarns. When the old schoolmaster first interrupts Sut's **"Trapping a Sheriff,"** and then asks George, "Is not that person slightly deranged?" George replies:

> "Oh, no, not at all, he is only troubled at times with violent attacks of durn'd fool."

> "He is laboring under one *now,* is he not?"

> I nodded my head. "Go on, Sut."

Only once does George crack. In **"Eaves-Dropping a Lodge of Free-Masons"** George begins, in somber, nostalgic tones, a story of his own boyhood adventures, only to be interrupted by Sut, who claims he will tell the tale himself, without any "durn'd nonsince, 'bout echo's an grapes, an warnit trees." As Sut reaches the climax of the tale and his imagination begins to outrun history, George protests:

> "The ole man made a wicked cirklin lick at him wif his orful nakid wepun [a sword]. 'Voop,' hit went, an' cut the flat crown outen his cap, smoof es yu cud onkiver a huckleberry pie wif a case-knife."

> "That part's not true, Mr. Sut," said I.

> "Yes hit am, fur yu see he dun hit so slick that the crown whirl'd roun like a tin plate in the ar, six foot abuv yer hed, went faster nur yu did, an' lit afore yu, es yu flew down stars fas' es yu were gwine. Oh, littil hoss, *he did du hit,* an' ef he'd lower'd his sites jus a scrimpshun he'd a-saved a pow'ful site ove meat an' bread frum bein wasted, an' curius pepil wud a-been now a-readin ove yur vartu's frum a lyin stone newspaper stuck in the yeath ove the graveyard yu wer a-blatherin about jus' now.

Having been interrupted, Sut switches from the third person to the second, directly addressing George in answer to the challenge. He also changes the tone of the tale, increasing the grotesquerie and the exaggeration:

> "An I haint told all, fur in yer skeer a-gwine away frum that orful place, yu run over the spot whar a fancy hous' 'bout five foot squar hed been upsot, slunged in up to yur eyebrows, amungst the slush

in the hole, broke fur the krick, lunged in, onbottoned yer shut collar, dove plum thru that ar crownless cap—hit cum ofen yer heels like a hoop—swum outen yer clothes, an' jus' let every durn'd rag float away, an' then went home es nakid es a well-scraped hog, but not half es clean. The pepil what yu passed on yer way tu the krick tho't yu wer the cholery acumin, an' burn't tar in thar yards an' stuff'd ole rags onder thar doors, an' into the keyholes; an' es yu sneaked back nakid frum the krick, they tho't yu wer the ghost of a skin'd bullfrog, ur a forewarnin ove cumin famin."

By the end of this passage the story sounds like the tales of Sut's own misadventures. What began as a humorous anecdote about his friend's boyhood has become a tall tale: not an outrageous impossibility, but a tall tale nonetheless. That some of it stretches the facts we know from George's interruptions; that it is intended not as a serious lie but as entertainment for "the crowd" in the bar we know from George's introductory statements and Sut's asides to the audience. As in all the stories, the framing sections emphasize that these are tales told rather than actions performed. (pp. 74-80)

Sut also frequently adopts the traditional tall tale structural technique of beginning with realistically described events that seem probable, as well as possible, and gradually expanding the tale into the realm of the incredible. In **"Hen Baily's Reformation,"** even George conspires to give the story a mock air of factuality and solemnity by beginning with a tongue-in-cheek headnote:

> This truthful narrative is particularly recommended to the careful consideration of the Rev. Mr. Stiggins, and his disciples, of the Brick Lane Branch of the Grand Junction Ebenezer Temperance Association. This mode of treatment can be fully relied upon.

Sut's story begins with a warning about drinking from gourds. The action of the tale then moves from Hen's mistakenly drinking turpentine to his swallowing an eight-inch lizard that had hidden in a drinking gourd, and on through his desperate acrobatics as he tries vainly to get the lizard up. Finally, when a mole sent up his trouser leg comes out his mouth on the tail of the scurrying lizard, we know we have been sold.

Once we are alert to them, tall tale characteristics abound in the **Yarns.** Sut maintains strictly his pose of truthfulness and plausibility when George attempts to catch him off guard. How did the quilting turn out? George asks, and Sut replies, "How the hell du yu 'speck me tu know? I warn't thar eny more." When he can get away with it, however, Sut inserts the knowledge of an omniscient narrator into otherwise first-person accounts of his adventures. In **"Assisting at a Negro Night-Meeting,"** for example, Sut tells George what the preachers were thinking:

> The suckit rider tuk hit [a beef bladder filled with "carburated hydorgen"] tu be the breast ove a fat roas hen, an the Baptis thot hit wer the bulge ove a jug.

And in **"Old Burns's Bull Ride"** Sut gives a detailed account of Burns's adventure without explaining how he happens to know the details when he had already "put the mountain atwixt" himself and the Burns's "plantashun."

Mixed with this mock-historical accuracy is a good deal of

tall tale exaggeration. Describing his mother's encounter with a sand-hill crane, Sut claims that she "outrun her shadder thuty yards in cummin half a mile." In **"Dad's Dog School,"** the pretended factuality of a folk tale is undercut by similar exaggeration. In an attempt to convey the grotesque proportions of the Squire's nose, Sut claims that once "a feller broke a dorg-wood hanspike ur a chesnut fence rail, I'se forgot which, acrost that nose, an' twenty-seven bats, an' three kingfishers flew outen hit." Sut's uncertainty about the exact weapon used on the Squire's nose typifies a tall tale technique in which humor arises from the conjunction of gross exaggeration and a pretended concern for historical accuracy. Minute absurd details also characterize the tall tale, and Harris sprinkles these about the yarns as well:

> [Sut's dad] seemed to run jis adzactly as fas' es a ho'net cud fly; hit were the titest race I ever seed, fur wun hoss to git all the whippin. Down thru a saige field they all went, the ho'nets makin hit look like thar were smoke roun' dad's bald hed, an' he wif nuffin on the green yeath in the way ove close about im, but the bridil, an' ni ontu a yard ove plow line sailin behine, wif a tir'd out ho'net ridin on the pint ove hit.

Such precise detail simultaneously brings these exaggerations to life and points out that they are fictions.

While some of the tales contain only one or two clues to their tallness, many obvious tall tale characteristics appear in one of Harris' most popular tales—**"Sicily Burns's Wedding."** Perhaps it is because so many clues are given that most modern readers can recognize the story as a *story* and thus comfortably enjoy the humor. In this yarn, folkloric sources are suggested by the bull-ride motif. Harris also prepares the reader for a tall tale by first allowing Sut a straight-faced comic monologue on several topics having little to do with the story he eventually tells. Like the storytellers Mark Twain describes in "How to Tell a Story," Sut "strings incongruities and absurdities together" as if they were utterly serious and important.

> I'll jus' gin yu leave tu go tu the devil ha'f hamon, if I didn't make fewer tracks tu the mile, an' more to the minit, than were ever made by eny human body, since Bark Wilson beat the saw-log frum the top ove the Frog Mountain intu the Oconee River, an dove, an' dodged hit at las'. I hes allers look'd ontu that performance of Bark's as onekel'd in history, allers givin way to dad's hon'et race, however.

> "George, every livin thing hes hits pint, a pint ove sum sort. Ole Bullen's pint is a durn'ed fust rate, three bladed, dubbil barril'd, warter-proof hypockracy, an' a never-tirein appertite fur bal'face [liquor]. Sicily Burns's pint am tu drive men folks plum crazy, an' then bring em too agin. Gin em a rale Orleans fever in five minits, an' then in five minits more, gin them a Floridy ager. Durn her, she's down on her heels flatfooted now. Dad's pint is tu be king ove all durn'd fools, ever since the day ove that feller what cribb'd up so much co'n down in Yegipt, long time ago, (he run outen his coat yu minds). The Bibil tells us hu wer the stronges' man—hu wer the bes' man—hu wer the meekis man, an' hu wer the wises' man, but leaves yu to guess hu wer the bigges' fool. . . ."

As the real action of the story begins, Sut liberally tosses in absurd details typical of the tall tale. The bee-covered bull, for example, backs into a tall Dutch clock, "bustin' hits runnin geer outen hit, the little wheels a-trundlin over the floor, an the bees even chasin them." Sut also assigns to the bees the kind of exaggerated malice and intellect that most tall tale insects seem to possess: "they am pow'ful quick tempered littil critters, enyhow. The air wer dark wif 'em, an' Sock were kivered all over, from snout tu tail, so clost yu cudent a-sot down a grain ove wheat fur bees, an' they wer a-fiting one anuther in the air, fur a place on the bull." Because the tall language draws attention to itself and away from the distress of bull and humans, the net effect is comic. Sut also employs understatements which are reminiscent of oral tall tales. After describing the wedding guests' frantic attempts to escape the bees, Sut remarks, "liveliest folks I ever did see." In a more extended use of comic understatement, Sut praises old Burns' skill with a basket: "I swar old Burns kin beat eny man on top ove the yeath a-fiting bees wif a baskit. Jis set 'im a-straddil ove a mad bull, an let thar be bees enuf tu exhite the ole man, an' the man what beats him kin break me."

The tall tale is also, of course, suggested by the near-impossibility of some of the story's main events: the bull piling all the tables on top of one another, with Mrs. Clapshaw perched on top of the pile; old Burns being thrown onto the bull's back and later (in the sequel, **"Old Burns's Bull Ride"**) thrown off and caught in a tree, dangling by his heels. Quite possible but clearly a stretcher is Sut's claim that "they is huntin' me tu kill me, I is fear'd."

At the end of the wedding story, Sut slips quickly into more general remarks and a lament on his foolishness:

> "Hit am an orful thing, George, tu be a nat'ral born durn'd fool. Yu'se never 'sperienced hit pussonally, hev yu? Hits made pow'fully agin our famerly, an all owin tu dad. . . ."

Like many tall tale narrators, in order to lend an air of credibility to his story and maintain a facade of seriousness, Sut ends not with a punch line but with a solemn statement about the significance of the action or with a transition to another topic of conversation.

Each of Sut's stories contains such tall tale elements, though the tallness is not equally obvious in all of the tales. In the collected *Yarns,* the better tales provide a guide for reading the lesser ones, and the book as a whole can be read as a collection of tall tales. Probably Sut is a rough joker; perhaps he does get into scrapes and live in an undercivilized world. But in his tales, these exaggerated or invented accounts of his escapades, the reader is intended to laugh not so much at the discomfiture of Sut's victims, but at his vivid comic language and at the outrageous, exaggerated relation between cause and effect, action and reaction. The initiated reader delights in seeing those exaggerated events illuminated by Sut's pyrotechnic language, and he feels liberated by the wild comic disorder at the same time that he admires Sut's imposition of artistic control on a disorderly world. (pp. 80-4)

Because he tells tall tales, Sut's pranks and social defects are not limited to the realm of the possible and the likely, and he uses this freedom deliberately to manipulate his audience. As he exaggerates the grotesqueness of his adventures and pushes on the limits of our credibility, he also approaches the limits of our ability to believe that other men are animals or machines and that pain is comic. Sut's yarns, then, offer the typical tall tale challenge: enjoy these tall tales and be, for the time at least, one of the boys (a society of free spirits) or be

offended by them and be, like the schoolmaster and encyclopedia salesman, an outsider and an effete social conformist. The naïve, overly squeamish listener (or reader) aligns himself with the victims of Sut's social aggression: Clapshaw, Sheriff Doltin, Parson Bullen, Mrs. Yardley. True, Sut sometimes victimizes the downtrodden and innocent as well as the socially smug. He disrupts a Negro camp meeting, terrorizes an Irish tramp, torments a turpentine-poisoned drunk, and kills or maims several animals. Nonetheless, these are tall tales, and the listeners or readers who fail to recognize them as such and grant an undue amount of pity to the imaginary victims become victims themselves: first, because they have identified themselves with the squeamish middle-class hypocrites of Sut's tales; second, because they suffer the discomforts of being offended rather than being entertained or relieved of psychic pressures; and, finally, because they have been fooled into believing a fiction.

While giving Sut a kind of immediate power over his listeners and readers, his yarns also give him power over the world he lives in. The absurdity of that world, not entirely generated by Sut's pranks and not entirely imaginary, impinges on Sut as well as on the other characters. As a means of coping with the stupidity of his father, the temptations of Sicily Burns, the interferences of the clergy, the hypocrisy of the middle class, and the general disorder around him, Sut creates tales which accentuate these stresses. In tales like **"Parson John Bullen's Lizards"** and **"Trapping a Sheriff,"** Sut's triumph is obvious. The prank brings pain and humiliation to the victim, the story's form and context allow Sut to exaggerate his success, and the comic tone brings further humiliation as the victim becomes the butt of a humorous tale. In tales where Sut himself is the victim (**"Sut's New Fangled Shirt," "Blown up with Soda," "Taurus in Lynchburg Market"**) and in the tales where Sut's primary function is merely to observe and report the workings of an unruly world (**"Sut Lovingood's Daddy, Acting Horse," "A Razor-Grinder in a Thunder-Storm," "Bart Davis's Dance," "Dad's Dog School"**), Sut masters his world by re-creating it in his own image. Sut the tall tale artist controls his fictional world more surely than Sut the prankster could ever hope to control the real world. Even the affliction of Sut's own durn'd fooledness can be mitigated through storytelling:

> "Why, Sut, what's wrong now? you look sick."
>
> "Heaps wrong, durn my skin—no my haslets—ef I haint mos' ded, an' my looks don't lie when they hints I'se sick. I is sick—I'se skin'd."
>
> "Who skinned you—old Bullen?"
>
> "No, hoss, a durnder fool nor Bullen did hit; I jis skin'd mysef."
>
> "What in the name of common sense did you do it for?"
>
> "Didn't du hit in the name ove common sense; did hit in the name, an' wif the sperit, ove plum natral born durn fool.
>
> "Lite ofen that ar hoss, an' take a ho'n; I wants two ove 'em, (shaking his constant companion, a whiskey flask, at me,) an' plant yersef ontu that ar log, an' I'll tell ef I kin, but hit's a'mos beyant tellin.
>
> "I'se a durnder fool nor enybody outside a As-

salum, ur Kongriss, 'sceptin ove my own dad, fur he actid hoss, an' I haint tried that yet."

Then follows the story of how Sut became stuck inside a freshly starched shirt and lost a good deal of his hide in getting out of it. He ends with this warning:

> "Now George, ef a red-heded 'oman wif a reel foot axes yu to marry her, yu *may* du hit; ef an 'oman wants yu tu kill her husban, yu *may* du hit; ef a gal axes yu tu rob the bank, an' take her tu Californy, yu *may* du hit; ef wun on em wants yu tu quit whisky, yu *mout* even du that. But ef ever an 'oman, ole ur yung, purty es a sunflower ur ugly es a skin'd hoss, offers yu a shut aninted wif paste tu put on, jis' yu kill her in her tracks, an' burn the cussed pisnus shut rite thar. Take a ho'n?"

In orthodox tall tale style and spirit, Sut exaggerates life's difficulties and conquers them by laughing at them.

Behind the character Sut is George Washington Harris exaggerating, laughing, and conquering as he spins tall tales for his readers. In Sut Lovingood, Harris exaggerated the common notion of a poor white southern mountaineer much as, in oral lore, a farmer may exaggerate the poverty of his land, the appetite of the local insects, and the ferocity of the weather for the benefit of the tourist. Harris' use of Sut as a narrator for his anti-Lincoln pieces indicates just whom Harris was trying to offend, fool, and exclude, and whom he intended to amuse. He had begun writing political articles in 1839 and was active in secessionist politics through the fifties. The first of his Sut stories, **"Sut Lovingood's Daddy, Acting Horse,"** appeared in the *Spirit of the Times* in 1854, but thereafter the yarns were published in Democratic newspapers of the South. Though the book *Sut Lovingood* was published in New York in 1867, the Lincoln pieces and other obvious satires were not included.

For Harris, Sut is a regional characteristic to be flaunted, a weapon to be wielded. Sut represents the lowest elements of southern culture—the white trash whose shiftlessness, sexual promiscuity, cruelty to the Negro, personal filth, and disrespect for the laws and values of Christian civilization would have chilled the very bones of any Yankee who met him. In the Sut Lovingood pieces, Harris the Southerner fought the battle against the North, industrial society, and the Republican party, not with the romantic agrarianism of a John Pendleton Kennedy or a John Esten Cooke, but with the aggressive humor of the tall tale. Even so, like all tall tales, these stories are primarily humorous, and Harris, like Sut, must have taken a great deal of delight in telling his **Yarns.** (pp. 85-8)

> Carolyn S. Brown, *"Sut Lovingood: A Nat'ral Born Durn'd Yarnspinner,"* in her The Tall Tale in American Folklore and Literature, *The University of Tennessee Press, Knoxville, 1987, pp. 74-88.*

ADDITIONAL BIBLIOGRAPHY

Arnold, St. George Tucker, Jr. "Sut Lovingood, the Animals, and the Great White Trash Chain of Being." *Thalia* 1, No. 3 (Winter 1978-79): 33-41.
  Describes Sut's relations with animals, delineating his place in the Great Chain of Being.

Blair, Walter. "Civil War Humor—Fools for Propaganda." In his *Horse Sense in American Humor from Benjamin Franklin to Ogden Nash,* pp. 149-71. Chicago: University of Chicago Press, 1942.
  Examines Harris as a member of a group of writers of the Civil War era, explaining how he presented his political beliefs.

———, and Hill, Hamlin. "Sut Lovingood and the End of the World." In their *America's Humor from Poor Richard to Doonesbury,* pp. 213-21. New York: Oxford University Press, 1978.
  Contrasts opposing critical views of Sut in attempting to define his philosophy.

Covici, Pascal, Jr. *Mark Twain's Humor: The Image of a World.* Dallas: Southern Methodist University Press, 1962, 266 p.
  A study of Mark Twain's humor that makes several references to Harris, including a comparison of narrative technique in his story "Eaves-Dropping a Lodge of Masons" and Twain's work.

Current-Garcia, Eugene. "Sut Lovingood's Rare Ripe Southern Garden." *Studies in Short Fiction* IX, No. 2 (Spring 1972): 117-29.
  Describes and comments on the individual stories in *Sut Lovingood's Yarns.*

Day, Donald. "The Political Satires of George W. Harris." *Tennessee Historical Quarterly* IV, No. 4 (December 1945): 320-38.
  An analysis and interpretation of Harris's political satires, written by a noted Harris scholar.

———. "The Life of George Washington Harris." *Tennessee Historical Quarterly* 6 (March 1947): 3-38.
  A biographical study respected for its accuracy and thorough documentation.

Gardiner, Elaine. "Sut Lovingood: Backwoods Existentialist." *Southern Studies* XXII, No. 2 (Summer 1983): 177-89.
  Argues that Sut can be viewed as a prototype of the existentialist antihero.

Hauck, Richard Boyd. "From the Absurd Frontier." In his *A Cheerful Nihilism: Confidence and "The Absurd" in American Humorous Fiction,* pp. 40-76. Bloomington: Indiana University Press, 1971.
  Discusses Harris and other Southwestern frontier humorists as part of a tradition of the absurd in American fiction.

Hubbell, Jay B. "George W. Harris." In his *The South in American Literature, 1607-1900,* pp. 678-79. Durham, N.C.: Duke University Press, 1954.
  A brief overview of Harris and his creation, Sut.

Inge, M. Thomas. "William Faulkner and George Washington Harris: In the Tradition of Southwestern Humor." *Tennessee Studies in Literature* VII (1962): 47-59.
  Points out similarities in the writings of Harris and Faulkner.

———. Introduction to *Sut Lovingood's Yarns,* by George Washington Harris, edited by M. Thomas Inge, pp. 9-24. New Haven, Conn.: College & University Press, 1966.
  A biographical and critical introduction to Harris and the Sut Lovingood stories.

Leary, Lewis. "The Lovingoods: Notes toward a Genealogy." In his *Southern Excursions: Essays on Mark Twain and Others,* pp. 111-30. Baton Rouge: Louisiana State University Press, 1971.
  Creates a genealogy for Sut, turning to the stories to describe his family and then tracing his descendents in the works of subsequent writers.

Lenz, William E. "Sensuality, Revenge, and Freedom: Women in

Sut Lovingood's Yarns." Studies in American Humor n.s. 1, No. 3 (February 1983): 173-80.

Examines Harris's depiction of women in the Sut Lovingood stories, emphasizing their capacity for sensuality and ability to inspire revenge.

The Lovingood Papers. 4 vols. Edited by Ben Harris McClary. Athens, Tenn.: Tennessee Wesleyan College, 1962; Knoxville, Tenn.: The University of Tennessee Press, 1963-65.

A four-volume series that includes both original stories by Harris first published in periodicals and not previously collected in book form as well as critical articles on Harris by various commentators. In addition, the first volume contains an article by Brom Weber in which he challenges Wilson's interpretation of the Sut Lovingood stories and his treatment of Weber's editorial approach to Harris's work (see excerpts by Weber and Wilson dated 1954 and 1962, respectively).

Lynn, Kenneth S. "The Volcano—Part II." In his *Mark Twain and Southwestern Humor,* pp. 112-39. Boston: Little, Brown and Co., 1959.

Discusses Harris in relation to the tradition of Southwestern humor.

McClary, Ben Harris. "The Real Sut." *American Literature* 27, No. 1 (March 1955): 105-06.

Suggests that Harris modeled his character Sut after an acquaintance named William (Sut) Miller.

Penrod, James H. "Folk Humor in *Sut Lovingood's Yarns." Tennessee Folklore Society Bulletin* XVI, No. 4 (December 1950): 76-84.

Identifies the elements in Harris's stories that tie them to the tradition of folk humor, outlining his use of folk customs, tall talk, rambling narration, and comic sayings.

———. "The Folk Hero as Prankster in the Old Southwestern Yarns." *Kentucky Folklore Record* II, No. 1 (January-March 1956): 5-12.

Surveys Southwestern tall tales to elucidate the role of pranksters, claiming that Sut is "the uncrowned king of pranksters in native American humor."

Plater, Ormonde. "Before Sut: Folklore in the Early Works of George Washington Harris." *Southern Folklore Quarterly* XXXIV, No. 2 (June 1970): 104-15.

Traces the folklore elements in the early stories of Harris.

Rickels, Milton. "George Washington Harris's Newspaper Grotesques." *The University of Mississippi Studies in English* n.s. 2 (1981): 15-24.

Contends that Harris's use of the newspaper format allowed him more freedom to explore folk culture.

Ross, Stephen M. "Jason Compson and Sut Lovingood: Southwestern Humor as Stream of Consciousness." *Studies in the Novel* VIII, No. 3 (Fall 1976): 278-90.

Points out similarities between Sut Lovingood and Jason Compson in William Faulkner's *The Sound and the Fury* (1929).

Wenke, John. "*Sut Lovingood's Yarns* and the Politics of Performance." *Studies in American Fiction* 15, No. 2 (Autumn 1987): 199-210.

Views the *Yarns* as a performance, dividing Sut's roles into that of actor, director, polemicist, and storyteller.

Young, Thomas Daniel. "A Nat'ral Born Durn'd Fool." *Thalia* VI, No. 2 (Fall-Winter 1983-84): 51-6.

Critiques the story "Parson John Bullen's Lizards" to illustrate Harris's skill as a humorist.

Nathaniel Hawthorne

1804-1864

(Born Nathaniel Hathorne) American novelist, short story writer, and essayist.

The following entry presents criticism of Hawthorne's novel *The Marble Faun; or, The Romance of Monte Beni* (1860); also published as *The Transformation; or, The Romance of Monte Beni* (1860). For information on Hawthorne's complete career, see *NCLC*, Vol. 2; for criticism devoted to his novels *The Scarlet Letter* and *The Blithedale Romance,* see *NCLC*, Vol. 10 and *NCLC*, Vol. 17, respectively.

The last of Hawthorne's great novels, *The Marble Faun* addresses his common theme of the effects of sin and guilt on the human psyche. Unique among Hawthorne's novels in its European setting, *The Marble Faun* compellingly evokes his vision of Rome, depicting the splendor of its historical and legendary past, the magnificence of its artistic treasures, and the blended grandeur and squalor of life there in the midnineteenth century. Long considered Hawthorne's most enigmatic novel—"my own moonshiny Romance," as the author called it—*The Marble Faun* has challenged readers to penetrate its unresolved mysteries of both plot and theme for well over one hundred years.

The Marble Faun was Hawthorne's last completed novel; by the early 1850s all his other major works of fiction had been published, including his short stories, *The Scarlet Letter,* and *The House of the Seven Gables.* However, as Hawthorne had never been able to live on the proceeds of his writings, he accepted employment as the American consul to England, traveling to Liverpool in 1853. He remained in England until the spring of 1858, when he journeyed with his wife, Sophia, and their children to Italy. The Hawthornes spent most of their time in Rome, where their sight-seeing took them on an extensive tour of the city's art galleries and museums. Hawthorne chronicled his Italian experiences in a journal later published as *Passages from the French and Italian Notebooks of Nathaniel Hawthorne,* describing in great detail the art, scenery, and people he observed; many passages of lush description were taken directly from his *Italian Notebooks* and incorporated into *The Marble Faun.* Among the art works that made an impression on him was a statue of a mythical faun done by Praxiteles, the Athenian sculptor of the fourth century B.C. "It seems to me," Hawthorne wrote, "that a story, with all sorts of fun and pathos in it, might be contrived on the idea of their species having become intermingled with the human race. . . ." It was not until 1859, however, while he was again living in England, that Hawthorne wrote the bulk of the novel that would become *The Marble Faun.* The romance was published the following year, appearing in England as *The Transformation* (a title chosen by the publishers over Hawthorne's objections) and in America as *The Marble Faun,* subtitled in both instances *The Romance of Monte Beni*.

In the preface to *The Marble Faun,* Hawthorne wrote (speaking of himself in the third person), "Italy, as the site of his Romance, was chiefly valuable to him as affording a sort of poetic or fairy precinct, where actualities would not be so ter-

ribly insisted upon as they are, and must needs be, in America. . . . Romance and poetry, ivy, lichens, and wallflowers, need ruin to make them grow." The only one of Hawthorne's novels not set in his native New England, *The Marble Faun* reflects its author's conflicting personal feelings toward Rome, about which he wrote: "no place ever took so strong a hold of my being . . . , nor ever seemed so close to me and so strangely familiar. I seem to know it better than my birthplace, and to have known it longer; and though I have been very miserable there, and languid with the effects of the atmosphere, and disgusted with a thousand things in its daily life, still I cannot say I hate it, perhaps might fairly own a love for it. But life being too short for such questionable and troublesome enjoyments, I desire never to set eyes on it again. . . . " Thus, he introduces the four main characters of *The Marble Faun*—Hilda, Kenyon, Miriam, and Donatello—into a city of mingled beauty and decadence. The former two are artists from New England: the pure and innocent Hilda is a sensitive and adept copyist of the masters, while Kenyon, who is in love with Hilda, is a sculptor. In contrast to their ingenuous American friends, Miriam and Donatello are Europeans surrounded by mystery and legend. A beautiful and passionate woman, Miriam has come to Rome to escape the taint of an unrevealed crime in which she was closely implicated but of which she was apparently not guilty. (Most commentators, noting Hawthorne's repeated insistence on linking Miriam with a portrait of Beatrice Cenci, an Italian noblewoman of the Renaissance who was executed for complicity in the murder of her sexually abusive father, surmise that the shadowy sin involves incest.) Donatello carries the mixed blood of humanity and of the ancient, legendary race of fauns. He delights the others with his natural innocence and goodness, though it is hinted that his youthful freshness will degenerate into sensual coarseness as he grows older. Donatello loves Miriam, but his affection cannot mitigate the aura of sadness and incipient danger that surrounds her. The novel's atmosphere of gloom and peril soon deepens when Miriam encounters a mysterious Capuchin monk who alludes darkly to a sordid event in their shared past and begins, inexplicably and threateningly, to haunt her, following wherever she goes. Matters reach a crisis one evening on the Tarpeian Rock, where Miriam and Donatello are again disturbed by the monk's brooding presence and the faun, goaded by rage, seizes the interloper. He then looks imploringly at Miriam for guidance and she silently acquiesces with her eyes: Donatello hurls the monk off the cliff to his death.

The rapturous sense of freedom and mutual passionate love the crime initially engenders in Miriam and Donatello is quickly replaced by crushing guilt. Unable to find comfort in one another's company, the two part—Donatello retreats to his ancestral estate of Monte Beni, where he mourns the loss of his carefree innocence; Miriam disappears for a time, plagued by her conviction that she has been the instrument of Donatello's moral destruction. Unbeknownst to the perpetrators, their deed had been witnessed by Hilda, whose horror is so great that she feels guilty even though she had no part in the act. She recoils from Miriam when her friend seeks comfort, becoming obsessively concerned with purging the stain she feels on her own soul. Disconsolate, Hilda is eventually drawn to the Church, where she, staunch Puritan though she is, derives spiritual solace from Catholic confession. Donatello and Miriam are eventually reunited in Rome, he a sadder, more perceptive and contemplative being. The novel's ending leaves their ultimate fate unclear, though it is hinted that after a term in prison Donatello will return to Miriam and the two will live a life of repentance. Hilda and Kenyon return to America, where they are to be married.

Commentators generally agree that the central theme of *The Marble Faun* is stated explicitly in Miriam's query to Kenyon: "The story of the Fall of Man! Is it not repeated in our Romance of Monte Beni? And may we follow the analogy yet farther? Was that very sin—into which Adam precipitated himself and all his race—was it the destined means by which, over a long pathway of toil and sorrow, we are to attain a higher, brighter, and profounder happiness, than our lost birthright gave?" At issue is the question of the *felix culpa,* or fortunate fall. According to this theory, Adam and Eve's fall from grace in Genesis was not tragic but beneficial, for it is not the ignorance of innocence but the experience of sin that makes humans truly moral beings. The issue with regard to *The Marble Faun,* therefore, is whether the protagonists are ennobled, made wiser and more fully human, by their fall from innocence, initiation into sin, and subsequent repentance. While the question obviously applies most closely to Donatello—not only as the one who commits the crime but as the creature who before it typifies humankind in a state of prelapsarian innocence—it also applies to each of the other characters to some extent. Miriam is morally, if not technically, guilty, Hilda suffers guilt by association, and Kenyon,

personally less involved than the others, struggles to understand the experience as he observes and comments upon the action. There is no critical consensus regarding the attitude Hawthorne took toward the fortunate fall. It has been variously argued that he affirmed the doctrine, that he denied it, that he was unable to decide the issue, and that he deliberately chose not to resolve it.

Much of the controversy about the fortunate fall centers around the issue of which of the novel's characters, if any, speaks for the author. Is it Miriam, who advances and embraces the theory? Or is it Hilda, who rejects it absolutely? Scholars disagree also about the significance of Kenyon's attitude; clearly drawn to the idea when Miriam proposes it, he instantly repudiates it when he sees how the theory horrifies Hilda, crying in panic: "I never did believe it! . . . Oh, Hilda, guide me home!" Hilda's character, in fact, is a main stumbling block for critics, who frequently debate whether she is the book's moral standard or its moral failure, whether she is fundamentally meant to be a sympathetic character or not. While most critics agree that she is insufferable in her Puritan stuffiness and spotless purity, it is unclear whether Hawthorne intended her to be so. Some contend that Hawthorne considered Hilda's careful regard for her own purity commendable, while others assert that he meant to show how her excessive self-righteousness causes her to forsake simple human decency: fearing all contact with sin (which is after all a necessary component of the postlapsarian human condition), she refuses contact with Miriam when her friend needs her most. Either she is right to preserve her position on a higher moral plane, or her purity is too self-absorbed and she errs in her refusal to become engaged with the rest of sinful, suffering humanity.

Although the central meaning of *The Marble Faun* remains thus unresolved, other aspects of the novel have received critical attention, primarily the role of aesthetics and art criticism in the book and the tension between European and American values. Recent critics have also explored the sexual overtones of *The Marble Faun,* commenting not only on the underlying theme of incest but on the dichotomy between Miriam's implied eroticism and Hilda's chaste, some argue repressed, sexuality.

"[If] I have written anything well," Hawthorne wrote to his friend William D. Ticknor shortly after the publication of *The Marble Faun,* "it should be this Romance; for I have never thought or felt more deeply, or taken more pains." The current of critical opinion, however, which has remained fairly constant over the years, contradicts the author's own assessment: such masterpieces as *The Scarlet Letter* and *The House of the Seven Gables* continue to overshadow *The Marble Faun* in Hawthorne's canon. What Henry James referred to as the novel's "almost fatal vagueness" has been a recurring complaint, as most commentators find the novel unnecessarily obscure and maddeningly mystifying. The book's allusiveness, too, has generated much discussion; though earlier critics tended to find more elaborate allegorical constructs in the novel than do their modern counterparts, recent scholars remark that the work's symbolic, mythic qualities sometimes blend uneasily with its realistic ones. Yet, *The Marble Faun* is considered an important work by a major American novelist. From the time of its first publication, *The Marble Faun* has been admired for its articulation of complex moral and theological issues. Not Hawthorne's best work, *The Marble Faun* is nonetheless one of his most ambitious in its probing of his recurring themes of the nature of innocence and knowledge, purity and sin, guilt and redemption.

(See also *Short Story Criticism,* Vol. 3; *Dictionary of Literary Biography,* Vol. 1: *The American Renaissance in New England; Concise Dictionary of American Literary Biography: Colonialization to the American Renaissance, 1640-1865;* and *Yesterday's Authors of Books for Children,* Vol. 2.)

NATHANIEL HAWTHORNE   (letter date 1859)

[*Writing to his friend James T. Fields, Hawthorne reports on the progress of* The Marble Faun. *Hawthorne's letter was first printed in 1872 in Fields's* Yesterdays with Authors.]

"The romance is almost finished, a great heap of manuscript being already accumulated, and only a few concluding chapters remaining behind. . . . I have found far more work to do upon it than I anticipated. To confess the truth, I admire it exceedingly at intervals, but am liable to cold fits, during which I think it the most infernal nonsense. You ask for the title. I have not yet fixed upon one, but here are some that have occurred to me; neither of them exactly meets my idea: 'Monte Beni; or, The Faun. A Romance.' 'The Romance of a Faun.' 'The Faun of Monte Beni.' 'Monte Beni: a Romance.' 'Miriam: a Romance.' 'Hilda: a Romance.' 'Donatello: a Romance.' 'The Faun: a Romance.' 'Marble and Man: a Romance.' When you have read the work (which I especially wish you to do before it goes to press), you will be able to select one of them, or imagine something better. There is an objection in my mind to an Italian name, though perhaps Monte Beni might do. Neither do I wish, if I can help it, to make the fantastic aspect of the book too prominent by putting the Faun into the title-page.

Nathaniel Hawthorne, in an extract from a letter to James T. Fields on October 10, 1859, in Hawthorne among His Contemporaries: A Harvest of Estimates, Insights, and Anecdotes from the Victorian Literary World *by Kenneth Walter Cameron, Transcendental Books, 1968, p. 321.*

[HENRY F. CHORLEY]   (essay date 1860)

[*An English man of letters, Chorley regularly reviewed Hawthorne's works in the* Athenaeum. *Here, he praises the descriptive power and moral theme of* The Marble Faun (*Chorley refers to the work by its English title*), *but finds the characters derivative and objects to the obscurity of the novel's conclusion. For Sophia and Nathaniel Hawthorne's response to Chorley's criticism, see excerpt dated 1860.*]

Not with impunity can a novelist produce two such books—each, of its class, perfect—as *The Scarlet Letter* and *The House of the Seven Gables.* He is expected to go on; and his third and fourth romances will be measured by their two predecessors, without reference to the fact that there may be slow growth and solitary perfection in works of genius. The yew and the locust-tree have different natural habits. Then, for one to whom all Europe is looking for a part of its pleasure, to stop the course of his labours is a piece of independence hard to forgive. Thirdly, there is hazard in an attempt to change the scale of creative exercise when an artist has shown himself perfect in the one originally adopted. The mas-

ters of cabinet-painting whom it would be wise to commission to cover a ceiling are not many. Raphael could produce the Pitti Ezekiel and the Cartoons, it is true; Rembrandt could paint the Temple scene in Jerusalem, which England possesses, as also the gigantic Duke of Gueldres in the Berlin Gallery; but Raphaels and Rembrandts are few.

It is only fit, fair, and friendly that the above three considerations should be allowed their full weight in adjudging the merit of Mr. Hawthorne's fourth and longest work of fiction [*Transformation; or, the Romance of Monte Beni*], produced after the pause of many years. It would be idle to appeal to them were the production which calls them forth not a remarkable one—one of the most remarkable novels that 1860 is likely to give us, whether from English, French, or American sources. Such an Italian tale we have not had since Herr Andersen wrote his *Improvisatore.* How potent is the spell of the South, as filling the memories and quickening the imagination of the stranger! how powerless over her own strongest sons in literary works of Art and Fancy we have occasion to see almost as often as we take up an Italian novel. Mr. Hawthorne has drunk in the spirit of Italian beauty at every pore. The scene of this romance is principally at Rome, and the writer's intense yearning to reproduce and accumulate his recollections of that wonderful city appears to have again and again possessed itself of heart and pen, to the suspense, not damage, of his story. (pp. 296-97)

Most of all do we enjoy Mr. Hawthorne's sympathy with the world's cathedral, St. Peter's, having rebelled for years against the bigotry with which sticklers for pointed arches or unlearned constructions have decried this gorgeous centre of the Roman Catholic rite, as a place mundane, theatrical, and "out of style." For such censors Art, Nature, and Beauty have no existence, save by the complacent favour of their own vanity!

We have inadvertently touched on the great scenic power and beauty of this Italian Romance ere offering a word on its matter and argument. Whether the elevating influences of remorse on certain natures have ever been taken as the theme of a story so fearlessly as here, may be questioned. Casuists and moralists must discuss the truth of the data. To Mr. Hawthorne truth always seems to arrive through the medium of his imagination;—some far-off phantasy to suggest a train of thought and circumstance out of which philosophies are evolved and characters grow. His hero, the Count of Monte Beni, would never have lived had not the Faun of Praxiteles stirred the author's admiration; and this mythical creature so engaged the dreamer's mind, that he draws out of the past the fancy of an old family endowed with certain constant attributes of Sylvan gaiety and careless, semi-animal enjoyments such as belonged to the dances and sunshine of Arcady. Such is Donatello at the beginning of the tale; and with these qualities are mixed up unquestioning, simple love and fidelity, which can take a form of unreasoning animal fury in a moment of emergency. He is hurried into sudden murder for the sake of the woman he loves; and with that the Faun nature dies out, and the sad, conscience-stricken human being begins, in the writhings of pain, to think, to feel,—lastly, to aspire. This, in a few words, is the meaning of "Transformation"; and for the first moiety of the romance the story turns slowly, with windings clearly to be traced, yet powerfully, round its principal figure. The other characters Mr. Hawthorne must bear to be told are not new to a tale of his. Miriam, the mysterious, with her hideous tormentor, was indicated in the *Zenobia* of **The Blithedale Romance,**—Hilda, the pure and innocent, is own cousin to *Phoebe* in **The House of the Seven Gables,**—Kenyon, the sculptor, though carefully wrought out, is a stone image, with little that appeals to our experience of men. These are all the characters; and when it is added that Miriam is a magnificent paintress with a mystery, that Hilda is a copyist of pictures from New England, and that Kenyon is her countryman, enough has been told to define the brain creatures who figure in the wild **Romance of Monte Beni.**

Mr. Hawthorne must be reckoned with for the second moiety of his book. In spite of the delicious Italian pictures, noble speculations, and snatches of arresting incident, which it contains, we know of little in Romance more inconclusive and hazy than the manner in which the tale is brought to its close. Hints will not suffice to satisfy interest which has been excited to voracity. Every incident need not lead to a mathematical conclusion nor *coup de théâtre* (as in the comedies of M. Scribe), but the utter uncertainty which hangs about every one and every thing concerned in the strong emotions and combinations of half of this romance, makes us part company with them, as though we were awaking from a dream,—not bidding tearful farewell at the scaffold's foot to the convict,—not saying "Go in peace" to the penitent who enters a religious house for the purposes of superstitious expiation,—not acquiring such late knowledge of the past as makes us lenient to crime, wrought by feeble human nature under the goad of long-drawn torture; and thus willing to forgive and accept the solution here proposed in so shadowy a fashion. Hilda and Kenyon marry, as it was to be seen they would do in the first page; but the secret of Miriam's agony and unrest, the manner of final extrication from it, for herself, and the gay Faun, who shed blood to defend her, then grew sad and human under the consciousness of the stain, are all left too vaporously involved in suggestion to satisfy any one whose blood has turned back at the admirable, clear and forcible last scenes of **The Scarlet Letter.** (p. 297)

> [*Henry F. Chorley*], *in a review of "Transformation; or, The Romance of Monte Beni," in* The Athenaeum, *No. 1688, March 3, 1860, pp. 296-97.*

SOPHIA HAWTHORNE AND NATHANIEL HAWTHORNE (letter date 1860)

[*While Henry F. Chorley's review of* The Marble Faun *in the* Athenaeum *(see excerpt dated 1860) was largely favorable, his criticism that the novel's characters were imitative of earlier Hawthorne characters irked Sophia Hawthorne, who defended her husband's work in the letter excerpted below. Hawthorne appended his own message to Chorley at the bottom of his wife's letter.*]

MY DEAR CHORLEY:—

Why do you run with your fine lance directly into the face of Hilda? You were so fierce and wrathful at being shut out from the mysteries (for which we are all disappointed), that you struck in your spurs and plunged with your visor down. For indeed and in truth Hilda is not Phoebe, no more than a wild rose is a calla lily. They are alike only in purity and innocence; and I am sure you will see this whenever you read the romance a second time. I am very much grieved that *Mr. Chorley* should seem not to be nicely discriminating; for what are we to do in that case? The artistic, pensive, reserved, contemplative, delicately appreciative Hilda can in no wise be re-

lated to the enchanting little housewife, whose energy, radiance, and eglantine sweetness fill her daily homely duties with joy, animation, and fragrance. Tell me, then, is it not so? I utterly protest against being supposed partial because I am Mrs. Hawthorne. But it is so very naughty of you to demolish this new growth in such a hurry, that I cannot help a disclaimer; and I am so sure of your friendliness and largeness, that I am not in the least afraid. You took all the fright out of me by that exquisite, gem-like, aesthetic dinner and tea which you gave us at the fairest of houses last summer. It was a prettier and more *mignonne* thing than I thought could happen in London; so safe, and so quiet, and so very satisfactory, with the light of thought playing all about. I have a good deal of fight left in me still about Kenyon, and the 'of-course' union of Kenyon and Hilda; but I will not say more, except that Mr. Hawthorne had no idea that they were destined for each other. Mr. Hawthorne is driven by his Muse, but does not drive her; and I have known him to be in inextricable doubt in the midst of a book or sketch as to its probable issue, waiting upon the Muse for the rounding in of the sphere which every work of true art is. I am surprised to find that Mr. Hawthorne was so absorbed in Italy that he had no idea that the story, as such, was interesting! and, therefore, is somewhat absolved from having ruthlessly 'excited our interest to voracity.' (pp. 160-61)

I dare say you are laughing (gently) at my explosion of small muskets. But I feel more comfortable now I have discharged a little of my opposition.

With sincere regard, I am, dear Mr. Chorley, yours,

SOPHIA HAWTHORNE.

• • • • •

DEAR MR. CHORLEY:—

You see how fortunate I am in having a critic close at hand, whose favorable verdict consoles me for any lack of appreciation in other quarters. Really, I think you were wrong in assaulting the individuality of my poor Hilda. If her portrait bears any resemblance to that of Phoebe, it must be the fault of my mannerism as a painter. But I thank you for the kind spirit of your notice; and if you had found ten times as much fault, you are amply entitled to do so, by the quantity of generous praise heretofore bestowed.

Sincerely yours,
NATH. HAWTHORNE.
(p. 161)

> *Sophia Hawthorne and Nathaniel Hawthorne, in a letter to Henry Fothergill Chorley on March 5, 1860, in* Hawthorne among His Contemporaries: A Harvest of Estimates, Insights, and Anecdotes from the Victorian Literary World *by Kenneth Walter Cameron, Transcendental Books, 1968, pp. 160-61.*

JOHN LOTHROP MOTLEY (letter date 1860)

[*Motley was a prominent American historian and diplomat. In the following excerpt from a letter to his friend Hawthorne, he expresses his admiration for* The Marble Faun. *Hawthorne showed his appreciation for Motley's remarks in a letter dated 1 April 1860 (see excerpt below).*]

Everything that you have ever written, I believe, I have read many times, and I am particularly vain of having admired

"Sights from a Steeple," when I first read it in the Boston *Token,* several hundred years ago, when we were both younger than we are now; of having detected and cherished, at a later day, an old Apple-Dealer, whom, I believe, you have unhandsomely thrust out of your presence, now that you are grown so great. But the **Romance of Monte Beni** has the additional charm for me, that it is the first book of yours that I have read since I had the privilege of making your personal acquaintance. My memory goes back at once to those walks (alas, not too frequent) we used to take along the Tiber, or in the Campagna; . . . and it is delightful to get hold of the book now, and know that it is impossible for you any longer, after waving your wand as you occasionally did then, indicating where the treasure was hidden, to sink it again beyond plummet's sound.

I admire the book exceedingly. . . . It is one which, for the first reading, at least, I didn't like to hear aloud. . . . If I were composing an article for a review, of course, I should feel obliged to show cause for my admiration; but I am only obeying an impulse. Permit me to say, however, that your style seems, if possible, more perfect than ever. Where, O where is the godmother who gave you to talk pearls and diamonds? . . . . Believe me, I don't say to you half what I say behind your back; and I have said a dozen times that nobody can write English but you. With regard to the story, which has been somewhat criticised, I can only say that to me it is quite satisfactory. I like those shadowy, weird, fantastic, Hawthornesque shapes flitting through the golden gloom, which is the atmosphere of the book. I like the misty way in which the story is indicated rather than revealed; the outlines are quite definite enough from the beginning to the end to those who have imagination enough to follow you in your airy flights; and to those who complain, I suppose that nothing less than an illustrated edition, with a large gallows on the last page, with Donatello in the most pensile of attitudes,—his ears revealed through a white nightcap,—would be satisfactory. I beg your pardon for such profanation, but it really moves my spleen that people should wish to bring down the volatile figures of your romance to the level of an every-day romance. . . . The way in which the two victims dance through the Carnival on the last day is very striking. It is like a Greek tragedy in its effect, without being in the least Greek. (pp. 261-63)

> *John Lothrop Motley, in an extract from a letter to Nathaniel Hawthorne on March 29, 1860, in* A Study of Hawthorne *by George Parsons Lathrop, 1876. Reprint by AMS Press, 1969, pp. 261-63.*

NATHANIEL HAWTHORNE   (letter date 1860)

[*In the following excerpt from a letter to John Lothrop Motley, Hawthorne responds to Motley's letter praising* The Marble Faun *(see excerpt above dated 1860) and thanks his friend for being one of the few to understand the novel.*]

You are certainly that Gentle Reader for whom all my books were exclusively written. Nobody else (my wife excepted, who speaks so near me that I cannot tell her voice from my own) has ever said exactly what I loved to hear. It is most satisfactory to be hit upon the raw, to be shot straight through the heart. It is not the quantity of your praise that I care so much about (though I gather it all up most carefully, lavish as you are of it), but the kind, for you take the book precisely as I meant it; and if your note had come a few days sooner,

I believe I would have printed it in a postscript which I have added to the second edition [see essay dated 1860], because it explains better than I found possible to do the way in which my romance ought to be taken. . . . Now don't suppose that I fancy the book to be a tenth part as good as you say it is. You work out my imperfect efforts, and half make the book with your warm imagination; and see what I myself saw, but could only hint at. Well, the romance is a success, even if it never finds another reader. (p. 263)

> *Nathaniel Hawthorne, in an extract from a letter to John Lothrop Motley on April 1, 1860, in* A Study of Hawthorne *by George Parsons Lathrop, 1876. Reprint by AMS Press, 1969, pp. 263-64.*

THE TIMES, LONDON   (essay date 1860)

[*This reviewer focuses on the imaginative, mythological power of* The Marble Faun *(referred to by the critic as* Transformation, *the title it was published under in England).*]

It may be tempting to make sport of a poet's dream, and the occasion is here ready to our inclinations. Mr. Hawthorne is a poet, and his **Transformation** is a dream, airy and illusory, enticing us to hot pursuit or leaving us to a sense of emptiness and ridicule. What is our proper province in a case like this? What have *we* to do with shadows or ethereal semblances? Even art has more solid materials for our investigation and opinion. We have, at all events, a shadow or rarefaction here, evoked by a poetical imagination from its contact with known facts. It may be tempting, as we have said, to keep within the domain of these facts, and to pour a contemptuous commentary on the fancies which have sprung out of them. But it is a temptation which we shall wisely resist in the interests of a higher art than comes ordinarily to the reader's closet or the critic's tribunal. We will only state as a preliminary that this is an ideal romance, of which the dust of modern Rome is something more than the background, and in which its hoary monuments each play their part. The expectants of satire will understand our abstinence when we tell them that, among other transcendental processes, the Faun of Praxiteles walks down from its pedestal and becomes the most prominent of the *dramatis personae.* On the other hand, those who welcome a work of pure phantasy will appreciate the ideal with reference to which it was moulded. A familiar marble statue is endued with a soul, and this soul is rigorously burdened with moral responsibilities beneath which it tends steadily to grow and develope itself. Strange as it may sound, this conception is not altogether new. The principle of this Roman dream is an echo of other dreams, and the **Transformation** of Mr. Hawthorne, thus freely effected, combines the feat of Pygmalion with the life ordeal of Undine.

We may wish to pass a balanced judgment on the artistic result, or at least to give the true *rationale* of the process. But when a work of imagination differs from the ordinary standard the task of the critic may be easy or it may be exceedingly difficult. It is easy to note and condemn certain deviations, which are unequivocal lapses, and the eccentricity, which is both an aberration and a weakness. The singularities of infirmity are the easiest blots to hit, for, like other blotches and distortions, they simply disfigure a type, and have nothing to commend their harsh departures from nature. But there are cases in which natural types have been and may be set aside for airy conceptions to which the world rightfully renders homage. Such conceptions belong to a truly ideal sphere, and

their congruities of grace and proportion sufficiently vindicate their author's audacity. Criticism abdicates part of its
functions, and accepts such conceptions as types, models—
existences independent and absolute. It allows a true creative
capacity to be a law to itself, nor does it dream of insisting
on the anomalies of tricksy Ariels or Pucks or the impossible
combination of qualities in an Apollo Belvedere.

The art which attains this high impunity is so subtle that it
defies analysis, and yet so definite in its manifestation that it
admits of no dispute. In a book like this before us we at once
admit its presence, perplexing and yet pleasing us, startling
and leading us captive. As far as our knowledge of the world's
present literature extends Mr. Hawthorne possesses more of
this rare capacity than any living writer. His art of expression
is equal to the idealism of his conceptions, and his pure flexible English beguiles his readers into accepting them as among
the sum of probable and natural things. But, none the less,
they are pure transcendentalisms, impalpable to common
sense and unamenable to law. Or rather, as we said, they are
a law to themselves, beyond the convenanted rules and formulas of art, and externally independent of the critical
scheme and dispensation.

If we conceive we are not entitled to assert our jurisdiction
at their expense, we may nevertheless consider the *rationale*
of their origin. There is a peculiar type of the American mind
which is strongly in revolt against American utilities, and
which is predisposed by the very monotony of its surroundings to hues of contrast and attitudes of antagonism. . . .
This impulse induces them to become vagrants in imagination and reality, tourists in the old world of Europe, dreamers
and artificers in the older world of poetry and romance; and
the contrast of that to which they attach themselves, as compared with that which they fly from, is more stimulating than
early association with such influences is to us. We have, in
truth, no parallel among ourselves to the freshness of their enthusiasm and no equivalent to its literary restlessness or *élan.*
Send Mr. Thackeray to Rome, and he goes and comes with
the average impressions of a man of the world, to whom art,
history, and poetry are very passable *entrées,* in addition to,
the ordinary pabulum of a 'fogey' or 'fat contributor.' But the
American artist finds himself in Rome with eyes full of innocent wonder, and a heart thumping against his breast like that
of Aladdin in the cave. He comes, as he observes, from a
country where 'there is no shadow, no antiquity, no mystery,
no picturesque and gloomy wrong nor, anything but a commonplace prosperity, in broad and simple daylight;' and he
stands in the centre of the ruins of the historic world till their
very dust, as it floats in the air, intoxicates him like wine—till
the ghosts of the Capitol dance before him in infinite confusion, like the night concourse of spectres which the magician
of the Coliseum displayed to the excited gaze of Benvenuto
Cellini. The statues and pictures take form and walk, as their
subjects quicken; or at least they seem to the poet's eye to be
struggling out of the tombs into which they are crushed by
a vast heap of vague and ponderous remembrances.

We can easily conceive that Mr. Hawthorne had no intention
at the outset of working such impressions into a story or picture of his own constructing. In fact, from the extent to which
he has introduced descriptions of various Italian objects, antique, pictorial, and statuesque, and, from the very miscellaneous nature of these items, we should rather infer that, in
the first instance, he contemplated a work of descriptive criticism. Be this as it may, there is no work, even of this class,

on Rome and its treasures which brings their details so closely and vividly before us. It is worth all the guide-books we
ever met with, as regards the gems of Italian art, the characteristic features of Roman edifices, and the atmosphere of
Roman life. In fact, we conceive it calculated, in many instances, to impart new views of objects with which travellers
may have imagined themselves already too familiar.

But, as we said, all these artistic and panoramic performances
might have been easily turned to other account, and were
probably sketched with another object, until Mr. Hawthorne,
standing within the gallery of the Capitol, conceived [his]
pregnant theory of the Faun of Praxiteles. . . .

Around this *pedestal,* as it were, of his conception, Mr. Hawthorne weaves a variety of suggestive legends and Arcadian
fillets appropriate to the main figure; and his dream of a modern Faun in the person of Donatello, the last Count of Monte
Beni, actually grows into a portrait by the marvellous skill
and consistency with which it is elaborated. At a later period
we have a picture of Donatello in his Tuscan home, with accessories such as Horace may have cherished at his Sabine
farm, and with the same internal light of a calm rustic felicity.
But the description of Donatello in the gardens of the Villa
Borghese is a more quotable specimen of the ingenious art
which sustains Mr. Hawthorne in his extravagant
audacity. . . .

The association of these two personages is the scaffolding by
which Mr. Hawthorne proceeds to the 'Transformation' of
the Faun's nature on a theory which seems to pervade his
works, that you may so change any nature by burdening it
with heavy responsibilities. It is represented of Miriam that
she has been equivocally involved in some awful catastrophe,
on account of which she is living in retirement and isolation.
A sort of half-mad priest is the depositary of her secret, and
persecutes her incessantly in spite of warnings and prayers.
Donatello is a witness to one of these interviews on the brink
of the Tarpeian Rock, and at a signal of half assent from
Miriam he murders the priest by throwing him headlong.
Thenceforth he and Miriam are bound together by the consciousness of their common crime, while this consciousness
subdues and shatters the nature of Donatello and leads up by
degrees to his so-called 'Transformation.' The last steps of
this process are not very happy, nor is their result clear, but
the harmony of the conception is sustained even when its outlines are blurred and Donatello is losing his affinity to the
wild creatures of the woods. . . .

From this point, which is midway in the second volume, Mr.
Hawthorne's purpose evidently falters, and there is comparatively a falling short of the intended result. The attentive
reader cannot fail to perceive this miscarriage. . . .

Thus, as we infer, Mr. Hawthorne has avowedly left us a vigorous sketch, instead of a finished work of art. His Transformation was too subtle a process for his skill to perfect in the
range of pure mythological existences; or, possibly, he was
conscious of a strain in contrasting such supernatural being
with the common every-day life of the Rome around him. At
all events, it is a startling effect to be got out of galleries and
museums, from the hints and suggestions of classified, catalogued art. Our astonishment is moved by the near approach to a great composition under such conditions, and out
of such rigid materials. We are more impressed by Mr. Hawthorne's success up to a certain point than by the shortcomings which render this success imperfect; and, like the gazers

on the sky in mythologic times, we are surprised that the wings of Icarus should bear him so far, instead of being amazed that they should dissolve so soon.

There is another female character, introduced as a foil to Miriam, and the happy issue of her intercourse with Kenyon is obviously designed as a contrast to the misery of the union which commences in crime. Otherwise Hilda is not worth much in our eyes, nor, we suspect, in Mr. Hawthorne's. Nor is there any explanation of the mystery which surrounds Miriam herself, which may or may not be considered a fault, at the option of the reader. Minor intricacies we do not remark, and minor blemishes we are indifferent to. Our desire has been to arrive at the central principle of a work of exceptional aim and singular beauty, and to convey this idea definitely to our readers. We find here the nucleus of a clear conception, which is for the most part luminous, though in its outer diffusion it lapses into vapour. So we recognize the power of an artistic Prospero over the cloudy forms and hues of dreamland; while there is so much originality in the shapes into which he attempts to mould them that, though the effect is incomplete, the effort is a work of genius.

A review of "Transformation," in The Times, *London, April 7, 1860, p. 5.*

NATHANIEL HAWTHORNE   (letter date 1860)

[*In this excerpt from a letter to James T. Fields, Hawthorne comments on the early critical reaction to* The Marble Faun. *This letter was first published in 1872 in Fields's* Yesterdays with Authors.]

[*The Marble Faun*] has done better than I thought it would; for you will have discovered, by this time, that it is an audacious attempt to impose a tissue of absurdities upon the public by the mere art of style of narrative. I hardly hoped that it would go down with John Bull; but then it is always my best point of writing, to undertake such a task, and I really put what strength I have into many parts of this book.

The English critics generally (with two or three unimportant exceptions) have been sufficiently favorable, and the review in the *Times* [see excerpt dated 1860] awarded the highest praise of all. At home, too, the notices have been very kind, so far as they have come under my eye. Lowell had a good one in the *Atlantic Monthly* [see excerpt dated 1860 in *NCLC,* Vol. 2], and Hillard an excellent one in the *Courier;* and yesterday I received a sheet of the May number of the *Atlantic* containing a really keen and profound article by Whipple [see excerpt dated 1860 in *NCLC,* Vol. 2], in which he goes over all my works, and recognizes that element of unpopularity which (as nobody knows better than myself) pervades them all. I agree with almost all he says, except that I am conscious of not deserving nearly so much praise. When I get home, I will try to write a more genial book; but the Devil himself always seems to get into my inkstand, and I can only exorcise him by penful at a time.

Nathaniel Hawthorne, in an extract from a letter to James T. Fields in April, 1860, in Hawthorne among His Contemporaries: A Harvest of Estimates, Insights, and Anecdotes from the Victorian Literary World *by Kenneth Walter Cameron, Transcendental Books, 1968, p. 322.*

NATHANIEL HAWTHORNE   (essay date 1860)

[*Hawthorne appended this explanatory postscript to the second edition of* The Marble Faun *in response to readers who had found the novel too obscure.*]

There comes to the Author, from many readers of the foregoing pages, a demand for further elucidations respecting the mysteries of the story.

He reluctantly avails himself of the opportunity afforded by a new edition, to explain such incidents and passages as may have been left too much in the dark; reluctantly, he repeats, because the necessity makes him sensible that he can have succeeded but imperfectly, at best, in throwing about this Romance the kind of atmosphere essential to the effect at which he aimed. He designed the story and the characters to bear, of course, a certain relation to human nature and human life, but still to be so artfully and airily removed from our mundane sphere, that some laws and properties of their own should be implicitly and insensibly acknowledged.

The idea of the modern Faun, for example, loses all the poetry and beauty which the Author fancied in it, and becomes nothing better than a grotesque absurdity, if we bring it into the actual light of day. He had hoped to mystify this anomalous creature between the Real and the Fantastic, in such a manner that the reader's sympathies might be excited to a certain pleasurable degree, without impelling him to ask how Cuvier would have classified poor Donatello, or to insist upon being told, in so many words, whether he had furry ears or no. As respects all who ask such questions, the book is, to that extent, a failure.

Nevertheless, the Author fortunately has it in his power to throw light upon several matters in which some of his readers appear to feel an interest. To confess the truth, he was himself troubled with a curiosity similar to that which he has just deprecated on the part of his readers, and once took occasion to cross-examine his friends, Hilda and the sculptor, and to pry into several dark recesses of the story, with which they had heretofore imperfectly acquainted him.

We three had climbed to the top of Saint Peter's, and were looking down upon the Rome which we were soon to leave, but which (having already sinned sufficiently in that way) it is not my purpose further to describe. It occurred to me that, being so remote in the upper air, my friends might safely utter, here, the secrets which it would be perilous even to whisper on lower earth.

"Hilda," I began, "can you tell me the contents of the mysterious pacquet which Miriam entrusted to your charge, and which was addressed to 'Signor Luca Barboni, at the Palazzo Cenci'?"

"I never had any further knowledge of it," replied Hilda, "nor felt it right to let myself be curious upon the subject."

"As to its precise contents," interposed Kenyon, "it is impossible to speak. But Miriam, isolated as she seemed, had family connections in Rome, one of whom, there is reason to believe, occupied a position in the Papal Government. This Signor Luca Barboni was either the assumed name of the personage in question, or the medium of communication between that individual and Miriam. Now, under such a government as that of Rome, it is obvious that Miriam's privacy and isolated life could only be maintained through the connivance and support of some influential person, connected with the administration of affairs. Free and self-controlled as she appeared, her every movement was watched and investigated far more thoroughly by the priestly rulers than by her dearest friends. Miriam, if I mistake not, had a purpose to withdraw herself from this irksome scrutiny, and to seek real obscurity in another land; and the pacquet, to be delivered long after her departure, contained a reference to this design, besides certain family documents, which were to be imparted to her relative as from one dead and gone."

"Yes; it is clear as a London fog," I remarked. "On this head no further elucidation can be desired. But when Hilda went quietly to deliver the pacquet, why did she so mysteriously vanish?"

"You must recollect," replied Kenyon, with a glance of friendly commiseration at my obtuseness, "that Miriam had utterly disappeared, leaving no trace by which her whereabout could be known. In the mean time, the municipal authorities had become aware of the murder of the Capuchin; and, from many preceding circumstances, such as his strange persecution of Miriam, they must have been led to see an obvious connection between herself and that tragical event. Furthermore, there is reason to believe that Miriam was suspected of implication with some plot or political intrigue, of which there may have been tokens in the pacquet. And when Hilda appeared as the bearer of this missive, it was really quite a matter of course, under a despotic government, that she should be detained."

"Ah! quite a matter of course, as you say," answered I. "How excessively stupid in me not to have seen it sooner! But there are other riddles. On the night of the extinction of the lamp, you met Donatello in a penitent's garb, and afterwards saw and spoke to Miriam, in a coach, with a gem glowing on her bosom. What was the business of these two guilty ones in Rome? And who was Miriam's companion?"

"Who?" repeated Kenyon. "Why, her official relative, to be sure; and as to their business, Donatello's still gnawing remorse had brought him hitherward, in spite of Miriam's entreaties, and kept him lingering in the neighborhood of Rome, with the ultimate purpose of delivering himself up to justice. Hilda's disappearance, which took place the day before, was known to them through a secret channel, and had brought them into the city, where Miriam, as I surmise, began to make arrangements, even then, for that sad frolic of the Carnival."

"And where was Hilda, all that dreary time between?" inquired I.

"Where were you, Hilda?" asked Kenyon, smiling.

Hilda threw her eyes on all sides, and seeing that there was not even a bird of the air to fly away with the secret, nor any human being nearer than the loiterers by the obelisk, in the piazza below, she told us about her mysterious abode.

"I was a prisoner in the Convent of the Sacré Coeur, in the Trinità de' Monti," said she; "but in such kindly custody of pious maidens, and watched over by such a dear old priest, that—had it not been for one or two disturbing recollections, and also because I am a daughter of the Puritans—I could willingly have dwelt there forever. My entanglement with Miriam's misfortunes, and the good Abbate's mistaken hope

of a proselyte, seem to me a sufficient clue to the whole mystery."

"The atmosphere is getting delightfully lucid," observed I, "but there are one or two things that still puzzle me. Could you tell me—and it shall be kept a profound secret, I assure you—what were Miriam's real name and rank, and precisely the nature of the trouble that led to all these direful consequences?"

"Is it possible that you need an answer to these questions?" exclaimed Kenyon, with an aspect of vast surprise. "Have you not even surmised Miriam's name? Think awhile, and you will assuredly remember it. If not, I congratulate you most sincerely; for it indicates that your feelings have never been harrowed by one of the most dreadful and mysterious events that have occurred within the present century."

"Well," resumed I, after an interval of deep consideration, "I have but few things more to ask. Where, at this moment, is Donatello?"

"In prison," said Kenyon, sadly.

"And why, then, is Miriam at large?" I asked.

"Call it cruelty, if you like—not mercy!" answered Kenyon. "But, after all, her crime lay merely in a glance; she did no murder."

"Only one question more," said I, with intense earnestness. "Did Donatello's ears resemble those of the Faun of Praxiteles?"

"I know, but may not tell," replied Kenyon, smiling mysteriously. "On that point, at all events, there shall be not one word of explanation." (pp. 463-67)

> *Nathaniel Hawthorne, in a postscript to his* The Marble Faun; or, The Romance of Monte Beni, *1860. Reprint by Ohio State University Press, 1968, pp. 463-67.*

[MARTHA T. GALE]   (essay date 1861)

[*Gale interprets* The Marble Faun *as a religious allegory.*]

It is not surprising that the writings of Nathaniel Hawthorne should be little read, and less liked, by the mass of straightforward, common-sense people, of Calvinistic views,—for while he seldom directly opposes the orthodox doctrines of religion, we look in vain for any recognition of them in his works. In fact the class of readers who thoroughly appreciate and enjoy them is small. The complaint is almost universally made, that his views of life are altogether too gloomy and morbid.

For ourselves, while he evinces so little conception of the remedial system which God has provided for the sins and sorrows of mankind; while he dwells so much upon gloomy wrongs, and portrays the horrors of remorse, without showing its only legitimate relief,—hope of pardon through an atoning Saviour,—we do not consider him a healthy writer, and cannot recommend the perusal of his works to immature and undiscriminating minds. Yet to reflective, imaginative readers, for whom Hawthorne more especially writes, his works are richly suggestive, though not always a source of unqualified enjoyment. But even among these, we suspect there are many who fail to penetrate the hidden meaning which generally lurks beneath his fanciful tales. We think this must be especially true with reference to his latest work,—*The Marble Faun*,—for though great admiration is expressed for the exquisite descriptions of art and nature which it contains, we hear continual complaint of the obscurity of the story, and its strange and unsatisfactory conclusion. Taking it merely as a story, no doubt there is ground for such complaints, but we must remember that Hawthorne is no mere novelist; many of his stories are allegories, unfolding some ethereal fancy, or important truth. (pp. 860-61)

We understand that the four principal characters in the story personify the different elements which we perceive in our strangely-molded natures; the Soul or Will, whichever we may call it; the Conscience or Intuitive power; the Reason or Intellect; and lastly, the Animal Nature, or Body. These four we find united in companionship, and in a state of comparative isolation from all others. They form, so to speak, a little world in themselves, and are all, for the time being, sojourners in the ancient city of Rome, at a distance from their homes.

The beautiful and courageous Miriam represents the *Soul;* her judicious and honorable friend, the sculptor Kenyon, is the *Reason.* She ever finds in him a wise counselor, but he is too cold and austere to secure her full confidence, or to give her, in her great trial, the warm sympathy she seeks. Rightly is he represented as a worker in marble, even as the Reason deals with truths in their naked severity and coldness. The fair and lovely Hilda admirably personates the *Conscience,* and sustains, throughout, the purity and loftiness of so elevated a character. Sympathizing and kind, tender and true, though dignified and somewhat reserved, she dwells apart, in the summit of a lofty tower, above the dust and miasma of the city; and though she comes down, and walks the filthy streets of Rome, her white robe is unsoiled, and she returns at night to feed her companions, the white doves, (pure thoughts and desires), and to keep the flame burning on the altar of Prayer. The others often refer to her as having a finer perception of the beautiful and true, than themselves; and though they sometimes complain that her standard of virtue is too high for them to reach, and her judgment upon their opinions and conduct too severe, yet they are never satisfied that theirs is correct, unless it coincides with hers.

Miriam and Hilda are both artists, for our nature was formed to enjoy and to produce the beautiful, although Hilda does not now originate pictures, as in her native home, but copies from the old masters; that is, the Conscience refers us to the eternal standards of Right and Wrong. Associated with these high-souled friends, we find a gay and thoughtless youth, so simple-minded and careless that they regard him as a mere child in understanding, yet his graceful beauty and mirthfulness, and especially his affectionate and winning manners, afford them so much pleasure that they admit him to constant companionship. This is Donatello, who represents the *Animal Nature.* Kenyon woos Hilda with an admiration bordering upon reverence, and Donatello passionately loves Miriam, though neither finds his affection at first fully reciprocated; Miriam indeed often regards the childishness of Donatello with contempt. But after Hilda has sprained her delicate wrist, she grasps the strong hand of Kenyon; and when Miriam finds herself cast off by Hilda, and regarded with suspicion by Kenyon, she clings tenaciously to the tenderness yet remaining for her in the heart of Donatello. That is, when the Conscience has been weakened by intercourse

with guilt, it is glad to lean somewhat upon the understanding; and after the Soul has become debased by crime, she loses much of her dignity and delicacy, and is even willing to confess, in the most humiliating manner, her subjection to the Body, and dependence upon it for happiness. "I lost all pride," says Miriam, "when Hilda cast me off."

Before his contact with guilt, Donatello is in a state of perfect, though childlike, enjoyment. He is in sympathy with the animal creation; understands the language of beasts and birds, and they come at his call. Whether he has really pointed and furry ears, being himself only an improved animal, we are left in doubt even at the end of the story.

That mysterious verse in the third chapter of Genesis: "And the Lord God said, Behold the man has become as one of us, to know good and evil; and now lest he put forth his hand and take also of the tree of life, and eat, and live forever;" appears to have started in the mind of our author the question, "Whether sin has not been the means of bringing a simple and imperfect nature to a point of feeling and intelligence, which it could have reached in no other way?" This idea he introduces again and again; but he evidently sees the great objections to which it is liable, for he represents Kenyon (the *Reason*) as replying to Miriam, when she asks this question: "I dare not follow you into the unfathomable abyss, whither you are tending. Mortal man has no right to tread where you now set your feet." And again, when Kenyon asks Hilda, "Is sin then, like sorrow, merely an element of human education, through which we struggle to a higher and purer state than we could otherwise have attained?"—the Conscience answers: "Do you not perceive what a mockery such a creed makes not only of all religious sentiments, but of moral law, and how it annuls and obliterates whatever precepts of heaven are written deepest within us? You have shocked me beyond words!"

In the very outset of the story, our party of four together visit the Catacombs. Prompted by a vain curiosity, the ill-fated Miriam wanders from her companions, and is for a moment lost in that labyrinth of tombs. In those sepulchral caverns she meets with a hideous mendicant monk, wandering there for penance, who now emerges with her into the light of day. He appears acquainted with her early history, alludes to crimes committed in the past with which they are both in some way connected, and declares that now he has found her, he will never again lose sight of her. He keeps his word, following her, from that day forward, like her very shadow, and darkening with his repulsive aspect every path she treads. Sometimes he stands suddenly before her, in the midst of the gayest dance; again, she seeks his dark features reflected from over her shoulder, in a moonlit fountain. Often he waits for her, at nightfall, in the obscurity of some ruined arch, and follows her stealthily home in the dusk of twilight. Though he is not always near her, being absent sometimes for days together, yet she is ever liable to his intrusion, and cannot by any entreaties prevail upon him to leave her entirely. So haunted is she by his disagreeable features, that they creep, imperceptibly to her, even into her best pictures, and injure the effect, so that not only is her life embittered by his persecution, but her prospect of excelling in her art seems blighted. Wandering in darkness, the soul has encountered the demon of *Temptation,* who, for some unexplained reason hidden in the past, some political crime of her ancestors, it is suggested, (the allusion is evidently to the sin of Adam), claims the right to pursue her.

We are taught that sin came at first through the animal nature, (Eve ate an apple), and the inducements to many of its forms are still presented through the bodily appetites. They are always more or less excited by temptation, but the soul can restrain them, and does, when she remains true to her high trust. So we see Donatello exasperated whenever the monk appears; but Miriam continually soothes and quiets him, and prevents any violent outbreak of passion. At last, however, when both are irritated to the utmost degree by his persistent intrusion, Donatello, with an animal rage, holds the hated man over the brink of the precipice, at the Tarpeian rock, and looks to Miriam for permission to throw him off.

They are alone—without the restraining presence of either Hilda or Kenyon. In her excitement, Miriam forgets to restrain herself, or exercise her usual control over him who turns to her for guidance. By a look of sympathy and encouragement, she consents,—and the dreadful deed of murder is done, which, afterwards, they would give worlds to undo.

The soul, by its silent acquiescence, must consent, or there can be no transgression of moral law. Temptation has done its work; the deadly sin has been committed; we next behold its consequences. For a moment, Miriam and Donatello exulted in that brief sense of freedom which violators of law always at first enjoy; but this is quickly followed by an unutterable horror in view of their crime, which gives place only to a life-long remorse. This remorse is, for a time, alleviated by a sense of companionship in sin. The author has here shown the subtlest analysis of thought and feeling. Is not the consideration that we are not alone in sin, the first and only relief that comes to the mind aroused to a sense of guilt? We mean, of course, aside from any hope of pardon. We say immediately: "we are not alone! there are others as guilty as ourselves." But this very thought soon turns to a new instrument of torture. There is companionship, indeed,—but what terrible companionship! To use the words of Hawthorne: "A crowded thoroughfare, and jostling throng of criminals. It is a terrible thought that an individual wrong-doing melts into the great mass of human crime, and makes us—who dreamed only of our own little separate sin—makes us guilty of the whole. And thus Miriam and her lover were not an insulated pair, but members of an innumerable confraternity of guilty ones, all shuddering at each other."

The next day they meet Kenyon, by appointment, at the church of the Capuchins, before Guido's picture of the Archangel Michael setting his foot upon the Tempter, for the purpose of ascertaining whether the face of the demon does not resemble that of Miriam's tormentor. Here they find themselves confronted by the evidence of their guilt in the corpse of the murdered monk, laid out in the garb of a Capuchin friar, with his cross and rosary, and candles burning around him. In the scene which follows, our author has not only faithfully delineated the courage and endurance which the soul develops in emergencies, but has shown his nice observation of its most hidden workings.

Though appalled at the awful spectacle, Miriam leads the shuddering Donatello close to the side of the dead monk, saying: "The only way in such cases, is to stare the ugly horror right in the face. Never a sidelong glance, nor a half-look, for those are what show a frightful thing in its frightfulest aspect. Lean on me, dearest friend; my heart is strong for both of us."

More than this, she goes back alone, and confronts the severe, reproachful glances that come from the half closed eyes of the murdered man; yes, even touches the cold hands of the corpse, to assure herself that the likeness to her former enemy is not an illusion.

Thus the soul cannot, if it would, ignore its guilt. Painful as is the theme, the thoughts are perpetually recurring to it; so that after vaguely hoping for a while that it is some dreadful dream that haunts us, some illusion that will presently vanish, we generally conclude, either in case of any overwhelming sorrow or oppressive sense of sin, that it is wisest to contemplate it steadily, till we have calmly decided just how much is real, and how much imaginary, and then brace ourselves to bear the worst.

Miriam and Donatello supposed themselves to be alone when he threw the monk over the precipice, (but the conscience is ever watchful over the soul, and especially in its hour of trial), and Hilda had noticed the monk gliding stealthily after Miriam, and returned to seek her friend. Through the half-opened gate of the court-yard she witnessed the deed of blood; then hurried away, with that deathly sickness of heart which the innocent suffer when they discover guilt in those whom they have loved and trusted, to stretch her hands towards heaven, and tell her disappointment only to her God.

The next interview between these friends, the meeting of the Soul and Conscience after sin, is beautifully delineated, and shows how innocence suffers from the mere knowledge of sin in others, and much more from direct contact with guilt. Up to this time they had delighted in each other's society. Miriam had said, "Nothing insures me such delightful and innocent dreams, as a talk late at night with Hilda." Now she fears, while she longs to meet that "white-robed friend," whose kind approval can give the soul a purer joy than the applause of all the world beside. But with truly noble courage she stills her beating heart, and climbs the long stairway of Hilda's tower.

With what a grieved severity Hilda motions her away, and warns her that their intimacy is now at an end! With what accuracy she explains to her the nature and extent of her guilt, replying to her inquiry, "What have I done?" "Ah, Miriam, that look!" "Donatello paused," she says, recounting the events of the night, "while one might draw a breath, but that look, ah, Miriam, that look!"

"It is enough!" replied the now convicted Miriam, bowing her head like a condemned criminal; "you have satisfied my mind on a point where it was greatly disturbed. Henceforward I shall be quiet. Thank you, Hilda."

The Soul, enlightened by Conscience, sees when, where, and just how far she has offended.

It is a well-known fact, that the capacity of pure and innocent physical enjoyment is paralyzed, often destroyed, by vice.

Here notice how completely our poor Donatello is changed. Before, he was the merriest creature in the world, and thought if Miriam could but deign to receive his love, he should be transcendently happy. But now, stupefied with horror at the crime he had committed, he has become incapable of pleasure, and though Miriam (the Soul) is so far degraded as to seek comfort and diversion from him, he can in no way console her. Benumbed and cold, he lies down in hopeless despair, while Miriam vainly strives to rouse him from his stupor, by lavishing upon him every expression of endearment. At last, finding that her presence must augment his grief, by constantly reminding him of his crime, she constrains herself to bid him a sad farewell.

Before sin, we saw him amid the gardens of Rome, reveling in the enjoyment of nature. But now he retires to his lonely castle, and confines himself in apartments formerly used as a prison, spending his days and nights in penance and remorse; that is, in weariness and pain. He no longer drinks the refreshing and fragrant wine of sunshine, for his hope and gladness, or animal spirits, are all gone. Feeling himself unworthy to enjoy the elevated society of his former friends, he exiles himself entirely from them.

"But why," the reader may ask, "are Miriam and Donatello, while so truly attached, so long separated? Can Soul and Body part, before the final division by death?" Certainly not; though they may be, to a certain extent, oblivious of each other. But we find that they were not widely separated. Miriam had followed Donatello to his retirement, though she does not intrude herself upon him, but occupies the stately and long unused apartments of the castle, while he remains secluded in his prison tower. Her presence is indicated to him, however, by the winning melody of her evening song, by which she wooes his return to her; an invitation which he longs, yet fears to accept.

We think Hawthorne here introduces the figure which Bunyan has elaborated in his allegory of the "Holy War," in the town of Mansoul. The nobler faculties of man are a constant reproof to any animal excess, and remind the fallen one of his debasement, so that any lapse into vice must necessarily interrupt all sweet communion between the inferior nature and the higher powers of the soul. When a man has yielded to his base passions he shrinks from reflection, nor does he wish to hold converse with his reason or his conscience.

But Kenyon visits Donatello and draws him forth to a better life. After much patient instruction, and many endeavors, he is enabled, under the blessing of heaven, to bring about a reunion between those who had been partially alienated, but who could not but be miserable in estrangement. They are united; but it is "for mutual support, for one another's final good, for effort, for sacrifice, but not for earthly happiness." To sinful man happiness is no longer a legitimate aim; those who seek it, chase a phantom which ever eludes their grasp. It comes, if it comes at all, as a "wayside flower, springing along a path that leads to higher ends."

Meanwhile, Hilda is left alone in Rome, and we are now shown the effect of sin upon the conscience. The loss of confidence in her friend has robbed her life of its joy; her guide and support, the Reason, is also absent. The pestilential air affects her with a dreamy languor; a torpor creeps over her spirit. She wanders gloomily through the vast galleries of art, in which she had formerly delighted, feeling that her keen insight into the spirit of the old masters is dimmed, and her enjoyment of their works wholly gone. She even questions whether they were ever so true and beautiful as she once supposed; for sin sometimes leads us to doubt whether there be any real goodness in the world. At last she throws off some portion of the burden that oppresses her spirits, by confessing her knowledge of the murder to the church. Remembering that Miriam had entrusted to her care a packet of important papers, she goes at the appointed time to deliver it to the authorities of Rome. She then mysteriously disappears, having

been detained by the ministers of justice, until at the return of Miriam and Donatello, full explanation and satisfaction are made. Conscience keeps the moral accounts of the soul, and will present them sooner or later at the tribunal of justice. But conscience herself becomes morbid, and is often brought under bondage to superstition, while sin remains unpunished or unpardoned.

Kenyon, after leaving Miriam and Donatello again united, hastens to seek Hilda in Rome. He finds her at St. Peter's, in the moment when she has relieved her burdened mind at the confessional. He is greatly disturbed to find her so much under the influence of superstition, and still more distressed at her speedy disappearance. For the first time in years, the lamp goes out upon the virgin's shrine, for now prayer is interrupted. He seeks her everywhere in vain, and can obtain no information concerning her until he meets with Miriam, who assures him of her safety and approaching restoration. Miriam, when Kenyon first meets her, appears beautiful as ever, richly dressed as a nobleman's daughter with the bright gem (of *forgiveness*) shining on her breast. He meets her again with Donatello, who has also regained his former grace and beauty, upon the Campagna, where they are spending a few brief days of happiness before their final separation.

The finding of the Venus, which is here narrated, what does it signify? "Beauty for ashes;" joy out of sorrow; *love,* which though mutilated and defaced with clinging earthliness still retains a divine purity and beauty; the only flower of Eden that has survived the fall, and still blossoms on its ruins.

Though manifesting a tender melancholy, both Miriam and Donatello seem now to have attained that state of elevated and tranquil enjoyment which lifts the pardoned soul above all earthly misfortune. For when the heart has gained that great bliss which springs from a sense of forgiveness, it grows so large, so rich, and so variously endowed, that it can bestow smiles on the joys of those around it, give tears to their woes—yes, shed them for sorrows of its own, and still retain a sweet peace throughout all. Yet Donatello continued to wear the penitent's robe, and is determined to give himself up to justice; for though the soul may obtain pardon, neither repentance nor reformation can save the body from suffering for sin, or remit its penalty, which is death. They cling most lovingly together at the last, knowing that their union must be short. And in the midst of the carnival,—for the world may all be merrymaking when our souls and bodies silently part,—there was a little stir among one portion of the crowd, and they were separated; the one to be imprisoned in the dungeons of the tomb; the other to wander lonely, disembodied, we know not how long, but not without hope of a final reunion. "Hilda had a hopeful soul, and saw sunlight on the mountain-tops."

Kenyon finds Hilda, who is released when Donatello surrenders himself to justice, and happy in wedded love they return to their native land. For the land of art and beauty has grown dark to both, since they behold it in the shadow of a crime, and their souls yearn for the home of their childhood. Are not the higher powers of our nature heaven-born, and when united in harmony, and obedience to divine law, should they not tend thitherward?

In his conclusion, the author speaks of a strangely sad event, which has harrowed the feelings of many, with which Miriam was connected. If this be intended as a part of the allegory, we suppose it refers to the Fall of Man. We infer from his narration that the soul is forgiven, but we look in vain for any mention of the merits of an *atoning Saviour.* It cannot be that he deems *remorse* can cancel sin! Why then does he never shed the light of faith over his gloomy pictures of despair? (pp. 861-70)

We wish he would cultivate the simplicity and cheerfulness of Bunyan. The immortal allegory is easily understood, and no doubt one of its great charms, with the multitude, is that the Pilgrim gets safely by the lions, escapes from the Giant Despair, defeats Apolyon, and having left all his burden at the cross, passes hopefully over the river into light. (p. 870)

[*Martha T. Gale*], *in a review of "The Marble Faun," in* The New Englander, *Vol. XIX, No. LXXVI, October, 1861, pp. 860-70.*

JESSIE KINGSLEY CURTIS   (essay date 1892)

[*Curtis interprets* The Marble Faun *as primarily an allegory of the conflict between Puritanism and Roman Catholicism.*]

Nathaniel Hawthorne was sometimes compared by admiring correspondents to Shakespeare. Wherein lay this resemblance? Could two styles be more diverse? With Shakespeare words leap and bound, scream and shriek, moan and groan; but with Hawthorne words march with a magic and musical tread along the pages. His style is a serenade of sounds, but as serene as a summer evening. We must remember that Shakespeare is ever dealing with humanity, and words with him throb with human pulse-beats; while Hawthorne is dealing with the attributes of humanity, and words lose their substance in the sentence that enshrines them.

In characters, Shakespeare has run the entire gamut of human passion, mastering alike the "base and the sublime." Nathaniel Hawthorne has given only a few characters, all related. Phoebe and Hilda, Kenyon and Coverdale, Zenobia and Miriam, Chillingworth and the Monk, Arthur and Clifford, Pansy and Pearl,—how they pair off like twin gems in different settings. Yet in one respect Hawthorne belongs with all the greatest literatures. There is an unknown quantity which the reader must discover for himself, and this algebraic value may vary with the individual. As every sect reads into Scripture its own sectarianism, as every speculator reads into Shakespeare his own speculations, so every thinker can read into Hawthorne his own thoughts. This is particularly true of *The Marble Faun* or *The Transformation,* over which hangs a mystery that the author has left for the reader to penetrate.

One vital mistake has been made by many. They have taken *The Marble Faun* as a guide to Rome; almost as a picture of Italy. It gives neither Rome nor Italy. (p. 139)

Nathaniel Hawthorne is too original and too patriotic to write historical novels, such as Scott's and Bulwer's, unless they be American. He is too intensely imbued with the sentiments of the New World to enjoy and appreciate the real sentiments of the Old World. He has certain problems of life that he is seeking to solve, and these are more important to him and to us than any pictures of places. This is the problem of the Puritan—sin; hence *The Marble Faun* has its own aesthetic and ethical value, but it has no value as a piece of art-criticism or as portrait history. It shows the New World gaz-

ing on the Old World, but keeping itself apart. It is Puritanism facing Popery.

In *The Marble Faun,* Hawthorne has almost returned to his first thought, and a parallel might be drawn with *The Scarlet Letter.* Four characters form the story. Sin is the source of thought. In *The Scarlet Letter* the sin is in the past; remorse, revenge, and repentance are in the present. We are studying the progress of these passions, their effect upon each other as well as upon individuals. In *The Marble Faun* the sin is told in the story; and we are studying the changes in character wrought by wrong. One evil genius haunts the story and, finally, leads two persons to crime. In *The Scarlet Letter,* we have the penetrating power of sin and its effect upon society; in *The Marble Faun* we have sin suddenly changing into crime, and the effect of crime on character. *The Scarlet Letter* gives the social attitude towards sin; *The Marble Faun,* the personal attitude towards crime. Both make sin the source of sympathy, and repentance the only road of development. Both have a symbolic meaning behind the story as well as philosophic thought in the story.

The great mystery of *The Marble Faun* is the evil genius that haunts all the scenes, that sometimes seems a person and ofttimes a myth. Who is this ugly, horrid being that emerges from the dismal catacombs and haunts the steps of Miriam? Mr. Lathrop suggests that it is Miriam's father, and that her story is the Cenci story; hence the murder is just human judgment translated as divine justice. This is the only plausible excuse for spending so much time over Guido's pictures. But the later chapters seem to imply that he is a lunatic cousin-lover. There seems to have been some hideous sin in the past. This sin, over which Zola might gloat, Hawthorne scarcely touches. It is the sinner, not the sin, that he would study. It is the effect of sin on mortals that he seeks to explain. Miriam, from the past, has felt its influence by some bitter and baneful experience. Pictures portray more than form to her. Even Guido can furnish thought, for the Beatrice suggests herself. Of all this little company, she only, like Eve, has "tasted of the tree of knowledge," and its bitterness and beguilements furnish ideas. Miriam has a wondrous and bewitching beauty. She possesses great personal charms, but she lacks in soul. She too often obtrudes herself, like Zenobia. Miriam is sweetest and tenderest after her crime, when there is a soul to save,—the soul she has led astray. When her life is given up, her new life-work is begun,—the salvation of the Faun.

The Faun is a being without soul, not like Miriam, by distance from nature, but by nearness to nature. The trees are his sisters; the birds are his brothers; the tiny insects gather over him in love. The voice of nature is his voice; and all the creations of nature understand his tongue. Art has no ideas for him. Life has but one call,—pleasure. Every step is a blithesome bound. Every look is a gladsome glance. Yet this being sins, sins to save another. From this time the old self is laid aside and a new self arises,—soul, manhood. He has now a life-work, penitence; he has the means of growth, salvation of self. The thoughtless is made thoughtful; the dreamer a doer; the lover of nature rises into the lover of men.

Hilda is the pure, exquisite being,—soul personified. She so makes herself a part of what she sees that she can transfer the diverse and idiomatic in early art to new canvases in a new era, while each picture keeps its special individuality and complete identity. Hilda is the perfect copyist because her own soul has become permeated with the aspirations of other souls. As the clean, white sheet receives most readily the rays through the camera, so the purity of Hilda's soul makes her an imitator rather than an inventor. Here she contrasts with Miriam, who is always casting her own sorrow-scrawled soul upon the waiting canvas. She always looks beyond the artist into ideas he failed to furnish. Hilda keeps to this character after the crime, which she simply sees, does not commit. Yet to see crime, to the pure, is to become criminal. To touch the soul with evil is to taint it. Silence may be falsehood, the burdened heart must unburden itself. Then there is the quick conscience, the Puritan girl, purifying herself from the sins of others. What a picture is that,—this new world of ours standing at the confessional in old St. Peter's! Sin makes the sameness of the centuries. Sin binds all nations, all religions, into one brotherhood, and penitence is the only progress, confession the only conquest. Hilda, in her horror of Miriam, the sinful, shows the pathless space that lies between men and angels, the need of a divine being to bridge the way from humanity to heaven; the atonement that shall bind sinner and sinless by a chain never forged upon the earth.

Kenyon is just a looker on; a teacher in times of trial; an earth guide, through the labyrinth of life. He is a friend to all.

Such is the story taken simply as a story. But here, as elsewhere, Hawthorne has a symbolic meaning. Miriam is the Roman Catholic Church, with "its revenues levied on the imagination," beautiful and brilliant, ever appealing to the eye, to the artistic rather than to the moral sense. Crimes have sheltered themselves under her name, but she herself is not a criminal, though, alas, often was she a tempter. And many men, like the Faun, have fallen for her sake. These sins, committed in her name, are forever haunting her soul. The bracelet of seven brilliant jewels, taken from seven sepulchres, what are they but the seven dead churches of Asia out of which Roman Catholicism had its birth and its being? Miriam's charms are of the beautiful and bewitching type, gorgeous and grand, but seldom soothing to the soul. The brilliant jewel which Miriam wears upon her breast, after this secret and solemn union with the Faun, is ritualism, her present glory.

Hilda is Puritanism, the soul superseding all its externals, New England her natural birthplace, purity preceding love in all the relations of life. The dove, symbol of the Holy Spirit, hovers about her abiding place. The lonely tower, reaching heavenward, is her home. The lamp, ever burning before the shrine, symbolizes prayer. Lofty are her longings, solitary is her summer, stern is she towards the criminal, repentless are her judgments. She cannot "look upon sin with any degree of allowance." Hating all idolatry, she would make herself a god by her own inexorable standards. Again do we see New England, but in a new form. Not Puritanism facing a single sinner, as in *The Scarlet Letter,* but Puritanism facing the church that she believes to be false. Never does she taunt, but always does she hold herself aloof "in silent and shivering solitude." That awful cry of her agonized sister, "Help, friends, help," never touches her stony ear. As the ice is hard and the snow is cold, yet both are pure, even when they freeze this body of ours, such also is the human heart when it has no look of love, no help for sinning man; such, also, is Puritanism when presented as authority, as conscience. Hilda receives the long preserved packet from Miriam and carries it to a lonely castle. What is this but the Bible which Catholicism preserved, but Puritanism took to the printer in his lonely castle? Again, she wears as her sole ornament that marvelous bracelet; just as Puritanism claims those seven old

churches, not ritualism, as her sole ornament. This she wears upon her wrist, the wrist of the hand of power. Again, she is hidden for a season, as Puritanism was persecuted when she first revealed the evils of Catholicism, but she returns in the midst of the Carnival, and, amid the mad rush of men, she tosses the rose, a pure and perfect flower,—love of truth,— and it is caught by Kenyon on the Corso, by Reason in the midst of riot.

The Faun is the early Greek, the old heathen world, nature personified; joyous in his life, heir to the "sunshine," ever glad and gay, he is also beauty personified. Then he becomes bound to the Roman Catholic Church, not by marriage, but by crime, as Paganism and Romanism are joined together in the sin of idolatry, a sin which Puritanism most of all dreaded and despised. At last this Faun drags out his life in some subterranean vault of Rome; as Greek statues are shut up in Roman churches and palaces, as the old pagan temples lie beneath or within the Roman churches.

Kenyon, the sculptor, working in marble cold and clear, changing the ideal into form and fitness for this human vision of ours, is Reason. And this Reason, that at first seemed a mere spectator, now becomes the guide to all,—to pure but pitiless Puritanism, to gorgeous and grieving Romanism, to once happy now sorrowing Paganism. He finally chooses, as a bride, Puritanism, and leads her out to a larger look upon life. Puritanism wedded to Reason shows a new mercy and a deeper tenderness for the fallen friends.

Who, then, is that dark and dreaded being who haunts Miriam as model and as monk, ever threatening, often protecting, at last slain,—slain by a glance? Is not this Tradition? He comes from the Catacombs, where Christian Rome began, and which Catholic Rome robbed of its innocent young life. Miriam is forever asserting her innocence; but crime haunts her history, and Tradition follows her everywhere, to the studio where Catholicism has done her grandest and most gracious work, out to the fountains and the fields, gifts from the popes to the Roman people. His first haunt is the catacombs, his last is the Coliseum; both places Catholicism has claimed from Fate. This spirit of Tradition has been forever spending itself on Rome, has often threatened it like old Fate itself, with danger and destruction, but at last is dashed to pieces on the Tarpeian rock, History. Rome rides along in her carriage, Paganism is buried in the vault of her church, Ritualism, regal as a jewel, shines upon her breast, while Tradition is dead, because history marks the descent of Time.

The statue of love, found by Reason, begrimed and broken with earth-injuries, is next viewed by Catholicism and Paganism. In the desolation of the Campagna, these three unite in their admiration and joy over this legacy from the past. Puritanism is not present. She does not find the earth-love until she has wedded Reason; although she clung with a love beyond that of earth to her own ideals, prayer, purity, conscience.

Thus while *The Marble Faun* fails as a faithful portrait of Rome, sole harbor of the ages of the arts, it is most faithful as a symbolic picture of Rome as a religion: Rome descendant of the Jew, Paganism her subject, Tradition ever following her; Rome longing for the aid of Reason, yet failing to seek it when Reason would have saved her; and lastly, Rome the horror of the Puritan.

The real story and the symbolic often run into one, and Hawthorne means they should. It is not a mixed metaphor, but one great truth entering into each. Bunyan's allegories are like axioms, self-evident truths. Hawthorne's are always problems, profound and occult, and to be fully understood they require as much study as Shakespeare. You must discover for yourself their interpretation, for Nathaniel Hawthorne never supplies brains to his readers. Most delightful are they simply as stories, yet read only as stories you lose their deepest meaning; just as when you make the Scriptures too literal and thus lose the largeness of their thought.

In studying Hawthorne we must remember that he is the exponent of Puritanism; that he is first and foremost an American. (pp. 141-46)

While Nathaniel Hawthorne belongs to all time, he is of one time. Long has the world claimed him, but he remains always a New Englander, "an absolute, solitary, and original genius," and our very own. He is ever searching for humanity, and he is always finding Puritanism. This Puritanism he gives with all its awful faults, with all its vital truths, with all its intense nature. Born on July 4, he is of right the highest literary exponent of America's greatest gift to the world. What Abraham Lincoln has furnished in manhood, that Nathaniel Hawthorne has furnished in literature.

> New birth of the new soil, the first American.

Mr. James repeatedly repeats, in his Hawthorne volume, the adjective "provincial" [see excerpt dated 1879 in *NCLC*, Vol. 2]. Perhaps this word is more goodly than it seems. If to be the best outcome of a country, to be the true representative of its highest thought, is to be provincial, then Hawthorne should be ranked with Homer, Dante, Shakespeare, Goethe, Burns, Balzac,—men so intensely national that they become universal, so permeated with place that they possess infinity. Greek, Tuscan, Saxon, German, Scot, French,—with these America has taken her place. Shall we be ashamed of our Puritanic provincialism when we have added the seventh in the masters of human passion? That seventh is Nathaniel Hawthorne. (pp. 146-47)

> *Jessie Kingsley Curtis, in a review of "The Marble Faun," in* The Andover Review, *Vol. XVIII, No. CIV, August, 1892, pp. 139-47.*

CARL VAN DOREN   (essay date 1920)

[*Van Doren is considered one of the most perceptive American critics of the first half of the twentieth century. He worked for many years as a professor of English at Columbia University and served as literary editor and critic for the* Nation *and the* Century *during the 1920s. A founder of the Literary Guild, Van Doren wrote and edited several American literary histories and was a critically acclaimed historian and biographer. Howard Moss wrote of him: "His virtues, honesty, clarity, and tolerance, are rare. His vices, occasional dullness and a somewhat monotonous rhetoric, are merely, in most places, the reverse coin of his excellence." In the following excerpt, Van Doren discusses the Puritan elements in* The Marble Faun.]

The Marble Faun is a sort of visitors' guidebook to Rome. And yet ***The Marble Faun,*** though set in an environment so amply pagan and Catholic, is in some respects the most Puritan of all Hawthorne's romances. He who under the gray skies of New England had created Hester and Zenobia, when he came to a world in which they and their kind might have grown to their intended stature, seems to have turned partial-

ly back to an austerer code. Among the children of the Renaissance he missed that sense of sin which in his native province had been as regularly present as sea and hills. Genial as were the pagan survivals in this many-stranded city, cheerful as were the Roman Christians, light-hearted as were the artists, Hawthorne's imagination would not expand unreservedly. It asked itself what would happen if sin and conscience should invade these charming precincts. It invented a story, suggested to it by the Faun of Praxiteles, "on the idea of [the faun's] species having become intermingled with the human race: a family with the faun blood in them having prolonged itself from the classic era till our own day" [see excerpt dated 1859 in *NCLC,* Vol. 2]. At first struck chiefly by the fanciful possibilities of the theme, Hawthorne deepened it into another *Paradise Lost*—of a sort. Once more pagan than the Puritans, he was now more Puritan than the pagans. He would not let even Donatello play forever, but brings him down from his tower in the Apennines to this pleasant Rome, where through sin he estranges himself from his careless Eden and enters the human confraternity of guilt. Miriam, on whose behalf he sins, sins with him by not preventing him; and having in this fashion shared a sin they find themselves indissolubly married by its spiritual consequences, whatever their outer fortunes may be. An accidental witness of their sin, Hilda, whose conscience grew in New England, in another degree also acquires the responsibility, which tortures her until she rises above her Puritan prejudices to a universal mood and unburdens herself at the confessional which her own creed has disallowed. How many charms fly at the mere touch of the Puritan philosophy! Yet there is more than Puritanism in Hawthorne's prophecy that if Donatello had gone on as he was he would gradually have lost his generous youth and then have "become sensual, addicted to gross pleasures, heavy, unsympathetic, and indulated within the narrow limits of a surly selfishness." There is more than Puritanism, too, in the speculation of one of the other characters: "Is sin, then, . . . like sorrow, merely an element of human education, through which we struggle to a higher and purer state than we could otherwise have reached?" This is almost as much as to wonder whether experience itself, evil as well as good, does not civilize us, as it civilized Donatello. Even where Hawthorne's language is the old language of sin and conscience, there lurk in his romances certain questions the answers to which conduct to the most spacious regions of morals and imagination. (p. 650)

> *Carl Van Doren, "The Flower of Puritanism," in* The Nation, *New York, Vol. CXI, No. 2892, December 8, 1920, pp. 649-50.*

AUSTIN WARREN   (essay date 1934)

[*In this excerpt from his wide-ranging introduction to his selected edition of Hawthorne's work, Warren argues that in* The Marble Faun *Hawthorne rejected the idea that humankind's fall from innocence was a fortunate occurrence.*]

The philosophical *motif* of ***The Marble Faun*** is the genesis of sin. In the last chapters of the novel Hawthorne allows himself, through the medium of his characters, some free speculation concerning the significance of the Fall. (p. xxviii)

The audacity of Hawthorne's speculation has been greatly exaggerated by his critics. The novelist takes full advantage of his *dramatis personae* to put his unorthodox inquiries into their minds; and not content with having these daring inquiries challenged by other characters, he silences them by speaking (after the Victorian convention) in his own person.

Thus, toward the end of **The Marble Faun,** Miriam, the most audacious of the characters, is allowed to speculate on the career of Donatello, who, by sinning, has become a man, "sadder but wiser." Yet even Miriam, drawn as she is to this conclusion, confesses, "I tremble at my own thoughts," while yet she must "probe them to their depths. Was the crime . . . a blessing, in that strange disguise? Was it a means of education, bringing a simple and imperfect nature to a point of feeling and intelligence which it could have reached under no other discipline?"

Kenyon (the male counterpart, for purity and timidity, to Hilda) replies, "You stir up deep and perilous matter. . . . I dare not follow you into the unfathomable abysses whither you are tending." To which Miriam rejoins, "I delight to brood on the verge of this great mystery. . . ." And then she turns to its obvious archetype: "The story of the fall of man! Is it not repeated in our romance of Monte Beni? And may we not follow the analogy yet further? Was that very sin,— into which Adam precipitated himself and all his race,—was it the destined means by which, over a long pathway of toil and sorrow, we are to attain a higher, brighter, and profounder happiness, than our lost birthright gave? Will not this idea account for the permitted existence of sin, as no other theory can?" *O felix culpa!*

"It is too dangerous," Kenyon again rejoins. "Mortal man has no right to tread on the ground where you now set your feet." And though Miriam is not silenced, but concludes: "At least . . . that sin which man chose instead of good—has been so beneficently handled by omniscience and omnipotence, that, whereas our dark enemy sought to destroy us by it, it has really become an instrument most effective in the education of intellect and soul," yet Hawthorne himself has the last word in the chapter. Tomorrow, Miriam and Donatello, "a remorseful man and woman, linked by a marriage-bond of crime," would "set forth towards an inevitable goal."

Three chapters later, Hawthorne reopens the same speculative discussion. This time the interlocutors are Hilda and Kenyon. Kenyon has entertained Miriam's "too dangerous" hypothesis: "Sin has educated Donatello, and elevated him. Is sin, then,—which we deem such a dreadful blackness in the universe,—is it, like sorrow, merely an element of human education, through which we struggle to a higher and purer state than we could otherwise have attained? Did Adam fall, that we might ultimately rise to a far loftier paradise than his?" Was the Fall really a Rise?

And now Hilda takes over Kenyon's old rôle and shrinks from this audacity with an expression of horror. "Do you not perceive what a mockery your creed makes, not only of all religious sentiments, but of moral law? and how it annuls and obliterates whatever precepts of Heaven are written deepest within us? You have shocked me beyond words!" "I was only playing with fancies," rejoins the distressed Kenyon, alarmed at having entertained such dangerous notions. "I never did believe it. But the mind wanders wide and wild. . . ." And here Hawthorne leaves the matter. He has speculated, but he has drawn back from the abysses his speculation opened up. The Fall is still the Fall. (pp. xxix-xxxi)

Austin Warren, in an introduction to Representative Selections *by Nathaniel Hawthorne, edited by*

Austin Warren, American Book Company, 1934, pp. xi-lxxiii.

F. O. MATTHIESSEN (essay date 1941)

[*A respected American literary scholar, Matthiessen is best known for* American Renaissance: Art and Expression in the Age of Emerson and Whitman, *a comprehensive study of the emergence of a uniquely American literature. While Matthiessen did not write a complete essay on* The Marble Faun, *his comments on the novel in* American Renaissance *are frequently cited by other critics as original and insightful. In the following excerpt, he disputes the notion that the theme of* The Marble Faun *is that "the fall of man was really his rise."*]

When Miriam has grown unbearably oppressed by the ambiguous power that her model holds over her—the nature of which she has been unable to confide to anyone—he appears stalking behind her and her friends that night in the Coliseum. She can stand the tension no longer, and shrinking into the shadow of an arch, and 'fancying herself wholly unseen,' she begins 'to gesticulate extravagantly, gnashing her teeth, flinging her arms wildly abroad, stamping with her foot. It was as if she had stepped aside for an instant, solely to snatch the relief of a brief fit of madness.' (p. 308)

Miriam has not been unobserved, since Donatello's inarticulate devotion to her is as faithful in its watch as that of a hound. Up to this point, even in the extremity of her solitude, she has felt that it would be a sin to stain his innocently joyous nature with the blackness of a woe like hers. But now, though perceiving how ironical it is that, in her utmost need, her beauty and gifts have brought her 'only this poor simple boy,' she decides that since he has seen so much, to-morrow she will tell him all.

At this moment they are rejoined by Kenyon and Hilda and the rest of the group. As they resume their walk, the sculptor speculates about the exact location of the spot where, according to the legend, Curtius plunged himself into a chasm in the earth in the belief that he might save his countrymen by this act of expiation. But to Miriam, though she has regained her self-control, this legend comes with a special application. Hawthorne almost suggests the words of Pascal when he makes her say that this 'chasm was merely one of the orifices of that pit of blackness that lies beneath us, everywhere. The firmest substance of human happiness is but a thin crust spread over it, with just reality enough to bear up the illusive stage-scenery amid which we tread. It needs no earthquake to open the chasm. A footstep, a little heavier than ordinary, will serve; and we must step very daintily, not to break through the crust at any moment. By and by, we inevitably sink!' Conventional Hilda is horrified at such thoughts, for it seems to her that there is no 'hideous emptiness under our feet, except what the evil within us digs'; and if there should be such a chasm, the one thing to do would be to bridge it over 'with good thoughts and deeds.'

As they continue to talk, Miriam suddenly draws the girl close to her, whispering, 'Hilda, my religious Hilda, do you know how it is with me? I would give all I have or hope—my life, oh how freely—for one instant of your trust in God! You little guess my need of it.' Hilda is then doubly frightened by her friend's doubt of Providence. Hawthorne only mentions this doubt in glancing fashion, but it lies behind the tragic event that transpires.

They have come finally to the Tarpeian rock, for Kenyon, a good American, is a walking Baedeker. Without realizing that the others have gone on, Miriam and Donatello linger on the precipice, since he has begun to ask her, with unexpected earnestness, about the kind of men who were punished here. She tells him that they were those who 'cumbered the world . . . men who poisoned the air, which is the common breath of all, for their own selfish purposes.' When he asks her again whether it was well done to fling them from the edge, she answers yes, for 'innocent persons were saved by the destruction of a guilty one, who deserved his doom.'

What happened next remained indistinct in her mind. She could seem to remember that as a figure approached her from the shadows, she had fallen in desperation on her knees; but in the wild moment that followed she could hardly distinguish afterwards whether she had been an actor or a sufferer. Donatello, in the fierce energy that had suddenly kindled him from a boy into a man, insisted that he had done only what her eyes bade him do. And she could no more deny that a kind of joy had flamed up in her heart as she beheld her persecutor in mortal peril, than she could say whether this feeling had been one of horror, or of ecstasy, or of both. She pressed Donatello to her in a clinging embrace, and in their first minutes together, they experienced a kind of rapture, a drunkenness like that of Adam and Eve after the temptation, the insane sense of release that is 'the foremost result of a broken law.' As their spirits rose 'to the solemn madness of the occasion,' they went down into the city, not stealthily, or fearfully, but with a stately and majestic stride. 'Passion lent them (as it does to meaner shapes) its brief nobility of carriage.' Their first union seemed closer than a marriage bond, so intimate that it annihilated all other ties. They felt that they were liberated 'from the chain of humanity; a new sphere, a special law had been created for them alone. The world could not come near them; they were safe!'

But if Hawthorne understood thus the nature of *hubris,* the understanding of *nemesis* came always more instinctively to the descendant of Puritans. There 'exhaled upward (out of their dark sympathy, at the base of which lay a human corpse) a bliss, or an insanity, which the unhappy pair imagined to be well worth the sleepy innocence that was forever lost to them.' But just then they heard below them the singing of the group who had so recently been their companions, the rising and falling of voices that had accorded with theirs. Then they knew they were alone. And even though, as they passed the site of Pompey's forum, Miriam's bravery reminded Donatello that a great deed had been done there, 'a deed of blood like ours!' she also knew, once these words were spoken—and recoiled from the thought—that they two together were now likewise of the fraternity of all other murderers.

Against the background of these unmistakable implications, it seems strange that so many critics have taken out of its context one of Miriam's speculations near the end of the book, in order to assert that Hawthorne's theme here is that the fall of man was really his rise. She argues to Kenyon that since Donatello's crime seems to have been the means of educating his simple nature to a level of feeling and intelligence that it would not have reached under any other discipline, may it not be that Adam's sin 'was the destined means by which, over a long pathway of toil and sorrow, we are to attain a higher, brighter, and profounder happiness than any our lost birthright gave? Will not this idea account for the permitted existence of sin, as no other theory can?' *'O felix culpa,'* declares the Exultet for the Holy Saturday Mass, *'quae talem et tantum meruit habere redemptorem'*.

But hardly more than the Church does Hawthorne hold this to be the whole truth. Miriam herself trembles at these irrepressible thoughts on regeneration through sin. Hawthorne declares that Kenyon 'rightly felt' them to be too perilous. But the novelist did not need to make this open comment, for the whole course of his action bears out that hardly more than Milton was he 'of the Devil's party without knowing it.' That comment on *Paradise Lost* was made by the greatest of the English romantics, Blake, and was subscribed to by Shelley in his equal fascination with the character of Lucifer. But what this interpretation ignores is the cumulative effect of the whole poem, the gradual decay and final degradation of the former Prince of Heaven, as the consequences of his fall from grace work themselves out inevitably in debasing his nature.

In comparable fashion, an understanding of **The Marble Faun** depends on being aware of the work as a whole. We must not overlook the circumstances in which Miriam's speculation occurs, for it is during the Roman Carnival, with its vestiges of the old pagan rite of spring. Miriam and Donatello have seized on the disguise of a masquerade for a moment of gay forgetfulness of their destiny. But when they encounter Kenyon, this is brought again, unavoidably, to the fore. It strikes the sculptor that these two have reached 'a wayside paradise,' but to-morrow—and here the analogy with the closing lines of *Paradise Lost* could hardly be more marked— 'a remorseful man and woman, linked by a marriage-bond of crime, they would set forth towards an inevitable goal.' Nor is that goal left shrouded in any doubt, for it is made explicit at the end that her life is to be spent in penitence, his in prison. (pp. 308-12)

[Hawthorne] clearly intended Kenyon and Hilda to be attractive: an earnest young sculptor of promise and 'quick sensibility,' who, as the era deemed appropriate, believed reverently that the girl he loved was 'a little more than mortal.' In his treatment of their relationship Hawthorne has obviously interwoven many strands of his own relations with his wife; but the unintended impression of self-righteousness and priggishness that exudes from these characters brings to the fore some extreme limitations of the standards that Hawthorne took for granted.

We need look no farther than two critical scenes with Miriam, before and after the murder of her model. In the first she has been driven by her 'weary restlessness' to visit Kenyon in his studio, in the half-formed hope that he may be able to counsel her how to escape from her desperate situation. At the sight of his Cleopatra, she is so impressed by his intuitive grasp of woman's nature that she turns impulsively to him: 'Oh, my friend, will you be my friend indeed? I am lonely, lonely, lonely. There is a secret in my heart that burns me,—that tortures me! Sometimes I fear to go mad of it; sometimes I hope to die of it; but neither of the two happens. Ah, if I could but whisper it to only one human soul!' He bids her speak, but with a hidden reserve and alarm, which her suffering can detect. For his cool reasonableness knows that if she does pour out her heart, and he then fails to respond with just the sympathy she wants, it will be worse than if she had remained silent. ' "Ah, I shall hate you!" cried she, echoing the thought which he had not spoken; she was half choked with the gush of passion that was thus turned back upon her. "You are as cold and pitiless as your own marble." '

It does no good for him to protest, as Miles Coverdale might also have done, that he is 'full of sympathy, God knows,' for his ineffectual scrupulosity has driven her away. The very evening after this visit the terrible event takes place.

Of this event Hilda, who had turned back from the other walkers to rejoin Miriam and Donatello, became thus unwittingly the only observer. In deliberately creating in her the ideal innocence of a New England girl, Hawthorne set himself to examine a nature that, as Miriam recognizes, might endure a great burden of sorrow, but 'of sin, not a feather's weight.' One source of Hawthorne's knowledge of such a problem is suggested by Elizabeth Peabody's remark that with all her sister Sophia's bravery in the face of much suffering, 'there was one kind of thing she could not bear, and that was, moral evil.' The result in Hilda is terrifying: Kenyon's nature is broad as a barn in comparison. What is uppermost in the single interview she allows herself with Miriam after the murder is her dread that she, too, may be stained with guilt. Her dearest friend has 'no existence for her any more,' and she wonders if she can even talk to her 'without violating a spiritual law.'

Miriam urges, in her despair, that she is still a woman as she was yesterday, 'endowed with the same truth of nature, the same warmth of heart, the same genuine and earnest love, which you have always known in me. In any regard that concerns yourself, I am not changed . . . But, have I sinned against God and man, and deeply sinned? Then be more my friend than ever, for I need you more.' But as the girl recoils from her, Miriam adds: 'I always said, Hilda, that you were merciless; for I had a perception of it, even while you loved me best. You have no sin, nor any conception of what it is; and therefore you are so terribly severe! As an angel, you are not amiss; but as a human creature, and a woman among earthly men and women, you need a sin to soften you.'

To this Hilda's only answer is that she prays God may forgive her if she has spoken 'a needlessly cruel word,' for 'while there is a single guilty person in the universe, each innocent one must feel his innocence tortured by that guilt. Your deed, Miriam, has darkened the whole sky!'

To such a dazzling extreme does the daughter of the Puritans merit Kenyon's tribute to 'the white shining purity' of her nature as 'a thing apart.' At one point much later in the narrative she thinks remorsefully, 'Miriam loved me well, and I failed her at her sorest need.' But Kenyon, though observing that Hilda's unworldly separation between the good and the bad cuts like a steel blade, and that she is incapable of mercy since in need of none herself, still defends to Miriam her 'just severity.' Its justice is accepted by the novelist, and even by Miriam. Yet she repeats that if Kenyon had not been cold to her confidence, if she had obeyed her first impulse, 'all would have turned out differently.' She knows too that both her friends, by their lack of active sympathy, have allowed the unreleased energies of her heart to grind destructively on herself.

The dilemma that Hawthorne has run into here through his determination to keep the scales of justice exact is due to his limited ability to create characters instead of states of mind. We can accept the position that since Miriam has sinned, or has at least been implicated in Donatello's act, her retribution must run its course. For we know that moral laws, whether under the aegis of Destiny or of Providence, are by their nature relentlessly inhuman. But what we cannot accept is that Kenyon and Hilda should be such correct mouthpieces for justice. They become thereby appallingly conscious of the significance of events in which their own human fallibility would be more confusedly involved, and they thus take on an air of insufferable superiority.

Still worse things remain to be seen in Hilda. Chilled into torpor by the fact of having to bear the knowledge of Miriam's guilt, she feels utterly alone in the Rome which Kenyon has left for the summer. In this state she begins to be drawn by the magnet of Catholicism, by its apparent comfort on all occasions for the pent-up heart. She asks herself whether its universal blessings may not belong to her as well, whether the New England faith in which she was born and bred can be perfect, 'if it leave a weak girl like me to wander, desolate, with this great trouble crushing me down?' Her struggle brings her compellingly to St. Peter's, to a confessional booth, *Pro Anglica Lingua.* But when she has poured out her whole story, and the priest asks her in some perplexity, whether, though born a heretic, she is reconciled to the Church, her answer is 'Never.' ' "And, that being the case," demanded the old man, "on what ground, my daughter, have you sought to avail yourself of these blessed privileges, confined exclusively to members of the one true Church, of confession and absolution?"

' "Absolution, father?" exclaimed Hilda, shrinking back. "Oh no, no! I never dreamed of that! Only our Heavenly Father can forgive my sins . . ." ' This instinctive determination of Hilda's to eat her cake and have it too is, one must admit, as American as the strip-tease, of which it forms the spiritual counterpart.

To be sure, though Hilda tells the priest that she will never return to the confessional, she also says that she will hold the cathedral in 'loving remembrance' as long as she lives, as the spot where she found 'infinite peace after infinite trouble.' But by then she has decided that it was 'the sin of others that drove me thither; not my own, though it almost seemed so.' She has also finally begun to accept Kenyon's long hopeless love; and, at last, it is he who turns to her for guidance, since his mind has been entangling itself in the intricate problem of wherein Donatello has been educated and elevated by his sin. The sculptor feels that in his own lonely life and work his thought has wandered dangerously wide, and adds: 'Were you my guide, my counsellor, my inmost friend, with that white wisdom that clothes you as a celestial garment, all would go well. O Hilda, guide me home!'

She disclaims any such wisdom, but they start back to New England together, and though she wonders what Miriam's life is to be and where Donatello is, still 'Hilda had a hopeful soul, and saw sunlight on the mountain-tops.' Those were the final words of the book until Hawthorne yielded to the demand for a more explicit account of the destinies of the two who remained in Rome. In its original form the end coincides curiously with the bright vision in the final sentence of *Walden,* and with the rising light that Whitman, even more than Emerson, envisaged as flooding his America. (pp. 356-60)

That is not to say that Hilda's voice remains dominant even at the end of *The Marble Faun.* Although she gets the last word, Kenyon's somber reflections just before are more in keeping with the prevailing tone of the whole. He thinks that such genial natures as the Faun's 'have no longer any business on earth . . . Life has grown so sadly serious, that such men must change their nature, or else perish, like the antediluvian creatures, that required, as the condition of their existence, a more summer-like atmosphere than ours.' Melville marked that and also double-scored a passage earlier in the book where Hawthorne was meditating likewise on the theme of cheerless decay. Hawthorne was always aware of how in his Yankee world, 'no life now wanders like an unfettered stream; there is a mill-wheel for the tiniest rivulet to turn. We go all wrong, by too strenuous a resolution to go all right.' (pp. 360-61)

> F. O. Matthiessen, "Allegory and Symbolism" and "Dark Necessity," in his American Renaissance: Art and Expression in the Age of Emerson and Whitman, Oxford University Press, 1941, pp. 242-315, 316-70.

MARK VAN DOREN (essay date 1949)

[Van Doren was one of the most prolific men of letters in twentieth-century American writing. His work includes poetry (for which he won the Pulitzer Prize in 1939), novels, short stories, drama, criticism, social commentary, and the editing of a number of popular anthologies. Van Doren's criticism is aimed at the general reader, rather than the scholar or specialist, and is noted for its lively perception and wide interest. In the following excerpt from his study of Hawthorne, Van Doren praises isolated aspects of The Marble Faun but finds the overall effect of the novel marred by mystification and irresolution.]

The Marble Faun (or Transformation, as it is still entitled in England) was better received than The Blithedale Romance, but a vagueness in its conclusion—a vagueness Hawthorne did not substantially correct by writing several supplementary pages—prevented it then, and prevents it now, from matching The Scarlet Letter. It stands, with The House of the Seven Gables, high among his works of the second level. It has many beauties rather than one, as it has many morals whose sum is no substitute for a single meaning. He contrived, rather than was possessed, to write this tale of an innocent creature educated by sin. The idea is valuable, but since there are no innocent creatures it cannot be stated in a novel—even, by Hawthorne's definition, in a romance, for his romances never aimed at being unearthly poetry. In 1850 he had explained to Lewis Mansfield, who sent him a long poem to criticize, how it is that the very finest ideas need to be anchored in fact lest they drift off into the haze of the unverifiable. So in The Marble Faun he labored to build a real world about the central figure of his myth. The scene was Rome, and he wrote down Rome as he found it in his note-books. He did this so thoroughly that the book has been a Baedeker for generations of tourists. But the more of it he did, the more risk he ran that the abstraction of his myth should seem to be only an abstraction, irrelevant and uncaused. He never rose clear of the risk. The Marble Faun is still two stories—of an idea and of some people.

The idea is great and difficult. Paradise Lost fails with it too, and for the same reason. Woe comes into the world, and human nature as we know it is created. "The story of the fall of man!" cries Miriam. "Is it not repeated in our romance of Monte Beni? And may we follow the analogy yet further? Was that very sin—into which Adam precipitated himself and all his race—was it the destined means by which, over a long pathway of toil and sorrow, we are to attain a higher, brighter, and profounder happiness, than our lost birthright gave? Will not this idea account for the permitted existence of sin, as no other theory can?" Milton puts similar words into the mouth of an archangel, and he does not take them back; Miriam later on is moved to say, "I never did believe it!" But in both poems realism wars with truth; psychology, supposed to buttress theology, ends by undermining it, with the double result that we neither wholly understand nor simply believe.

Hawthorne asks us to believe that in our time—which is to say, in time—a young man exists who never participated in the Fall. He has yet to experience "sin, sorrow, or morality itself." He has "no conscience, no remorse, no burden on the heart, no troublesome recollections of any sort." He survives out of an age of fauns and nymphs before mankind was guilty of Rome. Hence he would seem to have "no dark future" before him. Yet his future darkens when he meets and falls in love with Miriam, a beautiful woman of our world whose past is gloomy with some secret guilt and whose present is haunted by reminders, in the form of a man who shares that guilt, of the fact that she will never be free. The faun-youth, Donatello, murders this man to make her free, but discovers then that he is bound not only to Miriam in the marriage of a secret guilt but to the fate of all humanity, the fate of having henceforth to stoop under the burden of morality, to walk in the perpetual dusk of deeds remembered and regretted. The narrative ends when their penance has begun in the separate places to which confession has condemned them.

If we cannot believe this with perfect simplicity, the reason is partly that no long narrative could make us do so. It could be believed if it could be understood, but only parables induce such understanding. The Marble Faun is too long for a parable, too circumstantial for a myth. The circumstances are beautiful, and have their own reality, but it is not a reality that serves Hawthorne's high purpose. If his meditations concerning sin were never so complex before, or in themselves so interesting, it is all the more a pity that he complicates his plot to a point beyond which it can carry them. He contrives another couple, the sculptor Kenyon and the copyist Hilda, to reinforce his vision. They only ramify it. They are Americans, as it happens; he has done a "Cleopatra" like Story's, and she has Sophia's incapacity—a thing Hawthorne loved in his wife—to imagine evil; especially evil when it is mixed in one mind with good, for that, says Hilda, is "almost more shocking than pure evil." Hilda exemplifies yet another moral: the "discovery that sin is in the world" agonizes even innocent persons, and dooms them to the misery of an "awful loneliness"; "every crime destroys more Edens than our own." It is one of Hawthorne's minor triumphs that he saves Hilda from seeming to be a prig; but neither she nor the colorless Kenyon, a kind of Coverdale whose presence is necessary to the plot, in turn saves The Marble Faun from missing its lofty mark.

Many things are here that were in The Scarlet Letter. Two solitary lovers are brought together by a guilt they cannot share with the multitude about them. The multitude, the crowd, exists in full force again: at Perugia, in the marketplace where Miriam and Donatello meet—"and there they stood, the beautiful man, the beautiful woman, united forever, as they felt, in the presence of these thousand eyewitnesses who gazed so curiously at the unintelligible scene"—and at Rome where "the uproar of the Carnival swept like a tempestuous sea over the spot which they had included within their small circle of isolated feeling." This, like a hundred other things in *The Marble Faun,* is very fine. Yet the relevance is gone that read such terrible ironies into the Election Day of *The Scarlet Letter.* Hawthorne's crowd does not recognize now the individuals it engulfs; if it sees them at all, it finds them "unintelligible." Hawthorne does not concentrate his power, as indeed he seldom did. He loses half of it, for instance, when he transfers the necessity for confession from one of his principal to one of his secondary characters. It is Hilda, tortured by her knowledge of Miriam's sin, who must go to St. Peter's, though she is not a Catholic, and pour out her secret to a priest. This is one of the most interesting moments in *The Marble Faun,* and it is rightly famous, among other reasons for its revelation of the extent to which the religion of Rome had come to fascinate Hawthorne; but it does not take place, as everything does in *The Scarlet Letter,* at the heart of the story. This story has no heart; its meaning is distributed, as its emphasis is vague.

Hawthorne damned those readers who complained of his mystifications, but the readers were right. We never learn what guilt it was that blasted Miriam before she came to Rome; we never see the face of the man who haunts her there, or discover his relation to the unforgettable crime she cannot flee. She suffers fatally, as Zenobia does, from lack of definition. She is better than Zenobia because she is in a better book, but she is inferior to Hester because Hawthorne has not reduced her to clarity. He had not reduced his thought to the same indispensable point. That was why he needed to perform so many peripheral tasks; to write, for one thing, a guide-book to Rome; or simply to write—for *The Marble Faun* is beautifully written. We do not say this of the greatest stories.

Yet *The Marble Faun* has many rewards for the reader. If they are incidental, they are nevertheless splendid. Donatello on his tower, or in the forest where he utters his "wild, sorrowful cry" because the animals have ceased to trust him; Hilda in *her* tower, surrounded by white doves which as symbols of her purity might be ridiculous and yet are not—they are lovely, as she is in the same unaccountable way; the night scene at the Coliseum, the day scene by the Fountain of Trevi; the Carnival, and the rosebud thrown to Kenyon; the dead monk—these and dozens of other things as good have scarcely been surpassed among the embroideries of fiction. Also, Hawthorne has somehow mastered the delicate atmospheres of myth. Donatello's world is undefined, but the dew on it is fresh. Hawthorne himself seems unable to decide whether it is altogether well that sin has produced a world wherein "the entire system of man's affairs . . . is built up purposely to exclude the careless and happy soul." We are all, he says, "parts of a complicated scheme of progress, which can only result in our arrival at a colder and drearier region than we were born in." Not for nothing has he, a Puritan at heart, visited the pagan antipodes. The sweetness of this new world, but it is the oldest of worlds as well, both softens him and pains him. The result is a romance the very resonance of whose charm is consistent with its lack of resolution. Only one thing would have been better: the resolution, deeper than charm, which we call tragedy. (pp. 226-31)

Mark Van Doren, in his Nathaniel Hawthorne, *1949. Reprint by The Viking Press, 1957, 279 p.*

RICHARD HARTER FOGLE   (essay date 1952)

[Fogle discusses the unresolved tension between simplicity and complexity in The Marble Faun.*]*

The crucial problem of *The Marble Faun* is far-reaching in its implications. Has the faun Donatello been ruined or ennobled by his human crime? Miriam, the comrade of his fall, succinctly states the issue and its broadest relationship:

> The story of the fall of man! Is it not repeated in our romance of Monte Beni? And may we follow the analogy yet further? Was that very sin,—into which Adam precipitated himself and all his race,—was it the destined means by which, over a long pathway of toil and sorrow, we are to attain a higher, brighter, and profounder happiness, than our lost birthright gave? Will not this idea account for the permitted existence of sin, as no other theory can?

From this perilous moral the sculptor Kenyon, who may with some caution be taken as speaking for Hawthorne, recoils. " 'It is too dangerous, Miriam! I cannot follow you!' . . . 'Mortal man has no right to tread on the ground where you now set your feet.' " Nevertheless, we find him a few pages later advancing the same idea to the innocent Hilda:

> "Here comes my perplexity," continued Kenyon. "Sin has educated Donatello, and elevated him. Is sin, then,—which we deem such a dreadful blackness in the universe,—is it, like sorrow, merely an element of human education, through which we struggle to a higher and purer state than we could otherwise have attained? Did Adam fall, that we might ultimately rise to a far loftier paradise than his?"

Hilda repudiates the notion with horror. The pattern of advance and retreat is the same in both instances. Most commentators on *The Marble Faun,* however, have accepted the speculation itself, rather than the withdrawal, as representing Hawthorne's true intention. This interpretation leaves us with the doctrine of "the fortunate fall," according to which man's sin and expulsion from Eden is in reality a proof of God's mercy and concealed benevolence. On the other hand Austin Warren, in his excellent introduction to his selections from Hawthorne [see excerpt dated 1934], argues stoutly for the opposite view. Hawthorne, he maintains, is orthodox (Calvinistically orthodox, that is) in his thinking about human nature and himself retreats from and rejects the full possibilities of his speculation. Mr. Warren's opinion is the sounder of the two and is very cogently presented. Yet he errs in presuming that in the fictional substance of *The Marble Faun* the choice is made at all. Rather, it is only offered. Hawthorne neither accepts nor rejects; it is not his habit to come to ultimate conclusions. In the body of his works there are too many references to "the fortunate fall" to dismiss the idea with safety, while there are none which, read in context, would enable us to accept it as a doctrine. He leaves the question in suspension, which in *The Marble Faun* becomes the central mystery of man.

The suspension between opposite beliefs is the life-principle of *The Marble Faun,* embodied in imagery and symbolism, in character, in setting, and in movement or progression. I shall have most to say about the figurative patterns of imagery and symbol. The central suspension of *The Marble Faun* is an opposition between simplicity and complexity, which rests deliberately unresolved at the end. Simplicity is Donatello the faun in his original innocence, complexity is Donatello humanized, matured, and saddened. Simplicity is the Golden Age, the Arcadia which is the Faun's proper setting; complexity is the nineteenth century in which he is misplaced. Simplicity is the rural life of Tuscany, whence Donatello comes; complexity is Rome, the greatest of cities, where he meets with love and sin. Simplicity is Eden before the serpent and the flaming sword; complexity is the wide world of the exile, the real world of Hawthorne's characters. Simplicity is heaven itself (which will cause us most difficulty); complexity is human earth. Simplicity is, in fact, either sub- or super-human, while complexity is the stuff of humanity.

The simplicity of Donatello is that of a subhuman being, who is yet capable of virtues which humans have not. In his prototype the Faun of Praxiteles "the characteristics of the brute creation meet and combine with those of humanity." (pp. 162-64)

The Faun of Monte Beni, it appears, is both more and less than human in his simplicity. The fit setting for this creature is the Golden Age, or Arcadia, to which there are more than twenty explicit references in *The Marble Faun.* (p. 166)

This value of simplicity is neither dismissed nor supplanted in *The Marble Faun;* manifestly incomplete, it yet remains with an enchantment never dimmed. Donatello is humanized and refined, but with real loss. Hawthorne twice suggests the

The faun sculpted by Praxiteles.

place of this happy innocence in a state of ideal perfection, but the hinted synthesis is a perfection not of earth. " 'Nature needed, and still needs, this beautiful creature,' " says the sculptor Kenyon, " 'standing betwixt man and animal, sympathizing with each. . . . ' " Again, with reference to the vexed question of Donatello's hidden ears, it is remarked, ". . . into what regions of rich mystery would it extend Donatello's sympathies, to be thus linked (and by no monstrous chain) with what we call the inferior tribes of being, whose simplicity, mingled with his human intelligence, might partly restore what man has lost of the divine!"

Linked with the simplicity of Arcadia and the Golden Age is the simplicity of Eden before the Fall. The Borghese garden "is like Eden in its loveliness; like Eden, too, in the fatal spell [in this instance malaria] that removes it beyond the scope of man's actual possessions." Kenyon finds Edenlike the groves of Monte Beni. . . . Eden is the Christian counterpart of the pagan Golden Age. Hawthorne does not venture to identify the two, Eden having always a special sanctity, but in *The Marble Faun* they are clearly copresent, simplicities of similar import. Eden occurs far less in direct reference than do the Golden Age and Arcadia, but the story of the Fall is pervasive throughout.

The final and most difficult emblem of simplicity is heaven itself, in *The Marble Faun* most frequently embodied in the character of Hilda, the dove. It is the most difficult symbol since it cannot be distinguished from the lower simplicities of Eden and the Golden Age. They are beginnings; heaven is a culmination. They represent a term of the problem, a pole to be reconciled with its opposite; heaven should be solution and reconcilement. In Eden and the Age of Gold complexity has not yet appeared. The simplicity of heaven should include and resolve complexity. Yet it does not.

This problem is to be found not only in Hawthorne and *The Marble Faun,* but universally. It is a characteristically but not solely Christian problem. Heaven, which should be the resolution of complexity, appears instead to fall back upon avoidance and negation. For most imaginations the dilemma is, "Who wants to play on a harp, anyway?" Beatitude is difficult to envision. We know that Milton's hell is more impressive than his heaven, that the *Inferno* outweighs the *Paradiso,* and that Mr. Eliot evokes his Wasteland more convincingly than he escapes from it. In literature the problem is to achieve Plato's unmixed virtue without sacrificing probability. Most of us, I presume, would side with Aristotle, who prefers the faulty Achilles of the *Iliad.*

This consideration returns us to the character of Hilda as a symbol for heaven, which unquestionably she is. She lives among doves in a tower, a Christian vestal virgin tending an eternal flame. She is seen most typically robed in white, the white of simplicity and innocence. Her proper atmosphere is her tower room above the streets of ancient, human, sinful Rome: "Only the domes of churches ascend into this airy region, and hold up their golden crosses on a level with her eye. . . . " She has a "perfect simplicity." She lives amid "pure thoughts and innocent enthusiasms." A finely gifted copyist of painting, her closest affinity is with Fra Angelico, her favorite picture Guido's unruffled Michael slaying an inadequate dragon. Transfigured with sudden happiness, she "suggests how angels come by their beauty." Kenyon compares her to a spirit and wishes humbly, and with some sense of impiety, " 'that I might draw her down to an earthly fireside!' " Amid the evil of Rome she walks untouched. . . . (pp. 167-70)

As representative of heaven's simplicity, she consistently rejects the complex. Despite her gentleness, her moral judgments are relentless. " 'O Hilda,' exclaims Miriam, 'your innocence is like a sharp sword! . . . Your judgments are often terribly severe, though you seem all made up of gentleness and mercy.' " This statement is made before Miriam has exposed herself to her friend's eyes; she has no later cause to change her mind. After her sin and misfortune Miriam feels some bitterness, some sense of unfairness in Hilda's gentle but complete rejection of her. Kenyon's defense of the sinners is totally unacceptable to Hilda, and he charges her with lack of mercy.

" 'Ah, Hilda,' replied Kenyon, 'you do not know, for you could never learn it from your own heart, which is all purity and rectitude, what a mixture of good there may be in things evil.' " She answers, " ' . . . there is, I believe, only one right and one wrong; and I do not understand, and may God keep me from ever understanding, how two things so totally unlike can be mistaken for one another. . . .' " To this he concludes, " 'I always felt you, my dear friend, a terribly severe judge, and have been perplexed to conceive how such tender sympathy could coexist with the remorselessness of a steel blade. You need no mercy, and therefore know not how to show any.' " It is interesting to notice the repetition of the metaphor of the sharp sword of innocence. Could it bear a relation to the flaming sword of the expulsion, which occurs several times in *The Marble Faun?*

The simplicity of Hilda is inadequate for a complete judgment of human motives and values; this lack is felt in her by persons themselves not wholly qualified, and yet to be respected. Donatello, saddened and transformed by sin, makes the case against Hilda when Kenyon urges him to view some pictures by Fra Angelico:

> "You have shown me some of Fra Angelico's pictures, I remember," answered Donatello; "his angels look as if they had never taken a flight out of heaven; and his saints seem to have been born saints, and always to have lived so. Young maidens, and all innocent persons, I doubt not, may find great delight and profit in looking at such holy pictures. But they are not for me." "Your criticism, I fancy, has great moral depth," replied Kenyon: "and I see in it the reason why Hilda so highly appreciates Fra Angelico's pictures."
>
> (pp. 170-71)

While Hilda is the symbol of the simplicity of heaven, we cannot accept her judgment of earthly values, though we cannot finally reject it either. One answer lies in the lack of differentiation between the innocence of Eden and the innocence of heaven. Hilda is a child of Eden, to whom at Miriam's sin "Adam falls anew, and Paradise, heretofore in unfaded bloom, is lost again, and closed forever, with the fiery swords gleaming at its gates." Hilda, however, remains substantially unaltered by her contact with sin, despite her genuine and deep distress. We have seen that she walks amid evil untouched; a child of Eden she remains, bearing with her her paradise.

Another explanation is the inevitable confusion in Hilda of

human and superhuman, earth and heaven. To Miriam's plea for understanding and forgiveness she is forced to answer:

> If I were one of God's angels, with a nature incapable of stain, and garments that could never be spotted, I would keep ever at your side, and try to lead you upward. But I am a poor, lonely girl, whom God has set here in an evil world, and given her only a white robe, and bid her wear it back to Him, as white as when she put it on. Your powerful magnetism would be too much for me. The pure, white atmosphere, in which I try to discern what things are good and true, would be discolored.

Miriam rejoins, " 'As an angel, you are not amiss; but, as a human creature, and a woman among earthly men and women, you need a sin to soften you.' " One sees the complication; Hilda is at once human and divine. She is the emblem of heaven, yet her limitation hints faintly at a higher simplicity which embraces all humanity, instead of, like her, rejecting much of life. Hawthorne intends to go no further; engrossed in the idea of divine perfection, he yet draws a line beyond which his speculation does not trespass. Hilda represents for him a real, valuable, and attractive aspect of human life, which also is fortunately tinctured with divinity. He believes that there are such women as she—his own wife, for example—that they are significant and representative, and that they are worthy not only of reverence but of love.

As a literary character Hilda is not wholly unbelievable, but in isolation she fails to satisfy. Her limited perfection makes her inflexible and her actions too predictable. She is justifiable as one among other elements in the balance of a Hawthorne novel. One must feel, however, that Hawthorne was mistaken in making her the center of interest for a long section of the book. (Here one might notice at the same time an apparent design of fairly apportioning the emphasis among the four principal characters.) Hilda cannot act, but is only acted upon, since action is imperfection. One can believe in the spiritual misery arising from her knowledge of the crime of Miriam and Donatello, which drives this "daughter of the Puritans" to confession to a Catholic priest; but one cannot fully sympathize with her. Hilda is too strong in her simplicity for us to accept her dilemma as more than temporary. Likewise we cannot share Kenyon's anxiety at her sudden disappearance, despite Hawthorne's not wholly serious efforts to frighten us with suggestions about the terrible things that can happen to a virgin in Rome. Not to Hilda; we have been convinced of her invulnerability.

Against the simplicities of Donatello, the Golden Age and Arcadia, Eden, heaven, and its saintly Hilda stand the complexities of the present, of Miriam, of modern Rome, of ancient Rome which it evokes, and of the Roman Church. First, the refined but saddened nineteenth century of Kenyon and Miriam are directly opposed to the Golden Age of Donatello and the timeless Eden of Hilda. (pp. 172-74)

Rome, consummate creation of humanity and time, possesses both the horror and the fascination of complexity. (p. 175)

Rome, the human and complex, is the antithesis of the Arcadian seclusion of Monte Beni's groves. Donatello, it is fancifully said, wilts in the oppressive air of the city. Its august child, the Roman Catholic Church, is also a symbol of complexity. It offends against the simplicity of worship, and also from an excess of humanity, since in it the human masquerades as superhuman. Its complex hierarchy and multiplicity of forms contrast directly with the simplicity of Puritan worship in which Hilda was reared. It arouses a complex mixture of affection, reverence, and disgust. . . . Catholicism "marvellously adapts itself to every human need." It "supplies a multitude of external forms, in which the spiritual may be clothed and manifested." For Hawthorne the abiding flaw is its excessive admixture of the human: "If there were but angels to work it, instead of the very different class of engineers who now manage its cranks and safety-valves, the system would soon vindicate the dignity and holiness of its origin." (pp. 175-76)

Hilda, a "daughter of the Puritans," is tempted by the advantages of Catholicism and in confessing her secret to a priest receives them in part, but she remains faithful to the "white light" of a simpler and more purely supernatural communion.

Complexity is a human attribute, failing, and endowment. An important element in the complex of human nineteenth-century Rome is the ponderous memory of its ancient ancestor, the apotheosis of the human. Everywhere the "massive old stones and indestructible bricks of imperial Rome" are physically present and spiritually oppressive. The Rome of today "seems like nothing but a heap of broken rubbish, thrown into the great chasm between our own days and the Empire, merely to fill it up." In a significant and constantly recurring image, old Rome "lies like the dead corpse of a giant, decaying for centuries, with no survivor mighty enough even to bury it." The tremendous tombs of the Appian Way are emblems of the doom of human grandeur: "Nothing remains to the dishonored sepulchres, except their massiveness." Its most perfect embodiment is the equestrian statue of Marcus Aurelius on the Capitoline Hill. . . . (p. 177)

Human grandeur of character can reach no higher. A still better spiritual force, however, emanates from the "grand benignity" of the statue of Pope Julius in Perugia, which blesses the union of Miriam and Donatello, "stretching out the hand of benediction over . . . this guilty and repentant pair." An emblem of the Church, as Aurelius is of ancient Rome, the pontiff outweighs the emperor through a greater, though still imperfect, admixture of the divine.

The conception of the Renaissance also enters into the treatment of human values. The Renaissance is present in the great Roman palaces and in art, particularly painting. These palaces, like the ruins of the ancients, present an ironic portrait of the vanity of human achievement in their grandeur and squalor, their splendor and lack of comfort. There is, perhaps, an added reproach of perversity, since they were built by Christian cardinals as well as princes, who had better things before their eyes. Similarly, the paintings of the masters have an all-too-human taint. Titian is perhaps the type of the merely human; Raphael, half-divine, mingles his earthly loves with the likenesses of heaven:

> And who can trust the religious sentiment of Raphael, or receive any of his Virgins as heaven-descended likenesses, after seeing, for example, the Fornarina of the Barberini Palace, and feeling how sensual the artist must have been to paint such a brazen trollop of his own accord, and lovingly? Would the Blessed Mary reveal herself to his spiritual vision, and favor him with sittings alternately with that type of glowing earthliness, the Fornarina?

Here we run the danger of upsetting Hawthorne's balance. This condemnation occurs in a section which is as a whole a defense of Italian Renaissance painting. The criticism is immediately qualified, and is in any event a dramatic reflection of Hilda's momentary depression of spirit. The indictment remains, however, along with its qualifications.

There is in **The Marble Faun** an "organic" theory of art which extends in its application into all other problems of the book. In every discussion of painting and sculpture the individual work is judged according to the degree in which it possesses a unifying life and light. The meritless work, or the falsely fine, as Flemish genre painting, is empty technique, mere copy, dead mass. (pp. 178-79)

In describing Hilda's gifts as a copyist, Hawthorne makes the Coleridgean distinction between *copy* and *imitation,* a distinction parallel to *mechanical* and *organic.* Hilda, by a "guiding light of sympathy," is able to go "straight to the central point, in which the master had conceived his work." She achieves not merely the letter but the spirit of the original. She attains to what Coleridge terms imitation; others achieve a copy only. . . . (p. 179)

Truly organic art imitates from deep within; it has a life and soul, and thus it is immortal. The notion of organic imitation expressed in **The Marble Faun** is thoroughly Platonic and Christian. Art is always the imperfect imitation of a higher reality. The conception is loftier than the completed work. Thus Hilda is successful because she follows "precisely the same process step by step through which the original painter had trodden to the development of his idea." In Chapter XV, "An Aesthetic Company," rough sketches by the great masters are found more interesting than the paintings for which they are preliminary studies. "There is an effluence of divinity in the first sketch; and there, if anywhere, you find the pure light of inspiration, which the subsequent toil of the artist serves to bring out in stronger lustre, indeed, but likewise adulterates it with what belongs to an inferior mood." (p. 180)

The corresponding defect of art is literal, uninspired imitation. . . .

This conception of art is paralleled in other topics and fields of imagery. Rome itself, the Roman Church, and various Italian institutions all err in perpetuating mere mass when the life has vanished, so that the dead hand of the past is stiflingly heavy upon the weak human spirit. Forms once pervaded with life now slowly rot untouched and poison existence in their decay. Matter bulks larger than spirit, and the odor of human mortality is everywhere. The recurrent image of ancient Rome as a gigantic, unburied corpse is a case in point; the graveyard of the Capuchin monks in a subterranean crypt beneath their church is a single vivid instance. Skeletons lie everywhere, with skulls, "some quite bare, and others still covered with yellow skin, and hair that has known the earth-damps." The weight of mortality is overpowering. . . . (p. 181)

Now the life which is the value of art and of human institutions clearly comes from heaven. To some extent complexity = humanity = mortality = dead matter in **The Marble Faun,** while simplicity = divinity = immortality = life and light; but once again we must qualify and redress the balance. Art is represented by the Renaissance, not by the Primitives, although Hawthorne is aware of Giotto and Cimabue. The Roman Church is by no means condemned. The humanity of ancient Rome is more powerful still than following ages, and Hawthorne enlists our sympathies with the complex Miriam and against the simple Hilda. If one considers this problem, we may do well before finding Hilda overrighteous to heed the adjuration, "Clear your mind of cant!" How many of us would be willing to condone a particularly terrible murder committed before our eyes? Would we wish to go further than Hilda, who keeps the secret while breaking off relations with the murderers? That the question seldom arises in this light is evidence of Hawthorne's skill in framing the problem and certainly reveals his sympathy with the guilty.

In the symbols of art complexity as well as simplicity may be imbued with life. On the opening page, among the wonders of the Capitol we find a "symbol of the Human Soul . . . in the pretty figure of a child, clasping a dove to her bosom, but assaulted by a snake"—a symbol which fitly preludes the book. Kenyon's sculpture of Cleopatra, the embodiment of human complexity, is a vital masterpiece:

> In a word, all Cleopatra—fierce, voluptuous, passionate, tender, wicked, terrible, and full of poisonous and rapturous enchantment—was kneaded into what, only a week or two before, had been a lump of wet clay from the Tiber. Soon, apotheosized in an indestructible material, she would be one of the images that men keep forever, finding a heat in them which does not cool down, throughout the centuries.

Another immortal symbol of complexity is the Laocoon group, "which, in its immortal agony, impressed Kenyon as a type of the long, fierce struggle of man, involved in the knotted entanglements of Error and Evil, those two snakes, which, if no divine help intervene, will be sure to strangle him and his children in the end." Human complexity is real and is not to be passed over. The "knotted entanglement" exists, tempered by the simplicity of the divine. Hawthorne portrays the entanglement and dilemma, and its palliation, without venturing beyond the boundaries into preachment or prophecy. (pp. 182-83)

> *Richard Harter Fogle, in his* Hawthorne's Fiction: The Light & the Dark, *University of Oklahoma Press, 1952, 219 p.*

MERLE E. BROWN   (essay date 1956)

[*In the following excerpt from a discussion of* The Marble Faun's *structure, Brown examines the parallel moral development of the novel's four main characters. Charles R. Smith, Jr. later elaborated on the ideas offered by Brown (see excerpt dated 1962).*]

The Marble Faun by Nathaniel Hawthorne has suffered a plethora of interpretations, largely, I believe, because its design has never been fixed firmly and clearly. (p. 302)

[To] my way of reading, no part of the novel has been criticized so poorly as its design. What most critics say, or at least imply, is that the design, though drawn in firm outline, is too narrow to contain all that Hawthorne wished to put into the novel, that, as a result, part of the novel is packed together as a compact unity, but the rest is a large, amorphous mass dangling purposelessly from that stout framework. A less popular, less acute, and even harsher condemnation is that the novel has no design at all, that the entire "story" is simply a group of events unintentionally arousing expectations which are never fulfilled. This notion is rightly taken, I should say, as the confession of a failure in understanding. But it is my belief that the other criticism misses the truth too. The design of *The Marble Faun* is not obvious, to be sure, for the novel is a completed edifice, not merely the blueprint of one; but the design can be discovered, and, when it is scrutinized, I believe it will appear broad enough to encompass all that Hawthorne wished to include. And once the design is agreed upon, I think the dominant theme will be evident.

One must confess that the design of *The Marble Faun* is rather curious: it is a single idea, the transformation from innocence to experience, repeated, with no major deviations, four times. Considering that the novel was entitled *Transformation* when first published in England, it is not surprising that the idea itself, the transformation, has been noticed before. But to my knowledge the idea has been observed only as related to the career of Donatello, the young Italian count. It has not been recognized before that the transformation is repeated, that all four important characters undergo a similar change, and that Hawthorne has divided the novel into four overlapping parts each of which is primarily concerned with the change of one of the four characters. Of course, each part of the novel affects those which follow it: the climax of the first part leads to the climax of the second, the first and the second lead to the third, and the first three lead to the fourth. Furthermore, there is a concluding resolution, of all the events of the novel, in which all four characters take part. Thus, the entire novel moves in a single line of development, even though it is divided into four parts running parallel courses. I shall analyze each part separately from the others, in order to be clear, for the pattern, as it is repeated, becomes rather complicated, breaking as it does into at least five distinct stages.

The first part of the novel (Chapters I through XXIII), which is by far the longest part because it not only presents the first transformation but also prepares for the other three, is devoted to Miriam. When the novel opens she is living in close artistic communion with her two American friends, Kenyon and Hilda, and as a goddess to the enamored Donatello. The first stage in Miriam's career is a state of anguish which descends upon her when she accidentally stumbles upon a hirsute creature in the catacomb of St. Calixtus. This satyrical man comes out of the catacomb at Miriam's heels and trails her every footstep from then on. Gradually we learn that this hairy man, whom Miriam allows to serve as model for some of her paintings, took part in a mysterious past she lived before coming to Rome and meeting her present friends. The model's presence tortures Miriam because he committed a crime the circumstances of which suggest that she also was implicated. Legally Miriam was innocent of the crime, but the model has the power to destroy her reputation by innuendo. Under this constant threat, Miriam builds up in her mind an image of herself as Innocence Persecuted: pure herself, she has been unjustly fated to suffer over and over the threat of this wicked, untouchable man. Her sense of the injustice of her position, then, torments her as much as the threat itself does. Miriam can endure the wickedness of the model himself, for she has come to accept the existence of evil in the world; but what she cannot endure is the idea that there is any evil in herself. Content to be tormented, what she fears is the model's power to draw her over to the side of the tormenters.

Her futile efforts to escape the agony which the model's unexpected appearance in Rome causes her make up the second stage in Miriam's career. By drawing sketches of violence, she tries to purge herself of the model's presence, but she fails by recognizing that the violence she imagines would be even more wicked if practiced than anything the model himself has done. She visits her two artistic friends, in turn, hoping one of them will listen to her story sympathetically, praise her unstained purity, and thus grant relief for her fear and sorrow. But Miriam quickly and rightly estimates that in their inexperienced delicacy both Hilda and Kenyon would impute guilt where they saw only sorrow caused by guilt, and therefore she retreats from both without opening her mouth further. Although she does find relief by dancing wildly through the Borghese gardens with the simple Donatello, it is only momentary, for the hairy model catches up with them, the stringed instruments become discordant, and the dancers turn away.

But one night Miriam sets out on a ramble through Rome with an "aesthetic company," and this apparently frivolous tour of the city, as the third step in her journey, proves to be the situation which issues in her liberation. As the aesthetes wander carefree through the ruins of Rome, Miriam continues her futile efforts to escape the agony which the model's uninterrupted presence causes her. At the Fountain of the Trevi she scoops up a handful of water, throws it in his face, and cries, "In the name of all the Saints, vanish Demon, and let me be free of you now and forever!" Exorcism, however, does not prove effective in the nineteenth century. Madness helps some, however, as Miriam throws a fit in the shadows of the Coliseum. But she is too strong, her mind does not give way, and she returns to her agony once more. Minutes afterwards she has been inadvertently left alone on the edge of a precipice contemplating suicide.

This is the moment of the climax and fourth movement of the first section of the novel, the murder of the hairy model by Donatello. This murder, which serves as the origin of the careers of Donatello and Hilda, liberates Miriam from her agony and miraculously transforms her into a mature adult wise in the ways of the world. Giving up her innocent isolation from the corruption all about her, stepping out of the enchanted white circle into the surrounding darkness, she takes responsibility for the murder even though uncertain that she contributed in any way to it. Suddenly her vision penetrates the façade of ordinary life and she recognizes the bond between herself and Caesar's murderers and, for that matter, all other sinners in the world. Because of her newly acquired wisdom, which is the fifth and last stage in her career, she displays virtues never before released in her. For on the day after the murder, when visiting a dismal Capuchin church, Miriam is brought face to face with the dead model, magically changed into a pious monk lying sanctimoniously below the altar and accusingly bleeding upon her approach, and she courageously outbraves her reproachful tormenter with a vow that she will not fear to face him before the Judgment Seat. Immediately after this intrepid display of defiance, moreover, she forgives him all the wrong he has done her and gives the sacristan of the church money to be used for masses to save the soul of this man who sought to damn her.

To her new courage and mercy Miriam adds a power of self-sacrifice not hinted at in her character before. Having committed a murder for her, Donatello changed Miriam's contempt for him into the deepest love; but when her presence seems to torment the remorseful youth, Miriam gives up her only remaining purpose in life, that is, comforting him, and leaves him, never to return unless called for. After this repudiation Miriam heads for another by visiting Hilda, who had seen the murder by chance and departed unobserved by the others. Hardly able to endure Miriam's presence, Hilda accuses her of being too filthy to communicate with so pure and delicate a creature as herself. Miriam not only forgives Hilda her harshness but also helps her decide with whom she should share the burdensome secret of the murder.

Thus the first part of the novel ends with Miriam changed from an innocent young woman tormented by the slightest imputation of guilt and wholly selfish in her efforts to keep her fair repute into a mature woman who accepts her sinfulness and the bond linking her to all the criminals of the world and with this acceptance becomes virtuous in her new courage, loyalty, compassion, and charity.

In the second part (Chapters XXIV through XXXV) Donatello follows a course much like Miriam's. In the beginning he has fled from Rome to Monte Beni, the home of his innocent, carefree youth, as if pursued by the Furies themselves, though actually only the phantom of the model tracks him down, as the model himself hunted Miriam. Although every moment of his life is now full of torment, just as Miriam's was at the outset of the first part, Donatello's pain is caused not by an impossible commitment to his own purity, but by an exaggerated conviction that he is the wickedest man alive. Although Donatello's agony differs from Miriam's in this way, both states are isolating, both keep the characters aloof from other men. Probably Donatello's initial state resembles most closely the model's just after he committed his first crime. Indirectly Hawthorne suggests that, somewhat like young Goodman Brown, the model hated himself so intensely after his first serious failing that he was blind to the possibility of Grace, considered himself damned, and became an inveterate criminal. Hating himself, too, Donatello is in grave danger of this same suicidal despair.

Donatello, however, is still pliable enough to take the second step in his career, that is, to seek escape from his hateful position. He performs one kind of penance after another: he imprisons himself in an antique tower with only two owls and the ghost of a monk as company; he undertakes regular self-flagellation; he studies the most abstruse sciences and, against his nature, becomes a stargazer to induce equanimity; and he even fixes upon certain morbid rituals which include peering contemplatively at an ugly death's-head. But, of course, Donatello could not have chosen less likely means to extricate himself, and he totters on the brink of final despair.

The third movement of Donatello's career begins when Kenyon, who has been visiting at Monte Beni, decides to divert the remorseful youth by a random sightseeing tour through Umbria. Hawthorne presents this tour in a most haphazard fashion so that it seems to go nowhere, in the same way Miriam's ramble through Rome did. Actually, however, on this trip Donatello's observations convince him that among ordinary adults there is no more pure wickedness than there is pure virtue, that an evil action like his crime is not necessarily wholly evil and does not damn him as utterly evil, and that even the poor and mean beggar children along the wayside can be as rich in happiness as the wealthiest and fattest. Thus, when the tour ends in the square of Perugia, Donatello is ready to take his fourth step, that is, he is in a state to be saved.

He is saved by the appearance of Miriam, the very one whose presence had seemed to cause him the sharpest anguish but a few months before. At the sight of her Donatello suddenly stops thinking only of himself, calls to her, and, realizing that her need is like his own, asks her to marry him. Kenyon then declares the two joined, in what is very like a wedding ceremony, under the blessing of the statue of Pope Julius II, and the second part of the novel concludes with Donatello renewed and wiser, much as Miriam was at the end of the first part. He has accepted a place within the community of sinful mortals, and, though he does not confirm his wisdom by performing a sublime sacrifice, he is prepared to and will before the end of the story.

The third and fourth sections, which are shorter than the first two and can therefore be described more briefly, follow the same pattern: the torment, the futility of the efforts to escape leading to despair, the situation which does not seem to offer help but actually does, the climax in which relief is procured by help of another, and finally the wisdom gained from the experience.

In the third section (Chapters XXXVI through XLII) Hilda, who is alone in Rome for the summer, suffers so much from her secret knowledge of the murder that she feels herself besmirched by it. She seeks escape from her torment by contemplating her favorite paintings and statues in the galleries and churches at hand, but these have lost the consecration they once had for her. She even kneels before idols of the Virgin Mary, whom she has always adored, in hope of relief; but these idols now look more like voluptuous mistresses loved by the sculptors than representations of the Divine Mother. Then one day, in her anguish, Hilda wanders into St. Peter's Cathedral, and the situation which is to lead to her relief develops. Since she is a righteous Puritan, Hilda cannot be expected to accept this nest of Catholicism in a religious way, even though she has shown affection for Mary. Yet when she passes a confessional and sees the joy of a woman just leaving her burdens behind, Hilda is almost magically impelled into the booth herself. Having whispered the secret of the murder to the priest, Hilda proudly assures him that, being a Puritan, she has no intention of receiving absolution from his earthy hands, to which he replies that since she did not confess according to the rules he is not obliged to keep what she said secret. Even though Hilda defiantly scolds the priest for his quite reasonable retort, when she leaves him her whole being radiates joy, for, unconventional as her confession was, it has relieved her of her misery.

Unfortunately Hilda learns less from this climactic confession than she ought. Admitting afterward to Kenyon, who has just rushed back to Rome from Perugia, that she had to confess in order not to go mad, she ought to have realized that in slightly different circumstances she might have accepted a political crime as a way out of her trouble instead of a religious heresy. Then it should have occurred to her that the gulf between herself and Miriam was narrower than it had seemed before, that she herself was weak and even sinful. Although Hilda fails to learn quite this much, she does begin to question whether she had been just in casting Miriam off so ruthlessly. And this slight sign of regret leads her to remember a packet of Miriam's which she had promised to deliver that very day at the Palazzo Cenci. Hilda's efforts to deliver the packet develop directly into the fourth part of the

novel (Chapters XLIII through L), in which Kenyon is the central character, and to an incident which completes Hilda's education.

The day after Hilda sets out for the Palazzo Cenci, Kenyon waits in vain for her in the galleries of the Vatican. He goes to her living quarters but finds that she is not there either. In an agony he realizes that she must have been kidnaped. For weeks, then, he searches Rome vainly, quizzing everyone who has known Hilda ever so slightly, calling in the municipal police to help, and even questioning the priest to whom Hilda had confessed. This failure to find Hilda convinces Kenyon at last that the girl was not utterly self-sufficient. Before this time, he had never pressed his affection upon her, or even declared it to her in so many words. Believing she had no need or interest in him, Kenyon had carved a marble replica of her hand and worshiped it in place of the hand itself; that is, he had withdrawn from life, living among marble beings instead of human ones.

Kenyon's weakness, which Hawthorne has hinted at time after time before this fourth section, is very much like the weaknesses of the other three characters. For Miriam in her innocence had denied any connection between herself and the evil of the model, and Hilda had refused any contact with the tainted Miriam herself: while Donatello, who had been mightily repulsed by anything shadowy as long as he was innocent, after the murder believed himself unfit to live among ordinary men. Thus in similar ways all four characters refused to join in intercourse with other mortals, and only toward the end of their respective careers recognized the wrongfulness of their refusal.

Though Kenyon learned this truth, he was still helpless to discover Hilda; but the needed kind of deceptive situation develops for him as it did for the other three. Miriam, who has returned to Rome with Donatello, calls Kenyon to her and instructs him to join the crowd in the Roman Carnival the next day and to move with it until he reaches a certain house on the Corso. Following her instructions Kenyon is swept up in a hilarious crowd of ridiculously masked Romans, certainly the last kind of gathering in which to expect the quiet and restrained Hilda. Yet it is here, on a balcony of the designated house, that Hilda appears; and it is in the midst of this crowd that she expresses, by means of a rose tossed to Kenyon, her new knowledge of her need to live among ordinary mortals, even at the risk of a stain or two.

During the few days after Hilda's climactic reappearance, the wiser and more forward Kenyon presses the advantage of her tenderer and more pliable ways until, as the final climax of the entire novel, the two of them, standing within the Pantheon and under a very significant benediction by Miriam, agree to marry. Although it is obvious that this moment is crucial for Kenyon and Hilda, only the benediction indicates that Miriam and Donatello are still concerned. But, as suggested by a number of hints in the last few chapters, the benediction is indicative that Miriam and Donatello are actually responsible for the very opportunity of Kenyon and Hilda to marry.

That Hilda's release during the Carnival was contingent upon Donatello's and Miriam's giving themselves up to the police as murderers is suggested by the fact that the two Italians are arrested just before Hilda appears and also by Hawthorne's suggestion that the entire affair must have been arranged by the fitful imagination of a very distressed woman, that is, by Miriam. The happiness of the two Americans is thus dependent upon the grief of the two Italians, for while Hilda and Kenyon start out upon their married life Donatello languishes in prison and Miriam, though released by the police, endures a lonely life of miserable longing. This fact that the final happiness of the novel depends upon a grief no less intense is in harmony with Hawthorne's over-all design and also with his dominant theme.

Each of the four climaxes before the fifth and last one gave relief to one person at the expense of another's grief. Miriam's release from the model was purchased by the remorse of Donatello; Donatello's escape from the dreary region of remorse came at the expense of Kenyon, who was kept by the aid he gave the youth from being in Rome to share Hilda's secret, and thus save her from the sinful confession. Hilda's confession revealed the murder by Donatello and Miriam (though the priest does tell Hilda the proper authorities already know about it), violated her own Puritan integrity, and grieved the misled Kenyon, who believed Hilda had been ensnared by the Catholics. And the fourth part, which is closely linked with the ending, results in Hilda's release at the expense of Donatello's arrest.

Kenyon and Hilda are not made to appear wrong, however, in enjoying their own happiness at the expense of others, because Hawthorne has made it abundantly clear that every mature human experience is qualified by both good and evil, both pleasure and pain. The entire novel insists, indirectly of course, that one must accept this fact simply because it is a fact. The very aloofness one maintains in order not to lose his purity leads him into events as much evil as good. But Hawthorne goes beyond this idea to suggest that only after one accepts his place among the community of sinners can he become virtuous and possibly even happy. Miriam's virtue was displayed quite grandly the day after the murder and her recognition of her own sinfulness; Donatello's great triumph of virtue came only when he gave himself up to the corrupt police of Rome; while both Kenyon and Hilda, who have just entered into an active life among sinful mortals, are certainly taking a more compassionate view toward Miriam and Donatello than they did before, though actually these two Americans are not given the opportunity to manifest their newly acquired potentiality for virtue.

It is very important, I believe, that the dominant theme of **The Marble Faun,** as just described, be distinguished from the one attributed to the novel by several earlier critics, the idea that sin itself leads to virtue and happiness. The claim of these critics can be sustained only if it is decided that before the murder Donatello was in exactly the state Adam was in before the Fall. Then Miriam's suggestions about Donatello near the end of the novel would be taken as a comprehensive and exact statement of the theme: she thinks that as Donatello became more sensitive and intelligent after the murder than before, so Adam became better after the Fall than before. But actually, though Miriam's comments are by no means irrelevant, they are not complete; for Donatello is made to appear much more like a faun than like Adam, and, furthermore, in his amoral innocence, he lives surrounded by the corruptions of civilized humanity, which puts him in a different predicament from Adam's. **The Marble Faun,** then, is not merely another retelling of the parable of the Fall, and thus the dominant theme of the novel is not that the Fall was either fortunate or unfortunate.

Hawthorne is not coaxing us to commit murders in order to rise above our present state. What he is suggesting everywhere in the novel is the simple fact that sin is a condition of all human life, that we are all sinners whether we like or admit the fact or not. Although it is impossible not to sin, it is very easy, as the novel implies, to deny one's sinfulness, as Miriam does; or, having recognized one's own sinfulness, to deny like Donatello that anyone else could perform so dark a deed as he; or to substitute some facsimile for living with other adults, as Kenyon shyly does, on the pretext that one simply was not made for such intercourse; or, finally, to waste away with Hilda in a tower aloof from all men, proud of one's apparent but illusory purity, and spurning the begrimed specters of all men who dare approach one. Thus, Hawthorne implies that neither avoiding a sin nor committing one is going to lead a person to a better or happier life than that of one's infantile innocence. But he also suggests that refusing to recognize one's already existent sinfulness is a presumption more sinful than that sin one denies, and makes impossible the attainment of that virtue and happiness which is accessible to grown mortals. The potentiality for goodness is born in a person only with his awareness that he is one of an all-inclusive brotherhood of human beings, a relationship not of blood, of parentage, or by contract, but of sin and inadequacy, and requiring the mutual dependence of everyone. (pp. 302-12)

Merle E. Brown, "The Structure of 'The Marble Faun'," in *American Literature*, Vol. XXVII, No. 3, November, 1956, pp. 302-13.

ROY R. MALE   (essay date 1957)

[*Male examines the parallels between art and life in* The Marble Faun.]

Many readers, even those who appreciate Hawthorne's other works, have found **The Marble Faun** slow going. Its defects as a novel have often been observed. No coherent structure is immediately apparent; particularly in the opening chapters, Hawthorne is guilty of awkward transitions and clumsily playful author-to-reader comments; the narrative seems to bog down in the lengthy descriptions of Rome and its art objects. Of the four characters, only Miriam and Donatello show any signs of vitality. To make matters worse, Hawthorne teases the reader into looking at the wrong side of the tapestry; he supplies clues about Miriam and the model, for instance, that prompt precisely the kind of investigation he deplores in the conclusion.

The book's almost complete failure as novel inevitably limits its worth as romance, and I think **The Marble Faun** must finally be reckoned the least successful of Hawthorne's finished works. Yet with all its defects, the book deserves a sympathetic rereading, since its complex framework embraces Hawthorne's fullest explorations of morality and art. Indeed, its shortcomings result mainly from the grandeur of his aim. Never before had he tried to achieve so much in his medium; never before had he pressed the romance to its breaking point, as he does with Hilda in this book. His own comments reflect this gap between achievement and goal. "The thing is a failure," he said, in a mood of despair; yet he also called **The Marble Faun** his "best work."

Hawthorne's subject, once again, is the "riddle of the soul's growth." How does man develop his full human potential? How do incarnation, conversion, transfiguration take place? The central figures in this process are already familiar to us [from Hawthorne's earlier works]: the young man who frolics in timeless spatial freedom and innocence; the woman inexorably linked with time and guilt but also with a redemptive ideal; and the union between them, with its attendant shocks and recognitions. In *The House of the Seven Gables* Hawthorne involved the individual with his immediate cultural and familial ancestry; here he plunges the innocent into all time, confronts him with the totality of the past and with the very "model," the prototype of evil.

Some of Hawthorne's difficulties resulted from his efforts to achieve a density he felt to be lacking in his earlier work. In this book he strove to make the observer-commentator, Kenyon, a more substantial figure than Miles Coverdale; he tried to make Hilda both an allegorical ideal and a character; and he aimed at fusing action and setting in a structure more complex than any he had hitherto attempted. In this last intention he was quite successful, though the book's structure is discernible only after careful reading.

As the opening and concluding chapters indicate, the book is about four characters—Miriam, Hilda, Kenyon, and Donatello—who undergo a threefold process of transformation. The simplest way of grasping the book's structure is to envisage a circle divided into four parts revolving about a center. This center, or central experience, is expressed in various ways throughout the book. It is the way of conversion, in art and in life. Hawthorne discerns a "threefold analogy,—the clay model, the Life; the plaster cast, the Death; and the sculptured marble, the Resurrection." Indeed, all of Rome itself seems designed after this analogy. Its grimy streets swarm with intricate, colorful life; its pavements cover a grave; and its towers and churches stretch heavenward. "Everywhere . . . a Cross,—and nastiness at the foot of it."

The history of Rome and its environs follows the same pattern. The first stage was the innocent "sylvan life of Etruria, while Italy was yet guiltless of Rome"; the second was the sin and fall of Rome; the third, of course, was the rise of Christianity from the labyrinthine depths of the fall. These three periods are marked by cultural "peaks": Etruria in the Faun of Praxiteles in Chapter I; Rome in the statue of Marcus Aurelius in Chapter XVIII (which is entitled "On the Edge of the Precipice" and concludes with the "fall" of the model and of Donatello); and Christianity in the statue of Pope Julius in Chapter XXXV.

To combine the four characters and the threefold process is to arrive at the mystic number seven, which receives much attention in the book. The seven-branched candlestick that was lost at the Ponte Moll during Constantine's reign suggests to Hilda "an admirable idea for a mystic story or parable, or seven-branched allegory, full of poetry, art, philosophy, and religion." The whole ritual of transformation is summed up in Miriam's bridal gift to Hilda, an Etruscan bracelet, "the connecting bond of a series of seven wondrous tales, all of which, as they were dug out of seven sepulchres, were characterized by a seven-fold sepulchral gloom." In its "entire circle," the bracelet is the symbol of a "sad mystery," though there is a gleam of hope at the end.

In someone else's fiction we might dismiss these recurrent allusions to a seven-branched allegory as idle fancy, but Hawthorne seldom if ever labors a point unless it has meaning. Looking back over the book, we discover that every seventh chapter contains a recognition scene in which an individual is transfigured by a vital bond with the past. These sacramental "rites" do not follow the orthodox order prescribed by the

Roman Catholics, nor do we expect them to. What Hawthorne does insist upon is the real presence of the past and the need for communion with it if transformation is to occur. The first of these scenes occurs, of course, in Chapter I, when the three artists detect Donatello's striking resemblance to the statue and name him the "very Faun of Praxiteles." In Chapter VII Hilda is startled to observe that Miriam's expression has become almost exactly that of Beatrice Cenci. The corpse of the dead Capuchin, with the blood oozing from its nostrils, assumes the likeness of all evil for Miriam in Chapter XXI. It symbolizes "the deadly iteration with which she was doomed to behold the image of her crime reflected back upon her in a thousand ways." By this time Donatello has assumed a similar burden from the past, and his new awareness of its weight is typified in Chapter XXVIII when he takes up the alabaster skull of his ancestor and explains its meaning to Kenyon. Having done penance, Miriam and Donatello find their union blessed at "high noon" in Chapter XXXV, when the statue of Pope Julius seems to become "endowed with spiritual life." It is now Hilda's turn to recognize the bond, and in Chapter XLII she realizes for the first time the harshness of her earlier attitude toward Miriam. Now she is able to see the resemblance between herself and her former friend, and she makes what amounts to a penitential journey to the Palazzo Cenci, haunted by the "lovely shade of Beatrice."

The final "incarnation" takes place during the magnificent carnival scene of Chapter XLIX. Though Kenyon has been intellectually aware of the past, he has cherished a spiritual love for Hilda that has insulated him from the shocks of vital experience; he has resisted any real involvement with Miriam's trouble; and he has retreated from her suggested analogy between their story and the Fall of man. Now, in spite of himself, he becomes a part of the carnival. He finds his Hilda only after an exaggerated re-enactment of the Fall of man. A giant Eve, a female figure "seven feet tall," singles out the sculptor and makes "a ponderous assault on his heart." Failing in her first attempts, she shoots him in the heart with a popgun, "covering Kenyon with a cloud of lime-dust." This affair is "like a feverish dream," a surrealistic version of Adam's reduction to human clay, but it qualifies Kenyon for union with the multifoliate rosebud, the spirit incarnate in Hilda. (pp. 157-61)

In *The Marble Faun,* the parallel between sculpture and life is introduced in the title, established in the first paragraph, and maintained throughout the book. The process of transfiguration is as central in art as it is in life. The three stages of sculpture—clay, plaster cast, and marble—are, as we have already noted, analogous to life, death, and resurrection. Hawthorne begins by describing the marble statues in the sculpture room at the Capitol, "shining in the undiminished majesty and beauty of their ideal life," but at the same time "corroded by the damp earth." In the statue of a child "clasping a dove to her bosom, but assaulted by a snake" is prefigured the choice between "Innocence or Evil"—a choice that will affect the lives of the four individuals standing in the room.

The whole problem of evil, of reconciling "the incongruity of Divine Omnipotence and outraged, suffering Humanity," is in fact summed up in Kenyon's natural comparison of God to a sculptor who "held the new, imperfect earth in his hand, and modelled it." In creating the world, God was subject to the limitations of his art form, the imperfect clay in which he worked. Clay is, as Miriam says, earthy and human.

Kenyon's clay model captures "all Cleopatra—fierce, voluptuous, passionate, tender, wicked, terrible, and full of poisonous and rapturous enchantment." His clay bust of Donatello similarly expresses the mixture of good and evil that characterizes human life. Flexible, warm, impure, the intricate shape of clay seems "more interesting than even the final marble, as being the intimate production of the sculptor himself, moulded throughout with his loving hands, and nearest to his imagination and heart."

The beauty and life of the clay model disappear in the plaster cast. Imbued with mortality, it has no celestial hopes; it has the rigidity of marble with none of its purity. The skull in Donatello's room is carved "in gray alabaster, most skillfully done to the death, with accurate imitation of the teeth, the sutures, the empty eye-caverns, and the fragile little bones of the nose." The corpse of the dead Capuchin congeals into a ghastly waxen hardness that fits it into this grisly category. Like the macabre skulls in the Capuchin cemetery, the corpse seems a malevolent mockery of man's hopes for a future life.

But out of the clay and the plaster emerges the pure, white, undecaying figure done in marble, which assumes a sacred character. "It insures immortality to whatever is wrought in it, and therefore makes it a religious obligation to commit no idea to its mighty guardianship, save such as may repay the marble for its faithful care, its incorruptible fidelity, by warming it with an ethereal life." Yet though the marble should resolve the feverish activity of life into a cool repose—"a blessed change," as Miriam calls it—too often it appears rigid, harsh, and remote from human concerns. "You are as cold and pitiless as your own marble," she exclaims, as she detects Kenyon's reluctance to become entangled in her affairs.

With this basic resemblance between sculpture and moral growth established, we may now proceed to Hawthorne's distinction between sculpture and painting. Sculpture, as he views it in this book, is essentially a masculine art form. It freezes an image in space and has nothing temporal about it. "Flitting moments," Kenyon observes, "ought not to be incrusted with the eternal repose of marble." A sculptural subject, therefore, ought to be in a "moral standstill." Painting, on the other hand, is essentially feminine. "Your frozen art," Miriam gibes, "has nothing like the scope and freedom of Hilda's and mine. In painting there is no similar objection to the representation of brief snatches of time." Painting, she adds, is a warmer, more heartfelt medium.

The man, therefore, is a sculptor, while the two women are painters. But the fact that Hilda is a "copyist" requires further comment if we are to understand the initial artistic situation. To put it schematically, at the outset Donatello is nature, Hilda is spirit, and Miriam and Kenyon are the two working artists. Donatello, obviously, is the object: he is all matter, though a spiritual potential may be discerned. Hilda, as spirit, sees *sub specie aeternitatis*. She looks right through the surface of paintings to the central point or aim of the artist; she works religiously; but she can create nothing new. Donatello is the origin, Hilda the "end." To be converted into art, Donatello must "unearth"; Hilda must "earth-stain." Viewed from this perspective, the crucial moment comes late in the book when Donatello unearths the earth-stained statue of Venus de' Medici—a statue that reminds Kenyon of his quest for Hilda.

Truly creative art, therefore, requires both penetrative insight and sympathetic investment. Without the humane clothing of a sympathetic imagination, penetrative insight is like rigorous Freudian literary criticism; it plumbs the surface, but it leaves us with a nude, or at its worst, with a skull. On Hilda's religious plane it results simply in a pure copy of an unchanging idea. But investment without insight produces mechanical superficial copies far inferior to Hilda's spiritual imitations. Transformation of material into art must ultimately remain a mystery, a miracle. Like human conversion, it is consummated in a moment of immediate apprehension that comes as a reward for intellectual discipline and sympathetic understanding. The final product, the "genial moment" in which the inner germ finds the perfection of its outward form, is not entirely preconceived. With both his Cleopatra and his bust of Donatello, Kenyon begins hopefully with his conscious intentions, lives through a period of despair, and finally achieves the vital expression "independent of his own will." (pp. 163-66)

The discussions of art can be fully understood only as part of the book's thematic structure. Its action we have outlined as an ever widening four-part circle, revolving about a threefold central experience. After rebelling against her destined role as woman, Miriam discovers her bond with time and the specter of guilt; Donatello becomes passionately entangled with Miriam and her guilt; Hilda becomes involved (though vicariously) with Miriam, Donatello, and their guilt; and finally Kenyon (in an even more diluted mode) recognizes his relation to Miriam, Donatello, Hilda, and the total burden of humanity.

It is fitting that Miriam should be the major figure in the first part of the book, for she potentially offers what Rome does—"all time." A prototype of womanhood like Beatrice Rappaccini, Hester, and Zenobia, she seems to contain all races in her rich, mysterious origins. There is "an ambiguity about this young lady": linked like Eve and Pandora to the very model of evil, she also bears the seed of maturity and benediction. (p. 167)

We know that her mother died when Miriam was an infant and that a marriage unsuitable for the daughter but convenient for the family fortunes had been arranged. Miriam's fiancé had been her cousin, a man whose character "betrayed traits so evil, so treacherous, so vile, and yet so strangely subtle, as could only be accounted for by the insanity which often develops itself in old, close-kept races of men, when long unmixed with newer blood." She revolted against her father, repudiating the marriage contract. Then followed the nameless crime (probably, judging from the parallel with Beatrice Cenci, the murder of her father). (p. 168)

Legally innocent but morally guilty, affianced to satanic evil, Miriam obviously bears more than casual resemblance to Eve after her first depravity. Her original crime, like Eve's, was rebellion against the father ("Miriam" originally meant "rebellion"). Like Hester and Zenobia, however, she is linked not only to guilt but also to the vessel of purification; she is potentially a second Eve (again her name is significant: "Mary," of course, derives from Greek "Mariam," Hebrew "Miryam"). Hilda is Miriam's closest friend; they are like "sisters of the same blood," containing between them the essence of womanhood. But unlike Pearl, who is Hester's seed and effectively bruises the head of the serpent, Hilda does not function very well as a narrative embodiment of woman's redemptive qualities. We note the meaning of her separation from Miriam and their eventual reunion, but it is not dramatically convincing.

Miriam's efforts to expunge her guilt, to find "new hopes, new joys," can only lead to further extension of her Original Sin. Once the man has fixed his lot with her, he is, as Milton says, "certain to undergo like doom." Donatello, whose transformation appropriately occupies the central portion of the book, is first introduced as the ultimate of primitive innocence. Free to gambol in space, he "has nothing to do with time." In his animal-like youth, he enjoys the peak of intuitive sympathy with all forms of life. In order to mature, he must be educated through the heart by Miriam. But he educates her as well. She needs the ritual of the romp through the Borghese Eden, a refreshment from the fountain of simplicity in order to assume her proper role as woman. When she asks why he follows her, he answers simply, "Because I love you." There is no other way to say it, and he saves her from moving into a brittle existence where such sentiments, if uttered at all, would be verbalized into something like, "Our emotional impulses are integrated, and we show promise of attaining a moral and intellectual continuum." He saves her, in short, from the rigid refinement of a Kenyon.

The first fruit of Donatello's "marriage" with Miriam is a feeling of fiery intoxication distilled out of their mutual guilt. In a passage reminiscent of the forest scene in *The Scarlet Letter*, Miriam urges Donatello to fling the past behind him. "Forget it! Cast it all behind you," she urges. "The deed has done its office, and has no existence any more." But it soon becomes apparent that the specter of guilt is not buried this easily. Donatello, like the fallen Adam, now repels the woman. He returns to his parental home to make that agonizing reappraisal of his own heritage which is one of the first consequences of the union between man and woman. He has lost his unity with nature; Miriam has lost her friendship with Hilda.

Like Dimmesdale, Donatello now finds it necessary to avoid men's eyes; he contemplates turning inward to a monkish cell; he is overwhelmed by an exaggerated sense of the past. But he has developed a new dignity, so that his title, the Count of Monte Beni, now seems a more appropriate name. Here in his native land, he and Kenyon educate each other, the sculptor attempting to clarify the Count's muddled thoughts after his shock of recognition, and the Count implicitly demonstrating to Kenyon the difference between vital involvement with the past and mere intellectual apprehension of it. The whole process of moral growth reveals itself to Kenyon from Donatello's tower, as he gazes out over the valley . . . . (pp. 169-71)

The Count's great danger now, as his guide points out, is that he will be hypnotized by the vision of evil. Like Vergil advising Dante in Canto XXX of the *Inferno,* Kenyon tells Donatello that "it was needful for you to pass through that dark valley, but it is infinitely dangerous to linger there too long; there is poison in the atmosphere, when we sit down and brood in it!" Though he is a wise counselor, Kenyon prefers not to become too deeply involved himself. He watches the process of treading out the wine press; he sees the laborer's feet and garments dyed red as with blood; but he declines a sample of the Tuscan wine. "He had tried a similar draught . . . in years past, and was little inclined to make proof of it again; for he knew that it would be a sour and bitter juice, a wine of woe and tribulation, and that the more a man drinks of such liquor, the sorrier he is likely to be."

Donatello emerges from the valley and finds blessing when he rejoins Miriam under the statue of Pope Julius. Kenyon's remarks on their reunion are pontifical—he is, in effect, speaking for the Pope—but they make their point:

> Not for earthly bliss, but for mutual elevation, and encouragement towards a severe and painful life, you take each other's hands. And if, out of toil, sacrifice, prayer, penitence, and earnest effort towards right things, there comes, at length, a sombre and thoughtful happiness, taste it, and thank Heaven! So that you live not for it,—so that it be wayside flower, springing along a path that leads to higher ends,—it will be Heaven's gracious gift, and a token that it recognizes your union here below.

As the Faun, the original type of man, finds his soul and struggles with it "towards the light of heaven," the heavenly vision is brought down to earth. The incarnation of the Holy Spirit in the Dove is, as most readers have agreed, the most ineffective portion of the book. We do not boggle at the dove symbol in Eliot's *Four Quartets;* and we might accept Hilda in a medieval dream vision, but in fiction she is impossible. She needs to be either more adult or else a child, like Pearl, Ibrahim, or little Joe in "Ethan Brand." If she must be pictured as an adult, Hilda ought to be an ideal who is merely glimpsed at the end. When Hawthorne brings her out of her tower and involves her in the streets of Rome, we expect her to be more human than she can possibly be if she is to retain her allegorical function as spiritual purity. "It is like flinging a block of marble up into the air, and, by some trick of enchantment, causing it to stick there. You feel that it ought to come down, and are dissatisfied that it does not obey the natural law." This is Kenyon's observation about the timeless repose of marble, but it fits the problem of Hilda perfectly. She is associated throughout with the purity of marble. Even the marble image of her hand—the birthmark, the earthy part of Hilda that is all Kenyon can grasp—assumes its share of her remote divinity. Hawthorne apparently expected the reader to sense her icy rigidity and yet to sympathize with her. Thus he is forced into the excessive sentiment of such statements as "Poor sufferer for another's sin."

Nevertheless, this portion of the book has its high points: the description of Sodoma's Christ, with its parallel to Hilda's utter isolation in her vicarious atonement; her reaction to St. Peter's Cathedral; and, above all, her confession to the priest. As she yearns for the relief of the confessional, she sees the inscription *'Pro Anglica Lingua.'* It is "the word in season"; it is Hilda's opportunity to become part of the time-burdened human race; and here, for once, she is "softened out of the chillness of her virgin pride." That Hawthorne intended her to be delicately transformed into a woman from this point onward is clear when Kenyon finds the Venus Donatello has already unearthed. "What a discovery is here," he says. "I seek for Hilda, and find a marble woman! Is the omen good or ill?" The fact that the Venus is "slightly corroded" should supply his answer. But Hilda's purity is never more apparent and never more repulsive than it is in the final scenes with Kenyon.

Part of this is Kenyon's fault. If he is more substantial than Miles Coverdale, he is also much more stuffy. Hawthorne undoubtedly intended to portray the rigidity of the refined intellectual, but surely he did not mean Kenyon to be as insufferable as the modern reader finds him. (pp. 171-73)

Both Hilda and Kenyon, therefore, convince us of the loss that occurs in refinement. Kenyon, who apparently but not convincingly has earlier suffered through a tragic experience, is now content to distill life in his art and in his Hilda, who has her refined sculptor and her religion, which, like her art, is borrowed. Both ultimately remain spectators of the central experience of the book: the wedding of ultimate innocence—Etruria and the living Faun—with all time and all evil—Miriam and Rome.

Thus we are returned to the problem that has provoked much discussion: Does Hawthorne accept or reject the idea of the Fortunate Fall? (pp. 173-74)

[Almost] every page of the book indicates that without sin and suffering, moral growth rarely, if ever, results. With the examples of Miriam and Donatello fresh in our minds, it is difficult to see how any other interpretation is possible. Donatello is plunged "into those dark caverns, into which all men must descend, if they would know anything beneath the superficial and illusive pleasures of existence. And when they emerge, though dazzled and blinded by the first glare of daylight, they take truer and sadder views of life forever afterwards." Every human life, if it ascends to truth or delves down to reality, must undergo a similar change." This progression is presented historically, with the glimpse back into the Golden Age, "before mankind was burdened with sin and sorrow, and before pleasure had been darkened with those shadows that bring it into high relief, and make it happiness." It is presented scenically, when Kenyon beholds the sunshine, the shadow, the tempest, and finally the sunny splendor. And . . . it is presented dramatically.

How, then, can so acute a critic as Waggoner argue that Hawthorne did not intend this meaning? Surely Waggoner is right when he says that Hawthorne, with Hilda, would reject the "line of reasoning" that is implied in the phrase "the Fortunate Fall." But he is just as surely wrong in saying that the narrative embodiment of the idea of redemption through sin is confined to Miriam; that she runs away with the book so that the achieved meaning differs from the intended meaning. The point is that Hawthorne and Hilda reject Kenyon's argument precisely because it is a line of reasoning. Take the narrative element out of the Christian story; make a logical formula (the Fortunate Fall) of it; remove the temporal lag between Adam's sin and Christ's redemption and it becomes a frozen creed that is at best a paradox, at worst a mockery of true morality. We recall that one of the main points of *The Scarlet Letter* was that moral truth must be apprehended as a narrative, a parable, an allegory—not as a line of reasoning. This of course, is only another way of expressing what Christians mean when they speak of "living by Christ." It is what Hawthorne meant when he found theological libraries to be a "stupendous impertinence." (pp. 175-76)

In Hawthorne's view no automatic formula suffices for meeting problems of the spirit. In this imperfect world some rise by sin and some fall by virtue. "Sometimes the instruction comes without the sorrow," but Hawthorne is dubious about this possibility. "Oftener the sorrow teaches no lesson that abides with us." Dimmesdale ascends as a consequence of his sin; Young Goodman Brown's dying hour is gloom. Like Dimmesdale, Donatello rises spiritually and intellectually, although his flesh is incarcerated; Ethan Brand plunges into the pit. In order to develop his full human potential, man must become fully involved with time yet retain his unique ability to stand aside from its fleeting onrush and contemplate the eternal. This is the tragic vision of Hawthorne's fiction. (p. 177)

Roy R. Male, in his Hawthorne's Tragic Vision, *University of Texas Press, 1957, 187 p.*

MURRAY KRIEGER   (essay date 1961)

[*In the following excerpt from an essay first published in 1961, Krieger links the moral ambiguity of* The Marble Faun *to Hawthorne's ambivalence toward European aesthetics and ethics as revealed in his* Italian Notebooks.]

The Marble Faun, of all Nathaniel Hawthorne's fiction, may be the clearest acknowledgment of the uncertainty with which its author maintained his famed Puritanical morality. If the novel has been seriously underestimated, as I believe it has, it is because critics have commonly drained off its life by applying to it an *a priori* notion of Hawthorne's moral austerity which the novel itself does not justify. It is unfortunate that commentators have failed to accord to Hawthorne the benefits of the critical generosity usually reserved for Henry James in his later versions of "the international theme" that makes its earlier and influential appearance in **The Marble Faun.** Even writers who concede that James was indebted to this novel in his formulating this theme and who normally allow to James the controlled transcendence of his moral opposition between American and European values continue to see Hawthorne as the priggish provincial who condescends to his Italian experience and idolatrously creates cold New England saints to protect himself from it and purge it from his pages. However, it is not only that in Hawthorne, as later in James, the novel is grounded in a profound conflict between the limited claims of American moralism and of European aestheticism, but also that in Hawthorne, as later in James, the totality of the novel in its multi-dimensionality sees round any single restrictive moral vantage point. The earlier as well as the later writer is aware, in the moral-aesthetic polarity, of an irresolvable *either/or* and displays an ambivalence toward either pole that forces any total choice to be made only with a tragic sense of loss. It is as much a mistake to deny Hawthorne a finally cosmopolitan awareness of the mutual attractions and disadvantages of his alternatives as it is to deny him the awareness of the conflict itself.

None of this is to deny that his heroine Hilda is, for the most part, an intolerably pallid New England version of a human being; but it is to deny that, to the total neglect of Miriam's claims, we can blandly identify Hilda with Hawthorne's conception of the human ideal and thus can rub off her insufficiencies on him. After all, some of James' ambassadors from Woollett, Massachusetts, are no more humanly satisfying, and yet we see the total structure of the novel revealing an awareness that towers over their dwarfed sensibilities. It is risky to assume that Hawthorne was so much less an artist, that he projected his limitations so single-mindedly that we can turn our reactions to Hilda upon her creator, when he has really protected himself against them by seeing her inadequacies, intending them to be seen as such, and containing them within a structure that defines and judges them in the full dramatic density of their human relevance.

But are Hilda's limitations in fact Hawthorne's? Even before we reach **The Marble Faun** itself, our expectations concerning his New Englander's insularity may lead us to underestimate the depth of the experience described in his *Italian Notebooks,* to dismiss his Italian experience by assuming that he self-righteously dismissed it. It is this experience, and the problems revealed in it, that are projected onto the novel. The complexity of one is clue to the complexity of the other. Thus it is worth stopping to observe the tensions revealed in the journal since they make their way, equally unresolved, into the novel.

The journal continually shows Hawthorne profoundly perplexed by the art and the sense of the past which engulf him in the seat of Catholicism. This is not to say, as some have, that his experience was refracted through a narrowly provincial Puritan mind which would allow no value to anything it encountered. At the same time it is certainly true that there was much in Italy of which he was contemptuous, even much that he hated. This is truer in his earlier pages, written in days and nights of physical discomfort; but throughout the journal we see him bored by the endless and wearying exhibition of art, shocked by the pagan nudity of the sculpture, and morally outraged by the general corruption and filth of Rome and its people. But as he comes more and more to be captivated by certain works of painting and sculpture and forced into admiration for certain aspects of Catholicism, we become increasingly aware of another side to this sensitive New Englander. Finally, he could not quite make up his mind about Italy, but unquestionably he saw that he could not reject it uncritically, that he could not bring himself to spit it out even if he never dared swallow it.

Thus it is with a sense of unavoidable loss that, at the end, he takes up his Americanism and tries to forget the enigma that Rome became for him. . . . (pp. 79-81)

His moral consciousness, his scrupulosity, never leave him utterly, so that at best his attitude is ambivalent. The tradition and age of Rome sometimes impress him favorably, even arousing his admiration as an inheritor of Western culture and his envy as a patriotic and apologetic American; but at the same time he sees this enormous burden of the past oppressing the present with the massive legacy of centuries that have multiplied sin with brutality. The very aesthetic heritage which draws him to the Church binds it irrevocably to the paganism which Catholicism superseded (or, Hawthorne might prefer to say, adapted) in Rome. He is profoundly struck by what in the novel he calls (and not always condescendingly) the "convenience" of Catholicism, by the unfailing understanding through which the Church has adapted itself to all human weakness and all human needs, by the easy and pleasant and beautiful comfort it has made of religion. What better evidence of how moved he is than that he allows the inviolable Hilda, Puritanism itself, to avail herself of this "convenience," the Confessional, at a most crucial moment—and to be saved by it! Still never quite absent from his awareness is the feeling that this very paternal solicitude, however humanly soothing, contains an impurity and a corruption which can be avoided only by a hard and severe, individual and immediate religion, without worldly priestly intruders, illuminated by the light of heaven unfiltered by the deceptive man-made splendor of the stained-glass window.

Hawthorne's unresolved double vision in the *Notebooks* should warn us to expect no simple thematic resolution in *The Marble Faun.* The writer of the journal could hardly produce a partisan victory. And the closeness of the novel to the journal is striking in detail as well as in the larger thematic

concerns that we have been observing. Since Hawthorne thought of himself as a romancer rather than a realistic reporter and since he indeed was a most inventive storyteller, a maker of fables, it is surprising to find so much material carried over from the *Notebooks* into the novel without being significantly reshaped to fulfill a uniquely fictional purpose. And when we recognize the thematic and even symbolic use to which borrowings from the *Notebooks* are put, our surprise at the similarity of fact and fiction, of personal reaction and aesthetic creation, increases. These occurrences suggest that Hawthorne in his original autobiographical involvement was already thinking in the thematic and symbolic terms out of which the novel later emerged. And our observations have tended to confirm this suggestion. (pp. 82-3)

Even if we view the *Notebooks* as a sort of apprenticeship to the central issues of the novel, still we must wonder why the materials were not forced to respond more plastically to the demands of Hawthorne's "romance," which, according to his own prescriptions, must create a reality of its own distinct from that of ordinary existence. And the major difficulty in *The Marble Faun,* the weakness probably responsible for its unfortunate neglect, stems from his inability to create a unique realm of being for the characters and incidents in the romance; that is, his inability to decide whether the novel's reality was to stem from the Italian actualities borrowed from the *Notebooks* or from a special, fabulous world created in terms of its own symbolic necessities.

In his famous metaphorical definition of a romance in the lengthy introductory chapter to *The Scarlet Letter,* Hawthorne has told us of the romancer's power to "dream strange things and make them look like truth." He can manage this power because his romance is an independent, specially illuminated world, "a neutral territory, somewhere between the real world and fairyland, where the Actual and the Imaginary may meet, and each imbue itself with the nature of the other." In Hawthorne's metaphor familiar, even commonplace objects are acted on first by the cold lucidity of moonlight and secondly by the genial domesticity of a dim coal fire. The first transforms the objects into intellectual abstractions; the second informs those abstractions with the warmth of life, turning them "from snow-images into men and women." It is perhaps this metaphor Henry James refers to in his book on Hawthorne when he objects to unjustifiably abstract or allegorical elements in his predecessor by complaining of them as "moonshine" or as the products of a "lunar" mist [see excerpt dated 1879 in *NCLC,* Vol. 2].

The failings of *The Marble Faun* are mainly of this kind, but they occur because Hawthorne tries to ground his "lunar" elements in the precise and detailed realities provided by his *Notebooks.* Despite his intentions, his work, alas, is only half romance, and it cannot satisfy two realms of probabilities at once. An author is quite justified in establishing his own world, with its special laws, if he will not remind us too much of ours. But fantasy is difficult to follow or allow when it takes place before so vividly reported a backdrop as Hawthorne's Rome. He needs Rome and its many masterpieces which give meaning to the action and allow conversations which importantly reflect the speakers. But he must pay the price in realism for his use of this scenery. It is here that he becomes half-hearted, unable to make his fantasy literally sensible and not quite unwilling to try. He multiplies coincidences that often, with his encouragement, seem mystically induced and then belatedly and without conviction tries to account for them.

He cannot manage to make Miriam's persecutor either man or Satan, although on differing occasions he tries to make him both, even as these several occasions and their presuppositions about the persecutor are mutually contradictory. He has a similar problem with Donatello as man and/or faun.

Finally, the very source of the action depends on an ever-deepening mystery about Miriam's family and personal history and her relations with her persecutor. The intrusion of vague Gothic elements which remind us of unspeakable and unholy terror—a metaphysical horror which makes *any* action possible—cannot satisfy us. We simply do not believe that Hawthorne can satisfy us, that any literal reality can satisfy the supernatural requirements he has placed on his situation, and we can believe that the terror remains unspeakable only because the author dare not speak lest it evaporate before the breath of a reality that he cannot make impressive enough. So we never do find out the details. Late in the novel we are told that Kenyon has been the author's narrator and his sole source of information, even though only an omniscient author could have told us much of the story that has preceded. But Hawthorne introduces this narrator in this *ad hoc* way in order to impose this limit upon his omniscience so that we shall excuse him for not knowing what we must never find out. When he feels pressed by exasperated readers to add his chapter of "Conclusion," he apologizes for his Gothic vagueness by reinvoking his definition of romance and then, with regrettable coyness, at once provides inadequate explanations and introduces further mystifications to cover up for them. And again we feel the futility of this attempt at a romance in which, perhaps thanks to the borrowings from the realities of the *Notebooks,* he cannot totally believe. He cannot root his allegory in bedrock reality, even though it is biographical and geographical reality which permits it to take shape.

It is in the Preface to the novel that Hawthorne relates his notions about romance to his opposition between Italy and America, feeling that especially in Italy history can provide mystification (or mythification):

> No author, without a trial, can conceive of the difficulty of writing a romance about a country where there is no shadow, no antiquity, no mystery, no picturesque and gloomy wrong, nor anything but a commonplace prosperity in broad and simple daylight, as is happily the case with my dear native land. It will be very long, I trust, before romance-writers may find congenial and easily handled themes within the annals of our stalwart republic, or in any characteristic and probable events of our individual lives. Romance and poetry, ivy, lichens, and wall-flowers need ruin to make them grow.

This passage, dedicated to the distinction between realism and romance, fact and fancy, the literal and the symbolic, also returns us to Hawthorne's duality of attitude toward the old world and the new. And as we recall my earlier discussion of the aesthetic-moral conflict between these worlds and my observation that his original definition of romance in *The Scarlet Letter* at once opposed the real to the allegorical and human warmth to cold intellectual abstraction, we may be permitted to wonder whether the aesthetic difficulties we have seen him fall prey to in the novel are not the reverse side of the moral perplexities and indecisiveness we have seen him fall prey to in Italy. Could it not be that his inability to choose consistently between actuality and symbolic overlay or to synthesize them into his "neutral" realm of romance is a re-

flection of his inability to choose consistently between the inhuman austerity of New England moralism and the all-too-human license of aged Italian aestheticism or to synthesize these? Thus the relation of the *Notebooks* to the novel, of both of these to his notion of romance in contrast with reality, and of all these to the conflict between corrupt warmth and intellectual frigidity reveals how unified the aesthetic and thematic dimensions—and difficulties—of *The Marble Faun* come to be.

Hawthorne's own aesthetic, as we can derive it from what he says about the romance, indicates how much he concedes to the need for human warmth and how clearly he relates this need to the need for historical depth, even as the latter brings sin in its wake. The warmth of the hearth is the romancer's only protection against sheer moonshine, the only way to bring men and women out of snow-images. Hawthorne gives to Kenyon, his American sculptor in *The Marble Faun,* a similar artistic problem. Working in marble, he must imbue his objects with the warmth of humanity. And in moments of despondence he fears that after all the cold severity of his medium has proved too much for him. When his American moral overscrupulosity leads him to turn aside from Miriam in her need to confess to him, she cries, "You are as cold and pitiless as your own marble." Again Hawthorne's equation of the unfeeling virtue of moral severity with coldness and the yielding grace of faulty humanity with warmth. And again his aesthetic problem and his thematic problem are seen to join, his aesthetic sense conditioning his moral sense in broadening his awareness as a romancer even as it did in broadening his reactions to his Italian experience.

The structure of the novel is primarily controlled by the dramatic terms given the oppositions which have been concerning us, and with about the same ultimate indecisiveness, which explains why I quarrel with the common relegation of the novel and with the facile disposition of Hilda's place in it. Hilda must rather be seen as a person who is in one sense admirable, if not saintly, but in another sense seriously incomplete. Again it is the grim confrontation of cold and warmth, together with the grimmer insistence that there is no acceptable bridge between them. Each has the derivative qualities we have noticed: warmth has Catholicism, aestheticism, and tradition; cold has Protestantism, moral simplicity, and immediacy. Each set of qualities has its desirable and undesirable consequences: Catholicism is "convenient" but corrupt, aestheticism is enriching but pagan, and tradition is profound but carries along its burden of sin. The alternative qualities invert these attributes, correcting the moral deficiencies but losing their relevance to the needs of the human heart. Thus Protestantism is seen as a religion for angels and Catholicism as a religion for men. If the former will not bend to man to help him in his need, the latter cannot raise him so as to obliterate that need.

It is of course in Miriam and Hilda that this opposition realizes itself. Miriam not only is the essence of Rome but is made its literal incarnation. If Rome, home of the universal and traditional religion and of the pagan world's universal state is an exquisite choice as the symbol of warmth, Miriam is an exquisite choice as the symbol of Rome. She is beautiful, brilliant, charming—attractive in every way. Yet there is a fatality about her which is inevitably associated with her sin-ridden heritage. In the not quite idyllic early scene in the Villa Borghese, Rome's bloody inheritance from the ages and its own fatality, together with its beauty, are juxtaposed to hers. Rome is likened to Eden, but it is like Eden in its fatality—here represented by malaria—as in its loveliness. Immediately after this description Miriam warns Donatello to protect his innocence by avoiding her. He answers, "I would as soon think of fearing the air we breathe." Her reply completes the metaphor: "And well you may, for it is full of malaria. . . . Those who come too near me are in danger of great mischiefs, I do assure you." The murder she commits through Donatello is consistent with this metaphor. He hurls the persecutor-model from the Tarpeian Rock in what amounts to a pagan execution ceremony. Not only has Miriam given the assent of her eyes, but just before the act she has defended the principle behind the ancient Roman use of the Rock. Thus her crime, initially precipitated by an evil to which she was born but of which she was innocent, is committed in a manner similarly dictated by history.

If Miriam is the Roman ideal, certainly Hilda is the Puritan. She is as spotless and as unearthly as the doves who at once symbolize and accompany her. But despite her transcendent moral perfection, she is humanly insufficient. At the start she has no knowledge of sin, and when its existence is forced upon her, her sole reaction is fear of contamination. She fears that, once mixed, evil will appropriate good rather than good evil. In her severity she fails Miriam irrevocably and crucially as a friend. Miriam forcefully and repeatedly charges her willful blindness to the evil principle and her austere refusal to acknowledge and combat it with being serious human, if not moral, shortcomings. Her moralistic lover Kenyon joins in making these accusations, on occasion with surprising intensity; and even Hilda herself acknowledges their justness. All insist, however, that her action is right for her, that her nature makes it inevitable. Still there remains the unmistakable implication that this nature of hers is woefully inadequate. (pp. 83-8)

[The] contrast between our alternative heroines is perhaps seen most clearly in their reactions to Guido's *Archangel.* Miriam has never cared for the picture which moves Hilda to ecstasy. Only Hilda can appreciate the placid disdain of Michael in his triumph over Satan (or is it Miriam's persecutor-model?). Miriam, on the other hand, herself involved, sees this conflict between good and evil as bloody and cruelly fought with a complete commitment on both sides, even if she is heretically uncertain about who will finally win. Guido's painting seems totally inadequate to her. Her magnificently frightening description of what the picture should have been so moves Kenyon that even this conservative commentator begs Miriam to paint it. And Kenyon's word ought to be rather good authority to persuade us that Miriam has some share of truth in her view and that Hilda, after all, can be as optimistic as she is only because, out of fear of the Manichaean alternative, she can never give due credit to the existence of evil.

The Donatello story, obviously enough, is a parable of the fall of man. Through him the problem is clearly put to us at the end: was the Fall fortunate? If it was, then the existence of evil is theologically justified since good will come of it. And Puritan insufficiency, as represented by Hilda's refusal to compromise with the human state, is indeed proved to be insufficient. As we might expect, Miriam believes the Fall was fortunate, Hilda is shocked at the very notion, and Kenyon vacillates. Here again, as in the other opposed alternatives Hawthorne has treated, the answer is not definitive and any gain carries its consequent loss along with it. The loss of Don-

Hawthorne's wife, Sophia.

atello's perfect but amoral and unintellectual innocence must be mourned; but the moral consciousness and intellectual awareness which replaced it have brought him a new richness of person. Only his crime could have effected this transformation. And before he gives himself up to punishment, we find him for a moment both a Faun and a sensitive human being. Even his final imprisonment cannot shake our belief in what is after all a spiritual development. But at what a price! Perhaps Kenyon gives us a compromise, if compromising, answer in his statement that in the present world the innocence of Eden is an impossible incongruity. Thus Donatello's fall could be inevitable, and even fortunate, in view of the demands of reality, without forcing us to view the original Fall in this way. Of course, "the hopeful and happy-natured Hilda" cannot accept this modest formulation either.

Obviously this quarrel still concerns the problem of mixing good and evil. Are we to have Hilda's Michael, Miriam's Michael, or Satan? Will good remain aloof, will it struggle with evil and win, or will it struggle and be overcome? Indeed, can it struggle without being overcome in the process, win or lose? This is to ask whether we can have Miriam's Michael without having him inevitably transformed to Satan. The development of Donatello would seem to be clear evidence that for Hawthorne some good can come from evil. It would then be evidence, too, that for Hawthorne Hilda again fails as an all-encompassing ideal. She is, in the end, as she has always been, only half the story and half its meaning, even if the two halves continually overlap and cross over. Forced into a choice, we may have to choose her in the end, however great our losses, but only with the great sorrow of having been shown that our novel has made a choice necessary. (pp. 88-90)

> *Murray Krieger, " 'The Marble Faun' and the International Theme," in his* The Play and Place of Criticism, *The Johns Hopkins Press, 1967, pp. 79-90.*

CHARLES R. SMITH, JR.   (essay date 1962)

[*Drawing upon Merle E. Brown's study of structure in* The Marble Faun *(see excerpt dated 1956), Smith analyzes the thematic implications of the novel's design.*]

Very little of the critical attention paid to Hawthorne's *The Marble Faun* has centered on its structure. (p. 32)

The only article devoted exclusively to structural analysis is Merle E. Brown's "The Structure of *The Marble Faun.*" Brown believes the book to be constructed around "a single idea, the transformation from innocence to experience, repeated, with no major deviations, four times." He traces this transformation in each of the major characters: Miriam's immediately after the murder of the model, Donatello's after a long period of soul searching, Hilda's after unburdening herself in the confessional, and Kenyon's only after the disappearance of Hilda in the final chapters.

Although Brown is fairer to the novel than the other critics, his analysis still leaves a great deal unexplained. It does not satisfactorily account for the arrangement of the chapters before the murder scene, a part of the book under particularly heavy critical attack. Nor does it account for the order in which the changes take place. Finally, there are quite major deviations in the kinds of transformations and in the characters, both before and after.

Brown's interpretation seems somewhat oversimplified. The transformations do take place, and in the order he traces, but they seem not the structural principle in themselves but a part of a more complex structure. This oversimplification may result from a misreading of the novel's central theme. Brown states it as "the simple fact that sin is a condition of all human life, that we are all sinners whether we like or admit the fact or not." It is true that Hawthorne was aware of the constant presence of sin in humankind, but this is not all that he was saying in the novel. Probably the clearest explanation of the central theme can be found in Donald A. Ringe's "Hawthorne's Psychology of the Head and Heart" [see Additional Bibliography]. Ringe sees the theme as Hawthorne's attempt to present the two alternative courses of action for man living in a world in which evil exists:

> In *The Marble Faun,* then, Hawthorne presents both of his solutions to the problem of life. Men can act in either of two ways in this evil world, and each way entails its own sacrifices and its own reward. If man is to develop the noblest qualities of mind and heart and so achieve true and profound insight into the problem of human existence, he must sin, incur the perilous state of isolation and sacrifice whatever happiness can be achieved in a troubled world. On the other hand, he may seek his earthly blisses and sacrifice his individuality in the common anonymity of ordinary life.

Miriam and Donatello represent the first of these alternatives, Hilda and Kenyon the second. This understanding of the theme can lead to a more accurate understanding of the way the novel is constructed.

The action of *The Marble Faun* falls into seven major sections:

1. Initial characterization of Miriam, Hilda, Kenyon, and Donatello.

2. Explanation of the relationships between the characters.

3. Increase in the intensity of the Miriam-Donatello-model triangle, culminating in the murder scene, the novel's pivotal action.

4. Immediate after-effects of the murder: Miriam's transformation, Hilda's withdrawal, Donatello's exultation and despair.

At this point the story ceases to follow the characters as a group. The structure can be likened to the effect of a stone dropped into a pool. The effects of the murder are shown first on those most immediately concerned, Miriam and Donatello, then on Hilda, the observer, and finally on Kenyon, the one farthest removed from it.

5. The full course of Donatello's transformation from faun to a human being of superior sensibility.

6. Hilda's gradual acceptance of the fact of evil, loss of artistic ability, and awakening to Kenyon's love.

7. Kenyon's loss of artistic ability and complete dedication to ordinary human emotion.

The final chapter brings all the characters together again in Rome, restating the theme in terms of the probable fate of each couple, and of the degree of insight which each is capable of attaining.

In the first section, Chapters I through VIII, the four main characters are introduced and fully described, so that the stage of intellectual and emotional development each has reached at the beginning of the action is made clear. Donatello's similarity to Praxiteles' statue of the faun is pointed out in the first chapter and further explored in the second. He remains throughout the first section as a happy, not quite human creature, worshipping Miriam as a dog might its mistress. His antipathy towards the model, for example, Hawthorne calls "not so much a human dislike or hatred, as one of those instinctive, unreasoning antipathies which the lower animals sometimes display."

Miriam first appears to the reader as a dark and passionate beauty, shadowed by the sense of foreboding that pervades her fantastic explanation of the model. She is supplied with a vague but threatening past. (pp. 32-4)

Miriam's visit to Hilda's studio shows the contrasts between the two women. Hilda is also isolated: physically, in her tower dedicated to virginity, and spiritually in her complete innocence, which Miriam calls "a sharp steel sword." It is this militant innocence which lets her see in the portrait of Beatrice Cenci only sorrow, while the experienced Miriam sees also a consciousness of sin.

Of Kenyon we learn little in the first section, save that he is a sculptor of some ability. A thoughtful man, he is the one among them who seriously ponders the plight of Donatello, a faun in nineteenth-century Rome. The reader learns of his incipient love for Hilda only through a brief reference in

Chapter VII: "Kenyon the sculptor . . . took note of [Hilda's] ethereal kiss, and wished that he could have caught it in the air and got Hilda's leave to keep it."

The second section, Chapters IX through XIV, concentrates on the relationships which are developing between the major characters. The section follows the figure of Miriam as she wanders from one to another, trying to find some understanding and consolation. First she meets Donatello in the Borghese gardens.

Unable to convince Donatello that he should attempt to break off his attachment for her, Miriam decides to enter his world for a while. "Well, then, for this one hour, let me be such as he imagines me. . . . He shall make me as natural as himself for this one hour." They revel in the "Sylvan Dance," which is described in the Arcadian imagery constantly associated with Donatello during the period before the murder. The model appears again, breaking into Miriam's temporary escape from care and arousing again Donatello's animal hatred. For the first time, Miriam comes to fear the savagery which inspires him to say, "Shall I clutch him by the throat? . . . Bid me do so and we are rid of him forever." The link between the model and Miriam—some dark crime with which they were both connected—is now revealed, and Miriam predicts that only death will come of their meeting. As they leave, the scene shifts to show Hilda and Kenyon in the role they are to follow for most of the novel, observers of the relationship between Miriam and Donatello. Hilda can see no possibility that Miriam will ever love Donatello; Kenyon can, but he despairs of Hilda's ever loving him. As he tells Miriam when she visits his studio, Hilda seems more than humanly perfect.

During the visit, Miriam attempts to unburden herself to Kenyon, but finally keeps her silence, unable to believe that he has the sort of sympathy that would really reach out to help her. Nor can she turn to Hilda, because "Of sorrow, slender as she seems, Hilda might bear a great burden; of sin, not a feather's weight." Feeling utterly alone, Miriam experiences "this perception of an infinite, shivering solitude, amid which we cannot come close enough to human beings to be warmed by them, and where they turn to cold, chilly shapes of mist."

Now that the situation is fully revealed, Hawthorne proceeds to the evening of the murder in the third section, Chapters XV through XVIII. Things begin quietly enough at an artists' party, but the face of the model turns up among some old drawings, and the model himself accosts Miriam as the group takes a sightseeing walk through the city. Again Donatello wants to kill him, but Miriam restrains him as she might have "a faithful hound." But when the model appears yet again in the Coliseum, Miriam's control slips and she goes almost mad for a moment. When Donatello stays with her even through this and her warnings, she resolves to unburden herself to him the next day. Relieved by her decision, she goes with the rest of the party to the Tarpeian Rock, lingering to answer Donatello's questions as the rest go on ahead.

> "Who are they . . . who have been flung over here in days gone by?" "Men that cumbered the world," she replied. "Men whose lives were the bane of their fellow creatures. . . ." "Was it well done? . . ." "It was well done."

The model appears and approaches. Donatello springs at him, glances at Miriam, and throws him over the edge. Haw-

thorne has very carefully built the emotional tone between Miriam and Donatello, so that the murder seems believable but the responsibility almost impossible to fix. Miriam felt goaded beyond endurance; Donatello had been swayed by what she had just said, already hated the model, and perhaps was not human enough to know right from wrong. He sprang like an animal, saw permission in Miriam's eyes, and pushed. Miriam knew that she feared and hated the model, but did not know what had been in her eyes at the crucial moment. Who is culpable? Or is either?

The next section, Chapters XIX through XXIII, deals with the immediate effect of the murder on those concerned. Donatello was no longer the faun; now he was:

> the young man, whose form seemed to have dilated, and whose eyes blazed with the fierce energy that had suddenly inspired him. It had kindled him into a man; it had developed within him an intelligence which was no native characteristic of the Donatello whom we have heretofore known. But that simple and joyous creature was gone forever.

Immediately after the murder, Donatello felt only a wild exultation, a joy that he and Miriam were now bound together by love and guilt. But by the next day, after seeing the model's body transfigured into that of a saintly monk, his new-found intelligence had made him despair of his soul because of his sin, and almost hate Miriam for her part in it.

Miriam had felt the same exultation, and she had accepted her love for Donatello and her responsibility for his act. No longer thinking only of herself, she is able to go against her own instincts and send him away, so that he might forget both her and his deed. Going to see Hilda, she discovers that Hilda had seen the murder, and seen in Miriam's eyes "a look of hatred, triumph, vengeance, and, as it were, joy at some unhoped-for relief." Hilda can offer neither sympathy nor relief, feeling that just her knowledge of the crime has destroyed the innocence of the world. Oppressed by her knowledge, Hilda feels she cannot seek help from Kenyon, for he wishes to love her. Kenyon's role in this section is quite small. Not directly connected to the murder, he has no part to play here.

The fifth section, Chapters XXIV through XXXV, shows the whole of Donatello's change from faun to man and his ascent from despair to a limited hope. Through Kenyon, the observer, the reader learns the family history and Donatello's original state. Donatello's loss of ability to communicate with the animals underscores his humanity, as his musings in the tower do his state of despair. He who was once so much a part of nature now cannot feel its beauty even as much as Kenyon. Through remorse and penitence, he gradually rises from his depth of isolation and despair. By the time he is united again with Miriam in Perugia, he has come to hope for at least forgiveness.

Chapters XXXVI through XLII shift back to Hilda in Rome. She undergoes a cycle of despair similar to Donatello's. Her splendid isolation destroyed by her brush with sin, she loses both the sympathy she once had for the old masters and her ability as a copyist. Searching for someone to share what she feels is guilty knowledge, she begins to long for Kenyon's affection. He arrives just after she had eased her soul by confession in St. Peter's, and she begins to show some stirrings of love for him. Hilda starts to regret her brusque treatment of Miriam, who had come to her in need of help. She is beginning to share in the common emotions of love and pity, and she is spirited away by the plot machinery to finish her transformation.

The next section, Chapters XLIII to XLIX, covers the period of Hilda's disappearance and centers on Kenyon. Before he realizes that Hilda is missing, he meets Miriam and Donatello, and he cannot understand why they should risk their happiness by returning to Rome, although he can see Donatello's penitent's costume. Discovering that Hilda is really gone, he becomes more and more worried, realizing at last that she is not the idealized woman he had thought, but an inexperienced girl who might have encountered numberless accidents in Rome. Concerned only for Hilda, he cannot even develop a real interest in a newly discovered Venus, and Hawthorne comments, "He could hardly, we fear, be reckoned a consummate artist, because there was something dearer to him than his art." Meeting Miriam and Donatello again, he fails to understand them or the apparent connection between their surrender and Hilda's release. When Miriam poses the question of the Fortunate Fall—that sin may be a necessary means for salvation—he can neither refute nor reject it, but he refuses to admit that man has the right to even consider such an idea. "It is too dangerous, Miriam! I cannot follow you. . . . Mortal man has no right to tread on the ground where you now set your feet." He doesn't even notice the arrest of Miriam and Donatello at the moment of Hilda's reappearance. Concerned solely with his beloved, Kenyon can no longer feel the claims of art or of wider or deeper human sympathy.

The last chapter bears the same title as the first, "Miriam, Hilda, Kenyon, Donatello." It considers the probable fates of the two couples. Hilda and Kenyon are to become a happily married New England pair. He will never be a "consummate artist," but will probably be a respected carver of buttonholes. When he offers Hilda Miriam's idea of the Fortunate Fall, she is shocked and disgusted, and they reject it in favor of happy orthodoxy.

What will become of Miriam and Donatello is left in mystery, but it is almost certain that their lives will contain little of ordinary human happiness. Unlike Hilda and Kenyon, however, they have not been afraid to look deep into human nature, no matter how strange and unsettling the things they see. So each couple's story illustrates one of Hawthorne's alternatives: Hilda and Kenyon find earthly happiness at the cost of losing profound insight and the chance of creating great art; Miriam and Donatello gain profound insight at the cost of happiness.

Seen in this perspective, the careful structure of the novel is evident. The murder of the model is the pivotal event. The three sections before it presented the characters, their relationships, and the buildup of emotional tension which precipitated the murder. The four sections following show the changes brought about by it, progressing from the most immediately concerned to the farthest removed. Each character underwent a profound change, but the transformations were as various as the characters themselves.

The novel's content is complex, and so, necessarily, is its form. The structure is complex, but it is a structure and not the chaos it has so often been called. (pp. 34-8)

Charles R. Smith, Jr., "The Structural Principle of 'The Marble Faun'," in Thoth, Vol. III, No. 1, Winter, 1962, pp. 32-8.

HYATT H. WAGGONER   (essay date 1963)

[In the following excerpt from his seminal study of Hawthorne's works, Waggoner focuses on the concept of the fortunate fall in The Marble Faun.*]*

Hawthorne's whole career had prepared him to write **The Marble Faun,** his "story of the fall of man." Loss of innocence, initiation into the complexities of experience in a world of ambiguously mingled good and evil, experiences of guilt so obscurely related to specific acts as to seem more "original" and necessary than avoidable, these had been his subjects in story after story. Eden had never been far in the background, whether he was writing of life in a decayed mansion in Salem or of the attempts of reformers to undo the fall in a utopian community. The analogy with the Garden of Biblical myth had supplied the basic metaphor in **"Rappaccini's Daughter."** When, just after his marriage, he had experienced a happiness greater than he had ever known before, he inevitably thought of Sophia and himself in the Old Manse as a new Adam and Eve in an unfallen world.

Several of his stories that we generally think of as stories of initiation are equally stories of the fall. Robin's encounter with sin becomes a fortunate fall in **"My Kinsman, Major Molineux."** The innocence of this self-reliant and naïve country boy proves inadequate to guide him to his destination through the mazes of the city's streets, but thanks to a kindly Providence, he finds he may rise, after his fall, without the help he sought. Young Goodman Brown's experience in the forest was a less fortunate fall. Whether the evil he found universal there was only a dream, or a mirage contrived by the Devil to destroy him, or a false conclusion based on his inability to see the significance of his being there himself, at any rate he was destroyed by it when he lost faith in the reality of the good. From being an Innocent, he became a Cynic and so was lost because he could not accept the world as it really is. He prepares us for Giovanni in **"Rappaccini's Daughter,"** who cannot accept the ambiguous mixture of good and evil he finds in the garden. Brown's Faith wore pink ribbons until he lost it entirely; it never became mature. So Giovanni first thought Beatrice an angel, then decided she was a fiend, but never could accept her as a human being. The Adamic falls re-enacted by Brown and Giovanni led to no subsequent rise. **"My Kinsman"** is perhaps the only story Hawthorne ever wrote in which there is a fall that is clearly fortunate. **"Roger Malvin's Burial"** ends in a reunion with God and man after isolation, to be sure, but whatever "rise" there is here is a very sad one. The vision of life it implies remains tragic.

The last story reminds us of another way in which Hawthorne's career had prepared him to write **The Marble Faun.** Hawthorne had so obscured Reuben's guilt as to make it seem like a general human condition rather than the result of a specific act which he might well have avoided. All men, Hawthorne had implied, rationalize their self interest as Reuben does, and none of us tells all the truth all the time—though in the end our evasions catch up with us, as Reuben's did with him, until at last we are guilty in fact, by a kind of negative choice, as well as by virtue of our sharing the human condition. Our sin, in short, is both "original" and everrenewed. We are like the later Pyncheons, in part victims of the house, in part perpetrators of fresh sins—until love releases us from our inheritance. Hawthorne was more interested in guilt as a necessary human condition than he was in any specific sinful act. So he treated the central action in **The Marble Faun** in such a way that it is just as impossible to decide that Donatello is really responsible for the murder he committed as it is to decide that Reuben clearly did wrong when he left Roger Malvin to die. Miriam, herself a victim of a dreadful evil, is at least as responsible as Donatello, and the murdered man both invited and deserved his fate. All Rome, all history, made the crime inevitable, and its spreading effects leave no one untouched, not even the spotless Hilda. This murder is no ordinary crime but a re-enactment of the archetypal fall.

If Hawthorne had told this story many times before, he had never told it quite so directly or with so conscious an effort to determine its ultimate significance. It had generally been in the background, perhaps not consciously intended at all, as in **"Young Goodman Brown,"** or suggested in the form of enriching allusions, as in *The House of the Seven Gables.* Now it was made the explicit subject—the too explicit subject, the modern reader is likely to decide. When innocent, faun-like Donatello, who has grown up in a rural Arcadia where he has been "close to nature," encounters evil in the corrupt city and ends by committing a murder, but is apparently deepened and matured by the experience, Miriam sees the analogy with Eden and asks the question it prompts:

> The story of the fall of man! Is it not repeated in our romance of Monte Beni? And may we follow the analogy yet further? Was that very sin,—into which Adam precipitated himself and all his race,—was it the destined means by which, over a long pathway of toil and sorrow, we are to attain a higher, brighter, and more profound happiness, than our lost birthright gave?

Should we think of Adam's sin as a Fortunate Fall, and therefore perhaps of each man's re-enactment of the Fall as equally fortunate? Was Donatello's murder, in fact, a blessing in disguise? "Was it a means of education, bringing a simple and imperfect nature to a point of feeling and intelligence which it could have reached under no other discipline?" If sin is not educational, how else account for the fact that God permits it?

Kenyon, to whom Miriam addresses these questions, replies that he finds this line of speculation "too dangerous." He will not follow her into such "unfathomable abysses." Yet a little later, contemplating the significance of the fact that Donatello since his crime has perceptibly changed for the better, he *does* follow her:

> "Here comes my perplexity," continued Kenyon. "Sin has educated Donatello, and elevated him. Is sin, then,—which we deem such a dreadful blackness in the universe,—is it, like sorrow, merely an element of human education, through which we struggle to a higher and purer state than we could otherwise have attained? Did Adam fall, that we might ultimately rise to a far loftier paradise than his?"

When Hilda demonstrates "the white shining purity" of her nature and the orthodoxy of her religious faith by responding to the sculptor's questions with horror, declaring herself shocked beyond words, he quickly retracts, asks her forgiveness, and declares he never did really believe it. He is in love with Hilda and has no answer ready to give to the question she asks him. "Do not you perceive what a mockery your creed makes, not only of all religious sentiments, but of moral

law? and how it annuls and obliterates whatever precepts of Heaven are written deepest within us?"

For once, in this reply to Kenyon, Hilda may seem to the modern reader to demonstrate that moral sensitivity and insight that Hawthorne so emphatically, and to us for the most part so unaccountably, attributes to her. For she seems to have realized that one of the implications of the version of the old idea of the Fortunate Fall that both Miriam and Kenyon have put forth is that, since sin is educational, we *ought* to violate our consciences in order to attain the improvement in us that will result. In effect, whether she knows it or not, she sees that her friends are confusing history and myth. The myth describes the constant human condition: sin is "original" in man's nature, shared by all alike, present even in those not clearly guilty of any specific sin. It has nothing to say about what man ought to do about this fact. Only when it is taken as history does the question arise, Ought we then to imitate Adam and sin deliberately, so that Christ, the Second Adam, may come to redeem us? The idea of the Fortunate Fall arose when devout men contemplated the story of the old and new covenants as interpreted by Christians and felt a need to express their gratitude to God for the way He had brought good out of evil. Man had fallen but God had raised him again. Calamity had turned out, then, because "God so loved the world," to have unforeseeable, fortunate consequences: God sent His only son to die on the cross for our sins. Fortunately, the Atonement does for us what we cannot do for ourselves. The idea of the Fortunate Fall has immense theological implications, but no moral ones at all, or else the wrong ones, just as Hilda says.

The question as posed by Miriam and Kenyon is never resolved in the novel. It could not be without violating both Hawthorne's sense of the truth of life as he understood it and his sense of the limitations of words and rational thought in such areas, his sense of the mystery in which man finds himself. True, Miriam, who implies that she believes the fall *is* fortunate, is a sympathetic character and often speaks for the darker side of Hawthorne's mind, but she cannot be taken as always Hawthorne's spokesman. Hawthorne presents her as warped by her tragic experience even while he gives her his full sympathy. If her view of life is closer to Hawthorne's own than is Hilda's, Hawthorne admired Hilda more and wished he might more fully share her unquestioning faith. Miriam raised a question which Hawthorne too had pondered, and decided, apparently, he could not answer, at least not with a *yes* or a *no*.

Kenyon is much more a spokesman for Hawthorne than is Miriam, and Kenyon too rejects the implication of his own and Miriam's question. A good deal of the time in the novel there is very little distance between Kenyon and Hawthorne. Essentially, Kenyon and Hilda are Nathaniel and Sophia. When Hilda rebukes him for his speculation and he explains that he never really believed it, Kenyon goes on to explain his vagary:

> But the mind wanders wild and wide; and, so lonely as I live and work, I have neither polestar above nor light of cottage windows here below, to bring me home. Were you my guide, my counsellor, my inmost friend, with that white wisdom which clothes you as a celestial garment, all would go well. O Hilda, guide me home!

The parallel between this and many of Hawthorne's love letters to Sophia is very close. One of the things Hawthorne must have meant when he declared himself "saved" by his marriage was that he had found Sophia's buoyant faith a needed counterbalance to his own dark questionings. So Kenyon might be wiser in the ways of the world but Hilda, as we are often reminded, was wiser in religious truth. Kenyon might well ask her to guide him home, in Hawthorne's view of the matter. His refusal to carry on his line of speculation had Hawthorne's approval.

Depending on which aspect of it we look at, the plot either supports or does not support the rejection by Hilda and Kenyon of the idea of the Fortunate Fall. Though Donatello has been matured and humanized by his suffering, he must go to prison. Though Miriam has been ennobled by love, she ends in sad penitence, without hope of happiness with Donatello. Kenyon and Hilda decide to leave Rome, thus in effect putting the problem behind them. The plot gives no clear answer to the largest question explicitly posed by the novel.

But perhaps the question itself is illegitimate, impossible to answer. Hawthorne has Kenyon say, after he has looked from Donatello's tower at the landscape mottled with patches of sunlight and shadow and seen it as a symbol of life, "It is a great mistake to try to put our best thoughts into human language. When we ascend into the higher regions of emotion and spiritual enjoyment, they are only expressible by such grand hieroglyphics as these around us." By symbols, in short, and myths. Speaking in his own person as narrator, Hawthorne has already noted the loss now that man has grown beyond the archaic expressiveness of gestures, and "words have been feebly substituted in the place of signs and symbols." What words cannot do, the visual arts sometimes can. Speaking again in his own person, in one of the passages lifted from the Notebooks, Hawthorne says of Sodoma's Christ bound to a pillar that it shows what "pictorial art, devoutly exercised, might effect in behalf of religious truth; involving, as it does, deeper mysteries of revelation, and bringing them closer to man's heart, and making him tenderer to be impressed by them, than the most eloquent words of preacher or prophet." In his first chapter, describing the Faun, who was "neither man nor animal, and yet no monster," Hawthorne has despaired of putting his basic idea into abstract language: "The idea grows coarse as we handle it, and hardens in our grasp." The idea of the Faun, he decides, "may have been no dream, but rather a poet's reminiscence of a period when man's affinity with nature was more strict, and his fellowship with every living thing more intimate and dear." To discover what the novel finally, at its deepest level, means, then, we should turn from a consideration of the questions framed by Miriam and Kenyon to the myths which Hawthorne uses to shape his story.

Almost exactly in the center of his book Hawthorne has placed a chapter he calls simply "Myths." In it he gives us what Miriam, on another occasion, demands of Donatello, "the latest news from Arcady," which is, in effect, that nature has no cure for what ails us. However beautiful the old Arcadian myths are, however sad it is that we have lost our innocence, they are not true any longer in a fallen world. (In Hawthorne's terminology, the old pagan legends are "myths," the Biblical story in Genesis a symbolic truth, perhaps not literally true historically but true as a type of the human condition. He never refers to the Genesis story as a "myth.") Donatello, now that he has known sin, cannot re-enter Arcadia.

The chief substance of the chapter is the legend of Donatello's spring, which one of his ancestors found to be animated by a beautiful maiden, the spirit of the water, with whom he fell in love. On summer days she would cool his brow with her touch or make rainbows around him. Kenyon interrupts the story at this point with a skeptical comment:

> It is a delightful story for the hot noon of your Tuscan summer . . . But the deportment of the watery lady must have had a most chilling influence in midwinter.

If this criticism seems the product only of the skeptical mind, another is implicit in the story itself. Eventually the dryad refused to appear to her lover, and Donatello explains that her refusal was caused by the effort of his ancestor to wash off a bloodstain in the water. While summer and innocence last, in short, being "close to nature" is perhaps enough; at least, Hawthorne says elsewhere, it is a very beautiful idea. But winter and guilt come, death and sin are in the world, and Arcadianism does not know how to deal with them. Attempting to communicate with the wild creatures as he once had, Donatello calls to them in the "voice and utterance of the natural man," but he is frustrated when a brown lizard "of the tarantula species" makes its appearance. "To all present appearance, this venomous reptile was the only creature that had responded to the young Count's efforts to renew his intercourse with the lower orders of nature." Donatello falls to the ground and Kenyon, alarmed, asks what has happened to him. " 'Death, death!' sobbed Donatello."

Kenyon himself supplies sufficient comment on the legend of the spring: "He understood it as an apologue, typifying the soothing and genial effects of an habitual intercourse with nature, in all ordinary cares and griefs; while, on the other hand, her mild influences fall short in their effect upon the ruder passions, and are altogether powerless in the dread fever-fit or deadly chill of guilt." After a little more talk, the two friends part, Donatello to climb up in his tower once more, Kenyon to go inside to read "an antique edition of Dante." We have met the venomous reptile and heard Donatello's answer to Kenyon before, in Rappaccini's garden, where Hawthorne also alluded to Dante to help us to get our metaphorical bearings. Sin and death have entered the world, to spoil the Arcadian dream. Whether the fall is "fortunate" or not may be impossible to answer, but at least the world we know is no unfallen earthly paradise. Evil is in it, and nature itself offers no satisfactory cure.

The cure, insofar as there is any, lies partly in repentance and love in this world, and partly in the hope of another life. These meanings emerge from the plot considered as symbolic action or myth and from the implications of the leading images with which Hawthorne supports his myth. The plot gives us three of the characters at least, and perhaps by intention four, growing in moral and spiritual stature as they experience sin and suffering. Miriam ceases to suffer in isolation and think only of herself, falls in love with Donatello, and dedicates her life to penitence and to the service of the one she has wronged. Donatello gains in wisdom and understanding, becomes in fact human. Hilda comes down from the tower of her perfect rectitude, repents having turned away Miriam in her need, and becomes human enough to marry Kenyon. All, in fact, come down from the isolation of their towers; all fall in love. That there is no cure for suffering is clear from the careers of Miriam and Donatello, but that suffering and acknowledgment of mutual complicity in guilt are necessary preludes to any redemption possible to man is clear from the careers of all of them.

The "higher hopes" of another life that will rectify the wrongs of this one are implied in Kenyon's deference to Hilda, in his plea that she lead him home, and in Hawthorne's own too often expressed admiration of her. Hilda is "the religious girl" as well as the girl of a shining purity of character, Kenyon the "thinker," potentially the skeptic. Not just Kenyon but the whole novel stands in awe of Hilda, whose precise function is to keep the lamp of religious faith, with its higher hopes, burning. (She can let the flame of the old Catholic lamp go out at the end because she herself in her own person emanates a better and purer light.)

Hilda is supported in her task of guarding religious faith and hope by much of the imagery, sometimes with images that Hawthorne makes very emphatic, sometimes with what seem mere reflexes of his habitual style. I shall give just two examples. At the end of the chapter called "The Owl Tower," in which Kenyon and Donatello have climbed to the top of Donatello's tower and Kenyon has had his vision of the symbolic landscape, Kenyon finds, growing out of the masonry of the tower, seemingly out of the very stone itself, "a little shrub, with green and glossy leaves." Donatello thinks, "If the wide valley has a great meaning, the plant ought to have at least a little one." Kenyon asks Donatello if he sees any meaning here and Donatello says he sees none, but, looking at the plant, he adds, "But here was a worm that would have killed it; an ugly creature, which I will fling over the battlements."

Kenyon does not voice the meaning he sees, and Hawthorne makes no comment. But the context makes reasonably clear what Donatello missed. We are reminded of Melville's "Bartleby the Scrivener," in which, in the Tombs, green grass could be seen by Bartleby if he would only turn his face from the wall. Kenyon's view of the valley has increased his "reliance on His providence" (whereas Donatello has seen only "sunshine on one spot, and cloud in another, and no reason for it in either case"), and he has just explained to Donatello that he "cannot preach": words will not express his "best" thoughts, that is, his religious thoughts. He has seen, as he looked at the earth spread below them, something of the way of "His dealings with mankind." Now, in the rarefied "upper atmosphere" of the tower, he finds a green shrub, the meaning of which he does not even attempt to state for his companion. Green is the traditional color of hope, and the plant is growing in a very unlikely place: "Heaven knows how its seeds had ever been planted . . ." But not only Heaven knew: Hawthorne knew how the seeds of such hope as he cherished had been planted. The chapter ends with Donatello's destruction of the "worm" that would destroy the plant.

My second example comes at the end of chapter three, "Subterranean Reminiscences," in which the four friends have been exploring one of the catacombs, where they "wandered by torchlight through a sort of dream." Hilda and Donatello, both Innocents, find the darkness especially repellent: their experience of life has in no way prepared them for it. Miriam thinks that "the most awful idea connected with the catacombs is their interminable extent, and the possibility of going astray in this labyrinth of darkness . . ." When Kenyon wonders whether in fact anyone has ever been lost in the place, he is told of "a pagan of old Rome, who hid himself in order to spy out the blessed saints, who then dwelt and worshipped in these dismal places." The pagan has been "groping in the darkness" ever since, unable to find his way out.

At this point the party reaches a chapel carved out of the walls and stops to look at it; "and while their collected torches illuminated this one small, consecrated spot, the great darkness spread all round it, like that immenser mystery which envelops our little life, and into which friends vanish from us, one by one." Miriam, it turns out, has "vanished into the great darkness, even while they were shuddering at the remote possibility of such a misfortune." Miriam shares Hilda's strict orthodoxy even less than Kenyon, who at least longs for and admires what is not as much his as he would like it to be. She has something in common with the pagan of old Rome; she is not held by the brightly illuminated consecrated spot. (As it turns out, though, she is more a victim of persecution than an unbeliever.)

We are reminded of the brightly lighted chamber in **"Night Sketches,"** with the cold darkness all around, or of the darkness that seemed to press in on the little company at Blithedale. In the latter case, though, the hope suggested by the warmth and light was a secular one. Here everything about the context unites to suggest a purely "religious" hope—in the sense of a hope for immortality. The darkness into which our friends vanish is the darkness of death. Later, Kenyon will protest the presence of a skull in Donatello's bedroom: "It is absurdly monstrous, my dear friend, thus to fling the dead-weight of our mortality upon our immortal hopes. While we live on earth, 'tis true, we must needs carry our skeletons about with us; but, for Heaven's sake, do not let us burden our spirits with them, in our feeble efforts to soar upward." (Kenyon's higher hopes may have seemed to him feeble, but Hawthorne characterizes him elsewhere as he would have characterized himself, "a devout man in his way.") Those who know the extent of "the blackness that lies beneath us everywhere," who know that we are "dreaming on the edge of a precipice," who know that sinking into nature is equivalent to sinking into the grave and have explored the "dark caverns" of experience, will not need to keep a skull in the bedroom to remind them of man's mortality.

They will be likely to agree with the point of Hawthorne's moral and theological criticism of Sodoma's Siena fresco of Christ bound to a pillar. Hawthorne felt sure the picture sprang from sincere religious feeling: a shallow or worldly man could not have painted it. The picture is "inexpressibly touching" in its portrayal of the weariness and loneliness of the Savior:

> You behold Christ deserted both in heaven and earth; that despair is in him which wrung forth the saddest utterance man ever made, "Why hast Thou forsaken me?" Even in this extremity, however, he is still divine . . . He is as much, and as visibly, our Redeemer, there bound, there fainting, and bleeding from the scourge, with the cross in view, as if he sat on his throne of glory in the heavens! Sodoma, in this matchless picture, has done more towards reconciling the incongruity of Divine Omnipotence and outraged, suffering Humanity, combined in one person, than the theologians ever did.

The Marble Faun ought to have been Hawthorne's finest novel. His career had pointed toward it from the beginning. In it the heart imagery that is implicit in **"The Hollow of the Three Hills"** has become the underground world of Rome, the catacombs, the tomb or dungeon of the heart and of dreams. In it Robin's initiation has become consciously archetypal, to be seen in the dimensions of its largest significance. In it the implications of **"Earth's Holocaust"** and **"The Celestial Railroad"** have been combined within the framework of man's basic myth. The most persistent preoccupations and the recurrent images of a lifetime of writing have been brought together in what ought to have been a definitive recapitulation.

Instead, the novel is clearly inferior to **The Scarlet Letter** and even, it seems to me, to **The House of the Seven Gables.** Richer in many respects than **Blithedale,** it is less consistently interesting: there are frequent stretches of it one wants to skip. There is a very large gap in it between intended and achieved meaning. Hawthorne failed with Rome, and he failed with Hilda, and both were essential to the achievement of his intention.

Hilda is at once a nineteenth century stereotype and Hawthorne's tribute to Sophia. The only way of interpreting her that will "save" Hawthorne and his novel is to take the portrait ironically, but this will not do if we consider all the evidence. True, Miriam points out that Hilda's innocence is like "a sharp steel sword"; so white a purity makes for judgments that are "terribly severe." And Miriam often speaks for Hawthorne. Here we should probably assume that he thought so too. But this is only a minor qualification of what, for Hawthorne, is Hilda's awe-inspiring virtue and compelling attractiveness. Once again, as in the case of Miriam's implied assent to the idea of the Fortunate Fall, we may not assume that Hawthorne is completely committed to Miriam as his spokesman. In his own person, as narrator, he pays Hilda lavish, and tiresomely repetitious, tribute, and as Kenyon he marries her and asks her to guide him home.

Yet to the modern reader Hilda is either ridiculous or, if we can take her seriously, self-righteous and uncharitable. She is not only a far less impressive character, as a literary character, than Miriam, she is far less attractive, and even less "good," as a person. Throughout most of the course of the novel her chief concern is to protect the spotlessness of the innocence assumed by her and asserted by Hawthorne. She finds everyone else's faith and everyone else's conduct corrupt. When called upon for help, she turns her friend away lest she be stained by the contact. Though the idea would have shocked Hawthorne immeasurably, it is impossible not to see her as a feminine version of the man of adamant—at least until the very end, when the rigor of her moralism is softened somewhat.

There is no consistent or effective irony in the portrait. Though this "daughter of the Puritans," as Hawthorne repeatedly calls her, comes down from her tower to marry Kenyon, the change is not so much one from spiritual pride to humility as from priestess to goddess: "Another hand must henceforth trim the lamp before the Virgin's shrine; for Hilda was coming down from her old tower, to be herself enshrined and worshipped as a household saint, in the light of her husband's fireside." It is true that Hilda thought right and wrong completely distinct, never in any degree mingled or ambiguous—the error of judgment that Hawthorne's innocent young men have to grow out of, the idea they have to unlearn by painful experience. But Hawthorne thought such an error—if indeed error it was, as he would have said—charming and admirable in innocent young girls. Hilda is like young Robin before his "evening of ambiguity and weariness"; the difference between them is that Hawthorne does

not require that young girls should grow in knowledge of the world.

His century placed women on a pedestal just *because,* in their role of guardian of values that were being threatened, they knew nothing of the world. If their innocence rendered them helpless to deal with reality, it was nevertheless to be both protected and admired, for reality was very nasty. If they did not truly partake of the human condition, it was a good thing they didn't. A comment Hawthorne makes in the novel on a work of art, without suggesting any connection with his portrait of Hilda, suggests the chief reason for his failure with his heroine: "It was one of the few works of antique sculpture in which we recognize womanhood, and that, moreover, without prejudice to its divinity." Womanhood's "divinity"? Since Hilda was more than normally pretty and good, no wonder her destiny was to be "enshrined and worshipped" at the fireside.

As he depended greatly on Hilda to give his novel an affirmative meaning, so Hawthorne depended chiefly on Rome and its art treasures to give it thematic density. Here too he failed, though for quite different reasons. Again, recent efforts to "save" the novel do not really work. To be sure, Hawthorne anticipates James in developing the Europe versus America theme: Rome is the past, experience, culture, and corruption, in contrast with America's present, ideals, morality, and innocence: Miriam versus Hilda. This is fine, theoretically. But Hawthorne too often simply lifts long passages of description from the Notebooks, and the passages remain inert in the novel. There is too *much* of Rome, and too much about art. They are a burden the story is simply incapable of carrying.

Examples could easily be given of passages in which Hawthorne succeeds in making his comments on art and descriptions of Rome work for his story. Perhaps the best one is Miriam's comment on Guido's "dapper" Archangel, whose feathers are unruffled in his struggle with Satan: "Is it thus that virtue looks the moment after its death-struggle with evil? . . . A full third of the Archangel's feathers should have been torn from his wings . . ." But for page after page there is nothing like this, nothing in fact that is not very tedious. And Hawthorne seems to know it. At least he keeps apologizing for his descriptions while the story halts, sometimes for a chapter at a time, to accommodate them. This is simply awkward novel writing and no amount of demonstration that, where there are symbolic implications in the Notebook material they are consistent with the general theme, will really save the romance as a work of art. Thematic considerations alone cannot save any novel.

The effect on the reader of all this inert material is to suggest that Hawthorne was not sufficiently interested in his *story*—an effect reinforced by his embarrassed and coy protestations at the end, in the added conclusion, when he refused to make more than a slight gesture toward clearing up the mysteries of his plot. What he is really saying in his "Conclusion" is that he doesn't *care* whether Donatello had furry ears or not or who detained Hilda, and we the readers shouldn't either. But he had cared about Hester, and Hepzibah, and Zenobia, cared about them as people and not merely as allegoric or mythic symbols. Despite the elaborate density of its background, it might well be argued that **The Marble Faun** is more allegorical than any of the three preceding romances.

Still, if it is true that the work has been generally underestimated, as I think it has, the reason is not hard to find. Its weaknesses are very obvious, impossible I should think to overlook, while its strength is subtle and delicate. It is easy to read this work in which "Adam falls anew, and Paradise . . . is lost again" without responding to a good deal of its multiple suggestiveness. There is nothing in its period quite like the way it plays theological, philosophical, and psychological perspectives against each other in the image of the catacombs. Here the characters wandered in "a sort of dream," a dark labyrinth of guilt, an "ugly dream" indeed: "For, in dreams, the conscience sleeps, and we often stain ourselves with guilt of which we should be incapable in our waking moments." The "dark caverns" of experience in Hawthorne's novel are so richly meaningful that we should have to read the work for this if there were nothing else to draw us.

There is of course much else. The scene at the precipice (we are all, in some sense, "dreaming on the edge of a precipice"), the whole series of chapters laid in Donatello's country, where the serpent is discovered in nature's garden, the descriptions of the several studios (Miriam's is said to be "the outward type of a poet's haunted imagination," and the description justifies the comment)—all these parts of the work, and more, make it more worth reading than most American novels of the nineteenth century, even if we are not already committed to Hawthorne before we start it.

If we are, we shall find it an even more rewarding failure. For on the thematic level it is, for the most part, such *good* Hawthorne. It is not just Donatello but all of us who "travel in a circle, as all things heavenly and earthly do." The loss of innocence is very sad, but it is at least naïve and may be disastrous to suppose that we haven't lost it. Guilt is original, a necessary aspect of the human condition, not something that sets conspicuous sinners apart from the rest of us. And it is mutual, so that in our inevitable complicity we may not relieve ourselves of its burden by pointing the finger, casting the stone. Still, we need not despair if only we will acknowledge our complicity and enter the human circle.

"Outraged, suffering humanity" must learn to live with "the blackness that lies beneath us, everywhere," but Kenyon, taking the long view from the height of Donatello's tower, saw, above the stormy valley, "within the domain of chaos, as it were,—hill-tops . . . brightening in the sunshine; they looked like fragments of the world, broken adrift and based on nothingness, or like portions of a sphere destined to exist, but not yet finally compacted." Kenyon's images give us Hawthorne's answer to the question whether the fall was fortunate or not, an answer that springs from his "best thought" and that was otherwise inexpressible. (pp. 209-25)

Hyatt H. Waggoner, in his Hawthorne: A Critical Study, *revised edition, Cambridge, Mass.: The Belknap Press of Harvard University Press, 1963, 278 p.*

FREDERICK CREWS (essay date 1966)

[*Rejecting the common interpretation of* The Marble Faun *as a novel primarily about the fall of humankind, Crews examines the underlying sexual themes that he believes pervade the work.*]

Hawthorne's moral interpreters have been very sure of what his last complete romance, **The Marble Faun,** is really about. The theme is man's lapse from primal innocence and his pos-

sible regeneration. "Did Adam fall," asks the sculptor Kenyon, "that we might ultimately rise to a far loftier paradise than his?" It is scarcely noticed that Kenyon shrinks from the implications of his question and decides to drop the whole matter; the theologically oriented critic can give an answer without Kenyon's help. The "crucial problem" of *felix culpa* is resolved (but in divergent ways) by reference to a mixture of genuine evidence and "the background of Christian thinking on the subject" or "the central meaning of Christianity." Though the critics when taken together leave us bewildered, they do concur in feeling indulgent toward the book's artistic defects. "For on the thematic level it is, for the most part, such *good* Hawthorne." "For **The Marble Faun** is concerned with the way in which nature and spirit, innocence and evil, time and eternity may be conquered and reconciled in a moment of incarnation."

Such an emphasis misrepresents Hawthorne, not only because it credits him with more conviction than he has, but because it treats only a tiny fraction of his book. Instead of saying that he has affirmed or refuted a certain religious doctrine, it would be more appropriate to say that he found it hard to sustain his interest in such niceties. The theological speculations that his characters timidly raise and abandon are placed amid authorial comments that approach nihilism. The rude fact of death keeps reappearing to erase distinctions between good and evil, truth and falsehood; and all life is seen in a backward glance from the brink of nothingness. (pp. 213-14)

Weariness and despair are the real keynotes of **The Marble Faun,** beginning with Hawthorne's confession in his Preface that he no longer believes in the Gentle Reader's existence and continuing until the pathetic apologies and evasions in the subsequently appended Conclusion [see essay dated 1860]. His dark mood is reflected in countless little remarks about the "demon of weariness" that haunts gallery-goers, the loneliness and heartsickness of expatriates, and the remorse of old age, "when the accumulated sins are many and the remaining temptations few." The absurdity of much of his plot—the heaping-up of useful coincidences and the cheap mystification that is never justified or explained—appears as a further confession of despair, oblique but unmistakable. "When we find ourselves fading into shadows and unrealities, it seems hardly worth while to be sad, but rather to laugh as gayly as we may, and ask little reason wherefore." The fictional equivalent of forced gaiety is a book which no longer tries to capture human character with honest fullness, as in **The Scarlet Letter,** but slides off into patent allegory on one side and chatty circumstantiality on the other.

We must also question whether **The Marble Faun** is "such *good* Hawthorne" on the thematic level. It is true that all his former concerns are present, but they are handled with timid ambiguity. This is most obviously true of the *felix culpa* theme, but it applies to every other as well. Depending on the passages he cares to stress, the reader can see **The Marble Faun** as a Rousseauistic tract about man's decline from a golden age or an Emersonian tract about man's ascent to the ideal; as an attack on Roman Catholicism or a prelude to conversion; as a work of homage to Western history or a declaration of independence from it; as a hymn to America or a satire on its moral fastidiousness; as an allegory of artistic truth or yet another indictment of the creative imagination; as a tribute to feminine purity or a muted plea against sexual hypocrisy. Each irresolute theme is eventually submerged in gloomy ambivalence.

As we might almost be able to predict, the chief focus of this ambivalence is a choice between an overblown, oversexed, aggressive woman and a fragile, childlike, impregnable and impenetrable maiden. In Hawthorne's conscious view all merit belongs to the virgin Hilda. There is a general assumption in the romance, shared even by the characters who supposedly represent "experience," that femininity and absolute purity of imagination are synonymous—in other words, that Hilda *must* prevail over Miriam. As an embodiment of Mr. Podsnap's idea of chastity Hilda could easily be a comic figure. Her characteristic response to reality is the following: " 'It perplexes me,' said Hilda, thoughtfully, and shrinking a little; 'neither do I quite like to think about it'." And yet her "elastic faculty of throwing off such recollections as would be too painful for endurance" is precisely what Hawthorne feels increasingly necessary for himself. In creating Hilda and insisting, against his plain misgivings, that her vaccination against bodily thoughts is a moral virtue, he has provided himself with a (very inadequate) refuge from those same thoughts.

It is true, of course, that Hilda is to some extent an allegorical character, standing for Purity or the Ideal or Heaven or the American Girl or the Muse of Art or the Virgin Mary; all these identities can be justified through explication of the symbolic props that attend her. Insofar as she is allegorical, it is idle to criticize Hawthorne for having made her one-dimensional. Yet beyond all her allegorical roles Hilda is a human character within the romance's human plot, and Hawthorne is asking us to believe that her behavior toward her friends is above criticism. To do this he must, in effect, convince himself that misfortune and entrapment in the world's evil deserve no sympathy, for this is Hilda's own position. Her friend Miriam has been gratuitously tormented beyond endurance and has involved herself in a crime—the murder of the "model" or "monk" who has pursued her—through a moment of acquiescence in the deed. Miriam is considerably more sinned against than sinning, and in her remorse and anguish she needs Hilda's pity. When Hilda turns her back on Miriam, Hawthorne does his best to condone her—and so do all the other characters. Even Hilda's relenting, long after it might have been useful, is taken not as evidence that she was formerly wrong but as a proof of virtually divine magnanimity.

It should go without saying, by now, that when Hawthorne (or indeed, any writer) takes extraordinary pains to emphasize the asexuality of a girl, he is preoccupied with the general sexuality of women. In Hilda's case, as is appropriate to the most insistent exaggeration of purity in all his fiction, sexual symbolism and sexual innuendo follow the heroine wherever she goes. I do not mean that her lofty tower, like the Man of Adamant's cave, represents what she cannot face; that may be true, but Hawthorne does not employ his characteristic *doubles entrendres* in describing the tower. He does, however, create an intricately detailed analogy between sexuality and crime, so that the murder which Hilda witnesses becomes a kind of vicarious sexual initiation. Though she is pure, Hilda is susceptible to what she repeatedly calls "stain"; she does not wear "garments that never could be spotted." God, she says, wants her to return the robe He gave her "as white as when [I] put it on." The ambiguous stain is significantly associated with the stain of Beatrice Cenci, who happened to have been raped by her father before she had him murdered; and

while this lurid fact is never mentioned directly, Hawthorne's readers certainly knew it. When Hilda, contemplating Guido Reni's portrait of Beatrice, asks, "Am I, too, stained with guilt?", the double reference is maintained; and interestingly enough, the portrait does resemble Hilda's own face. Later, a young Italian artist paints Hilda as "gazing with sad and earnest horror at a blood-spot which she seemed just then to have discovered on her white robe." The picture, which connoisseurs take to be inspired by Guido's Beatrice, is called by others, "Innocence, dying of a blood-stain!"

Such language does not, of course, suggest that Hilda really is "guilty" of having been deflowered, any more than it proves her a criminal. At most it reveals a sexual fascination on Hawthorne's own part when he ponders the "dark pitfall" and "fathomless abyss" separating Hilda from Miriam. On the whole it is futile to try to match Hilda's rendered character against the prurient imagery that surrounds it; the latter serves almost as a Mercutio voice to sneer at the unreal perfection of the former.

This, I fear, is a comment that holds for characterization in *The Marble Faun* generally. Any attempt to discuss Hawthorne's people in literal terms, or even according to their apparent allegorical values, must falsify the prevailing air of self-contradiction. The virgin Hilda resembles Beatrice Cenci and therefore is associated with the Beatrice-like Miriam, her supposed opposite; Miriam occasionally acts with Hilda-like altruism, and can find "none but pure motives" in her heart; Donatello is simultaneously as voluptuous as Miriam and as easily shocked as Hilda; and the sculptor Kenyon—at once a prude and a freethinker—mediates among his three friends with an ease that proves their estrangement to be only provisional, however "abysmal" it may appear. The only clear point is that some private discomfort has made all Hawthorne's portraits insincere.

In order to arrive at the significance of this peculiarity we must follow the direction of Hawthorne's images. His Rome is an incessant reminder of the unconscious pit beneath his characters' surface banalities. We are asked to think of ruined pagan temples under the "evanescent and visionary" Christian world; catacombs which suggest "the possibility of going astray into this labyrinth of darkness" or the re-emergence of some "fiendish malignity" of ancient days; chasms which are among "the orifices of that pit of blackness that lies beneath us, everywhere"; and dungeons, into one of which Donatello will be committed at his own request after failing to carry his burden of guilt unacknowledged in the upper world. And these heavily symbolic locales of action are scarcely distinguishable from other, sheerly figurative, representations of the human mind. The model's past relation to Miriam emerges from "subterranean reminiscences"; Donatello learns how to master his emotions and thrust them once again "down into the prison-cells where he usually kept them confined"; Hilda's glimpse of evil has "allowed a throng of torturing recollections to escape from their dungeons into the pure air and white radiance of her soul"; she has been helplessly "straying farther into the intricate passages of our nature"; and Donatello "had already had glimpses of strange and subtle matters in those dark caverns, into which all men must descend, if they would know anything beneath the surface and illusive pleasures of existence." Is it fortuitous that all these figures for the terrible unknown are hidden cavities, and that female sexuality is the taboo of the surface Hawthornian world? In a backhanded way Hawthorne enjoins us not to be satisfied with his own and his characters' disinfectant ideals, but rather to mark their emergence from and protection against an all-consuming sexual obsession.

In one sense we can agree with those critics who have found *The Marble Faun* to be a book about man's fall, about initiation into evil and the consequences of that initiation. If we formulate that theme in strictly literal terms, however, we must confine the central plot to Miriam and Donatello. It is more comprehensive to say that the book deals with initiation into a *sense* of evil, whether real or only vicarious, and that this sense is ultimately a euphemism for knowledge of sexuality. For *The Marble Faun*—like *The Blithedale Romance* but without its irony toward an obsessed protagonist—dwells on the very existence of sexual passion as if this were the most hideous of the world's evils. All Hawthorne's major characters, even the latest counterpart of Zenobia, share the author's distaste for the idea which somehow insinuates itself into all their doings. The single committed crime which has to bear the weight of four characters' brooding about guilt is powerfully sexual in itself, not only in its traumatizing effect on its virgin witness, Hilda, but in its essential circumstances and emotional atmosphere. The victim is in some way perceived as a sexual rival, and in killing him Donatello does make a tie of erotic guilt between Miriam and himself. The murder is an act of mutual consent, of guilty impulse which should not have been gratified, of "passion," and it produces both "horror" and "ecstasy" in the woman who has consented. Like Milton's Adam and Eve after a similarly ambiguous misdeed, the offending couple at first feel an intimacy "closer than a marriage-bond." . . . (pp. 214-20)

When second thoughts begin to urge the folly of the act, Miriam and Donatello still have the consolation of knowing "how close, and ever closer, did the breadth of the immeasurable waste, that lay between them and all brotherhood or sisterhood, now press them one within the other!" And finally this suggestive coupling is seen with disgust: Donatello begins to envision "the ever-increasing loathsomeness of a union that consists in guilt. Cemented with blood, which would corrupt and grow more noisome forever and forever, but bind them none the less strictly for that." When Miriam argues, "Surely, it is no crime that we have committed," she has assumed Hester Prynne's role before Arthur Dimmesdale. The chief point of difference is that Hawthorne's sum of frankness has now dwindled to the point where even the Hester-figure, though surrounded with hints of a long sexual history, remains technically chaste and shares in the general hypersensitivity and reticence.

The sexual connotations of the murder scene alone might not be strong enough to support the reading we have given, but they are the culmination of multiple innuendoes about Miriam's symbolic nature. Without ever saying directly that she is sexually stained, Hawthorne has labored ingeniously to ensure that we get that impression. He uses the fact that "nobody knew anything about Miriam, either for good or evil" to speculate whether her "freedom of intercourse" might mean that one could easily "develop a casual acquaintance into intimacy" with her. If, as Hawthorne goes on to suggest, this supposition is false, it is not because of Miriam's chastity but because "by some subtle quality, she kept people at a distance." That is to say, people recognize something fearful in her—the "abyss" from whose brink they timidly withdraw. The lack of rapport between Miriam and the others is thus a factor of their inexperience, not her coldness; and

throughout the romance she is the victim of Hawthorne's paradox that intense passion places one beyond the community of respectable lovers. Like Hester and Zenobia, Miriam is not an outcast *and* oversexed but an outcast *because* she is oversexed. And like them, she is driven by her enforced isolation into occasional questionings of man-made law.

The mystery over her family background and personal troubles is well calculated to reinforce Miriam's aura of sexuality. Hawthorne manages to draw upon racial fears which in our own time have led to genocide: Miriam is not only part English and part Italian, but part Jewish as well, and it is rumored that she also has "one burning drop of African blood in her veins." The equation of obscure, esoteric origins with promiscuity is already familiar to us from the metaphorically "Oriental" character of Hester and Zenobia, and Miriam too, in addition to her literal ancestry, has "a certain rich Oriental character in her face." As for her Jewishness, Hawthorne reveals what he thinks of that when he describes Hilda's trip through the Jewish ghetto—"the foulest and ugliest part of Rome . . . where thousands of Jews are crowded within a narrow compass, and lead a close, unclean, and multitudinous life, resembling that of maggots when they overpopulate a decaying cheese." Such prose, which reminds us more of *Mein Kampf* than of the theological works that are usually adduced to explain Hawthorne's ideas, vividly demonstrates that Jewishness, earthliness, filth, and sexuality are symbolically interchangeable in his imagination. Miriam's fate in the plot of the romance is to be the scapegoat for a sexual nausea that Hawthorne, along with his other characters, prefers to vent upon the foreign temptress and her sensual race.

The chief character for whom Miriam's sexuality is oppressive is Kenyon, who occupies approximately the same place in this romance that Holgrave and Coverdale did in previous ones. That is to say, he is the artist-figure who is closest to Hawthorne himself, and who escapes from dangerous fantasies and radical opinions by giving himself over to a Sophia-figure: Hilda is the new Phoebe or Priscilla. Kenyon's rebellious leanings are, of course, considerably milder than his predecessors', as is appropriate to the generally greater repression in *The Marble Faun.* He is so prudish that "he almost reproached himself when sometimes his imagination pictured in detail the sweet years that [he and Hilda] might spend together." But the fact that he does have such an imagination, capable of picturing marriage "in detail," leaves him subject to intimidation by the idea of Miriam and consequently very much in need of antiseptic Hilda. He must respond to Miriam's proffered confidences with "a certain reserve and alarm," and later must declare that Hilda was right to spurn her. "The white shining purity of Hilda's nature," he explains to Miriam with pitiless pomposity, "is a thing apart; and she is bound, by the undefiled material of which God moulded her, to keep that severity which I, as well as you, have recognized."

In any previous work a figure like Kenyon would be subject to the incisive irony which Hawthorne reserves for the characters who most closely resemble himself. There is, indeed, more than a hint of satire behind Kenyon's extravagant and unsubstantiated fear of "that mass of unspeakable corruption, the Roman Church," and toward the end of the book his unconscious misogyny gets mocked by the "gay persecutors" of the Roman Carnival. Yet Hawthorne is too involved in Kenyon's uneasiness to sustain an ironic distance from it;

the Carnival must be set aside as "a feverish dream" from which one awakens to Hilda and the fireside. (pp. 220-23)

The other important male character, Donatello, has a closer yet more shifting relation to Miriam than Kenyon does. Loving her in a doggy way at first, then shrinking from her with "shuddering repugnance" after the murder, and finally joining her in a brief fellowship of guilt, he exemplifies the whole range of attitudes that might be appropriate to her sexual meaning—from ignorant devotion through the terror of discovery to a mature reconciliation with reality. Beneath the obvious metamorphosis of "the sylvan Faun" into "the man of feeling and intelligence" lies an implied mastery of the "fear" and "disgust" which first assault him, significantly, not at the time of the murder but when he sees Miriam's self-revealing sketches depicting the beheading of men by vengeful females. In terms of the symbolism we have been following, Donatello may be said to survive the crisis of adolescence that Kenyon, with Hawthorne's encouragement, refuses to undergo.

Needless to say, however, this development on Donatello's part takes place *only* in symbolism, and is further compromised by the uncertainty of Hawthorne's attitude toward him. Is natural impulse inherently corrupt or not? Hawthorne cannot decide, and so he teases us desperately with innuendoes about Donatello's ears, his supposed tail, his gross ancestors, his resemblance to a voluptuous statue—and yet insists that his innocence prior to the murder is total. The net result is a smutty equivocation.

It may now be appreciated that our critical task is not to find moral or religious consistency in *The Marble Faun,* but to grasp the connection between its pervasive anxiety and its overt story and themes. If Hawthorne's religious musings are at once inconclusive and pathetically sincere, it must be because he has tacitly supplied a real basis for his characters' seemingly exaggerated guilt-feelings, and one which no expiation will suffice to remove. It is clearly not enough to say that those characters have been made uneasy about sexuality; mere uneasiness does not call up Hawthorne's grim vision of "the crown of thorns, the hammer and nails, the pincers, the spear, the sponge." There is in *The Marble Faun* a remarkable savagery of self-punishment and, accompanying it, a perverse and persistent sense of renewed criminality. Our expectation, drawn from comparable instances elsewhere in Hawthorne's career, is that the nature of this criminality will be indicated both by a symbolic configuration of the main group of characters and by the nature of the central action they perform.

Let us first note that in a certain sense Hawthorne's four main characters share the same predicament. Hilda and Donatello are repeatedly described as children, and the four together make a troupe of siblings: Miriam sees Hilda as a "younger sister," Kenyon offers Miriam "brotherly counsel," and so on. All four, furthermore, are isolated from parents. Hilda is an orphan with no near relatives; Kenyon has no discernible family ties; Donatello is the only surviving member of the Monte Beni line; and Miriam, having "lost her English mother" at an early age, seems to have been victimized by the dictates of a father who is conspicuously omitted from direct mention.

By now every reader will know what to expect when he comes across a Hawthornian orphan—to say nothing of a quartet of them. The absence of literal parents will entail, not a sense of playful freedom, but a dual obsession, a feeling of vague parental tyranny and a longing for an ideal parent-figure to restore security and forgive offenses. The removal of the literal parent makes way for the dichotomized fantasy-parents, the creatures of disjoined accusation and remorse.

In *The Marble Faun* there is an excellent candidate for the role of ogre-father in the bearded, ageless specter who emerges simultaneously from Miriam's past and from her hidden thoughts. His reappearance to remind her that "our fates cross and are entangled" may be correlated with the mystery of silence about her family in general and her father in particular. Indeed, at two moments Hawthorne unaccountably refers to him as "Father" when the context calls for "Brother." His bizarre double role as satyr-like villain and penitent monk is appropriate to the child's idea of sexual excess and remorse in the offending parent. None of these facts, of course, proves that the model *is* Miriam's father; the point is that Hawthorne, having symbolically regarded his other characters as siblings, appears to have endowed the model with traits that would justify filial resentment.

The model's haunting effect, as we might anticipate after such relationships as those between Major Molineaux and Robin, Jaffrey Pyncheon and Holgrave, applies not only to Miriam (who *may* be his daughter) but also to a male character who is distinctly not his literal son: Donatello. The "instinctive, unreasoning" antipathy that Donatello feels for the model when the latter first interferes with his childlike frolicking with Miriam may be regarded as Oedipal if we take Hawthorne's family symbolism seriously. And there is every encouragement to do so. For the principal deed of *The Marble Faun* is the joint murder of this same villain by Miriam and Donatello—a murder which separates them from "all brotherhood and sisterhood," clearing the way for a later ambiguous union but at the same time demanding an eventual repentance. Surely it is no coincidence that this obscure figure from Miriam's earlier days is thought to be the one obstacle between Donatello and Miriam's love, and that the very act of his murder is rendered in the sexual imagery we have examined. The consummation which appears to be made possible by the model's death, but which cannot be forthrightly mentioned, is an act of incest in Hawthorne's mind if not in the minds of his characters.

Thus we gather that Hawthorne has taken the Cenci case, which figures so prominently in the allusive symbolism of *The Marble Faun,* and in his scarcely perceptible way has given it a twist that his predecessor Shelley would have appreciated. In both versions the paternal figure is evidently guilty of sexual misconduct toward the daughter-figure; the bond between the model and Miriam "must have been forged in some such unhallowed furnace as is only kindled by evil passions and fed by evil deeds," and Miriam confesses that "with one word he could have blasted me in the belief of all the world." In both cases, too, the "Beatrice" is joined in the murder by a "brother" who is equally anxious that the "father" die. The novelty comes in Hawthorne's implication of a sexual advantage in this death; the removal of an incestuous tyrant only provides the circumstances for still further hints of wicked love.

Let me repeat, lest I be misunderstood, that these are conclusions not about Hawthorne's characters but about their meaning within a pattern of authorial obsession. Like *The House of the Seven Gables* and *The Blithedale Romance, The Marble Faun* does not treat a literal instance of incest, or even of incest-temptation; it exploits a rather slender story for its vague and bizarre incestuous overtones. As in the former romances, Hawthorne's characters are neither consciously aware of this fantasy-meaning nor free from its distorting effects; they display an outlandish prudery and guilt whose source in incest-fear can only be located in Hawthorne himself. And so, too, they must make amends proportionate to the imagined misdeed. The greater part of *The Marble Faun* may be said to explore various avenues of possible escape, not from the guilt that has been objectively incurred in the plot, but from the incestuous theme behind that plot. (pp. 224-28)

Art theory in *The Marble Faun* is not really separable from Hawthorne's omnipresent brooding about sex. As its title implies, the book deals in an oxymoronic marriage of marble and faun, of cold artistic stasis and the raw passion which it imprisons. Thus in Kenyon's sensitive reaction to the Laocoön, form and passion are in perfect equilibrium. The Laocoön

> impressed Kenyon as a type of the long, fierce struggle of man, involved in the knotted entanglements of Error and Evil, those two snakes, which, if no divine help intervene, will be sure to strangle him and his children in the end. What he most admired was the strange calmness diffused through this bitter strife; so that it resembled the rage of the sea made calm by its immensity, or the tumult of Niagara which ceases to be tumult because it lasts forever.

The symbolism of family entanglement here, with its suggestion of an unrelenting sexual threat, can hardly be seen as fortuitous after all we have found in *The Marble Faun;* and it is evident that in Hawthorne's view artistic form is cast into the struggle on the side of control. Art is a way of managing too-powerful feelings. And thus Miriam, the oversexed one, can say enviously to Kenyon, "You turn feverish men into cool, quiet marble. What a blessed change for them! Would you could do as much for me!"

At the same time, however, art is a means of registering anxiety. Miriam's expressionistic works, which are "ugly phantoms that stole out of my mind . . . things that haunt me," plainly serve this purpose, and when she tries instead to produce trite scenes from common life she is invariably compelled to portray a likeness of herself spying at lovers through a window or "between the branches of a shrubbery." This accusation of vicarious sexuality helps to explain Hawthorne's emphasis on artistic *shame,* and particularly on the hypocrisy of sensualists who revel in female nudity with the pretext of creating worshipful Madonnas. But more important . . . is the implication, fostered by both Miriam and Kenyon, that the artist cannot contain himself. If he has no choice but to reveal his sexual fears in his art, then the only way to prevent such revelation is to give up art altogether. And if Kenyon is permitted to escape this logic and continue his pursuit of banal ideality, I suggest that Hawthorne himself was not. The unfinished romances that follow *The Marble Faun* consist of innumerable false starts in which formerly serviceable clichés of plotting get contaminated by sexual fantasy and are therefore abandoned.

Hilda's arrival to rescue the bewildered sculptor in *The Marble Faun* powerfully reinforces the whole erotic meaning of Hawthornian art. I refer not so much to the scene in the Corso as to the earlier one where her safety is first announced to Kenyon. There, out on the Campagna, Kenyon makes one last descent into the caverns of the unconscious whose antithesis is Hilda. A "cellar-like cavity" within "old subterranean walls" is the setting, which "might have been the ruins of a bath-room, or some other apartment that was required to be wholly or partly under ground." The ruins of a bath-room!—indeed a spot where one is likely to hit upon "some discovery which would attract all eyes." What Kenyon finds are the parts of a lovely antique Venus who, when her limbs are reassembled, "showed that she retained her modest instincts to the last. She had perished with [her arms], and snatched them back at the moment of revival. For these long-buried hands immediately disposed themselves in the manner that nature prompts, as the antique artist knew, and as all the world has seen, in the Venus de' Medici." With this graceful gesture the statue calls attention to the genital obsession of the entire scene, an obsession bearing an obvious relevance to the fears for Hilda, who was last seen heading for the Cenci Palace.

To find Hilda intact, in other words, one must get this Venus, with its "lovely crevice of the lips," out of one's mind. The figure is not only a woman, however, but a masterful work of sculpture as well; it ought to appeal to Kenyon, who is alleged to be a sculptor himself. Yet having created a work of art which charmingly embodies both normal erotic feeling and normal modesty, Hawthorne dismantles it in loyalty to the amply demonstrated need for Hilda. After a first show of interest Kenyon lapses into apathy. . . . (pp. 236-39)

Hawthorne remains duplicitous to the end. He seems to be saying that Kenyon's human love is supplanting his cold aesthetic taste—an economy that further implies a vicarious erotic function for art, since direct love makes art seem empty. Yet when we reflect that vapid Hilda is here dethroning a supple and lovely Venus, the surface meaning becomes exactly reversed. The remainder of the scene shows that in his clandestine way Hawthorne has not abandoned his awareness that commitment to Hilda is simply a form of panic. Only after forswearing any interest in the Venus is Kenyon entitled to hear the good news that Hilda will be safely returned to him. And though Hawthorne is bound, for reasons that are at once conventional and personal, to make the dreary exchange of Venus for Hilda, he cannot resist the honest impulse to count his loss, and Kenyon's. "Does it not frighten you a little," teases Miriam, alluding to the statue—"like the apparition of a lovely woman that lived of old, and has long lain in the grave?" "Ah, Miriam! I cannot respond to you," says Kenyon. "Imagination and the love of art have both died out of me." (p. 239)

> *Frederick Crews, in his* The Sins of the Fathers: Hawthorne's Psychological Themes, *Oxford University Press, 1966, 279 p.*

CLARE R. GOLDFARB (essay date 1969)

[*Goldfarb considers Hilda and Kenyon symbolic of misguided American isolationism.*]

As an artist Hawthorne continually complained that his homeland lacked the elements needed to create art; in particular, America lacked a romantic atmosphere. Hawthorne's most notable complaint appears in the "Preface" to *The Marble Faun.*

> No author . . . can conceive of the difficulty of writing a romance about a country where there is no shadow, no antiquity, no mystery, no pictur-

esque and gloomy wrong, nor anything but a commonplace prosperity, in broad and simple daylight, as is happily the case with my dear native land [see excerpt dated 1859 in *NCLC,* Vol. 2].

In Italy he had found the atmosphere he wanted, a true contrast to the "grassy" and "elm-shadowed wayside" of a New England village. In an atmosphere of "shadow," "antiquity," and "mystery," he places two American artists, Hilda, the Puritan maiden, and Kenyon, the sculptor; with them are two Europeans, Miriam, the painter, and Donatello, Count of Monte Beni. By examining each member of this quartet, Hawthorne comments on the ambiguous qualities of innocence and experience; his comments form a critique of American life and art.

Comparing the two Americans to the two Europeans naturally reveals similarities and differences. If the partners change places, other important similarities and differences appear. In such an exchange, Hilda and Donatello emerge as archetypal innocents; Miriam and Kenyon as finer intelligences, as point-of-view characters. Comparing American artists to each other and comparing their reactions to European art show only one side of the coin. Contrasting American and European initiation experiences and contrasting reactions to these experiences show the other side.

When we divide the characters traditionally into Americans and Europeans, we must consider Hilda and Kenyon and their reactions to European art. Hilda's reaction is idolatrous: she becomes a slave to it. While a student in America, her teachers had proclaimed her "genius for the pictorial art." Although her skill lacked a "darker and more forcible touch," she might one day produce "original works worthy to hang in that gallery of native art which, we hope, is destined to extend its rich length through many future centuries." Preparing for that eventuality, Hilda comes to Italy. Certainly Italy could provide that "darker and more forcible touch." But instead of developing her own genius, Hilda chooses to sacrifice it to the old masters. She chooses to become a slave because of a missing ingredient in her temperament. A lack of artistic commitment, not a lack of talent, causes her servitude—causes her to become a copyist. With her natural gifts, she produces extraordinary copies of masterpieces. In fact, Hilda seems to be a medium through whom the dead artists live in the present. "The spirits of the old masters" hover over her and guide "her delicate white hand." Her copies seem to suggest more than the original; that is, what the great master had in his imagination. The girl seems "a finer instrument, a more exquisitely effective piece of mechanism, by the help of which the spirit of some great departed painter now first achieved his ideal, centuries after his own earthly hand, that other tool, had turned to dust." At the end of the novel when Hilda returns to Kenyon after a mysterious absence, the reader is told to "fancy that she had been snatched away to a land of picture" where she conversed with great artists and beheld the works they had done in heaven. Absorbing European art, Hilda has not transformed it into something better; what she has absorbed has overwhelmed her. The result is a dehumanized woman, an impression reinforced by her white dresses and her abode high in a tower away from the bustle of human life.

Hawthorne insists that Hilda is noble because she has sacrificed herself to the masters whose achievements she cannot approach. His rationalization does not erase the fact that Hilda is an artistic coward who has surrendered her soul to the already accepted and esteemed excellence of the Borghese, the Corsini, and the Sciarra. She has denied the fledgling galleries of art in her homeland, which demand a commitment to the unknown and unproven, a commitment she is too feeble to give.

It is impossible to separate Hilda's lack of artistic achievement from her lack of humanity. As she is an incomplete artist, so is she incomplete in her human relationships. Refusing to give herself to live human beings and devoting herself to dead ones, she prefers to remain detached and aloof.

Her attitude to Miriam is, of course, the main indictment of Hilda's inhumanity. At the beginning of *The Marble Faun* Hilda announces her friendship with Miriam loudly and clearly. And yet when she is given the chance to prove it, she shrinks from the contact. She is unable to give of herself to another human being because there is nothing left. Hilda is a shell; her soul has gone to the service of dead artists.

Hilda's soul(less) mate is the man of marble, Kenyon. As a sculptor who works in marble, Kenyon's achievement is certainly not a small one. We admire his pearl fisher, his Milton, his model of Hilda's hand, and his best work, Cleopatra. European art has not subjugated him as it has Hilda. At the same time, his commitment to art is insincere and incomplete. While Kenyon draws and plans the models for his statues, other men chisel out the figures from the white marble. He is at a distance from his own art. "The finished statuary which art lovers admire so extravagantly is in harsh reality the work of some nameless machine in human shape."

Kenyon is even less involved with the human beings around him than he is with his art. He is literally and symbolically a man of marble whose love for Hilda takes the form of the white stone of his profession. It is significant that one of his finest marble creations is Hilda's hand kept in an exquisite box in his desk. And it is also significant that while searching for Hilda on the Campagna, Kenyon finds, instead, a marble woman. As he is unable to make contact with his art so he is unable to form a relationship with Hilda: he does win her at the end of the novel but he wins a "household saint"—not that earthly creature, a wife.

Kenyon keeps his distance from his beloved and also from his friend, Miriam. Hilda shrinks from Miriam and complicity in Miriam's guilt; so does Kenyon, less violently, but no less completely, shrink from listening to Miriam confess her dark secret. Both Hilda and Kenyon deny Miriam the comfort of meaningful friendship. Both lack total commitment to life and to art; they are incomplete human beings and artists.

Through Hilda and Kenyon Hawthorne criticizes American life and art. He creates two American expatriate artists and ships them to Italy. By doing so, he suggests that American experience in isolation is not enough for the artist who would be great. Kenyon, Hilda, and America need the "dark," "forcible" touch that European experience can provide. That touch may be dangerous. Like many Americans from Tom Paine to Ralph Waldo Emerson, Hawthorne presents the traditional view of Europe and America in parent-child relationship. He warns that dependence on European values can stifle original talent and stop the quest for a new art. Witness Europe's destruction of Hilda's art.

Even more ambiguity exists in the relation of Europe and America. Hawthorne reveals it by placing Hilda and Kenyon next to their European counterparts, Miriam and Donatello.

Ready to be initiated into the experiences of the world, at the beginning of *The Marble Faun* Donatello and Hilda are innocents. Although Donatello's past is deeply rooted in history, like Hilda he is an orphan and the last of his line. Obviously meant to represent man before the Fall, Donatello is full of the joy of life but devoid of "moral severity." Miriam treats him more like a lap dog than a suitor despite his adoration. When his feelings for Miriam lead him to commit a murder, Donatello changes; he gains a soul. The crime educates him for better or worse and creates a major theme of the book: a human soul may realize itself by engagement with evil. This theme puts us in the familiar territory of Donatello's transformation and involves the argument for or against the theory of the Fortunate Fall. Rather than argue, I prefer to point out two important effects of the crime. It joins Donatello with Miriam and it teaches him "moral severity." His new thoughts display an awareness of right and wrong and a desire for justice—empty abstractions to him before the murder.

As the principal actor in the murder Donatello immerses himself in elements which create and destroy; Hilda, his innocent counterpart and the star witness of the murder, refuses to immerse herself in anything except self-pity. Unmindful of the misery Miriam and Donatello endure, Hilda beats her breast and wanders in search of a friend to help her. "Why should not there be a woman to listen to the prayers of women? A mother in heaven for all motherless girls like me." She finds peace in the Catholic confessional. When the priest discovers that she is not of the faith, he demands an explanation for Hilda's sacrilege. She speaks in egotistical terms. Her only concern is her own purity:

> I am a motherless girl, and a stranger here in Italy. I had only God to take care of me, and be my closest friend; and the terrible, terrible crime, which I have revealed to you, thrust itself between him and me; so that I groped for him in the darkness, as it were, and found him not—found nothing but a dreadful solitude, and this crime in the midst of it! I could not bear it. It seemed as if I made the awful guilt my own, by keeping it hidden in my heart. I grew a fearful thing to myself. I was going mad!

Surely Hilda knows that Miriam is also a stranger in Italy and also in need of help—but not a word of pity or sympathy is asked in the confessional for her. To Hilda, the murder was a crime and a sin. No explanation can soften the black and white facts. Since Hilda's only concern is to be relieved of any complicity with Miriam and Donatello, she wants no part of their burden of guilt. The confession relieves and restores Hilda: "her bosom was as pure now as in her childhood. She was a girl again."

By analyzing Hilda's comment and release, Hawthorne makes a statement about American experience. If he is juxtaposing Hilda's with America's, he is showing that Americans are immature and overly concerned with remaining uninvolved; he is also showing that American isolationism is hypocritical. At the same time that Hilda reaches out to Catholicism, an old world institution, for comfort, she cherishes her brand of isolationism. The parallel with America may be drawn: at the same time that the young country proclaims its isolationism, its determination to rely only on itself, it needs the old world as a spiritual reservoir or a regenerative force.

Hawthorne shows his new and old world innocents, Hilda and Donatello, in their reactions to crime and passion. He also shows them by their relations with the people who love them. Kenyon and Miriam comment on the action of *The Marble Faun;* they also present in and by themselves further development of the subject of American experience. Seeking an escape from her past, Miriam tries to establish a life for herself as an artist in Rome. When a person from her past and reminiscent of its terrors discovers her, her attempt fails. A symbol of sheer malevolence, the man haunts Miriam's life as closely as she is pursued by that symbol of sheer animal innocence, Donatello. When he inevitably confronts Miriam's tormentor, he murders him—the act making him a part of Miriam's life.

Soon after the murder, Donatello returns to his family estate. Kenyon visits it and discerns the change in the Count. Although he does not know about the murder, Kenyon urges Donatello to throw off his gloom and come into the sunlight once again. Sensitive enough to notice that Donatello has grown a soul, Kenyon fails to use this perception for his own moral development. That role is left to Miriam.

Before Miriam and Donatello give themselves up to human justice, Miriam comments on the change that has come over Donatello. She thinks the "experience of pain" has changed and improved him. With thoughts racing far and deep she disparages human justice and disagrees with Donatello's compulsion to be punished by man. An embryonic Raskolnikov, Miriam travels in realms of thought which shock her listener Kenyon. He is afraid to follow her: "Mortal man has no right to tread on the ground where you now set your feet."

Contrasting Miriam and Kenyon reinforces a major idea of *The Marble Faun:* immersion in the darker elements of man's existence heightens perceptions and awareness. Miriam is immersed in dark elements: her perceptions have deepened, and self-pity has dissolved before her concern for Donatello and his fate. On the other hand, Kenyon who has refused to take the plunge remains unchanged, the man of marble. By making Kenyon and Miriam point-of-view characters at the end of *The Marble Faun,* Hawthorne reveals the weakness of Kenyon and the dangerous strength of Miriam.

Kenyon's timid spirit makes him a fit companion for Hilda whom he finally wins for a household saint. As a parting gesture, Miriam sends Hilda a wedding gift, a priceless bracelet composed of Etruscan gems dug out of seven sepulchres—each gem having belonged to a royal person who lived an "immemorial time ago." This symbolic act gives the pair, especially Hilda, one last chance to gain some lesson from the experience of the past. It only brings tears to the girl's eyes as a remembrance of Miriam. Hilda and Kenyon have each other now and except for a few feeble tongue cluckings, they look back neither to the darkness of St. Angelo, Donatello's dungeon, nor to the lifelong pilgrimage of Miriam; they see only the "sunlight on the mountaintops." Then the lovers leave the past behind them and return to America, the new world. They come out of their experience in European tradition and the past little changed, yet ironically brought together by an experience in tragedy and passion. Optimistic and cheery, they cannot comprehend, nor do they wish to, the more tragic aspect of life.

The thesis the reader must draw from their experience—from their inability to cope with Miriam and Donatello—from Hilda's total subjugation to European art—from Kenyon's lack of involvement with art and life—urges America to commit herself to life and to understand that life by understanding Europe; it warns that Europe means a dark past entangled with sin, horror, and crime; that Europe may enslave but may also liberate the artist and the man. The alternatives to that experience are a stunted development and shallow, imperfect examples of art and life. The answers to *what* America should become and *how* she should become are ambiguous. Isolationism is empty, but involvement may bring disaster. Isolationism is inadequate, but involvement may bring servitude. In spite of the ambiguities, the scales tip on the side of involvement with Europe. (pp. 19-22)

> *Clare R. Goldfarb, " 'The Marble Faun' and Emersonian Self-Reliance," in* American Transcendental Quarterly, *No. 1, Part 1, 1969, pp. 19-23.*

NINA BAYM (essay date 1976)

[*Baym reads* The Marble Faun *as an exploration of the tension between art and civilization, eroticism and repression.*]

The Marble Faun is by far the most complex and ambitious of Hawthorne's mature romances. It records the distorting effect of repressive institutions on human life. It attempts to discover the origins of reverence for the authoritarian within the psyche. It postulates art as the expression of an erotic counterforce to civilization, and chronicles the struggle between them. It carries its investigation of all these concerns beyond the bounds of the earlier romances and comes to conclusions even more anguished. It is especially forceful in its articulation of the dilemma of the modern artist. Like *The House of the Seven Gables* and *The Blithedale Romance,* and also *The Scarlet Letter* in part, *The Marble Faun* is the story of a failed artist. But the implication of *The Blithedale Romance*—that artists fail because society will not permit strong art to exist—is much more explicit subject of *The Marble Faun.*

Kenyon is greatly superior to Coverdale in the vigor and scope of his talent. He is a truly promising American artist. His failure results directly from his acceptance of the social view (represented by Hilda) that great art is inferior to genteel art, because it is too crude, coarse, and unmannerly for a polished and improved civilization. Classical and Renaissance art is great because it is not civilized art or, at least, is much less civilized than modern art. But modern civilization is an indisputable improvement over civilizations of the past, and therefore has no place for these less civil productions. Kenyon's tragedy is that he accepts this popular rationale without believing it, because he cannot live without the love and approval of one who embodies this belief herself. (pp. 229-30)

The Marble Faun . . . has no suggestion of a true historical progress toward individualism. It is suggested that the modern age is more repressive than earlier times, and that the modern age justifies its own repressions by labeling them social refinements and advances. Modern society is built on the foundation of a great hypocrisy about human nature, and it offers its hypocrisy as a virtue. Is such a civilization really an advance? Each artist must answer this question as he can. If he feels it to be real progress, he must regard great art as an expression of the childhood of the race and define his own genteel productions as superior. If he feels classical art to be manifestly greater than anything attainable by the contemporary artist, he must see his own civilization as a decline and accept an irrevocable sense of separation from the compla-

cent contemporary culture. At the end of *The Marble Faun* Kenyon finds himself unable to sustain the degree of social criticism and isolation that goes with acknowledging the greatness of art of the past. He abandons his position, and Hawthorne finds it a tragedy for modern art.

The Marble Faun is designed as a sequence of parallels and contrasts between two couples. Kenyon and Hilda are modern Americans who represent socialized beings. The obscure, ancient origins of Donatello and Miriam link them to the beginning of human history. Although it is clearly impossible that any presocial beings should actually exist in the present, Hawthorne comes as close as he can to the idea of such a being in Donatello. Newly arrived from the country, Donatello is certainly not civilized at the story's outset. Through his attachment to Miriam, however, he is initiated into the civilized human condition. This story is only a segment of the romance, for it is contained within the larger story of Kenyon's comprehension of, and response to, Donatello's fate.

Ultimately, all the events of the romance fall into place as aspects of Kenyon's experience. According to how he makes use of his experience, he will become a great artist or he will not. At first open and responsive to the lessons he is learning, he panics and draws back when he discovers that the value system implied in Donatello's history is incompatible with Hilda's values. If he accepts Donatello, he must lose Hilda. Like Hawthorne's other protagonists under pressure, Kenyon is too socialized a man to endure long without the iron framework of familiar institutions. With some regret, but more relief, he leaves his intellectual wanderings to come home to Hilda. Donatello and Miriam are safely stowed behind their labels as penitent sinners; there, like Hester behind her *A,* they represent no further threat to the values of the group. (pp. 231-32)

The romance falls into three parts of roughly equal length. The first, which runs through chapter 19, introduces all the characters, themes, and symbols, and closes with the chief event of the story: Donatello's murder of Miriam's phantom persecutor. The second section chronicles Donatello's inner struggle after the event, his growth, maturation, and eventual reconciliation with Miriam in chapter 35. At the same time, and more importantly, this section shows Kenyon's role in Donatello's development—his support and guidance—which implicates him in Donatello's story. For much of the section Donatello is in a severe mental depression, given over to guilt and self-loathing. But Kenyon intuitively perceives the murder as an inevitable rite of passage and even an act of heroism. He quite deliberately guides the despairing hero back to the light, and arranges for Miriam to meet them in Perugia. At this reunion, under the benign eye of the statue of Pope Julian, the story of Donatello and Miriam comes to a logical, and a happy, ending. It is at least possible that chapter 35 was originally designed to conclude the romance. The chapter has a heavy oratorical rhetoric like the last scaffold scene in *The Scarlet Letter* and the conclusion to *The House of the Seven Gables,* and at thirty-five chapters *The Marble Faun* was already the longest work Hawthorne had written. With Miriam and Donatello brought together, and Kenyon hastening off to Rome and Hilda, the reader might anticipate a second happy union and close the book contented.

But in the last third of the romance Hawthorne in a sense begins again, following Kenyon back to Rome and through his mental crisis as he now suffers the consequences of his sympathetic participation in Donatello's "crime." Hilda disappears, and Kenyon cannot live without her. Like Dimmesdale returned from the forest, Kenyon finds the clarity of his moral vision dissipated in the context of civilization. The issue that connects Donatello's act to Kenyon's is what has been identified repeatedly in the criticism as the "fortunate fall." Miltonic (and Dantean) echoes abound in *The Marble Faun,* but the issue is really just like that in *The Scarlet Letter.* A certain act is stigmatized by society as a crime. It is experienced psychologically as a sin—that is, it produces guilt. But is it really a sin in an absolute sense? Without a divinity present to make his commandments clearly known, and with society claiming, but by no means demonstrating, divine sanction for its judgments, the question remains open. Each "sinner" must work the problem out in solitude and suffering.

Now it might appear that a murder would belong to the small category of acts clearly and absolutely evil, so that Donatello would be unquestionably a sinful man. But the penumbra of allusions surrounding his act prevents one from coming to this conclusion. The persecutor comes to life in the catacombs when the friends are touring them, and he thereafter follows Miriam about like a vengeful ghost. Posing as her model, he is a maniac and a specter of evil; her thralldom is horrifying. Because the model is characterized as a living phantom, his murder does not strike one as the taking of a life. Donatello's act is assimilated into the heroic tradition wherein innocent maidens are rescued from monsters, ogres, and demons. In *A Wonder Book* and *Tanglewood Tales* Hawthorne presented five examples of heroic monster-slayers: Jason, Theseus, Perseus, Hercules, and Bellerophon. He knew that such slayers are never criminals, always heroes. Guido's painting of the archangel Michael as slayer of the monster Satan carries the pagan tradition into a Christian context; and when he invents a drawing of the painting in which Satan has the model's face, Hawthorne puts Donatello into the tradition as well. (pp. 233-34)

By making the model a Capuchin monk Hawthorne links him to the Roman power structure and turns his murder into a crime against the state. The power structure, associated with the great weight and age of Rome (the model is persistently identified with each antique sight in the city), becomes a symbol of the "fathers" in the sense of elders. The idea of patriarchy is of course embodied in priestly nomenclature. To the elders are opposed the passion and spontaneity of the young Miriam and Donatello, their sheer wish to live, to love, to express themselves. The wish, and the behavior it occasions, are harmless in themselves but, forbidden by society, involve defiance of the rules.

Self-expressive behavior, then, is not evil in an absolute sense. It is defined that way by a power structure that sees such behavior as a threat. If in fact such behavior really threatens the power structure we do not know; of course, it becomes threatening in the circumstances, because it defies authority. Thus, the authorities create the situation that threatens them. Despite the move across the ocean and into an entirely different symbolic vocabulary, the symbol system is precisely the same in *The Marble Faun* as in *The Scarlet Letter.* The Puritan and Catholic oligarchies are one and the same.

Miriam plays much the same role in regard to Donatello that Hester did for Dimmesdale. She is, in fact, much less developed as an independent character, and is much more a functional figure in relation to others, than Hester was. She is another representative of passion, creativity, and spontaneity, also like Zenobia although less flawed. She is supposed to be the most beautiful woman in the world. As a woman she stands for the full idea of womanhood that must be accepted if man is to do her justice and grow to his own fullest expression. Like Hester in the forest, or Zenobia at the outset of *The Blithedale Romance,* she suggests a richer and more generous humanity than that permitted under the sterile patriarchy (in the case of a Catholic hierarchy, the sterility is more than metaphorical). And she may also stand for an alienated part of the masculine psyche—aspects of tenderness and passion that the male has repressed and needs to recover to be a whole person. For although there is a certain appeal in Donatello as a faun, there is also something contemptible about him. The many animal allusions state plainly that he is not quite human. He is a case of arrested development, a curiosity. His feelings for Miriam are the agency by which he is transformed from monstrously overgrown child to adult. (pp. 235-36)

[We] have to ask why Donatello, who is not a socialized man like Coverdale and Dimmesdale, feels guilty after he has committed the deed. Both Coverdale and Dimmesdale start as social products and cannot break through in any sustained way to a condition of inner freedom. But Donatello has passed his life outside society. He should be able, if anyone can, to escape the recoil into guilt. But because Miriam is deeply bound up in the social order, Donatello is implicated in society through his feelings for her. The model materializes as a consequence of Donatello's growing passion for Miriam; he is the symbol of the guilt that shadows sexuality. Thus, the crux of Donatello's deed is not murder but sex.

The fall of man, in Judeo-Christian tradition, has of course long been associated with the awakening of human sexuality. After the murder Miriam and Donatello spend the night together, and we may assume that they become lovers. Then it turns out that the model is only "apparently" dead; his corpse bleeds in their presence the next morning, and thereafter he assumes a greater reality, as punishing agent in Donatello's mind, than he ever possessed when he simply followed Miriam about. For Hawthorne in *The Marble Faun* the human being—or more precisely the human male, since the female, as we shall see, has a different development—is not adult unless his life has sexual expression. But sexual expression in the modern world is necessarily accompanied by the profound ambivalence that modern culture feels toward sex. Guilt, therefore, is an aspect of adulthood in modern society.

Guiltless sex, which once existed—the testimony of antique sculpture is clear on this point, and the Monte Beni males have been enjoying a promiscuous existence for centuries—is no longer attainable; to avoid guilt one must avoid sex, in which case one exists as an incomplete or puerile human being. The fall of man, then, lies in the event that makes him perceive sex as shameful. Once sex is perceived in this way, man can be expected to create his own repressive social institutions. Because he wishes to punish himself, and to suppress his offending sexuality, he invents the patriarchy. But what has taken place in human history to charge the sex act with this dire import?

At first glance, the text might appear to support an Oedipal interpretation like that constructed by Freud in *Moses and Monotheism.* The youth kills his father in order to possess the mother, and then feels a guilt that is nothing more than the fear of being punished. Because he is a primitive being, the young man believes that the dead have the power to avenge themselves, and therefore the fact that he has killed the enemy augments rather than relieves his anxiety. Some sort of incest motif is certainly implied in the layer of Cenci allusions, and in the initial relationship of Donatello to Miriam, which is so patently that of a small boy to his mother. Yet the explanation works only partially, for it does not explain the transition from guilt-free early social structures to the guilt-ridden organization of modern society.

Once the patriarchal society has been constructed—however that comes about—the sex act becomes even more guilt-ridden because it is now hedged round with social prohibitions. Most important, sex means a surrender to female power that, however temporary, and while perfectly natural in a matriarchy, is abhorrent in a patriarchy and indeed a threat to it. Every sexual act in modern times represents, for the male, the momentary triumph of the archaic and outlawed power of the female. Donatello's story, then, embodies that crucial—and, so far as I can see, unexplained—moment in history when sex (either in fact or in fancy understood as the union with the mother) ceased to be a joy for the male and became instead a horror. That moment is the fall of man, and there is no returning to the innocent ages preceding it. The question for modern man is whether he will be able to transcend that fall or will forever remain its victim.

Donatello's first impulse is to get as far away from Miriam, whom he now sees as the instigator, as he possibly can. But in returning to prepatriarchal Monte Beni he actually enters her kingdom. Her presence is felt all around the grounds, whose fertility and subtropical sunshine are associated with her. She even has a shrine in the manor, where, it seems, "the sun was magically imprisoned, and must always shine." To escape, Donatello climbs the ancient, masculine tower which reaches away from nature and earth but symbolizes neither enlightenment nor freedom. It is a cold, dark, cheerless monument to death. The dynamics of Donatello's guilt, as it pushes him toward a punitive authoritarian superstructure as well as patriarchal celibacy, are seen in his new, obsessive Catholicism. He decides to become a monk. Thereby he will repudiate his sexuality and take on the role (the model, too, was a monk) of Miriam's oppressor instead of her liberator.

And yet, even at the height of his alienation from Miriam, Donatello repeats his crime. At the top of his tower a green plant grows, existing mysteriously in an ambience that would appear to offer it absolutely no support. Kenyon, the teacher and guide, asks Donatello what lesson he can draw from the little shrub. " 'It teaches me nothing,' said the simple Donatello, stooping over the plant, and perplexing himself with a minute scrutiny. 'But here was a worm that would have killed it; an ugly creature, which I will fling over the battlements'." Miriam, like the plant, is life. If it is a crime to defend her, it is suicide to deny her.

While Donatello struggles in this morass, Kenyon enters his story as the apparent embodiment of an enlightened, liberal view. Kenyon came to Rome naively believing that Victorian "ideal" art was the culmination of artistic progress through the centuries. At home in America he had industriously and profitably turned out a series of busts of public men of the day. But in the presence of classical art the true artist in him emerges; he recognizes its greatness and is inspired by it. He also knows at least on an intuitive level that he cannot achieve this greatness himself simply by imitation. He must re-create classical goals by modern means of expression. He cannot, for example, sculpture nude figures as the Greeks did, because

modern people differ from ancient Greeks in their perception of the body. Now although classical art is superior for precisely those qualities that genteel art congratulates itself on having surpassed, Kenyon at first thinks he can succeed in his aim. His conviction that modern times are compatible with great art parallels his belief that Donatello can be reconciled to Miriam within the precincts of the patriarchy.

It looks at first as though Kenyon's optimism is justified. His Cleopatra actually succeeds as he wants it to. Remaining within the limits of decorum (the statue, for example, is fully and magnificently clothed), it still celebrates the anarchic eroticism of the queen. When he begins work on the bust of Donatello, he advances beyond simple eroticism into more complex and timely ideas. He perceives, and represents, beauty and virtue in the very qualities of Donatello that have separated him from the faun he earlier was: in suffering, in self-knowledge, in self-consciousness. The bust is Kenyon's formulation of the "fortunate fall." The fall begins a process through which man grows—or can grow—beyond the pretty simplicity of childhood into a rich and complex awareness of his life in history and time.

Of course, if the man does not grow, but remains paralyzed by his guilt, there is no fortune in the fall. That is why Kenyon is at such trouble to bring out in the real Donatello what he has put into his sculpture. He is continually exhorting him, through the second third of the book, to leave off his slothful remorse and his self-indulgent penitences (much like Dimmesdale's) and go about the business of becoming a man. It is he who persuades Donatello to leave Monte Beni at last, and he directs Miriam to meet them beneath the Pope's statue in Perugia. The couple is reunited there under the apparent blessing of papal authority symbolized in the statue of Pope Julian.

To end at this point must have been a temptation to Hawthorne, for it is a conclusion in accord with Kenyon's optimism and Hawthorne's hopes for the future of art. But he must have felt that its sanguine character was unjustified, for the last third of *The Marble Faun* utterly undoes it. The statue of Pope Julian is not a real ruler, but an artist's dream of one; it corresponds to the truth of the heart's craving but to no actual pontiff. Donatello's fall will be interpreted as a crime, and no art but genteel art will be permissible in modern times.

When Kenyon returns to Rome he arrives just in time to observe Hilda on her knees at the confessional, and, although his Yankee soul is dismayed, he has too much respect for Hilda to argue with her at length. Indeed, he is afraid to risk her displeasure. The myth that we have been following in Donatello's case is exclusively masculine. Woman's situation is necessarily quite different. The advent of the patriarchy means a radical change in the way woman is perceived. The idea of woman as a self disappears, and she is viewed only in terms of her relation to man. She is repressed as a means of controlling the male. So far as a woman is sexually attractive she inspires fear and persecution. (pp. 236-41)

[Hilda is] a deliberate contrast to Miriam. Like Priscilla, she is a social product who has internalized social rules and restrictions. But Priscilla represents woman as man's servant while Hilda represents her as his chaste ideal, his inward monitor. The incident at St. Peter's implies no new development in her character—she has always worshiped the fathers. She did, however, mistakenly think that the Old Masters, the

Renaissance artists whom she so reverently copied (while bowdlerizing their work), were the proper authority. She misunderstood them, because she was innocent. The great achievement of Renaissance art in Hawthorne's interpretation here is the way in which it succeeds in celebrating Eros within the forms of an antierotic culture. Pretending to paint the Virgin, the Renaissance master in fact painted his mistress. Hilda's special talent as a copyist is called the spiritualizing of such paintings. She selects a small detail (here is the miniaturizing impulse again, which Hawthorne always associates with genteel art) and reproduces it in a chaster, more ideal redaction. That is, she makes the painter's mistress truly into the Virgin. Obviously, she misses the point of the painting. But the culture is delighted with her sort of work, for through it the unsocial energies of these unmistakably great paintings can be assimilated into the social matrix.

However, Hilda loses her naive talent when she witnesses the murder, and gains an unhappy enlightenment. She now has the same opportunity that the murder gives Donatello, to grow beyond her narrow reach into a fuller humanity. But she cannot do this, and she resolutely determines to keep an innocence that in fact she no longer has. Her conflict is expressed as a polarity between concepts of art-mothers and church fathers. Miriam offers her, as she offers Donatello, an example, but it is rejected with fear and loathing. (Observe the contrast between Miriam's original, honest, and very feminine art—dealing with women's subjects from a woman's point of view—and Hilda's exclusive devotion to male painters.) Hilda's despairing progress toward the confessional is impeded not, as she believes, by her Puritanism (in the symbol system of *The Marble Faun* Catholicism and Puritanism are identical), but by the restraining spirit of her mother, whose presence she feels "weeping to behold her ensnared by these gaudy superstitions."

Hilda bemoans her motherless plight throughout the romance, and it is certain that a mother might have stood as buffer between the girl and the exclusive influence of the fathers. But as a result of the latter influence, Hilda repeatedly rejects all images of maternity that are presented to her. No mother is good enough for her. Miriam, called her older sister, is a case in point; and Hawthorne treats the subject in art imagery as he follows Hilda's quest, in chapter 38, for a satisfactory picture of the Virgin. Although Hilda says she is looking for a mother, in fact she is looking for a virgin, and since mothers are not virgins, she must reject each image. "She never found just the Virgin Mother she needed," Hawthorne comments.

The symbolism of tower, dove, and shrine implies Hilda's devotion to the idea of chastity. But her devotion is founded on fear. Under stress she reveals that her true motive is less a conviction of the beauty of chastity than her desire to be good and obedient: "I am a poor, lonely girl, whom God has set here in an evil world, and given her only a white robe, and bid her wear it back to Him, as white as when she put it on." And, she continues (for she is here casting off Miriam), "Your powerful magnetism would be too much for me. The pure, white atmosphere, in which I try to discern what things are good and true, would be discoloured." In another part of the romance a portrait is made of her, which shows Hilda "gazing, with sad and earnest horrour, at a blood-spot which she seemed just then to have discovered on her white robe."

The menstrual and defloration imagery betrays Hilda's intense sexual anxiety.

Hilda then is deeply implicated in the sexual morbidity underlying the structure of guilt, remorse, misery, inhibition, repression, and hypocrisy that is the social atmosphere of *The Marble Faun.* Her dedication to the Virgin shows her longing to escape sexuality, as does her rejection of the sexual nature of her own mother. She would like to think herself the product of a virgin birth, miraculously free of the curse of a sexual nature. Her meditations on the portrait of Beatrice Cenci show her need to believe that one can remain sinless in a fallen world. In her words with Miriam she envisions herself as a child of the father, not of the mother; her ideals are based on an intransigent refusal to know the facts of life. But of course she does know them, so her refusal is hypocritical. Yet she honestly believes that her hypocrisy is a high moral attitude, and the culture supports her belief. To deny the existence of evil is a kind of good.

After the murder, Hilda's ability to deny evil is sorely tested. It turns out that she can deny evil in herself only by imputing it to others. She is driven by anxiety and fear to expose her friends as a means of absolving herself. Using the confessional for this purpose, she patently perverts the intentions of that ritual, which require the penitent to confess one's own sins. Instead, she confesses the sins of others and fiercely insists that she is blameless. Her psychological structure is too rigid and fragile to permit the incorporation of an idea of fault or error in herself. Tattling rather than confessing, she exemplifies the way in which socialized people act as cultural police. She delivers up Miriam and Donatello to the authorities.

And so does Kenyon. The last third of the romance explores his mental collapse and recovery as he loses and regains Hilda. When he explains to her something of the new insights that Donatello's story has given him, she disappears. Miriam and Donatello, now a composite figure, return; they can no longer coexist with Hilda. Kenyon must choose between them. Miriam and Donatello offer him the promise of great artistic achievement. He cannot accept it if Hilda is the price, and she is. He rejects the couple and they give themselves up to the authorities in exchange for Hilda, who returns when they are arrested. Thus Hawthorne shows that neither of his young Americans can rise to the complex lessons that Europe is offering them.

Hawthorne takes an entirely different approach to Miriam and Donatello in this last section of the book; they seem much less real, more remote and fanciful. In effect, the story of the characters Miriam and Donatello has come to an end, and the two figures in the last third of the romance are aspects of Kenyon's drama, phantoms in his consciousness. They are the beautiful man and woman he has created out of his artistic and erotic energies. Now he has to give them up.

In a strangely mythic and magic episode on the campagna, this significant exchange takes place. The scene of their meeting is a sunken spot in the fields, at once underground and in the sun, in the country away from Rome and yet within the enclosure of a Roman ruin. A magic animal leads Kenyon to this sacred spot, where he unearths and assembles the fragments of an exquisite antique Venus. The goddess of love and mother of Eros, she is a symbol of the matriarchy and an example of the greatest art. The order in which Kenyon puts together the pieces of this shattered work—torso, arms, head—represents the progressive embodiment of the fundamental erotic force, an epitome of the artistic process of creation. The Venus is a work that Kenyon discovers, that he digs up, that he re-creates.

As Kenyon completes his work he is joined by Miriam and Donatello, who inform him that they had discovered the statue and left it for him to put together. They are like Surveyor Pue and Hester in the Custom House, the source and symbol of Hawthorne's artistry. But Kenyon is not Hawthorne. He rationalizes his disaffection by explaining that the statue is cold marble, while his lost Hilda is life. But all the rhetoric of the romance contradicts him. As Frederick Crews has expressed it, Hawthorne "seems to be saying that Kenyon's human love is supplanting his cold aesthetic taste. . . . Yet when we reflect that vapid Hilda is here dethroning a supple and lovely Venus, the surface meaning becomes exactly reversed" [see excerpt dated 1966]. The "surface meaning" is no more than Kenyon's uneasy defense. Victim of his age's malaise, he chooses the virgin over Venus, a choice resulting from the same panic that drove Hilda into the church.

Yet Kenyon's fear is absolutely justified—this is Hawthorne's most bitter perception—for without Hilda he will certainly go mad. He cannot survive without her. He has already endured a period of protracted mental depression. He has already ceased to be an artist. "Ah, Miriam, I cannot respond to you," he says crossly. "Imagination and the love of art have both died out of me." He does not have the stamina to be the artist he wanted to be. The carnival scene shows him at lowest ebb, and Hilda is restored to him in the nick of time. The carnival scene recalls moments in Hawthorne's fiction stretching all the way back to **"My Kinsman, Major Molineux."** Dimmesdale's return from the forest; the phantasmagoric chapter woven about the corpse of Pyncheon; the bitter pageant of repudiation at Blithedale—each romance has had such a climactic scene, but the Roman Carnival is the most grotesque of all. The psyche in a state of anarchic turbulence throws up into the light of consciousness a host of horrible fears and fantasies symbolized by a succession of grotesque, partly sexual, dream figures. If Kenyon sinks into this swamp, he is lost forever.

At the close of this scene, Miriam and Donatello take a formal farewell of their friend. "Donatello here extended his hand, (not that which was clasping Miriam's,) and she, too, put her free one into the sculptor's left; so that they were a linked circle of three, with many reminiscences and forebodings flashing through their hearts. Kenyon knew intuitively that these once familiar friends were parting with him, now. 'Farewell!' they all three said, in the same breath." Soon after, Kenyon hears that they have been arrested, and "just as the last words were spoken, he was hit by . . . a single rosebud, so fresh that it seemed that moment gathered." This dewy messenger signifies the end of Kenyon's feverish season in purgatory. Hilda is back; he is safe. At the same moment he is also hit by a cauliflower, a gratuitous expression of the author's disgust that yet another surrogate has been unable to survive social pressure.

Whether or not Kenyon will actually give up art in his American future, he will certainly produce no more feline Cleopatras or broodingly beautiful fauns. In his Roman weeks before Hilda's disappearance, the nature of his art was already beginning to change; while his artisans were at work turning the Cleopatra into marble, he modeled "a beautiful little statue of Maidenhood, gathering a snow-drop." The energy and vigor of his monumental productions are shrinking into the delicate, miniaturing craftsmanship of the genteel artist. Kenyon will emerge from his ordeal another artist of the beautiful. He is already becoming impatient and disenchanted with his Cleopatra: "I should like," he tells Hilda, "to hit poor Cleopatra a bitter blow on her Egyptian nose, with this mallet." The act of consigning Miriam and Donatello to the lifelong status of sinners represents just such a bitter blow to the values of art, as it defaces and discolors the image of "the beautiful man, the beautiful woman," which the romance had so lovingly developed.

Kenyon rejects these two figures; but does not Hawthorne also? We can, of course, dismiss the contention of some critics that Hawthorne is creating a dichotomy between life and art, rejecting art in favor of life; because, . . . [in] all the major romances, art and life stand together and are rejected together in favor of inhibition and security. But it is Hawthorne's act as author that permits Miriam and Donatello to vanish from the sunlight of the romance, and he who gives Hilda the last, horrified criticism of the theory of the fortunate fall. Is Hawthorne himself thus retreating from the bold position he had staked out?

In a sense, he most certainly is. But I am inclined to think that the gesture represents not so much timidity as realism. Hawthorne concluded that society would not permit such a pair to exist uncensured or knowingly entertain an art that celebrated them. The dark finale represents his clear-sighted estimate of their chances for survival. Ultimately, society is to blame for making serious artistry so psychologically strenuous. (pp. 241-47)

On the other hand, the authorial treatment of Hilda certainly suggests a divided loyalty. She is narrow, she is merciless, she is finally inhuman, but Hawthorne nowhere summons the rhetoric to condemn her. Miriam makes a few complaints about her, but is sternly rebuked by Kenyon; and Hawthorne permits Kenyon to have the last word. Hilda is the culture's most cherished stereotype; the author who would openly attack her certainly runs a terrible professional risk. But Hawthorne's attitude toward Hilda is less duplicitous than genuinely ambivalent. Great art is unquestionably the product of human imperfection; if it were possible for mankind to advance into the serene atmosphere of moral perfection, then perhaps art might be a small sacrifice. The question revolves around the place of an ideal of perfection in a situation where perfection is unattainable. Is such an ideal, unattainable though it is, useful because it spurs men on to better things? Or is it not only useless but pernicious because it keeps men from recognizing the reality of their condition and from progressing within that reality? But even if the ideal is pernicious in practice, might it still not be beautiful in itself? Such questions keep Hawthorne from making the final judgment on Hilda that the narrative presses upon him. (p. 248)

Nina Baym, in her The Shape of Hawthorne's Career, *Cornell University Press, 1976, 283 p.*

ALLAN GARDNER LLOYD SMITH (essay date 1983)

[*Lloyd Smith links the theme of artistic expression in* The Marble Faun *to the novel's ethical meanings.*]

In *The Marble Faun* sculpture is distinguished from the other arts by its several separate stages of production, one of which is implicated in the broader economics of the society. First come some hastily scrawled figures on the whitewash of the wall. These "are probably the sculptor's earliest glimpses of ideas that may hereafter be solidified into imperishable stone, or perhaps may remain as impalpable as a dream. Next there are a few very roughly modelled little figures in clay or plaster, exhibiting the second stage of the Idea as it advances towards a marble immortality; and then is seen the exquisitely designed shape of clay, more interesting than even the final marble, as being the intimate production of the sculptor himself, moulded throughout with his loving hands, and nearest to his imagination and heart. In the plaister-cast, from this clay-model, the beauty of the statue strangely disappears, to shine forth again, with pure, white radiance, in the precious marble of Carrara." . . . Behind the coldness and purity of the marble, then, is a great distance back to the original conception, and the interposition of other hands, making the finished product just that, a *product* of a series of almost industrial actions by nameless machines in human shape. Against this procedure the narrator posits an aesthetic of sincerity, familiar to any readers in late eighteenth and early nineteenth century theorists of art: the work of art is "true" insofar as it corresponds to the artist's state of mind, it receives its authenticity from the immediate impress of his thought and feeling, like the clay-model, and loses this authenticity insofar as it becomes a mechanical copy. Against this cliche of Romantic and Victorian thought, however, is played off the suggestion that the sculptor tell his craftsmen "that the figure is embedded in the stone, and must be freed from its encumbering superfluities", another touchstone of Romantic aesthetics in which art is naturalized by the claim of inevitability. What should be the divine inspiration of the artist, to intuit the figure in the stone, becomes an instruction to human machines to rid the figure of its encrustations. In Italy, the home of the art most revered by Americans of Hawthorne's generation, the Romantic concepts of inspiration and natural genius were put under some stress by the recognition of the role of craftsmen both in sculpture and in the early schools of painting ("in the manner of . . ."). But Hawthorne finds the notion of the preexistence of the form too susceptible of moralizing to dispense with it, for after this he writes that "it was impossible not to think that the outer marble was merely an extraneous environment; the human countenance, within its embrace, must have existed there since the limestone ledges of Carrara were first made"; thus suggesting both a natural hieroglyphics within the interior of the landscape, and the doctrine of predestination. "As these busts in the block of marble," thought Miriam, "so does our individual fate exist in the limestone of Time. We fancy that we carve it out; but its ultimate shape is prior to all our action." So the artist's lost intimacy with his own work is compensated by the fulfillment of a greater plan than his, working equally through his inspiration and the craftsman's instructions. Small comfort exists for Miriam in these rocky doctrines, or, for that matter, in the "finely cut features" of Kenyon, which look "as if already marble." The "inspiration" of Romantic theory is transmuted to the severity of a harsh predestinarian dogma, although (perhaps to rehabilitate Kenyon?), the thought is given to Miriam here. A further, slightly recherche attempt to humanise the sculptor for the ensuing scene comes when he emerges to meet Miriam and says, "I will not offer you my hand . . . it is grimy with Cleopatra's clay" and is met by the response "No; I will not touch clay; it is earthy and human."

The episode of Kenyon and his Cleopatra (Galathea) contains a suppressed sexuality denied in the marble hand; but which is paralleled late in the novel in his discovery of the beautiful classic Venus which, because of his "love" for the

missing Hilda, fails to arouse his full artistic admiration. It seems "to fall asunder again, and become only a heap of worthless fragments." One aspect particularly of his discovery requires contemplation: "protruding from the loose earth, however, Kenyon beheld the fingers of a marble hand; it was still appended to its arm, and a little further search enabled him to find the other." Replaced, the hands automatically take up a position of natural modesty, a gesture which deepens the significance of the marble hand of Hilda's that the sculptor so reverences. What the hand hides is what the hand "stands for"; and it is possible to read the "hands" of **"Rappaccini's Daughter"** and **"The Birthmark"** as similar instances of synechdoche. Marble is the extreme example of covering over traces in *The Marble Faun* as it bears mute testimony to an absent passion which still controls the form when freed of its material "clay."

In the broken statue Kenyon confronts the dismembered body of his own desire: it is another version of the passion of Miriam, originally transmuted into the fierce voluptuous Cleopatra which, even in marble, is "fervid to the touch with fiery life," and against which (to placate Hilda?), he contemplates an act of disguised sexual aggression; "I should like to hit poor Cleopatra a bitter blow on her Egyptian nose, with this mallet." His imaginary exorcism performed, Kenyon has yet to encounter the deeper threat of the classic statue, the forgotten beauty of the goddess enshrined in art:

> In a corner of the excavation, lay a small round block of stone, much incrusted with earth that had dried and hardened upon it. So, at least, you would have described this object, until the sculptor lifted it, turning it hither and thither, in his hands, brushed off the clinging soil, and finally placed it on the slender neck of the newly discovered statue. The effect was magical. It immediately lighted up and vivified the whole figure, endowing it with personality, soul, and intelligence. The beautiful Idea at once asserted its immortality, and converted that heap of fragments into a whole, as perfect to the mind, if not to the eye, as when the new marble gleamed with snowy lustre; nor was the impression marred by the earth that still hung upon the exquisitely graceful limbs, and even filled the lovely crevice of the lips. Kenyon cleared it away from between them, and almost deemed himself rewarded with a living smile.

After reconstituting this beautiful statue, Kenyon finds it difficult to fix his mind upon it; and the magic departs as "the divine statue seemed to fall asunder again, and become only a heap of worthless fragments." The narrator comments: "He could hardly, we fear, be reckoned a consummate artist, because there was something dearer to him than his art," but the ease and silence of this victory of repression over libido may occasion suspicion that it is incomplete, as Miriam suggests when she asks: "Does it not frighten you a little, like the apparition of a lovely woman that lived of old, and has long lain in the grave?"

The movement from blank and meaningless stone, into beauty and life, and back again into senseless material recurs constantly in *The Marble Faun.* It happens in the revivified Venus and it also occurs in the figure of the Faun. . . . It is repeated when Kenyon and Hilda examine his Cleopatra; she responding that she is "ashamed to tell" him how much she admires the statue; he maintaining that it has become for him "a mere lump of senseless stone." This movement recapitulates the arc of sexual desire in a rather morbid form, and invites careful examination of the way in which Miriam may lie behind both Cleopatra and the broken Venus.

"What I most marvel at," said Miriam, "is the womanhood that you have so thoroughly mixed up with all those seemingly discordant elements. Where did you get that secret? You never found it in your gentle Hilda. Yet I recognise its truth." Kenyon agrees that "it was not in Hilda" whose "womanhood is of the ethereal type," thus strongly suggesting to the reader that it must therefore be from the other woman in the artist's circle, who has all the features of Cleopatra (except the Egyptian physiognomy), that he learned the "secret." And this is the chapter in which Miriam is drawn (almost) to part with her own "secret" truth to one who might understand her. She subsides on realizing his lack of sympathy, and says, "You can do nothing for me, unless you petrify me into a marble companion for your Cleopatra there; and I am not of her sisterhood, I do assure you!" There is an ambiguity in this reference: Miriam may mean that she is not statue-like, that is, subdued; or that she is not sensuous and passionate, that is, indecorous or possibly licentious; at least not any longer. But the denial surely does suggest a recognition of her own qualities here, if only some of them.

The fullest description of Miriam herself also occurs in the description of another art work, her own portrait: "there appeared the portrait of a beautiful woman, such as one sees only two or three, if even so many, in all a lifetime; so beautiful, that she seemed to get into your consciousness and memory, and could never afterwards be shut out, but haunted your dreams, for pleasure or for pain; holding your inner realm as a captured territory, though without deigning to make herself at home there." She is very youthful, and has a Jewish aspect, neither roseate nor pale; eyes of a depth that cannot be sounded, and black abundant hair, which is not glossy but is Jewish, "a dark glory such as crowns no Christian maiden's head." (pp. 131-36)

The process of vitalizing and devitalizing the stone of sculpture repeats the arc of suppressed, emergent, and resuppressed sexual desire which Hawthorne introduces always in terms of its inaccessibility (here presented as Jewishness), but also uses to explore the experience of life and death, and as a metaphor for emergent spiritual consciousness. Hawthorne supposes that the reader is acquainted with Thorwaldsen's threefold analogy: "the Clay-model, the Life, the Plaister-Cast, the Death; and the sculptured Marble, the Resurrection"; which seems to be attested to by the "lambent flame of spirit that kindles up Donatello's features in Kenyon's unfinished bust. The face gives an impression of a "soul . . . being breathed into him," which may be merely the "chance result of the bust being just so far shaped out, in the marble, as the process of moral growth had advanced, in the original." Kenyon agrees with Hilda to leave it in that state, propounding "the riddle of the Soul's growth, taking its first impulse amid remorse and pain, and struggling through the incrustations of the senses." The model emerges from the Catacombs to haunt Miriam, is killed and returns to the calcifications of the cemetery of the Capuchins, in which his bones will be used as stones, like the skeletons of dead monks made into arches; his fitful embodiment is reiterated in the trickle of blood that flows from his dead body in the Church, and in the effect upon her imagination: "as if a strange and unknown corpse had miraculously, while she was gazing at it, assumed the likeness of that face, so terrible henceforth in her remembrance." Donatello's arc is also incomplete: he is immured in the prison, but not fully caught in Kenyon's marble, for that would be blasphemously final in this structure. This is the area of possibility in sculpture that seems to interest Hawthorne: the intimacy of the clay-model, touched by the artist's hands; the incompleteness that is more suggestive than the finished product; the "Idea" that organizes even the fragments of a beautiful statue: a Romantic aesthetic of the fragment, incompletion and "sincerity" that also incorporates a moral perspective regarding the transience of life, beauty and earthly affairs. But the element that is incomplete, or fragmentary and suggestive is as potentially dangerous as sex or crime.

In the aesthetics of painting in *The Marble Faun* is a comparable anxiety. Inspiration is privileged over the final product in the sketches of "An Aesthetic Company" where the rude daubs of the Old Masters demonstrate the superiority of the "Idea" over time and the decay of its vehicle. (pp. 137-38)

Miriam's paintings are powerful examples of expressiveness in art, for they body out her feelings in tableaus of women, "acting the part of a revengeful mischief towards man." Her pictures are of Jael, driving the nail through the temples of Sisera, dashed off as if Miriam were herself Jael; of Judith, holding the head of Holofernes, in almost a parody of Allori's version, or of Herod's daughter, receiving the head of John the Baptist, and everlasting remorse with it. The descriptions attempt to neutralize the force of Miriam's work by adopting a humourous tone: "The head of Holofernes, (which, by-the-by, had a pair of twisted moustachios, like those of a certain potentate of the day)," and by instant moralizing: "in one form or another, grotesque, or sternly sad—she failed not to bring out the moral, that woman must strike through her own heart to reach a human life, whatever were the motive that impelled her"; but the effect that these paintings have on Donatello is allowed to be definitive. He responds with trouble, fear and disgust, and Miriam admits: "They are ugly phantoms that stole out of my mind; not things that I created, but things that haunt me." Yet even in her more conventional, sentimental studies of the winning of love, the stages of wedded affection, or the poetry of an infant's shoe, "productions of a beautiful imagination, dealing with the warm and pure suggestions of a woman's heart"; even these intimations of a "force and variety of imaginative sympathies" contain an expressive trace: a "figure portrayed apart", peeping through the branches of a shrubbery, through a frosted window, or leaning from a chariot "always depicted with an expression of deep sadness" and bearing the traits of Miriam's own face and form. Just as Kenyon's statuary bore the ineffaceable traces of his secret life, so Miriam's trouble always emerges, if only in a small figure, set off to the side like a signature, in her paintings. Art is a mirror, in which the uncanny—that which should not have been allowed to be seen but has become visible, according to Schelling—irrupts into the public arena. In *The Marble Faun* art endlessly repeats the hidden faces of its creators and its observers: Miriam and Hilda both appear as the subjects of paintings; and both are seen to resemble the Guido portrait of Beatrice Cenci; Donatello is seen as the marble faun, and is later revealed in his new essence through the idle workings of the clay in Kenyon's hands, and the accidental incompleteness of his marble bust; Kenyon is revealed through his sculptures and the figure he "discovers," and the model appears as the Demon in Guido's sketch for the St Michael. Innumerable other instances of "trace" exist in the narrative, in, for example, Miriam's question to Hilda, "Do you see it written in my face, or painted in my eyes?" she asks, or in the message her eyes contain when Donatello has the model in his power on the Tarpeian Rock, a message so clear that Hilda reads it too, before the deed "took but that little time to grave itself in the eternal adamant." But painting is a special case of that "engraving" for it is here that the obverse of the Romantic dictum of "sincerity" has its effect: if the artist is not sincere, he had better beware the magic mirror which reveals all that he wishes to hide.

"On the emptiness of Picture galleries" criticizes the Italian masters from that point of view, through Hilda's disillusionment after she experiences the terror of witnessing a murder committed by her closest friends. "She saw beauty less vividly, but felt truth, or the lack of it, more profoundly. She began to suspect that some, at least, of her venerated painters, had left an inevitable hollowness in their works, because, in the most renowned of them, they essayed to express to the world what they had not in their own souls. They deified their light and wandering affections, and were continually playing off the tremendous jest . . . of offering the features of some venal beauty to be enshrined in the holiest places." For "what is deepest" these painters substituted a keen intellectual perception and a knack of external arrangement "instead of the live sympathy and sentiment which should have been their inspiration." Exceptions to the grand tradition of passing off a harlot as the Madonna (Hawthorne's own sleight of hand in *The Scarlet Letter* perhaps), are only to be found in the "humble aspiration" of Fra Angelico (Perugino), whose Virgin "revealed herself to him in loftier and sweeter faces of celestial womanhood" than even Raphael could imagine, or Sodoma who, "beyond a question, both prayed and wept, while painting his fresco, at Siena, of Christ bound to a pillar." It will be seen that Hawthorne had not escaped from the paradox inherent in his theory of art: the work must be sincere, but if sincere it is likely to express too much, the harlot will be substituted for the Madonna, the secret will emerge, the statue come to life, the marble lose its chastity. Only the devout escape, with Sodoma. The devout; and Hilda.

Expressive art has the advantage of authenticity, but what it expresses may be too dangerous to confront: Kenyon is afraid of his statue of Cleopatra, Donatello terrified by what he sees in Miriam's paintings. Hilda's art, copying, has the advantage that it does not reveal the artist but only brings out another facet of the prototype. In part this may be seen as a clash between romantic and classicist aesthetics: as Miriam humourously argues to Kenyon, "There are not—as you will own—more than half-a-dozen positively original statues or groups in the world, and these few are of immemorial antiquity," an accusation which, at least implicitly, extends into the realm of painting and is acknowledged in Hilda's choice to be not "a minor enchantress within a circle of her own" but the "handmaid of those old magicians." Would it have been worth Hilda's while, asks the skeptical narrator, "to relinquish this office for the sake of giving the world a picture or two which it would call original; pretty fancies of snow and moonlight; the counterpart in picture, of so many feminine achievements in literature!" The exclamation mark suggests that there is to be no appeal from this judgement, but Hawthorne's anti-feminist animus should not totally dispel the issue of originality that is at stake. Miriam's originality consists in enthusiastic re-imaginings of traditional subjects; Kenyon too works with stereotypical figures: a certain amount of secondariness is evident even in these examples of the expressive techniques. Authenticity seems to reside in

these works only in their guiltiness. Within the deliberately limited frame of this perspective, Hilda's work as a copyist takes on some significance: she feels deeply, and works religiously to recapture the spirit of her old masters, so that "From the dark, chill corner of a gallery—from some curtain chapel in a church, where the light came seldom and aslant—from the prince's carefully guarded cabinet, where not one eye in thousands was permitted to behold it—she brought the wondrous picture into daylight, and gave all its magic splendour for the enjoyment of the world."

The accuracy of Hilda's eye is related to the accuracy of her moral perception: the one sinks into the picture, seeing it fully, and seizing its subtle mystery, even photographing it, the other probes her friends like a sharp steel sword. After her revelation of the evil close at hand, the "gifted simplicity of vision" required for the appreciation of great art is lost, and she ceases to perform as an artist at all. But indeed, the possibility of such an apprehension was always there, contained in the pictures Hilda chose to allow into her "heart" and, specifically, in the portrait of Beatrice Cenci. Day after day Hilda sits before that picture (which it is forbidden to copy) until it is "photographed" in her heart. But this, of all pictures, is not innocent, at least not to the voyeuristic eyes of its nineteenth century admirers. . . . Nothing in the picture offers the reading which the story of Beatrice imposes upon it: in fact, the picture contradicts that story, for, "Who, indeed, can look at that mouth—with its lips half-apart, as innocent as a baby's that has been crying—and not pronounce Beatrice sinless!" But if the observer brings to the picture all the appalled fascination which it is claimed to inspire, why is the innocent Hilda so absorbed in it? Surely she participates with narcissistic masochism in the thrill this painting allows. This is implied also in the scene after the crime, when Hilda sees her own face and the Beatrice reflected in the same looking glass, and fancies "that Beatrice's expression seen aside and vanishing in a moment, had been depicted in her own face, likewise . . ." The painting's profoundest expression "eludes a straightforward gaze"; it can only be caught by side glimpses, or when seen casually, "even as if the painted face had a life and consciousness of its own, and, resolving not to betray its secret of grief or guilt, permitted the true token to come forth, only when it imagined itself unseen." The Cenci portrait then, is an ultimate expression in art of the idea of essence, it is exactly what it is not, can only be seen when it is not seen. . . . Hilda's identification with the portrait which antedates her awareness of the crime of Miriam and Donatello, and its relation to incest and parricide, suggests an ambiguity at some very deep level of her identity which the surface of the text energetically denies. The choice even of what to copy may be a revelation in the magic mirror. But this meaning, it may be more accurate to say is not Hilda's but imposed upon her from outside, by the exigencies of construction or, the self-revelation of its creator who exposes himself in the mirror of the book.

The problem of originality is, cast another way, the problem of repetition, the avoidance of imitation. *The Marble Faun* is concerned with this problem in art, the life of the individual, the life of the species and the history of societies. Hilda chooses the supplement, thus trying to circumvent it; by conscious repetition she will preempt *un*conscious repetition, become the handmaiden of Raphael instead of another feminine scribbler in paint. But the model she chooses is so full of duplicity as to reintroduce the problem: in avoiding accidental *imitation* she enters an accidental *emulation*. This is an eddy from the larger pattern of the novel which touches everyone. The question proposed by the larger pattern has been called the "fortunate fall": is it better than Donatello should sin, and thus gain spiritually, than that he should have remained innocent and incapable of moral and spiritual development? By extension, therefore, is it better that mankind should have "fallen" into experience and the possibility of spiritual growth, than have remained in a golden age of innocence and ignorance? Kenyon and more especially Hilda, have upset readers by their unwillingness to admit this apparently reasonable proposition. When Kenyon hears Miriam ask "Was the crime—in which he and I were wedded—was it a blessing in that strange disguise? Was it a means of education, bringing a simple and imperfect nature to a point of feeling and intelligence, which it could have reached under no other discipline?" he replies "You stir up deep and perilous matter, Miriam . . . I dare not follow you into the unfathomable abysses whither you are tending." Miriam will not be put off, and follows her question to its logical conclusion. "Was that very sin—into which Adam precipitated himself and all his race—was it the destined means by which, over a long pathway of toil and sorrow, we are to attain to a higher, brighter, and profounder happiness than our lost birthright gave? Will not this idea account for the permitted existence of sin, as no other theory can." But Kenyon repeats, "It is too dangerous, Miriam! I cannot follow you! Mortal man has no right to tread on the ground where you now set your feet." Critics . . . have delighted in condemning the reaction of Kenyon and the "hopeful and happy-natured" Hilda from the secure perspective of Hawthorne's assumed standpoint . . . But the question of the "fortunate fall" is deeper than these easy assumptions allow. Hilda's reaction to Kenyon's exposition of the theory is not as laughable as such critics would suppose: "This is terrible and I could weep for you, if you indeed believe it. Do not you perceive what a mockery your creed makes, not only of all religious sentiments, but of moral law, and how it annuls and obliterates whatever precepts of heaven are written deepest within us? You have shocked me beyond words." Behind the Augustan doctrine is the gnostic heresy: if the fall was fortunate then the serpent was the agent of good, and the God of the garden was evil. (pp. 139-46)

Hawthorne's awareness of gnostic allegory (and he read widely in religious sources), would mean that the doctrine of the fortunate fall was indeed a dangerous doctrine, provocative of Satanic inversions and ultimately, as in **The Marble Faun,** implying an acceptance of incest, parricide and murder as the origins of good. No wonder that Hilda calls for silence from Kenyon, and sees the threat to those precepts which are necessarily claimed to be "written deepest within us"; the precepts that are the naturalised creators of human society. Rome is itself a "sermon in stones" on the consequences of abandoning those precepts; there is crime and blood everywhere and the vision of the city is nightmarish whether in daylight or darkness. In daylight, as the opening paragraph of "Hilda's Tower" describes it, Rome is a "long decaying corpse, retaining a trace of the noble shape it was, but with accumulated dust and a fungous growth overspreading all its more admirable features"; in moonlight it is summed up by the descriptions of the legend of Curtius and the gulf "beneath us, everywhere." Kenyon, his imagination excited by the idea of the chasm, continues the theme of the crimes of Roman history: "Doubtless too . . . all the blood that the Romans shed, whether on battlefields, or in the Coliseum, or on the cross—in whatever public or private murder—ran into

this fatal gulf, and formed a mighty subterranean lake of gore, right beneath our feet." These are the consequences of the "fortunate fall." (pp. 146-47)

> *Allan Gardner Lloyd Smith, in his* Eve Tempted: Writing and Sexuality in Hawthorne's Fiction, *Croom Helm, 1983, 182 p.*

ADDITIONAL BIBLIOGRAPHY

Abel, Darrel. "A Masque of Love and Death." *University of Toronto Quarterly* XXIII, No. 1 (October 1953): 9-25.
    Investigates how the characters of *The Marble Faun* symbolically illustrate aspects of Hawthorne's moral vision.

Barnett, Gene A. "Art as Setting in *The Marble Faun.*" *Transactions of the Wisconsin Academy of Sciences, Arts and Letters* LIV (1965): 231-47.
    Contends that Hawthorne "organically and functionally" integrated descriptions of Roman art into the plot, characterization, and theme of *The Marble Faun.*

Beidler, Peter G. "Theme of the Fortunate Fall in *The Marble Faun.*" *The Emerson Society Quarterly,* No. 47 (1967): 56-62.
    Recapitulates the critical debate regarding the theme of the fortunate fall in *The Marble Faun,* attempting to clarify and define the central questions of the argument.

Bercovitch, Sacvan. "The Frontier Fable of Hawthorne's *Marble Faun.*" *The South Dakota Review* 4, No. 2 (Summer 1966): 44-50.
    Posits that *The Marble Faun* is "a fable of the American West, in which the European setting becomes a metaphor for America."

Berthold, Dennis. "Hawthorne, Ruskin, and the Gothic Revival: Transcendent Gothic in *The Marble Faun.*" *The Emerson Society Quarterly* 20, No. 1 (1974): 15-32.
    Delineates the influence of the Gothic on *The Marble Faun* and relates this to the novel's theme.

Bewley, Marius. "Hawthorne and Henry James: *The Marble Faun* and *The Wings of the Dove.*" In his *The Complex Fate: Hawthorne, Henry James and Some Other American Writers,* pp. 31-54. New York: Grove Press, 1954.
    Traces the influence of *The Marble Faun* on Henry James's work, particularly his conception of Milly Theale in *The Wings of the Dove* (1902).

Bicknell, John W. "The *Marble Faun* Reconsidered." *The University of Kansas City Review* XX, No. 2 (Spring 1954): 193-99.
    Identifies Hawthorne's increasing pessimism as the reason why *The Marble Faun* is morally and artistically inferior to his earlier work.

Blow, Suzanne. "Pre-Raphaelite Allegory in *The Marble Faun.*" *American Literature* XLIV, No. 1 (March 1972): 122-27.
    Treats the connection between *The Marble Faun* and Pre-Raphaelite art.

Boswell, Jeanetta. *Nathaniel Hawthorne and the Critics: A Checklist of Criticism, 1900-1978.* The Scarecrow Author Bibliographies, no. 57. Metuchen, N.J.: Scarecrow Press, 1982, 273 p.
    A bibliography of Hawthorne criticism.

Brodtkorb, Paul, Jr. "Art Allegory in *The Marble Faun.*" *PMLA* LXXVII, No. 3 (June 1962): 254-67.
    A consideration of Hawthorne's use of art allegory in the novel.

Byers, John R., and Owen, James J. *A Concordance to the Five Novels of Nathaniel Hawthorne.* 2 vols. New York: Garland Publishing, 1979.

A concordance to Hawthorne's five novels.

Cameron, Kenneth Walter, ed. *Hawthorne among His Contemporaries: A Harvest of Estimates, Insights, and Anecdotes from the Victorian Literary World.* Hartford: Transcendental Books, 1968, 560 p.

A collection of nineteenth-century criticism, both formal and informal, of Hawthorne's works.

Carpenter, Frederic I. "Puritans Preferred Blondes: The Heroines of Melville and Hawthorne." *The New England Quarterly* IX (June 1936): 253-72.

Explores the dichotomy between dark-haired women of experience and blonde women who embody the ideal of purity in the fiction of Hawthorne and Herman Melville. Carpenter also suggests that Hawthorne's ultimate preference for Hilda in *The Marble Faun* constitutes his denial of the creative impulse.

Clarke, Graham. "To Transform and Transfigure: The Aesthetic Play of Hawthorne's *The Marble Faun.*" In *Nathaniel Hawthorne: New Critical Essays,* edited by A. Robert Lee, pp. 131-47. London: Vision Press, 1982.

A study of Hawthorne's concern with the artistic process in *The Marble Faun.*

Crowley, J. Donald, ed. *Hawthorne: The Critical Heritage.* The Critical Heritage Series, edited by B. C. Southam. London: Routledge & Kegan Paul, 1970, 532 p.

Excerpts nineteenth-century critical commentary on Hawthorne's works, including *The Marble Faun.*

Darnell, Donald G. " 'Doctrine by Ensample': The Emblem and *The Marble Faun.*" *Texas Studies in Literature and Language* XV, No. 2 (Summer 1973): 301-10.

Establishes parallels between the emblem tradition (defined by E. N. S. Thompson as "a combination of motto, picture, and short poem used collectively to expound some moral or ethical truth") and Hawthorne's descriptive technique in *The Marble Faun.*

Elder, Marjorie J. "Hawthorne's Aesthetic Practices: *The Scarlet Letter* and *The Marble Faun.*" In her *Nathaniel Hawthorne: Transcendental Symbolist,* pp. 121-70. Athens: Ohio University Press, 1969.

Concludes that in *The Marble Faun* "Hawthorne's artistry in all its phases evidences the Transcendental aesthetic."

——. "Hawthorne's *The Marble Faun:* A Gothic Structure." *Costerus* 1 (1972): 81-8.

Examines aspects of Gothicism in *The Marble Faun.*

Fogle, Richard Harter. "*The Marble Faun.*" In his *Hawthorne's Imagery: The "Proper Light and Shadow" in the Major Romances,* pp. 125-72. Norman: University of Oklahoma Press, 1969.

Analyzes images of light and darkness in *The Marble Faun.*

Gollin, Rita K. "Painting and Character in *The Marble Faun.*" *The Emerson Society Quarterly* 21, No. 1 (1975): 1-10.

Explores Hawthorne's attitude toward art through a study of his *French and Italian Notebooks* and through interpretation of Hilda's and Miriam's views of art in *The Marble Faun.*

Hall, Spencer. "Beatrice Cenci: Symbol and Vision in *The Marble Faun.*" *Nineteenth-Century Fiction* 25, No. 1 (June 1970): 85-95.

Illuminates the role and significance of Guido Reni's portrait of Beatrice Cenci in *The Marble Faun,* finding the picture symbolic of the bond that unites Miriam and Hilda.

Hawthorne, Julian. "*The Marble Faun.*" In his *Nathaniel Hawthorne and His Wife: A Biography,* Vol. II, pp. 236-61. Cambridge: Houghton, Mifflin and Co., Riverside Press, 1893.

A description, by Hawthorne's son, of contemporary response to *The Marble Faun.* The chapter includes excerpts from both reviews and personal letters.

Howard, David. "The Fortunate Fall and Hawthorne's *The Marble Faun.*" In *Romantic Mythologies,* edited by Ian Fletcher, pp. 97-136. London: Routledge & Kegan Paul, 1967.

Distinguishes the American perspective of Hilda and Kenyon from the European one of Miriam and Donatello in an extended analysis of the theme of the fortunate fall in *The Marble Faun.*

Huzzard, John A. "Hawthorne's *The Marble Faun.*" *Italica* XXXV, No. 2 (June 1958): 119-24.

Considers Hawthorne's depiction of Italy in *The Marble Faun,* finding that the setting has "a greater importance in the novel than either the plot or the theme."

Johnson, Claudia D. " 'There Was Something Dearer to Him than His Art': *The Marble Faun.*" In her *The Productive Tension of Hawthorne's Art,* pp. 103-23. University: University of Alabama Press, 1981.

Examines moral, artistic, and imaginative themes in *The Marble Faun.*

Jones, Marga Cottino. "*The Marble Faun* and a Writer's Crisis." *Studi Americani* 16 (1970): 81-123.

Attributes the artistic inferiority of *The Marble Faun* and Hawthorne's other works of the period to the author's uncharacteristic use of European settings. The result, according to Jones, is fragmentation and inconsistency in both substance and style.

Kesterson, David B. "Journey to Perugia: Dantean Parallels in *The Marble Faun.*" *The Emerson Society Quarterly* 19, No. 2 (1973): 94-104.

Details the Dantean influence on *The Marble Faun.*

——, ed. *Studies in "The Marble Faun."* Charles E. Merrill Studies, edited by Matthew J. Bruccoli and Joseph Katz. Columbus: Charles E. Merrill Publishing Co., 1971, 118 p.

A collection of previously published essays on *The Marble Faun,* from the earliest reviews to modern assessments.

"*The Marble Faun:* Completed." *The Knickerbocker* LVI, No. 1 (July 1860): 65-73.

A parody of *The Marble Faun* that ridicules the novel's obscurity.

Levy, Leo B. "*The Marble Faun:* Hawthorne's Landscape of the Fall." *American Literature* XLII, No. 2 (May 1970): 139-56.

Explicates the thematic significance of the Italian setting in *The Marble Faun,* emphasizing the dichotomy between Rome as aesthetic treasure and Rome as decaying ruin.

Lewis, R. W. B. "The Return into Time: Hawthorne." In his *The American Adam: Innocence, Tragedy and Tradition in the Nineteenth Century,* pp. 110-26. Chicago: University of Chicago Press, Phoenix Books, 1955.

Investigates the element of time and the role of the artist in *The Marble Faun.*

Liebman, Sheldon W. "The Design of *The Marble Faun.*" *The New England Quarterly* XL, No. 1 (March 1967): 61-78.

Contends that the ruling motif of *The Marble Faun* is that of the sarcophagus.

McCarthy, Harold T. "Hawthorne's Dialogue with Rome." In his *The Expatriate Perspective: American Novelists and the Idea of America,* pp. 62-78. Rutherford, N.J.: Fairleigh Dickinson University Press, 1974.

A largely biographical essay elucidating the significance of Rome to Hawthorne personally and thus to his composition of *The Marble Faun.*

McPherson, Hugo. "*The Marble Faun.*" In his *Hawthorne as Myth-*

Maker: A Study in Imagination, pp. 158-69. Toronto: University of Toronto Press, 1969.

Emphasizes the "initiation into human imperfection" of Kenyon and Hilda.

Meyers, Jeffrey. "Guido Reni and *The Marble Faun.*" In his *Painting and the Novel,* pp. 6-18. Manchester: Manchester University Press, 1975.

Regards incest as the "repressed theme" of *The Marble Faun* and discusses its relation to Guido Reni's painting of Beatrice Cenci.

Moss, Sidney P. "The Problem of Theme in *The Marble Faun.*" *Nineteenth-Century Fiction* 18, No. 4 (March 1964): 393-99.

Suggests that *The Marble Faun* offers no unambiguous answers to the novel's central question of Hawthorne's attitude toward the fortunate fall.

———. "The Symbolism of the Italian Background in *The Marble Faun.*" *Nineteenth-Century Fiction* 23, No. 3 (December 1968): 332-36.

Maintains that the Italian setting of the novel mirrors and amplifies the thematic progression of innocence-sin-redemption embodied in Donatello's experience.

Pattison, Joseph C. "The Guilt of the Innocent Donatello." *The Emerson Society Quarterly,* No. 31 (1963): 66-8.

Contends that Donatello must be held morally accountable for his crime.

[Peabody, Elizabeth Palmer]. "The Genius of Hawthorne." *The Atlantic Monthly* XXII, No. CXXXI (September 1868): 359-74.

An analysis, by Hawthorne's sister-in-law, of ethical and religious themes in *The Marble Faun.*

Pearce, Roy Harvey. "Hawthorne and the Twilight of Romance." *The Yale Review* XXXVII, No. 3 (March 1948): 487-506.

Contends that *The Marble Faun* fails on its own terms and as a representation of the nineteenth-century romance genre.

Ringe, Donald A. "Hawthorne's Psychology of the Head and Heart." *PMLA* LXV, No. 2 (March 1950): 120-32.

Argues that in his fiction Hawthorne proposed two alternatives for human life: a regeneration through the experiences of sin, isolation, and sacrifice, or an ordinary, happy existence untroubled by deeper knowledge. Ringe contends that Donatello and

Miriam exemplify the former choice, Hilda and Kenyon the latter.

Schneider, Daniel J. "The Allegory and Symbolism of Hawthorne's *The Marble Faun.*" *Studies in the Novel* 1, No. 1 (Spring 1969): 38-50.

Sees *The Marble Faun* as a symbolic rendering of the human need to strike a balance between the polarities of spirit vs. flesh, ideal vs. material, and essence vs. existence.

Scrimgeour, Gary J. "*The Marble Faun:* Hawthorne's Faery Land." *American Literature* XXXVI, No. 3 (November 1964): 271-87.

Posits that the Italian setting of *The Marble Faun* is integral to its moral themes.

Simpson, Claude M. Introduction to *The Marble Faun; or, The Romance of Monte Beni,* by Nathaniel Hawthorne, edited by William Charvat, Roy Harvey Pearce, Claude M. Simpson, and others, pp. xix-xliv. Columbus: Ohio State University Press, 1968.

Describes the composition, publication, and critical history of *The Marble Faun.*

Strout, Cushing. "Hawthorne's International Novel." *Nineteenth-Century Fiction* 24, No. 2 (September 1969): 169-81.

Highlights the importance of the tension between Europe and America as a theme in *The Marble Faun.*

Turner, Arlin. *Nathaniel Hawthorne: A Biography.* New York: Oxford University Press, 1980, 457 p.

An important biography.

Waples, Dorothy. "Suggestions for Interpreting *The Marble Faun.*" *American Literature* 13, No. 3 (November 1941): 224-39.

Links five psychological theories of Sigmund Freud to mental states described in *The Marble Faun:* "timelessness as a characteristic of the unconscious; the connection between myth or symbol and the unconscious; repetition-compulsion; the existence of a death instinct; the contest for the soul between life and death."

Zivkovic, Peter D. "The Evil of the Isolated Intellect: Hilda, in *The Marble Faun.*" *The Personalist* XLIII, No. 2 (April 1962): 202-13.

Examines Hilda's moral flaw of self-imposed isolation.

Charlotte Ramsay Lennox

1729 or 1730-1804

English novelist, critic, playwright, poet, and translator.

Lennox was a distinguished and versatile woman of letters who wrote in a wide range of genres, including drama, poetry, criticism, and, most importantly, the novel. Several of Lennox's novels gained recognition in her day, but it was her second, *The Female Quixote; or, The Adventures of Arabella,* that achieved the greatest critical and popular success and assured her literary reputation. Regarded as one of the finest of the numerous satirical imitations of Miguel de Cervantes's *Don Quixote* to appear during the mid-eighteenth century, *The Female Quixote* depicts the adventures of an eccentric heroine, Arabella, who lives in a private world constructed out of seventeenth-century French romances. Critics generally concur that the novel successfully combines Cervantes's conception of the burlesque with the moralizing pathos of Samuel Richardson and other writers of the sentimental novel. Apart from their interest in *The Female Quixote,* commentators cite Lennox's study *Shakespear Illustrated* as one of the first critiques of Shakespeare's dramas to analyze his use of a wide range of sources. Today, however, Lennox is still primarily known for *The Female Quixote.*

Lennox's early life is not well documented. Biographers nevertheless generally agree that she was born in 1729 or 1730, possibly in Gibraltar, where her father, James Ramsay, was a captain-lieutenant in an English regiment. The family appears to have moved to New York province in 1739 when Ramsay was appointed captain of an independent foot company in the British colonial army. In later years, Lennox claimed that her father had been the "Royalist Governor" of the province of New York, but biographers state that in actuality he was stationed at various frontier outposts, primarily at Albany, then an isolated village. Although Lennox's life in Albany proved to be a source of inspiration for the scenery and imagery in her novels *The Life of Harriot Stuart* and *Euphemia,* little is known about the time she spent there, and the nature of her youthful education remains a mystery. Scholars surmise from her works, however, that she must have been well-read, particularly in seventeenth-century French romances. Sometime between 1743 and 1746 James Ramsay died. Lennox then returned to England, and discovered that her relations were not in a position to provide for her; Lennox's subsequent pursuit of a literary career has been attributed in part to economic necessity.

Lennox's first work, a volume of poetry entitled *Poems on Several Occasions,* was published in 1747 to moderate acclaim. In the same year she married Alexander Lennox, a Scotchman with publishing connections. The two settled in London, where Lennox lived for the remainder of her life. Between 1747 and 1751, Lennox began to establish herself in the city's literary circles. Among the famous authors whose acquaintance she made at this time was Samuel Johnson, who befriended her and arranged an all-night celebration at the Ivy Lane Club upon the completion of her first novel, *The Life of Harriot Stuart,* which was published in December of 1750. Johnson's overall contribution to Lennox's career was to be crucial. As her chief literary mentor, he wrote dedica-

tions for her, suggested ideas for works, and assisted her with translations. The years 1751-54 marked the apogee of Lennox's early career. In 1751 she met Richardson, who advised her in the writing of *The Female Quixote.* Published in March 1752, the novel was an immediate critical and popular success. In 1753-54, Lennox's critical study *Shakespear Illustrated* appeared, but neither this work nor *The Female Quixote* brought her sufficient income. In the decade following the publication of these major works, therefore, Lennox continued to write prolifically under the pressure of economic necessity. Two new novels appeared: *Henrietta* in 1758 and *Sophia* in 1762. She also began to write dramas, produced several translations of works by popular French writers, and from 1761 to 1762 was the principal contributor and chief editor of a women's magazine entitled *The Lady's Museum.* The remaining decades of Lennox's life were comparatively unproductive. She continued publishing translations, and her final novel, *Euphemia,* appeared in 1790. Although she planned a number of new literary projects, none of these were realized, for in her last years family and monetary problems completely distracted her. Her husband had proved to be financially irresponsible, and by around 1792 they had separated. Lennox's poverty was extreme enough to permit the Royal Literary Fund to award her financial assistance, which she received until 1804, when she died penniless.

Although Lennox's literary accomplishments were diverse, she is best known for her novels, particularly *The Female Quixote,* and for *Shakespear Illustrated.* Lennox's novels, written in the sentimental tradition, display the influence of Richardson and invariably feature sentimental heroines who combine extreme sensibility with absolute goodness. Her plots closely follow the conventions of sentimental fiction in their portrayal of virtuous young women who undergo dramatic adventures with a series of suitors before finally finding happiness in marriage. Lennox's prose style is considered just as conventional, for she paid close attention to the reigning neoclassical rules of decorum and restraint formulated in the seventeenth century. Aside from *The Female Quixote, Henrietta* is often cited as Lennox's best novel, distinguished from her other less important works of fiction by its carefully delineated plot, stylistic purity, and detailed scenes of eighteenth-century society life. Commentators have also remarked upon the historical and biographical interest of *Harriot Stuart* and *Euphemia,* noting that Lennox's use of American subject matter and scenery was largely unprecedented.

The Female Quixote, critics agree, possesses a degree of originality and sophistication noticeably lacking in all of Lennox's other works. *The Female Quixote* is the story of Arabella, the only child of a marquis, who has been raised alone by her father in a castle remote from society. After discovering her father's extensive collection of historical romances, particularly those written by Gauthier de Costes de La Calprenède and Madeleine de Scudéry, Arabella accepts their chivalric ideals as the proper guide for her behavior in society. The novel essentially consists of a series of adventures, first in the countryside, and later in Bath and London, where Arabella is pursued by an elegant but artificial knight, Sir George Bellmour, and also by her aristocratic cousin, Sir Charles Glanville. Throughout, Arabella interprets the actions of her suitors as if they were living in the medieval France of La Calprenède and Mlle. de Scudéry, which results in the creation of many comic and farcical situations. However, Arabella is finally "cured" of her romantic delusions by a learned cleric, whereupon she recognizes her folly and marries Glanville. Although the plot structure of *The Female Quixote* derives from *Don Quixote,* which is similarly broken up into discrete comedic episodes, Lennox's novel provides a very different kind of comedic effect because it substitutes a woman for the traditional male quixotic hero. The often catastrophic results of Arabella's distorted perceptions have been seen by many commentators as evidence of a serious didactic intent: to persuade young women of the dangers of becoming too absorbed in the unreal world characteristic of popular romance. Critics point out that Lennox in this instance used a literary model not merely for convention's sake, but for the particular purpose of deflating the importance of these romances for women. In the process, she mocked Cervantes's chivalric idealism, simultaneously underscoring the problem of feminine isolation from everyday reality in a male-dominated society. Lennox produced only one other work that is acknowledged as having a similar degree of originality and critical interest, her study *Shakespear Illustrated.* Johnson had suggested to Lennox the basic idea: an original study of Shakespeare's sources and his use of them in his dramas. Lennox accomplished exactly that, doing all of the translations of the sources herself. However, she added her own largely negative critical commentary on the aesthetic merits of Shakespeare's dramas, basing her judgments on such classical principles as Aristotle's three unities and seventeenth-century notions of probability, decorum, and poetic justice.

The critical history of Lennox's works is almost entirely that of *The Female Quixote,* although *Shakespear Illustrated* has always been recognized as an innovative work. In the eighteenth century, *The Female Quixote* was judged for its conformity to current literary convention: its genteel and dignified language, noble and virtuous heroine, and, most importantly, reliance upon Cervantes's *Don Quixote* for its satirical theme were assiduously noted and appreciated by reviewers. The novel remained popular through the latter half of the eighteenth century, but with the shift in the early nineteenth-century English novel towards a more sophisticated treatment of social and moral themes, many critics came to regard *The Female Quixote* as outmoded and discussed it primarily as a skillfully written period piece. In the early twentieth century, the novel continued to be discussed by historians of the English novel, usually in much the same terms. In the late twentieth century, however, critics have discovered a number of formal oppositions operating in the novel that give it richness and complexity. Feminist critics, for instance, have examined several issues arising from Arabella's attempt to impose her distorted perceptions on external reality, including the tension between realism and romantic convention in the narrative and the presence in the novel of conflicting levels of discourse that reflect the struggle of women to be recognized in a male-controlled society. Other critics have addressed the opposition of literary forms in *The Female Quixote,* those, for example, between the novel and the romance, or the burlesque and the ironic comedy. Still other commentators have taken a psychological approach, exploring the conflict in Arabella between having to conform to normal social behavior and wishing to express her true, inner feelings. *Shakespear Illustrated* has not evoked a similarly complex critical response over the years. In her own day, reviewers in popular magazines lauded Lennox's careful and innovative study of sources, but they generally dismissed her criticism as pseudoclassical and overly academic. This appraisal of Lennox's work has been attributed to the fact that *Shakespear Illustrated* appeared at the beginning of a new phase in Shakespeare commentary led by such critics as Johnson and Joseph Wharton, who explored the inner logic of Shakespeare's art rather than basing their judgments—like Lennox—on a declining aesthetic theory. In the nineteenth century, the originality of Lennox's study of Shakespeare's sources was remarked upon by critics, yet for the most part they considered her approach anachronistic, or simply misguided. Today, *Shakespear Illustrated* is largely unknown and little discussed, despite the fact that scholars acknowledge it as a ground-breaking work. The considerable body of criticism that has recently appeared on *The Female Quixote,* however, suggests that interest in Lennox's central work will continue in the future, maintaining her status as a minor but distinctive figure in eighteenth-century English literature.

PRINCIPAL WORKS

Poems on Several Occasions (poetry) 1747
The Life of Harriot Stuart (novel) 1750
The Female Quixote; or, The Adventures of Arabella (novel) 1752
Shakespear Illustrated; or, The Novels and Histories on Which

the *Plays of Shakespear Are Founded, Collected, and Translated*. 3 vols. (criticism) 1753-54
Philander: A Dramatic Pastoral [first publication] (verse drama) 1757
Henrietta (novel) 1758
Sophia (novel) 1762
**The Sister* (drama) 1769
***Old City Manners* (drama) 1775
Euphemia (novel) 1790

*This drama is an adaptation of Lennox's novel *Henrietta*.

**This drama is a reworking of the comedy *Eastward Hoe!* by George Chapman, Ben Johnson, and John Marston.

MONTHLY REVIEW, LONDON (essay date 1750)

[*In this excerpt from a review of* The Life of Harriot Stuart, *the critic admires the naturalness of the novel's style, but disparages its lack of originality.*]

We are persuaded that [*The Life of Harriot Stuart*] is really the produce of a female pen; and therefore some may think it intitled to our more favourable regard. However, without a compliment to the author, we may safely venture to pronounce her work to be the best in the novel way that has been lately published. Her language is pretty good, and the manners of her persons, together with the incidents of her story, are most of them within the bounds of nature, and agreeable to what we daily see in common life. But at the same time it must be owned that this work affords nothing great, or noble, or useful, or very entertaining. Here are no striking characters, no interesting events, nor in short any thing that will strongly fix the attention, or greatly improve the morals of the reader.

> *A review of "The Life of Harriot Stuart," in* Monthly Review, *London, Vol. IV, December, 1750, p. 160.*

SAMUEL RICHARDSON (letter date 1751)

[*Considered the originator of the modern English novel, Richardson is credited with introducing to his eighteenth-century audience the first tragic novel,* Clarissa; or, The History of a Young Lady (1747-48) *and the first novel of manners,* The History of Sir Charles Grandison (1753-54). *Richardson's novelistic intent was avowedly didactic; his best-known work,* Pamela; or, Virtue Rewarded (1741), *recounts the adventures of a virtuous young woman who, after repeatedly and successfully resisting the sexual advances of her employer, is rewarded by his offer of marriage. Richardson met Lennox in 1750, shortly after the appearance of her first work of fiction,* The Life of Harriot Stuart. *He encouraged her to continue writing, became her friend, and furthered her career by acting as critic and business advisor. In the following excerpt from a letter to Lennox, Richardson comments favorably on a late manuscript of the first volume of* The Female Quixote *while suggesting she revise the genealogy of the character Sir George.*]

I am quite charm'd with the lovely Visionary's [Lady Arabella, in *The Female Quixote*] Absurdit[ies]y (and the Perplexi-

ty which follows it, to Sir Charles to Glanville and her self) on her supposing Sir Charles in Love with her.

But I think, that Sir Georges's [*sic*] Story, and his Pretensions to the Kingdom of Kent, is carried too far. He ought not at least to have made his Claim so recent—He might have made a Discovery of his Genealogy from the Saxons and the Heptarchy, without so immediately interesting his Father and Grandfather in it. It is impossible, but she must know, that there had not been a Kingdom of Kent for many Generations. And it was too gross for Mr. Glanville to bear, who had been sollicitous that Sir George should not play upon Arabella. . . .

The story of the Highway-Men, and Arabella's Absurdity on their Appearance, very pretty—

You have very pretty Scenes before you, Madam, at Bath and London. (p. 338)

> *Samuel Richardson, in a letter to Charlotte Lennox in November, 1751, in* Harvard Library Bulletin, *Vol. XVIII, No. 4, October, 1970, pp. 337-38.*

LADY MARY WORTLEY MONTAGU (letter date 1752)

[*Montagu is celebrated as a consummate writer of intelligent, witty, candid—and frequently scandalous—letters. A cosmopolitan woman who spent much of her life in Italy and one of the first Europeans to study Turkish culture, Montagu moved with ease in prominent social and literary circles, counting among her many friends and admirers Alexander Pope. Spanning the years 1708 to 1762, Montagu's correspondence is addressed to a wide variety of recipients and is considered remarkable for its versatility and range. In the following excerpt from a letter to her daughter Mary, the Countess of Bute, Montagu attacks the protagonist of* The Life of Harriot Stuart *for her absurdity and artificiality. Furthermore, she objects to the character Lady Cecilia Isabella as an unflattering portrayal of her friend Lady Belle Finch.*]

I could relate many speeches of his [Sir John Rawdon] of equal beauty, but I believe you are already tired of hearing of him, as much as I was with the memoirs of Miss H. Stuart [*The Life of Harriot Stuart*]; who, being intended for an example of wit and virtue, is a jilt and a fool in every page. But while I was indolently perusing the marvellous figures she exhibits, no more resembling anything in human nature than the wooden cut in the Seven Champions, I was roused into great surprise and indignation by the monstrous abuse of one of the very few women I have a real value for; I mean Lady B. F. [Belle Finch]; who is not only clearly meant by the mention of her library (she being the only lady at court that has one), but her very name at length, she being christened Cecilia Isabella, though she chooses to be called by the latter. I always thought her conduct, in every light, so irreproachable, I did not think she had an enemy upon earth; I now see 'tis impossible to avoid them, especially in her situation. It is one of the misfortunes of a supposed court interest (perhaps you may know it by experience), even the people you have obliged hate you, if they do not think you have served to the utmost extent of a power that they fancy you are possessed of; which it may be is only imaginary. (p. 221)

> *Lady Mary Wortley Montagu, in a letter to the Countess of Bute on March 1, 1752, in* The Letters and Works of Lady Mary Wortley Montagu, Vol.

II, *revised edition, edited by Lord Wharncliffe, Swan Sonnenschein & Co., 1893, pp. 220-23.*

SIR ALEXANDER DRAWCANSIR [PSEUDONYM OF HENRY FIELDING] (essay date 1752)

[*Fielding is often considered the most important contributor to the development of the English novel in the eighteenth century. With his* The History of the Adventures of Joseph Andrews *(1742) and* The History of Tom Jones, Foundling *(1749), the genre matured as an art form. Eschewing the didacticism and exoticism of his contemporaries' work, Fielding depicted the natural world and designed his fiction to "laugh mankind out of their favourite follies and vices." His novels, noted for their complexity, humor, compassion, and moral lessons, present a vivid, entertaining view of eighteenth-century English life. Fielding was acquainted with Lennox early in her literary career. In the following excerpt, he compares* The Female Quixote *with its prototype, Miguel de Cervantes's* Don Quixote *(1605-15), praising Lennox's novel for its greater sense of realism and its instructional value for young women. Fielding's remarks were first published 24 March 1752 in* The Covent-Garden Journal.*]

I have perused a Book called, **The Female Quixote, or The Adventures of Arabella;** and I shall give my Opinion of it with no less Sincerity than Candour.

This is an Imitation of the famous Romance of Cervantes called *The Life and Actions of that ingenious Gentleman Don Quixote of the Mancha,* &c. A Work originally written in Spanish, and which hath been translated into most of the Languages, and admired in most of the Countries in Europe.

I will here very frankly declare my Opinion in what Particulars the Imitation falls short; in what it equals, and in what it excels its illustrious Original.

In the first Place, Cervantes hath the Advantage of being the Original; and consequently is intitled to that Honour of Invention, which can never be attributed to any Copy however excellent. An Advantage which Homer will always claim, and which is perhaps the only one that he can claim, over Virgil and Milton.

In the next Place Cervantes is to be considered as an Author who intended not only the Diversion, but the Instruction and Reformation of his Countrymen: With this Intention he levelled his Ridicule at a vicious Folly, which in his Time universally prevailed in Spain, and had almost converted a civilized People in a Nation of Cut-throats.

In this Design he imitated the three glorious Poets I have mentioned. The first of whom placed the particular Good of Greece, the second the Honour of Rome, and the third the great Cause of Christianity before their Eyes, when they planned their several Poems. And the Success of none of them was perhaps equal to that of Cervantes.

Here again the Spanish Romance hath the Advantage of the English.

Thirdly, the Character of Don Quixote himself, as well as that of Sancho Pancha, are superior to those of Arabella and her Maid.

Fourthly, some of the Incidents in the Original are more exquisitely ridiculous than any which we find in the Copy. And those I think, are all the Particulars in which an impartial Critic can give the Preference to the Spaniard. And as to the two last, I cannot help observing, they may possibly be rather owing to that Advantage, which the Actions of Men give to the Writer beyond those of Women, than to any Superiority of Genius. Don Quixote is ridiculous in performing Feats of Absurdity himself; Arabella can only become so, in provoking and admiring the Absurdities of others. In the former Case, the Ridicule hath all the Force of a Representation; it is in a Manner subjected to the Eyes; in the latter it is conveyed, as it were, through our Ears, and partakes of the Coldness of History or Narration.

I come now to speak of those Parts in which the two Authors appear to me upon an Equality. So they seem to be in that Care which both have taken to preserve the Affection of their Readers for their principal Characters, in the midst of all the Follies of which they are guilty. Both Characters are accordingly represented as Persons of good Sense, and of great natural Parts, and in all Cases, except one, of a very sound Judgement, and what is much more endearing, as Persons of great Innocence, Integrity and Honour, and of the highest Benevolence. Again the Fidelity and Simplicity of Sancho Pancha, are well matched by these Qualities in Arabella's Handmaid. Tho' as I have before observed, I do not think the Character of Sancho is here equalled. It is perhaps a Masterpiece in Humour of which we never have, nor ever shall see the like.

There are probably more Instances under this Head, which I shall leave to the discerning Reader. I will proceed in the last Place to those Particulars, in which, I think, our Countrywoman hath excelled the Spanish Writer.

And this I am not afraid to declare, she hath done in my Opinion, in all the following Particulars.

First, as we are to grant in both Performances, that the Head of a very sensible Person is entirely subverted by reading Romances, this Concession seems to me more easy to be granted in the Case of a young Lady than of an old Gentleman. Nor can I help observing with what perfect Judgment and Art this Subversion of Brain in Arabella is accounted for by her peculiar Circumstances, and Education. To say Truth, I make no Doubt but that most young Women of the same Vivacity, and of the same innocent good Disposition, in the same Situation, and with the same Studies, would be able to make a large Progress in the same Follies.

Secondly, the Character of Arabella is more endearing than that of Quixote. This will undoubtedly be the Case between a beautiful young Lady and an old Fellow, where equal Virtues in both become Candidates for our Favour.

Thirdly, the Situation of Arabella is more interesting. Our Hearts are engaged very early in good Wishes for the Success of Mr. Glanville; a Character entirely well drawn, as are indeed many others; for in this Particular, the English Author hath doubtless the Preference.

Fourthly, here is a regular Story, which, tho' possibly it is not pursued with that Epic Regularity which would give it the Name of an Action, comes much nearer to that Perfection than the loose unconnected Adventures in Don Quixote; of which you may transverse the Order as you please, without any Injury to the whole.

Fifthly, the Incidents, or, if you please, the Adventures, are much less extravagant and incredible in the English than in the Spanish Performance. The latter, in many Instances, approaches very near to the Romances which he ridicules. Such are the Stories of Cardenio and Dorothea, Ferdinand and Lucinda, &c. In the former, their is nothing except the Absurdities of the Heroine herself, which is carried beyond Common-Life; nor is there any Thing even in her Character, which the Brain a little distempered may not account for. She conceives indeed somewhat preposterously of the Ranks and Conditions of Men; that is to say, mistakes one Man for another; but never advances towards the Absurdity of imagining Windmills and Wine-Bags to be human Creatures, or Flocks of Sheep to be Armies.

I might add more on this Subject, but I will pursue it no further; having already, I apprehend, given a larger Dose to Malice, Envy, and Ignorance, than they will care to swallow; but I cannot omit observing, that tho' the Humour of Romance, which is principally ridiculed in this Work, be not at present greatly in fashion in this Kingdom, our Author hath taken such Care throughout her Work, to expose all those Vices and Follies in her Sex which are chiefly predominant in our Days, that it will afford very useful Lessons to all those young Ladies who will peruse it with proper Attention.

Upon the whole, I do very earnestly recommend it, as a most extraordinary and most excellent Performance. It is indeed a Work of true Humour, and cannot fail of giving a rational, as well as very pleasing, Amusement to a sensible Reader, who will at once be instructed and very highly diverted. Some Faults perhaps there may be, but I shall leave the unpleasing Task of pointing them out to those who will have more Pleasure in the Office. This Caution, however, I think proper to premise, that no Persons presume to find many: For if they do, I promise them, the Critic and not the Author *will be to blame.* (pp. 279-82)

> *Sir Alexander Drawcansir [pseudonym of Henry Fielding], "Review of 'The Female Quixote'," in* The Covent-Garden Journal, Vol. I, *edited by Gerard Edward Jensen, Yale University Press, 1915, pp. 279-82.*

[SAMUEL JOHNSON]   (essay date 1752)

[*A remarkably versatile and distinguished man of letters, Johnson was the major literary figure of the second half of the eighteenth century; his monumental* A Dictionary of the English Language *(1755) standardized for the first time English spelling and pronunciation, while his moralistic criticism strongly influenced contemporary tastes. In the following excerpt, Johnson praises the comedic aspects of* The Female Quixote, *concluding his remarks by referring to Henry Fielding's review of the novel (see excerpt dated 1752).*]

The solemn manner in which [Arabella, in *The Female Quixote*] treats the most common and trivial occurrences, the romantic expectations she forms, and the absurdities which she commits herself, and produces in others, afford a most entertaining series of circumstances and events. Mr. Fielding, however emulous of Cervantes, and jealous of a rival, acknowledges in his paper of the 24th, that in many instances this copy excels the original; and though he has no connection with the author, he concludes his encomium on the work, by earnestly recommending it as a most extraordinary, and most excellent performance.

> [*Samuel Johnson*], *in a review of "The Female Quixote; or, The Adventures of Arabella," in* The Gen-

tleman's Magazine and Historical Chronicle, *Vol. XXII, March, 1752, p. 146.*

DAVID GARRICK   (letter date 1753)

[*An English actor, dramatist, and theater manager, Garrick was one of the most important theatrical innovators of the eighteenth century. His immense popularity as an actor was largely due to his naturalness, which sharply contrasted with the declamatory style customary in his day. His contribution as a dramatist consists primarily of such farces as* The Lying Valet *(1741) and* Miss in Her Teens *(1747). Once a pupil of Samuel Johnson, Garrick was acquainted with most of the leading political and literary figures of his era and met Lennox through Johnson's circle. His contribution to Lennox's career as a dramatist was notable, for in 1775 he successfully produced her comedy* Old City Manners. *In the following excerpt from a letter to Lennox, Garrick disparages her negative appraisal of Shakespeare in* Shakespear Illustrated.]

In the Whole [of *Shakespear Illustrated*] I imagin'd that you had betray'd a greater desire of Exposing his Errors than of *illustrating* his Beauties—there appeared to me (and indeed to many others) a kind of severe Levity & Ridicule, which might with Justice have been exercis'd upon Tom Durfey, but (I think) is somewhat unjustifiable, when us'd against so great and so Excellent an Author. . . . (p. 41)

> *David Garrick, in a letter to Charlotte Lennox on August 12, 1753, in* Harvard Library Bulletin, *Vol. XIX, No. 1, January, 1971, pp. 40-1.*

THE CRITICAL REVIEW, LONDON   (essay date 1758)

[*In this excerpt from a review of* Henrietta, *the critic discusses the plot, style, and characterization of the novel, as well as its sensitive treatment of religious subjects.*]

Mrs. Lennox has forfeited no part of her reputation by this publication [*Henrietta*]; which we warmly recommend as one of the best and most pleasing novels that has appeared for some years. The story is simple, uniform and interesting; the stile equal, easy, and well kept up, sinking no where below the level of genteel life, a compliment which cannot be paid to one of the most celebrated novel-writers we have. The characters are natural and properly supported.—Tho' the reputation of Henrietta is chiefly founded on her steady adherence to the principles to the protestant religion; that preference is given with a delicacy, that, not the most bigotted Roman-catholic could be offended at; the heroine no where betrays the rudeness of party, or the malevolence of religious attachment. The whole is interspersed with some short and spirited reflections aptly introduced, and here and there are some light sketches of humour very entertaining. (p. 130)

> *A review of "Henrietta," in* The Critical Review, *London, Vol. 5, February, 1758, pp. 122-30.*

THE CRITICAL REVIEW, LONDON   (essay date 1762)

[*In this review of* Sophia, *the critic emphasizes that the novel is a valuable moral lesson for women.*]

In this little history [*Sophia*] is exemplified the triumph of wit and virtue over beauty, with that delicacy peculiar to all the novels of the ingenious Mrs. Lennox. The lesson is instructive, the story interesting, the language chaste, the reflections natural, and the general moral such as we must recommend to the attention of all our female readers. It is commonly asserted, that women are sooner corrupted by the vicious of their own sex, than of ours; we have before us an instance, which evinces they are more agreeably instructed. A woman only can enter justly into all the scruples and refinements of female manners. (pp. 434-35)

> *A review of "Sophia," in* The Critical Review, *London, Vol. 13, May, 1762, pp. 434-35.*

CLARA REEVE   (essay date 1785)

[*Reeve was an eighteenth-century English novelist and critic who is now best known for her Gothic romance* The Old English Baron *(1778). Immensely popular during the eighteenth century,* The Old English Baron *remains important for its role in the development of the Gothic genre. Reeve pursued her interest in the romance genre in her* The Progress of Romance, *a history of the romance and novel constructed around a series of dialogues between three fictional Greek characters named Hortensius, Sophronia, and Euphrasia. In the following excerpt from* The Progress of Romance, *Euphrasia remarks that* The Female Quixote *effectively satirizes seventeenth-century French romances, while Sophronia points out that the taste for those romances had already disappeared by the time Lennox published her work.*]

Euphrasia. **The Female Quixote** was published in the year 1752.—In this ingenious work the passion for the French Romances of the last Century, and the effect of them upon the manners is finely exposed and ridiculed.—The Author of it is since well known as one of the distinguished female writers this age has produced among us—Mrs. *Lennox.*

Sophronia. That circumstance is so well known, that I shall not be thought to detract from her merit, if I venture to remark, that the Satire of the **Female Quixote** seems in great measure to have lost its aim, because at the time it first appeared, the taste for those Romances was extinct, and the books exploded.

Euphrasia. Your remark is just,—this book came thirty or forty years too late.—But Mrs. *Lennox*'s character is established upon works of a superior kind, which are above our retrospect, though we can only speak here of her Novels.

—She wrote two others, one called **Henrietta,** and the other **Sophia**—both of indisputable merit. (pp. 6-7)

> *Clara Reeve, "Evening IX," in her* The Progress of Romance, Vol. I, *1785. Reprint by The Facsimile Text Society, 1930, pp. 6-7.*

THE CRITICAL REVIEW, LONDON   (essay date 1790)

[*In this excerpt from a review of* Euphemia, *the critic notes the novel's effective descriptive passages and skilled characterization.*]

If we enlarge in our account of this pleasing work [***Euphemia***], it is chiefly because we think it uncommon in its construction, and interesting from some of its descriptions; accounts of a country which, though long in our possession, has scarcely ever been described in a picturesque narrative. Euphemia does not appear, at first, the most striking personage of the history. We begin where novels usually end, by her marriage; a marriage dictated by duty and convenience rather than affection. The character of Mr. Neville, her husband, is

drawn only in the little incidents of Euphemia's correspondence; and it seems to be copied from nature, where similar inconsistencies are sometimes found. Haughty, positive, feeling a rational well grounded affection, which his lordly pride will not always permit him to acknowledge, eager to be distinguished as well as to command, his failings are the source of Euphemia's distress, and afford her not only an opportunity of establishing her own character, but of giving a striking example to wives in similar situations: yet the conclusion does not leave the mind wholly at rest: the trials of our heroine are not at an end; and, though in possession of many sources of happiness, the whole may be tainted by the inconsiderate, hasty conduct of such a husband. But Mrs. Neville's story affords no instance of sudden attachments, of improper connections, or romantic adventure. If historic truth (for we see many reasons to lead us to think this story a copy from real life), had not prevented, we could have wished Mr. Neville had been sent to sleep with his fathers, and a more suitable companion provided for the gentle, the benevolent, the affectionate Euphemia. The loss of her son, her again recovering him, and the incidents which happened during the separation, are told with great feeling, and are highly interesting. The description of the Bellenden family, of Mr. C. and of lieutenant Blood, are well drawn sketches, seemingly from real life; and the history of Mrs. Freeman, in many respects, truly interesting and pathetic. . . . The account too of the family being confined in a distant house by a sudden fall of snow, in consequence of the premature commencement of winter, and in danger of famishing, with the circumstance of their relief, is not less attractive. . . . (p. 81)

The history of Euphemia's friend, miss Harley, approaches more nearly to the general style of novels, but it exceeds the greater number, though it does not reach the first of the first rank. The characters, however, though drawn without any splendid traits, are sufficiently distinct, and very ably supported: indeed, in every part of these volumes, we see characters delineated with so much apparent fidelity, and preserved with such strict consistency, that we almost forget we are reading a novel. This last work of Mrs. Charlotte Lennox, if it should prove her last, will not sully her fame. If she does not shine with meridian splendor, she sets with a mild radiance, more pleasing and more attractive. (p. 83)

> *A review of "Euphemia," in* The Critical Review, *London, Vol. LXX, July, 1790, pp. 81-3.*

THE EUROPEAN MAGAZINE, AND LONDON REVIEW (essay date 1790)

[*In this review of* Euphemia, *the critic notes Lennox's successful use of the epistolary form, the naturalness of her characterization, and her skill at descriptive prose.*]

The epistolary form of writing, when applied to the subject of Fictitious History, renders, in general, the narrative extremely languid, by delaying that quick succession of events in which the charm of romance is made at present principally to consist. In the work now before us [***Euphemia***], however, this defect is judiciously avoided by confining the correspondence between two persons only, each of whom are made to disclose a different story in such a manner as to form a kind of double plot, intricated with great art, and unravelled with an ingenuity that produces a very pleasing effect. The scenes are very correct representations of *real life;* and to those who feel domestic comfort, an important ingredient in the cup of human bliss, the incidents will be peculiarly interesting. Mr. Neville, the husband of Euphemia, is a character, the resemblance of which we have frequently seen in *the World,* but never before to our recollection in *a Novel,* and furnishes a useful lesson to the numerous progeny of novel-writers, that a discriminating attention to the variety of the species is the true school of Genius and Originality. The character of Euphemia is a model of female excellence: not that she is arrayed in that abundant perfection which distinguishes and adorns the heroines of modern romance; but, possessing a moderate portion of reason and good sense, she exercises them in the discharge of her duty, to the disappointment of adversity, the enjoyment of virtue, and the attainment of happiness. Among the traits which distinguish the character of old Harley, we now and then perceive a glimmering resemblance of Mr. Western in *Tom Jones;* particularly in the unconquerable partiality he feels for his lovely niece; and his sudden transitions from the transports of rage and resentment to the feelings of tenderness and reconciliation.—The picturesque beauties of the province of New York, the manners and customs of its inhabitants, together with the vagrant life of the savages, are described, in the course of this correspondence, with great beauty and effect. As to the general merits of the work, we may truly say, that if it be, as it most certainly is, the duty of a Novelist "to convey instruction, to paint human life and manners, to expose the errors into which we are betrayed by our passions, to render virtue amiable, and vice odious," Mrs. Lennox has performed the important task with no inconsiderable degree of success; and although it may perhaps appear less brilliant than the former productions of her sensible and entertaining pen, to us the mild radiance of a setting sun is more agreeable than the intense heat of its meridian beams. (pp. 121-22)

A review of "Euphemia: A Novel," in The European Magazine, and London Review, *Vol. 18, August, 1790, pp. 121-22.*

JANE AUSTEN   (letter date 1807)

[*Jane Austen is considered one of the finest prose stylists of nineteenth-century English literature. Her novels depict the life of the landed gentry in the English countryside from a social and moral perspective, and* Pride and Prejudice *(1813),* Mansfield Park *(1814), and* Emma *(1816) are considered classics of the genre. Austen apparently held Lennox's work in high esteem and evidently modeled her Gothic satire* Northanger Abbey *(1818) in part on* The Female Quixote. *In the following excerpt from a letter to her sister Cassandra, Austen indicates her preference for* The Female Quixote *over a translation of Madame de Genlis's romance* Alphonsine.]

Alphonsine did not do. We were disgusted in twenty pages, as, independent of a bad translation, it has indelicacies which disgrace a pen hitherto so pure; and we changed it for the *Female Quixote,* which now makes our evening amusement; to me a very high one, as I find the work quite equal to what I remembered it. (p. 173)

Jane Austen, in a letter to Cassandra Austen on January 7, 1807, in Jane Austen's Letters to Her Sister Cassandra and Others: 1796-1809, *Vol. I, edited by R. W. Chapman, Oxford at the Clarendon Press, 1932, pp. 170-75.*

AUSTIN DOBSON   (essay date 1892)

[*In the following excerpt, Dobson criticizes* The Female Quixote *for the repetitiveness of Arabella's romantic conceits, its lack of eighteenth-century social context, and its unnatural characterization.*]

Mrs. Lennox's fundamental idea [in *The Female Quixote; or, the Adventures of Arabella*], no doubt, is a good one, although the character of the heroine has its feminine prototypes in the *Précieuses Ridicules* of Molière and the Biddy Tipkin of Steele's *Tender Husband.* It may be conceded, too, that some of the manifold complications which arise from her bringing every incident of her career to the touchstone of the high-falutin' romances of the Sieur de la Calprenède, and that 'grave and virtuous virgin,' Madeleine de Scudéry, are diverting enough. The lamentable predicament of the lover, Mr. Glanville, who is convicted of imperfect application to the pages of *Cassandra,* by his hopeless ignorance of the elementary fact that the Orontes and Oroondates of that performance are one and the same person; the case of the luckless dipper into Thucydides and Herodotus at Bath who is confronted, to his utter discomfiture, with 'History as She is wrote' in *Clelia* and *Cleopatra;* the persistence of Arabella in finding princes in gardeners, and rescuers in highwaymen—are things not ill-invented. But repeated they pall; and not all the insistence upon her natural good sense and her personal charms, nor (as compared with such concurrent efforts as Mrs. Haywood's *Betsy Thoughtless*) the inoffensive tone of the book itself, can reconcile us to a heroine who is unable to pass the sugar-tongs without a reference to Parisatis, Princess of Persia, or Cleobuline, Princess of Corinth;—who holds with the illustrious Mandana that, even after ten years of the most faithful services and concealed torments, it is still presumptuous for a monarch to aspire to her hand;—and who, upon the slightest provocation, plunges into tirades of this sort: 'Had you persevered in your Affection, and continued your Pursuit of that Fair-one, you would, perhaps, ere this, have found her sleeping under the Shade of a Tree in some lone Forest, as *Philodaspes* did his admirable *Delia,* or disguised in a Slave's Habit, as *Ariobarsanes* saw his Divine *Olympia;* or bound haply in a Chariot, and have had the Glory of freeing her, as *Ambriomer* did the beauteous *Agione;* or in a Ship in the Hands of Pirates, like the incomparable *Eliza;* or'—at which point she is fortunately interrupted. In another place she fancies her uncle is in love with her, and thereupon, 'wiping some Tears from her fine Eyes,' apostrophises that elderly and astounded relative in this wise—'Go then, unfortunate and lamented Uncle; go, and endeavour by Reason and Absence to recover thy Repose; and be assured, whenever you can convince me you have triumphed over these Sentiments which now cause both our Unhappiness, you shall have no Cause to complain of my Conduct towards you.' There is an air of unreality about all this which, one would think, should have impeded its popularity in its own day. In the Spain of Don Quixote it is conceivable; it is intolerable in the England of Arabella. But there are other reasons which help to account for the oblivion into which the book has fallen. One is, that by neglecting to preserve the atmosphere of the age in which it was written, it has missed an element of vitality which is retained even by such fugitive efforts as Coventry's *Pompey the Little.* Indeed, beyond . . . references to Johnson and Richardson, and an obscure allusion to the beautiful Miss Gunnings who, at this date, divided the Talk of the Town with the Earthquake, there is scarcely any light thrown upon contemporary life and manners throughout the whole of Arabella's history. Another, and a graver objection (as one of her critics, whose own admirable 'Amelia' had been but recently published, should have known better than any one) is that, in spite of the humour of some of the situations, the characters of the book are colourless and mechanical. Fielding's Captain Booth and his wife, Mrs. Bennet and Serjeant Atkinson, Dr. Harrison and Colonel Bath, are breathing and moving human beings: the Glanvilles and Sir Charleses and Sir Georges of Mrs. Charlotte Lennox are little more than shrill-voiced and wire-jointed 'High-Life' puppets. (pp. 64-7)

> *Austin Dobson, " 'The Female Quixote',," in his* Eighteenth Century Vignettes, first series, *Dodd, Mead and Company, 1892, pp. 55-67.*

THOMAS R. LOUNSBURY   (essay date 1901)

[*Lounsbury discusses* Shakespear Illustrated, *noting the originality of Lennox's research and the general competence displayed in the work. However, he suggests that Lennox's critical stance belongs more to the late seventeenth century than to the eighteenth.*]

It was during the years 1753 and 1754 that Mrs. Lennox brought out a work of a new kind entitled *Shakespeare Illustrated, or the Novels and Histories, on which the Plays of Shakespeare are Founded, collected and translated from the Original Authors with Critical Remarks*. . . . The collection she made of sources was the first of a number of similar ones, which owe their existence purely to the interest inspired by the writings of the dramatist. It therefore serves the double purpose of exemplifying the growth of the poet's reputation and the way in which it was occasionally assailed. The information it furnished, though far from complete and long since superseded, was in general sufficiently satisfactory so far as it went. It was the critical observations with which the work was supplied, that have given it whatever interest or distinction it now possesses. Rymer had led the way for them by asserting that *Othello* had been altered from the original of Cinthio in several particulars, but always for the worse. In this style of criticism Mrs. Lennox left her predecessor far behind. She made it clear that in his adaptations from previous writers Shakespeare almost invariably fell below them. Whatever he touched he deformed. Anything that was particularly good in what he borrowed he contrived to make bad; everything that was bad he changed to worse. He added to the events in the stories, upon which he founded his plays, useless incidents, unnecessary characters, and absurd and improbable intrigues. Even when we admire the beauty of any new passage he introduced, we are usually struck by its inappropriateness. Occasionally she relented; the tenderness of the woman prevailed over the severity of the judge. In a few instances guarded praise was given the dramatist for improvement in certain details. Still, as a general rule, the epithets most frequently employed to describe the variations made by him from his originals were the adjectives "absurd" and "ridiculous." (pp. 289-91)

[Outside] of periodical criticism, the attitude taken and the views expressed in [*Shakespeare Illustrated*] met with but scant favor. It reacted, indeed, injuriously at a later period upon Mrs. Lennox's own literary undertakings. The ill-success of her play of *The Sister,* which was brought out at Covent Garden in February, 1770, but withdrawn after the first night, was attributed by some to the indignation and re-

sentment which her remarks upon Shakespeare had aroused. Whether this be true or not, the publication of her work furnishes another exemplification of a melancholy fact which, the longer we live, forces itself more persistently upon our observation. There is nothing more to be deplored in the fortunes of individuals than the hard lot that befalls some in having been born at the wrong time or in the wrong country. . . . Such was the unhappy fate of Mrs. Lennox in regard to Shakespeare. She missed her century. Had she flourished in the period immediately following the Restoration, she would have found herself in a far more congenial atmosphere. She would have been enrolled as a distinguished figure in a set which would have sympathized with her opinions and exalted her uncommon learning and critical acumen. Had she in addition become Mrs. Rymer, the conjunction of these two stars, shooting madly from their spheres in the Shakespearean firmament, would have attracted the attention of observers for all time. (pp. 291-92)

> *Thomas R. Lounsbury, "Late Seventeenth-Century Controversies about Shakespeare," in his* Shakespeare as a Dramatic Artist: With an Account of His Reputation at Various Periods, *Charles Scribner's Sons, 1901, pp. 257-92.*

MIRIAM ROSSITER SMALL   (essay date 1935)

[*Small's* Charlotte Ramsay Lennox *is the only full-length study of the author's life and writings. In the following excerpt from this work, Small discusses the salient elements of narration, theme, and characterization in* The Life of Harriot Stuart, Henrietta, Sophia, *and* Euphemia.]

[*The Life of Harriot Stuart*] shows a distinct narrative power; it moves along rapidly and coherently, and most of the incidents are clearly presented though they lack originality. The novel suffers from lack of characterization. All the gallants are exactly alike: Dumont, Belmein, Campbel, Clayton, differ not in the slightest degree, save that one declares his passion more fluently or more respectfully or more poetically than another. We see no possible reason why Harriot should not love Dumont, then Belmein, Dumont again, Campbel, and finally Dumont at the end; for, except for the names, they are one character,—and that the dimmest sort of character. The young ladies are likewise taken from one pattern, except the members of Harriot's family, who are rather more clearly distinguished. Mrs. Dormer is but a continuation of Mrs. Blandon, blessed with a little higher station in life. The only characters that we feel are real at all are those whom we have reason to think Mrs. Lennox took from her own experience. Harriot's father has a definite personality and a very attractive one. We can almost feel a daughter's pride and love shining through the portrayal of this gracious, dignified officer. The mother, too, while less clear, is a real person, though she has much more sympathy with her elder, practical-minded daughter than with the flighty, poetical, romantic heroine. The other two characters whom we might choose to rescue from the charge of being merely names are the Lady Cecilia, who seems to assume a certain reality, even though it is an unpleasant one, and Repeti, the French tutor. He is vain, clever, and deceitful, capable of an inexorable malice against anyone who once offends him. In the cases of the characters where she had living models Mrs. Lennox was successful in achieving a reality in portrayal; otherwise we have types acting mechanically, mere puppets drawn by the strings of a young girl's romantic fancy.

The scenes from the novel which have most interest are those in which Mrs. Lennox drops her romancing and gives simple descriptions of things which, in all probability, she witnessed herself. Such is her father's arrival in Albany.

> My father was received with much respect by the inhabitants of A—, who had impatiently expected us. We were saluted by all the ships in the harbour, who had their flags and streamers out; and the mayor, with the principal persons of the city, waited our landing, and conducted us to the fort, in which was a very fine house, where the commanding officer always resided.

> (pp. 122-23)

The motive of surprise is never used in the novel; it is always expectation. Each event is ushered in by some such lugubrious foreboding as this: "Little did I realize what horrid experiences this step would involve me in." Or "I left her so sensibly affected with this little parting, that I could not help expressing my surprise at it. Alas! I did not foresee that it would be long ere I should see her again, and that fortune was preparing the severest afflictions for me!"

The novel partakes of the sentimental nature of its heroine. Extraordinarily vain and forever conscious of the impression that her looks and speeches are going to make upon others, Harriot is also unfailingly moral and lacking in all sense of humor. In this respect there is a further similarity between her and the whole book, which does not contain one iota of legitimate humor. The modern reader may extract some from the extreme sensibility or silliness of Harriot, her pursuits by unworthy, dishonorable men, and her own conventionally virtuous romance. We tire of the theme, and the story lacks virility. There is certainly a little influence of *Clarissa Harlowe* in the sufferings of the virtuous maiden reflected here. For the most part, however, we have Mrs. Lennox experimenting. She takes a little background from her own experience,—the most natural, real parts of the novel—and lards all this over with the romantic fancy of a young, rather foolish girl somewhat spoiled by early appreciation of her literary powers and beauty. Most of the incidents which bear any stamp of originality redound to the advantage of Harriot and furnish her with an opportunity to appear as a great martyr, a great saint, a lady of remarkable virtue or remarkable courage. It is easy to believe that this is the first novel of a young lady, for there is a certain seriousness about unimportant things, an overemphasis upon what are really rather inconsequential interests of the young—especially the young of Harriot's sex—which stamps it as essentially a puerile production. (p. 125)

[*The Life of Harriot Stuart*] is gracefully written in a simple, straightforward style, especially noticeable in the narrative portions, but, except for the interesting light on American Colonial manners in Albany, there is little that is not too trivial and inconsequential to be considered worth writing. (pp. 126-27)

In [*Henrietta*] we find Mrs. Lennox more worldly wise than in her two earlier novels. She is constantly alive to the advantages that the world gives to wealth over virtue, beauty, and even birth. Many references to this subject show bitterness and resentment on the part of the author, and a disillusioned attitude toward the eighteenth century world of fashion. The men and women of society who are introduced are represented as vain, shallow, and mercenary. Even the countess who is Henrietta's benefactress selfishly watches out for her own and her son's material welfare. The silly, hollow ideals of society are laid bare in all their sordid unpleasantness. Henrietta, whose sufferings we follow, is too much the paragon of beauty and virtue to win our wholehearted sympathy. She is too conscious of her virtue and of the sins of others, and she never hesitates to inform her acquaintances how they might improve themselves—not infrequently, it turns out, by following her excellent example. In her character we see the influence of Richardson. Much more time is given to delineating her emotions and reactions than to the actual events of the story. We have seen that in her two earlier novels Mrs. Lennox showed a certain power in narration, in clear telling of a story. We miss that here, where the desire to present a moral heroine and her reactions under her trials has slowed the tale.

The characterization in this novel is stronger than in *Harriot Stuart.* Mr. Bale is a pleasant old gentleman and his son is rather interesting, too, in his sheepish attempt at wickedness. Miss Belmour, Miss Woodby, and Miss Cordwain are typical women of fashion who show the hollowness and futility of their lives, bounded by the petty interests of the day and governed by the dictates of a mercenary code. Their sole cause for living seems to be to fall in and out of love and to make a prosperous match. The gallants are moulded from the same pattern as those in *Harriot Stuart* with a little less sentimentality in their portrayal. (pp. 132-33)

Henrietta met with general favor in the reviews and was commended for its gentility. The *Monthly Review* is most lavish in its praise, though the review is short.

> We look upon this to be the best novel that has appeared since *Pompey the Little* [by Frank Coventry, 1751]. The incidents are probable and interesting; the characters duly varied and well supported; the dialogue and conversation-scenes, spirited and natural, both in genteel and low life; the satire generally just; and the moral exemplary and important.

This is higher praise than this magazine accords to any other of Mrs. Lennox's novels. *The Critical Review* also commends it, especially in its treatment of religious subjects [see excerpt dated 1758.] (p. 136)

It is interesting that both these reviews cite *Henrietta* as the best novel in some years. There is a certain dignity about the work which won it respect. Not silly as was *Harriot Stuart,* lacking the ingenuity of *The Female Quixote,* it yet possesses an economy of style, a clearness of plot, and a sensible criticism of eighteenth century fashionable life which entitle it to second place among the novels of Mrs. Lennox. Though Henrietta does the conventional things—faints, blushes, is easily alarmed, and enlarges upon her virtue—she has courage and initiative. Her unquestionable intellectual powers and her independence of others' opinions where principle is concerned, combined with swiftness and lack of hesitation in action, give her strength. The novel acquires further distinction from the unusual or amusing minor characters and from the ease with which Mrs. Lennox writes. The experience of many translations besides her own creative work has given her familiarity with the language and a wide vocabulary which she employs with skill and often with grace. She never indulges in great scenes of emotion; these are passed over rapidly or told about in a few words. She doubtless realized her limitations and did not attempt heights which she had not the power to attain. For this, credit should be given her. The general note of the novel is restraint and economy both of incident and of moral reflection.

Mrs. Lennox's next novel was *Sophia* or *Harriot and Sophia.* It appeared in Mrs. Lennox's periodical publication, *The Lady's Museum* (1760-1), and in book form in 1762. (p. 137)

Sophia was translated into French and the translation published in London and Paris in 1770. In the preface the translator, after paying high honor to the art of novel-writing in England under Richardson and Fielding, exonerates this novel from being merely an imitation of these two great novelists as most succeeding English novels have been, and makes great claims for the charm of its heroine. She need not rely upon the fame of her creator, Mrs. Lennox, well known though she be in the world of letters, since "il suffit de la connoître pour l'aimer, et d'être vertueux pour chercher à l'imiter."

To a twentieth century eye Sophia's charm is less obvious, even though by her "unwearied application to reading, her mind became a beautiful store-house of ideas: hence she derived the power and the habit of constant reflection, which at once enlarged her understanding, and confirmed her in the principles of piety and virtue." (pp. 138-39)

We hear much of the wit and charm of Sophia but we seldom experience them. Her great learning and piety bore us as she buoys herself up through her hardships by the "modest approbation" of her own virtues. It is difficult to take a scene like the following seriously.

> The wretched fallen Harriot was proud! the diamonds that glittered in her hair, the gilt chariot, and the luxurious table; these monuments of her disgrace contributed to keep up the insolence of a woman, who by the loss of her honour was lower than the meanest of her servants, who could boast of an uncorrupted virtue.
>
> Sophia received her with the modest dignity of conscious virtue, and Harriot, tho' incapable of much reflection, yet soon perceived the miserable figure she made, in the presence of such a character, and stood silent and abashed, while Sophia contemplated her finery with an eye of pity and anguish.

The Man of Feeling is anticipated in the excessive sensibility of our hero.

> 'Angelick creature!' exclaimed Sir Charles, with his eyes swimming in tears,; (or) —while her surprise kept her motionless, he threw himself at her feet, and taking one of her hands, pressed it respectfully to his lips, tears at the same time falling from his eyes.

Sophia is the least successful of all Mrs. Lennox's heroines. She has little of the sweet natural charm which Arabella possessed, and she lacks the independence and occasional pertness of Henrietta. The mother is like Harriot's mother in *Harriot Stuart.* Mr. Herbert is the Mr. Bale of *Henrietta* more distinctly drawn and given more opportunity to exploit his kindliness and moralistic views. Mrs. Howard reminds us of the Lady Cecilia in *Harriot Stuart* save that the more detailed picture given here shows her as a more actively unpleasant and despicable character. Mrs. Lennox must have known and hated the prototype of such ladies, for she draws

them with a vigor and energy which argue personal resentment. Mrs. Gibbon rides a hobby as did Mrs. Autumn in *Henrietta;* her attempt to use long words and her subsequent mistakes put her in the class which includes such delightful figures as Mistress Quickly and Mrs. Slipslop earlier, Tabitha Bramble later, and which reaches its apotheosis in Mrs. Malaprop.

> '—she declared she would never more have any *collection* with such vulgar creatures . . . from that moment she broke off any *treatise* of marriage between her nephew and me.' . . . 'and to *felicitate* your success, I will let her know that I am willing to receive the honour of a visit from her.' . . . 'You see, Madam,' said she, 'what *affluence* your commands have over me:'

In condemning the book for lack of characterization, we should have to except Mrs. Howard, Mrs. Gibbon, and the more slightly sketched figures of the Lawsons. *Sophia* belongs in the same class with *Henrietta,* but it is greatly inferior in style, characterization, and narrative. There is something in the situation of the two daughters and the mother which reminds one dimly of Mrs. Dashwood and her two daughters, Elinor and Marianne, in *Sense and Sensibility.* Jane Austen suggests the same general relation, but she has humanized them all and made the folly of Marianne romantic rather than vicious, to say nothing of the charm which she has bestowed upon the affectionate but weak mother and the generous, sensible Elinor. If she knew *The Female Quixote* so well [see excerpt dated 1807], it is possible that she had read other novels of Mrs. Lennox and found something that appealed to her in the situation depicted in *Sophia.* (pp. 139-41)

Sophia even more than *Henrietta* places Mrs. Lennox in the class of the novelists who write for the "propagation of virtue". In *Humphry Clinker* Smollett says of contemporary novelists.

> Tim had made shift to live for many years by writing novels at the rate of five pounds a volume; but that branch of business is now engrossed by female authors, who publish merely for the propagation of virtue, with so much ease, and spirit, and delicacy, and knowledge of the human heart, and all in the serene tranquillity of high life, that the reader is not only enchanted by their genius, but reformed by their morality.

Smollett's recipe for success, substituting sentimental morality for literary value, is carried out better in *Sophia* than in any other of Mrs. Lennox's novels.

Mrs. Lennox's later novel, *Euphemia,* comes toward the close of her literary career, in 1790. . . . It is significant that, forty years after her first novel, Mrs. Lennox was able to write one which met with a fair amount of favor, at least in the reviews. (pp. 142-43)

There is little consistent story [in *Euphemia*]. The book is made up of pictures of life or of tiny incidents almost as though it were a book of reminiscences. As most of the story is laid in America, and as those are the scenes most simply and faithfully presented, it is easy to surmise that we here have Mrs. Lennox going back in spirit to the scenes of her childhood and recreating them with an old person's exact memory of the early part of his life. The renewed interest in strange lands and peoples and the theme of the "noble savage" may have suggested to her that a presentation of what she had actually seen would be acceptable. Besides this biographical element in the settings, one cannot help feeling that Mr. Neville is Mr. Lennox. There is an intimacy about the way his character is presented that makes us feel that the writer certainly knew such a person and knew him in the relation here presented. The fact that there is nothing inconsistent with the little we know about Mr. Lennox in this portrayal—on the other hand, that he is just what we should imagine him, especially in his relation with his son— substantiates this surmise. (pp. 145-46)

Much of this novel of little incident is taken up with moral axiom; both Euphemia and Mrs. Benson are prone to reflect upon the imminence of death and the wages of sin. Many of the short reflections have a Johnsonian flavor; some are briefly and effectively phrased. For example:

> The life of a good man is a continual prayer.
>
> Conversation, said she, has been properly stiled the air of the soul; they who value the health and ease of the mind, ought to chuse an element pure and serene for it to breathe in.

Especially in the last two volumes occurs more and more of this tendency to philosophize and pause to reflect upon general truths. It gives the work rather the effect of an essay than a novel.

There are many scenes in America which are authentically and simply described. That Mrs. Lennox is calling upon her memory is evident for two reasons: many of the descriptions are practically the same as those in *Harriot Stuart;* all the background is early Colonial and not contemporary with the time Mrs. Lennox was writing, when, of course, everything was quite changed. (pp. 146-47)

There are a few signs of Mrs. Lennox's being alive to the tendencies of her own time. One is shown in the description of nature; here is a picture of the Hudson and its banks.

> but in the morning we were again becalmed, and as we moved slowly along the liquid plain, which was as smooth as glass, we were at leisure to admire the magnificent scene that presented itself to our eyes.—The river here being very narrow, running between a ridge of mountains on each side, whose tops covered with groves of lofty trees, seemed to hide their heads in the clouds, while their sloping sides were adorned with the most beautiful verdure, and trees of many species unknown to us. The awful gloom from the surrounding shades, the solemn stillness, inspired a soft and pleasing melancholy, which we enjoyed in silence, being, as the poet says, 'rapt in pensive musing'.

Such words as "groves", "verdures", "gloom", and "melancholy" remind us of Mrs. Ann Radcliffe and the sort of nature which she presents. Only one of her novels, *The Castles of Athlin and Dunbayne,* had appeared as yet, and this came out the year before *Euphemia,* in September, 1789. (p. 148)

[Another] similarity between the two books is in the recognition scenes of the two young men. In *The Castles of Athlin and Dunbayne* the Baroness thus recognizes her son:

> 'It is,—it is my Philip!' said she, with strong emotion; 'I have, indeed, found my long lost child; that strawberry on his arm confirms the decision.'

In *Euphemia* Mrs. Lennox is more original, and the mark by which Euphemia recognizes her son is the print of a bow and arrow on his breast, caused by a fright she received from an Indian before Edward was born. This method of certain recognition is by no means new: the strawberry mark at once reminds us of *Joseph Andrews* and the general device may be traced in English fiction to the mark of a lion's paw on the neck of a character in Sidney's *Arcadia* and to the bright cross on Havelok's back in *The Lay of Havelok the Dane.*

In taking over the letter form, Mrs. Lennox may have been encouraged by the success of such books as *Evelina* (1788) and *Julia de Roubigné* (1777). Thus in many respects we see Mrs. Lennox reflecting tendencies of the closing decades of the eighteenth century. She reminds us a little of Mrs. Radcliffe in her nature descriptions. She shows the influence of the belief in the natural goodness of the savage, a theory which had begun early in the century but had received especial impetus from Rousseau's *Emile* (1762). She adheres still to the earlier sentimentality but tinges it with didacticism as the fashion is. Finally, she uses the letter form, which is just on the verge of decline. Mingled with all these contemporary fashions is a large element of biographical detail, both of Mrs. Lennox's life as a child in Albany, and of some of her experiences as a wife and mother. There is a mellowness about the flavor of the whole, a rather gentle detachment, as of one now losing interest in life except through the halo of reminiscence, which lends the book a distinctive charm. (pp. 149-50)

The contributions which Mrs. Lennox made to the advancement of the novel are not many, chiefly because she followed so closely the tendencies of the period in which she was writing. Even *The Female Quixote,* the plot of which is original with her, is in general character suggested by a noticeable bent in eighteenth century writers to copy from Cervantes and the quixotic character. In her other novels we have instances of the sentimental heroine: in *Henrietta* done with considerable success; in *Sophia* with little to distinguish it from the ordinary novel of the time. It is in the American scenes of *Harriot Stuart* and *Euphemia* that we find something original with Mrs. Lennox and interesting historically and biographically. The accurate simple accounts of a passage up the Hudson and of life in the fort at Albany with occasional excursions into the surrounding country are the most valuable and unusual portions of these novels. Mrs. Lennox is most successful, both in scenes and characters, when she is drawing upon her personal experience. She possesses little originality and is easily influenced by prevailing fashions of writing. She has, however, a natural ease in telling a story, and her narratives are, in general, good. In *Euphemia,* which contains more philosophizing than any other novel of hers, there is dignity and succinctness in the expression of the aphorisms. Her early heroines have an independence of mind and action which sets them off from many of their prototypes and gives them charm, even today. In addition—and what mattered especially to an eighteenth century critic—all her novels pay strict attention to the rules of decorum and are characterized by excessive gentility. This acts to the detriment of humor, of which, comparatively speaking, her novels contain little. They seek rather to instruct than to amuse, except in the case of *The Female Quixote,* and of separate minor characters in the other novels. On the whole, it is this tendency to instruct which detracts from the vitality of the works and relegates them to obscurity. The parts which have freshness today are a few characters like Colonel Stuart, Henrietta, Mrs. Howard, and Mr. Neville, and the Colonial scenes drawn from Mrs. Lennox's childhood experience. (pp. 152-53)

Miriam Rossiter Small, in her Charlotte Ramsay Lennox: An Eighteenth Century Lady of Letters, *Yale University Press, 1935, 268 p.*

GUSTAVUS HOWARD MAYNADIER   (essay date 1940)

[*In the following excerpt, Maynadier discusses character and scene development and plot resolution in* The Life of Harriot Stuart *and* The Female Quixote. *Maynadier also comments on the inordinate length of the novels.*]

Besides her two novels with American scenes [*Harriot Stuart* and *Euphemia*] Mrs. Lennox wrote three, perhaps four, others, of which far and away the best is *The Female Quixote: or, The Adventures of Arabella,* her one work still interesting by virtue of intrinsic merit. Published only a year and a quarter after *Harriot Stuart,* it is so superior to that effort as to seem hardly by the same hand. Indeed if *The Female Quixote* were sufficiently shortened, it would be not merely good but very good. No wonder Jane Austen admired it [see excerpt dated 1807], as her letters show, for it has scenes of excellent humor and a situation which she thought fit to duplicate in *Northanger Abbey*—a lovable young girl absurdly misjudging everyday happenings because she views them in the light of the preposterous romances which she has read. Only Lady Arabella, the heroine of *The Female Quixote,* knows even less of life than Miss Austen's Catherine Morland and reads romances even more extravagant, with the result that her fantastic ideas, unlike Catherine's, often go too far beyond probability. (pp. 36-7)

Arabella herself critics have generally praised for her womanly reality, not of the first order surely, yet enough to make her a lady of true delicacy, lovable and charming in spite of her illusions. In this she resembles her literary successor already mentioned, Catherine Morland, and in some ways, too, another novel-reading young lady, Lydia Languish. She is further like Miss Languish in her repugnance to accepting a husband who has been picked out for her—in each case the hero of the tale—and also, it may not be too trifling to observe, in having a maid named Lucy, though the two Lucys have nothing in common. Other characters occasionally gleam into reality, but the majority are lifeless, even the hero for the most part, exemplary and sensible young man though he is, and admirably patient with the vagaries of his lovely cousin whom he finally marries.

A serious fault of the novel which commentators have pointed out is the clumsy way in which at last Arabella's conversion to good sense is brought about. It is chiefly by the arguments and exhortations of a dry-as-dust parson in the longest chapter of the book. Probably the dullest too, despite Mrs. Lennox's entitling it, 'Being in the author's opinion, the best chapter in this history.' Dr. Johnson, it seems probable, wrote most of the chapter because of his high regard for Mrs. Lennox; and it was a sign of her high regard for him that she not only entitled the chapter as she did, but also inserted a clause in one of the sentences, referring to him as 'the greatest genius in the present age.' A still graver fault of the novel is the length. Arabella's incessant pointing to the behavior of her favorite romantic heroines becomes tedious in the extreme. If all her adventures, which vary in interest greatly, had the interest of the best, there would still be too many. And too many, as already remarked, are beyond the bounds of proba-

bility. Even so, Macaulay was not justified in declaring that if we consider *The Female Quixote* 'as a picture of life and manners, we must pronounce it more absurd than any of the romances which it was designed to ridicule.'

Such a charge might with much more reason have been brought against *Harriot Stuart* which, with its bewildering mass of improbabilities, seems at times almost burlesque. Obviously Mrs. Lennox never so intended it. All seriously she sought to portray her Harriot as a thoughtless girl whose coquettish vanity was the cause of many of her trials, yet gifted and affectionate, with generous feelings, and finally sense enough to laugh at her youthful folly. To this study of character, unskilful and almost buried out of sight by Harriot's adventures, Mrs. Lennox had the originality to add those scenes based on her own experiences in America which constitute the novelty of the book and its greatest interest. Only Mrs. Lennox herself had read too many romances; *The Female Quixote* shows that at one time she must have been a prodigious reader of them. *Harriot Stuart* was her first novel, and the art of the new kind of fiction—character more important than adventure—was itself young. Mrs. Lennox was still too near lifeless, formless models. She never learned to write a compact story, she never attained complete reality of characters or scenes, but after her first experiment she did make an advance in her second novel, later by only fifteen months, that is marvelous. If she never wrote so well again, she was at least able to give considerable reality to the beginning of *Henrietta,* her third novel, and in *Euphemia,* when she was seventy, to rouse some interest by psychological study. (pp. 42-6)

Gustavus Howard Maynadier, in his The First American Novelist? *Cambridge, Mass.: Harvard University Press, 1940, 79 p.*

RONALD PAULSON   (essay date 1967)

[*In the following excerpt, Paulson discusses the predominant theme he sees in* The Female Quixote: *the conflict between decorous forms of behavior and subjective feeling expressed in the character of Arabella.*]

Charlotte Lennox' novel, *The Female Quixote,* derives from Marivaux' *Don Quixote Moderne,* in which both male and female Quixotes appear. The fixation of these Quixotes is courtly love with its conventions of the imperious lady, abject servant-lover, and the rest. Mrs. Lennox increases the role of the female (Mlle. Babet), producing her heroine Arabella, and reduces that of the male (Jean Bagnol), until all that remains is the pretended chivalry of Sir George. Arabella contains both aspects of the Quixote syndrome, vice and corrective.

As a villain, Arabella represents the female attitude that Fielding would probably have called prudery—the refusal to recognize her feelings or desires, her very humanity, and the consequent destruction of innocent people because they do not conform to the stereotype she carries in her head. Thus at the end of Book IV Arabella is sufficiently carried away to cry to Lucy (her Sancho-like maid):

> Do you think I have any cause to accuse myself, though five thousand men were to die for me! It is very certain my beauty has produced very deplorable effects; the unhappy Harvey has expiated, by his death, the violence his too-desperate passion forced him to meditate against me: the no less guilty, the noble unknown Edward, is wandering

about the world, in a tormenting despair, and stands exposed to the vengeance of my cousin, who has vowed his death. My charms have made another person, whose character ought to be sacred to me, forget all the ties of consanguinity, and become the rival of his son, whose interest he once endeavoured to support: and lastly, the unfortunate Bellmour consumes away in an hopeless passion.

The effect of transplanting the female half of the courtly love code in the eighteenth century is to produce a monster of egotism or self-sufficiency, who can say and believe that "It is impossible to think" that Sir George won't die "since he has not so much as received a command from me to live."

The satire on French romances is less important as a theme than the more general one of form vs. feeling. Quixotism in Arabella means a rigidity of behavior—her favorite word is "questionless"; there is no doubt as to her rightness and everyone else's wrongness. In the central instance of Mr. Glanville, the romance forms stand between Arabella and her feelings and of course thwart Glanville's feelings. Mrs. Lennox' novel demonstrates what happens when a woman is given the Quixote role. There is a great difference between Quixote as a funny-looking old man and as a beautiful young girl. Being female, Arabella has to remain passive: her actions are largely blocking ones rather than the active, questing ones of her male counterpart. Insofar as she remains passive, she appears a prude, wrapped in neuroses; and to the extent that she is an active Quixote, one feels (as in the scene where she makes Glanville read) that if she is not merely atrociously selfish, she is, in fact, out of her mind. In other words, she comes across much more as a character than as a satiric symbol; the reader takes her seriously and asks questions.

There are several reasons for this effect. First, *The Female Quixote* has a small cast of characters and is tightly knit, with unity of place through most of it and few digressions. The episodes are longer and more fully developed than in other Quixotic novels (*The Female Quixote* is closer in this way, as in others, to the Richardsonian novel). So much time is spent on the Glanville courtship, and necessarily in conversation, that the focus appears to be on the heroine's mind and the way it operates. Second, Glanville and Arabella's father try so hard to understand her that the reader also sees her as demented. The characteristic reaction to her from relations or close friends is sympathy or annoyance. As Sir Charles Glanville says, "I should be sorry to have a daughter-in-law for whom I should blush as often as she opened her mouth." Finally, there is no ironic observer like Fielding's narrator to distance Arabella; she is merely described.

However, in Book VII, as if she remembered it was expected of her, Mrs. Lennox takes her characters to Bath and London, introducing Arabella to a wider circle of acquaintance, and it is at this point that the book almost breaks. The intense psychological scrutiny of Arabella made possible by the small circle and the single locale is replaced by a rather clumsy attempt at the rapid satiric survey of society. On the one hand Arabella is presented as the Quixotic fool, and on the other she is the Quixotic observer and ideal. Such scenes as the one in which Arabella and Charlotte Glanville misunderstand each other over the meaning of "adventure" present the positive half of the Quixote syndrome. To Arabella "adventure" is a romantic platonic love; to Charlotte, a sordid affair, probably like Miss Groves'. To Charlotte "favors" are kisses or very probably worse, while to Arabella they are offerings of

scarves or bracelets as tokens to her "servant." Here Arabella becomes the ideal or, at least, a corrective, and her Quixotism shows how far the world has fallen from the idealism of courtly romance. In "a chapter of the satirical kind" she becomes a satirist of Bath:

> What room, I pray you, does a lady give for high and noble adventures, who consumes her days in dressing, dancing, listening to songs, and ranging the walks with people as thoughtless as herself? How mean and contemptible a figure must a life spent in such idle amusements make in history?

"History" is a perspective that shrinks the business of Bath. She goes on to ridicule the effeminate men (vs. her heroes of romance) and the dress- and fashion-conscious men and women (vs. the Service of Love)—all "wholly unworthy of a hero." She concludes (and this applies equally to the scenes with Charlotte): "When actions are a censure upon themselves, the reciter will always be considered as a satirist." Later, apropos of Charlotte, she says, "But with him who is incapable of any violent attraction, and whose heart is chilled by a general indifference, precept or example will have no force." She is opposing indifference to her own strong feelings about what is proper, what is good and evil: "For there is nothing at so great a distance from true and heroic virtue, as that indifference which obliges some people to be pleased with all things or nothing."

Thus if Arabella represents as Quixotic villain the constricting aspect of courtly love conventions, as heroine she represents their liberating aspect. J. M. S. Tompkins is probably correct to include *The Female Quixote* among preromantic novels rather than satiric; Mrs. Lennox does not satirize Arabella's romances as much as use this form as a convenient vehicle for introducing romance into the humdrum life of Arabella and her readers. Nevertheless, *The Female Quixote* is a remote anticipation of the world of manners. In spite of her madness, Arabella has the special quality and beauty of a Harriet Byron, Catherine Morland, or Elizabeth Bennet. Her madness is related to that special quality of imagination that sets Austen's heroines off from the other women in her novels, and the blindness that goes with Arabella's madness is at least analogous to the blind spot in the Elizabeth Bennets and Emma Woodhouses. And then Glanville resembles the Darcys who persevere in the face of the heroine's misunderstanding (and annoying qualities such as arrogance or prejudice), and Charlotte Glanville is the other woman (in *Pride and Prejudice,* Bingley's sister) who is after the man who loves the heroine and who is both jealous and unable to believe that he can really love her rival.

The effect of such scenes as the one with Arabella, Miss Groves, and her woman, Mrs. Norris, is to produce comic clash of manners—the artificial, book-learned manners of Arabella; the realistic, cynical ones of Mrs. Norris, who thinks she can get money out of Arabella for the information she has to impart; and the shallow city sophistication of Miss Groves (as artificial as Arabella's manners). The scene in which Arabella and Charlotte talk at cross-purposes about the word "adventure" operates in the same way. Manners are, of course, crucial in a man's approach to Arabella. Sir George is *not* rebuffed on his first meeting with Arabella because, with Charlotte pressing all her attentions upon him, he has no opportunity to attempt "a piece of gallantry which could undoubtedly have procured him a banishment from her presence." The comedy then arises from misunderstandings:

Arabella talks on one level, Charlotte on another (as Don Quixote and Sancho do), much as the representative of one class talks with another, and the resulting misunderstandings make up the fabric of the novel. Mrs. Lennox' novel ultimately comes down to the subject of how the mating ceremony should be carried out: what is decorous, and how much should form give way to feeling? (pp. 275-79)

Ronald Paulson, "The Novel of Manners," in his Satire and the Novel in Eighteenth-Century England, Yale University Press, 1967, pp. 266-310.

MARGARET DALZIEL (essay date 1970)

[In the following preface to her edition of The Female Quixote, Dalziel compares and contrasts Lennox's work with Miguel de Cervantes's Don Quixote (1605-15), focusing in particular on the divergent attitudes displayed in the two novels towards chivalric codes of behavior.]

Like Cervantes in Don Quixote, Charlotte Lennox in The Female Quixote made one special kind of romance—the French heroic romance of the seventeenth century—the object of her burlesque. Her heroine Arabella does once mention an English imitation, Roger Boyle's Parthenissa, but her mind has been nourished on the works of La Calprenède (Cassandra, Cleopatra, Pharamond) and Mlle de Scudéry (Clelia, and Artamenes, which is better known as The Grand Cyrus). She accepts as true the image of human action and character presented in these romances, and forms her expectations of life accordingly.

Now the French romances are typical of the genre, in that they take love and war as their subjects and represent them in what we recognize as ideal rather than real forms; but they have certain specific qualities which make it plausible that they should be accepted by a young lady as guides to conduct. Mlle de Scudéry in particular concentrates on love rather than war, and makes the experience of her heroines very important. They are pictured in ideal terms; they are of high birth, and impossibly beautiful, wise, and good; they are the objects of universal admiration and love but, though apparently endowed by fortune with every imaginable gift, are destined to suffer a great variety of distresses before achieving a happiness which is as perfect as everything else about them. Mrs. Lennox's heroine, therefore, being conventionally young, well-born, lovely, intelligent, and virtuous, and in addition brought up in great seclusion, can be credibly represented as identifying herself with the heroines of French romance. From this arise in her story many situations analogous to those in Don Quixote. But, unlike Don Quixote, Arabella is also created to be the heroine of a serious love-story, a story with the conventional romantic characters and the conventional romantic ending, a marriage which is a union of 'Fortunes, Equipages, Titles, and Expence', of 'every Virtue and laudable Affection of the Mind'. Hence in part the marked difference between Mrs. Lennox's novel and its prototype.

It is true that Cervantes's hero and Mrs. Lennox's heroine share certain illusions and experiences. Both quote their romances as authorities, and expect their own adventures to be the subject of future histories, yet both are represented as being perfectly rational, indeed very sensible and intelligent, when they can forget their books. Both think they are much more fallen in love with than is the case; both tend to think that the ladies of their acquaintance are in danger of being abducted by villains. Each of them has a servant whose devotion, naiveté, and simple common sense contribute not only to the humour of the story, but also to exposing what is implied by the mania of master or mistress. Episodes like Arabella's rescue of the thieving gardener Edward from being beaten recall similar episodes in the life of Don Quixote, as when he rescues the shepherd boy from being beaten by his master; the threatened burning of the books in The Female Quixote is the counterpart of the actual bonfire in Don Quixote; Arabella's attempts to befriend Miss Groves and the pretty girl at Vauxhall are faint copies of Don Quixote's acts of knight-errantry; and the canon's long discourse at the end of Part I of Don Quixote has its analogue in the more successful effort made by the Doctor at the end of The Female Quixote to undo the spells binding Arabella.

But the very mention of knight-errantry stresses the difference between the two books. The first chapter of Don Quixote tells us that the hero's purpose is to roam through the whole world 'redressing all manner of Grievances, and exposing himself to Danger on all occasions', so that 'at last after a happy conclusion of his Enterprizes, he might purchase everlasting Honour and Renown'. Likewise, Sorel's extravagant shepherd, Scarron's Destiny and Star, Marivaux's Pharsamond are inhabitants of a larger world, able to travel abroad in search of adventures. But Mrs. Lennox could not send the conventional heroine of an eighteenth-century novel, virtuous and gently-bred, to wander about looking for adventures. Her heroine's life must be confined within the bounds of literal possibility set by her social and economic position, and the range of possible predicaments in which her romantic illusions can involve her is restricted. On the other hand, she has to grow and change as she learns what life is really like. Since Mrs. Lennox's purpose, unlike that of Cervantes, is wholly comic, Arabella's disillusionment, her improved understanding of the world and the acceptance of her proper place in it, must be achieved without too much emphasis on the suffering inevitable to such growth.

One way in which Mrs. Lennox achieves this is by presenting the world of the French romances as completely ridiculous, so that when Arabella finally rejects it neither she nor the reader is afflicted with a sense of loss. Arabella is led at first to accept it by her belief that the romances, describing as they do the fortunes of such characters as Cyrus, Alexander the Great, Roxana, Augustus, and Cleopatra, are histories; therefore, as history, except perhaps for a certain degeneration in modern times, is uniform, they are reliable guides to life in eighteenth-century England. 'These things happen every Day,' she says, of a lover's disguising himself as a gardener to be near his mistress, words echoed by Sir George Bellmour about the frequency with which men die of unrequited love. 'Do not the same Things happen now, that did formerly?' she asks her uncle, when he doubts the likelihood of her being forcibly carried away into Turkey. Glanville and the Countess, humouring her, make no direct attack on this belief, though both insist, in Glanville's words, that 'the World is quite different to what it was in those Days'; it takes the Doctor to go to the root of the matter, demolish her belief that the romances are historical, and destroy the whole illusion.

This intellectual error might have been shown up as merely absurd; but Mrs. Lennox is even more explicit than Cervantes in exposing its moral consequences. From her notion of history, as composed of the adventures of heroes and heroines, Arabella has formed an ideal of heroic behaviour that is strongly attacked. The book reveals that this idea includes, for the heroine, disobedience to her natural guardians, tyranny over lovers, and being responsible, however passively, for countless deaths; and while for the hero it enjoins courage and courtesy, it also entails slavish and exclusive devotion to his lady, irrespective of his duties to parents and country.

The total rejection of the morality of the romances is significant in two ways. However critical Cervantes may be of the chivalric code, he yet shows that obedience to it leads Don Quixote to perform heroic and gracious deeds which win our sympathy; but Mrs. Lennox, when Arabella attempts similar deeds, concentrates our attention on her folly. Where Don Quixote can claim that 'since my being a Knight-Errant, I am brave, courteous, bountiful, well bred, generous, civil, bold, affable, patient, a sufferer of Hardships, Imprisonment, and Enchantments', and the reader agrees that in a sense this is true, the best Arabella can say for the romances in her conversation with the Doctor is that she has read them without injury to her judgment or virtue. By the very title of her novel, Mrs. Lennox invites comparison with *Don Quixote;* it is hard not to think that in contrast with Cervantes she has over-simplified the experience of her central character, and lost opportunities of giving her positive and endearing qualities.

The second conclusion to be drawn from her onslaught on the romances is that she has no sympathy with the changing views which were to lead to the publication, only two years after *The Female Quixote,* of Thomas Warton's *Observations on the Fairy Queen,* of two editions of *The Faerie Queene* in 1758, and of Bishop Hurd's *Letters on Chivalry and Romance* in 1762; and which were to lead later writers like Dr. John Gregory and Clara Reeve to stress the ennobling influence of romances. Mrs. Lennox's attitude is typical of the earlier rather than the latter half of the eighteenth century. She makes fun of Arabella's insistence that her books 'give us the most shining Examples of Generosity, Courage, Virtue and Love; . . . regulate our Actions, form our Manners, and inspire us with a noble Desire of emulating those great, heroic, and virtuous Actions, which made those Persons so glorious in their Age, and so worthy Imitation is ours; and instead adopts the canon's view that 'all the Books of Knight-Errantry are false, fabulous, useless, and prejudicial to the Publick'. They are false in fact, and they embody immoral beliefs and attitudes. Mrs. Lennox's views are made explicit in the book through the characters of the Countess and the Doctor, and are implied particularly in the attention paid to the meaning of the words *history, adventure,* and *hero* (with its derivatives).

Throughout most of *The Female Quixote,* this concern with the immorality of the French romances (despite the uniformly chaste conduct of heroes and heroines) is nicely balanced by Mrs. Lennox's keen sense of their absurdity. She was perhaps encouraged in this by the gay attacks on their verisimilitude made by French writers from Sorel to Marivaux, including Subligny, whose *Mock-Clelia . . . In imitation of Dom* [*sic*] *Quixote* may have influenced also her choice of events, since it ends with the heroine's riding her horse into a canal in imitation of Clelia's swimming the Tiber. Like these writers, Charlotte Lennox laughs at the romances for the repetitive improbability of their events, the perennial youth and unlikely perfection of their characters, their inflated diction and their jargon of superlatives, peppered with words like *questionless, doubtless,* and *haply.* At times her attitude is purely

sportive, as in the description of Arabella's eccentric (though becoming) clothes, her way of being everywhere accompanied by her 'women', and her poor opinion of the attractions of London as contrasted with those of the cities of romance. More often she makes us laugh, but shudder also to see the dangers which threaten Arabella and sometimes overwhelm her. Some are material dangers, as when, running away from the supposed designs of Edward the gardener, she accepts a ride from a 'Generous Stranger', who is 'extremely glad at having so beautiful a Creature in his Power. From dangers of this kind she is always rescued; on this occasion, the stranger's chariot suffers a fortunate accident. She does not escape so easily from the moral dangers which attend her delusion, dangers such as a sense of arrogant superiority over those who, like Miss Glanville, fall short of the heroic ideal; the vulgarity, however innocent, of encouraging Miss Groves's confidant to betray her mistress's secrets; the real though unintentional unkindness of her failure to visit Glanville when he is ill, contrasted with the serious impropriety of her plan to visit Sir George Bellmour when she thinks he is ill; and the vanity of supposing that so many men, from the gardener and her uncle to Mr. Tinsel and Mr. Selvin, are in love with her. All these situations Mrs. Lennox manages to make plausible by giving her heroine a very secluded upbringing, as well as by showing the effects of her reading, and they are among the best things in the novel. They give scope to Mrs. Lennox's talent for inventing likely sources of misunderstanding among the characters, they display human nature in its mixed and varied quality, and they are described in a pleasantly ironical style, or through lively natural dialogue.

These are some of the qualities which made *The Female Quixote* so well-liked in its day, and which help to account for Fielding's remarkably eulogistic review of it in the *Covent Garden Journal* [see excerpt dated 1752]. Another reason for its popularity was that although Richardson, Fielding, and Smollett were writing at this time, there were few other novelists worth reading. It is clear too that the French romances were still being read; we know, for example, that people as disparate in station and taste as Fielding, Johnson, Horace Walpole, and Mrs. Chapone all read them in their youth, and were no doubt typical of many others who would enjoy the jokes in *The Female Quixote* with full understanding. *Don Quixote* too was far better known then than it is now, so that the characters and fortunes of Arabella and Lucy would gain by the reader's ability to compare them with those of their prototypes. Add to this the competence with which Mrs. Lennox delineates minor and mixed characters like Miss Glanville and Sir George Bellmour, and her easy, lively style, and one can well understand why the novel appeared in several editions during the eighteenth and early nineteenth centuries and was translated into French, German, and Spanish.

Later readers are likely to be troubled by its undoubted weaknesses. They may find it repetitive; Arabella's long accounts of episodes in the romances may irritate them as much as they irritate her hearers in the book; the important character of Glanville is hardly equal to his part in the story; and the ending should have been more artistically contrived. In this last point they would agree with Mrs. Barbauld, who made some perceptive remarks in the introduction to her edition of *The Female Quixote.* She found it

> rather spun out too much, and not very well wound
> up. The grave moralizing of a clergyman is not the
> means by which the heroine should have been

cured of her reveries. She should have been recovered by the sense of ridicule, by falling into some
absurd mistake, or by finding herself on the brink
of becoming the prey of some romantic footman,
like the ladies in Moliere's piece of *Les Précieuses
Ridicules,* the ridicule of which has pretty much the
same bearing.

None the less, **The Female Quixote** is still extremely readable
for its own sake. And it has an interesting place in the history
of English fiction, being formed on two ideas which have produced so many good novels: the burlesque of a genre that has
come to seem absurd, and the adventures of a young girl
when first she is introduced into society. (pp. xiii-xviii)

> *Margaret Dalziel, in an introduction to* The Female
> Quixote; or, The Adventures of Arabella *by Char-
> lotte Lennox, edited by Margaret Dalziel, Oxford
> University Press, London, 1970, pp. xiii-xviii.*

SUSAN G. AUTY (essay date 1975)

[*In the following excerpt, Auty compares* The Female Quixote
with Miguel de Cervantes's Don Quixote (1605-15), *focusing
on Lennox's portrayal of Arabella and her use of humorous
and ironic devices that raise the novel from the level of burlesque to that of true human comedy.*]

To compare **The Female Quixote** with Cervantes' incomparable original would be an unthinkable offence against literary decorum today. Yet in the more casual critical climate
of the mid-eighteenth century, Fielding discussed quite freely
the likenesses of the two books and, even more surprisingly,
managed to come up with several points in Mrs. Lennox's
favor—the plausibility and attractiveness of the heroine, the
regularity and interest of the story [see excerpt dated 1752].
As the one most responsible for the eighteenth century's new
found affection for Don Quixote, Fielding would have been
extremely interested in this new variation of the worthy but
unworldly knight. For like the Don, Arabella is unfailingly
self-redeeming: her charm far overpowers her outrageous
blindness; and like *Don Quixote,* **The Female Quixote** escapes
the limitations of burlesque on the open wings of its main
character. Indeed, a comparison of the novels is not unseemly
when one sees both as burlesques which were betrayed by
their author's concern for humanity into becoming comic
novels.

The points of similarity between the two works are really
quite numerous, if superficial finally in any consideration of
their value. Arabella too has had her head turned by a constant and very rich diet of Romances. The seclusion of her
family estates makes her delusion seem more natural than the
Don's (a nicety much commended by Fielding), but Arabella's belated experiences with the world have as little effect on
her understanding as do the knight errant's. She is, we are
told many times and occasionally shown, extremely sensible
and witty if one can avoid any mention of her favorite topic.
Like Don Quixote, she is in a position to surround herself
with people who are inclined to go along with her strange
ways, so that within the confines of her own world she does
not seem extraordinarily ridiculous. Her maid performs the
role of squire with great innocence and respect; Glanville,
who loves her too dearly to upset her, provides her with the
intelligent conversation that the curate and the barber supply
in the original. The romantic young girl, like the chivalrous
knight, is made to carry the author's satiric messages in her
own ridiculous speeches. What Arabella misses in the way of
adventures as a house-bound young lady, she makes up for
with her imagination and her ingenious ability to implicate
the most innocent people in her fantasies. Though she has no
occasion to tilt at windmills, she readily supposes that a gardener caught in the act of stealing carp from the pond is a
young nobleman in disguise about to throw himself in the
pond out of secret love for her.

The fineness of Arabella's imagination is, for all the other
similarities of structure and plot, the only meaningful basis
for establishing a relationship between the quixotic female
and the knight. In both, it is the source of their absurdity and
distinction; even more, it is the delicate instrument against
which the world must be tuned to make a place for them, to
accommodate their ideas of reality that are both right and
wrong, silly and sensitive at the same time. In both works the
quixotic imagination, by ranging freely between the ridiculous and the grand, is the source of the special comedy that
distinguishes them today.

Like Cervantes, Mrs. Lennox had satiric observations to
make about society and used her Quixote figure to mock fos-
sils of literature and culture through burlesque writing and
didactic episodes as he did (and Fielding after him). In her
innocence, Arabella unwittingly acts as chief prosecutor
against the Romances: her requirements for life are based on
literary models, and in giving her specifications to her maid
Lucy for the contents of her "history" she cannot help revealing the absurdity of these works:

> Well! exclaimed *Arabella:* I am certainly the most
> unfortunate Woman in the World! Every thing
> happens to me in a contrary manner from any other
> Person! Here, instead of my desiring you to soften
> those Parts of my History where you have greatest
> room to flatter; and to conceal, if possible, some of
> those Disorders my Beauty has occasioned; you ask
> me to tell you what you must say; as if it was not
> necessary you should know as well as myself, and
> be able, not only to recount all my Words and Ac-
> tions, even the smallest and most inconsiderable,
> but also all my Thoughts, however instantaneous;
> relate exactly every Change of my Countenance;
> number all my Smiles, Half-smiles, Blushes, Turn-
> ings pale, Glances, Pauses, Full-stops, Interrup-
> tions; the Rise and Falling of my Voice; every Mo-
> tion of my Eyes; and every Gesture which I have
> used for these Ten Years past; nor omit the slightest
> Circumstance that relates to me.

Not only does she talk in a high-toned manner that could
only be learned from bad fiction—this she always does—but
she happily catalogues the coquetries of Romance, which are
no different from the ones she spurns in her "real" life.
Whereas Arabella is unable to recognize the simple stupidity
of numbering the smiles on a girl's face and calling it her history, we see Mrs. Lennox's smile quite clearly.

John Warner, in an unpublished thesis, comments on Mrs.
Lennox's skillful use of Arabella's comical deficiencies to
pointedly satiric ends. He notes that Arabella's naivete "allows Mrs. Lennox to make implicit, rather than overtly didactic, contrasts between her heroine's innocent delusion and
the sophisticated hypocrisy of society. Without allowing Arabella to assume a satiric pose inconsistent with her romantic
role, Mrs. Lennox secures her points by juxtaposing society
against her heroine." The contrast is clear when Arabella
protects a mistreated prostitute in the mistaken and comical

belief that she is a great lady suffering at the hands of a ravisher. The Female Quixote makes us see what society is unable to discern, that it really makes no difference if the ravished woman is a tramp or a lady. Arabella's standard inflexible assumption is as true as if it were a sensible assessment of the situation: "questionless" the man is ravishing the woman and one must be "base" to leave her "in the Power of that Man."

Arabella's blindness necessarily sharpens our vision of reality; her blurry focus must be corrected by our awareness of the true picture. The difference is often satirically instructive, as when the demure young heroine exempts the laws of love from the laws of the land on the strength of the widely followed code of honor, which allows one to "hunt your Enemy thro' the World, in order to sacrifice him to your Vengeance." Her logical deduction that the conventions of love may contradict the conventions of justice rests clearly on the false assumption about honor that was still commonly made in the eighteenth century. Mrs. Lennox uses Arabella's befuddled mind here (a mind which we have seen treats the idea of death more lightly than a kiss on the hand) to deal a humorous but effective blow to the practice of dueling, which was then in the process of dying its own form of slow death.

Though we may still appreciate the aim and thrust of Mrs. Lennox's satiric stabs, many of which are out of date, the book would not still give pleasure without the comedy that so frequently arises from Arabella's addiction to the heroic mode of life. The romantically inclined heroine's habitual insistence on life's conformity with her own imaginative construction is balanced by Mrs. Lennox's equally strong insistence on telling what Aldous Huxley calls the "Whole Truth." Homer is Huxley's model for (and Fielding a later example of) a teller of the Whole Truth, and from his essay one sees that he is simply distinguishing the comic perspective from the more focused vision of tragedy: "[Homer] knew that even the most cruelly bereaved must eat; that hunger is stronger than sorrow and that its satisfaction takes precedence even of tears. He knew that, when the belly is full (and only when the belly is full) men can afford to grieve. In a word, Homer refused to treat the theme tragically. He preferred to tell the Whole Truth."

Arabella's tragic expectations are constantly disappointed by her very human lovers. Glanville's distress could not possibly be genuine in her eyes, since as she says, "that Uneasiness has neither made you thinner, nor paler, I don't think you ought to be pitied: For to say the truth, in these Sort of Matters, a Person's bare Testimony has but little Weight." Although Glanville has not starved himself simply because he has been parted from his lovely cousin for a few months, we know that Arabella's truth is far too demanding to be applicable to the frail beings that human heroes are and that Glanville has, indeed, felt as much distress as is fair to expect on such an occasion.

As often as her innocently arrogant heroine commands her suitors to live or die, Mrs. Lennox counters her commands with the facts of reality. Glanville's fever increases even after Arabella makes known her desire on the matter. Nevertheless she congratulates herself on her lover's eventual recovery, but must then deal with the disconcerting fact of Miss Glanville's indifference to her accomplishment. In fact, throughout the novel, much to Arabella's continual surprise no one gives her due credit for the survival of various lovers and no one actually dies or even suffers extreme discomfort as a result of love—not counting the embarrassment and mortification that Glan-

ville goes through, which Arabella of course does not recognize. Only the Marquis dies, of very natural causes over which his daughter admittedly has no powers. Mrs. Lennox makes it clear that living men do not expire simply to satisfy the rapacities of a lovely young lady's imagination.

The humor, however, is by no means always at the expense of the heroine's flighty mind. The nonromantics become ridiculous in their own way, as they engage in the heroic feat of "educating" Arabella. The adults of the novel always try to force hard reality into Arabella's fantasy world, the domain of which is real enough—her father's sequestered castle. But the castle walls of her mind are more difficult to scale, almost impossible, and the attempts of Glanville's father, Sir Charles, to do so result in the reader's great amusement if not Arabella's enlightenment. Miriam Small, author of the only full-length book on Mrs. Lennox [see excerpt dated 1935], judges the humor of *The Female Quixote* to be "most successful when it is obtained by presenting Arabella's idiosyncrasies in their effect upon some stolid and unimaginative person whom they leave in hopeless confusion."

Because the representatives of the real world are so unimaginative themselves, Arabella's sprightliness in comparison allows us to preserve our affection even while laughing at her. When Sir Charles's sceptical question draws a typically positive answer from the authoritative heroine, we laugh at him for taking Arabella so seriously:

> For Heaven's sake, Niece, said Sir *Charles,* How come such improbable Things into your Head? Is it such an easy Matter, think you, to conquer Kingdoms, that you can flatter a young Man, who has neither Fleets nor Armies, with such strange Hopes?
>
> The great *Artaban,* Sir, resumed *Arabella,* had neither Fleets nor Armies, and was Master only of a single Sword; yet he soon saw himself greater than any King, disposing the Destinies of Monarchs by his Will, and deciding the Fates of Empires by a single Word.

It is somehow pleasing to the reader that Arabella's imagination can supply her with such splendid facts about man's ability to accomplish what he sets out to do. Her conviction is of course absurd, but her optimism is contagious. Obstacles, physical or mental, do not exist in a heroic realm, for the imagination amends them, accounting for the ease with which heroes carry out their lives. The tales are unintentionally comic, for while they deal exclusively in large and noble happenings and are peopled with impossibly courageous heroes, all of which has nothing to do with the comic universe, the expedition with which the hero reaches his goal is naturally comic and is what makes the romantic genre so appealing to ordinary mortals. Even death is reduced to inconsequential proportions by the very frequency of its occurrence (indeed, the true hero will eschew suicide because it is so easy, choosing instead to pine away in a forest unbeknownst to his loved one). One cannot help being charmed by the world of heroic tragedy; how very stolid Sir Charles sounds and how much more preferable are the absurdities of Arabella. Just as the inn becomes, for the reader as for Don Quixote, a real castle, so when Arabella answers her uncle's objections we admire her and wonder why he is not able to see things so imaginatively.

The very figure of Arabella serves the comedy of the work, for even while she is exposing the affectations of the fashionable world, she is drawing attention to her own naturally fine qualities. Admitting to Miss Glanville that her observations of society might be construed satirically, she nevertheless shuns the character of a satirist: "When Actions are a Censure upon themselves, the Reciter will always be consider'd as a Satirist." She is right to reject the label, for her manner is such that the recitation always impresses the reader more with her own modesty and natural sense than with its barbed implications:

> What room, I pray you, does a Lady give for high and noble Adventures, who consumes her Days in Dressing, Dancing, listening to Songs, and ranging the Walks with People as thoughtless as herself? How mean and contemptible a Figure must a Life spent in such idle Amusements make in History? Or rather, Are not such Persons always buried in Oblivion, and can any Pen be found who would condescend to record such inconsiderable Actions?

This speech is not so much satire as a more mundane statement of Keats's assertion that "a man's life of any worth is a continual allegory." In the same way, Arabella's extraordinary appearance at the ball in a dress styled after the "gallant" Princess Julia's, a dress that suits her own features perfectly, is not a slap in the face to the other ladies present (though they take it as one) but a recommendation of good taste and individuality. In turn, our admiration for Arabella, a comic response, overshadows our scorn for the empty-witted ladies, a satiric response.

Only when Arabella herself becomes tiresome, stubbornly positive of her superior understanding, does the comedy fail. When she imposes endlessly on the sensible and loving Glanville, the reader stops appreciating her fantastic visions and starts wishing that she would venture out of her fortified mind long enough to see the lively possibilities of reality. Her arrogance becomes as unbearable to the reader as it is to the other characters, especially when in the eighth book (of nine) she is still quick to assume that a beau, whose taste is more for her fashionable cousin, must have chosen to fall upon his sword to "put an End to his Life and Miseries at once" after she denied him the favor of loving her: "How, Sir, interrupted *Arabella*, is he dead then already? Alas! why had he not the Satisfaction of seeing me before he expir'd, that his Soul might have departed in Peace! He would have been assur'd not only of my Pardon, but Pity also; and that Assurance would have made him happy in his last Moments." Like Sir Charles, one wishes to cry out in despair in the middle of the endlessly long discourse that follows:

> I am very sorry, Madam, said Sir *Charles,* to hear you talk in this Manner: 'Tis really enough to make one suspect you are—
>
> You do me great injustice, Sir, interrupted *Arabella,* if you suspect me to be guilty of an unbecoming weakness for this Man: If barely expressing my Compassion for his Misfortunes be esteem'd so great a Favour, what would you have thought if I had supported his Head on my Knees while he was dying, shed Tears over him, and discover'd all the Tokens of a sincere Affliction for him?—
>
> Good God! said Sir Charles lifting up his Eyes, Did any body hear of any thing like this?

Arabella's self-assurance allows her to make assumptions that support her peculiar cast of mind; she habitually interrupts with her own version of a person's thoughts. In the past

she has even convinced herself that the elder Glanville was violently in love with her and trying to usurp his son's place, when in fact he was trying to advance it. It is maddeningly inconceivable to her on this occasion that Sir Charles might want to suggest that she is out of her wits. That he grows peevish along with the reader is what saves the comedy from degenerating too much. With a rapid transfer of loyalties, the reader makes answers for Sir Charles that will end the matter before Arabella has a chance to misconstrue his words again. If Mrs. Lennox had not given us the company of reluctant listeners within the book, we would not have been able to bear not only Arabella's nonsense but also the fact that those around her were tolerating it. Throughout the novel we are reassured by the down-to-earth people who surround the Female Quixote that there is a limit to even the most creative and liberating imaginings, that improbabilities are boring when they have no enlightening relation to real life. Yet as we sense that Sir Charles still respects Arabella's intelligence and admires her character as much as ever, we do not like the extravagant heroine any less.

In addition to Arabella's occasionally tiresome character, there are faults of timing which impair the usually smooth narrative: the repetition of an observation in different forms, the protraction of an event that is only mildly amusing, the inclusion of an unnecessary speech are all misjudgments that disturb the comedy on occasion. Yet Mrs. Lennox's control over the tone of her work is apparent in her handling of the burlesque material. The long central section in which Sir George, a friend of Glanville's, sets out to win Arabella from him by indulging her heroic predilections with a "history" of himself as a young prince, might well have been only a satiric digression were the tone not so perfectly suited—more affectionate than mocking—to the whole novel. Mrs. Lennox's inventive imagination, which is at least as extravagant as Arabella's, together with her ear for the portentous gravity of the Romance style, serve both the originals and her parody well.

One has the chance in this section to get inside a romantic tale, to become as involved with the fantasy as Arabella perpetually is, to be enchanted as well as diverted. Mrs. Lennox has managed to combine the ludicrous aspects of the stories—the dungeons, the wicked brothers, the exiles—with their appealing qualities—the nobility of the heroes, the variety and excitement of the storybook world—and thus to make us laugh and keep us fascinated at the same time. A brief extract is all that is needed to convey the peculiar flavor of both the original and the parody:

> Then, taking leave of me with much Tenderness, she went out of the Prison, leaving *Toxares* with me, who assisted me to dress, and conducted me out of that miserable Place, where I had passed so many sad, and also joyful Hours. At a Gate to which he brought me, I found a Horse waiting; and, having embraced this faithful Confidant, with many Expressions of Gratitude, I bestowed a Ring of some Value upon him to remember me by; and, mounting my Horse, with a breaking Heart, I took the first Road which presented itself to my Eyes, and galloped away, without knowing whither I went. I rode the whole Night, so totally engrossed by my Despair, that I did not perceive my Horse was so tired, it could hardly carry me a Step farther; At last the poor Beast fell down under me, so that I was obliged to dismount; and, looking about

me, perceived I was in a Forest, without seeing the
least Appearance of any Habitation.

The striking features of romantic prose are its humorlessness,
its verbiage, its concentration on extremities of emotion, its
grim determination to carry the reader along with the hero
and reproduce in him identically heightened feelings. Mrs.
Lennox matches the luxuriousness of the style, dwelling on
the exact quality of the action or emotion as lovingly as the
writer of genuine Romance. Rather than lightening the prose
with obvious burlesque, she has, like Pope in *The Dunciad,*
harnessed the self-parodying features of the original to do the
job for her; in this way the reader has the experience of both.
We meditate upon the knight's mixed emotions, the "sad, and
also the joyful" hours spent in that "miserable Place"—
paradox sustains the lively imagination. We appreciate that
the value of the ring was considerable, but not unseemly—all
this is carried in the word "some," which is given force by
one's notions of heroic beneficence. We feel the discomfort of
the "poor Beast" and understand the urgency of the situation
that necessitated the neglect of that animal. Yet, at the same
time, our image of the teller, the careless and frivolous Sir
George, and our consciousness of the context, which is maintained by the sceptical questions of Sir Charles (who has understandably been thrown into a state of confusion by the
sudden elevation of his son's friend to the post of "young
prince of Kent"), make the sentiment and the ominous air of
Fortune and Fate that hangs over the tale seem palpably ridiculous. *The Female Quixote* is both enlivened and enriched
by Mrs. Lennox's sensitive ear, which was able to reproduce
accurately the absurd and yet captivating works of the Romantic imagination.

The nonburlesque narration perpetuates the lightheartedness
that is aroused in the parody. The ironic teller of Arabella's
history manages her business so gently as to be almost unno-
ticeable; indeed, Ronald Paulson insists she is not there:
"There is no ironic observer like Fielding's narrator to distance Arabella; she is merely described" [see excerpt dated
1967]. One may have to refer to Meredith's highly literate
definition of irony to appreciate Mrs. Lennox's delicate treatment of her character, which has been adjusted to the temperament of her Female Quixote and to the understated jest of
the work as a whole. According to Meredith, "if, instead of
falling foul of the ridiculous person with a satiric rod, to make
him writhe and shriek aloud [as Fielding and Smollett often
do to their minor characters], you prefer to sting him under
a semi-caress, by which he shall in his anguish be rendered
dubious whether indeed anything has hurt him, you are an
engine of Irony." In *The Female Quixote,* the caress almost
fully relieves the sting:

> Having said this, with one of her fair Hands she
> cover'd her Face, to hide the Blushes which so
> compassionate a Speech had caus'd—Holding the
> other extended with a careless Air, supposing he
> would kneel to kiss it, and bathe it with his Tears,
> as was the Custom on such melancholy Occasions,
> her Head at the same Time turned another Way, as
> if reluctantly and with Confusion she granted this
> Favour.—But after standing a Moment in this Pos-
> ture, and finding her Hand untouch'd, she conclud-
> ed that Grief had depriv'd him of his Senses.

Mrs. Lennox's restraint amounts to irony; her very lack of
commentary is a comment when supported by the suggestions concerning Arabella's state of mind, the "supposing"
and "as if reluctantly" revealing the degree to which she de-

ludes herself. The reader sees clearly that she is not so innocent as to be entirely without guile and vanity. In addition,
the "so compassionate" and "such melancholy Occasions"
are straightforwardly ironic descriptions that make Arabella's exaggerations seem absurd. Although the author does not
stop to mention that she is sorry to have to inform us of the
weaknesses in her favorite character, the loving mockery is
as clear as it is in Fielding's novels. (pp. 66-75)

[In] reading *The Female Quixote,* we never sense any ironic
betrayal by the author of her characters; there are no poisoned darts to shape our opinion. Mrs. Lennox takes care to
suit the tone to her subject, and as the only real villains in *The
Female Quixote* are the invisible writers of Romance, not
even the Romances themselves, the narration is gentle
throughout and provocative of the kindly smiles one senses
to be always present on the face of the author herself.

Only towards the end of the novel does the prose seem to reflect an occasionally humorless expression. Mrs. Lennox is almost as successful at resisting the temptation to moralize as
she is at refraining from satire and on the whole maintains
a nice distance both from sermon and scorn. But just as her
timing once or twice slips, her ear is guilty of similar insensi-
tivities (or possibly her admiration for Johnson leads her at
times to misappropriate his style). Arabella's diatribe against
satire, so far from being satirical itself, is too evidently a sermon presented by the author:

> The Ugliness of Vice, reply'd *Arabella,* ought only
> to be represented to the Vicious; to whom Satire,
> like a magnifying Glass, may aggravate every De-
> fect, in order to make its Deformity appear more
> hideous; but since its End is only to reprove and
> amend, it should never be address'd to any but
> those who come within its Correction, and may be
> the better for it: A virtuous Mind need not be
> shewn the Deformity of Vice, to make it hated and
> avoided; the more pure and uncorrupted our Ideas
> are, the less shall we be influenc'd by Example.

Even the echo from Swift's Preface to *The Battle of the Books*
has been couched in morality at the expense of its irony. The
straightforward declarative sentences, dull unless handled by
a master of diction, fall flat upon the audience as well as
the company; we are forced to agree entirely with Miss Glanville's observation, "You are so very grave, and talk upon
such high-flown Subjects."

The gravity and subject of the penultimate chapter, however,
prove a far greater threat to the humor of the work as a
whole. A serious suggestion made in 1843 attributing this
chapter to Johnson himself has been accepted by many scholars since then as plausible. The least one can say, on the evidence of the style, is that Mrs. Lennox was writing what she
thought would please and compliment her eminent and gracious friend. Thus the corrections of the "good Divine" are
all offered in the sweeping sentences of Johnsonian truths:

> The only Excellence of Falsehood, answered he, is
> its Resemblance to Truth; as therefore any Narra-
> tive is more liable to be confuted by its Inconsisten-
> cy with known Facts, it is at a greater Distance
> from the Perfection of Fiction; for there can be no
> Difficulty in framing a Tale, if we are left at Liberty
> to invert all History and Nature for our own Con-
> veniency. When a Crime is to be concealed, it is
> easy to cover it with an imaginary Word. When
> Virtue is to be rewarded, a Nation with a new

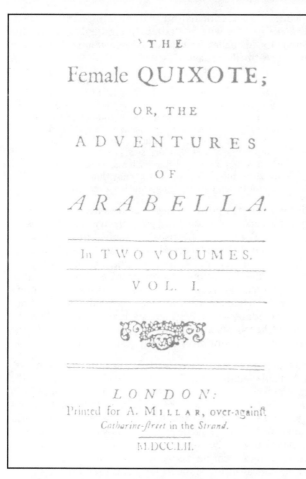

Title page for an early edition of The Female Quixote.

Name may, without an Expence of Invention, raise
her to the Throne.

The weight is almost too much for the comedy to bear: the
ending simply does not spring naturally from the delightfully
light story that precedes it. Only the efficiency with which it
is accomplished is comical about Arabella's cure, and one
would not comment on that fact except as a justification, for,
Mrs. Lennox's need to be efficient (to avoid excessive
length—a specific recommendation from Richardson, no less
accounts for the chapter's jarring artificiality and senten-
tiousness.

However, the substance of Mrs. Lennox's last chapter, even
more troubling to the comedy than the tone, is finally the
most regrettable feature of the concluding section. It is here
that the fragile connection between the sublime original and
the clever offspring is most endangered. . . . Whereas in
Don Quixote, the deathbed recantation is accompanied by
the narrator's reaffirmation of his character's worthiness,
mad or sane, in ***The Female Quixote*** Arabella's shame at her
past is so great as to repudiate all that we found charming.
No one speaks in honor of the childlike heroine now newly
grown-up as Cervantes does of Don Quixote now the ordinary Alonso Quixano. He notes that whether as a knight or
a plain man, Quixote "had always shew'd himself such a good
natur'd man, and of so agreeable a behavior, that he was not
only belov'd by his family, but by every one that knew him."

Charlotte Lennox neglects to praise her sprightly heroine for
the entertainment she has offered along with the vexation.
She does not contradict Arabella's cries about having "trifled
away" her time. The omission is a sin against the very comedy she has so imaginatively engendered from the hearty stock
of Cervantes' incomparable (Fielding's opinion notwithstanding) work. Fortunately, the reader does not require any
justification for the facts of Arabella's life; her quixotic imagination is provocative of a comic pleasure that raises the novel
from the realm of the "historically interesting" to one which
merits the consideration given to works that accurately record, with cheerfulness, the complexity of human nature.
(pp. 75-8)

> *Susan G. Auty, "Fielding's Followers," in her* The
> Comic Spirit of Eighteenth-Century Novels, *Ken-
> nikat Press, 1975, pp. 55-102.*

LELAND E. WARREN   (essay date 1982)

[*In the following excerpt, Warren addresses the significance of
Arabella's romantic fantasies in* The Female Quixote *through
an analysis of conversational conventions as they existed in
male-dominated eighteenth-century English society.*]

> The glory of women is, to make themselves but lit-
> tle talked of: very different from men, who play,
> with an unabashed countenance, upon the great
> theatre of the world, all the parts which the pas-
> sions dispose them to. Women should only act, as
> one may say, behind the curtains: they cannot ap-
> pear upon the stage until particular circumstances
> lead them there.

As a conventional mid-eighteenth-century view of a woman's
proper public life, this passage helps us to see the particular
madness of the Lady Arabella, Charlotte Lennox's ***Female
Quixote.*** Gorging herself on French romances in bad translations, "she was taught to believe, that Love was the ruling
Principle of the World; that every other Passion was subordinate to this; and that it caused all the Happiness and Miseries
of Life. Her Glass, which she often consulted, always showed
her a Form so extremely lovely, that, not finding herself engaged in such Adventures as were common to Heroines in the
Romances she read, she often complained of the Insensibility
of Mankind, upon whom her charms seemed to have so little
Influence." Curing her is difficult, for she has "such a strange
Facility in reconciling every Incident to her own fantastic
Ideas that every new Object added Strength to the fatal Deception she laboured under." Her conduct then exemplifies
an eighteenth-century view of madness. Madmen, Locke
wrote, "err as men do that argue right from wrong principles.
For by the violence of their imaginations, having taken their
fancies for realities, they make right deductions from them.
But Arabella's fantasy, if comic, is potentially more dangerous than such commonly cited cases as those of the man who
wouldn't urinate for fear he would drown the world or of the
man who refused contact with others because he thought
himself made of glass. For Arabella's fantasy is a shareable
one, and the novel's satire on romance could have a point
only because its audience could see romance's false vision as
contagious. The female mind, the novel implies, will all too
easily embrace a fantasy that subverts the role women are expected to play.

But Arabella's story also outlines the conditions of female life
that encourage the production of fantasy. A victim of her fa-

ther's determination to create a paragon who will offset memories of the hopelessly corrupt world that has forced him into a bitter retirement, she is reared in complete isolation. At seventeen, when her story begins, she is beautiful and intelligent, but also mad; for by effectively emptying her life of people and events with which she might have fashioned a self-image, her father has driven her to romances for the materials of such a definition. Convinced that she is a haughty and domineering heroine, Arabella now speaks the fantastic language of romance, establishing a mental dissociation paralleling the physical dissociation forced upon her by a well-meaning father. In his effort to keep out all corruption, her father has also excluded the "weight" of reality that, as we shall see, was thought particularly necessary to keep a woman from derangement.

Miriam Rossiter Small has lamented the "aura of romanticism" that prevents *The Female Quixote* from treating "characters, especially people of fashion . . . more incisively." Of course, the story does read more like a fable than a novel of manners, but there is evidence that Arabella's situation, its causes, and her response to it are grounded in social reality. If Arabella must resort to a ready-made fantasy to find a discourse through which she can shape her life, eighteenth-century women were similarly driven toward isolating modes of speaking by being denied access to the language of public affairs. And the confused motives for the male-dominated world's forcing women toward inert discourse is reflected in the actions of the various male characters in the novel who, intentionally or not, help maintain Arabella's delirium. Finally, this male ambivalence suggests that for the eighteenth century, female discourse was forced to represent an aspect of human speech that was simultaneously desired and despised. Female conversation fascinates because in reaching toward the condition of pure art it offers glimpses of a world free from the confusions of reality. But this fascination is also proof that women's speech must be set apart. Otherwise, we are asked to see, women's ways with words might seduce all speech to the condition of fantasy to which it naturally threatens to sink anyway.

A central irony of Arabella's story is that as she learns not to expect our disenchanted world to provide the kind of adventures necessary for a romantic heroine, she is shown to be a genuine heroine, one whose quality is revealed through the subtle exercise of intelligence and grace in social relationships. "Singular as some of her sentiments" are, we are told, her conversation is "far superior to [that of] most other ladies." People are "charm'd into an Extacy" by her talk and made to forget "her former extravagances" whenever the matter of romances can be avoided. "Disgusted" at the "insipid Discourse" of ladies who talk only of fashion, she is also a worthy intellectual match for the learned divine who finally effects her cure. Glanville, her suitor, realizes that Arabella will make an ideal wife if she can be cured of her one flaw, and we are to see it as being to his credit that even the "downright frenz(ies)" to which her delirium drives her cannot blind him to her essential perfection. Consequently, in hopes that she will cure herself, he indulges her by taking on the "Air of great Distance and Respect" proper to a romantic lover.

Glanville convinces Arabella's father to go along with this game, and both temporarily accept a fantastic inversion by which female dictates to male because Glanville rightly believes that Arabella's apparent madness is in fact the surest

evidence of a superior nature that, once properly directed, will make her the wife he desires. Interestingly enough, the grounds for his belief are best stated in a Johnsonian speech made by Arabella herself:

> . . . I am inclin'd to conceive a greater Hope of a Man, who in the Beginning of his Life is hurry'd away by some evil Habit, than one that fastens on nothing. . . . I am persuaded that Indifference is generally the inseparable Companion of a weak and imperfect Judgment. . . . But certain it is that this lukewarmness of Soul, which sends forth but feeble Desires, sends also but feeble Lights; so that those who are guilty of it, not knowing any thing clearly, cannot fasten on any thing with Perseverance.

This view that the power of desire creates the "light" necessary for a person to know "things(s) clearly" and to "fasten on any thing" raises problems when applied to Arabella, because though she has "fastened on nothing," her mind is the opposite of indifferent. Neither the characters, places, and events nor the values found in romances have any weight in eighteenth-century reality, but Arabella uses these empty counters to articulate a world that mirrors the power of her desire. To adapt Arabella's image, Glanville knows that the matter of her articulation is nothing, but he is drawn to the high degree of desire revealed in its expression.

It has long been argued that Mrs. Lennox blundered in having Arabella finally cured, in Mrs. Barbauld's words, by "the Grave moralizing of a clergyman," that it would have been artistically and didactically better had the heroine "been recovered by the sense of ridicule; by falling into some absurd mistake, or by finding herself . . . the prey of some romantic footman." But if the story's conclusion is, novelistically, a failure, it does seem necessary to the work's effort to show how male idealization of the female helps to enforce isolation. Glanville is not unaware that ridicule might cure his future wife quickly, but what of the side effects?

> Sometimes he fansied Company, and an Acquaintance with the World, would produce the Alteration he wished: Yet he dreaded to see her exposed to Ridicule by her fantastical Behaviour, and become the Jest of Persons who were not possessed of half her Understanding.

This fear of contamination by the world suggests Glanville's belief that the brilliance he perceives in Arabella is in part a function of her separation from a reality that might repress desire.

We might compare Glanville's willingness to indulge Arabella's fantasy lest the shock of ridicule taint her perfection with the comic villainy of one Sir George, who enters as fully as he can into the heroine's beliefs in order to seduce her. Unlike Glanville, who merely refuses to contradict his beloved, Sir George studies to portray himself as a romantic hero by conversing, writing letters, and even constructing an autobiography based upon his hasty review of his object's favorite reading matter. Wishing to confirm Arabella in her madness so that he might possess her physically, Sir George might have been the kind of threat Mrs. Barbauld had in mind, had he been more intelligent. But I would argue that although Sir George is introduced as a foil for Glanville—Glanville sincere, pure, courageous, with honorable intentions toward Arabella; Sir George a devious, lustful, cowardly seducer—they are alike in wishing to delay their common object's awakening. Sir George thinks that awake Arabella will be more capable of resisting his advances; Glanville fears that awake Arabella will not be the woman he loves.

Ronald Paulson has called our attention to parallels between Arabella and Jane Austen's most fascinating characters [see excerpt dated 1967]. Arabella's "madness," he writes, "is related to that special quality of imagination that sets Austen's heroines off from other women in her novels, and the blindness that goes with Arabella's madness is at least analogous to the blind spots in the Elizabeth Bennets and Emma Woodhouses." We are likely to use this perception merely as another way of arguing the quality of Austen's art, an art capable of showing Emma to be both maddeningly blind and worthy of our regard, while a figure like Arabella remains a wooden image with labels. But without denying the evident superiority of Emma as a literary creation, I think there is something to be said for Lennox's dualistic way of drawing Arabella. By separating completely the two sides of her character—the one so fully congruent with society's expectations, the other revealing the character's individual desire—Lennox draws attention to a doubleness that forces itself upon eighteenth-century women. And since Arabella's private vision is confessed to be madness, Lennox has room to express the degree of anger latent in women as a result of the enforced split. The particular form of Arabella's delusion allows her to express anger rather bluntly by encouraging lovers to (probably) futile quests on which she assumes some will die. Patricia Meyer Spacks has cited Lord Kames's observation that "it is not difficult to keep females within bounds; for they are trained to reserve and to suppress their desires." Arabella, of course, has received no such training and continually exceeds the bounds of proper conduct, but it is notable that such a threatening female must be shown as insane. The manual I quoted in opening insists that women are to "reign . . . by insinuating ways," their "character marked by mildness and cheerfulness." Arabella rejects insinuation and rules by command; nor is there mildness or cheerfulness in her tyranny.

But the novel offers much evidence that there is a kind of method in this madness, that Arabella is fending off an inevitable suppression or concealment of the language through which she defines herself. We have already suggested how one of her sane speeches provides a rationale for turning her madness into a sign of special potential, as though the public and private selves do somehow communicate to one another. But most significant are passages equating the end of her delusion with personal oblivion. When Arabella, in an attempt to save the apparently dying Glanville, agrees to "give him permission to love her," Lennox writes, "when that important step is taken, and (the lover's) constancy put to a few years more trial; when he has killed all his Rivals, and rescued her from a thousand Dangers; she at last condescends to reward him with her Hand; and all her Adventures are at an end for the future." Marriage, the end of her adventures, will, Arabella fears, force her to become like the fashionable ladies she sees at Bath: "How mean and contemptible a Figure must a life spent in idle Amusements make in History? Or rather, Art not such Persons always buried in Oblivion, and can any Pen be found who would condescend to record such inconsiderable Actions?"

This passage, like others in the novel, functions both in the account of the heroine's madness and in the novel's satire of contemporary English women. Arabella *is* ridiculous to assume that a life should be ordered by the standards of romancers, but so too are the idle amusements of fashionable ladies contemptible. Such passages point up Arabella's dilemma; she can be someone in a nonexistent world, or she can become like the females she sees around her and be a nobody in the real world. At this point Lennox introduces a Countess to suggest an alternative to either mad heroism or worthless busyness. Unlike the other Bath ladies, the Countess perceives Arabella's inner value and moves to befriend her. Arabella, in turn, recognizes a superior quality in the Countess, and, as we would expect, asks for a narrative of the Countess's adventures.

> The Word Adventure (the Countess replies) carries in it so free and licentious a Sound in the Apprehension of People at this Period of Time, that it can hardly with Propriety be apply'd to those few and natural Incidents which compose the History of a Woman of Honour. And when I tell you . . . that I was born and christen'd, had a useful and proper Education, receiv'd the Address of my Lord—— through the Recommendation of my Parents, and marry'd him with their Consent and my own Inclination, and that since we have liv'd in great Harmony together, I have told you all the material Passages of my Life, which upon Enquiry you will find differ very little from those of other Women of the same Rank, who have a moderate Share of Sense, Prudence and Virtue.

The Countess, of course, foreshadows what Arabella is to become. Intelligent, accomplished, and sensitive to female merit, she is the one woman Arabella encounters who does not immediately offend by her frivolity and whom Arabella could accept as a model. But the bond between them is also based on their ability to share the discourse of romance. While others gape at the inflated greeting Arabella offers, "the Countess who had not forgot the language of Romance, return'd the Compliment in a Strain as heroick as hers." For the Countess's autobiography quoted above is not the whole story; "she herself had when very young, been deep read in Romances; and but for an early Acquaintance with the World, and being directed to other studies, was likely to have been as much a Heroine as Lady Bella." Thus if the Countess is a role model for women and a promising physician for Arabella, she also emphasizes the novel's implication that to the extent a woman has the capacity to rise above the triviality of most women's existence, she becomes susceptible to a discourse of fantasy.

Because the Countess, like Glanville, both sees the basic worth of the enchanted lady and fears the consequence of waking her too abruptly, she decides to enter into Arabella's discourse in order to lead her gradually back to truth, the public discourse. She implies that though heroes and heroines did once exist and that their values and conduct were once appropriate, times have changed. Such adventures as heroines once underwent would today bring "an Imputation on (a lady's) Chastity," and "judging of (heroes) as Christians, we shall find them impious and base, and directly opposite to our present Notion of moral and relative Duties." The Countess's strategy here is to initiate the process of separation between Arabella and her fantasy but to do so in a relatively painless way. Here the world of romance is not fantasy, nothing; it is simply the past. The Countess would hope to have Arabella accept the actual woman's world, the world of the Countess's idealized autobiography, before forcing her to admit the absolute emptiness of the images presented by romance. She would provide a new discourse before taking away the old.

The Female Quixote probably owed much of its original success to its application in a fairly explicit way of two conventional eighteenth-century tenets to the specific condition of young women. First, adolescent females show particularly well the dangers of solitude—"That nurse of private vice, and private woe." If one is not subjected to the world (i.e., other people), he risks the madness of giving himself up to private fantasy. Youth is "the dangerous age" because the young, not yet having had the chance to interact adequately with others to learn the limits reality imposes upon the self, are especially vulnerable; young females, often intentionally shielded from truth, are most vulnerable of all. Second, the novel takes its place in the eighteenth-century attack on or redefinition of the heroic. The Countess's comments on heroes echo a theme outlined in Steele's *The Christian Hero* (1701) and repeated throughout the century; the true hero is one who embodies Christian principles in the mundane affairs of life; the false view of the hero as a self-regarding figure of boundless physical force is evidence only of the continuing seductive power of classical literature. It is particularly important that a young woman learn these two lessons since, seduced by private fantasy, she is likely to embrace a life antithetical to the domestic, unobserved heroism she is expected to undertake.

But I want to emphasize that both of these popular themes are bound up with attitudes toward conversation. (pp. 367-73)

Arabella shows both her innate superiority and her folly through her talk. Those who surround her are continually shocked and dumbfounded at the inflated utterances of our heroine, utterances that make conversation impossible since they allow no sane response, and those who care most for her wish she would simply remain silent. Glanville, in particular, is aware that she illustrates all too well Bordelon's dictum on "The Tongue of Women": "Women would not be so much despised by men, if they did not say so many things that deserve to be despised." But Arabella's talk is not the kind of woman's talk Bordelon had in mind; he refers to the trivial chatter of fashion and parties attacked by social critics of the day and loathed by Arabella herself. On the other hand, it is Arabella's nonromantic speeches that Lennox expects us to see as proof of her character's superior merit. But these Johnsonian speeches that so impress her hearers have little to do with Arabella herself. This is not to say that she is insincere in making them or that Mrs. Lennox doesn't regard them as statements of general truths, but it is the discourse of romance that allows the individual to come alive, just as trivial women's talk, however despised, is the means by which most women around Arabella define themselves. That trivial talk is conversation, albeit at a low level, and serves therefore to maintain and demonstrate the sanity of its participants. But such talk is hateful to Arabella because she sees it as the normal mode of expression for those willing to accept oblivion.

But what choice is open to a woman who rejects the kind of talk for which her sex is ritually condemned? Those who wrote on conversation in the eighteenth century had little doubt that woman's speech was different from man's, though they differed as to whether it was necessarily so. (p. 374)

When reading [eighteenth-century] prescriptions for female conversation, we notice a paradox. On the one hand, women's talk is admired because of its lightness, because it

seems unbound by the harsh realities of daily life that make gaiety difficult for men. But there is also a recognition that those things particularly expected of women—guiding a social conversation in paths that will give pleasure to all and cause no uneasiness, running a domestic establishment smoothly while remaining unnoticed—require great art and a fine understanding of the subtleties of human relationships. Women, then, are allotted two opposed spaces: one quite apart from the realities of life, the other so deeply buried in the most minute details of social and domestic life that they can never touch anything major. Placing women in either space, of course, effectively cuts them off from the arena in which men are to act in running the world. But what such logically discordant positions imply, finally, is that women are simply incomprehensible to those prescribing for them. (p. 376)

But perhaps the most important function of this conversation so carefully set apart from truth or reality is that it implies another discourse. Behind the descriptions of or formulas for women's conversation lurks the implication that women are to talk in their own way in order to help prove that there is another kind of talk, carried on by men, that can engage reality. Women's talk can have a special charm because their words are not hedged in by reality, and since it is the use of language to give pleasure by covering over or diverting the attention from unpleasant reality, women's conversation always partakes of fantasy. Harmless, because it confesses its lack of connection with reality and, delegated to women, never threatens male centers of power, this ideal discourse serves both to point up the gap between the world experienced and the world spoken and to build confidence that masculine discourse, accepting the burden of truth, may close the gap.

Perhaps the most quixotic thing our Female Quixote does is to refuse the role allotted to women and to insist on becoming an active participant in the discourse of truth usually reserved for men. We have already noted the recurrent criticism of Mrs. Lennox for not having Arabella cured by ridicule, and I must confess disappointment at the novel's not allowing the Countess to lead Arabella from her fantasy by a kind of protoanalysis. But by introducing a male authority figure in the person of a "pious and learned" divine who cures Arabella through logical argument, Lennox allows her heroine to confront masculine speech and to force a confession of the tenuousness of its relation with reality.

The clergyman, secure in the "authority of his function," is brought in to convince the young woman by logic of the utter falseness of romances and of their danger to society. At first he too feels the mixed admiration and anxiety in the presence of Arabella: "Tho' he saw much to praise in her Discourse, he was afraid of confirming her obstinacy by Commendation: And tho' he also found much to blame, he dreaded to give Pain to a Delicacy he rever'd." Soon, though, he realizes that Arabella's mind is strong enough to bear his most powerful and bluntest arguments, and that only through such arguments can he hope to sway her. The ensuing dialogue covers various questions about the proper role of narratives in helping us to know the world, all of which will be familiar to those who know Johnson's theories of history and fiction. Though Arabella does not easily give up her convictions, she finally admits that romances carry no truth and that her belief in them has endangered her own life and the lives of others. Her "Heart yields to the Force of Truth," and now aware of the

"Obligations" Glanville's "generous Affection had laid (her) under," she undertakes to become the model wife.

But while it is true that the novel's conclusion shows a re-assertion of the rational male authority temporarily threat-ened by female fantasy, true that Arabella will apparently as-sume a properly unobtrusive role, she does not yield without forcing her mentor to admit the power of her fantasy. Al-though the clergyman gives most of his attention to proving romances absurd fictions, he cannot deny either that they may show a world better than that he would have Arabella accept or that since they may have consequences in his real world they have a kind of reality. He must appeal, finally, to human sympathy:

> It is impossible to read these Tales without lessen-ing part of that Humility, which by preserving in us a Sense of our Alliance with all human nature, keeps us awake to Tenderness and Sympathy, or without impairing that Compassion which is im-planted in us as an Incentive to Acts of Kindness.

The test of romances finally is not whether they describe a true or a desirable world; the question is, do they help to in-volve their readers in the common discourse of society or do they encourage fragmentation by helping each individual to his self-glorifying language? Arabella's romances fail the test badly, urging the reader to imagine herself "a haughty Beau-ty who sits a calm Spectatress of the Ruin and Desolation, Bloodshed and Misery, incited by herself." Fortunately for the clergyman, Arabella does possess that native sympathy whose existence is essential to the case against romance. Oth-erwise she might ask why the vision of woman offered by ro-mance is more insane than the various postures assumed by men in their domination of the public realm.

Though *The Female Quixote* is ostensibly a satire on seven-teenth-century romances, it is, more significantly, a caution-ary tale on the dangers of the self-isolating discourses to which women were thought to be highly susceptible. But Ar-abella's experience and a reading of eighteenth-century books on women's conversation suggest that it was only in such fan-tasies that women could assume the freedom and independ-ence of action that men exercised freely. What's more, if the male determination to see the language of women as only obliquely connected with reality is in part an act of oppres-sion, it is also the result of an idealization that helps to define actuality. The underlying pathos of this comic novel is that, driven to an ideal world by being denied actuality, its heroine must then deny the self she has created in order to be allowed once more a place in actuality. Having shown her potential by mastering one language, she must now deny all meaning to those words. But if, her glory passed, she must now assume the discourse of a wife whose object is to be "always buried in oblivion," her adventures have not been without point. They help us to see that the projection upon women of a weakness for fantasy was an attempt to trace a clear line be-tween an ideal language without content, the language of madness, and the language with which we must confront the world. The hopelessness of such a project can help us under-stand the energy with which it was pursued. In a sense, Ara-bella represents actual women who were sent in spite of them-selves on adventures to the frontier of language. (pp. 377-79)

Leland E. Warren, "Of the Conversation of Women: 'The Female Quixote' and the Dream of Perfec-

tion," in Studies in Eighteenth-Century Culture, *Vol. 11, 1982, pp. 367-80.*

LAURIE LANGBAUER (essay date 1984)

[*In the following excerpt, Langbauer analyzes, from a feminist viewpoint, the conceptual boundaries between the novel and ro-mance she perceives operating in* The Female Quixote.]

Charlotte Lennox's *The Female Quixote: or, the Adventures of Arabella* structures its story on the contrast between the novel and romance. Its heroine, Arabella, is a female qui-xote—a girl so affected by her reading of romances that they seem to have driven her mad. Yet Arabella's excesses of be-havior actually reflect what is wrong with romance. She acts the way she does because she believes in romance and is sim-ply acting out its conventions. Through her, *The Female Qui-xote* shows that romance is excessive fiction, so excessive that *it* is nonsensical, ultimately mad. The silly extravagances of romance that Arabella illustrates are meant as a foil for the novel's strengths.

More than simply providing a contrast to the novel, romance acts as a displacement of the novel's problems. Lennox does not explicitly define her novel against romance. Instead, she condemns romance as specious fiction, and covers up the fic-tiveness of her own form, implying by her blindness to it as a form, that it is real and true. Yet Lennox's equation of ro-mance and fiction attests to a tacit recognition that the prob-lems of romance are the problems of fiction, the novel's as well. By deriding romance, construing it as the realm of ex-cess and nonsense, *The Female Quixote* veils its own excess-es, tries to appear stable and controlled. One way to read Ara-bella's madness is as a danger the novelist wants to displace, the novelist's own hidden danger. What takes Arabella over are the powerful, subversive forces not just of one genre, ro-mance, but of all writing.

Even eighteenth-century critics recognized the female qui-xote's danger was no longer real by the time of Lennox's book, if it ever had been:

> . . .the Satire of the *Female Quixote* [writes Clara Reeve in 1785] seems in great measure to have lost its aim, because at the time it first appeared, the taste for those Romances was extinct, and the books exploded. . . . This book came some thirty or forty years too late. . . . Romances at this time were quite out of fashion, and the press groaned under the weight of Novels, which sprung up like Mushrooms every year [see excerpt above].

Readers had lost their taste for romances: there were no Ara-bellas who would believe in them. For writers, it was a differ-ent story; there were Charlottes (and Claras) whose novels, like mushrooms, needed dead wood out of which to spring. Underlying the novel's covert need for romance as a means of displacement is an even more submerged tension—an at-traction to romance as the very source of writing. Another way to read the mad Arabella is as the novelist's fantasy of wish-fulfillment. She is the ideal reader, completely given over to the sway of the text, attesting to the power of ro-mance, a power the novelist desires for her form too. But be-cause that power resides in "everything we do not under-stand," the novelist is caught in a double-bind; she tries to cast out from her writing exactly that power which she also envies and wishes to usurp.

In the act of casting out, Lennox is drawn into what she rejects. What Lennox sees as the themes and conventions of romance give form to her novel, just as do those she adopts as antidote to them. Margaret Dalziel has suggested that, "unlike Don Quixote, Arabella is also created to be the heroine of a serious love-story, a story with the conventional romantic characters, and the conventional romantic ending" [see excerpt dated 1970]. Ronald Paulson adds: "Mrs. Lennox does not satirize Arabella's romances as much as use this form as a convenient vehicle for introducing romance into the humdrum life of Arabella and her readers" [see excerpt dated 1967]. The novel uses romance to define itself, but the opposition breaks down, and subverts that definition. *The Female Quixote* both mocks and lauds its heroine's quixotism, and the way it ridicules romance actually exposes the attractions of that form. What it locates as romance's problems—the disorder and rigidity of its form, the ambiguities of its language—become its own.

What *The Female Quixote* says about romance is useful because it provides a definition of the novel, one that zeroes in on elements that are troubling because also generative of form and meaning. But romance is troubling in another way as well; it acts as a lightning rod for the anxieties about *gender* at the heart of every depiction of the sexes. Romance has traditionally been considered a woman's form. The novel's very definition of romance echoes the way patriarchy defines women: they are both seen as marginal, the negative of the defining agents. *The Female Quixote*'s derision of Arabella lends extra force to its subordination of romance, for, as a *female* quixote, she is already subordinate—a subordinate character in the novel's social world, a subordinate sign in its formal one.

But Lennox rewrites the conventional derisive association of women and romance. Although she attacks romance for its feminine excesses, she also tries to dissociate it from women by educating Arabella out of it. Yet the novel ultimately shows that women and romance are so bound that separating the two ends the story. It suggests a positive, although wistful, alignment of them—if romance were available to women unmediated, it might be a source of power, and a ground from which they could speak. (pp. 29-31)

Instead of being in control of romance, the novel is drawn into and repeats it. It does so especially in its depiction of Arabella. Although presented as a spoof, she is very much a romance heroine herself. Like them, she is an impossible paragon—"the Perfection of Beauty, Wit, and Virtue." The book actually affirms her identification with romance heroines, that identification imperceptibly taking over from the mockery. At what should be her greatest public disgraces—the Ball and Vauxhall gardens—the ridicule dissolves. Arabella confronts the "design'ed Ridicule of the Whole Assembly," but

> Scarce had the first tumultuous Whisper escap'd the Lips of each Individual, when they found themselves aw'd to Respect by that irresistable Charm in the Person of *Arabella,* which commanded Reverence and Love from all who beheld her.

The tone of the book changes into the same tone it has been belittling before as romantic. Arabella and the crowd are frozen in uneasy, wishful moments—uneasy because the romance within the novel comes out of hiding, wishful because such moments acknowledge a fantasy the novel can't acknowledge elsewhere. In these moments, the line between the novel and romance disappears. Arabella *is* a romance heroine, and receives the respect and obeisance that are a romance heroine's due. (pp. 31-2)

Crucial to the book's depiction of her, and its derision of romance, is its assertion of a natural, sensible Arabella, superior to and distinct from her romantic self. This essential self is not very convincing, however, since the book mostly tells us it exists rather than shows us. Our access to this Arabella, like Glanville's, is supposed to be through her conversation, which, "when it did not turn upon any Incident in her Romances, was perfectly fine, easy, and entertaining." But we get very little of Arabella's conversation that is not romantic, and the little we do get shows an Arabella no more "real" because less literary than the self drawn from romance. The speeches which are to impress us are, if anything, even more artificial—set-pieces modelled on historical writers or moral essays. (pp. 32-3)

Ridicule is the tool the novel uses against Arabella and, through her, romance. During her climactic renunciation of romance, it is only when Arabella recognizes that she can be absurd (and has been in regard to the rules of the debate about romance between her and the Doctor) that her "Heart [can yield] to the Force of Truth," and she can see the absurdity in romance and in her romantic behavior. What convinces her to give up romance is not so much the Doctor's logic as her own shame, and it is later "Reflections on the Absurdity of her past Behaviour, and the Contempt and Ridicule to which she now saw plainly she had exposed herself" which clinch her rehabilitation.

Yet the function of ridicule in this novel is not as simple as it seems. Ridicule seems to be something the book *does;* it holds up Arabella and romance for our laughter and derision. But actually, ridicule is not so much what the book does as what it is *about.* Over the course of the story, we notice that we are not so much laughing at Arabella; we are watching the other characters laughing. Again and again, just at moments when Arabella causes them great uneasiness, they can barely choke back their laughter at her absurdity. This ongoing laugh-track may at first seem like an unsophisticated cue, Lennox telling her readers: laugh here, this is funny. Yet what it does is subtly to change the effect of the laughter. Because the characters laugh first, the author and the readers are slightly dissociated from the ridicule.

Ridicule is set up as an issue, rather than used as a tactic, as something we consider rather than participate in, from the first page, when we learn of Arabella's father's unjustified public disgrace. Ridicule most explicitly stands out as an issue when Arabella lectures about it in her disquisition on raillery. What Arabella says there suggests the way raillery works in this book. She says that

> the Talent of Raillery ought to be born with a Person; no Art can infuse it, and those who endeavour to railly in spite of Nature, will be so far from diverting others, that they will become the Objects of Ridicule themselves.

Although Lennox blunts her statement by imagining some ideal of raillery (which obviously doesn't exist if, as Glanville suggests, *Arabella* is meant to exemplify it), this passage suggests that Lennox recognizes ridicule as tricky and shifting, a form of scapegoating that rebounds on the one who does it. That ridicule can especially be a form of literary scapegoating is affirmed by Glanville, when he accuses Sir George of

> Rail[ing] with premeditated Malice at the *Rambler;* and, for the want of Faults, turn[ing] even its inimitable Beauties into Ridicule; The Language, because it reaches to Perfection, may be called stiff, laboured, and pedantic; the Criticisms, when they let in more Light than your weak Judgment can bear, superficial and ostentatious Glitter; and because those Papers contain the finest System of Ethics yet extant, [you] damn the queer Fellow, for overpropping Virtue.

If, as Glanville suggests, ridicule works to hide the attractions of a literary form, what are the attractions of ridiculed romance?

Perhaps the answer lies in romance's diversion. "Diverting" is the word the novel uses most to describe Arabella's romantic absurdities, and the word suggests not just that they are funny, but that they distract us from something else. The Doctor gives us the key to what we are diverted from when he says about romances, "If they are at any Time read with Safety, [they] owe their Innocence only to their Absurdity." Lennox's mockery of romance allows us to partake of it *innocently* in her novel, to feel at a distance from what is actually the source of our pleasure. What we especially enjoy, the Doctor tells us, is fantasy. The novel projects onto romance all the titillation and wish-fulfillment of fiction:

> But who can forbear to throw away the Story that gives to one Man the Strength of Thousands; that puts Life or Death in a Smile or a Frown; that recounts Labours and Sufferings to which the Powers of Humanity are utterly unequal.

Fielding, in his review of *The Female Quixote* [see excerpt dated 1752], sees the attraction slightly differently:

> [*The Female Quixote*] is indeed a Work of true Humour, and cannot fail of giving a rational, as well as very pleasing, Amusement to a sensible Reader, who will at once be instructed and very highly diverted.

Fielding's emphasis on the rational, sensible, and instructive suggests that what the humor of this novel diverts the reader from acknowledging are the pleasures of the irrational, mocked in the novel as romantic foolery. Figuring fantasy and the irrational as romance, the novel seems safely to encapsulate them, to cast them from itself, while still relying on their attractions.

The novel cannot admit it has such forces in its midst because having them there is dangerous, dangerous because disordering. Disorder is certainly the effect they have had on Arabella. Encountering them in romance has disordered her brain, driven her "out of her senses." . . . Order is what makes Fielding prefer *The Female Quixote* to *Don Quixote* as a response to romance:

> here is a regular Story, which, tho' possibly it is not pursued with that Epic Regularity which would give it the Name of an Action, comes much nearer to that Perfection than the loose unconnected Adventures in *Don Quixote;* of which you may transverse the Order as you please, without any Injury to the whole.

It is not simply that Arabella is out of her senses, but that the irregularities and improbabilities of romance are ravings, "senseless Fictions."

Yet the formal problems of romance are exactly what Lennox worried about most in writing her own novel. Length is what she attacks romance for most effectively (certainly the most quoted scene from the book is the one in which Glanville, to please Arabella, attempts some romances, but "counting the Pages, he was quite terrified at the Number, and could not prevail upon himself to read them." And length is what plagued her most in writing her book. Her letters to Richardson, perhaps not the best advisor in this matter, consult him about the problem: how to fill volumes without being prolix? According to her critics, it is a problem he did not help her resolve. Mrs. Barbauld is one of the first to find *The Female Quixote* "rather spun out too much and not very well wound up." And romance's other formal excesses make their way into the novel. In having Arabella enumerate romances, Lennox goes too far. Arabella conjures up too many characters, cites too many texts, repeats too many similar scenes, so that her recourse to romances ultimately takes away from the *novel's* order, makes *it* digress. In the end, romance splits the book wide open: Lennox's attempts to evict romance are loose-ended—she introduces the Countess only to whisk her away—and ultimately fracturing—the Doctor comes out of nowhere and introduces a chapter that jars with the rest of the story, rather than smoothly resolving it.

That the novel cannot escape from what it casts as the madness of romance is already evident in its own treatment of madness. What the novel shows us is that Arabella's madness is contagious; part of its threat to Glanville is that it will make *him* mad: Arabella's confusion and disorder leave him in confusion and disorder. His perpetual cry is "You will make me mad!" As Glanville's threatened madness shows, to define madness is already in some part to include and reflect it. To repudiate romance is to subject oneself to its essential disorder.

The disorder of romance, its failure to stay within bounds, is one of the ways the novel figures its madness. But another part of romance's madness is just how strictly bound it is. Through Arabella, the novel mocks romance's intricate and unbendable rules. As Ronald Paulson writes: "Quixotism in Arabella means a rigidity of behavior." Arabella's relation to romance is a form of repetition compulsion; she forever re-enacts the same romance conventions in the face of wildly different experiences. Romance's especial madness is that its rules are so rigid and yet so empty: that the novel sets it up as a form without sense becomes clear in Arabella's explanation of its special provinces, love and honor:

> The Empire of Love, said she, like the Empire of Honour, is govern'd by Laws of its own, which have no Dependence upon, or Relation to any other.

It is an empire "dependent upon nothing but itself," and it is that kind of empty relationality the novel attacks. Romance is mad because it elevates rules for their own sake—and, in fact, we see that Arabella is attracted not just to the laws of romance, but to law in any form. It is she who insists upon and dwells upon the laws of disputation in her discussion with the Doctor.

The problem with romance is that it suggests that writing can be made up of non-referential relations, and that rule and form can be attractive in themselves. This is a dangerous suggestion, and Lennox tries to get around it in her own book by foisting it onto romance. Yet what informs this novel is a structure fully as formal as romance's. Lennox's playful treatment of Richardson's *Clarissa* suggests how much the rules of the *novel* are on her mind, and suggests too that the novel is not simply a mirror of the world but, like romance, has rules—conventions . . . Lennox attests to the importance of novelistic convention in her initial plan for Arabella's cure. Duncan Isles has argued that the Countess, whose appearance is such a loose thread in the book's final version, was initially to be the agent of Arabella's cure, and to affect it by having her read *Clarissa*. The conventions of the novel were (perhaps too) explicitly to be the antidote for the conventions of romance.

The novel suggests that language is most at fault in romance: to halt Sir George's romancing, Glanville admonishes, "Pray, Sir *George* . . . lay aside this pompous style," suggesting that romance *is* its style, that one disappears with the other. . . . The novel makes a sharp distinction between its own "plain *English*" and the language of romance, which it establishes as the offender through parody.

The Countess, in reasoning with Arabella, confronts this problem of language:

> Tho' the Natures of Virtue or Vice cannot be changed . . . , yet they may be mistaken; and different Principles, Customs, and Education, may probably change their Names, if not their Natures.

Sophistry is what the Countess is criticizing here, the sophistry of romance, which speciously makes distinctions on the basis of names, not natures. When first presented with Mr. Glanville, Arabella employs romance with such sophism:

> What Lady in Romance ever married the Man that was chose for her? In those Cases the Remonstrances of a Parent are called Persecutions; obstinate Resistance, Constancy and Courage; and an Aptitude to dislike the Person proposed to them, a noble Freedom of Mind which disdains to love or hate by the Caprice of others.

The foundation underlying this kind of irony is the belief that words have easily accessible, stable meanings and are transparently referential to them. One of Lennox's very few discursive footnotes, in fact, objects to romance precisely because it does *not* use language this way:

> This Enigmatical Way of speaking upon such Occasions, is of great Use in the voluminous *French* Romances; since the Doubt and Confusion it is the Cause of, both to the Accus'd and Accuser, gives Rise to a great Number of succeeding Mistakes, and consequently Adventures.

Romance is especially damned because enigmatic language is not just an element of it, but its very source and impetus, the basis for its adventures. And not only does Lennox wish to argue against the uncertainty of language being the foundation for fictional texts, she even suggests that language regulates, brings multiple meanings and erring associations back into line: chiding Arabella for her cockeyed, extravagant notions, the Doctor tells her: "Your Imaginations, Madam . . . are too quick for Language," suggesting the very casting into words will organize and rationalize her fancy. (pp. 33-8)

[The novel attests] to the power of language by attesting to the spoken word. Just as Arabella makes a firm distinction

between being loved and being *told* she is loved, the novel itself also emphasizes the force of talking. Glanville, for instance, is able to counter Arabella's ravings with words of his own, to talk people into believing her sane. Similarly, it is for her words that he depends on the Countess, trusting that "the Conversation of so admirable a Woman would be of the utmost use to *Arabella*." And it is ultimately conversation that cures Arabella—the Doctor talks her out of her delusion at the end. With this thematic recognition of the importance of language to its own story, the novel once again winds up confirming what it has initially criticized as romantic.

The novel buttresses its genre distinctions with gender. It associates the dangers of romance with sins of women, and through this association clinches its derision of the form. Romance's faults—lack of restraint, irrationality, and silliness—are also women's faults. Fielding makes this connection in his review of *The Female Quixote*, where he finds that novel better than Cervantes's because more credible. A woman *would* be drawn into romances:

> as we are to grant in both Performances, that the Head of a very sensible Person is entirely subverted by reading Romances, this Concession seems to me more easy to be granted in the Case of a young Lady than of an old Gentleman. . . . To say Truth, I make no Doubt but that most young Women . . . in the same Situation, and with the same Studies, would be able to make a large Progress in the same Follies.

To Fielding, the strength of *The Female Quixote* is that it tells us something not just about romance or Arabella, but about all women. Genre and gender collapse into each other; by exposing romance, *The Female Quixote* exposes women:

> . . . tho' the Humour of Romance, which is principally ridiculed in this Work, be not at present greatly in fashion in this Kingdom, our Author hath taken such Care throughout her Work to expose all those Vices and Follies in her Sex which are chiefly predominant in Our Days, that it will afford very useful Lessons to all those young Ladies who will peruse it with proper attention.

In fact, what Fielding identifies as its relation to "those Vices and Follies in her Sex" is what expressly underwrites romance as unrealistic and irrational. (pp. 39-40)

The Female Quixote does in part agree with Fielding's reading of it; it equates romance and women's sexuality by focusing on romance's improprieties, emphasizing how romance's wildness offends against sexual decorum. When Arabella asks the Countess to narrate her adventures, the Countess is properly shocked at the romantic term. She answers:

> The Word Adventure carries in it so free and licentious a Sound in the Apprehensions of People at this Period of Time, that it can hardly with Propriety be apply'd to those few and natural Incidents which compose the History of a Woman of Honour.

And the book affirms that the only history or adventures a woman can have are sexual ones: when Arabella *does* hear the adventures of other characters, as she does about Miss Groves from her maid and about people at the ball from Mr. Tinsel, what she hears is scandal. The sharp-eyed Miss Glanville points out that the madness romance has caused in Arabella is definitely sexual. Arabella's romantic behavior is a way of "exposing" herself, of displaying sexual signs. . . . And this sexual madness is seen as particularly dangerous. Although Arabella refrains from going to routs with Miss Glanville, romance prompts her to have routs of her own. She creates a scene in the gardens over a woman disguised as a man:

> Mr. *Glanville* almost mad with Vexation, endeavour'd to get *Arabella* away.
>
> Are you mad, Madam, said he in a Whisper, to make all this Rout about a Prostitute?

While Miss Glanville indulges her sexuality in the carefully controlled world of London parties, the license of romance makes Arabella's indulgences extreme, links her with a prostitute. Her routs are not the consoling, appropriated domestications Miss Glanville enjoys; in Arabella's case, the hint of revolution is now back in the word; it contains the power of overthrow associated with any return of the repressed.

On this level, Lennox accepts the derision of romance; her strategy is to separate Arabella from it, to educate her out of romance and dissociate her from its realm. (pp. 40-1)

Yet, in **The Female Quixote,** the parallel between women and romance is so complete that a woman cannot take herself out of romance without disappearing altogether. The text shows that Arabella's only escape from romance is to stop being a woman. Indeed, Arabella's association with women is tenuous throughout the book: she is really a man's woman. Women are jealous of and reject her; men are attracted and sympathetic. The men view her identification with romance's heroines as something from which they must reclaim her, and that reclamation involves her complete identification with men. We are told that Arabella's romanticism reflects very badly on Glanville; he fears that her absurdity makes *him* ridiculous. Instead of casting light on him, she needs to become sane in order to be his reflection. At the end of the book, Arabella *is* inaugurated into man's realm and becomes indistinguishable from the men in it. She leaves romance by participating in the patriarchal discourse of moral law, and in that discussion loses her voice; her words become literally undistinguishable from those of the Doctor. (pp. 41-2)

And in **The Female Quixote,** there is a price for renouncing romance and acceding to male order. With Arabella's foreswearing of romance and her rehabilitation by the Doctor, the story—abruptly—ends. That the story must end with the end of romance is something the book has consistently foreshadowed. . . . Book Three ends with some words of Arabella's which forecast the end of the novel: explaining the laws of romance to Glanville, Arabella tells him that a heroine puts off marriage about twenty years, for when "she at last condescends to reward him with her Hand . . . all her Adventures are at an End for the future." (pp. 43-4)

The entire novel is about Arabella's conviction that romance is an appropriate sphere for her. The reason it is attractive is because it is empowering, not imprisoning. No matter how much the novel travesties romance, it also presents romance as what gets Arabella out of the boredom and seclusion of her father's house, and when she abandons romance at the conventionally happy ending, she is trapped again, into marriage and submission. Ellen Moers has looked at the association of romance and female power; she suggests that women writers and readers don't see romance as a male prison but as a woman's form, and find in that recognition a source of femi-

nism. It is *male* writers, reacting to the association of women and romance, who have degraded the form, identified its heroines as passive, and erotic in their passivity. Nancy Miller, too, looks at the ways women's fiction rejects the passivity and eroticism conventionally read into them. A repressed content underlies eroticism, a content with all the customary charge and evasiveness of an unconscious desire. Miller sees that content as

> not erotic impulses, but an impulse to power: a fantasy of power that would revise the social grammar in which women are never defined as subjects; a fantasy of power that disdains a sexual exchange in which women can only participate as objects of circulation.

The Female Quixote quite clearly makes fun of romance's emphasis on the erotic. Not so clearly, however, it is compelled by an underlying emphasis on what Miller calls "disdain." Arabella is obsessed with the disdainful ladies, the lordly ladies, of romance not simply because she is obsessed with sex, but because even more deeply she yearns for power. As we have seen with Arabella's routs, the association of women and romance touches on revolution, and it hints at a rebellion of the oppressed as well as the repressed, at women's ambitious as well as erotic fantasies. (pp. 44-5)

Female power is an issue from the opening of the novel—it is the Marquis's loss of power, his disgrace at court and subsequent withdrawal, that allows the story to begin. The Marquis indeed falls "a Sacrifice to . . . Plots," especially to the plot of this novel, which gets its impetus for its story about a woman from this symbolic diminution of male authority, an authority seen as exclusive, as precluding any woman's power. (p. 45)

Lennox weakens the men around Arabella in order to give her strength: Glanville, for example, must sicken in order for Arabella to feel herself powerful enough to risk admitting him as a lover. It is perhaps a measure of Lennox's world that in her book female power can exist only as a delusion; only as long as Arabella sticks to romance and remains blind to reality, can she have her own way. Significantly, to make her abjure this power, Lennox must have Arabella herself eventually sicken. The last scene of the book depicts the invalid Arabella renouncing romance, as the rejuvenated men gather around her bed. But in saying that power resides in delusion, Lennox is indicating what is partly also compensation for women's weakness. Arabella's madness does keep her world in an uproar: a subversive power exists in playing upon the hidden delusions which reside in and undo any seemingly fixed order and logic. (p. 46)

Arabella's romances are an inheritance from her mother. Such an inheritance seems to be an indictment of women; in the innocent retreat the Marquis has tried to provide, corrupt culture and sexuality intrude through the (even absent) mother; it is she who introduces Arabella into the realm of language and convention through the romances she passes down to her daughter. But underlying this indictment is a wistful picture of romance as a women's form, providing a bond between women. The book's depiction of the Countess—Arabella's surrogate mother—grows out of this same longing. When Arabella talks to the Countess, we're surprised to realize that she simply hasn't had anyone she could really *talk* to (which also explains Lucy's importance to her). She and the Countess can understand each other because they have both read romance; it gives them a common language.

In this bond between Arabella and the Countess, Lennox's mockery of romance disappears; for a moment she explicitly values it: Arabella and the Countess, alike because they have read romance, are also alike paragons of virtue. Those outside romance's influence, like Miss Glanville and the women of London, are empty-headed, selfish, and ordinary.

Yet Lennox's positive alignment of women and romance is wistful because she recognizes how tenuous that position is. Her treatment of romance reflects her feelings about the novel's possibilities, and by locating a woman's form in romance, she is placing it in what her form, the novel, cannot admit and casts out. This placement recognizes that women have no real place, and Lennox's novel figures their ostracism repeatedly: women precursors are largely absent—Arabella's mother is dead, the Countess almost immediately leaves her, called away by her own mother's "Indisposition" (from the Latin, the state of placelessness), and the literary precursors Lennox calls on are all male: Young, Richardson, Johnson. And not only are women exiled to romance, but even that possibility, when not derided, is appropriated by patriarchy: when the book opens, the Marquis has taken his wife's romances out of her closet and put them in his library; the writers of romance, Calprenade and Scudery, are men; even though Lennox herself makes up a romance in this novel, she puts it into the mouth of Sir George.

The Female Quixote needs romance to set itself up as a novel, but, when prodded, romance deconstructs and merges into the novel. Gender categories in the book are just as shifting and soluble. The novel uses romance to try to stabilize gender—in romance, women are beautiful and men are brave—but the world of the novel shows that formula is too simple. (pp. 47-8)

[Romance's] effect on Arabella's sexual image is contradictory. On the one hand, it goes against what is seen as the very essence of woman: silent, submissive, invisible. Arabella believes instead that a lady's reputation depends "upon the Noise and Bustle she makes in the World." But on the other hand, it makes her especially womanly, not just because it allows her to play up her sexual attractions, but because its influence distinguishes her as the best of women.

Whether Lennox is emphasizing the link between romance and women's sexuality or romance and women's power, the structural parallel between romance and women remains. Each is the name for qualities the status quo finds transgressive and threatening, and attempts to dispel by projecting into a separate genre or gender. By doing so, the novel or patriarchy shores up its stability, emphasizes its boundaries—romance and women are in the no-novel's no-man's land outside; their very exile is what gives the others shape. Yet such distinctions are consoling fictions. What *The Female Quixote* ultimately shows us is not what romance is and how the novel differs from it, or what woman is and how patriarchy is opposed to her. When we try to pinpoint romance or woman we are left empty-handed; what remains basic to them is only that they stand for whatever the defining agent rejects or taboos. They highlight the ways it is divided from itself, and unsettle and fascinate it in consequence. (p. 49)

Laurie Langbauer, "Romance Revised: Charlotte Lennox's 'The Female Quixote'," in Novel: A Forum on Fiction, *Vol. 18, No. 1, Fall, 1984, pp. 29-49.*

DALE SPENDER   (essay date 1986)

[In the following excerpt from her study of women writers before Jane Austen, Spender argues that Lennox's place among eighteenth-century English women novelists has been underestimated.]

By 1755, Charlotte Lennox 'was one of the most famous and highly praised writers in London', and to my mind her reputation was well deserved. I am impressed by her literary achievement but I am also fascinated by the way she fits into the female tradition, for in the writing of Charlotte Lennox we have one of the 'links in the chain'.

When Charlotte Lennox is placed in context—with Aphra Behn and Delarivière Manley before, and with Fanny Burney, Maria Edgeworth and Jane Austen yet to come—when she is placed alongside Eliza Haywood, we can see her writing helping to form part of that 'continuum' of women's writing to which Elaine Showalter referred. In the work of Charlotte Lennox we find some of the vigour of Aphra Behn, the barbed wit and the bathos of Delarivière Manley, and the plot pace of Penelope Aubin; we find some of the seeds that will bloom in the writing of Fanny Burney, Maria Edgeworth and Jane Austen. And we can see that *The Life of Harriot Stuart* shares much in common with [Eliza Haywood's] *The History of Betsy Thoughtless* which was published not long afterwards.

Harriot Stuart is another lively young woman but she has the added romantic dimensions of 'New World' vivacity and 'New World' adventures. (Charlotte Lennox's account of the Indians, and the dangers, parallels those of her predecessor, Aphra Behn, in *Oroonoko,* and of course gave rise to comparable scepticism about the veracity of the writer.) Harriot is careless; in such a new country it is relatively easy to neglect some of the 'old forms' but there is a price to be paid for such negligence: Harriot's actions are often misconstrued as she flirts and fancies and flaunts some of the most cherished social practices of the day, including those of being a docile and dutiful daughter. Harriot is not quite so 'thoughtless' as Betsy, but she is definitely more determined. And although, like Evelina (who was to make her appearance almost thirty years later) (*Evelina,* Fanny Burney, 1778), Harriot too learns from experience, she has few of the sober and reflective qualities that were to stand Evelina in such good stead when that young lady made her entrance into the world.

But Harriot is a warm and likeable (as distinct from admirable) character, and as with many of the other heroines in the writing of Charlotte Lennox, there can be no doubting her authenticity. One critic, Philippe Séjourné, has been struck by this. While I am always suspicious of claims which would have a particular woman as 'the first' in any field of literary endeavour (because it is often nothing other than evidence that their predecessors have been forgotten or ignored), in terms of today's realism, there is some justification for Philippe Séjourné's stand that in *Harriot Stuart* we have the first real portrayal of a woman, by a woman:

> Harriot herself, like Eliza Haywood's Betsy Thoughtless the same year, is drawn with considerable art. As readers we are carried along because of her compelling personality. Fielding's Sophia, Richardson's Pamela and Clarissa were men's creations but she is one of the first portraits by a woman, and she is so convincing, in spite of all the incredible elements in the novel, that we may go one step further and ask ourselves whether this is

not one of the first, if not the first self portrait of a woman in fiction?

As Harriot Stuart did precede Betsy Thoughtless, it may well be that it is Harriot rather than Betsy who should take pride of place in the gallery of women characters who embody some of the experiences of their creators. But it is not an essential exercise—and perhaps not even a useful exercise—to attempt to establish who was 'the first'. I am cautious about accepting such assertions. Not just because I have not read *all* Eliza Haywood's earlier novels (I do not even pretend to know whether I am aware of *all* her earlier novels), or because I have not read *all* of the novels by other women who preceded her, but because to insist on Charlotte Lennox as the first woman writer to present a self-portrait, is to overlook the contribution of Delarivière Manley in *Rivella,* to put aside Cynthia and Octavia in the writing of Sarah Fielding, and to ignore the 'personal' dimensions in women's letter writing and epistolary novels from the Duchess of Newcastle to Mary Davys.

Whether Charlotte Lennox is even the first novelist of North America is in a sense a 'side-issue'. . . . It is more important to establish the cross-links in women's literary tradition than to establish a series of starting posts.

And with Charlotte Lennox there are many links to be found between her work and that of other women writers. There is the link with Susanna Rowson and Frances Brooke who wrote about the New World—from firsthand experience. There is the link with Frances Sheridan who wrote about women's disillusionment with marriage—from firsthand experience. In 1761, Frances Sheridan's *Memoirs of Miss Sidney Biddulph* appeared and in this three-volume novel we have a heroine who marries to please her mother and who lives to regret her choice of husband. Charlotte Lennox declared her indebtedness to Frances Sheridan's literary contribution, and in her own novel, *Euphemia* we are presented with a plot which has its parallels with *Miss Biddulph* for Euphemia, too, marries to please her mother rather than herself, and both heroines find themselves tested to their limits by the stupid and boorish behaviour of their husbands.

But it would be possible to make too much of this link. It could be that for very many middle class girls, the practice of pleasing a mother and of gaining a dreadful husband was a common one indeed. If both Frances Sheridan and Charlotte Lennox were concerned to portray some of the realities of women's lives, the similarities in their novels might well be no more than an understandable coincidence.

It is neither *Harriot Stuart* nor *Euphemia,* however, on which I would want to base the case for Charlotte Lennox's achievement: while both are good, they are nevertheless surpassed by *The Female Quixote.* In this novel Charlotte Lennox writes a 'romance' in which she mocks romance, and not only are her characters well drawn but her style is satirically comical and her structure distinctly clever. The novel has been criticised for its unevenness—some sections are considered too long and some too short—and although there are some grounds for complaint there are also extenuating circumstances (Charlotte Lennox was very much at the mercy of her publisher and her own pressing financial needs), and overall, I do not think that the so-called unevenness detracts from her considerable achievement. (pp. 199-202)

There are some excruciatingly embarrassing yet comic scenes when Arabella banishes for life a man who pays her a compli-

ment, when she is convinced that she is the cause of some poor man's death because she has spoken harshly to him, when she believes that the highwaymen who hold her up are noble courtiers—in disguise, of course. The reader cannot help but feel frustration with Arabella's inability to put two and two together in the 'real' world. Because she makes sense of the world in such an unconventional way she repeatedly makes herself very vulnerable as she enters upon the most 'ludicrous' mistakes—as is the case when she attends a race meeting and transforms it in her own terms into an Olympic Games of old, where the jockeys are riding for the favours of women.

But with all her faults, Arabella is more than endearing. This is partly because Charlotte Lennox is able to cultivate such empathy with her heroine that there are few problems with 'identification' and the reader becomes distressed with Arabella's continued 'perversity'. When will she discover the error of her ways and see the true worth of Mr. Glanville—and live happily ever after? She pushes his patience so far, she comes so close to losing him for he is at his wit's end what to do with her when so many of his schemes for disavowing her of her romanticism fail to have the desired effect.

There are serious concerns in the novel as well. There is of course the issue of what constitutes a good education and the question of how far fiction can corrupt young minds. But more important, as far as I am concerned, is the exploration of the nature of *reality;* what is it, how is it acquired, how does it work? How can human beings construct such different views of the world from the same evidence?

Charlotte Lennox raises so many fascinating psychological issues which are the subtext throughout the novel, and which give it an added dimension. Yet surprisingly, virtually no one has commented on this aspect of *The Female Quixote,* which is for me one of its most salient and intriguing features. Even in contemporary times it still serves as a remarkable 'case study' on the vagaries of the human mind. I found the novel marvellously satisfying at a variety of levels—for its satire, its humour, its tensions, and its insights into the human condition. It is astonishing that this novel, which has no peer in the works of Daniel Defoe, Henry Fielding or Samuel Richardson, should not be part of our literary heritage, although admittedly it might benefit from some abridgment.

So when Henry Fielding, Samuel Richardson and Dr Johnson declare that Charlotte Lennox is a genius, that her work is original, provocative, and psychologically penetrating, and that she is a great writer, I have no difficulty accepting their judgment [see excerpts dated 1751 and 1752]. I would rate her in much the same terms myself.

That all her work is not of the same calibre as *The Female Quixote* does not detract from its excellence, and perhaps if she had enjoyed greater financial resources and stability, Charlotte Lennox would have gone on to write more novels on a par with *The Female Quixote.* But as it was, she was always pushed for money and she pushed her pen accordingly. (pp. 202-03)

Her literary skills were many and varied and by any standards other than those used by 'the men of letters', Charlotte Lennox would be ranked among the great and influential writers of the eighteenth century. She should be granted unchallenged status as one of the mothers of the novel. Her eclipse constitutes a significant gap, not just in the literary traditions of women, but in the cultural heritage of society.

It is wearying to be obliged to record . . . that Charlotte Lennox's reputation owes more to the commentary on the lives of Henry Fielding, Samuel Richardson and Dr Johnson—and the way in which her boisterous and boyish American manners won them to her cause—than it does to her writing. And the literary tradition would be enriched not simply by the inclusion of Charlotte Lennox but by the exclusion of such gratuitous and irrelevant insult which all too frequently substitutes for criticism of the woman writer. Without the distraction of the consideration of her merits as a woman we would be free to concentrate on her merits as a writer—and to grant her a distinguished role in the rise of the novel. (pp. 204-05)

Dale Spender, "Charlotte Lennox and North America," in her Mothers of the Novel: 100 Good Women Writers before Jane Austen, *Pandora Press, 1986, pp. 194-205.*

JANE SPENCER (essay date 1986)

[*In the following excerpt, Spencer shows how Arabella's projection of an imaginary romance world onto a male-dominated society finally vindicates her lofty ideals, making her a virtuous heroine who retains her individuality by writing her own history.*]

No-one understood the appeal of romance better than Charlotte Lennox, whose novel *The Female Quixote; or, the Adventures of Arabella* is an analysis of romance as a fantasy of female power. Like its model, *Don Quixote,* it has a protagonist captivated by the visions of romance and comically blind to the real world. The difference is that the romances which have deluded Arabella are the seventeenth-century French romances with their pictures of the romantic heroine's absolute power over her lovers. Arabella's story is thus closely related to the reformed coquette tradition. Like the coquette, she is reluctant to give up the woman's power in the courtship game; and also like the coquette, she has a lover-mentor who tries to guide her into a more realistic frame of mind. Realism for Arabella, as for Amoranda or Betsy Thoughtless, means giving up the illusion of power and accepting the proper, subordinate role of the young woman in society. In the didactic tradition to which all these novels belong, there is a connection between the anti-romantic and the anti-feminist elements.

Arabella, brought up in the country by her widowed father, has seen nothing of the world, and she believes that the romances she reads are reflections of life. Her entry into wider society, in Bath and later in London, provides opportunities for satirical contrast between her ideals and reality, in which fashionable society is Lennox's target as much as romantic illusion. Eventually Arabella, cured of her delusions, marries her cousin Glanville, who has been patiently waiting for her to come to terms with the real world.

Comedy in *The Female Quixote* is generated by Arabella's application of the expectations, moral standards and elevated diction of the French romances to the incidents of everyday life. When one of her father's gardeners is caught trying to steal fish from the pond, Arabella insists on believing him to be a young nobleman in disguise, trying to drown himself out of hopeless love for her. When a young gentleman rides towards her with perfectly innocent intentions, she accuses him of trying to abduct her. The comedy has its serious side, as Lennox indicates the moral dangers in Arabella's attitude.

Quixotism leads the heroine not to the sexual 'ruin' that anti-romantic moralists predicted for female readers, but to a perversion of her naturally likeable personality. Centring all her thoughts on her imaginary vision of herself, she loses all touch with the real feelings of the people around her. Believing it to be a fatal necessity that heroines' beauty must kill, she contemplates with serenity the supposed deaths of rejected lovers, or Glanville's risking his life in a duel, and when Glanville is dangerously ill of a fever she imperiously commands him to live. To her, his illness 'is no more than what all do suffer, who are possessed of a violent Passion; and few Lovers ever arrive to the Possession of their Mistresses, without being several times brought almost to their Graves'. (pp. 187-88)

Lennox handles Arabella throughout with a sympathy the self-centred heroine may seem at first not to deserve. We can understand and share this sympathy if we examine how Lennox portrays Arabella's preposterous imaginary world as her refuge from a reality that deprives women of power. Arabella's belief in the despotic power of her charms makes up to her for her lack of power in real life. In fact, she is the obedient daughter of a man who keeps her in isolation. Going to church is a privilege that the Marquis 'sometimes allow[s] her', and an occasional ride in the countryside attended by servants is described as 'the only Diversion she was allowed, or ever experienced'. Her notion of her power over her lovers comes up against her father's mundane plans for her marriage. He recommends her as a suitable wife to her cousin Glanville, and expects the courtship to take 'a few Weeks'. Arabella is attracted towards her cousin, but she expects years of silent devotion before a proposal. While she is still unsure whether she ought to grant him the favour of walking alone with her, he, to her horror, declares his love. Her ideas about a heroine's prerogative and a lover's duties are challenged at every turn. When she is offended with Glanville, she orders him out of the house, but her father makes her write and ask him back again. Her claim that Glanville has performed none of the services required of a hero in romances meets her father's insistence on reality. 'What Stuff is this you talk of? . . . I perceive you have no real Objection to make to him', he tells her.

Male-centred reality keeps on imposing itself on Arabella's feminocentric fictions. When Glanville learns that Arabella's notions are taken from romances about the distant past, he dismisses them, assuring her that 'The World is quite different to what it was in those Days'. As he courts Arabella, he posits unheroic, male-dominated modernity against 'the illustrious Heroines of Antiquity'. Romances, in his view, 'contradicted the known Facts in History, and assign'd the most ridiculous Causes for Things of the greatest Importance'. He asserts the primacy of the masculine realm of politics and war, 'Things of the greatest Importance', and derides the notion that they are governed by the feminine influence of love. He tries to lead Arabella from feminine 'error' to masculine 'truth'.

When Arabella does give up her illusions, she gives up her power. There is nothing left for her to do but accept Glanville and submit to real life. Lennox makes it clear that this will be far less exciting than the fictions she has used to challenge it. The reality she is going to have to come to terms with is described by the benevolent Countess, who, trying to argue

Arabella out of her romantic obsession, presents her own calm, uneventful life as a model of female experience:

> when I tell you . . . that I was born and christen'd, had a useful and proper Education, receiv'd the Addresses of my Lord—through the Recommendation of my Parents, and marry'd him with their Consents and my own Inclination, and that since we have liv'd in great Harmony together, I have told you all the material Passages of my Life, which upon Enquiry you will find differ very little from those of other Women of the same Rank, who have a moderate Share of Sense, Prudence and Virtue.

In effect, the Countess is telling Arabella (and by implication every woman) not to be a heroine. This smooth ideal of a woman's life is disrupted not only in Arabella's romances but in every eighteenth-century novel which centres on the heroine. Whether deprived of parents and guardians or persecuted by them, whether she defies authority to marry the man of her choice or becomes a martyr to duty, the young woman in the novel becomes a heroine only by departing from this uneventful norm: otherwise there would be nothing to say about her.

Of course the ideal woman in eighteenth-century society is the woman about whom there is nothing to say. Deluded Arabella thinks that a heroine's good reputation depends on the 'Noise and Bustle she makes in the World', but she has to learn a woman's best fame is to be unknown. In eighteenth-century parlance the very word *adventures* in connection with a woman implies a loss of virtue. In Arabella's romance-world, a heroine's adventures mean abductions, disguises, and escapes, none of which derogate at all from her honour; but in reality, the Countess tells her, a woman's adventures can only be illicit sexual relations: 'The Word Adventures carries in it so free and licentious a Sound in the Apprehensions of People at this Period of Time, that it can hardly with Propriety be apply'd to those few and natural Incidents which compose the History of a Woman of Honour. To retain her virtue, Arabella must relinquish her adventures: but as we can see from the subtitle of the novel, **The Adventures of Arabella,** this means giving up the story of her life and her identity as heroine. The Countess's advice to Arabella implies the most extreme anti-feminist attitude to women's fictions: any woman whose life is eventful enough to be the subject of romance has compromised feminine virtue. The ideals offered to Arabella are silence, anonymity, and the end of the story—or rather, no story at all.

But that ideal cannot possibly be attained in a novel. Arabella *is* a heroine and she does have a story. Like Don Quixote, she has heroic as well as ridiculous qualities: in contrast to the vanity and spite of the fashionable young lady Miss Glanville, Arabella's idealism appears in a positive light.

Like Don Quixote, too, she has some power to impose her romantic visions on the real world. She turns Glanville's courtship into something closer to the long-term devotion required in romance than to the business-like few weeks projected by her father. When Glanville realizes that Arabella is modelling herself on the romance heroine, he knows that 'the Oddity of her Humour would throw innumerable Difficulties in his Way, before he should be able to obtain her', and being really in love with her, he rises to the challenge. For all his intention of weaning her from her romantic follies he finds himself acting the part of a romantic hero, and though at first this is an assumed role, it tends to come closer and closer to

the reality of his feelings, and we soon learn that 'he stood in such Awe of her, and dreaded so much another Banishment, that he did not dare, otherwise than by distant Hints, to mention his Passion'. Here, Lennox parodies the terms of romance, but her hero is beginning to take them seriously.

Glanville's endeavours to guide Arabella towards truth lead him deeper into romantic fiction. When they are out riding together, Arabella sees a former admirer, who, she believes, is trying to kidnap her. She wants to know if Glanville is brave enough to defend her. He almost loses his temper as he tells her that no-one is trying to harm her, but when Arabella rides away, and the supposed kidnapper jokes that she is 'fit for a Mad-house', Glanville fights with the man for insulting her. Arabella has the gratification of seeing her lover literally (though luckily not fatally) shed blood in her defence. . . . Arabella relinquishes her role as heroine, but not until she is sure of love from a man who offers all the devotion of a hero.

The Female Quixote is not only a satire on Arabella's adventures, it is the story of her actual courtship and marriage, and she is necessarily at the centre of it. The novel has some of the same kind of appeal as the romance it mocks. At one point, Arabella promises Miss Glanville her story:

> another time, you shall know my History; which will explain many things you seem to be surprised at, at present.
>
> Your History, said Miss *Glanville!* Why, will you write your own History then?
>
> I shall not write it, said *Arabella;* tho', questionless, it will be written after my Death.
>
> And must I wait till then for it, resumed Miss *Glanville,* gaily?
>
> No, no, interrupted *Arabella:* I mean to gratify your Curiosity sooner; but it will not be yet a good time; and, haply, not till you have acquainted me with yours.
>
> Mine! said Miss *Glanville:* It would not be worth your hearing; for really I have nothing to tell, that would make an History.

Miss Glanville, like the Countess's sensible young woman, has no history; but as readers we can see that this is because she is insipid and unheroic. Arabella, on the other hand, is a heroine and her history, of course, has been written as she anticipates. Therefore she is an example that a woman can be essentially virtuous and yet escape the anonymity the Countess advocates. Despite Lennox's conservative moral view, **The Female Quixote** with its romance appeal gives its virtuous woman power, importance and a history. (pp. 188-92)

> Jane Spencer, "Romance Heroines: The Tradition of Escape," in her The Rise of the Woman Novelist: From Aphra Behn to Jane Austen, *Basil Blackwell, 1986, pp. 181-212.*

JAMES J. LYNCH   (essay date 1987)

[*In the following excerpt, Lynch investigates how elements of realism and the narrative conventions of romance combine in* The Female Quixote *to produce a "displaced romance form."*]

Charlotte Lennox's **The Female Quixote,** like Cervantes' *Don*

Quixote, pre-supposes that romance distorts truth and that the dangers of such distortions can be exposed by placing a character who is deluded by romance into a fictionally real world. Lennox's principal concern is to ridicule heroic romances in the same way Cervantes ridiculed chivalric romances. What is more interesting about the novel, however, is that the realistic plot, by which Lennox exposes the unreality of heroic romances, itself employs many of the same narrative conventions that had become clichés in the heroic novels. Lennox's novel demonstrates that the codes of behavior conventional to eighteenth-century realism are not all that far removed from the romance behavior which most eighteenth-century novelists condemn as improbable.

Like any imitator of *Don Quixote,* Lennox creates two kinds of fiction: the "romance" world of quixotic delusion and the "real" world in which those delusions are set. "Romance" in this context refers to those literary works, such as chivalric novels and heroic novels, which, to use Clara Reeve's distinction between romance and the novel, describe "in lofty language . . . what never happened or is likely to happen." Romance opposes a more realistic kind of fiction whose primary assumption, again to quote Reeve, "is to represent every scene in so easy and natural a manner and to make them appear so probable as to deceive us into a persuasion (at least while we are reading) that all is real, until we are affected by the joys or distresses of the person in the story as if they were our own." Reeve's definition emphasizes what perhaps needs no emphasis—that even a fictionally real world is a rhetorical manipulation that causes readers to identify with the characters and thus participate in the characters' turmoils. It is important to keep this fact in mind because the fictionally real world that exposes romance improbability is essentially different in Lennox's and Cervantes' novels. Whereas Cervantes merely asks the reader to witness Alonso Quijano's delusions, Lennox asks the reader to enter into a fictional world that is suggestive of realism, yet is largely a sentimental displacement of the romance world.

In Cervantes' attack on chivalric romances, the fictionally real world is primarily low mimetic. That is, it is a world in which windmills are merely windmills, sheep merely sheep, wine-bags merely wine-bags, and delusion merely delusion. The inserted tales of Cardenio and Dorothea and of Fernando and Lucinda do suggest romance assumptions, and, indeed, the Canon of Toledo does outline an ideal way of writing romance so that it delights and instructs as poetry does. Yet the narrative frame Cervantes uses owes its allegiance to history, to empirical truth.

The fictionally real world of *The Female Quixote* also owes its allegiance to empirical truth, but it is essentially different from the framework of Cervantes' novel. In *Don Quixote,* Quijano's delusions provide the principal source of complication and thus dictate the structure of the novel. A middle-aged man is deluded by romances; his delusions come into conflict with the real world; and eventually he is returned to sanity. Lennox uses the same formula in her novel. However, the fictionally real plot is complicated not only by the absurdities of a young woman's befuddlement with heroic romance, but also by complications conventional to eighteenth-century sentimental novels. This "realism" may be regarded as a displacement of romance because it is predicated on the assumption, common to many eighteenth-century novels, that ideal happiness can be found by lovers who, though separated by contingent circumstances, will find their reward in

the conventional reunion and marriage. Because Lennox is ridiculing the peculiar fascination that female readers, such as Arabella, had for the heroic romances, one might assume that the displaced romance is merely another form of female fantasy. While I shall point out parallels between Arabella's fascination with romance and that of female readers of contemporary paperback romances, I contend that that displaced romance in *The Female Quixote* is more the product of accepted practices of eighteenth-century sentimentalism than it is the product of a female novelist pretending to attack romance while at once preserving its fantasy.

In Lennox's novel, the realistic story line—what I call the displaced romance—exhibits qualities typical of the sentimental novel: the love of a hero and a rival (the one motivated by true affection, the other by greed) for a heroine who, although initially swayed by appearances, eventually recognizes the hero's true heart. Henry Fielding, in his review of *The Female Quixote* in *The Covent-Garden Journal,* is evidently attracted to the qualities of displaced romance in the novel [see excerpt dated 1752]. He notes that it is "more interesting" than Cervantes' novel, for it engages "our hearts . . . very early in good Wishes for the Success" of the hero. Undoubtedly, the love story also prompted Fielding to observe that Lennox's novel, unlike Cervantes', has a "regular Story."

In a typical sentimental novel of the eighteenth century, narrative interest is not so much centered on the hero's physical prowess or on his military glory as it is in the heroic novels. Rather, it focuses on the hero's capacity for faithful love. The form of such a novel thus differs from the romance form in that it focuses on internal worth rather than heroic triumph. It concentrates our interest on the heroine's initial resistance to a character whom we know is suitable for her (because of our omniscience and our rhetorical expectations of such a plot). Suspense in the sentimental novel tradition arises from the consequences of a hero or a heroine's failure to see the other's true heart. Thus conventionally there are not the same kind of dramatic conflicts characteristic of the "adventures" in romance fiction. Setting aside the complications arising from Lennox's imitation of *Don Quixote,* the plot of *The Female Quixote* depends upon the heroine's inability to see the "sensible" worth of the hero: his generosity, faithful love, and good nature. Because Glanville tries valiantly to convince Arabella of his worth, he is tested as much as any character in the heroic romances.

Ironically, the complications of the realistic story line in *The Female Quixote* involve the very act of reading romances. Because of her infatuation with romance, Arabella misreads the desirable qualities evident to us in Glanville's character. She mistakes the trappings and clichés of glorified romance behavior for the inner qualities which these stylistic tropes signify. Her quixotism is to impose the language of love and honor that she has learned from La Calprenède and Scudéry upon a hero who measures up to the substance but not the style of her expectations. The conflicts in the novel are thus semantic confusions that are ultimately resolved when Arabella is able to "read" properly Glanville's behavior and that of his duplicitous rival, Sir George. Lennox thus advocates a fictional world in which the qualities of love and fidelity—made into clichés in the heroic novel—find a more realistic though no less ideal, mode of expression.

Unlike Don Quixote's, Arabella's sallies are closet adventures, created by ironic, though logically consistent, misreadings of fact as fancy. One of her first adventures illustrates the method. In book I, chapter 7, Arabella supposes that Edward, the head gardener's servant, is a disguised nobleman secretly in love with her. The narrator's description establishes the facts that Arabella misreads:

> he had a good Face; was tolerably genteel; and, having an Understanding something above his Condition, join'd to a great deal of *secondhand* Politeness, which he had contracted while he lived at London, he appeared a very extraordinary Person among the Rustics who were his Fellow-Servants.

Although the only features that distinguished Edward from Arabella's more countrified servants are the manners he acquired as a servant in more urban surroundings, Arabella interprets these distinctions as signs of a mysterious romance birth:

> His Person and Air had something, she thought, very distinguishing. When she condescended to speak to him about any Business he was employed in, she took Notice, that his Answers were framed in a Language vastly superior to his Condition; and the Respect he paid her had quite another Air from that of the awkward Civility of the other Servants.

Since she presupposes she is a romance heroine, it is easy for her to imagine that Edward, like an Oroodates or an Artamènes, must be a romance lover:

> Having discerned so many Marks of his Birth far from being mean, she easily passed from an Opinion that he was a Gentleman, to a Belief that he was something more; and every new Sight of him adding Strength to her Suspicions, she remained, in a little time, perfectly convinced that he was a Person of Quality, who, disguised in the Habit of a Gardener, had introduced himself into her Father's Service, in order to have an Opportunity of declaring a Passion to her, which must certainly be great, since it had forced him to assume an Appearance so unworthy of his noble Extraction.

Once Arabella has translated Edward into a disguised lover, she is able to translate the reality of his actions into romance behavior. She attributes his awkwardness as a gardener, for instance, not to inexperience or to ineptitude (more likely reasons), but to his disguised nobility and secret passion for her. More absurdly, she sees his frustrated attempt to poach carp from the estate's pond as heroic sighs of pining love, and when he is caught in the act of poaching, she assumes that he was going to drown himself in heroic despair. (pp. 51-4)

All of Arabella's later quixotic actions depend upon the same ironic confusion of fact and fancy established in this early episode. Because she supposes that her life is guided by the same principles as the heroic romances, she imagines that no character enters her life coincidentally. This simple irony makes her absurd to all the fictionally real characters she encounters. When those characters begin to complicate the fictionally real plot, however, the simple irony becomes complex.

Although Arabella's adventures are probable, it is important to note that the very basis for the fictionally real plot owes much to the romance tradition. Arabella is raised, for example, in a secluded "Castle" which her father purchased after political intrigues forced his removal from Court. Her seclusion and ignorance of contemporary life lend probability to her quixotic misreadings, but they also provide fertile grounds for romance adventures. She is as far removed from contemporary society as the heroines of La Calprenède's and

Scudéry's novels were from seventeenth-century society. Thus, when her father introduces Glanville as a prospective match, her isolation from society causes her to suppose he is one of a type with such characters as Artamènes, who enter the protected worlds of heroines and fall desperately in love with them. Later, when Glanville's rival, Sir George Bellmour, appears on the scene, he quickly recognizes Arabella's madness and pretends to be the kind of heroic suitor he assumes to be the norm. Sir George's duplicity contrasts Glanville's honesty and sets in motion a conflict between false and true honor that parallels the conflict between romance and realism. Arabella's quixotism thus not only confuses fact and fancy, but it also creates complications in the fictionally real plot that can be resolved only by straightening out the imagined romance dilemma first.

To make matters even more complex, Lennox arranges the story in such a way as to create potential conflicts that could exist both in the most outlandish romances and the most probable eighteenth-century novels. When Arabella's father dies, for example, he makes Glanville's father, Sir Charles, the heroine's guardian and stipulates that, should Arabella choose not to marry Glanville, Glanville will inherit a portion of his estate. This twist sets up the potential conflict of parental tyranny, common both to romances and to contemporary novels such as *Tom Jones* and *Clarissa*. Although Glanville actually is the best possible husband for the heroine (unlike those suitors whom tyrannical fathers or guardians impose on romance heroines), the potential shape of the conflict nevertheless prompts Arabella to doubt Glanville's love. Her scorn sets up the principal narrative obstacle Glanville must overcome.

Arabella's infatuation with heroic romances implicitly invites a psychological interpretation of her character. In this regard, Janice A. Radway's recent study of the psychological and sociological functions of contemporary Harlequin and Silhouette romances provides an interesting paradigm for Arabella's reading habits. Radway argues that contemporary paperback romances fulfill "certain basic psychological needs for women that have been induced by culture and its social structures, but that often remain unmet in day-to-day existence as the result of concomitant restrictions on female activity." The romances compensate women in two ways: (1) "by prompting identification between the reader and a fictional heroine whose identity as a woman is always confirmed by the romantic and sexual attentions of an ideal male"; (2) by filling "a woman's mental world with the varied details of simulated travel." Arabella recognizes the improbability of romances at various points in the novel, yet, like the women Radway studied, she still insists on their autonomous reality. She thus finds in the works of La Calprenède and Scudéry a utopian fantasy that allows her to escape from her day-to-day existence and to act out fears that are the consequence of her role as a daughter and woman in the realistic world. The ever-present violence in the heroic novels perhaps even permits her to act out a revenge fantasy in which she, identifying with a heroine, manages to bring the hero grovelling to his knees in abject love for her.

Arabella's vicarious desire to imagine that her world is identical with the romance world constitutes a desire to be transported from an isolated and disappointing environment. Her father has immured himself and his family into a remote castle to protect himself from court politics. Arabella's fantasies about heroes who inevitably triumph in a supremely masculine way thus enact for the daughter the conflicts which her father has avoided. More strikingly, Arabella's mother died shortly after Arabella's birth, thus not only depriving the heroine of maternal nurturance, but also causing her to be educated solely by her "grave and melancholy" father. Notably, the romances Arabella soon grows to love had been purchased by her mother "to soften a Solitude which she found very disagreeable." Her father, true to the Cervantine convention, eventually wants to burn these books.

Like the women in Radway's study and like her own mother, Arabella seeks to escape solitude by reading romances. More strikingly, however, her longing for adventures manifests unexpressed fears about her own future. Although her father attempts to cultivate her learning, it becomes apparent that she must marry in terms set forth by the prevailing patriarchal culture. Notably, she is seventeen when her adventures begin. Her father's introducing Glanville as a suitor places her father in a role similar to the tyrannical father of romance who attempts to force his daughter to marry a convenient—and, in the romances, altogether unsuitable—prospect. This suggestion of conventional parental tyranny, in fact, is sustained even after Arabella's father dies. Sir Charles Glanville, the hero's father, becomes the heroine's guardian, thus doubling the potential threat. Even though Sir Charles has no desire to impose his will otherwise than Arabella wishes it, the latent fear of superior masculine authority undoubtedly exists.

We must keep in mind, of course, that unlike Radway's readers, Arabella is fictional. Nevertheless, romances function for her in much the same way as they do in the case study of actual female readers. Seeking a romance fantasy allows Arabella at once to act out her fears and, ultimately, to control her imagined destiny. Indeed, more often than not, Arabella imitates those heroines who cause their suitors to undertake elaborate exploits to prove their love. In this respect, Arabella wishes to uncover both the worth of her prospective husband and her own worth as a woman capable of inspiring love.

The operation of this psychological attempt both to encounter and control her own unexpressed fears is particularly evident immediately after Glanville first declares his love for her—in plain language, not the exalted language she wishes to hear. Speculating, contrary to what we know to be true, that Glanville might rape her or that her father might force Glanville upon her, Arabella contemplates escape. In doing so, however, she must mentally rewrite romance convention to suit her particular anxieties:

> The Want of a Precedent, indeed, for an Action of this Nature, held her for a few Moments in Suspense; for she did not remember to have read of any Heroine that voluntarily left her Father's House, however persecuted she might be; but she considered, that there was not any of the Ladies in Romances, in the same Circumstances with herself who was without a favoured Lover, for whose sake it might have been believed she had made an Elopement, which would have been highly prejudicial to her Glory; and, as there was no Foundation for any Suspicion of that Kind in her Case, she thought there was nothing to hinder her from withdrawing from a tyrannical Exertion of parental Authority, and the secret Machinations of a Lover, whose Aim was to take away her Liberty, either by obliging her to marry him, or making her a Prisoner.

Since there is no "favoured Lover" to whom she might escape, her romances fail her. But her desire to escape, if only

from imagined tyranny, is real. It is a fear of marriage itself and the consequent loss of "Liberty" and subjection to another.

However irrelevant it may seem to impute modern psychology to Arabella's romance reading, the suggestion that she identifies with a romance heroine's archetypal struggles is important to an understanding of the displaced romance plot in *The Female Quixote.* In this plot, Glanville unwittingly and Sir George quite overtly act out romance incidents that ultimately teach Arabella to "read" realistic characters as probingly as she has read the romances.

In terms of the realistic plot, Glanville is a sentimental lover whose desire for Arabella is honorable (a fact confirmed by his persistence even after the terms of her father's will are revealed). Although he is illiterate in romances and fails miserably when the heroine attempts to correct his education by assigning a lengthy passage from the *Cassandre,* he soon learns to detect when Arabella is riding her hobby-horse and when she is not. Indeed, despite her extravagancies, he admires her for her sentimental qualities, the "Elegance and Simplicity of Manners" and the "Benevolence of Heart" that set her apart from other women.

Sir George, on the other hand, epitomizes the hypocrisy of modern gentility. Interested in Arabella only for her money, he feeds her vanity by letting her assume that her romance fancies are real. His ready knowledge of romance literature underscores his duplicity and contrasts him with Glanville who, though unschooled in romance, nevertheless possesses the honor and fidelity that are made into clichés by the French heroic romances. As if to underscore Sir George's duplicity and Arabella's quixotism, Lennox adds a further complication by introducing Miss Glanville, the hero's sister, as a rival for Sir George's affection. Miss Glanville, in her own quixotic way, misinterprets George's behavior towards Arabella as affection for herself: she thinks he ridicules Arabella to endear himself to her. Indeed, Sir George plays fast and loose with Miss Glanville in order to keep in contact with Arabella.

Notably, Sir George's manipulation of the language of heroic love causes two different sets of complications: (1) it urges Arabella to draw further conclusions based on the premise that romances depict real life; (2) it sets up realistic conflicts between him and Glanville that eventually force Glanville to play the role of a romance hero against his better judgment. Shortly after Sir George first meets the heroine and discovers her romance hobby-horse, for example, he feeds her quixotic vanity by speaking in the hyperbolic manner of a heroic lover:

> If he walked with her in the Gardens, he would observe, that the Flowers, which were before languishing and pale, bloomed with fresh Beauty at her Approach; that the Sun shined out with double Brightness, to exceed, if possible, the Lustre of her Eyes; and that the Wind, fond of kissing her celestial Countenance, played with her Hair; and by gentle Murmurs, declared it Happiness.

The hyperboles reconfirm Arabella's belief in romance language and thereby provide a framework for her to make further logical deductions based on this false language.

Later, her romance deductions lead to a series of episodes in which Glanville's love and patience are tested and in which Sir George's duplicity is exposed. Despite Glanville's ability to recognize when Arabella is riding her hobby-horse, he be-

A frontispiece from an eighteenth-century edition of The Female Quixote.

comes jealous of Sir George and, in the final book of the novel, nearly kills him. The reality of this act finally awakens Arabella from her dream world and restores order to the semantic disorder she created.

To understand how the realistic plot resembles episodes in romance, we need to examine a sequence of events that begins about midway through the novel. During one of her short-lived periods of sanity, Arabella participates in a hunt with Glanville, Sir George, and others. While Glanville and Arabella are alone, the heroine sees a man, Mr. Hervey, who had played a role in one of Arabella's earlier closet adventures. Presupposing that Hervey's presence at this point could be no mere coincidence, she supposes he is going to ravish her and thus urges Glanville to do battle with him while she rides off to get help. In the interim, Glanville nearly falls to blows with Hervey because that gentleman teased Glanville about her eccentricities. When Arabella returns, with Sir George and the others, Glanville and the ravisher have disappeared. Glanville had returned home in shame and frustration at having been nearly swept up in Arabella's madness. Arabella, however, deduces that Glanville must have set off on a heroic quest in order to punish Hervey. Her misreading of facts allows Sir George to embellish his own role:

Mr. Glanville is already so happy in your Opinion, said Sir George, with a very profound Sigh, that there is no need of his rendering you this small Service, to increase your Esteem: But, if my Prayers are heard, the Punishment of your Ravisher will be reserved for a Person less fortunate, indeed, than Mr. Glanville, tho' not less devoted to your Interest, and concerned in your Preservation.

Sir George's litotical "less fortunate" and "not less devoted" perfectly accords with the indirectness of romance rhetoric. Yet, although Sir George is skilled at romance hyperbole, his attempt at the complementary rhetorical device, litotes, is less successful. Arabella interprets his studied indirectness as a direct avowal of love and is naturally offended.

The offense Arabella imagines at Sir George's behavior precipitates quixotic episodes that first create semantic confusions for Glanville and his father and then actually prompt Sir George to contrive an embellished recital of his own adventures. The episode is worth recounting, for it shows how extensively the romance confusions affect realistic conflicts.

It begins with Sir Charles's reaction to Sir George's behavior towards Arabella. He witnessed the offense Arabella took, even though he did not hear what Sir George said. Taking his role as Arabella's guardian too seriously, Sir Charles thus vows to redress the wrong. Arabella, however, infers that her guardian's zeal is actually an indirect expression of his own love for her, and she accordingly scorns him as well. Even after Sir Charles is satisfied that Bellmour has committed no real harm, Arabella continues to think of Sir Charles as an unwelcome suitor. This confusion is enhanced by the exigencies of the realistic plot. Impatient that Arabella and Glanville's relationship is at a stand still, Sir Charles makes it his mission to convince Arabella to marry his son. Yet because he is unwilling to become a tyrannical guardian, he speaks indirectly, hinting what he expects she already knows: that he wishes her to marry Glanville. Indirectness, however, is so much a part of Arabella's twisted romance logic that she supposes he is making further overtures of his love. This confusion is cleared up when Glanville, whom Arabella now sees as a treacherous accomplice of his father, makes sense of Arabella's misreading. Ironically, though, the episode is not finished until Arabella commands Sir Charles to be silent about his passion and he, in order to curb his anger, remains silent—an indirectness prompted by rage not convention.

The resolution of the subplot momentarily sets both the romance and the fictionally real plots on an even keel, but Sir George, in order to press his suit for Arabella's hand, quickly initiates another romance deception. From this point on, the realistic plot—the conflict between Sir George and Glanville—will be controlled by the rival's ability to manipulate romance appearances. Almost in spite of Arabella's quixotism, Sir George's deception forces Glanville to act as a heroic lover. At the end of book IV, for example, he writes Arabella a letter in which he tells her he intends to die as a punishment for his presuming to love her. Sir George's letter prompts Arabella to conclude that she must visit the apparently despairing suitor and, with all her imagined power as a romance heroine, command him to live. When Glanville learns of this he becomes enraged and acts, in the heroine's eyes, according to the fiery temper of La Calprenède's Orontes. If she insists on going to Sir George, he tells her, he will die at her feet! Thus, in trying to reason with Arabella on her own terms, Glanville becomes entrapped into romance cliché The episode is resolved harmlessly enough by Arabella's decision to write rather than visit Sir George, but when Sir George reappears and tries to play the role of a pining suitor, he and Glanville nearly come to blows because the hero thinks Sir George is again mocking Arabella.

From this point in the novel onward, Sir George's manipulation of romance cliché becomes a source of complications in the realistic plot. Shortly after Sir George's feigned suicidal despair, he attempts to rectify his romance stature in Arabella's eyes by reciting the history of his own adventures. His recital, which itself mocks the absurdity of interpolated stories in romances, quickens complications of the realistic plot in two ways. First, it encourages Miss Glanville to interpret Sir George's tale as a mockery of Arabella and thus a further indication of his affection for her. Second, the recital itself backfires. In order to get Arabella to perceive him as a heroic lover, he spins a gloriously improbable tale about his love for a lady to whom he was betrothed but who was abducted by a rival. Attempting to gain Arabella's pity, he notes that he has searched for her at great length and finally given up in despair. Instead of pity—a quality more realistic in a sentimental novel—Sir George earns scorn. Arabella clings to the improbable logic of romance and condemns him for not continuing his search, or for at least not dying in despair. If there is poetic justice in a novel that attacks literature where poetic justice is a prerequisite, Sir George's comeuppance is poetically just, for the end of his history forces him to remove himself from Arabella's presence or live with her scorn.

It is precisely this unofficial exile from Arabella that precipitates the final conflicts of the realistic plot. In the final book of the novel, Sir George creates yet another fictional romance episode by which he hopes to discredit Glanville in the same way he discredited himself. The episode occurs when the heroine, Glanville, and his sister are staying near Richmond after Arabella found the realities of London unsuitable for romance. Sir George arranges for a woman, assuming the name Cynecia, to recite her adventures to Arabella in conventional romance fashion. Cynecia tells of her love for Ariamènes, who, in order to win her hand has set forth on a heroic conquest with hopes of proving, as Artamènes did in the *Grand Cyrus,* that he is worthy of her. Cynecia's story once again convinces Arabella of the reality of romances and, indeed, feeds her vanity by providing her with an audience to whom she might recite her own adventures. When Arabella does so and confesses, in the indirect fashion of a romance hero, that she "does not hate Glanville," Cynecia reveals that Glanville is none other than Ariamènes.

Eventually, Sir George's contrivance backfires, just as his own recital did, but ironically it fails because Glanville becomes more and more like a romance hero. The ruse causes Glanville to be like Artamènes and scores of other romance heroes who are unjustly accused of infidelity as a result of a rival's malice. Correctly supposing that Sir George has initiated the confusion, he remains secluded in the house at Richmond, even after she commands him to remove himself. Meanwhile, she sets off across the Thames to Twickenham in order to search for Cynecia. There she quixotically misperceives a group of horsemen as ravishers and nearly drowns herself by trying to swim across the river to escape them, just as the heroine of Scudéry's *Clélie* swam across the Tiber. In the meantime, Miss Glanville discovers that Sir George has secretly arrived at Richmond. Deducing that his intention is to see Arabella, Miss Glanville dresses up in Arabella's clothing and meets Sir George in the garden. When Glanville, un-

aware of Arabella's absence, sees a female form in Arabella's eccentric costume and supposes it to be Arabella, he rushes out, sword in hand, and wounds Sir George. The romance ruse is thus foiled by displaced romance behavior.

Arabella's irrational behavior in attempting to swim the Thames results from her belief that she could perform a feat as improbable as one in romance. Glanville's behavior, however, results from a different, although no less irrational source. Letting his heart get the better of his head, he attempts to be Arabella's heroic champion and, as a result, nearly commits murder. His action demonstrates the proximity of heroic and sentimental codes of honor. Caught up in conventions that he accepts as fact, just as Arabella is caught up in romance conventions, he thus behaves in a way analogous to one of Arabella's romance figures.

Eventually, Arabella is cured of her madness, just as Don Quixote was cured of his, but the reality to which she returns is still a modified romance world. Indeed, Lennox seems to be suggesting that what is wrong with Arabella's imagination is not that she seeks escape into a fictional world, but that the kind of fiction she escapes to is wrongheaded. In the penultimate chapter of the novel, the heroine debates with a doctor of divinity whether heroic novels are false, absurd, and harmful. He convinces her that the works from which she has taken so much delight and instruction portray patent falseness as truth and encourage readers to expect love to be heroic and therefore fatal. When the doctor convinces her that events she thought requisite for heroic behavior lead, in real life, to bloodshed, she realizes how far the stylized portrayal of these events in romances led her astray from reason.

Significantly enough, the doctor does not condemn all fiction. He recommends the work of "an admirable Writer of our own Time," identified in Lennox's footnote as Samuel Richardson, who "has found a way to convey the most solid Instructions, the noblest Sentiments, and the most exalted Piety, in the pleasing Dress of a Novel." It is no coincidence that Richardson should be accorded such praise, since he offered Lennox encouragement and advice as she composed the novel [see excerpt dated 1751]. Yet, even without the influence of a prominent novelist, it is clear that Lennox has been advocating throughout that truth may take on "the pleasing Dress of a Novel."

Thus recalled from the language of fancy back to the language of sentimental fact, Arabella is able to recognize Sir George's deceptiveness and to see actualized in Glanville the love, devotion, and sensibility she thought possible only in romancified forms. True to romance and sentimental conventions, the heroine marries Glanville, and Sir George, "entangled in his own Artifices," marries Miss Glanville. This dual marriage points out what seems to be Lennox's final comment on the conventions of romance and realism. The marriage of Sir George and Miss Glanville clearly belongs to the realistic world; they are "married," according to Lennox, "only . . . in the common Acceptation of the Word; that is they were privileged to join Fortunes, Equipages, Titles, and Expence." Glanville and Arabella, on the other hand, were united "as well as in these, as in every Virtue and laudable Affection of the Mind." Their union celebrates the ideals of sentimentalism and in so doing implies a displaced romance form that, while donning the "pleasing Dress of a Novel," inevitably transcends the merely realistic. (pp. 54-61)

James J. Lynch, "Romance and Realism in Char-

lotte Lennox's 'The Female Quixote'," in Essays in
Literature, *Vol. 14, No. 1, Spring, 1987, pp. 51-63.*

MARGARET ANNE DOODY   (essay date 1987)

[*In the following excerpt, Doody reappraises, from a feminist
viewpoint, the critical acuity of* Shakespear Illustrated.]

In the past two centuries, the view of **Shakespear Illustrated**
has been largely negative—a view the more readily taken because of an increasing Shakespeare idolatry since the Romantic age. It has been customary to believe that Lennox's remarks exhibit a personal lack of literary insight, and that her
dullness is complicated by an unfortunate cultural manifestation of an outdated aesthetic. For instance, Thomas R.
Lounsbury, professor of English at Yale in 1901, sarcastically
found Lennox suffering the "unhappy fate" of being "born at
the wrong time": "She missed her century. Had she flourished in the period immediately following the Restoration,
she would have found herself in a far more congenial
atmosphere. . . . Had she in addition become Mrs. Rymer,
the conjunction of these two stars . . . would have attracted
the attention of observers for all time" [see excerpt dated
1901]. More recently, in 1935, Charlotte Lennox's biographer, Miriam Rossiter Small, also dismissed Lennox's judgments as mistaken and embarrassing:

> Having finished the drudgery of finding and pre-
> senting the sources, the lady unfortunately wished
> to express her own opinions, and profited by her
> hours of toil to display all the erudition of which
> she could make herself mistress. Having concen-
> trated upon the plots almost entirely, she naturally
> tended to regard only the plots of Shakespeare's
> plays. Therefore, arming herself with the pseudo-
> classical standards of Probability, Decorum, and
> Poetical Justice, Mrs. Lennox advanced upon the
> plays of Shakespeare. Dire were the results of her
> invasion to her reputation as a Shakespearean critic
> and a judge of true values.

An inferior critic, a mere "lady" advancing on Shakespeare,
a lady who, moreover, adheres blindly to mistaken old "pseu-
do-classical" standards—this is the author of **Shakespear Illustrated** according to one kind of judgment. There is no need
for us to accept that judgment. In our own period, when critics like Janet Adelman, Janice Jardine, and Coppelia Kahn
have also advanced upon the plays of Shakespeare, and when
Shakespeare seems to us, as to Lennox, not such a repository
of pure "true values" as to be above social and psychosexual
criticism, the work of Lennox may seem fresh and interesting. I believe that something of importance—of importance
to the eighteenth century and to ourselves—is at issue in Lennox's Shakespeare criticism, and that a consideration of the
kind of criticism contained in the "Critical Remarks" can explain Lennox's motives in going through the "drudgery" of
producing the sources. Lennox's critical comments also illustrate her other works for us; her remarks on Shakespeare's
plays cast a direct light upon her best-known novel, *The Female Quixote.* (p. 297)

For a while, in the later seventeenth century, it had seemed
that romances, read avidly by men and women alike, supplied
a common and large-scale world of literary reference where
women could be at home. Katherine Philips not only gave
herself a romantic name ("Orinda") and thus a *persona*
speaking out of the heart of romance, she also gave her
friends new romance names. The "real world" could be as-

similated to that other one which gives the woman authority
and poetic presence. Women's poetry, including that of the
pious Elizabeth Rowe, is decorated with innumerable pastoral Myrtillos and Amaryllises, the classically-rooted florets of
romance. Women could hope that this public and conventional poetic tradition might be acceptable. Women writers
did not adopt these romance elements merely as a matter of
strategy. The romantic mode was for them the available public language and form which might convey private experience. They borrowed from it even when their writing was not
public—as in the case of Mrs. Delany's autobiography. When
in the 1740s Mrs. Delany (née Mary Granville) began to tell
the story of her early life to her friend, the Duchess of Port-
land, she did so in a series of letters encoded in the terms of
the romance. The romance was of great importance because
it allegorized every woman's life for her.

But by the middle of the eighteenth century any writer of intelligence and ambition had to realize that other frames of
reference and other modes of thinking had gained control.
Romance and romance codes would not do any more—
romance had gone out, and with it women's whole literary
experience for two generations. The new ethos was satiric and
classical, public and authoritative—the Augustan modes and
manners were much harder for women to maneuver in. *The
Female Quixote* brings these matters into the open. It is the
best comic novel by an Englishwoman before Burney and
Austen, and its effectivenes is related to the importance of its
subject and the tensions within it. It exhibits the conflicts between Romance and Augustan reality, between an older
world and modern times, and between feminine and masculine views and experience. The heroine, Arabella, finds that
her view of the world and the way in which she wishes to
order that world are helpless against the male and modern
powers. The books formerly purchased by her mother to assuage loneliness represent the only inheritance from her
mother, and these fictions prove of no avail. Like most heroines in novels by women, Arabella is in an ironic relationship
to the mother and to the female inheritance which customari-
ly proves a trap as well as a bond. In the conflict staged between Romance and the feminine tradition on the one hand
and Augustan views and masculine authority on the other,
the "wrong side" represented by Arabella is doomed from the
start.

Arabella is, however, destined to gain the reader's sympathy.
The heroine is wrong but romantic; the victorious characters
and views are in a sense always right but—if not repulsive—
at least dull. The heroine is not inferior to the men she
meets—she merely believes that her feminine tradition is
true. She has a sense of history, even if the history she has
learned is called false. There is something dreadfully stodgy
about the real world which Arabella is told she should enter,
and where she should know her place. This real world is simply a realm where she has no power. She does not, for instance, have the right to command men away by a significant
gesture, as her heroines do. The author may even subtly stress
the bitterness of the story's message, its realization. There is
a cold shudder in the center of the novel when the Countess
explains to Arabella that nice women never have adventures
or histories. "The Word Adventures carries in it so free and
licentious a Sound . . . at this Period of Time, that it can
hardly with Propriety be apply'd to those few and natural Incidents which compose the History of a Woman of Honour."
This is something the adventurous poet Harriot Stuart would
never have believed. Charlotte Lennox did not want to be-

lieve it—and still, I think, felt that this dull middle-class complacency which is the timid Augustan's notion of realism was horribly false. But a truth had to be faced: that women's tradition, their lore and language, are all considered false and must be given up. The good if unimaginative hero and the good clergymen do their Augustan work on Arabella—that is, the author does her in, assisted by Dr. Johnson, who is commonly supposed to have written the remarks of the clergyman that convert the heroine to right thinking. Parts of the conversion conversation sound like the most melancholy brainwashing, the removal of excitement: "He cannot carry you to any of these dreadful Places, because there is no such Castle, Desert, Cavern, or Lake."

The comedy of this novel, like all good comedies, arises from serious tensions and conflicts. The novel is a hidden drama of relinquishment, of bidding farewell to poetic hopes—the author's hopes, not just Arabella's. There can be no more Delias and Damons, no more tempest-tossed Harriots. Women's old literary tradition, essentially the Romance tradition, has been shown up as false—or perhaps just declared to be false and foolish. The modern men have a knack of not reading the texts that would explain Romance to them: "For Heaven's sake, Cousin, resumed *Arabella,* laughing, how have you spent your Time; and to what Studies have you devoted all your Hours, that you could find none to spare for the Perusal of Books from which all useful Knowledge may be drawn?"

Arabella gives her cousin and admirer, Mr. Glanville, some romances to read, but though he pretends obedience, he will not attempt the texts: "counting the Pages, he was quite terrified at the Number, and could not prevail upon himself to read them: Therefore, glancing them over, he pretended to be deeply engaged in reading, when, in Reality, he was contemplating the surprising Effect these Books had produced in the Mind of his Cousin." But, we might ask, how can Glanville contemplate the effects without any real knowledge of the cause? He refuses such knowledge, for these antiquated romances (standing for a past age and also for the feminine tradition) are beneath him. In the discussion or examination that ensues, Glanville tries to lie and finesse, pretending to know what he does not know, but he gives himself away:

> This unlucky Question immediately informed *Arabella,* that she had been all this time the Dupe of her Cousin; who, if he had read a single Page, would have known that *Orontes* and *Oroondates* was the same Person. . . .
>
> The Shame and Rage she conceived at so glaring a proof of his Disrespect . . . were so great, that she could not find words severe enough to express her Resentment.

The satire here is not altogether against Arabella. Do people read or know the kind of stories they condemn? Later, Arabella encounters Sir George, who really has read romances, as he proves when, in order to impress her and gain her favor, he invents his own story with glib efficiency. In making up his romance about himself, however, Sir George shows that he never got the point, never understood women's place (or Woman's place) in the romance. Arabella, incensed at his tale of errant infidelity, rebukes him:

> your suffering so tamely the Loss of this last Beauty, and allowing her to remain in the Hands of her Ravisher, while you permit another Affection to take Possession of your Soul, is such an Outrage to all Truth and Constancy, that you deserve to be

ranked among the falsest of Mankind. . . . looking upon myself, as dishonoured by those often prostituted Vows you have offered me, I am to tell you, that I am highly disobliged; and forbid you to appear in my Presence again, till you have resumed those Thoughts, which are worthy your noble Extraction; and are capable of treating me with that Respect, that is my Due.

> Saying this, she . . . walked very majestically out of the Room, leaving Sir *George* overwhelmed with Shame and Vexation at having conducted the latter Part of his Narration so ill.

It seems no accident that Lennox's next work is the **Shakespear Illustrated,** which deals at length with the reading and use of romances and novels. It is quite evident that Lennox and Dr. Johnson have different views as to the precise nature of the book. Johnson wrote the "Dedication" to Lord Orrery, as from the pen of Charlotte Lennox herself.

> How much the Translation of the following Novels will add to the Reputation of *Shakespear,* or take away from it, You, my Lord . . . must now determine. Some Danger, as I am informed, there is, lest his Admirers should think him injured, by this Attempt, and clamour as at the Diminution of the Honour of the Nation. . . .
>
> That no such Enemies may arise against me . . . I am far from being too confident, for who can fix Bounds to Bigotry and Folly? My *Sex,* my *Age,* have not given me many Opportunities of mingling in the World; there may be in it many a Species of Absurdity which I have never seen, and among them such Vanity as pleases itself with false Praise bestowed on another, and such Superstition as worships Idols, without supposing them to be Gods.

Johnson rests his case on the soundness of truth; we should acknowledge the facts, not pretend that Shakespeare was utterly original—nor even, in plotting, very inventive. But Johnson (masquerading as Lennox) in this dedication confidently claims that it scarcely matters; Shakespeare's reputation cannot really be diminished by our discovery of mere sources of plot. "*Shakespear's* Excellence is not the Fiction of a Tale, but the Representation of Life; and his Reputation is therefore safe, till Human Nature shall be changed."

There is a great disjunction between Johnson's dedication and Lennox's text. Lennox in her own true voice gives us no assurances. She insists that plot does matter, that it is intimately related to the way characters are handled and to their significance. Over and over again, she finds fault with Shakespeare's handling of the "Fiction of a Tale." As far as she is concerned, his reputation is not safe, but rather abides our question. Lennox, I believe, is really carrying the war into the enemy camp by turning not on a poor weak deluded Arabella, a safe target of mockery, but on the highest idol now enshrined in the English Augustan pantheon; she turns also on the safe and assured Augustan readers—genteel and fashionable readers—who take admiration of Shakespeare now for granted.

It is part of Lennox's point that Shakespeare read romances and novels. Charlotte Ramsay's own reading in girlhood had evidently consisted of an enormous number of romances and novellas. Margaret Dalziel, editor of the Oxford English Novels edition of **The Female Quixote,** sees nothing in that work but a cheerful rational burlesque of what is obviously absurd, and even concludes from this "onslaught on the romances" that Lennox "has no sympathy with the changing views which were to lead to the publication . . . of . . . Bishop Hurd's *Letters on Chivalry and Romance* . . . and which were to lead later writers . . . to stress the ennobling influence of romances. Mrs. Lennox's attitude is typical of the earlier rather than the latter half of the eighteenth century" [see excerpt dated 1970]. That is, her editor faults Lennox for being, in her best work, rather too Augustan. This is not a helpful reading of the novel. It never seems to occur to Dalziel to wonder how the author came to know so many romances so well. She seems to believe Charlotte Lennox "mugged up" the subject for the sake of the satire, rather than comprehending that such an extensive and detailed treatment speaks of long acquaintance with the genre. It seems likely that Lennox had read, as well as the romances of Scudéry and her contemporaries, some of the many translations of novellas such as those by Cinthio or Boccaccio or Bandello. She evidently noticed very early that Shakespeare too had read romances, and her own reading served a scholarly purpose in turning her in that direction. She is, in her critical book, making a point of the fact. Shakespeare—the safe, the idolized Shakespeare—had been guilty of reading what were in effect romances, and, really, of writing them. Lennox turns the tables in showing that the English author now thought of as most admirable had dealt in what was most (unjustly) despised in the new age. At the same time, Shakespeare fails to meet either the demands of the new Augustan criterion—originality—or the standards of moral and emotional honesty set by the romances.

I believe we can hear in **Shakespear Illustrated** the sound of two axes being ground. First, Lennox is writing as romance-reader and romance-writer—and as novel reader. She is a defender of romance and novels, willing to listen attentively to what the original artist in narrative fiction was trying to do. Unlike her contemporaries, who are content with insulting the sources when they notice them, and passing on, she will try to make us read them, as Arabella tried to make Glanville read Scudéry. It seems to Charlotte Lennox that Shakespeare (like his modern adulators) is guilty of the same fault as the male characters in **The Female Quixote**—he reads romances and stories wrongly, inefficiently, without full comprehension. And when he tries to re-work them, he usually bungles the matter. "It has been mentioned as a great Praise to *Shakespear* that the old paltry Story of *Dorastus* and *Fawnia* served him for a Winter's Tale, but if we compare the Conduct of the Incidents in the Play with the paltry Story on which it is founded, we shall find the Original much less absurd and ridiculous."

The phrase "old paltry Story" evidently aroused Lennox's wrath and contempt. Later we discover that the phrase is derived from Hanmer's condescending remark, which Lennox attacks after having done her own demolition job on Shakespeare's use of the story. In criticizing Shakespeare, Lennox invokes not only the new standard of originality, but also the older Augustan criteria of probability and decorum, as well as "poetical justice." The author who did not worry slavishly about realistic probabilities in designing **Harriot Stuart** here makes herself into an ultra-Augustan, turning against the literary hero the sort of phrases so often and so conveniently used to attack romances and the modern novel (idle and improbable romances, absurd novels). Lennox keeps reminding her readers that if these are the criteria, Shakespeare, for all

our idolatry, fails the tests over and over again, doing worse in fact than the romance writer, as in *The Winter's Tale:*

> The extravagant Effects of the King's Rage and Jealousy are carried far enough in all Conscience in the Novel, and *Shakespear* is not a Whit more moderate; only he has altered a Circumstance which entirely destroys the little Probability the Novelist had preserved in the Relation. . . .
>
> *Shakespear* makes the King in the Heighth of his Frenzy of Jealousy send himself to the Oracle of Apollo, and in the mean time commit the most barbarous Cruelties on his Queen and Child. How inconsistent is this! . . . The Request comes very naturally from the Queen in the Novel, and the King's Compliance with it is very well accounted for, but in the Play nothing can be more absurd than that the King should be reasonable enough to consult voluntarily the Gods concerning the Infidelity of his Wife; and while the Answer was expected, and her Guilt yet doubtful, punish her with as much Rigour as if the Oracle had declared her an Adultress. Here again the paltry Story has the Advantage of the Play.

And lastly, what about the effect of the closing scene?

> The Novel makes the Wife of the jealous King die through Affliction for the Loss of her Son; *Shakespear* seems to have preserved her alive for the sake of her representing her own Statue in the last Scene; a mean and absurd Contrivance; for how can it be imagined that *Hermione,* a virtuous and affectionate Wife, would conceal herself during sixteen Years in a solitary House, though she was sensible that her repentant Husband was all that time consuming away with Grief and Remorse for her Death; and what Reason could she have for chusing to live in such a miserable Confinement, when she might have been happy in the Possession of her Husband's Affection and have shared his Throne: how ridiculous also in a great Queen, on so interresting [sic] an Occasion, to submit to such Buffoonery as standing on a Pedestal, motionless, her eyes fixed, and at last to be conjured down by this magical Command of *Paulina.* . . .
>
> To bring about this Scene, ridiculous as it is, *Shakespear* has been guilty of many Absurdities, which would be too tedious to mention, and which are too glaring to escape the Observation of the most careless Reader.

It is noticeable that Lennox, though she had theatrical ambitions herself, first as an actress and later as a playwright, makes no allowance for a difference between narrative and mimetic fiction, and never considers stage effect as distinct from reading effect. "The Novel has nothing in it half so low and improbable as this Contrivance of the Statue; and indeed wherever *Shakespear* has altered or invented, his *Winter's Tale* is greatly inferior to the old paltry Story that furnished him with the Subject of it." Lennox's comments on Hermione indicate that the critic thinks Shakespeare has done the character an injustice. And that is my second point—the second axe that I hear Lennox grinding. Shakespeare, like the men in **The Female Quixote,** reads romances badly, or misreads, or bungles, partly or even largely because, Lennox suspects, Shakespeare is not interested in doing women justice. She evidently suspects him of wishing to deprive the female characters of power and authority. Why *should* Hermione give up her position as queen for sixteen years? Why should she make herself ridiculous in acting out that charade as a statue?

If we look at the pattern of procedure in *Shakespear Illustrated,* we can see that it runs parallel to *The Female Quixote*—and the longer we look at the two works, the more closely they seem related. In general, the pattern of *The Female Quixote* is to give us a chapter exhibiting an absurd romantic action of Arabella, followed by another short chapter giving the reaction of the commonsensical Augustan characters, with authorial commentary interwoven. The pattern of *Shakespear Illustrated* is generally in accord, with similar divisions. The first section gives us the translation of or a version of the major source. This is followed by a section typically entitled "Observations on the Use Shakespeare has made of the foregoing Novel in his [name of play]." That is, in the critical book, the romances or novellas take the place of Arabella, and Shakespeare and his play the place of the sensible modern Augustans. But now the Arabella-like stories are shown as superior, and the Shakespearean plays, now representing Augustan respectability and good sense (like the hero who remakes and re-interprets Arabella) are seen as defective. Arabella wins vicariously in this book at last, and both the feminine literary tradition (the romance and the story) and the female characters are vindicated against Shakespeare.

The bulk of Lennox's critical remarks address themselves in some way to the problems of the female characters in Shakespeare, and to the problems of their characterization. In her discussion of *King Lear,* for instance, Lennox spends a large proportion of her commentary on Cordelia, and particularly on the use and effect of Cordelia's big scene at the beginning. The source story makes sense; the prince might be impressed by seeing Cordelia's noble honesty, even if she were disinherited. But Shakespeare deprives Cordelia of any chance to make an impression, leaving an improbability:

> *Shakespear* does not introduce this Prince till after the absurd Trial *Lear* made of his Daughters Affection is over. The Lover who is made to Marry the disinherited *Cordelia* on account of her Virtue, is very injudiciously contrived to be Absent when she gave so glorious a Testimony of it, and is touch'd by a cold Justification of her Fame, and that from herself, when he might have been charm'd with a shining Instance of her Greatness of Soul, and inviolable Regard to Truth.
>
> So unartfully has the Poet managed this Incident, that *Cordelia*'s noble Disinterestedness is apparent to all but him who was to be the most influenced by it. In the Eyes of her Lover she is debased, not exalted; reduced to the abject Necessity of defending her own Character, and seeking rather to free herself from the Suspicion of Guilt, than modestly enjoying the conscious Sense of superior Virtue.

Miriam Small complains that "Mrs. Lennox brings up a minor point and overemphasizes it in its relation to the rest of the story. . . . In thus running off on a tangent, Mrs. Lennox vitiates the general dignity of her work. Small has not, however, noticed the running argument in favor of women. Lennox is entirely consistent in her discussion of play after play. Among the Shakespearean female characters that she discusses only Beatrice and Lady Macbeth seem to meet her unqualified approval. In general, she feels that the female characters are much prouder, freer, stronger, and more effective in the source stories. Her comment on Cordelia is not

tangential. Shakespeare, she suspects, wants to debase women and make them "abject"; instead of dramatizing the heroines of the stories he replaces them with female weaklings of his own. Thus, Shakespeare will not follow Cinthio, whose Epitia offers the heroic sacrifice; Shakespeare makes Isabella, his heroine in *Measure for Measure,* "a mere Vixen in her Virtue," an "affected Prude," whereas Mariana languishes in faithful love for a man who certainly does not deserve it: "That *Shakespear* made a wrong Choice of his Subject, since he was resolved to torture it into a Comedy, appears by the low Contrivance, absurd Intrigue, and improbable Incidents, he was obliged to introduce, in order to bring about three or four Weddings, instead of one good Beheading, which was the Consequence naturally expected. Shakespeare tends to let men off for vice, while making women suffer. Worse than that, Shakespeare consistently makes the women weaker than they are in the romantic narrative sources, as in the typical case of Helena in *All's Well.*

> The Character of the Heroine is more exalted in the Original than the Copy.
>
> In *Boccace* we see her, after her Marriage and the cruel Flight of her Husband, taking the Government of the Province in her own Hands, and behaving with so much Wisdom, Prudence and Magnanimity, as acquired her the Love and Esteem of the People, who all murmured against the Injustice of their Lord in not being sensible to so much Merit. . . .
>
> *Shakespear* shews her oppressed with Despair at the Absence of the Count, incapable of either Advice or Consolation; giving unnecessary Pain to the good Countess her Mother-in-law (a Character entirely of his own Invention) by alarming her with a pretended Design of killing herself.

The Romances show women as rulers, as powers in their own right, capable of "Magnanimity." The dramatist is interested in them only as they are pathetic. Shakespeare the modern, thought by modern Augustan critics to be the realist of English greatness and to represent the most thorough understanding of "the crouded World," is in Lennox's view an anti-romantic anti-feminist. He tends too often, in her opinion, to diminish women into lovesick minxes or neurotic weaklings, taking from them the power and the moral independence which the old romances and novels had given them. His misreading of the stories means he tends to humiliate his women. Charlotte Lennox's fervent favoring of "poetical Justice" in *Shakespear Illustrated* seems closely related to her feeling that Shakespeare sometimes lets the men off very lightly, whereas if anyone gets punished or hurt or pushed out of our view it is the woman, who should be the heroine but who is given such an unheroic part to play. Even when the lady is supposed to be greatly loved by the hero, he lacks that fidelity which the romances inculcate. Consider the anticlimactic case of Ophelia:

> The accidental killing of her Father, and her Distraction, which was caused by it, is all his own Invention, and would have made a very affecting Episode if the Lady had been more modest in her Frenzy, and her Lover more uniformly afflicted for her Death; for at his first hearing it he expresses only a slight Emotion; presently he jumps into her Grave, fiercely demands to be buried with her,

fights with her Brother for professing to love her, then grows calm, and never thinks of her any more.

Such behavior is, as Arabella would have told Hamlet, "an Outrage to all Truth and Constancy." In his dedication at the front of **Shakespear Illustrated,** Johnson praises Shakespeare for presenting real characters—*"His Heroes are Men"*—and for making "the love and Hatred, the Hopes and Fears of his chief personages—seem as are common to other human Beings." Charlotte Lennox seems implicitly to retort that Shakespeare should have understood love better when it was the business of a play, and she appears also to complain that all of Shakespeare's heroes are *"Men"* in the more restricted sense.

We do not have to believe Charlotte Lennox on Shakespeare, whose position now seems even safer than it was in 1753. It may yet be admitted without absolute heresy that her tart remarks can be refreshing after so much elaborate praise, in the Romantic age and after, of the beauty of Shakespeare's heroines—praise started and chiefly articulated by men. Charlotte Lennox may be a solitary dissenter, but her critical remarks are not stupid. Her whole scholarly labor is an achievement of which any professional academic might well be proud. It strikes me that she deserves yet more crowns of bays; she is the first woman to produce a scholarly work on English literature, and the first feminist critic of a major author. **Shakespear Illustrated**—at the very least the sections of "Observations"—ought to be reprinted in an accessible form. The book has some importance in the history of criticism, and something to offer anyone who studies the eighteenth century. It is an important work in Lennox's career, uniquely and overtly polemical—as **The Female Quixote** is covertly polemical beneath its facade of compliance and conformity. In **Shakespear Illustrated** we find a last defense of the old "paltry stories," the romance and the romance tradition—the female tradition which Augustans have pooh-poohed. It was certainly no accident that it was a woman who had such command of this old shadowy source material. Ostensibly Augustan, the book says "No" rather viciously to certain assumptions, pointing out absurdities with a force not uninspired by some rage. In **Shakespear Illustrated** Charlotte Lennox took revenge for her ridiculed, chastened Arabella. The critical work seems the work of an Arabella unreformed. (pp. 298-307)

> *Margaret Anne Doody, "Shakespeare's Novels: Charlotte Lennox Illustrated," in* Studies in the Novel, *Vol. XIX, No. 3, Fall, 1987, pp. 296-310.*

ADDITIONAL BIBLIOGRAPHY

Bradbrook, Frank W. "The Feminist Tradition." In his *Jane Austen and Her Predecessors,* pp. 90-119. Cambridge: Cambridge University Press, 1966.

Surveys the feminist tradition in the English novel, contending that *The Female Quixote* was an important influence on Jane Austen's *Northanger Abbey* (1818).

Butt, John. "Other Prose Fiction." In his *The Mid-Eighteenth Century,* edited by Geoffrey Carnall, pp. 449-94. The Oxford History of English Literature, vol. VIII. Oxford: Clarendon Press, 1979.

Discusses the moral implications of Arabella's behavior in *The Female Quixote* and describes the role of the female protagonists in *The Life of Harriot Stuart* and *Henrietta.*

Hazen, Allen T. *Samuel Johnson's Prefaces and Dedications.* New Haven: Yale University Press, 1937, 257 p.

Contains dedications written by Samuel Johnson for Lennox, historical documentation of their collaboration, and bibliographical descriptions of Lennox's works.

Horner, Joyce M. "The 'Lady' Novelist." In her *The English Women Novelists and Their Connection with the Feminist Movement (1688-1797),* pp. 24-47. Smith College Studies in Modern Languages, vol. XI, nos. 1, 2, & 3. Northampton, Mass.: George Banta Publishing Co., Collegiate Press, 1930.

Examines autobiographical elements in *The Life of Harriot Stuart, The Female Quixote,* and *Euphemia,* comparing Lennox's success as a writer with that of her female contemporaries in England.

MacCarthy, B. G. "The Novel of Sentiment and of Sensibility." In her *The Later Women Novelists, 1744-1818,* pp. 31-86. Cork, Ireland: Cork University Press, 1948.

Contends that *The Female Quixote* is inferior to its prototype, Miguel de Cervantes's *Don Quixote,* both in thematic structure and parodic effect.

Mayo, Robert D. *The English Novel in the Magazines, 1740-1815: With a Catalogue of 1375 Magazine Novels and Novelettes.* Evanston, Ill.: Northwestern University Press, 1962, 695 p.

Contains a discussion of Lennox's contribution to the field of eighteenth-century women's magazines, as well as scattered references to contemporary commentary on Lennox and her works.

Reynolds, Myra. "General Learning and Literary Work." In her *The Learned Lady in England, 1650-1760,* pp. 137-257. Vassar Semi-Centennial Series. Boston: Houghton Mifflin Co., Riverside Press, 1920.

Summarizes Lennox's literary career, emphasizing the diversity of her work.

Ross, Deborah. "Mirror, Mirror: The Didactic Dilemma of *The Female Quixote.*" *Studies in English Literature 1500-1900* 27, No. 3 (Summer 1987): 455-73.

Argues that the conflict between romance and realism in *The Female Quixote* is necessitated by Arabella's frustrated inner life; the novel, according to Ross, is "both a romance and a satire of romance."

Spacks, Patricia Meyer. "Sisters." In *Fetter'd or Free? British Women Novelists, 1670-1815,* edited by Mary Anne Schofield and Cecilia Macheski, pp. 136-51. Athens: Ohio University Press, 1986.

Analyzes the moral and didactic implications of sibling rivalry in *Sophia.*

Charles (James) Lever

1806-1872

(Also wrote under the pseudonyms Harry Lorrequer and Cornelius O'Dowd) Irish novelist, journalist, and essayist.

Lever was one of the most popular novelists in mid-nineteenth-century England. Writing lighthearted, adventurous tales about Irish country life and the military, he achieved immediate success with the English reading public with his earliest novels, *The Confessions of Harry Lorrequer, Charles O'Malley, the Irish Dragoon, Jack Hinton, the Guardsman,* and *Tom Burke of "Ours"*. Most contemporary English critics, however, while delighting in the spontaneity, humor, and excitement of these works, belittled their artistry, faulting them as carelessly written, repetitious, and often unoriginal. In successive works, Lever became increasingly concerned with his artistic technique, devoting more attention to plot construction and character development; he also dealt more seriously with Ireland's social and political problems, which many Irish critics argued had been misrepresented and treated with undue levity in Lever's early works as a result of his English sympathies. Lever's audience reacted unfavorably to these changes, and his popularity steadily declined in England. In the twentieth century, Lever's novels have received relatively little attention; only recently have Irish commentators begun to reassess his social and political ideas.

The second son of an English father and an Irish mother, Lever was born and raised in Dublin, where he attended various preparatory schools. In his youth, Lever earned a reputation as a prankster and an able storyteller, and was little interested in his studies, except for his fencing and dancing classes. Nevertheless, aided by coaching from his studious older brother, Lever entered Trinity College, Dublin, at the age of sixteen. He experimented with writing while in college, and in 1826 his first published work, an essay on opium entitled "Recollections in the Night," appeared in a short-lived Cork magazine. When he received his bachelor of arts degree in 1827, he was undecided on a profession and travelled to Canada, where he toured the frontier for several months. The following year he went to Germany to study medicine at universities in Göttingen and Heidelberg, but withdrew from school to visit Vienna, Weimar, and Paris. Lever then returned to Dublin and finished his medical degree in 1831 at Trinity College. Later that year, he married Kate Butler, a woman he had known since childhood. They eventually had four children, three daughters and a son.

A man of extravagant tastes and habits, Lever was perpetually in need of money and was anxious to establish himself in the medical profession. He worked for the County Clare Board of Health during a cholera epidemic in 1832 and later received a position at a dispensary in Portstewart, a resort town in Ulster. Here, in 1835, he became friends with William Hamilton Maxwell, an author who was famous for his adventurous hunting and military tales. Maxwell encouraged Lever to write again, and in 1836, the *Dublin University Magazine* published a story by Lever entitled "The Black Mask," a historical romance set in Budapest. Late in 1836, Lever developed plans for a series of sketches consisting of anecdotes mainly about Irish and military life told to and by a character

named Harry Lorrequer. Keeping Lever's authorship a secret, the *Dublin University Magazine* published the first of the sketches in February of 1837; other sketches appeared intermittently in the periodical over the next two years, during which time Lever accepted a post as doctor to the English colony in Brussels. Lever's stories proved extremely popular and ultimately became his first novel, *The Confessions of Harry Lorrequer,* which was published in book form in 1839 with illustrations by Hablôt K. Browne, better known as "Phiz," the illustrator of many of Charles Dickens's novels. Lever's first success prompted him to begin a second novel in 1840; published serially in the *Dublin University Magazine, Charles O'Malley, the Irish Dragoon* is Lever's best-known work. The popularity of these two novels greatly increased the circulation of the *Dublin University Magazine,* and in 1842, Lever was offered its editorship.

Abandoning his medical career, Lever returned to Dublin to assume his duties as editor. He moved his family into Templeogue House, a Jacobean mansion outside of Dublin, where he often lavishly entertained visitors, among them the writers William Makepeace Thackeray, G. P. R. James, and Anthony Trollope. Despite the generous salary paid him by the magazine, Lever's excessive spending and gambling debts forced him to work doubly hard writing. Finishing his third novel, *Jack Hinton,* in late 1842, he immediately began working simultaneously on his next two, *Tom Burke of "Ours"* and *Arthur O'Leary, His Wanderings and Ponderings in Many Lands,* both of which he finished by the end of 1843. The following year, Lever wrote two more novels, *The O'Donoghue: A Tale of Ireland Fifty Years Ago* and *St. Patrick's Eve,* as well as several essays for the *Dublin University Magazine.* The stress of writing and editing weighed heavily on Lever, who had taken over the magazine while a controversy raged between Irish nationalist and Anglo-Irish writers over English rule of Ireland. The *Dublin University Magazine,* an Anglo-Irish periodical that had traditionally supported Protestantism and English rule, came under constant attack by the Dublin *Nation,* a pro-Catholic, anti-English newspaper. Lever, however, was disinterested in the political dispute, and he attempted to reconcile both sides by softening the Anglo-Irish bias of the magazine. However, he only succeeded in drawing attacks from Irish and Anglo-Irish writers alike. Early in 1845, he gave up the struggle in disgust and left Dublin for the Continent, where he remained for the rest of his life.

Over the next two years, Lever and his family lived in various countries, including Belgium, Germany, Austria, and Italy. Eventually settling in Florence, Lever continued to live extravagantly, frequently hosting private theatricals and parties at his home for the English residents in the city. Constantly in debt, Lever published novel after novel, usually writing two at a time, one for the London publisher Chapman and Hall and one for the *Dublin University Magazine.* Critics often attribute the faults of his style to the haste with which he wrote; continually under a deadline from at least one of his publishers, Lever rarely corrected or revised his manuscripts, many of which were lost in the mail, requiring him to rewrite them from memory because he never kept notes or made copies.

Lever's last years were marked by a series of misfortunes. In 1858, he received a long-desired appointment from the British government as Vice Consul at Spezia, Italy. The post, however, disappointed Lever, who found the pay insufficient and the work dull. In 1859, he began corresponding with Charles Dickens, who offered him generous terms to write a serialized novel for Dickens's periodical, *All the Year Round.* First appearing in June of 1860, the novel, *A Day's Ride: A Life's Romance,* was a dismal failure, and Dickens was forced to run his own novel, *Great Expectations,* simultaneously to boost faltering sales of his publication. Personal misfortune also plagued Lever. In 1861, his wife became an invalid, and late in 1863, his son died. Four years later, Lever was appointed Consul at Trieste, Italy. He hoped to retire from novel writing and live off the income from this position, supplemented by the money that he received for essays he was writing regularly for *Blackwood's Magazine* under the name Cornelius O'Dowd. However, he was disillusioned to learn that his assistant's salary was to be paid out of his own, leaving him less money than he made while Vice Consul at Spezia. The greatest hardship of his life struck in 1870, when his wife died. Although in his final years Lever suffered bouts of illness and depression, he still wrote, completing his last novel, *Lord Kilgobbin,* in March of 1872. He died in his sleep the following June.

Lever wrote over thirty novels during his career. His first four, *Harry Lorrequer, Charles O'Malley, Jack Hinton,* and *Tom Burke of "Ours",* were by far his most popular. Often described as "slapdash" and "rollicking," these works portray the life of the Irish gentry during the late eighteenth and early nineteenth centuries and are replete with thrilling scenes of duelling and combat and boisterous descriptions of dining and drinking. Similar in style and construction, the novels all have simple plots, which join together amusing anecdotes that Lever heard from friends or derived from his experiences. Each work begins in Ireland, where the title character falls in love with the heroine. Believing his feelings unrequited, the hero enters the army and proves his strength and courage on the battlefield. After several perilous adventures, he returns home and wins the hand of the heroine. While contemporary critics continually praised Lever's ability to tell vigorous, exciting stories, most agreed that the novels had little artistic merit. Critics complained that his stories were repetitive, his anecdotes unoriginal, and his characters superficial. His loosely constructed plots were also widely condemned, with several critics remarking that many of the incidents related had no bearing on the outcome of the story. In a caustic review of *Charles O'Malley,* Edgar Allan Poe used the novel to show that, as a rule, the most popular books are the least artistic; according to Poe, "drinking wine, telling anecdotes, and devouring 'devilled kidneys' may be considered the sum total, as the *thesis* of the book." Despite censure from Poe and others, Lever's works were indeed popular. As one early critic noted, "such a profusion of fun, adventure, and rollicking hearty enjoyment wins its way into the tastes of the most various readers."

Responding to criticism of his literary talents, Lever worked to improve his artistic technique in his later novels: he attempted to construct his plots so that incidents proceeded in a logical sequence to the story's conclusion, and he strove to portray his characters with greater sympathy and understanding. These changes were gradual and, indeed, his last novel, *Lord Kilgobbin,* is generally considered his most polished work. Lever also began focusing on different subjects in his later novels; they contain very few military adventures, dealing instead with social and political themes. For example, *The Dodd Family Abroad,* based on his own experiences, portrays the problems faced by an Irish family as they travel on the Continent. In other novels, including *The Fortunes of Glencore* and *Sir Brook Fossbrooke,* Lever continued to depict scenes of Irish life, but much of the levity characteristic of his early novels was supplanted by a serious tone evincing Lever's broadening interest in Ireland's political conflicts with England. While nineteenth- and early twentieth-century English critics praised Lever's artistic improvement in his later novels, many thought that they were less enjoyable and lacked the vitality and humor of his early works.

Although most contemporary English critics acknowledged that Lever's early novels were entertaining, many Irish commentators, notably the author William Carleton, were infuriated by them. Lever drew most of the novels' protagonists from Ireland's predominantly Anglo-Irish landlord class, which was notorious for exploiting its tenants. Irish critics insisted that Lever had ignored this exploitation and that his buoyant depictions of Irish life were false. Furthermore, Irish critics argued that many of Lever's minor characters, including Charles O'Malley's well-known comic servant, Mickey Free, popularized a degrading, clownish stereotype known as the "stage Irishman." These attitudes toward Lever's works were common during the Irish Literary Renaissance of the late nineteenth century, when renowned Irish poet and critic William Butler Yeats asserted that Lever and Samuel Lover, another Irish author, "wrote ever with one eye toward London. They never wrote for the people, and neither have they ever . . . written faithfully of the people." For most of the twentieth century, Irish commentators neglected Lever's works, but lately they have begun to reexamine them. Some recent Irish scholars have defended Lever against the charge that he was overly sympathetic to the English, pointing out that in his novels, particularly the later ones, he described the cruelty and decadence of the landlords and blamed them for ignoring their responsibilities to their suffering tenants. Arguing that Yeats and other critics had based their judgment of Lever solely on his earliest novels, A. Norman Jeffares stated: "Lever loved his country; he surveyed its politics sardonically, at times detachedly; . . . and he had a sharp awareness of the differences in Irish and English sensibilities. How could Yeats (and a horde of lesser writers after him) have got hold of the wrong Lever?"

(See also *Dictionary of Literary Biography,* Vol. 21: *Victorian Novelists before 1885.*)

*PRINCIPAL WORKS

The Confessions of Harry Lorrequer (novel) 1839
Charles O'Malley, the Irish Dragoon [as Harry Lorrequer] (novel) 1841
Jack Hinton, the Guardsman (novel) 1843
Tom Burke of "Ours" (novel) 1843
Arthur O'Leary, His Wanderings and Ponderings in Many Lands (novel) 1844
The O'Donoghue: A Tale of Ireland Fifty Years Ago (novel) 1845
St. Patrick's Eve (novel) 1845
The Knight of Gwynne: A Tale of the Time of the Union (novel) 1847
Confessions of Con Cregan, the Irish Gil Blas (novel) 1850
Roland Cashel (novel) 1850
The Daltons; or, Three Roads in Life (novel) 1852
The Dodd Family Abroad (novel) 1854
The Martins of Cro' Martin (novel) 1856
The Fortunes of Glencore (novel) 1857
Davenport Dunn: A Man of Our Day (novel) 1859
One of Them (novel) 1861
A Day's Ride: A Life's Romance (novel) 1863
Cornelius O'Dowd upon Men and Women and Other Things in General. 3 vols. [as Cornelius O'Dowd] (essays) 1864-65
Luttrell of Arran (novel) 1865
Sir Brook Fossbrooke (novel) 1866
The Bramleighs of Bishop's Folly (novel) 1868
Lord Kilgobbin: A Tale of Ireland in Our Own Time (novel) 1872
The Novels of Charles Lever. 37 vols. (novels) 1897-99

*Most of Lever's works were first published serially in periodicals.

MORGAN RATTLER [PSEUDONYM OF **PERCIVAL W. BANKS**] (essay date 1840)

[*Asserting that Lever fittingly avoids artistic pretensions in* The

Confessions of Harry Lorrequer, *Banks praises the work as pure entertainment.*]

The Confessions of Harry Lorrequer is an extremely well-chosen title. It possesses the rare merit of alike suiting the interests of the publisher and the author, generally, as Sir Walter Scott has explained, so discordant. It is sufficiently attractive, without being too communicative—without being calculated to raise, in the mind of the most imaginative, a preconception of what the work is to be. It therefore lays no ground for disappointment, and in no sort compromises the author. But it has another merit: it *individualises* the work. It declares to you most plainly that you are neither to expect novel nor romance; and it comforts you with the assurance that you will not be vexed by an abortive attempt at either. You are only to have such snatches of one man's life and adventures as he is pleased to give you. You are only of necessity to have *one* full-drawn character—the "I" of the narrative; all the rest, without destroying the effect, *may* be sketches, and the majority of them in outline. . . . To three classes of writers . . . the form of work adopted by the author of the ***Confessions of Harry Lorrequer*** is peculiarly advantageous,—to the *young* man who writes for fame—to the man engaged in a profession, and who can only devote leisure hours to the cultivation of literature—and, thirdly, to the man who writes for money, and cares for reputation (mere vanity apart, which flattery so easily bought can satisfy), precisely as the thief in the story did for character, and that was to make a better market for it. (pp. 321-22)

Our author . . . belongs to the two first-named classes; and has accordingly chosen wisely, and, as we shall see, acted wisely upon his choice. His story is a story of pure out-and-out fun; and in its quaint, occasionally rather coarse, and invariably "rollicking" Irish way, it is, though seen through an atmosphere something misty, brilliant after its kind as Beaumarchais's *Figaro,* which, from its sparkling wit, blazing out sentence after sentence, has not been inaptly compared to a display of fireworks. Harry Lorrequer advisedly passes over all the darker passages which might be naturally introduced into his confessions. He never, in search of the sentimental or the sublime, goes beyond the object he proposed to himself. He does not attempt to give you the "mirth and laughter," and the "sermons and soda-water," in the same dose. . . . He strives to produce the mirth and laughter, first by the humorous collocation of incidents, in which, perhaps, lies his greatest merit; next, in the delineation of character, in which he is not so happy, for, with the exception of his hero, and one or two other persons, the sketches are exaggerated into caricature; and, lastly, by his dialogue and narrative, which is exceedingly light, bright, and buoyant. It has the charm of freshness, and unaffectedness, and perfect ease. There is no imitation of this, that, or the other approved style of jocose composition—no turn of phrase, or trick of verbal humour, borrowed from Fielding, from Goldsmith, or from Sterne—there is no mannerism, no straining after effect, no intellectual posture-making—no struggle to say smart or fine things; and, lastly, there is no stumbling, or tripping, or knocking, or clapping, or daisy-cutting—there is no break in the easy pace; it is like your best hack's hand-gallop, that will take you to cover as though you were in an arm-chair, at the rate of twenty miles an hour, and pull you every yard of the way. Then, dealing with things farcical, and making his characters for the most part in farce—or, if you will, grotesque comedy—he has the good sense never to attempt pathos. No man of less transcendant power than Shakspeare, Molière, or

Scott, ever yet succeeded in intermingling the grotesque with the pathetic. Molière may deepen and darken his comedy, so as to cause the shadow to fall upon your heart, and make you sad the whilst you smile, and wiser, more merciful, and more tolerant of your weak fellow-mortals for the sadness. Scott may fling shadows thicker and more dread around the doomed Master of Ravenswood, by the broad ludicrousness of Caleb's shifts—by the cynical merriment of the creature, half-fiddler, half-sexton—a fleshly apparition, flitting betwixt life and death—the wedding and the burial—human joy and human sorrow—a mockery upon all. Shakspeare may freeze the blood as he listeth with his terrible contrasts—the din of preparation in the household of the Capulet—the sacrificial silence of one chamber—the lewd old nurse, prattling over the bed of true Juliet—the drunken porter, vomiting forth his ribald jests at the gate of that castle on whose battlements the raven is hoarse with croaking. But when any man of less genius attempts such like things in any degree, he is sure to fail miserably, and the more ludicrously if the endeavour be to rise from the grotesque and farcical to the tragic, and not the contrary. You can have no sympathy with the miseries or heroics of any body at whom you have been accustomed to laugh. (pp. 322-23)

I give Lorrequer, accordingly, uncommon credit for his abstinence from fine writing, and the more because I am convinced he must have withstood strong temptation; and this, in a young writer, is something at least equal to the chastity of Scipio, who, perhaps, only declined cracking commandments with a black woman, after all. But how do I come to the above conclusion about Lorrequer? Thus! There are only two or three serious passages in the whole volume, and these are written with great vigour and intense feeling. . . . *The Confessions* [are] made by one who tells of a great many queer things, and sundry thereof of doubtful morality, but yet appears to be no heart-broken penitent. But then Mr. Lorrequer is a soldier. Nor need you wonder, gentle reader, at an Irish civilian's choosing a military hero. There is no country in the world in which the military are so popular as in Ireland, or in which they are on such terms of familiar intercourse with the gentry. (p. 323)

[Let] us pause to consider him a little in the abstract. To do this we must revert to him as a creation of the author's. He is the only elaborated character in the work; the rest are sketches drawn with more or less pains, but all with a free and generally an able hand; and indubitably all are, notwithstanding farcical exaggeration, from the life. Now the character of the hero is interesting to an Irishman in a degree which no Englishman, not very familiar with Ireland and Irishmen, can comprehend, much less appreciate; and this, startling as it may seem to you, gentle reader, . . . is because of its reality! . . . Harry Lorrequer is the most *real* Irish character that was, perhaps, ever drawn. I have known and do know a hundred *young* Irishmen in many leading characteristics *like* Lorrequer. If I were to summon up all these before my mind's eye together, and take from each those traits which would be available to me in a generalising process, whereby I should hope to make a representative morally of the whole number, the result of that experiment would be something in its main features closely resembling Harry Lorrequer; or, in other words, an exemplar of the CLASS, "*Young Irish gentlemen.*" The prominent points of this character for good or evil are well known; it will be admitted, too, by the candid, that some of the worst vices are but virtues pushed into extremes—as generosity into prodigality, hospitality into profu-

sion, and courage, which, with a gentleman, is a *feeling*, into what alone becomes a gladiator, a *sense*. But the nicer traits of the Irish character have rarely been touched upon, and never developed fully; and yet, perhaps, they are more fatal than those with which Irishmen are commonly reproached when the vulgar are their assailants.—Such as an inordinate love of conviviality, fun, frolic, practical joking, rows; a reckless indifference, at the least, with respect to mortal quarrels, an inveterate improvidence, a heedlessness as to consequences, a thoughtlessness of things to come; but the nicer traits lie too deep for the casual observer. They are to be caught only by anxious examination of one's own past life, and of the lives and characters of others, his intimate associates; and thus, no doubt, were they seized by the author of *Harry Lorrequer.* (p. 327)

[The faults of Irishmen spring from] infirmity of purpose, insecurity of will, easiness of temptation, facility of receiving impressions from that which is present and disregard of that which is afar, whether it be in place or time; a strong disposition to consider scarcely any future sacrifice too great to secure the gratification of the moment, or the moment's freedom from annoyance; a superstitious belief in Fate and Fortune, which seems engendered of the climate, for it prevails from the cabin to the castle. The peasant proclaims his faith in the divinity of what he styles "Luck;" the gentleman even of learning and genius has, like Napoleon, his star; or if not, if he disavow the superstition and deny it even to himself, a feeling of fatalism is lurking in his mind, ready upon some signal occasion to blaze forth. Childhood, from the impressions it receives in such a country as the green land of song, of legend, and of mysteries, is very potent in such matters!

It is before some one or more of these causes seldom clearly to be seen, often not at all to be noticed, but haunting their victim like an evil spirit, that the energy and industry, the valour, the knowledge, and the genius of Irishmen, have most frequently fallen. In the *Confessions of Harry Lorrequer,* most, if not all, these enemies of the young Irishman's fortunes are laid bare in a series of most humorous scrapes, into which having got himself without necessity, he usually gets himself out with adroitness; or if not, luck is sure to do it for him. It would be out of my power, were it even desirable, to attempt any formal allusion to the several adventures in which he is engaged, from his falling in love with Lady Jane Callonby to his marriage with that charming fair. Let me, however, take occasion here to remark, that sundry of those characteristics of which I have been specially speaking just now, are exhibited by Master Harry in his intercourse with the sex. Adoring the earl's daughter as he does, he nevertheless makes love to Heaven knows how many; but makes love and proposes to no less than two other ladies whilst he is "severed from her," and *near* either of them:—

> Oh, 'tis pleasant to think that wherever we rove
> We are sure to find something that's blissful and
>   dear;
> And that when we're away from the lips that we
>   love,
> We need only make love to the lips we are near.

This is pre-eminently Irish! and it is the principle upon which all young Irishmen act. To talk of Irishmen generally as fortune-hunters, is a vulgar, stupid error. There are no men in the world, with the average allowance of brains, who make such confounded fools of themselves about women as Irishmen do, and are constantly doing, and will be everlastingly doing, and this without being paid a single stiver for the performance. Even age does not cure them of this failing. (pp. 327-28)

As a specimen of our author's power of writing seriously and earnestly, I would gladly, if space allowed, quote his account of a trial for murder, in an assize town. I would gladly follow him into France and Germany; as it is, I shall wind up with an apologue. The electors of the city of Cork have, in their choice of members to represent them in parliament, shewn great discrimination, and a laudable pride, in the occupation which the majority of them pursue. They evidently, in the way of business, plume themselves upon porter, potatoes, and pigs, as in the way of pleasure they do upon poetry, punch, and politics; and have evinced this by exporting, as their contribution to the collective wisdom, a couple of Corcagian gentlemen, who, like themselves, are attached to the provision trade, and think a fat pig the most interesting animal, and a hogshead of porter one of the noblest objects in creation. . . . Of the two M.P.'s, Mr. Callaghan especially patronises and presides over the pigs; Mr. Beamish is a brewer of porter. Thanks to Johnny Robinson's excellent story, styled *"the Bāmishes,"* the latter senator's name, even without the aid of Harry Lorrequer, is much more generally known in the convivial circles of this metropolis than his porter; whilst on the other hand, not only throughout his native Cork, but, moreover, in the counties of Kerry and Clare, Tipperary and Limerick, the person is no better than an abstraction, and the name is only used to designate a particular species of stout,—and right good stout it is, and high is the esteem with which it is regarded. Neither "Guiness's," nor even "Dan O'Connell's," nor any other potatory composition of a milder character, has a chance with it. Nor can any other be palmed off upon the humblest connoisseur of the beverage throughout the south of Ireland, so long "as reason holds her seat;" and no landlord, however, thievish, ventures to try it. The greater number of them, however, keep a weaker and less generous porter than "Bamishes;" and when they have their customers well *"screwed,"* they, doubtless from a regard for their nervous system, administer the milder and washier potation to them.

> "Are they," exclaims a landlord famous for his 'Bamish,'—"are they drunk enough, Tim, for 'Clancy' yet?"
>
> "No, maisther, dear! not yet; they're only singing."
>
> "What is it they're at now, Tim, *agra?*"
>
> "Oh, maisther, 'tis hugg'n and kiss'n they are, and call'n for more 'Bamish.'"
>
> "The thieves of the world, 'tis long they were coming to it! They've ruined me in 'Bamish!' Now, Molly, my jewel, shovel 'Clancy' into them!"

The author of the *Confessions of Harry Lorrequer* has, in his own country at least, the mirth-loving public at the hugg'n and kiss'n point. But I have read the two first numbers of his new work, *Charles O'Malley, the Irish Dragoon,* and he is not "shovelling Clancy" into them. On the contrary, there is more strength and higher flavour in the fresh tap of his "Bamish" than in that which before won praise. (pp. 335-36)

> Morgan Rattler [*pseudonym of Percival W. Banks*], *"'The Confessions of Harry Lorrequer' Considered,"* in Fraser's Magazine for Town & Country,

Vol. XXII, No. CXXIX, September, 1840, pp. 320-36.

[WILLIAM MAGINN?]   (essay date 1842)

[*One of the most prominent journalists in England during the first half of the nineteenth century, Maginn wrote prolifically for a variety of English periodicals. His articles range from burlesques in verse to literary criticism and contain a rich blend of farcical humor, classical allusions, and political commentary. The following excerpt is from an unsigned review in Fraser's Magazine that has been attributed to Maginn by Lever's first biographer, W. J. Fitzpatrick. Although Maginn commends* Charles O'Malley *as buoyant, humorous, and vividly descriptive, he qualifies his praise, faulting Lever's tendency to exaggerate and calling the novel "light literature."*]

Charles Lever, the author of *Harry Lorrequer* and *Charles O'Malley,* again shines forth in culmination over the fun-loving world of London. (p. 448)

Notwithstanding the difficulties that stood in the way of *Harry Lorrequer* as an Irish production, every page of which was redolent of turf and whisky,—notwithstanding its being born an *alien,* as all works be that are issued to the light beyond the sound of Bow bells, and the regions of fog and puffery,—notwithstanding the prevailing taste for the literature and philosophy of Cockaigne—for the popular perry, which it was seriously argued by the "best possible public instructors" was preferable to champagne—notwithstanding all these impediments *Harry Lorrequer* achieved a most brilliant success. REGINA [*Fraser's Magazine*], who disdains all sordid motives, lent her aid to a just appreciation of a work of merit, without considering how, or where, or why, or by whom, it had been published [see excerpt dated 1840],—REGINA, without caring that the chapters of *Harry Lorrequer* appeared first in the columns of another magazine, was most anxious when the work came forth in its complete form, to see that it had a fair start in the race for popular favour. No such effort is in the least required on behalf of *Charles O'Malley.* It comes before us as the production of an author on whom the public have conferred their well-considered approbation, and as such we deal with it.

We have conferred, and we still propose to confer, high praise upon Mr. Lever; but we beg distinctly to have it understood that it is only meant to be comparative. We think he is the best of the mere monthly writers, but no more. . . .

All great novelists, from the days of Xenophon down to those of Hope, were men of genius and learning. The popular monthly effusionists nowadays are neither. But now for *Charles O'Malley.*

The title pretty clearly expresses what we have to expect from the two volumes. An Irish Dragoon—a bold dragoon, and moreover, a regular slap-up, swell dragsman,—a type of a large class; for Ireland gives considerably more than half the officers to our cavalry. (p. 449)

The incidents under which Charles O'Malley is introduced to us whilst at home are common enough in Irish novels—a fox-chase, an after-dinner quarrel, a duel, a contested election, and, of course, a falling head-foremost in love with a young lady, who is to be the hero's destiny throughout his career, and his reward at its close. Without conferring much of an original aspect upon these pages, Mr. Lever makes them, nevertheless, interesting by the great buoyancy of spirit with which he narrates them. But his exaggerations sometimes, when, in the Yankee phrase, he wants to pile up an agony of interest, are pushed beyond taste and judgment. A real fox-chase in Galway is a splendid thing to see and an admirable subject to describe. Why, therefore, have recourse to feats and falls that are ludicrously impossible in the eyes of every man who has been accustomed to ride to hounds and is familiar with the capabilities of horses, and who is satisfied that gentlemen's heads are not quite as thick as those of buffaloes? The sketch of the election is pleasant enough, but a vast deal more might have been made of it. And the attempt of some of the O'Malley freeholders to carry off Sir George Dashwood's (the rival candidate) carriage, and on being disappointed in this, to fling his daughter, the lady of Master Charley's love, over a bridge into a mountain-torrent, together with the jumping over of the horses, and the rescue of the girl by the hero, and his getting his skull cracked for his trouble, might be mitigated in all its marvellous details with considerable advantage. The whole affair, too, is despicably un-Irish. What! an Irishman throw a pretty girl into a river! Oh *meelagh murther!* what an atrocious calumny on one who

> Loves all that is lovely,
> Loves all that he can.

'Ifaith, doctor, I would not like to be in your breeches if they should ever visit Connaught. The air of Galway, in fact, is too keen, even in fancy, for Lever. It has something like an intoxicating effect on him, and his imagination runs riot with a vengeance. This fault of extreme exaggeration, however, it is but fair to say, is not peculiar to Lever amongst the novelists of the day. On the contrary, we know not one who is free from it, while few possess the redeeming qualities of the author of **Harry Lorrequer.** But, to proceed; the future dragoon leaves Galway for Trinity College, Dublin. . . . There are descriptions of scenes alleged to have taken place there which it is ridiculous to imagine could have taken place in any college in the world, much less in one where the discipline is peculiarly strict, and speedily and vigorously enforced. In fact, the caricaturing is so gross and so incompatible with the scenes in which it is laid, that it has not even the slightest touch of fun in it. The stories about Dr. Barrett and Mooney had been told in print a hundred times before and a thousand times better. Mr. Lever says in *l'envoi* to his kind readers:—

> Others again have fallen foul of me for treating of things, places, and people, with which I had no opportunity of becoming personally acquainted. Thus one of my critics has shewn that I could not be a Trinity College-man; and another has denied my military matriculation. Now, although both my Latin and learning are on the peace establishment, and, if examined in the movements for cavalry, it is perfectly possible I should be cautioned, yet as I have both a degree and a commission, I might have been spared this reproach.

We can only say with reference to the demonstration of the first critic, of whom we know nothing, except through Mr. Lever, that he would seem to have no bad grounds to go upon. A Trinity College-man would scarcely talk of an officer who does not exist in the University,—namely, "*the proctor.*" He would have known than in T.C.D. the duties of the *proctors* are discharged by the *dean,* and those of the *bull-dogs* by the *porters.* He would probably, when he was using technical or slang terms peculiar to the college, such as "*chum,*" meaning fellow-lodger in the same set of chambers, and "*jib*" for junior freshman, have said *skip,* and not *servant.* Would any

Trinity Collegeman describe a pair of "*jibs*" leading such a life as this?—"Under Webber's directions, there was no hour of the day that hung heavily on our hands. We rose about eleven and breakfasted; after which succeeded fencing, sparring, billiards, or tennis in the park." Now, to stop a moment, tennis was never played in the park; there was plenty of hurling, cricketing, foot-ball, racket-playing, hand-ball (fives) playing, but no such thing as tennis was ever heard of. The fencing and sparring in men's rooms is right enough, so is the billiards *in town,* at Earl Street, or Hayes's, or the like places. The college authorities never patronised that beautiful game by building a table for the amusement of the students. But, to proceed:

> About three we got on horseback [the old hour, by the way, for Commons in the dininghall], and either cantered in the Phoenix or about the squares till visiting time; after which, made our calls, and then dressed for dinner, which we never thought of taking at Commons', but had it from Morrison's, we both being reported sick in the dean's list, [a T.C.D.-man would simply say, "on the sick-list"], and thereby exempt from *the meagre fare of the fellows' table.* In the evening our occupations became still more pressing, there were balls, suppers, whist-parties, rows at the theatres, shindies in the street, devilled-drumsticks at Hayes's, select oyster-parties at the Carlingford; in fact, every known method of remaining up all night, and appearing both pale and penitent the following morning.

Surely Mr. Lever must have mistaken the college for a caravansery, through whose open gates men can come and go at all hours unquestioned and uncontrolled. (pp. 452-54)

We conclude that the assertion "He has a degree and a commission" to be a mere mystification. We know he "never set a squadron in the field" any more than Maurice Quill, of whose name, adventures, and stories, he makes so liberal an use. We presume that as a medical student, who perhaps attended the lectures on anatomy, physiology, &c. chemistry, and botany, given by the university professors, but open to all who pay for the courses, he picked up some names of persons and things and some old stories; but that he really knew nothing of college life or of the university he has held up to ridicule. We have thought it not amiss to make these observations, and one of our strongest reasons sprung from the popularity—the great and deserved, and increasing popularity—of Mr. Lever's writings amongst the idle lovers of light literature in this country. Thousands who have no personal knowledge of the three universities, nor, peradventure, any just notion of them, but, perhaps, prejudices, bitter as ignorant against their names,—will read **Charles O'Malley** and be disposed to take the author's outrageous caricatures, for which there is not the slightest foundation in possibility, as more than highly-coloured sketches of what had been within the experience of him, a College-man, or might have been within his judgment. Thus in the estimation of this multitude of persons, the Dublin university, instead of being regarded as a venerable seat of religion and learning—as a well-ordered and well-disciplined institution, in which decency and decorum, and gentlemanly conduct and demeanour, are enforced, and morality and piety inculcated—as a benign mother that offers to the children she rears every advantage that can possibly be extended to the student, and therefore deserves his eternal gratitude, his most affectionate and reverent remembrance—would come to be regarded as a place in which there was no touch or tincture of religion, or morality, or learning, or gentlemanly conduct or feeling, but in their stead, noise, idleness, drunkenness, profaneness, black-guardism, and debauchery enough to make it an abomination upon the face of the earth. Having now endeavoured to neutralise an evil which might, amongst a large class, give birth to one prejudice more against Ireland, we proceed with a lighter spirit. The author's humorous style of sketching character, and his inimitable tact and drollery in telling a story, are amongst his highest recommendations. (pp. 454-55)

The praise that Doctor Johnson confers upon Shakspeare's Falstaff, viewing the character in one aspect, might be applied in nearly the same words to Lever's Monsoon. There is another personage a great promoter of fun, one Mickey Free, Master Charley's own man. The conception of the character is what one might fantastically style stereotyped. Everybody who writes novels about Irish people has his or her Micky Free. . . . But though the conception be not original, the execution is first-rate. Micky Free is one of the very best of his class. (p. 458)

There is, also, in the more serious passages of the work, wherein the struggles and triumphs of the British arms are treated of, great vividness of description, and a show of honest fervour which carries the reader forward in a state of thrilling excitement. Certainly it is not to the mere novelist we would go for the true description of one of our great battles. In Napier we have an historian worthy of the great deeds he celebrates—one that can take his place as the inspired depicter of the battle-field beside those mighty word-painters, who have given eternal blazon to the deeds of our predecessors in all earthly glory and supremacy—Sallust, Livy, Tacitus, and "mightiest Julius." But as the work of a romancer, there are many passages of stern fight described, which, to the uncritical eye of a civilian, are bright with interest. Take the following. The scene is Talavera:—

> A signal gun from the French boomed heavily through the still air. The last echo was growing fainter and the heavy smoke breaking into mist, when the most deafening thunder ever my ears heard came pealing around us. Eighty pieces of artillery had opened upon us, sending a very tempest of bullets upon our line, whilst midst the smoke and dust we could see the light troops advancing at a run, followed by the broad and massive column in all the terror and majesty of war. 'What a splendid attack! How gallantly they come on!' cried an old veteran officer beside me, forgetting all rivalry in his noble admiration of our enemy. The intervening space was soon passed, and the tirailleurs falling back as the column came on, the towering masses bore down upon Campbell's division with a loud cry of defiance. Silently and steadily the English infantry awaited the attack and returning the fire with one withering volley, were ordered to charge. Scarcely were the bayonets lowered when the head of the advancing column broke and fled, while Mackenzie's brigade overlapping the flank pushed boldly forward, and a scene of frightful carnage followed. For a moment a hand-to-hand combat was sustained; but the unbroken files and impregnable bayonets of the British conquered, and the French fled back leaving six guns behind them.
>
> (pp. 460-61)

This, it will be easily conceded, is well done for a novelist; and yet how unsatisfactory it is even with all the freedom of its details as compared with the truth, stronger than fiction, as

narrated by the great historians of the two great empires, Rome and England. (pp. 461-62)

The hero's adventures after all [his] campaigning, as we foresee from the first, lead him to the haven of peace as the husband of Lucy Dashwood; and the bold dragoon subsides into a resident landlord, with a Galway tenantry under his command. Joy to his wedlock, prosperity to his efforts on behalf of his fellow-countrymen. He has led us through many pleasant scenes; he has often made us stare at his bouncers and matchless intrepidity of assertion in matters of taste and fact; but he has never for a moment made us drowsy, never bored us with seedy sentimentality and maudlin morality. In a word, we had rather, speaking metaphorically, or in parable, or in a phasis of fun—we cannot hit upon the right term for it—we had rather borrow money to drink with the author of *Charles O'Malley,* than get drunk at the costliest expense of any other scribbler in the light brigade of flimsy literature.

Some eight numbers of *Jack Hinton* have been published. They are written with untiring energy, and we look forward to its progress with anticipations of pleasure. To be sure the leading characters are, in the essence, still the same with those in *Harry Lorrequer* and *Charles O'Malley;* but the scenes, and, above all, the stories recounted by the various personages, will be different. (p. 463)

> [*William Maginn?*], *"Charles O'Malley and Jack Hinton: Irish Dragoons and English Guardsmen,"* in Fraser's Magazine for Town & Country, *Vol. XXVI, No. CLIV, October, 1842, pp. 447-65.*

EDGAR ALLAN POE   (essay date 1842)

[*Considered one of America's most outstanding men of letters, Poe was a distinguished poet, novelist, essayist, journalist, short story writer, editor, and critic. Poe stressed an analytical, rather than emotive, approach to literature, emphasizing the technical details of a work instead of its ideological statement. Although Poe and his literary criticism were controversial in his lifetime, he is now valued for his literary theories. Here, Poe attacks* Charles O'Malley, *which he considers vulgar in both thought and execution. Poe's remarks were first published in* Graham's Magazine *in March 1842.*]

The first point to be observed in the consideration of *Charles O'Malley* is the great *popularity* of the work. We believe that in this respect it has surpassed even the inimitable compositions of Mr. Dickens. At all events it has met with a most extensive sale; and, although the graver journals have avoided its discussion, the ephemeral press has been nearly if not quite unanimous in its praise. To be sure, the commendation, although unqualified, cannot be said to have abounded in specification, or to have been, in any regard, of a satisfactory character to one seeking precise ideas on the topic of the book's particular merit. It appears to us, in fact, that the cabalistical words "fun" "rollicking" and "devil-may-care," if indeed words they be, have been made to stand in good stead of all critical comment in the case of the work now under review. We first saw these dexterous expressions in a fly-leaf of "Opinions of the Press" appended to the renowned *Harry Lorrequer* by his publisher in Dublin. Thence transmitted, with complacent echo, from critic to critic, through daily, weekly and monthly journals without number, they have come at length to form a pendant and a portion of our author's celebrity—have come to be regarded as sufficient response to the few ignoramuses who, obstinate as ignorant, and fool-hardy as obstinate, venture to propound a question or two about the true claims of **Harry Lorrequer** or the justice of the pretensions of **Charles O'Malley.**

We shall not insult our readers by supposing any one of them unaware of the fact, that a book may be even exceedingly *popular* without *any* legitimate literary merit. This fact can be proven by numerous examples which, now and here, it will be unnecessary and perhaps indecorous to mention. The dogma, then, is absurdly false, that the popularity of a work is *primâ facie* evidence of its excellence in some respects; that is to say, the dogma is false if we confine the meaning of excellence (as here of course it must be confined) to excellence in a literary sense. The truth is, that the popularity of a book is *primâ facie* evidence of just the converse of the proposition—it is evidence of the book's *demerit,* inasmuch as it shows a "stooping to conquer"—inasmuch as it shows that the author has dealt largely, if not altogether, in matters which are susceptible of appreciation by the mass of mankind—by uneducated thought, by uncultivated taste, by unrefined and unguided passion. So long as the world retains its present point of civilization, so long will it be almost an axiom that no extensively *popular* book, in the right application of the term, can be a work of high merit, *as regards those particulars of the work which are popular.* (pp. 311-12)

[The popularity of **Charles O'Malley**] must not be considered in any degree as the measure of its merit; but should rather be understood as indicating a deficiency in this respect, when we bear in mind, as we should do, the highest aims of intellect in fiction. A slight examination of the work, (for in truth it is worth no more,) will sustain us in what we have said. The plot is exceedingly meagre. Charles O'Malley, the hero, is a young orphan Irishman, living in Galway county, Ireland, in the house of his uncle, Godfrey, to whose sadly encumbered estates the youth is heir apparent and presumptive. He becomes enamoured, while on a visit to a neighbor, of Miss Lucy Dashwood, and finds a rival in a Captain Hammersley. Some words carelessly spoken by Lucy, inspire him with a desire for military renown. After sojourning, therefore, for a brief period, at Dublin University, he obtains a commission and proceeds to the Peninsula, with the British army under Wellington. Here he distinguishes himself; is promoted; and meets frequently with Miss Dashwood, whom obstinately, and in spite of the lady's own acknowledgment of love for himself, he supposes in love with Hammersley. Upon the storming of Ciudad Rodrigo he returns home; finds his uncle, of course, *just* dead; and sells his commission to disencumber the estate. Presently Napoleon escapes from Elba, and our hero, obtaining a staff appointment under Picton, returns to the Peninsula, is present at Waterloo, (where Hammersley is killed) saves the life of Lucy's father, for the second time, as he has already twice saved that of Lucy herself; is rewarded by the hand of the latter; and, making his way back to O'Malley Castle, "lives happily all the rest of his days."

In and about this plot (if such it may be called) there are more absurdities than we have patience to enumerate. The author, or narrator, for example, is supposed to be Harry Lorrequer as far as the end of the preface, which by the way, is one of the best portions of the book. O'Malley then tells his own story. But the publishing office of the *Dublin University Magazine* (in which the narrative originally appeared) having been burned down, there ensues a sad confusion of identity between O'Malley and Lorrequer, so that it is difficult, for the nonce, to say which is which. In the want of copy consequent

upon the disaster, James, the novelist, comes in to the relief of Lorrequer, or perhaps of O'Malley, with one of the flattest and most irrelevant of love-tales. Meantime, in the story proper are repetitions without end. We have already said that the hero *saves the life of his mistress twice, and of her father twice.* But not content with this, he has *two* mistresses, and *saves the life of both, at different periods, in precisely the same manner*—that is to say, by causing his horse, in each instance, to perform a Munchausen side-leap, at the moment when a spring forward would have impelled him upon his beloved. And then we have one unending, undeviating succession of junketings, in which "devilled kidneys" are never by any accident found wanting. The unction and pertinacity with which the author discusses what he chooses to denominate "devilled kidneys" are indeed edifying, to say no more. The truth is, that drinking wine, telling anecdotes, and devouring "devilled kidneys" may be considered as the sum total, as the *thesis* of the book. Never in the whole course of his eventful life, does Mr. O'Malley get "two or three assembled together" without seducing them forthwith to a table, and placing before them a dozen of wine and a dish of "devilled kidneys." This accomplished, the parties begin what seems to be the business of the author's existence—the narration of unusually *broad tales*—like those of the Southdown mutton. And here, in fact, we have the *plan* of that whole work of which the *United Service Gazette* has been pleased to vow it "would rather be the author than of all the *Pickwick*s and *Nickleby*s in the world"—a sentiment which we really blush to say has been echoed by many respectable members of our own press. The general plot or narrative is a mere thread upon which after-dinner anecdotes, some good, some bad, some utterly worthless, and *not one truly original,* are strung with about as much method, and about half as much dexterity, as we see ragged urchins employ in stringing the kernels of nuts.

It would, indeed, be difficult to convey to one who has not examined this production for himself, any idea of the exceedingly rough, clumsy, and inartistical manner in which even this bald conception is carried out. The stories are absolutely dragged in by the ears. So far from finding them result naturally or plausibly from the conversation of the interlocutors, even the blindest reader may perceive the author's struggling and blundering effort to introduce them. It is rendered quite evident that they were originally "on hand," and that *O'Malley* has been concocted for their introduction. Among other *niaïseries* we observe the silly trick of whetting appetite by delay. The conversation over the "kidneys" is brought, for example, to such a pass that one of the speakers is called upon for a story, which he forthwith declines for any reason, or for none. At a subsequent "broil" he is again pressed, and again refuses, and it is not until the reader's patience is fairly exhausted, and he has consigned both the story and its author to Hades, that the gentleman in question is prevailed upon to discourse. The only conceivable result of this *fanfarronade* is the ruin of the tale when told, through exaggerating anticipation respecting it.

The anecdotes thus narrated being the staple of the book, and the awkward manner of their interlocution having been pointed out, it but remains to be seen what the anecdotes are, in themselves, and what is the merit of their narration. And here, let it not be supposed that we have any design to deprive the devil of his due. There are several very excellent anecdotes in **Charles O'Malley** very cleverly and pungently told. Many of the scenes in which Monsoon figures are rich—less, however, from the scenes themselves than from the piquant, but by no means original character of Monsoon—a drunken, maudlin, dishonest old Major, given to communicativeness and mock morality over his cups, and not over careful in detailing adventures which tell against himself. One or two of the college pictures are unquestionably good—but might have been better. In general, the reader is made to feel that fine subjects have fallen into unskilful hands. By way of instancing this assertion, and at the same time of conveying an idea of the tone and character of the stories, we will quote one of the shortest, and assuredly one of the best.

"Ah, by-the-by, how's the Major?"

"Charmingly: only a little bit in a scrape just now. Sir Arthur—Lord Wellington, I mean—had him up for his fellows being caught pillaging, and gave him a devil of a rowing a few days ago.

" 'Very disorderly corps yours, Major O'Shaugnessy,' said the general; 'more men up for punishment than any regiment in the service.'

"Shaugh muttered something, but his voice was lost in a loud cock-a-doo-doo-doo, that some bold chanticleer set up at the moment.

" 'If the officers do their duty Major O'Shaugnessy, these acts of insubordination do not occur.'

"Cock-a-doo-doo-doo, was the reply. Some of the staff found it hard not to laugh; but the general went on—

" 'If, therefore, the practice does not cease, I'll draft the men into West India regiments.'

" 'Cock-a-doo-doo-doo!'

" 'And if any articles pillaged from the inhabitants are detected in the quarters, or about the persons of the troops—'

" 'Cock-a-doo-doo-*doo*!' screamed louder here than ever.

" 'Damn that cock—where is it?'

"There was a general look around on all sides, which seemed in vain; when a tremendous repetition of the cry resounded from O'Shaughnessy's coat-pocket: thus detecting the valiant Major himself in the very practice of his corps. There was no standing this: every one burst out into a peal of laughter; and Lord Wellington himself could not resist, but turned away, muttering to himself as he went—'Damned robbers every man of them,' while a final war-note from the Major's pocket closed the interview."

Now this is an anecdote at which every one will laugh; but its effect might have been vastly heightened by putting a few words of grave morality and reprobation of the conduct of his troops, into the mouth of O'Shaughnessy, upon whose character they would have told well. The cock, in interrupting the thread of his discourse, would thus have afforded an excellent context. We have scarcely a reader, moreover, who will fail to perceive the want of *tact* shown in dwelling upon the *mirth* which the anecdote occasioned. The error here is precisely like that of a man's laughing at his own spoken jokes. Our author is uniformly guilty of this mistake. He has an absurd fashion, also, of informing the reader, at the conclusion of each of his anecdotes, that, however, good the anecdote might be, he (the reader) cannot enjoy it to the full extent in

default of the *manner* in which it was orally narrated. He has no business to say anything of this kind. It is his duty to convey the manner not less than the matter of his narratives.

But we may say of these latter that, in general, they have the air of being *remembered* rather than invented. No man who has seen much of the rough life of the camp will fail to recognize among them many very old acquaintances. Some of them are as ancient as the hills, and have been, time out of mind, the common property of the bivouac. They have been narrated orally all the world over. The chief merit of the writer is, that he has been the first to collect and to print them. It is observable, in fact, that the second volume of the work is very far inferior to the first. The author seems to have exhausted his whole hoarded store in the beginning. His conclusion is barren indeed, and but for the historical details (for which he has no claim to merit) would be especially prosy and dull. *Now the true invention never exhausts itself.* It is mere cant and ignorance to talk of the possibility of the really imaginative man's "writing himself out." His soul but derives nourishment from the streams that flow therefrom. . . . So long as the universe of thought shall furnish matter for novel combinations, so long will the spirit of true genius be original, be exhaustless—be itself.

A few cursory observations. The book is filled to overflowing with songs of very doubtful excellence, the most of which are put into the mouth of one Micky Free, an amusing Irish servant of O'Malley's, and are given as his impromptu effusions. The subject of the improvisos is always the matter in hand at the moment of composition. The author evidently prides himself upon his poetical powers, about which the less we say the better; but if anything were wanting to assure us of his absurd ignorance and inappreciation of Art, we should find the fullest assurance in the mode in which these doggerel verses are introduced.

The occasional sentiment with which the volumes are interspersed there is an absolute necessity for skipping.

Can anybody tell us what is meant by the affectation of the word *L'envoy* which is made the heading of two prefaces?

That portion of the account of the battle of Waterloo which gives O'Malley's experiences while a prisoner, and in close juxta-position to Napoleon, bears evident traces of having been translated, and very literally too, from a French manuscript.

The English of the work is sometimes even amusing. We have continually, for example, *eat,* the present, for *ate,* the perfect. . . . [We] have this delightful sentence—"Captain Hammersley, however, *never* took further notice of me, but continued to recount, for the amusement of those *about,* several excellent stories of his military career, which I confess were heard with every *test* of delight by all save me." . . . [We] have some sage talk about "the entire of the army;" and . . . the accomplished O'Malley speaks of "*drawing* a last look upon his sweetheart." These things arrest our attention as we open the book at random. It abounds in them, and in vulgarisms even much worse than they.

But why speak of vulgarisms of language? There is a disgusting vulgarism of thought which pervades and contaminates this whole production, and from which a delicate or lofty mind will shrink as from a pestilence. Not the least repulsive manifestation of this leprosy is to be found in the author's blind and grovelling worship of mere rank. Of the Prince Regent, that filthy compound of all that is bestial—that lazar-house of all moral corruption—he scruples not to speak in terms of the grossest adulation—sneering at Edmund Burke in the same villainous breath in which he extols the talents, the graces and *the virtues* of George the Fourth! That any man, to-day, can be found so degraded in heart as to style this reprobate, "one who, in every feeling of his nature, and in every feature of his deportment was every inch a prince"—is matter for grave reflection and sorrowful debate. The American, at least, who shall peruse the concluding pages of the book now under review, and not turn in disgust from the base sycophancy which infects them, is unworthy of his country and his name. But the truth is, that a gross and contracted soul renders itself unquestionably manifest in almost every line of the composition.

And this—*this* is the *work,* in respect to which its author, aping the airs of intellect, prates about his "haggard check," his "sunken eye," his "aching and tired head," his "nights of toil" and (Good Heavens!) his "days of *thought!*" That the thing is popular we grant—while that we cannot deny the fact, we grieve. But the career of true taste is onward—and now more vigorously onward than ever—and the period, perhaps, is not hopelessly distant, when, in decrying the mere balderdash of such matters as **Charles O'Malley,** we shall do less violence to the feelings and judgment even of the populace, than, we much fear, has been done to-day. (pp. 314-20)

Edgar Allan Poe, "Charles James Lever," in his Essays and Reviews, *edited by G. R. Thompson, Literary Classics of the U.S., 1984, pp. 311-20.*

WILLIAM MAKEPEACE THACKERAY (essay date 1845)

[*A famed Victorian author, Thackeray is best known for his satiric sketches and novels of upper- and middle-class English life.* Vanity Fair: A Novel without a Hero *(1848), a panorama of early nineteenth-century English society, is generally considered his masterpiece. Thackeray was also a friend of Lever, to whom he dedicated* The Irish Sketchbook *(1843). Here Thackeray uses the publication of* St. Patrick's Eve *as an occasion to condemn the practice of moralizing on political and economic issues in fiction. Thackeray's comments were first published in the London* Morning Chronicle *on 3 April 1845. For a parody of Lever's novels by Thackeray, see excerpt dated 1847.*]

Since the days of Aesop, comic philosophy has not been cultivated so much as at present. The chief of our pleasant writers—Mr. Jerrold, Mr. Dickens, Mr. Lever—are assiduously following this branch of writing; and the first-named jocular sage, whose apologues adorned our spelling-books in youth, was not more careful to append a wholesome piece of instruction to his fable than our modern teachers now are to give their volumes a moral ballast. To some readers—callous, perhaps, or indifferent to virtue or to sermons—this morality is occasionally too obtrusive. Such sceptics will cry out—We are children no longer; we no longer want to be told that the fable of the dog in the manger is a satire against greediness and envy; or that the wolf and the lamb are types of Polk gobbling up a meek Aberdeen, or innocence being devoured by oppression. These truths have been learned by us already. If we want instruction, we prefer to take it from fact rather than from fiction. We like to hear sermons from his reverence at church; to get our notions of trade, crime, politics, and other national statistics, from the proper papers and figures; but when suddenly, out of the gilt pages of a pretty picture book,

a comic moralist rushes forward, and takes occasion to tell us that society is diseased, the laws unjust, the rich ruthless, the poor martyrs, the world lop-sided, and *vice versâ,* persons who wish to lead an easy life are inclined to remonstrate against this literary ambuscadoe. (pp. 70-1)

Mr. Lever is by far the most gentle of the comic satirists: he is not only gentle and kindly in his appreciation of the poor man, but kindly and gentle in regard to the rich, whom certain of Mr. Lever's brother moralists belabour so hardly; and if occasion is here taken of [*St. Patrick's Eve*] to enter a protest against sentimental politics altogether, it is not because this author is more sinful on this score than any other, but because the practice amongst novelists is prodigiously on the increase, and can tend, as we fancy, to little good. You cannot have a question fairly debated in this way. You can't allow an author to invent incidents, motives, and characters, in order that he may attack them subsequently. . . . The landlords may be wickedly to blame; the monsters get two per cent for their land; they roll about in carriages, do nothing, and drink champagne; while the poor labourer remains at home and works and starves;—but we had better have some other opinion than that of the novelist to decide upon the dispute between them. He can exaggerate the indolence and luxury of the one, or the miseries and privations of the other, as his fancy leads him. In the days of Marmontel and Florian it was the fashion to depict shepherds and shepherdesses in pink ribbons and laced petticoats, piping to their flocks all day, and dancing and serenading all night; in our time writers give a very different view of the peasant. Crime, poverty, death, pursue him: the gamekeeper shoots him or banishes him from his home and little ones; the agent grinds him down; the callous landlord pockets the rent which has been squeezed out of the vitals of his victim, and goes home and drinks a cool bottle of claret after church. Much of this may be true as regards the luckless peasant of the present time—but what remedy or contrast has the political novelist to propose? An outcry against the landlords. His easy philosophy has led him no farther. Has any sentimental writer organized any feasible scheme for bettering the poor? Has any one of them, after weeping over poor Jack, and turning my lord to ridicule, devised anything for the substantial benefit of the former. . . . When Cobden thunders against the landlords, he flings figures and facts into their faces, as missiles with which he assails them; he offers, as he believes, a better law than their's as a substitute for that which they uphold. When Sir Robert Peel resists or denies or takes up the standard which he has planted, and runs away, it is because he has cogent prudential reasons for his conduct of the day. But on one side and the other it is a serious contest which is taking place in the press and Parliament over the "Condition of England question." The novelist as it appears to us, ought to be a non-combatant. But if he persists in taking a side, don't let him go into the contest unarmed; let him do something more effectual than call the enemy names. The cause of either party in this great quarrel requires a stronger championship than this, and merits a more earnest warfare.

We have said that the landlords in Ireland are by no means maltreated by Mr. Lever; indeed his remedy for the national evils is of the mildest sort and such as could not possibly do harm to that or any other afflicted country. The persons who, it is proposed, shall administer the prescribed remedies, viz., the absentees, who are called upon to return to Tipperary and elsewhere, might not at first relish the being brought so near the patient; but for the sick man himself, there can be no doubt that the application of a landlord would not injure him, any more than that of a leech in a case of apoplexy, or of a teaspoon full of milk and water in a fever. That the medicine would be sufficiently powerful is another question. It has been proposed by many persons: by Miss Edgeworth, by Mr. Carleton, and others, as well as Mr. Lever; but we fancy it would not answer one-hundredth part of the purpose for which it is intended; besides that, the landlords obstinately decline being put forward for the experiment.

The aim of our author's book is, he says, to show that absentees should return; that "prosperity has as many duties as adversity has sorrows; and that those to whom Providence has accorded many blessings are but the stewards of heaven's bounty to the poor."

As a general proposition none can be more amiable and undeniable than this; but we deny that Mr. Lever has worked it well, or has so constructed his story as especially to illustrate this simple moral. His purpose is very good, but his end, when he defines it, is frequently entirely preposterous. (pp. 72-5)

In Mr. Lever's story, the hero (a tenant) in the first place gets a farm *for nothing*. He does not better himself; but takes to drink and idleness, and the landlord is rebuked because he is not there to be kind and didactic to him, and teach him how he should go.

In the second part of the story the tenant is turned out of his farm, drinks worse than ever, and finally agrees to *murder* the landlord's agent; but before this crime is committed the landlord returns, the tenant marries the young person to whom he is attached, all parties are reconciled, and all live happily ever after.

Now, have we not a right to protest against morals of this kind, and to put in a word for the landlord, just for novelty's sake? A man gets a farm for nothing (a gentleman surely cannot well let his ground for *less*), and who but the landlord is blamed because his idle tenant does not prosper? The tenant determines on murdering the agent, and the argument is, "Poor fellow! why was not the landlord there to teach him better?" Writers who mount the bench as judges in the great philanthropic suit now pending, have surely no right to deliver such preposterous sentences as these. Here we have an Irish judge convicting the landlords of "*guilt,* in deriving all the appliances of his ease and enjoyment from those whose struggles to supply them were made under the pressure of disease and hunger." Why not hunger? Without hunger there would be no work. We have just seen Mr. Lever's peasant, idling and drinking when he got his farm for nothing, and when he is to pay his landlord, the latter is straightway brought in *guilty.* What a verdict is this! All property may similarly be declared iniquitous, and all capital criminal. Let fundholders and manufacturers look out—Judge Jerrold will show them no favour, Chief Baron Boz has charged dead against them, and so we see it has been ruled in Ireland by the chief authority of the literary bench.

A friend who comes in, and has read both ***Saint Patrick's Eve*** and the above observations, declares that the story has nothing to do with politics; that no critic has a right to judge it in a political sense; and that it is to be tested by its descriptive, its humorous, its pathetic, or romantic merits.

An illustration depicting the title character of The Confessions of Harry Lorrequer.

If such be the case (and we have our doubts), a great deal may be said in praise, and a little in blame of Mr. Lever's new story. In the first place, the writing is often exceedingly careless. The printer or some one else has somehow left out a verb in the very first sentence, by which the whole fabric falls to pieces. . . . Periods are violently torn asunder. Accusatives are wrenched from their guardian verbs, which are left atrociously mangled. A regard for that mother whom the critic and the novelist ought to revere equally, the venerable English grammar, binds us to protest against this careless treatment of her. In regard of the merits, the narrative has the animated, rapid, easy style which is the charm of the author's writing, the kindly and affectionate humour (which appears in this volume to greater advantage, because it is not *over laughed* by the boisterous jocularity which we find in some of his other works), and the gay and brilliant manner of depicting figure and landscape, which distinguishes Mr. Lever's dexterous and facile hand. Parts of the tale are told with exceeding pathos and sweetness; and he who begins must needs go through it, with interest and with unabated pleasure. (pp. 76-7)

William Makepeace Thackeray, "Lever's 'St. Patrick's Eve'—Comic Politics," in his Contributions to the Morning Chronicle, *edited by Gordon N. Ray, University of Illinois Press, 1955, pp. 70-7.*

HARRY ROLLICKER [PSEUDONYM OF WILLIAM MAKEPEACE THACKERAY] (essay date 1847)

[*The following excerpt is from* Phil Fogarty: A Tale of the Fighting Onety-Oneth, *a parody of Lever's novels that Thackeray, under the pseudonym Harry Rollicker, wrote for* Punch *magazine in 1847. For critical commentary by Thackeray, see excerpt dated 1845.*]

I.

The gabion was ours. After two hours' fighting we were in possession of the first embrasure, and made ourselves as comfortable as circumstances would admit. Jack Delamere, Tom Delancy, Jerry Blake, the Doctor, and myself, sat down under a pontoon, and our servants laid out a hasty supper on a tumbrel. Though Cambacères had escaped me so provokingly after I cut him down, his spoils were mine; a cold fowl and a Bologna sausage were found in the Marshal's holsters; and in the haversack of a French private who lay a corpse on the glacis, we found a loaf of bread, his three days' ration. Instead of salt, we had gunpowder; and you may be sure, wherever the Doctor was, a flask of good brandy was behind him in his instrument-case. We sat down and made a soldier's supper. The Doctor pulled a few of the delicious fruit from the lemon-trees growing near (and round which the Carabineers and the 24th Leger had made a desperate rally), and punch was brewed in Jack Delamere's helmet.

"'Faith, it never had so much wit in it before," said the Doctor, as he ladled out the drink. We all roared with laughing, except the guardsman, who was as savage as a Turk at a christening.

"Buvez-en," said old Sawbones to our French prisoner; "ça vous fera du bien, mon vieux coq!" and the Colonel, whose wound had been just dressed, eagerly grasped at the proffered cup, and drained it with a health to the donors.

How strange are the chances of war! But half an hour before he and I were engaged in mortal combat, and our prisoner was all but my conqueror. Grappling with Cambacères, whom I knocked from his horse, and was about to despatch, I felt a lunge behind, which luckily was parried by my sabretache; a herculean grasp was at the next instant at my throat—I was on the ground—my prisoner had escaped, and a gigantic warrior in the uniform of a colonel of the regiment of Artois glaring over me with pointed sword.

"Rends-toi, coquin!" said he.

"Allez au Diable!" said I: "a Fogarty never surrenders."

I thought of my poor mother and my sisters, at the old house in Killaloo—I felt the tip of his blade between my teeth—I breathed a prayer, and shut my eyes—when the tables were turned—the butt-end of Lanty Clancy's musket knocked the sword up and broke the arm that held it.

"Thonamoundiaoul nabochlish," said the French officer, with a curse in the purest Irish. It was lucky I stopped laughing time enough to bid Lanty hold his hand, for the honest fellow would else have brained my gallant adversary. We were the better friends for our combat, as what gallant hearts are not?

The breach was to be stormed at sunset, and like true soldiers we sat down to make the most of our time. The rogue of a Doctor took the liver-wing for his share—we gave the other to our guest, a prisoner; those scoundrels Jack Delamere and

Tom Delancy took the legs—and, 'faith, poor I was put off with the Pope's nose and a bit of the back.

"How d'ye like his Holiness's *fayture?*" said Jerry Blake.

"Anyhow you'll have a *merry thought,*" cried the incorrigible Doctor, and all the party shrieked at the witticism.

"De mortuis nil nisi bonum," said Jack, holding up the drumstick clean.

"'Faith, there's not enough of it to make us *chicken-hearted,* anyhow," said I; "come, boys, let's have a song."

"Here goes," said Tom Delancy, and sung the following lyric, of his own composition:—

> Dear Jack, this white mug that with Guinness I fill,
> And drink to the health of sweet Nan of the Hill,
> Was once Tommy Tosspot's, as jovial a sot,
> As e'er drew a spigot, or drain'd a full pot—
> In drinking all round 'twas his joy to surpass,
> And with all merry tipplers he swigg'd off his glass.
>
> One morning in summer, while seated so snug,
> In the porch of his garden, discussing his jug,
> Stern Death, on a sudden, to Tom did appear,
> And said, "Honest Thomas, come take your last bier;"
> We kneaded his clay in the shape of this can,
> From which let us drink to the health of my Nan.

"Psha!" said the Doctor, "I've heard that song before; here's a new one for you, boys!" and Sawbones began, in a rich Corkagian voice—

> You've all heard of Larry O'Toole,
> Of the beautiful town of Drumgoole;
>   He had but one eye,
>   To ogle ye by—
> Oh, murther, but that was a jew'l!
>   A fool
> He made of de girls, dis O'Toole.
>
> 'Twas he was the boy didn't fail,
> That tuck down pataties and mail;
>   He never would shrink
>   From any sthrong dthrink,
> Was it whisky or Drogheda ale;
>   I'm bail
> This Larry would swallow a pail.
>
> Oh, many a night at the bowl,
> With Larry I've sot cheek by jowl;
>   He's gone to his rest,
>   Where there's dthrink of the best,
> And so let us give his old sow
>   A howl,
> For 'twas he made the noggin to rowl.

I observed the French Colonel's eye glistened as he heard these well-known accents of his country; but we were too well-bred to pretend to remark his emotion.

The sun was setting behind the mountains as our songs were finished, and each began to look out with some anxiety for the preconcerted signal, the rocket from Sir Hussey Vivian's quarters, which was to announce the recommencement of hostilities. It came just as the moon rose in her silver splendor, and ere the rocket-stick fell quivering to the earth at the feet of General Picton and Sir Lowry Cole, who were at their posts at the head of the storming-parties, nine hundred and ninety nine guns in position opened their fire from our batter-ies, which were answered by a tremendous cannonade from the fort. (pp. 26-8)

Our embrasure was luckily bomb-proof, and the detachment of the Onety-oneth under my orders suffered comparatively little. "Be cool, boys," I said; "it will be hot enough work for you ere long." The honest fellows answered with an Irish cheer. I saw that it affected our prisoner.

"Countryman," said I, "I know you; but an Irishman was never a traitor."

"Taisez-vous!" said he, putting his finger to his lip. "C'est la fortune de la guerre: if ever you come to Paris, ask for the Marquis d' O'Mahony, and I may render you the hospitality which your tyrannous laws prevent me from exercising in the ancestral halls of my own race."

I shook him warmly by the hand as a tear bedimmed his eye. It was, then, the celebrated colonel of the Irish Brigade, created a Marquis by Napoleon on the field of Austerlitz!

"Marquis," said I, "the country which disowns you is proud of you; but—ha! here, if I mistake not, comes our signal to advance." (p. 29)

The second rocket flew up.

"Forward, Onety-oneth!" cried I, in a voice of thunder. "Killaloo boys, follow your captain!" and with a shrill hurray, that sounded above the tremendous fire from the fort, we sprung upon the steep; Bowser with the brave Ninety-ninth, and the bold Potztausend, keeping well up with us. We passed the demilune, we passed the culverin, bayoneting the artillerymen at their guns; we advanced across the two tremendous demilunes which flank the counterscarp, and prepared for the final spring upon the citadel. Soult I could see quite pale on the wall; and the scoundrel Cambacères, who had been so nearly my prisoner that day, trembled as he cheered his men. "On, boys, on!" I hoarsely exclaimed. "Hurroo!" said the fighting Onety-oneth.

But there was a movement among the enemy. An officer, glittering with orders, and another in a gray coat and a cocked hat, came to the wall, and I recognized the Emperor Napoleon and the famous Joachim Murat.

"We are hardly pressed, methinks," Napoleon said sternly. "I must exercise my old trade as an artilleryman;" and Murat loaded, and the Emperor pointed the only hundred-and-twenty-four-pounder that had not been silenced by our fire.

"Hurray, Killaloo boys!" shouted I. The next moment a sensation of numbness and death seized me, and I lay like a corpse upon the rampart.

II.

"Hush!" said a voice, which I recognized to be that of the Marquis d' O'Mahony. "Heaven be praised, reason has returned to you. For six weeks those are the only sane words I have heard from you."

"Faix, and 'tis thrue for you, Colonel dear," cried another voice, with which I was even more familiar; 'twas that of my honest and gallant Lanty Clancy, who was blubbering at my bedside overjoyed at his master's recovery.

"O musha, Masther Phil agrah! but this will be the great day intirely, when I send off the news, which I would, barrin' I can't write, to the lady your mother and your sisters at Castle

Fogarty; and 'tis his Riv'rence Father Luke will jump for joy thin, when he reads the letther! Six weeks ravin' and roarin' as bould as a lion, and as mad as Mick Malony's pig, that mistuck Mick's wig for a cabbage, and died of atin' it!"

"And have I then lost my senses?" I exclaimed feebly.

"Sure, didn't ye call me your beautiful Donna Anna only yesterday, and catch hould of me whiskers as if they were the Signora's jet-black ringlets?" Lanty cried.

At this moment, and blushing deeply, the most beautiful young creature I ever set my eyes upon, rose from a chair at the foot of the bed, and sailed out of the room.

"Confusion, you blundering rogue," I cried; "who is that lovely lady whom you frightened away by your impertinence? Donna Anna? Where am I?"

"You are in good hands, Philip," said the Colonel; "you are at my house in the Place Vendôme, at Paris, of which I am the military Governor. You and Lanty were knocked down by the wind of the cannon-ball at Burgos. Do not be ashamed: 'twas the Emperor pointed the gun;" and the Colonel took off his hat as he mentioned the name darling to France. "When our troops returned from the sally in which your gallant storming party was driven back, you were found on the glacis, and I had you brought into the City. Your reason had left you, however, when you returned to life; but, unwilling to desert the son of my old friend, Philip Fogarty, who saved my life in '98, I brought you in my carriage to Paris."

"And many's the time you tried to jump out of the windy, Masther Phil," said Clancy.

"Brought you to Paris," resumed the Colonel, smiling; "where, by the soins of my friends Broussais, Esquirol, and Baron Larrey, you have been restored to health, thank heaven!"

"And that lovely angel who quitted the apartment?" I cried.

"That lovely angel is the Lady Blanche Sarsfield, my ward, a descendant of the gallant Lucan, and who may be, when she chooses, Madame la Maréchale de Cambacères, Duchess of Illyria." (pp. 29-31)

From that day I began to mend rapidly, with all the elasticity of youth's happy time. Blanche—the enchanting Blanche—ministered henceforth to me, for I would take no medicine but from her lily hand. And what were the effects? 'Faith, ere a month was past, the patient was over head and ears in love with the doctor; and as for Baron Larrey, and Broussais, and Esquirol, they were sent to the right-about. In a short time I was in a situation to do justice to the *gigot aux navets,* the *boeuf aux cornichons,* and the other delicious *entremets* of the Marquis's board, with an appetite that astonished some of the Frenchmen who frequented it.

"Wait till he's quite well, Miss," said Lanty, who waited always behind me. " 'Faith! when he's in health, I'd back him to ate a cow, barrin' the horns and teel." I sent a decanter at the rogue's head, by way of answer to his impertinence.

Although the disgusting Cambacères did his best to have my parole withdrawn from me, and to cause me to be sent to the English depot of prisoners at Verdun, the Marquis's interest with the Emperor prevailed, and I was allowed to remain at Paris, the happiest of prisoners, at the Colonel's hotel at the Place Vendôme. I here had the opportunity (an opportunity not lost, I flatter myself, on a young fellow with the accomplishments of Philip Fogarty, Esq.) of mixing with the *élite* of French society, and meeting with many of the great, the beautiful, and the brave. Talleyrand was a frequent guest of the Marquis's. His *bon-mots* used to keep the table in a roar. Ney frequently took his chop with us; Murat, when in town, constantly dropt in for a cup of tea and friendly round game. Alas! who would have thought those two gallant heads would be so soon laid low? My wife has a pair of earrings which the latter, who always wore them, presented to her—but we are advancing matters. Anybody could see, "*avec un demioeil,*" as the Prince of Benevento remarked, how affairs went between me and Blanche; but though she loathed him for his cruelties and the odiousness of his person, the brutal Cambacères still pursued his designs upon her.

I recollect it was on St. Patrick's Day. My lovely friend had procured, from the gardens of the Empress Josephine, at Malmaison (whom we loved a thousand times more than her Austrian successor, a sandy-haired woman, between ourselves, with an odious squint), a quantity of shamrock wherewith to garnish the hotel, and all the Irish in Paris were invited to the national festival.

I and Prince Talleyrand danced a double hornpipe with Pauline Bonaparte and Madame de Staël; Marshal Soult went down a couple of sets with Madame Récamier; and Robespierre's widow—an excellent, gentle creature, quite unlike her husband—stood up with the Austrian ambassador. Besides, the famous artists Baron Gros, David and Nicholas Poussin, and Canova, who was in town making a statute of the Emperor for Leo X., and, in a word, all the celebrities of Paris—as my gifted countrywoman, the wild Irish girl, calls them—were assembled in the Marquis's elegant receiving-rooms.

At last a great outcry was raised for *La Gigue Irlandaise! La Gigue Irlandaise!* a dance which had made a *fureur* amongst the Parisians ever since the lovely Blanche Sarsfield had danced it. She stepped forward and took me for a partner, and amidst the bravoes of the crowd, in which stood Ney, Murat, Lannes, the Prince of Wagram, and the Austrian ambassador, we showed to the *beau monde* of the French capital, I flatter myself, a not unfavorable specimen of the dance of our country.

As I was cutting the double-shuffle, and toe-and-heeling it in the "rail" style, Blanche danced up to me, smiling, and said, "Be on your guard; I see Cambacères talking to Fouché, the Duke of Otranto, about us; and when Otranto turns his eyes upon a man, they bode him no good."

"Cambacères is jealous," said I. "I have it," says she; "I'll make him dance a turn with me." So, presently, as the music was going like mad all this time, I pretended fatigue from my late wounds, and sat down. The lovely Blanche went up smiling, and brought out Cambacères as a second partner.

The Marshal is a lusty man, who makes desperate efforts to give himself a waist, and the effect of the exercise upon him was speedily visible. He puffed and snorted like a walrus, drops trickled down his purple face, while my lovely mischief of a Blanche went on dancing at treble quick, till she fairly danced him down.

"Who'll take the flure with me?" said the charming girl, animated by the sport.

"Faix, den, 'tis I, Lanty Clancy!" cried my rascal, who had been mad with excitement at the scene; and, stepping in with a whoop and a hurroo, he began to dance with such rapidity as made all present stare.

As the couple were footing it, there was a noise as of a rapid cavalcade traversing the Place Vendôme, and stopping at the Marquis's door. A crowd appeared to mount the stair; the great doors of the reception-room were flung open, and two pages announced their Majesties the Emperor and the Empress. So engaged were Lanty and Blanche, that they never heard the tumult occasioned by the august approach.

It was indeed the Emperor, who, returning from the Théâtre Français, and seeing the Marquis's windows lighted up, proposed to the Empress to drop in on the party. He made signs to the musicians to continue: and the conqueror of Marengo and Friedland watched with interest the simple evolutions of two happy Irish people. Even the Empress smiled; and, seeing this, all the courtiers, including Naples and Talleyrand, were delighted.

"Is not this a great day for Ireland?" said the Marquis, with a tear trickling down his noble face. "O Ireland! O my country! But no more of that. Go up, Phil, you divvle, and offer her Majesty the choice of punch or negus."

Among the young fellows with whom I was most intimate in Paris was Eugène Beauharnais, the son of the ill-used and unhappy Josephine by her former marriage with a French gentleman of good family. Having a smack of the old blood in him, Eugène's manners were much more refined than those of the new-fangled dignitaries of the Emperor's Court, where (for my knife and fork were regularly laid at the Tuileries) I have seen my poor friend Murat repeatedly mistake a fork for a toothpick, and the gallant Massena devour pease by means of his knife, in a way more innocent than graceful. Talleyrand, Eugène, and I used often to laugh at these eccentricities of our brave friends; who certainly did not shine in the drawing-room, however brilliant they were in the field of battle. The Emperor always asked me to take wine with him, and was full of kindness and attention.

"I like Eugène," he would say, pinching my ear confidentially, as his way was—"I like Eugène to keep company with such young fellows as you; you have manners; you have principles; my rogues from the camp have none. And I like you, Philip my boy," he added, "for being so attentive to my poor wife—the Empress Josephine, I mean." All these honors made my friends at the Marquis's very proud, and my enemies at Court *crever* with envy. Among these, the atrocious Cambacères was not the least active and envenomed.

The cause of the many attentions which were paid to me, and which, like a vain coxcomb, I had chosen to attribute to my own personal amiability, soon was apparent. Having formed a good opinion of my gallantry from my conduct in various actions and forlorn hopes during the war, the Emperor was most anxious to attach me to his service. The Grand Cross of St. Louis, the title of Count, the command of a crack cavalry regiment, the 14me Chevaux Marins, were the bribes that were actually offered to me; and must I say it? Blanche, the lovely, the perfidious Blanche, was one of the agents employed to tempt me to commit this act of treason.

"Object to enter a foreign service!" she said, in reply to my refusal. "It is you, Philip, who are in a foreign service. The Irish nation is in exile, and in the territories of its French allies. Irish traitors are not here; they march alone under the accursed flag of the Saxon, whom the great Napoleon would have swept from the face of the earth, but for the fatal valor of Irish mercenaries! Accept this offer, and my heart, my hand, my all are yours. Refuse it, Philip, and we part."

"To wed the abominable Cambacères!" I cried, stung with rage. "To wear a duchess's coronet, Blanche! Ha, ha! Mushrooms, instead of strawberry-leaves, should decorate the brows of the upstart French nobility. I shall withdraw my parole. I demand to be sent to prison—to be exchanged—to die—anything rather than be a traitor, and the tool of a traitress!" Taking up my hat, I left the room in a fury; and flinging open the door tumbled over Cambacères, who was listening at the key-hole, and must have overheard every word of our conversation.

We tumbled over each other, as Blanche was shrieking with laughter at our mutual discomfiture. Her scorn only made me more mad; and, having spurs on, I began digging them into Cambacères' fat sides as we rolled on the carpet, until the Marshal howled with rage and anger.

"This insult must be avenged with blood!" roared the Duke of Illyria.

"I have already drawn it," says I, "with my spurs."

"Malheur et malédiction!" roared the Marshal.

"Hadn't you better settle your wig?" says I, offering it to him on the tip of my cane, "and we'll arrange time and place when you have put your jasey in order." I shall never forget the look of revenge which he cast at me, as I was thus turning him into ridicule before his mistress.

"Lady Blanche," I continued bitterly, "as you look to share the Duke's coronet, hadn't you better see to his wig?" and so saying, I cocked my hat, and walked out of the Marquis's place, whistling "Garryowen."

I knew my man would not be long in following me, and waited for him in the Place Vendôme, where I luckily met Eugène too, who was looking at the picture-shop in the corner. I explained to him my affair in a twinkling. He at once agreed to go with me to the ground, and commended me, rather than otherwise, for refusing the offer which had been made to me. "I knew it would be so," he said, kindly; "I told my father you wouldn't. A man with the blood of the Fogarties, Phil my boy, doesn't wheel about like those fellows of yesterday." So, when Cambacères came out, which he did presently, with a more furious air than before, I handed him at once over to Eugène, who begged him to name a friend, and an early hour for the meeting to take place.

"Can you make it before eleven, Phil?" said Beauharnais. "The Emperor reviews the troops in the Bois de Boulogne at that hour, and we might fight there handy before the review."

"Done!" said I. "I want of all things to see the newly-arrived Saxon cavalry manoeuvre:" on which Cambacères, giving me a look, as much as to say, "See sights! Watch cavalry manoeuvres! Make your soul, and take measure for a coffin, my boy!" walked away, naming our mutual acquaintance, Marshal Ney, to Eugène, as his second in the business.

I had purchased from Murat a very fine Irish horse, Bugaboo, out of Smithereens, by Fadladeen, which ran into the French ranks at Salamanca, with poor Jack Clonakilty, of the 13th, dead, on the top of him. Bugaboo was too much and too ugly an animal for the King of Naples, who, though a showy horseman, was a bad rider across country; and I got the horse for a song. A wickeder and uglier brute never wore pig-skin; and I never put my leg over such a timber-jumper in my life. I rode the horse down to the Bois de Boulogne on the morning that the affair with Cambacères was to come off, and Lanty held him as I went in, "sure to win," as they say in the ring.

Cambacères was known to be the best shot in the French army; but I, who am a pretty good hand at a snipe, thought a man was bigger, and that I could wing him if I had a mind. As soon as Ney gave the word, we both fired: I felt a whiz past my left ear, and putting up my hand there, found a large piece of my whiskers gone; whereas at the same moment, and shrieking a horrible malediction, my adversary reeled and fell.

"Mon Dieu, il est mort!" cried Ney.

"Pas de tout," said Beauharnais. "Ecoute; il jure toujours."

And such, indeed, was the fact; the supposed dead man lay on the ground cursing most frightfully. We went up to him: he was blind with the loss of blood, and my ball had carried off the bridge of his nose. He recovered; but he was always called the Prince of Ponterotto in the French army, afterwards. The surgeon in attendance having taken charge of this unfortunate warrior, we rode off to the review where Ney and Eugène were on duty at the head of their respective divisions; and where, by the way, Cambacères, as the French say, "se faisait désirer."

It was arranged that Cambacères' division of six battalions and nine-and-twenty squadrons should execute a *richochet* movement, supported by artillery in the intervals, and converging by different *épaulements* on the light infantry, that formed, as usual, the centre of the line. It was by this famous manoeuvre that at Arcola, at Montenotte, at Friedland, and subsequently at Mazagran, Suwaroff, Prince Charles, and General Castanos were defeated with such victorious slaughter: but it is a movement which, I need not tell every military man, requires the greatest delicacy of execution, and which, if it fails, plunges an army into confusion.

"Where is the Duke of Illyria?" Napoleon asked. "At the head of his division, no doubt," said Murat: at which Eugène, giving me an arch look, put his hand to his nose, and caused me almost to fall off my horse with laughter. Napoleon looked sternly at me; but at this moment the troops getting in motion, the celebrated manoeuvre began, and his Majesty's attention was taken off from my impudence.

Milhaud's Dragoons, their bands playing "Vive Henri Quatre," their cuirasses gleaming in the sunshine, moved upon their own centre from the left flank in the most brilliant order, while the Carbineers of Foy, and the Grenadiers of the Guard under Drouet d'Erlon, executed a carambolade on the right, with the precision which became those veteran troops; but the Chasseurs of the young guard, marching by twos instead of threes, bore consequently upon the Bavarian Uhlans (an ill-disciplined and ill-affected body), and then, falling back in disorder, became entangled with the artillery and the left centre of the line, and in one instant thirty thousand men were in inextricable confusion.

"Clubbed, by Jabers!" roared out Lanty Clancy. "I wish we could show 'em the Fighting Onety-oneth, Captain darling."

"Silence, fellow!" I exclaimed. I never saw the face of man express passion so vividly as now did the livid countenance of Napoleon. He tore off General Milhaud's epaulettes, which he flung into Foy's face. He glared about him wildly, like a demon, and shouted hoarsely for the Duke of Illyria. "He is wounded, Sire," said General Foy, wiping a tear from his eye, which was blackened by the force of the blow, "he was wounded an hour since in a duel, Sire, by a young English prisoner, Monsieur de Fogarty."

"Wounded! a marshal of France wounded! Where is the Englishman? Bring him out, and let a file of grenadiers—"

"Sire!" interposed Eugène.

"Let him be shot!" shrieked the Emperor, shaking his spyglass at me with the fury of a fiend.

This was too much. "Here goes!" said I, and rode slap at him.

There was a shriek of terror from the whole of the French army, and I should think at least forty thousand guns were leveled at me in an instant. But as the muskets were not loaded, and the cannon had only wadding in them, these facts, I presume, saved the life of Phil Fogarty from this discharge.

Knowing my horse, I put him at the Emperor's head, and Bugaboo went at it like a shot. He was riding his famous white Arab, and turned quite pale as I came up and went over the horse and the Emperor, scarcely brushing the cockade which he wore.

"Bravo!" said Murat, bursting into enthusiasm at the leap.

"Cut him down!" said Siéyès, once an Abbé, but now a gigantic Cuirassier; and he made a pass at me with his sword. But he little knew an Irishman on an Irish horse. Bugaboo cleared Siéyès, and fetched the monster a slap with his near hind hoof which sent him reeling from his saddle,—and away I went, with an army of a hundred and seventy-three thousand eight hundred men at my heels. (pp. 31-8)

> *Harry Rollicker [pseudonym of William Makepeace Thackeray], "Phil Fogarty," in* Burlesques, *by William Makepeace Thackeray, Merrill and Baker, n.d., pp. 26-38.*

[MARGARET OLIPHANT]   (essay date 1855)

[*A prolific nineteenth-century Scottish novelist, critic, biographer, and historian, Oliphant published nearly one hundred novels. Many of them were tales of Scottish and English provincial life, including her most popular work, a series of novels known as the* Chronicles of Carlingford *(1863-76). She was also a regular contributor to Blackwood's Magazine, from which this excerpt is taken. Oliphant praises Lever's works, which she believes have been undervalued because they lack philosophical and psychological depth.*]

Our renewed acquaintance with war, and the universal interest we have in everything which illustrates to us the life of our gallant representatives in the field, will no doubt renew, to a considerable degree, the first freshness of approbation with which the public hailed the works of Mr. Lever. Though these brisk and lively narratives are considerably like each other, we do not desire to see a more animated and interesting story than *Charles O'Malley*—a book which bears a second

reading; and they all show, more or less, its characteristic qualities. It is not Mr. Lever's forte perhaps, to dive into the secret heart of things, or analyse his heroes and his heroines; but who can take a standing leap like the author of *Harry Lorrequer?* Who can witch the world with such noble horsemanship? He has the true spring of Irish humour and Irish shrewdness in him. Mickey Free is as merry and honest a rogue as every happy fancy invented; and all the secondary bits of life and character in the home-country are admirable. We have a very undue propensity to underrate these stories of adventure; but we think it remains to be proved that our books of emotion and sentiment are really of a higher class, as they certainly are not of a healthier. It is good to be the favourite of youth—good to awake the eager interest, the laugh which rings from the heart; and now that the trumpet sounds in our ears once more, it is time to throw off our supercilious contempt for those manly feats of strength and daring which delight a boy. After all, life as it goes on in the world is sometimes quite as elevated, and occasionally a more important matter for our observation than that life in the heart which we love so much to dwell upon and disclose. A campaign against the national enemy, agitating a thousand brave souls and widening its influence to embrace a thousand homes, and to touch every rank of the community, is a greater thing than the campaign of a king or queen of hearts, even though it be a quite successful one, and result in a few blighted lives, and long-winded miseries. There is no dulness in Mr. Lever's dashing, daring, rapid books. Of their kind they are capital—almost as exciting still as even these letters from the Crimea which we seize so eagerly. A strange change has passed upon the thoughts of this peace-loving nation. What piece of abstract literature, though its writer were laureated poet or throned philosopher, would not be put aside to-day for the simple letter of some poor private from the fated seat of war? (pp. 565-66)

> [*Margaret Oliphant*], *"Modern Novelists—Great and Small," in* Blackwood's Edinburgh Magazine, *Vol. LXXVII, No. CCCCLXXV, May, 1855, pp. 554-68.*

THE NATIONAL REVIEW, LONDON   (essay date 1857)

[*This anonymous critic lauds Lever's adventurous early works, but notes a steady decline in his ability to sustain the reader's interest in novels written after* Tom Burke of "Ours".]

The issue of a cheap edition of those old favourites, *Harry Lorrequer* and his successors, tempts us to say a few words on the style and subjects of Mr. Levers' novels. It is not only the young ensign or the schoolboy that has taken delight in these exciting and graphic tales. Such a profusion of fun, adventure, and rollicking hearty enjoyment wins its way to the taste of the most various readers. These stories are the true type, in the present day, of the novel which seeks only to fulfil the primary aim of all novels, that of amusing. To read them is pure relaxation. As it is said of good claret, that there is not a headache in a hogshead of it, so it may be said of romances like Mr. Lever's earlier stories, that there is not a moral lesson in a dozen of them. There are no concealed sermons, there is no sentimentalism, no philosophy, no politics, in the biographies of those dashing lieutenants whom he has made the subjects of his fictions. All is simple unadulterated comedy. We are transported into the gayest and most charming world, where every one eats, and drinks, and is merry; and we are never suffered to leave it until the last page has been read. If, therefore, it may be considered one chief purpose of works of fiction to relieve men from the burden of ordinary life by offering the contrast of imaginary pleasures, every one must acknowledge that this purpose has been most successfully achieved by Mr. Lever. (pp. 1-2)

He supplies us with the excitement which professed books of travel used to afford, while the reader was still at the mercy of the writer, and humbly believed whatever he found written. We now keep the most severe check on writers of travel, and a man can no more romance about Lake Tchad or Lake Ngami than he can about the Serpentine. But we must allow a novelist to have free play; and if he can but make us believe in a *tierra incognita,* we like him to fill it with wonders. Mr. Lever takes us to the unknown regions of Galway, and finds in that remote country "an opportunity of showing his parts, without incurring any danger of being examined and contradicted." He is master of the situation; he can work his will with us, and we submit with a pleased patience to hear what he is kind enough to narrate. His art teaches him to give a coherence and unity to the whole series of wonders, and we get quite used to, and at home in, the land of romance which he describes. His heroes may do any thing, bear any thing, say any thing, and it all seems quite natural and indisputable. He charms us by the harmony of his fiction. We do not wish to ask, whether his scenes are true, or probable. . . . This is the secret of Mr. Lever's success, the great merit of his works. He takes us away to his own enchanted ground of marvels, and there shows "the copiousness of his invention and the greatness of his genius."

Harry Lorrequer was the first, and is in many respects the best, of Mr. Lever's stories. It displays all his excellencies in the highest perfection; it takes us completely into the marvelous land which he has made his own, and through which he travels with so much ease and satisfaction. All the pleasures of life are spread before us; wit, wine, and women, fighting and loving, daring leaps, absurd hoaxes, mad Irishmen. We are led from story to story, and have good things thrown before us in profusion; and it is all done so pleasantly. The monkeys who stay at home cannot help liking to hear the travelled monkey talk; and we are obliged to a writer who can almost persuade us, that the life painted in *Harry Lorrequer* is a real or a possible life. (pp. 2-3)

He strings together a number of stories, each of which has probably some foundation in fact; and he arranges these as if the occurrences forming their subject-matter had happened consecutively, within a very short space of time, to the same person. The stories are so well told, and told at so great a length, that one by one they absorb our attention, and it hardly enters our head to remember how very odd it is that so many curious things should turn up so quickly. (p. 3)

[The] thread of the narrative has very little to do with the real substance of the book. It is literally a thread, and nothing more, and only serves to support a surprising burden of anecdote. Each incident of Harry Lorrequer's short career is made the subject of a separate history; and is so expanded, and polished, and garnished, that it is made most skilfully to have an independent interest, and to last page after page, to the great amusement of the reader, and the great credit of the writer. There are also a great number of subsidiary or digressive stories, and it taxes the art of Mr. Lever to introduce them neatly and plausibly. Sometimes, we must own, the mode of introduction is rather bold. In journeying from Paris to Strasburg, for instance, Lorrequer falls in with an Irish-

man whom he unintentionally offends; and, having slightly mentioned the circumstance, he continues: "Delighted to have thus fallen upon a character, as the Irishman evidently appeared, I moved my chair towards him; and finding he was not half-pleased at the manner in which my acquaintance had been made with him, and knowing his country's susceptibility of being taken by a story, I resolved to make my advances by narrating a circumstance," &c. &c. Certainly, if a man's not liking you is a reason for telling him a story, there can never be much difficulty in a story-teller fulfilling his vocation. It is curious to see what is the story with which Lorrequer propitiates the wrath of an entire stranger. It turns upon an adventure of some English officers, who go an excursion to Pera. There they occupy a kiosk that appears to be deserted, and begin luncheon. The owner of the kiosk sends to say that he and his suite would like to witness the repast. The Turks come, and the officers present each of them with a glass of champagne. All decline in silence except one very ferocious Turk, who curses the abomination. Shortly after the procession has left the visitors to themselves, the ferocious Turk comes back, and, seeing all safe, exclaims: "I'll taste your wine, gentlemen, an' it be pleasing to you." The story is so well told in the book, that we scarcely think of any thing but the manner of telling it; but if we go back, and look only at the manner in which it is introduced, we have to suppose Lorrequer saying to himself: "That man, whom I never saw before, does not seem to wish to know me; I will tell him a story of a drunken Irishman pretending to be a Turk, and then we shall be good friends."

No one can make more of a story than Mr. Lever can. He knows the secret of dwelling on each minute part, amplifying and spicing it so as to delay, and enhance the value of, the final wind-up of the anecdote. The story which we have just abridged lasts in the book through two closely printed pages. The view is described, and the kiosk, and we are told what an excellent meal the officers had, and what the Turks looked like, and how they behaved; and lastly, the account of the change of appearance in the Turk, who returns back as an Irishman, makes almost half-a-page in itself. "The dark complexion," we read, "the long and bushy beard, were there; but instead of the sleepy and solemn character of the Oriental, with heavy eye and closed lip, there was a droll half-devilry in the look," and so on, by all which our expectation is wound up to the highest pitch; and the concluding exclamation of the Irishman, which is not very amusing in itself, is made the most of. Mr. Lever also knows one or two other secrets of his art, and he uses his knowledge freely. For instance, he is well aware that the probability of a story depends very much more on the writer than on the matter of the story itself. If an almost impossible incident is treated as of an easy and ordinary occurrence, it makes its own way with the reader, and commends itself to him in the very teeth of his common sense. There is a long story in *Harry Lorrequer* of a counsel who wished to get rid of a jury, that he thought unequal to try an important case. He accordingly quoted the beautiful line of the Greek poet, *"Vacuus viator cantabit ante latronem."* The judge said that it was Juvenal's Latin; the counsel insisted it was the Greek of Hergesius, and at last said, that if the judge were to submit this question to the jury, "it would be Greek to every man of them." Common sense tells us that the judge would have told the counsel to proceed with his case, and not waste the time of the court; but the story-teller takes care that his story shall not end in this way, and goes on as if it were the simplest matter in the world to say, "The look, the voice, and the peculiar emphasis with which Peter gave these words were perfectly successful. The acute judge anticipated the wish of the counsel, and the jury were dismissed."

Story-tellers have always this advantage, that they can stop when they like, and dismiss all their fictitious personages when their purpose has been served. In real life there is never any stopping, and many of the most funny anecdotes would have an unpleasant ending if the whole of the circumstances were related. But an adept takes care that actions shall seem to have no consequences which he does not wish us to dwell on, and would have us believe that all ends when he ceases to relate. In ***Harry Lorrequer,*** for instance, we have a story of an Irish gentleman, who went to a Dublin theatre when some Red Indians were exhibited. The friend who accompanied him, on leaving the theatre shortly after this gentleman had quitted his place, found him beating the box-keeper. It appeared that the cause of his anger was that the box-keeper, thinking it a compliment to reveal the mysteries of the establishment, had informed him that the Red Indians really came from Galway. "The words were no sooner out of his lips," says the narrator, "than Burke, who immediately took them as a piece of direct insolence to himself and his country, felled him to the earth, and was in the act of continuing the discipline when I arrived on the field of battle." Here the story ends, and very conveniently. Perhaps if the story-teller had gone further, the joke would have ceased to be a joke. It is very funny that the gentleman should have beaten the box-keeper; but it would not have been quite so funny that the box-keeper should have called for assistance, and beaten the gentleman; that a row should have ensued, and then the police have interfered.

Mr. Lever has recourse to one expedient to make his stories effective, the legitimacy of which is, perhaps, doubtful. He tells us when to laugh; and he does this by simply describing the vast mirth and overpowering fits of laughter which the incidents of the story produced on the actual spectators. Harry Lorrequer, we are told, was acting some private theatricals, and, the curtain drawing up too soon, was discovered by the audience in a state of deshabille. We cannot doubt that this is very funny, when we read in conclusion, "The shouts of laughter are yet in my ears, the loud roar of inextinguishable mirth, which, after the first brief pause of astonishment gave way, shook the entire building." (pp. 4-7)

The occasions for all this laughter, so carefully chronicled, are very frequent, and Harry and his friends lead the gayest of lives. No wonder that young gentlemen who learn that regimental life is one round of unceasing merriment, should long ardently to select this life as their own. No wonder, also, that the parents of Harry Lorrequer should find the taste an expensive one. There is no pause in the merriment, devilry, fun and wit which officers are represented as enjoying. The hero has, of course, a serious love-affair, to which he devotes himself occasionally, and the uncertainties of which are supposed to cause him some uneasiness. Otherwise he is free from care, and never feels any surfeit, repentance, or responsibility. The only sorrow to which human flesh is represented as liable, is that of being sent in detachment to some stupid little country village. The feelings which such a change awaken are of course awful: "The surrender of your capital mess, with its well-appointed equipments, your jovial brother-officers, your West-India Madeira, your cool Lafitte, your daily, hourly, and half-hourly flirtations with the whole female population, not to speak of your matches at trotting, coursing, and pigeon-shooting,—to surrender all these for a country inn, with

bacon to eat, whisky to drink, and the priest or constabulary chief to get drunk with, and your only affair of the heart being the occasional ogling of the apothecary's daughter opposite,"—this is indeed a dreadful change. We are aware, indeed, that in the story the detachment-duty is not really going to be dull, and that the removal to country quarters is only the prelude to some exciting adventure. But even to persons not so sure of adventures as Harry Lorrequer, detachment-duty is held out as almost the only evil they need seriously fear.

It will be observed, that Harry, in the passage we have just quoted, treats getting drunk as a matter of course, and that the alternative is only between getting drunk on good liquor in good company, and getting drunk on bad liquor in bad company. There never was an author more fond of giving his characters something to drink than Mr. Lever. The whole set of people, men and women, are as thirsty as fish, and are always after the foaming champagne or the real poteen. It is said that more champagne is drunk on the Derby day than is grown in France, and Mr. Lever's military heroes and heroines live in a world where every body goes to the Derby every day. The young soldiers may, indeed, be said to divide their time between two kinds of entertainment. The first is graced by the presence of ladies. The serious love of the story does not appear, for she is above it, and remains mostly in the background, contributing little more to the progress of the story than the occasional appearance of her lovely face and genteel manners, and the ground she furnishes the hero for romantic outbursts in his maudlin moments. But all the minor beauties are there; the young ladies whom the hero takes up for the moment, with their mammas, and one or two oddities to furnish amusement to the party. At the entertainments of this first kind the gentlemen remain more or less sober, and champagne, with appropriate conversation, forms the main feature of the occasion. . . . At the other kind of feasts the ladies are absent, and then the gentlemen become openly and avowedly intoxicated. Harry Lorrequer begins with a banquet of this description; and there is no reserve or disguise about the effects. "When I first returned to consciousness," says Harry, "I found myself lying exactly where I had fallen. Around me lay heaps of slain." He then describes how he dreaded going down a flight of stairs, and how his fears were ended by his falling, and coming upon an alderman who lay drunk at the bottom. It is all told with the most perfect ease and confidence; and the young gentleman never feels a moment's shame, or reflects that he has been making himself a beast.

There is, however, a delusively tragic side to all this comedy. Harry Lorrequer and his friends indulge in one pastime more serious than popping champagne corks. On the slightest provocation a duel is got up; and Lorrequer fights two without having in either case the slightest notion why he is fighting, or any cause whatever for quarrelling with his opponent. We have an anticipatory conviction that it will never suit so merry a book that these encounters should end fatally, and they are touched in with as light and sportive a hand as possible. (pp. 7-9)

Charles O'Malley was the successor of ***Harry Lorrequer.*** In this work, which may be taken as the standard type of all the best of Mr. Lever's productions, an attempt was made to substitute adventure and connected thread of incident for the detached anecdotes of which ***Harry Lorrequer*** had mainly consisted. The hero figures in the two great theatres of action which Mr. Lever delights to depict—the wild country of the west of Ireland, and the Peninsular war. He is here in his glory. . . . He can tell us what he pleases, and he revels in his license of romance. If he chooses to describe men with their heads under their shoulders, we have but to sit and listen. It is true that we soon become used to it all, and the sense of the marvellous wears off. . . . But still the general impression certainly remains, that any one who lived like Charles O'Malley would lead a most wonderful life.

We are introduced to this young gentleman at the early age of seventeen. Speaking of himself at this period of his career, he modestly says: "I rode boldly with fox-hounds; I was about the best shot within twenty miles of us. I could swim the Shannon at Holy Island; I drove four-in-hand better than the coachman himself." This precocious stripling is sent to a neighbouring house to canvass for the county on behalf of his uncle; an employment admirably adapted to his mature years and experience. He there meets with the serious love of the story (with the sweetest blue eyes that ever beamed beneath a forehead of snowy whiteness, &c. &c.). . . . (pp. 9-10)

The gentleman with whom he is staying, and whom he is visiting for the purpose of an election-canvass, has been already secured by a rival candidate. A grand dinner is given, when the health of the future member is proposed; and Charles, thinking his uncle is meant, rises to return thanks. This naturally exposes him to some ridicule, and more especially from a Mr. Bodkin, who assures him that "by the rock of Cashel, we will carry our man against all the O'Malleys that ever cheated the sheriff." This was quite enough for the furious Charles. "Scarcely were the words uttered, when I seized my wine-glass, and hurled it with all my force at his head; so sudden was the act, and so true the aim, that Mr. Bodkin measured his length upon the floor." We may venture to observe, that nothing could have been more creditable to Charles's strength, and that bringing down a giant with a smooth stone from a brook was nothing to finishing off an enemy with a wine-glass. A duel of course follows; and terrible as are the duels in *Harry Lorrequer,* they are nothing to the duels in *Charles O'Malley.* But, as we might expect, the hero escapes. "My eye glanced towards my opponent, I raised my pistol and fired. My hat turned half round upon my head, and Bodkin fell motionless to the earth." The perils of O'Malley are not, however, over. His second hurries him to the Shannon, where a boat is lying in readiness. They embark, and are pursued by a party of infuriated supporters of Mr. Bodkin. A thunderstorm adds a little additional interest to the scene; and yet so great is their skill, that amidst the wildest fury of the elements they steer their boat through an imperceptible aperture between sunken rocks, and thus escape, their pursuers being unable to catch persons so securely protected by the exigencies of the story.

Hardly is this excitement well over, when one even stranger begins. The election-day arrives, when his uncle and the father of Miss Dashwood, the young lady on whom he has set his heart, are to contest the county. The fortunes of the fight enable him to render the most signal service to the fair Lucy, and thus to create an interest in his favour, which might have sooner rewarded his ardour with the possession of her charms had he been of a marriageable age. Some of his uncle's followers thought it a fair stroke of election warfare to seize on the carriage in which Miss Dashwood was seated, and to drive it in the direction of a most dangerous bridge. It does not ap-

Phiz's frontispiece for Charles O'Malley.

pear what bearing on the contest the feat could have had, even if perfectly successful. But it gave Charles an opportunity of distinguishing himself. He galloped wildly in pursuit, and arrived at the bridge just in time to see the carriage arrested half-way across, and a ruffian poised on the box-seat, prepared to throw Miss Dashwood into the Lurra-garh, "a torrent that ran deep and boisterously beneath." . . . Our readers are aware that the works of Mr. Lever had, on their first appearance, the advantage of profuse illustrations. The drawing that commemorates the rescue of Miss Dashwood is eminently characteristic of the class of romances to which *Charles O'Malley* belongs; and if any one unacquainted with Mr. Lever's writings wished to know the sort of matter he was to expect if he studied them, he could not have a better way of estimating their adventurous side at a glance than by bestowing a moment's attention on this striking design. A low bridge crosses a frightful gulf, over which a man is hanging, attached apparently by no better support than a handkerchief, which has happened to catch at the top of the wall, and in some marvellous way is sufficiently strong to keep him suspended over the abyss. Two horses are twisted into the most frantic contortions over the parapet of the bridge, and in the exact centre of the picture is the box-seat of a carriage otherwise unseen. Raised with one foot on the seat and the other on the splash-board, a gigantic prize-fighter holds high above his head a female form, while Charles is seen on the point of dealing destruction with his formidable whip. We shudder; and so awful is the confusion, and so fierce the struggle indicated, that we are not surprised, on turning the page, to find the next chapter beginning, "Nearly three weeks followed the event I have just narrated, ere I again was restored to consciousness." What became of the ruffian, how the man holding on by the handkerchief ever got up again, and how Miss Dashwood or any of the party ever got home, we are not told. A veil is drawn over these immaterial trifles, and fancy may revel in the void.

The west of Ireland is not, however, the only scene of O'Malley's exploits. He hears Miss Dashwood intimate that she could never love any one but a dragoon, and so a dragoon he determines to become. He goes with his regiment to the Peninsula, and is there from the first coming of Sir Arthur Wellesley to the fall of Ciudad Rodrigo. He passes through unnumbered perils, and is present at battle after battle. Mr. Lever shows great skill in the manner in which he mixes up the narrative of a particular officer with the record of the leading events of the war. We have at once a military history, as intelligible and impressive as most military histories, and interspersed is a series of the escapes, combats, carouses and flirtations of Charles O'Malley. He is accompanied by an Irish servant, who contributes very considerably to the amusement; and the Peninsula portion of the work is at once entertaining and tolerably quiet and unpretending. The known current of the history of the war keeps the imagination of the novelist within bounds. Certainly Charles is a great fire-eater; but then, that is his profession. He manages to take the place of a wounded officer at the storming of Ciudad Rodrigo, and there performs feats of the highest gallantry. (pp. 11-13)

At the end of the tale, the hero is rewarded not only with honour and fame, . . . but also with the hand of the heroine. Mr. Lever does not show the fertility and ingenuity in his love-scenes which we might have expected. The love-passages of Harry Lorrequer and his successor are, indeed, almost exactly alike. The young ladies appear willing from the first, and there is no very good reason why they should not be wooed and won at any time; but the heroes prevent so abrupt and happy a termination of their courtship by their peculiar manner of making a declaration. They never give the lady time to speak her mind; like jesting Pilate, they will not wait for an answer. Charles O'Malley is always pledging himself to love for ever and ever; and then dashing his spurs into his horse, and galloping away frantic with the agony of thinking his love rejected. Now we know, as well as Miss Dashwood did, that he need only have kept quiet a moment longer to have had all he wanted; and it is rather hard upon a willing young lady and sympathising readers, that he will not take the goods which the gods give him. The two works conclude with a chapter of almost similar construction. The hero bids farewell, and then the heroine blushes and trembles in the most encouraging manner; but it is of no use. The hero insists on an eternal farewell, which, as we can feel that only four or five pages are left, we know to be nonsense. However away he goes, and then he comes back once or twice to have another last despairing farewell; until, at length, the lady catches his eye, and then a glance reveals the truth, and he is blest beyond belief. It argues a greater poverty of invention than we should have expected in Mr. Lever, that he should have made two warriors so equally timid, and two lovers so equally unable to see that they need only wait for a very ready answer.

Charles O'Malley was quickly followed by two other tales of a very similar character, *Jack Hinton* and *Tom Burke*. The first of the two exactly copies *Charles O'Malley*, in having

the scene first laid in the West of Ireland, and then in the Peninsular War. The usual lovely young lady is, as usual, prevented by circumstances from following the dictates of her heart; and she consoles herself, for being denied to a lover who is longing to have her, by admiring his feats in duelling and riding. It is all Charles O'Malley over again. The most exciting part is the description of a steeple-chase, followed of course by a little pistol-shooting between the hero and his competitor. The duels in Mr. Lever's works are sufficiently numerous to give scope for a careful induction of particulars; and, by a studious comparison of the various encounters, we arrive at two great general facts: one, that the hero's assailant is indisputably and grossly in the wrong and wears a malignant scowl, the symbol of a still more malignant heart; and the other, that he is invariably hit on the hip, while the hero escapes. Exceptions prove the rule; and the duel in *Jack Hinton* which apparently invades, really strengthens, the general principle. The hero does not escape; but then, how is this brought about? He does escape from his enemy's fire, for the ball just grazes his cheek; but his enemy (shot, *en règle,* through the hip) throws his discharged pistol in Jack Hinton's face, stuns him, and lays him up for three weeks. Hinton is then carried, as an interesting invalid, into the neighbourhood of the serious love; and the story is greatly benefited by the unhandsome conduct of his opponent. But the fundamental law that, being a hero, no amount of pistol-bullets can hurt him, remains unbroken. (pp. 15-16)

We will only notice one character in *Jack Hinton,* and we do so because he is the best type of a class very prominent in these tales. This is Father Tom Loftus, a rollicking, loose, drunken, fine-hearted Irish priest. This sort of priest appears to be an indispensable appendage of a Galway tale, and goes a great way to justify the remark, so frequent in the mouths of the personages of these romances, that Galway is a very strange and exceptional region. (p. 18)

In *Tom Burke* the rich vein of Mr. Lever's fancy is beginning to fail. There is a faint smack of the old Galway leaven about the book, but there is not much more. Still *Tom Burke* deserves to be classed with the tales written in Mr. Lever's genuine style. The hero goes into Napoleon's army instead of Wellington's, and the scene during three-fourths of the story is laid in France. It is the old thing in a new dress; and an Irish chasseur is as good fun as an Irish ensign, so long as they do the same things. In the beginning of *Tom Burke* the old familiar faces and the old kind of Irish talk welcome us. . . . But the purely Irish part is soon over; and although the foreign life, and the career of a French officer, are made tolerably interesting, and the soldiering is like the soldiering of *Harry Lorrequer,* yet there is want of raciness and zest, and the spirit and fun are gone.

After we have done with *Tom Burke,* we enter on a series of tales on which we do not care to touch in detail. Every now and then there is a gleam of the former merriment and wonder-working power, but the whole is flat and dull. How is it possible that any one should have an exhaustless fund of good stories? Let us suppose that [if] a genial sociable man, with a good memory and a turn for exaggeration, picks up as many as two hundred new funny anecdotes, he is certainly endowed far above his neighbours; but if he once begins to print, he must come, sooner or later, to the end of his treasure. Then, again, the sphere of possible variety is necessarily limited when there is but one field for the author to display his powers in. Galway, as a remote country, is capitally suited for the localisation of all that is marvellous, but a certain sort of sameness must creep over even Galway fictions. If the hero is to fight a duel, and he is not to be killed or seriously wounded, there is no alternative; he must escape. If he is to ride over rough country, his animal may be more or less obstreperous, the walls may be ten or twenty feet high, his rival may or may not glare at him with a demon glance, but the whole thing is substantially the same. It is but a certain amount of riding under difficulties. The young lady who is the day-dream of the lieutenant's boyhood and the guiding-star of his proud and lonely manhood, as she is never suffered to speak, or to act otherwise than a marriageable lay-figure, cannot admit of much difference of treatment. No wonder, then, that the day came when Mr. Lever had over-written himself. Sometimes succeeding a little better, sometimes failing a little more decidedly, he has gone on getting further and further away from the richness and strength of his early writings, until at length he has got down to the *Fortunes of Glencore.*

It is curious that a writer of Mr. Lever's undoubted ability and sense should have given this unfortunate novel to the world at the same time that his early works were being reprinted, and not have seen how painful is the contrast. Mr. Lever tells us in the preface to the *Fortunes of Glencore,* that it has been his object in that story to depict the shifting play of character, to analyse motives, and to examine the secrets of the human heart. As might be expected from this announcement, the book is insipid and conventional beyond endurance, never irradiated by a spark of fun, with no adventures, no Galway wonders, no Irish sports and feats. It is one dead level of the trivialities of minor continental society, and the moral tortuosities of an invalid peer and a satirical diplomat, his friend. We will not linger over a subject which must lead us into dispraise of a writer who has so often amused and delighted us as Mr. Lever has. Only we cannot forbear an expression of surprise that Mr. Lever should not see how good his early works were, and how disappointed any one must be who, full of the charms of his first stories, takes up the *Fortunes of Glencore.* The unhappy reader comes fresh with the recollection of the good things of *Charles O'Malley;* and then, on being offered a novel containing "an analysis of character," can scarcely help feeling a sensation like that of the Red-Indian chiefs, who, appearing before the United-States officials on the day when they had been accustomed to receive a yearly present, and being greeted instead with a moral and edifying lecture, exclaimed, "We came to get tobacco and to be made drunk, and not to hear sermons." If we cannot have new novels like the old ones, let us go back to the first-fruits of Mr. Lever's genius. Let us wander with him in the remote country of which he used to tell in such pleasant traveller's stories, and believe as heartily as we can in the Galway of Charles O'Malley. (pp. 18-20)

> *"Mr. Lever's Novels," in* The National Review, *London, Vol. V, No. IX, July, 1857, pp. 1-20.*

CHARLES DICKENS   (letter date 1860)

[*Dickens, a nineteenth-century English novelist, short story writer, and dramatist, is one of the greatest and most popular novelists in world literature. His works display his comic gifts, his deep social concerns, and his extraordinary talent for characterization. Also a well-known journalist, Dickens acquired his friend Lever's* A Day's Ride *for weekly publication in his magazine* All the Year Round. *In this excerpt from a letter to Lever, Dickens compliments the first few unpublished install-*

ments of the novel, seeing them as promising. For more commentary by Dickens, see letter dated 6 October 1860.]

My Dear Lever.

Having got your proofs [of *A Day's Ride*] from the Printer's, I have read them. And I hasten to say that I firmly believe you had no warrant whatsoever for depreciating what you were doing, and that it is full of life, vivacity, originality, and humour. The only suggestion I have to make (and that arises solely out of the *manner* of publication) is, that we ought to get at the action of the story, in the first No. and that I therefore would, by a little condensation there, and a little enlargement of the quantity given in the first week, get at the invitation to the dinner, *as the end to the first weekly part.* I think the rising of invention in the drunken young man, extraordinarily humourous; it made me laugh to an extent and with a heartiness that I should like you to have seen and heard. Go on and prosper! You have opened an excellent vein, as it seems to me, and have a rich working before you. (pp. 19-20)

> *Charles Dickens, in a letter to Charles Lever on June 21, 1860, in* Charles Dickens's Letters to Charles Lever, *edited by Flora V. Livingston, Cambridge, Mass: Harvard University Press, 1933, pp. 19-20.*

CHARLES DICKENS   (letter date 1860)

[*Writing once again to Lever, Dickens reveals that* A Day's Ride *has not fulfilled his expectations for its success and that he has decided to run his own novel,* Great Expectations *(1861), in* All the Year Round *to boost declining sales of the journal. In an unexcerpted letter written later the same month, Dickens attributes the failure of* A Day's Ride *to the strictures of weekly publication, which demand that the audience's interest be captured immediately, rather than to the work itself, of which he writes, "I value it exactly as I valued it when we first corresponded about it." For Dickens's initial praise of* A Day's Ride, *see preceding letter dated 21 June 1860.*]

My Dear Lever.

I have a business report to make, that I fear I can hardly render agreeable to you. The best thing I can say in the beginning, is, that it is not otherwise disagreeable to *me* than as it imposes this note upon me. It causes me no other uneasiness or regret.

We drop, rapidly and continuously, with **The Day's Ride.** Whether it is too detached and discursive in its interest for the audience and the form of publication, I can not say positively; but it does not *take hold.* The consequence is, that the circulation becomes affected, and that the subscribers complain. I have waited week after week, for these three or four weeks, watching for any sign of encouragement. The least sign would have been enough. But all the tokens that appear, are in the other direction; and therefore I have been driven upon the necessity of considering how to act, and of writing to you.

There is but one thing to be done. I had begun a book [*Great Expectations*] which I intended for one of my long twenty number serials. I must abandon that design and forego it's profit (a very serious consideration, you may believe), and shape the story for these pages. I must get into these pages, as soon as possible, and must consequently begin my story in the No. for the 1st. of December. For as long a time as you continue afterwards, we must go on together.

This is the whole case. If the publication were to go steadily down, too long, it would be very, very, very difficult to raise again. I do not fear the difficulty at all, by taking this early and vigorous action. But without it there is not a doubt that the position would be serious.

Now do, pray, I entreat you, lay it well to heart that this might have happened with any writer. . . . The difficulties and discouragements of such an undertaking are enormous, and the man who surmounts them today may be beaten by them tomorrow. (pp. 23-5)

> *Charles Dickens, in a letter to Charles Lever on October 6, 1860, in* Charles Dickens's Letters to Charles Lever, *edited by Flora V. Livingston, Cambridge, Mass: Harvard University Press, 1933, pp. 23-5.*

[ROBERT B. LYTTON] (essay date 1862)

[*A minor English poet and statesman, Lytton was the son of Edward Bulwer-Lytton and an acquaintance of Lever. In the following excerpt, Lytton extols the liveliness of Lever's early novels but finds his later works, especially* The Dodd Family Abroad, *of greater artistic worth despite their repetitive focus on vice and corruption in society.*]

The name of Charles Lever is still chiefly associated with those novels by which his popularity as a writer was first secured, and by which, perhaps, his subsequent literary reputation has been in some measure overpowered. These works have probably met with a more cordial reception from the public than from the critics. Their author may, in a certain sense, defy criticism by exclaiming, like Horace, "*Pueris canto!*" He has been the biographer of boyhood. . . . It would undoubtedly be as ungracious to reproach the author of **Charles O'Malley** with the absence of those pretensions to literary dignity which he himself disclaims with so merry a laugh at dignities of every sort, as to denounce the Greek lyrist for his resolute refusal to celebrate the exploits of Atrides. (p. 452)

Mr. Lever's blooming young heroes, if not invariably blameless, are at least exceedingly joyful. . . . To watch them from the beaten highroad of tame and ordinary experience, dashing and glittering through a stupendous steeple-chase of astounding and never-ending adventure, literally takes away our breath. We cannot but sigh as we ask ourselves, "Was life indeed, then, at any time, such an uncommonly pleasant holiday?" Has not the world itself grown older and colder since those jaunty days when the dazzling Mr. Lorrequer drove his four-in-hand through all the proprieties? . . . The fact is, that times are changed with us. Napoleon's Paladins are *pulvis et umbra*. Beau Brummel has paid his last debt. Duelling is a thing forsworn. . . . And Harry Lorrequer, and Charles O'Malley, and Jack Hinton, and Tom Burke, and Bagenal Daly, look down upon us from the distance of an age no longer ours. We have no hope ever again to meet them cantering in the Phoenix Park, or swaggering down Sackville Street, or dancing at Dublin Castle. They are all "gone *proiapsoi* to the Stygian shore." (pp. 452-53)

Mr. Lever has, himself, survived his first progeny. That in growing an older, he had also grown a wiser, and in some respects a sadder man, his more recent writings bear witness. Job's second batch of sons and daughters, who were, doubtless, a much steadier set of young people than the first, could

not have differed from that jovial crew who were overwhelmed in a whirlwind whilst "eating and drinking wine," more strongly than Mr. Lever's later works differ from his earlier ones.

The author of **Harry Lorrequer** has given unquestionable proof of powers matured by time, and enriched by cultivation. His more recent novels evince a greater mastery in the craft of authorship, a larger experience, and more skilled faculty of construction. But whether these qualities exist in so great a degree as entirely to compensate the reader for the absence of that vivacity, freshness, and continuous flow of high animal spirits, which have rendered Mr. Lever's first books so widely and so justly popular, is a question which we shall presently have occasion to consider. (p. 453)

We believe that Mr. Lever's later novels are, on the whole, less generally popular than those by which his reputation as a writer was first acquired. This is natural, for many reasons quite independent of the merits or defects of the works themselves. The public is seldom of one mind with an author in comparing the relative merit of his works, especially where such comparison is between early and subsequent efforts. . . . A previous success is often the greatest hindrance to a subsequent reputation. People are sometimes startled into applause by the first revelation of an original mind; they are generally on their guard against any inconsiderate approval of a second. And as the process by which the mind of an author passes from one phase into another is usually gradual, and marked by various stages of development more or less imperfect and unsatisfactory, the advance made is not always immediately noticeable, and the recognition accorded to it is naturally slow and dubious. This must be especially the case with an author who has introduced himself to the public rather as a boon-companion than a moralist. We have often heard it said of Mr. Lever that he is much less funny than he used to be; which is indeed true. But when it is asked why he does not resort to the style and matter of his early novels, and implied that he should write nothing but **Harry Lorrequers** and **Charles O'Malleys,** we must express the conviction that compliance with any such demand, even if it were not purely impossible, would be altogether unadvisable. We could not ourselves bring to the perusal of repeated **Harry Lorrequers** an undiminished capacity to be amused by them. . . . We cannot blame Mr. Lever for abandoning a vein of humour which he has the merit of having exhausted: but it is nevertheless obvious, that in relinquishing that particular kind of fiction in which he is allowed to have excelled, Mr. Lever has withdrawn from a territory of which he was sole and undisputed proprietor, and entered upon one in which, whatever the acquirements he may bring to the cultivation of it, he is not without competitors.

It must be conceded that what we miss in Mr. Lever's later publications is that freshness, vivacity, and exuberant wealth of animal spirits, which gave to his earlier novels their chief charm. Although the relative merit of his recent works is decidedly unequal, some of them being much better than others, and all of them being better in one part than in another; yet there is in the majority of them a sameness of subject and material which does not give fair play to the powers employed upon them. Upon this point we shall speak more fully by-and-by; but whatever objections we may presently have to make in detail to some of Mr. Lever's last books, we have no hesitation in expressing the opinion, that amongst these books are to be found proofs of a genius richer, maturer, and more pleasing than any which is apparent in the earlier works of the same author. Indeed, *The Dodd Family Abroad,* which has not been published many years, is in our opinion the best of all Mr. Lever's works. He has written nothing at any time comparable to the letters of Henry Dodd; nor could there be any better evidence than what is afforded throughout the pages of this delightful and good-humoured satire, that the genius of the author, if it has lost much of that physical animation which is the arbitrary gift of youth, has acquired with years that thoughtful and more pleasing humour which is the result of enlarged experience and deeper sympathy with mankind. . . . If the dramatic power exist in the capacity to realise and express with an accuracy, too great for mere conjecture, other people's habits of thought and feeling, Mr. Lever has shown in this book more of such power than in anything else he has ever written. The humour of his earlier books is almost entirely superficial. It deals purely with external things, and is little more than an extraordinarily acute sense of the ludicrous in situation and circumstance. In this book the humour is of that rarer kind which plays less with external and accidental peculiarities than with men's modes of thought, and the manner in which different minds are impressed by the same facts, or operated on by the same influences. The difference of the result in each case is great. The highest humour is inseparable from a profound sympathy with human nature, and is therefore always tinged with sadness. For man is too grand a subject, after all, for eternal practical jokes, and even the most defaced and misfeatured humanity should be safe from unmitigated laughter. The fun which abounds, however, in Mr. Lever's more youthful writings, ignores the existence of sorrow in any sense but that of a hateful deformity, to be contemplated as little as possible; and consequently this sort of fun, incompatible as it is with any deep sympathy, is never quite free from a certain element of cruelty, inherent to the strong animal life of early youth. But what is most delightful in the letters of "K. I." is that loving, tender capacity to feel for and with humanity in all the forms of its imperfection and weakness—that tendency to live in the life of others, and to draw from the various thoughts and acts and manners of mankind constant food for reflection, which breathe through the playful satire, and furnish material to the genial humour of those charming letters. And though the author appears to have given fuller scope both to his own sentiments and his own experience in the letters of "K. I.," yet the same spirit of kindly humour, and the same shrewd appreciation of social characteristics, are apparent in all the epistles, even where the drollery most approaches to caricature, as in those of the Irish servant-girl who complains to her friends at home of being like "a pelican on a dissolute island." (pp. 460-62)

The adventures of a vulgar Irish family abroad in search of economy combined with pretension and display, afford Mr. Lever a good opportunity for satirising the social and political condition of a great number of foreign States. In doing this he has shown not only an affluent experience of Continental life, and a quick perception of all social phenomena, but also a very uncommon amount of shrewd common-sense and sound political judgment. We must say the satire is well deserved and unerringly aimed. Nothing escapes. The state of society, the conduct of government, the foreign and domestic policy, the administration of justice, the civil and military jurisdictions, the morals and manners of Continental capitals, are sharply canvassed. The character, too, of Kenny Dodd, in its strange admixture of childishness and wisdom, ignorance of the world and knowledge of mankind, and that

subdued humorous consciousness which it betrays of the utter worthlessness of those influences to which it is ever an easy victim, greatly facilitates the indulgence of that moralising vein in which Mr. Lever reviews almost every possible aspect of society. From the moment in which K. I. discovers that "shamelessness is the grand characteristic of foreign life," and that "one picks up the indecency much easier than the irregular verbs," the wisdom of his private reflections keeps pace with the folly of his public proceedings. (p. 463)

[K.I.] is fond of drawing political deductions from social facts. He attributes the failure of all attempted rebellions in Ireland to the fact that Paddy is so fond of a row for its own sake, that he never remembers it is only a means to an end. He traces the capacity of Englishmen for constitutional government to that habit of self-control, mutual forbearance, and providence for others, which they instinctively acquire from the practice of those home-duties which hardly exist on the Continent, and shrewdly infers that cafés are hostile to constitutions. But he has something to say, and what he says is generally suggestive, upon all possible subjects, from Verdi's music to the "Mind of Man." . . . In short, humanity, in all its operations, external and internal, is his constant and congenial theme. His knowledge of human nature is so extensive, and his theories of how to deal with it so shrewd and practical, that one would almost think him capable of managing the Austrian empire, were it not that he so good-humouredly reveals to us, with a quaint mixture of pathos and drollery, that all his theoretical wisdom is chiefly the result of successive and lamentable failures in family legislation. In this contrast, indeed, between the follies he is ever committing, and the wisdom with which he moralises over them, the humour of the character is contained. (p. 466)

K. I. has certainly no pretension to be a faultless philosopher, but he is a very pleasant one. . . . He has so large a sympathy for human nature, that his own claim upon that of the reader is irresistible; and so kindly and compassionate a feeling for the imperfections of mankind, that we follow him with undiminished affection through all the faults and follies that he so frankly attributes to himself. . . . Even the subordinate characters of this charming fiction are full of merit and individuality. . . . Mr. Lever is indeed so happy in the management of dialogue, and in the art of allowing his characters to evolve themselves without interference from the author, that there is every reason to think he would be successful in the comic drama; and were he to exercise his genius in that direction, we have little doubt but what he would do much to rescue the English stage from its present discreditable obligation to the charity of third-rate French playwrights. . . . [It] is our sincere opinion that Mr. Lever has written nothing comparable to this book. . . . (pp. 467-68)

The *Dodd Family* is an elaborate denunciation of the folly of "people living upon false pretences;" and *Davenport Dunn,* which deals with the crimes rather than the follies of society, exposes with considerable power, and an extraordinary knowledge of the dark side of modern civilization, the innumerable "fraudulent pretences" of roguery in every rank of life. The character of Dunn himself, which is that of the brilliant commercial swindler, the Robert Law of these days, whose roguery is on a magnificent scale, is carefully drawn; and Mr. Lever has certainly the merit of never allowing himself to be tempted into conventional exaggeration of this character. . . . But the best and most powerful character in this book—a character in which Mr. Lever has shown, in addition to his ordinary knowledge of the world, no ordinary knowledge of human nature—is that of Grog Davis, the professional "sporting swindler." This man, a vulgar blackleg, and in all his dealings with society a most unmitigated scoundrel, nevertheless affects us with a sense of power, and secures from us a degree of interest which it would be impossible to feel for a character of which the delineation was less true to the deepest realities of nature. The whole conception of this character is indeed of the highest order. The one redeeming point in the much-defaced humanity of this man, and the secret of the strong dramatic interest which he excites, lies in his devoted and absorbing affection for his daughter. (p. 468)

There are some admirable characters in Mr. Lever's [*One of Them*]. Mrs. Penthony Morris is excellent. So, in another way, is Mr. Ogden, the bully of a public office, the sycophant of secretaries of state, and the tyrant of junior clerks, the pedant of Downing Street, and the bore of all society. . . . Layton, the lost man of genius, is of a higher range, and there is considerable power, and not a little pathos, in Mr. Lever's vigorous sketch of this character. But perhaps the best-sustained character in the book is that of the Yankee, Leonidas Shaver Quakenboss.

In the delineation of this character Mr. Lever has evinced one merit, for which, perhaps, he can hardly hope to receive due appreciation from the majority of readers. Quakenboss is, so far as we know, almost the only Yankee of English manufacture in whose figures of speech the purely Yankee idiom, peculiar to the New England States, is not constantly confounded with the slang of the South and West. Mr. Lever is also deserving of approval for not having allowed the merely ludicrous in a subject so obviously open to coarse caricature, to overpower his finer perception of what are the better and worthier qualities of the Yankee character. In this respect, however, he has been anticipated by Sir E. Lytton.

There is certainly no lack of power in Mr. Lever's later novels. On the contrary, they contain writing of great power, and evince qualities which belong to genius of a higher order, than we discover in his earlier and still, perhaps, more popular books. Had he never written anything but the *Dodd Family,* that work alone would have entitled him to take undisputed rank amongst the humorists of England; and had that work been the first of a hitherto unknown writer, the sensation he would have excited must have been very great. But familiarity, if it does not breed contempt, often induces indifference. . . . Popularity is an alms which, the more cheerfully it is accorded to a first appeal, the more churlishly it is conceded to a second from the same quarter. . . . Still there are undoubtedly drawbacks to the claim of Mr. Lever's later works on general sympathy and approval for which he is himself responsible; and we have reserved to the last the few remarks which we have to make of an unfavourable nature in reference to these works, because the cordial recognition which we have already expressed of their author's ability will be the best guarantee for our sincerity in objecting to the subjects on which that ability is sometimes exercised. There is a sameness of subject about the majority of Mr. Lever's younger novels, which is partly counterbalanced by the fact that such sameness lies at least within the sphere of a more or less national interest, such as the portraiture of Irish life. But the continued repetition of scenes representative of a kind of society which is neither familiar nor pleasing to a large class of English readers, which is the characteristic of nearly all Mr. Lever's later works, is under any circumstances a mis-

take. The frivolity of Continental society, the vulgarity and mistakes of English travellers abroad, and the tricks and deceptions of sharpers and adventurers, is a very legitimate subject for satire; but it has really been exhausted with great success in the *Dodd Family,* and we regret to see it enter so largely into the staple material of Mr. Lever's subsequent novels. (pp. 470-71)

In such works as *Davenport Dunn* and *One of Them,* the genius of the author carries everything before it. But the subject of such a story as *The Daltons* can, we should think, have little interest for the mass of the public. We need not defend these remarks from the imputation of a false and vulgar morality which would exclude from fiction its legitimate sources of interest in the delineation of crime and the analysis of evil. Nothing in human nature can be alien to art, which derives from nature all its materials. All we ask from an author is to preserve the balance and proportion of the emotions to which he appeals. To be continually poring over the blots and failures of humanity, or the vices and corruption of any social state, is neither profitable nor pleasant. . . . As we close one after the other of such books, we feel like men returning from a hell. Our gains are not equivalent to the unpleasurable process of their acquirement, and we long for some more wholesome intercourse with mankind. The highest and most truthful art must occasionally hold intercourse with evil, but it is a mistake in art to make that intercourse habitual. . . . We attribute this defect to what is perhaps in itself a conscientious quality. We think that Mr. Lever is apt to be content to draw his materials for fiction too exclusively from *observation.* Human nature is indeed inexhaustible, but no one man's observation of human nature can be so. The widest experience is limited, and the limit of it must be reached at last. There is only one inexhaustible source for fiction, and that is the Imagination.

But the imagination itself is an engine which cannot be kept in frequent operation without being frequently supplied with fuel. It cannot act without being first acted upon. And the fault we are inclined to attribute to the majority of our modern writers of romance is, that they give out too much and take in too little. Let men say what they will about native originality, man is not really a creator. He changes, improves, and extends, that is all. . . . Those authors who rely chiefly upon personal observation and experience for the materials of fiction, cannot be too careful to vary their point of sight pretty often. (pp. 471-72)

If Mr. Lever is disposed to dispute the justice of these observations, or, at any rate, their special application to himself, he may certainly refer to the extraordinary sameness of a vast number of his contemporary novelists, who do not seem, on that account, to enjoy less popularity. One set of writers can talk of nothing but governesses, tutors, and athletic curates, who love fly-fishing and abhor Strauss. The domestic novel happens to be in fashion, and we certainly have enough of it. Others are never happy out of the precincts of Pall-Mall and the Clubs, unless it be at a fashionable-watering place; and some can give no flavour to English fiction without importing it from Florence or Rome, or borrowing their intrigue from the secret societies, and their sentiment from Mazzinian manifestoes. But Mr. Lever is immeasurably richer in imagination and power than all such writers; and if he would occasionally emigrate to "fresh fields and pastures new," he has already all that is needful in the way of stock and capital. He may be contented with his present reputation, which is extensive, and likely to be permanent; but we believe that it is in his own power to elevate and enlarge it. (p. 472)

[*Robert B. Lytton*], in a review of *"Works of Charles Lever,"* in Blackwood's Edinburgh Magazine, *Vol. XCI, No. DLVIII, April, 1862, pp. 452-72.*

CHARLES LEVER (essay date 1872)

[*Lever reflects on his most popular work,* Charles O'Malley, *in this excerpt from his preface to an 1872 edition of the novel.*]

The success of *Harry Lorrequer* was the reason for writing *Charles O'Malley.* That I myself was in no wise prepared for the favor the public bestowed on my first attempt is easily enough understood. The ease with which I strung my stories together,—and in reality the *Confessions of Harry Lorrequer* are little other than a note-book of absurd and laughable incidents,—led me to believe that I could draw on this vein of composition without any limit whatever. I felt, or thought I felt, an inexhaustible store of fun and buoyancy within me, and I began to have a misty, half-confused impression that Englishmen generally labored under a sad-colored temperament, took depressing views of life, and were proportionately grateful to any one who would rally them even passingly out of their despondency, and give them a laugh without much trouble for going in search of it.

When I set to work to write *Charles O'Malley* I was, as I have ever been, very low with fortune, and the success of a new venture was pretty much as eventful to me as the turn of the right color at *rouge-et-noir.* At the same time I had then an amount of spring in my temperament, and a power of enjoying life which I can honestly say I never found surpassed. The world had for me all the interest of an admirable comedy, in which the part allotted myself, if not a high or a foreground one, was eminently suited to my taste, and brought me, besides, sufficiently often on the stage to enable me to follow all the fortunes of the piece. Brussels, where I was then living, was adorned at the period by a most agreeable English society. Some leaders of the fashionable world of London had come there to refit and recruit, both in body and estate. There were several pleasant and a great number of pretty people among them; and so far as I could judge, the fashionable dramas of Belgrave Square and its vicinity were being performed in the Rue Royale and the Boulevard de Waterloo with very considerable success. There were dinners, balls, déjeûners, and picnics in the Bois de Cambre, excursions to Waterloo, and select little parties to Bois-fort,—a charming little resort in the forest whose intense cockneyism became perfectly inoffensive as being in a foreign land, and remote from the invasion of home-bred vulgarity. I mention all these things to show the adjuncts by which I was aided, and the rattle of gayety by which I was, as it were, "accompanied," when I next tried my voice.

The soldier element tinctured strongly our society, and I will say most agreeably. Among those whom I remember best were several old Peninsulars. Lord Combermere was of this number, and another of our set was an officer who accompanied, if indeed he did not command, the first boat party who crossed the Douro. It is needless to say how I cultivated a society so full of all the storied details I was eager to obtain, and how generously disposed were they to give me all the information I needed. On topography especially were they valuable to me, and with such good result that I have been more than once complimented on the accuracy of my descriptions of places which I have never seen and whose features I have derived entirely from the narratives of my friends.

When, therefore, my publishers asked me could I write a story in the Lorrequer vein, in which active service and military adventure could figure more prominently than mere civilian life, and where the achievements of a British army might form the staple of the narrative,—when this question was propounded me, I was ready to reply: Not one, but fifty. Do not mistake me, and suppose that any overweening confidence in my literary powers would have emboldened me to make this reply; my whole strength lay in the fact that I could not recognize anything like literary effort in the matter. If the world would only condescend to read that which I wrote precisely as I was in the habit of talking, nothing could be easier than for me to occupy them. Not alone was it very easy to me, but it was intensely interesting and amusing to myself, to be so engaged.

The success of *Harry Lorrequer* had been freely wafted across the German ocean, but even in its mildest accents it was very intoxicating incense to me; and I set to work on my second book with a thrill of hope as regards the world's favor which—and it is no small thing to say it—I can yet recall.

I can recall, too, and I am afraid more vividly still, some of the difficulties of my task when I endeavored to form anything like an accurate or precise idea of some campaigning incident or some passage of arms from the narratives of two distinct and separate "eye-witnesses." What mistrust I conceived for all eye-witnesses from my own brief experience of their testimonies! What an impulse did it lend me to study the nature and the temperament of narrator, as indicative of the peculiar coloring he might lend his narrative; and how it taught me to know the force of the French epigram that has declared how it was entirely the alternating popularity of Marshall Soult that decided whether he won or lost the battle of Toulouse.

While, however, I was sifting these evidences, and separating, as well as I might, the wheat from the chaff, I was in a measure training myself for what, without my then knowing it, was to become my career in life. This was not therefore altogether without a certain degree of labor, but so light and pleasant withal, so full of picturesque peeps at character and humorous views of human nature, that it would be the very rankest ingratitude of me if I did not own that I gained all my earlier experiences of the world in very pleasant company,—highly enjoyable at the time, and with matter for charming souvenirs long after.

That certain traits of my acquaintances found themselves embodied in some of the characters of this story I do not seek to deny. The principal of natural selection adapts itself to novels as to Nature, and it would have demanded an effort above my strength to have disabused myself at the desk of all the impressions of the dinner-table, and to have forgotten features which interested or amused me.

One of the personages of my tale I drew, however, with very little aid from fancy. I would go so far as to say that I took him from the life, if my memory did not confront me with the lamentable inferiority of my picture to the great original it was meant to portray.

With the exception of the quality of courage, I never met a man who contained within himself so many of the traits of

Falstaff as the individual who furnished me with Major Monsoon. But the major—I must call him so, though that rank was far beneath his own—was a man of unquestionable bravery. His powers as a story-teller were to my thinking unrivalled; the peculiar reflections on life which he would passingly introduce, the wise apothegms, were after a morality essentially of his own invention. Then he would indulge in the unsparing exhibition of himself in situations such as other men would never have confessed to, all blended up with a racy enjoyment of life, dashed occasionally with sorrow that our tenure of it was short of patriarchal. All these, accompanied by a face redolent of intense humor, and a voice whose modulations were managed with the skill of a consummate artist,—all these, I say, were above me to convey; nor indeed as I re-read any of the adventures in which he figures, am I other than ashamed at the weakness of my drawing and the poverty of my coloring. (pp. vii-x)

[Frank Webber] was one of my earliest friends, my chum in college, and in the very chambers where I have located Charles O'Malley, in Old Trinity. He was a man of the highest order of abilities, and with a memory that never forgot, but ruined and run to seed by the idleness that came of a discursive, uncertain temperament. Capable of anything, he spent his youth in follies and eccentricities; every one of which, however, gave indications of a mind inexhaustible in resources, and abounding in devices and contrivances that none other but himself would have thought of. (p. xv)

[Of Mickey Free] I had not one but one thousand types. Indeed, I am not quite sure that in my last visit to Dublin, I did not chance on a living specimen of the "Free" family, much readier in repartée, quicker with an apropos, and droller in illustration than my own Mickey. This fellow was "boots" at a great hotel in Sackville Street; and I owe him more amusement and some heartier laughs than it has been always my fortune to enjoy in a party of wits. His criticisms on my sketches of Irish character were about the shrewdest and the best I ever listened to; and that I am not bribed to this by any flattery, I may remark that they were more often severe than complimentary, and that he hit every blunder of image, every mistake in figure, of my peasant characters, with an acuteness and correctness which made me very grateful to know that his daily occupations were limited to blacking boots, and not polishing off authors.

I believe I have now done with my confessions, except I should like to own that this story was the means of according me a more heartfelt glow of satisfaction, a more gratifying sense of pride, than anything I ever have or ever shall write, and in this wise. My brother, at that time the rector of an Irish parish, once forwarded to me a letter from a lady unknown to him, but who had heard he was the brother of "Harry Lorrequer," and who addressed him not knowing where a letter might be directed to myself. The letter was the grateful expression of a mother, who said,

> I am the widow of a field officer, and with an only son, for whom I obtained a presentation to Woolwich; but seeing in my boy's nature certain traits of nervousness and timidity which induced me to hesitate on embarking him in the career of a soldier, I became very unhappy and uncertain which course to decide on.

> While in this state of uncertainty, I chanced to make him a birthday present of *Charles O'Malley*, the reading of which seemed to act like a charm on his whole character, inspiring him with a passion for movement and adventure, and spiriting him to an eager desire for a military life. Seeing that this was no passing enthusiasm, but a decided and determined bent, I accepted the cadetship for him; and his career has been not alone distinguished as a student, but one which has marked him out for an almost hare-brained courage, and for a dash and heroism that give high promise for his future.

> Thank your brother for me, . . . a mother's thanks for the welfare of an only son; and say how I wish that my best wishes for him and his could recompense him for what I owe him.

I humbly hope that it may not be imputed to me as unpardonable vanity,—the recording of this incident. It gave me an intense pleasure when I heard it; and now, as I look back on it, it invests this story for myself with an interest which nothing else that I have written can afford me.

I have now but to repeat what I have declared in former editions, my sincere gratitude for the favor the public still continues to bestow on me,—a favor which probably associates the memory of this book with whatever I have since done successfully, and compels me to remember that to the popularity of *Charles O'Malley* I am indebted for a great share of that kindliness in criticism, and that geniality in judgment, which—for more than a quarter of a century—my countrymen have graciously bestowed on their faithful friend and servant, Charles Lever. (pp. xv-xvii)

> *Charles Lever, in a preface to his* Charles O'Malley: The Irish Dragoon, *Vol. I, Little Brown, and Company, 1903, pp. vii-xvii.*

[FRANCES CASHEL HOEY] (essay date 1872)

[*Despite faulting many aspects of Lever's novels, particularly their representation of Catholic priests, Hoey gives an essentially favorable overview of them.*]

General incredulity attends the announcement of last appearances. The world looks with a cheerful confidence for the advent of some circumstance which shall induce the singer or the actor, the lecturer or the public personage who has made her final curtsey or his valedictory oration, to reconsider the determination which is to hide them thenceforth from its eyes and ears. (p. 379)

Mr. Lever has just concluded a novel, of which he speaks as a final effort, and, while we believe and hope that this will prove an example of the last appearance as popularly understood, the occasion seems favourable for a brief consideration of his achievements, in the long and highly successful career which began with *Harry Lorrequer,* and of which *Lord Kilgobbin* is the latest stage. In a survey of this kind it is necessary to consider not only the specialties of the writer, but the taste and manners of the period at which he first made his mark. This is especially called for in the case of Mr. Lever, because tastes and manners, in later times, have undergone so decided a change that the mere mechanism of his early works, perfectly acceptable and accepted when they were written, would be now accounted gravely defective. "Slapdash" is out of fashion. . . . A beginner who should try the slapdash style would inevitably fail; he would rudely jar the public taste; but it constituted a great portion of the charm of the *Harry Lorrequer* novels. The wonderful "go" in them, the buoyant animal spirits, the confident audacity, the romance, flimsy enough when it is examined critically, which it never was by Mr. Lever's readers in those days, were irresistible. (pp. 380-81)

There is no eminent writer of fiction in whom the defects of his qualities are more strongly marked. In some respects the contrast amounts to paradox. With great versatility he combines sameness by which any other writer would long ago have wearied his public, and with all this sameness, which, with quite audacious carelessness, he maintains unrelieved, he is not monotonous. He has a lively and brilliant imagination, but he allows it to run into exaggerations, which injure its best efforts; and he is so habitually disdainful of proportion and consistency, that not one of his works is really fine as a whole. They are like unfinished pictures, with grand masses of colour, but full of faults in drawing and incongruous grouping; in their first effect bright and charming, but with serious defects on close examination. And yet, let that examination be ever so close, it does not decrease even the critic's pleasure in books which, though constantly offending against his judgment, always appeal successfully to his fancy, and never fail to awaken some of the old gleefulness which accompanied the first reading of them. Mr. Lever's materials are as easily reducible to a catalogue as the contents of an artist's colourbox, and his manner is as recognizable for its mannerisms as that of Mr. Dickens or Mr. Wilkie Collins; but he uses his materials deftly, changing their position, and flashing them about so dazzlingly, that he disguises their sameness with great general success, and his mannerisms are not very objectionable. The long catalogue of Mr. Lever's works—for he has been very industrious in his vocation—may be divided into three sections, the component parts of each differing from those of the others in form, spirit, meaning, and *mise-en-scène*, and yet all bearing a genuine resemblance to each other, having similar characteristic merits and identical defects. If we name these three sections respectively the military, the social, and the politico-social, our readers will be able to follow the exposition of their sameness in variety, their variety in sameness.

The military novels, which were so successful, so widely popular when they appeared many years ago, and which are still read with pleasure and appreciation gratifying to observe amid the general debasement of fiction and the public taste for it, are *Harry Lorrequer, Charles O'Malley, Tom Burke,* and *Jack Hinton. Maurice Tiernay* belongs, strictly speaking, to this category; but that work is inferior to all the others, possesses hardly any trace of their special merit, is vulgar in style, in many instances is the merest literal translation from dubious French memoirs, and is disfigured by the worst defects of the others so much exaggerated, that we reluctantly admit its place and record its authorship.

The social novels are, *The Knight of Gwynne, The O'Donoghue, The Martins, The Daltons, The Dodd Family Abroad, Roland Cashel, One of Them, Barrington, Davenport Dunn, The Fortunes of Glencore, Luttrell of Arran,* and *That Boy of Norcott's.* To this category also there belongs a work which Mr. Lever's admirers would much rather he had never written, which does him no credit in any way. It is *Sir Jasper Carew,* a conception at once so crude and so extravagant that it is difficult to believe it can have come from even his " 'prentice hand," and incredible but that it must have

been written long before the time at which it appeared, when the author's reputation was firmly established.

The politico-social novels are, *Tony Butler, Sir Brook Fossbrooke, The Bramleighs,* and *Lord Kilgobbin.* Beside these, and the papers contributed to *Blackwood's Magazine* under the name of Cornelius O'Dowd, which we do not propose to include in our attempt at an appreciation of Mr. Lever, there are some nondescript productions which are not worthy of being classed even with *Maurice Tiernay* and *Sir Jasper Carew.* They are called *A Rent in a Cloud* and *A Day's Ride,* and we never yet heard of any one who pretended to know what either of them means. Perhaps no writer of eminence who has enjoyed a prolonged career has escaped the production of something which it would have been better for his fame and his memory that he had left unwritten. . . . Mr. Lever is not, in this respect, an exception, but he is a forcible example.

The military novels had, on their first appearance, the great charm of novelty. . . . Mr. Lever had a fair, uninterrupted field, and from the first found favour. He has had fewer imitators than any other popular novelist; he would be more difficult of imitation than any. Spurious-grotesque copies of Mr. Dickens, mock-cynical copies of Mr. Thackeray, there have been in plenty; but though he is not on the same line with either, Mr. Lever is more difficult of even coarse imitation than the great humorist, or the great ethical novelist. His very faults and absurdities would be hard to catch, while the charm of his writings is lent by a quality of mind and tone of spirits not to be simulated. Mr. Trollope writes good hunting stories, but they are just a little too technical, and Mr. Whyte Melville can describe a steeplechase sufficiently well to satisfy the readers who know all about it, without boring the readers who do not; but no one except Mr. Lever could tell the story of the hunt in which Captain Hammersley's "English mare, that was such a beauty this morning," was killed at the sunk fence, or of the steeplechase which Tipperary Joe won for Jack Hinton. In both these instances, as in several others which might be selected from his earlier works, he exhibits great art. The scenes are full of stir, of interest, of excitement; there are the noise, the exertion, the bustle, all the outward characteristics of the sporting scene, and all kept up well. But there is also the intense, sustained strife of human passion, on which the reader's attention is riveted, and in the latter case there is one of the most beautiful and pathetic bits of character-drawing to be found in fiction, and, in our opinion, the finest thing in that way Mr. Lever has ever done. (pp. 381-84)

In his first work [*Harry Lorrequer*] almost all the mannerisms which Mr. Lever has persisted in ever since are to be found. The gorgeous upholstery, the constant eating and drinking, the affection of a perfect connoisseurship in cookery by his heroes, who describe all their meals as "appetizing," and all their loves as "superbly beautiful," and possessed of wonderful feet; the lavish prodigality of wealth, especially in the case of people who are picturesquely ruined; the versatility of emotions, which fulfil the whole Shaksperian category within a page; the constant use of the generic term "passion" for the specific term "anger," and the invariable representation of people of rank in attitudes of haughty "insolence," and people of no rank in attitudes of curiosity and cringing; we find them all in *Harry Lorrequer.* We also find them all in *Lord Kilgobbin,* and in every intervening novel of the long series, sometimes more, sometimes less disagreeably promi-

Charles O'Malley rescuing the heroine.

nent, but always there, and always giving an impression of vulgarity which is provoking, and of which one longs, vainly, to get rid. These things come between the reader and a hearty sympathy with the author, but they do not prevent a cordial admiration. In *Harry Lorrequer,* some of his best effects are produced by slight touches of description, contrasting pleasantly with the daub which is as much a characteristic of his general style as its dash. For instance, Emily Bingham is capitally drawn, as no inferior artist could draw her,—a flirt without a suggestion of impropriety; and no one can fail to recognize the adroitness with which her girl friends are generalized as "of that school of young ladies who admire the *Corsair* and Kingstown, and say, 'Ah, don't!' " In *Harry Lorrequer* we find the prototype of that wonderful person who is always turning up in Mr. Lever's novels, the kind-hearted, choleric, amusing Irishman, whom no one ever saw at any time off the stage, and now never sees on it—the man who flies into a rage and breaks things. Mr. O'Leary's conduct in the French gaming-house, where he upsets the croupier, chair and all, with one sudden jerk upon the floor, and giving a tremendous kick to the cassette, sends all the five-franc pieces flying over him, then jumps upon the table, and brandishing his black-thorn through the ormolu lustre, scatters the wax-lights on all sides, accompanying the exploit by a yell that would have called up all Connemara at midnight, is milder than that of many of his successors. Mr. Dodd, a very estimable person, and the author's favourite among all his creations, returns unexpectedly on two occasions to his place of abode, and finding, on each, a large and distinguished party assembled without his knowledge, proceeds to beat the attendants and smash the furniture, lamps, and table equipage, as a gentle hint to his wife and daughters that he does not approve of the festivities. Mr. O'Shea (in *One of Them*) is frequently "about to" hurl articles of brittle fabric at his servant's head; the military heroes get knocked down into insensibility almost as frequently as the superbly beautiful heroines faint; a glass of wine "dashed" into the face of an opponent is an ordinary incident;—on the whole, there is a surprising amount of assault and battery distributed through these volumes, and yet, the riot in them is not rowdy, and the life is not low. There is in Mr. Lever's pictures of Irish life and character genuine, racy, exuberant humour, so captivating, that, if the reader cannot ignore, he is forced to forgive the extravagances which accompany it. When he began to write, the old school—which cultivated the emotions, and dealt in gestures and changes of complexion—had not utterly ceased to exist. . . . We must not, therefore, condemn the violent emotions to which Mr. Lever constantly appeals in his earlier novels, as such completely ludicrous machinery for producing effects, as they would certainly appear if employed by a writer of the present time; but neither are they to be quite overlooked, for no fashion can ever have prevented them from being bad art, and no toleration can disguise the fact that they are very tiresome. Roars of laughter; bursts of laughter; convulsive merriment; shouts of laughter which make the glasses ring and shake the table; peals of laughter rising beyond all control; unrestrained mirth; hardly-contained laughter; people who repress with difficulty an almost irresistible inclination, not simply to laugh, but to burst into laughter. These are only a selection from the phrases which stud the pages of the Irish novels; and they alternate with faces darkened by passion, bursting hearts, and hearts which are only almost bursting, eyes blazing with rage, features convulsed with misery, eyes brimming with scalding tears, frames quivering with emotion, eyes covered by trembling hands, lips blanched with agony, brows lifted in disdain, lips curled in indignant pride, convulsed faces hidden in ready handkerchiefs, and wonderful lashes drooping over wonderful eyes in which there is a "world" of something or other much too tremendous for words—fortunately too tremendous, for if the utterances of all these people were only equal to their contortions, if their language were as expressive as their looks, one would be swept away before such a "reg'lar knock-down of talent." One of the best bits of one of his best books—the meeting of Charles O'Malley and Mickey Free at Brussels after Waterloo—is turned into a positive absurdity by one passage, a perfect sample of the convulsive-tempestuous style in which Mr. Lever deals with the emotions: "Regardless of everybody, Mickey burst his way through the dense mass. 'Oh, murther! Oh, Mary! Oh, Moses! Is he safe here after all?' The poor fellow could say no more, but *burst* into a *torrent* of tears. A *roar* of laughter around him soon, however, turned the *current* of his emotions; when, *dashing* the *scalding* drops from his eyelids, he *glared fiercely like a tiger on every side.* " The physical feats of the people in these books are no less sudden, surprising, and swift-succeeding than their emotional paroxysms. They are always rushing, dashing, galloping at the top of their horses' speed, waving rapid adieux, clearing fences or hedges at a bound, getting terrible wounds of which they are unconscious, fracturing their limbs and getting over it with wonderful celerity, springing down staircases or out of windows, flinging themselves into the saddle and disappearing, getting into tremendous difficulties for want of common sense and discretion, and rushing away from them, half mad, rather than take time and pains to explain. Their love-making is very funny. The fair ones always have long and heavy "tresses," which "droop" across the manly bosom of the devoted dragoon; and they always faint, when they do not utter an "insolent" dismissal, unless when they combine those lines of action. Then the devoted dragoon sprinkles the pale face with a few drops of water, and the conversation goes on quite as naturally as before,—that is to say, very unlike nature indeed. (pp. 386-88)

The materials of which the military novels are constructed have been selected somewhat after the fashion in which M. Alexandre Dumas chose the stuff whereon he laid his cumbrous and gorgeous embroideries. They are, like the *Trois Mousquetaires* and their fellows, quasi-historical; and they have a certain sequence as well as an undisguised likeness. We prefer, for the sake of the writer's fame, to put **Maurice Tiernay** out of account, and to consider only those works in which Mr. Lever illustrates Irish life on the one hand, and, on the other, the stirring military events which made memorable the beginning of the present century. To estimate them and their effects rightly, we must bear in mind that they appeared in a time of profound peace, when the strife they recalled was a tradition, and young people regarded any war as a thing which their parents had seen, which, after a shabby sort, might be seen in India and elsewhere among "blacks," but which was replaced, in their time, by home politics and exhibitions. War was just far enough removed to be capable of endowment by so skillful a writer with the romance, the dash, the daring, the personal heroism, the individual interest, which it has no longer, now that the horrible and gigantic mechanism of it is displayed before us, on a scale which utterly drawfs the campaigns through which Charley O'Malley and Fred Power, Jack Hinton and Phil O'Grady, Tom Burke and Tascher dashed and slashed, loved and laughed, played the hero and occasionally the buffoon. The fighting scenes are very brilliant—full of life, colour, and movement, instinct with the pride, the excitement, and the romance of war. We do not believe in the romance of war now, but these pages make us almost believe in it again, and even in the fun of it, still more incredible. The pictures are all drawn from the officer's point of view, and the artist's; they are the precise antithesis of the Erckmann-Chatrian pictures; they are brim full of dash and humour, and they are most fascinating. The grimness of war is not here, though its sad and solemn side is not utterly ignored either, but the "long sword, saddle, bridle, whack, rowdydow!" predominate. The animal spirit, the glee, the extravagance which make the scenes of Irish life so delightful and so impossible, are rife on the fields of the Peninsula, where more things were possible than in Galway; and Dr. Quill and Major Monsoon are sufficient in themselves to render the book which has to tell of them famous. Mr. Lever is very skilful in his combination of the real and the imaginary; thus he places the Major and the Doctor in fictitious circumstances, which admirably develop the characteristics of the two well-known originals. *Harry Lorrequer* and *Charles O'Malley* are, indeed, little more than the cleverly-contrived medium for the telling of a number of good stories, of which some were widely and well known, and others had a more restricted currency. . . . [These] stories, whether those which tell of Ireland thirty or seventy years ago, are equally novel and strange to the readers of to-day, who compare them with the Ireland of the present time. In *Charles O'Malley* the best examples of the author's skill, both in the real and in the imaginary, are found. . . . The Peninsular scenes are of first-rate merit, it is impossible to read them without a kindling of enthusiasm, a *verve* something like the

author's own; and the glimpses they afford of the great historical personages engaged remain upon the mental vision more clearly than any formal presentments of them. The Wellington, Picton, and Uxbridge of Mr. Lever—even the sketchy Napoleon—are to his readers Wellington, Picton, Uxbridge, and Napoleon, as truly as Scott's Graham of Claverhouse is their "bonnie Dundee," and Scott's Duke of Burgundy is their Charles le Téméraire. Even Erckmann-Chatrian cannot destroy the impression of Tom Burke's First Consul and *Petit Caporal.*

In *Charles O'Malley* we find the two best samples of Mr. Lever's humour, and, indeed, we do not think Frank Webber and Mickey Free have ever been surpassed by any writer. For pure unmitigated fun, the extravagant ebullition of animal spirits, for extreme irresistible drollery, Frank Webber has no compeer; and the happiest idea that ever occurred to any writer is, surely, his sham despatch upon the capture of the college pump, and its arrival in the midst of the terrible earnest of the taking of Ciudad Rodrigo. The Trinity College scenes are incomparably ludicrous, and Frank Webber sustains his character to the last. Mickey Free is, in our opinion, a far superior conception to Sam Weller: he is more true to nature, as all Irish readers well know—none but an Irishman could have drawn the character,—his humour is much more real and brilliant, and his fidelity to his master has nothing of the haphazard, good-eating-and-drinking-secured complexion, which is all Mr. Dickens has invested Sam with; besides, he is consistent even in his absurdities. Sam Weller is inconsistent with his first introduction to Mr. Pickwick, and with his father's situation in life. Next in force and vitality, and in strong contrast, comes Corney Delaney, but the interval is wide. We do not know of any parallels for them in English fiction in merit and humour except Andrew Fairservice and Caleb Balderstone. . . . Mickey Free is the only singer of comic songs who is not a bore; and, though there is one feature in his fun to which we shall presently take grave exception, his humour is never tiresome or misplaced, because the true depth of feeling is never wanting to modify and adorn it. (pp. 390-93)

Corney Delany, the plague of Phil O'Grady's life; Tate Sullivan, the fine old man, whose solitary ramble among the family portraits in the picture gallery at Gwynne Abbey, gives one touch of pathos to a book which, with plenty of room for it, is singularly deficient in that element; Darby M'Keown, the piper and conspirator who rescues Tom Burke; Kerry O'Leary, whose relations with Mrs. Branagan the cook, supply all the fun to be found in *The O'Donoghue,*—on the whole, the dreariest book written by Mr. Lever;—and others, too numerous to name, who are old servants or retainers to the always ruined and yet uprising Irishmen, old and young, with whom he deals, are very amusing, but not one of them equals Mickey Free. And yet it is chiefly by means of Mickey Free that Mr. Lever has most grievously offended a large number of his admirers, and done discredit to his own taste and breeding, while sinning against the truth to an extent of which it is impossible he can be unconscious. Is there only one class of his countrymen of whom Mr. Lever is so entirely ignorant, that his attempt to represent them agreeably is fraught with injustice and insult? We should hold him in more esteem if we could believe this, but, unfortunately, we cannot; and we are forced to see, in his systematic and coarse misrepresentation of the Catholic priesthood, a bid for popularity, based upon an intimate knowledge of the ignorant prejudices of Irish Protestants, to whom anything which turns the vows of the priesthood into ridicule, and casts suspicion on the conduct of priests, is welcome; and the ignorant indifference of English Protestants, who have a kind of general notion that what an Irishman, with so extensive a knowledge of Irish character, has to say of Irish priests, must be as true as it is humorous. This is none the less unworthy because Mr. Lever tries to secure himself against the disgust and indignation which his priests are calculated to excite in our minds, by such epithets as "the good priest," "honest Father Tom," &c.; and by depicting such a scene—full of power and pathos as it is—as the anguish of Father Tom Loftus by the deathbed of the unshriven murderer. The whole thing is untrue, unseemly, and impossible; the tragedy as false as the farce; the priest weeping, praying, and gesticulating in the cabin as the priest gambling and drinking, cracking loose jokes, and telling stories of successful cajolery of his bishop in the canal-boat. This sort of thing, sufficiently offensive in the case of Jack Hinton's clerical friend, Tom Loftus, becomes still more so when conveyed through the medium of Mickey Free, who is made to heap ridicule, by his stories and his songs, not only on priests, but on the tenets of the Catholic religion, in confirmation of the lowest and most ignorant prejudices. (pp. 393-94)

It may be said that it is absurd to reckon such things as these—the broad farce of the book, the red-hot poker and flour-bag business of the bustling pantomime—as causes of offence. But that is not quite true, at least it is not all the truth. We do not see the fun of them, even granting that fun, if it existed, could excuse their bad taste and coarseness; and, under their farcical extravagance there is a deliberate and malignant purpose. From the scandalous priest in **Jack Hinton**—the one fine and pathetic episode in whose career, the scene of Shaun's death, merely serves to render the picture more insidiously mischievous—to the flirting, flattering Monsignori who fish for such fashionable converts as Lady Grace Twining and Lady Augusta Bramleigh, there is in every portrait drawn by Mr. Lever's pen, in every sketch, in every reference, misrepresentation and insinuation. The taunts are thrown out jestingly, the charges are cleverly manipulated, but they amount to this—that ignorance, scheming, bullying, excess in eating and drinking, extortion and lying, are the general characteristics of the Catholic priesthood; and that the system of the Catholic church is one of tyranny, venality, and superstition, of gross falsehood, and of barter and sale. No doubt there are persons who, having no means of knowing better, actually believe that such is the case. With them we have, we can have no quarrel. But as it is hardly possible to credit Mr. Lever with so much invincible ignorance, he lays himself open to the reproach of courting a low kind of popularity by a mean order of misrepresentation.

In his power of describing natural scenery, of bringing the localities in which his people play their parts vividly before his readers, we consider that Mr. Lever comes next to Sir Walter Scott among novelists; and he does not overdo this portion of his task, as Sir Walter sometimes did; for instance, in *Guy Mannering* and *The Monastery*. In **Charles O'Malley** there are many exquisite pictures of Irish scenery; and **Jack Hinton** is yet more rich in them. The journey of the aide-de-camp and the priest, in which the episode of Shaun occurs, is a fine, picturesque, and impressive piece of writing; and the dull and improbable story of **Luttrell of Arran,** is redeemed by descriptions of the scenery of the Ulster coast and the islands, which will bear comparision with the picture of the Orkneys

in *The Pirate*. Nothing can be more admirable than the description of Gwynne Abbey, the Corvy, and the wild and picturesque coast of Coleraine. . . . He has caught the spirit, the peculiar tone and significance of Irish scenery, as he has caught certain characteristics of the Irish peasantry, which he presents with unexaggerated truth and force. In both these respects **Roland Cashel** is one of his best works. The description of Tubbermore and its tenants, especially of Tom Keane, is most admirable. It is a pity that the writer spoiled so excellent a book by tacking on to the natural catastrophe a number of merely sensational incidents, neither interesting in themselves, artistically contrived, nor in harmony with the tone of the preceding portions. Some of his happiest effects are made in this novel. (pp. 396-97)

No writer of fiction, with the exception of Mr. Anthony Trollope, has ventured to repeat similar combinations of character, situation, and incident so often as Mr. Lever. The ruined Irish gentleman, of old family, whose habitual extravagance is described as a very splendid characteristic, with the drawback of insolvency as a consequence, sooner or later, but generally later, is to be found in Godfrey O'Malley, Maurice Darcy, Martin of Cro'Martin, O'Donoghue, Dalton, Barrington, Luttrell, and Kellett. There is no difference in kind in these pictures, and there is not much in degree. That the Knight of Gwynne should be so very charming and high-minded, and yet so totally unprincipled, is calculated to create surprise, but Mr. Lever puts the case with a persuasive gorgeousness which drives away scruples. So it is with Godfrey O'Malley. Then there is the universal second—the fighting friend—as indispensable as Tilburina's confidant. He is Count Considine, Bagenal Daly, Grog Davis, Mr. O'Shea, and others. There is the scheming villain of the story—Ulick Burke, Davenport Dunn, "honest" Tom Gleeson, Old Hickman, the Abbé Esmonde, Mehée de la Touche, Nick Holmes, Tom Linton (who is a Carker in a higher grade), Captain Hemsworth, and as many others as there are books, and they all scheme much in the same way, and are not so much acute and clever as their victims are credulous or careless, or inconceivably absent-minded and given to make blunders. (p. 398)

The dashing dragoon and his equally dashing friend, who is always supposed to be in love with the leading lady—Fred Power with Lucy Dashwood, Phil O'Grady with Louisa Bellew, De Beauvais with Marie D'Auvergne—is not more omnipresent than the shrewd, wealthy attorney, with his good stories, his sharp practice, and his vulgar, handsome, worldly wife, who comes of a better family than his, and never allows him to forget her origin. Mr. Lever relies much on men of law for the action and also for the fun of his novels. . . . Then there is always the young lady who understands farming and administers the out-at-elbows estate; and the high-spirited brother, who must have money, and who gets it somehow, who is exceedingly arrogant and detestably vulgar, but of whom the reader happily sees very little. Mr. Lever's dealings with money are truly magnificent—he confers estates with a generosity equal to that of Miss Flite, and never are his people so superbly lavish as when they are in hopeless difficulties. Then do they give magnificent entertainments, buy thoroughbred horses, respond with alacrity to every demand of friendship and every appeal for charity, dash about in post-chaises and stimulate postboys with guineas, live in profuse luxury, and exhibit a faultless taste in cookery. The amount of eating and drinking in Mr. Lever's books is only to be equalled by the perpetual breakfasts, luncheons, and suppers of the modern English drama, and all his people talk about it, as they "sip claret," "sit over burgundy," or "quaff champagne," for there is an appropriate form for each feat. (pp. 398-99)

All the *jeunes premiers* run over *menus* as glibly as so many *garçons de restaurant,* and discuss wine with the science and earnestness of so many tasters. If Mr. Lever's young men are surprising, his old men are still more astonishing. In the first place, they are so very old. Nothing under eighty is sufficiently wonderful. Count Considine is eighty-two, and he is only a little older than Godfrey O'Malley, and the charming pair of friends cheat bailiffs, defy debtors, entertain the county and the hunt, tell boisterous stories, send belligerent letters, and are utter scamps and roysterers, in theory at all events, at that venerable time of life. (p. 400)

His young ladies are stagy and silly, with very few exceptions, but they are perfectly free from the vulgarity of Miss Braddon's or the pagan lawlessness of Miss Broughton's heroines, young persons for whom one would like to prescribe solitary imprisonment and periodical whipping. He never degrades his ideal to the mere mercenary tricks, the mere low appetites, the shallow and repulsive passions, provoked mainly by bigness of stature, brutality of manners, perpetual smoking, and rowdyism in dress, which have been of late the main characteristics of our heroines of fiction. Chivalrous respect for women lends a pleasant flavour to his writings, which most readers learn to appreciate more and more as it becomes rarer in the highly-spiced novels of so-called real life, which seem to us designed to teach that there is nothing so little worthy of respect as women, especially when interpreted by women. The beautiful girls, with whom the dashing dragoons, or the brilliant *attachés,* or the rising young politicians fall in love after a headlong fashion, are all as grand, as dignified, as pure, as elevated, as the princesses of old romance for whom brave knights fought in the lists, and were rewarded by a smile, or at most a glove or a scarf. "I have never," says Mr. Lever, in his preface to *Charles O'Malley,* "written one line to disparage the good cause of honour and true manliness, nor have I said a syllable, so far as I know, to heighten the colour on the purest cheek of maidenhood." That which the author claims for himself in those words we gladly acknowledge. Not only are his works void of offence of the kind in which modern fiction abounds,—offence which renders that fiction so dangerous to the young, and which makes it incumbent on Catholic parents to exercise strict supervision over their daughters' reading,—but his ideal of womanhood is lofty and refined, his estimate of home, its duties, its virtues, and its pleasures, is high, and pure, and good. He can seldom touch any subject without exaggeration, and therefore he sometimes borders on the absurd even in this particular; as, for instance, when he makes General Hinton conceal the fact of his ruined fortunes from Lady Charlotte, and persuade her that he accepts a foreign command to oblige a royal highness; but it is impossible not to admire the standard of courtesy, consideration, and deference for women which he sets up. . . . The semi-savages of the O'Donoghue household, the gloom of Kilgobbin, the sensational extravagance of life at Tubbermore, the ruin and heartbreak at Cro'Martin, the senseless, riotous profusion at Gwynne Abbey, are all tempered and dignified by the respect paid to the presence of women. This element of beauty, purity, and decorum is hardly ever wanting in Mr. Lever's works; when it is wanting, as, for instance, in *The Dodd Family,* in which all the women are comic caricatures, (except Caroline Dodd, who is a phan-

tom), the book is unsatisfactory, and we miss the touch that would harmonize the whole. (pp. 401-03)

In Mr. Lever's preference for *The Dodds,* we do not coincide. There is more broad fun in it, more "high jinks," more sheer animal spirits, than in any of his works since the initiatory series; but it is a case, not of more wit, only of more laughter. It is broad farce; it is a picture without shadows; and every one writes in exactly the same smart style, except the sententious Caroline. Mary Anne Dodd and Betty Cobb, Kenny and his wife, all turn into accomplished letter-writers; and though they are amusing, the incongruity cannot be overlooked, from a critical point of view. James Dodd is a tiresome absurdity. His sister expresses in her first letter a doubt whether he can spell sufficiently well to correspond with his friend, and yet he writes letters full of all the smartest "knowingness" of low and loose Continental life from the start.

We are disposed to give Grog Davis and Annesley Beecher the precedence over their numerous brethren in originality and in merit. Before Davenport Dunn's time the humour which distinguished Mr. Lever's earlier works had begun to decline. By that time there was little more than smartness left. Another kind of humour developed itself later, but this was a transition period. *Davenport Dunn* is a wonderfully smart production: everybody says smart things, and the action of the story is smart. But that is all. (p. 404)

When Mr. Lever's works are regarded *en masse,* there is too much clever humbug in them; but, of course, they do not produce the same effect in detail. He demands too freely our interest in schemers, our admiration for their schemes. It is quite true that he upholds courage, honour, and manliness, especially in his earlier works. There is some declension of the standard in the later ones. The military heroes were finer fellows than the *jeunes premiers* of the politico-social series. But he takes shallow views of life generally, and there is too much of the "agreeable rattle" about his men in office and in responsible social positions. Not that we admire political dogmatism or didacticism in novels, but that there is a way of touching serious subjects seriously, and that Mr. Lever has, for the most part, missed it, and fallen into the smooth, epigrammatic line, which "makes things comfortable" without much trouble. His dashing dragoons were real soldiers, his statesmen and diplomatists are not real. . . . Only a short portion of Mr. Lever's life has been passed in Ireland, and the tendency of his mind, natural to a writer of fiction, is to seize upon the picturesque and the paradoxical. He found both in plenty, he has reproduced them; but he has gone no farther, and no deeper. True sympathy with the Irish people he does not feel. It could not exist together with ignorance of their religion, which implies the absence of true patriotism. An Irishman who is not a Catholic may love Ireland well and even wisely, but he cannot love her well or wisely if he regards the Catholic Faith with contempt which sometimes tries to be good-natured, and an affected magnanimity which represents to instructed minds that they really ought to be glad these poor people, with their vivid imagination and superstitious turn, can derive harmless consolation from the worship of images. There are a few finely-worded passages in Mr. Lever's works, which may seem to Protestants quite liberal and sympathetic, but, when examined, they will be found to mean simply this. His sketches of the peasantry are adorned with many beautiful touches of pathos, and the brightest, best, heartiest of his humour is lavished upon them. The funeral of Godfrey O'Malley, the scene on the course at

Loughrea, the denunciation of Mark O'Donoghue by the widow, the funeral of Shaun the murderer, are among the finest examples of the former. The gathering of Sir Marmaduke Travers's tenants, and the whole picture of the old home of *The Martins* are two specially striking instances of the latter; but each of Mr. Lever's readers will recall numerous others without difficulty. He is particularly happy in episodes, many of which will outlive that of the stories in which they occur. Miss Judy Macan's arrival at General Dashwood's ball, and the story of Frank Webber's dialogue with the man in the sewer, Miss O'Shea, Arthur O'Leary's *rencontre* with Mrs. Ram, the unlucky "Aunt Fanny" called to the Kennyfeck Council, and Peter O'Gorman, brought up express to inquire Roland Cashel's "intentions," but sent back to Galway when Aunt Fanny reports that Cashel "will 'blaze' for the asking," Lady Mary Boyle's device for keeping Billy Curtis from going to the poll, the story of Freney the robber; these and many more examples, present themselves at once to confirm this observation. Many of his comic personages have all the individuality with which Mr. Dickens inspired his, without their grotesqueness. Among the most amusing of his originals are to be found some specimens of the country doctor, old Hickman, Doctor Roach, and Doctor Dill.

There is a strange contradiction between the perennial, untamed buoyancy of Mr. Lever's spirits, and his belief in the efficacy and the prevalence of charlatanism. He is untouched with world-weariness, and yet, what could be supposed more surely calculated to inspire it than the notion prevalent in his works, that it is a world of "seems!"

In one respect Mr. Lever differs widely from other great or considerable writers, his contemporaries. He has not fallen away from the point of excellence which he attained. It was not so elevated as it might have been, had his views been sounder, his sympathies wider, his convictions more profound, and his self-confidence less active and sufficing. Those works of his which we willingly ignore are not his later performances. The fame which he achieved by his first novels is in no way impaired by *Lord Kilgobbin:* he will live as the bards of the gleeful time live, and be regarded as, "if not the first, on the very first line" of the novelists of the nineteenth century. (pp. 406-08)

> [*Frances Cashel Hoey*], *"The Works of Charles Lever," in* The Dublin Review, *n.s. Vol. 18, second quarter, 1872, pp. 379-408.*

MACMILLAN'S MAGAZINE (essay date 1872)

[*Writing soon after Lever's death, this anonymous critic laments the literary world's loss of a unique and powerful writer.*]

On the first day of June last, at the hour of noon, in the Villa Gasteiger at Trieste, passed away from this world one of the most genial, the most kindly, and the most brilliant of those spirits which of late years illumined our literary horizon.

For well-nigh forty years the name of Lever has been familiar to us as one of the most popular of British novelists, occupying a field upon which scarcely any other ventured to enter. Almost the creator of a style in which he was singularly successful, and the depicter of scenes and characters which he treated in a manner peculiarly his own, he delighted us with a flow of narrative, bright, sparkling, humorous, pathetic, and vivacious, that seemed as inexhaustible as it was perennial, and that ran as strongly from the fountain of his genius

during the last months of his life, as it did in the far-away days when *The Confessions of Harry Lorrequer* first attracted public attention, and gave the world promise of a writer of original power. (p. 337)

With Charles Lever passes away a style of novel peculiarly his own. Indeed it required all his genius and established reputation to enable it to hold its ground against new forms of thought and construction. Still his writings will long be popular. He is never sensational, in the sense in which that phrase has become descriptive of a class of novels in which the enormities of human nature—outrageous crimes and abdominable sins—are essentials. Nor, on the other hand, is he the depictor of calm, real life, extracting its interest from the discharge of daily duties and the sentiments and passions of ordinary people. He paints neither stormy seas, nor savagely grand scenery, luridly lighted up by the lightning flash or the conflagration; nor yet the placid lake or the sunny meadows with their unchanging though unexciting loveliness. He has, however, his own peculiar style, neither still life nor life in convulsions—the life of dramatic action, full of movement, incident, situation, pageant, and, if we may use the illustration, of stage effect. Into this he throws the energy of a lively genius, a joyous temperament, a ready wit, a keen appreciation of character, a good deal of sagacity, and a large experience of mankind.

To the honour of Lever be it ever remembered, that, like Dickens and Thackeray, he has written nothing to raise the blush of shame or of offended modesty. No impure word sullies his page; no impure thought is suggested by his freest sallies.

While he never shrank from censuring social immorality or false modes of fashionable life, no man knew better how to treat with equal delicacy and truth the vices or the failings which he wished to reprove. He did not love to expose the social sore so as to disgust or offend, but with singular skill he knew how to suggest the presence of the ulcer by an illustration or an anecdote. (pp. 343-44)

While a marked resemblance runs through all the writings of Lever—a thoroughly pronounced individuality that separates him from the other novelists of his time—we find, as might be expected in one whose labours extend over so many years, a change, growing gradually no doubt, yet sufficiently distinct at long intervals of time. And he who compares *Harry Lorrequer* with *The Daltons,* or with *Lord Kilgobbin,* will see as much difference in the compositions as he will see between the exuberance of youth, the fulness of manhood, and the maturity of age in the same individual. Lever, like the great painters, had his various manners. In the first, there is high colouring, the glare of sunlight, the flush of life: in the second, more sobriety of tones, more shadow, and somewhat of repose: in the third—the political and social novel, of which *The Dodd Family* and *Lord Kilgobbin* are the best illustrations—we find the highest finish, the most elaboration, the greatest breadth and depth. Here it is—to pass from metaphor—that he exhibits the ripeness of long years of observation and reflection, a carefulness of composition, an enlarged knowledge of mankind, and an intimate acquaintance with the politics of the world that make him in some of his utterances as epigrammatic as Rochefoucauld and as sagacious as Talleyrand. (p. 344)

"Charles James Lever," in Macmillan's Magazine, *Vol. XXVI, No. 154, August, 1872, pp. 337-44.*

ANTHONY TROLLOPE   (essay date 1876)

[*A distinguished Victorian novelist, Trollope is best known for his* Barsetshire Chronicles (*1855-67*), *a series of novels that realistically and humorously depicts English provincial life. In this excerpt from his autobiography, written in 1876, Trollope remembers his friend Lever as a great wit.*]

How shall I speak of my dear old friend Charles Lever, and his rattling, jolly, joyous, swearing Irishmen. Surely never did a sense of vitality come so constantly from a man's pen, nor from man's voice, as from his! I knew him well for many years, and whether in sickness or in health I have never come across him without finding him to be running over with wit and fun. Of all the men I have encountered, he was the surest fund of drollery. I have known many witty men, many who could say good things, many who would sometimes be ready to say them when wanted, though they would sometimes fail—but he never failed. Rouse him in the middle of the night, and wit would come from him before he was half awake. And yet he never monopolized the talk, was never a bore. He would take no more than his own share of the words spoken, and would yet seem to brighten all that was said during the night. His earlier novels—the later I have not read—are just like his conversation. The fun never flags, and to me, when I read them, they were never tedious. As to character, he can hardly be said to have produced it. Corney Delaney, the old man-servant, may perhaps be named as an exception.

Lever's novels will not live long, even if they may be said to be alive now, because it is so. What was his manner of working I do not know, but I should think it must have been very quick, and that he never troubled himself on the subject, except when he was seated with a pen in his hand. (pp. 226-27)

Anthony Trollope, "On English Novelists of the Present Day," in An Autobiography, *Harper & Brothers, 1883, pp. 219-34.*

W. B. YEATS   (essay date 1889)

[*The leading figure of the Irish Renaissance and a major poet in twentieth-century literature, Yeats was also an active critic of his contemporaries' works. As a critic he judged the works of others according to his own poetic values of sincerity, passion, and vital imagination. In the following excerpt from an essay entitled "Popular Ballad Poetry in Ireland," which was first published in November 1889 in* Leisure Hour, *Yeats explains why he did not include the works of Thomas Moore, Samuel Lover, and Lever in his study. For further commentary by Yeats, see excerpt dated 1891; for critical reaction to Yeats's opinions, see excerpt by A. Norman Jeffares dated 1980.*]

The English reader may be surprised to find no mention of Moore, or the verses of Lever and Lover. They were never poets of the people. Moore lived in the drawing-rooms, and still finds his audience therein. Lever and Lover, kept apart by opinion from the body of the nation, wrote ever with one eye on London. They never wrote for the people, and neither have they ever, therefore, in prose or verse, written faithfully of the people. Ireland was a metaphor to Moore, to Lever and Lover a merry harlequin, sometimes even pathetic, to be patted and pitied and laughed at so long as he said "your hon-

our," and presumed in nowise to be considered a serious or tragic person. (pp. 161-62)

W. B. Yeats, "Popular Ballad Poetry of Ireland," in his Uncollected Prose: First Reviews and Articles, 1886-1896, *Vol. 1, edited by John P. Frayne, Columbia University Press, 1970, pp. 146-62.*

W. B. YEATS   (essay date 1891)

[*In this excerpt from his introduction to* Representative Irish Tales, *first published in 1891, Yeats, while finding Lever's works humorous, states that they defame the Irish peasant. For further criticism by Yeats, see excerpt dated 1889; for an opposing viewpoint to Yeats's commentary on Lever, see excerpt by A. Norman Jeffares dated 1980.*]

I notice very distinctly in all Irish literature two different accents—the accent of the gentry, and the less polished accent of the peasantry and those near them; a division roughly into the voice of those who lived lightly and gayly, and those who took man and his fortunes with much seriousness and even at times mournfully. The one has found its most typical embodiment in the tales and novels of Croker, Lover, and Lever, and the other in the ruder but deeper work of Carleton, Kickham, and the two Banims.

There is perhaps no other country in the world the style and nature of whose writers have been so completely governed by their birth and social standing. Lever and Lover, and those like them, show constantly the ideals of a class that held its acres once at the sword's point, and a little later were pleased by the tinsel villainy of the Hell Fire Club—a class whose existence has, on the whole, been a pleasant thing enough for the world. It introduced a new wit—a humour whose essence was dare-devilry and good-comradeship, half real, half assumed. For Ireland, on the other hand, it has been almost entirely an evil, and not the least of its sins against her has been the creation in the narrow circle of its dependants of the pattern used later on for that strange being called sometimes 'the stage Irishman'. They had found the serious passions and convictions of the true peasant troublesome, and longed for a servant who would make them laugh, a tenant who would always appear merry in his checkered rags. The result was that there grew up round about the big houses a queer mixture of buffoonery and chicanery tempered by plentiful gleams of better things—hearts, grown crooked, where laughter was no less mercenary than the knavery. The true peasant remained always in disfavour as 'plotter', 'rebel', or man in some way unfaithful to his landlord. The knave type flourished till the decay of the gentry themselves, and is now extant in the boatmen, guides, and mendicant hordes that gather round tourists, while they are careful to trouble at no time any one belonging to the neighbourhood with their century-old jokes. The tourist has read of the Irish peasant in the only novels of Irish life he knows, those written by and for an alien gentry. He has expectations to be fulfilled. The mendicants follow him for fear he might be disappointed. He thinks they are types of Irish poor people. He does not know that they are merely a portion of the velvet of aristocracy now fallen in the dust. (pp. 25-6)

Charles Lever . . . wrote mainly for his own class. His books are quite sufficiently truthful, but more than any other Irish writer has he caught the ear of the world and come to stand for the entire nation. The vices and virtues of his characters are alike those of the gentry—a gentry such as Ireland has had, with no more sense of responsibility, as a class, than have the *dullahans, thivishes, sowlths, bowas,* and *water she-ries* of the spirit-ridden peasantry. His characters, however, are in no way lacking in the qualities of their defects—having at most times a hospitable, genial, good soldier-like disposi-tion.

Croker and Lover and Lever were as humorists go, great fel-lows. They must always leave some kind of recollection; but, to my mind, there is one thing lacking among them. I miss the deep earth song of the peasant's laughter. Maginn went nearer to attain it than they did. In "Father Tom and the Pope" he put himself into the shoes of an old peasant hedge school-master, and added to the wild humour of the people one crowning perfection—irresponsibility. In matters where irresponsibleness is a hindrance the Irish gentry have done little. They have never had a poet. Poetry needs a God, a cause, or a country. But witty have they been beyond ques-tion. If one excepts *The Traits and Stories,* all the most laugh-able Irish books have been by them. (p. 27)

W. B. Yeats, in an introduction to Representative Irish Tales, *edited by W. B. Yeats, Colin Smythe, 1979, pp. 25-32.*

THE ACADEMY   (essay date 1897)

[*This critic appreciates Lever's works primarily for their spon-taneity, humor, and faithful depictions of Irish character.*]

Nowadays, when half the novels read as if they had been writ-ten during the influenza, animal spirits are cheap at any price, and nowhere are they to be had so easily as in a volume of Lever.

That is Lever's essential quality, the stock-in-trade with which he started; one has only to re-read his first book, **Harry Lorrequer,** to be quite sure about this. . . . It is always he himself who provides the entertainment; one never forgets Lever in his characters. With the most extraordinary fertility of brilliant improvisation, he was incapable, or almost inca-pable, of sustained invention. **Harry Lorrequer** began as a se-ries of detached sketches; and scarcely any of his novels at-tained to the dignity of a compact and developed plot. Like Scott, he began a story without knowing where it was going; but, unlike Scott, he had not the art to draw the whole into a unity of action. His best novels are simply the recital of scenes in the life of a particular person, not connected by any continuous thread or intrigue; and in a chief faculty of the artist, the art of construction, he must be pronounced almost wholly deficient. You may begin to read him wherever you like and it will make very little difference to your enjoyment; but, after all, the important thing is that he remains enjoy-able.

A great many people talk about Lever as if he were fit only for the schoolroom. In most cases that is because they have not re-read him; if it were a genuine opinion it would argue stupidity. Lever, it is true, belonged to a generation which had a robust taste in humour; he lived in the era of practical jokes; and in addition to that he had the fortune or misfortune to be illustrated by Phiz, who accentuated the horseplay and the farcical types of his characters. But the buffoonery is only an excrescence; he had above all the personal magnetism of a born storyteller, that easy flow of light description, which, without tedium or hurry, leads up to the point; and that ex-traordinary memory for stories which left his imagination

nothing to do but to fill in picturesque details. A gentleman who lived at Portstewart when **Harry Lorrequer** was coming out in monthly parts remembers how he used to conquer the extreme shyness of his boyhood and creep into the drawing-room when Dr. Lever was there, to hear him rattling on in just the same pleasant way as in the printed pages. Lever's early attempts confined themselves chiefly to humorous nar-rative, in which he had felt his feet; but even in **Harry Lorre-quer** there is already one masterpiece of grave storytelling—the adventure of Trevanion, an English officer, who dealt with a French duellist during the occupation of Paris. Anoth-er master of narrative, William Napier, has told the story—a true one—in one of the letters printed in his life; and to com-pare the two is to get a good notion of the vivid little inven-tions by which Lever brings the scene before one. As he made his hand, he widened his choice of themes; pathos and even tragedy came well within his range, quite real in their way. Even Dickens could scarcely have done anything more grim than the death-bed scenes which open **Tom Burke.** Lever could draw a very convincing villain.

He has an Irishman's prejudices and prepossessions; conviv-ial qualities weigh with him, perhaps, more than they ought to; and he does not appreciate the commercial virtues. He could not write the romance of a merchant's honour, as Bal-zac did in *César Birotteau* and Daudet in *Risler ainé;* but if you want a roguish attorney or a pretentious upstart Lever is the very man to do it for you.

Yet, with all that, he has a large and humane tolerance even for his rogues; he likes the twinkle in the eye of a county hor-sedealer, or the suave manners of a continental swindler. In-deed, Lever is hard only on the people who bore him, espe-cially upon the stupidity of arrogance. He delights to show the condescending Englishmen outwitted by the mere Irish. When he draws them, as he drew, for instance, Walpole in **Lord Kilgobbin,** the portrait is telling enough, but it lacks moderation. Indignation puts too much gall into his ink. He is best with his own people, for with them he is never wholly out of sympathy, unless, indeed, they are bailiffs or, worse still, mortgagors who have ousted an old family. In this, as in so many other ways, he is profoundly Irish.

It has become the fashion to say that he misrepresented Irish character; but the charge is unreasonable. Writers of to-day insist upon the Celtic melancholy, but the Celtic gaiety is quite as characteristic; and the melancholy is most conspicu-ous among the peasants, who only interested him by their love of adventure and sport, and by their undeniable humour and quickness of tongue. Mickey Free is not a literally truth-ful representation, but he is artistically true—a dexterously heightened rendering of a familiar type. . . . All that Lever aspired to do was to sketch the amusing or the grotesque side of the people, their conscious or their unconscious humour, and he took the best types for his purpose; not the most char-acteristically Celtic nor the most poetic, but simply the most amusing. The bulk of his figures, however, belong either to the landlord class, which in the west and south remains very much as he painted it, or to that middle stratum which in Ire-land consists almost exclusively of solicitors and priests. Lever painted society as he saw it, and a room in which Lever found himself was not likely to remain gloomy, and was ex-ceedingly likely to become convivial. His own temperament throws a cheerful reflection on all his sketches; but they are not the less true for that. As an artist, he did not take himself seriously, he shunned all manner of filing work upon his productions, and would not even be at the pains to correct his proofs; but everywhere in his pages there is a genial and spontaneous humour, combined with a real knowledge of life, and a power of presenting character which increased steadily through his long career of writing. Lever never did anything better than the scene between Lord Kilgobbin and Miss Betty O'Shea in his last novel; and, above all, there is an ease of narration and a delight in the humour of his own situations which it would be hard to parallel except in the work of Dumas *père*. Perhaps the best way to praise Lever is to say that of all novelists he is the one who has most affinity with the creator of Chicot and D'Artagnan. (pp. 404-05)

"Charles Lever," in The Academy, *Vol. LI, No. 1301, April 10, 1897, pp. 404-05.*

LEWIS MELVILLE [PSEUDONYM OF LEWIS S. BENJAMIN] (essay date 1906)

[*Melville describes Lever's works, distinguishing between his bold, high-spirited early novels and his more subdued, artistically improved later ones.*]

With just so much right as Scotsmen claim Sir Walter Scott as their national novelist, many admirers of Charles James Lever demand that the latter be regarded as the national Irish romancer. But while the works of Scott are beloved by his compatriots, those of Lever are by no means popular with his countrymen. The reasons are not far to seek: Scott glorified his characters, making his heroes and heroines the noblest of their race; Lever, the possessor of a sense of humor far keener than that of the greater writer, sacrificed everything in the endeavor to amuse. Those of Lever's detractors who hail from the Emerald Isle complain bitterly that he has done much "to perpetuate the current errors as to Irish character," yet it cannot truthfully be asserted that he has on the whole been guilty of gross misrepresentation; and the various accusations, carefully examined, amount to little more than a charge of having depicted only certain classes of society. It is true that except *en passant,* as in the opening chapters of *Tom Burke of "Ours,"* Lever did not treat of the political aspect of the Irish question; but that was not because he was unpatriotic, but because he had little interest in the problem; and it must be admitted that he did not portray the hardworking clerk or the honest business man of everyday life. He was at his best when describing the men who drank deep, rowed hard, gamed heavily, fought bravely, and led a devil-may-care life; but also he depicted with graphic pen the wretched state of the peasantry, and drew with no unskilful hand the pitiful lot of the decayed Irish gentleman.

The humorist cannot but poke kindly fun at the weaknesses of his fellows, and Lever could not refrain from good-humored laughter at his countrymen's foibles. In his earlier books he made fun of most things, but he never wrote irreverently of sacred subjects, and always showed himself keenly alive to the holiness of the affection between parents and children, and to the beauty of love between man and woman. He wrote of youth and its joys: of the days *qu'on est bien à vingt ans,* when ambition is much but love is more, when frankness has not given place to diplomacy, when rash bravery rather than discretion is the rule. He wrote not of philosophy, nor of morality, but of the joyous times before high-spirited men come to forty year, and abandon "wine, woman, and song" for the serious business of life. He wrote, it must be remembered, of an era when existence was not so strenuous as it is

now, when less was expected from a man and less consequently was forthcoming, when the duel was of frequent occurrence, drunkenness regarded only as a venial fault, and practical joking an everyday occurrence.

It has been well said that Lever rollicked through life rather than lived, and when writing his books there is no doubt he drew largely on his experiences. One hears of his establishing in Dublin a *Burschenschaft,* the members of which wore scarlet vests with gilt buttons and a red skull-cap adorned with white tassels when they assembled for the suppers, songs, and conversational jousts that formed the staple of the night's entertainment. One hears how he took a party of friends to a ball at a house some miles distant in a furniture van, a hearse, and a mourning carriage; and of how, when practising as a doctor at Coleraine, and riding to visit a patient, he leaped his horse over a turf-cart that blocked the way. This latter exploit is introduced into many of the stories, and was cleverly parodied by Thackeray and Bret Harte [see excerpt by William Makepeace Thackeray dated 1847]. (pp. 649-50)

Lever studied medicine at Göttingen and Dublin, took his degree at the university in the latter city in 1831, and afterwards practised for some years in various parts of Ireland. It does not appear that he served any apprenticeship to letters, and, so far as it is known, he began his artistic career by the contribution to the *Dublin University Magazine* in 1837 of some sketches, afterwards issued in monthly parts with numerous additions as well as with illustrations by "Phiz," and in 1839 published in book form. This was, of course, *The Confessions of Harry Lorrequer,* which almost at once secured a favorable review in *Fraser's Magazine* [see excerpt by Percival W. Banks dated 1840]. (p. 651)

Lever was not yet prepared to abandon his original profession, and an opening being found for him to practise in Brussels, he repaired thither. He had thought he would be appointed physician to the English Embassy, but in this he was disappointed, although he secured a fair number of patients; and being discontented, was easily seduced by the offer of the shrewd manager of the *Dublin University Magazine* to return to the Irish metropolis to edit that periodical at the handsome salary of twelve hundred a year. The manager was moved to this proposal by the success of the story Lever wrote for him while in Brussels, *Charles O'Malley, the Irish Dragoon,* and the desire to retain for the magazine the services of the popular writer. He never had cause to regret the step, while the success of *Jack Hinton, the Guardsman* must have removed any lingering doubt he may have had as to the wisdom of the course he had taken. (pp. 651-52)

Following *Jack Hinton* came in quick succession *Tom Burke of "Ours," The Adventures of Arthur O'Leary,* and *The O'Donoghue,* with the publication of which terminated the author's connection with the *Dublin University Magazine.* It may be said at once that all these books lack plot. "Story! God bless you, I have none to tell, Sir," is the quotation prefixed to *Harry Lorrequer,* and this might as well have been taken for the motto of the rest, which are absolutely formless, and consist merely of a great number of stories hung together upon the slightest connecting thread possible.

Charles O'Malley is, perhaps, the most popular of the early books. The characters are unusually bright, even for Lever, and each has an amazing super-abundance of animal spirits, while the verses interspersed through the volumes are fresh and merry, and the anecdotes are related with peculiar gusto.

Nowhere are there better stories than that which tells how Lady Boyle won the election for Tom Butler, and than that of "the man in the sewer," while the episode of the undergraduate has been thought worthy of repetition, with slight variations, by almost every novelist who has since portrayed life at a university. The gem of the book is the account of the pretended death and mock funeral of Godfrey O'Malley, a device adopted to enable that worthy man to escape his creditors and seek re-election for his constituency: and most amusing is the letter in which the news is conveyed to his nephew,

> Your uncle Godfrey, whose debts (God pardon him!) are more numerous than the hairs of his wig, was obliged to die here last night. We did the thing for him completely; and all doubts as to the reality of the event are silenced by the circumstantial detail of the newspaper "that he was confined six weeks to his bed, from a cold he caught ten days ago while on guard"; repeat this, for it's better we had all the same story, till he comes to life again, which maybe will not take place before Tuesday or Wednesday. At the same time, canvass the country for him, and say he'll be with his friends next week, and up in Woodford and the Seariff barony: say he died a true Catholic; it will serve him on the hustings. Meet us in Athlone on Saturday, and bring your uncle's mare with you—he says he'd rather ride home; and tell Father MacShane to have a bit of dinner ready about four o'clock, for the corpse can get nothing after he leaves Mountmellick.

Lever most nearly approached failure with **Arthur O'Leary,** a sort of Baedeker's guide to the Continent, hopelessly overweighted with very long and rather tiresome interpolated narratives. On the other hand, the best of the books already mentioned—the best, perhaps, of all the books Lever ever wrote is **Tom Burke of "Ours."** In that story there is a great variety of scenes and graphic descriptions, especially of Paris in 1806 and the Court at the Tuileries; while the whole is more than usually dramatic in treatment. . . . This is an historical novel of the old school, in which an obscure Irishman mixes in the best society, is always on the spot at the right moment, and is invariably in the confidence of his generals. Napoleon—the Napoleon of fiction, tender at one moment, cruel at the next—figures largely in the tale, and Tom is frequently in his presence, on one occasion actually saves his life, and at the end meets him by accident at Fontainebleau on the eve of his abdication. (pp. 652-53)

In each of these books is a dashing hero, in spite of the author's intention not always a gentleman, and often not far removed from a scamp, doing things that are unpardonable, and behaving in a way that no other novelist's hero ever does. The fact of the matter is, as has already been said, Lever subordinated everything to humor, and without a twinge of compunction would make a "bounder" of his best-beloved character for the sake of a good story. There is, too, a strong family likeness about the heroes. Each gets into trouble, usually when he is in no way to blame; each falls invariably on his feet; each fights duels with the most famous swordsman or the most renowned shot, and at worst escapes with a more or less severe wound; and each seems to be unsuccessful in love, but never fails—in the last chapter—to win for his wife the woman he desires. In each book there is also one villain—for choice, a scoundrelly attorney; and numberless officers, army doctors, priests, briefless barristers, horse-dealers, and smugglers, all of whom have "yarns" to relate, practical jokes to engineer, and a marvellous, never flagging flow of high

Mickey Free in a scene from Charles O'Malley.

spirits. The female characters rarely emerge from shadow, and, though but barely outlined, are usually of one of two types: the rather worldly-minded woman, and the well brought up, pure, honest, and, it must be confessed, generally uninteresting young girl; though occasionally he extended his limits, as when he drew the *vivandière* Minette, the laughable Madame Lefevbre, and the inimitable Mrs. O'Reilly. When dealing with men, however, his characterization, though never subtle, was frequently vigorous; and he has given us the delightful Bubbleton, who could never open his mouth but to utter some absurdity; the humorous Major Monsoon; the Knight of Gwynne, one of the most lovable and pathetic figures ever depicted; and the wily, cunning, humorous Mickey Free—by which last portrait Lever may be content to stand or fall as a creator. (p. 654)

The books of Lever's second period differ considerably from those written in earlier years. The style is less rugged, the construction better, the characters more carefully drawn, and the author's greater experience of life is evident throughout. But the anecdotes are fewer, there are none of the delightful songs; the martial scenes, dashing heroes, rollicking officers, and jolly priests have disappeared; and to most readers without these Lever is not Lever. The high spirits have gone, too, and the amusing practical joke and the merry quip and crank are things of the past; but the old humor is there, not so gay, indeed, and more reflective, but not a whit less agreeable, though appealing perhaps to a more delicate taste in letters.

Roland Cashel shows Lever in a state of transition, between his two manners, and with **The Fortunes of Glencore,** which followed it, he reached for the first time the later style. Then came **Davenport Dunn,** the story of a clever commercial swindler of that name and of Grog Davis, a "lag" who is almost redeemed by the great love he bore his daughter. **Davenport Dunn** is good, but best of all is **The Dodd Family Abroad,**

a series of letters written by members of an average middle-class Irish family, with no unusual gifts and few special opportunities for observation, who have gone on the continent with crude and ridiculous notions of what awaited them there. (p. 656)

The Dodd family consists of a husband and wife, a son, James, and two daughters, Mary Anne and Catherine. The husband is a fairly sensible man, brought away rather against his will, level-headed enough as a rule, but somewhat thrown off his balance by the complete change of surroundings; the wife is a silly woman who dearly loves a lord, in which particular she is resembled by James, a weak young man, inclining to dandyism, extravagant, and entirely inexperienced. Mary Anne is a splendid example of the *genus* snob, who cuts an old friend because he looks dowdy, and is for ever complaining that Dublin is "terribly behind the world in all that regards civilization and *ton*"; delighting to flirt with all and sundry—but there fate gets even with her by letting her "carry on" with a *table d'hôte* acquaintance who turns out to be not the nobleman whose title she assumes, but a common thief. It is a relief to turn to Catherine, agreeable, sensible, retined, tender—Lever's favorite female character, said to have been drawn from his wife. The great merit of **The Dodd Family Abroad** is the way in which each person, while chronicling the doings of the party, is made to expose his or her character. Lever believed he never wrote anything to equal this book, and certainly without fear of contradiction it may be said he never wrote anything better. Indeed, for sustained interest, quiet satire, reflective humor, and brilliant analysis of character it stands among his works unrivalled.

Humor rather than pathos was Lever's *forte*. He admitted that his stories were wanting in scenes of touching and pathetic interest, but he consoled himself, as he characteristically told his readers, remembering to have heard of an author whose paraphrase of the Book of Job was refused by a publisher if he could not throw into it a little more humor. . . . But Lever could write well enough of tender incidents, and with a delicacy not equalled by many authors whose fame rests upon novels of misery or sad sentiments. Take, for example, the description of Tom Burke's thoughts as his father lay dying.

> I am writing now of the far-off past—of the long years ago, of my youth—since which my seared heart has had many a sore and scalding lesson; yet I cannot think of that night, fixed and graven as it lies in my memory, without a touch of boyish softness. I remember every waking thought that crossed my mind—my very dream is still before me. It was of my mother. I thought of her, as she lay on a sofa in the old drawing-room, the window open, and the blinds drawn—the gentle breeze of a June morning flapping them lazily to and fro, as I knelt beside her to repeat my little hymn, the first I ever learned; and how at each moment my eyes would turn and my thoughts stray to that open casement through which the odor of flowers and the sweet song of birds were pouring; and my little heart was panting for liberty, while her gentle smile and faint words bade me remember where I was. And now I was straying away through the old garden, where the very sunlight fell scantily through the thick-woven branches loaded with perfumed blossoms; the blackbirds hopped fearlessly from twig to twig, mingling their clear notes with the breezy murmur of the summer bees. How happy was I then! and why cannot such happiness be last-

ing? Why cannot we shelter ourselves from the base contamination of worldly cares, and live on amid pleasures pure as these, with hearts as holy and desires as simple as in childhood?

Lever was well aware of his faults. "I wrote as I felt—sometimes in good spirits—sometimes in bad—always carelessly—for, God help me! I can do no better," he said at the beginning of his career in **Harry Lorrequer**. . . . [Though] it has more than once been pleaded in extenuation, it was not haste that gave him a loose style, although Lever himself wondered if he had written less he would have written better. This was, in great part, due to lack of revision, and he would not revise his manuscript because, knowing himself not to be a capable artist, he dreaded lest possibly he might at first, by happy chance, make the right impression, and then carefully improve it away. On the other hand, Lever possessed imagination of no mean order, rising at times to outbursts of real poetry; he had considerable descriptive power, and drew splendid pen-pictures of landscape and seascape, besides depicting vividly scenes in Irish and French life; and he was *facile princeps* in his particular field—the narration of humorous incident. There can be no doubt—although at present a spirit of reaction is evident in critical circles—that, in spite of all their faults of omission and commission, by virtue of the genuine raciness that inspired them, the easy humor, the natural tenderness, the best of Lever's rollicking, madcap stories will for all time have an honored place in English literature. (pp. 656-58)

Lewis Melville [pseudonym of Lewis S. Benjamin],
"Charles Lever," in The Living Age, *Vol. CCL, No.*
3245, September 15, 1906, pp. 649-58.

BERNARD SHAW   (essay date 1906)

> [*Shaw is generally considered the greatest and best-known dramatist to write in the English language since Shakespeare. He is closely identified with the intellectual revival of the British theater, and in his dramatic theory he advocates eliminating romantic conventions in favor of a theater of ideas grounded in realism. During the late nineteenth century, Shaw was a prominent literary, art, music, and drama critic, and his reviews were known for their biting wit and brilliance. In this excerpt from his preface to* Major Barbara, *he acknowledges the influence of* A Day's Ride *on his ideas. Shaw's remarks were written in 1906.*]

About half a century ago, an Irish novelist, Charles Lever, wrote a story entitled **A Day's Ride: A Life's Romance.** It was published by Charles Dickens in *Household Words* [*A Day's Ride* was actually published in Dickens's *All the Year Round*], and proved so strange to the public taste that Dickens pressed Lever to make short work of it. I read scraps of this novel when I was a child; and it made an enduring impression on me. The hero was a very romantic hero, trying to live bravely, chivalrously, and powerfully by dint of mere romance-fed imagination, without courage, without means, without knowledge, without skill, without anything real except his bodily appetites. Even in my childhood I found in this poor devil's unsuccessful encounters with the facts of life, a poignant quality that romantic fiction lacked. The book, in spite of its first failure, is not dead: I saw its title the other day in the catalogue of Tauchnitz.

Now why is it that when I also deal in the tragi-comic irony of the conflict between real life and the romantic imagination, critics never affiliate me to my countryman and immediate forerunner, Charles Lever, whilst they confidently derive me from a Norwegian author of whose language I do not know three words, and of whom I knew nothing until years after the Shavian *Anschauung* was already unequivocally declared in books full of what came, ten years later, to be perfunctorily labelled Ibsenism? I was not Ibsenist even at second hand; for Lever, though he may have read Henri Beyle, *alias* Stendhal, certainly never read Ibsen. Of the books that made Lever popular, such as *Charles O'Malley* and *Harry Lorrequer,* I know nothing but the names and some of the illustrations. But the story of the day's ride and life's romance of Potts (claiming alliance with Pozzo di Borgo) caught me and fascinated me as something strange and significant, though I already knew all about Alnaschar and Don Quixote and Simon Tappertit and many another romantic hero mocked by reality. From the plays of Aristophanes to the tales of Stevenson that mockery has been made familiar to all who are properly saturated with letters.

Where, then, was the novelty in Lever's tale? Partly, I think, in a new seriousness in dealing with Potts's disease. Formerly, the contrast between madness and sanity was deemed comic: Hogarth shews us how fashionable people went in parties to Bedlam to laugh at the lunatics. I myself have had a village idiot exhibited to me as something irresistibly funny. On the stage the madman was once a regular comic figure: that was how Hamlet got his opportunity before Shakespear touched him. The originality of Shakespear's version lay in his taking the lunatic sympathetically and seriously, and thereby making an advance towards the eastern consciousness of the fact that lunacy may be inspiration in disguise, since a man who has more brains than his fellows necessarily appears as mad to them as one who has less. But Shakespear did not do for Pistol and Parolles what he did for Hamlet. The particular sort of madman they represented, the romantic make-believer, lay outside the pale of sympathy in literature: he was pitilessly despised and ridiculed here as he was in the east under the name of Alnaschar, and was doomed to be, centuries later, under the name of Simon Tappertit. When Cervantes relented over Don Quixote, and Dickens relented over Pickwick, they did not become impartial: they simply changed sides, and became friends and apologists where they had formerly been mockers.

In Lever's story there is a real change of attitude. There is no relenting towards Potts: he never gains our affections like Don Quixote and Pickwick: he has not even the infatuate courage of Tappertit. But we dare not laugh at him, because, somehow, we recognize ourselves in Potts. We may, some of us, have enough nerve, enough muscle, enough luck, enough tact or skill or address or knowledge to carry things off better than he did; to impose on the people who saw through him; to fascinate Katinka (who cut Potts so ruthlessly at the end of the story); but for all that, we know that Potts plays an enormous part in ourselves and in the world, and that the social problem is not a problem of story-book heroes of the older pattern, but a problem of Pottses, and of how to make men of them. To fall back on my old phrase, we have the feeling—one that Alnaschar, Pistol, Parolles, and Tappertit never gave us—that Potts is a piece of really scientific natural history as distinguished from funny story telling. His author is not throwing a stone at a creature of another and inferior order, but making a confession, with the effect that the stone hits each of us full in the conscience and causes our self-esteem to smart very sorely. Hence the failure of Lever's book to please the readers of *Household Words.* That pain in the

self-esteem nowadays causes critics to raise a cry of Ibsenism. I therefore assure them that the sensation first came to me from Lever and may have come to him from Beyle, or at least out of the Stendhalian atmosphere. I exclude the hypothesis of complete originality on Lever's part, because a man can no more be completely original in that sense than a tree can grow out of air. (pp. 9-11)

> *Bernard Shaw, in a preface to his* Major Barbara, *Penguin Books, 1946, pp. 9-49.*

HUGH WALKER   (essay date 1910)

[*Walker describes Lever's strengths and weaknesses and explains his preference for the novelist's early works.*]

There are multitudes of Englishmen whose conception of Irish life and of the Irish character is drawn from Lever, and who, when they think of the Irishman, do so through the medium of Lever's stories. And yet it is plain that the characters are little better than farcical caricatures, and that Lever only skims the surface of Irish life. His superficiality may have been partly due to the fact that by blood he was more English than Irish. His father migrated from Manchester to Ireland, and his mother too was of a family originally English. (pp. 636-37)

To [his] early years belong what have certainly been Lever's most popular novels, *Harry Lorrequer, Charles O'Malley, Jack Hinton* and *Tom Burke of Ours.* In later days Lever's books showed an advance in literary skill, and, though he was never a careful writer, he worked in a less reckless style than he did in the beginning of his career. For these reasons some, himself among the number, have preferred certain of his later stories, such as *Tony Butler* and *Sir Brook Fossbrooke.* But the superior popularity of the early tales, and especially of *Charles O'Malley,* seems to be well deserved. No degree of care or labour could ever have made Lever a great novelist. His conception of character was crude and shallow, and he had little power of construction. Even in his later days the change is, after all, only superficial. "You ask me how I write," he says to Blackwood as late as 1863; "my reply is, just as I live—from hand to mouth." And the reply is an exact statement of the truth, and an explanation at once of Lever's merits and of his defects. Not only did he write rapidly, but he instantly forgot what he had written. His letters from Spezzia and Trieste to the Blackwoods are full of lamentations over 'copy' which he fears has gone astray. It would not be difficult to write something new, but to write what would fit in to the part before and the part after—*hic labor, hoc opus est.* In particular, he never could wind up satisfactorily. The characters of a book, he says, "are like the tiresome people who keep you wishing them good-night till you wish them at the devil. They won't go—the step of the hall-door would seem to have bird-lime on it." Naturally therefore when the influence of the time induced Lever to attempt analysis the result was unsatisfactory. His charm goes as he becomes more consciously literary, and his own preference for these later stories seems to be rather the attempt at self-persuasion of a man who suspects that his day is over than a genuine opinion.

There is however sound self-criticism in the opinion Lever expresses of the series of miscellaneous papers entitled *Cornelius O'Dowd upon Men, Women, and other Things.* "They are," he says, "the sort of things I can do best. I have seen a great deal of life, and have a tolerably good memory for strange and out-of-the-way people, and I am sure such sketches are far more my 'speciality' than story-writing." Just for this reason the early stories, reckless and planless, are the best. The qualities which give Lever's works their value are the lively narrative, the humour and the "rollick." He stands supreme for unfailing flow of spirits. In the early tales these qualities are unrestrained, and neither facts, nor character, nor plot is allowed to interfere with them. Harry Lorrequer and Charles O'Malley go where the whim of the author decides, and do whatever most tends to entertainment. Lever naturally took first the cream of that experience of life and knowledge of strange characters of which he speaks. Many of the most eccentric characters and not a few of the most surprising adventures were real. Major Monsoon was an officer in the British army, who by a legal deed, for the sum of four napoleons, assigned to Lever the right to make what use he pleased of himself and his adventures, or what he described as his adventures.

Charles O'Malley is a story not merely of Irish life, but of the great struggle which was convulsing Europe during Lever's childhood; and when Thackeray parodied Lever in *Phil Fogarty* [see excerpt dated 1847], the fighting element was one of the principal points upon which he directed his good-natured satire. Lever thus belongs not only to the Irish group, but to the class of military novelists, whom the stir and excitement, the glory and the sufferings of the Napoleonic wars called into existence. He was not the earliest of the class, but he was the best, because he was most successful in welding fiction with history, or perhaps rather because he firmly resolved to subordinate history to fiction; for the historical element in Lever's lively tales is very slight indeed. (pp. 637-39)

> *Hugh Walker, "After Scott," in his* The Literature of the Victorian Era, *1910. Reprint by Cambridge at the University Press, 1940, pp. 612-59.*

J. M. SPAIGHT (essay date 1930)

[*Reassessing Lever's novels, Spaight asserts that the best of his works,* Jack Hinton, Charles O'Malley, Harry Lorrequer, The Knight of Gwynne, *and* Tom Burke, *will continue to be read by those who love an exciting, vigorous tale.*]

To understand Lever the writer one must understand Lever the man. His personal history furnishes the clue to much that is puzzling in his literary career. Judged by his best, he was a great and original humorous writer; by his worst, he was a hack-novelist of the most uninspired type. He was both the one and the other mainly because of the facts of his life. (p. 679)

He was perpetually in need of money, extravagant, careless about ways and means, an inveterate gambler at cards (not at the tables), an indifferent manager of his business affairs, yet happy withal. When his first great grief came to him in the death of his only son in 1863, he had difficulty in finding the money needed for the burial expenses. (p. 680)

It is necessary to draw attention to this side of Lever's life and character, for one finds here a determining factor of his career as a writer. He wrote his novels to pay his bills, and, because his bills were heavy and pressing, he wrote usually against time, often against the grain, worriedly, hurriedly, without focal intervals of thought. Most of his novels were issued in monthly parts, and sometimes he wrote on, after all that he

really had to say was said, simply because a given number of parts had to be completed. (p. 681)

The fact is that under the pressure of monetary needs he wrote too much and too quickly. . . . Sometimes he had two stories on hand at the same time. He was writing *The Daltons* simultaneously with *Con Cregan* in 1849 and with *Maurice Tiernay* in 1850. Frequently before he had finished one novel he began another, and he was inclined to lose interest in the book already in hand. The result was occasionally a complaint from his publisher or his editor; Dickens, to whose periodical *All the Year Round* Lever contributed *A Day's Ride,* was among the complainants.

In another way also the chances of Lever's personal career had a profound influence upon his literary career. By leaving Ireland he really cut himself off from his best source of inspiration. He continued to write about Irish characters and Irish themes, but he had now to rely more and more upon memory and imagination and less and less upon current observation. "Now and then," he said in February 1865, "I feel as I were only manufacturing out of old wearables, like the devil's dust folk at Manchester." He was essentially an Irish novelist. His Irish novels are beyond question the most successful. The Irish characters in his novels as a whole are the truest to life. He seems never to have understood, at any rate he never succeeded in portraying convincingly, the character of people of other races. There is something wrong about most of his foreigners. They do not live. Even in his analysis of Irish types he does not show himself capable of probing very deeply into hidden motive and undisclosed impulse. But he does give, on broad lines, a true picture of certain types of the Irish men and women of his time as they appeared to an understanding, if not profound or subtle, observer. One feels that he knew them, and especially the 'oddities' among them, as he never knew the people of other lands.

He left Ireland in 1837. In 1842 he returned, to take up the editorship of the *Dublin University Magazine*. In 1845 he quitted Ireland for the last time, returning only for two brief visits in later years. His three years' sojourn at Templeogue, near Dublin, from 1842 to 1845, was an unhappy experience, embittered by quarrels with William Carleton and others. For his own comfort—and one has only one life to live, and it is brief—he probably did well to turn to Italy and the sunshine. It may be, nevertheless, that if he had taken the other course, if he had hardened his heart and remained in Ireland, quarrels or no quarrels, he would have consulted his own interests as a writer better. He might then have given us, out of his riper experience, a finer novel of Irish life than any of those which he in fact wrote. As it was, his quality as a novelist steadily deteriorated. (pp. 682-83)

Mention of the Carleton quarrel suggests yet another head of criticism of Lever's characterisation. He was accused in his own day, and since, of taking a delight in portraying the 'stage Irishman'—a travesty of the real Irishman. That criticism has some substance in it, but in so far as it implies that Lever deliberately tried to vilify his countrymen and hold them up as laughing-stocks to the world, it is an unfair criticism. Some of Lever's portraits of Irish men and women are undoubtedly caricatures; but so are many of his portraits of people of other races. He painted the Irish peasants as he knew them. He did not know them as well as Carleton, who was himself of peasant stock. Lever was not; he was to that extent handicapped in writing of them; but then he had the advantage—or the disadvantage—of understanding another

Irish class far better than Carleton ever knew it. It was for that class he wrote. One must grasp this fact if one is to understand Lever's literary position.

Lever belonged to the Irish upper middle class, and wrote always with an eye fixed on an Irish upper middle-class audience. There is no middle class, of course, in Ireland, and equally, of course—because one is speaking of Ireland,—it is the Irish middle class which is the most vital element of the Irish race. It has given both Ireland and the British Empire many of its most illustrious servants. From it, in particular, has sprung a long line of Army officers whose names are linked with the story of British arms. The soldier's life has always had a powerful attraction for young men of this class, largely, but by no means exclusively, men in whose veins runs a mixed current of Irish and English blood. Lever was of this class, and wrote for it. That is why his novels are so full of military history. He knew that those for whom he wrote would love, as he did, a gallant stirring tale. He reflected, in fact, an authentic Irish spirit of his time, albeit a sectional one, no doubt. (pp. 683-84)

Lever, born and bred in Ireland, saw himself always as a citizen of the world. For him Ireland and Irish affairs were part of and related to a larger community and a more complex economy. This attitude of his to Irish interests and Irish politics is reflected in all his books. To condemn him for it, even if justifiable, beside the point. One has to take him as he was, and what is important is that it *was* his attitude, in actual fact.

Having this wider outlook, Lever refused to recognise the validity of the injunction, *De Hibernis nil nisi bonum*. It is a stupid injunction, the sign of an inferiority complex. Why should we be exempt from criticism? Lever saw his country's faults. He loved it, but in something of the bantering way in which the defunct relative, Jones M'Carthy, of his own Mrs Kenny James Dodd loved it. "He loved his country, and it was a treat to hear him praise it. 'Ah!' he would say, 'there's but one blot on her—the Judges is rogues, the Government's rogues, the Grand Jury's rogues, and the People is villains!' "

Lever has been reproached with giving a false and misleading impression of the typical Irish gentleman of his day—by no means, it is contended, the happy-go-lucky irresponsible person whom Lever represents him as being. It is true that Lever's portraits are highly coloured and perhaps overdrawn, but that they had real prototypes I have little doubt. (pp. 684-85)

At any rate, it was the "man for Galway" type of man, "with debts galore but fun far more," who appealed to Lever and whom he loved to draw. Mostly his character drawing is poor. His young men of fashion might have stepped out of the later pages of Ouida. His great ladies are grotesque, frigid, abominably rude to inferiors, impossible persons. His elderly maiden ladies, such as Miss Maria Daly and Miss Dinah Barrington, are violent termagants. His young ladies are mostly female prigs, talking high-falutin' twaddle. (p. 685)

In truth Lever was, as a society novelist, a failure. His most ambitious books are *Davenport Dunn* and *The Daltons,* both novels of great length. In them he brings upon a crowded canvas a host of characters, exalted personages, adventurers, blacklegs, respectable people, nondescripts, thrown together in the cosmopolitan society of various Continental towns, and, in *Davenport Dunn,* in the Ireland of the period of the Encumbered Estates Court. The result is in each case a picture which is pretentious and wholly unconvincing. A few

good things there are in each book. The scene in which Davenport Dunn saves the Ossory Bank when a 'run' is made upon it is effectively described, but most of the characters in the book—Annesley Beecher, Grog Davis the 'Leg,' 'Holy Paul' Classon, Davenport Dunn himself—are unpleasant and rather boring; and one can never quite believe in the 'good' characters such as Charles Conway, Sybella Kellett, and Lizzie Davis. In *The Daltons* the background of fighting in the Milanais is vividly suggested, but on the whole the book fails to grip the attention. The closing scene in it—an Assize trial which begins with the indictment of one man for murder and ends with the conviction of another (who started as a witness!)—is simply fantastic. (pp. 685-86)

It is doubtful whether any of Lever's later stories will survive or will deserve to survive. *Luttrell of Arran* is typical of them. It is a poor performance. The girl Kate O'Hara (Luttrell) and the old diplomatist are drawn sympathetically enough, but they are not really vitalised. The lawyer M'Kinlay's mishaps ought to be diverting, but are not. The Vyners, Grenfell, Ladarelle, and the Luttrells, father and son, are all characters in whom it is difficult to believe or to take any sustained interest. *The Dodd Family Abroad* is amusing in parts, and the account which it gives of the life of an Irish family in Brussels, Bonn, Como, Florence, and other places is not without interest even to-day; in its own day the book must have been a useful guide-book of the chatty story-telling type since popularised by C. N. and A. M. Williamson. But most of the later books make tedious reading. There is little in them of the racy humour, the keen joy of life, the rollicking fun of the earlier novels. In characterisation and design they are uniformly commonplace.

It is by the early novels that Lever's fame will stand. He never improved on them. Which is the best it is hard to say, and in any case a comparison of them is not easy. As a novel of military life and adventure *Tom Burke* seems to me to stand high. Lever wrote it after he had steeped himself in the history of the Napoleonic wars, for the purpose, afterwards abandoned, of writing a life of Napoleon. Some of the descriptions of the fighting in which Tom Burke takes part in the French service are thrilling. The campaigns of Austerlitz, Jena, and Auerstadt are vividly sketched; so, too, is the life of the Paris of 1806. The great marshals of France—Berthier, Murat, Bernadotte, Davoust, Lannes, Oudinot, Ney—pass with Napoloen himself across the stage, dim figures, but impressive in their shadowy outline. Lever was always a hero-worshipper. We see the great armies of France on the move and in action—the voltigeurs, tirailleurs, cuirassiers, chasseurs of the guard. Lever never did anything better in this category of descriptive writing.

Tom Burke seems to have been in the nature of an experiment; it was at any rate a deviation from Lever's former line of country. He harked back to the old line in *The O'Donoghue* and *The Knight of Gwynne*. . . . Of these the latter seems to me to be much the more successful book. The scene of both is laid in Ireland—in the one case in the wild country on the Cork-Kerry borders, in the other in Connaught, Ulster, and Dublin. *The O'Donoghue* is a depressing book, relieved hardly at all by Lever's accustomed gaiety and exuberant spirits. Mark O'Donoghue, the hero, is an ill-conditioned churl. The young Guardsman, Frederick Travers, is a paladin and a paragon, but a figure of pure cardboard in which there is no breath of life. The female characters are, as usual, unreal in the extreme.

In *The Knight of Gwynne* we have an achievement of a very different order. Lever himself ranked it as "the best of the breed," and it was financially his most successful book. His faults are there, but his merits are there too, and in stronger measure. The book would make a fine film play. (pp. 688-89)

The Knight of Gwynne was really the last book of Lever's first—and best—period. His two earliest books, *Harry Lorrequer* and *Charles O'Malley,* are probably the most popular of all, and are certainly the best known. In both the story is told in a collection of loosely strung episodes. Both books are weak in design, construction, and plot. Neither is a well-finished novel; but both are gloriously amusing. *Harry Lorrequer,* the book by which Lever made his name, is full of roaring fun, outrageous adventures, and comic situations, but on the whole it is distinctly amateurish. (p. 690)

Charles O'Malley . . . is only a little less amateurish than *Harry Lorrequer,* but with all its faults it is perhaps the most thoroughly enjoyable of all Lever's books. Mickey Free is a genuine creation. To every old Trinity man the picture which the book gives (supplemented by some further glimpses in *The Martins* and later books) of the College life of the day is a lasting joy. The pranks of Frank Webber are a sheer delight. Webber was drawn from two originals, Robert Torrens Boyle and John Ottiwell, but at least one of Lever's own adventures is worked into the story of his escapades. (pp. 690-91)

Lever's third book, *Jack Hinton,* is, in the opinion of many judges, the best of all. The hero, an English Guardsman, is, it must be confessed, as great a 'stick' as all Lever's other Guardsmen, but he is a gallant 'stick' and a likeable. Some of the other characters are the best which Lever ever drew. Mr and Mrs Paul Rooney are delightful exaggerations. Father Tom Loftus of Murranakilty is glorious. The description of his game of cards with the other passengers in the cabin of the canal boat between Dublin and Port Shannon is beyond price. (p. 691)

It is hard to believe that there will not always be a public, limited but loyal, for the best in Lever. Such books as *Jack Hinton, The Knight of Gwynne, Tom Burke, Harry Lorrequer,* and *Charles O'Malley* must continue to have their readers. However serious and sober-minded the world becomes, there will always be people who love a rattling tale. They will not, perhaps, be over-critical readers. It would be absurd to say that Lever was a great novelist. To deep psychological insight, to subtle analysis of character, to the intellectual power which amazes and enslaves a reader's understanding, his pages show amply that he has no claim. He is surpassed by a host of other writers in the qualities which go to make the great masters of fiction. He was not faultless even on the executive side of literary craftsmanship. He was too prolix, and he had little capacity for discrimination and selection. But he had one or two merits which cover a multitude of defects—he could make men laugh, and he loved, and could make his readers love, a breathless, gallant tale of adventure and arms—a tale that seems to swing along to "the cavalry canter of 'Bonnie Dundee.' " Furthermore, he could reproduce as no one else the life and atmosphere of an old Ireland which has now passed for ever.

It is to young men, and especially young men of his own good Irish stock, that Lever makes his appeal. There is a call for

them—a call of laughter and bugles—in his headlong pages. One must have something in one's composition of his own qualities, of light-heartedness, high spirits, irresponsibility, gaiety, love of a fight, fully to appreciate him. There will always be people of that kidney, be the world never so super-civilised and the spirit of war never so completely exorcised. (pp. 692-93)

J. M. Spaight, "Charles Lever Re-Read," in Blackwood's Magazine, *Vol. CCXXVII, No. MCCCLXXV, May, 1930, pp. 679-93.*

A. NORMAN JEFFARES (essay date 1980)

[*Jeffares is an Irish educator whose interests range from the poetry of Geoffrey Chaucer to twentieth-century literature. His major scholarly concern, though, is the life and works of William Butler Yeats, about whom he has written several critical works. In this excerpt, Jeffares examines Lever's attitudes toward Ireland and its people as expressed in his novels, disputing Yeats's contention that Lever was an English sympathizer. For a sampling of Yeats's comments on Lever, see excerpts dated 1889 and 1891.*]

[Lever's last novel, *Lord Kilgobbin,*] demonstrates the fierce dislike he had formed for English rule [of Ireland]. His novels from the 'forties onward show this increasingly critical spirit, a sense of impending disaster no less acute than Yeats's own. And yet Yeats and most Irish critics have labelled him a mere creator of the stage Irishman, a hearty, a garrison writer. The only conclusion one is forced to is that they accepted the fashionable labels and read no further than *Harry Lorrequer* and *Charles O'Malley.* They got hold of the wrong Lever.

In Lever's thirty-three novels we have a fascinating insight into eighteenth and nineteenth century Irish life—history and politics as well as social, economic, military and sporting details, in addition to interpretations of Irish character in speech and action, for Lever, like all Irishmen, was deeply conscious of the different ways the Irish and the English speak and think. These novels were written by a man who travelled widely, was well read and highly intelligent, and knew rural Ireland's poverty and bravery as perhaps only a dispensary doctor could. Lever came to understand how government, or rather British party politics, worked; he wanted—increasingly—to put his own point of view, and provided a rich range of character as well as historical background and physical locale in his writings. He created convincing examples of both the dashing, feckless ascendancy and the self-deluding romantic, being himself a subtle blend of romantic and realist.

It is clear to a contemporary reader approaching *Charles O'Malley* detachedly that Lever ran into unduly sensitive nationalist attitudes. Even Shaw, who paid handsome tribute to Lever [see excerpt dated 1906], and whose criticism ought to be taken as an antidote to Yeats's, has recorded some misgivings or reservations about Mickey Free, O'Malley's servant. But is the stage Irishry of this character so different from the stage cockney of, say, Sam Weller? It is possible that the excessively nationalist bias of critics neglected the harsh criticism of Irish political life and social life dropped incidentally in this novel. While the faked death of Charles O'Malley's uncle is primarily amusing it also reflects upon typical attitudes of landowners to debt and mortgages, when an incidental passage shows the casual attitude young officers adopted to the bills they ran up with tradespeople.

However, the first sign of direct criticism of English attitudes to Ireland comes in *Jack Hinton* where Lever placed a young Englishman in Ireland as an A.D.C. This was a device originally developed by Maria Edgeworth, from whose novels—and whose advice—Lever learned so much. Jack Hinton is shown the wretchedness of Ireland, and told that it is caused by English misrule. The English, argues Father Tom Loftus, do not know, or will not know the Irish: 'More prone to punish than prevent, you are satisfied with the working of the law and not shocked by the accumulation of crime; and, when broken by poverty and paralysed by famine, a gloomy desolation spreads over the land, you meet in terms of congratulations to talk over tranquillized Ireland'. The priest argues that English laws and institutions are inadequate and unsuitable for Irish conditions, and maintains that the Irish see them as sources of their misery and instruments of tyranny. The picture is Swiftian in its analysis, because it argues that the Irish do not help themselves. Dublin is shown as it was after the Union, with a nostalgic look at the glories of the late eighteenth century 'when the names of Burke, Sheridan, Grattan and Curran start up'. The heroine's father, Sir Simon Bellew, deals with

> the brightest period in Ireland's history—when wealth and genius were rife in the land, and when the joyous traits of Irish character were elicited in all their force by prosperity and happiness. It was then shone forth in all their brilliancy the great spirits whose flashing wit and glittering fancy have cast a sunlight over their native country, that even now in the twilight of the past, continues to illuminate it. Alas! they have had no heritors to their fame—they have left no successors behind them.

The Viceregal court is degenerate—when drunk, the Viceroy knights O'Grady's servant Corny Delany (an event based on a real incident). The social life of Dublin is being invaded by *nouveaux riches*. But there is a larger aim behind the novel which Lever later described. Provoked by characteristically disparaging remarks on Ireland and Irishmen in the London press, he decided not only to show an Englishman misjudging Irish people but also to demonstrate that the Irish squire, priest and peasant were unlike anything in the larger island, that the Dublin professional men, officials and shopkeepers had traits and distinctions entirely their own. He saw Irish habits of quizzical speech playing on the credulity of visitors; he stressed the virtues of Irishwomen who were not overcome by 'the fatigues of fashionable life' and retained an enjoyment of society. Lever, his youth affected by the loss of the capital's former vitality caused by the effects of the Union, had come to see that Dublin had not necessarily lost so much. His hero speaks of 'the supercilious cant and unimpassioned coldness of London manners'.

Jack Hinton is, relatively speaking, an early novel, begun in Brussels. What of those which Lever wrote while in Dublin, while editing the *Dublin University Magazine?* If we read *Tom Burke of Ours* we find this so-called garrison writer taking as his hero a 14 year old orphan who is caught up with loathing for British rule in Ireland, witnesses the savagery of the yeomanry after 1798, and escapes from trial in Dublin to arrive in France, join the Polytechnique and become an officer in Napoleon's army. Disgusted by the arrogance of the French in victory and the suspicion attaching to him, he resigns his commission and returns to Ireland. Here he is again

arrested, and is lucky to be acquitted. His trial reveals the duplicity and the degradation of informers and *agents provocateurs*. He returns to France to fight for Napoleon and the romantic ends, of what is largely a military-historical novel, are tied up. This is an anti-Castle, anti-British novel. Although the hero is befriended at several points in the story by an eccentric English officer the latter is shown as someone who utterly misunderstands the Irish as a race.

In 1845 Lever also published *St Patrick's Eve,* which deals with the cholera epidemic of 1832, as it affected the population around Lough Corrib. Here we find Lever describing the poverty, 'the same dull routine of toil and privation', of small farmers and peasants, punctuated by faction fights. He illustrates the relations between landlords, their agents and the tenantry. There is both sympathy for those in adversity and a stern warning that prosperity has its duties.

In the 1872 Introduction to *The O'Donoghue* Lever doubted whether it had been right to extinguish the old feudalism which bound peasant to landlord before preparing for the new relationship of gain and loss currently coming into being. And he wrote a superb account (in the same preface) of this feudal aristocracy, wondering whether they could change:

> Between the great families—the old houses of the land and the present race of proprietors—there lay a couple of generations of men, who with all the traditions and many of the pretentions of truth and fortune, had really become in ideas, modes of life, and habits, very little above the peasantry around them. They inhabited, it is true, 'the great house', and they were in name the owners of the soil, but crippled by debt and overbourne by mortgages, they subsisted in a shifty conflict with their creditors, rack-renting their miserable tenants to maintain it. Survivors of everything but pride of family, they stood there like the stumps, blackened and charred, the last remnants of a burnt forest, their proportions attesting the noble growth that had preceded them. What would the descendants of these men prove when, destitute of fortune and helpless, they were thrown upon a world that actually regarded them as blameable for the unhappy condition of Ireland?

Here Lever attacks 'duty work', and the exaction of 'gifts' by unscrupulous agents which led to 'the great man' being felt to be an oppressor.

This novel repeats Lever's increasing contempt for 'Castle society' and for the administration. In *The Knight of Gwynne* he showed how the Union and the destruction of the Irish parliament in Dublin, once decided upon in England, had been pushed through by 'gross corruption' and 'trafficking for title and place'. Here Lever picked out as a reason for the fall of the Ascendancy, a 'fatal taste for prodigality'. The gentry were 'reckless, wasteful, extravagant'; they lived beyond their means; they were without foresight or prudence—which they would have regarded as meanness—while believing they were sustaining the honour of the country, they were sapping the foundations of its prosperity. The English in England, however, were also to blame. For instance, they simply had not faced the reasons for the disastrous famine of the mid-century. In *The Dodd Family Abroad* one of Lever's characters attacks the English view that the peasantry's laziness had caused the famine:

Ask him, did he ever try to cut turf with two meals of wet potatoes *per diem* . . .

. . . The whole ingenuity of mankind would seem devoted to ascertaining how much a bullock can eat, and how little will feed a labourer. Stuff one and starve the other, and you may be the President of an Agricultural Society and Chairman of your Union [workhouse].

Lever continued his analysis of the Ascendancy's situation in **The Martins of Cro' Martin,** where he again dealt with the cholera epidemic of 1832, giving affectionate praise to the 'poor famished and forgotten people' of Clare. In this novel he pictured the old relationship between landlords and tenants collapsing and estrangement between the two classes deepening. Despite mistakes, however, he thought more generosity and forbearance was emerging on both sides. Later he saw the post-famine period as one of transition, and in his preface to the 1872 edition he wrote that

There was not at that time the armed resistance to rents, nor the threatening letter system to which we are afterwards to become accustomed, still less was there the thought that the Legislature would interfere to legalize the demands by which the tenant was able to coerce his landlord; and for a brief interval there did seem a possibility of rewriting once again by the ties of benefit and gratitude, the two 'classes whose real welfare depends on concern and harmony'.

In **Barrington** Lever further explored the Ascendancy in decline. Barrington, a former pre-Union Dublin parliamentarian, and his sister, a belle in Castle Society, try to manage an Inn in the country, she apparently accepting her role as hostess of a little wayside inn, he romantically pretending that the clients are guests, and pouring the remnants of their money into useless law suits. The return of brother and sister to the once fashionable and now decaying Reynolds Hotel in Dominick Street in Dublin echoes Maria Edgeworth's picture of the former capital's faded glories in *The Absentee.* Lever, however, treats this Anglo-Irish nostalgia for the past with detachment.

His steadily increasing dislike of English administrators and Dublin Castle Society emerges here and there in **Sir Brook Fossbrooke,** a novel with a complex plot and increased depth in portrayal of character. He includes in this novel attacks on jobbery, police spying, the use of informers, the invention of 'treason-felony'. Lever had developed his capacity for irony; and he also continued to speculate on the differences between Irish and English characters:

Plodding unadorned ability, even of a high order, meets little favour in Ireland, while on the other side of the Channel Irish quickness is accounted as levity, and the rapid appreciation of a question without the detail of long labour and thought, is set down as the lucky hit of a lively but very idle intelligence.

He expressed direct scorn for those English officials in Ireland, from whose rudeness he had himself suffered:

Is it fancy, or am I right in supposing that English officials have a manner specially assumed for Ireland and the Irish—a thing like the fur cloak a man wears in Russia, or the snowshoes he puts on in Lapland not intended for other latitudes, but admirably adapted for the locality it is made for? . . .

A portrait of Lever in later life.

I do not say it is a bad manner—a presuming manner—a manner of depreciation towards those it is used to, or a manner indicative of indifference in him who uses it. I simply say that they who employ it keep it as especially Ireland as they keep their Mackintosh capes for wet weather, and would no more think of displaying it in England than they would go to her Majesty's levee in a shooting-jacket.

Lever's last novel—and the best of them—**Lord Kilgobbin** illustrates in sombre fashion how Ireland was misgoverned and ready to explode, in his words 'uneasy disquieted and angry'. Here are the views of Molyneux and Swift given fresh life: here is fierce indignation at the ineptitude of English politicians who vacillated between repression and submission to terrorism; here, too, is a vacuum, for the Anglo-Irish had lost their power, indeed their will to govern the country. The landlords were decadent, the Fenians inefficient, and he disliked the new citified commercial class that was emerging out of the poverty of the country people, so weakened by the effects of famine and by continuing emigration. Despite anger and despair, despite his feeling of impending catastrophe, Lever loved his country; he surveyed its politics sardonically, at times detachedly; he was Anglo-Irish in his enjoyment of scenery and complexity of character; and he had a sharp awareness of differences in Irish and English sensibilities.

How could Yeats (and a horde of lesser writers after him) have got hold of the wrong Lever? (pp. 104-10)

> *A. Norman Jeffares, "Yeats and the Wrong Lever," in* Yeats, Sligo and Ireland: Essays to Mark the 21st Yeats International Summer School, *edited by A. Norman Jeffares, Barnes & Noble Books, 1980, pp. 98-111.*

ANTHONY CRONIN (essay date 1983)

[*Cronin surveys Lever's novels, emphasizing the author's broadening interest in Ireland's political and social problems.*]

> To drink a toast,
> A proctor boast,
> Or bailiff as the case is;
> To kiss your wife,
> Or take your life
> At ten or fifteen paces;
> To keep game cocks, to hunt the fox,
> To drink in punch the Solway,
> With debts galore, but fun far more;
> Oh, that's "the man for Galway".

The lines, about a Galway landlord and Member of Parliament, Giles Eyre, come from one of Charles Lever's few successful forays into verse; and they make one thing about him immediately plain. He was not the inventor nor the celebrator of the "stage Irishman". That dubious distinction belongs to his contemporary Samuel Lover. . . . (p. 51)

Lever was the inventor, laureate and celebrator of an almost equally durable breed, "the stage Anglo-Irishman", whose pedigree carries on through the lesser work of Somerville and Ross into the "hard-drinking country gentlemen" of Yeats's rather rambunctious and sometimes less than honest last poems.

In fact when the Irish people, or, to avoid begging questions, the lower orders of the population of the island, appear in Lever they represent, as often as not, a vein of realism. His ear for the speech of those lower orders is coolly accurate; his respect for their general shrewdness not inconsiderable. Because Lever wrote, and for a long time wrote successfully, for a foreign—that is, a British—audience, his stock-in-trade was, like that of many later Irish writers, the picturesque, the outlandish and the comic. Ireland was, to him as to them, an island of "quare goings on" and laughable surprises; but although Mickey Free following after the heels of the horses provides some of them, the majority are provided by the members of Lever's own class and their hangers-on. They are in fact the Rackrents, their boon companions and their political associates broadened and, in terms of literary technique, coarsened for comic purposes; but dealt with, as perhaps everything that is seen as comic must be dealt with, generously and affectionately, so that there are really two modes of distortion, the comic and the affectionate. And when, in the later books, a genuine disgust and cruelty of portraiture becomes apparent, it is reserved for the lawyers and the middlemen who are seen to have dragged that class down.

The hall-mark of the Rackrents' world was the make-shift: the broken-down sidecar used as a gate, the pillow case that replaces the glass in the upper windows; and the element of the make-shift was strong both in Lever's life and in his literary technique. He seems to have become everything he did become by a sort of accident. He became a doctor (of sorts), a magazine editor (of sorts), and a novelist (again only of sorts) because there was nothing better at hand to become; and he wound up as a consular official in an obscure Continental seaport, the appointment having been made in very haphazard fashion by an unthinking aristocratic patron. Although he hated the place, it was there that he died.

Since his death his reputation has declined further than that of any comparable Victorian figure; but that too is partly an accident. Lever writes of a world whose cruelties and shortcomings have become all too apparent to later generations; and when we expect him to be apologetic he is, on the contrary, full of zest and glee. It comes as something of a surprise to find that he was born in Dublin as late as 1806; and that he is writing, for much of the time, about a world that had vanished before he was even born. The Peninsular War, which preoccupies him so much, was over before he was in his teens. What he knew about it he had heard from hearsay and anecdote and the same largely applies to the Ireland of all except a few later books. It is a ramshackle, corrupt, jovial Ireland. . . . He is not a realist; he is an artist in nostalgia. He is a perfect example of a writer whose class orientation is so complete as to colour his vision of nearly everything. (The Rooneys in *Jack Hinton* are, consciously, caricature *parvenus;* but in delineating them Lever is unconsciously caricaturing the aristocratic view: Mrs Rooney has the "coarse expression which high living and a voluptuous life is sure to impress upon those not born to be great".) And he is, in his own aristocratic, ascendancy way, a patriot. (pp. 51-3)

[Lever's first novel, *Harry Lorrequer,*] consists almost entirely of rambling, inconsequentially jointed stories of the kind that were bandied about in the bar library (Lever might have made a better lawyer than doctor); in Trinity common rooms; in garrison towns (he might have made a better soldier than either); in big houses and country inns. Much of it is horseplay at its most unbearable. It was a rip-roaring success; it confirmed Lever's image in the public eye; and it may well be his worst novel.

Yet even here we must not underestimate him. There are fascinating glimpses of Irish life during the eighteen hundred and teens. The parish priest of Kilrush, for example, to which assemblage of mud huts and its benighted inn Harry is exiled by his superior officer for his sins, breakfasts from a snow-white cloth on newly-taken trout and buttered toast, has all the metropolitan morning papers airing upon the hearth, offers his guest a choice of tea or coffee and adds: "There's the rum if you like your coffee *chassé.*"

Lever followed *Harry Lorrequer* with a multitude of novels all in the same vein: *Charles O'Malley, Jack Hinton* and *Tom Burke of "Ours."* etc. The public, for a while, could not have enough, Lever needed the money. The scene usually alternates between the Ireland of the first years of the century and the Spain of the Peninsular War which was largely fought by Irish regiments or regiments officered by the type of reckless, misfortunate, game-for-anything type of young Irish subaltern that Lever made his hero.

Charles O'Malley is probably the best of these. Some of the opening scenes: the hunt, the country-house dinner, the duel, the election, the review of the Phoenix Park are superbly energetic and often truly funny. But once again we are stuck in the past, in the era before the Act of Union, "the most brilliant period of my country's history" as the dedication calls it. "The rain was dashing in torrents against the windowpanes, and the wind sweeping in fitful gusts along the dreary and deserted streets, as a party of three persons sat over their wine, in that stately old pile which once formed the resort of the Irish Members, in College Green, Dublin, and went by the name of Daly's Club House" it begins; though we are soon off to the wars, lightheartedly marching to the treble of the fifes on the breeze, drinking, dicing, looting and philandering as befits our station; and if the reader can forget about the grimmer realities beyond Lever's ken or caring he can follow our hero's adventures at Fuentes D'Onoro, Almeida and the Azava happily enough. Of course our author never was a soldier. The Peninsula with its dark-eyed beauties and its opportunities for glory had been a distant place of rumoured adventure in his boyhood. Yet in certain ways nobody has ever written better, even if we say "superficially" or "heartlessly" about military life or the exigencies of campaign psychology: and right enough he did claim to have had adventures on the warring frontiers of the new world, including a spell among the Indians.

Soon after *Charles O'Malley* Lever made a characteristically haphazard attempt to edit the magazine whose fortunes he had made. Then, in debt as usual, he departed for the Continent, and most of the rest of his life was peregrination.

Not so oddly perhaps, divorced from Ireland he began to treat it more seriously; and he certainly made efforts to become a novelist rather than a grand outpourer of stored anecdote. In *The Knight of Gwynne,* published in 1847, almost half a century after the event, he is still brooding over the Act of Union; but there is a difference in his attitude now: in spite of the light-hearted tone which he attempts to maintain he sees it very plainly as a calamity and one for which he must seriously find a reason. The extraordinary thing to our eyes, though, must be the fact that in "black 'forty-seven", with the people dying in their hundreds of thousands from the famine of which most contemporaries saw the Union as the cause, it is not the people who matter to Lever, but his own class, its dishonour and its loss. The opposing title page of the original edition (by the great Phiz) shows Ireland as a maiden balancing a harp upon a mound of earth. She is trampling underfoot a scroll called "Agitation" and behind her is a city which is doubtless meant to be Dublin, but has more of a look of London about it. The river of this great port is full of shipping, so it is evidently prosperous; and indeed the surround tells us that someplace or other is GREAT in the development of her resources; GLORIOUS in the happiness of her people; FREE from poverty, misery and anarchy.

Given the year that was in it, it was all a little unfortunate; and indeed the illustrator and the publishers of this "Tale of the Time of the Union" had somewhat simplified Lever's final admission and hope, which went:

> Of the period which we have endeavoured to picture some meagre resemblance, unhappily, the few traces remaining are those most to be deplored. The Poverty, the Misery, and the Anarchy survive; the Genial Hospitality, the warm attachment to Country; the cordial generosity of Irish feeling, have sadly declined. Let us hope that from the depth of our present sufferings better days are about to dawn, and a period approaching when Ireland shall be "Great" in the happiness of her people, "Glorious" in the development of her inexhaustible resources, and "Free" by that best of freedom, free from the trammels of an unmeaning party warfare,

which has ever subjected the welfare of the country to the miserable intrigues of a few adventurers.

Even this, however, comes as a bit of a surprise in view of the fact that the happiness, and, even more so, the wishes of the people seem to have been the least of Lever's concerns throughout. There is a Dublin slum scene which makes us regret that his interests were so much narrower than Dickens's until it becomes apparent that his sympathies are so narrow that he could never have written about the Dublin poor with any worthwhile degree of creative enthusiasm: like all apologists for aristocracy he prefers the rural variety and understands it better. The "mob" makes a brief appearance in support of one of the gentlemen who will not vote for the Union and is treated by him with the contempt it deserves:

> The crowd which, growing as it went, followed him from place to place throughout the city, would break forth at intervals into some spontaneous shout of admiration, and a cheer for Bagenal Daly, commanded by some deep throat, would be answered by a deafening roar of voices. Then would Daly turn and, as the moving mass fell back, scowl upon their unwashed faces with such a look of scorn, that even they half felt the insult.

Taunted by a supporter of the government with the possession of such unwashed friends, Daly answers, "Aye and by my soul, for the turning of a straw, I'd make them your enemies"; but suppresses the impulse almost immediately:

> For a second or two Daly's face brightened, and his eyes sparkled with the fire of enterprise, and he gazed on the countless mass with a look of indecision, but suddenly folding his arms, he dropped his head and muttered, "No, no, it wouldn't do, robbery and pillage would be the whole of it," and without raising his eyes again, walked slowly homewards.

The scene makes us realise how deep the memory of Emmet's insurrection and the "mob" unleashed for a moment must have gone. Even more so it is borne in on us that Lever regards the argument about the Union and the fate of Ireland as a quarrel between gentlemen; indeed the whole burden of the story is whether or not the government can manoeuvre the Knight of Gwynne into a position which makes it impossible for him, for honour's sake, to abstain or vote against the measure. And while the Knight agonises about his honour, Lever agonises over the question of how the class he loved had been brought to yield up its country so easily:

> Each day revealed some desertion from the popular party of men who, up to that moment, had rejected all the seductions of the Crown, country gentlemen, hitherto supposed inaccessible to all the temptations of bribery, were found suddenly addressing speculative letters to their constituencies wherein they ingeniously discussed all the contingencies of a measure they had once opposed without qualification. Noblemen of high rank and fortune were seen to pay long visits at the Castle, and by a strange fatality were found to have modified their opinions exactly at the period selected by the Crown to bestow on them designations of honour or situations of trust and dignity. Lawyers in high practice at the bar, men esteemed by their profession, and held in honour by the public, were seen to abandon their position of proud independence, and accept government appointments, in many

cases inferior both in profit and rank to what they had surrendered.

> There seemed a kind of panic abroad. Men feared to walk without the protective mantle of the Crown being extended over them; the barriers of shame were broken down by the extent to which corruption had spread.

The "proud independence" of the lawyers is a particularly strange notion, but except for its historical interest, the whole thing would scarcely be worth the attention of a modern reader were it not for one brilliant and malign portrait, done with a subtlety and care which is surprising in the hitherto nearly always unsubtle and slapdash Lever. Con Heffernan is a politician without office or the desire for office, the sort of parasite on power that exists in all societies. As his name implies, he is probably of lowly enough origin; nobody seems to know. He is, "in secret, far from esteeming the high and entitled associates with whom his daily life brought him in contact" but yet "no man ever went through a longer or more searching trial unscathed, nor could an expression be quoted, or an act mentioned, in which he derogated, even for a moment from the habits of 'his order' ". In other words, Heffernan too obeys the code of honour and therefore reveals a doubt somewhere in Lever of its sufficiency. His role, in the politics of the plot, is to instruct Castlereagh in the weak points of every man who has to be bribed, or bullied or pressured into voting for the Union. His purpose, in Lever's scheme of things, is to explain the fact that the ascendancy betrayed itself. To do this he must be, pretty nearly, evil personified; but fortunately Lever's interest in the matter is so great that he is moved to create a human being of very nearly epic dimensions; and in the moral test in which they are engaged he ends by finding the player far more interesting than the gentlemen.

But not all the Con Heffernans in the world could make *The Knight of Gwynne* into a serious work of art. Lever simply did not have that sort of thing in him. What he does do is to give this first of the plot-constructed novels of Lever's maturity an unusual readability, which is more than *The Confessions of Con Cregan* or *Roland Cashel* have; though—or perhaps because—they continue the transition from the loosely jointed, rambling, picaresque works of his youth to the considerably tighter and, as they say, better constructed ones he wrote towards the end. And as he wandered over the Continent with servants and family, the whole disorderly household posting on from stage to stage in their own carriage and often being taken for a band of circus people by sober citizens, he turned his attention more and more to "the Irish question", or rather to a series of Irish questions: land tenure, repeal, Fenianism. His interest in these matters was probably motivated by little more than a search for a new sort of "Oirishness" to replace the old. He was gaming away and there was not, in truth, much demand now for elopements and duellings. The Irish question, with all its endless ramifications, had become of interest to anxious, sincere, middle-class, late-Victorian men and women; and Lever, like a host of others, undertook to explain it. Far away from Trinity and the clubs of Dublin though he was, he trots out the clichés: the natural, feudal loyalty of the peasantry, often to an eccentric with a Gaelic name; the wicked agents and middlemen who come between the landlord and those to whom he recognises a feudal obligation.

But a strange thing was happening to him; and by the time "in breaking health and broken spirits" he came to write his last book, *Lord Kilgobbin,* it was fairly evident. Writing during the passage of the first land act and the disestablishment and disendowment of the Church of Ireland, but before Gladstone's Irish policy was fully formed and Balfour's, of course, dreamed of, he is at last able to separate the interests of the landed class from the interests of England and to foresee the betrayal and abandonment by the British policy and politicians of the aristocracy over whom he had thrown, in the long ago, the mantle of his own sort of patriotism, the heroes of which are no longer the expansive duellists who had put on their top-boots and ridden up to Dublin to vote against the Union seventy years before; the object of which, astonishingly enough, is a freedom and betterment which includes the people.

Nothing is more remarkable about this remarkable novel than the sympathetic portrait of the intelligent and articulate "headcentre" of the Fenian brotherhood, Dan Donegan. Lever had always been a political novelist—he had always had the Irish passion for "pure" politics, the ins and outs of it, and how votes are won and lost—but that even he should have become so perspicacious and analytic is evidence of how political the whole of nineteenth-century Irish literature was: indeed it may not be far-fetched to see the lack of politics in the literature of the twentieth century as a reaction against the endless earlier discussions of the causes of agrarian outrage and Irish discontent. Most of it is repetitious and cliché-ridden. Lever's originality and broadness of view came to him late.

Lord Kilgobbin is undoubtedly a curious book, full of good stuff, including a new kind of satirical, anti-establishment humour—the scene in which the Viceroy recommends his aide to take up a post in Guatemala is not far short of Evelyn Waugh—but unfortunately it is not quite the novel some of its most enthusiastic admirers have claimed it to be. Lever could do nothing by halves. Having decided to write novels of causative and linked event, he entirely over-did it. There is too much plot in *Lord Kilgobbin;* too much "construction" of the most obvious novelistic sort; too much coincidence and all the rest of it. "If I have never disguised from myself", he said,

> the ground of any humble success I have attained to as a writer of fiction; if I have always had before me the fact that to movement and action, the stir of incident and a certain light-heartedness and gaiety of temperament, more easy to impart to others than to repress in oneself, I have owed much, if not all, of whatever popularity I have enjoyed;—I have yet felt that it would be in the delineation of very different emotions that I should reap what I would reckon as a real success. Time has but confirmed me in the notion, that any skill I possess lies in the detection of character and the unravelment of that tangled skein which makes up human motives.

But unfortunately it is the unravelment of that tangled skein which the novelist has deliberately tangled up with a view to unravelling it that is the basis of most of the later books. And though some of the characterisation in *Lord Kilgobbin* is, on a sketchbook level anyway, quite brilliant—the Irish adventurer, Joe Attlee, who has elements of both Tim Healy and Oscar Wilde, though neither of them had yet been heard of; the cynical English politician, Lord Danesbury, who reminds one of the philosophical Balfour and the indolent Roseberry, though they too were in the womb of time—event and character, event and motive seem often unrelated and even at cross-purposes. (Of course they sometimes are in life, as the novelists of character-motivated event cannot admit; but in **Lord Kilgobbin** it is the novelist's hand which too obviously plays the part of drift, or circumstance or social destiny or whatever).

Still, it is nice to think that he kept some of the best wine till last and produced it though he was beholden to the British government for the consular job. He ended his days in Trieste on the Adriatic, a post he had received from Lord Derby, who said, "Here is six hundred pounds a year for doing nothing and you are just the man to do it", from which remark one surmises that his lordship may not have thought the writing of novels amounted to a day's work. His last years were ironically saddened by the fact that his son had an unfortunate career in that army which he had imagined as full of scapegrace heroes, and by the boy's death. Also he disliked Trieste, though he wrote **Lord Kilgobbin,** which is high-spirited and optimistic enough, there. He is buried in the British cemetery, near to Wincklemann the archaeologist. One hopes that James Joyce, who went into voluntary exile in the same city, may have made a pilgrimage or two to his grave. They had, strange to say, quite a lot in common: an unorthodox patriotism; a good deal of contempt for the plot-making process; and, above all, of course, a sense of humour. (pp. 53-60)

> Anthony Cronin, "Charles Lever: Enter the Stage Anglo-Irishman," in his Heritage Now: Irish Literature in the English Language, *St. Martin's Press, 1983, pp. 51-60.*

ADDITIONAL BIBLIOGRAPHY

Alexander, Doris. "Eugene O'Neill and Charles Lever." *Modern Drama* V, No. 4 (February 1963): 415-20.

> Argues that Lever's novels provided O'Neill with the historical background for his drama *A Touch of the Poet* (1957).

Colum, Padraic. "*A Day's Ride.*" In his *A Half-Day's Ride; or, Estates in Corsica,* pp. 1-7. New York: Macmillan Co., 1932.

> An impressionistic interpretation of *A Day's Ride.*

Downey, Edmund. *Charles Lever: His Life in His Letters.* 2 vols. Edinburgh: William Blackwood and Sons, 1906.

> Lever's letters to various friends and associates, connected by Downey's biographical narrative. This work also reprints eight prefaces that Lever wrote in late 1871 and early 1872 for a new edition of his novels.

Fitzpatrick, W. J. *The Life of Charles Lever.* 2 vols. London: Chapman and Hall, 1879.

> The first book-length biography of Lever.

Friswell, J. Hain. "Mr. Charles Lever." In his *Modern Men of Letters Honestly Criticised,* pp. 171-80. London: Hodder and Stoughton, 1870.

> Comments on the style, subjects, and themes of Lever's novels.

Graves, C. L. "The Lighter Side of Irish Life." *The Quarterly Review* 219, No. 436 (July 1913): 26-47.

> Summarizes the general characteristics of Lever's novels.

Hale, J. R. "Charles Lever and Italy." *English Miscellany* 10 (1959): 233-47.

> Explores Lever's use of Italian settings.

Hennig, John. "Charles Lever and Rodolphe Toepffer." *The Modern Language Review* XLIII, No. 1 (January 1948): 88-92.

> A textual comparison of a chapter from *Arthur O'Leary* and Toepffer's story "Le lac de gers" (1839). Hennig suggests that Lever plagiarized from the earlier work.

Jeffares, A. Norman. "Lever's *Lord Kilgobbin.*" *Essays and Studies* 28 (1975): 47-57.

> A study of *Lord Kilgobbin* highlighting Lever's awareness of Ireland's social and political problems. Jeffares defends Lever from previous critics who dismissed his depictions of Irish life as superficial and tainted by English prejudices.

Rolfe, Franklin P. "Letters of Charles Lever to His Wife and Daughter." *Huntington Library Bulletin,* No. 10 (October 1936): 149-84.

> Discusses a collection of some 300 unpublished letters by Lever in the possession of the Huntington Library in San Marino, California.

Stevenson, Lionel. *Dr. Quicksilver: The Life of Charles Lever.* 1939. Reprint. New York: Russel and Russel, 1969, 308 p.

> An important and comprehensive biographical study intended to remedy the inadequacies of earlier biographies by W. J. Fitzpatrick and Edmund Downey [see entries above].

Sutherland, J. A. "Lever and Ainsworth: Missing the First Rank." In his *Victorian Novelists and Publishers,* pp. 152-65. Chicago: University of Chicago Press, 1976.

> An analysis of Lever's dealings with Chapman and Hall, the publisher for whom he wrote *The Knight of Gwynne.* The article suggests that this work's failure marked the downfall of his career.

Wagenknecht, Edward. "Charles Lever and the Anglicized Irish." In his *Cavalcade of the English Novel from Elizabeth to George VI,* pp. 187-92. New York: Henry Holt and Company, 1948.

> A brief survey of Lever's novels.

Weintraub, Stanley. "Bernard Shaw, Charles Lever and *Immaturity.*" *The Shaw Bulletin* II, No. 1 (January 1957): 11-15.

> Asserts that Shaw's first novel, *Immaturity* (1879), is early evidence of the influence of *A Day's Ride* on his works. Shaw himself noted his debt to Lever in the preface to his play *Major Barbara* [see excerpt dated 1906].

Charlotte (Turner) Smith

1749-1806

English novelist, poet, translator, and author of children's books.

Smith was an extremely popular late eighteenth-century writer who, although renowned as a poet in her own day, is primarily remembered for her sentimental adventure novels. Her first three novels, *Emmeline, the Orphan of the Castle, Ethelinde; or, The Recluse of the Lake,* and *Celestina,* while of historical interest for their place in the sentimental tradition, are also considered the first English narratives to incorporate romantic landscape description, a technique borrowed by Smith's better-known contemporary, Ann Radcliffe, for her highly influential Gothic romances. Of Smith's subsequent novels, only *Desmond* and *The Old Manor House* have received significant critical attention. *Desmond* is regarded as Smith's most outspoken expression of her liberal political beliefs, *The Old Manor House* as her greatest artistic success.

Smith's literary career evolved out of her struggle to surmount the adversity she faced following her marriage. She was born in London to wealthy, landed parents. When Smith was three, her mother died, and afterward she was raised by her father and maternal aunt. Educated at schools in Chichester and Kensington, and then at home by private tutors, Smith studied French, acting, drawing, and writing. On her own, she read voraciously and composed poetry, an activity her father strongly encouraged. Smith's misfortunes began in 1765, when she entered into an arranged marriage with the son of a wealthy West Indian merchant, Benjamin Smith, who very soon after the wedding revealed himself to be extravagant and dissolute. They had several children together, and his irresponsibility often placed the large family in financial distress. In 1776, Smith's father-in-law died, leaving a will intended to benefit Smith and her children; however, the document was so complex that lawyers could not establish a definite claim to the inheritance, which was valued at 36,000 pounds. Embittered by her inability to obtain this desperately needed money, Smith was to later openly denounce the injustice of the English legal system in the prefaces to her novels.

Smith turned to writing as a career in an attempt to support her family. In December of 1783, her husband was sent to debtors' prison. During his seven month incarceration, she collected the various poems she had written over the years into *Elegiac Sonnets, and Other Essays.* Published at her own expense in 1784, the book was a great success, going through two editions within a year. In the winter of 1785, Smith's husband fled to France to escape creditors. Smith accompanied him, and while there she translated into English Abbé Prévost's novel *Manon Lescaut,* publishing the work after her return to England the following summer. In 1787, she obtained a legal separation from her husband, resolving to provide for her children by writing. Finding translation tedious and unrewarding and her poetic inspiration too erratic to guarantee a steady income, she attempted a novel. *Emmeline* appeared in 1788 and met with both popular and critical acclaim. Smith's popularity continued throughout her career, during which she produced nine more novels and two additional volumes of poetry. Late in her career, Smith turned to writing

books for children, primarily didactic works designed to teach such virtues as charity, fortitude, and humility. Smith often expressed the desire to stop writing, hoping that each successive work would bring her the financial stability needed to retire, but the requirements of her large family prevented it. She died in 1806. Six months later, a settlement was finally reached on her father-in-law's will. Because none of her children claimed the inheritance, it was bestowed upon her husband's niece.

During Smith's lifetime, her poetry attracted a large audience and was commended by several prominent literary figures, including William Cowper. However, contemporary commentary focused on her novels, and it is for these that she is principally remembered. Generally placed by critics in the tradition of the sentimental novel, Smith's works reflect the influence of her predecessor in the genre, Samuel Richardson. This influence is particularly noted in her first three novels, *Emmeline, Ethelinde,* and *Celestina,* each of which relates the adventures of a virtuous young heroine in distress who is separated from her lover by a series of mishaps. Smith's poetic landscape descriptions in these works, however, also link her with the Gothic tradition: many critics credit her with introducing to the English novel the use of picturesque scenery to create an atmosphere sympathetic with the emotions of her characters. This essentially romantic technique had a significant influence on Radcliffe, who made it a standard feature of the Gothic novel.

Smith's subsequent works are more varied in plot and style than her first three novels. Her fourth novel, *Desmond,* is her first and most strident attempt to discuss political issues. As a woman writing in the eighteenth century, she realized that she strayed from convention in discussing political ideas, but in her preface to *Desmond* she defends the right of women to do so: "But women it is said have no business with politics— Why not? . . . Even in the commonest course of female education, they are expected to acquire some knowledge of history; and yet, if they are to have no opinion of what *is* passing, it avails little that they should be informed of what *has* passed. . . ." Commentators note that the plot of this work, which revolves around the French Revolution of 1789, is secondary to the expression of Smith's political sympathies for the revolutionaries. Critics have speculated that because Smith lost favor with some of her readers for her liberal opinions, she tempered her outspokenness on political issues in succeeding works. For example, her next novel, *The Old Manor House,* contains very little political discussion, although it does criticize the English government's handling of the American Revolution, and her last novel, *The Young Philosopher,* concerns itself only with the intellectual theories behind revolution. *The Old Manor House,* generally judged Smith's best work, tells of the growing love between Orlando and Monimia, whose attempts to unite are continually foiled by Orlando's domineering cousin, Mrs. Rayland. *The Old Manor House* is praised for showing a greater attention to plot construction, particularly in the first half of the work, than Smith's other novels. In addition, critics have concurred with Sir Walter Scott in labeling the portrait of Mrs. Rayland, whom Smith uses to satirize social snobbism, as "without a rival" in the literature of the period.

Early reviews of Smith's novels were generally positive, with critics praising her fluent prose, vivid landscape descriptions, and well-drawn characters who spoke in appropriate dialects. Though some commentators faulted her works for failing to teach an adequate moral, many found them superior to other contemporary novels in this respect. Some reviewers took an autobiographical approach to Smith's fiction, pointing out that the afflictions suffered by her heroines often resulted from marriages to profligate husbands or from the actions of dishonest lawyers. In addition, critics cited the influence of Smith's personal difficulties on the melancholy tone of her works. Commentators also attributed Smith's implausible plots—she frequently concluded overwhelmingly depressing stories with happy endings—to her personal circumstances, many noting that she did not have time to thoroughly revise because she was forced by monetary concerns to meet a constant succession of publisher's deadlines.

Since the early twentieth century, critics have often viewed Smith's works from a historical perspective, examining them in relation to both the sentimental and Gothic traditions. While some recent commentators have also traced the influence of her works on such nineteenth-century novelists as Jane Austen and Charlotte Brontë, others have focused on the eighteenth-century conventions that inhibited and restricted Smith and other female novelists of the period. Today, however, Smith's works are of interest primarily to scholars, who continue to note the impact of their romantic landscape descriptions on the development of the English novel.

(See also *Dictionary of Literary Biography,* Vol. 39: *British Novelists, 1660-1800.*)

PRINCIPAL WORKS

Elegiac Sonnets, and Other Essays (poetry) 1784
Manon Lescaut [translator; from *Manon Lescaut* by Abbé Prévost] (novel) 1785
Emmeline, the Orphan of the Castle (novel) 1788
Ethelinde; or, The Recluse of the Lake (novel) 1789
Celestina (novel) 1791
Desmond (novel) 1792
The Emigrants (poetry) 1793
The Old Manor House (novel) 1793
The Banished Man (novel) 1794
The Wanderings of Warwick (novel) 1794
Montalbert (novel) 1795
Marchmont (novel) 1796
The Young Philosopher (novel) 1798
Conversations Introducing Poetry, Chiefly on Subjects of Natural History, for the Use of Children and Young Persons (fictional dialogues and poetry) 1804
Beachy Head, with Other Poems (poetry) 1807

THE GENTLEMAN'S MAGAZINE AND HISTORICAL CHRONICLE (essay date 1786)

[*This anonymous critic briefly reviews* Elegiac Sonnets, and Other Essays.]

A very trifling compliment is paid to Mrs. Smith, when it is observed how much her Sonnets exceed those of *Shakespeare* and *Milton.* She has undoubtedly conferred honour on a species of poetry which most of her predecessors in this country have disgraced.—The pieces, however, which are the genuine offspring of her own fancy, are by far the most interesting in her whole collection [***Elegiac Sonnets, and Other Essays***]. The wretched suicide *Werter* is too much flattered by her notice; and the strains of *Petrarch* are more talked of than imitated, even in the country that produced them. (p. 334)

> A review of "Sonnets," in The Gentleman's Magazine and Historical Chronicle, *Vol. LVI, No. 4, April, 1786, pp. 333-34.*

[MARY WOLLSTONECRAFT] (essay date 1788)

[*Wollstonecraft, an eighteenth-century English author, is best known for her* A Vindication of the Rights of Woman *(1792), now considered the first great feminist document. In this excerpt from a review of* Emmeline, *Wollstonecraft censures the work for providing a poor model for young readers to follow.*]

Few of the numerous productions termed novels, claim any attention; and while we distinguish [***Emmeline, the Orphan of the Castle***], we cannot help lamenting that it has the same tendency as the generality, whose preposterous sentiments our young females imbibe with such avidity. Vanity thus fostered, takes deep root in the forming mind, and affectation banishes natural graces, or at least obscures them. We do not mean to confound affectation and vice, or allude to those pernicious writings that obviously vitiate the heart, while they lead the understanding astray. But we must observe, that the false expectations these wild scenes excite, tend to debauch the mind, and throw an insipid kind of uniformity over the moderate and rational prospects of life, consequently *adventures* are sought for and created, when duties are neglected, and content despised.

We will venture to ask any young girl if Lady Adelina's theatrical contrition did not catch her attention, while Mrs. Stafford's rational resignation escaped her notice? Lady Adelina is indeed a character as absurd as dangerous. Despair is not repentance, nor is contrition of any use when it does not serve to strengthen resolutions of amendment. The being who indulges useless sorrow, instead of fulfilling the duties of life, may claim our pity, but should never excite admiration; for in such characters there is no true greatness of soul, or just sentiments of religion; indeed this kind of sorrow is rather the offspring of romantic notions and false refinement, than of sensibility and a nice sense of duty. Mrs. Stafford, when disappointed in her husband, turned to her children. We mention this character because it deserves praise.

We have not observed many touches of nature in the delineation of the passions, except the emotions which the descriptions of romantic views gave rise to; in them the poetical talents of the author appear, as well as in some sonnets interspersed in the work. Indeed some of the descriptions are so interesting and beautiful that we would give a specimen, if they could be separated from the woven web without injuring them. . . . (p. 333)

> [*Mary Wollstonecraft*], *in a review of "Emmeline, the Orphan of the Castle," in* The Analytical Review, *Vol. LXXVIII, July, 1788, pp. 327-33.*

THE MONTHLY REVIEW, LONDON   (essay date 1788)

[*This reviewer acclaims* Emmeline, *considering it superior to most contemporary novels.*]

Novel-writing having for its object a delineation of the manners and characters of men, is, necessarily, a difficult task; yet it is a province in which the tyro in literature is ever eager to try his skill. He views, perhaps, the production of some distinguished genius with astonishment and delight: then hastily and rapturously exclaiming with Corregio, *Ed io anche son pittore!* he presently commences a writer of novels. But, alas! he has mistaken inclination for ability; he has forgotten the precept of an eminent poet—totally forgotten that he is to

> Admire superior sense, and doubt his own.

Hence the many trifling, the many wretched productions in the line in question, which have recently come before us: for though—to continue the allusion we set out with—a painter may have produced the foam he found it difficult to represent, by throwing his pencil in anger at the picture he was about to finish; yet it is not by accident, it is not by a casual dash of the *pen,* that a literary work is to be perfected, and fitted for the eye of the world. It must be the result of attention, of a long and laborious study.

Thus much premised, our sentiments thus made known, the censure we have so frequently passed on the modern novelist

will scarcely be considered as *severe.* But we have here a task very different to that in which we have been lately engaged.

Mrs. Smith, the ingenious, and (knowing her only by her writings) we will venture to add the *amiable* authoress of [*Emmeline*]—since almost every page of it breathes the purest and most benevolent affections—has long since distinguished herself in the poetical character. Having wandered for some time in woods and wilds with the tuneful Maids, she now steps forth with courage into the haunts and resorts of men. Possessing a nice and accurate judgment, her drawing is elegant and correct. All is graceful and pleasing to the sight: all, in short, is simple, femininely beautiful and chaste. Let it not be urged, in objection to this, that grandeur and sublimity are the surer indications of genius; and that in the walks of nature, the greatest objects are the most deserving of our particular regard. To many, indeed, the wild but magnificent scenery of Salvator Rosa is much less pleasing than the calm, the regular compositions of Claude Lorraine. But a difference in taste will distinguish the connoisseur, as well as the professional artist.

To follow the agreeable Biographer of Emmeline through the course of her work, or to attend to the order and disposition of its several parts, as the incidents are various and many, would employ by far too great a portion of our time. We must therefore content ourselves with observing, in general terms,—that the whole is conducted with a considerable degree of art; that the characters are natural, and well discriminated: that the fable is uncommonly interesting; and that the moral is forcible and just. (pp. 241-43)

> *A review of "Emmeline, the Orphan of the Castle," in* The Monthly Review, *London, Vol. LXXIX, September, 1788, pp. 241-44.*

ANNA SEWARD   (letter date 1788)

[*In this excerpt from a letter written to a Reverend Berwick, Seward, a popular poet known as "The Swan of Lichfield," faults Smith's sonnets as imitative.*]

Popular as have been [Mrs Smith's] sonnets, they always appeared to me as a mere flow of melancholy and harmonious numbers, full of notorious plagiarisms, barren of original ideas and poetical imagery. You observe, that, till Mrs Smith's sonnets appeared, you had considered the sonnet as a light and trivial composition. Boileau says that "Apollo, tired with votaries who assumed the name of poet, on the slight pretence of tagging flimsy rhymes, invented the strict, the rigorous sonnet as a test of skill;"—but it was the legitimate sonnet which Boileau meant, not that facile form of verse which Mrs Smith has taken, three elegiac stanzas closing with a couplet. Petrarch's, and Milton's, and Warton's sonnets are legitimate. (pp. 162-63)

Of Mrs Smith's sonnets, I must observe, that I have only seen the first edition [*Elegiac Sonnets, and Other Essays*]; in the preface to which she says, "If, in these sonnets, there are any lines taken from other poets, I am unconscious of the theft." The first of these sonnets concludes:

> Ah! then how dear the muses' favours cost,
> If those paint sorrow best who feel it most.

Pope's concluding line in his Eloisa to Abelard, is:

He best shall paint them who shall feel them most.

There is a pretty image in Mrs Smith's second sonnet, but it is taken from Collins:

> Till spring again shall call forth every bell,
> And dress, with humid hands, her wreaths
> agains.—*Mrs S.*

> Till spring, with dewy fingers cold,
> Returns to deck their hallow'd mould.—*Collins.*

That second sonnet concludes thus:

> Ah! why has happines no second spring?

This conclusion is a very inferior imitation of Beattie's "Hermit's Complaint," of which the ensuing lines form the last verse:

> Nor yet for the ravage of winter I mourn,
> Kind nature the embryo blossoms will save:
> But when shall spring visit the mouldering urn;
> O! when will she dawn on the night of the grave.

Mrs Smith asking the question of *happiness,* which Beattie asks of *the spring,* proves the mischiefs of injudicious imitation. (pp. 163-64)

> *Anna Seward, in a letter to Rev. Berwick on October 6, 1788, in her* Letters of Anna Seward: Written Between the Years 1784 and 1807, *Vol. II, Archibald Constable and Company, 1811, pp. 161-66.*

[WILLIAM ENFIELD]   (essay date 1791)

[Apart from noting what he calls a few "trivial defects," Enfield highly praises Smith's Celestina.*]*

The modern Novel, well executed, possessing the essential characters of poetry, perhaps even more perfectly than the ancient Romance, certainly deserves a place among the works of genius:—nor ought the multiplicity of insignificant or contemptible pieces, which are poured forth under this title, to preclude from notice such as possess superior merit. This circumstance rather furnishes a reason for taking some pains to bring them forward out of the promiscuous crowd, in which they first appear, and to give them that distinction, to which, in every walk of literature, genius is entitled.

Such distinction we judge to be due to the author of [*Celestina*], who has already given several pleasing proofs of her ready invention and elegant taste. (p. 287)

[*Celestina*] is natural, and well conceived; and the whole business is so artfully conducted, as to give the narrative a general air of probability. Some few circumstances are, perhaps, liable to objection. Particularly, it may be thought,—at least by those who have never heard, or who have forgotten, that it is one of the characters of love "to hope, though hope itself were lost,"—that Montague Thorold's inflexible perseverance is improbable;—that the sudden transfer, which he makes of his affections, from Celestina, after her marriage, to her cousin Anzoletta, on account of her likeness to Celestina, is incredible;—and that there is no foundation for supposing such a likeness, as Celestina's father (to whom her resemblance was so great as to strike his sister Lady H. Howard, at their casual interview,) was not related either to the father or mother of Anzoletta: but, notwithstanding these and a few other trivial defects, the incidents of this novel are happily

imagined, and judiciously disposed. The characters, particularly those of Willoughby and Celestina, Vavasour, Montague Thorold, Lady Castlenorth, and Mrs. Molyneux, are distinctly marked and well supported: the sentiments are such as could only have been dictated by true sensibility: the descriptions of natural scenes are elegant and picturesque; and the language is natural, easy, and, as the subject requires, familiar, ornamented, or pathetic. (p. 289)

> [*William Enfield*], *in a review of "Celestina," in* The Monthly Review, *London, Vol. VI, September, 1791, pp. 286-91.*

CHARLOTTE SMITH   (essay date 1792)

[In this excerpt from her preface to Desmond, *Smith defends the novel from anticipated censure of its plot and, especially, its political themes.]*

In sending into the world a work so unlike those of my former writing, which have been honored by its approbation, I feel some degree of that apprehension which an Author is sensible of on a first publication.

This arises partly from my doubts of succeeding so well in letters as in narrative; and partly from a supposition, that there are Readers, to whom the fictitious occurrences, and others to whom the political remarks in these volumes may be displeasing.

To the first I beg leave to suggest, that in representing a young man, nourishing an ardent but concealed passion for a married woman; I certainly do not mean to encourage or justify such attachments; but no delineation of character appears to me more interesting, than that of a man capable of such a passion so generous and disinterested as to seek only the good of its object; nor any story more moral, than one that represents the existence of an affection so regulated.

As to the political passages dispersed through the work, they are for the most part, drawn from conversations to which I have been a witness, in England, and France, during the last twelve months. In carrying on my story in those countries, and at a period when their political situation (but particularly that of the latter) is the general topic of discourse in both; I have given to my imaginary characters the arguments I have heard on both sides; and if those in favor of one party have evidently the advantage, it is not owing to my partial representation, but to the predominant power of truth and reason, which can neither be altered nor concealed.

But women it is said have no business with politics—Why not?—Have they no interest in the scenes that are acting around them, in which they have fathers, brothers, husbands, sons, or friends engaged?—Even in the commonest course of female education, they are expected to acquire some knowledge of history; and yet, if they are to have no opinion of what *is* passing, it avails little that they should be informed of what *has passed,* in a world where they are subject to such mental degradation; where they are censured as affecting masculine knowledge if they happen to have any understanding; or despised as insignificant triflers if they have none.

Knowledge, which qualifies women to speak or to write on any other than the most common and trivial subjects, is supposed to be of so difficult attainment, that it cannot be acquired but by the sacrifice of domestic virtues, or the neglect of domestic virtues, or the neglect of domestic duties.—*I* however may safely say, that it was in the *observance,* not in the *breach* of duty, *I* became an Author; and it has happened, that the circumstances which have compelled me to write, have introduced me to those scenes of life, and those varieties of character which I should otherwise never have seen: Tho' alas! it is from thence, that I am too well enabled to describe from *immediate* observation,

> The proud man's contumely, th'oppressors wrong;
> The laws delay, the insolence of office.

But, while in consequence of the affairs of my family, being most unhappily in the power of men who *seem to exercise all these with impunity,* I am become an *Author by profession,* and feel every year more acutely, *"that hope delayed maketh the heart sick."* (pp. i-v)

For that asperity of remark, which will arise on the part of those whose political tenets I may offend, I am prepared; those who object to the matter, will probably arraign the manner, and exclaim against the impropriety of making a book of entertainment the vehicle of political discussion. I am however conscious that in making these slight sketches, of manners and opinions, as they fluctuated around me; I have not sacrificed truth to any party—Nothing appears to me more respectable than national pride; nothing so absurd as national prejudice—And in the faithful representation of the manners of other countries, surely Englishmen may find abundant reason to indulge the one, while they conquer the other. To those however who still cherish the idea of our having a *natural* enemy in the French nation; and that they are still more *naturally* our foes, because they have dared to be freemen, I can only say, that against the phalanx of prejudice kept in constant pay, and under strict discipline by interest, the slight skirmishing of a novel writer can have no effect: we see it remains hitherto unbroken against the powerful efforts of learning and genius—though united in that cause which *must* finally triumph—the cause of truth, reason, and humanity. (pp. viii-ix)

> *Charlotte Smith, in a preface to her* Desmond: A Novel, *Vol. I, G. G. J. and J. Robinson, 1792, pp. i-ix.*

THE CRITICAL REVIEW, LONDON   (essay date 1792)

[*This reviewer disagrees with Smith's sympathetic view of the French Revolution but considers* Desmond *entertaining and well written.*]

Mrs. Smith has exhausted various plans in the department of novel-writing, and has now attempted a new one [in *Desmond*]. The tale is simple. . . . (p. 99)

While the attention, though constantly directed to the principal personages, is not rivetted by various changes of fortune, or harrassed by a tale artfully perplexed; and a suspense, where the event is carefully concealed, the mind is kept in a pleasing agitation by numerous episodes, introduced with skill, and characters well developed, or artfully contrasted. That of Waverly is correctly drawn, and consistently supported: a young man, whose mind is incapable of one fixed serious resolution, whose opinions are changed by every person's persuasion, whose conduct is the sport of every contingence. Bethel, the friend of Desmond, is not introduced only to correspond with. The serious thoughtfulness of his mind, the effect of disappointment, is seldom tinctured by improper

gloom, or shaken by petulant resentments. Montfleuri is the lively, elegant, Frenchman, as Frenchmen were. Desmond himself is eager and impetuous only in the service of his Geraldine; in other respects calm, attentive, and benevolent. Geraldine is 'patience on a monument.' She feels the whole of Verney's insults and misconduct, but forgets not, in any instance, that she is a wife and a mother. The subordinate characters we need not particularly mention, though they add to the entertainment of the reader, and do not suffer his attention to fail. The conduct of the story is sometimes exceptionable: in the second volume it seems to proceed slowly and heavily. The connection of Desmond with madame Bossbelle is unnecessarily introduced; for the only purpose it answers, viz. to increase the perplexity previous to the catastrophe, is scarcely perceived among the more affecting circumstances of the other events. Besides: we may be romantic; but we felt our esteem for Desmond in some degree lessened by it.

The principal novelty in the conduct of this tale is the introduction of French politics, and a more happy description of French manners than we usually meet with in similar publications. Our author's residence in France has furnished her with these additions, which will be differently judged of according to the taste, more properly, according to the political opinions of the readers. The more varied descriptions will, in every view, be found to add to the merit of the work; and the concluding scenes, when Geraldine is in pursuit of Verney, are conducted with so much skill, and worked up with so much terror and pathos, as to fix the rank of this last work of Mrs. Smith in the very first class. Indeed, in all her novels, the descriptions of scenery and situation are peculiarly excellent. Her politics we cannot always approve of. Connected with the reformers, and the revolutionists, she has borrowed her colouring from them, and represented their conduct in the most favourable light. If an aristocrate is introduced, he is either to be confuted or ridiculed. We know not if this be a fault: Mrs. Smith has spoken as she thought, and represented the conduct and sentiments of the democrats as they appeared to her. History may confirm her sentiments, and confute ours. The principal subject of enquiry is how far they ought to be introduced into a work of this kind. We have often had occasion to observe, that the opportunities of modern fine ladies for information are so few, that every means of their obtaining it, incidentally, should be approved of. On the other hand, it may be asked, ought not the state of the question, in such situations, to be given more impartially, or at least the arguments on each side fairly stated? It may be replied that Mrs. Smith is certainly too eager, even though it be in pursuit of truth; nor does she always, when the argument on the other side appears to be just, enforce it with her usual energy. To this, indeed, it may be fairly answered, that the last objection has only considerable weight, when the question is previously begged, and truth supposed to be only on one side. (pp. 99-100)

> *A review of "Desmond: A Novel," in* The Critical Review, *London, n.s. Vol. VI, September, 1792, pp. 99-105.*

THE CRITICAL REVIEW, LONDON   (essay date 1793)

[*While acknowledging Smith's eloquent prose style and arresting descriptions, this reviewer faults the moral, characters, plot, and length of* The Old Manor House.]

[He] who aspires to pre-eminence as a novelist, or looks forward with fond expectations to future applause, must possess very superior qualifications, both mental and acquired, before he can obtain that celebrity which can secure him a temporary fame, or recommend him to the attention of posterity. To conduct a series of familiar events so as to route and preserve attention, without a violation of nature and probability; to draw and support the different characters necessary for an animated and varied drama in just and glowing colours; to hold up the mirror of truth in the moment of youthful intemperance, and to interweave amidst the web of fable, pictures to instruct, and morals to reform, requires such strength of genius; such stores of wit, humour, and original fancy; such nice discrimination of character, and such intimate and universal knowledge of the world, as very seldom fall to the lot of humanity in the same individual. (p. 45)

We shall now take a general view of the merits of Mrs. Smith's last production [the *Old Manor House*], compared with the requisites which we have already specified, and which we conceive indispensible in the formation of a good novel.

After a perusal of these four volumes we are forced to confess, that though we have found much to commend, we have also found much to disapprove. From the name of Mrs. Charlotte Smith we certainly were led to expect something above the common love cant of novels; some novelty in the delineation of character; some new and interesting description; some artful concealment of plot; some happy and ingenious development and design.—At all events, we fully persuaded ourselves we should not wander long in search of what is exemplary and amiable in the eye of virtue; and that, whatever deficiencies might appear in regard to taste or invention, the picture of moral rectitude would never be defaced, nor the colouring of honourable sentiment ever obscured. How much we were disappointed in these expectations may be collected from the . . . leading circumstances in the *Old Manor House.* (pp. 45-6)

[We] ask Mrs. Smith, or any novel writer or reader, what possible benefit can accrue to society, and to youth in particular, from a perusal of scenes so repugnant to decorum and virtue? To draw characters where the follies, the passions, and the vices of mankind are finally productive of calamity is proper painting; because, from the ill success and punishment of imprudence and criminality, an excellent moral is deduced. But is this the colouring of Mrs. Smith's pictures? No such thing. On the contrary we find, that while youthful thoughtlessness and intemperance are crowned with success, ingratitude and the most complicated villany remain unpunished. The old colonel is reconciled to Warrick, and leaves him his whole fortune.—The infamous Rokers, and their accomplice the bishop, are only obliged to refund what they had procured by fraud, and Mrs. Lennard, the grand instrument of evil to the Somerive family, and the tyrant of poor Monimia, is taken home and placed in her former station in Rayland-hall, where she is cherished and caressed by those whom she strove by the blackest arts to ruin. With regard to *character* in this novel, we find little that can be said to leave a clear and distinct image on the mind.—We sometimes think we see Philip Somerive, and his unhappy father—but the one, the authoress has kept so much in the back ground of the piece as to be seldom visible; and the other, who unquestionably is the most respectable and amiable personage in the group, she has thought it expedient to put out of the way by making him die of a broken heart. We are afraid we can say little of *plot,* for

there seems to be none but the *concealment of a will,* and still less of the *denouement,* which, in our opinion, is 'most lame and impotent.' Why did not Mrs. Lennard, when she dipped so deep in treachery, burn the real will; and what at the time of her apostacy could have been her motives for preserving that which could alone detect the infamy of the transaction?—The conclusion is wound up in such a hasty and improbable manner; and every thing is so instantaneously reversed, that it reminds us of those pantomimical entertainments where the whole scenery is changed by a stroke of harlequin's sword. We were in expectation, that, as an apology for Orlando's misplaced affection, and as an explanation of Mrs. Lennard's unaccountable harshness to Monimia, the heroine of the piece would have turned out a very different personage—but no; she still remains the obscure niece of Mrs. Lennard, and Orlando's conduct is, of course, held up as an example for all young gentlemen of family and fortune to marry any pretty servant maid they chuse.

To deny Mrs. Smith merit in other respects would be unjust. She certainly possesses in no inferior degree the power to arrest and command attention, by a happy description of circumstances and objects awful, terrific, and sublime; and discovers such fertility of imagination, as often to multiply incident on incident, even when there appears no necessity for it. The pathetic, or the tender, we do not think is Mrs. Smith's forte; but the bold, the manly, the intrepid, and the dignified sentiments of the human breast are touched with no unskilful hand. The work is likewise, on the whole, written in an easy flowing style, and except a few *prettinesses,* such as, 'books never disturbed in their long slumber'—'a tear *blistered the paper'*—'iron prudery'—'massive dignity'—'infant April,' &c. is free from that affectation and turgidity which of late have disgraced modern compositions of this kind. The letters between old Mr. Somerive and Orlando, relative to the impending duel, are elegant examples of epistolary writing. (pp. 51-3)

The whole of the story might have been comprised in *two* volumes. Were novelists a little more merciful to their readers, perhaps we Reviewers, who are obliged to read *all* they write, would be more patient.—But when we find the most ordinary and trivial occurrences in life drawn out to whole chapters, and the eternal theme of love and sentiment spun out to *thirteen hundred pages,* can it be wondered at if we sometimes yawn, and exclaim in the words of Hotspur, 'Oh! it is as tedious as a tired horse or a scolding wife?' (p. 54)

A review of "The Old Manor House," in The Critical Review, *London, n.s. Vol. VIII, May, 1793, pp. 44-54.*

[WILLIAM ENFIELD] (essay date 1793)

[*Enfield favorably views Smith's* The Old Manor House, *but does not consider it superior to her previous novels.*]

Mrs. Smith's talents for novel-writing are already well known to the public; and we have had repeated occasions to acknowledge her merit in a species of composition, which, when executed with judgment and ability, in a moral view, is useful, as well as pleasant to those who read only for amusement: it is therefore the less necessary for us to undertake an elaborate examination of [*The Old Manor House*]: but we shall not dismiss it without giving a brief outline of its plan.

The principal scene of the tale is one of those spacious ancient halls, or manor houses, which fill the warm imagination with romantic ideas, and which at once invite and favour adventure. The possessor of the mansion is an ancient maiden lady, the sole heiress of a great family. A favourite kinsman, a youth of seventeen, whose family resides in the neighbourhood, is permitted to visit the hall; and, when winter arrives, to sleep in a little tapestry room, next to the old library, in a wing of the house far remote from the division inhabited by the female part of the family. The confidential servant, or companion of the old lady, had been permitted to take into the house an orphan niece, nearly of the same age with the young hero of the tale, and the apartment allotted to her is in a turret which terminates one wing of the house. This young pair, Orlando and Monimia, who find opportunities for frequent interviews, entertain a tender and innocent attachment for each other. The principal business of the piece is to exhibit the embarrassments which attend their concealed passion during Orlando's residence at home, and the difficulties and distresses through which they afterward pass. The main plot is diversified with many collateral occurrences, which all contribute to give unity to the whole. The narrative, if not in every particular guided by probability, is however too well filled up with incident to suffer the reader's attention to flag. The characters are drawn with strength and discrimination, and speak their own appropriate language.

This novel particularly contains many very successful imitations of the ordinary language of people in different classes of the inferior ranks, which may in some instances remind the reader of that great painter of manners, Henry Fielding. Several humourous scenes in higher life are also represented. . . . (pp. 150-51)

The reader is not to infer . . . that the novel is entirely, nor chiefly, of the humourous kind. In many parts it is sentimental; sometimes, though not frequently, it becomes pathetic; and once or twice, but very sparingly, political ideas and opinions are introduced, and the author takes occasion to express that generous spirit of freedom, which is displayed more at large in her *Desmond.* In fine, though we cannot say that we think the present novel *superior* to those which Mrs. S. has formerly produced, yet it discovers, in a considerable degree, facility of invention, knowledge of life, and command of language. (p. 153)

> [*William Enfield*], *in a review of "The Old Manor House," in* The Monthly Review, *London, Vol. XI, June, 1793, pp. 150-53.*

SIR WALTER SCOTT (essay date 1834)

> [*A Scottish novelist, poet, historian, biographer, and critic of the Romantic period, Scott is best known for his historical novels, which were great popular successes. Here, Scott offers a sympathetic assessment of Smith's novels, emphasizing her personal misfortune and its effect upon her work.*]

We must . . . take the liberty somewhat to differ from the . . . [opinion that Mrs Smith's prose is] much inferior to her poetry. We allow the great beauty of the sonnets, nor are we at all moved by the pedantic objection, that their structure, in two elegiac quatrains, terminated by a couplet, differs from that of the legitimate sonnet invented by the Italians, and imitated by Milton, and other English authors, from their literature. The quality of the poetry appears to us of much more importance than the structure of the verse; and the more simple model of Mrs Smith's sonnets is equally or better fitted

for the theme, generally melancholy and sentimental, which she loves to exercise her genius upon, than would have been the complicated and involved form of the regular Italian sonnet. But, while we allow high praise to the sweet and sad effusions of Mrs Smith's muse, we cannot admit that by these alone she could ever have risen to the height of eminence which we are disposed to claim for her as authoress of her prose narratives. The elegance, the polish, the taste, and the feeling of this highly-gifted lady, may no doubt be traced in Mrs Charlotte Smith's poetry. But for her invention, that highest property of genius, her knowledge of the human bosom, her power of natural description, her wit, and her satire, the reader must seek in her prose narratives.

We remember well the impression made on the public by the appearance of *Emmeline, or the Orphan of the Castle,* a tale of love and passion, happily conceived, and told in a most interesting manner. It contained a happy mixture of humour, and of bitter satire mingled with pathos, while the characters, both of sentiment and of manners, were sketched with a firmness of pencil, and liveliness of colouring, which belong to the highest branch of fictitious narrative. One fault, we well remember, struck us, and other young readers such as we then were. There is (or at least was, for it may have passed away since we experienced such sensations) a strain of chivalrous feeling in the mind of youth, which objects to all change and shadow of turning on the part of the hero and the heroine of the novel. As the favoured youth is expected to be

> A knight of love, who never broke a vow;

so the lady, on her side, must be not only true of promise, but, under every temptation, faithful to her first affection. So much is this the case, that we have not known any instance in which the heroine is made to pass through the purgatory of a previous marriage ere the end of the work assigned her to her first well-beloved, which has not, for that reason, given sore offence to the reader. Now Emmeline (completely justified, we acknowledge, in reason, and still more in prudence) breaks off her engagement with the fiery, high-spirited, but noble and generous Delamere, to attach herself to a certain Mr Godolphin, of whose merits we are indeed told much, but in whom we do not feel half so much interested as in poor Delamere; perhaps because we are acquainted with the faults as well as virtues of the last, and pity him for the misfortunes to which the authoress condemns him in partiality for her favourite.

It may be said by some, that this is a boarding-school objection. All we can answer is, that we felt it natural at the time when we read the book. It may be said, also, that passion, and sacrifices to passion, are a dangerous theme, when addressed to youth; yet we cannot help thinking that prudence, as it is in a distinguished manner the virtue, so it is in some sense the vice of the present time; and that there is little chance of Cupid, king of gods and men, recovering any very perilous share of his influence during an age in which selfishness is so predominant. It seems at least hard that the novelists of the present day should be amongst the first to uplift the heel against the poor little blind boy, who is naturally their tutelar deity. . . . (pp. 59-61)

The *Recluse of the Lake,* though the love tale be less interesting, owing to a sort of fantastic romance attached to the hero Montgomery, is in other respects altogether fit to stand beside the *Orphan of the Castle.* The cold-hearted, yet coquettish woman of fashion, Lady Newenden, who becomes vicious out of mere *ennui,* is very well drawn, and so are the female horse-jockey and the brutal buck.

Mrs Smith's powers of satire were great, but they seldom exhibit a playful or light character. Her experience had unfortunately led her to see life in its most melancholy features, so that follies, which form the jest of the fortunate, had to her been the source of disquiet and even distress. The characters we have just enumerated, with others to be found in her works, are so drawn as to be detested rather than laughed at; and at the sporting parson and some others less darkly shaded, we smile in scorn, but without sympathy. The perplexed circumstances in which her family affairs were placed, induced Mrs Smith to judge with severity the trustees who had the management of these matters; and the introduction of one or two legal characters (men of business, as they are called) into her popular novels, left them little to congratulate themselves on having had to do with a lady whose pen wore so sharp a point. Even Mr Smith's foibles did not escape. In spite of "awful rule and right supremacy," we recognise him in the whimsical projector, who hoped to make a fortune by manuring his estate with old wigs. This satire may not have been uniformly well merited; for ladies who see sharply and feel keenly are desirous sometimes to arrive at their point, without passing through the forms which the law, rather than lawyers, throws in the way. A bitter excess of irritability will, however, be readily excused by those who [are aware of] . . . the agitating, provoking, and distressing circumstances, in which Mrs Smith was involved during the greater part of her existence. Her literary life also had its own peculiar plagues, to the character of which she has borne sufficient testimony in one of her later novels. There is an admirable correspondence between a literary lady and some gentlemen of the trade, which illustrates the uncertainty and vexation to which the life of an author is subjected.

The *chef-d'oeuvre* of Mrs Smith's works is, according to our recollection, the **Old Manor-House,** especially the first part of the story, where the scene lies about the ancient mansion and its vicinity. Old Mrs Rayland is without a rival; a Queen Elizabeth in private life, jealous of her immediate dignities and possessions, and still more jealous of the power of bequeathing them. Her letter to Mr Somerive, in which she intimates rather than expresses her desire to keep young Orlando at the Hall, while she is so careful to avoid committing herself by any direct expression of her intentions with respect to him, is a masterpiece of diplomacy, equal to what she of Tudor could have composed on a similar occasion. The love of the young people thrown together so naturally, its innocence and purity, and the sort of perils with which they are beset, cannot fail deeply to interest all those who are interested by this peculiar species of literature. The unexpected interview with Jonas the smuggler furnishes an opportunity for varying the tale with a fine scene of natural terror, drawn with a masterly hand.

In the **Old Manor-House** there are also some excellent sketches of description; but such are indeed to be found in all Mrs Smith's works; and it is remarkable that the sea-coast scenery of Dorset and Devon, with which she must have been familiar, is scarce painted with more accuracy of description, than the tower upon a rugged headland on the coast of Caithness, which she could only become acquainted with by report. So readily does the plastic power of genius weave into a wreath materials, whether collected by the artist or by other hands. It may be remarked, that Mrs Smith not only preserves in her landscapes the truth and precision of a painter, but that they sometimes evince marks of her own favourite pursuits and studies. The plants and flowers are described by their Linnaean names, as well as by their vulgar epithets; and in speaking of the denizens of air, the terms of natural history are often introduced. Something like this may be observed in Mr Crabbe's poems; but neither in these nor in Mrs Smith's novels does it strike the reader that there is pedantry in such details; an objection which certainly would occur, were such scientific ornaments to be used by a meaner hand.

The most deficient part of Mrs Smith's novels, is unquestionably the plot, or narrative, which, in general, bears the appearance of having been hastily *run up,* as the phrase goes, without much attention to probability or accuracy of combination. This was not owing to any deficiency in invention; for when Charlotte Smith had leisure, and chose to employ it to the purpose, her story, as in the **Orphan of the Castle,** is conducted with unexceptionable ingenuity. But she was too often summoned to her literary labours by the inexorable voice of necessity, which obliged her to write for the daily supply of the press, without having previously adjusted, perhaps without having even rough-hewn, the course of incidents which she intended to detail. Hence the hurry and want of connexion which may be observed in some of her stories, and hence, too, instances, in which we can see that the character of the tale has changed, while it was yet in the author's imagination, and has in the end become different from what she herself had originally proposed. This is apt to arise either from the author having forgotten the thread of the story, or her having, in the progress of the narrative, found it more difficult to disentangle it skilfully than her first concoction of the tale had induced her to hope. This desertion of the story is, no doubt, an imperfection; for few of the merits which a novel usually boasts are to be preferred to an interesting and well-arranged story. But then this merit, however great, has never been considered as indispensable to fictitious narrative. On the contrary, in many of the best specimens of that class of composition—*Gil Blas,* for example, *Peregrine Pickle, Roderick Random,* and many others of the first eminence—no effort whatever is made to attain the praise belonging to a compact system of adventures, in which the volumes which succeed the first, like the months of summer maturing the flowers and fruit which have germinated in spring, slowly conduct the tale to the maturity at which it arrives upon its conclusion, as autumn gathers in the produce of the year. On the contrary, the adventures, however delightful in themselves, are but

Like orient pearls at random strung,

and are not connected together, otherwise than as having occurred to one individual, and in the course of one man's life. In fine, whatever may be the vote of the severer critics, we are afraid that many of the labourers in this walk of literature will conclude with Bayes, by asking, "What is the use of the plot but to bring in fine things?" And, truly, if the fine things really deserve the name, we think there is pedantry in censuring the works where they occur, merely because productions of genius are not also adorned with a regularity of conception, carrying skilfully forward the conclusion of the story, which we may safely pronounce one of the rarest attainments of art.

The characters of Mrs Smith are conceived with truth and force, though we do not recollect any one which bears the stamp of actual novelty; and indeed, an effort at introducing such, unless the author is powerfully gifted with the inventive faculty, is more likely to produce monsters than models of composition. She is uniformly happy in supplying them with language fitted to their station in life; nor are there any dialogues to be found which are at once so entertaining, and approach so nearly to truth and reality. The evanescent tone of the highest fashionable society is not easily caught, nor perhaps is it desirable it should be, considering the care which is taken in these elevated regions to deprive conversation of every thing approaching to the emphasis of passion, or even of serious interest. But of every other species of dialogue, from the higher to the lower classes of her countrymen, Mrs Smith's works exhibit happy specimens; and her portraits of foreigners, owing to her long residence abroad, are not less striking than those of Britons.

There is yet another attribute of Mrs Smith's fictitious narratives, which may be a recommendation, or the contrary, as it affects readers of various temperaments, or the same reader in a different mood of mind. We allude to the general tone of melancholy which pervades her composition. . . . The conclusions of her novels, it is true, are generally fortunate, and she has spared her readers, who have probably enough arising out of their own concerns to make them anxious and unhappy, the uncomfortable feeling of having wasted their hour of leisure upon making themselves yet more sad and uncomfortable than before, by the unpleasant conclusion of a tale which they had taken up for amusement. The sky, though it uniformly lours upon us through Mrs Smith's narrations, breaks forth on the conclusion, and cheers the scene when we are about to part from it. Still, however, we long for a few sunny glimpses to enliven the landscape in the course of the story, and with these we are rarely supplied; so that the general influence of melancholy can scarce be removed by the assurance, that our favourites are at length married and prosperous. The hasty and happy catastrophe seems so inconsistent with the uniform persecutions of Fortune, through the course of the story, that we cannot help doubting whether adversity had exhausted her vial, or whether she had not farther misfortunes in store for them after the curtain was dropped by the Authoress. Those who have few sorrows of their own, as Coleridge beautifully expresses it, love the tales which call forth a sympathy for which their own feelings give little occasion; while others, exhausted by the actual distresses of life, relish better those narratives which steal them from a sense of sorrow. But every one, whether of sad or gay temperament, must regret that the tone of melancholy which pervades Mrs Smith's compositions, was derived too surely from the circumstances and feelings of the amiable Authoress. . . . Nothing saddens the heart so much as that sort of literary labour which depends on the imagination, when it is undertaken unwillingly, and from a sense of compulsion. The galley-slave may sing when he is unchained, but it would be uncommon equanimity which could induce him to do so when he is actually bound to his oar. If there is a mental drudgery which lowers the spirits and lacerates the nerves, like the toil of the slave, it is that which is exacted by literary composition when the heart is not in unison with the work upon which the head is employed. Add to the unhappy author's task, sickness, sorrow, or the pressure of unfavourable circumstances, and the labour of the bondsman becomes light in comparison. (pp. 61-9)

Sir Walter Scott, "Charlotte Smith," in his Biographical Memoirs of Eminent Novelists, and Other Distinguished Persons, Vol. II, *Robert Cadell, 1834, pp. 20-70.*

LEIGH HUNT　(essay date 1847)

[*An English poet and essayist, Hunt is remembered as a literary critic who encouraged and influenced several Romantic poets, especially John Keats and Percy Bysshe Shelley. Although his critical works were overshadowed by those of more prominent Romantic critics, including his friends Samuel Taylor Coleridge and Charles Lamb, his essays are considered both insightful and generous to the fledgling writers he supported. In the following excerpt, Hunt briefly comments on Smith's poetry and novels.*]

Some of [Charlotte Smith's] novels will last, and her sonnets with them, each perhaps aided by the other. There is nothing great in her; but she is natural and touching, and has hit, in the music of her sorrows, upon some of those chords which have been awakened equally, though not so well, in all human bosoms. (p. 139)

Mrs. Smith's love of botany, as Mr. Dyce observes, "has led her, in several of her pieces, to paint a variety of flowers with a minuteness and delicacy rarely equalled." This is very true. No young lady, fond of books and flowers, would be without Charlotte Smith's poems, if once acquainted with them. The following couplet, from the piece entitled **"Saint Monica,"** shows her tendency to this agreeable miniature painting:—

> From the *mapp'd* lichen, to the *plumed* weed;
> From *thready* mosses to the *veined* flow'r.

Mrs. Smith suffered bitterly from the failure of her husband's mercantile speculations, and the consequent troubles they both incurred from the law; which, according to her representations, were aggravated in a scandalous manner by guardians and executors. Lawyers cut a remarkable figure in her novels; and her complaints upon these her domestic grievances, overflow, in a singular, though not unpardonable or unmoving manner, in her prefaces. To one of the later editions of her poems, published when she was alive, is prefixed a portrait of her, under which, with a pretty feminine pathos, which a generous reader would be loth to call vanity, she has quoted the following lines from Shakespeare:—

> Oh, Grief has chang'd me since you saw me last;
> And heavy hours, with Time's deforming hand,
> Have written strange defeatures on my face.

(pp. 140-41)

Leigh Hunt, "Specimens of British Poetesses, No. II," in his Men, Women and Books: A Selection of Sketches, Essays, and Critical Memoirs from His Uncollected Prose Writings, Vol. II, *Smith, Elder and Co., 1847, pp. 129-143.*

THE AMERICAN REVIEW: A WHIG JOURNAL DEVOTED TO POLITICS AND LITERATURE　(essay date 1849)

[*In a survey of six of Smith's novels, this critic for an American journal praises the vividness of her characters and landscape descriptions.*]

[Smith's first novel, **Emmeline, the Orphan of the Castle,** was] published in 1788, in four volumes. The first edition, of fifteen hundred, sold immediately, and the copy before me bears date 1789, and is one of the third edition. This is emphatically a most interesting story, simple in style, attractive in the plot, and containing exquisite descriptions of scenery. Emmeline's simple charms are very fascinating,

> Her soul awakening every grace
> Is all abroad upon her face.

The account of her childhood, passed in the old castle in Wales—the marine scenery in the Isle of Wight—the fine character of Godolphin, possessed a charm new in novels. Wonderful it was, that in the midst of cares and unceasing harassments, her fancy should have been so bright—her eye so observing, her imagination so creative. She opened a rich mine, and year after year, with a surprising felicity and untiring power, she poured forth her treasures, "riches fineless." All her characters speak in language appropriate to them. We have the good old housekeeper, Mrs. Carey—the vulgar Mrs. Garnet—the interesting Mrs. Stafford, the fiery Delamere, his affectionate sister, Augusta, and the plotting Crofts. Beautifully does Sir E. Brydges enumerate the traits which characterize every heroine delineated by Charlotte Smith [see Additional Bibliography]. An elevated simplicity, an unaffected purity of heart, of ardent and sublime affections, delighting in the scenery of nature, and flying from the sophisticated and vicious commerce of the world; but capable, when necessity calls it forth, of displaying a vigorous sagacity and a lofty fortitude which appals vice and dignifies adversity. Can we doubt that the innocent and enchanting childhood of Emmeline, or the angelic affections of Celestina, were familiar to the heart of the author? (pp. 624-25)

Ethelinde, or the Recluse of the Lake, in five volumes, was published in London in 1789. It is sufficient to say that it equalled *Emmeline* in the public estimation. We have a splendid specimen of a man in Sir Edward Newenden, unhappily wedded to "a vain, unquiet, glittering, wretched thing:"—a Miss Newenden, whose time is almost entirely occupied by the stable or the kennel, and whose dress was usually such as only distinguished her from a man, by the petticoat, and who had imbibed a notion that "to possess a good horse, was the first point requisite to human happiness, and to be able to ride well, the first of human perfections." The history of Mrs. Montgomery is very interesting. The dignified deportment of Colonel Chesterville, contrasts well with the vulgarity of Mr. Ludford and his vulgar family. How many imaginary sufferings poor Miss Clarinthia Ludford endures with her sentimental loves, and her determination to marry against the wishes of her parents. Ethelinde Chesterville is the charm of the work,

> It shineth as a precious diamond set
> In my poor round of thought.
>   Barry Cornwall.

Her paternal affection—her sincerity—the goodness of her heart—her sound sense—her firmness—her delicacy—her fortitude—the absence of all selfishness, endear her to every reader, and we follow her in her career with all the interest that we would take in that of a dear friend. Her love for Montgomery, and its growth, is touchingly described. How entrancing that first beam of intelligence between one's self and the being we adore! Ere memory extends in the heart with hope, ere the eloquence of words has sought to depict our feelings, there is, in these first hours of love, some indefinite and mysterious charm, more fleeting, but more heavenly than even happiness itself. Some of the scenes of this novel are laid by Grasmere Water; the following description is po-

etical and true to nature: "It was now evening; the last rays of the sun gave a dull purple hue to the points of the fells which rose along the water and the park; while the rest, all in deep shadow, looked gloomily sublime. Just above the tallest, which was rendered yet more dark by the wood that covered its side, the evening star arose, and was reflected on the bosom of the lake, now perfectly still and unruffled. Not a breeze sighed among the hills, and nothing was heard but the low murmur of two or three distant waterfalls, and at intervals the short soft notes of the woodlark, the only bird that sings at this season in the evening." (It was the middle of August.)

Celestina, four volumes, appeared in 1791. There are a number of characters in this novel which give a full scope to the talents of its accomplished author; the sensible and considerate Mrs. Willoughby; a Lord Castlenorth, one of those unfortunate beings who have been brought up never to have a wish ungratified; Miss Fitz Hayman, proud and cold; Matilda Molyneux, vain, foolish, and vindictive; Arabella Thorold, silly and affected; the romantic Montagu Thorold, and his brother, Captain Thorold, whose whole soul is taken up with his uniform; Mrs. Elphinstone, sad and resigned; the unfortunate Emily Cathcart, good even in ruin; Lady Horatia Howard, mild and lady-like; the purse-proud merchant, Jedwin; Jessie Woodburn, sweet as her own name; the angelic Celestina, and her lover, George Willoughby, are sketched with the pencil of a master. Some descriptions of the Hebrides, "placed far amid the melancholy main," their lonely rocks, scant verdure, and terrific storms, are painted in the tone and with the force of Johnson or Boswell. . . . The picturesque wanderings of Willoughby among the Pyrenees are written with a zest that creates a longing to visit them. (pp. 625-26)

Desmond, in three volumes, appeared in 1792. In the preface to this novel Mrs. Smith observes: "In sending into the world a work so unlike those of my former writings, which have been honored by its approbation, I feel some degree of that apprehension which an author is sensible of on a first publication. This arises partly from my doubts of succeeding so well in letters as in narrative; and partly from a supposition, that there are readers to whom the fictitous occurrences, and others to whom the political remarks in these volumes may be displeasing" [see excerpt dated 1792]. . . .

It is not to be wondered at that the novel of *Desmond* gave offense to many of Mrs. Smith's aristocratic friends, for her fervid zeal gave great energy to her style, and sharpened her observation. I cannot perceive that she has set down aught in malice. The abuses under the kingly and priestly government in France are denounced in the most unsparing manner. The horrible outrages perpetrated under the game laws come in for their full share of indignant reproof and abhorrence. The character of Desmond is an exquisite one, generous, manly, tender, and sincere. Geraldine Verney is one of the very best of Mrs. Smith's female portraits, a meek, patient sufferer under the brutality of a reckless, vicious husband. A bad husband Mrs. Smith drew to the life, for her own always served her for a model. (p. 627)

Mrs. Smith had become highly interested in the French Revolution, and expressed her opinions freely, by which she gave much offense to her aristrocratic friends; but the publication of *The Old Manor House,* 1793, instantly regained her the public favor. It is one of the very best novels in any language, and on which Charlotte Smith can securely rest her fame—"a wreath that cannot fade." (p. 628)

Orlando Somerive and Monimia are the hero and heroine of the work. Orlando serves under Burgoyne in the American war as an ensign; this war meets with no favor at the hands of Mrs. Smith. Orlando returns to England after much suffering, and finds Rayland Hall deserted, his benefactors dead, and those that knew him in the days of his prosperity turn coldly from him. The plot is a most interesting one; the characters true to life. Mr. and Mrs. Somerive, the kind parents; Phil Somerive, heartless and unprincipled; Woodford, low-bred, and aping the fashions, are life-like, "and finished more through happiness than pains." (p. 629)

There appeared to be no limit to [Mrs. Smith's] mental resources, and every succeeding work displayed more ripened powers. **Montalbert** appeared shortly after the **Old Manor House.** This novel is full of incidents and romantic interest, and beautifully written, interspersed with fine descriptions of rich, luxuriant Italy and Sicily—opposed to the green and undulating hills of England. Rosalie, the pure, gentle and affectionate girl, and the proud and impetuous Montalbert greatly interest the reader. Mrs. Smith's novels are essentially moral. **Marchmont, The Wanderings of Warwick,** and the **Banished Man,** I have never read.

Charlotte Smith's history and disposition can be best gathered from her productions. I feel grateful for the amusement and instruction she has afforded me. Her works I have read at intervals during the past winter, and the dreary day and evening have been frequently cheered by her genius. (pp. 629-30)

> "Charlotte Smith," in The American Review: A Whig Journal Devoted to Politics and Literature, No. XVIII, June, 1849, pp. 619-30.

WILLIAM WORDSWORTH   (essay date 1850?)

[*Wordsworth is considered by many scholars to be the greatest and most influential English Romantic poet. In the following excerpt, he acknowledges his indebtedness to Smith for the form of his "Stanzas Suggested in a Steamboat off St. Bees' Head, off the Coast of Cumberland" (1833). Because information about when these comments were written was not found, the essay date given is the year of Wordsworth's death.*]

The form of stanza in this Poem ["Stanzas Suggested in a Steamboat off St. Bees' Head, off the Coast of Cumberland"], and something in the style of versification, are adopted from the **"St. Monica,"** a poem of much beauty upon a monastic subject, by Charlotte Smith: a lady to whom English verse is under greater obligations than are likely to be either acknowledged or remembered. She wrote little, and that little unambitiously, but with true feeling for rural Nature, at a time when Nature was not much regarded by English Poets; for in point of time her earlier writings preceded, I believe, those of Cowper and Burns. (p. 151)

> William Wordsworth, in his The Prose Works of William Wordsworth: Critical and Ethical, Vol. III, edited by Rev. Alexander B. Grosart, Edward Moxon, Son, and Co., 1876, 516 p.

JULIA KAVANAGH   (essay date 1863)

[*Examining three of Smith's novels—Emmeline, Ethelinde, and The Old Manor House—Kavanagh suggests the reason for the decline of her literary reputation.*]

Mrs. Charlotte Smith enjoyed a combination of powers which rarely fail to acquire for their owner a present reputation, and seldom secure a lasting fame. She knew how to tell a story, and make it interesting; she could sketch character with shrewdness and truth; she had feeling, and selected her affecting incidents with judgment; her eye for nature was true, and her descriptions were always fresh, vivid, and natural. But she possessed not one of these gifts in its fulness. It is not moderation, but excess that strikes the public, and even posterity. Miss Burney verged on caricature, yet she holds a far higher place than Mrs. Smith; Mrs. Radcliffe was natural in nothing, her terror, her landscapes, are utterly beyond all truth, yet she can still charm the imagination and win forgiveness for her sins. It is Mrs. Smith's fault that she has none, and yet is not perfect. Her best stories are tinged with a sort of mediocrity, which often looks like the effect of haste, and suggests that her powers were never fairly developed. It is hard to think that she who kept so clear from romantic folly and worldly coldness, who could paint pleasing and natural characters, and sketch such fresh and charming landscapes, could not have done better under more favourable circumstances. Even as it is, the place she holds in English literature is worthy of a record. She is a connecting link between opposite schools, and the most characteristic representative of the modern domestic novel. She is quite distinct in this respect from the writers of her times, and the combination, though in an inferior degree, of merits so different, is her claim to originality. She wrote much, and with unequal success. **Emmeline, Ethelinda,** and **The Old Manor House** are three of her best and most agreeable works. They are fully sufficient to shew us the bent and strength of her mind in fiction.

In **Emmeline** we have the graceful story of an orphan girl pining under the stigma of illegitimate birth and the miseries of dependance. The course of events at length restores her to her genuine rank, and her long alienated inheritance, and makes her happy with the man she loves, after many trials, brought on by the circumstances of her position, and the impetuosity of a man whose passion she pities, but never shares. Neither the story nor the characters show much vigour, the incidents are often utterly improbable, as, for instance, the manner in which the legitimacy of Emmeline's birth remains so long undiscovered. The cast of the tale, moreover, belongs to a school that never was good—the school of distressed maidens, missing fathers, children changed at nurse, &c.—a school to which even [Miss Burney's] vivacious Evelina fell a victim; but for all that, **Emmeline** has many pleasing and tender passages we could find in no other writer of the times.

In **The Old Manor House** Orlando, the hero, is the interesting character, but in **Emmeline,** as in **Ethelinda,** the heroine it is who wins and attracts. (pp. 194-96)

Mrs. Smith's heroines are . . . generally poor, and in depressed circumstances; their importance is not that of birth, wealth, or fashion—it is that of intellect and refined manners. They are ladies—young ladies, and the most perfect prototype of the lady in the modern novels of to-day. Emmeline is a gentle and sensitive girl, who likes to read by the seashore, or on the banks of quiet lakes. We feel the spirit of

Thomson, of Gray, and Cowper in the tranquil scenes where she likes to move. She is beautiful, but beauty is her least attraction. She is thoughtful, amiable, modest, and intellectual; such a girl as any wise man would wish to marry. (pp. 200-01)

[We] think that, among the infinite varieties of heroines to which feminine literature has given birth in England, Mrs. Smith's may claim to be the earliest and most successful in personations of the lady—not the elegant, well-bred, fashionable lady, but the lady of delicate feelings, accomplished mind, and good manners—the lady who will make a country gentleman's wife. Emmeline and Ethelinda are far beyond anything similar in contemporary literature, French or English. They have been imitated until their successors have grown commonplace and tame, but the charm of the original models is still such as can be felt. Strength or depth of feeling or character we must not ask from them, the time is not come yet for either quality to display itself in the heroine; but they are not mere figures of flesh and blood—they are women amiable and accomplished, somewhat sad and pensive—the daughters of a gentle and meditative race, whom the sorrows of life affect indeed, but for whom the charms of intellect are ever in store.

In *Evelina* and *Cecilia* it is the world that lies before the heroines, with its changing, lively scenes; we see it but little, and under its gloomiest colours, in all that Mrs. Charlotte Smith, herself a woman of many sorrows, wrote. But if too much bitterness tinges her account of a society which Miss Burney represented with such comfortable powers of sarcasm, she had a tenderness which the authoress of *Evelina* never reached. There is great beauty and pathos in many parts of **Emmeline;** and especially affecting is the passage in which Emmeline's uncle—not unkind at heart, not unjust by will, but rendered harsh and exacting by prosperity—takes up from her table the portrait which he supposes to be his son's, and feels his anger melt away on beholding the well-remembered features of his long-lost brother, looking at him with sad eyes, that seem to reproach him for such severity to his unprotected orphan child.

Ethelinda shows far more power than **Emmeline.** The characters are better drawn, the scenes more vivid, than in Mrs. Smith's first novel, but the tale is not so pleasing. Ethelinda is the poor cousin of Lady Newenden, and accompanies her and Sir Edward Newenden on a visit to their ancestral mansion near Grasmere. Ethelinda has, like Emmeline, a tender and pensive turn. She likes poetry, she likes, too, the lovely lake scenery. There is great freshness in the short glimpses which we get of the mountain region; no set scenes, no set descriptions are these, but clear, vivid pictures, that make the evening star rise once more above the mountain's ruddy peak, that make us feel the coolness of the rippling lake, and bring the pleasant sound of the mountain waterfalls. (pp. 203-05)

The heroine is subordinate in **The Old Manor House,** Mrs. Smith's finest imaginative effort, but it has other merits. It is her best and most interesting novel, though, like all she wrote, it is tinged with despondency and sadness. In vain does she make heroes and heroines happy in the end: the spirit of disappointment ever broods over the tale. (p. 209)

The great merit of this tale, as of all Mrs. Charlotte Smith wrote, lies in its truth. Mrs. Grace Rayland is one of the most finely drawn characters in the English fiction of the eighteenth century, and, we will venture to add, to Sir Walter Scott's praise, "old Mrs. Rayland is without a rival" [see excerpt dated 1834], that none, save Mrs. Smith, could have portrayed her. Miss Burney would have exaggerated, and Mrs. Inchbald would have satirized her. That truth, which gives Mrs. Charlotte Smith a Cowper-like fidelity of description in natural objects, also saved her from the worst of all unreal delineations—that which deals with human beings. As a general rule, her personages are all living and real; she was liable but to one mistake, and into this she was led by her own embittered temper—her heartless people are too open in their heartlessness. They have not enough of the decent hypocrisy of life and society, and lay themselves out with too much complaisance to our contempt and abhorrence. We feel that when they say or do anything selfish or ill-natured it is to waken our detestation. Akin to this mistake is that of incidents too harassing and painful. There is a grandeur in tragic sorrows, a holiness in death; but the mere anxieties of daily life are wearisome and small, and must enter sparingly into the elements of fiction. They narrow the bounds of that wonderful world, and the reality they possess is not that great reality on which the novelist can build safely—that broad truth which comes home to every heart.

In another attribute of the novelist, description, Mrs. Charlotte Smith is more at home. She was one of the first to wield that wonderful power, unknown to the humourists, and to their successor, Miss Burney. In her that power was very great. Whatever she painted, a room, a house, a landscape, became visible to the eye. And hers was not, like Mrs. Radcliffe's, an ideal and romantic nature, it was the nature we all know, with her woods, her waters, her skies, and her mute appeals to the wayward heart. (pp. 227-29)

This association between our secret feeling and the eternal, immutable nature which surrounds us, is one of the aspects of modern fiction, but it was long the attribute of poetry; and it was only towards the close of the eighteenth century that it passed into prose in the writings of Rousseau and Bernardin de Saint Pierre in France, and of Mrs. Charlotte Smith and Mrs. Radcliffe in England. Mrs. Smith, no doubt, felt the tendency of her age, and yielded to it; but her power is too genuine for its originality to be doubted—freshness, vigour, and truth still mark her efforts, and have left their stamp on all she wrote. A few faults, great faults, though her contemporaries thought them slight, have contributed to make her be too soon forgotten. First of all, Mrs. Smith was not genial: few women are; just as few women have the true comic power. The very keenness of their perceptions seem to make them reach ridicule at once, and too surely, for that good-humour without which there is no comic power, to remain and co-exist. The same subtlety makes women too sensitive; they suffer because they are too quick to detect sorrow and to feel it. That sensitiveness embittered Mrs. Smith's temper—we miss a gentle, lenient, and kindly spirit in her writings. She could not forget her sufferings and her wrongs; rebellion was rife in her, and revolt, though it may give momentary power, secures no lasting fame. Calmness is the attribute of fine minds and of great natures. They feel deeply, as they see far, but the serenity of strength, and the steadiness of conscious power, are ever with them. Miss Burney, Mrs. Inchbald, Mrs. Radcliffe especially, had their share of that high intellectual attribute. Mrs. Smith had not. Fitful, impatient, and wearied, she sought for relief in composition; and though she was too superior a woman not to write much that was excellent, not to produce entertaining books, full of genuine matter and interest, she failed in what she had talent enough to accomplish—in producing a good story. There is something like personal animosity in her delineation of her hateful characters, and this is a fault, and a great one; there is decidedly bad temper, a sin that can rarely be forgiven. Truth, her great charm, her gift and her power, is thus not without frequent alloy. She is not all true—who is?—and there is no vivid imagination, no sparkling wit, no gaiety of mind or heart, no commanding style, to atone for the inevitable coldness, not to say bitterness, which is the tone of her writings. They remain amongst the most remarkable but least read productions of the time to which she belonged, stamped with the melancholy fiat—above mediocrity, but below genius. (pp. 231-34)

> *Julia Kavanagh, " 'Emmeline'—'Ethelinda'—'The Old Manor House'," in her* English Women of Letters: Biographical Sketches, Vol. I, *Hurst and Blackett, Publishers, 1863, pp. 194-234.*

ALLENE GREGORY (essay date 1915)

[*Gregory traces the liberal political opinions expressed in* Desmond, The Old Manor House, *and* The Young Philosopher.]

[A] literary lady who has left in her novels some expression of her liberal political convictions is Mrs. Charlotte Turner Smith. (p. 213)

There are certain circumstances in her life which may have influenced her political opinions: a residence of some years in France, made necessary by her husband's financial difficulties, and the marriage of one of her daughters to a French *émigré.* Her connexion with the little circle of Radicals in London probably did not extend beyond a mere acquaintance with one or two of them.

The first and fullest expression of Charlotte Smith's Revolutionary politics was her novel **Desmond.** The preface gives interesting evidence as to the source of Mrs. Smith's Revolutionism [see excerpt dated 1792]. (p. 214)

The plot is simpler than is usual in novels in letter form. Desmond, a young man of virtue and sensibility, has a Wertherlike platonic passion for an unhappily married lady, Mrs. Geraldine Verney. He goes to France to endeavour to forget her, attracted thither by his interest in the Revolution. He visits a young French nobleman of republican sympathies, Count Montfleuri, and his uncle, of intense aristocratic prejudices, Count d'Hauteville. His observations on the actual conditions of the country, as contrasted with the lurid reports that reach England, are detailed in his letters to his friends.

Meanwhile, Mrs. Verney's husband has ruined himself at cards and gone to France, leaving her unprotected with three children to care for. Desmond, returning to England, manages to help her secretly. Her husband sends for her to meet him in France, and she dutifully obeys. She falls into the hands of one of the wild bands of royalist marauders. Desmond rescues her. She learns that her husband was among these bandits, but had been mortally wounded some time before. She and Desmond find him and care for him. He dies, leaving Desmond the guardian of his children. Desmond, of course, marries his Geraldine, and his friend Montfleuri marries her younger sister Fanny.

The letters devoted to the actual narrative would scarcely fill more than one of the three volumes. The rest is devoted to conversations and arguments about the Revolution. One feels that the author is really giving a pretty fair representation of the political conversations afloat in English society at the time. It all has a very natural sound. The young enthusiast Desmond, sure that the Revolution is really ushering in a new era, that all discouraging reports from France are merely misrepresentations by parties interested in preserving despotism; his friend Bethel, older and less sanguine, republican in his sympathies but not so sure of the successful outcome of the present struggle; and the young French nobleman, Montfleuri, with his accurate knowledge of the old régime to balance the mistakes of the new: these represent the radical side. Opposing them, there are all shades of opinion: General Wallingford, irascible, vituperative, who regards the French as the natural enemies of England; Lord Newminster, a young fop, who "wishes the King and Lords may smash them all—and be cursed to them"; a Bishop who defends order, the Establishment, and Church properties; a London merchant, who "wishes the whole race were extirpated, and we were in possession of their country, as in justice it is certain we ought to be," and a host of others. There is a narrative of a (supposedly typical) French farmer whose life is made intolerable by the game laws and special privileges of his overlord. Montfleuri gives an interesting analysis of the historical causes leading up to the Revolution, and of its philosophies. . . . (pp. 215-16)

Desmond has long discussions with various opponents of Revolutionism, in which he answers the characteristic conservative arguments. The ultra aristocratic Count d'Hauteville advances an argument which (the author says in a footnote) "has been called unanswerable." "You consider your footman on an equality with yourself,—Why then is he your footman?" Desmond answers very concisely that abolishing an aristocracy of birth does not necessarily mean introducing social or economic equality. This is a crucial point in Revolutionism. It is to be observed that Charlotte Smith's answer is the answer of early commonsense Revolutionism, not of later philosophic and religious Revolutionism. (pp. 217-18)

The general conclusions of the book are something like the following: "A revolution in the government of France was absolutely necessary; and, that it has been accomplished at less expense of blood, than any other event." English opposition to the French Revolution is due to three principal causes: (1) The ancient hatred to France, as England's natural enemy; (2) misunderstandings, party prejudice, and "the apathy of people who, at ease themselves, indolently acquiesce in evils that do not affect them"; and finally, (3) the vast numbers of people "whose interest, which is what wholly decides their opinions, is diametrically opposite to all reform, and of course, to the reception of those truths which may promote it." Desmond and his friends agree in criticizing the English government. The counts against it are three: (1) Inequality of representation and corrupt elections; (2) penal laws, with capital punishment for slight offences, and unspeakable prison conditions; (3) slow, uncertain and inefficient legal procedure, especially in the Courts of Equity and Chancery. But the immediate establishment of a republic in England is considered neither necessary nor desirable. Conditions are radically different from those in France.

Charlotte Smith's next novel, **The Old Manor House,** contains no direct references to the French Revolution, and few distinctively doctrinary passages. Nevertheless, it has a certain interest for us. The first part is a satire on pride of birth. Mrs. Rayland, an eccentric old lady of noble family and great wealth, disowns her humble cousin. She is induced, however, to allow his young son Orlando to visit her, and gradually becomes attached to the boy. The plot concerns itself chiefly with the manoeuvrings of Mrs. Rayland to keep Orlando in her power without definitely promising to make him her heir, and with Orlando's love for the housekeeper's gentle niece. Orlando obtains an ensign's commission, and is sent to the war in America. Here follow scathing satires on governmental bad policy, corrupt motives, and general mismanagement in the war with the colonies. Of course, on Orlando's return he finds that Mrs. Rayland has died and left a will in his favour after all.

The last of Mrs. Smith's novels which has any significance for us is **The Young Philosopher, Nature his Law and God his Guide**. At this stage of events Charlotte Smith's Revolutionism has lost some of its optimism and complacent belief in the efficacy of reforms. There is a new note of bitterness in her satire of existing conditions. At the same time, she is much more interested in the philosophic aspect of Revolutionism than she was at the beginning. Evidently she feels the need of an intellectual justification for her liberal principles, now that practical justification in the form of a successful republican government in France has failed.

The preface says with some bitterness that the author is well qualified to describe the "evils arising from oppression, fraud, and chicanery." . . . In closing she disclaims any personal responsibility for the sentiments of her characters and declares that her only moral is "to show the ill consequences of detraction and the sad effects of parental resentment." The year 1798 was not so propitious as the year 1792 had been for the frank avowal of radical political views.

The plot centres in the misfortunes of a young man of Rousseauistic education and principles, in a state of society where he is regarded as being, at best, harmlessly insane. He wishes to settle down as a contented farmer but finds that the abuses of the world fairly force themselves upon him in his retreat, and demand that he do his best to spread the truths which are their only remedy. From the time he is a boy at Eton he is forced into a Shelley-like rebellion against cruelty and oppression. . . . He began to read the writings of the French philosophers, "who have been supposed to have contributed to the production of the great and awful changes that were approaching." Finally, prejudice and persecution, together with his own too keen perception of the miseries under the surface of society, make England intolerable to the young philosopher; he departs for the wilds of America.

These three novels represent distinct stages in English Revolutionism. **Desmond** was written when, in spite of decided opposition in high places, the tide of popular opinion had not yet fully turned against France. Revolutionary sympathizers, of whom there were many, hoped that the worst was passed and that the progress of reform in England might suffer no check from the example of a neighbouring conflict. In 1793 the Reaction set in in full force, war was declared, and the situation looked black for Radicals of all sorts. In her novel of this year, Charlotte Smith drops the question of the French Revolution altogether, and goes back to safe Whig ground. In 1798 she ventures again upon the subject, with renewed fervour. But the emphasis is changed. She has lost faith in reform, and is now a philosophic Revolutionist. (pp. 218-22)

Allene Gregory, "Some Typical Lady Novelists of the Revolution," in her The French Revolution and

the English Novel, *G. P. Putnam's Sons, 1915, pp. 191-230.*

JAMES R. FOSTER   (essay date 1928)

[*Foster credits Smith with introducing romantic landscape description to the English novel and marks her influence on the works of Ann Radcliffe.*]

Time and the critics have dealt but scurvily with Charlotte Smith, since she has been completely forgotten, being neither as bad as the Minerva Press nor as striking as Ann Radcliffe. The relative position these two novelists held in the years before the publication of *Udolpho* has been exactly reversed, and this is perhaps an injustice since no little of Ann Radcliffe's success was due to the help and example of her rival. (p. 463)

It is to the line of sentimental novels that began with Richardson and then became more romanesque and adventure-like because of the influence of Prevost that Charlotte Smith belongs. In her early poems which she dedicated to William Hayley, disciple of Cowper, after warning us in the preface that her sonnets will find readers only "among the few, who to sensibility of heart join simplicity of taste" we find that she continually strikes the note of melancholy. The poetess is a "poor wearied pilgrim in this toiling scene" who because of her keener sensibility and superior talent must bear the pain of a festering thorn in her breast. Not even the beauty of the South Downs can "teach a breaking heart to throb no more." Three of the sonnets are supposed to be written by Werther, "passion's helpless slave" who, "scorning reason's mild and sober light pursues the path that leads but to the Grave."

Certainly some of this is pose. Later the author had a better right to such a dark view when life actually visited her with more misfortunes than befell the lot of many a heroine of fiction. She was left motherless in early girlhood and was delivered over to the care of an aunt who tried to give her a fashionable education, with the result that she read novels and wrote verse instead of following a sane educational plan. At sixteen she was married to the son of a wealthy West Indian merchant and introduced to the "dissipation of London." She separated from her husband after bearing him twelve children. Most of her married life had been a Gypsy-like wandering from place to place: Southgate, Lys Farm, a gloomy ruin of a chateau in Normandy, Woodlading and the King's Bench itself, where Mr. Smith's "affairs" brought him. (pp. 465-66)

Doubtless our author often thought of herself as a romantic heroine in what was then called an "interesting" situation, and this is seemingly corroborated by her constant recurrence to the theme of a badly married wife helped by a thoughtful *sensible* lover. We admire her pluck in attacking the pettifoggers, but pity her indiscretion in publically ridiculing her husband. While he always cut a ridiculous figure in a novel, she drew quite flattering pictures of herself as a contrast.

Yet she did not let sentimental pathos completely veil reality; a strain of the matter-of-fact shows itself now and again. This was the side of her that took pleasure in Fanny Burney's social satire. . . . (p. 467)

The Old Manor House, while not without romantic elements, is the best expression of this more matter-of-fact vein. The heroine is an orphan—a genuine orphan who neither turns out to be of noble extraction nor an heiress, the dour old Mrs. Rayland is almost worthy of Jane Austen, and there is more than a hint of real English flavor in the setting. In other novels when the official robes of the high priestess of sensibility slip away, she strikes chords quite out of harmony with the usual strain. For example, Geraldine is made to say of Lovelace: "that character does not exist now; there is no modern man of fashion who would take a hundredth part of the trouble that Richardson makes Lovelace take, to obtain Helen herself, if she were to return to earth." Or Ethelinde refuses to marry her faithful but poverty-stricken lover because such a union would only bring "poor brats into the world."

Akin to this realism is the satire modelled after that in [Burney's] *Evelina* and *Cecilia;* yet she manages to keep this element subordinate. Social satire of a kind is one of the natural developments of sensibility, since it is founded on the idea of contrast in capabilities of "feeling": callous heart and cold reason clash with the high-strung susceptibility of the aristocrats of emotion. Thus Anna Howe's lampooning of Solmes and the Harlowes may be considered a precedent for Burney's Brangtons, the immediate model for Mrs. Smith's *nouveau riche* Ludfords, the Woodfords, the Misses Crofts and the like. But the lawyers, insists our author, come from real life. Fanny Burney's novels themselves are not free from sentimentality, as is clear from characters like Macartney and Belfield, and situations like that of Cecilia's losing her way in London.

While satire allies the Smith novel with neo-classical tendencies, the exotic and poetic landscapes are romantic, and here we find our author an innovator, for while Frances Brooke (1745-1789) introduced American scenery and Rousseauian countrysides, and Walpole, Clara Reeve and Sophia Lee tenebrous castles, grottos and subterranean passages with other romantic accessories, she was the first in England to give an appreciable attention to romantic landscape description.

She was acquainted with the descriptions of Gessner, Rousseau, Marmontel, Florian and Mme. de Genlis, and like the first of these was fond of the pastoral, the exotic, the sublime; like the last she fostered a taste for the tenebrous as well. Her characters feel a strange sympathy with the chill and hollow night wind as it groans in the leafless trees, the cemeteries and the corridors of deserted chateaux, or when it whips the waves to fury and piles high lightning-illumined clouds. "Such was the gloomy temper of my soul, that I was pleased only with horrors," declares Mrs. Vyvian, who haunted the catacombs of an ancient convent. In an old chapel on the Isle of Skye "the ground sounded hollow beneath their feet, and a mournful echo ran around the damp walls. The moon, darting for a moment through the ruined stone-work of the dismantled window showed them a broken table that had once been an altar, on which some pieces of Gothic ornaments of the chapel were scattered. . . . " There is an air of terror, gloom and sublimity thrown over her old castles, tombstones of the past and symbols of feudal oppression which she preferably locates in Spain, France or Italy. She attempted the sublime and beautiful in her mountain scenery of the Alps and the Pyrenees, and landscapes of Italy, Languedoc, America and the Hebrides. In *Desmond* and *Celestina* we see the France of Rousseau; there are happy peasants dancing beneath a smiling sky and surrounded by romantic scenery. The play of color and shade on a mountain side is noted, and even the names of the exotic flora indicated. "The landscapes of

Mrs. Radcliffe are far from equal in accuracy and truth to those of her contemporary Mrs. Charlotte Smith, whose sketches are so very graphical, that an artist would find little difficulty in painting from them," wrote Walter Scott. Yet she is not always accurate, for she moved the Louisiana of *Manon Lescaut* north to the St. Lawrence [in *The Old Manor House*], but if she went slightly amiss in her exotic scenery, she made up for it in her English landscapes, which are as accurate as they are poetic.

Charlotte Smith wrote three successful novels before Ann Radcliffe fixed the public eye with her first long narrative in 1791. . . . There is a distant resemblance [in Smith's first novel, *Emmeline, the Orphan of the Castle*] to *Cecilia,* but the tone and conception is different, since the chief purpose is to follow the pathetic trials of a *sensible* heroine delivered over to the persecution of an insistent and impetuous lover, and heir to the calamities incident to an unprotected existence in an unfeeling and adventurous world. For example, the apology for Adelina, the victim of "unrestrained sensibility" and mother of an illegitimate child, . . . is certainly not in the Burney vein. *Emmeline* is notable for two things: the innovation of the romantic description of the Isle of Wight, and the fact that its method and plan is that employed in the later novels of Mrs. Smith and the most successful ones of Ann Radcliffe. [The critic adds in a footnote: Of course, the old castle, that necessary article, is found here.] (pp. 467-70)

The question put [in the second novel, *Ethelinde*], "What response should be made to the love of a virtuous and *sensible* man who had married the wrong woman" is asked here twice. Lady Newenden hates Westmoreland scenery, the ruinous condition of her husband's country seat, Grasmere Abbey,—a great cold place that struck her as damp as a family vault—and languishes for London and Bath. What more could be said to confirm us in the certainty of her depravity? We are not surprised when she absconds with the licentious lord who had formerly been so troublesome to Ethelinde. To repay Newenden's benevolence to her wild brother and her weak father, Ethelinde cares for his children. Her lover, the poor recluse of the lake, gone to India to make his fortune, is reported dead. Should Ethelinde marry Newenden who is now a widower? She works herself into a passion trying to make a decision; amid the terrible accompaniment of thunder she imagines her father's ghost visits her with a consoling message. Her lover does return, and with him a rich uncle like Warner in *Sidney Bidulph,* and the poor Newenden is forced to add the virtue of renunciation to his already lengthy list.

There is more romantic landscape than in *Emmeline.* Metastasio is quoted in the description of the lake which is quite as noteworthy as that of the sea off Dorset, the castle in the storm, and the family graveyard with its cypress, mouldering walls and wind "murmuring hollow among the ruinous buildings." The atmospheric preparation for the appearance of the ghost is exactly like that which became famous as "Radcliffian" and which really is as old as *Cleveland,* if not older, and illustrates the usual combining of states of high sentimental tension with the melodramatic terror of ghosts. Consequently the novel of terror is also a novel of sensibility as written by the female novelists of this period.

Celestina, the last of the Smith novels that need be described here, since it is the last to appear before Ann Radcliffe's first success, *The Romance of the Forest,* is still more romantic than its predecessors. One part consists of a description of the

Pyrenees, quite in the spirit of the Rocks of Meillerie, a graphic picture of the old castle of Rochemorte, and the Gothic story that explains the origin of the heroine.

The love-sick Willoughby, medicining his sick soul with the sublimities of the Pyrenees, happens on the castle of Rochemorte, late the seat of a proud, ferocious and superstitious old baron who had cast his own son into the Bastille. Willoughby meets this son, lately liberated. He is a typical hero of sensibility:

> . . . . his face, pale, sallow, and emaciated as it was, was marked with such a peculiar expression, that all the adventures of his life seemed to be written there. When he spoke, his dark eyes were full of fire and vivacity, yet at times they were wild; and at others, heavy and glazed—his brows were a little contracted, and hollowness about his temples and cheeks, and the strong muscles of his whole face, seemed to bear the harsh impressions of the hand of adversity.

This is De Bellegarde, who had run away from Rochemorte to the wars. Hearing that his sister is persecuted by a priest, a favorite of the baron, De Bellegarde returns secretly with an English friend Ormond. They manage to talk with the sister, Genevieve, who is accompanied by her friend Jacqueline. All four are mutually smitten with love, are secretly married, and to avoid the suspicious priests and populace, live in a ruined wing of the castle. A monk betrays them, and the furious baron puts his son in prison, Jacqueline in a convent, and takes Genevieve's baby from her. The evil priest now gains complete control, marries his sister to the old baron, and turns Rochemorte into a licentious palace. Finally De Bellegarde is released to fight in America, where he finds the dying Ormond. When the baron dies, De Bellegarde returns, hoping to take his wife from the convent. Celestina is Genevieve's child: she had been taken from a convent by the charitable Mrs. Willoughby.

This tale of cruelty and priestly lust with its setting in the Romance lands was exactly to the taste of the "tender-hearted" readers of the time. The other part of the story is nearly as romantic. Willoughby is prevented from marrying Celestina by the scheming Lady Castlenorth, who tells him such a union would be incest. He wanders disconsolately through France and Spain, while Celestina follows friends to the romantic Isle of Skye, where "images of horror, the wild and dreary scenes" are agreeable to her soul. A Des Grieux-like lover follows her even here, but is forced to be satisfied with Celestina's cousin when Willoughby returns, having proven Lady Castlenorth a liar.

Celestina is typical of the sentimental adventure novel of the time, and in point of influence is perhaps the most important of Mrs. Smith's tales. *The Romance of the Forest* would never have taken the form it did had not *Celestina* been written. The greater part of Mrs. Smith's work was written after this novel, but no entirely new elements were added, and often she fell below her standard of achievement. (pp. 470-73)

A certain restraint that usually stopped her short of sheer melodrama, a style in its happiest moments clear, rapid and readable, although sometimes too poetic or slightly affected, and a facility in construction raises Charlotte Smith much above the average novelist of her day. Her greatest innovation was description, since Sophia Lee, Clara Reeve and other English imitators of Prevost and D'Arnaud had already introduced French sensibility. With Mrs. Smith the pictorial, whether macabre, exotic or pastoral, became an important element in the novel. Her influence was immediate, and is most noteworthy in the work of Ann Radcliffe.

This writer could have obtained neither her romantic landscape nor the pattern of a long sentimental adventure novel from *Otranto*. Consequently it is necessary to look elsewhere, to the *Recess* of her Bath schoolmistress [Sophia Lee], and to Charlotte Smith, for her models. In these one meets the same general conception and plan, the same treatment of the supernatural, and often the same situations, themes and characters. The sensibility of the Radcliffian heroine is manifested by the intensity of her passion, by the love of nature and retirement, and by her almost pathological craving for experiencing fear. The emphasizing of the last element and the building of an elaborate technique for it, is the chief difference between Mrs. Radcliffe and her predecessors. She borrowed ideas and situations from Mrs. Smith, but the chief indebtedness is on the score of description. While Gilpin's essays gave encouragement, and Mrs. Piozzi and Swinburne were levied upon, the precedent for introducing such material in the novel was given by Mrs. Smith, whose *Celestina,* praised highly for its descriptions of Languedoc and Gascony, was published just before the *Romance of the Forest,* the first Radcliffian work to make much of landscape description and to be of the usual three-volume length.

In fact, this novel is full of reminiscences of **Emmeline, Ethelinde** and **Celestina,** and attention later given to the machinery of the pseudo-supernatural is paid here to states of "extreme susceptibility." The unrequited lover Louis La Motte is another Montague Thorold, Switzerland plays the same rôle as the Isle of Skye in **Celestina,** while the primary situation is not unlike **Emmeline.**

Furthermore, borrowings in the later novels indicate Radcliffe's habitual recourse to the narratives of her rival. Montoni's marriage with Emily's aunt is not unlike Roker's marriage of Leonard, the ghosts of Bangy castle prove to be the smugglers of the **Old Manor House,** while the recovery of Ludovico reminds one of the banditti scene in **Desmond.** Schedoni of the *Italian* is undoubtedly Lewis' *Monk,* but is also like D'Aucheterre of **Celestina,** one of the descendants of the evil priest in *Cleveland.*

My purpose in balancing Ann Radcliffe's account book is not the rehabilitation of Charlotte Smith, for her works are dead, and justly so. Rather it is an attempt to describe the sentimental adventure narrative as it was before the German *Schauerroman* made itself felt in England and converted a novel already open to satire into one richly deserving Jane Austen's ridicule. (pp. 474-75)

James R. Foster, "Charlotte Smith, Pre-Romantic Novelist," in PMLA, Vol. XLIII, No. 2, June, 1928, pp. 463-75.

ERNEST A. BAKER (essay date 1934)

[*Baker surveys Smith's novels, arguing that they incorporate elements both reminiscent of earlier domestic novels and anticipatory of later Gothic romances.*]

Mrs Charlotte Smith is not generally thought of among the exponents of Gothic romanticism, nor as one who preceded and gave useful ideas to Mrs Radcliffe. She wrote domestic fiction having a family resemblance to Richardson's, modified by what she learned from Fanny Burney. But Mrs Smith, especially after she separated from her ne'er-do-well husband and had the sole care of her dozen children, was a most industrious writer, and among her numerous novels several of the best evidently drew their romantic furnishings from Prévost, indulged in heterogeneous adventure after the same pattern, including similar mysterious and terrifying occurrences afterwards explained away, and painted sentimental landscapes in tune with the sentimental moods, in the more recent manner of Rousseau and of the *Adèle et Théodore* (1782) of Madame de Genlis. This was a great stride in the direction to be taken in a short while by Mrs Radcliffe. If Mrs Smith is not a typical Gothic novelist, or not exclusively that, she was right on the borderline.

Apart from some early poems, her first published work was a translation of *Manon Lescaut.* It was followed by a novel, **Emmeline, the orphan of the castle,** which might be summed up as of the *Cecilia* type [by Burney], with reminiscences of [Richardson's] *Clarissa.* The blameless young lady is the reputed illegitimate daughter of the dead elder brother of Lord Montreville. This arrogant and ambitious nobleman, with a more arrogant and ambitious wife, might be compared with Mr Delvile, except that he turns softhearted in extremity, and also is not an occasion for humour. As in *Cecilia,* the eldest son, Lord Delamere (Lord, when the ambitious father becomes a marquess), falls violently in love with Emmeline, who sets propriety and an almost excessive dutifulness before self-interest and a budding attachment, and steadily repulses him. The story is complicated and leisurely. Only in the fourth volume does Emmeline discover the marriage certificate in the casket proving that she is legitimate and the vast Mowbray property hers. By that time, she has a steadier and less intractable lover in Godolphin, whom she marries.

Most of the characters are aristocrats or at least very genteel. Except a few having objectionable rôles, they merit the description of "persons as respectable for their virtues as their station." One of the best is Lady Adelina, who, a very Clarissa, repulses the dissolute betrayer who is the father of her child. There is also a rejection scene boldly abridged from Sir Hargreaves Pollexfen's famous proposal to Miss Byron: Emmeline answering falteringly

> That to his person there could be no objection, he goes on:
> "To his fortune?"
> It was undoubtedly more than situated as she was she could expect.
> "To his family?"
> It was a family whose alliance must confer honour.
> "What then?" vehemently continued the Chevalier—"what then, charming Emmeline, occasions this long reserve, this barbarous coldness?"

So it continues, in a style often copied; even Maria Edgeworth did so in *Belinda.* The story is skilfully planned, and apart from the slowness, which was probably an asset to leisured readers, it is well narrated. Humour is alleged by the author, but must be taken for granted. Emmeline's propriety, though a general trait in heroines of her social class, is overpowering. She comes almost as near to breaking a blood-vessel as Mrs Delvile in the prize scene in *Cecilia,* when the nefarious Mr Crofts calls her a little prude and tries to snatch a kiss. Just such a gentle, shrinking, refined, and strong-minded figure of beautiful girlhood was to hold the centre of the picture and

rivet the sympathies of sentimental readers in all Mrs Radcliffe's novels.

But the background of harmonious landscape was as essential as the human element; Mrs Smith's successor was to accept not a single heroine failing in a proper devotion to scenery. Description is at a minimum in **Emmeline,** though there are a few seaside and woodland scenes; in the next novel, **Ethelinde, or the recluse of the lake,** she took great pains, however, with her setting at Grasmere amid the lake mountains, and in **Celestina** with the rural beauties of Provence. Here is a passage prophetic of [Radcliffe's] *The Romance of the Forest* and *The Mysteries of Udolpho:*

> Celestina, who was in that disposition of mind to which horrors are congenial, walked slowly on notwithstanding; but quitting the cliffs, on account of the gales of wind which blew from the sea, she went along a narrow pass, where there was a cairn or heap of stones loosely piled together, the work of the first wild natives of the country; and as that was as far as she thought it proper to venture from the house, though it was not more than eight o'clock, she leaned pensively against it, and watched with some surprise the fluctuations of the clouds that were wildly driven by the wind across the disk of the moon, and listened with a kind of chill awe, to the loud yet hollow echo of the wind among the hills, which sometimes sobbed with stormy violence for a moment and then suddenly sinking, was succeeded by a pause more terrible. It was in one of those moments of alarming silence that Celestina thought she saw the shadow of a human form for a moment on the ground, as if the person was behind her who occasioned it.

In **Desmond,** a contemptible husband tries to induce his wife to become the mistress of a wealthy duke. She indignantly takes flight; and, when her mother turns her away, is protected by Desmond. Both are too high-minded to take advantage of the situation. Geraldine returns and nurses her dying husband, who had thrown in his lot with a troop of bandits and been shot in a skirmish, and completes her year of mourning before she marries her lover. The novel is largely composed of letters from Desmond travelling in France, and he describes the state of things at that period. Mrs Smith's sympathies were with the revolutionaries, and neither the outspoken discussions on freedom and equality nor the strictures on the policy of the British Government met with much approval in England. Desmond, it is to be noted, is a lover of the Werther stamp; the new leaven was working and turning even the novel of sensibility towards ideas.

All these diversified ingredients are combined in **The Old Manor House,** which may be accepted as the type novel of Charlotte Smith. It is domestic fiction, branching off into intrigues and adventures, and exhibiting her political bias in some satire on pride of birth and in her sympathy with the other side when the young hero is sent to fight against the American revolutionaries. The rambling old mansion, with its hidden passages and stairways, haunted not by ghosts but by smugglers, the gruesome incidents of red Indian warfare and the hairbreadth escapes, along with the sentimental evocation of ominous scenery, are all features of Gothic romance. Other components are a reminder that Fanny Burney had recently been handling similar domestic problems. But Fanny Burney did not show the same consciousness that the industrial revolution was in full swing, and that the rich merchant and mill-owner were in the act of ousting the old aristocracy from their pre-eminence.

A great house and estate, the ancient patrimony of the Raylands, are now in the hands of an aged lady, last representative of the male line. The presumptive heirs are descended from the female side; and this imperious old woman, a great lady, in spite of her prejudices and caprices, regards them as debased and adulterated by their connexion with trade, and, further, as offspring of the regicides against whom her ancestors drew their swords. It is noteworthy that the age of snobbishness is beginning, though the peculiar British snobbery of the nineteenth century, based on the inferiority complex, differing from French *snobisme* which is based on the superiority complex, is not yet in sight. It is still the insolence of birth and wealth, like the French *morgue,* scorn for natural deficiencies, jealousy of the rank which pretenders are trying to undermine. Mrs Smith is as incensed as Bage against the purse-proud grandee, and not less against the moneyed upstart, such as Stockton, who gathers round him a rabble of gamesters and debauchees, in an old castle which his huge fortune gained in commerce has enabled him to buy, who shoots all over the county, hunts down the rustic lasses, and drinks himself into the grave. Naturally, the jealous old lady hates the parvenu more virulently than even her encroaching kindred the Somerives, and any intercourse with him is sure to jeopardize their hopes of succeeding; for, although Mr Somerive is next-of-kin, she can dispose of the estate freely by will.

Such is the posture of affairs. Orlando is the second son of Mr Somerive, but the eldest is a rake and a spendthrift, and has ruined his chances with Mrs Rayland. Orlando, on the contrary, is the all-too-perfect young man, the romantic hero. He wins the old lady's affections, not for mercenary reasons, but rather because he is good-natured, and still more because he is in love with Monimia, the ill-used niece of her housekeeper and confidant. The lovers meet in the secret apartments of the old fabric, and are scared by noises and mysterious sights, afterwards traced to the band of smugglers who have their storehouse in the vaults. But Orlando is given a commission, and serves in the American war. Captured by the Indians, he presently falls into the hands of the French, and a long period elapses before he escapes and at last finds himself in England again. He arrives in a destitute condition, to find his father dead, his mother and sisters in poverty, the old manor house in the hands of strangers, and Monimia vanished. The fourth and last volume deals with his feverish quest for his lost love, with the exposure of the intrigues by which a fraudulent will had been substituted for the one that left him principal heir, and with the rediscovery of Monimia. It is all fairly exciting. Mrs Smith recounts facts without realism; that was all she was competent to do. She could not draw a striking character; but she had a sound knowledge of human nature in general, and her creations act upon reasonable and well-defined motives. Her criticism of the state of society is also effective. She does not make much of the war. But her pro-American feeling causes her to exaggerate the perils of Orlando and the English troops, and the sufferings due to the rascality of contractors supplying the fleet and army. Profligate aristocrats such as the baronet who tries to capture Monimia; or the general who fails to seduce Orlando's sister, and when he prepares to marry her is cut out by his own nephew: all supply something corresponding on the one hand to the Lovelace

and Pollexfen business in Richardson's novels, and on the other suiting Mrs Smith's book as a social reformer.

Her use of scenery is thoroughly romantic. The decayed house, set against deep woods, with a broad sheet of water in front that looks mysterious in the moonlight, responds to the more picturesque incidents and the feelings of the harried lovers. As Orlando listens to the low wind sounding hollow through the firs and "stone pines," and faintly sighing among the reeds, he is "impressed with those feelings which inspire poetic effusions. Nature appeared to pause, and to ask the turbulent and troubled heart of man, whether his silly pursuits were worth the toil he undertook for them? Peace and tranquility seemed here to have retired to a transient abode." He sees, "by the faint light which the old Gothic casements afforded at that hour of the evening," Monimia sitting alone. When he arrives in London, the throng of coaches, the dirt and fog, and the deafening noise, fill him with mournful reflections, and remind him that amidst these multitudes "there was not one interested for him." There are not many such set pieces, however, and no such symphonic painting of nature as those in which Mrs Radcliffe afterwards excelled; still the setting is adequately prepared, and contrasts well with the baldness of less imaginative novelists.

Mrs Smith returned to domestic problems and portraiture of character in **The Banished Man,** and to full-blooded romance in **Montalbert.** But the only one among her later novels worthy of note is **The Young Philosopher, Nature his law and God his guide,** the object of which is to present "a just picture of a man so calm, as to be injured by fraud and offended by folly, and who shall yet preserve his equality of temper." Disillusioned and embittered by the ill-success of the revolutionary movement in France and of reform in England, she recounts the unfortunate career of a disciple of Rousseau, who meets with the usual fate of the idealist in a refractory world, and is driven at last to seek a better way of life in the American backwoods. Though in the main a discussion novel or a near approach thereto, this has a good deal of description of Scottish scenery; and Mrs Smith has by this time developed such a passion for nature that in footnotes she gives the botanical names of the flowers that adorn the scene. Mrs Radcliffe was to be more artistic. (pp. 187-92)

> *Ernest A. Baker, "The Gothic Novel," in his* The History of the English Novel: The Novel of Sentiment and the Gothic Romance, *Vol. 5, H. F. & G. Witherby, 1934, pp. 175-227.*

ANNE HENRY EHRENPREIS   (essay date 1969)

[Ehrenpreis discusses the strengths and weaknesses of The Old Manor House.*]*

He who would aspire to pre-eminence as a novelist, wrote one early reviewer of **The Old Manor House,** must have the following aims [see *Critical Review* excerpt dated 1793]:

> To conduct a series of familiar events so as to rouse and preserve attention, without a violation of nature and probability; to draw and support the different characters necessary for an animated and varied drama in just and glowing colours; to hold up the mirror of truth in the moment of youthful intemperance, and to interweave amidst the web of fable, pictures to instruct, and morals to reform.

The late eighteenth-century critic was less concerned than his modern counterpart with the novel's structure, and did not apply rigid standards to the shaping of a plot. He valued the ability to 'rouse and preserve attention' more than a logical development of events. By these criteria, the structure of *The Old Manor House* holds up well enough, though the modern reader finds it indubitably the novel's weakest point. Mrs. Smith's contemporaries would have seen nothing odd, for instance, in the digressions on the American war, Indians, and Negro slaves in Volume III, nor would the change of tone there have troubled them. But the conclusion of the whole work appeared hasty and unsatisfactory even to the reviewer quoted above, and it is obvious that the first two volumes are much more carefully wrought than the second half of the story. By keeping her focus on Orlando, Mrs. Smith is forced to follow him to America, where she is clearly out of her element, and she then must introduce a monumental letter from Monimia to catch the reader up on events back home. The succession of arbitrary obstacles confronting Orlando before the reunion with his beloved in the final volume, and the implausible delays in telling his mother of their secret marriage, are more apt to try the reader's credulity than pique his interest. Neither is much skill to be seen in the summary disposal of Philip Somerive (opening Orlando's way to his inheritance) or in the hocus-pocus surrounding the will.

However she may mishandle suspense in the final volume, Mrs. Smith employs it to good effect in the earlier half of the novel. The clandestine meetings of Monimia and her lover are threatened by continual dangers; each crisis is a little different, and the excitement is sustained through the end of Volume II, when the growing suspicions thrown on their relationship make a change of scene necessary. The 'Gothic' interlude in the chapel (which gave Ann Radcliffe the idea of smugglers for *The Mysteries of Udolpho*) is carefully prepared in the lovers' first secret meeting: Monimia tells Orlando all about the ghost, but they encounter none. Happily, the mystery is not spun out too long, for—unlike Mrs. Radcliffe—Mrs. Smith relieves the reader's curiosity before it has tired.

Since these two ladies have been widely compared for their descriptions of landscape, it is unfortunate that *The Old Manor House* includes a bold exception to Mrs. Smith's normal excellence in this respect. Spring in the Canadian wilderness is pictured as arriving abruptly in a luxuriant savannah alive with magnolia, cypress, and other tropical growth. More than one American critic, finding this passage irresistibly funny, has singled it out for ridicule. I think the author here was misguidedly following William Bartram's *Travels through North and South Carolina;* apart from this blunder, however, she drew her landscapes from life, with loving exactitude. Her English scenes have a natural, realistic charm that is nowhere to be found in her rival novelist's tenebrous panoramas. As one of Mrs. Smith's earliest enthusiasts observes, 'In Mrs. Radcliffe's works . . . the narrative is often of little use but to introduce the description to which it is subservient; in Mrs. Smith's, the description is only used to illustrate the story, and never forced into the service: it is always natural.' If Mrs. Radcliffe's landscapes have been aptly compared to the romantic canvasses of Salvator Rosa, Mrs. Smith's may perhaps be likened to the quiet water-colours of Paul Sandby.

Even Mrs. Radcliffe's most devoted apologists do not claim much for her powers of characterization. Indeed, the supreme defect of the eighteenth-century novel, according to its most knowledgeable analyst, is the disconnection between character and action. But several of Charlotte Smith's creations in this novel are made to act in ways wholly consistent with their established natures. In the first half of the story, the plot is moved forward less by artificial devices than by actions which derive directly from the people concerned. Betty Richards's selfish vanity in lingering on in the village brings about the subsequent encounter with Sir John Belgrave and its disastrous consequences for Orlando and Monimia. Old Pattenson's mistaken jealousy of Orlando causes Betty's dismissal from the Hall (after some close calls for the hero), and the reduction of his own claims on his lady's fortune. Mrs. Rayland's pride makes her put off announcing her chosen heir, thus creating the backbone of the whole story. Mrs. Rayland is Charlotte Smith's masterpiece. Domineering, capricious, an inveterate snob, she has been admired by many critics, including Sir Walter Scott, who thought her 'without a rival' [see excerpt dated 1834]. Her incredulity at finding the intruder on her land to be a baronet, her close inquiries as to what the parvenu Stockton serves at table—these are elegant touches in the creation of a fully realized individual.

One of Mrs. Smith's greatest virtues is making her characters speak in appropriate dialogue. Scott finds her 'uniformly happy in supplying them with language fitted to their station in life'. Her varied gallery of humble characters is particularly striking in this respect. Orlando and Monimia, pasteboard figures by contrast, often speak in the hollow rhetoric that was conventional for sentimental scenes ('Charming girl! how every sentence you utter, every sentiment of your pure and innocent mind delight me!'); but even they are sometimes allowed to converse in an unusually natural style. The insolence of Belgrave and Stockton, the hearty vulgarity of Philip Somerive, the man-of-the-world bravado of General Tracy (one of her most solid creations), are consistently conveyed in their speech.

These gifts of characterization and the author's technical skill in handling a big complicated scene are best displayed in what is perhaps the high point of the novel, the tenants' feast. Against a backdrop of the groaning board, the family portraits, and the waxed oaken floors of Rayland Hall, a little drama of intrigue and cross-purpose is played out. Each of the players is busied with some scheme that runs counter to the moves of others. Orlando, aching to bring about the secret meeting between his sister and his beloved, is struck with the egregious Miss Hollybourn, who has reasons of her own for wishing to detain him. The Archdeacon, all eagerness to impress his hostess on his daughter's account, runs foul of the old lady's sense of family and fails to realize that 'Mrs. Rayland, though she loved her own money, loved nobody the better for having or affecting to have as much'. Philip Somerive, hot in pursuit of Betty and drink, unwittingly frustrates his brother's plans and creates more confusion. The various strands of this well-sustained comedy are carefully interwoven. The whole scene—couched in the admirable prose of which the author was capable—makes one devoutly wish that Mrs. Smith had had the leisure to write more often with a comparable degree of care.

The *Critical* reviewer quoted above, who demanded of a novel, as was conventional, 'pictures to instruct, and morals to reform', found *The Old Manor House* painfully lacking in this respect. According to him, the clandestine meetings in Monimia's turret were immoral (they are patently innocent), Orlando's connivance at Warwick's secret marriage was a blot on his character, and the ending unaccountably left villainy—particularly Mrs. Lennard's—unpunished. The reviewer indignantly concludes that Orlando's conduct is 'held up as an example for all young gentlemen of family and fortune to marry any pretty servant maid they chuse'. That the critic remains blind to the author's form of moral justice in this novel is perhaps, by this late point in the eighteenth century, more of a commentary on him than on the conventions of the age. Even so blinkered a moralist might have found comfort in the fact that the hero never gives pain to others in order to gratify himself—a lesson which Mrs. Smith carefully reiterates. By refusing the temptation to take Monimia with him to America, he avoids grieving his family, and he is finally reunited with her while on an errand of mercy for his friend Fleming. Mrs. Lennard is restored to Rayland Hall by the niece she has wronged only after an obviously retributive interlude where she is incarcerated by her villainous husband and forced to steal pen and ink just as she had made Monimia do.

What was lacking in Mrs. Smith was not a sense of moral fitness but a stereotyped view of good and evil. For all her vindictive castigation of lawyers and her heavy-handed satirical treatment of hypocritical clergymen and others whom she clearly despised, she possessed an underlying tolerance. This reveals itself not only in 'a greater tenderness to frailty, a less rigid distribution of justice', but in an unwillingness to see humanity in simple blacks and whites. Thus the first person to show Orlando any kindness, on his return from the war, is the mistress of a friend of the reprehensible Stockton: a girl who 'wanted neither understanding nor humanity, however deficient she might be in other virtues'. Mrs. Smith's treatment of her favourite convictions—the stupidity of national prejudice, the inhumanity of slavery—demonstrates the same moral realism. In the course of her didactic passages on the wicked behaviour of the British during the American war, she reprimands them for deceiving their Indian allies; but a few pages later she lets these same Indians plunder defenceless villages and massacre women and children. The Wolfhunter saves Orlando's life, but he remains a blood-thirsty savage none the less. Perseus, the Negro slave who becomes Orlando's servant, is endowed with intelligence, courage, and loyalty; but when the crippled old soldier knocks at the door with vital news for his master, Perseus 'would not believe, like a smutty-faced son of a b—h as he is, that such a poor cripple as I could have to do to speak with you'.

Like Fielding, Mrs. Smith is intolerant of cant and pretension in all forms; and if she found in lawyers the heaviest concentration of both qualities, she had his example to draw on as well as her own experience. In her social criticism she is equally hard on the pretension of the aristocratic Mrs. Rayland, who represents an obsolescent order of society, and of the vulgar Stockton, whose kind is about to take over. Lacking Fielding's benevolence, she is apt to let her satire descend into caricature, her criticism become invective. But while her surface waspishness is perfectly apparent and has been repeatedly censured, her liberal spirit is more subtle. An ironic appreciation of human variety and a deep concern with man's cruelty to man are qualities that command approbation in any writer; in one who received little of the world's charity during a bleak, necessitous life, they demand our respect. (pp. xiv-xix)

> *Anne Henry Ehrenpreis, in an introduction to* The Old Manor House *by Charlotte Smith, Oxford University Press, London, 1969, pp. vii-xix.*

CARROLL LEE FRY   (essay date 1970)

[*In the following excerpt from the conclusion to his book-length study* Charlotte Smith, Popular Novelist, *Fry argues why Smith's novels should be read and remembered today. Fry's remarks were written in 1970.*]

Charlotte Smith's novels are seldom remembered, even by literary historians. When they are discussed, it is often in the context in which Jane Austen's Miss Stanley and Kitty speak of them in "Catherine or the Bower." Miss Stanley, a highly accomplished young lady, refers to Mrs. Smith's novels as "the sweetest things in the world" and finds ***Emmeline*** "*so much* better than any of the others." When Mrs. Smith is remembered at all, it is often as a sentimental novelist whose works are "the sweetest things in the world." This situation is understandable, especially since the early novels, those which Kitty and Miss Stanley discuss, seem to be intended to appeal to popular taste. It would seem, therefore, that "What is Charlotte Smith's achievement?" and "Why read a Charlotte Smith novel?" are questions that would be pertinent in the . . . study of a writer so seldom and so imperfectly remembered.

One reason for reading a Charlotte Smith novel is the fact that her fiction is highly representative of the subject matter, themes, and conventions of the fiction of her day. And if the fiction of the period from 1771 to 1814 lacks the greatness that was to come in the nineteenth century, it is none the less important in literary history. Among the writers of this period, Miss Tompkins points out, "there are no names which posterity has consented to call great." But, she continues, this fiction "fed the appetite of the reading public, reflected and shaped their imaginations, and sometimes broke into experiment and creative adventure." It was, in short, the "leaf mould" from which a more talented generation of writers was to spring. Charlotte Smith's novels are a mirror of the subject matter, conventions, and themes of the fiction of her day. Indeed, . . . she was often an innovator in the development of new approaches in the fiction of the 1790's.

Perhaps, then, Mrs. Smith's achievement should be measured to some extent in terms of what she helped to set in motion. She was skillful enough as a writer to use the gothic mode with a new effectiveness, even though she disliked the excesses that developed in the 1790's. Her genuine joy in physical nature seems evident in both her poetry and fiction, and she probably helped to make descriptions of natural scenery popular in fiction. . . . She uses the conventional characters that had been developed by writers of sentimental fiction not only to radiate their joys at viewing sublime or picturesque scenery, their terrors in dark corridors, and their distress at complications in their love lives, but to try to inspire the reader to their own outrage at a system that permits, or in some cases, facilitates, social injustice. One can only wonder, in fact, why the authorities in England permitted her to speak out against these injustices when Thomas Holcroft was tried for treason and Thomas Paine had to leave England hurriedly.

It should also be observed that the fiction to which Mrs. Smith brought innovations serves as an excellent illustration of that change in taste and values in the last half of the eighteenth century that is called pre-romanticism by literary historians. Professor Noyes, after admitting that the term is "not strictly definable," states that pre-romanticism includes a return to nature, a taste for melancholy, primitivism, sentimentalism, individualism and exoticism, the medieval revival, revolution, and humanitarianism and idealism. ***Desmond, The Old Manor House, The Banished Man,*** and ***The Young Philosopher*** illustrate almost all of these characteristics. Almost point for point, this list describes the attitudes and tastes of the sentimentalist in Mrs. Smith's fiction. Desmond might be used as an example. He feeds his melancholy by returning to England to be near Geraldine, and he enjoys the sadness that proximity to her brings. He is capable of "feeling," as a sentimentalist, for the plight of the French peasants under the monarchy in France, and he has proper "taste" in natural scenery. Indeed, in his taste for nature, which shows "so much genuine enthusiasm," and in his capacity for feeling, he shows himself to be highly individual—even alienated. He reacts properly to ruins, the remains of medieval culture, and tells his friend Bethel that he loves "everything ancient, unless it be ancient prejudice." . . . If he does not make a direct statement regarding primitivism, he does comment on the nature of man in ways which show that he would agree with Bage in *Hermsprong* or Elizabeth Inchbald in *Nature and Art* that man is inherently good and only bad when the establishment makes him so. This belief is shown when he disagrees with the view that only veteran statesmen are able to govern a nation: "That they [the new French leaders] may be unlearned in the detestable chicane of politics is certain, but they are also uncorrupted by the odious and pernicious maxims of the unfeeling tools of despotism." This assumption of man's basic goodness, if "uncorrupted by . . . despotism," is fundamental to both primitivism and to the revolutionary ethos at the end of the century.

But while her fiction does contain most of the elements of this change in taste, it is still apparent that Mrs. Smith is the daughter of the age of reason. She no doubt found the emphasis on feeling in *La Nouvelle Héloïse* and *The Sorrows of Young Werther* delightful. . . . [Several] of her sonnets use Werther as a speaker. But if she found these characters attractive, she none the less stresses reason as a balance for strong feeling. George Delmont, in ***The Young Philosopher,*** is called a philosopher because he is able to explode prejudices through reason, and Orlando Somerive uses reason to combat superstition and social injustice. Those characters in Mrs. Smith's novels who give full sway to feeling, characters such as Adelina in ***Emmeline,*** Sir Edward Newenden in ***Ethelinde,*** and Laura Glenmorris in ***The Young Philosopher,*** are inevitably punished. Thus, in her insistence on a proper balance between reason and feeling, Mrs. Smith shows herself to be a transition figure between the enlightenment and the so-called romantic movement.

But perhaps the best reason for reading a Charlotte Smith novel is that she is the best novelist of the period between the death of Smollett and the publication of *Waverly.* It is true that many faults can be found with her fiction. She too often goes into lengthy digressions that are specifically autobiographical and not especially pertinent to the work. And she sometimes follows literary conventions that proved to be ephemeral, simply to please an undiscriminating audience. It has often been observed that her plots are poorly planned. But if she is guilty of poor plotting and if she created wooden characters as heroes and heroines, these are qualities common to the novel of the period. In Mrs. Smith's favor, it must be said that she was always at the forefront in the development of new themes and subject matter for prose fiction, and that to some extent she helped to expand the horizons of the novel. In her best work she created memorable characters, and she made the novel of sentiment more relevant to the

world of the late eighteenth century. She deserves to be remembered in literary history as "the most respectable novelist of the period." (pp. 200-05)

Carroll Lee Fry, in his Charlotte Smith, Popular Novelist, *Arno Press, 1980, 239 p.*

KATHARINE M. ROGERS   (essay date 1977)

[*Rogers argues that while established patterns for the eighteenth-century "feminine" novel encouraged many women to write, they also hindered such authors as Smith and Elizabeth Inchbald from acheiving their potential. This article originally appeared in* Eighteenth-Century Studies *with full documentation and explanatory notes.*]

By the later eighteenth century women dominated the field of novel writing in quantity and held their own with men in quality. Among the conditions which made this development possible, such as improved education for women and more mixed social gatherings, perhaps the most important was the emergence of a pattern for a "feminine" novel—a sort of novel that women were both qualified and encouraged to write. It had to be a male author, Samuel Richardson, who established the form within which women authors could congenially work, since women themselves had not yet acquired the confidence to try something new. Richardson's novels focus on internal experience, particularly in the minds of women. (p. 63)

Telling his stories entirely or primarily from a woman's point of view, Richardson necessarily made his heroine an independent entity, not one who exists merely in relationship to men; he expressed her way of seeing, so that he presented manners, morals, human relationships as they affect women. . . . This precedent that a woman's consciousness was worth examining was invaluable to women authors. (pp. 63-4)

The existence of the pattern set by Richardson greatly helped women whose natural talents and interests fitted it, such as Frances Brooke and Frances Sheridan. Without the model set by him and developed by generations of women authors, we might not have the achievement of Jane Austen.

But, like any pattern, it could degenerate from a model to a set of constrictions. Once an area of "women's material" was established, they were expected to stay within it. Granted, they alone knew women's experience at first hand, but that came to mean that they were supposed to write of nothing else. Granted, they were credited with knowing more about intuition, delicate feelings, subtle social interaction, but that tended to restrict them to a subjective world where feelings were all-important and practical concerns vulgar and irrelevant. The result was often a hothouse atmosphere of contrived situations and artificially protracted agonies, lacking the realism of serious art. (p. 64)

The requirement to keep beyond moral reproach combined with the pressure to focus on a female protagonist disastrously to flatten women's novels. For the chastity, propriety, sense of duty, delicacy enjoined on women in real life were doubly enjoined on the fictitious woman who was not worthy to be a heroine if she could not serve as a model. Moreover, since the main concern was to keep the heroine beyond criticism by the most rigorous standard of female virtue, the emphasis tends to fall on the errors she avoids rather than the good qualities she has. Her chastity must not only keep her chaste but keep her from strong feelings for any man to whom she is not married, her prudence must keep her from entering any situation wherein she might conceivably be compromised, her modesty must keep her from showing even the least sign of egotism. Hence she is too dull to engage our interest and sympathy, as well as too unreal. To insure maximum innocence, heroines were made extremely young; they range from eighteen down to fourteen (Charlotte Smith's Monimia). This increases the dullness, because teen-agers are less interesting than mature women, and the unreality, because these girls must act with the prudence and judgment of grown people.

Since the heroines are so flat, interest in their stories must be generated by distressing plot circumstances. And since a flawless person cannot have any responsibility for the misfortunes which befall her, we have the dissociation of plot from character which has been noticed as a critical weakness in the later eighteenth-century novel. (pp. 65-6)

The plots are almost forced into melodrama, since those who suffer from realistic misfortunes generally contribute to them. A real woman might compromise herself with a man, but then she would cease to be perfect; a totally innocent one might be kidnapped by a seducing scoundrel, but that is not very likely. Since the heroine must have the birth and refinement of a lady—that was part of the feminine ideal—and at the same time be eligible for pity and melodramatic adventures (not very likely if she enjoyed the protection of an upper-class family), the circumstances of her birth were usually peculiar. She was almost always "a lovely orphan," and thus deprived of the secure social position which would protect her from kidnappers or designing seducers. (An added advantage of orphan status is that it left her free to make her own choice of husband; otherwise, well-conducted as she was, she would have had to wait until her parents chose.) A suspicion of illegitimacy helped in generating difficulties, since she could then be a nobleman's child (and thus inherit the good breeding which was part of female perfection) and still retain the advantages of isolation and oppression. But this suspicion had to be cleared up by the end of the novel, since a lapse in chastity on her mother's part would, by hereditary influence, have blemished the flawless purity required in the heroine. These are the circumstances of Burney's Evelina and Charlotte Smith's Celestina and Emmeline, "the Orphan of the Castle."

Recognizing this weakness in contemporary fiction, a writer in the *Critical Review* (June 1788) expressed his longing "to see a female character drawn with faults and virtues, to see her feel the effects of misconduct, which does not proceed from a bad heart or corrupted inclinations, and to see her in the end happy, in consequence of her reformation; in short to see a female Jones, or another Evelina, with faults equally embarrassing, yet as venial." The criticism is just, but it reveals the radically different standards applied to male and female characters.

Tom Jones's faults are plain to see. But where are Evelina's? There is only social inexperience, which is hardly a fault since she is just seventeen and was brought up in seclusion. Still, Fanny Burney should get credit for some realism in giving her adolescent heroine the awkwardness of adolescence. Charlotte Smith's Emmeline, who is only fifteen and was brought up by servants in an isolated castle, is endowed with "a kind of intuitive knowledge" which enables her to teach herself all a lady's accomplishments as well as to demonstrate flawless poise in the most trying social situations. Evelina's

blunders in etiquette, her paralysis when trying to make conversation with Lord Orville, the clumsiness which gives Sir Clement his opportunities to torment her, make her a refreshingly realistic comic heroine for her time.

In some ways, however, Burney's novels did suffer from contemporary expectations for ladies' fiction. She felt impelled to introduce the contrived agonies of Evelina's reunion with her father and of Cecilia's brain fever; she flattened her second heroine, Cecilia, into a paragon too unfailingly correct to be implicated in the social satire which was what really interested her. The accepted pattern was far more destructive to two other gifted women novelists of the period, Charlotte Smith and Elizabeth Inchbald. (Both women's association with political radicalism may have contributed to their uneasiness with moral and literary convention.) Smith followed the pattern without conviction, so that most of her novels nominally center on an insipid heroine, and we must look for interest and realistic life in peripheral areas. Sparked by indignation at political abuses or derision of social pretentiousness, her writing is original and forceful; but applied to the sentimental distresses of a well-conducted young lady, it goes dead. Inchbald ignored the convention in her best work, the first half of *A Simple Story* (1791), and followed it to the destruction of interest and plausibility in the second part.

The heroine of the first part, Miss Milner, not only fails to meet the conventional feminine ideal, but has serious faults which lead her into a foredoomed and tragic sexual relationship. She is a beautiful heiress who falls in love with her guardian, Dorriforth, an upright but rigid Roman Catholic priest. After he is released from his vows (in order to perpetuate an earldom), he realizes he loves her. But even in the courtship period there is trouble, since she insists on having her own way and he insists on exerting rational control over her.

Miss Milner is far indeed from the feminine ideal represented by Emmeline or even Richardson's Anna Howe: she is thoughtless, self-willed, defiant of authority, fond of power and admiration, impulsive and imprudent. And yet Inchbald shows her to be a lovable as well as attractive woman. Lacking the negative virtues of feminine propriety, she has all the outgoing ones which transcend that ideal—passionate love, generosity, warm reckless sympathy. She defies her stern guardian's wishes to bring into his home the young nephew whom he has unjustly repudiated. She loves her guardian, before he has even proposed to her, "with all the passion of a mistress," as well as "all the tenderness of a wife." (pp. 66-9)

In the second part of the novel, Inchbald reverts completely to the conventional pattern, with consequent loss of originality and conviction. Miss Milner's daughter, Matilda, the heroine of this section, is totally blameless, subjected to loneliness and oppression only because her father refuses to see her and a predatory squire seeks to take advantage of her unprotected situation. This young woman shows no evidence of self-will, feels no love for a man until it is duly authorized by her father, and effusively worships the father who has disowned her for her mother's fault.

The failure of nerve which weakened the second part of *A Simple Story* is even more evident in Inchbald's curiously diffident preface. Though she must have realized the superiority of her work to most contemporary novels, her tone is consistently apologetic. She deplores the cruel necessity which has forced her, against her inclination and capacity, to become an author; she defensively claims she wrote solely because of financial need and attributes her success entirely to good fortune.

Charlotte Smith was more assertive: her prefaces defend her right to portray and to criticize and imply pride in her work, though she too constantly reminded her readers that she wrote from necessity. Indeed she did write under relentless financial pressure, having nine children to support. This forced her to attend to what was acceptable in ladies' fiction, to which her talent and inclinations were even less suited than were Inchbald's, although she did sometimes incur criticism by deviating from the accepted pattern.

Emmeline, her first novel, was a very successful work modeled on Burney's *Cecilia:* it competently followed the formula while bringing in just enough fresh observation to provide variety without upsetting convention. Emmeline herself is the typical heroine of the period—a neglected orphan who ultimately proves to be the legitimate daughter of a nobleman, an untaught fifteen-year-old who is nevertheless able to conduct herself impeccably in high society, a woman who is supposed to combine spirited intelligence with delicacy and the strongest regard for propriety. She is pursued by six suitors, three presentable and three unpresentable; but her never-failing rectitude protects her from incorrect behavior with anyone. Immune to imprudent passions, she agrees to marry Delamere only because he is wildly in love with her, to make him happy rather than to gratify herself. She suffers from the usual series of harrowing and undeserved misfortunes, but we know that her calm consciousness of behaving properly at all times will pull her through. Her disciplined mind and clear conscience "enabled her to support, with the dignity of conscious worth, those undeserved evils with which many of her years were embittered."

Emmeline herself has little interest for us today, but the book does contain some penetrating social satire, mostly directed against male self-centeredness and conceit. Although Delamere, the hero, is exaggerated, Smith does effectively expose his selfishness as he tries to force marriage on the woman he loves without bothering to find out whether she loves him, or gaily disregards the fact that a young man may defy censure and slander as a dependent young woman cannot. Smith neatly ticks off masculine conceit when she notes that a man of fashion who took pride in making fun of some socially aspiring women was "influenced by a vanity as silly as that he delighted to expose."

But what is more interesting in Charlotte Smith is her protests against the novel form which she felt it necessary to follow. In the preface to *The Banished Man* she suggested she might try "the experiment that has often been talked of, but has never yet been hazarded . . . to make a novel without love in it." Although she did not in fact hazard it, the main emphasis in *The Banished Man* is on the French Revolution, the problems of the émigrés who fled to England, and those of Charlotte Denzil, a middle-aged mother of a family and hard-pressed author like herself. Through her, Smith derides the kind of rarefied fiction which women with real problems had to write: Mrs. Denzil goes to her writing desk after listening to Mr. Tough's importunate demands that she pay his bill—"precious recipe to animate the imagination and exalt the fancy!" Here "she must write a tender dialogue between some damsel" of innumerable perfections "and her hero, who, to the bravery and talents of Caesar, adds the gentleness of Sir Charles Grandison, and the wit of Lovelace. But Mr. Tough's . . . rude threats . . . have totally sunk her spirits; nor are they elevated by hearing that the small beer is almost out" and "the pigs of . . . her next neighbour, have broke into the garden." When she finally gets to bed, she lies awake worrying whether the scarlet fever in a nearby cottage will strike her own children.

Smith was so impatient with the unreality demanded of the main characters that she sometimes longed to stop writing fiction. In *Marchmont* she protested against the limitations of the contemporary heroine: "very young women have no striking traits of character to distinguish them. . . . How difficult then is it for a novelist to give to one of his heroines any very marked feature which shall not disfigure her!" He is not free to give her any "other virtues than gentleness, pity, filial obedience, or faithful attachment." Smith tried to make the heroine of this novel a more forceful and interesting character. She tells us that Althea's unusual misfortunes produced "that fortitude and strength of mind which gave energy to an understanding, naturally of the first class." But unfortunately she failed to demonstrate energy or any other distinguishing characteristic in Althea's actions. Though Smith recognized the problem, she was not prepared to solve it. She was unable or unwilling to create a heroine with a strongly marked character. . . . (pp. 71-4)

Though Smith failed to provide interesting heroines, she deviated from convention both in the subjects she introduced into her novels and her attitudes toward them. Well aware that politics was not considered a subject fit for ladies, she explicitly justified her presentation of the French Revolution in *Desmond:* have women "no interest in the scenes that are acting around them, in which they see fathers, brothers, husbands, sons, or friends engaged?" She went on to a general protest against a system which despised women "as insignificant triflers" if they were ignorant, but censured them "as affecting masculine knowledge if they happen[ed] to have any understanding." Convention claims that "knowledge, which qualifies women to speak or write on any other than the most common and trivial subjects, is . . . of so difficult attainment, that it cannot be acquired but by the sacrifice of domestic virtues, or the neglect of domestic duties" [see excerpt dated 1792]. But actually she herself has been forced by duty to her family both to become an author and to acquire experience in the masculine world of business, since her husband was incapable of supporting them. As a woman who had to struggle constantly with legal and financial problems, she bitterly satirized lawyers for snubbing women who tried to do business.

Not only did Smith argue politics in *Desmond,* she dared to fly in the face of respectable public opinion by vigorously defending the French Revolution. Still, despite her political radicalism and some effective satire on unthinking opponents of the Revolution, the central situation of the book is drearily conventional, dripping with sentimental distress and tied to narrow morality. The virtuous heroine, married to a worthless husband, blindly obeys and sacrifices everything for him; we are supposed to admire her resolve "to be a complete martyr to [her conjugal] duty."

On the other hand, Smith took a relatively liberal view of lapses from conventional morality in women as long as they were not her heroines. In several novels she represented kept mistresses as kind and generous, and she showed wives committing adultery not because they were vicious but because they were pushed into marriages before they knew men or themselves, because their education had provided them with no inner resources, because their husbands neglected and exploited them while another man showed tender consideration. (It is significant, however, that these marital situations which lead wives to adultery are kept off-stage, never directly dramatized.)

Because it emphasizes the subjects Smith was really interested in—social and political abuses, the absurd incongruities of human character—*The Old Manor House* is much her best novel. The heroine is, as usual, young, innocent, refined, distressed, and uninteresting; but we do not see much of her. The hero, Orlando, is hardly a colorful character; but he does hold our interest and, incidentally, shows the advantages of a male protagonist. For one thing, because he is a man, he can have interesting experiences in the outside world. He goes as an officer to fight the American colonists in the Revolution, which gives him the opportunity to observe the appalling conditions on an English troop transport and the horrors inflicted on the colonists, and even to make friends with an Indian warrior and get to know something about his culture. As a man who has seen war, Orlando can reflect convincingly on the senselessness of military glory in general and the American War in particular, and marvel at the attitude of a more experienced fellow officer who, though a humane and intelligent man, assures him it is not a soldier's business to look into the justice of the cause in which he fights.

Moreover, although Orlando is good in the same way the heroines are good—he is gentle, considerate, ever mindful of his obligations to his family, willing to sacrifice his own interests or put aside his own concerns to help others—these virtues are more moving in him because they are the effect of conscious choice. A good woman, according to convention, necessarily acted in this way. Her intuitive delicacy and rectitude forced her to; her practice of the feminine virtues was not a matter of choice and therefore arouses no interest. We feel that Orlando is exerting his will to be such a good son and brother, and we like and admire him accordingly.

But the figures who stand out in *The Old Manor House* are not the idealized young couple but humorously satiric characters like Mrs. Rayland, the selfish old woman who tyrannizes over everyone because of her wealth and family. The contrast between her self-confidence and her ignorance, between her self-satisfaction and her total lack of good feelings, between the power she has and her unfitness to wield it, is both comic and appalling. Imbued with the military glory of her ancestors, she rejoices that Orlando is going to fight a duel, even though he is the only human being for whom she has any affection; and she insinuates that his parents are distressed only because their side of the family has an admixture of plebeian blood. Hearing that a newly rich man has bought a neighboring estate, she laments that "money does every thing"—totally oblivious of the fact that every bit of her own consequence derives from her wealth.

Orlando's sister Isabella is an interestingly mixed character, fluctuating between innocence and natural affection on the one hand, vanity and worldly tastes on the other. When the old rake General Tracy proposed to her, she accepted because she could not resist the money and rank he offered. But as she began to hear about his sex life, she wanted to break the engagement—"and yet she knew not how to retract, and was not always sure that she wished it." Almost on the eve of marriage, she tried on her new pearl necklace and reflected that it did not really make her look prettier than her plain ribbon had. Her natural feelings burst out, and she ran away and

married his nephew. Isabella is thoughtless, flippant, and frivolous, but, although obviously not ideal, comes across as attractive and, in essentials, virtuous. Because she is not the heroine, Smith can represent her as a realistic seventeen-year-old.

Smith and Inchbald owed little, directly, to the tradition of the feminine novel. However it did help both writers by giving them confidence to express their perceptions as women. Their distinctively feminine point of view led them to important new themes, such as Inchbald's sympathy with her heroine's resentment of male authoritarianism even when right, and to small but new insights, such as Smith's evaluation of Rosalie's self-questioning in *Montalbert.* Finding herself bored, Rosalie wonders whether the fault is within or outside of herself: early in life "she became conscious, that such sort of people as she was usually thrown among . . . who only escape from dullness by flying to defamation, were extremely tiresome to her, though she saw that nobody else thought so, and suspected herself of being fastidious and perverse." Before the feminine novel had developed, a woman's boredom would have been ignored as unimportant, and a girl who grew restive in the social circle where she was placed would simply have been dismissed as selfish, not shown conscientiously examining her motives.

Nevertheless, it seems clear that this tradition, which authorized but also restricted, blocked both writers from achieving what they could have. It is risky to speculate about unfulfilled potential, but the unevenness of their works—the discrepancies between brilliant characterization and unconvincing stereotype, between original thought and timid moralizing, between stimulating idea and failure to realize it in the fiction—suggests that they could have written better and more integrated novels if it were not for the repressive forces on women writers in their time. Economic pressure from publishers and buying public, and, more subtly compelling, the internalized social pressure which would have limited the authors' own views of what was proper and moral, kept both women working in an uncongenial pattern. . . . The result was that Inchbald cut off what could have been a brilliant, original analysis of an incompatible marriage; and Smith's gifts for humor, characterization, and satire were dissociated from the main plots of her novels. (pp. 74-8)

Katharine M. Rogers, "Inhibitions on Eighteenth-Century Women Novelists: Elizabeth Inchbald and Charlotte Smith," in Eighteenth-Century Studies, *Vol. 11, No. 1, Fall, 1977, pp. 63-78.*

DIANA BOWSTEAD (essay date 1986)

[*Bowstead discusses the political and domestic themes of* Desmond, *arguing that Smith intended her readers to draw parallels between the governmental injustices the French suffered under the ancien régime and the abuses her heroine suffers in marriage.*]

Charlotte Smith's *Desmond* is remarkable for being the only epistolary novel among the ten Smith published between 1788 and 1798. It is also remarkable for being among the most successful of early attempts at a fully realized political novel in English. Although the central plot of *Desmond* is firmly grounded in the sentimental tradition, and, in fact, is very similar to the plot George Eliot describes in "Silly Novels by Lady Novelists," the thrust of the novel is nonetheless realistic, radical, and incisive. Throughout the novel, the political debates and observations that fill many of the letters tie injustice in the government of nations to injustice in the government of families. Quite overtly, by way of the "sentiments"—that is, the ideas and opinions—expressed by each of the correspondents, the domestic tyranny of which Geraldine Verney, the putative heroine, is an acquiescent victim is treated as analogous to political tyranny in France prior to the Revolution. More insidiously, the striking juxtaposition of a sentimental narrative and lengthy discussions among the correspondents of evils implicit in autocracy induces a reflective reader to notice that the conventions of popular romantic fiction are themselves informed by questionable tenets about the exercise of power: that is, a notion of eroticism characterized by contemptuous dominion, on the one hand, and obeisant delicacy, on the other. (p. 237)

The novel begins when Desmond sets out to visit France. He has two reasons for traveling. First, he wants to put distance between himself and the married woman he loves, Geraldine Verney. Second, he is something of a Jacobin, and wants to see at firsthand the consequences of the Revolution in France. (p. 240)

Beginning the novel by geographically separating her main characters, Smith of course precludes conventional exposition of character and any initial complications of situation. Instead she begins with exposition of a different sort: of her political subject matter, in scenes that are peopled by "embodied arguments." Apparently unrelated encounters between Desmond and individuals he meets along his route incrementally define what Smith puts forth as the central issue in the politics of the period: the disposition of property. Later, the romantic action of the novel draws the institution of marriage into a, by then, carefully ordered "grouping" of opinions about the ownership and government of property and invites readers to compare analogues—that is, to consider wives, too, as a kind of property—and themselves make inferences about the moral implications of such comparisons. Smith's literary tact is such that only once in the novel is the connection overtly made: when Geraldine refers to herself, in passing, while describing her husband, the "unfortunate man whose property I am."

Smith's strategy is to establish thematic connections between what initially seem to be no more than narrated anecdotes. She does so by means of recurrent episodes that involve the consumption, distribution, and production of food so that the ideas her characters express seem, with a certain dramatic inevitability, to inform and determine their behavior. She uses table manners, gourmandizing, indulgence of sexual appetites, treatment of poachers, farming practices, estate management, and more to animate characters in ways that seem consonant with their political principles, and either attractive or repulsive to suit Smith's bias.

Smith begins with the very first stop Desmond makes before crossing the English Channel. It is in Margate, where he meets two members of Parliament: Lord Newminster, who sits in the House of Lords, and General Wallingford, in Commons. This event is reported in a letter to [Erasmus Bethel, Desmond's ex-guardian and friend] . . . , and is the first instance in which conservative opinion is presented to the reader. General Wallingford arrives at a house in which Desmond and Lord Newminster have spent the afternoon to announce the latest news from France, that, "by a decree passed the nineteenth of June, these low wretches, this collection of dirty fellows, have abolished all titles, and abolished the very name

of nobility." As important in characterizing Lord Newminster's political posture as any more serious defense of privilege that he offers is the scene in which Smith shows him engaged with his dog. Before refreshments are cleared, Newminster orders his servant to bring him the remains of the hot chocolate and a plate of bread and butter. "The man obeyed, and the noble gentleman poured the chocolate over the plate, and gave it altogether to the . . . dog—'was it hungry?' cried he—'was it hungry, a lovely dear?—I would rather all the old women in the country should fast for a month, than thou shouldest not have thy bellyful'." This speech expresses the insensitivity that Smith proposes is at the root of his politics. Conservative opinion about who should eat is subsequently shown as, at the least, socially irresponsible, if not also cruelly egocentric. (pp. 241-42)

All such variants on the theme of the greedy gratification of appetites by men of means anticipate or echo two set pieces about the abuse of large land holdings, one in England and the other in France. Bethel reports to Desmond on "improvements" initiated by Stamford, who, having begun as Bethel's lawyer, has become a member of Parliament and very wealthy: profiting from sinecures and shady investments. In order to sustain the lavish table that draws influential people to his house in London, he quite literally puts a modest, but elegant, estate—formerly the Verneys'—entirely in the service of appetite. (p. 243)

In France, the home of the Compte d'Hauteville serves as an eerie image of the ultimate consequences of socially irresponsible land management: a magnificent gothic edifice within an agricultural wasteland. . . . The castle itself is a meeting place for those aristocrats who refuse to accept the Revolution and who intrigue to enlist the aid of other European monarchs for a counter-revolutionary invasion of France. As such it is a "residence, where mortified and discomfitted tyranny seems to have taken up its full station; and with impotent indignation to colour with its own gloomy hand every surrounding object." Thus, the house stands almost as an expressionistic emblem of the nocuous chagrin of its owner and tenants. (p. 244)

In contrast stands the estate of d'Hauteville's nephew, the former Marquis de Montfleuri, an aristocrat sympathetic to the spirit of revolution and in all respects an ideal "governor," even if himself something of an epicure. Desmond describes him as "a man in whom the fire of that ardent imagination, so common among his countrymen, is tempered by sound reason." Montfleuri has begun a program of reform on his own estates, which Desmond visits, anticipating and precluding violence among his dependents by correcting abuses and amending iniquities in the traditional agrarian system. . . . Montfleuri's reforms have been sound and effective because he understands the causes of disaffection among the lower classes as well as among the middle class, as he demonstrates in explaining some of them to Desmond.

Montfleuri's function as a character in this fiction turns on the fact that reforms on his estate are an expression of his radical beliefs. He first embodies, as exemplar, Smith's implicit thematic subject; then he articulates, as knowledgeable partisan, her explicit political statement in support of the Revolutionary cause. By way of Montfleuri's speech in defense of the Revolution, as Desmond records it, Smith gives her readers an extraordinarily concise review of French history from the Jacobin point of view. Montfleuri goes as far back in time as the reign of Henry III, and concentrates on the policies and practices of subsequent monarchs insofar as they affected the quality of life in France. (pp. 244-45)

Smith, by means of Montfleuri's "sentiments," offers her readers a persuasive essay on the political, economic, intellectual, and military circumstances in France that, from the radical point of view, invited rebellion and by implication condone it.

Unlike the monarchy that historically exploited the country at the expense of the populace, unlike Stamford in England and d'Hauteville in France who exploit the land at the expense of those who live on it, Montfleuri sees his own interests best served when the people who work his estate benefit from enlightened, morally responsible management. As a character, Montfleuri serves as an attractive, sympathetic spokesman for the Jacobin cause inasmuch as he is motivated by a humane, moral appreciation of the obligations a man of property ought to assume to promote conscientious government and far-sighted husbandry.

Just as the opinions and behavior of individual landholders serve, in this novel, as specific manifestations in the private sphere of its political subject, so too does its romantic plot illustrate the continuity between ideology and action. Ways of governing erotic and/or romantic inclinations and of cultivating equitable, consensual relationships between men and women are explored within Smith's unusually simple—both for her and for the time—narrative. Rather than developing a large cast of paired lovers—her usual practice—Smith puts Desmond at the center of a romantic triangle of sorts, which provides the means for a simple contrast between the two women to whom Desmond is drawn. The dramatic structure of the novel, although significant for what it allows Smith to say about women and marriage, is not, however, totally successful.

Contemporary critics quite rightly took exception to a subplot that is, in fact, too much a function of thematic design and of too little use in promoting the narrative. In effect, Smith doubles her heroine, introducing Josephine de Boisbelle, Montfleuri's sister, midway through the first volume of the novel. She, like Geraldine, suffers in consequence of a marriage arranged for her without due attention to the character and principles of the bridegroom. Whereas Geraldine is chaste, even in thought, and the proper object of Desmond's deep and distant reverence, Josephine acknowledges her sensual feelings and freely enters into an illicit relationship with him; neither claims to love the other—Josephine too has a first love, from whom she has been separated since forced to marry de Boisbelle. Smith uses Josephine to propose that the sentimental heroine may, herself, have sexual appetites and to imagine for her readers the consequences when she chooses to satisfy them: in this case, an unwanted pregnancy, but no public shame or private guilt because Josephine's enlightened brother and honest lover cooperate to protect her reputation. The price she pays for her indiscretion is no higher than that required of Desmond. (pp. 246-47)

Although Smith seems to acquiesce to generally accepted social and literary proprieties of her time in the broad outlines of Geraldine Verney's story, she introduces ironic overtones that color the effect of the novel by positing a second "heroine," equally sympathetic, whose behavior deviates significantly from approved norms.

The second volume of **Desmond** is largely given over to Geraldine and the romantic plot in which she figures as suffering heroine. Smith works here with and through conventions common in eighteenth-century sentimental fiction. Geraldine's story might well be what George Eliot satirizes in "Silly Novels by Lady Novelists" when she says that the typical heroine of such novels

> as often as not marries the wrong person to begin with, and she suffers terribly from the plots and intrigues of the vicious baronet; but even death has a soft place in his heart for such a paragon, and remedies all mistakes for her just at the right moment. The vicious baronet is sure to be killed in a duel, and the tedious husband dies in his bed requesting his wife, as a particular favour to him, to marry the man she loves best, and having already dispatched a note to the lover informing him of the comfortable arrangement.

Only two features of Geraldine Verney's situation differ from Eliot's typical plot. The novel begins, not when Geraldine enters society, but when she is already married, a phenomenon rare enough to have been considered a novelty of its plot even though it had been done first by Henry Fielding in *Amelia*. Second, Geraldine is never seen to sparkle as the reigning beauty and wit of her social set, nor is she ever seen so comfortably provided for that "we have the satisfaction of knowing that her sorrows are wept into embroidered pocket-handkerchiefs" and "that her fainting form reclines on the very best embroidered upholstery." The Verneys' financial straits keep Geraldine at home; opulence is far beyond their means.

For all that threatens to become maudlin in a plot otherwise quite close to Eliot's summary, the thrust of the novel is nevertheless away from excessive sentimentality. Eliciting pity is in this novel a means rather than an end. The reader's pity for Geraldine is not supposed to become awe at virtue's transcendent capacity for self-immolation. . . . Rather, it is supposed to become indignation on her behalf and on behalf of all victims of institutionally authorized oppression. And these emotions are supposed to motivate critical insight into wrongful and inhumane presuppositions that are used to rationalize servility on the one hand and to justify privilege on the other.

Inasmuch as Geraldine Verney's story is played off against the French Revolution, the domestic tyranny of which she is the victim has analogues in political tyranny in France. Hence the reader is forced to consider, insofar as he is sympathetic to her sorrows and distress, whether she should be submissive or rebellious. The subplot of the novel suggests an alternative to submission. Josephine leaves her husband (as Smith herself did). For Josephine, honor and integrity demand an assertion of self-worth and independence. What is more, her virtue is not, like Geraldine's, inviolable. Her audacity and ardor cast a none-too-flattering shadow over Geraldine's diffidence and chastity. The final effect of the romantic plot in **Desmond** derives from its ironic structure. Since a happy ending for Geraldine seems to be achieved at Josephine's expense, Josephine's bitter lot is a nagging reminder that all such stories need not end as the conventions of sentimental fiction dictate. Although Geraldine is a "distressed heroine" and suffers as nobly as any of her breed, the reader is finally not altogether certain that abjection is a heroic posture. The disposition of subject matter—the contiguity of two such similar stories—raises questions about the relationship between resignation and integrity in a morally responsible individual, even when that individual is a woman.

In spite of its conventional aspects, Geraldine's story serves to bring a kind of realism into fiction that was new to the novel in 1792. Although the tale of Geraldine's trials ends with spectacular melodrama, the distress this heroine suffers throughout most of the novel offers no appealing titillation. Admittedly, the threat of lascivious seduction and of rape echoes in the background of some scenes, but the possibility of either coming to pass is denied as often as it is suggested. Geraldine insists that such dangers are peculiar to the fiction of an earlier time—there are references to *Clarissa, Sir Charles Grandison,* and *Evelina*—and not to contemporary real life. (pp. 252-53)

Geraldine's distress is of a psychologically wearing kind: she worries about money; she worries about her children's present confusion about the absence of their father and the numerous changes in residence; she worries about their future security should Verney squander money they ought to inherit; she worries about whether she should go on nursing the youngest child since her anxiety seems to affect his health. In addition, she worries about her dangerously irresponsible brother, who, had he been otherwise, might have served as her protector.

Geraldine's predicament is not at all the kind that sentimental heroines suffer. Melodramatic resolution at the end of the novel notwithstanding, Geraldine's story is about the dismal facts of wretched marriages, and especially of those (like Smith's) that have been arranged by self-absorbed parents. Geraldine's difficulties are never, until the end of the novel, dramatic or extravagant enough to be captivating.

In the third volume of the novel, issues that until now have been treated quite separately: the merits of democratic government, the proper management of estates and the kind of arrangements that ought to exist between husband and wife are brought together in a rather remarkable sequence of three contiguous letters. Avoiding polemic, Smith instead relies on the reader to appreciate what is meaningful about the juxtaposition of subjects and about the imagery they share. The broad, political issue that links them is overtly aired in the third letter, although it is implied earlier: whether there is, or can be, any rationale for oppression—at the extreme, for slavery.

The first of the three letters is from Geraldine Verney, recently arrived in France, to her sister. She writes that circumstances in and around Paris are not as bad as rumors reaching England suggest, and that she is persuaded that reforms benefiting the French peasants are in progress. She then observes that her sympathy for those who effected a greater democratization of French politics

> must be from conviction, for it cannot be from the prejudice of education—*we* were always brought up as if we were designed for wives to the Vicars of Bray—My father, indeed, would not condescend to suppose that our sentiments were worth forming or consulting; and with all my respect for his memory, I cannot help recollecting that he was a very Turk in principle, and hardly allowed women any pretensions to souls, or thought them worth more care than he bestowed on his horses, which were to look sleek, and do their paces well.

The aside, in which daughters are equated with horses, seems

gratuitous, but leads directly to the next letter, in which Geraldine perceives herself as legally held captive because she is, for all practical purposes, Verney's property.

Geraldine has, in the interim between this and the next letter, taken a house in the suburbs of Paris while waiting for her husband to arrange to have her brought to him. She has every reason to believe that he intends to sell her services to some of his powerful friends in return for the money and patronage he desperately needs, having already spent both her fortune and hers on various forms of debauchery, some of which are indistinguishable from depravity. If her husband does indeed plan to venture into the white slave trade, she is already on her way to market; against the advice of friends, she has insisted that it is her moral duty to join Verney in the interior of France when he summons her. While waiting to continue the journey, she writes to her sister:

> You, my Fanny— . . . have never been unhappy, and have never known . . . the strange and, perhaps, capricious feelings of the *irretrievably* wretched—Since I have found myself so, I have taken up a notion that I do not breathe freely, while I am within the house; and like the poor maniac, who wandered about in the neighborhood of Bristol, I fancy 'that nothing is good but liberty and fresh air.'

Her claustrophobia is emblematic of a psychological rebellion against surrendering herself to Verney's purposes, even if morally she feels compelled to.

The notion that she is a prisoner is then developed indirectly by means of the creatures her son captures in the garden. Because Geraldine feels incarcerated indoors, she lives

> all day about the gardens; while the sun is high, Peggy attends me with the three children, in some shady part of them; and George often amuses himself with catching the little brown lizards which abound in the grass, and among the tufts of low shrubs on this dry soil—He brings them to me—I bid him take great care not to hurt them—I explained to him, that they have the same sense of pain as he has, and suffer equally under pressure and confinement—He looks very grave, as I endeavour to impress this on his mind; and then gently putting them down, cries, "no! no! indeed! I will not hurt you, poor little things!"

Geraldine's fears, both for herself and for her children, develop around the analogy to the helpless lizards so that the child seems both the antithesis of the husband who has made her "suffer . . . under pressure and confinement" and he seems as vulnerable as these creatures are:

> How much a tone, a look, an almost imperceptible expression of countenance will awaken to new anguish an heart always oppressed like mine!—As, liberating his prisoners, he says this—I look round on him, his sweet sister, and his baby-brother, and internally sighing, say, 'Oh! would I were sure, if ever your poor mamma is torn from you, that nobody will hurt *you*, poor little things!'

Geraldine and her children are in danger because they are, according to the courts, the church, and the morality of the drawing room, bound to suffer the consequences of Verney's neglect or abuse of them.

The issue of the slave trade and its relevance to the marriage market are then, respectively, the explicit and implicit subjects of the third letter. Writing to Bethel, Desmond records a conversation with a member of Parliament who owns an estate in the West Indies. Desmond has been arguing the morality of treating human beings like cattle. The member of Parliament replies,

> You are young . . . and have but little considered the importance of this trade to the prosperity of the British nation; besides, give me leave to tell you, that you know nothing of the condition of the negroes neither, nor of their nature—They are not fit to be treated otherwise than as slaves, for they have not the same senses and feeling as we have. . . . They have no understanding to qualify them for any rank in society above slaves: and, indeed, are not to be called men—they are monkies.

The reference to monkeys evokes earlier references to horses; between the two analogous allusions is the fablelike episode of the lizards. If the reader identifies with Geraldine's plight as a potential victim of the white slave trade, he or she has been given every reason to see the plight of a Negro slave from the same perspective. And, of course, the analogy works the other way as well; those who oppose the institution of slavery for political or moral reasons are invited to consider the position of women in so civilized a country as England. (pp. 254-57)

As an experiment in political fiction, *Desmond* is at least as extraordinary as William Godwin's *Caleb Williams*. The sophisticated use of juxtaposition and metaphoric connection described above is only one of several insidious and seditious strategies that Smith uses to make her point. Unlike *Caleb Williams*, *Desmond* is not an exciting, suspenseful novel. Both its "matter" and its "manner" are relatively untheatrical. Smith concedes to popular taste in Geraldine's bizarre adventures on her way to her husband. When she does find Verney, he is fortuitously dying, repentant, and anxious to charge Desmond with the responsibility for her care and protection; the novel ends in a gush of sentiment. Otherwise, *Desmond* is almost entirely a discussion of questions raised by events in France and a description of events in Geraldine's marriage: the two subjects reflecting on each other by way of common themes, especially slavery.

Smith does not allow her treatment of marriage to take shape as articulated polemic, as the political issues she raises do. None of the correspondents, least of all Geraldine, takes an ideological position on the rights of women or the iniquities of the law. Rather, Smith uses Geraldine's letters to show her trying to come to terms with her situation. Insofar as the reader is appalled at the consequences of such an attempt, the novel succeeds as persuasion in the way fiction should: by effectively rendering the extremes to which an individual might be driven by "things as they are."

Interesting in terms of what is possible within the epistolary form is the psychological and moral confusion that Geraldine's letters betray. Smith shows her reaching for and rationalizing a moral construct that will allow her to keep some remnant of dignity in a world in which the law of the country and her mother and brother agree that her husband has the right to govern his affairs and his family however he sees fit. Geraldine's letters, in the third volume of the novel, describe the terms on which she hopes to salvage some degree of integrity even as the circumstances of her marriage force her toward the ultimate degradation: that she be compelled by her

husband to bed with his friends. Having conceded as much to Verney's demands as she feels she can, she finally decides that she will not allow him to use her as property, that she cannot be made to consider herself "his slave." Even so, she wills herself to serve Verney's needs in every other way. (p. 259)

Although Smith then brings her story to a close with Geraldine safely in Desmond's protection, her virtue in every respect intact—that is, although she provides the happy ending that reviewers and readers found morally and aesthetically satisfying—there is a nagging dissonance that runs through the last volume of this novel. Smith suggests a much darker variant of the story, in which women like Geraldine, having contracted bad marriages, destroy themselves trying to reconcile notions of personal honor and virtue with the behavior required of them by the men who govern their lives. By way of Geraldine, Smith reveals the psychological disintegration that is the likely consequence.

Although Smith does not show Geraldine engaged in an overt act of rebellion against Verney, the radicalization of her heroine is complete by the end of the novel, and must be taken as its central action, although it is a psychological, moral, and political reversal rather than a dramatic one. She understands that she has been taken for "property" and that she must not again seem a willing slave. Having extended her sympathies for French peasants and slaves to include a perception of her own position as wife, she allies herself in her second marriage to a man of the right political principles. Smith intends her readers to see that the security of Geraldine's position in the household Desmond governs depends on his honest intention to translate his ideological opposition to political autocracy into reasonably democratic domestic policies.

Because the plot involves so little dramatic action, *Desmond* is very much out of the mainstream of the English novel as that channel was carved out during the nineteenth century. It is easy to understand why *Desmond* has until now been neglected. It is difficult to understand why those interested in political, and especially feminist, literature have turned their attention recently so exclusively to Mary Wollstonecraft's clumsy, stridently partisan fiction when there is also Charlotte Smith's decorous and devastating *Desmond* to speak for the times. (pp. 260-61)

> *Diana Bowstead, "Charlotte Smith's 'Desmond': The Epistolary Novel as Ideological Argument," in* Fetter'd or Free? British Women Novelists, 1670-1815, *edited by Mary Anne Schofield and Cecilia Macheski, Ohio University Press, 1986, pp. 237-63.*

ADDITIONAL BIBLIOGRAPHY

Brydges, Sir Egerton. "Charlotte Smith." In his *Imaginative Biography*, Vol. II, pp. 75-101. London: Saunders and Otley, 1834.
    A biographical sketch.

Bushnell, Nelson S. "Artistic Economy in *Jane Eyre*: A Contrast with *The Old Manor House*." *English Language Notes* V, No. 3 (March 1968): 197-202.
    Uses parallel incidents in Smith's *The Old Manor House* and

Charlotte Brontë's *Jane Eyre* (1847) to demonstrate the stylistic differences between the two authors.

Cary, Meredith. "New Roles in Old Societies." In her *Different Drummers: A Study of Cultural Alternatives in Fiction,* pp. 134-79. Metuchen, N.J.: Scarecrow Press, 1984.

Views the hero of *The Old Manor House* as unconventional.

Ehrenpreis, Anne Henry. "*Northanger Abbey:* Jane Austen and Charlotte Smith." *Nineteenth-Century Fiction* 25, No. 3 (December 1970): 343-48.

Examines the influence of *Ethelinde* on Jane Austen's *Northanger Abbey* (1818).

———. Introduction to *Emmeline: The Orphan of the Castle,* by Charlotte Smith, edited by Anne Henry Ehrenpreis, pp. vii-xv. London: Oxford University Press, 1971.

Combines an analysis of *Emmeline* with a survey of the novel's contemporary critical reception.

Heilman, Robert Bechtold. *America in English Fiction, 1760-1800: The Influences of the American Revolution.* Louisiana State University Studies, no. 33. Baton Rouge: Louisiana State University Press, 1937, 480 p.

Traces the influence of the American Revolution on English fiction. Discussions of Smith's novels are interspersed throughout Heilman's study.

Hilbish, Florence May Anna. *Charlotte Smith, Poet and Novelist (1749-1806).* Philadelphia: University of Pennsylvania, 1941, 634 p.

An important biography of Smith containing extended critical study of her works.

Hunt, Bishop C., Jr. "Wordsworth and Charlotte Smith." *The Wordsworth Circle* 1, No. 3 (Summer 1970): 85-103.

Posits that Smith's poetry influenced William Wordsworth.

Magee, William H. "The Happy Marriage: The Influence of Charlotte Smith on Jane Austen." *Studies in the Novel* VII, No. 1 (Spring 1975): 120-32.

Asserts that Jane Austen borrowed and reworked some characters, situations, and themes from Smith's novels.

McKillop, Alan Dugald. "Charlotte Smith's Letters." *The Huntington Library Quarterly* XV, No. 3 (May 1952): 237-55.

Describes the contents of forty-five letters by Smith housed at the Huntington Library in San Marino, California.

Pollin, Burton R. "Keats, Charlotte Smith, and the Nightingale." *Notes and Queries* n.s. 13, No. 5 (May 1966): 180-81.

Claims that Smith's sonnet "On the Departure of the Nightingale" was a source of ideas and diction for John Keats's "Ode to a Nightingale."

St. Cyres, Viscount. "The Sorrows of Mrs. Charlotte Smith." *The Cornhill Magazine* XV, No. 89 (November 1903): 683-96.

A biographical and critical study examining the effects of Smith's personal afflictions on her poetry.

Stendhal

1783-1842

(Pseudonym of Marie-Henri Beyle; also wrote under pseudonyms Louis-Alexandre-César Bombet, Henri Brulard, and M. B. A. A., among others) French novelist, autobiographer, travel writer, essayist, critic, and novella writer.

The quintessential egoist, Stendhal depicted the individual's lifelong quest for self-knowledge and perpetual search for love in writings admired as early and incisive examples of modern psychological realism. In a spare, understated prose style, his two principal works, the novels *Le rouge et le noir* (*The Red and the Black*) and *La chartreuse de Parme* (*The Charterhouse of Parma*), describe his characters' examinations of their mental and emotional states. Stendhal's introspective fictional characters mirror their author, whose indefatigable self-analysis is recorded in such autobiographical works as *Vie de Henri Brulard* (*The Life of Henri Brulard*) and *Souvenirs d'égotisme* (*Memoirs of an Egotist*). Virtually ignored by his contemporaries, Stendhal became the object of literary hero worship in the 1880s and is today regarded as one of the greatest authors of nineteenth-century France.

Born Marie-Henri Beyle in Grenoble, Stendhal adored his mother, and her death when he was seven was the first misfortune of his lonely and embittered childhood. He was left thereafter in the care of people he detested: his father, a prosperous middle-class lawyer whom he always referred to as "the bastard," his Aunt Séraphie, and his tutor, Abbé Raillane—all, to Stendhal's mind, conservative, bourgeois, pious hypocrites. Grenoble, too, he found stultifying and provincial. In reaction to this environment, Stendhal adopted a liberal political stance and became an atheist. Stendhal was finally able to escape his family and Grenoble at the age of nineteen, when, because of his remarkable proficiency in mathematics, he was sent to Paris to enroll at the École Polytechnique. Stendhal quickly lost interest, however, and never matriculated. Nonetheless, many biographers link his early skill in mathematics to his enduring attraction to logic and precision. In 1800 Stendhal obtained a commission in the French army through the influence of his cousins, the Darus, and was stationed in Milan, the city he came to love above all others. The rest of Stendhal's life was divided between France and Italy; he supported himself with a series of minor government posts.

An understanding of Stendhal's emotional and intellectual life, scholars stress, is essential to an appreciation of his work. Stendhal's absorbing interests were always himself, love, and writing. The love affairs of the never-married Stendhal, which were many, passionate, and generally short-lived, have received much attention from biographers and literary critics. Perpetually in love, Stendhal considered the emotion a transcendent experience. He maintained a contradictory attitude toward women, as revealed in his many autobiographical writings: inclined to idealize the objects of his affections, at the same time Stendhal fancied himself a conquering, cynical seducer. Of related importance in Stendhal's life was his longing for social success. An admitted egoist, yet often painfully shy and self-conscious, Stendhal, was acutely sensitive to the impression he made upon others and frequently adopted the

persona of the satirical wit to amuse companions and hide his own insecurity. Always partial to mystery and disguise (he employed over two hundred pseudonyms in his published works and correspondence), Stendhal became increasingly secretive, almost paranoid, in later years. Critics remark that for all his romances, Stendhal was ultimately a solitary man; toward the end of his life, he wrote that he was "sad to have nothing to love." Stendhal died at the age of 59, hours after collapsing in a Paris street following a stroke. Only three people attended his funeral. In accordance with his wishes, on his tombstone was inscribed *"Arrigo Beyle, Milanese. Visse, scrisse, amo"* ("Henri Beyle, Milanese. He lived, he wrote, he loved").

The themes of Stendhal's work are those of his life: the quest for self-knowledge and for love. Indeed, the titles of two of his minor works, *Memoirs of an Egotist* and *De l'amour* (*On Love*), could stand as descriptive designations of his entire oeuvre. Many scholars agree that each of Stendhal's heroes is, in some sense and to varying degrees, Stendhal himself, a "reconstituted Beyle," according to Albert Thibaudet. Stendhal's preoccupation with the psychology of self and the task of attaining self-knowledge is shared by his protagonists, who endlessly analyze their own actions, motivations, perceptions, and emotions. Further, they, like their author, are impelled, willingly or unwillingly, by love. His characters are thus ruled, in Stendhal's terms, by two principles that at times conflict: *la logique,* rational, precise, scientific thought, and *espagnolisme,* a tendency toward impulsive, passionate, and occasionally violent behavior.

Stendhal began his literary career inauspiciously, publishing biographies, criticism, and travel essays. These early pieces contain traces of his trademark introspection, and critics agree that personal remarks and allusions constitute the primary interest of such derivative (frequently plagiarized) books as *Vies de Haydn* (*The Life of Haydn*), *Rome, Naples, et Florence* (*Rome, Naples, and Florence*), *Histoire de la peinture en Italie,* and *Promenades dans Rome* (*A Roman Journal*). Stendhal's essay *Racine et Shakespeare* (*Racine and Shakespeare*), a comparative analysis in which he expresses his preference for the "Romantic" dramas of William Shakespeare over the neoclassical works of Jean Racine, is of some interest to scholars insofar as it reveals his literary theory. *Racine and Shakespeare,* evidencing Stendhal's primary concern with emotional states, is often cited in studies of his relationship to Romanticism. However, he diverged from the movement not only in his psychological realism but in his forging of a different stylistic ideal: clear, concise, dispassionate writing. Stendhal turned to the subject that enthralled him in *On Love,* an analytical treatise. Within a scientific, clinical framework that is interrupted by personal reflections and allusions, Stendhal defined seven varieties of love, declared his preference for *amour-passion* ("passionate love"), and catalogued the phases of the experience. This work contains his well-known theory of "crystallization," a metaphor—drawn from the scientific phenomenon of a tree branch becoming covered with crystals when left in a salt mine—describing the initial phases of love. Stendhal was in his mid-forties before he published his first novel, *Armance,* a psychological study of two highly sensitive and morally scrupulous young people in love.

The Red and the Black appeared in 1831, but attracted little attention. Now considered one of Stendhal's masterpieces, the novel boasts one of the most memorable and compelling protagonists in French literature—Julien Sorel. Stendhal himself usually referred to *The Red and the Black* simply as "Julien," and critics agree that the character dominates the novel, forming the central enigma of what has long been acknowledged a mystifying book. The very title of *The Red and the Black* was a puzzle to early readers, though it is now generally recognized that the colors represent the two main avenues of social mobility in nineteenth-century France: red refers to the army, black to the church. The son of working-class parents, Julien is ambitious, calculating, and morbidly sensitive. Because he comes of age too late to participate in the military glory of France under Napoleon (his hero and Stendhal's own), he looks to the church for the social and economic advancement he desires. Consciously modeling himself on Tartuffe, the arch-hypocrite of Molière's 1664 play of the same name, Julien is on the threshold of his desired success, achieved through a combination of intelligence, charm, and seduction, when he destroys it all by an impetuous, emotional act of violence. Stendhal culled the basic plot of *The Red and the Black* from newspaper accounts of Antoine Berthet, a seminary student who, employed as a tutor in two successive households, seduced the wife of his first employer and the daughter of his second. Later, believing that his first lover was responsible for his blighted career, Berthet shot her, for which crime he was executed. The melodramatic

action is typical, critics note, of the Romantic tendency of the period, but they add that Stendhal was not interested, as were other Romantic novelists, in dramatic effect for its own sake. Indeed, in this work as in Stendhal's others, he avoided sensational description. The interest of Stendhal's novel thus lies in his exploration of his characters' psychological states, his depiction of the emotional duress that precipitates the melodrama.

During the 1830s Stendhal began several autobiographies and two novels, *Lucien Leuwen* and *Lamiel,* all of which remained unfinished and were not published until years after his death; he also composed several novellas. Of the autobiographies, *The Life of Henri Brulard* recounts, in frank, intimate detail, the first eighteen years of Stendhal's life, while the *Journal* and *Memoirs of an Egotist* cover later periods. All three were written quickly, with no revision, for Stendhal believed that reflection and revision would compromise the sincerity and integrity of his accounts. *Lucien Leuwen* and *Lamiel* both have love as a major theme. In addition, *Lucien Leuwen* probes the nature of its title character's conscience while *Lamiel,* unique in Stendhal's work in its female protagonist, showcases an intelligent and independent woman determined to succeed in life on her own terms. Stendhal's novellas, based on historical chronicles, are tales of subterfuge and passion set in Renaissance Italy.

Stendhal wrote *The Charterhouse of Parma,* today ranked with *The Red and the Black* as one of his greatest works, in only seven weeks in 1839. Comparing the two classics, Howard Clewes wrote: "*Le Rouge* is a young man's anguish—a shout of rage and defiance; *La Chartreuse* is the ironic daydream of one who, if not content, is at least mollified." Urbane irony pervades *The Charterhouse of Parma,* a novel of political intrigue set in Italy. The ostensible main character of the book, Fabrizio (or Fabrice) del Dongo, is generally accounted uninteresting in comparison with the complex, fiery Julien Sorel. From the novel's beginning, with its famous description of Fabrizio's confusion in the chaotic battle of Waterloo, to its conclusion, when he withdraws to the monastery of the title, Fabrizio is a passive rather than active character. Even in his consuming love for Clélia, he is more one who reacts than one who acts. In this novel, unlike *The Red and the Black,* it is not the young idealist who draws the reader's attention but the mature, worldly, even cynical characters. Fabrizio and Clélia's love is set in apposition to that of Gina, Duchess of Sansévérina, and Count Mosca, the former beautiful, intelligent, self-assured, and ruthless in the cause of her unrequited love for her nephew Fabrizio, and the latter, Gina's lover, a wily, Machiavellian statesman with a heart. A knowing and satirical analysis of politics and a penetrating exploration of love, *The Charterhouse of Parma* is a panoramic, complex book, dedicated, as Stendhal wrote, "To the Happy Few."

As his dedication indicates, Stendhal believed that he wrote only for a select few capable of appreciating his work. Indeed, his writings were almost entirely neglected by his contemporaries. Some of his early biographies, criticism, and travel books had a modest success, but *On Love* sold only seventeen copies in eleven years, and the novels were similarly ignored. Stendhal found a powerful champion in the great French novelist Honoré de Balzac, who in 1840 wrote a lengthy, highly laudatory review of *The Charterhouse of Parma,* calling it "a book in which sublimity glows." Balzac also commented, however, that few would be the readers able to recognize the novel's genius, and in fact this proved to be true of Stendhal's canon as a whole. Stendhal, then, was a literary nonentity during his lifetime and for forty-odd years after his death. *Je serais célèbre vers 1880* ("I will be famous around 1880"), Stendhal once remarked, and his prediction proved true. In the late 1880s Stendhal's works began to attract widespread attention, beginning with the discovery of the forgotten writer's unpublished work in a Grenoble library. Over the next few years, as his autobiographies and *Lamiel* and *Lucien Leuwen* were published for the first time, a cult of admirers—known as Stendhalians, or Beylists—formed. Within a very short time, Stendhal had attained national recognition as one of France's greatest novelists and a significant precursor of psychological realism in fiction. Critics praised his merits as an astute observer of humanity, arguing that Stendhal was a psychologist as well as a writer, remarkable for his penetrating insight into the human mind and emotions. "Beylism"—a rather vaguely defined philosophy encompassing, among other elements, intense concern with self, uncompromising individualism, preoccupation with romantic love, and an energetic, idealistic devotion to the *chasse au bonheur* ("pursuit of happiness")—became highly fashionable in France. English-speaking readers were somewhat less enthusiastic, though from the turn of the century criticism of Stendhal increased markedly. Recognizing Stendhal's work as essentially an extension of his own personality but finding it difficult to like the self thus exposed, English-language commentators, while admitting the power and fascination of Stendhal's writing, were disturbed by what George Saintsbury described as its "disagreeable" tone. The perceived immorality of such characters as Julien Sorel, Gina Sansévérina, and Mosca created a barrier to a full appreciation of Stendhal.

Gradually, however, these moral objections lost their force, and since the mid-twentieth century British and American critics have agreed with their French counterparts in designating Stendhal one of the most significant and influential writers of nineteenth-century France. Recent critics, while echoing earlier commentators in their assessment of Stendhal's psychological insight, compelling characterization, and realistic method, have discovered new aspects of modernity in his work. Frequently discussed, for example, is the theme of the individual in conflict with society. Examining Stendhal's isolated protagonists, critics analyze the sociopolitical, moral, and personal implications of their alienation. Paradoxically, as criticism of the author's work explores a broader spectrum of themes and issues, Stendhal remains as elusive to readers as he was to himself—and as fascinating a subject for study. As Warner Berthoff wrote in 1986: "It is as if, no matter how many good and true things have been said about his rendering of human experience . . . [Stendhal] retains a power to surprise the next round of readers and to convince them that something essential to the whole performance remains critically undefined."

PRINCIPAL WORKS

Lettres écrites de Vienne en Austriche, sur le célèbre compositeur Jh Haydn, suivies d'une vie de Mozart, et de considérations sur Métastase et l'état présent de la musique en France et en Italie [as Louis-Alexandre-César Bombet] (biographies) 1814; also published as *Vies de Haydn, de Mozart, et de Métastase,* 1854
  [*The Life of Haydn, in a Series of Letters Written at Vienna, followed by the Life of Mozart, with Observa-*

tions on Metastasio, and on the Present State of Music in France and Italy, 1817]
Histoire de la peinture en Italie (essay) 1817
Rome, Naples, et Florence en 1817; ou, Esquisses sur l'état actuel de la société, des moeurs, des arts, de la littérature, etc. de ces villes célèbres (travel essay) 1817; revised and enlarged edition, 1826
  [*Rome, Naples, and Florence in 1817: Sketches of the Present State of Society, Manners, Arts, Literature, &c. in These Celebrated Cities,* 1818; revised and enlarged edition, 1959]
De l'amour (essay) 1822
  [*On Love,* 1915]
Racine et Shakespeare (criticism) 1823
  ["Racine and Shakespeare" published in *Racine and Shakespeare,* 1962]
Vie de Rossini (biography) 1824
  [*Memoirs of Rossini,* 1824]
Racine et Shakespeare no. II; ou, Réponse au manifeste contre le romantisme prononce par M. Auger dans une scéance solenell de l'Institut (criticism) 1825
  ["Racine and Shakespeare II" published in *Racine and Shakespeare,* 1962]
Armance; ou, Quelques scènes d'un salon de Paris en 1827 (novel) 1827
  [*Armance* published in *The Abbess of Castro, and Other Tales,* 1926]
Promenades dans Rome (travel essay) 1829
  [*A Roman Journal,* 1957]
Le rouge et le noir: Chronique du dix-neuvième siècle (novel) 1831
  [*Red and Black: A Chronicle of the Nineteenth Century,* 1898; also published as *The Red and the Black,* 1914]
Mémoires d'un touriste (travel essay) 1838
  [*Memoirs of a Tourist,* 1962]
L'abbesse de Castro (novellas) 1839; also published as *Chroniques italiennes* [enlarged edition], 1855
La chartreuse de Parme (novel) 1839
  [*The Charterhouse of Parma,* 1902]
Correspondance inédite (letters) 1855
Vie de Napoléon (unfinished biography) 1876
  [*A Life of Napoleon,* 1956]
Journal de Stendhal . . ., 1801-1814 (journal) 1888
*Lamiel (unfinished novel) 1889
  [*Lamiel; or, The Ways of the Heart,* 1929]
**Vie de Henri Brulard (unfinished autobiography) 1890
  [*The Life of Henri Brulard,* 1925]
***Souvenirs d'égotisme (unfinished autobiography) 1892
  [*Memoirs of an Egotist,* 1949]
****Lucien Leuwen (unfinished novel) 1901
  [*Lucien Leuwen,* 1951]
The Abbess of Castro, and Other Tales (novel and novellas) 1926
The Works of Stendhal. 7 vols. (novels, novellas, and essay) 1926-28
Stendhal. 79 vols. (novels, unfinished novels, unfinished autobiographies, journal, novellas, essays, biographies, criticism, and letters) 1927-37
To the Happy Few: Selected Letters of Stendhal (letters) 1952
The Private Diaries of Stendhal (journal) 1954

*This work was primarily written October-December 1839.
**This work was written November 1835-April 1836.

***This work was written June-July 1832.
****This work was written June 1834-November 1835.

HONORÉ DE BALZAC   (essay date 1840)

[*Balzac is considered by many scholars one of the world's great-est novelists. He intended his* Comédie humaine, *a series of ninety-one novels and stories written over a period of twenty years, to be a complete fictional portrayal of his era. The result is a masterpiece incorporating more than 2,000 characters who embody the social, philosophical, moral, and emotional condi-tions of nineteenth-century France. Balzac's supremacy as a novelist, according to critics, is due to his boundless imagina-tion, the realistic sureness of his observations, and the univer-sality of his delineations of character and the human passions. Balzac was virtually the only contemporary of Stendhal to rec-ognize the latter's talent; his well-known review of* The Charterhouse of Parma, *first published in the* Revue Parisi-enne *on 25 September 1840 and excerpted below, lauded the novel as a work of genius. (For Stendhal's appreciative re-sponse, see excerpt below.) Despite Balzac's stature, however, the review did little to augment Stendhal's reputation.*]

If I have so long delayed, in spite of its importance, in speak-ing of [*La Chartreuse de Parme*], you must understand that it was difficult for me to acquire a sort of impartiality. Even now I am not certain that I can retain it, so extraordinary, after a third, leisurely and thoughtful reading, do I find this work.

I can imagine all the mockery which my admiration for it will provoke. There will be an outcry, of course, at my infatua-tion, when I am simply still filled with enthusiasm after the point at which enthusiasm should have died. Men of imagina-tion, it will be said, conceive as promptly as they forget their affection for certain works of which the common herd arro-gantly and ironically protest that they can understand noth-ing. Simple-minded, or even intelligent persons who with their proud gaze sweep the surface of things, will say that I amuse myself with paradox, that I have, like M. Sainte-Beuve, my *chers inconnus*. I am incapable of compromise with the truth, that is all.

M. Beyle has written a book in which sublimity glows from chapter after chapter. He has produced, at an age when men rarely *find* monumental subjects and after having written a score of extremely intelligent volumes, a work which can be appreciated only by minds and men that are truly superior. In short, he has written *The Prince up to date,* the novel that Machiavelli would write if he were living banished from Italy in the nineteenth century.

And so the chief obstacle to the renown which M. Beyle de-serves lies in the fact that *La Chartreuse de Parme* can find readers fitted to enjoy it only among diplomats, ministers, ob-servers, the leaders of society, the most distinguished artists; in a word, among the twelve or fifteen hundred persons who are at the head of things in Europe. Do not be surprised, therefore, if, in the ten months since this surprising work was published, there has not been a single journalist who has ei-ther read, or understood, or studied it, who has announced, analysed and praised it, who has even alluded to it. I, who, I think, have some understanding of the matter, I have read it for the third time in the last few days: I have found the book finer even than before, and have felt in my heart the kind of

happiness that comes from the opportunity of doing a good action.

Is it not doing a good action to try to do justice to a man of immense talent, who will appear to have genius only in the eyes of a few privileged beings and whom the transcendency of his ideas deprives of that immediate but fleeting popularity which the courtiers of the public seek and which great souls despise? If the mediocre knew that they had a chance of rais-ing themselves to the level of the sublime by understanding them, *La Chartreuse de Parme* would have as many readers as *Clarissa Harlowe* had on its first appearance.

There are in admiration that is made legitimate by conscience ineffable delights. Therefore all that I am going to say here I address to the pure and noble hearts which, in spite of cer-tain pessimistic declamations, exist in every country, like un-discovered pleiads, among the families of minds devoted to the worship of art. Has not humanity, from generation to generation, has it not here below its constellations of souls, its heaven, its angels, to use the favourite expression of the great Swedish prophet, Swedenborg, a chosen people for whom true artists work and whose judgments make them ready to accept privation, the insolence of upstarts and the indifference of governments? (pp. 85-6)

This is what happened to me. At the first reading, which took me quite by surprise, I found faults in the book. On my read-ing it again, the *longueurs* vanished, I saw the necessity for the detail which, at first, had seemed to me too long or too diffuse. To give you a good account of it, I ran through the book once more. Captivated then by the execution, I spent more time than I had intended in the contemplation of this fine book, and everything struck me as most harmonious, connected naturally or by artifice but concordantly.

Here, however, are the errors which I pick out, not so much from the point of view of art as in view of the sacrifices which every author must learn to make to the majority.

If I found confusion on first reading the book, my impression will be that of the public, and therefore evidently this book is lacking in method. M. Beyle has indeed disposed the events as they happened, or as they ought to have happened; but he has committed, in his arrangement of the facts, a mistake which many authors commit, by taking a subject true in na-ture which is not true in art. When he sees a landscape, a great painter takes care not to copy it slavishly, he has to give us not so much its letter as its spirit. So, in his simple, artless and unstudied manner of telling his story, M. Beyle has run the risk of appearing confused. Merit which requires to be studied is in danger of remaining unperceived. And so I could wish, in the interest of the book, that the author had begun with his magnificent sketch of the battle of Waterloo, that he had reduced everything which precedes it to some account given by Fabrizio or about Fabrizio while he is lying in the village in Flanders where he arrives wounded. Certainly, the work would gain in lightness. The del Dongo father and son, the details about Milan, all these things are not part of the book: the drama is at Parma, the principal characters are the Prince and his son, Mosca, Rassi, the Duchessa, Ferrante Palla, Lodovico, Clelia, her father, the Raversi, Giletti, Mari-etta. Skilled advisers or friends endowed with simple com-mon sense might have procured the development of certain portions which the author has not supposed to be as interest-ing as they are, and would have called for the excision of sev-eral details, superfluous in spite of their fineness. For instance, the work would lose nothing if the Priore Blanès were to disappear entirely.

I will go farther, and will make no compromise, in favour of this fine work, over the true principles of art. The law which governs everything is that of unity in composition; whether you place this unity in the central idea or in the plan of the book, without it there can be only confusion. So, in spite of its title, the work is ended when Conte and Contessa Mosca return to Parma and Fabrizio is Archbishop. The great comedy of the court is finished. (pp. 128-30)

If, beneath the Roman purple and with a mitre on his head, Fabrizio loves Clelia, become Marchesa Crescenzi, and if you were telling us about it, you would then wish to make the life of this young man the subject of your book. But if you wished to describe the whole of Fabrizio's life, you ought, being a man of such sagacity, to call your book *Fabrizio, or the Italian in the Nineteenth Century.* In launching himself upon such a career, Fabrizio ought not to have found himself outshone by figures so typical, so poetical as are those of the two Princes, the Sanseverina, Mosca, Ferrante Palla. Fabrizio ought to have represented the young Italian of to-day. In making this young man the principal figure of the drama, the author was under an obligation to give him a large mind, to endow him with a feeling which would make him superior to the men of genius who surround him, and which he lacks. Feeling, in short, is equivalent to talent. *To feel* is the rival of *to understand* as *to act* is the opposite of *to think.* The friend of a man of genius can raise himself to his level by affection, by understanding. In matters of the heart, an inferior man may prevail over the greatest artist. There lies the justification of those women who fall in love with imbeciles. So, in a drama, one of the most ingenious resources of the artist is (in the case in which we suppose M. Beyle to be) to make a hero superior by his feeling when he cannot by genius compete with the people among whom he is placed. In this respect, Fabrizio's part requires recasting. The genius of Catholicism ought to urge him with its divine hand towards the *Charterhouse of Parma,* and that genius ought from time to time to overwhelm him with the tidings of heavenly grace. But then the Priore Blanès could not perform this part, for it is impossible to cultivate judicial astrology and to be a saint according to the Church. The book ought therefore to be either shorter or longer.

Possibly the slowness of the beginning, possibly that ending which begins a new book and in which the subject is abruptly strangled, will damage its success, possibly they have already damaged it. M. Beyle has moreover allowed himself certain repetitions, perceptible only to those who know his earlier books; but such readers themselves are necessarily connoisseurs, and so fastidious. M. Beyle, keeping in mind that great principle: "Unlucky in love, as in the arts, who says too much!" ought not to repeat himself, he, always concise and leaving much to be guessed. In spite of his sphinx-like habit, he is less enigmatic here than in his other works, and his true friends will congratulate him on this.

The portraits are brief. A few words are enough for M. Beyle, who paints his characters both by action and by dialogue; he does not weary one with descriptions, he hastens to the drama and arrives at it by a word, by a thought. His landscapes, traced with a somewhat dry touch which, however, is suited to the country, are lightly done. He takes his stand by a tree, on the spot where he happens to be; he shews you the lines of the Alps which on all sides enclose the scene of

action, and the landscape is complete. The book is particularly valuable to travellers who have strolled by the Lake of Como, over the Brianza, who have passed under the outermost bastions of the Alps and crossed the plains of Lombardy. The spirit of those scenes is finely revealed, their beauty is well felt. One can see them.

The weak part of this book is the style, in so far as the arrangement of the words goes, for the thought, which is eminently French, sustains the sentences. The mistakes that M. Beyle makes are purely grammatical; he is careless, incorrect, after the manner of seventeenth-century writers. . . . In one place, a discord of tenses between verbs, sometimes the absence of a verb; here, again, sequences of *c'est,* of *ce que,* of *que,* which weary the reader, and have the effect on his mind of a journey in a badly hung carriage over a French road. These quite glaring faults indicate a scamping of work. But, if the French language is a varnish spread over thought, we ought to be as indulgent towards those in whom it covers fine paintings as we are severe to those who shew nothing but the varnish. If, in M. Beyle, this varnish is a little yellow in places and inclined to scale off in others, he does at least let us see a sequence of thoughts which are derived from one another according to the laws of logic. His long sentence is ill constructed, his short sentence lacks polish. He writes more or less in the style of Diderot, who was not a writer; but the conception is great and strong; the thought is original, and often well rendered. This system is not one to be imitated. It would be too dangerous to allow authors to imagine themselves to be profound thinkers.

M. Beyle is saved by the deep feeling that animates his thought. All those to whom Italy is dear, who have studied or understood her, will read **La Chartreuse de Parme** with delight. The spirit, the genius, the customs, the soul of that beautiful country live in this long drama that is always engaging, in this vast fresco so well painted, so strongly coloured, which moves the heart profoundly and satisfies the most difficult, the most exacting mind. The Sanseverina is the Italian woman, a figure as happily portrayed as Carlo Dolci's famous head of *Poetry,* Allori's *Judith,* or Guercino's *Sibyl* in the Manfredini gallery. In Mosca he paints the man of genius in politics at grips with love. It is indeed love without speech (the speeches are the weak point in *Clarisse*), active love, always true to its own type, love stronger than the call of duty, love, such as women dream of, such as gives an additional interest to the least things in life. Fabrizio is quite the young Italian of to-day at grips with the distinctly clumsy despotism which suppresses the imagination of that fine country; but . . . the dominant thought or the feeling which urges him to lay aside his dignities and to end his life in a Charterhouse needs development. This book is admirably expressive of love as it is felt in the South. Obviously the North does not love in this way. All these characters have a heat, a fever of the blood, a vivacity of hand, a rapidity of mind which is not to be found in the English nor in the Germans nor in the Russians, who arrive at the same results only by processes of revery, by the reasonings of a smitten heart, by the slow rising of their sap. M. Beyle has in this respect given this book the profound meaning, the feeling which guarantees the survival of a literary conception. But unfortunately it is almost a secret doctrine, which requires laborious study. **La Chartreuse de Parme** is placed at such a height, it requires in the reader so perfect a knowledge of the court, the place, the people that I am by no means astonished at the absolute silence with which such a book has been greeted. That is the lot that awaits all books in which there is nothing vulgar. The secret ballot in which vote one by one and slowly the superior minds who make the name of such works, is not counted until long afterwards. (pp. 130-33)

After the courage to criticise comes the courage to praise. Certainly it is time someone did justice to M. Beyle's merit. Our age owes him much: was it not he who first revealed to us Rossini, the finest genius in music? He has pleaded constantly for that glory which France had not the intelligence to make her own. Let us in turn plead for the writer who knows Italy best, who avenges her for the calumnies of her conquerors, who has so well explained her spirit and her genius. (p. 133)

M. Beyle is one of the superior men of our time. It is difficult to explain how this observer of the first order, this profound diplomat who, whether in his writings or in his speech, has furnished so many proofs of the loftiness of his ideas and the extent of his practical knowledge should find himself nothing more than Consul at Civita-vecchia. No one could be better qualified to represent France at Rome. M. Mérimée knew M. Beyle early and takes after him; but the master is more elegant and has more ease. M. Beyle's works are many in number and are remarkable for fineness of observation and for the abundance of their ideas. Almost all of them deal with Italy. He was the first to give us exact information about the terrible case of the Cenci; but he has not sufficiently explained the causes of the execution, which was independent of the trial, and due to factional clamour, to the demands of avarice. His book *De l'amour* is superior to M. de Sénancour's, he shews affinity to the great doctrines of Cabanis and the School of Paris; but he fails by the lack of method which, as I have already said, spoils *La Chartreuse de Parme.* (pp. 134-35)

M. de Chateaubriand said, in a preface to the eleventh edition of *Atala,* that his book in no way resembled the previous editions, so thoroughly had he revised it. M. le Comte de Maistre admits having rewritten *Le Lépreux de la vallée d'Aoste* seventeen times. I hope that M. Beyle also will set to work going over, polishing *La Chartreuse de Parme,* and will stamp it with the imprint of perfection, the emblem of irreproachable beauty which MM. de Chateaubriand and de Maistre have given to their precious books. (p. 135)

> *Honoré de Balzac, "Stendhal," in* Novelists on Novelists: An Anthology, *edited by Louis Kronenberger, Doubleday & Company, Inc., 1962, pp. 85-136.*

STENDHAL   (letter date 1840)

[*In the following excerpt from Stendhal's letter to Honoré de Balzac expressing his appreciation for the latter's favorable review of* The Charterhouse of Parma (*see excerpt above*), *Stendhal describes his own writing ideals.*]

Yesterday evening, monsieur, I had a great surprise. I do not think that anybody has ever been so treated in a review, and by the best judge of the matter. You have taken pity on an orphan abandoned in the middle of the street. I have responded worthily to such kindness: I received the review yesterday evening, and this morning I reduced the first fifty-four pages of the work whose worldly success you are so greatly fostering, to four or five pages.

The laborious kitchen of literature might well have given me a distaste for the pleasure of writing: I have postponed my hope of the satisfactions of authorship to twenty or thirty years hence. A literary botcher might then discover the works whose merit you so strangely exaggerate. (p. 370)

Since you have taken the trouble to read this novel three times, I shall have a deal of questions to ask you at our first encounter on the boulevard:

> (1) Is it permissible to call Fabrice "our hero"? My object was to avoid repeating the name "Fabrice" too often.
>
> (2) Should I omit the Fausta episode, which became too long in the course of writing? Fabrice seizes the offered opportunity of demonstrating to the Duchess that he is not susceptible of *love.*
>
> (3) The fifty-four first pages seemed to me a graceful introduction. I did indeed feel some remorse whilst correcting the proofs, but I thought of Walter Scott's tedious first half-volumes and the long preamble to the divine *Princesse de Clèves.*

I abhor the involved style, and I must confess to you that many pages of the *Chartreuse* are published as originally dictated. I shall say, like a child: "I won't do it again." I believe, however, that since the destruction of the Court in 1792, form has daily played a more meagre part. If M. Villemain, whom I mention as the most distinguished of the academicians, were to translate the *Chartreuse* into French, he would take three volumes to express what has been presented in two. Since most rascals are given to over-emphasis and eloquence, the declamatory tone will come to be detested. At the age of seventeen I almost fought a duel over M. de Chateaubriand's "the indeterminate crest of the forests", which numbered many admirers amongst the 6th Dragoons. I have never read *La Chaumière indienne,* I cannot endure M. de Maistre.

My Homer is the *Mémoires* of Marshal Gouvion Saint-Cyr. Montesquieu and Fénelon's *Dialogues* seem to me well written. Except for Madame de Mortsauf and her fellows, I have read nothing published in the last thirty years. I read Ariosto, whose stories I love. The Duchess is copied from Correggio. I see the future history of French letters in the history of painting. We have reached the stage of the pupils of Pietro de Cortone, who worked fast and indulged in violently exaggerated expression, like Mme Cottin when she causes the ashlars of the Borromaean isles to "walk". After this novel, I did not. . . . Whilst writing the *Chartreuse,* in order to acquire the correct tone I read every morning two or three pages of the Civil Code.

Permit me to employ an obscenity. I do not wish to f——g the reader's soul. The poor reader lets pass such ambitious expressions as "the wind uprooting the waves", but they come back to him when the moment of emotion has gone by. For my part, I hope that if the reader thinks of Count Mosca, he will find nothing to reject.

> (4) I shall have Rassi and Riscara appear in the foyer of the Opera, having been sent to Paris as spies after Waterloo by Ernest IV. Fabrice, returning from Amiens, will notice their Italian look and their "thick" Milanese, which these observers suppose nobody can understand. Everybody tells me that one must introduce one's characters. I shall devote much less space to the good Abbé Blanès. I thought it was necessary to have characters who took no part in the action but simply touched the

reader's soul and removed the sense of romanticism.

I shall seem to you a monster of conceit. Our great academicians would have had the public raving about their writings, if they had been born in 1780. Their hopes of greatness depended upon the ancien régime.

As half-fools become more and more numerous, the part played by *form* diminishes. If the *Chartreuse* had been translated into French by Mme Sand, she would have had some success, but to express what is told in the two present volumes she would have needed three or four. Carefully weigh this excuse.

The half-fool cleaves especially to the verse of Racine, for he can tell when a line is not finished; but Racine's versification daily becomes a smaller part of his merit. The public, as it grows more numerous and less sheep-like, calls for a greater number of "little true touches" concerning a passion, a situation taken from life, etc. We know to how great an extent Voltaire, Racine, etc.—indeed, all except Corneille—are compelled to write lines "padded" for the sake of rhyme. Well, these lines occupy the place that was legitimately owed to such little true touches.

In fifty years M. Bignon, and the Bignons of prose, will have bored everyone so much with productions devoid of any merit except elegance that the half-fools will be in a quandary. Since their vanity will insist that they continue to talk about literature and make a show of being able to think, what will become of them when they can no longer cling to form? They will end by making a god of Voltaire. Wit endures only two hundred years: in 1978 Voltaire will be Voiture; but *Le Père Goriot* will always be *Le Père Goriot*. Perhaps the half-fools will be so upset at no longer having their beloved rules to admire that they will conceive a distaste for literature and turn religious. Since all the rogues of politics have the declamatory and eloquent tone, people in 1880 will be disgusted with it. Then perhaps they will read the *Chartreuse.*

The part played by *"form"* becomes daily more meagre. Think of Hume: imagine a history of France, from 1780 to 1840, written with Hume's good sense. People would read it even if it were written in patois: in fact, it would be written like the Civil Code. I shall correct the style of the *Chartreuse,* since it offends you, but I shall have great difficulty. I do not admire the style now in fashion, I am out of patience with it. I am confronted with Claudians, Senecas, Ausoniuses. I have been told for the past year that I must sometimes give the reader a rest by describing landscape, clothes, etc. Such descriptions have bored me so much when written by others! But I shall try.

As for contemporary success, of which I should never have dreamed but for the *Revue Parisienne,* I told myself at least fifteen years ago that I would become a candidate for the Académie if I won the hand of Mlle Bertin, who would have had my praises sung thrice a week. When society is no longer "spotted" with vulgar newly-rich, who value nobility above all else, precisely because they themselves are ignoble, it will no longer be on its knees before the journal of the aristocracy. Before 1793, good society was the true judge of books; now it is dreaming of the return of '93, it is afraid, it is no longer a judge. Take a look at the catalogue of a little bookshop near Saint-Thomas d'Aquin (rue du Bac, about no. 110), a catalogue which it lends to the neighbouring nobility. It is the

most convincing argument I know of the impossibility of finding favour with these poltroons numbed by idleness.

I have nowhere portrayed Herr von Metternich, whom I have not seen since I saw him in 1810 at Saint-Cloud, when he wore a bracelet of the hair of Caroline Murat, who at that time was so beautiful. I never regret what was fated not to happen. I am a fatalist, and I hide it. I dream that perhaps I shall have some success about 1860 or '80. By then there will be little talk of Herr von Metternich, and still less of the small prince. Who was Prime Minister in England at the time of Malherbe? Unless by any chance his name was Cromwell, I am at a loss for an answer. (pp. 370-73)

I take a character well known to me, I leave him with the habits he has contracted in the art of going off every morning in pursuit of pleasure, and next I give him more wit. . . .

Your amazing article, such as no writer has ever received from another, caused me—I now dare to confess it—to burst into laughter as I read it, whenever I came upon a somewhat excessive piece of praise, which I did at every step. I could imagine the faces my friends would pull as they read it. (p. 374)

> *Stendhal, in an extract from a letter to Honoré de Balzac on October 16, 1840, in* To the Happy Few: Selected Letters of Stendhal, *translated by Norman Cameron, 1952. Reprint by Hyperion Press, Inc., 1979, pp. 370-74.*

ELIZABETH BARRETT [LATER ELIZABETH BARRETT BROWNING] (letter date 1845)

[*A leading Victorian poet, Browning is best known for her cycle of love poetry,* Sonnets from the Portuguese *(1850). In this excerpt from a letter to her friend Mary Russell Mitford, she testifies to the fascination and power of* The Red and the Black.]

I must beg you to order and read *Le rouge et le noir* by a M. de Stendhal . . . a 'nom de guerre' I fancy. I wish I knew the names of any other books written by him. This, which I should not dare to name to a person in the world except you, so dark and deep is the colouring, is very striking and powerful and full of deep significance. I beg you to read it as soon as possible. Balzac could scarcely put out a stronger hand. It is, as to simple power, a first-class book—according to my impression—though painful and noxious in many ways. But it is a book for you to read at all risks—you must certainly read it for the power's sake. It has ridden me like an incubus for several days. (p. 240)

> *Elizabeth Barrett [later Elizabeth Barrett Browning], in a letter to Mary Russell Mitford in April, 1845, in her* Elizabeth Barrett to Miss Mitford: The Unpublished Letters of Elizabeth Barrett to Mary Russell Mitford, *edited by Betty Miller, John Murray, 1954, pp. 240-42.*

CHARLES AUGUSTIN SAINTE-BEUVE (essay date 1854)

[*Sainte-Beuve is considered the foremost French literary critic of the nineteenth century. Of his extensive body of critical writings, the best known are his "lundis"—weekly newspaper articles that appeared every Monday morning over a period of two decades. While Sainte-Beuve began his career as a champion of Romanticism, he eventually formulated a psychological method of criticism. Asserting that the critic cannot separate a work of literature from the artist, Sainte-Beuve considered recognition of an author's life and character essential to the comprehension of his or her work. Though he usually treated his subjects with respect, he dealt harshly with several, notably François Chateaubriand and Honoré de Balzac. In the twentieth century, Sainte-Beuve's treatment of Balzac provoked the ire of Marcel Proust and inspired* Contre Sainte-Beuve (1954; By Way of Sainte-Beuve), *in which Proust contested the validity of Sainte-Beuve's analytical method. Other twentieth-century critics praise Sainte-Beuve's analytical method, but question his biographical approach. The following excerpt is taken from his notoriously unfavorable assessment of Stendhal. Here, in remarks first published in January 1854 as one of his "lundis," Sainte-Beuve enumerates his objections to Stendhal's novels and shorter fiction.*]

Beyle had a certain success as a novelist. I have recently re-read most of his novels. The first in date was **Armance ou quelques scènes d'un salon de Paris,** published in 1827. It was not successful and was little understood. The Duchesse de Duras had shortly before composed pleasant novels or novelettes which were much appreciated in high society; in addition, she had given a reading of an unpublished short piece entitled *Olivier.* Inaccurate accounts of this reading fired people's imaginations, and there was a kind of malicious competition in treating what was wrongly supposed to have been the subject of *Olivier.* Beyle, following Latouche, made the mistake of attacking the same theme—a theme impossible to repeat and anything but pleasant to understand. His Octave, a rich, blasé, bored young man is, we are told, of superior intelligence, but capricious, impractical, and capable only of causing suffering to those who love him. He succeeds in being odious and arouses the reader's impatience. The salons the author had in mind are not portrayed truthfully in this work, for the simple reason that Beyle did not know them. . . . His novel is enigmatic with respect to its subject and without truth with respect to detail, and as such exhibited neither genius nor powers of invention.

The Red and the Black, so titled no one knows why, referring to some emblem we can only guess at, was scheduled for 1830, but was not published until the following year. It is at least a novel with action. The first volume is interesting, despite the manner and the implausibilities. The author sets out to portray classes and parties as they existed before 1830. He begins by picturing a pretty little town in the Franche-Comté. There is M. de Rênal, the royalist mayor, a rich and influential man of less than average intelligence; his lovely wife is unsophisticated; they have two fine children. He wants a private tutor for the children, so as to outdo a local rival. The tutor chosen for this post is Julien, the nineteen-year-old son of a cabinetmaker, who knows Latin and is studying to be a priest. One morning Julien appears at the mayor's gate in a very white shirt, with a spotless lavender coat under his arm. . . . The introduction of this timid young man into a society to which he was not brought up, but had coveted from a distance; the streak of vanity which distorts all his feelings so that even in the touching tenderness of a weak woman he sees merely an opportunity for coming into possession of the pleasures and luxuries of a superior caste; the contemptuous, tyrannical attitude he quickly adopts toward the woman whom he should serve and honor; the protracted illusions about him on the part of his fragile, interesting victim, Mme. de Rênal—all this is or at least would have been well rendered, if the author had been less restless and less epigrammatic in his manner of telling it. Beyle's deficiency as a novelist was due to his taking up this type of composition only after he had been a

critic, so that he follows certain preconceived ideas; nature did not endow him with the talent for composing narratives in which the characters are at home and behave spontaneously, acting according to the course of things. He forms characters by combining two or three ideas which he believes to be correct and above all *piquant,* as he reminds us at every step. They are not living beings, but cleverly constructed automatons; almost at every move they make, we hear the machinery grinding and realize the author is outside them, turning the crank. With the two or three ideas the author has given Julien, he very soon appears no more than an odious little monster, a criminal of the Robespierre type, who operates in ordinary life in terms of domestic intrigue. And in fact he ends on the scaffold. The author's portrayal of the parties and cabals of the period also lack the coherence and moderation in development which alone can make for a real novel of manners. I venture to suggest that Beyle had seen too much of Italy, that he had gained too deep an insight into the Rome and Florence of the fifteenth century, that he had read too much Machiavelli, not only *The Prince* but also his life of the clever tyrant Castruccio, and that all this had a harmful influence on him and made him misunderstand France, so that he was unable to offer her pictures of herself such as she likes and applauds. Although perfectly honest and honorable in his private manners and behavior, as a writer he applied moral standards different from ours. He saw hypocrisy where there was no more than a legitimate sense of propriety, nature reasonably and honestly observed—as we like to find it even in the portrayal of passions.

He did better in his novels and stories with Italian subjects. . . . *L'Abbesse de Castro* is a good example of the narrative of banditry, a genre popular in Rome, but we feel, literarily, that it becomes a genre like any other, and that it should not be done to death. . . . [In **San Francesco a Ripa**] the scene is laid early in the eighteenth century: a jealous young princess takes revenge on an unfaithful French lover. The narrative is lively, raw, and abrupt. At the end there is a profusion of bullets. The faithless man and his valet were "each pierced with more than twenty bullets," such was the fear lest the master escape. In the more classical genre of Dido and Ariadne, in novels of the tone of *La Princesse de Clèves,* bullets and deathly blows are used less lavishly. Instead we have elegiac monologues, delicate thoughts, and fine shades of feeling. When we have exhausted one of the genres, we pass gladly to another to renew our appetite; but if we must choose between two abuses, a certain poetic excess of tender effusiveness is less tiresome to read.

The Charterhouse of Parma is of all Beyle's novels the one that gave a few persons the greatest idea of his talent in this genre. The opening is graceful and genuinely charming. It gives a picture of Milan between 1796, the year of the first Italian campaign, and 1813, when the brilliant court of Prince Eugène came to an end. It was a happy inspiration to show us the young Fabrice, all fire and enthusiasm, running away from home on hearing that Napoleon had landed at Juan-les-Pins in 1815, to fight in France under the imperial eagles. But his bizarre Odyssey has nothing artificial about it—Beyle took his idea from a book of recollections by an English "soldier of the 74th regiment," a man who witnessed the Battle of Vittoria without understanding any of it, more or less as Fabrice witnessed the Battle of Waterloo wondering afterward whether he had really been in a battle and whether he could say that he had actually fought in it. Along with his recollections of that book Beyle combined personal recollections of his youth, such as when he had left Geneva on horse-back to witness the Battle of Marengo. I like this beginning a great deal, though I cannot say the same of what follows. The novel is less a novel than memoirs of the life of Fabrice and his aunt, Mme. de Pietranera, who becomes the duchess de Sanseverina. Italian morality, which Beyle abuses a bit, is decidedly too different from ours. Fabrice, after his brilliant beginnings and his flash of enthusiasm in 1815, might have become one of those distinguished Italian liberals who nobly and perhaps vainly aspire to a regeneration of their country, but who, by their scholarly labors and unselfishness, share in our ideals (Santarosa, Cesare Balbo, Capponi). But Beyle did not so conceive his hero—lest he relapse into what is commonplace on this side of the Alps. He made Fabrice a pure-blooded Italian, bishop-coadjutor at an early age and then an archbishop without vocation, mediocrely and indolently witty, libertine, weak (even cowardly). A perpetual pleasure seeker, he falls in love with one Marietta, a provincial actress, and goes about with her everywhere without shame, without consideration for himself or his status, without regard for his family or for the aunt who loves him too much. I am well aware that Beyle posits as a principle that a pure Italian is totally unlike a Frenchman and has no vanity, that he does not feign love when he does not feel it, that he endeavors neither to please nor to surprise, nor to make a good impression, and that he is content to be himself in perfect freedom. However, what Fabrice is and appears to be for almost the entire novel, despite his good looks and figure, is very ugly, very insipid, very vulgar. Nowhere does he conduct himself like a man, but like an animal at the mercy of his appetites or a libertine child who indulges his every whim. There is no morality, no principle of honor: he is only determined not to simulate love when he is not in love. Similarly, at the end, when he falls in love with Clélia, the daughter of a dreary general, Fabio Conti, he sacrifices everything to her, even good manners and gratitude to his aunt. In earlier writings Beyle had defined *amour passioné* as almost the specific characteristic of the Italian and southern temperament generally; Fabrice is a character who supports that theory. He goes out every morning in search of love and only at the end is he allowed to experience it. Fabrice sacrifices everything to it, just as earlier he had sacrificed everything to pleasure. The pretty descriptions of landscapes, especially of Lake Como and its vicinity, cannot, in view of the rest, ennoble a character so little worthy of interest, so incapable of honor, so ready to do anything—even to commit murder—for his momentary gain and for passion. In fact, the one time Fabrice does kill, he does it in self-defense. He fights in a rather ignoble manner on the highway with a certain Giletti, the actor protector of Marietta, who regards Fabrice as her favorite. If we were to go into the plausibility of the events in the novel, we might ask why this highway accident has such a great influence on Fabrice's future fate; we might ask why he, the friend of the Prince of Parma and of his prime minister (or so he can consider himself), a bishop-coadjutor and very influential in the little state, runs away like a criminal because he happens to kill in self-defense, before witnesses, a lowly actor who threatened and attacked him. Fabrice's behavior, his extravagant flight, and the consequences the author draws from it are all inexplicable if we were to look for plausibility or logic in this novel, which, except for the beginning, is nothing but a witty Italian masquerade. The love scenes, some of them rather good—those with the duchess who is Fabrice's aunt, and with the young Clélia—only half-redeem the impossibilities which leap to the eye and shock common sense. Truth there may well be in matters of detail,

but it does not suffice to make me look upon this world as anything but a fantasied world, fabricated to the same extent as it is observed by a very intelligent man who has composed an Italian *marivaudage* in his own manner. The affectation and grotesqueness of the genre grow more marked as the novel develops. When I have finished it, I feel the need to re-read some very simple, even-keeled work of fiction, which gives a broad, kindly portrait of human nature, in which aunts are not infatuated with their nephews, bishops are not as libertine and hypocritical as the Cardinal de Retz may have been as a young man, and are much less brilliant; where poisoning, lies, anonymous letters, and base actions of every kind are not part of ordinary behavior and are not all but taken for granted; in which, under the pretext of simplicity and avoidance of effects, I am not thrown into incredibly tortuous complications and intrigues more alarming than the labyrinth of ancient Crete.

Ever since Beyle began to chide France for the feelings we display in our literature and our society, I have more than once felt the desire to defend them. One of his principal theories, in accordance with which he wrote his novels, is that love is all but unknown in France—that is to say, love worthy of the name, as he understands it: *amour passion,* a lovesickness, which by its nature is something as special as is crystallization in the mineral kingdom (the comparison is his). But when I see what this love-passion develops into under Beyle's pen, in beings he seems to propose to us as models, in Fabrice when he finally attains to it, in the Abbess of Castro, in the Princess of Campobasso, in Mina de Wangel (another of his novellas), I am persuaded that I like and respect love in the French manner. Though physical attraction certainly plays its part, still there are also moral elements—taste and inclination, well-mannered gallantry, mutual esteem, enthusiasm, even reason and intelligence. Such love retains a little common sense; society is not entirely forgotten, nor is duty sacrificed to blind instinct and ignorance. Corneille's Pauline, in my opinion, embodies the ideal of this type of love fairly well. Though many diverse feelings are included in it, honor and idealism are not silenced. Looking for somewhat less exalted examples, we should find at least kindness and a certain decency, whether in true loves or liaisons, perhaps even respectful, affectionate attachments—what we call it is not very important. Love-passion, such as immortal poets depicted it in Medea, in Phaedra, and in Dido, is moving to see, thanks to them. But I have no patience with the love-passion which has become systematic in Beyle. A kind of animal sickness such as Fabrice serves to symbolize at the end of his career is very ugly, and there is nothing attractive about its semi-demented conclusion. After you have read this, you turn back very naturally, it seems to me, to the French genre of novelistic composition or at least to a genre fuller in scope, which provides an element of reason and sound emotion, true simplicity such as is found in Manzoni's *I Promessi Sposi,* in every good novel by Walter Scott, in some quite uncomplicated but adorable short story by Xavier de Maistre. The rest is merely the work of an intelligent man who went out of his way to devise unexpected, piquant analytical paradoxes, but the characters were not really products of his heart or imagination. They do not live.

You can see how far I am from sharing M. de Balzac's enthusiasm for *The Charterhouse of Parma* [see excerpt dated 1840]. Balzac, to put it plainly, spoke of Beyle the novelist as he would have liked to be spoken of himself. (pp. 225-33)

For his part, M. de Balzac found something lacking in Beyle's style, and so do we. Beyle either dictated or wrote hastily himself, just the way he talked. Whenever he attempted to revise or correct his first draft, he started all over again, rewriting entirely—sometimes a third time—yet without necessarily improving on the first draft. What he had not got down the first time, he was never able to capture or develop later. Though his style might gain in emphasis thereby, his thought was not clarified in consequence. He had singular ideas about how writers approach their task: "When I set out to write," he says, "I am not at all concerned for the ideal beauty of my words. I am assailed by ideas which I feel the need of setting down. I suppose that M. Villemain is assailed by the forms of phrases, and that what is called a poet, a M. Delille or a Racine, is assailed by verse forms. Corneille was mainly interested in forms of dialogue." In short, he goes to a great deal of trouble to understand a very simple thing; he was not one of those to whom the image is suggested by the thought, or in whom lyrical, eloquent feelings burst forth and flow in natural, harmonious development. His early studies did nothing to correct this inadequacy; he had no teacher, no professor of rhetoric—something it is always a good thing to have had, even if one has to rebel against him later. In spite of his elaborate theories on this score, he was well aware that something was lacking. While he seemed to scorn style, he was really very much preoccupied with it.

Though I have been criticizing Beyle's novels with some outspokenness, I am far from wishing he had never written them. If masterpieces are ever to be created again, writers have to be willing to take risks—even to produce essentially unfinished works. Beyle has this kind of courage. (pp. 233-34)

[Whenever] Beyle had an idea, he took a piece of paper and wrote—not worrying about what others would say and never soliciting praise. In this he was a true gentleman. His novels are what they are, but they are not vulgar; like his criticism, they are destined primarily for other novelists. They have fresh ideas and blaze new trails. In studying the possibilities they open up, a novelist of talent may be helped to find himself. (p. 235)

Charles Augustin Sainte-Beuve, "Stendhal," in his Selected Essays, *edited and translated by Francis Steegmuller and Norbert Guterman, Doubleday & Company, Inc., 1963, pp. 209-39.*

HENRY JAMES (essay date 1874)

[*James was an American-born English novelist, short story writer, critic, and essayist of the late nineteenth and early twentieth centuries. He is regarded as one of the greatest novelists of the English language and admired as a lucid and insightful critic. His commentary is informed by his sensitivity to European culture, particularly English and French literature of the late nineteenth century. James was a frequent contributor to several prominent American journals, including the* North American Review, *the* Nation, *and the* Atlantic Monthly. *In this excerpt from an essay that originally appeared in the* Nation *on 17 September 1874, James assesses Stendhal as a writer, designating* The Charterhouse of Parma *as his masterpiece, though an "immoral" one.*]

Beyle is always interesting and often divertingly so, but his merit, to our sense, is not in his powers of entertainment, greater or less, but simply in his instinctive method. What this method was, and how instinctive it was, is suggested by this passage in a letter to his sister, written in his twenty-first year:

> I like *examples,* and not, like Montesquieu, Buffon, and Rousseau, systems . . . . Help me to know provincial manners and passions; describe me the manners in the drawing-room of Madame——. I need examples and facts. Write quickly, without seeking fine phrases . . . . Contribute to my knowledge of women, facts, facts! I have a passionate desire to know human nature, and a great mind to live in a boarding-house, where people cannot conceal their real characters . . . . Borrow and read Sallust; you will find there thirty superb characters.

Later, he advises the same young lady to make a list of the good and bad passions, and then to write opposite each category a description of such examples as she had observed. By perseverance in this course, she would find that she had discovered treasures of knowledge of human nature. It was this absorbing passion for example, anecdote, and illustration that constituted Beyle's distinctive genius, and is the ground of the fresh claims put forth on his behalf by his recent eloquent apostle, M. Taine. Beyle felt, as soon as he began to observe, that character, manners, and civilization are explained by circumstances, and that in the way of observing and collecting circumstances there was a great work to be done. He devoted himself as far as possible to doing it, and on the whole, with his profound mistrust of systems, left the theory of the matter very much to take care of itself. M. Taine follows, with a genius for theory, and erects a symmetrical system on Beyle's unordered *data*. It is interesting to observe that in his attempts to theorize, Beyle is always flimsy and erratic; and that in his attempts to collect small facts in the manner of Beyle (as in *Monsieur Graindorge*), M. Taine is generally ponderous and infelicitous. (pp. 152-53)

Stendhal was apparently very industrious, though he worked in a desultory and disjointed manner, wrote (or published, at least) because he had to do so for bread, and affected to be as little as possible a littérateur by profession. He ought to have considered, however, that the character was made honorable by the danger which he persisted in fancying attached to it. He published everything under a false name (he had half a dozen), travestied his own on his tombstone, and is known to fame by a disguise. He professed an entire indifference to literary fame, except as consisting in mere conciseness. He boasts that the ***Chartreuse de Parme*** is written in the style of the Civil Code. He borrowed largely, especially in his early writings, and transferred long passages from other books without acknowledgment. One may say roughly that his subject is always Italy. He had a number of affectations, but his passion for Italy is evidently profoundly sincere, and will serve to keep his memory sweet to many minds and his authority unquestioned. This subject he treated under a number of different forms; most successfully, toward the end of his life, in a novel which will always be numbered among the dozen finest novels we possess; in a number of short tales, founded on fact, and extracted from the manuscript archives of Italian families, of many of whom Stendahl purchased the privilege of transcribing for a certain number of mornings in their libraries—just as in some parts of the Rhineland one may obtain for a small fee the right to spend an hour in a vineyard or orchard, and retire carrying as much fruit as possible about one's person, as the phrase is; and in a series of loosely connected notes, descriptive, reflective, anecdotic, and epigrammatic, on monuments and pictures, manners and morals (such as *Rome, Naples et Florence* and the *Promenades dans Rome*). To these last may be added his *Histoire de la Peinture en Italie* and various pamphlets—the *Vie de Rossini* and *Racine et Shakespeare*. The *History of Painting* is an ambitious name for a string of desultory though often acute suggestive dissertations on matters nearly and remotely connected with Italian art. It is no history, and, with much suggestiveness, it has to our mind little value. Stendhal as an art-critic is inveterately beside the mark, and it is striking evidence of the development of the science of taste within the last forty years that with his extreme "sensibility," as he would call it, and his excellent opportunities for study, he should seem to us nowadays to belong to so false a school. (pp. 155-56)

[Beyle] was a strange mixture of genius and pretension, of amiability and arrogance, of fine intuitions and patent follies. He condemned his genius to utter more foolish things than it seems to us a wise man was ever before responsible for. He practised contempt on a wholesale, a really grotesque scale, and considered, or pretended to consider, all mankind an aggregation of "*sots,*" except a small class endowed like himself with "sensibility." We have spoken of his method; it was excellent, but we may say on the whole that it was better than any use he made of it—save only when he wrote the *Chartreuse de Parme.* His notion was that *passion,* the power to surrender one's self sincerely and consistently to the feeling of the hour, was the finest thing in the world, and it seemed to him that he had discovered a mine of it in the old Italian character. In the French, passion was abortive, through the action of vanity and the fear of the neighbors' opinion—a state of things with which he is never weary of expressing his disgust. It is easy to perceive that this doctrine held itself quite irresponsible to our old moralistic canons, for *naïveté* of sentiment in any direction, combined with great energy, was considered absolutely its own justification. In the *Chartreuse de Parme,* where every one is grossly immoral, and the heroine is a kind of monster, there is so little attempt to offer any other, that through the magnificently sustained pauses of the narrative we feel at last the influence of the writer's cynicism, regard it as amiable, and enjoy serenely his clear vision of the mechanism of character, unclouded by the mists of prejudice. Among writers called immoral there is no doubt that he best deserves the charge; the others, beside him, are spotlessly innocent. But his immorality seems vicious and harsh only according to the subjects he handles. *Le Rouge et le Noir, L'Amour,* and certain passages in his other writings have an air of unredeemed corruption—a quality which in the novel amounts to a positive blight and dreariness. For the rest, Stendhal professed a passionate love of the beautiful *per se,* and there is every reason to suppose that it was sincere. He was an entertaining mixture of sentiment and cynicism. He describes his heroes and heroines in perfect good faith as "sublime," in appearance and fact, in the midst of the most disreputable actions, and it seems to him that one may perfectly well live a scandalous life and sit up half the night reading Dante in a glow of pure rapture. In repudiating Mr. Paton's assumption that he is a light writer [see Additional Bibliography], we would fain express that singular something which is fairly described neither as serious nor as solemn—a kind of painful tension of feeling under the disguise of the coolest and easiest style. It is the tension, in part, of conceit—the conceit which leads him with every tenth phrase to prophesy in the most trenchant manner the pass to which "les sots" will have brought things within such and such a peri-

od—and in part of aspiration, of deep enjoyment of some bold touch of nature or some fine stroke of art. This bespeaks the restlessness of a superior mind, and makes our total feeling for Beyle a kindly one. We recommend his books to persons of "sensibility" whose moral convictions have somewhat solidified. (pp. 156-57)

    Henry James, "Henry Beyle," in his Literary Reviews   and Essays on American, English, and   French Literature, *edited by Albert Mordell, Vista*   House Publishers, 1957, pp. 151-57.

GEORGE BRANDES (essay date 1882)

[*Brandes, a Danish literary critic and biographer, was the principal leader of the intellectual movement that helped to bring an end to Scandinavian cultural isolation. Writing during the latter part of the nineteenth and the early part of the twentieth century, he departed from the influence of G. W. F. Hegel and developed the psychological criticism of Charles Augustin Sainte-Beuve and the sociological criticism of Hippolyte Taine. Brandes believed that literature reflects the spirit and problems of its time and that it must be understood within its social and aesthetic context. His major critical work,* Hovedstrømninger i det 19de aarhundredes litteratur (1872-90; Main Currents in Nineteenth Century Literature), *traces the development of European literature in terms of writers' reactions to eighteenth-century thought. Brandes discusses Stendhal at length in his* Main Currents, *providing a biography, examining his character, and comparing him with Prosper Mérimée. In the following excerpt from a chapter assessing Stendhal as a novelist, Brandes analyzes characterization in* The Charterhouse of Parma and The Red and the Black, *commenting as well on Stendhal's style and his position in nineteenth-century intellectual history.*]

Both [*Le Rouge et le Noir* and *La Chartreuse de Parme*] deal with the period immediately succeeding Napoleon's fall, and both deal with it in the same spirit. The motto of both might be the passage from De Musset's *Confession d'un Enfant du Siècle* quoted in *The Reaction in France:* "And when the young men talked of glory they were answered: Become priests! and when they talked of honour: Become priests! and when they talked of hope, of love, of power, of life, it was always the same: Become priests!" The scene of *Rouge et Noir* is laid in France, that of *La Chartreuse* in Italy, but in both books the principal character is a young man with a secret enthusiasm for Napoleon, who would have been happy if he could have fought and distinguished himself under his hero in the bright sunlight of life, but who, now that that hero has fallen, has no chance of making a career except by playing the hypocrite. In this art the two young men gradually develop a remarkable degree of skill. Julien and Fabrice are cut out for cavalry officers; nevertheless both become ecclesiastics; the one passes through a Catholic seminary, the other rises to be a bishop. Not without reason have Beyle's novels been called handbooks of hypocrisy. The fundamental idea inspiring them is the profound disgust and indignation which the spectacle of triumphant hypocrisy aroused in their author. Desiring to work off this feeling he gave vent to it by simply, without any display of indignation, representing hypocrisy as the ruling power of the day, to which every one who desired to rise was compelled to do homage. And he tries to play the modern Macchiavelli by frequently applauding his heroes when their attempts at impenetrable hypocrisy succeed, and expressing disapproval when they allow themselves to be surprised or carried away, and unguardedly show themselves as they are. A certain unpleasant forcedness is inseparable from this ironic style of narration.

As Beyle's was essentially a reasoning mind, with a gift of purely philosophic observation, externalities did not impress him strongly, and he had little skill in depicting them. His one interest is in emotional and intellectual processes, and, himself an adept in the observation of these processes, he endows almost all his characters with the same skill. They as a rule have an understanding of what is happening in their own souls which far surpasses that derived by ordinary mortals from experience. This conditions the peculiar construction of Beyle's novels, which consist in great part of connected monologues that are at times several pages long. He reveals all the silent working of his characters' minds, and lends words to their inmost thoughts. His monologues are never the lyric, dithyrambic outbursts which George Sand's often are; they are the questions and answers—short and concise, though entering into minute details—by which silent reflection progresses.

The fundamental characteristic of Beyle's principal personages, who, measured by the current standards of morality, have no conscience and no morals, is, that they have evolved a moral standard for themselves. This is what every human being ought to be capable of doing, but what only the most highly developed attain to; and it is this capacity of theirs which gives Beyle's characters their remarkable superiority over other characters whom we have met with in books or in real life. They keep an ideal, which they have created for themselves, constantly before their eyes, endeavour to follow it, and have no peace until they have won self-respect. Hence Julien, who is executed for an atrocious attempt to murder a defenceless woman, is able to comfort himself in the hour of his death with the thought that his life has not been a lonely life; the idea of "duty" has been constantly present with him.

It is evident that Beyle found this feature which he has bestowed on his heroes in his own character. In a letter written in 1820, after remarking that he detests large hotels because of the incivility shown in them to travellers, he adds: "A day in the course of which I have been in a passion is a lost day for me; and yet when I am insolently treated I imagine that I shall be despised if I do not get angry." This is precisely the manner in which Julien and Fabrice reason. With some such thought in his mind Julien compels himself to lay his hand caressingly on Madame de Rênal's, Fabrice compels himself defiantly to repeat the true but contemptuous words he had used in speaking of the flight of the French soldiers at Waterloo. Julien is French, and acts with full consciousness of what he is about; Fabrice is Italian and naïve, but they both possess the quality to which we may give the name of moral productivity. Julien says to himself in prison: "The duty which I, rightly or wrongly, prescribed to myself, has been like the trunk of a strong tree against which I have leaned during the storm"; the light-hearted Fabrice, reproaching himself with a momentary feeling of fear, says to himself: "My aunt tells me that what I need most is to learn to forgive myself. I am always comparing myself with a perfect model, a being who cannot possibly exist." Mademoiselle de la Mole in *Rouge et Noir* and Mosca in *La Chartreuse de Parme* are distinguished by the same superiority and self-reliance. Mosca, a character in whom Beyle's contemporaries naïvely saw a portrait of Metternich, is, in spite of his position as prime minister of a small legitimist state, quite as free from prejudice in his views

of the system he serves as Beyle's young heroes are. The object of his private hero-worship is Napoleon, in whose army he held a commission in his youth. He jests as he puts on the broad yellow ribbon of his order. "It is not for us to destroy the prestige of power; the French newspapers are doing that quite fast enough; *the reverence mania* will scarcely last out our time."

But whether the personages described be eminently or only ordinarily gifted human beings, the manner in which their inner life is revealed is unique. We not only see into their souls, but we perceive (as in the writings of no other author) the psychological laws which oblige them to act or feel as they do. No other novelist offers his readers so much of the pleasure which is produced by perfect understanding.

Madame de Rênal loves Julien, her children's tutor. We are told that "she discovered with shame and alarm that she loved her children more than ever *because they were so devoted to Julien.*" Mathilde de la Mole tortures Julien by confiding to him her feelings for her former lovers. "If molten lead had been injected into his veins he would not have suffered so much. How was the poor fellow to guess that it was *because she was talking to him* that it gave Mademoiselle de la Mole so much pleasure to recall her flirtations with Monsieur de Caylus and Monsieur de Luz?" Both these passages elucidate a psychological law.

Julien has entered the Church from ambitious motives, and secretly detests the profession he has embraced. On the occasion of some festival he sees a young bishop kneeling in the village church, surrounded by charming young girls who are lost in admiration of his beautiful lace, his distinguished manners, and his refined, gentle face. "At this sight the last remnant of our hero's reason vanished. *At that moment he would, in all good faith, have fought in the cause of the Inquisition.*" The addition "in all good faith" is especially admirable. A parallel passage is to be found in *La Chartreuse.* After the death of a Prince whom he has always despised and who has actually been poisoned by his (Mosca's) mistress, Mosca has been obliged to put himself at the head of the troops and quell a revolt against the young Prince, whose character is as despicable as his predecessor's. In the letter in which he communicates the occurrence to his mistress, he writes: "But the comical part of the matter is that I, at my age, actually had a moment of enthusiasm whilst I was making my speech to the guard and tearing the epaulettes from the shoulders of that coward, General P. *At that moment I would, without hesitation, have given my life for the Prince.* I confess now that it would have been a very foolish way of ending it." In both these passages we are shown with remarkable sagacity how an artificial enthusiasm dazzles and is, as it were, caught by infection.

No other novelist approaches Beyle in the gift of unveiling the secret struggles of ideas and of the emotions which the ideas produce. He shows us, as if through a microscope, or in an anatomical preparation where the minutest veins are made visible by the injection of colouring matter, the fluctuations of the feelings of happiness and unhappiness in acting, suffering human beings, and also their relative strength. Mosca has received an anonymous letter which tells him that his mistress loves another. This information, which he has several reasons for believing to be correct, at first utterly unmans him. Then, as a sensible man and a diplomatist, he involuntarily begins to take the letter itself into consideration and to speculate as to its probable writer. He determines that it has been composed by the Prince. "This problem solved, *the little feeling of pleasure produced by the obviously correct guess* was soon effaced by the return in full force of the painful mental apparition of his rival's fresh, youthful grace." Beyle has not neglected to note the momentary interruption of the pangs of jealousy by the satisfaction of discovery.—In the course of a few days Julien is to be executed. Meanwhile he is receiving constant visits from the woman he loves, but from whom he has been separated for years, and is absorbed by love to the exclusion of all thought of his imminent fate. "One strange effect of this strong and perfectly unfeigned passion was *that Madame de Rênal almost shared his carelessness and gentle gaiety.*" This last bold touch speaks to me of extraordinarily profound observation. Beyle has correctly felt and expressed the power of a happy, absorbing passion to banish all gloomy thoughts (even the thought of certain death) as soon as they attempt to intrude themselves; he knows that passion wrestling with the idea of approaching calamity renders it powerless, when it does not succeed in dismissing it as utterly incredible. It is such passages as these which make other novelists seem shallow in comparison with Beyle.

His characters are never simple, straightforward beings; yet he manages to impart to them, to the women as well as the men, a peculiar imprint of nobility. They possess a certain genuine, though distorted heroism, a certain strength of aspiration which elevates all their emotions; and in the hour of trial they show that they have finer feelings and stouter hearts than the generality of human beings. Observe some of the little characteristics with which he stamps his women. Of Madame de Rênal in *Rouge et Noir* we are told: "Hers was one of those noble and enthusiastic souls which feel almost as keen remorse for not having performed a magnanimous action of which they have perceived the possibility, as for having committed a crime." Mathilde de la Mole says: "I feel myself on a plane with everything that is audacious and great. . . . What great action has not seemed foolishness at the moment when it was being ventured on? It is not till it is accomplished that it seems possible to the ordinary mortal." In these two short quotations, two uncommon female characters of opposite types, the self-sacrificing and the foolhardy, are outlined with the hand of a master. We feel that Beyle was absolutely correct when, in his letter to Balzac, he defines his artistic method as follows: "I take some person or other whom I know well; I allow him or her to retain the fundamental traits of his or her character—*ensuite je lui donne plus d'esprit*" [see excerpt dated 1840].

Of the two novels, *Le Rouge et le Noir,* the scene of which is laid in France, is unmistakably the better; in *La Chartreuse de Parme* we only occasionally feel that we are treading the firm ground of reality. Beyle constructed his own Italy upon the foundation of the fantastically interpreted experiences of his youth, and upon us moderns this Italy produces an impression of untrustworthiness. Both in his novel and in his essays he shows that the Italian mind, by reason of its quality of vivid imagination, is much more plagued by suspicions and delusions than the French, but that in compensation its pleasures are more intense and more lasting, and that it possesses a keener sense of beauty and less vanity. We are every now and then surprised by observations in the domain of racial psychology, which, provided they are correct (which I believe them to be), are extraordinarily acute. We are told, for instance, of the Duchess of Sanseverina, that, although she herself had employed poison to make away with an enemy, she was almost beside herself with horror when she heard that

the man she loved was in danger of being poisoned. "The moral reflection did not occur to her which would at once have suggested itself to a woman educated in one of those religions of the North which permit personal examination: 'I employed poison and am therefore punished by poison.' In Italy this species of reflection in a moment of tragic passion would seem as foolishly out of place as a pun would in Paris in similar circumstances." What evidently attracted Beyle most profoundly in the Italian character was its purely pagan basis, which none of the ancient or medieval religions had really affected. But, in spite of the excellence of its racial psychology, *La Chartreuse de Parme* is less to the taste of the modern reader than *Le Rouge et le Noir* from the fact of its containing more of the purely extrinsic Romanticism of its day in the shape of disguises, poisonings and assassinations, prison and flight scenes, &c. A deeper-seated, intrinsic Romanticism is common to both books.

In many ways Beyle is extremely modern; his constant prophecy, "I shall be read about 1880," has been accurately fulfilled; nevertheless, both in his emotional life and in his delineation of character, he is distinctly a Romanticist. It is to be observed, however, that his Romanticism is the Romanticism of a powerful and of a critical mind; it is the element of enthusiasm to the verge of madness and of tenderness to the pitch of self-sacrifice, that is sometimes found in characters the distinguishing features of which are sense and firmness. In Beyle's essentially self-conscious characters this Romanticism acts like a powerful explosive. It is enclosed in a hard, firm body, but there it retains its power. A blow, and the dynamite shatters its casing and spreads death and destruction around—*vide* Julien, the Duchess of Sanseverina, &c. At times these characters appear rather to belong to that sixteenth century which Beyle studied so devoutly than to the nineteenth. Beyle himself remarks of Fabrice that his first inspiration was quite in the spirit of the sixteenth century; and Mathilde is represented as living her whole life in that spirit. But with this Romanticism of energy and daring deeds Beyle combines the form of Romantic enthusiasm peculiar to the France of 1830. His Julien, the gifted plebeian who is kept from rising by the spirit of the Restoration period, who feels himself eclipsed by the all-prevailing gilded mediocrity, is consumed by hunger and thirst for adventures and impressions, and employs, when he is reduced to impotent hatred, every possible means to raise himself above his original social position, but remains, even when he is for the moment successful, at war with his surroundings and unsatisfied. As the melancholic rebel, as the vengeance-breathing plebeian, as *l'homme malheureux en guerre avec la société* (Beyle's own name for him), he is a brother, about the same age but more prudent, of the step-children of society whom Hugo paints—Didier, Gilbert, Ruy Blas; of the hero of Alexandre Dumas' youth, Antony the bastard; of De Musset's Frank, George Sand's Lélia, and Balzac's Rastignac.

As a stylist, Beyle is directly descended from the prose writers of the seventeenth and eighteenth centuries. He formed his style upon Montesquieu's; he occasionally reminds us of Chamfort; he is an admirer of Paul Louis Courier, who, like himself, exchanged a military for a literary career, and whose perspicuous, classic simplicity of style strongly commended itself to him. But when Courier made it his chief aim to attain to perfect harmony and pellucidity of style, when, praising an ancient author, he said of him that he would have let Pompey win the battle of Pharsalus if he could thereby have rounded his own period better, he adopted the standpoint farthest removed from Beyle's. Beyle the stylist has no sense for either colour or form. He neither could nor would write for the eye; the picture was nothing to him in comparison with the thought; he never made even the slightest attempt to write in the manner of Chateaubriand or Hugo. And just as little did he appeal to the ear; poetic prose was an abomination to him; he detested the style of Madame de Staël's *Corinne,* and scoffed at that of George Sand's novels. . . . Nevertheless, Beyle has artistic qualities. Though the construction of his books is wretched—the drawing of them, so to speak, bad—many of the details are painted with a masterly touch. Though his style is not in the least musical—which is curious in the case of such a worshipper of Italian music—unforgettable sentences abound in his pages. He was not master of the art of writing a page, but he had the genius which sets its stamp on a word or a descriptive phrase. In this respect he is the antipodes of George Sand; her page is always much superior to her word; Beyle's word is far better than his page. He had a genuine admiration for Balzac, but a horror of his style. In **Mémoires d'un Touriste** he expresses the opinion that Balzac first wrote his novels in sensible language, and then decked them out in the ornamental Romantic style with such phrases as "The snow is falling in my heart," &c. Beyle's own style has the merits and the defects which are the inevitable results of his philosophic and abruptly intermittent mode of thought. It is rich in ideas and guiltless of ornamentation, but it is slipshod and jerky. A horror of emptiness and vagueness is its distinguishing and truly great virtue; writing so full of well-digested matter as his is rare.

Beyle often said that only pedants and priests talk about death; he was not afraid of it, but he looked upon it as a sad and ugly thing of which it becomes us best to speak as little as possible. When in 1842 he died suddenly, as he had hoped he might, his name was almost unknown to the public. Only three people attended his funeral, at which not a word was spoken. Such notices of him as appeared in the newspapers, though well-intentioned, only proved how little understood he was by those who appreciated him most. But since then his fame has steadily increased. At first he was regarded as a more or less affectedly eccentric original; and at a later period, when his great gifts were acknowledged, he was still looked upon as an isolated figure, as a paradoxical, unfruitful genius. I, for my part, see in him not only one of the chief representatives of the generation of 1830, but a necessary link in the great intellectual movement of the century; for as a psychologist his successor and the continuer of his work was no less a man than Taine, and as an author his successor and disciple was Prosper Mérimée. (pp. 228-38)

> *George Brandes, "Beyle," in his* Main Currents in Nineteenth Century Literature: The Romantic School in France, Vol. V, *translated by Diana White and Mary Morison, William Heinemann, 1904, pp. 228-38.*

FRIEDRICH NIETZSCHE (essay date 1886)

[*Nietzsche is considered one of the most important philosophers of the nineteenth and twentieth centuries. His thought has influenced nearly every aspect of modern culture. Among his many achievements, he is acknowledged as a forerunner of existentialism, the first philosopher to recognize nihilism as a historical phenomenon, and an important psychological theorist. The following excerpt is taken from his* Beyond Good and

Evil, *first published in German in 1886. Here, in the midst of a discussion of the arts of different nations, Nietzsche parenthetically pays tribute to Stendhal.*]

As antithesis to German inexperience and innocence *in voluptate psychologica,* which is not too distantly related to the boringness of German company—and as the most successful expression of a genuine French curiosity and inventiveness in [the] domain of delicate thrills, one should observe Henri Beyle, that remarkable anticipator and forerunner who ran with a Napoleonic tempo through *his* Europe, through several centuries of the European soul, as a detector and discoverer of this soul—it needed two generations to *overtake* him, to divine once more some of the riddles which tormented and delighted him; this strange Epicurean and question-mark who was France's last great psychologist—. (p. 168)

> *Friedrich Nietzsche, "Peoples and Fatherlands," in his* Beyond Good and Evil: Prelude to a Philosophy of the Future, *translated by R. J. Hollingdale, Penguin Books, 1973, pp. 151-72.*

THE CRITIC, NEW YORK (essay date 1895)

[*In this excerpt from an anonymous review of* The Charterhouse of Parma, *the writer notes the novel's faults of immorality and excessive detail.*]

As a romancer, Stendhal will never be popular with English-speaking readers, though in his native land the taper of his fame burns with increasing brightness. *La Chartreuse* is a cynical, depressing story of illicit love and petty court intrigue, with scarcely a scene or a character that one remembers with unalloyed pleasure. As a pitilessly truthful "human document" it has undoubted value, though its moral tone is hopelessly, because unconsciously, degraded. The hero is a Catholic priest who successfully resists the fascinations of his aunt, devoting himself in preference to a married woman who is not of his own blood. This sort of thing is treated as though it were a matter of course, and one's sympathy is invited for Fabrice and his Claire, who are made as amiable as the author knows how.

Stendhal's prime fault as a writer of fiction was his tendency to overload his narrative with details. In this he was true to his own belief that "il n'est point de sensibilité sans détails," and that "the public wants little, true facts about a passion or a situation in life." One may grant so much, without admitting the fitness of Stendhal's method. It is the romancer's business to select and emphasise such details as are characteristic or significant, leaving something to the reader's imagination. Such a process would have improved **La Chartreuse de Parme,** in which at present one cannot see the wood for the trees. Even so fervent an admirer as Balzac regretted that the author had not used the pruning-knife on this book [see excerpt dated 1840]. Yet, if the strong situations and affecting crises had been treated with proper emphasis, the fault complained of would have been less conspicuous. But the low relief in which these are depicted gives one the impression that small things and great are alike unimportant—the moral of Ecclesiastes, untempered by a faith in Providence. Beyle declared that his irony was a mask assumed in order to conceal his tender sensibility. With less of self-consciousness, he might have dispensed with a mask so unpleasing. It is notable that the Waterloo campaign, described with a grotesque and harrowing realism, gave occasion for some of the best-remembered scenes of the novel. When a Frenchman can mock at military glory, his illusions have perished indeed.

A review of "La Chartreuse de Parme," in The Critic, *New York, Vol. XXIV, No. 722, December 21, 1895, p. 425.*

EMILE FAGUET (essay date 1899)

[*Faguet was an influential French literary historian and critic of the late nineteenth and early twentieth centuries. His critical writings are recognized for their emphasis on the work itself and their understanding of the history and evolution of French poetry. Although his favorite period was the seventeenth century, he was interested in and wrote extensively on many eras of French literature, from the Pléiade poets to the Romantics. In the following excerpt from an essay originally published in French in 1899, Faguet analyzes* The Red and the Black *and* The Charterhouse of Parma, *focusing on the extent to which Stendhal's novels are "true."*]

Stendhal left two novels worthy of a place in posterity: *Le Rouge et le Noir (Scarlet and Black)* and *La Chartreuse de Parme (The Charterhouse of Parma).* The latter is a second edition of the former, corrected and, at the same time, impaired. I will deal with the former first.

Scarlet and Black is a work big in conception and significance. Its title makes its subject clear; *Scarlet and Black*—soldier and priest, military ambition and ecclesiastical ambition, one succeeding the other; warlike energy and intriguing diplomacy, the latter seeking to realize the dream of power which the former has conceived. Although vast, the title is still a little narrow for the idea of the work. I should prefer that the book had as its title its date, 1830; that is the title of *Scarlet and Black.* The century is thirty years old. It was born to the sound of arms; its thoughts fed at first upon the conquest of the world. Two things absolutely unknown to the preceding century became its two fixed ideas: the admission of all French people to all possible employments, if they knew how to undertake them; and sovereign power, even over the whole of Europe, offered to the first comer who should know how to conquer it. These things are absolutely new. They could not have been dreamed of forty years earlier. They are true; they are facts, and recent facts. The future will show that, although true, they are practically illusions however; that they are only realities to the advantage of one or two of Fortune's favorites, and that they are exceptional realities; but the future has not yet come, and, on the strength of recent facts, these things have an immense hold upon the imagination. They are profoundly corrupting. The usual effect of big historical upheavals has manifested itself: a sudden and profound demoralization. Two things have been shown to be possible: to achieve everything and to achieve quickly. . . . [The] middle classes, better-class peasants, obscure provincials, workers, all the common world, is eaten up with ambition. He who later will depict them, Balzac, will give them almost only that passion under different forms. Their social ideas, if they are worthy to be called ideas—hate of the clergy and hate of the nobility—arise only from impatience against these two obstacles, or remnants of obstacles, which they believe still prevent them from having access to everything. Their only political idea, which they are to realize in the middle of the century, universal suffrage, is only the same fixed idea: that it is possible to attain to everything, and that it is possible to arrive quickly.

The aim in *Scarlet and Black* was to show to us the effect produced by these restlessnesses, these impatiences, these desires, in a passionate soul united to a superior intelligence. It is the novel of the century. Julien Sorel saw the Empire in the sense that he was brought up by a captain who served under Napoleon. Regret for this time, when one could be a general at thirty, and when one was treated as *an emperor* in France or, at least, a king in Sweden, formed all his thoughts during childhood. From regret he quickly passed to ambition: for he is energetic and, in the end, all the paths to success are not closed; but it is an ambition of a particular character, special to that period and one which many young people must have had between 1815 and 1830. All the paths to success are not closed; but those which remain are devious. One can no longer achieve things by warlike energy; one achieves by intrigue—that is to say, an energy made up of presence of mind, sustained application, obstinate prudence and ingenious fraud. This is doubtless a fine field of activity, but it is humiliating and mortifying. Certain souls, under the old régime and under the new, find themselves completely in their natural element there and do not have any qualms about it; but the man "born to be a colonel under Napoleon," while resigning himself to such proceedings—for one must succeed: it is a duty—will be so ashamed of them that he will hate furiously those whom he will be forced to use as stepping-stones to success—that is to say, all his benefactors.

This is the man of the century, or at least this is Julien Sorel. His is not a wicked soul. He likes the people of his class, if only they were not entirely brutes. He likes his companion, the wood merchant. At one moment, in conversation with him, he gets away from blessed mediocrity and feels himself tempted. He has not a vulgar soul; for one moment, in the mountains, as the day is slowly drawing to a close, he feels himself intoxicated by the penetrating charm of the solitude, by that exquisite enchantment which is nothing more than the liberation of the soul, and he becomes for a quarter of an hour a veritable Chateaubriand in America. This boy, a plebeian with delicate skin and beautiful burning eyes, would be a Rousseau of the Charmettes under the Revolution and the Empire. But now that is out of the question. We are in 1818. A mad hope has run across the world. Each plebeian believes he has, wants to have, or is furious at no longer having, his marshal's truncheon in his knapsack. Julien's soul is neither wicked nor vulgar; it is depraved. He wants to succeed, cost what it may, and he hates from the bottom of his soul those who come between him and his aim. He detests them for preserving a state of society in which he is forced to treat them with respect in order to succeed, and to be a hypocrite in order to carry out his profession of aspirant. If he finds his Madame de Warens he will detest her while loving her, will make her suffer while giving her happiness, and, above all, will see in her a conquest flattering to his angered and embittered vanity. If he finds a girl from the leading classes, as proud as he, whom he loves and who loves him, the love between these two will be a terrible drama, in which each, from the moment that his love is declared, feels that he is giving himself away and is humbling himself, dreads the other's pride, immediately reproves himself and regains possession of himself, endures and causes to be endured all the tortures that pride can inflict upon love, and thus passes in turn through all the agonies of humiliation, revolt, "impotent hate" and satisfied hate.

It is a magnificent character, profoundly true and admirably shown up into its very depths; a true character of an individual truth and, at the same time, representative of a whole epoch, nay, more, of a whole class at any time that a violent social upheaval shall have opened up to it all hopes of success without removing all the obstacles in the way.

The detail is even more beautiful than the general conception. Certain scenes, by their moderation, by the clear, dry way in which they are sketched, by their energetic and rather broad precision, are marvels of psychological analysis and what might be called moral dissection. Julien in peasant's clothes meeting Mme de Renal at the gate; Julien *wanting* to take Mme de Renal's hand in the garden; Julien in the café at Besançon; Julien preparing his nocturnal visit to Mlle de La Môle and scaling up to her window as one would go to storm a fortress; all the struggle of pride between Mlle de La Môle and Julien—all these are exquisite passages, of surprising depth and, at the same time, perfect clearness, one of the triumphs of that "moral literature" of the French, so curious, so learned, so expert, so incisive, which has perhaps no other rival in the world. How well they know themselves! How well they know their fellows! When one thinks that Stendhal could not bear Racine!

There are things that are bad in this masterpiece, bad and incomprehensible. It is easy to understand the love of Mme de Renal for Julien. Mme de Renal has not loved; she is thirty; Julien appears; she feels the need to protect him against the dull arrogance of M. de Renal; she talks gently to him; she entrusts her children to him; the children are fond of Julien; so the chaste and perilous intimacy is established. It is much less easy to understand the love of Mlle de La Môle for Julien. The proud Mathilde in love with this little secretary, son of a sawyer—this will pass; and confessing this love to herself —this too will pass; but, throwing herself into the arms of the secretary—no, this is too much!

Stendhal, singularly discreet in this carefully thought-out work, felt the objection and tried to forestall it by explaining Mathilde's feelings. For this he must first be congratulated: most novelists just neglect to tell us, or to help us to guess, the *why* of the loves of their heroes. Joan loves Peter, they will tell us at great length: and they give us the adventures of Peter and Joan. Stendhal explained at length why Mathilde loves Julien. But his explanation causes surprise. Why does Mathilde love this passionate plebeian? It is precisely because he is plebeian and because she feels he is passionate. At least he does not resemble the others, the insipid young men who surround her. Perhaps he is a Danton. "Could he be a Danton?" Here is why Mathilde loves Julien. And then comes a very clever and extremely interesting analysis of intellectual love, love through the imagination, and that sort of love which places a living person in a framework prepared long in advance by a series of dreamings, meditations and idealizings. The analysis is good: but it does not elucidate Mathilde's case. Mathilde's pride is aristocratic pride, and Stendhal has marked it with traits so strong that no mistake can be made about it; Mathilde's pride and admiration are all for her ancestors, the La Môles, who were beheaded under Charles IX. and Louis XIII. And therefore the adolescent dreamings which prepared her for love will most certainly be, will have to be, peopled by figures of great men of action, with high ambitions, but always gentlemen, great lords. It will never enter her head that a plebeian could be a great man. So, if she falls in love with a plebeian, it will not be as a result of her previous dreamings, as a result of the preliminary working of her imagination: there will be some other reason. In other words,

Mathilde must not be made to experience intellectual love, love through the imagination, but, on the contrary, quite another sort of love, sensual or sentimental, for example, counteracting in her all the work of her imagination, as well as of her education and her prejudices.

This mistake gives something artificial and forced to the beginnings of the love affairs of Mathilde. Stendhal wanted to make a study of intellectual love; he chose a poor example.

It must be added that, as soon as Mathilde's love has been declared and is considered as an accomplished fact by the reader, when there is no further question of the struggle between her pride and her love, then the work is admirable.

The ending of *Scarlet and Black* is curious, and, in truth, a little more false than is permissible. The impression of a French reader of 1900, or even of 1860, is that at the conclusion of *Scarlet and Black* the characters lose their heads. You recall the situation: Julien has become the lover of Mlle de La Môle, and Mlle de La Môle is with child. This is not all; as favourite secretary of M. de La Môle, Julien has been made confidant, accomplice and servant to a political conspiracy— which, by the way, is the most complicated and annoying thing in the world. However, Julien is absolutely master of the situation: he holds all the forts. M. de La Môle, weak and very sensitive to the coaxing of his daughter, cannot but resign himself to accept Julien as his son-in-law. And, actually, he is made gradually to resign himself, to furnish Julien with a noble title and an officer's commission; Julien is getting on. Suddenly something happens to put all these people in an extraordinary state. A married woman writes that Julien has formerly been her lover. From that moment all is broken off, ruined, hopeless. Mlle de La Môle exclaims and writes: "All is lost!" M. de La Môle does not want to hear anything more about it, nor to resign himself to anything; he takes back all that he has given; he becomes implacable. Julien, the impeccable aspirant, the man of appalling coolness and imperturbable will-power, is the most mad of them all. Really, he only needs to wait. However curious the effect produced by Mme de Renal's revelation upon Mlle de La Môle, M. de La Môle will have to recover his composure and face the necessities of the situation. All Julien need do is to wait. He does not wait. He rushes straight to Mme de Renal and shoots her dead with a pistol.

I say that everybody loses his head without any reason. First, Mme de Renal. If necessary, she might be made to denounce Julien in an access of jealousy. But no, she is made to do so in an access of devotion. On the part of a woman not only very much in love, not only very generous, but rendered very intelligent by love, and who has employed superior diplomacy to extricate herself from the business of the anonymous letter in the first part of the novel, this proceeding, done from such a motive, is absolutely incomprehensible. It could never have entered the head of Mme de Renal: it only entered the head of our anti-clerical Stendhal. As for M. de La Môle, he becomes very suddenly puritan and foolish; and Mathilde very suddenly hopeless; and Julien very suddenly distracted. They are none of them any longer recognizable. Herein is a condemnation of the author.

I believe that I see the reasons for this extraordinary weakness at the end of a story conducted up to that point with so much skill and such understanding of truth; and I believe there are two reasons for it. First, we are in 1830, and, however much Stendhal wants to be impervious, there is nobody, especially when it comes to writing a novel, who is not influenced by the fashion. Now in 1830 a novel might accord with truth as far as its ending, exclusively. In its ending at least it must be romantic—that is to say, adventurous, extraordinary and, generally speaking, tragic. . . . From 1830 to 1850 every novel had to have at least blows at the end. Another reason, more important, is to be found in Stendhal's character and the twist of his imagination, such as we know them. Stendhal is, on the one hand, a man who likes truth and knows how to distinguish it; on the other hand, he is a man who adores "energy," and we know what he means by an energetic deed. In writing *Scarlet and Black,* or, rather, in composing it in his mind, his observant instincts and his psychologist's tastes were completely satisfied, but his idolatry of "energy" was not. He saw Julien Sorel, patient, persevering, discreet, tenacious, bold when necessary; but not at all *energetic*—that is to say, giving a good stab in the Italian fashion. And he must have despaired at sight of him proceeding towards a bourgeois ending, towards success, a fine marriage and a regiment or legation. This conclusion, since up to that point the novel had been so good, was the true, almost the necessary, inevitable conclusion. But it distressed Stendhal. It was painful to him to think that his dear Julien could not kill somebody, could not do what a Lafargue had done. So as to make Julien into a Lafargue, Stendhal threw into disorder and spoiled his whole novel. He switched it completely off its proper track. So as to give Julien a chance to let off a pistol, or a pretext for doing so, Stendhal suddenly changed the characters of Mme de Renal, of Mathilde, of M. de La Môle and of Julien. The cult of energy caused Stendhal to say many stupid things and, in this case, made him do a stupid thing.

This is much to be regretted. It puts an accidental ending to a "true" novel. The two real endings to *Scarlet and Black* from which Stendhal had to choose were these: either Julien could marry Mathilde, with her father's consent, and become gradually, very quickly even, a violent aristocrat, implacably hard upon his inferiors; or Julien could marry Mathilde against the father's wishes, and drag her down into the depths, where they would both become envious, bitter, rebel "déclassés." The novel, in either case, would then have had the complete and deep significance which it lacks, or rather seems to lack, and which its actual conclusion hides and causes us to forget, instead of confirming and bringing it forcefully to our notice.

Scarlet and Black is, however, a great work, worthy to have been, like most great works, practically overlooked when it first appeared, and to have earned the attention of posterity like all works, even stupid, which are based on a big and universal truth.

The Charterhouse of Parma is a kind of counterfeit of *Scarlet and Black.* The general idea and the characters are similar; the setting and the scenery are different; but the general idea is presented with less force and the characters are, so to say, blunted and filed down, while the thoughts and descriptions are given in less relief. It is a second test for ideas that are already well worn. *Scarlet and Black* is the story of a young ambitious Frenchman of 1815, *The Charterhouse of Parma* is that of a young ambitious Italian of 1815. The young Frenchman became an enthusiast for Napoleon, and drank in the "Napoleonic spirit" by talking with a soldier of the Empire; the young Italian, son of one of the victors of Marengo, witnessed the last effort of the Empire and fought at Wa-

A portrait of Stendhal's father, Chérubin Beyle.

terloo. What happens to the one in France at the time of the Restoration is *Scarlet and Black;* what happens to the other in the Italy of the Holy Alliance is *The Charterhouse of Parma.* Both have their protectors, M. de La Môle and the minister Mosca, who are extremely like each other; both at twenty have lady friends of thirty, Mme de Renal and the Duchess Sanséverina, who at least as lovers are exactly alike; both fall in love with young women, Mlle de La Môle and Clelia Conti, who, I admit, do not resemble each other but who have one thing in common, that they are both disappointing and conventional, one as an aristocratic French beauty, the other not much better than a German sheep, for Stendhal, who did admirable portraits of the women of thirty, was not so sure of himself in those of the young women.

The basis, then, and many details are the same in these works. *The Charterhouse of Parma* is remarkable for a kind of obliteration or deadening of everything which can be felt after reading *Scarlet and Black.* Like Julien, Fabrice, after his warlike enthusiasm, determines upon an ecclesiastical career and upon following the devious ways of intrigue, thus becoming a hypocrite and a diplomat after the style of Cardinal de Retz. But, as a member of the aristocracy by birth and protected by the mistress of a minister, he does not have to make the same effort as Julien, nor to express the same feelings. In him there is no tension of the will, none of the passion of envy, hate and defiance. Hence he has no significance, or more truthfully one would say he has no character. With Julien it is the difficulties of his struggle and his remoteness from his goal, combined with his ambition, which make his character. Julien is all the time active; Fabrice is almost passive. All sorts of things happen to him; but what is interesting is what people do, not what happens to them. The greatest fault of

The Charterhouse of Parma is this extreme insignificance of the principal character and the little interest he arouses.

On the other hand, the Duchess Sanséverina is a vigorously drawn and impressive figure. She is energetic and clever, clumsy also, and imprudent at the beginning of her success, by reason of those two very feminine characteristics of too much self-confidence and hastiness. This young Agrippina does great honour to Stendhal. The trouble is that the author has right at the beginning put Fabrice too much in the lime-light as leading actor in the piece, and thus it is rather difficult for us to turn upon the Duchess the interest which we expect Fabrice to arouse and which he scarcely ever does.

Another trouble which is of little importance to most readers is that the part of the Duchess is morally of very little significance. What is the meaning of this Duchess and all her doings? That beautiful and intelligent women have an immense place in monarchic societies? Of course, this is true, but it is of no particular interest now. For us there is more attraction in such themes as the coming of the plebeian classes, their effort to succeed and the feelings which accompany this effort.

Finally, just as everything is duller, less spirited, in *Chartreuse* than in *Scarlet and Black,* so the conclusion is flatter, duller. It must be added that it is truer and better satisfies our logical instinct. In *Scarlet and Black* everybody goes mad; in *Chartreuse* everybody is resigned. The Duchess, still loving her nephew, gives up the life of intrigue and, sweet and melancholy, goes off to live in bourgeois comfort at Naples with her minister, who gives up his ambitions. Fabrice, become a Bishop, is steeped in the gloomy calm of a love-habit, a bit furtive and shameful, which is like an old man's liaison.

This ending is very interesting for the study of Stendhal, both as a novelist and as a man. We are in 1839 now and not 1830. As a man, Stendhal seems less attached to his dear "energy," to his bursts of violent and unbridled passion. As a novelist, in spite of all the picaresque or chivalrous adventures with which he has filled *Chartreuse,* Stendhal inclines more and more to realism. This ending to *Chartreuse* at least is entirely realistic. He seems to be saying to us: this enthusiasm, these big hopes, this frenzy for greatness, this Napoleonic spirit, so general after the great crisis of the European upheaval, where are they going to end in the near future? In resignation, in the tranquillity of a bourgeois life, monotonous and selfish. This story begins with the heroic escapade of the young Fabrice at Waterloo and ends with the cautious, discreet and regular adultery of Mgr Fabrice del Dongo with Mme Clelia Crescenzi. And so are the lives of all of us. We all have our escapade at Waterloo to begin with, something similar to the bishopric of Parma to continue, until we make for ourselves a "chartreuse" in solitude and silence at the end.

The Charterhouse of Parma, less powerful and deep than *Scarlet and Black,* is, however, a distinguished work in parts. It contains that admirable picture of the battle of Waterloo which has become classic as a true account, as vividly impressive and spectacular as the *Enlèvement de la Redoute;* it contains a sketch of the "Court of Parma," very living, very lively and in fine relief; and it has an ending powerful and sober and true in its melancholy. It is annoying that half the book is unreadable. All Fabrice's adventures after the murder of the comedian, and then the whole of Fabrice's stay at the citadel, bore the reader to death. In these are a very marked absence of invention and a most cruel monotony. There was nobody with less genius for writing an epic than Stendhal. Little

significant facts of a state of mind, details of habits, studies in psychology—this is where he excels. Away from these he sinks to an indifferent level. (pp. 55-66)

Stendhal was a realist. He is that essentially, in spite of his taste for "energy" and for stabbing. He did not always succeed in painting true characters, but he wanted to do so and did not always fail. He knows how to see and to observe; he can analyse. He has the essential gift for doing this; he can come out of himself and enter into the head of another, seeing something there, often very distinctly. In this respect the creator of Julien Sorel, Mme de Renal and the Duchess Sanséverina is the earliest of our realists. He is more correctly so than Balzac, who was able to observe, but rather as a visionary, and was a realist still encumbered by the clumsiest and most vulgar sort of romanticism. He is more correctly so than Mérimée, who, it is true, was almost free from romanticism, but was a realist who always had, either from timidity or some other cause, a taste for letting his observation go astray, for showing us customs always in some way rather foreign and to a certain extent incapable of assimilation by us. In *Memories of a Tourist* and *Scarlet and Black* Stendhal had the audacity, or the sincerity, or at least the originality, to present to us average French customs, average characters born of our soil and shaped by our history, at a particular date, without the violent exaggerations of a too crowded brain, without in any way discreetly changing, cleverly displacing and ingeniously ignoring the perspective. In the decline of romanticism, in the unjust but fatal disgust which followed about 1850 upon half-a-century's fashion, Stendhal appeared justly as the most anti-romantic of the whole romantic, lyric and elegiac epoch. This lingerer from another epoch became, as naturally happens in the play of literary actions and reactions, a herald, and a realist school came into being just in the nick of time to enable him to become its ancestor. Thus his impermeability was rewarded, as he had foretold, though without expecting much from it. And if to these facts you add that his ideas and irreligious tendencies, so out of place in the period in which he lived, were not at all scandalous or unacceptable to the people of the second half of the nineteenth century, who had, as a matter of fact, other reasons for enjoying them, then you will understand this phenomenon—not uncommon in literary history—of an author much more widely read, and especially much more admired, by the generation after him than by his own.

Considering him without further reference to his inclusion in or exclusion from any particular school of thought, Stendhal remains an eminent figure in the history of our literature. He represents the eighteenth century, among such as Duclos, Helvétius, Destutt de Tracy and Cabanis; a man dry of soul, intellectually bright, positivist in his turn of mind, and of a rather coarse sensuality. But he represents the eighteenth century—how shall I say?—perverted, or rather hardened, and rendered more brutal by the Revolution and the Empire. The eighteenth century, even at its dryest and most vulgar, had its little glimpses of the ideal which must never be forgotten. Positivist, sensualist, believing only in material happiness and preaching only the "search for happiness"; even so, Stendhal wanted the happiness for everyone; even so, he *dreamed on behalf of humanity;* even so, he saw before him an era of prosperity and sweet voluptuousness which he thought he was preparing for all men and which he invited the whole human race to share. Stendhal's only belief is in sensation, though he does not think that it is within everybody's reach. He is an epicurean without having the hope or nourishing the dream of universal epicurism. He seems always to say: "Seek happiness, do not seek anything else; there is scarcely anything else." In a word, he belongs to the eighteenth century but lacks its optimism. He represents an eighteenth century which has passed through a terrible period of brutality and violence, which has been hardened and saddened, and which has kept all its ideas without its dream. Hence the dryness, the hardness and the gloom of all the work of this lingering Holbach. Hence comes Julien Sorel, "who is not the equal of Valmont"—I mean who is worth even less—whose leading idea is that life on earth is a search for pleasure, and that pleasure is reserved for a small number of very strong, very energetic and very implacable egoists. The dream of the eighteenth century was *the establishment of happiness;* Stendhal's idea was *the search for happiness,* which quickly became *the struggle for happiness.* Here is what Stendhal, grandson of M. Gagnon, and creator of Julien Sorel, did: he transformed by a touch of his hand epicurean optimism into pessimistic epicurism.

From the more particular point of view of literary history we have already seen how important Stendhal is. It is quite true that he is the restorer of realism in France, and certainly if the realist school of 1850 had not existed he would have had less fame; but all the same he would have had his merits. He would have remained isolated in history, as he was, indeed, in the literary world of his time, as representative of an art which is French *par excellence*—that of examining those around him, of taking stock of them and of creating one or two characters which reproduce them faithfully, but are more compact, more alive, more striking than the originals. This was a lost art which he found again. If he had been alone in practising it, all the more would it be necessary to mark him out and honour him. But since he came before Balzac, and did it better than he—by which I mean with less power but more truth—since he came before Mérimée and as writer is infinitely superior to him—though less keen as observer—he was the restorer of a style that was to be of such importance in the century that literary history has in him not only an object for study, but one of its most important, most essential turning-points. One can dislike him; one can laugh at him. He lends himself to each of these two forms of hostility. He is unsympathetic as a man, very dry and very pretentious. He is ridiculous first for his great pretentiousness, then for his hint of ingenuousness, and, finally, for the extreme narrowness and limitation of his general ideas. But he is original, he is quite himself. He observed and saw certain things well. He is loyal, sincere and conscientious in his profession of observer. He has taste for the truthful detail, seen close at hand and faithfully reported, and he gave back to us this taste which we had lost in some extraordinary way. That shows that he was fond of truth, and for this a man is always worthy of respect and recognition. And Providence keeps a reward for those who love truth. To Stendhal she gave the gift of writing "some infinitely ingenious volumes," as Balzac said [see excerpt dated 1840], and above all, perhaps, the most solid, the fullest and the most lively novel which was published between the appearances of *Adolphe* and *Mme Bovary,* as a reward for his having thought and said "that a novel is a mirror wandering along a highroad." (pp. 67-70)

Emile Faguet, "Stendhal," in his Politicians & Moralists of the Nineteenth Century, *translated by Dorothy Galton, Ernest Benn Limited, 1928, pp. 23-70.*

JEAN CARRÈRE   (essay date 1902-04)

[*In this excerpt from an essay originally published in the* Revue hebdomadaire *sometime between 1902 and 1904, Carrère observes a ubiquitous quality of pure "wickedness" in Stendhal's work.*]

[It] is an indisputable fact that Stendhal has had, and still has, a profound influence upon later generations. Less vast and less animated than that of Balzac, perhaps inferior in talent and charm, his bold, dry work has, nevertheless, an unquestionable originality. It is impossible for us to read it without being moved in the mysterious and unexplored depths of our being. His genius goes neither high nor far, but he goes deep; and it is in the most secret recesses of our nature that he wields his narrow, yet all the more persistent, power.

And the frame of mind which Stendhal provokes is not difficult to determine. It may be summed up in a single word, a word much used nowadays, to which we should like to restore all its primitive moral vigour—wickedness.

Wickedness is, obviously, the contrary of goodness. We know fairly well what goodness is in life, and we know that the finest work of the human mind is impregnated with it. The sincere love of our neighbour, care never to hurt him, an ardent desire to assuage the sufferings of others, the pain which another's misfortune gives us, pity for the weak, indulgence for the man who falls, forgiveness of injury, the thirst for justice, enthusiasm for all that is beautiful, the communion of our heart with the whole of humanity—are not these and other sentiments what we mean by "goodness"? And is it not in these virtues that, after a hundred years of experience, we recognise the indisputable nobleness of human nature? We have at least, in proof of it, the masterpieces of the poets, from Valmîki to Tolstoi, from Orpheus to Hugo. Goodness in the *Iliad* is Achilles shedding tears with the father of his vanquished enemy; in the *Odyssey* it is the profoundly human chant in which we see Menelaus and Helena reconciled on the threshold of age; in Sophocles it is the old men of Athens receiving Antigone and Oedipus; it is Socrates in the *Phaedo;* it is the whole of Vergil with that trembling pity which extends even to the tears of things; it is Dante drawn to the very torments of his Francesca; it is Rabelais overflowing with indulgence and mercy; it is Balzac flinging into space, for all the disinherited of life, the last appeal of the divinised Séraphita; it is, from its mysterious sources lost in the mists of history to our own time, a great unbroken stream that flows on from age to age, ever broader and deeper, pouring into our eternal pain the eternal solace which Shakespeare called "the milk of human kindness."

There is one whose lips seem never to have touched this sacred milk which all great geniuses drink—Stendhal. It is impossible to imagine a man and a work in which everything conspires more surely to produce the exact opposite of goodness. (pp. 89-91)

Now, his work has, morally, an admirable and a formidable unity. Here there is no hesitation or slow development; no contradiction in the conception of the world. Stendhal is consistent from one end to the other, and the ideas he inspires are always and everywhere the opposite of all that is generous and good.

All the heroes he flung into life, "all his world," as he used to say, are unscrupulous egoists, determined to do anything whatever to procure, at any cost, an hour of pleasure or power. For them existence has no other purpose than the satisfaction of all their desires. They have no ideal except the ardour of an over-excited passion. They are, naturally, like Stendhal himself, superior beings; they are endowed even beyond measure with all the faculties of genius. Shall I say that they are handsome and seductive? More than that; they are beauty and seduction incarnate. They are fine, they are loved by women, they are envied and hated by the majority of men and served fanatically by a few. How can an obscure poor devil help but admire these magnificent creatures? Yes, let us admire them, and wish to be in their place, and be drawn into their brilliant circle.

Young Fabrizio del Dongo, the hero of the *Chartreuse de Parme,* is adorned with every shining grace. He is chivalrous, enthusiastic, courageous, bold, tender, eloquent. What does he do with so many virtues? He uses them solely in the pursuit of his passions from year to year, day to day, hour to hour. During his short career he does as much evil around him as it is physically possible to do; and he does it ingenuously, a smile upon his lips, innocent as a jaguar amongst gazelles. Then there is Count Mosca, the man of genius, the great politician. For the caprice of a woman he gambles with the kingdom confided to him; strews a few insignificant corpses here and there; robs the public treasury and betrays the State; then ends his edifying life in a peaceful retreat near Pompeii, surrounded by esteem and respect.

These are the best, the models! If, by some chance, the handsome young man was not born in a palace, and had not the love of duchesses and protection of the powerful for viaticum on his way to happiness, we have a still more magnificent hero, Stendhal's favourite hero, the beloved child of his genius, the ambitious and passionate plebeian, the wolf let loose in the social forest. We have Julien Sorel, one of the most finished types in French literature. But what a type! What gall!

The Red and the Black is Stendhal's masterpiece, perhaps the only work of his that will survive, certainly the work into which he has put his whole self, and which has most influence. In every enduring creative work the poet projects himself into his hero, and projects his hero into the reader. (pp. 92-4)

Julien Sorel is for Stendhal a powerful lens by means of which his concentrated rays burn and parch all that they touch. There is no other work so evidently desolating; and it is such by the sovereign will of its author. Sorel is the most finished incarnation of hatred; and he embodies it with so much genius that in the end he communicates the poison to us. Strange power of literary art! This envious and base creature, this hypocritical valet, this youthless calculator who begins by serving others in the hope that he will one day command, this plebeian who detests his family, despises his fellows, and hates all that is above him, this lackey dying because he cannot be an emperor, this badly emancipated slave dragging along all the rancour of the *ergastulum,* this unbridled and cunning blackguard, succeeds in the end in gaining our affection. We hang upon his fortunes, follow his adventures with beating hearts, suffer at his defeat, and weep over his death. Yes, we love him. We are with him against the whole world; or, rather, in the end it is he who lives in us.

It is because Stendhal has adorned his favourite hero with all the graces of his own mind. He has armed Sorel with his own

ruthless logic, and by this he has made him all the more disturbing and dangerous. (pp. 94-5)

How odious this Julien is; how vile and fundamentally ignoble; how we should despise him if we could examine him coolly! But can anyone examine the hero of a novel in cold blood? Can anyone escape the charm with which the author invests him? For Julien has all the luck. Instead of being punished for his hatred and pride, the author awards him what will seem to the sensitive reader the most radiant of crowns—an heroic and romantic death. After that, is it any use trying to prevent young and weak souls from admiring this particular specimen of humanity? Poets are responsible for their heroes. Stendhal's hero is, as far as my knowledge goes, the most pernicious of all, because he inspires misanthropy. (p. 95)

Listen, now, to the last monologue of Julien as he is about to die, in which he haughtily resumes his philosophic calm:

> There is no such thing as a *natural right.* The word is nothing but a piece of ancient folly. . . . There is no *right* except where there is a law forbidding us to do a certain thing under threat of punishment. Before the law nothing is *natural* except the strength of the lion and the need of the creature that is hungry, or is cold; *need,* in a word. . . . No, the people who are honoured are merely scoundrels who have had the good fortune never to have been caught red-handed. . . . Hypocrisy, or at least charlatanry, everywhere, even amongst the most virtuous and the greatest. . . . No, man cannot trust man.

Here it is man who is hated, and the hate is incurable.

What is likely to be the effect of such a theory, set in all the seduction of a captivating story, on the mind of young men? There are few who do not in their youth have their fits of misanthropy: whether it be from disappointment at his own lot or disillusion as to the glamour of the world, the man who is entering life feels the accents of anger or indignation murmuring in him. At twenty one is always more or less Alcestis. And the higher one's powers are, the more one has to suffer. In that case one sees what ravages the creation of a Julien Sorel may make in strong imaginations. One easily conceives oneself equal to him in superior merit, and so one naturally becomes like him in his pride and his unbridled ambition. How many young men of generous soul I have myself known who have been disturbed by it throughout youth, sometimes throughout life!

In this deliberate corruption of characters we have—heavy as the word may seem—a real crime on the part of Stendhal. (pp. 96-7)

In the whole of French literature Stendhal's work is the most conspicuous in having an influence that is opposed to every ideal. It is infinitely more unhealthy than that of Balzac, because it is unhealthy everywhere, always, indisputably, without the least tendency to good anywhere. Certainly Balzac created a deplorable frame of mind in fostering, by his seductive exaltation of the conquerors of life, the cult of success and of money; but, if he failed in his work, he did at least set before himself a magnificent task, and the short flights of his unfinished heroes bear witness that they wanted to rise toward the brightness of the sun.

Balzac's fault was to allow himself to be dazed by the pretentious splendour of social life, and to linger too long, with his fine men of ambition, over the material intoxications of the world. He sinned from weakness and lack of serenity. Stendhal, on the other hand, deliberately urges us to evil. He is disturbing and unhealthy of set purpose; he is so furiously; he has no other aim but that, until it becomes a sort of proud disinterestedness. He peers into the depths of our hearts for obscure instincts which we would not ourselves dare to discover. He stirs them with a fierce pleasure. He shakes them, and desperately enjoys seeing them rise to the surface. Listening to him, we are surprised and disturbed to find in ourselves things of which we were ignorant. Then, if we have a hesitating soul and a poorly tempered character, we begin to be astonished at the revelations that issue from our subconscious depths. We stand open-mouthed with vague admiration before the singular revealer, and we are ready to accept the direction which his deliberate philosophy would give us in regard to these larval instincts he reveals in us.

For the souls of men in our time it is plainly a disquieting symptom that such work should have fanatical admirers amongst us. (pp. 98-9)

Jean Carrère, "Henri Beyle (Stendhal)," in his Degeneration in the Great French Masters, *translated by Joseph McCabe, T. Fisher Unwin, Limited, 1922, pp. 87-99.*

LYTTON STRACHEY   (essay date 1914)

[*Strachey was an early twentieth-century English biographer, critic, essayist, and short story writer. He is best known for his biographies* Eminent Victorians *(1918),* Queen Victoria *(1921), and* Elizabeth and Essex: A Tragic History *(1928). Critics agree that these iconoclastic reexaminations of historical figures, in which Strachey integrated established facts, speculative psychological interpretations, and imaginative recreations of his subjects' thoughts and actions, revolutionized the course of modern biographical writing. Strachey's literary criticism is also considered incisive. In the following excerpt from an essay written in 1914, he comments on Stendhal's compressed classical style and simultaneous intensity of feeling.*]

It was as a novelist that Beyle first gained his celebrity, and it is still as a novelist—or rather as the author of *Le Rouge et Le Noir* and *La Chartreuse de Parme* (for an earlier work, *Armance,* some short stories, and some later posthumous fragments may be left out of account) that he is most widely known to-day. These two remarkable works lose none of their significance if we consider the time at which they were composed. It was in the full flood of the Romantic revival, that marvellous hour in the history of French literature when the tyranny of two centuries was shattered for ever, and a boundless wealth of inspirations, possibilities, and beauties before undreamt-of suddenly burst upon the view. It was the hour of Hugo, Vigny, Musset, Gautier, Balzac, with their new sonorities and golden cadences, their new lyric passion and dramatic stress, their new virtuosities, their new impulse towards the strange and the magnificent, their new desire for diversity and the manifold comprehension of life. But, if we turn to the contemporaneous pages of Stendhal, what do we find? We find a succession of colourless, unemphatic sentences; we find cold reasoning and exact narrative; we find polite irony and dry wit. The spirit of the eighteenth century is everywhere. . . . It is true that Beyle joined the ranks of the Romantics for a moment with a *brochure* attacking Racine at the expense of Shakespeare; but this was merely one of those contradictory changes of front which were inherent in his nature; and in reality the whole Romantic movement meant

nothing to him. . . . To him the whole apparatus of "fine writing"—the emphatic phrase, the picturesque epithet, the rounded rhythm—was anathema. The charm that such ornaments might bring was in reality only a cloak for loose thinking and feeble observation. Even the style of the eighteenth century was not quite his ideal; it was too elegant; there was an artificial neatness about the form which imposed itself upon the substance, and degraded it. No, there was only one example of the perfect style, and that was the *Code Napoléon;* for there alone everything was subordinated to the exact and complete expression of what was to be said. A statement of law can have no place for irrelevant beauties, or the vagueness of personal feeling; by its very nature, it must resemble a sheet of plate glass through which every object may be seen with absolute distinctness, in its true shape. (pp. 275-77)

This attempt to reach the exactitude and the detachment of an official document was not limited to Beyle's style; it runs through the whole tissue of his work. He wished to present life dispassionately and intellectually, and if he could have reduced his novels to a series of mathematical symbols, he would have been charmed. The contrast between his method and that of Balzac is remarkable. That wonderful art of materialisation, of the sensuous evocation of the forms, the qualities, the very stuff and substance of things, which was perhaps Balzac's greatest discovery, Beyle neither possessed nor wished to possess. Such matters were to him of the most subordinate importance, which it was no small part of the novelist's duty to keep very severely in their place. In the earlier chapters of *Le Rouge et Le Noir,* for instance, he is concerned with almost the same subject as Balzac in the opening of *Les Illusions Perdues*—the position of a young man in a provincial town, brought suddenly from the humblest surroundings into the midst of the leading society of the place through his intimate relations with a woman of refinement. But while in Balzac's pages what emerges is the concrete vision of provincial life down to the last pimple on the nose of the lowest footman, Beyle concentrates his whole attention on the personal problem, hints in a few rapid strokes at what Balzac has spent all his genius in describing, and reveals to us instead, with the precision of a surgeon at an operation, the inmost fibres of his hero's mind. In fact, Beyle's method is the classical method—the method of selection, of omission, of unification, with the object of creating a central impression of supreme reality. Zola criticises him for disregarding "le milieu." . . . Zola, with his statistical conception of art, could not understand that you could tell a story properly unless you described in detail every contingent fact. He could not see that Beyle was able, by simply using the symbol "nuit," to suggest the "milieu" at once to the reader's imagination. Everybody knows all about the night's accessories— "ses odeurs, ses voix, ses voluptés molles"; and what a relief it is to be spared, for once in a way, an elaborate expatiation upon them! And Beyle is perpetually evoking the gratitude of his readers in this way. "Comme il insiste peu!" as M. Gide exclaims. Perhaps the best test of a man's intelligence is his capacity for making a summary. Beyle knew this, and his novels are full of passages which read like nothing so much as extraordinarily able summaries of some enormous original narrative which has been lost.

It was not that he was lacking in observation, that he had no eye for detail, or no power of expressing it; on the contrary, his vision was of the sharpest, and his pen could call up pictorial images of startling vividness, when he wished. But he very rarely did wish: it was apt to involve a tiresome insistence. In his narratives he is like a brilliant talker in a sympa-thetic circle, skimming swiftly from point to point, taking for granted the intelligence of his audience, not afraid here and there to throw out a vague "etc." when the rest of the sen-tence is too obvious to state; always plain of speech, never self-assertive, and taking care above all things never to force the note. His famous description of the Battle of Waterloo in *La Chartreuse de Parme* is certainly the finest example of this side of his art. Here he produces an indelible impression by a series of light touches applied with unerring skill. Unlike Zola, unlike Tolstoi, he shows us neither the loathsomeness nor the devastation of a battlefield, but its insignificance, its irrelevant detail, its unmeaning grotesquenesses and indigni-ties, its incoherence, and its empty weariness. Remembering his own experience at Bautzen, he has made his hero—a young Italian impelled by Napoleonic enthusiasm to join the French army as a volunteer on the eve of the battle—go through the great day in such a state of vague perplexity that in the end he can never feel quite certain that he really *was* at Waterloo. He experiences a succession of trivial and un-pleasant incidents, culminating in his being hoisted off his horse by two of his comrades, in order that a general, who has had his own shot from under him, might be supplied with a mount; for the rest, he crosses and recrosses some fields, comes upon a dead body in a ditch, drinks brandy with a *vi-vandière,* gallops over a field covered with dying men, has an indefinite skirmish in a wood—and it is over. (pp. 278-81)

It is . . . in his psychological studies that the detached and intellectual nature of Beyle's method is most clearly seen. When he is describing, for instance, the development of Ju-lien Sorel's mind in *Le Rouge et Le Noir,* when he shows us the soul of the young peasant with its ignorance, its ambition, its pride, going step by step into the whirling vortex of life—then we seem to be witnessing not so much the presentment of a fiction as the unfolding of some scientific fact. The proce-dure is almost mathematical: a proposition is established, the inference is drawn, the next proposition follows, and so on until the demonstration is complete. Here the influence of the eighteenth century is very strongly marked. Beyle had drunk deeply of that fountain of syllogism and analysis that flows through the now forgotten pages of Helvétius and Condillac; he was an ardent votary of logic in its austerest form—"la lo-gique" he used to call it, dividing the syllables in a kind of awe-inspired emphasis; and he considered the ratiocinative style of Montesquieu almost as good as that of the *Code Civil.*

If this had been all, if we could sum him up simply as an acute and brilliant writer who displays the scientific and prosaic sides of the French genius in an extreme degree, Beyle's posi-tion in literature would present very little difficulty. He would take his place at once as a late—an abnormally late—product of the eighteenth century. But he was not that. In his blood there was a virus which had never tingled in the veins of Vol-taire. It was the virus of modern life—that new sensibility, that new passionateness, which Rousseau had first made known to the world, and which had won its way over Europe behind the thunder of Napoleon's artillery. Beyle had passed his youth within earshot of that mighty roar, and his inmost spirit could never lose the echo of it. It was in vain that he studied Condillac and modelled his style on the Code; in vain that he sang the praises of *la Lo-gique,* shrugged his shoulders at the Romantics, and turned the cold eye of a scientific inves-tigator upon the phenomena of life; he remained essentially a man of feeling. . . . In short, as he himself admitted, he never could resist "le Beau" in whatever form he found it. *Le*

Beau! The phrase is characteristic of the peculiar species of ingenuous sensibility which so oddly agitated this sceptical man of the world. His whole vision of life was coloured by it. His sense of values was impregnated with what he called his "espagnolisme"—his immense admiration for the noble and the high-resounding in speech or act or character—an admiration which landed him often enough in hysterics and absurdity. Yet this was the soil in which a temperament of caustic reasonableness had somehow implanted itself. The contrast is surprising, because it is so extreme. Other men have been by turns sensible and enthusiastic: but who before or since has combined the emotionalism of a schoolgirl with the cold penetration of a judge on the bench? . . . Such were the contradictions of his double nature, in which the ele-ments, instead of being mixed, came together, as it were, in layers, like superimposed strata of chalk and flint.

In his novels this cohabitation of opposites is responsible both for what is best and what is worst. When the two forces work in unison the result is sometimes of extraordinary value—a product of a kind which it would be difficult to parallel in any other author. An eye of icy gaze is turned upon the tumultu-ous secrets of passion, and the pangs of love are recorded in the language of Euclid. The image of the surgeon inevitably suggests itself—the hand with the iron nerve and the swift knife laying bare the trembling mysteries within. It is the in-tensity of Beyle's observation, joined with such an exactitude of exposition, that makes his dry pages sometimes more thrilling than the wildest tale of adventure or all the marvels of high romance. The passage in *La Chartreuse de Parme* de-scribing Count Mosca's jealousy has this quality, which ap-pears even more clearly in the chapters of *Le Rouge et Le Noir* concerning Julien Sorel and Mathilde de la Mole. Here Beyle has a subject after his own heart. The loves of the peas-ant youth and the aristocratic girl, traversed and agitated by their overweening pride, and triumphing at last rather over themselves than over each other—these things make up a gladiatorial combat of "espagnolismes," which is displayed to the reader with a supreme incisiveness. The climax is reached when Mathilde at last gives way to her passion, and throws herself into the arms of Julien, who forces himself to make no response. . . . (pp. 282-85)

[This scene] contains the concentrated essence of Beyle's ge-nius, and . . . , in its combination of high passion, intellectual intensity and dramatic force, may claim comparison with the great dialogues of Corneille. (p. 286)

At times his desire for dryness becomes a mannerism and fills whole pages with tedious and obscure argumentation. And, at other times, his sensibility gets the upper hand, throws off all control, and revels in an orgy of melodrama and "es-pagnolisme." Do what he will, he cannot keep up a consis-tently critical attitude towards the creatures of his imagina-tion: he depreciates his heroes with extreme care, but in the end they get the better of him and sweep him off his feet. When, in *La Chartreuse de Parme,* Fabrice kills a man in a duel, his first action is to rush to a looking-glass to see wheth-er his beauty has been injured by a cut in the face; and Beyle does not laugh at this; he is impressed by it. In the same book he lavishes all his art on the creation of the brilliant, worldly, sceptical Duchesse de Sanseverina, and then, not quite satis-fied, he makes her concoct and carry out the murder of the reigning Prince in order to satisfy a desire for amorous re-venge. This really makes her perfect. But the most striking example of Beyle's inability to resist the temptation of sacrificing his head to his heart is in the conclusion of *Le Rouge et Le Noir,* where Julien, to be revenged on a former mistress who defames him, deliberately goes down into the country, buys a pistol, and shoots the lady in church. Not only is Beyle entranced by the *bravura* of this senseless piece of brutality, but he destroys at a blow the whole atmosphere of impartial observation which fills the rest of the book, lavishes upon his hero the blindest admiration, and at last, at the moment of Julien's execution, even forgets himself so far as to write a sentence in the romantic style: "Jamais cette tête n'avait été aussi poétique qu'au moment où elle allait tomber." Just as Beyle, in his contrary mood, carries to an extreme the French love of logical precision, so in these rhapsodies he expresses in an exaggerated form a very different but an equally characteristic quality of his compatriots—their instinctive responsiveness to fine poses. (pp. 286-87)

Lytton Strachey, "Henri Beyle," in his Books and Characters: French & English, *Harcourt Brace Jovanovich, 1922, pp. 267-93.*

LÉON BLUM   (essay date 1914)

[*A Socialist statesman who served as premier of France during the 1930s, Blum was also a prominent literary critic. In the following excerpt from an essay that appeared in the* Revue de Paris *in 1914 and was later included in his influential* Stendhal et le Beylisme *(1947), Blum explicates Stendhal's personal system of philosophy: "Beylism."*]

The life of Stendhal testifies that his System ["Beylism"], applied to his own needs, procured him but imperfect results. Such is the usual case with theoreticians and moralists: their lives explain their theories, often inspire them, but rarely confirm them. Nonetheless Stendhal never stopped believing in the practical effectiveness of his System, and this penchant which seems fundamental to him was reinforced by the all-powerful influence exercised on his mind by the reasoners of the eighteenth century and the *idéologues* of the Empire. Montesquieu, de Tracy, and Helvétius figure, along with Shakespeare, among his youthful idols. He maintained that Helvétius was "the greatest philosopher that France has had," and when, around 1820, he recalled this opinion, he professed to believe it still. He considered as one of the cardinal events of his life his encounter with Condillac's *Logic,* about which his mathematics teacher at *l'École Centrale,* M. Dupuy, used to say to him: "Study it well, my boy; it's the basis of everything." As for Destutt de Tracy, whose book he knew by heart, he was so choked with admiration the first time he found himself in his presence that he could not speak. Faith in philosophical theories, with most people, is rarely more than an illusion or a brief infatuation of youth. Stendhal held on to this neophyte's enthusiasm all his life. Mérimée once noted that the very word *logic* was enough to fill up his mouth. "We must, in all things, be guided by *Lo-Gic,* he would say, leaving an interval between the first syllable and the rest of the word."

Like Helvétius and like Condillac, he was an empiricist, a sensualist, and a rationalist; like them, he made the senses the basis of all knowledge; like them, he believed that ideas come out of controlled and generalized sensations; like them, while limiting the role of reason to the logical classification of experience, he believed in its total power over Nature. He thus reduced the universe to a sort of mechanistic unity which could englobe states of consciousness as well as exterior phenomena

and which submits the problems of the heart to the usual rules of experimental method. If we wanted to bring in proof of this logical, in short, scientific tendency in Stendhal, we would be obliged to quote half his works. (pp. 101-02)

Thus the immediate characteristic of "Beylism" is the belief in the general applicability of the System, the implicit affirmation that it governs emotive states and the moral universe like the other phenomena of Nature, and, consequently, that the conquest of happiness operates according to the same laws as the search for truth. But this first principle, although incontestable, cannot be conceived or applied by the common herd. In order to acquire an impartial knowledge of oneself, in order resolutely to adapt one's conduct to the peculiar exigencies of one's nature, one must give proof of rarer gifts: independence of mind and strength of will. Thus the second characteristic of "Beylism" is that it relates exclusively to an elite. Stendhal writes and thinks only for "the happy few," for the small number of original personalities who dare to violate "the great principle of the epoch: be like everyone else." The sheeplike mass who are the slaves of the great law of social propriety, the flabby souls who make no distinction between happiness and tranquillity or stability, have nothing to do but turn away as quickly as possible from a teaching that is not made for them, and every page of Stendhal reiterates this warning to the unworthy reader. Despite all the differences, "Beylism" is based on a vision analogous to Nietzsche's. Certain ideas are the meat of masters and others the pasturage of slaves. The masters are those who dare to be themselves, who neither bow down nor conform, who, against all wear and tear and all compromise, preserve the impulsive vigor of their original instincts.

But Nietzsche, who places his superman sometimes in heroic action, sometimes in the monastic life of the thinker, was able to conceive of his victory in an ideal sense. Stendhal, on the contrary, confronts his elite with daily reality; he plunges them into social life, into that routine of exchanges, tedious obligations, and minor relations that the world imposes on us; that is to say, instead of imagining, like Nietzsche, a triumphant elite, he starts from a plagued and almost persecuted elite. The world does not permit of differences; originality offends it as much as rebellion, and, if it cannot really crush originality, it punishes it. In any case, the conditions of life in society are not exactly propitious to the flowering of original personalities. Young men brought up by society know how to dress themselves with tact, to relate anecdotes with finesse, to enter a café gracefully, but any idea that is not handed down to them, that is to say hackneyed, seems to them an impropriety, and any strong feeling, a lack of taste. The small number of generous souls to whom "Beylism" addresses itself must thus develop themselves, in all likelihood, outside of those elegant circles where we must suppose them placed through some fortuitous circumstance, and thus where their singularity must be doubly offensive, being that of inferiors and intruders. Even Lucien Leuwen, though the son of a banker, is disconcerting to the society of the *Chaussée d'Antin.* Similarly Octave, who is the only son of the Count de Malivert, surprises the society of the *faubourg Saint-Germain.* Since their virtue is not cut along the common measure, it is not acceptable, and is turned to ridicule. All the more so for a Julien Sorel, son of a woodcutter, who is rather the typical case! It must follow logically that preliminary efforts, according to the System, must move toward formulating some sort of defensive tactics. Before embarking upon the "quest for happiness," the elite will have to defend itself against the world, that is to say, insure its personality against the wear and tear of interaction with others, protect its sensibilities against injury from contacts, and preserve its pride against the humiliation of showing pain.

To this end, the first rule is to practice a systematic mistrust and to create a *tabula rasa* through universal doubt. It is necessary to challenge all authorities, believe only in that which one could have verified by oneself, presuppose that the friend one is listening to has some interest in deceiving, that the author one reads is a flunky paid to spread lies. The member of this elite who lives in society is beset by hostile intrigues and false conceptions; he must parry the former, and cast aside the latter by means of a permanent skepticism which he must be careful not to display: "One must be mistrustful, most men deserve it, but be very careful not to reveal one's mistrust." A fatal error, the first into which generous spirits are likely to fall, is to judge others according to ourselves and to attribute to their acts the motives which determine our own. The System can protect us against faulty judgment, the source of inevitable deceptions. Each individual must be looked upon as a distinct reality, and explained by the totality of the facts we can relate to him. The fact, the cold and naked fact, is the only basis for a knowledge of the world. "Give me lots and lots of facts," the young Stendhal had written to his sister Pauline. And like the experimentation practiced by the scientist, the observations we make on men should be free from all emotional or moral prejudices. We must look at things with a clear eye, shunning all misleading appearances; "error is in all things the obstacle to happiness." But in this battle one must be careful not to allow to the world the same advantage one has taken over it. The very veils we withdraw from others must remain tightly closed around our own inner secret. The very protective necessities which command caution also prescribe dissembling. When you write frankly and openly, the police are lying in wait; when you act or when you think, public opinion is on the lookout. Thus you must deceive the world as you would throw spies off the track; to this purpose you fill your private papers with pseudonyms, words with special meanings, and intentional contradictions; you conceal your actions under an apparent submission to the laws of society, and your emotions under the impassive air of someone "a thousand miles from the immediate emotion." We have already stated it: for the member of the elite, oppressed or threatened by a hostile world, hypocrisy is the only means of maintaining independence. Let us hide our originality and our differences from society; yield to it the concessions it demands; then, our peace once assured by this dissimulation, let us live secretly, according to our own inclinations and our own law. (pp. 102-04)

The character of count Mosca, in *La Chartreuse de Parme*, is little more than the putting into practice of these rules of conduct. Their value, according to Stendhal, must be held to be general, and whoever observes them rigorously will preserve both his freedom of action and the integrity of his personality. But it goes without saying that the details of application will depend on individual natures. In spite of common traits, the elite is composed of an infinite number of distinct types; it is up to every individual to determine precisely his own weak points, the learnings and the weaknesses which expose him most dangerously to the world, and then, once recognized, he must correct them, harden himself. For Stendhal, for example, the weak point is vanity, the fear of ridicule, the perpetual feeling of being seen. This anxiety of his is so consistent that he preserves it, as M. Faguet has observed, even

toward his readers; hence, his incessant dialogue with his "Dear reader" and the continual warnings: "I am jumping forward twenty pages here. . . . All of this development is terribly boring, etc., etc." But introspection, practiced with the very vigor of a clinical examination, has permitted a sure diagnosis. Stendhal knows the disease; he has determined the cause, which is not overweening pride or native insociability, but a hypertrophied sensibility. . . . The method which has allowed the localization and explanation of the disease shall furnish the possible remedy: turn upon vanity, convince it that it misunderstands its own interest, that this concern for the opinion of others grants too much importance to the common herd, to those fools one despises and that it is necessary to rise above them under pain of "impertinence toward oneself." When one has seen to the bottom of one's vice or weakness, a statement which touches to the quick, an appropriate argument directed at the part of the soul in question, can suffice for a cure. If the effort fails, since it is important above all "not to show oneself inferior" there is still the "System" to be turned to, in order to dissimulate one's misfortune and one's suffering. It is thus that Stendhal will dissimulate to the very end his susceptibility and his emotionalism which had proved incurable: "I have learned to hide all this under an irony which is imperceptible"—he means "impenetrable"— "to the vulgar herd."

Introspection and inward experimentation thus furnish the means to limit the effects of the outside world on our sensibilities and also those of our own natural weaknesses. Through the application of the same devices, the will, upon reflection, is able effectively to work out exercises to counter melancholy, for example, or boredom. But the method is not only a critical or defensive one; it also assumes a positive and expansive character. It allows us to direct all our actions toward their real goal, which is happiness. Along with Helvétius, La Rochefoucauld, or Bentham, Stendhal maintains that our self-interest, that is to say, our own particular notion of happiness, is the sole motive of our resolutions, and that instrumentality to happiness is the sole reason for deciding between courses of action. In his eyes happiness is not a fantastical notion or an ideal conception, but rather a tangible object which is ours to attain. Our instincts lead us to it: it suffices to enlighten them through the use of reason, and to reinforce them through the will. The System will teach us that kind of impartial clear-sightedness which will allow us to recognize the contrary forces in ourselves and to set up a battle-plan; it will persuade us that the vital force of our personality should serve the real necessities of our own happiness, and not be turned to the profit of the usual hackneyed common conceptions. When we have become fully aware of the essential demands of our personality, when we have concentrated all our active will to this end, when we have resolutely rejected the false principles of accepted morality or of religion, the false promises of society, then happiness can be logically obtained, through necessary stages, like a mathematical proof. In this proceeding, we will come up against the eternal enemy: society, but we will know how to combat it, that is to say, to deceive it. As soon as the appropriate tactics have rid us of its hold, happiness will depend on nothing other than our own lucidity and courage: it is necessary to see clearly, and to dare.

In this generally accurate, though somewhat systematized analysis, for which the *Correspondance* or the diaries of Stendhal have furnished all the elements, it is the heir of the eighteenth century whom we have discovered, the student, not of

Voltaire, whom Stendhal knew early but never liked, but of the logicians and Encyclopedists. Stendhal takes from them the conception of a life subjected to critical attention and to system, of which all the logically connected actions leading up to a concrete and tangible goal are governed by a purely human idea. But the thinkers and the novelists of the eighteenth century were extremely consistent with themselves when they formulated this mathematics of action. The final ends of human action being, according to them, purely material interests or purely sensual pleasure, their system was exactly in tune with their ethic and one could imagine that a well-defined code, a rigorous system of practical guides, could be set down for the use of the ambitious, the voluptuary, or the libertine. The deep-seated originality of "Beylism" is to have directed this strategy toward an entirely new object: happiness. It is to have proposed to passionate souls a logic that was conceived only for sterile hearts and positive ambitions. A mechanics of happiness and not of pleasure: this formula contains a profound innovation. Stendhal takes off from Condillac and Helvétius, philosophers who explain all knowledge by the senses and reduce all reality to matter; but he crowns them with a conception of happiness into which sensual and material elements no longer enter. Happiness, as Stendhal understands it, goes far beyond a mere titillation of the senses; it brings into play the profound vital forces of the soul; it implies a leap, a risk, a gift of self in which the whole personality is involved. It is independent of action and has nothing in common with good fortune or success. No external contrivance can procure it, because it is not the satisfaction of a desire. It is a blooming-forth, a moment of total forgetfulness and perfect consciousness, a spiritual ecstasy where all the mediocrity of reality is destroyed. The most intense states of love, the joy that works of art may give can furnish some idea of it; whatever is not this is nothing, and barely deserves the name of pleasure. "Beylism" is not made for those second-rate "bons vivants" who search out pleasure in a mere flattery of the senses, but for the exigent spirits who crave the combined satisfaction of the intellect, the imagination, and the will. (pp. 105-07)

Very early, in the time of his youthful admiration for Helvétius, he had already forseen the flaw of his System: "Helvétius drew with great truth for cold hearts and with even greater falsity for ardent souls." Now the ardor of the passions is the indispensable condition of happiness and marks the real distinction between men. Later, going over the memories of his beginnings in Paris and trying to find out what happy influence had preserved him from the pettiness of the milieu and "the bad taste of liking Delille," we hear him answer himself: "It was this personal doctrine founded on true, deep, and self-conscious pleasure, extending to happiness, which Shakespeare and Corneille gave me." As for the roads that had led him to that notion of happiness, by this point we have already gone over them more than once. The imagination, swollen with reading, had conceived of life as a beautiful book, had seduced the unsuspecting soul with enchanted promises, and adorned reality with all the fantastical invention of poets. This romantic habit was reinforced by "Espagnolism," that is to say, by that lofty feeling for one's inner dignity that scorns petty rewards and wishes naught for the soul but the highest objects. Abstention and renunciation are preferable to struggling for vulgar satisfactions. . . . Only happiness can make life pay, and only those intense emotions for which one would pay with his life create happiness.

Here again, it was in the eighteenth century that this passion-

ate ethic originated. This part of the code, however, connects Stendhal, not with the logicians and the materialists, but with the man who was their most avowed enemy: Rousseau. There were no ardent souls in France before "the immortal Jean-Jacques" and the Revolution. Jean-Jacques was our professor of passion, of raptured enthusiasm, and Stendhal is merely picking up his lesson. Thus Stendhal blends, in his work and in his System, the two opposing currents of the century: that which Romanticism had cut off, and that which Romanticism had drawn out and developed. Between these two tendencies—the mechanism borrowed from Helvétius and Romantic individualism after the manner of Rousseau—there is nonetheless a manifest contradiction. The scientific precision of observation and logical rigor in one's conduct may open avenues toward pleasure or success, but not toward happiness understood in this way. To be sure, "Beylism" furnishes an effectual method for tempering the soul against the world, for the protection of the sensibilities or self-esteem; we can even find in it what Stendhal himself would have refused to see—a practical handbook for success, a course in the ways of arriving. But what logical progression could lead us to a happiness which is a gift, a form of Grace, something like an ecstasy of tenderness or of dream? What link between the concerted proceedings of the intelligence or of the will, and this poetic and almost mystical transport of the heart? It is possible to provoke and to cultivate pleasure, to go through the different stages, to learn to handle it like a sensitive instrument; but no effort of will can create happiness, and no operation of the mind can dissect and analyze it. Emotion and passion constitute the most spontaneous reactions in a human being, and the ones that are the hardest to understand, and, far from being able to determine or to follow these mysterious workings, a logical system would make them forever impossible in a spirit entirely given over to it. The two tendencies that Stendhal attempts to combine are placed, in reality, at the most opposite poles of thought and of action, and when one verbally sets forth the simple formulas: "system of happiness," or "mechanics of happiness," the contradiction descends even into the words.

This contradiction, however, lies at the very heart of "Beylism"; better still, it is the essence of it, and, by bringing it to light, we feel we are touching upon and pointing out the very secret of Stendhal. One feels persisting in him this juvenile mixture of forces that life ordinarily separates before they are put into action: the early presumptions of the intellect which pretends to bring all under its sway; the youthful ambitions of the heart that wishes to experience all. By a miracle all his own, the co-existence of these refractory elements lives on in Stendhal through the bubbling turmoil of the years of apprenticeship. The demands of System did not dry up passion; nor did passion allay or discourage intellectual faith. Through the effect of a double influence and of a double revolt, it is possible to follow to the very end in his works the combination of a heart and a mind that contradict each other; of an intellect that believes in the necessity of order and the effectiveness of logic, that subjects everything to rational explanation and empirical verification; and of a sensibility that thirsts for, and values, only disinterested exaltation, free movement, and ineffable emotion. That this fundamental opposition compromises the solidity of the system is very possible; but it is the artist, not the philosopher, that we are looking for in Stendhal, and a work of art can conciliate opposites much better than dialectics. What is unique and undefinable in his charm comes from this happy fault. Like those young faces of which it might be said that life has not yet specialized their attractiveness, one finds in him hints of many things, promises of still others; he excites in the reader at the same time forces of curiosity and of sympathy that no other author has been able to concentrate. He awakens, excites, flatters, caresses everything, and—the secret of his charm—without ever satisfying. The contradiction which remains carries perfect satisfaction over into a "beyond," and his works are thus crowned by the poetic prestige of the unfinished and the elusive.

This same antinomy should furnish the key to Stendhal's characters, if it is true . . . that their creator constantly incarnated himself in his creatures. Thus can be explained the fact that their behavior conforms to the needs of a boundless sensibility, that the inward thrusts of passion bring forth, during all the intense moments of their story, an unbroken surface of reason, and that one perceives in their conduct neither design without indiscretion nor enthusiasm without design. It should also furnish the key to his opinions, if it is true, as we believe, that his opinions in everything were drawn exclusively from his personal experience. And thus can be explained that he should have counterposed on all important subjects two different opinions, one of which translates the conviction of the intellect where the other expresses the conflicting needs of the heart. The intellect, empiricist and positivist, professes the philosophy of utility and the religion of the fact. The character of Olivier in **Armance** is particularly significant in this respect, and, under the species of Olivier and of Lucien Leuwen, Stendhal seems, at moments, even to come close to Saint-Simonism. The heart, on the other hand, is repelled by the material satisfactions by which most men are contented and fooled—those petty interests which turn one away from the real life. In its distaste for anything profitable, for those large, well-cultivated tracts of land, for the kind of positive activity exemplified by the Swiss or Yankee personality, it turns back, with a nuance of regret, to the old courtly society as described by Duclos and Lauzun, whose graceful, free and easy carelessness is a form of elegance. In politics, all his thought-out convictions lead Stendhal to democracy. He held at once to the lessons of Montesquieu and of Rousseau. He was strong on the two Houses, and one remembers that Julien Sorel, in the seminary, exposed himself to the worst reprisals in order to read *Le Constitutionnel,* the liberal sheet of the times. But, while the reason recognizes democracy for the best of governments and protests against all social distinctions between men, the heart and the nerves demand those perfectly harmonious feelings that only the contact of an elite can procure. "I had, and still have the most aristocratic tastes. I would do anything for the happiness of the people, but I should prefer spending fifteen days out of each month in prison to living among shopkeepers." The same contradiction is found in his aesthetics: he held . . . that the devices of the artist constituted a definite and certain "technique," that is to say, a science; he considered the work of art as a determined phenomenon that the activity of natural laws, historic conditions, and physical temperaments controls, and this was the great innovation of his **Histoire de la peinture en Italie;** but, at the same time, creative inspiration and the ecstasy of contemplation of the Beautiful seemed to him the realization of a mystery, a pure emanation of the inner life, a sort of ineffable revelation which swells from the most secret regions of the heart. Even for the imitation of the coldest objects, the painter must have a "soul." Beauty is that which speaks to the soul, that which throws it into revery, that which transports it into "those noble distances" where it believes the happiness that reality keeps from it is to be found; and, if the notion of beauty varies through history, it is be-

cause all the generations of men have not agreed on the notion of happiness. Stendhal maintained in turn, or both at the same time, that the work of art is an almost pre-determined product, and the expression, that is to say, the spiritual life, is all of art.

The same contradiction holds in his manner of writing: purely logical when it is a question of explaining feelings or beings, purely poetic when it is a question of expressing them. This is why, when one calls Stendhal an analyst, when the analytical spirit has been seen as his *faculté maîtresse* in the sense that Taine attached to the term, the judgment is not incorrect; rather it is partial, incomplete, and only accounts for one aspect of his genius. Doubtless the material of his books was entirely furnished by introspection or inner experimentation, and he conceived this double work in the manner of the scientist who isolates the phenomenon in question, attempts to obtain it in the pure state, and then studies the variations of it under different reactions. He wished to see the heart just as it is, putting aside all the causes of error or illusion. Since he believed in the mechanical continuity of states of consciousness, since he held that the feelings just as well as the other phenomena of nature have each a sufficient reason, he schooled himself to place them in their proper order. Hence his characters' actions and emotions are always justified by their motive, and, as Paul Bourget has shown, he passes on to his characters themselves the task of justifying their conduct. Stendhal's heroes are soliloquizers. Let us note in passing that, if they carry on this perpetual discussion with themselves, it is not because they are affected by the "mania of self-dissection," it is not that Stendhal has made them "quibblers, scrutinizing their most intimate secrets, and reflecting upon themselves with the lucidity of a Maine de Biran or a Jouffroy." By a genial vision, which is the glory of his heroes and which places Stendhalian analysis high above the ordinary psychologies, Stendhal, in fact, conceived of critical self-curiosity and perspicacity as a necessary adjunct of personal scruples, of the feeling of honor. If his characters examine themselves, it is not to know themselves, but for self-control, to assure themselves, at each critical turning-point of their lives, that they are doing nothing unworthy of their own self-esteem. The problems they put to their consciences are moving, since their dignity and even their happiness are in the balance, and if they dissect themselves, it is not out of a pedantic attention or a morbid mania, but rather a kind of vital necessity. But, even in this work, Stendhal leaves voluntary gaps, which Zola has pointed up with rare perspicacity: those "analytical leaps," those "danses du personnage" which correspond to a sudden intuition, to the rapid jolt of the unforeseen. And above all—here is the essential point—he never maintained that in ordering the elements of a chapter or the motives of an action along the lines of deduction, a novelist would have exhausted all of his task.

The working out of a psychological novel involves a preliminary work, to which the name of analysis is appropriate, which consists in rounding up a certain number of facts and ideas through observation and reflection, in determining the relations between them—in a word, in establishing between the motives and the feelings of the characters the same kinds of apparent logical connections that a playwright tries to create between the events he is dealing with. This preparatory operation does not demand, strictly speaking, any properly literary talent, and does not presuppose any other faculties than those that the philosopher, the doctor, the politician, and even the businessman employ regularly in the practice of their profession. Where talent and art come in is in the putting to use, in the animation of the psychological raw materials thus assembled; and the real sign of talent, the very condition of art, is that the preliminary operation be absorbed in its result. It is no longer a question of explaining an emotion, but of communicating its quality and force; not of cataloguing the motives behind an act, but of bringing out its human signification or dramatic accent; not of listing the elements making up a character, but in making the very life and specific individuality felt. Analysis falls short of this task because to analyze means necessarily to generalize, to bring out the common principles of distinct realities. Only evocative synthesis, of which poetry is the most perfect mode, can bring us into communication with the pure emotion, with the real being, with the essential in life. Art begins with this synthesis, and Stendhal, at the same time that he is an analyst and a logician, is an artist.

Hence, he only held himself to the analytical method in stories composed for demonstrative purpose, like the one he placed at the end of the book, *De l'Amour.* Since his goal was to prove a theory by an example, to follow the development of a feeling along a predetermined route, he follows it in fact, step by step, with an explanation and a justification of the itinerary, the whole thing worked out in advance with prodigious care, and the effect being that of a prodigious aridity. This exception set aside, one feels him, once he has finished his preparation, to be searching out the wholly significant act which reveals the depth of a character, the shade of feeling that reveals the uniqueness of a being, the pointed fact or inspired word which brings to light the virgin states of the soul. Far from relying on the agency of causes and forces to express emotions, he confides to us his vexation that common language is incapable of translating them, and that it is impossible to pour the essence of life into the too rigid mold of words. In order to establish contact between his character and life, then between his character and the reader, he proceeds by shocks and jolts, by rapid and repeated suggestions. No commentary, no explanation, but on the contrary unforeseen grasps, sudden dashes which search out and find the intangible regions of feeling. Taine, who was the master of modern analysis, felt better than anyone else the purely emotive character of this manner. He even added that this virtue produces obscurity. "The reader," he said, "should be able to discover without their being explained to him, the relations and repercussions of such delicate, such strong feelings in characters so original and so great." Elsewhere he says, and admirably, relating Stendhal to Goethe, Byron, and Musset: "Each word is like a blow to the heart. The abruptness, the destructiveness, the mobility of the passions, all their turmoil, all the madness, all the oddness, all the profundities of human emotions, I feel them at once, not after study, by reflection, as when I read others, but right off, and in spite of myself." It is thanks to this search for substantial life, by this appeal to the passionate sympathy of the reader, to the feelings called forth in him, that Julien Sorel and Fabrice del Dongo have been cherished or hated like real people. Only the emotion of art can create such miracles. Moreover, did not Stendhal himself, conscious of his double nature, often feel that the invincible surges of his feelings were outweighing the perfect ordering of his logic? When he made himself re-read the Napoleonic Code each morning, was this anything other than the defense of Condillac's pupil against the sentimental excesses *à la Rousseau* into which he felt himself spontaneously drawn? "I make every possible effort to be dry. I want to impose silence on my heart which believes it has much to say.

I am forever trembling to have set down nothing more than a sigh when I think I have written a truth." Thus the logician was mistrustful of the poet, and the poet, likewise, in his moments of pure abandon, was mistrustful of logic and analysis. "Such tender feelings are spoiled if set forth in detail." That is the unfinished sentence on which the *Vie de Henry Brulard* ends, and on which one can only dream. (pp. 107-13)

*Léon Blum, "A Theoretical Outline of 'Beylism',"
translated by Richard L. Greeman, in* Stendhal: A
Collection of Critical Essays, *edited by Victor
Brombert, Prentice-Hall, Inc., 1962, pp. 101-13.*

ARTHUR SYMONS (essay date 1917)

[*Symons was an English critic, poet, dramatist, short story writer, and editor who first gained notoriety in the 1890s as an English decadent. Eventually, he established himself as one of the most important critics of the modern era. As a member of the iconoclastic generation of* fin de siècle *esthetes that included Aubrey Beardsley and Oscar Wilde, Symons wholeheartedly assumed the role of the world-weary cosmopolite and sensation hunter, composing verses in which he attempted to depict the bohemian world of the modern artist. He was also a gifted linguist whose sensitive translations from Paul Verlaine and Stéphane Mallarmé provided English poets with an introduction to the poetry of the French Symbolists. However, it was as a critic that Symons made what is considered his most important contribution to literature. His* The Symbolist Movement in Literature *(1899) provided his English contemporaries with an appropriate vocabulary with which to define their new aesthetic—one that communicated their concern with dreamlike states, imagination, and a reality that exists beyond the boundaries of the senses. In the following excerpt, Symons faults the style and characterization of* The Red and the Black.]

To Stendhal style was a kind of purgatory. He confesses the fact in his letter to Balzac. First he says: "In composing *La Chartreuse de Parme* to find the tone, I read every morning two or three pages of the Civil Code, so as to be always natural" [see excerpt dated 1840]. Then he goes on:

> I am going to seem to you a monster of pride! What, says your intimate sense, that animal there, not content with what I have done for him, an unexampled thing in this century, still wants to be praised in regard to style! One must hide nothing from one's doctor. Often have I reflected for a whole half-hour in order to place an adjective before or after its substantive. My only desire is to write with truth and with clearness all that comes to me out of my heart. I see only one rule: *to be clear.* If I am not clear, then my world is annihilated.

This is quite beautifully written; but does it explain the question of his actual style? To my mind he never, or rarely, attains that peculiarly French gift, the gift of exquisite speech, *argute loqui,* which I find equally in Rabelais as in Flaubert; equally in a stanza of Villon and in a stanza of Verlaine. (p. 296)

[Ask] yourself if Stendhal ever wove perfect rhythms into his prose. Rhythm has, if anything, more value in prose than style; not only because rhythm alone, and rhythm of a regular and recurrent kind only, distinguishes poetry from prose, but also because it is more like the flesh that covers the bones than the bones one sees only when the skin covers them. Again, a writer generally learns style as he often has to learn technique; but the sense of rhythm must be born in a great prose writer in the sense, yet in a different sense, from that of the poet. For it is no paradox to say: there is one thing prose cannot do—it cannot sing. (pp. 296-97)

I return to the question whether Stendhal has or has not a sense of rhythm. I cannot deny it; as I would be the last to say that Julien Sorel is not a creation, but that he is not a creation after the order of Balzac. Stendhal substituted the brain for the heart as the battle-place of the novel: not the brain as Balzac conceived it, a motive force of action, the mainspring of passion, the force by which a nature directs its accumulated energy; but a sterile sort of brain, set at a great distance from the heart, whose rhythm is too faint to disturb it.

For this reason one must search far and wide to find rhythms to one's liking in the prose of Stendhal. I choose for comparison what is really the crisis of *Le Rouge et le Noir:* the death-scene of Julien Sorel.

> Le mauvais air du cachot devenait insupportable à Julien. Par bonheur le jour où on annonça qu'il fallait mourir, un beau soleil réjouissait la nature, et Julien était en veine de courage. Marcher au grand air fut pour lui une sensation délicieuse comme la promenade à terre pour le navigateur qui longtemps a été à la mer. Allons, tout va bien, se dit-il, je ne manque point de courage. Jamais cette tête n'avait été aussi poètique qu'au moment où elle allait tomber. Les doux instants qu'il avait trouvés jadis dans les bois de Vergy, revenaient en foule à sa pensée et avec une extrême énergie. Tout se passa, simplement, convenablement, et de sa part sans aucune affectation.

This prose is essentially and effectively tragic; but is it entirely satisfying to one's ears as a form of exquisite rhythm? Does he touch to the quick the nerves of Julien on the last day of his life? I can but repeat what I wrote in Madrid, comparing Balzac's Valérie with Stendhal's Julien.

> But we have only to say "Valérie!" and the woman is before us. Stendhal, on the contrary, undresses Julien's soul in public with a deliberate effrontery. There is not a vein of which he does not trace the course, not a wrinkle to which he does not point. We know everything that passed through his mind, to result probably in some insignificant inaction. And at the end of the book we know as much about that particular intelligence as the anatomist knows about the body which he has dissected. But meanwhile the life has gone out of the body; and have we, after all, captured a living soul?
>
> (pp. 297-98)

Writing on Balzac in Madrid, I said: "Goriot, Valérie Marneffe, Pons, Grandet, Madame de Mortsauf even, are called up before us after the same manner as Othello or Don Quixote; their actions express them so significantly that they seem to be independent of their creator." Can one, I ask again, compare for an instant, with these characters I have named, certain of Stendhal's characters, such as Julien Sorel, Mathilde, Fabrice, even Mosca, who is said to have been made after Metternich? He writes wonderful things about them; but they are not wonderfully alive, they say no wonderful things. Are any of them absolutely visible to our vision?

Take, for instance, one of his most famous chapters in *Le Rouge et le Noir,* called "Une Heure du Matin." Notice how cold in observation, how calculated in manner, is Julien's seduction of Mathilde. The parts seem to have been interchanged; so cynical is the scene that it no more thrills us than

I imagine those strange lovers themselves were thrilled. "Il n'avait pas d'amour du tout." "Mais elle eût voulu racheter au prix d'une éternité de malheur le nécessité cruelle où elle se trouvait." Are not these tragic comedians, not quite in Meredith's sense of the words, for Lassalle had, imagined he had, passion, and Clotilde, who pretended to have it, had none? Yet, in spite of the undercurrent of sarcasm that one finds in this scene, it is redeemed, to my mind, by the cry of rage of Mathilde in the next chapter: "J'ai horreur de m'être livrée au premier venu!"

Caring, perhaps, as Stendhal thought, supremely for life, he never cared for that surprising, bewildering pantomime which life seems to be to those who watch its coloured movement, its flickering lights, its changing costumes, its powdered faces, without looking through the eyes into the hearts of the dancers. He never chose those hours of carnival when, for our allotted time, we put on masks and coloured dresses and dance a measure or two with strangers as an escape from life felt to be almost overpowering. Do we not, among ourselves, avoid the expression of a deeply-felt emotion in order that we may not intensify the emotion itself by giving it words?

These sensations and adventures being infinitely beyond his reach, he may have escaped into the crowd, to fancy that he lost sight of himself as he disappeared from the sight of others. But never can it be said of him (as I have said of a modern poet I have known) that the more he soiled himself at that gross contact, the farther would he seem to be from what beckoned to him in one vain illusion after another vain illusion, in the delicate places of the world. (pp. 300-01)

> *Arthur Symons, "Stendhal," in* The English Review, *Vol. XXV, October, 1917, pp. 294-301.*

ANATOLE FRANCE   (essay date 1921)

> [*France was a French novelist and critic of the late nineteenth and early twentieth centuries. According to contemporary literary historians, France's best work is characterized by clarity, control, irony, perceptive judgment of world affairs, and the Enlightenment traits of tolerance and justice. In the following excerpt from an essay originally published in the* Revue de Paris *and translated for* To-day *in 1921, France poses the question of whether Stendhal wrote well and offers a mixed reply.*]

There are some men of genius who, like Leibnitz, attract us more by their personality than by their works. There are others whose only interest lies in their writings; Le Sage, for example. I fancy that when we read Beyle, it is Beyle we are seeking, and that the man himself is more to us than the finest stories he ever wove. He was nevertheless an incomparable essayist and a very great novelist. His passion for the romantic, his contempt for verisimilitude, which he often sacrificed for some vague, indefinite "higher thing," are very remarkable. Beyle's method, so happily exemplified in *le Rouge et le Noir* and in *la Chartreuse,* in no sense foreshadows the style of romance which was to hold the field for the remainder of the nineteenth century. Beyle was much more nearly allied to Richardson, Jean-Jacques, Laclos, Benjamin Constant and Goethe, at all events in his desire to portray sentiment and nothing but sentiment. There is nothing in Beyle which suggests Balzac, his junior by sixteen years, but more precocious, more advanced than he, Balzac the prince of word-painters, Balzac who gives us such vivid, richly coloured pictures of men and things; nothing, either, that reminds us of Walter

Scott, who was the elder of both, of Walter Scott, with his wealth of description, whom we must certainly not forget since in those days he held dominion over every heart and every mind throughout the world.

It is well known that, though Stendhal worked out his plots with elaborate attention to detail, he never attempted to revise or correct. Are we to infer from that that he did not write well? Certainly we are not. Fénelon rarely corrected his work, and when he did, he spoilt it. Fénelon was regarded by Stendhal as the most engaging writer of the seventeenth century, and there are still many who share his opinion. Beyle, like Fénelon, held that, in style, the great thing was to be natural. We could only infer from that that he was not an artist, or at any rate, not more of an artist than Fénelon. In point of fact, everything goes to show that he was considerably less so. But there are several ways of writing, and a man may achieve conspicuous success without exercising any conscious artistry, and become a writer of high repute, after the fashion of Henri IV in his *Letters* and Saint-Simon in his *Memoirs,* without making so much as a single correction.

"Well," you ask once more, "did Beyle write well?" If I had to answer this question clearly and definitely, I should make answer that, in Beyle's day, no one wrote well; that the French language had gone to perdition and that every writer at the beginning of the nineteenth century, Chateaubriand as well as Marchangy, every writer, I repeat, wrote ill, with the solitary exception of Paul-Louis Courier, and his was a case apart. Paul-Louis Courier having noted that the French language had perished, fashioned for his own special use a medium composed of fragments culled from Amyot and La Fontaine. That is the exact opposite of what Stendhal did, and no two contemporaries could ever be less like one another.

"Yes, yes," I hear you say, "but come now, Beyle, did he write well, or did he not?"

Well, then, I say unto you, if you would find the French language, look for it in the chapters of Pantagruel, or in the essays of Montaigne, or in a page of old Amyot whose grace and charm Racine ever despaired of capturing, and you will forthwith perceive that, in the ages which followed, we shall seek in vain for a flower of such loveliness, for such inimitable elegance. Pass quickly on and search the great centuries that follow. If, then, you take as an example of good style the *Conversation du maréchal d'Hocquincourt avec le père Cannaye, le Roman comique,* Racine's *Letters sur les Imaginaires,* the *Caractères* of La Bruyère, the *Souvenirs* of Madame de Caylus, then you will say that Beyle is not a good writer. But if you compare him, as is equitable and just, with one of his contemporaries and the best among them, with the most talented and most gifted, you will say that he writes well, nay, very well indeed, and that he surpasses Chateaubriand in the clarity of his subject-matter and in the chastity of his diction. (pp. 125-29)

Anatole France, "Stendhal," in his Prefaces, Introductions and Other Uncollected Papers, *edited and translated by J. Lewis May, 1927. Reprint by Kennikat Press, 1970, pp. 101-31.*

STEFAN ZWEIG (essay date 1928)

[*An Austrian author, Zweig wrote popular biographies and novellas that were among the first to venture into the field of analytic psychology. In the following excerpt from an extended consideration of Stendhal's character, personality, and thought, he discusses the essence of Stendhal's art as the psychological exploration of his own ego.*]

[Stendhal] was forty-three when he began to write his first novel—*Le Rouge et le Noir* (for an earlier romance, **Armance,** is too slight to be taken seriously into consideration); at fifty, he wrote **Lucien Leuwen;** at fifty-four, **La Chartreuse de Parme.** Three novels are his whole literary accomplishment, three variations on one and the same original and elementary theme: the spiritual history of Henri Beyle's youth, a story the aging Beyle does not wish to see perish and must therefore continually renew. All three might bear the same title as the one adopted by Flaubert (who was born much later than Beyle, and was one of his most ardent detractors), *L'éducation sentimentale,* the education of the emotions.

The three young men—Julien, the ill-used son of a peasant, Fabrice, the pampered nobleman, and Lucien Leuwen, the son of a banker—are all born into a chill world, but they enter life with glowing hearts and immense idealism, are enthusiastic admirers of Napoleon, worship everything that is heroic and great and free. In the superabundance of their feeling, they seek a something better, a something more spiritual, a something more inspired than the actualities of life. All three bring a perplexed mind, and a pure heart filled with restrained passion, to lay at the feet of womankind; each is filled with the romanticism of youth unspotted as yet through contact with the common and calculating world of every day. Yet for each in turn comes a rude awakening, the terrible discovery that in a frozen and hostile environment the fires of the heart must be smothered, enthusiasm denied expression, the real self disguised. Their chivalrous impetus breaks against the mob mind of an epoch immersed in money-making, against the meanness and the poltroonery of "those others" (Stendhal's pet aversions!) Little by little they learn the tricks and dodges of their opponents, cleverness in intrigue, artful calculations; they become crafty, deceitful, cold men of the world. Or, worse still, they become knowing; as calculating and egotistic as Stendhal is in middle age; they become brilliant diplomatists, business geniuses, superlative bishops; in a word, they come to terms with reality and adapt themselves to their surroundings as soon as they feel that they have been thrust forth from their true spiritual world, the world of youth and genuine idealism.

In the sixth decade of his life, Henri Beyle sets himself to the writing of these novels, that he may gather the three young men around him; or, rather, that he himself may relive "sa vie à vingt ans," may passionately relive his youth, his youth when he harboured such shy, reserved, and glowing feelings within his breast, when he had such implicit faith in the world. Only when he himself has become informed, cool-headed, and disillusioned does he tell the story of his heart as a young man, does he portray the everlasting romance of the "beginning." Thus these novels unite in a wonderful manner the fundamental contrasts of his character, unite the lucidity of age with the noble perplexity of youth. Stendhal's lifelong struggle of spirit with feeling, of realism with romanticism, is at last liquidated in three unforgettable battles, each one of them as memorable as Marengo, Austerlitz, and Waterloo.

These three young men, though they experience different destinies and are of varying races and characters, are nevertheless brothers in the realm of feeling: their creator has endowed them all with his own romanticism, and has given this to them that they may develop it. There is the same tie uniting the three men into whom they grow up: Conte Mosca, Leuwen the banker, and Comte de la Môle; they are all Beyle himself, the intellectualist who has crystallized into pure spirit, the man who has become wise, out of whom every vestige of idealism has been burned by the fires of reason. These transfigurations are symbolical representations of what life makes of the young; they show us how the "exalté en tout genre se dégoute et s'éclaire peu à peu," as Henri Beyle writes of his own life. Heroic enthusiasm is dead, magical intoxication is replaced by a sad superiority of tactic and practice, and elemental passion has to yield to a cold pleasure in the game of life. The three men end by ruling the world; Conte Mosca in his principality, Leuwen on the stock exchange, Comte de la Môle in the realm of diplomacy; but they do not love the marionettes which dance to their pulling of the strings; they are full of scorn, because they know all the pitiable meannesses of their fellow mortals. They have not lost the power of appreciating beauty, have not ceased to thrill responsively to heroism; but the appreciation and the thrill remain in the realm of feeling, and can no longer be translated into action. Gladly enough would they exchange their worldly achievements for the obscure, confused yearnings of youth—which, though it has achieved nothing, can dream of achieving all. Just as Antonio Montecalino, the shrewd, dispassionate, and calculating aristocrat, contrasts with Torquato Tasso, the young and ardent poet, so do these men of maturer years, for whom daily life has become a matter of plain prose, contrast with the young men they themselves once were. Maturity contemplates youth with mixed feelings: would fain be helpful, and is none the less hostile; is somewhat contemptuous, and yet is moved to envy. It is the old antithesis between brain and heart, between the waking man and the dreamer.

Stendhal's universe oscillates between these two poles of human destiny, between the boy's vague yearning after beauty and the man's positive will-to-power, a will touched with irony. It is between the vicissitudes of manhood, between age and youth, between maturity and romanticism, that the surging current of feeling finds vent. Women confront these striplings, who though shy are burning with desire; women, by the music of their goodness, assuage the torment of unfulfilled craving. They provide a pure and glowing outlet for youthful passion, these women of Stendhal's, noble in character one and all, Madame de Rênal, Madame de Chasteller, La Duchessa di Sanseverina. But not even this hallowed surrender can preserve the young men's pristine purity of soul, for at every step forward into life they plunge deeper into the morass of human baseness. Here again we have a contrast. These heroic and aspiring women, capable of providing the spirit of youth with wings, are contraposed to the commonplace world of reality and of practical life, to the cunning and crafty brood of petty intrigues and placehunters, to mankind as Stendhal sees it through the spectacles of his contempt. In retrospect he contemplates these women with the eyes of his youth, and glorifies them, for even as an elderly man he is still in love with love; taking them gently by the hand, he leads these adorable idols forth from the most secret haven of his heart, and presents them to his heroes. At the same time, with all the vigour of his pent-up wrath, he thrusts the baser wretches down into the shambles. Out of offal and fire he creates his judges, his lawyers, his pettifogging ministers, his parade-ground officers, his chatterers of the salons; and all these creatures, sticky and malleable as mud, all these nullities, increase and multiply till they become the great majority of mankind, and succeed (as is ever the way on earth) in crushing the sublime. Throughout Stendhal's works, the tragical melancholy of an incurable enthusiast goes hand in hand with the keen-bladed irony of a disillusioned man. In his novels Stendhal depicts the world of reality with a hatred no less strong than the glowing passion with which he paints the world of his fancy; he is as great a master in the one field as in the other; he belongs to two worlds and is equally at home in either, whether it be the world of the intellect or that of the feelings.

Stendhal's novels probably owe a good deal of their charm and distinction to the fact that they are the product of a man in his maturity, a man whose memories are still fresh and whose survey of events has been well pondered before setting it to paper, whose writing is youthful in sentiment and impregnated with a wise deliberation as far as the thoughts are concerned. Distance alone is capable of imparting a creative interpretation to the meaning and the beauty of each passion. Does not Stendhal himself write: "Un homme dans les transports de la passion ne distingue pas les nuances"; a man cannot know the origin or the limits of his sensations? He may be able to voice his ecstasy in lyrical and hymnal form, sending it forth into limitless space; but he cannot, in the moment of passion, explain the ecstatic rapture and give it epic expression. Analysis demands clearness of vision, cool blood, alert understanding, a position which is above the passionate; it needs a certain lapse of time since the event, and a steady pulse so that the hand of the sculptor may not tremble. In his novels, Stendhal displays to a supreme degree all these requisites, both internal and external. He, the artist arrived at the boundary line which separates the rise from the fall in a man's life, consciously and knowledgeably portrays the world of the feelings; he recaptures the emotions of the past, understands them, and is able to bring them into the daylight, to express them while keeping them within due bounds. Stendhal's greatest delight, the impulse which urges him to the task of writing these novels, is the opportunity it affords him to contemplate this inner world of his revived emotions.

The outward husk, the technique of novel-writing, is of little importance to our artist; he improvises as he goes along. Indeed, having come to the end of a chapter, he has no idea what is to happen in the following. The episodes are not always compatible with the characters, and Goethe, who was one of the first to read Stendhal with appreciation, did not fail to point this out. In a word, the melodramatic side of the stories could have been concocted by Mr. Anybody. Stendhal is a genuine literary creator only in the passionate moments experienced by his heroes. His writings have artistic worth and vitality only insofar as they depict the inner currents of life. They are at their most beautiful where one feels that the author has spiritually participated; they are incomparable where Stendhal's own shy and reticent soul is allowed to speak through the words and deeds of his favourites, where he allows his characters to suffer on account of the cleavage within his own nature. The description of the battle of Waterloo in the *Chartreuse de Parme* is a masterly résumé of the years he spent in Italy as a youth. Just as Stendhal himself had been drawn to Italy, so his Julien is attracted to Napoleon, hoping to find upon the battlefields that spirit of heroism which he feels to be astir within his own soul. But the rude hand of reality tears the veils from his idealistic concept. Instead of clashing cavalry charges he experiences the senseless confusion of modern warfare; instead of the Grande Armée, he finds a rout of men fleeing before the foe; instead of heroes, he encounters cynical soldiers, as mediocre and second-rate in their fine uniforms as dozens of other men in drab coats. These disillusionments are limned with marvellous insight. No other artist has succeeded in depicting with such intimacy of touch the way in which the ecstasy of the soul is again and again bruised upon the rock of hard reality, until at length, too weary to rise, it resigns itself to its defeat. Stendhal's psychological genius triumphs precisely in those moments when the senses and the brain generate electric sparks through contact one with another, and when the two opposites in his disposition meet. He excels himself as an artist only when he makes his characters experience what he himself has experienced, and his portrayals are complete only when he is in perfect spiritual accord with his creations. His art, too, therefore, is autobiographical, and discloses the most intimate secrets of his personal life. "Quand il était sans émotion, il était sans esprit."

Yet strangely enough it is this quality of sympathetic understanding which Stendhal is at most pains to conceal. He is ashamed lest some casual reader shall detect how much of himself has gone to the making of Julien, Lucien, and Fabrice. No one must ever guess that his soul has been breathed into these imaginary beings. Stendhal, therefore, adopts the style of the dispassionate chronicler, of the police-court recorder: "Je fais tous les efforts pour être sec." He would have been nearer the truth had he written: "pour paraître sec." One must indeed be dull of perception not to detect behind this "dryness" the emotional participation of the author. Stendhal, so full of passion, is never cold in his writing. In truth he is an impassioned novelist, if ever a novelist was impassioned. But his passion is deliberately kept out of sight. Just as in daily life he is desperately concerned lest he shall "laisser deviner ses sentiments," so in his writings he tries to conceal his emotion beneath a veil of assumed impassivity. He refuses to wear his heart upon his sleeve, for nothing is more distasteful to him than the public display of emotion; his sense of spiritual discretion makes him shrink away in disgust from the man who tells his story in a voice choked with tears; he loathes the guttural "ton déclamatoire" of a Chateaubriand, who transfers the bombastic mouthings of the boards into the realm of literature. Better by far to appear hard than "larmoyant," better be lacking in art than become pathetic, better be logical rather than lyrical!

Stendhal therefore chews his every word to exhaustion before he spits it out into the world, and in order to acquire the style of his desire he assiduously cons the bourgeois code ere he sets himself to work in the morning. Nevertheless, dryness is far from being Stendhal's ideal. With his "amour exagéré de la logique," he aims at making his style as inconspicuous as possible so as not to obscure the vividness of his picture: "Le style doit être comme un vernis transparent: il ne doit pas altérer les couleurs ou les faits et pensées sur lesquels il est placé" The mere words are not to obtrude themselves upon our notice by assuming the lyrical form, the colorature, the "fiorituri" of Italian opera. On the contrary, the words must play second fiddle to the events and thoughts, or, to change the metaphor, they must, like a well-tailored suit, fit the situation so becomingly that they are forgotten, and only the spiritual movements they clothe find palpable expression. Clarity is Stendhal's chief aim. His Gallic instinct for lucidity makes him abhor everything which savours of muddleheadedness, of sentimentality, of pomposity, of turgescence: above all he dislikes that succulent sentimentalism which Rousseau introduced into French literature. Stendhal wants precision and

Stendhal around the age of nineteen.

truth to be part of every feeling, even the most confused; he wants clarity to penetrate into the labyrinthine ways of the heart. "Ecrire" spells for him "anatomiser," that is to say the dissection of every sensation into its component parts, the measurement of heat in degrees, the examination of the emotions with clinical accuracy as though they were an illness. In art, as in life, the only thing which bears no fruit is vagueness, confusion of thought. One who befuddles himself with emotion sinks into the quagmire of his own feelings. While he is sleeping off the fumes of intoxication, he misses the highest, the most spiritual form of enjoyment: consciousness of enjoyment. But he who plumbs his own depths with clearness of vision is able to relish these same depths, to contemplate them with manly and genuine appreciation. While realizing the confusion of his feelings he can simultaneously recognize their beauty. Thus Stendhal is fond of putting into practice the old Persian precept which tells us to ponder with the waking mind that which the ecstatic heart betrays in moments of passionate exaltation. He is at once the most blissful servant of the soul, and yet, by his clear-cut logic, he remains master of his emotions.

To know his own heart; by understanding, to enhance the mystery of the emotions because one has fathomed them— such is Stendhal's formula. The children of his fancy, his heroes, feel just as he feels. They, too, have no wish to be fooled, to be swept off their feet by emotion, but would fain keep watch over their feelings, hearken to them, plumb them, analyze them; they want to understand their emotions as well as to feel them. No phase, no mutation, is allowed to escape their vigilance; they test themselves to see whether their emotions are genuine or false, whether some other, still deeper feeling does not lie concealed behind. They are statisticians of their own hearts, alert and unsentimental observers of their own sentiments. They are continually asking themselves: "Do I love her already? Do I still love her? What did I feel then and why don't I feel the same now? Is my affection genuine or is it feigned? Am I merely play-acting where she is concerned?" They keep their fingers upon the pulse of their emotions and are instantly aware when excitement quickens the beat. Their self-scrutiny mercilessly confronts their self-surrender; with the precision of an insensate machine they reckon up the expenditure of feeling. In the very moment of rapturous fulfilment they pause to consider; "pensait-il" and "disait-il à soi-même," constantly crop up to impede the restless movement of the story. Every stretch of the muscles, every twitch of the nerves, is commented upon with the accuracy of a physicist or a physiologist. These peculiarities endow them all with the typical Stendhalian cleavage of character: they enthusiastically calculate their sensations, and with cool deliberation they make up their minds to experience an emotion just as if it were a business affair.

As an example I will cite the well known love scene in *Rouge et Noir.* Here, in the very moment of ecstasy, when the maiden he loves is about to give herself to him, Julien remains fully intellectualized, painfully wide-awake. He is risking his life in order, at one o'clock at night, to visit Mademoiselle de la Môle. To reach her, he has had to place a ladder near the open window of her mother's bedroom. Surely passion, the spirit of romance, should be supreme? But the critical intelligence is still dominant! "Julien was much perplexed, he was at a loss what to do, he felt not the smallest particle of love. In his bewilderment he thought it incumbent upon him to be bold, and he therefore made to embrace her. 'Fie!' said she, thrusting him away. Her repulse pleased him immensely. He hastened to cast a glance around the room." Thus intellectually conscious, thus cool and deliberate in thought, are Stendhal's heroes even at the height of their most daring adventures. Let us follow the scene to its close; let us see how, after all the reflections and meditations in the midst of the lovers' excitement, the young maid gives herself to her father's secretary. "Mathilde found it hard to address him with the familiar 'thou,' and, when she did, the word lacked tenderness and therefore gave Julien no pleasure. He was amazed to find that he had as yet no sensation of happiness. In order that he might experience this emotion he took refuge in deliberation, reminding himself that he was in the good grace of a young girl who was, in general, chary of her praise. The reflection brought him happiness, for it gratified his vanity." What are her thoughts meanwhile? "I must talk to him. One is supposed to talk to a lover." To paraphrase Gloster, did ever man and woman woo one another in such a vein? What other writer has ventured to allow his characters to control themselves, to calculate their actions with such composure, in circumstances of high tension? And Stendhal's characters are by no means persons of a fishy disposition!

Here we approach the innermost technique of his psychological exposition, a technique which smothers the fires and disintegrates feeling into its impulses. Stendhal never contemplates an emotion as an entity, but always as a compost of innumerable details; he examines its crystallizations under a lens. That which in the realm of reality takes place suddenly, in one spasmodic movement, is divided by his analytical mind into infinitesimal molecules of time; he shows us a slow-motion picture of the psychical actions, and thus permits us to comprehend them with greater intellectual accuracy. The events in Stendhal's novels take place almost entirely upon the psychical plane, and not in the earthly realm of time and space; they occur, not so much in the lists of objective reality, as in the tumultuous region of the nerves that interconnect heart and brain. Art for the first time is used as an instrument for the elucidation of unconscious functional action. *Le Rouge et le Noir* begins the series of the "roman expérimental," which is later to bring the science of psychology so closely into contact with imaginative writing. We are not surprised to find that Stendhal's contemporaries did not regard this newfangled art as art at all. On the contrary, they looked upon it as antipoetical, as a grossly mechanical and materialistic probing of the soul. Balzac, for instance, had something like a monomania for the study of the impulses, but he regarded them as unified, as integral. Stendhal, on the other hand, put them under the microscope, that he might examine the tiny germs, the true exciters of the strange disease known as love. Doubtless such elaborate methods impede the vehement course of the action, and many passages in Stendhal's works savour of laboratory sobriety, of the dispassionateness of the schoolroom. Nevertheless, Stendhal's furor artisticus is quite as creative as is Balzac's, though the former casts his into a logical mould, fanatically seeking after clarity, and displaying a determination to attain clairvoyance of the soul. His depiction of the world is no more than a medium for the comprehension of the soul; his portrayal of men is merely a preliminary essay for his portrait of himself. Stendhal, the arch-egoist, dispenses passion only that it may return to himself in a stronger and wiser form; he seeks to know mankind in order the better to know himself. "Art for art's sake," the objective delight in presentation, the discovery and the creation of personages for the sheer pleasure in the doing, was neither known to nor practised by Stendhal. Such were his limitations! This master of spiritual autoeroticism, this most self-absorbed of artists, was never able to merge himself wholeheartedly into the world-all, to throw wide his arms and exclaim: "Come, soul of the universe, and penetrate my being through and through." He was incapable of any such ecstatic self-abnegation. In spite of his amazing artistic penetration he was never, not in one single instance, able to understand the art of another man of letters when such an author drew his inspiration, not from the purely human, but from the primal sources of the cosmos—from chaos. The titanic, any cosmic emotion, any thought of being merged with the universe—these were terrifying to Stendhal. Rembrandt, Beethoven, Goethe, beauty that was stormy or belonged to the sombre realms of thought, these things were a closed book to him. His crystal-clear intelligence could apprehend beauty only when it presented itself in the Apollonian art, the luminous serenity of a Mozart and a Cimarosa, whose melodies are clear as spring water; or of a Rafael and a Guido Reni whose pictures are so engagingly simple and easy to understand. The mystery and suffering of the world, Dionysian art, mighty, strenuous, violently destructive, driven onward by daimonic forces, such art was beyond his ken. Nothing in the vast universe held his interest save the human factor; and that human factor consisted, in the last resort, of the microcosm called Stendhal.

To fathom this one entity he became a man of letters; he created characters in order to portray himself. Although genius made him a supreme artist, Stendhal never served art; he made use of art as a delicate and responsive instrument whereby he could measure the rapturous flight of the spirit and express this flight in the music of his prose. Art was never a goal for him, it was always a road leading to his one and only goal: the discovery of his ego, the joy of self-knowledge. (pp. 159-72)

Stefan Zweig, "Stendhal: The Artist," in his Master Builders, an Attempt at the Typology of the Spirit: Adepts in Self-Portraiture, Casanova, Stendhal, Tolstoy, Vol. 3, *translated by Eden Paul and Cedar Paul, 1928. Reprint by Cassell and Company Limited, 1952, pp. 154-72.*

CECIL ROBERTS   (essay date 1929)

[*Roberts records his pained disappointment with* Armance.]

The reader who discovers Stendhal through the pages of *Armance* will find himself wondering whether the distinguished admirers of this author have taken leave of their senses. The publication of this book is a witness of the severe penalties that afflict fame. With the *Charterhouse of Parma* Stendhal took rank among the masters, with *Armance* he steps down among the amateurs, for a more puerile story surely never got into a reprint. . . .

Henri Beyle, to give him his proper name, would probably be the first to suppress *Armance* if it were possible. He would rest content that Tolstoy had praised *The Charterhouse of Parma* and Mr. Compton Mackenzie had confessed to reading it nine times. It is probable that the reader of *Armance* will consider one reading is one too many. . . . One is shocked to find that, chronologically, it comes five years after *On Love* and twelve years before *The Charterhouse of Parma.* This bewildering piece of amateurism between two peaks of genius destroys any hope that it was an apprentice work, or the expiring cry of an emptied mind. . . .

The story is so slight that neither reader nor writer can take the slightest notice of it, but even the flimsiest, hackneyed material may shine with the light of genius irradiating its worn threads, although there is not a single moment of intuitive felicity. The whole ridiculous parade through the drawing-rooms of duchesses and relatives drags on, with chit-chat and fopperies of thought and conduct that fail to cover the poverty of thought and weakness of design.

Can this be Stendhal? one asks again and again. Could the pen that massed the marvels of *The Charterhouse of Parma* waver over such platitudinous passages? Or having wavered, could any writer with the slightest self-criticism allow such poor stuff to escape into print? . . .

[In] sorrow for Stendahl . . . , one passes this book in pained if surprised silence. One refuses to measure a man by his worst, especially such a man as Stendhal.

Cecil Roberts, "Stendhal," in The Bookman, *London, Vol. LXXVI, No. 452, May, 1929, p. 123.*

JOSEPH WOOD KRUTCH   (essay date 1930)

[*Krutch was one of America's most respected literary and drama critics. Noteworthy among his works are* The American Drama since 1918 *(1939), in which he analyzed the most important dramas of the 1920s and 1930s, and "Modernism" in* Modern Drama *(1953), in which he stressed the need for twentieth-century playwrights to infuse their works with traditional humanistic values. Here, Krutch relates Stendhal's heroes to*

their author, arguing that the protagonists of the novels are all projections of Beylism.]

Always the desire to be great in some respect had been with Stendhal more definite and more constant than the desire for greatness of any particular kind. He had abandoned one career after another and he had put off until his youth was past even those literary efforts which, since childhood, he had planned to make. He had been a soldier, business man, diplomat and lover without finding satisfaction in any capacity. His whole life had been a search for a role which he could play whole-heartedly. And now when he came to write novels he began to multiply his personalities—to give himself a multiplicity of lives with which to experiment—not only because the pleasure of watching himself live was the only one he had ever had, but also because in novels he could set according to his own will the conditions of the game. In life, unfortunately, these conditions had been set for him. (p. 234)

Of these *alter egos* who lived for him, Julien Sorel, hero of *The Red and the Black,* may be taken as typical and in him may be discovered Stendhal's dream of himself. Julien is of humble birth, son of a coarse-grained father whom he hates and, because of humiliations, fired with a double ambition—to succeed and to be loved. The external circumstances of his life are quite different from those of his creator but his character and his methods are the same. Like Stendhal he formulates a Machiavellian plan (in which conscious hypocrisy plays a large part) for the cultivation of his personality, and like Stendhal he is not wholly aware of the incompatibility between the ideals of the Saint Preux and the Don Juan. His character is purged of all that Stendhal recognized as potentially ridiculous in himself and his schemes are made more successful than Stendhal was ever able to make his own, but he remains essentially an *alter ego,* merely more perfectly Stendhalian than Stendhal himself.

And what may be said of Julien Sorel may, in general, be said also of the heroes of *The Charter House of Parma* and *Lucien Leuwen.* Both the settings and all the circumstances under which the characters make their *débuts* are varied, but the central figure is in each case the same romantic egotist seeking the same satisfactions through the same means. Stendhal did not care how completely the accident of birth varied the details of the problem to be solved—probably indeed he preferred to set it each time anew—and he even consented to give Lucien Leuwen an admirable father, but the problem must be always the same—how a young man, at once romantic and clear-sighted, may go about to win a knowledge of the human heart and through that knowledge achieve the kind of success which consists in the realization of self.

Moreover, his heroes are, again like himself, victims of a not wholly comprehended bitterness. They feel themselves invested with a certain right to move in a moral universe beyond good and evil, because something—unusual sensibilities and unusual, hardly defined, wrongs—sets them apart. The world is their oyster and they will open it ruthlessly, yet the pearl which they are always hoping to find is a delicate jewel—some great love or the opportunity for some dazzling ultimate heroism. And so it is that they too go about dishonourably in search of honour, and attempt to attain an ideal love by seducing and abandoning the wives or daughters of those who befriend them. Aristocratically disdainful of the vulgar, they are nevertheless champions of the people against their oppressor and this paradox is related to all the others. For at bottom their perversities are masquerading as the protests of a man who finds the world not good enough for him. Just as Stendhal himself felt relieved of any loyalty to the aims of Napoleon because the soldiers of Napoleon did not fulfil his idea of what military chivalry demanded, so his heroes abandon their mistresses because the latter are not quite worthy, and act the hypocrite because the world is too low to deserve honest treatment.

Thus whether "Beylism" be studied in the person of its creator or in that of one of his characters, it is not, as he supposed, a logical philosophy of life, but rather a complex of ideas, desires and quasi-ethical principles which attain such unity as they have, not because of any necessary relation of one to another, but because they found themselves together in the personality of Stendhal and were by him transferred to his characters. To be a Beylist one must believe (1) in romantic love, (2) in the cult of the ego, (3) in the morality of the superman, (4) in military glory and (5) in political liberalism. One need not act always in the direction which all of these beliefs would seem to recommend. The egotist may momentarily be lost in the lover; the cult of self and the morality of the superman may interfere with the lover of political justice. But one must at different times be aware of all these impulses and one must think of them not as essentially contradictory but as somehow fusible into a philosophy never quite grasped. (pp. 235-37)

Now in the case of Stendhal himself the psychological determinants in this *mélange* of warring elements are clearer than they ever are in the case of the characters to whom he transfers them. His own mental life may be explained in terms of a reaction to his earlier experiences, as an effort to divest himself of the fixations of his childhood and, while purging his hatreds away, to salve his wounds with the triumphal successes imagined during the period of his intensest humiliations. The death of the too well beloved mother had burdened him with a romantic longing which no actual person could satisfy, and the hatred of his father had generated in him that fixed delusion of persecution which seemed to justify an amoral struggle against an inimical world. Sheer negativism had made him a Jacobin in the midst of a conservative family, but he had, nevertheless, all those feelings of aristocratic superiority which are commonly cherished by morbidly sensitive souls who compensate by imagining themselves endowed with some capacity or some fineness of feeling belonging exclusively to those whom Stendhal loved to call "the happy few."

But however clear the psychology of Beylism may be when it is thought of as an attribute of Henri Beyle, it is less so when it is thought of in connection with the characters of his novels considered as persons entirely separate from him, and it is less clear for the simple reason that though Stendhal attributes to them all that he recognized as significant in himself he could not, because he himself did not thoroughly understand, explain their personalities on the basis of the factors which determined his own. Hence they appear as Beylists without having gone through the experiences which, in the case of its creator, generated that philosophy.

When a novelist draws his material, as Stendhal did, from himself, when he creates characters in his own image in order to put them through adventures emotionally satisfying to himself, he must, before his novels attain the full validity of art, detach them from their psychological origins and make them something capable of an existence independent of himself and of the purely individual needs they were created to

fulfil. So long as their interest or their significance is understandable only in relation to the author, they are documents (perhaps highly interesting ones) for the study of his personality, but they are not in any complete sense works of art and it must be confessed that the novels of Stendhal are, in this respect, inferior to those of other masters no more renowned than he. Nor is it merely that the virtue of the heroes (exaggerated by way of compensation for Stendhal's own bungling efforts) is often too remarkable for the taste of the reader. The fact is that the novels are too perfectly fitted to gratify the emotional needs of their creator to be wholly satisfying to anybody else and that the secret of the personality of the characters can never be unlocked with any key furnished by the works in which they are found. The key is Stendhal himself.

And yet, though these novels may not be wholly satisfactory as art, they have exercised a fascination over many minds and an influence upon novel writing which may be attributed in part to the interest of the man who half reveals himself in them and in part to the fact that, whether through accident or not, they furnish a sort of bridge between the romantic literature of his epoch and the psychological realism that was to follow. Perhaps a nature as unstable and chaotic as his, is not likely to produce perfect art, but its restless, rebellious eccentricity is very likely, on the other hand, to throw off hints and to discover new modes of sensibility. It is in minds like his that intellectual or emotional "sports" destined to play important roles take their rise, and so it was in his case. In the very heart of romanticism something antiromantic was born.

As to the romantic elements they are so obvious that it is hardly worth while to insist upon them. Not only is his tendency to revolve around the ideas of Love and Glory typically romantic but so too is that whole conception of the "storminess" of the superior character. And yet the ideal of analysis tends to replace that of ecstasy so that Beylism differs from, let us say, the philosophy of Rousseau by the presence of a certain cynical dryness, by the abstraction of all that is genuinely transcendental and the introduction of utilitarian principles which lead him to consider even the pleasures of romantic love as the result of an agreeable delusion—which a rational man may permit himself to use as he uses alcohol—rather than as a mysterious gift of God. (pp. 238-40)

And however inharmonious or unstable the particular combination of discordant elements which Stendhal called Beylism may be, his variations from the romantic were variations in the direction in which the temper of Europe was moving. Not only is there present in him that conflict between rationalism and romantic sensibility which was to destroy the latter but there is also clearly foreshadowed that moral nihilism into which the nineteenth century was unwillingly driven. His heroes were very imperfect supermen struggling desperately against their romantic impulse in the effort to achieve a Nietzschean morality and coming near enough to it to make Nietzsche one of the most enthusiastic of Stendhal's admirers [see excerpt dated 1886]. The experiences of the latter's infancy plus the literature upon which he nourished his morbid sensibilities fixed certain romantic conceptions indelibly upon him, but if one can imagine him with certain of the delusions to which he recurrently fell victim stripped away, he would be very nearly a contemporary man looking at the contemporary man's bleak world and wondering what may be found to take the place of all that we have outgrown.

In the course of some very brief remarks upon the novels of Stendhal, Croce let fall the phrase "unconscious irony," and it is, perhaps, the most pregnant one ever applied in an effort to describe these works. No writer since Stendhal has ever succeeded in completely resolving the conflicts which form the moral substance of his fiction. Romantic love persists in spite of all possible disillusion with it and the typical contemporary hero is one who, like Julien Sorel, gropes his way toward new standards and new ethics while he is still emotionally controlled by the world in which he half believes. But man, more and more convinced of his littleness, is more and more inclined to regard his predicament with bitter irony. The last delusion of grandeur gone, he is haunted by the suspicion that the play in which he is the protagonist is not tragedy but farce and so he finds in the heroes of Stendhal who still trail the remnants of the romantic robes an unconscious irony which the author never makes explicit because he never, except in flashes, perceived it. (pp. 241-42)

To say that *The Life of Henri Brulard* is Stendhal's best book, that the posterity to whom its author looked must find its direct revelations more completely satisfying than any of his imaginative treatments of his ego, is, of course, to say that in a measure he failed as a novelist. Yet the fact is hardly to be doubted. The reality which emerges from the pages of *Brulard* is more continuously fascinating than any fantasies he was able to create, the man more intriguing than any of the roles he allowed himself in imagination to play. He had never quite succeeded in transforming the personal into the universal, and while the amoral heroics of his characters seemed shocking to his contemporaries, they sometimes strike us as a little theatrical and forced. But *Henri Brulard* takes its place with the great confessions; it is a book as searching and honest as any a troubled man ever succeeded in writing about himself. (pp. 247-48)

Joseph Wood Krutch, "Stendhal," in his Five Masters: A Study in the Mutations of the Novel, *Jonathan Cape & Harrison Smith, 1930, pp. 175-249.*

PAUL VALÉRY   (essay date 1930)

[*Valéry was a prominent French poet whose work demonstrates the concern with artistic form characteristic of late nineteenth-century Symbolist aestheticism. Because Valéry desired to have total control over his literary creations from their conception through their composition, he directed his powers of analysis to the creative process itself. This fascination with the creative act is the impetus for much of his poetry and the subject of much of his prose. Valéry endorsed Edgar Allan Poe's dictum that a poet should create solely from his powers of concentration and intellect, rather than depending upon random inspiration. From this ideal, Valéry developed a theory that holds that literary composition, like science and mathematics, is valuable only as a mirror to the workings of the creative mind. In the following excerpt from an essay first published in* Variété II *in 1930, Valéry describes his reactions upon first reading* Lucien Leuwen *and sums up Stendhal's importance as "one of the demigods of our Letters."*]

[Until I read *Lucien Leuwen*], I had read nothing on love which did not bore me exceedingly and appear absurd or worthless. I placed love so high and so low in my youth that I found nothing strong enough or true enough or harsh enough or tender enough in the most illustrious works. But

in *Leuwen,* the extraordinarily delicate drawing of *Madame de Chasteller's* portrait, the noble and profound character of the hero's sentiment, the progress of an attachment which becomes all-powerful in a sort of silence; and the consummate art of holding it in, of keeping it uncertain of itself—all this captivated me and led me to re-read the book. Perhaps I had my reasons for being somewhat intimately touched by these indefinable qualities. Moreover, I was astonished to be touched; for I did not suffer, and I scarcely suffer now, from being beguiled by a written work to a point where I no longer clearly distinguish my own affections from those communicated to me by an author's craftsmanship. I see the pen and him who holds it. I care little for his emotions, I have no need of them. I ask him only to instruct me as to his means. But *Lucien Leuwen* performed in me the miracle of a confusion which I loathe.

As to the picture of provincial, Parisian, military, political, parliamentary and electoral life, and the charming caricature of the first years of the reign of Louis-Philippe, vivid and brilliant comedy, sometimes light comedy—as the *Chartreuse de Parme* sometimes suggests operetta—it provided me entertainment sparkling with traits of character and ideas. (pp. 102-04)

For me, Henri Beyle is a type of intelligence much more than he is a man of letters. He is too peculiarly himself to be reduced to a writer. It is in this that he pleases and displeases others, and pleases me.

I have seen Pierre Louÿs curse his deplorable prose, throw down *Le Rouge et Le Noir* and trample it with a strange and possibly justified fury.

But Stendhal, as he is and may be, has, in spite of the Muses, in spite of his pen, and almost in spite of himself, become one of the demigods of our Letters, a master of that abstract yet ardent literature, more frugal and lighter than any other, which is characteristic of France. It is a *genre* which takes account only of acts and ideas, which disdains settings, which make light of harmony and the balance of form. It is all in the stroke, the tone, the formula and the dart, it is prodigal of foreshortenings and vivid mental reactions. This *genre* is always swift and readily insolent. It seems to have no age and, to some extent, no matter. It is personal in the extreme, directly *centred* on the author, as disconcerting as a game abounding in give and take, and it fends off the dogmatic and the poetic which it detests equally.

One could never finish talking about Stendhal. I see no higher praise. (pp. 153-54)

Paul Valéry, "Stendhal," in his Variety: Second Series, *translated by William Aspenwall Bradley, Harcourt Brace Jovanovich, 1938, pp. 101-54.*

ERICH AUERBACH   (essay date 1942-45)

[*Auerbach was a German-born American philologist and critic. He is best known for his* Mimesis: Dargestellte Wirklichkeit in der abendländischen Literatur (*1946;* Mimesis: The Representation of Reality in Western Literature)*, a landmark study in which the critic explores the interpretation of reality through literary representation. The breadth of Auerbach's learning is evident in the scope of the work: he begins with an examination of literary imitation in the Bible and Homer's writings and progresses through literary history to an explication of the works of such modern writers as Marcel Proust and*

Virginia Woolf. Auerbach's discussion of nineteenth-century authors includes commentary on Stendhal, Gustave Flaubert, Johann Wolfgang von Goethe, Johann Christoph von Schiller, and Fedor Dostoevski. In the following excerpt from Mimesis, which was written between 1942 and 1945, Auerbach finds Stendhal's realism rooted in his novels' precise sense of historicity.]

Julien Sorel, the hero of Stendhal's novel *Le Rouge et le Noir,* an ambitious and passionate young man, son of an uneducated petty bourgeois from the Franche-Comté, is conducted by a series of circumstances from the seminary at Besançon, where he has been studying theology, to Paris and the position of secretary to a gentleman of rank, the Marquis de la Mole, whose confidence he gains. Mathilde, the Marquis's daughter, is a girl of nineteen, witty, spoiled, imaginative, and so arrogant that her own position and circle begin to bore her. The dawning of her passion for her father's *domestique* is one of Stendhal's masterpieces and has been greatly admired. One of the preparatory scenes, in which her interest in Julien begins to awaken, is the following, from volume 2, chapter 14:

> Un matin que l'abbé travaillait avec Julien, dans la bibliothèque du marquis, à l'éternel procès de Frilair:
>
> —Monsieur, dit Julien tout à coup, dîner tous les jours avec madame la marquise, est-ce un de mes devoirs, ou est-ce une bonté que l'on a pour moi?
>
> —C'est un honneur insigne! reprit l'abbé, scandalisé. Jamais M. N . . . l'académicien, qui, depuis quinze ans, fait une cour assidue, n'a pu l'obtenir pour son neveu M. Tanbeau.
>
> —C'est pour moi, monsieur, la partie la plus pénible de mon emploi. Je m'ennuyais moins au séminaire. Je vois bâiller quelquefois jusqu'à mademoiselle de La Mole, qui pourtant doit être accoutumée à l'amabilité des amis de la maison. J'ai peur de m'endormir. De grâce, obtenez-moi la permission d'aller dîner à quarante sous dans quelque auberge obscure.
>
> L'abbé, véritable parvenu, était fort sensible à l'honneur de dîner avec un grand seigneur. Pendant qu'il s'efforçait de faire comprendre ce sentiment par Julien, un léger bruit leur fit tourner la tête. Julien vit mademoiselle de La Mole qui écoutait. Il rougit. Elle était venue chercher un livre et avait tout entendu; elle prit quelque considération pour Julien. Celui-là n'est pas né à genoux, pensa-t-elle, comme ce vieil abbé. Dieu! qu'il est laid.
>
> A dîner, Julien n'osait pas regarder mademoiselle de La Mole, mais elle eut la bonté de lui adresser la parole. Ce jour-là, on attendait beaucoup de monde, elle l'engagea à rester. . . .

> (One morning while the Abbé was with Julien in the Marquis's library, working on the interminable Frilair suit:
>
> "Monsieur," said Julien suddenly, "is dining with Madame la Marquise every day one of my duties, or is it a favor to me?"
>
> "It is an extraordinary honor!" the Abbé corrected him, scandalized. "Monsieur N., the academician, who has been paying court here assiduously for fifteen years, was never able to manage it for his nephew, Monsieur Tanbeau."

> "For me, Monsieur, it is the most painful part of my position. Nothing at the seminary bored me so much. I even see Mademoiselle de la Mole yawning sometimes, yet she must be well inured to the amiabilities of the guests of this house. I am in dread of falling asleep. Do me the favor of getting me permission to eat a forty-sou dinner at some inn."

> The Abbé, a true parvenu, was extremely conscious of the honor of dining with a noble lord. While he was trying to inculcate this sentiment into Julien, a slight sound made them turn. Julien saw Mademoiselle de la Mole listening. He blushed. She had come for a book and had heard everything; she began to feel a certain esteem for Julien. He was not born on his knees, like that old Abbé, she thought. God, how ugly he is!

> At dinner Julien did not dare to look at Mademoiselle de la Mole, but she condescended to speak to him. A number of guests were expected that day, she asked him to stay. . . .)

The scene, as I said, is designed to prepare for a passionate and extremely tragic love intrigue. Its function and its psychological value we shall not here discuss; they lie outside of our subject. What interests us in the scene is this: it would be almost incomprehensible without a most accurate and detailed knowledge of the political situation, the social stratification, and the economic circumstances of a perfectly definite historical moment, namely, that in which France found itself just before the July Revolution; accordingly, the novel bears the subtitle, *Chronique de 1830.* Even the boredom which reigns in the dining room and salon of this noble house is no ordinary boredom. It does not arise from the fortuitous personal dullness of the people who are brought together there; among them there are highly educated, witty, and sometimes important people, and the master of the house is intelligent and amiable. Rather, we are confronted, in their boredom, by a phenomenon politically and ideologically characteristic of the Restoration period. In the seventeenth century, and even more in the eighteenth, the corresponding salons were anything but boring. But the inadequately implemented attempt which the Bourbon regime made to restore conditions long since made obsolete by events, creates, among its adherents in the official and ruling classes, an atmosphere of pure convention, of limitation, of constraint and lack of freedom, against which the intelligence and good will of the persons involved are powerless. In these salons the things which interest everyone—the political and religious problems of the present, and consequently most of the subjects of its literature or of that of the very recent past—could not be discussed, or at best could be discussed only in official phrases so mendacious that a man of taste and tact would rather avoid them. How different from the intellectual daring of the famous eighteenth-century salons, which, to be sure, did not dream of the dangers to their own existence which they were unleashing! Now the dangers are known, and life is governed by the fear that the catastrophe of 1793 might be repeated. As these people are conscious that they no longer themselves believe in the thing they represent, and that they are bound to be defeated in any public argument, they choose to talk of nothing but the weather, music, and court gossip. In addition, they are obliged to accept as allies snobbish and corrupt people from among the newly-rich bourgeoisie, who, with the unashamed baseness of their ambition and with their fear for their ill-gotten wealth, completely vitiate the atmosphere of society. So much for the pervading boredom.

But Julien's reaction, too, and the very fact that he and the former director of his seminary, the Abbé Pirard, are present at all in the house of the Marquis de la Mole, are only to be understood in terms of the actual historical moment. Julien's passionate and imaginative nature has from his earliest youth been filled with enthusiasm for the great ideas of the Revolution and of Rousseau, for the great events of the Napoleonic period; from his earliest youth he has felt nothing but loathing and scorn for the piddling hypocrisy and the petty lying corruption of the classes in power since Napoleon's fall. He is too imaginative, too ambitious, and too fond of power, to be satisfied with a mediocre life within the bourgeoisie, such as his friend Fouquet proposes to him. Having observed that a man of petty-bourgeois origin can attain to a situation of command only through the all-powerful Church, he has consciously and deliberately become a hypocrite; and his great talents would assure him a brilliant intellectual career, were not his real personal and political feelings, the direct passionateness of his nature, prone to burst forth at decisive moments. One such moment of self-betrayal we have in the passage before us, when Julien confides his feelings in the Marquise's salon to the Abbé Pirard, his former teacher and protector; for the intellectual freedom to which it testifies is unthinkable without an admixture of intellectual arrogance and a sense of inner superiority hardly becoming in a young ecclesiastic and protégé of the house. (In this particular instance his frankness does him no harm; the Abbé Pirard is his friend, and upon Mathilde, who happens to overhear him, his words make an entirely different impression from that which he must expect and fear.) The Abbé is here described as a true parvenu, who knows how highly the honor of sitting at a great man's table should be esteemed and hence disapproves of Julien's remarks; as another motive for the Abbé's disapproval Stendhal could have cited the fact that uncritical submission to the evil of this world, in full consciousness that it is evil, is a typical attitude for strict Jansenists; and the Abbé Pirard is a Jansenist. We know from the previous part of the novel that as director of the seminary at Besançon he had had to endure much persecution and much chicanery on account of his Jansenism and his strict piety which no intrigues could touch; for the clergy of the province were under the influence of the Jesuits. When the Marquis de la Mole's most powerful opponent, the Abbé de Frilair, a vicar-general to the bishop, had brought a suit against him, the Marquis had made the Abbé Pirard his confidant and had thus learned to value his intelligence and uprightness; so that finally, to free him from his untenable position at Besançon, the Marquis had procured him a benefice in Paris and somewhat later had taken the Abbé's favorite pupil, Julien Sorel, into his household as private secretary.

The characters, attitudes, and relationships of the dramatis personae, then, are very closely connected with contemporary historical circumstances; contemporary political and social conditions are woven into the action in a manner more detailed and more real than had been exhibited in any earlier novel, and indeed in any works of literary art except those expressly purporting to be politico-satirical tracts. So logically and systematically to situate the tragically conceived life of a man of low social position (as here that of Julien Sorel) within the most concrete kind of contemporary history and to develop it therefrom—this is an entirely new and highly significant phenomenon. The other circles in which Julien

Sorel moves—his father's family, the house of the mayor of Verrières, M. de Rênal, the seminary at Besançon—are sociologically defined in conformity with the historical moment with the same penetration as is the La Mole household; and not one of the minor characters—the old priest Chélan, for example, or the director of the *dépôt de mendicité,* Valenod—would be conceivable outside the particular historical situation of the Restoration period, in the manner in which they are set before us. The same laying of a contemporary foundation for events is to be found in Stendhal's other novels—still incomplete and too narrowly circumscribed in **Armance,** but fully developed in the later works: in the **Chartreuse de Parme** (which, however, since its setting is a place not yet greatly affected by modern development, sometimes gives the effect of being a historical novel), as also in **Lucien Leuwen,** a novel of the Louis Philippe period, which Stendhal left unfinished. In the latter, indeed, in the form in which it has come down to us, the element of current history and politics is too heavily emphasized: it is not always wholly integrated into the course of the action and is set forth in far too great detail in proportion to the principal theme; but perhaps in a final revision Stendhal would have achieved an organic articulation of the whole. Finally, his autobiographical works, despite the capricious and erratic "egotism" of their style and manner, are likewise far more closely, essentially, and concretely connected with the politics, sociology, and economics of the period than are, for example, the corresponding works of Rousseau or Goethe; one feels that the great events of contemporary history affected Stendhal much more directly than they did the other two; Rousseau did not live to see them, and Goethe had managed to keep aloof from them. (pp. 454-58)

We may ask ourselves how it came about that modern consciousness of reality began to find literary form for the first time precisely in Henri Beyle of Grenoble. Beyle-Stendhal was a man of keen intelligence, quick and alive, mentally independent and courageous, but not quite a great figure. His ideas are often forceful and inspired, but they are erratic, arbitrarily advanced, and, despite all their show of boldness, lacking in inward certainty and continuity. There is something unsettled about his whole nature: his fluctuation between realistic candor in general and silly mystification in particulars, between cold self-control, rapturous abandonment to sensual pleasures, and insecure and sometimes sentimental vaingloriousness, is not always easy to put up with; his literary style is very impressive and unmistakably original, but it is short-winded, not uniformly successful, and only seldom wholly takes possession of and fixes the subject. But, such as he was, he offered himself to the moment; circumstances seized him, tossed him about, and laid upon him a unique and unexpected destiny; they formed him so that he was compelled to come to terms with reality in a way which no one had done before him. (p. 459)

Stendhal's realistic writing grew out of his discomfort in the post-Napoleonic world and his consciousness that he did not belong to it and had no place in it. Discomfort in the given world and inability to become part of it is, to be sure, characteristic of Rousseauan romanticism and it is probable that Stendhal had something of that even in his youth; there is something of it in his congenital disposition, and the course of his youth can only have strengthened such tendencies, which, so to speak, harmonized with the tenor of life of his generation; on the other hand, he did not write his recollections of his youth, the **Vie de Henri Brulard,** until he was in his thirties, and we must allow for the possibility that, from the viewpoint of his later development, from the viewpoint of 1832, he overstressed such motifs of individualistic isolation. It is, in any case, certain that the motifs and expressions of his isolation and his problematic relation to society are wholly different from the corresponding phenomena in Rousseau and his early romantic disciples.

Stendhal, in contrast to Rousseau, had a bent for practical affairs and the requisite ability; he aspired to sensual enjoyment of life as given; he did not withdraw from practical reality from the outset, did not entirely condemn it from the outset—instead he attempted, and successfully at first, to master it. Material success and material enjoyments were desirable to him; he admires energy and the ability to master life, and even his cherished dreams (*le silence du bonheur*) are more sensual, more concrete, more dependent upon human society and human creations (Cimarosa, Mozart, Shakespeare, Italian art) than those of the *Promeneur Solitaire.* Not until success and pleasure began to slip away from him, not until practical circumstances threatened to cut the ground from under his feet, did the society of his time become a problem and a subject to him. Rousseau did not find himself at home in the social world he encountered, which did not appreciably change during his lifetime; he rose in it without thereby becoming happier or more reconciled to it, while it appeared to remain unchanged. Stendhal lived while one earthquake after another shook the foundations of society; one of the earthquakes jarred him out of the everyday course of life prescribed for men of his station, flung him, like many of his contemporaries, into previously inconceivable adventures, events, responsibilities, tests of himself, and experiences of freedom and power; another flung him back into a new everyday which he thought more boring, more stupid, and less attractive than the old; the most interesting thing about it was that it too gave no promise of enduring; new upheavals were in the air, and indeed broke out here and there even though not with the power of the first.

Because Stendhal's interest arose out of the experiences of his own life, it was held not by the structure of a possible society but by the changes in the society actually given. Temporal perspective is a factor of which he never loses sight, the concept of incessantly changing forms and manners of life dominates his thoughts—the more so as it holds a hope for him: In 1880 or 1930 I shall find readers who understand me! (pp. 461-62)

In his realistic writings, Stendhal everywhere deals with the reality which presents itself to him: *Je prends au hasard ce qui se trouve sur ma route,* he says . . .: in his effort to understand men, he does not pick and choose among them; this method, as Montaigne knew, is the best for eliminating the arbitrariness of one's own constructions, and for surrendering oneself to reality as given. But the reality which he encountered was so constituted that, without permanent reference to the immense changes of the immediate past and without a premonitory searching after the imminent changes of the future, one could not represent it; all the human figures and all the human events in his work appear upon a ground politically and socially disturbed. To bring the significance of this graphically before us, we have but to compare him with the best-known realistic writers of the pre-Revolutionary eighteenth century: with Lesage or the Abbé Prévost, with the preeminent Henry Fielding or with Goldsmith; we have but to consider how much more accurately and profoundly he enters into given contemporary reality than Voltaire, Rousseau,

and the youthful realistic work of Schiller, and upon how much broader a basis than Saint-Simon, whom, though in the very incomplete edition then available, he read assiduously. Insofar as the serious realism of modern times cannot represent man otherwise than as embedded in a total reality, political, social, and economic, which is concrete and constantly evolving—as is the case today in any novel or film—Stendhal is its founder.

However, the attitude from which Stendhal apprehends the world of event and attempts to reproduce it with all its interconnections is as yet hardly influenced by Historism—which, though it penetrated into France in his time, had little effect upon him. For that very reason we have referred in the last few pages to time-perspective and to a constant consciousness of changes and cataclysms, but not to a comprehension of evolutions. It is not too easy to describe Stendhal's inner attitude toward social phenomena. It is his aim to seize their every nuance; he most accurately represents the particular structure of any given milieu, he has no preconceived rationalistic system concerning the general factors which determine social life, nor any pattern-concept of how the ideal society ought to look; but in particulars his representation of events is oriented, wholly in the spirit of classic ethical psychology, upon an *analyse du coeur humain,* not upon discovery or premonitions of historical forces; we find rationalistic, empirical, sensual motifs in him, but hardly those of romantic Historism. Absolutism, religion and the Church, the privileges of rank, he regards very much as would an average protagonist of the Enlightenment, that is as a web of superstition, deceit, and intrigue; in general, artfully contrived intrigue (together with passion) plays a decisive role in his plot construction, while the historical forces which are the basis of it hardly appear. Naturally all this can be explained by his political viewpoint, which was democratic-republican; this alone sufficed to render him immune to romantic Historism; besides which the emphatic manner of such writers as Chateaubriand displeased him in the extreme. On the other hand, he treats even the classes of society which, according to his views, should be closest to him, extremely critically and without a trace of the emotional values which romanticism attached to the word people. The practically active bourgeoisie with its respectable money-making, inspires him with unconquerable boredom, he shudders at the *vertu républicaine* of the United States, and despite his ostensible lack of sentimentality he regrets the fall of the social culture of the *ancien régime.* . . . No longer is birth or intelligence or the self-cultivation of the *honnête homme* the deciding factor—it is ability in some profession. This is no world in which Stendhal-Dominique can live and breathe. Of course, like his heroes, he too can work and work efficiently, when that is what is called for. But how can one take anything like practical professional work seriously in the long run! Love, music, passion, intrigue, heroism—these are the things that make life worthwhile. . . .

Stendhal is an aristocratic son of the *ancien régime grande bourgeoisie,* he will and can be no nineteenth-century bourgeois. . . . Sometimes he has pronounced accesses of socialism: in 1811, he writes, energy was to be found only in the class *qui est en lutte avec les vrais besoins* (**Brulard**). But he finds the smell and the noise of the masses unendurable, and in his books, outspokenly realistic though they are in other respects, we find no "people," either in the romantic "folk" sense or in the socialist sense—only petty bourgeois, and occasional accessory figures such as soldiers, domestic servants, and coffee-house mademoiselles. Finally, he sees the individual man far less as the product of his historical situation and as taking part in it, than as an atom within it; a man seems to have been thrown almost by chance into the milieu in which he lives; it is a resistance with which he can deal more or less successfully, not really a culture-medium with which he is organically connected. In addition, Stendhal's conception of mankind is on the whole preponderantly materialistic and sensualistic. . . . But in Stendhal, happiness, even though highly organized human beings can find it only in the mind, in art, passion, or fame, always has a far more sensory and earthy coloring than in the romanticists. . . . His conception of *esprit* and of freedom is still entirely that of the pre-Revolutionary eighteenth century, although it is only with effort and a little spasmodically that he succeeds in realizing it in his own person. For freedom he has to pay the price of poverty and loneliness and his *esprit* easily becomes paradox, bitter and wounding. . . . His *esprit* no longer has the self-assurance of the Voltaire period; he manages neither his social life nor that particularly important part of it, his sexual relations, with the easy mastery of a gentleman of rank of the *ancien régime;* he even goes so far as to say that he cultivated *esprit* only to conceal his passion for a woman whom he did not possess. . . . Such traits make him appear a man born too late who tries in vain to realize the form of life of a past period; other elements of his character, the merciless objectivity of his realistic power, his courageous assertion of his personality against the triviality of the rising *juste milieu,* and much more, show him as the forerunner of certain later intellectual modes and forms of life; but he always feels and experiences the reality of his period as a resistance. That very thing makes his realism (though it proceeded, if at all, to only a very slight degree from a loving genetic comprehension of evolutions—that is, from the historistic attitude) so energetic and so closely connected with his own existence: the realism of this *cheval ombrageux* is a product of his fight for self-assertion. And this explains the fact that the stylistic level of his great realistic novels is much closer to the old great and heroic concept of tragedy than is that of most later realists— Julien Sorel is much more a "hero" than the characters of Balzac, to say nothing of Flaubert. (pp. 462-66)

Erich Auerbach, "In the Hôtel de la Mole," in his Mimesis: The Representation of Reality in Western Literature, *translated by Willard R. Trask, Princeton University Press, 1953, pp. 454-92.*

SIMONE DE BEAUVOIR   (essay date 1949)

[*One of the most prominent writers of her generation, Beauvoir was a member of the French left-wing intellectual circle associated with existentialist Jean-Paul Sartre. She is known as both a chronicler of that milieu and a literary explicator of existentialist philosophy. She also became identified as a leading feminist theorist with the publication of* Le deuxième sexe *(1949;* The Second Sex), *her comprehensive study of the secondary status of women throughout history. In the following excerpt from this work, Beauvoir examines Stendhal's attitude toward women and the themes they represent in his fiction.*]

Stendhal loved women sensually from childhood. . . . Women inspire his books, feminine figures people them; the fact is that he writes for them in large part. "I take my chance of being read in 1900 by the souls I love, the Mme Rolands, the Mélanie Guilberts. . . ." They were the very substance of his life. How did they come to have that preferment?

This tender friend of women does not believe in the feminine mystery, precisely because he loves them as they really are; no essence defines woman once for all; to him the idea of "the eternal feminine" seems pedantic and ridiculous. . . . The differences to be noted between men and women reflect the difference in their situations. (pp. 147-48)

The worst handicap [women] have is the besotting education imposed upon them; the oppressor always strives to dwarf the oppressed; man intentionally deprives women of their opportunities. . . . A great many women are doomed to idleness, when there is no happiness apart from work. This state of affairs makes Stendhal indignant, and he sees in it the source of all the faults for which women are reproached. They are not angels, nor demons, nor sphinxes: merely human beings reduced to semislavery by the imbecile ways of society.

It is precisely because they are oppressed that the best of them avoid the defects that disfigure their oppressors; they are in themselves neither inferior nor superior to man; but by a curious reversal their unhappy situation favors them. It is well known how Stendhal hated serious-mindedness: money, honors, rank, power seemed to him the most melancholy of idols; the vast majority of men sell themselves for profit; the pedant, the man of consequence, the bourgeois, the husband—all smother within them every spark of life and truth; larded with ready-made ideas and acquired sentiments and conformable to social routines, their personalities contain nothing but emptiness; a world peopled by these soulless creatures is a desert of ennui. There are many women, unfortunately, who wallow in the same dismal swamps; these are dolls with "narrow and Parisian ideas," or often hypocritical devotees. Stendhal experiences "a mortal disgust for respectable women and their indispensable hypocrisy"; they bring to their frivolous occupations the same seriousness that makes their husbands stiff with affectation; stupid from bad education, envious, vain, gossipy, worthless through idleness, cold, dry, pretentious, malicious, they populate Paris and the provinces; we see them swarming behind the noble figure of a Mme de Rênal, a Mme de Chasteller. The one Stendhal has painted with the most malevolent care is without doubt Mme Grandet, in whom he has set forth the exact negative of a Mme Roland, a Métilde. Beautiful but expressionless, scornful and without charm, she is formidable in her "celebrated virtue" but knows not the true modesty that comes from the soul; filled with admiration for herself, puffed up with her own importance, she can only copy the outer semblance of grandeur; fundamentally she is vulgar and base; "she has no character . . . she bores me," thinks M. Leuwen. "Perfectly reasonable, careful for the success of her plans," her whole ambition is to make her husband a cabinet minister; "her spirit is arid"; prudent, a conformist, she has always kept away from love, she is incapable of a generous act; when passion breaks out in that dry soul, there is burning but no illumination.

This picture need only be reversed to show clearly what Stendhal asks of women: it is first of all not to permit themselves to be caught in the snares of seriousness; and because of the fact that the things supposed to be of importance are out of their range, women run less risk than men of getting lost in them; they have better chances of preserving that naturalness, that naïveté, that generosity which Stendhal puts above all other merit. What he likes in them is what today we call their authenticity: that is the common trait in all the women he loved or lovingly invented; all are free and true beings. Some of them flaunt their freedom most conspicuously: Angela Pietragrua, "strumpet sublime, in the Italian manner, *à la* Lucretia Borgia," and Mme Azur, "strumpet *à la* Du Barry . . . one of the least vain and frivolous Frenchwomen I have met," scoff openly at social conventions. Lamiel laughs at customs, mores, laws; the Sanseverina joins ardently in intrigue and does not hesitate at crime. Others are raised above the vulgar by their vigor of spirit: such is Menta, and another is Mathilde de La Mole, who criticizes, disparages, and scorns the society around her and wants to be distinguished from it. With others, again, liberty assumes a quite negative aspect; the remarkable thing in Mme de Chasteller is her attitude of detachment from everything secondary; submissive to the will of her father and even to his opinions, she none the less disputes bourgeois values by the indifference which she is reproached for as childishness and which is the source of her insouciant gaiety. Clélia Conti also is distinguished for her reserve; balls and other usual amusements of young girls leave her cold; she always seems distant "whether through scorn for what is around her, or through regret for some absent chimera"; she passes judgment on the world, she is indignant at its baseness.

But it is in Mme de Rênal that independence of soul is most deeply hidden; she is herself unaware that she is not fully resigned to her lot; it is her extreme delicacy, her lively sensitivity, that show her repugnance for the vulgarity of the people around her; she is without hypocrisy; she has preserved a generous heart, capable of violent emotions, and she has a flair for happiness. The heat of this fire which is smoldering within her can hardly be felt from outside, but a breath would be enough to set her all ablaze.

These women are, quite simply, *alive;* they know that the source of true values is not in external things but in human hearts. This gives its charm to the world they live in: they banish ennui by the simple fact of their presence, with their dreams, their desires, their pleasures, their emotions, their ingenuities. The Sanseverina, that "active soul," dreads ennui more than death. To stagnate in ennui "is to keep from dying, she said, not to live"; she is "always impassioned over something, always in action, and gay, too." Thoughtless, childish or profound, gay or grave, daring or secretive, they all reject the heavy sleep in which humanity is mired. And these women who have been able to maintain their liberty—empty as it has been—will rise through passion to heroism once they find an objective worthy of them; their spiritual power, their energy, suggest the fierce purity of total dedication.

But liberty alone could hardly give them so many romantic attributes: pure liberty gives rise rather to esteem than to emotion; what touches the feelings is the effort to reach liberty through the obstructive forces that beat it down. It is the more moving in women in that the struggle is more difficult. Victory over mere external coercion is enough to delight Stendhal; in his *Chroniques italiennes* he immures his heroines deep within convents, he shuts them up in the palaces of jealous husbands. Thus they have to invent a thousand ruses to rejoin their lovers; secret doors, rope ladders, bloodstained chests, abductions, seclusions, assassinations, outbursts of passion and disobedience are treated with the most intelligent ingenuity; death and impending tortures add excitement to the audacities of the mad souls he depicts for us. Even in his maturer work Stendhal remains sensitive to this obvious romanticism: it is the outward manifestation of what springs

from the heart; they can be no more distinguished from each other than a mouth can be separated from its smile. Clélia invents love anew when she invents the alphabet that enables her to correspond with Fabrice. The Sanseverina is described for us as "an always sincere soul who never acted with prudence, who abandoned herself wholly to the impression of the moment"; it is when she plots, when she poisons the prince, and when she floods Parma that this soul is revealed to us: she is herself no more than the sublime and mad escapade she has chosen to live. The ladder that Mathilde de La Mole sets against her windowsill is no mere theatrical prop: it is, in tangible form, her proud imprudence, her taste for the extraordinary, her provocative courage. The qualities of these souls would not be displayed were they not surrounded by such inimical powers as prison walls, a ruler's will, a family's severity.

But the most difficult constraints to overcome are those which each person encounters within himself: here the adventure of liberty is most dubious, most poignant, most pungent. Clearly Stendhal's sympathy for his heroines is the greater the more closely they are confined. To be sure, he likes the strumpets, sublime or not, who have trampled upon the conventions once for all; but he cherishes Métilde more tenderly, held back as she is by her scruples and her modesty. Lucien Leuwen enjoys being with that free spirit Mme de Hocquincourt; but he passionately loves the chaste, reserved, and hesitant Mme de Chasteller; he admires the headstrong soul of the Sanseverina, who flinches at nothing; but he prefers Clélia to her, and it is the young girl who wins Fabrice's heart. And Mme de Rênal, fettered by her pride, her prejudices, and her ignorance, is of all the women created by Stendhal perhaps the one who most astounds him. He frequently locates his heroines in a provincial, limited environment, under the control of a husband or an imbecile father; he is pleased to make them uncultured and even full of false notions. Mme de Rênal and Mme de Chasteller are both obstinately legitimist; the former is timid and without experience; the latter has a brilliant intelligence but does not appreciate its value; thus they are not responsible for their mistakes, but rather they are as much the victims of them as of institutions and the mores; and it is from error that the romantic blossoms forth, as poetry from frustration.

A clear-headed person who decides upon his acts in full knowledge of the situation is to be curtly approved or blamed; whereas one admires with fear, pity, irony, love, the courage and the stratagems of a generous heart trying to make its way in the shadows. It is because women are baffled that we see flourishing in them such useless and charming virtues as their modesty, their pride, their extreme delicacy; in a sense these are faults, for they give rise to deception, oversensitiveness, fits of anger; but they are sufficiently accounted for by the situation in which women are placed. Women are led to take pride in little things or at least in "things of merely sentimental value" because all the things "regarded as important" are out of their reach. Their modesty results from their dependent condition: because they are forbidden to show their capabilities in action, they call in question their very being. It seems to them that the perception of others, especially that of their lover, reveals them truly as they are: they fear this and try to escape from it. A real regard for value is expressed in their flights, their hesitations, their revolts, and even in their lies; and this is what makes them worthy of respect; but it is expressed awkwardly, even in bad faith; and this is what makes them touching and even mildly comic. It is when liberty is taken in its own snares and cheats against itself that it is most deeply human and therefore to Stendhal most engaging.

Stendhal's women are touching when their hearts set them unforeseen problems: no law, no recipe, no reasoning, no example from without can any longer guide them; they have to decide for themselves, alone. This forlornness is the high point of freedom. Célia was brought up in an atmosphere of liberal ideas, she is lucid and reasonable; but opinions acquired from others, true or false, are of no avail in a moral conflict. Mme de Rênal loves Julien in spite of her morality, and Clélia saves Fabrice against her better judgment: there is in the two cases the same going beyond all recognized values. This hardihood is what arouses Stendhal's enthusiasm; but it is the more moving in that it scarcely dares to avow itself, and on this account it is more natural, more spontaneous, more authentic. In Mme de Rênal audacity is hidden under innocence: not knowing about love, she is unable to recognize it and so yields to it without resistance; it would seem that because of having lived in the dark she is defenseless against the flashing light of passion; she receives it, dazzled, whether it is against heaven and hell or not. When this flame dies down, she falls back into the shadows where husbands and priests are in control. She has no confidence in her own judgment, but whatever is clearly present overwhelms her; as soon as she finds Julien again, she gives him her soul once more. Her remorse and the letter that her confessor wrests from her show to what lengths this ardent and sincere soul had to go in order to escape from the prison where society shut her away and attain to the heaven of happiness.

In Clélia the conflict is more clearly conscious; she hesitates between her loyalty to her father and her amorous pity; she tries to think of arguments. The triumph of the values Stendhal believes in seems to him the more magnificent in that it is regarded as a defeat by the victims of a hypocritical civilization; and he is delighted to see them using trickery and bad faith to make the truth of passion and happiness prevail over the lies they believe in. Thus Clélia is at once laughable and deeply affecting when she promises the Madonna not to *see* Fabrice any more and then for two years accepts his kisses and embraces on condition that she keep her eyes shut!

With the same tender irony Stendhal considers Mme de Chasteller's hesitancies and Mathilde de La Mole's incoherencies; so many detours, reversals, scruples, hidden victories and defeats in order to arrive at certain simple and legitimate ends! All this is for him the most ravishing of comedies. There is drollery in these dramas because the actress is at once judge and culprit, because she is her own dupe, because she imposes roundabout ways upon herself when she need only decree that the Gordian knot be cut. But nevertheless these inner struggles reveal all the most worthy solicitude that could torture a noble soul: the actress wants to retain her self-respect; she puts her approbation of herself above that of others and thus becomes herself an absolute. These echoless, solitary debates are graver than a cabinet crisis; when Mme de Chasteller asks herself whether she is or is not going to respond to Lucien Leuwen's love, she is making a decision concerning herself and also the world. Can one, she asks, have confidence in others? Can one rely on one's own heart? What is the worth of love and human pledges? Is it foolish or generous to believe and to love?

Such interrogations put in question the very meaning of life, the life of each and of all. The so-called serious man is really futile, because he accepts ready-made justifications for his life; whereas a passionate and profound woman revises established values from moment to moment. She knows the constant tension of unsupported freedom; it puts her in constant danger: she can win or lose all in an instant. It is the anxious assumption of this risk that gives her story the colors of a heroic adventure. And the stakes are the highest there are: the very meaning of existence, this existence which is each one's portion, his only portion. Mina de Vanghel's escapade can in a sense seem absurd; but it involves a whole scheme of ethics. "Was her life a miscalculation? Her happiness had lasted eight months. Hers was a soul too ardent to be contented with the reality of life." Mathilde de La Mole is less sincere than Clélia or Mme de Chasteller; she regulates her actions according to the idea of herself which she has built up, not according to the clear actuality of love, of happiness: would it be more haughty and grand to save oneself than to be lost, to humiliate oneself before one's beloved than to resist him? She also is alone in the midst of her doubts, and she is risking that self-respect which means more to her than life. It is the ardent quest for valid reasons for living, the search through the darkness of ignorance, of prejudices, of frauds, in the shifting and feverish light of passion, it is the infinite risk of happiness or death, of grandeur or shame, that gives glory to these women's lives.

Woman is of course unaware of the seductiveness she spreads around her; to contemplate herself, to act the personage, is always an inauthentic attitude; Mme Grandet, comparing herself with Mme Roland, proves by the act that she is not like her. If Mathilde de La Mole remains engaging, it is because she gets herself involved in her comedies and because she is frequently the prey of her heart just when she thinks she is in control of it; she touches our feelings to the degree that she escapes her own will. But the purest heroines are quite unselfconscious. Mme de Rênal is unaware of her elegance, as Mme de Chasteller is of her intelligence. In this lies one of the deep joys of the lover, with whom both reader and author identify themselves; he is the witness through whom these secret riches come to light; he is alone in admiring that vivacity which Mme de Rênal's glances spread abroad, that "lively, mercurial, profound spirit" which Mme de Chasteller's entourage fails to appreciate; and even if others appreciate the Sanseverina's mind, he is the one who penetrates farthest into her soul.

Before woman, man tastes the pleasure of contemplation; he is enraptured with her as with a landscape or a painting; she sings in his heart and tints the sky. This revelation reveals him to himself: it is impossible to comprehend the delicacy of women, their sensitiveness, their ardor, without becoming a delicate, sensitive, and ardent soul; feminine sentiments create a world of nuances, of requirements the discovery of which enriches the lover: in the company of Mme de Rênal, Julien becomes a different person from that ambitious man he had resolved to be, he makes a new choice. If a man has only a superficial desire for a woman, he will find it amusing to seduce her. But true love really transfigures his life. "Love such as Werther's opens the soul . . . to sentiment and to the enjoyment of the *beautiful* under whatever form it presents itself, however ill-clothed. It brings happiness even without wealth. . . ." "It is a new aim in life to which everything is related and which changes the face of everything. Love-passion flings all nature with its sublimities before a man's eyes like a novelty just invented yesterday." Love breaks the everyday routine, drives ennui away, the ennui in which Stendhal sees such deep evil because it is the lack of any reason for living or dying; the lover has an aim and that is enough to turn each day into an adventure: what a pleasure for Stendhal to spend three days hidden in Menta's cave! Rope ladders, bloodstained caskets, and the like express in his novels this taste for the extraordinary. Love—that is to say, woman—makes apparent the true ends of existence: beauty, happiness, fresh sensations, and a new world. It tears out a man's soul and thereby gives him possession of it; the lover feels the same tension, knows the same risks as his mistress, and proves himself more authentically than in his professional career. When Julien hesitates at the foot of a ladder placed by Mathilde, he puts in question his entire destiny: in that moment his true measure is taken. It is through women, under their influence, in reaction to their behavior, that Julien, Fabrice, Lucien work out their apprenticeship in dealing with the world and themselves. Test, reward, judge, friend—woman truly is in Stendhal what Hegel was for a moment tempted to make of her: that other consciousness which in reciprocal recognition gives to the other subject the same truth that she receives from him. Two who know each other in love make a happy couple, defying time and the universe; such a couple is sufficient unto itself, it realizes the absolute.

But all this presupposes that woman is not pure alterity: she is subject in her own right. Stendhal never limits himself to describing his heroines as functions of his heroes: he gives them a destiny of their own. He has attempted a still rarer enterprise, one that I believe no novelist has before undertaken: he has projected himself into a female character. He does not hover over Lamiel like Marivaux over Marianne or Richardson over Clarissa Harlowe; he assumes her destiny just as he had assumed Julien's. On this account Lamiel's outline remains somewhat speculative, but it is singularly significant. Stendhal has raised all imaginable obstacles about the young girl: she is a poor peasant, ignorant, coarsely raised by people imbued with all the prejudices; but she clears from her path all moral barriers once she understands the full meaning of the little words: "that's silly." Her new freedom of mind allows her in her own fashion to act upon all the impulses of her curiosity, her ambition, her gaiety. Before so stout a heart, material obstacles could not but be smoothed away, and her only problem will be to shape a destiny worthy of her in a mediocre world. She must find fulfillment in crime and death; but this is also Julien's lot. There is no place for great souls in society as it exists. And men and women are in the same boat.

It is noteworthy that Stendhal should be at once so deeply romantic and so decidedly feministic; usually feminists are rational minds who in all matters take a universal point of view; but Stendhal demands woman's emancipation not only in the name of liberty in general but also in the name of individual happiness. Love, he believes, will have nothing to lose; on the contrary, it will be the more true as woman, being man's equal, is able to understand him the more completely. No doubt certain qualities admired in women will disappear; but their worth comes from the freedom they express. This will be manifested under other forms, and the romantic will not vanish from the world. Two separate beings, in different circumstances, face to face in freedom and seeking justification of their existence through one another, will always live an adventure full of risk and promise. Stendhal puts his trust in truth. To depart from it means a living death; but where it shines forth, there shine forth also beauty, happiness, love, and a joy that carries its own justification. That is why he re-

jects the mystifications of the serious, as he rejects the false poetry of the myths. Human reality suffices him. Woman according to him is simply a human being: nor could any shape of dreams be more enrapturing. (pp. 148-56)

Simone de Beauvoir, "Stendhal or the Romantic of Reality," in Stendhal: A Collection of Critical Essays, *edited by Victor Brombert, Prentice-Hall, Inc., 1962, pp. 147-56.*

HOWARD CLEWES   (essay date 1950)

[*Clewes discusses* The Charterhouse of Parma, *highlighting the novel's omnipresent irony.*]

La Chartreuse de Parme is sometimes said to be the best novel in the French language. Certainly it must be counted among the great flights of imagination in French, or indeed any other, literature. (p. 101)

The difference between the Stendhal who wrote **Le Rouge et Le Noir** and the man who wrote **La Chartreuse** is striking. **Le Rouge** is a young man's anguish—a shout of rage and defiance; **La Chartreuse** is the ironic day-dream of one who, if not content, is at least mollified. It is in many ways a finer piece of work, in some a lesser one, than **Le Rouge.** There is no analysis of the dark places of the human soul, in **La Chartreuse,** comparable with that for which one remembers the story of Julien Sorel. There is none of the unbearable tenseness which gives **Le Rouge** the stamp of having been wrung from its author drop by drop. If in some ways it represents an advance in technique—and it does—in others it is retrogressive. He has taught himself some new lessons, only to fling away the old ones. Infinitely more complex in its narrative, altogether wider and deeper in its awareness of the extent of human activity, **La Chartreuse** is almost too vast and too complex. That is not to say that Stendhal has abandoned his beliefs or preferences or philosophy. But they are differently applied. There is an urbanity about **La Chartreuse** which derives directly from Stendhal's own middle age. You feel he is no longer his own victim, torturing himself in order to record his own cries of pain. Even his hatred, virulent as it is, is seasoned with irony. Nor is he Fabrizio in the sense that he was Julien Sorel in the earlier novel.

It seems to me that Fabrizio, at any rate until he falls in love, is something of a cypher, and certainly a bore. He is the young man, the most common type in fiction, who is learning about life—the young man to whom things happen; and it is the things which happen to him that interest us, not the boy himself or even his reactions. And such also would appear to be the extent of Stendhal's participation in that character. But when Fabrizio falls in love and acquires some sort of purpose, a will-to-act of his own, he leaps into life and begins to dominate the action; for the first time he is interesting for his own sake. Even then, however, Stendhal identifies himself with his hero only in the boy's love for the girl, and it is not the harsh, immediate passion of Julien for Madame De Rênal. It is romantic love. Stendhal is writing wistfully, wishfully and tenderly, not of himself as he is or was, but as he might have been. It is with Mosca, if anybody, that Stendhal associates himself, for Mosca is in love with Gina, and so is Stendhal. Clelia even more than Fabrizio is a cypher; she has no character other than she acquires by her piety and her love. She is a dream, a vision.

The first major event described in **La Chartreuse** is the battle of Waterloo. Stendhal did not see the battle himself, but the accuracy of his detail is not in question; the fifty pages he gives to it are among the great imaginative descriptions of battle in the world's literature.

"Disguised" as a traveller in barometers, Fabrizio makes his way from Milan into France to join the standard of his hero, Napoleon. He arrives on the battlefield, after his release from arrest as a spy, to find himself straightway involved in the action. Thereafter there is no respite. The reader sees only with Fabrizio's eyes and experiences the battle only as he experiences it. And from start to finish Fabrizio is in complete ignorance about what is happening. He does not know whether he is riding the tide of victory or defeat or even who, individually, is fighting whom. He understands exactly as much of the battle, in fact, as any private soldier has ever understood of a battle before or since. He is tossed hither and thither like a leaf in a hurricane; he advances, retreats, gets hopelessly lost, finds himself attached to the staff of Marshal Ney, is rescued from tight corners by sundry corporals, is succoured by benevolent *vivandières,* vomits at the sight of a dead man's dirty feet, is ignominiously wounded by a deserter, performs little feats of heroism which, in their context, are only comic or silly, and then, when it is all over, asks: "Has the battle been fought yet?"—and hastens to buy a newspaper to find out who won. The private soldier of the Second World War switched on a field wireless for the same purpose.

Stendhal's battle was and remains a masterpiece of realistic writing. As such it is perhaps out of place in a novel whose story—though not its treatment—is in the main romantic. It is also said that it has little or nothing to do with the rest of the action. Both complaints are justified. Nevertheless *La Chartreuse* would be the lesser for its exclusion.

Balzac described the novel as the one Machiavelli would have written had he lived banished from Italy in the nineteenth century [see excerpt dated 1840]. The comment does Stendhal rather less than justice. If *La Chartreuse* is political and in that respect anti-social, amoral and essentially evil, it is also profoundly human. The criticism is in any case extremely superficial; Stendhal can hardly be said to approve of the political skulduggery he describes with such apparent objectivity; the whole picture is shot with bitter irony. But what has upset so many critics is not the irony of Stendhal so much as the additional irony of the characters themselves. What appears to irk is their acceptance of their own frightful turpitude with hardly a shrug of the shoulders. They know the difference between good and evil, right and wrong, but they also know that it is more important in this world to appear to be acting rightly than to act rightly in fact; you accept your own infamy with a smile of resignation: such is life, etc. This is the lesson that Count Mosca, like Leuwen *père* and *fils,* is at pains to teach Fabrizio. Stendhal himself has learned that whatever he himself might feel about the social and political scene of his day, he must, if he is to keep his Consulship, hold his peace and play the game according to the rules. Would he object to the rules of the game of whist? Mosca asks Fabrizio. Of course not. You play, and you try to win. And so Stendhal, in the shape of Mosca, takes Fabrizio by the hand and leads him through the labyrinth of intrigue and greed and fear which formed the background to nineteenth-century statesmanship. It is an ugly and fascinating picture, the more so that we see it this time from within, not, as in *Le Rouge,* from below and beneath. *La Chartreuse,* in fact, utters the same cry of pain as *Le Rouge,* but now the author is mocking his

own anguish. Nothing is real, nothing true, nothing sacred, nothing guileless; not even pain.

Stendhal's pursuit of something in himself in which he could wholeheartedly believe never ended. In *Lamiel,* his last novel, he carried it one stage further and, in Dr. Sansfin, seems to be deriding his own irony. It is as though his, Stendhal's, mind were composed of a series of assumed beliefs laid like masks one upon the other, and as with that pitiless, inward-seeing third eye he subjects each to its scrutiny, it is shown up as in some way bogus—as, in fact, a mask, and there is always another beneath. But concealing what? What are the features of the face which lies beneath the last of all? Is there nothing in which to believe? If there is, he does not find it. He is sincere only about love. And even this must be the highly idealised love of a Fabrizio for a Clelia.

La Chartreuse is primarily a love story. The action, whether political or functional or psychological, derives its impetus from love, or hate or jealousy arising out of love—the human interest so lacking in the political foreground of *Lucien Leuwen.* At the heart of it all lies the passion of Gina Sanseverina for her nephew, Fabrizio. (pp. 103-07)

Gina, Duchess Sanseverina, is Stendhal's most spectacular woman. It has been said that he modelled her on his own early love, Gina Pietragrua, and there is no doubt something more to support the theory than the similarity of name. But Gina Sanseverina is infinitely finer than the baker's daughter for whom Stendhal donned his striped trousers in Milan in 1811. She is a hymn to the type of woman Stendhal always admired, and she is a triumph. She has been described as a common strumpet, a murderess, an adulteress, a vulgar wanton, and she is all these things. But she is magnificently human. She is of the stuff of life. Her behaviour is irrational because it is passionate, and she remains true to her own belief, or Stendhal's, that passion is its own law. The book is redolent of her physical presence, her full-blooded loves and hates, her wit, her beauty, her splendour. As might be expected, once she has left the scene and disappeared into exile with the devoted Mosca, the rest of the story is somewhat anticlimactic. Clelia marries the man her father has chosen for her and Fabrizio takes his vows and becomes a distinguished churchman. And this seems to be the right place to end.

But it does not end—not by any means. Clelia meets Fabrizio again, drawn by gossip to the church at which he is preaching. Having assisted in Fabrizio's escape and thus in a measure betrayed her father, who was held responsible, she has sworn never again to meet her lover face to face. So she meets him in the dark. It is all rather absurd, no doubt intended to be satirical, but so remote from the rest of the story that one's interest flags or at least wilts under the strain of believing in such a situation. She bears him a child, Sandrino, who dies. The candles are lit over the child's cot and, by their light, she sees her lover. But the spell is broken and the incident does not register. Fabrizio retires to the Charterhouse of Parma, and the story trails away into silence.

It is not possible in a limited space to examine the detail of *La Chartreuse,* nor even more than a few of its many characters. One is tempted by all of them—by Ernesto and his youthful successor, by the richly drawn Rassi, by Raversi, by Ludovico, by Ferrante Palla, the young poet whom Gina Sanseverina uses to carry out the murder of the prince—it is an impressive gallery of portraits. There is one, however, who takes precedence over even Gina, and that is Count Mosca.

It has been said, inaccurately, that Mosca is drawn from Metternich. Stendhal detested Metternich, not only for what the latter stood for in society and politics, but as a personal enemy. It was Metternich who had twice had Stendhal ejected from Milan, Metternich who refused him the exequatur which would have confirmed his appointment as Consul-General of Trieste. It was the spirit and policy of Metternich against which Stendhal wrote, schemed and laboured all his life. He certainly did not model his most lovable character, Mosca, on a personage whom he took to be the fountainhead of his misfortunes. If Metternich is identifiable at all in *La Chartreuse* it is as the despotic Prince Ernesto Ranuccio IV who, like the Austrian, caused his bedchamber to be searched every night for malevolent liberals. Count Mosca was, or was intended to be, Stendhal himself—not a tortured, psychopathic Julien Sorel, nor even a dreamy, romantic Fabrizio, but a middle-aged statesman of realistic outlook, immense ability and dry humour, in love with Gina Sanseverina.

As a "working" statesman without private means, who has not used his position to feather his own nest, Mosca is bound to follow his own cynical advice to Fabrizio. But he is at heart a liberal and humane man and, while pandering to the despotism of the sovereign, endeavours quietly to mitigate its effects. He deplores his own moral callousness and condemns his gentle-heartedness, knowing the one to be evil and the other, in a statesman, a weakness. Yet he accepts both in himself with complete calm and knows that if it comes to the point, as it does, he will act in whatever may be his own best interests. For as well as the fact that his office of prime minister is also his bread and butter, he loves power for its own sake and is never happier than when using it. He prefers to use it benevolently, of course, because benevolence pays a higher dividend, but, while wishing that that which is in his own and his sovereign's best interests should also be morally right, he recognises that the two, or three, cannot always coincide. It is the use of power which intrigues him, not really the means to which it is put, and for all his revulsion from the despotism of his Prince, he can never quite resist the temptation to show the despot how best to be despotic; he advises Ernesto quite dispassionately, when the latter is vexed by the growth of carbonarism in Parma, that he must either butcher ten thousand souls immediately, or give in and make a few popular concessions. This is pure Machiavelli. But Stendhal recognises that even in statesmanship there is a human element and though Mosca has no sense of guilt, he has nevertheless a lively scrupulosity. He will stoop to the most heinous forms of political intrigue when they are expedient, yet he will suffer eternal remorse over a generous action which he could have taken and did not. On the surface, of course, he is the immaculate diplomat in every circumstance—bewigged and powdered, suave, bland, witty, discerning, calculating to a hair's breadth the methods and motives of those by whom he is opposed. He shows turmoil of spirit only in respect of his love for Gina.

Through Gina Sanseverina, and indeed on her instigation, he becomes involved in the fate of her nephew, Fabrizio. He contrives to maintain his equilibrium politically, but not emotionally. He is aware of the lady's passion for the boy, and he experiences a very hell of jealousy. Now, jealousy in an elderly or middle-aged statesman is a phenomenon which might well cause a giggle or at best an acknowledgment of its pa-

thos. In any event the man's stature would suffer a sudden reduction, one would say. But the effect in this instance is entirely the opposite. The man's character has been so firmly established by Stendhal, and the writing of the scenes in question so perfectly controlled, that Mosca loses neither stature nor credibility by this illumination of his capacity for ordinary human emotion. Indeed in the grip of jealousy he acquires a certain Shakespearean magnificence; he hovers on the edge of madness and murder, resists both, and is never, in the toils or in their aftermath, anything but impressive and moving. It is a flawless portrait. (pp. 108-11)

> *Howard Clewes, in his* Stendhal: An Introduction to the Novelist, *A. Barker, 1950, 128 p.*

MARTIN TURNELL (essay date 1951)

[*Turnell has written widely on French literature and has made significant translations of the works of Jean-Paul Sartre, Guy de Maupassant, Blaise Pascal, and Paul Valéry. In the following excerpt from his respected study of Stendhal, Turnell interprets social and psychological aspects of* The Red and the Black.]

The opening chapters of a novel by Stendhal must be read with the same care as the opening scenes of a comedy by Molière. They contain the essential clues to the understanding of the whole book. *Le Rouge et le noir* begins with a description of the little town of Verrières in which the novelist displays his admirable sensibility:

> La petite ville de Verrières peut passer pour l'une des plus jolies de la Franche-Comté. Ses maisons blanches avec leurs toits pointus de tuiles rouges s'étendent sur la pente d'une colline, dont les touffes de vigoureux châtaigniers marquent les moindres sinuosités. Le Doubs coule à quelques centaines de pieds au-dessous de ses fortifications, bâties jadis par les Espagnols, et maintenant ruinées.

> [The small town of Verrières may be regarded as one of the most attractive in the Franche-Comté. Its white houses with their high pitched roofs of red tiles are spread over the slope of a hill, the slightest contours of which are indicated by clumps of sturdy chestnuts. The Doubs runs some hundreds of feet below its fortifications, built in times past by the Spaniards and now in ruins.]

The little town nestling among the hills, with its 'habitants plus paysans que bourgeois' and its 'jeunes filles fraîches et jolies' who work in the mills, gives and is intended to give an impression of peacefulness. We must not overlook the 'fortifications'. In an earlier period, they had marked the limit reached by the invader. Nor is it without significance that they are 'ruined'. For Verrières will suffer from an 'invader' of another kind whose incursions will cause a considerable disturbance.

The novelist goes on to describe the industries of the place: the sawmills, the manufacture of 'painted tiles' and nails. Then we are introduced to M. de Rênal, Mayor of Verrières:

> At the sight of him every hat is quickly raised. His hair is turning grey, and he is dressed in grey. He is a Companion of several Orders, has a high forehead, an aquiline nose, and on the whole his face is not wanting in a certain regularity: indeed, the first impression formed of it may be that it com-

bines with the dignity of a village mayor that sort of charm which may still be found in a man of forty-eight or fifty. But soon the visitor from Paris is annoyed by a certain air of self-satisfaction and self-sufficiency mingled with a suggestion of limitations and want of originality. One feels, finally, that this man's talent is confined to securing the exact payment of whatever is owed to him and to postponing payment till the last possible moment when he is the debtor.

It is not simply the portrait of an individual; it is the portrait of a class. For M. de Rênal is the symbol of the privileged classes—genteel on the surface, hard as nails underneath—in their ruthless struggle with the unprivileged.

No one who has read Stendhal's principal works will have failed to notice that he was obsessed with prisons, secret police and spies. The casual reference to 'fortifications' in the first paragraph of the book is caught up three pages later by a reference to 'walls':

> You must not for a moment expect to find in France those picturesque gardens which enclose the manufacturing towns of Germany; Leipsic, Frankfort, Nuremberg, and the rest. In the Franche-Comté, the more *walls* a man builds, the more he makes his property bristle with stones piled one above another, the greater title he acquires to the respect of his neighbours.

'Walls' is one of the focal words of the novel. They are in the first place the ramparts which separate the two worlds of the privileged and the unprivileged. They are also the 'fortifications' which preserve the bourgeois world from the incursions of peasants and workers. In spite of their gentility and respectability, the privileged are far from being idle behind their fortifications; they wage a ceaseless war against those outside and are constantly thrusting their ramparts further forward and acquiring fresh territory:

> M. de Rênal's gardens, honeycombed with *walls,* are still further admired because he bought, for their weight in gold, certain minute scraps of ground which they cover. For example that sawmill, whose curious position on the bank of the Doubs struck you as you entered Verrières, and on which you noticed the name *Sorel* inscribed in huge letters on a board which overtops the roof, occupied, six years ago, the ground on which at this moment they are building the *wall* of the fourth terrace of M. de Rênal's gardens.

At this point the two worlds represented by M. de Rênal and Sorel—Julien's father—face one another directly. (pp. 141-43)

One of the central themes of **Le Rouge et le noir** is the 'class war'. Stendhal's conception of it was much wider than that of modern political theorists, but his book is the story of a parvenu who succeeds in penetrating the 'walls' which protect the privileged and in attaching himself to a class to which he does not belong. He penetrates not only the walls of M. de Rênal's estate, but the walls of the seminary and of the Hôtel de La Mole. In the end, society takes its revenge. With the same ease with which it casts the simple Abbé Chélan outside its walls, it finally shuts Julien behind prison walls and executes him not for slaying, or attempting to slay, one of its members, but for trying to usurp its privileges.

We must turn now to the character of the parvenu. Stendhal uses a number of different methods of creating character, but one of the most important is the description of his chief character's effect on other people. We are told of Julien at the seminary:

> Julien avait beau se faire petit et sot, il ne pouvait plaire, il était trop différent.

> [In vain might Julien make himself small and foolish, he could not give satisfaction, he was too different.]

The Abbé Pirard says to him:

> Avec ce je ne sais quoi d'indéfinissable, du moins pour moi qu'il y a dans votre caractère, si vous ne faites pas fortune, vous serez persécuté; il n'y a pas de moyen terme pour vous.

> [With this something indefinable that there is in your character, at any rate for me, if you do not make your fortune you will be persecuted. There is no middle way for you.]

He fares no better in his own family:

> Objet des mépris de tous à la maison, il haïssait ses frères et son père; dans les jeux du dimanche, sur la place publique, il était toujours battu.

> [An object of contempt to the rest of the household, he hated his brothers and father; in the games on Sundays, on the public square, he was invariably beaten.]

The Marquis de La Mole says of him:

> Mais au fond de ce caractère je trouve quelque chose d'effrayant. C'est l'impression qu'il produit sur tout le monde, donc il y a là quelque chose de réel.

> [But at the bottom of this character I find something frightening. It's the impression that he makes on everybody, so there must be something real about it.]

These observations reveal Julien from a number of different angles. We see him as he appeared to his proletarian family, to his fellow-seminarists, to his confessor and to aristocratic conservatives like M. de La Mole; but they have one thing in common. The *reader's* reactions are almost identical with those of the other *characters.* We, too, find Julien 'different', 'indefinable', 'difficult to place', 'frightening'. Stendhal certainly intended that we should, and he himself completes the evidence by describing him as 'un homme malheureux, en guerre avec toute la société'. For Julien is an *étranger* or 'outsider' in the society of his time.

Now this conception of character is of capital importance in Stendhal's work and something must be said of the *étranger* type and of the age which produced him. It is commonly assumed that there are resemblances between the Napoleonic age and our own, but it is easy to exaggerate them. In spite of revolution, war and devastation, the Europe which emerged from the Napoleonic wars was on the threshold of a great age of peace and plenty. At the same time, to a contemporary observer, it must have presented an appearance of considerable confusion. The Revolution had petered out in dictatorship; and dictatorship led not simply to monarchy, but to an extremely sordid, conventional and repressive monarchy. In politics, France was divided between conservatives

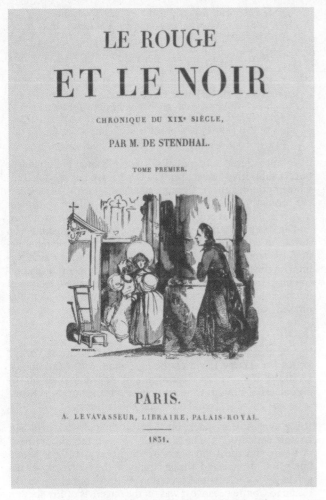

Title page of the first edition of Le rouge et le noir.

and liberals, but we often find it difficult to distinguish between their policies which appear equally confused.

A sensitive observer like Stendhal was struck by the muddle and lack of vitality of this society—it is the constant burden of his writings—and it is precisely in these conditions that the *étranger* makes his appearance. He is the Janus-face who emerges in periods when the sensitive individual cannot identify himself with any of the different groups of which society is composed. For the *étranger* has *no recognized mode of feeling.* In spite of his intelligence and his extraordinary calculations, he is continually swinging from one extreme of feeling to another and back again. 'Chez cet être singulier,' said Stendhal, 'c'était presque tous les jours tempête.'

The *étranger* is essentially an individualist at odds with society, but it must be recognized that he is an entirely new type in European fiction. He has little in common with the Romantic outcast or Flaubert's *ratés,* with Gide's *immoraliste* or Camus' 'outsider', who are all manifestations of a much more personal attitude. Stendhal's characters are the direct product of their age and are only comprehensible when seen in relation to it. They are left to work out their destiny in a chaotic society and their only supports are their own immense force of character and their own genius. In spite of their shortcomings, the way in which they set about their task

stamps their attitude as an heroic one. I think that we can go further than this and say that Julien Sorel is 'the modern hero'.

Stendhal's conception of character is an example of the way in which he discarded philosophical theories when they came into conflict with his artistic vision. The materialism implicit in the work of the philosophers whom he admired led logically to determinism, to the belief that character is nothing but the product of environment. It would be an understatement to say that Stendhal did not accept this view. *Le Rouge et le noir* is based on the contrary view—on the view that genius is absolute and inexplicable. Stendhal took his 'plot' from a newspaper account of a peasant who was executed for shooting his mistress and proceeded to transform it in the light of his own experience. There is nothing in Julien's upbringing or environment to account for his gifts. His instruction has been limited to a few Latin lessons with the *curé* and reading a life of Napoleon given to him by an old soldier. He has been bullied and obstructed in every possible way by his family, but when his chance comes he is ready to seize it with both hands. The lesson is obvious. The genius will either turn into Napoleon or be executed as a common criminal. The answer depends on the sort of society in which he finds himself and on the use he makes of his opportunities. In other words, environment does not determine a man's *character,* but it does determine his *fate.*

When this is grasped, it is easy to see what *Le Rouge et le noir* is 'about'. Julien's character is not, perhaps, drawn with the firmness of Fabrice's and there are moments when Stendhal slips into melodrama or reveals the unfortunate influence of Romanticism; but these are minor flaws in his great achievement. The book is a profound study of the impact of genius on a corrupt society. (pp. 143-46)

[The] first step in Julien's career is to discover not merely what sort of a man he is, but what sort of a man he must become in order to succeed. When we read the novels, we find that all Stendhal's principal characters are tormented by the novelist's own question: 'Qu'ai-je été, que suis-je?' They are perpetually interrogating themselves about their own feelings, wondering what they really feel for this woman, why that woman leaves them cold or asking themselves whether or not some defect in their make-up renders them incapable of loving at all.

> Il est dans l'essence de cette âme d'agir à la fois et
> de se regarder agir, de sentir et de se regarder sentir.

Paul Bourget's comment draws attention to an important difference between Stendhal and all his predecessors. Self-knowledge is not destructive as it was for Mme de La Fayette and Constant; it is not merely a prelude to action as it was for Laclos; in Stendhal action and analysis are simultaneous. All his characters realize that they can only exploit their genius by becoming something, by discovering some principle of unity within themselves. They must first of all rid themselves of the gnawing sense of anxiety which dogs them and become integrated personalities, and they can only become integrated personalities by observing their feelings at the actual moment of action. *Logique* and *espagnolisme* play a big part in the drama. The function of *logique* is to integrate personality, to control and direct the blind forces of *espagnolisme.* It is *logique* which is continually pulling them up, making them pause and ask themselves what they feel and why they feel as they do.

Although **Le Rouge et le noir** deals with the class war, I think that it will be apparent that the term *étranger* is not primarily a *social,* but a *psychological* distinction. The 'walls' are barriers between the different classes, but they also stand for the psychological barriers which cut the 'outsider' off from the rest of humanity. For the book is much more than a conflict between two social classes. It is a conflict between two irreconcilable ways of life. Julien would have been an 'outsider' in any class of society, and he is equally out of place in the world of his father, of the Rênals and the La Moles. The fact that he belongs socially to the proletariat simply provides a particular setting for the study of a much wider problem and creates an additional obstacle to Julien's success. There was not the slightest chance of his exercising his peculiar talents in his father's world, and a rise in the social scale is necessary to start him on his career.

He does not make the first breach in the 'walls' himself. M. de Rênal is prompted by vanity to engage a tutor for his children in order to score off his fellow-bourgeois. He approaches M. Sorel, knowing that he has a son who enjoys a certain reputation for learning. The bourgeois thus makes the first breach in his own walls which lets the outsider in. From this moment Julien's fortunes depend on himself. His attack is twofold. He has to impress the bourgeois, and he has to overcome his own feeling of anxiety by a personal success. There could be no better way than to persuade the bourgeois that he is a prodigy of learning and to seduce his employer's wife. Everything goes according to plan. (pp. 147-48)

Julien's success with Mme de Rênal is a form of apprenticeship in which for the first time he puts his theories into practice, and the account of his feelings is instructive:

> Cette main se retira bien vite; mais Julian pensa qu'il était de son *devoir* d'obtenir que l'on ne retirât pas cette main quand il la touchait. L'idée d'un devoir à accomplir, et d'un ridicule ou plutôt d'un sentiment d'infériorité à encourir si l'on n'y parvenait pas, éloigna sur-le-champ tout plaisir de son coeur.

> [The hand was hurriedly withdrawn; but Julian decided that it was his *duty* to secure that the hand should not be withdrawn when he touched it. The idea of a duty to be performed, and of making himself ridiculous, or rather being left with a sense of inferiority if he did not succeed in performing it, at once took all the pleasure from his heart.]

In the French analysis of emotion, said Rivière, 'la morale même devient un élément psychologique'. Stendhal's use of the word *devoir* is an excellent example. It is the focal word of the passage and he underlines it to make sure that its significance shall not escape us. It means something very different from Corneille's *devoir*. It is not a disinterested 'duty'; the imperative comes from Julien's subjective need to bolster up his own inner morale or, as Stendhal, very much in advance of his time, suggests, to rid himself of a *sentiment d'infériorité.*

This is how Stendhal describes his feelings after he has made a conquest of Mme de Rênal:

> Le lendemain on le réveilla à cinq heures; et, ce qui eût été cruel pour Mme de Rênal si elle l'eût su, à peine lui donna-t-il une pensée. Il avait fait *son devoir, et un devoir héroïque.* Rempli de bonheur par

ce sentiment, il s'enferma à clef dans sa chambre, et se livra avec un plaisir nouveau à la lecture des exploits de son héros.

> [Next morning he was called at five o'clock; and (what would have been a cruel blow to Madame de Rênal had she known of it) he barely gave her a thought. He had done *his duty, and a heroic duty.* Filled with joy by this sentiment, he turned the key in the door of his bedroom and gave himself up with an entirely new pleasure to reading about the exploits of his hero.]

The italics are again Stendhal's. Julien's feelings are no longer purely subjective and selfish. His experience has modified his whole outlook and the feelings which accompany his success are something entirely new for him. The *sentiment d'infériorité* has, at any rate for the time being, been exorcized and has been replaced by satisfaction over accomplishing 'son devoir, et un devoir héroïque'. There is an immense relief behind the words, a sense of release from something which was imprisoning him and preventing the development of his personality. Instead of being eaten up by a subjective feeling of inferiority, he has broken the vicious circle and identifies himself with the *public* figure of Napoleon.

• • • • •

'In contrast to the naturalness of the Rênal estate at Vergy,' writes Mr. Harry Levin of the love-affair with Mathilde de La Mole, 'her love has ripened in a library, nourished on the chronicles of Brantôme and Aubigné and the novels of Rousseau and Prévost' [see Additional Bibliography].

It is a suggestive remark, but I find it difficult to accept Mr. Levin's conclusions. The contrast between the 'naturalness' of Vergy and the atmosphere of the 'library' in Paris is certainly intentional and the meaning of the whole novel depends on a correct interpretation of it. Stendhal chose the Franche-Comté because it was on the outskirts of France and geographically remote from the sophisticated capital to which Julien will eventually graduate. It is the start of his career, the place at which the forward bastions of civilization are breached to admit the intruder.

Julien's career is a journey to the interior. When he leaves Verrières, we have the impression that he is entering a long, dark tunnel and that the 'fresh, deep valleys' which surround the 'little town' are the daylight receding behind him as he penetrates further and further into it. We are aware of a feeling of claustrophobia as the seminary doors close on him. Henceforth, the drama takes place not in the open air, but in the oppressive, airless seminary, in the library of M. de La Mole and at the secret session amid the candles and the sealing wax, the papers and the serious anonymous faces of the conspirators.

The physical journey is at the same time *a journey to the interior of the mind.* It is accompanied by a deepening of experience, a growing complexity of feeling. The outer world loses its importance; the 'action' shifts to the world within. (pp. 148-50)

The characters live in a dream world, entirely preoccupied with what is going on inside their own minds. . . . (p. 150)

Mathilde, too, is an *étrangère* in nineteenth-century society, and it is because she has failed to meet anyone like herself that, until Julien arrives, she spends her time in a private world of her own reading about the heroic exploits of her sixteenth-century ancestors. She is desperately bored and desperately out of place in a society of which she can say with some truth: 'Je ne vois que la condamnation à mort qui distingue un homme . . . c'est la seule chose qui ne s'achète pas.' . . .

It used to be fashionable at one time to debate the respective merits of **Le Rouge et le noir** and **La Chartreuse de Parme**. The **Chartreuse de Parme** may be the greater novel, but I do not think that Stendhal ever surpassed the account of the love affair between Julien and Mathilde. . . . (p. 151)

Their attraction-and-repulsion sounds at first like an episode in the sex war; but Stendhal's interpretation of this fundamental antipathy is much more profound than Laclos' in the *Liaisons dangereuses*. In the *Liaisons* it is inspired by a desire to dominate the opposite sex; in **Le Rouge et le noir** it is part of a larger war against society seen collectively. In spite of the violent conflict between them and the savage delight that they experience in humiliating one another's pride—always the vulnerable spot—Julien and Mathilde are allies against society and are united by a bond which goes far deeper than their antipathy. The words *singulier—singularité* must occur a hundred times in the second part of the novel, and they describe the link which unites Julien and Mathilde and separates them from everyone else.

The forty-sixth chapter, which describes the seduction of Julien by Mathilde, illustrates some of Stendhal's most remarkable qualities—his insight into conflicting and contradictory feelings, his blend of tenderness and irony and also his use of the Romantics' stock-in-trade to express an anti-romantic attitude. Julien has just climbed into Mathilde's bedroom:

> 'Vous voilà, monsieur,' lui dit Mathilde avec beaucoup d'émotion; 'je suis vos mouvements depuis une heure.'
>
> Julien était fort embarrassé, il ne savait comment se conduire, il n'avait pas d'amour du tout. Dans son embarras, il pensa qu'il fallait oser, il essaya d'embrasser Mathilde.
>
> 'Fi donc!' lui dit-elle en le repoussant.
>
> ['Here you are, sir,' Mathilde said to him with deep emotion; 'I have been following your movements for the last hour.'
>
> Julien was greatly embarrassed, he did not know how to behave, he did not feel the least vestige of love. In his embarrassment, he decided that he must show courage, he attempted to embrace Mathilde.
>
> 'Fie, sir!' she said, and thrust him from her.]

They are both extremely embarrassed, but for different reasons. Their mutual attraction is deeper than they realize, but Julien has engaged in the escapade largely out of bravado and because he is flattered by the invitation to visit the daughter of the house in the small hours. A Romantic hero would certainly have worked himself up into a fine frenzy by a torrent of words. Julien does his best, but Stendhal shows us with his customary lucidity that in reality he feels nothing and has no idea what to do.

Mathilde, too, is anxious for a 'big scene', but she is paralysed by the conflict between what is really admirable in her—her

boldness and *singularité*—and the conventional feelings against which she rebels. . . . (pp. 152-53)

Stendhal is remorseless in his exposure of their embarrassment:

> Mathilde faisait effort pour le tutoyer, elle était évidemment plus attentive à cette étrange façon de parler qu'au fond des choses qu'elle disait. . . .
>
> 'Il faut cependant que je lui parle,' dit-elle à la fin, 'cela est dans les convenances, on parle à son amant.'
>
> [Mathilde made an effort to use the more intimate form; she was evidently more attentive to this unusual way of speaking than to what she was saying. . . .
>
> 'I must speak to him, though,' she said to herself, finally, 'that is laid down in the rules, one speaks to one's lover.']

Then comes the final criticism of the Romantic attitude:

> Après de longues incertitudes, qui eussent pu paraître à un observateur superficiel l'effet de la haine la plus décidée . . . Mathilde finit par être pour lui une maîtresse aimable.
>
> A la vérité, ces transports étaient un peu *voulus*. L'amour passionné était encore plutôt un modèle qu'on imitait qu'une réalité.
>
> [After prolonged uncertainties, which might have appeared to a superficial observer to be due to the most decided hatred . . . Mathilde finally became his mistress.
>
> To tell the truth their ardours were a little artificial. Passionate love was still more of a model to be imitated than a reality.]
>
> (pp. 153-54)

The whole incident is related in a tone of ironic comedy, but we continually have the impression that Stendhal's words are *doing* more than they *say*. The hot, prickly embarrassment of the lovers is contagious and communicates itself to us; but we are aware of the underlying seriousness and we see far more deeply into the real impulses of the characters than they do themselves.

Stendhal's prose is, indeed, seen at its most impressive in the encounters between Julien and Mathilde. (p. 154)

Beneath its dry sparkle, his prose has tentacular roots which thrust downwards into the hidden places of the mind. He possessed the *vue directe* into the complexity of the human heart, the power of seizing feelings at the moment of their formation and translating them with an admirable lucidity:

> Ce tutoiement, dépouillé du ton de la tendresse, ne faisait aucun plaisir à Julien, il s'étonnait de l'absence du bonheur; enfin, pour le sentir, il eut recours à sa raison. Il se voyait estimé par cette jeune fille si fière, et qui n'accordait jamais de louanges sans restriction; avec ce raisonnement il parvint à un bonheur d'amour-propre.
>
> [This use of the singular form, stripped of the tone of affection, ceased, after a moment, to afford Julien any pleasure, he was astonished at the absence of happiness; finally, in order to feel it, he had re-

course to his reason. He saw himself highly esteemed by this girl who was so proud, and never bestowed unrestricted praise; by this line of reasoning he arrived at a gratification of his self-esteem.]

(pp. 156-57)

[The] prose performs the actions that it describes. The novelist suggests a feeling to us, then proceeds to peel away the outer layers in order to show us that it is not at all what it appears to be. The *tutoiement* should be a sign of *tendresse,* but is not. It gives Julien no 'pleasure', and he is 'astonished' at the absence of a *bonheur* which is normally a product of *tendresse* and *plaisir. Enfin* marks the characteristic change of direction. Julien sets to work to produce a substitute feeling of 'happiness' by the use of 'reason'. He tells himself that if there is no 'tenderness' in Mathilde's tone, at least this person who is proud and not given to overpraising anyone 'esteems' him. This argument, this manipulation of ideas, produces a fresh combination of feelings. We have watched the whole process from the beginning, have seen the feelings transformed. With the *bonheur d'amour-propre* everything suddenly falls neatly into place.

In other places Stendhal writes:

Deux mois de combats et de sensations nouvelles renouvelèrent pour ainsi dire tout son être moral.

Ce cruel soupçon changea toute la position morale de Julien. Cette idée trouva dans son coeur un commencement d'amour qu'elle n'eut pas de peine à détruire.

Ces souvenirs de bonheur passé s'emparaient de Julien et détruisaient bientôt tout l'ouvrage de la raison.

Son mot si franc, mais si stupide, vint tout changer en un instant: Mathilde, sûre d'être aimée, le méprisa parfaitement.

[Two months of struggle and of novel sensations had so to speak altered her whole moral nature.

This cruel suspicion completely changed Julien's moral attitude. The idea encountered in his heart a germ of love which it had no difficulty in destroying.

These memories of past happiness took possession of Julien, and rapidly undid all the work of reason.

This speech, so frank but so stupid, altered the whole situation in an instant: Mathilde, certain of being loved, despised him completely.]

In all these examples, the operative words are the verbs *changer, renouveller, détruire.* The verb—usually a transitive verb—is the pivot of Stendhal's most characteristic sentences because he is much more interested in mental *activity* than in mental *states.* These three verbs indicate the field of experience. His characters' feelings are constantly 'changing', are engaged in a continual process of 'renewal' and 'destruction'. They are not superficial changes of mood; they go to the roots of the 'moral being'. A sudden shock 'destroys' their moral stability; they set to work slowly and painfully to rebuild it. Another shock undoes the work of 'reason', and the whole process starts all over again. A final sentence completes the picture:

Mathilde était alors dans l'état où Julien se trouvait quelques jours auparavant.

[Mathilde was at that time in the state in which Julien had been a few days previously.]

Although they are bound to one another in the innermost depths of their being, Julien and Mathilde are practically never both in the same mood on the same day, and this produces the clash. It is a psychological obstacle race in which they take it in turns to be pursuer and pursued, executioner and victim.

One of the most interesting things about Stendhal's characters is the impression that they give that the whole of their lives, the whole of their being, is engaged in every action. . . . (pp. 157-58)

The life of Stendhal's characters is a process of *extension* which finally reaches the point at which not merely something, but *everything* gives way. It is because they are 'outsiders' that they can find no proper outlet for their great gifts. Their incredible calculations and their immensely sharpened sensibility, which result from this position, subject their personalities to an intolerable strain until they are driven to abandon the world of action and to withdraw completely into the world of contemplation. (p. 159)

When Julien reaches the prison at Besançon his sensibility is exhausted. The extended personality has reached the point at which it can no longer carry on, when there is nothing left for it in life. This explains Julien's attitude to Mathilde and Mme de Rênal. He cannot face the prospect of life together with Mathilde and he turns to the more restful figure of Mme de Rênal. She is of course the mother-image and the prison itself a symbol of the womb to which he wishes to return. Once in prison, he can give himself up to *rêverie.* The last thing he wants is to be acquitted or to escape or even to return to the world of action after a term of imprisonment. Mathilde's attempts to save him are simply exasperating and he takes good care that they fail.

I think we must add that the prison episode is also a profound study of the psychology of heroism. Julien appears to stick to his ideals, to go heroically to his death. In fact, he commits suicide; but he does not do so for the reasons suggested by his critics. The 'hero' lives at a far greater pitch of intensity than the general run of men, and what appears to be an heroic death in battle is probably in many instances a case of suicide dictated by an unconscious realization that he is 'finished'.

The account of the execution is a masterly example of Stendhal's power of understatement:

Tout se passa simplement, convenablement, et de sa part sans aucune affectation.

[Everything passed simply, decorously, and without affectation on his part.]

The last scene, in which Mathilde follows the funeral cortège with Julien's severed head on her knees, has perplexed Stendhal's critics. It seems to me to be a deliberately macabre piece of comedy. His admiration for the sixteenth century was deep-rooted, and he certainly approved this final display of Mathilde's *singularité,* which could only have appeared odd to an effete age. It was Stendhal's parting shot at the men of 1830. (pp. 159-60)

Martin Turnell, "Stendhal," in his The Novel in

France: Mme de La Fayette, Laclos, Constant, Stendhal, Balzac, Flaubert, Proust, *New Directions, 1951, pp. 123-208.*

RENÉ WELLEK (essay date 1955)

[*Wellek's* A History of Modern Criticism *(1955-65) is a major, comprehensive study of the literary critics of the last three centuries. Wellek's critical method, as demonstrated in* A History, *is one of describing, analyzing, and evaluating a work solely in terms of problems it poses for itself and how the writer solves them. For Wellek, biographical, historical, and psychological information are incidental. Although many of Wellek's critical methods are reflected in the work of the New Critics, he was not a member of that group and rejected their more formalistic tendencies. In this excerpt from* A History of Modern Criticism, *Wellek discusses Stendhal's theories of literary criticism.*]

Stendhal's mind is surely one of the most interesting and possibly oddest minds of the time. We know it now better than any contemporary could know it, since a large mass of letters, diaries, drafts of articles, marginalia, and thinly disguised autobiographical narratives have been unearthed. All through this mass of papers are scattered pronouncements on literature and books. They are most formal, though still light in tone, in the large number of reviews printed in English in three English magazines: the *New Monthly,* the *London Magazine,* and the *Athenaeum.* Stendhal, who is usually known for the slight piece **Racine et Shakespeare,** emerges in that as a critic of considerable intrinsic interest; he represents an attitude toward literature which could hardly be elsewhere documented so well and so entertainingly.

Stendhal was not an aesthetician and theorist of great consequence. Partly, he simply distrusted system and theory, because, in his mind, they were associated with the poetics of neoclassicism, with the pedantries of La Harpe and Marmontel. Partly he thought of aesthetics as the theories of ideal beauty formulated by Winckelmann and his disciples, and he had no use for their absolutism. In his **Histoire de la peinture en Italie** Stendhal tried rather dilettantishly to formulate his own theory of ideal beauty, using the temperament types of Cabanis and endorsing a historical relativism. Partly, he considered theory as the baneful pedantry of the new German romantics, especially A. W. Schlegel whom he heartily disliked. Stendhal is frankly and simply an Epicurean, a hedonist who judges and wants us to judge art by the pleasure it gives us. "Whoever we are, king or shepherd, on the throne or in a hovel, one has always reason to feel as one feels and to find beautiful that which gives pleasure." Thus, the "quantity of pleasure felt seems to [him] the only reasonable thermometer to judge of the merit of the artist." Also in music, "in order to be happy we don't have to be reduced to examining it: this is what the French will not understand; their manner of enjoying the arts is to judge them."

This does not promise well for criticism, but actually Stendhal's search for happiness is too self-consciously intellectual ever to deprive him of the strong framework of convictions and norms of taste which he holds almost instinctively. Harry Levin's telling definition of the essence of Beylism, "to keep one's head while losing one's heart" [see Additional Bibliography], applies also to Stendhal's literary opinions. Stendhal has a deep suspicion of mere emotionalism and a positive horror of the mystical and vague. His pleasure must be an intellectual pleasure, not the all-too-easy one of tears and laughter. It should be rather the delicious smile kindled by a Cervantes or a Lesage or a Mérimée. Thus we can easily predict his dislikes. He had no use for the expansive sentimentality of Madame de Staël, though he acknowledged the justness of many of her views. He despised the aesthetic religion of Chateaubriand, his florid style, his gross insincerity. He abominated most of his contemporaries for their pompous, loud, emphatic style and pretended, at least, to take the *Code civil* as the model of his own writing. He was sincerely shocked when Balzac, in his eulogy of the **Charterhouse of Parma,** thought that the weak part of the book was its style. He defended himself, saying that he may write badly only "out of an exaggerated love of logic."

We can understand why Stendhal had no use for German philosophy and ridiculed Kant and Schelling from hearsay. Plato was another writer he would not understand, as everything mystical and high flown smacked to him of obscurantism. Religion of any sort was a closed book to him, and anticlericalism was a basic instinct to a man who hated the Bourbon Restoration and the Austrian rule of Italy. Thus Lamartine cannot excite his admiration and Vigny is ridiculed for *Eloa.* The loves of the devil and the incarnation of a divine tear must have been inspired by "too copious potations of that famous Italian wine *Lachryma Christi.*"

It may be surprising that Stendhal showed much sympathy for one pronouncedly Catholic writer: Manzoni. He thought of him primarily as the author of the *Lettre à M. Chauvet,* from which he drew some arguments against the unities. He admired *Il cinque maggio* as one of the summits of modern poetry, surely also because it expressed his own feelings about Napoleon. He praised the tragedies, though they seemed to him to make too many concessions to classical conventions. He praised the *Inni sacri,* though he added that they have an antisocial, poisonous tendency. He thought the *Promessi sposi* much overrated. But there is always in Stendhal a special tenderness for his Italian contemporaries, particularly the romantic group in Milan from which he had originally learned to associate liberalism, patriotism, and romanticism.

Stendhal had no such restraints toward the Germans. He did not know their language and disliked the people. He admired Schiller and their historical tragedy on doctrinal grounds but usually joined in the disparagements of Goethe that he read in the *Edinburgh Review.* He disliked A. W. Schlegel most, though this may seem a paradox considering Schlegel's own exposition of dramatic romanticism. But Stendhal wanted to prove to himself and others that romanticism was not reactionary, not mystical, not German, and thus minimized his considerable agreement with many of Schlegel's theories. All the marginalia preserved are extremely uncomplimentary. Every other note calls Schlegel a "ridiculous pedant," empty, mystical, vague. Stendhal objects most to the disparagement of Molière and to the idolatry of every word in Dante, Shakespeare, and Calderón. He eagerly reproduced Hazlitt's introductory reflections to his review of Schlegel's *Lectures,* which criticized German scholarship and its desire for eminence at any price, but he apparently did not note that Hazlitt actually agreed with Schlegel's basic tenets. Stendhal saw in Jeffrey and Hazlitt, and even in Johnson, the expounders of the true romantic creed, which to him was largely a rejection of the French dramatic system. The new literature meant the historical drama, the modern satirical comedy, and it came to mean the new psychological novel which Stendhal was to write. Poetry is not in the center of things at all. At most Stendhal appreciated Byron when he was satirical and liberal, and Béranger because he was the singer of the French opposition. His admiration for Jeffrey and Johnson, whom he called the "father of romanticism," is thus not so surprising as it may seem. Stendhal knew Johnson's *Preface* to Shakespeare and could agree with his polemics against the unities and his conception of Shakespeare as a painter of men, a creator of characters rather than a poet or a playwright. Stendhal could admire Byron for personal and political reasons, but he was not too seriously interested in his poetry. He found the tragedies boring and too similar to the manner of Racine and Alfieri. He did not care for *Lara* or the *Corsair,* as they were foreign to French taste, his own taste, which preferred the delicate vein of satire (the *Lettres persanes, Candide,* Molière, and Beaumarchais) to pathos and passion. Stendhal remarks well that Byron tried to be both a lord and a great poet and that one must choose one of these two irreconcilable merits. Byron lacked the will to make the choice. Stendhal liked only the satirical poetry of the later Byron, which reminded him of Ariosto and the Venetian poet Buratti. If Stendhal had any poetical taste it was for the dialect poets of Italy, partly for reasons which were not literary. As a self-appointed Milanese, Stendhal sided violently in the *questione della lingua* with those who fought the exclusive dominance of Tuscan. He most enjoyed Tomasso Grossi, Carlo Porta from Milan, Giovanni Meli from Sicily, and Pietro Buratti from Venice. Stendhal thought of them as popular, "natural," and liberal poets, Italian Bérangers.

The center of Stendhal's literary interest was in the two genres he attempted himself: comedy and the novel. At first he put high hopes in comedy as a socially effective type and studied its technique closely, hoping to produce comedies himself. He commented on most of Molière's plays, went to performances, observing and counting the passages which aroused laughter, ranked them elaborately, and tried to fit them into a theory of laughter and into a scheme of evolution of literature in relation to society. Stendhal analyzed the sources of the comic in a court society and arrived at the conclusion that there are two: to be mistaken in the imitation of what is good taste at the Court, and to have some similarity in one's manners and conduct with a bourgeois. With the rise of the bourgeoisie around 1720 a third source of the comic appeared: the imperfect and awkward imitations of courtiers by the bourgeois themselves. The French comedy writers are fitted into this scheme; but Molière is condemned as immoral, in that his art is inspired by a horror of being different from the ruling society, by a desire for complete conformity. His *Femmes savantes* is immoral because it teaches women to beware of ideas. *Le Misanthrope,* though a great play, is not comic: the hero is a misplaced republican. The comedies ridiculing the physicians are not truly comic either, because the victims of the satire are made odious and arouse rather indignation than laughter. *Tartuffe* is not comic, because he exposes a danger and engages us too passionately to make us laugh: Jesuitism was still very much an issue of the day. Thus Molière is paradoxically shown to be neither moral nor truly comic. Regnard, on the other hand, is both, as he excites neither hatred nor indignation.

The social scheme of evolution which frames Stendhal's history of comedy forces him, as it did Hazlitt before, to the conclusion that our own time is not a good time for comedy. A republic kills laughter, because men seriously occupied cannot laugh. Modern society becomes uniform; class distinctions and thus distinctions of manners disappear. The sources of comedy dry up. But in practice Stendhal enjoyed the comedies of Picard and Scribe and many obscure playwrights of the time and reported about them with gusto to the English magazines. His own ambition to become a new Molière was dead by then.

All his hopes were put in the novel. The 19th century, he thought, will distinguish itself by its accurate depictions of human passion. In his own copy of *Le Rouge et le Noir,* Stendhal noted that the head of the *idéologues,* Destutt de Tracy, had told him "that truth could only be attained by means of the novel." The novel is the comedy of the 19th century. It is to be social and psychological, contemporaneous, even topical, but also universal, probing into the nature of man. At times Stendhal seems to speak like an advocate of photographic naturalism. The famous epigraph of a chapter in *Le Rouge et le Noir,* which defined the novel as a "mirror walking down a road," might give rise to such an interpretation, especially if we confront it with the earlier use of the same figure in the Preface to **Armance:** "is it the fault of the mirror that ugly people have passed in front of it? On whose side is a mirror?" But surely this emphasis on objectivity and on the need for inclusion of the ugly in the novel must be modified by Stendhal's frequent rejections of the horrible and dull. In refusing to describe the election in **Lucien Leuwen** he admits that "it is true, but true like the morgue, which is the kind of truth we leave to novels in duodecimo for chambermaids." Stendhal even defends the need for idealization in the novel. It must be the kind Raphael used to make his portraits more like the subject. Especially the heroine needs such treatment, as the reader has seen the woman he has loved only by idealizing her. At first, Stendhal welcomed the historical novel, such as Scott's, for Scott seemed "romantic," i.e. more real, more alive than the current productions of the sentimental or horrible novelists. But Stendhal was not blind to Scott's shortcomings. He recognized that he has no true historical imagination and always wrote only from the point of view of his own time. "He studies love in books and not in his own heart." In a manuscript piece entitled **"Walter Scott et *La Princesse de Clèves,"*** Stendhal expresses preference for the method of Madame de La Fayette, because it is "easier to describe the dress and the leather collar of a serf of the Middle Ages than the movements of the human heart." Still, he can ask elsewhere whether "the action of things on man is the particular domain of the novel," and surely his own practice of drawing on court documents and memoirs and calling his books "chronicles" seem to point in the direction of the later "documentary" novel. But this is again contradicted by his protest against the principle of imitation of nature and his bold assertion that "a work of art is always a beautiful lie." Hugo's *Han d'Islande* seemed to him "the most extraordinary and *ultra* horrible production of a disordered imagination," but Balzac's realistically pictured *Médecin en campagne* is also called "a dirty pamphlet."

There are many surface contradictions in Stendhal's pronouncements which, after all, were made over a long period of time, often on some polemical occasion, to score a point and to display his wit. But one should recognize the basic unity of his taste and see his peculiar and possibly unique position in a history of criticism. By his instinct for clarity, his rationalism in philosophy, his irony, his distrust of sentimentalism, and his love for understatement Stendhal derives from the 18th century, in spite of all his attacks on the courtly forms of French classicism. He engages in the romantic debate as an outsider, bringing from Italy the identification of romanticism with modernity and liberalism. Only his fierce individualism and his cult of passion associate him with the other romantics. He ignores or rejects the symbolic and mystical view of literature: he has no use for medievalism or even for Christianity. At times he anticipates the theories of realism, but he lacked the theoretical equipment to define more closely the great and astonishing novelty of his own practice. (pp. 246-52)

René Wellek, "Stendhal and Hugo," in his A History of Modern Criticism, 1750-1950: The Romantic Age, Vol. 2, *Yale University Press, 1955, pp. 241-58.*

ROBERT M. ADAMS (essay date 1959)

[*An American educator and critic, Adams is the author of works on religion, opera, and a variety of literary topics. In the following excerpt from his highly regarded* Stendhal: Notes on a Novelist, *he discusses Stendhal's minor novels* Armance, Lucien Leuwen, *and* Lamiel, *attributing their weakness primarily to the author's lack of narrative invention.*]

"With that audacity which never failed to distinguish him, the Baron Stendhal drove, in his first fiction, upon an impossible topic, and shattered the resources of his gallant cavalry against an impregnable position." Reports from the foothills of Parnassus rarely fail to speak in some such mournful metaphors as these of Stendhal's first skirmish with the art of the novel; and they are right, it is hard to present *Armance* as a triumphant encounter. The plain fact is that so long as one sees it under the aspect of a story about physical incapacity—impotence, in a word—it must necessarily appear grotesque. . . . Faced with the necessity of confessing his incapacity to his mistress (and so, perforce, to the patiently inquisitive reader), the hero of *Armance* blushes and blunders like a bashful school-boy; he resorts to desperate expedients, heroic evasions; writes short notes which he tears up without revealing what is in them; hints and blurts and retracts; confesses, but inaudibly; and so, fairly gagged on his own humiliation, finally removes himself from this mortal sphere, still unspeaking. . . . (pp. 142-43)

Numerous diagnoses of Octave de Malivert have been indicated; various practical alternatives to suicide have been suggested, some extremely ingenious, all giving a fine impression of French resourcefulness, aplomb, and finesse under awkward circumstances. Biographers and psycholiterary commentators, loth to overlook the rich implications of the topic, have hastened to explore the life of Henri Beyle for appropriate castration-fantasies, inversion-indices, and subnormal regressive anal-erotic libido fixations. Needless to say, they have found what they were looking for.

But if we put aside these juicy topics, for a moment anyhow; if we forget temporarily that Octave is impotent and that this fact has delicious implications in all conceivable directions, what have we left? Very much what the subtitle of *Armance* describes: "Quelques scènes d'un salon de Paris en 1827." This is not by any means a contemptible theme for a novel; indeed, the detailed satiric study of social manners furnishes at least half the materials which make up the *Rouge* and the *Chartreuse.* It may well be argued that in *Armance* this groundwork is pricked out with even more precision, point, and subtlety than in the later works. Every Stendhal novel is a concerto for passionate soloist and social orchestra; the solo

violin part in *Armance* is quite unplayable, but the orchestral score is almost a model of virile, satiric delicacy.

Paris in 1827—Stendhal is meticulous in indicating the precise stage in the development of hypocrisy and selfishness which his specimen-society has attained. (By 1830, when Julien Sorel traces his quick, brilliant orbit through the upper salons of Paris, their tone will have changed considerably. They will be darker, duller, more dogmatic, more in the hands of jesuits and fanatical legitimists. On the other hand, in 1834 and 1835, the period of *Lucien Leuwen,* society is once more in the hands of the dead-center, and fanatical royalist circles in dreary little provincial towns like Nancy are taking on a vaguely nostalgic, pseudo-chivalric set of snob values.) And the novel, without ever moving far outside its indicated theater of the salon, does in fact present a remarkable parade of social psychopaths, unsparingly rendered with a clinical objectivity which has reminded some commentators of Proust. There is Madame d'Aumale, featherheaded by a kind of sublime principle—so frantic in her avoidance of boredom that she never knows from minute to minute what she will do next. There is M. de Soubirane, the Commander, a hangover from 1789, bold, bluff, and stupid, in whom the fatuity of argument has simply replaced the affectation of youth. There are the Duchesse d'Ancre and her friend Madame de la Ronze, in whom malicious jealousy is forever frozen. There is the Chevalier de Bonnivet, a jesuit in the new style, malicious, ambitious, and reactionary, who at a moment's notice can interrupt the pleasures of a flirtation in order to read a moral lecture to the servants. There is Madame de Bonnivet herself, with an architect at her country estate who understands so intuitively when promotions to the Order of the Holy Spirit are to be announced, that his clients are always in the politic place at the politic moment. Madame de Bonnivet it is who is so infatuated with the new German metaphysics that to find a *rebellious nature* in need of reclamation is, for her, sheer ecstasy. She is, says Stendhal, like that "celebrated Doctor of the last century, [who], summoned to the bedside of a great nobleman, his friend, after examining the symptoms of the disease slowly and in silence, exclaimed in a sudden transport of joy: 'Ah! Monsieur le Marquis, it is a disease that has been lost for centuries! Vitreous phlegm! A superb disease, absolutely fatal. Ah! I have discovered it, I have discovered it!' Such was the joy of Madame de Bonnivet; it was in a sense the joy of an artist."

There is the apex of all French snobbery, a Duke with a gift for divining things or people that are going to become the fashion; a weekend invitation to his estate puts one automatically in line for a peerage. There is the half-pay lieutenant, M. Dolier, a firm and honorable man, who once served Napoleon and therefore has no hope of making any headway whatever in the new society of 1827. And finally, in the background behind these people, are the serried rows of new snobs and new arrivals, jealous of their petty distinctions and quite indistinguishable. There is the Napoleonic nobility, coarse, common, and invincibly complacent; there are the surly manufacturers, whose essential way of life is rude, clumsy, and competitive; there are the stupid manufacturers, who probably mean no harm, as they mean no good, but simply don't know how to behave. All are equally rich, equally unmannered. There are the obsequious deputies, who make awkward allusions in drawing-rooms to the money they are going to vote the people of quality; there are galaxies of mothers with daughters to dispose of; there are aunts with nieces to sell, and of course there are the innumerable, anonymous envious. *Armance* sets before us the whole range and run of a snob society invaded by vulgarians; it has some trouble putting these people in motion, but they are magnificently present; and from this aspect the novel is, indeed, something of a triumph.

Appearing as he does among all these mannered grotesques, it would be tempting to explain Octave de Malivert in terms appropriate to the creation of a modern novelist, writing with "The Waste Land," *The Sun Also Rises, Ulysses,* and *Lady Chatterley's Lover* in his immediate background. Clearly, then, Octave would symbolize the sterility of the culture which surrounds him. Unfortunately, there is not the slightest ground for supposing that anything like this notion ever crossed Beyle's mind, though various eager critics have undertaken to make it cross the reader's. Quite unjustifiably; for Octave is far from a languid, effete, or spiritless young man. On the contrary, he is in rebellion against the languor of his own class; he has just left the Ecole Polytechnique, he reads the utilitarian philosophers, and dallies with the idea of taking the name of Martin or Lenoir and getting a job as a chemical engineer or a valet. Various circumstances suggest that he has interesting difficulties in expressing his antipathy for the society in which accident has placed him, and placed him very well. He tends to cultivate with unnatural assiduity the society of people whom he is known to despise; he is perfectly obedient towards his mother and father, and painfully respectful of social opinion; after reading a liberal paper or book, he immediately and mechanically reads one of the opposite complexion. Yet alongside this almost parodic meekness flourish fits of unpredictable and uncontrollable rage. Irked at the vulgarity of a countess, he rushes out into the street and picks a sabre-fight with a couple of common soldiers; in the midst of a cheerful game of charades, he turns furiously on a footman and throws him out the window. These are known as the "migraines" of the young Vicomte de Malivert; and they have interesting social as well as psychological overtones. Boredom breeds violence; the frustration of feeling useless culminates in an aimless act of smashing. But that this charming and very modern syndrome has any bearing on his hero's impotence, Stendhal will not tell us.

It is not simply that he will not spell out the impact of helpless ambivalence on a sensitive organism; he appears to have in mind a different set of motivations altogether. Octave's difficulties apparently derive from, or are attributed to, an excess of sensibility, not an impasse. In the bread-and-butter terms of the everyday world, there is absolutely no reason why he cannot marry Mademoiselle Armance de Zohiloff, or live fraternally in her society, or reach any arrangement he wants to with her. His mother conspires to throw Armance at him; his father is willing; the young lady herself is, in a sublime way, agreeable. Society will accept anything—but loftiness of sentiment is carried to such extremes, on both sides, that all undertakings become quite impossible. Armance thinks that people will consider her a fortune-hunter if she likes Octave; Octave imagines people, especially Armance, will think him purse-proud if he continues to exist; and, in short, purity of motives is so much mooted by these very impurely motivated people, that one would welcome a breath of satire. Though it is liberally diffused elsewhere, there is none for the hero or his lady.

Chapter Nine introduces a theme which gives promise of producing some elementary illumination. Armance hotly accuses her lover of frequenting what can only be, though they are not overtly anything, houses of ill fame. He admits the charges are true, he offers no excuses or explanations, he merely promises never to appear in such places again. The subject is dropped, and disappears forever from the novel. All this is clearly noble as the dickens, but it gives us not the faintest idea of what our impotent is up to in these interesting circumstances. Does he go to the brothels merely to utter witticisms? To test his manhood or confirm his lack of it? If he goes out of boredom, does he find brothels more amusing than salons? Is it conceivable that he is not as impotent there as he is with Mademoiselle Armance? These are delightful questions with which to while away the weary hours, but Stendhal's novel, alas, gives no grounds for answering them. His correspondence suggests answers to a couple of them, but this circumstance merely underlines the incompleteness of the fiction.

All these considerations point toward the conclusion that the characters of *Armance* are under-activated and over-motivated; faults which coincide nicely with the general tendency of the writing itself to be over-emphatic. The fact that Octave is not impressed by coming into a fortune, the fact that Armance is indifferent to worldly pelf, the fact that maman de Malivert loves her son beyond all else in life—these points are made and remade and overmade, till they become impossibly intrusive. And meanwhile the narrative languishes. All very well to say that Stendhal's narrative technique is essentially episodic; but to introduce the Chevalier de Bonnivet, upon whom the novel's action is to hinge, at the beginning of Chapter 25, out of 31, is to abuse the privileges of authorship. And, broadly speaking, one of the great faults of *Armance* is a failure to dramatize. The book is discursive, not narrative; with the exception of several purely lyrical passages celebrating the airy, intimate delights of two perfectly attuned souls, its emotional and intellectual abstractions are not adequately embodied in metaphors of action. Instead of once acting out Octave's contempt for the nineteenth century, and being done with it, the author pounds it on the reader's nerves till they ache.

How to find an adequate vehicle for expressing and disposing of the hero's irritating hauteur? It is a problem in itself, a very adequate problem for a man writing his first novel at age 43, even without the additional embarrassments of the impotence-theme. . . . But there is an oddity about the ending which provides a far-fetched yet amusing alternative to this rather severe conclusion.

Having been tricked by circumstances into marrying Mlle. de Zohiloff without telling her of his condition, Octave makes an impressive, compensatory testament, and then embarks for the war of Greek independence with the firm intention of not returning. On the way to Greece he feigns illness in order to allay later suspicions, and then, on the last night out, consumes a mixture of opium and digitalis which wafts him on his way with a peaceful, heroic smile on his lips. Now a novel published in 1827 which wound up on this key could scarcely avoid reminding the contemporary reader of Lord Byron, who had perished quite as heroically and almost as uselessly, in the swamps of Missilonghi just three years before. The reminiscence is reinforced by a pair of epigraphs from *Don Juan;* and in point of fact, there is a good deal of peripheral similarity between Octave and Byron. They are both handsome, witty, brave, noble, rich, and young; both mysteriously melancholy, derisive of middle-class manners, bored and violent, capable of immense worldly success, but scorning it with lordly hauteur.

This is an interesting list of parallel characteristics; but surely it must founder completely when we juxtapose the impotence of Octave with the immense, priapic vigor of the English lord. But perhaps the sexual contrast merely modulates the parallel into a new key. If Beyle had meant to imply that at the heart of Byron's personal and literary promiscuity there was an essential sterility, he would not have been the first to feel this. Byron himself sensed and expressed it. His immense comic epic, *Don Juan*, was planned to parade its Jack-in-the-bed hero throughout Europe, from boudoir to boudoir and boredom to boredom, till his sins achieved their final and fitting punishment. He must be sent to hell, i.e., to England, and there frozen to death with respectability and cant. Octave de Malivert, to be sure, is not a blasé bankrupt like the Byron hero, whose essential attitude was finely expressed by Scott Fitzgerald under the metaphor of a man who was given a fixed sum of capital (a limited capacity for sensation) and spent it all by the age of thirty. So far as his impotence is given any distinct motivation at all, Octave seems to be suffering, as I have said, from an excess of sensibility. On the other hand, an excess and a deficiency of sensibility are not always at opposite ends of the spectrum; Octave's passion makes him incapable of love, Don Juan's immense talents and prolonged practice in love finally make him incapable of passion. The promiscuous figure is emotionally sterile; that is, ultimately, the reason for his promiscuity. The impotent figure is emotionally too deep and responsive; that is the indicated reason for his impotence.

Whether Beyle had all these paradoxes in mind when he produced *Armance* may be debated; within the novel itself he is not even explicit about the causes of Octave's impotence, though the motivations indicated within the novel mostly run this way, and Beyle's references to the topic outside the novel fully confirm it. . . . The Byron-parallel may be one of those gratuitous critical contributions of which we are, nowadays, properly suspicious. Had it been fortified only a little, it might have helped relate the social satire of the novel to the hero's peculiar psychological problems, and given the reader welcome grounds for deciding where, in Octave de Malivert, the healthy protest leaves off and the morbid reactions begin. (pp. 143-51)

Perhaps it is just as well that Beyle . . . found himself shunted off into other, and more active themes.

For nothing in *Armance* prepares us to think that the next fiction its author attempts will be a masterpiece, or even the particular sort of novel that the *Rouge* is—leaving aside the question of its merits. *Armance* is slow, strained, and choked; the *Rouge* is swift, confident, and full-throated. Octave is sometimes an amusing satiric talker but most often a pathetic sufferer; Julien unhesitatingly acts. Armance de Zohiloff is nothing more than highmindedness, personified but never animated; Madame de Rênal and Mathilde de la Mole are women, heroic and complete.

Authors are often known to undergo breakthroughs, transformations as startling as they are absolute; and Stendhal, whose art was in large measure an art of improvisation, was particularly dependent on the unpredictable fluctuations of his subconscious. But once he had broken through, the *Rouge* by no means placed him in the clear. Sharp outline and wiry bounding narrative line are as remote from *Lucien Leuwen*

and *Lamiel*, as they are from *Armance;* the active hero or heroine is still muddled by over-motivation, assertion and analysis are still asked to do duty for action, and clinical investigation still shades vaguely into satiric exposé. Above all, the sense of unpredictable and mysterious danger, which fills the two great novels with light and passionate energy, is replaced in *Lucien* and *Lamiel* by a sense of predictability and passivity in which the two protagonists repeat the weakest characteristic of Octave de Malivert.

Of all Stendhal's novels, *Lucien Leuwen* is undoubtedly the most nineteenth-century. The steam-engine, the telegraph, and the forms and formalities of public opinion have now combined to produce a new, dull, and narrow world within which Lucien, equipped with nothing but money and republican scorn, is asked to survive. Salons exist in this world but only on the fringe of that enormous, anonymous machinery which, whether one regards the way in which it really works or merely the way in which it is supposed to work, is greased only by the universal unction of human *bassesse*. Within this world, Napoleon is gone and forgotten, or all but forgotten; his memory lingers as a vague nostalgia among the veterans gone cynical and corrupt in the service of the Restoration; or as an ideal, still living but hopeless, in the hearts of one or two firm and honorable men, set to do the dirtiest chores of the new regime and cynical of any reward. The provinces are populated by uneasy grotesques, timid, greedy, gauche, and cynical; the capital is inhabited by ruthless and cynical manipulators. (pp. 151-52)

Stagnation is unforeseen, and stagnation occurs; in its first volume, at least, *Lucien Leuwen* is almost an epic of stagnation, in which the tepid, scummy pond of provincial life is endlessly poked and prodded by an idle young man who has neither the envious energy to make war on society like Julien, nor any need to take unscrupulous advantage of it, like Fabrizio. As soon as he sees Nancy, Lucien despises it; 300 pages later, he is still despising it. His great question in life is, What must one do to respect oneself? and in looking for the answer in the 27th Lancers, garrisoned at Nancy, he is clearly beside all the possible points. Only the incident of his falling in love with Mme. de Chasteller has caused the 300 pages of the first volume to move in any particular direction. Here, indeed, the sensitivity of Lucien, which in the world of practical affairs freezes him into a permanent posture of *mépris,* finds its proper element. In the entire canon, there is nothing in its own way quite so fine as Lucien's love for Mme. de Chasteller. Julien's love affairs are perhaps rather embittered by his role as outsider; his hypocrisy makes for several little comedies of misunderstanding and imperception, but it also casts a shadow over the moments of tenderness which punctuate the social struggle. Fabrizio in his passion for Clélia, on the other hand, is almost purely heroic. But Lucien is both comic and heroic at once, both sublime and ridiculous; his love is simultaneously airy and intimate; and the whole delineation of his passion has that quality, which Beyle admired so much in the *Matrimonio segreto,* of tenderness mingled with gaiety. The affection of François Leuwen for his son, which finds expression in a fine vein of disillusioned drollery, suggests something of the warm comic feeling which Lucien generates in this most inward and self-absorbed of love affairs. He is a fine, spirited young animal; but his political ambitions are stunted from the beginning by the crass dead-centrism of Louis Philippe's bourgeois monarchy and his own exquisite scruples. When the satire on provincial society has begun to languish for lack of fresh material, and the threads of Lucien's love affairs are finely snarled between his own prickly conscience and that of Mme. de Chasteller, one begins to wonder if the novel will ever get off the ground.

There are in *Lucien,* as in *Armance,* patches of brilliant social satire and subtle psychological analysis; there are devastating situations implicit in the relations between silly liberals, panicky ultras, and "dead-centers" whom everyone despises. There are special glints and avenues of satire in the hero's being himself a dead-center, for lack of anything more significant to be. But in a garrison regiment, Second Lieutenant Leuwen is almost as much stunted in his possibilities of change and development as Octave the impotent. He has nowhere to go. . . . [Stendhal] tended to start his characters at the end of a rope, and hope for inspiration to get them moving.

Some of the most disappointing things about *Lucien* are the fragments of fascinating social flotsam with which Stendhal evidently attempted to prime his pump. Milord Link, a mysterious English homosexual, turns up late in the first volume, and looks like a promising storm-center, but he drifts out of sight without getting himself involved in an action. Dr. du Poirier, who is an ultra in Nancy and gets his principles altered to those of a liberal in Paris, arrives on the scene as late as the Chevalier de Bonnivet in an action which he is to influence decisively; he is clearly a fascinating fellow, but his motivations are utterly indefinite, and having shown himself a liberal and a coward in Chapter 57, he quietly fades away. There is a lancer in the regiment, formerly a book-binder, actor, fencing-master, deserter, and almost a galley-slave; but Ménuel, after regaling us with his life-history for a few pages at the beginning of Chapter 8, also disappears for good. All the novels of Stendhal contain characters who turn up for a short stretch of time and then drop into the background; when the narrative stream is bearing strongly along, these passing encounters, which may or may not turn out to be significant later, give an immense sense of richness and hidden potentiality. But when the narrative is anemic, it is irritating to see potential sources of energy go to waste.

The best elements of *Lucien Leuwen* are found, undeniably, in the second volume. Lucien is transformed here into the secretary of a minister. . . . The satire cuts deeply and truly into French political life; the hero's self-disgust counterpoints enchantingly his genuine pride at playing a man's role in the actual, dirty world of men. He is a perfectly delightful sinner, only less so than his father. For meanwhile, M. Leuwen, taking the rules of democratic government at the foot of the letter, has organized a burlesque political party of obedient nonentities, "the legion of the *midi,*" whipped them into shape with promises, stupidities, and self-importance, and made himself a vigorous figure in the administration.

These are elegant and rollicking themes; as a maker of ministers and a Machiavellian ironist of government, the banker Leuwen is altogether peerless. His amorous and social advice to his son is a veritable model of French fatherly concern tempered with total sophistication; indeed, he is in a fair way toward running off with the novel entirely. But the picaresque adventures of these rich rascals, the Leuwens father and son, lead us ever farther from the strange, half-chivalric world inhabited by Bathilde de Chasteller. Lucien at least can only profit by having some of the sentimental bloom rubbed off him. In Chapter 67 we find him holding the swooning Madame Grandet in his arms and thinking about party politics—and in this role he is, momentarily at least, a worthy

successor to Julien Sorel. But though Stendhal had at least one perfectly elegant denouement in mind for his novel, he seems to have hesitated about working it out, and left the story unfinished from sheer indecision. Lucien's affair with Madame Grandet was to have been the keystone in a vast political stratagem of his father's; at the height of this plot, he was to desert Mme. Grandet, and find true understanding with Mme. de Chasteller at Nancy, or, perhaps after some further intrigues, at Rome. In a plot like this, Lucien's love, by triumphing over his own sardonic and his father's serious ambition, might take on a touch of the heroic. But, caught between this ending and several other possible ones, with a sense of weariness at the necessity for new characters, and a distaste for a hero who seemed to be nothing more than "a nail exposed to the blows of the hammer of fate," Stendhal gave up on his story entirely.

Despite fine touches, then, *Lucien Leuwen,* which was written after the *Rouge,* suffers from some of the same deficiencies as *Armance,* which was written before; and yet the *Rouge* itself is quite free from them. There seems to be no simpler way of accounting for this pattern than by Stendhal's need for a preexisting narrative framework. Fine as it is in spots, *Lucien* as a whole runs the constant risk of "turning out soggy" because there are not enough scenes involving "change of attitude." They were his own phrases, jotted on the MS as he went along or looked over what he had already written; and in another moment of misgiving, he wrote, "If this is worthless, one of the prime reasons will have been having to think of a plot." The fact is, that for a novelist who considered that "the business of a novel is to narrate," Stendhal had little capacity for devising extended and coherent actions. He sometimes tried to rationalize this deficiency into a merit, saying that it helped his invention, in writing, not to know from day to day or even from page to page what was going to happen next. "One never goes so far," in the words of an ancient proverb, "as when one does not know where one is going" (note on *Lucien Leuwen*). It is clear that very often this is indeed the character of his best writing, where the dialogue seems to spring from the immediate needs of the situation, and the action is directed as much by the whims, schemes, mistakes, and preconceptions of the characters themselves as by any intent of the author's. It is clear too that his first drafts were usually too voluminous by far; that he relied upon the last revisions to chasten his language, simplify his style, and give nerve to his prose. *Lucien,* never having undergone this process, cannot fairly be compared in point of economy with the corrected novels.

But for all these limitations and rationalizations, the fact remains that a novelist who does not know where he is going does not know what effects he is building toward, and is in no position to pick and choose among the economies and extravagances available to him. Lucien Leuwen is, if anything, too one-sided emotionally to be a successful protagonist; the only deep passion of his life is Madame de Chasteller, and if his father were one-tenth the Machiavellian he is made to seem, he would see that Lucien can only be led securely by this one cord. But the other characters in the fiction are wide-open possibilities. Dr. du Poirier is a rascal, clear enough, but a totally unpredictable rascal; we get one fix on him, deceiving Lucien about Mme. de Chasteller's "bastard"; we get another when he apostasizes to "liberalism"; still a third when he turns out to be a physical coward; but, were we ever to see him again, one cannot doubt that he would be miles away, on the track of another snipe altogether. So too with Milord

Link, or Mme. Grandet, or Louis-Philippe himself; any of these characters might be unexpectedly converted to serve any conceivable purpose in the novel. It is precisely because the bit players in the drama are too indefinite to give it a steady direction (in the words of M. Bardèche, they "never make up a system of forces on which the destiny of the hero will depend") that young Leuwen himself has to be tied down so tightly. And tying him down tightly almost forces him to be more pathetic than comic; deprives him of a field of maneuver, and reduces him, regrettably, to the stock sad young man of nineteenth-century fiction. Gide, who rather overestimated lack of impetus in a novel (surely it is excessive to hope that each chapter will seem like a fresh beginning to a story) thought *Armance* and *Lucien Leuwen* the finest of Stendhal's novels; but, as the world runs, this judgment tells us more of Gide than of Stendhal. (pp. 153-58)

If the point needed further making, *Lamiel* would suffice to show . . . the hesitant course of [Stendhal's] narrative instinct when unguided by a pre-formed plot. The raw materials of the novel represent a fantastic challenge. A hunchbacked sadistic doctor who fancies himself a Don Juan, and a handsome young girl, impatient of her sex yet resolved to trade upon it and ambitious for the supreme experiences of life—these are startling characters with whom to start a story. That they are capable of fine comic effects the story itself, as far as Stendhal carried it, brilliantly demonstrates. Bold, naïve, inquisitive, and unpredictable, Lamiel embarks on her travels with all the energy she is supposed to be seeking; infinite possibilities lie before her, including the wry one that she will discover energy in others only when she no longer has it herself. But over none of his novels did Stendhal ever hesitate more confusingly than over this one. There are several different notions of the central action; there are varying lists of subordinate characters; there are dozens of different time-schemes. Two or three versions of the opening passage were written; a number of different endings were contemplated. It is odd to find the man who had just written off the *Chartreuse* in one brilliant, uninterrupted surge of six weeks' work, paltering and hesitating over *Lamiel* like the most unpracticed of novices. And yet what could one expect? At the core of each of his other novels there is a solid bit of fact borrowed from someone else. . . . Only *Lamiel* is almost without a grain of sand for the pearl to grow around. There was to have been a brigand in open warfare with society, with whom Lamiel was to have fallen in love; and for him at least, Jean Prévost discovered a number of real-life originals. But a good deal of the novel as Stendhal first sketched it was original creation; like all his original work, it was curiously formless; and he never did decide how much of it would or would not be useful to him in carving out the ultimate intrigue.

Much more interesting than the obvious episodic deficiencies of a MS which, as it exists, was very likely nothing more than preliminary work for a story which never got written, is the extraordinary character of Dr. Sansfin. A brilliant and unscrupulous mind hidden in an ugly body, he dreams, like Beyle himself, of letting his spirit take possession of a handsome corpse. Finding Lamiel dying of boredom, he undertakes to seduce her by being entertaining; and he manages, single-handed, to make out of this frank and energetic Norman peasant-girl an accomplished Parisian hypocrite. His fate is one familiar to Pygmalions; having given Lamiel the spirit of a cold and deliberate adventurer in evil, he sees her seduce, or be seduced by, a good-looking simpleton. And

in one of the many fragments which clutter up the MS, Dr. Sansfin falls furiously on this young fellow with a dagger, and acts out his destruction in a fine symbolic way.

It may well be that in the dualism of hideous cynical Sansfin and lovely innocent Lamiel are represented two aspects of Henri Beyle, the coldly experienced and the naïvely ardent. If this were so, and one were set to seek evidences of the same contrast elsewhere in the novels of Stendhal, it would not be hard to fix on the division between Conte Mosca and Fabrizio in the *Chartreuse,* between Leuwen *père* and Leuwen *fils* in *Lucien,* and perhaps between M. de la Mole and Julien in the *Rouge.* Earlier than the *Rouge,* one is probably wandering among shadows; there is no one person who plays for Octave the role which, with steadily darkening overtones, M. de la Mole, François Leuwen, Mosca, and Dr. Sansfin play for their respective innocents. But the repetition of a dualism which sets black so distinctively against white—which is pregnant, as it were with Dr. Jekyll and Mr. Hyde as well as the two faces of Dorian Gray, Lafcadio and Fleurissoire, William Wilson and his double, and a whole string of schizophrenic romantic protagonists,—throws into relief the entire problem of Stendhal's pre-Freudian insights, as the biographers have delighted to call them. These can be usefully divided into complex analyses of psychic causation, which are good; and simple delineations of psychic pattern considered as a final effect, which are bad.

The trouble with Dr. Sansfin, squat like a toad by the ear of Lamiel, inoculating her with the first principles of Beylism, is that it brings us too quickly to the end of Sansfin; and the end of Sansfin imposes a whole fresh beginning on Lamiel, which is hard to avoid depicting as a regression, and over which, in fact, Stendhal consistently faltered. For the Stendhal hero (and heroine, too, be it understood) is a flexible and unpredictable creation precisely as he combines the passionate freshness of youth with the cynical experience of age. Any tendency to sort out these two elements, and embody them in separate *personae* leads at once to the stiffness of allegory and the embarrassment of confessional writing. Stendhal was by no means exempt from this fault of the two-dimensional, analytically-motivated character; but it afflicted him chiefly where he was most conscious of the oddity of his basic premise and desirous of throwing its consequences into high relief. The first two or three chapters of *Armance* recite, almost in textbook fashion, various clinical symptoms of the Vicomte de Malivert. Interesting as they are, in fact, just because they have a special clinical interest of their own, these symptoms remain unassimilated in the novel. Having been mentioned once, they never appear again; the author feels no obligation to make use of them. And so it is with Lamiel and Dr. Sansfin; his work in introducing her to the realities of life is mechanically performed; one may feel either grateful at having it out of the way, or irritated at having it so gracelessly in the foreground; but at best it merely postpones and complicates the evil hour when Lamiel must test on her own pulses, and prove through her own experience, the falsity of social convention, the reality of passion and energy. Prologue or epilogue, footnote or commentary, whatever one wants to call it, Beylism personified is outside a true Stendhal novel. (pp. 165-68)

Robert M. Adams, in his Stendhal: Notes on a Novelist, *The Noonday Press, 1959, 228 p.*

F. W. J. HEMMINGS   (essay date 1964)

[Hemmings considers the conclusion of The Red and the Black *appropriate to Julien's psychology, interpreting it as his "act of self-justification."]*

No incident in [*Le Rouge et le Noir*] has incurred so much criticism and aroused so much speculation as Julien's attempt on Mme de Rênal's life which, although unsuccessful, ruins a career of unlimited promise and delivers him to the executioner. The situation which Stendhal has reached in chapter XXXV of the second part of *Le Rouge et le Noir* can be summarized in a few lines. Mathilde, discovering that she is with child by Julien, tells her father that they must marry. The Marquis de La Mole, another 'homme à imagination', had dreamed of seeing his daughter marry into a ducal family. His fury is boundless but he is obliged to yield to the realities of the situation; to make the match socially a little more acceptable, he has a minor title conferred on Julien, procures him a commission in the hussars, and settles an income on him. He delays giving his final consent only in order to complete his inquiries into Julien's character. These inquiries result in a letter from Mme de Rênal in which Julien is described as an ambitious young man who profits by his sexual attractions in order to enslave and dishonour whatever woman has most credit in the household in which he is serving.

M. de La Mole warns Mathilde he will never consent to her marriage with a man of this type. Julien, having been shown Mme de Rênal's letter, tells Mathilde her father's decision is perfectly understandable. Without another word he takes horse for Verrières, where he arrives on a Sunday morning. He purchases a pair of pistols and tells the gunsmith to load them for him; enters the church as mass is being celebrated; and sees Mme de Rênal a few pews away. He hesitates for so long as she is clearly visible. But when she lowers her head Julien fires once at the kneeling figure bathed in the red light which streams through the crimson awnings hung over the windows of the church. With the first shot he misses; he fires again and she falls.

Émile Faguet, at the beginning of this century, was apparently the first commentator to complain that this train of incidents was in total contradiction with the psychology of the various characters involved in them [see excerpt dated 1899]. M. de La Mole ought to have reflected that little weight could be given to the denunciation of a jealous cast-off mistress. Mathilde, instead of sending Julien an agitated and despairing summons, ought to have waited for her father to come round to a more rational way of thinking. Julien, finally, ought to have seen that nothing was to be gained by assassinating his accuser. Whatever he may say or think, the Marquis is in no position to forbid or defer indefinitely his daughter's marriage to Julien.

Faguet suggests two reasons why Stendhal should have set plausibility at defiance here. In the first place, the fashion of the day required a melodramatic finish to a novel. There may be something in this, even though Stendhal had contented himself with an ending in a minor key for *Armance.* The successful novels—*Les Chouans, Notre-Dame de Paris, Indiana*—published in France about the same time as *Le Rouge et le Noir* were nothing if not sensational; and Stendhal was not indifferent to the claims of the contemporary romantic sensibility. His concessions to this taste, however, though real, are seldom so conspicuous, and they must be looked for in rather subtler touches. To take but one instance, a careful

reading of *Le Rouge et le Noir* allows one to detect traces of a kind of fate symbolism (admittedly more German than French in inspiration) which might be held to represent a passing obeisance to romanticism. Has it ever been observed how, on three crucial occasions, the hero finds himself *in a church hung with red draperies* of one sort or another? When he enters the church at Verrières with intent to murder, 'toutes les fenêtres hautes de l'édifice étaient voilées avec des rideaux cramoisis'. The detail echoes an earlier incident which took place in the cathedral at Besançon, the gothic pillars of which, in celebration of the Corpus Christi holiday, were encased in 'une sorte d'habit de damas rouge' rising to thirty feet; it was here, behind one of these red pillars, that Julien saw Mme de Rênal unexpectedly for the first time since he left Verrières. The shock of seeing him caused her to swoon away. Both these occasions are no doubt meant to recall the experience Julien had when he was on his way, for the first time, to the Rênals' house. On a whim, he entered the church—later to be the scene of his criminal attempt—and found it 'sombre et solitaire. A l'occasion d'une fête, toutes les croisées de l'édifice avaient été couvertes d'étoffe cramoisie. Il en résultait, aux rayons du soleil, un effet de lumière éblouissant, du caractère le plus imposant et le plus religieux.' Julien picks up a scrap of newspaper in the Rênal family pew. On one side are printed the words: 'Détails de l'exécution et des derniers moments de Louis Jeanrel, exécuté à Besançon, le . . .', and on the other the beginning of a sentence: 'Le premier pas . . .' Julien, on leaving the church, imagines he sees blood spilt on the floor. A closer inspection shows the illusion to have been created by drops of holy water which shine red in the red light which streams through the red curtains. So discreet a use of omens and portents does not suffice to make *Le Rouge et le Noir* a *schicksalsroman,* and perhaps, after all, bearing in mind Stendhal's literary preferences, it might be safer to trace such features to Shakespeare rather than to contemporary romantic literature. His admiration of *Macbeth* would have been strong enough to tempt him to this distant imitation.

Faguet's other suggestion is that Julien would not have been, as Stendhal wanted him to be, a second Laffargue, a man of 'energy', if he had not sooner or later tried to kill someone. Stendhal's conception of energy was a little more subtle than this: strength of character does not necessarily display itself in homicide. Nevertheless, the opinion that Stendhal's invention here was not altogether free received powerful reinforcement when the story of the seminarist of Brangues came to light. At the time Faguet was writing, Stendhal's incontrovertible use of this *cause célèbre* had not yet been fully established. Some of the most authoritative of his modern critics suppose that Stendhal's hand was in a sense forced by the necessity to dovetail Julien's career into the historical framework provided by Berthet's, even though Julien did not have Berthet's motives for murder or the character that might have led him to commit it. Other apologists suppose Julien to have lapsed, at this point in the story, into a psychopathic condition, and are prepared to back up this theory with a wealth of clinical detail.

In reality, it is unnecessary to suppose either that Stendhal was being clumsy or that Julien had taken leave of his senses. The incident, artistically desirable in that it provides a 'strong' climax, is also well-founded psychologically and, if the phrase may be used, poetically true.

Well-founded psychologically, because Julien's violent reaction is perfectly explainable as that of a man of spirit who has been, to use an expressive contemporary word, 'smeared'. The question is not whether Mme de Rênal's accusation is true or false; the question is not even whether Mme de Rênal believes what she has written (it emerges later that she composed the letter at the prompting of her confessor). The point, as Julien sees it, is that, in everyone's eyes but his own, the picture that has been drawn of him corresponds a shade too closely to reality. It is undeniably true that, in the two households in which he served, he 'dishonoured the woman who had most credit'. His motives were not ignoble, or not as ignoble as the letter suggests; but who will believe him, when the motives attributed to him are so plausible? The essence of a 'smear' is that it presents a portion of the truth and adds a degrading lie which nothing in what is known of the truth contradicts. Whatever protestations he may now make, and however M. de La Mole may profess to accept these protestations, Julien could never be sure that, in his heart, the Marquis will not continue to believe that he had been forced to yield his daughter to a scheming adventurer. Like Octave in this, Julien cannot endure not to be esteemed by those he respects. M. de La Mole himself, baffled by the enigmas in Julien's character, is convinced of at least one thing: 'il est impatient du mépris . . . [il] ne peut supporter le mépris à aucun prix.'

With absolute logic, Julien chooses the only course which can efface this suspicion, because it is the very last course of action that would be expected of an ambitious schemer: committing murder in broad daylight and insisting, when interrogated, that the crime was premeditated. It is not an act of despair, for Julien has no reason to despair: he can still marry the Marquis's daughter and progress to the summits of society on which after all there is room for men with far more on their conscience than the seduction, for mercenary reasons, of their employer's daughter. It is not an act of despair, it is not even an act of vengeance, as he pretends to Mathilde. It is an act of self-justification. It cuts short his life, ruins his hopes, but ensures at least that no man will think him a wily scoundrel.

The poetic truth of the episode lies in the opportunity it provided Stendhal to reveal in the end the authentic Julien, who had occasionally emerged in the early chapters, but who subsequently, in the 'little world' of the seminary and in the 'great world' of Paris, had drowned more and more deeply in a murk of artificiality. At Besançon he was still an apprentice in the art of suppressing his own personality. 'Après plusieurs mois d'application de tous les instants, Julien avait encore l'air de *penser*. Sa façon de remuer les yeux et de porter la bouche n'annonçait pas la foi implicite et prête à tout croire et à tout soutenir, même par le martyre.' But the more he committed himself to his ambition, the easier he found it to act the parts required of him: the part of the perfect secretary, the part of the intrepid horseman, the part of the confidential agent. M. de La Mole asks him to post himself at the door of the Opéra, at half past eleven every evening, to observe the deportment of young men of fashion, and imitate them. He forms a close friendship with a charming exquisite, the Chevalier de Beauvoisis, and learns so well the art of foppishness that in London, in the native land of dandyism, he eclipses all rivals. Later, he acts for weeks on end the part of devoted admirer of a pious prude in order to humiliate Mathilde and tame this notorious shrew. Stendhal, it is true, professes to admire the 'courage' with which Julien feigns indifference to his mistress and admiration for Mme de Fervaques; but is this

not another instance of the 'double irony', noted earlier, of the commentator who hides his deepest meaning under a screen of deceptive transparency?

All through the second part of this novel, Julien is becoming *civilized;* at the end of it, he is on the point of reaping civilization's rewards. 'My adventure is over,' he exclaims the evening he learns that he now ranks as a lieutenant of hussars; 'mon roman est fini, et à moi seul tout le mérite.' He sacrifices all these rewards by a single act of *energy*, making the most uncivilized, most ungentlemanly gesture of shooting down the woman who had impugned his honour, for all the world like a Corsican cut-throat.

He is recompensed by a serenity which he had never known before, save in brief snatches in the garden at Vergy and in the mountains above Verrières. His prison-cell is at the top of a tower, with a 'superb view', and here, writes Stendhal, 'son âme était calme . . . La vie n'était point ennuyeuse pour lui, il considérait toutes choses sous un nouvel aspect. Il n'avait plus d'ambition. Il pensait rarement à mademoiselle de La Mole';—instead, his mind reverts with persistence to Mme de Rênal, 'surtout pendant le silence des nuits, troublé seulement, dans ce donjon élevé, par le chant de l'orfraie'. The cry of the osprey—an unusually evocative touch which is premonitory of the zone of poetry into which Stendhal is now moving. . . . Julien, by the proximity of death, is suddenly aged, as though a man's age depended not on the number of years lived but on the time left for him to live.

The happiness of the dreamer takes charge, with this difference, that formerly his dreams were of the future, and of clashes with men, triumphs over women, the battle of the sexes, and the war of the classes. Now he has done with *the others*. He shuts his ears to news of the outside world; cuts as short as he decently can his conferences with defending counsel; is impatient with his faithful friend Fouqué, who is pathetically plotting his escape from prison, and even more impatient with Mathilde. 'A vrai dire il était fatigué d'héroïsme.' He implores them not to trouble him. . . . He barely conceals from Mathilde the fact that his first love fills his thoughts. Before the trial he had been flooded by memories of incidents thought forgotten; Verrières and Vergy had completely displaced Paris in his thoughts, and he was truly happy only when, left in complete solitude, he was free to relive that more distant past. In the court room only the presence of Mme Derville has power to draw him out of his glacial indifference to the proceedings: he imagines she is there as Mme de Rênal's emissary. The following day, in the condemned cell, he is woken by Mathilde, frantic with grief and with the sense of failure. He is silent when she seeks, by entreaty, argument, and invective, to dissuade him from refusing to appeal against his sentence. He is not listening to her. Instead, his imagination shows him, in a vision of hallucinatory intensity, Mme de Rênal's bedroom in the house at Verrières, the local newspaper, with the story of his execution emblazed on its front page, as it lies on the orange counterpane, Mme de Rênal's hand crumpling its pages convulsively, the tears coursing down her face. . . .

The undeserved and crowning happiness is when Mme de Rênal, braving scandal and her husband's interdict, visits him in prison. Stendhal implies, in the few brief scenes in which he shows them together, something which a younger novelist than he could never have suggested, at any rate with such conviction: that the transcendent enchantment of love comes with the sharing of the past in recollection.

The other incidents in this culminating drama—Mathilde's intriguing, her furious and helpless jealousy, the attempted bribery of justice, Julien's appearance in court and deliberate taunting of the jurymen to ensure they should not acquit him—all these seem vaguely unreal, for we see everything with minds clouded by the powerful emanation of Julien's enraptured dream-state. Even his bitter animadversions against society, his anguished speculations on the after-life, seem less important than the granting of this unforeseen happiness. They do, however, succeed in making his death seem real, the finality absolute, even though, when he reaches the moment of death, Stendhal avails himself of his supreme resource: silence.

> Jamais cette tête n'avait été aussi poétique qu'au moment où elle allait tomber. Les plus doux moments qu'il avait trouvés jadis dans les bois de Vergy revenaient en foule à sa pensée et avec une extrême énergie.

> Tout se passa simplement, convenablement, et de sa part sans aucune affectation.

The writer who was to narrate so scrupulously the gruesome tortures inflicted by her judges on Beatrice Cenci, says no more than this touching the execution of Julien Sorel.

He had not been allowed to refuse the consolations of religion, but had made it clear to the priest that he repented of nothing in his life. 'J'ai été ambitieux, je ne veux point me blâmer; alors, j'ai agi suivant les convenances du temps.' The words are addressed, on a deeper level, by Stendhal to the reader. If Julien was for most of his life misguided it is the ethos of his age that should be blamed. Napoleon is a symbol, a pretext, no more. The historical moment called for the kind of single-minded, resolute *arrivisme* that Julien did his best to display. One way or another, betrayal was inescapable: Julien's choice lay between betraying his soul through hardness and betraying his spirit through softness. Had he remained at Verrières, had he accepted the profitable partnership which Fouqué offered him in his timber business, he would perhaps have been happy, but he would not have been a hero; it is required of Aeneas that he leave Carthage and her queen, even though this Aeneas goes to found no new city. It would be naïve to write down *Le Rouge et le Noir* as a sermon on the folly of human ambitions; for things could not have been otherwise. But it is obviously far more than a piece of social satire; though it might not be altogether misplaced to speak of it as a piece of sublimated social history. Stendhal had perhaps something of the sort in mind when he gave his novel the sub-title *Chronique du XIXᵉ siècle*.

But any formula seems intolerably constricted. 'Every time you discuss Stendhal, you are left with the impression that you have said nothing at all, that he has eluded you, and that everything remains to be said. In the end you have to resign yourself and restore him to his unpredictable and miraculous utterance' [according to J. P. Richard]. *Le Rouge et le Noir* acts, in its own way, as Stendhal does in his larger fashion: the book, and the man, defy criticism, if criticism is the art of throwing a net of convincing approximations over the protean masterpiece or artist. It is not criticism merely to marvel. But in that case criticism is here powerless, for in the last resort there is nothing we can do but marvel at the sheer intellectual brilliance with which Stendhal has connected his several explosive themes in an ordered system, presented the complex totality lucidly and exhaustively, and irradiated the whole with that strange stark poetry which is peculiarly his own. (pp. 123-31)

> *F. W. J. Hemmings, in his* Stendhal: A Study of His Novels, *Oxford at the Clarendon Press, 1964, 232 p.*

LOUIS KRONENBERGER (essay date 1966)

[*A drama critic for* Time *from 1938 to 1961, Kronenberger was a distinguished historian, literary critic, and author highly regarded for his expertise in eighteenth-century English history and literature. Of his critical work, Kronenberger's* The Thread of Laughter: Chapters on English Stage Comedy from Jonson to Maugham *(1952) and* The Republic of Letters *(1955) contain some of his best literary commentaries. A prolific and versatile writer, he also wrote plays and novels and edited anthologies of the works of others. In the following excerpt from an essay first published in the* Michigan Quarterly Review *in July 1966, Kronenberger examines the "worldliness" of* The Charterhouse of Parma.]

For most discerning readers—there are those, to be sure, who find Stendhal uncongenial—*The Charterhouse of Parma* ranks among the greatest of novels; but scarcely anyone, I think, would deny it a place with the very greatest novels of worldliness. It is this for two substantial reasons: because of its tone—its attitude of an urbane, unillusioned, enormously perceptive *homme du monde;* and again because of the level at which the worldliness operates. Our very scene is the court of a small early nineteenth-century principality. We are concerned with, so to speak, *professional* worldlings, with courtiers and politicos, great ladies and ministers of state. One's every move, be it never so trivial, tends to be a calculated one—because any move, in an audience chamber or merely on a dance floor, may have consequences. One's every word, even the merest banter, needs to be weighed, for every word will be communicated to others. The favor of the prince is no sooner won than it may be lost again; the favorite of the prince is no sooner established than he may be dismissed. Every social occasion is endowed with political significance; every comic contretemps may have tragic repercussions; every forgotten indiscretion may be strategically brought to light. At any given moment, the ruler's policy may derive from the ruler's vanity, just as his personal fears may occasion his whole court's fright. Moreover, the worldliness is all the greater here, all the more concentrated, because the scene is so limited, the stage so small. At this miniature court of this toylike principality, everyone is the warier for being involved in the same wiles, for giving ear to the same gossip, for coveting the same places, for clinging to the same ropes, for being equally a contestant, a competitor, a conspirator. The whole thing has, in its blend of rather sinister worldly disguises and ticklish worldly missteps, now the sound of melodrama and now the tone of farce. But there are deeper sounds too, and profounder intimations—all that high comedy has to tell us, in its own way, of what is tragic in life.

For *The Charterhouse* goes beyond the usual worldling writer catching his worldling characters out; goes beyond a tearing off of masks and a mockery of pretenses, beyond even the most extensive representation of social stances and sophisticated gambits. One reason why it is so great a novel of worldliness is that, without relaxing its worldliness, it transcends it—not by introducing copybook figures of greater nobility or idealism, not by counterpoising booted-and-spurred abstractions of ethics or philosophy, but by creating three particular magnificent characters, one of whom—Count Mosca—sums up what can be said both for and against the enlightened worldling, two others of whom—the hero Fabrizio, and the incomparable Duchess of Sanseverina—stand less outside the worldly scene than above it. It is not so much that they are incapable of mastering its ways as unwilling to submit to its laws; as that they are moved, in the great crises of their lives, by grander personal desires, by more urgent personal visions. They do not evade, they do not in the didactic sense renounce the worldly life; they enlarge upon it.

But behind them is their creator; *in* them, indeed, is their creator, in each of the three there is one side or another of Stendhal. And Stendhal is more brilliantly endowed than even they are. E. M. Forster speaks somewhere of a not too happy encounter with Howard Sturgis, who conveyed the impression—Forster noted with amused malice—that Forster's books contained him and not he his books. Certainly Stendhal's books do not contain him, he contains them. We are particularly aware of this in *The Charterhouse,* aware not only of someone who can command a whole orchestra of human musical instruments, fiddles and flutes, trombones and tubas; who, again, can create an entire small state rich in history and geography alike, but someone who most of all can imbue the whole with something complex and multicolored, a kind of compass with all its varying points; a contradictory whole that subtly rejects what it seems to accept, makes comedy of what it seems to hold sacred, blithely stands on its head what it seems to have stood on a pedestal. It is a method that uses every kind of contrast as a form of criticism yet seems to find all forms of contrast inadequate as a guide—so that the final irony is the inadequacy of irony. (pp. 181-83)

The commonest approach of current criticism toward *The Charterhouse* is as a political novel, and certainly it is notable as just that: indeed, the very framework—of a small autocratic state where every one is jockeying for power—implies political action inside it. All the same, I think that a distinction needs to be made about *The Charterhouse* that so far as I know has not been: which is that it is essentially a novel of political *intrigue* rather than of political ideas, a kind of handbook on political tactics rather than a textbook of political thought. And in this sense it seems to me a political novel folded into something broader and more commodious: in other words, it is ultimately concerned with intrigue itself, with methods, with stratagems, whether political or social or sexual; whether inside ministries or throne rooms or boudoirs; whether in pursuit of power or position; whether a matter of false friendships or false vows. It is because *The Charterhouse* is concerned with worldly motives and ambitions on the political *and* the social *and* the personal side, having as much about it of Castiglione's *The Courtier* as of Machiavelli's *The Prince,* that it is a supreme novel of worldliness first, and a remarkable political novel secondarily.

Very much of the secondary, and sometimes primary, pleasure that the book provides has to do with political machinery no less than political machinations. One of the most delightful of creative enterprises for an author is setting up a history, a geography, a cosmology of his own; inventing a state, a capital, a dynasty such as Stendhal has done here, a miniature world which shall be made to seem real and in time take on more than factuality—take on depth and signifi-

cance. Stendhal's world has, in small compass, everything needed for Stendhal's purpose. Martin Turnell refers to it as a police state, and to the Prince as a dictator; but that, I think, gives it too purely modern a slant. Parma is rather a remnant of autocracy, of something despotic by inheritance, than a foretaste of totalitarianism, with its pretense of a welfare state and a usurper-despot. Indeed, what is so peculiarly operatic about the manner and even the events of *The Charterhouse* springs from how old-fashioned and ornate an autocracy it is; any police-state conception, even as opera, lies far in the future and the world of *verismo*. More important, a police state cannot easily ascend to high comedy, cannot explode at will into extravagance, or plummet into farce. What gives *The Charterhouse* both its Renaissance cunning and its rococo court life is its air of the ancien régime—and at a moment in the consciousness of Europe when the ancien régime has crystallized as precisely that: when a new order is challenging it and triumphing over it.

In this world of Parma, which a little recalls the old description of Russia under the Czars—"autocracy tempered by assassination"—the ultras and liberals intrigue against one another with the utmost unscrupulousness, the great difficulty being that they tend to function with the utmost impotence and that their political aims are mangled by their personal ambitions. The official chief Liberal is the governor of the Citadel, which is to say the head of the jail, and most of his prisoners are fellow Liberals whom he treats with all possible harshness. The farcically ironic use to which Stendhal puts the whole party system, the space he happily lavishes on all the stratagems of party functionaries, as against how little he does with beliefs and ideas, further stresses how much more this is a novel of political intrigue than of political thought. Mosca, who, though Prime Minister of the reactionary party, is Parma's best proponent of liberal tolerance—to *practice,* indeed, any kind of liberalism he must preach its opposite—even Mosca is concerned not with how best to persuade or convince Ernesto IV, but with how best to manage him: whether with coarse flattery or veiled threats, but in any case with the arts of the diplomat rather than the arguments of the statesman. And as the plot thickens, it becomes Mosca's problem to manage the Prince as much in terms of the Duchess and Fabrizio as of Parma's internal and foreign affairs. Moreover, at one of the great crises of the story, Mosca's horrible ministerial blunder constitutes one of Stendhal's most brilliant satiric triumphs. When the Duchess, as the price of her remaining in Parma, forces the Prince to remove the prison sentence he has imposed on Fabrizio, and astutely stipulates that "these unjust proceedings shall have no consequences in the future"—in other words, that Fabrizio shall go permanently free—Mosca, drawing up the document for the Prince to sign, from a form of diplomatic caution that has become second nature with him, omits the safeguarding phrase, and so gives the Prince the chance to throw Fabrizio into the Citadel. This way in which he instinctively serves the Prince's interest rather than that of the woman he passionately loves is a just insight into human conditioning. Certainly it would be possible, but I think unsound, to bring Freud into it and suggest that, by omitting the crucial phrase, Mosca is unconsciously conspiring the downfall of his rival with the Duchess.

The whole scene that culminates in Mosca's drawing up the document is full of the most adroit and delicious high comedy, one of the scenes that contribute generally to *The Charterhouse*'s high distinction, but more particularly to its definitive portrayal of worldliness and its comic verve and wit. (pp. 188-91)

Much of [the story], as we observed earlier, is operatic; almost all of it, which intensifies what is operatic, is Italian. Behind the uniforms and medals there are passionate bodies, and behind the masks, devious minds. In the course of the book Fabrizio kills a man; the Duchess has the ruler of Parma killed; the ruler himself kills whoever seems to menace him; the Duchess has the strongest amorous feelings for Fabrizio, as has Mosca for her, and Fabrizio for Clélia. Fabrizio escapes by a silken rope from a high tower; opportunists everywhere conspire, ruffians everywhere lie in wait, politicians everywhere bide their time. The effect of so much melodrama laced with so much urbanity is sometimes merely storybook, and at other times rather dreamlike and surrealist. At still other times, it becomes a particular type of opera—one in which the libretto runs to crude action but the music to refined commentary. Accompanying the flash of a stiletto will be an aria full of exquisite perception or ironic mockery. As the plot plunges into some new thicket of intrigue, the orchestra sounds chords of civilized ennui or despair. In a work like *The Charterhouse,* story and theme, action and reaction, surface and subsurface, present and past, often play antiphonal roles. And so, most of all, do the romantic and the realistic in Stendhal's cosmos—or perhaps we might better say the romancer and the psychologist in Stendhal. The story lets us revel in the merely witty, entertaining, thrilling, almost frivolous, only for us to suddenly find ourselves—with all the torches extinguished—in the dank vault of self-interest, hearing strange animal screeches of treachery and malignity. And this most operatic of stories is of course recounted in Stendhal's bare Code Napoleon style; amid all the sword flourishes and rapier thrusts of his characters, he himself uses a plain pen.

Having eaten our cake and enjoyed every rich crumb of the story, just what have we besides? I'm not sure just what: as no one can be more explicit than Stendhal, so no one at times seems more enigmatic. The sense of enigma derives, to some degree, from a total absence of dogma: the essence of Stendhal's urbane worldly-wiseness is that one can pose no lasting answers or solutions. It is as easy to blueprint an imaginary principality as it is hard to chart the course of man's emotional or moral destiny. And so, when most serious or engaged, Stendhal may turn most whimsical and flippant: balked of reality, he will permit himself to play the conjurer. Doors sometimes magically fly open in *The Charterhouse,* with no realistic concern about any hand or key to open them with. Stendhal in one way is immensely creative in *The Charterhouse,* and by different standards hardly creative at all. Thus there is no immediacy about his people, no sense of what we might call the next door neighbor; nor do characters or events come upon us as things known or seen. Stendhal, in other words, does not create in the sense that he seems to re-create, as Jane Austen does, or Fielding, or Tolstoy. Perhaps one reason why Stendhal does not do this is that from his inventing *everything*—even his own detailed history and geography—very little seems familiar or near at hand. Despite what a Mosca may owe to a Metternich, and even a fictitious Parma to a historical Modena, the book is a perfect tissue of the artificial and imaginary. In going so far outside ordinary nature, Stendhal is equally going inside his private self. And that, though at first it might not seem so, makes for less unity of effect than would the usual vision of the outside world. For where, by one's interpretation of things and view of life, one can harmo-

A portrait of Angela Pietragrua.

nize the diversities of the outside world, when it is the contradictions of one's own complex inner self that provide the substance of one's book, the result may well be clouded and enigmatic. What in other words we have in *The Charterhouse* is neither any sort of subjective or autobiographical novel on the one hand, nor any sort of objective and photographic novel on the other. We have instead a Stendhal who, however detached he may seem, is not so much detached as diffused. He has changed the banknote of his whole self into a number of coins, he has distributed himself among various characters—Mosca, Fabrizio, Palla, the Prince, the Duchess. Or say that there is a general flavor to the book in which we discern a variety of flavorings—this herb and that condiment, a certain strange syrup and some very old brandy—removing any of which would be to mar the taste. The enigma of Stendhal is not, I think, so much any failure to communicate his feelings or thoughts as the impossibility of consolidating them; the impossibility for the contradictions to be neatly resolved, for the coins to turn back into the banknote. *The Charterhouse* is perhaps the greatest of worldly novels because it comprehends all worldliness within itself, but itself emerges as more than a critique of worldliness. Indeed, simply by its projection of Stendhal's own intellect and nature, it points up the inadequacy of all general critiques; it stresses how much all answers can leave unanswered. Hence the final taste of the book has incongruous and disconcerting and unruly flavors.

Irony and comedy join hands, tragedy and farce embrace, passion sits cheek by jowl with mockery, charm with brutality, idealism with crime. The showman links arms with the philosopher, the fool with the sage; and along with torches that penetrate the darkness, fireworks glitter idly in the night. All this is perhaps not too far from Paul Valéry when he says that for him Stendhal is "a type of intelligence much more than he is a man of letters" [see excerpt dated 1930]—the wonderful play of Stendhal's mind and the way it becomes concrete through his characters and his cosmology; the way too, I myself would add, that it becomes a system of values by refusing, in any final sense, to formulate one.

The book's whole storybook setting is really an embodiment of Stendhal's mental universe; and it perhaps makes less for something enigmatic than for something too diversified to be defined. . . . We get the whole diversified Stendhal because he is projected by way of his substance, not his manner; of his story, not his storytelling; of his distributing, not his dramatizing, himself. (pp. 193-97)

Thus, in the book, where there is personal harmony there is no philosophical unity. The contrast in attitudes between, say, the Duchess and Mosca, between her purposefulness shaped by passion—what Stendhal calls *espagnolisme*—and his cautious sense of the world—what is half ironically called *logique*—creates a private conflict that is one of the eternal collisions of civilized morality: whether, one might say, to go at life on the other man's terms or on one's own; to go at it discreetly or defiantly; to keep as much as one can, or play for all or nothing. It is the opposition, no doubt, of the lion and the fox. We tend naturally to exalt the lion, and we do well to, except—and here the fox begins to speak—that if those who lack a lion's strength would themselves survive and serve others, they must needs take on some of the fox's cunning; for there are also wolves in the world, and vultures, and hyenas. In Stendhal, as in so many superior natures, the idealist and the enlightened worldling strive to complement each other, though at times their strife merely cripples both. In *The Charterhouse* it is Mosca, not the Duchess, who wins—Mosca who indeed wins the Duchess, without winning her heart or for that matter winning her for long; for she but a short while survives Fabrizio, who has had her heart always. Still, as we are told in that very last sentence of the book, in that mockery of a fairy-tale ending, Mosca was "immensely rich." And indeed he lived on, immensely powerful and useful and rich, when all the others were dead. And there is a kind of purely practical justice about his triumph. That the civilized man of sense, the benevolent compromiser who can use the world's weapons against the world, shall succeed is perhaps all we can realistically hope for in the world of politics. For if power corrupts, perhaps it is then best held by those who know it does, and are just a little corrupted—vaccinated, as it were, against corruption. And it is Mosca too, in the end, who alone of the great trio *understands* politics: the Duchess is impatient of its rules, Fabrizio is indifferent to its ends. The Duchess and Fabrizio represent at bottom the private life and what reflects Stendhal's inner world: the Duchess is an aspect of what is single-minded in the artist's aim, Fabrizio of what is inviolable in the artist's nature. The two of them are inseparably mingled in Stendhal's approach to things, as they are incestuously joined in Stendhal's story. Except that, as I'm not sure has ever been stressed, the whole problem of incest is oddly ironic for being actually illusory—Fabrizio is no blood nephew of the Duchess, and we have

here one more chance to speculate on appearance and reality, on what might be called the morality of mirage.

Here, then, is a novel of many and opposed attitudes; a hall of mirrors full of brilliant but conflicting lights. What gives it formal unity and workable proportions is the setting—the creation of a wonderfully compact small state that acts as a stout cord around a rather unwieldy bundle: for along with all the enchantments of make-believe go all the hardheaded involvements of politics and society. But beyond what is fantastic and what is all too realistic, there is something particular and grand, appertaining to Stendhal's "happy few," to his sense of an elite. That is what is so splendid about the book, that it deals convincingly with immensely superior people. Their superiority is not altogether a moral one—we know how ruthless on occasion they can be; even less a spiritual one—there is nothing exalted about them, no more a religious sense of sin than a mystical sense of sainthood. Their superiority is not humanitarian either; they are no more concerned with self-sacrifice than with sainthood. Their superiority is a matter of personal texture and stature, of something large, distinguished, aristocratic: they are, in the real right sense of the word, the best people, and their satisfaction lies in living for and with one another.

It is part of Stendhal's own nature, but also of the age he lived in, that these people impose themselves on us with a quick, assured sharpness; they do not go swathed in a latter-day, a Henry Jamesian or Virginia Woolfian, sensibility. As there is nothing gross or piglike about them, there is nothing birdpecking; they are unafraid of being vulgar, and so they *are* not vulgar. They are superior too, without being literary: they have not their author's manner, but the grand manner.

Not sensibility of the modern kind is what so enriches this book, but that gaiety which Stendhal considered a mark of healthy art, and that great eighteenth-century endowment which Valéry noted, "the priceless gift of vivacity." And Stendhal would have been amused, Valéry goes on to say, "had he been given a glimpse in a crystal globe of all his doctoral future—of how his witticisms were twisted into theories, his manias into precepts, of how his brief maxims were the basis for interminable commentaries, his few favorite motives the source of volumes of exegesis." Well, some exegesis is always indicated with a great writer, and much of it can be useful; but with Stendhal, I would venture to say, it has proved particularly tiresome and costly, by giving modest nourishment to others at the cost of dehydrating Stendhal himself—Stendhal, who of all writers perhaps loses most by dehydration, because his verve, his mockery, his mellowness, his impudence, his quick dancing impulses, his quick flashing insights, his ability to shadow the tragic in the sunlight of comedy, to glimpse the profound in the caperings of farce, are the very essence of his art. The element of quicksilver in him is the chiefest part of his artistic gold. *The Charterhouse of Parma* is not least operatic, in that it has something of the unparaphraseableness, the untranslatability, of music. (pp. 197-200)

Louis Kronenberger, " 'The Charterhouse of Parma', " *in his* The Polished Surface: Essays in the Literature of Worldliness, *Alfred A. Knopf, 1969, pp. 181-200.*

VICTOR BROMBERT   (essay date 1968)

[*Brombert is a prominent American scholar of nineteenth-century French literature. His studies of Stendhal include* Stendhal et la voie oblique *(1954) and* Stendhal: Fiction and the Themes of Freedom *(1968). In the following excerpt from the latter work, he discusses* Lucien Leuwen, *concentrating on the novel's themes of identity and freedom.*]

This massive, incompleted novel [*Lucien Leuwen*] is possibly Stendhal's most ambitious project. In *Le Rouge et le Noir,* politics and contemporary history constitute the background to the hero's private destiny. Some years later, in *La Chartreuse de Parme,* Stendhal was to achieve an astonishing poetic stylization of political and historical reality. In *Lucien Leuwen,* he undertook a systematic survey. The moral climate under Louis-Philippe's constitutional monarchy, the new political role of the army, the power of the financial world, the mores and maneuvers of ministers and deputies, the tactics of electoral campaigns, the growing tensions of class consciousness—all these Stendhal combined with the love story of a banker's son, frustrated in his amorous enterprises, in quest of himself. Private concerns and collective issues meet at a dramatic crossroad. *Lucien Leuwen* is a text that no history of literary realism can afford to neglect, yet it is at best a fascinating failure. (pp. 101-02)

The defects of the novel are obvious. Aside from its being now too sketchy and now too cluttered, the text is loose in construction and often lacks a clear focus. Satirical impulses tend to submerge the sentimental plot. Lengthy dialogues, especially in the second part, weigh down on the action and fail to live up to the author's witty intentions. Even worse, no apparent inner necessity propels either the protagonist or the external action. Artificially created hurdles, episodic figures, and digressions create a climate of diffusion and gratuitousness. Nowhere is Stendhal's narrative self-consciousness more acute. Nowhere does he appear in greater need of self-justification and self-consolation.

Yet the many tensions and frustrations of the novel also point to its human and literary qualities. "*I write upon the sensations of 1819,*" Stendhal jotted down in his peculiar English in the margin of the manuscript. These sensations, he added, were as fresh as those of yesterday, though fifteen years had elapsed. The allusion is clearly to the unhappy episode with Métilde Dembowski in Milan. Not that the novel grew out of a deliberate attempt to recapture the past; it was the activity of writing that resuscitated emotions. Involuntary memory was thus associated with the very process of creation. . . . The weakness, and also the strength, of the book is that the author, deprived of a preestablished plot line, literally does not quite know where he is going.

It is hardly surprising that the birth and growth of love should be evoked here with particular sharpness. In no other text does Stendhal stress so insistently the inhibiting *pudeur* of his heroine and the poetic appeal of her moral claustration. Nowhere is his unconscious search for retrospective compensation so clear. The feminine modesty of Mme de Chasteller and the timid clumsiness of Lucien permit, at every point, hypothetical and speculative glimpses into *what might have been.* This creation of fiction within fiction, this exploitation of the misunderstandings and doubts during the early stages of love, this atmosphere of meaningful incommunicability, make *Lucien Leuwen* Stendhal's most searching love story. It is also his most vehement affirmation of anti-Don Juan values. At critical moments, Lucien is paralyzed by self-consciousness. The greater his awareness of Mme de Chasteller's beauty, the less his ability to act and to seduce. The lover's inefficiency is thus in direct proportion to his ability to be deeply moved. His "raisonnements admiratifs" go hand in hand with a ridiculous ineptitude. But Lucien's awkwardness, though it often makes a fool of him, constitutes his charm and ennobles him. The author cruelly explains that Lucien did not exaggerate his own ineptness, but he also, almost in the same breath, explains that the only person in whose eyes he does not want to appear foolish holds an altogether favorable opinion of his gaucherie.

The secret, compensatory victory is, of course, visible only to the omniscient author's retrospective and re-creative glance and explains why he steadily glorifies his hero's naïveté and lack of proficiency. Nothing Lucien ever achieves is attributed to skill, and his inexperience guarantees the authenticity of his feelings. If ever he is adroit, it is not due to determination or talent, but to chance—"hasard tout pur." This systematic and paradoxical debunking parallels the poetry of unawareness that characterizes Stendhal's fiction. For Lucien is almost chronically unable to assess his own situation and is blind to his virtues and victories. He thus fails to realize that Mme de Chasteller has changed her manner toward him quite early in the game. After the ball, he is totally unable to notice the extent of his success. Sitting in front of her window, he is entirely blind to the fact that she loves him madly at that very moment. And of course he cannot know that she spends hours behind her shutters waiting for him to appear. Similarly, he cannot evaluate the impact of his letters, never suspects that she would willingly allow herself to be kissed by him, and systematically misinterprets her anger, which is aimed not at him but at herself. Above all, Lucien never guesses how easy it would be to force Mme de Chasteller to admit her love for him. The incredible ease with which he is duped by the wild stratagem of Docteur Du Poirier, who succeeds in making him believe that the woman he loves has just given birth to an illegitimate child, only confirms the mental climate of undiscernment.

Lucien's touching blindness, one of the meaningful themes in the novel, is part of a larger pattern of understated, lyric experience. As Lucien and Mme de Chasteller listen to Mozart in the rustic café, *Le Chasseur vert,* they experience one of those rare moments of Stendhalian felicity when everything contributes to a privileged and fleeting harmony. The soft, slow music echoes the "touching obscurity of the deep woods." Stendhal slyly observes that an enchanting evening such as this may be counted among the greatest enemies of frigidity. The intimacy of the amorous echo is ironically attributed by Stendhal to music and poetic trees, when it is, in fact, the boon of unjaded sensibilities. The result is an epiphany of immaterial pleasure. "It is for such rare moments that it is worth living." The fragile and subdued lyric experience is directly linked to a state of innocence and non-lucidity. The passage, stressing depth and obscurity, appropriately ends with a musical silence:

> Les cors bohèmes étaient délicieux à entendre dans
> le lointain. Il s'établit un profond silence.

This silence is the symbol of a meaning that transcends words and perspicuity.

There are also non-lyric qualities that provide the usual counterpoint of satire and indignation. The arrival of Lucien's regiment in Nancy is the pretext for a biting diagnosis of social tensions and turpitude. The clash between factions, social groups, and political interests has its comic side, but points above all to a climate of suspicion and hatred. The worst symptom of this social pathology is the profanation and steady degeneration of values, symbolized by the low status of the once glorious army, which has become an internal police arm of the government. Lieutenant Colonel Filloteau, a hero at Austerlitz and Marengo, now accepts bribes and speaks of the need to repress political rebels ("réprimer les factieux"). The disease is, of course, not new; corruption and degeneration have been slow. "Happy the heroes who died before 1804!" writes Stendhal.

The army, already discredited at the time Julien Sorel dreams of heroic deeds, is now a spy-ridden hotbed of secret agents. Delation is the least heinous activity (officers have received instructions not to read newspapers in public places). Far more depressing to Lucien than these professional informers is the shameful political role of the military, reduced to the function of a counterrevolutionary, antiproletarian tool of the *juste-milieu*. It is bad enough that a colonel suggests to a lieutenant the appropriateness of hanging an equestrian portrait of the bourgeois king Louis-Philippe over his commode. What makes it truly unpalatable to serve is that military service has become servitude—a servitude for the sake of a pernicious, totally unheroic tyranny. The cynical Docteur Du Poirier explains that the era of real wars is over, that from now on it will be the "guerre de tronçon de chou" against starving workers bold enough to protest their misery. Rue de Transnonain, where a popular uprising was brutally crushed in 1834, has replaced the nobler battlefield of Marengo.

Lucien's regiment is in fact sent to the town of N— where "seditious" workers have confederated and where a new version of military bravery may lead to a dishonored cross of the Legion of Honor. Lucien's sense of shame (he calls it "remords") is equalled only by his sense of pity at the sight of proletarian poverty and the squalid living conditions of the very people his unit is supposed to repress. The entire "campaign" ends with bitter irony, as the newspapers proclaim the glory of the regiment and the cowardice of the workers.

A typically Stendhalian question presses itself to the forefront: given the moral situation of present-day society, how is one to be moral? How, in a world of counterfeit, is one to preserve one's dignity and affirm one's courage? The question is put concretely by Lucien, as he is sent on a dubious governmental mission: "If I am courageous, what matters the form of the danger?" The scene of the election campaign is thus quite literally compared to a "battlefield." In Nancy, Lucien seems caught between the ineffectual utopianism of the Republicans and the elegant, though selfish nostalgia of the aristocrats for a world that no longer exists. The dilemma symbolizes Stendhal's own dissatisfaction with these equally appealing and equally unworkable options. And it is characteristic that the moral issue should be put so clearly in historical terms: "Am I fated to spend my days between mad, selfish and polite legitimists who adore the past, and mad, generous and boring republicans who adore the future?" Lucien's father opts for the world of the Ancien Régime. But that precisely is one of the major differences between father and son. Lucien sees no such choice. Neither nostalgia nor utopian dreams satisfy him. His acute, almost oversensitive awareness of the period does not permit him to escape out of time. He is committed to the *now* and yet is aware that he must strive

to remain morally free. No other work of Stendhal poses the dilemma of freedom in sharper terms. (pp. 102-08)

The themes of freedom are not presented as dramatically in *Lucien Leuwen* as they are in *Le Rouge et le Noir* and in *La Chartreuse de Parme,* where the prison image is a key metaphor. The prison motif in *Lucien Leuwen* is less important, although there are some evident variations: the jail from which Ménuel escapes, the strict monastery of La Trappe where Lucien dreams of seeking refuge from worldly turpitude, the claustration of the loved one, the cells of the state prison symbolizing tyranny. But although the image of internment is less central to this work, the dialectics of freedom and nonfreedom are developed with skill and considerable complexity. On the simplest level, the problem is posed in social, or even sociological terms. The new monied classes seem to have earned for themselves a hitherto unknown independence. Docteur Du Poirier may be a caricature of the self-made man ("I earned this fortune, not by taking the trouble to be born . . ."), but M. Leuwen, the witty banker, is also an upstart, though an infinitely elegant one, who has acquired power and the freedom to do as he pleases through money. If Docteur Du Poirier, the vulgar parvenu, manipulates the provincial nobility, M. Leuwen can afford to speak almost as an equal to the king, even to intimidate him. Money is an obtrusive presence in the novel because it symbolizes a pervasive force and a growing form of pride. The humiliated minister Count de Vaize puts it succinctly: "A decree by the king creates a minister, but a decree cannot create a man such as M. Leuwen." The extent of M. Leuwen's independence appears during the interview with the king, when he quite literally has no favor to ask.

But if money is a liberating force, it also brings about a new form of enslavement. Father and son are most clearly opposed on this point; it is not fortuitously that M. Leuwen's death is accompanied by bankruptcy. For Lucien, the banking business means fetters ("ma pensée devrait être constamment enchaînée . . ."), not because he fears the enclosure of an office ("cloué dans le comptoir . . .") but because he is repulsed by the vile *"métal."* This aristocratic distaste for money corresponds to Stendhal's notion that concern for lucre exposes one to vulgarity, making true independence impossible. And is not Lucien's primary and ultimate quest the achievement of a valid privacy? Stendhal here diagnoses the inner contradictions of bourgeois mentalilty and morality. No other work of his so readily lends itself to a Marxist critique.

Similar tensions and ambiguities also affirm themselves in the realm of political thought. Lucien starts out by being summarily dismissed from the Ecole Polytechnique for having participated in some Republican demonstrations. Yet this same Lucien, who is revolted by the army police action against the workers and who in Nancy can truly sympathize only with the Republican Gauthier, also falls in love with the most unyielding *ultra* lady in town, fights a duel to prove that he is not a Republican, and sets out to conquer the aristocratic society in his garrison town. Once again, incompatible orders of freedom clash. While it is true that on the one hand Lucien's "amour de la liberté" remains a vital force, blending with his outrage at the sordid deals of a régime he despises, it is also true, on the other hand, that he is the beneficiary of the very régime he condemns, that he knows it, and feels guilty about being its accomplice.

To avoid facing his own inauthenticity, Lucien characteristically shifts the moral issue to the esthetic level. Liberty and democracy may be fine; but they lead to a reign of mediocrity. In the United States of America, Lucien feels, one must succumb to boredom and inelegance; there one must pay court even to the corner grocer! The Ancien Régime was corrupt and encouraged corruption, but at least conversation was bright. America, a symbol of reason and equity, is also a symbol of vulgarity and the cult of the dollar. "I would prefer a hundred times the elegant mores of a corrupt court," concludes Lucien. By a twist in the argumentation, he thus establishes the priority of elegance ("civilization") over "liberty," because this liberty in a democracy is not of a spiritual or moral nature and implies the intolerable despotism of the newly rich. If the choice is between Talleyrand and the corner grocer, Lucien chooses sophistication rather than mercantile virtue. The implications of such a choice extend beyond the character of Lucien. Stendhal himself, in one of his interventions in the novel, ironically comments that liberty has unworthy lovers; in her magnanimity, she forgets all too often to ask those who come to her: *"D'où venez-vous?"* (pp. 116-19)

Neither an aristocrat nor a proletarian, Stendhal is the first of a long line of bourgeois writers attracted to the values they denounce, rebellious against their background, and, above all, aware of the bad conscience of their own social class. The political exploitation of symbols of liberty is particularly abhorrent to them. Thus Flaubert, in describing the sack of the Tuileries in *L'Education sentimentale,* ironically gives the allegorical pose of the Statue of Liberty to a slut.

Stendhal's notions of freedom must evidently be defined not in political terms, but in those of a self-protective disengagement from pressures. The difficulty is how to achieve immunity or obtain release. And the pressures of society and social behavior are the most difficult to elude. Affranchisement is here an altogether individual undertaking; no political régime can guarantee a meaningful moral freedom. Nor can any ethical system. Freedom must almost always be invented under the least auspicious circumstances. Can Lucien be free enough from silly moralistic prejudice to be a full-fledged rascal—a real "coquin"? That is the question M. Leuwen raises, as his son is about to accept the test of government service. The answer is implicit in the dual existence that Lucien proposes to lead while in the employ of the Minister of the Interior. "I have sold myself body and soul to His Excellency," he explains to the Count de Vaize, but this bargain extends only to daylight working hours. "My evenings belong to me." What is involved is a double moral life. Such patterns of duplicity occur with regularity throughout Stendhal's work. They explain the premium put on an intimacy of the happy few, for this intimacy (this "parfum de sincérité parfaite") is permanently threatened by social pressures to which, in order to survive, one must in part submit.

Love of pleasure and love of beauty are thus not frivolous indulgences; they are, so to speak, moral obligations. Lucien's first glimpse of Mme de Chasteller suffices to dispel all his "dark thoughts." And these dark thoughts, these "idées tristes," are focused precisely on the oppressive realities of social tensions and hostilities. Love, in the Stendhalian context, takes on a central importance, not simply because it echoes personal memories and dreams, but because it is the one area where private and social realities come into the sharpest clash. It is certainly not by sheer whim that Lucien's mind "crystallizes" for the sequestered and politically reactionary

Mme de Chasteller, just as it is not a coincidence that Julien Sorel seduces a woman of another social class, and that Fabrice falls in love with the daughter of his political enemy. Quite appropriately, Mme de Chasteller sits behind "hermetically closed" shutters; her symbolic claustration points simultaneously to feminine modesty and political prejudices. Symbolically, too, communication between the two lovers involves a permanent sense of distance.

But if Mme de Chasteller is the prisoner of her femininity and of her political opinions, Lucien is far from set free through the act of loving. Whereas Julien Sorel and Fabrice del Dongo achieve their most intense amorous fervor in prison, no literal prison of love exists in *Lucien Leuwen;* yet images of ensnarement and of entrapment in love occur repeatedly. Lucien, having discovered his own submission to Mme de Chasteller (his "slavery" to a political bigot), is compared to a "savage bird" caught in a net and set in a cage. Similarly, the inaccessible lady herself feels uncomfortably subjected to another consciousness. Loss of independence, fear of an intruding and disruptive "other," awareness of a restrictive and fettering relationship—these are the accompanying symptoms of the phenomenon called love. Even M. Leuwen complains of the unhappy bonds, loss of independence, and loss of sleep inherent in love. "The first of duperies is to love," he explains, for once in an almost serious tone, to his son.

Love and secrecy are intimately related in Stendhal's novels because silence and affective masquerade are the logical antidotes to this infringement on one's freedom. Hence Julien Sorel's dream to kiss Mathilde without her knowing it. The chief effort, defensive and on the whole inefficacious, is directed toward hiding one's vulnerability. "The main thing is that nobody notice my madness." It is in this light that one should assess the meaning of Lucien's renting a furnished apartment ("Here I am free") and of his toying with the idea of a false name, which only heightens the sense of emancipation. Stendhal does not hesitate to use the expression "the instinct of freedom."

It is clear that the themes of freedom in *Lucien Leuwen* have their most complex resonance at the psychological level. Lucien's very make-up remains perpetually fluid, as does the composition of the novel. Will he "gallop" toward the enemy or will he "run away"? He does not know. There is no way of predicting. Nor is there a definitive manner of assessing what has occurred. "Have I acted well or badly?" Again, he does not know. It is hardly surprising, then, that in a novel so concerned with the elusive problem of identity the father image predominates. Despite his encouragement, M. Leuwen represents indeed . . . a coercive force. The rental of the apartment is, in part at least, a gesture of rebellion against paternal encroachment. The assuming of a false name is an even more symbolic act. The father motif may well be the key to the entire novel. Though paternal figures recur in almost every novel of Stendhal, nowhere does the image of the father play such an important role as in *Lucien Leuwen.* (pp. 119-22)

The centrality of the father in *Lucien Leuwen* is attested to by the epigraph to Part I—a quotation attributed to Lord Byron, which Stendhal dedicates "To the happy few" and which extols the qualities of an exceptional *paterfamilias.* M. Leuwen, at first sight, seems an altogether different father from the vulgarian Sorel and the cowardly Marquis del Dongo. For once Stendhal grants his privileged hero the dream-father, witty, generous, and young in spirit, who treats his son like a peer. M. Leuwen repeatedly insists on preserving his son's freedom. "I in no way want to take advantage of my rights to *curtail* your freedom." Yet the threat to his son's independence, the difficulties inherent in their relationship, and above all the anxieties of the identity-search and the identity-affirmation are brought out with particular acuteness in this novel precisely to the extent that M. Leuwen, the father, is not a villain.

For there is irony in Lucien's being called an "enfant content." What this contentedness implies is an intolerable subjection. Though M. Leuwen wants his son to be happy, the happiness he conceives for him leaves Lucien little room for divergence of taste or opinion. It is only natural that Lucien is in a latent state of insurrection against this invasive affection. "I wish I did not have to rely at every moment on my father's resourcefulness." The truth is that M. Leuwen—though perhaps largely unaware of it himself—wishes to manipulate not only financial and political affairs but his son as well, Lucien resents his father's desire to make his son happy "*à sa façon.*" And indeed, his father deprives him quite literally of even the briefest moment of liberty. If he is so determined "not to leave a quarter of an hour of solitude" to his son, it is because, as Lucien points out, he is determined to wage war against the "petits quarts d'heure de liberté" the young man needs to protect his own privacy and dignity. No wonder he ultimately rebels against what he himself, in an impatient outburst, calls the "sollicitude paternelle."

Viewed in this light, the explosion is less shocking. It is not M. Leuwen specifically—he happens to be a warm and charming person—who is the target. Nor is Lucien a particularly ungrateful wretch. His remorse would redeem him. But the "grand remords" concerning his father is not so much for an act committed as for a state of feeling against which there is little recourse. "He [Lucien] felt no friendship for him [M. Leuwen]." The "intimate shame" of not loving has little to do with the specific quality of these two human beings. Similarly, the deep "chasm" between them marks not merely the polarity of enthusiasm and irony so typical in Stendhal, but the need for and also the impossibility of a relationship closely enmeshed with the identity quest.

The father-son relationship is made even more uncomfortable by M. Leuwen's unavoidable role as judge. "*Studiate la matematica,*" he writes to Lucien in Nancy. The painful allusion is to Jean-Jacques Rousseau's famous fiasco with the courtesan in Venice. Throughout the novel, the father and his substitutes, Coffe and Dévelroy, play the part of an external consciousness; and what they do have to say is hard for Lucien to take. Yet much as he would like to free himself, Lucien is bound to their judgment; he even yearns for it and constantly wishes to prove himself in their eyes ("Lucien tenait à prouver à son père et à Dévelroy . . ."); he hopes his father will have some "consideration" for him; he feels the need to "submit his mind to that of another and ask for advice."

The reason is clear: though afraid of the intruding presence of "another" and jealous of his own autonomy, Lucien cannot, by himself, catch hold of himself. His own personality, by dint of his existential freedom, escapes him. He is not only incapable of assessing his course of action or of understanding his own character but also of observing himself accurately in the art of becoming. He therefore *needs* a judge and interpreter. "Good God! Whom could I consult?" The most basic estimations elude him, "Did I act well or badly?"—"What opinion should I have of myself?" And he is perpetually puzzled by his own reactions ("Do I myself know what I think?"). Lucien Leuwen is a hero in search of his character.

The novel thus marks the impasse of a type of *Bildungsroman* in which the hero's primary apprenticeship is not that of the world but of the self. Stendhal's refusal to indulge in aprioristic conceptualizations of a given psychology here causes, however, the absence of an "essential" stability and direction. This conceptual vacuity is in large part responsible for the particular failure of this novel; it may well have contributed largely to Stendhal's inability to complete it. (pp. 123-25)

> *Victor Brombert, in his* Stendhal: Fiction and the Themes of Freedom, *Random House, 1968, 209 p.*

GÉRARD GENETTE (essay date 1969)

[*In this excerpt from a study first published in French in 1969, Genette uses a passage from* Rome, Naples, and Florence *to illustrate aspects of Stendhal's unusual narrative style.*]

> Some months ago a married woman of Melito, renowned as much for her ardent piety as for her rare beauty, had the weakness to grant her lover an assignation in a mountain forest, two leagues from the village. The lover was happy. After this moment of delight, however, the enormity of her sin oppressed the soul of the guilty woman: she remained plunged into gloomy silence. "Why are you so cold to me?" asks the lover. "I was thinking how we would see each other tomorrow; that abandoned hut, in the dark wood, is the most convenient place." The lover leaves her; the unhappy woman did not come back to the village, but spent the night in the forest, busy, as she admitted, praying and digging two ditches. The next morning the lover arrives and is killed at the hands of this woman whom he believed adored him. This unhappy victim of remorse buries her lover with the greatest care, comes back to the village, where she confesses to the priest and embraces her children. She returns to the forest, where she is found dead, lying in the ditch dug next to that of her lover.

This brief anecdote is a fairly representative example of what one might call, without exaggerating its specificity, *Stendhalian narrative.* We will not dwell on the (striking) illustration of the "Italian soul," a mandatory element in Beylist verisimilitude, but take a closer look at the characteristic elements of the narrative treatment by which this "little true fact" becomes a text by Stendhal.

The first of these features is no doubt the almost systematic displacement of the narrative in relation to the action, which results both in the elision of the principal events and the accentuation of the incidental circumstances. The act of adultery is designated three times by a sort of narrative metonymy: the assignation given to the lover; the lover's "happiness" (a banal figure, revivified here by the conciseness of the statement); the "moment of delight," qualified retrospectively on the basis of the virtuous state of conscience that follows. Not by itself, therefore, but by the events that lead up to it, accompany it, or follow it. The murder of the lover is subtly relegated, by an academic periphrasis, to a subordinate proposition the main stress of which is elsewhere. Lastly, and above all, the suicide of the young woman undergoes a complete ellipsis between her return to the forest and the moment when she is found dead; an ellipsis reinforced still further by the temporal ambiguity of the narrative present, and the absence of any adverb of time, which make the two verbs apparently simultaneous, thus eliminating the entire duration that separates the two actions.

This elision of the strong tenses is one of the features of Stendhalian narrative. In the *Chartreuse,* the first embrace of Fabrizio and Clelia, in the Farnese tower, is so discreet that it generally passes unnoticed ("She was so beautiful, with her gown half torn off, and stirred to such a pitch of passion, that Fabrizio could not refrain from following an almost unconscious impulse. No resistance was offered him"), and Gina's "sacrifice" with Ernesto-Ranuccio V disappears between two sentences: "He had the temerity to reappear, trembling all over and extremely miserable, at three minutes to ten. At half past ten the Duchessa stepped into her carriage and set off for Bologna." Fabrizio's death is implied rather than mentioned, on the last page: "She [Gina] lived for a very short time only after Fabrizio, whom she adored, and who spent but one year in his Charterhouse." In this case one may blame the forced mutilation of this epilogue, but in the *Rouge,* the execution of Julien, so long expected and prepared for, is eclipsed at the last moment: "Never had that head such poetic beauty than at the moment when it was about to fall. The sweetest moments he had known in the past in the woods of Vergy came thronging back into his mind with the most eager insistence.

"Everything passed off simply and decently, with no trace of affectation on his part." There follows a flashback (a method, on the contrary, very little used by Stendhal, who tends, seemingly, to accelerate duration rather than retard it), which contributes still more to this effacement of the death by resuscitating Julien for the space of half a page. Jean Prévost remarked quite rightly [in *La création chez Stendhal* (1951)] of these silent and nearly disguised deaths that they constitute a sort of "literary euthanasia."

This discretion concerning the cardinal functions of the narrative contrasts, obviously, with the importance given to incidental and almost technical details: the precise location of the forest, the abandoned hut, the digging of the two ditches. This "attention to small things," which Stendhal praised in Mérimée, is even more characteristic of his own manner: we have already met with some of the effects of this. Stendhal himself carries Mérimée's precision still further: " 'He helped her down from her horse on some pretext,' [Mérimée] would say. [Stendhal] says: 'He helped her down from her horse on the pretext that he had seen that the horse was losing one of its shoes and he wanted to fix it with a nail.' " But it should be noted above all that this attention to objects and circumstances—which is accompanied, however, as we know, with great disdain for description—almost always serves to mediate the evocation of important actions or situations by allowing various kinds of material substitutes to speak in their place. In the last scene of *Vanina Vanini,* the "cold, sharp chains" that hold Missirilli and separate him from Vanina's embraces, the "diamonds" and "little files," the traditional tools of escape, that she gives him and which in the end he throws to her "as much as his chains allow him," all these details shine with such intensity of presence, despite the dryness of their expression, that they eclipse the dialogue between the two lovers: they bear the meaning far more than the words exchanged.

Another form of ellipsis and perhaps an even more specific one might be called the ellipsis of intentions. It consists in reporting the actions of a character without informing the reader of their purpose, which will appear only after the event.

The second meeting arranged for the following day in the abandoned hut misleads the reader as much as it did the lover, and if the digging of two graves hardly leaves any doubt as to what will follow, the fact remains that the narrative is deliberately silent about the purpose that gives meaning to a series of actions (coming back to the village, confessing, embracing her children), leaving us the task of filling this gap retroactively. Thus, in *L'Abbesse de Castro,* Stendhal tells us that Vanina notices her father's anger against Branciforte. "She went at once," he adds, "and threw a little powder on the wood of the five magnificent arquebuses that her father had hanging next to his bed. She also covered with a light layer of dust his daggers and swords." The connection between the father's anger and the fact of throwing dust on his weapons is not obvious, and the function of this action remains obscure until the moment we read that "visiting her father's weapons that evening, she saw that two arquebuses had been loaded and that almost all the daggers had been handled": she had spread the dust in order to know what preparations her father was making, but the narrative carefully concealed this motivation from us. The most famous example of this Stendhalian habit is obviously the end of chapter 35 of the second part of *Le Rouge et le noir,* when we see Julien leave Mathilde, dash off in a post-chaise to Verrières, buy a brace of pocket-pistols from the gunsmith and enter the church, without our being informed of his intentions other than by their fulfillment in the line: "He fired a shot at her with one pistol and missed her. He fired a second shot; she fell."

We must stress here the necessarily deliberate character of the method: if the Stendhalian method were, like the later manner of Hemingway, a purely "objective" relation of the actions performed, with no incursion into the consciousness of the characters, the ellipsis of intentions would conform to the overall attitude, and therefore would be much less marked. But we know that Stendhal never confined himself to this "behaviorist" prejudice, and even that recourse to interior monologue is one of his innovations and one of his most constant habits. Here, he in no way refrains from informing the reader that "the enormity of her crime oppressed the soul of the guilty woman" and if Stendhal does not let the reader know more about his heroine's intentions it is obviously by voluntary omission. Similarly, when Vanina hears Missirilli announce that with the next defeat, he will abandon the cause of Carbonarism, Stendhal simply adds, that this word "threw a fatal light into her mind. He said to herself: "The Carbonari have received several thousand sequins from me. No one can doubt my devotion to the conspiracy.' " This interior monologue is as misleading as the narrative of the criminal-narrator in *The Murder of Roger Ackroyd,* for Stendhal, pretending to relate Vanina's thoughts at this point, is careful to conceal the most important thing, which is more or less, as we learn some pages later: "So I can denounce the sale without Pietro suspecting." The incidental, here again, is substituted for the essential, just as in the story about Melito the details concerning the abandoned hut conceal, for both the future victim and the reader, the planned murder.

This type of ellipsis implies great freedom in the choice of narrative point of view. Stendhal inaugurates the technique of the "restrictions of field," which consists in reducing the narrative field to the perceptions and thoughts of a single character. But he alters this choice, on the one hand, as we have just seen, by keeping from him some of his thoughts, often the most important ones; but also by frequently changing the focal character: even in a novel as centered on the character of the hero as the *Rouge,* the narration sometimes adopts the point of view of another character, such as Mme de Rênal, or Mathilde, or even M. de Rênal. Here, the focal point is almost constantly the heroine, but the narrative makes at least one incursion, and a retrospective one at that, into the consciousness of the lover ("this woman whom he believed adored him"). Lastly, and above all, the focusing of the narrative is disturbed, as it almost always is in Stendhal, by the practice of what Georges Blin has called [in *Stendhal et les problèmes du roman* (1954)] "the intrusion of the author," and which it would no doubt be better to call intervention of the *narrator,* making a distinction, particularly necessary in the case of Stendhal, between the identity of these two roles.

Nothing, in fact, is more difficult than to determine at each moment what the virtual source of the Stendhalian discourse is, the only two constants being that this source is highly variable and that it is rarely identical with the person of Stendhal. We know his almost hysterical taste for travesty, and we know for example that the supposed traveller of the *Mémoires d'un touriste* is a certain M. L . . . , a commercial traveller in hardware, whose opinions do not always coincide with those of Beyle. In the novels and novellas, the situation of the narrator is generally indeterminate. The *Rouge* and *Lamiel* begin with a chronicle told by a narrator-witness who belongs to the diegetic world: that of the *Rouge* is an anonymous inhabitant of Verrières who has often observed the valley of the Doubs from the promenade widened by M. de Rênal, and who praises the Mayor, "though he is on the extreme right, and I am a Liberal." The narrator of *Lamiel,* who is more precisely identified, is the son and grandson of Messrs. Lagier, notaries at Carville. The first slips away after a few pages without his disappearance being noticed by anyone, the second announces his departure with more fuss in these terms: "All these adventures . . . concern the young Lamiel girl. . . . And I have taken it into my head to write them down so that I may become a man of letters. So, O benevolent reader, farewell, you will hear no more of me." As for the *Chartreuse,* Stendhal certainly acknowledges, in antedating it, the writing of this "novella," but not without placing most of the responsibility for it on the shoulders of a supposed canon of Padua, whose memoirs he seems merely to have adapted. Which of the two assumes the "I" that appears three or four times at least, and always in an unexpected way, in the course of a chronicle that in principle is quite impersonal?

The situation of the *Chroniques italiennes,* and in particular *L'Abbesse de Castro,* is both clearer and more subtle, for Stendhal claims to be acting only as a translator, but an indiscreet and active translator, who does not deny himself the pleasure of commenting on the action ("Candor and uncouthness, the natural results of the liberty suffered by republics, and the habit of passions openly expressed, and not yet contained by the morals of monarchy, are revealed for all to see in the person of the Signior di Campireali as soon as he takes a step"), or of authenticating his sources ("Now, my sad task will be limited to providing a necessarily dry extract of the trial at the end of which Elena met her death. This trial, the report of which I read in a library, whose name I must not reveal, comprises no less than eight volumes in-folio"), or of judging the text that he is supposed to be recopying ("That evening, Elena wrote to her lover a naive and in my opinion very moving letter"), or even of practicing on several

occasions a rather insolent censorship: "I think I ought to pass over in silence many circumstances which, in turn, depict the morals of that period, but which seem to me sad to relate. The author of the Roman manuscript took infinite pains to arrive at the exact date of these details which I am suppressing."

It is often as if Stendhal had transported this *marginal* situation in relation to a text of which he is not supposed to be the author and for which he appears to accept no responsibility, from the *Chroniques* and the anecdotes collected in the first Italian essays, into his great works of fiction: Blin has shown the quite natural passage that leads from the supposed cuts of *L'Abbesse de Castro* to the famous etc.'s which, in the novels, cut short so many tirades supposedly regarded as too flat or boring. But what is true of censorship is equally so of the other forms of commentary and intervention. It is as if Stendhal, having got into the habit of annotating the texts of others, continues to gloss his own without seeing the difference. We know in particular how he burdens his young heroes with judgements, admonitions, and advice, but critics have also noticed the dubious sincerity of those paraphrases in which Stendhal sometimes seems to separate himself hypocritically from his favorite characters, to present as a defect or blunder what in actual fact he regards as sympathetic or admirable characteristics. "Why," he says in the sixth chapter of the *Chartreuse,*

> why should the chronicler who follows faithfully all the most trivial details of the story that has been told him be held up to blame? Is it his fault if his characters, led astray by passions which he, most *unfortunately* for himself, in no way shares, descend to actions that are profoundly immoral? It is true that things of this sort are no longer done in a country where the sole passion that has outlived all the rest is lust for money, that gives vanity its chance.

It is almost impossible in such examples to distinguish between the ironic intervention of the author and the supposed intervention of a narrator distinct from him whose style and opinion Stendhal is playing at counterfeiting. Antiphrasis, satirical parody, the *style indirect libre,* pastiche ("This Minister, in spite of his light-hearted air and his lively manners, did not possess a soul of the French type; he could not *forget* the things that grieved him. When there was a thorn in his pillow, he was obliged to break it off and to blunt its point while getting many a prick from it in his trembling limbs. (I must apologize for this extract, which is translated from the Italian)") follow one another and sometimes overlay one another in a counterpoint of which the opening pages of the *Chartreuse* form a characteristic example, mingling the epic bombast of the victory announcements published by the revolutionaries, the bitter or furious recriminations of the despotic party, the irony of the Voltairian observer, popular enthusiasm, the cautious expressions of administrative language, etc. With Stendhal, then, the image of the narrator is essentially problematic, and when the Stendhalian narrative gives way, however little, to discourse, it is often very difficult and sometimes impossible to answer the apparently quite simple question: *who is speaking?*

From this point of view, our text of reference is distinguished first of all by its sobriety of discourse, the absence of any explicit comment (this is what Stendhal calls "recounting narratively"). This absence is not insignificant: on the contrary, it has a great value, indeed, for any reader who is at all familiar with Stendhal's Italy, an obvious one. The silence of the narrative emphasizes most eloquently the grandeur and beauty of the action: it contributes therefore to describing it. It is a zero degree commentary, precisely the one that classical rhetoric recommended for *sublime* moments, when the event speaks for itself better than any sort of speech could; and we know that the sublime is not for Stendhal an academic category, but one of the most active terms in his system of values.

Discourse is not, however, totally absent from this narrative—such an exclusion is indeed only an academic hypothesis, almost impossible in narrative practice. Here, we should note first the initial temporal indicator "some months ago," which situates the event in relation to the instance of discourse constituted by the narration itself, in a relative time that emphasizes and authenticates the situation of the narrator—a single chronological point of reference. Also there is the testimonial formula "as she admitted," which connects, according to Roman Jakobson's categories, the process of the statement (the action), the process of the enunciation (the narrative), and "a process of stated enunciation": the evidence, or more specifically in this case the avowal, which it seems could only have been received during the confession mentioned below, a confession thus designated in an oblique way as the source of most of the narrative, and in particular of everything concerning the motivations of the action. These two "shifters" place the narrator therefore in the situation of a historian, in the etymological sense, that is to say, as investigator-reporter. Such a situation is quite normal in an ethnographical text like **Rome, Naples et Florence** (or the **Promenades,** or the **Mémoires d'un touriste**), but as we have seen Stendhal, perhaps simply out of habit, maintains certain signs of it even in his great works of "fiction"; hence such strange precautions as that "I think" which crops up quite naturally, it seems, in the middle of a chronicle in . . . **Le Rose et le vert,** but which reappears more surprisingly in a sentence like the following from **Leuwen** (it concerns Mlle Berchu's dress): "It was made of a material from Algiers, and had very wide stripes, brown, I think, and pale yellow," or from the **Chartreuse:** "The Contessa smiled—as a measure of precaution, I fancy."

The case of the demonstrative ("That unfortunate woman . . ."), of which Stendhal makes a very marked use, is rather more subtle, for it consists essentially (apart from its stylistic value as—perhaps Italianate—emphasis) of an anaphoric reference by the narrative back to itself (the unfortunate woman already mentioned): this reference back necessarily passing through the instance of discourse and therefore by the relay of the narrator, and consequently of the reader, who imperceptibly finds himself called upon as a witness. The same goes for the intensive "so," also typically Stendhalian, and which again implies a return of the text upon itself. Indeed the two turns of phrase are often frequently found together "that woman so tender. . . ."

As for expressions implying a measure of judgment, they remain, despite their discretion, difficult to assign. "The unfortunate woman," "unfortunate victim of remorse" may express Stendhal's sympathetic opinion, but "gave in," "sin," "guilty," and even "delight" involve a moral judgment that it would be very imprudent to attribute to him. These moralizing terms stem rather from the heroine herself, with a slight inflection of indirect discourse, though they may reflect the common opinion of the village, the vehicle of the anecdote, whose judgments Stendhal would not hesitate to reproduce

without necessarily agreeing with them, as when he reports in italics certain expressions borrowed from vulgar speech for which he refuses to take responsibility himself—too anxious to preserve a dignity that he lets us perceive without allowing us to judge it; faithful to his policy, which is to be always present, and always out of reach. (pp. 168-78)

Gérard Genette, " 'Stendhal'," in his Figures of Literary Discourse, *translated by Alan Sheridan, Columbia University Press, 1982, pp. 147-82.*

WALLACE FOWLIE (essay date 1969)

[*Fowlie is among the most respected scholars of French literature. His work includes translations of important French poets and dramatists (Molière, Charles Baudelaire, Arthur Rimbaud, Paul Claudel, Saint-John Perse) and critical studies of the major figures and movements of modern French letters (Stéphane Mallarmé, Marcel Proust, André Gide, the surrealists, among many others). In this excerpt from his* Stendhal, *Fowlie discusses the author's autobiographical writings.*]

In his art as novelist, Stendhal never uses directly the activities and adventures of his own life and never draws directly upon his personal suffering. The tone of self-complacency and the habit of the unabashed self-confession of the typical romantic writer are totally absent in Stendhal's novels. By means of the style and the plots of his books, he created a distance between himself and his readers. If in a fundamentally psychic sense he identifies himself with his heroes; his heroes are not recognizably Stendhal in any exterior sense. He separated his personal writings from his novels. His autobiography is to be found in two books: **Souvenirs d'égotisme** of 1832 and **Vie de Henry Brulard** of 1836.

The first of these writings, the **Souvenirs,** is a scrupulous self-analysis. With no desire to idealize his features or exalt his traits, Stendhal quite resolutely wrote about himself for the purpose of reaching some degree of self-knowledge. He had just begun his consulate service in Città Vecchia and had considerable leisure ahead of him, when he announced his intention of using this leisure (*pour employer mes loisirs*) in that foreign land for the purpose of writing out what happened to him during his Paris years of 1821 to 1830. Did he do all within his power to reach happiness at the time of the minor and major events in his life during those nine years? What kind of man had he become? What was the quality of his mind? His self-evaluation had varied so much from day to day, from month to month, that he now distrusted his judgments. He was struck by the fact that his judgments had varied as much as his disposition had fluctuated. . . . With these opening questions, Stendhal announced the frankness with which he hoped to write about himself and the rigorous tone reminiscent of a La Rochefoucauld with which he planned to consign his observations to paper.

This tone of honesty and scrupulosity with respect to difficult personal problems we have come to associate with the personal journal of the twentieth century, with André Gide, for example, and Julien Green. There is no reason to believe that Stendhal ever planned to publish his **Souvenirs d'égotisme,** but he did plan to leave it with his papers for the use of posterity.

The word *égotisme,* as used by Stendhal, has often been given a Nietzschean-like meaning, equivalent to a superman's drive to reach happiness at any cost. The worship of oneself, the cult of self-development, is a concept not applicable to Stendhal. The cult of the self, as found in such a romantic work as Musset's *Confession d'un enfant du siècle* and much later in the writings of Maurice Barrès, is not what Stendhal meant by egotism. Stendhal exhibits an interest in himself because of a greater interest in analysis itself, because of his belief that analysis is a therapeutic exercise by means of which a man's disposition can be understood and improved. Stendhal is not self-admiring, as Rousseau is, in his *Confessions*. He is not presenting himself as an exceptional human being whose sensitivity sets him apart from mankind, in the manner Chateaubriand develops in his autobiography *Mémoires d'outre-tombe.*

The two texts *Egotisme* and *Henry Brulard* are self-appraisals which have the value of documents, first, and of a literary art, second. As he wrote them, he had probably very little sense of the value they were to possess today, and yet they are the texts in which Stendhal's mind is the sharpest, in which his powers of observation are the most developed. In these two books, as well as in his letters and other personal writings, Stendhal appears the moralist, in the manner of a Montaigne and a Gide—a man inhabiting a moral world, who is determined to analyze his conduct in that world in terms of the prevalent moral conventions and in terms of the hypocrisy by which moral conventions are sustained. We see Stendhal play a social role and participate in the game of society, and at the same time we see him trying to preserve in himself and express his most spontaneous feelings and his noblest impulses. There is peril, obviously, in these two ways of behavior, both moral and social peril. Precisely these forms of peril are the substance of *Souvenirs d'égotisme* and *Vie de Henry Brulard.* Henri Beyle is the lonely hero of these two books, and he is actually far more lonely than his lonely heroes, Julien Sorel and Octave and Fabrice del Dongo. (pp. 141-43)

Vie de Henry Brulard is the story of his life through adolescence. It is the third of Stendhal's books to rally an impressive number of admirers who are anxious to announce the outstanding book: Is it *Le Rouge et le Noir* or *La Chartreuse de Parme* or *Vie de Henry Brulard?* Those who give first place to *Vie de Henry Brulard* base their claims on the boldness with which Stendhal explored his past and sought to recover time that had been lost. About to turn fifty (*je vais avoir cinquante ans*), Stendhal declared it was time to know himself, or to know the boy and the man he was. What was to count the most for him was simplicity and honesty in the narration. The determination to speak the truth explains why he took pen in hand. (p. 144)

He never rewrote or reworked any of the passages in the manuscript because of his belief that the first draft of such writing would be the most accurate, the most truthful. The portraits he gives of his childhood and adolescence are precious commentaries for an understanding of his work. The genesis and the development of his sensibility and his thought are carefully described and annotated.

Stendhal succeeds in resurrecting moments of his past and giving them a freshness as if they had been lived the day before he wrote, rather than thirty-five or forty years earlier. The facts of chronological time do not count as much as the power of the writer's memory which is able, on the most striking pages of *Vie de Henry Brulard* to reinstate the past within the present. . . .

Such a meticulous scholar as Paul Arbalet who has written extensively on the early years of Stendhal's life (*La Jeunesse de Stendhal*) has discovered errors in facts and dates in *Vie de Henry Brulard,* and he has proved quite conclusively that the portraits of the father, Chérubin Beyle and the priest Abbé Raillane, represented them as more sinister than they actually were. But such points, made in the name of historical truth, do not alter the veracity Stendhal records of the effect of such figures on the young boy Henri Beyle. The writer is concerned with relating the truthfulness of his reactions to people and events and to the city of Grenoble.

He yearned for affection and did not receive it. When, in the country setting of Les Echelles, he experienced happiness by simply being in close proximity to young women in beautiful dresses, the transport he felt was of such a nature that it was impossible to analyze. In narrating his life, Stendhal moves back and forth between sentiments of suspicion and despair, and sentiments of elation and daydreaming. The man is already in the child. The entire book is an explicit document on the explanation and the analysis of a temperament that was fully formed at a very early age. The memory of a sensation leads him to a very concrete scene he is able to recall. He trusts the sensation. He distrusts the judgments of others and his own judgments. Scrupulously he moves into his past and tries not to alter or embroider his memories. What happened to Henri Beyle we see happening at the moment when we are reading the text.

Souvenirs d'égotisme begins, in 1832, with the end of Stendhal's great love for Métilde Dembowska. But he is too close to that suffering to write about it. Throughout the book there are a large number of portraits. The meditations about himself are grouped especially at the beginning. The rest of the work is concerned with episodes and anecdotes.

The portraits undoubtedly suffer from a lack of rewriting. Those portraits that seem the best are based on models from whom Stendhal was the most detached emotionally. The proprietor of the Hôtel de Bruxelles, M. Petit, is a good example of a portrait Stendhal struck off that is successful because of an absence of any emotional involvement. Mérimée is clearly described in certain salon scenes, but the reason for his friendship with Beyle is not clear. Destutt de Tracy is given a fuller portrait, especially in his physical appearance and in the casualness of his conversation. Métilde Dembowska and her cousin Madame Traversi are only vaguely sketched.

The personal meditations, of which there are many, follow a similar pattern. They start up because of a need to write, and they proceed without plan, without organization. The themes are repetitive. The questions asked by the writer are numerous, but the answers given are few. The kind of writing, so obviously improvised in *Souvenirs,* does not permit Stendhal to judge himself, to judge the events of his past and to measure their importance. He oscillates too much from theme to theme, and without the necessary details, to reach any conclusions about the relative importance of events and thoughts.

Stendhal is more intriguing, more successful, in the purely narrative sections of *Souvenirs d'égotisme.* For the story of an event, he chooses details that are both important and vivid. These parts of the work do not need rewriting. His remarkable memory serves him well, as well as his power of imagination and his ability to imagine the circumstances of the scenes. Whenever his heart is involved, as with the appearance of Countess Curial in his life, he avoids any real analysis. This kind of commentary is reserved for the novels. The writing of *Souvenirs* was interrupted by Stendhal's activities in Cività Vecchia, but even if he had continued, he would probably not have written any real analyses of his loves and of his temptations to love. That part of his life remained within his memory, to be recast in his novels. The telling portraits he is able to write out so swiftly, the dream or meditation sequences and the constant check he makes on his mental attitudes—all of this is announced in *Souvenirs d'égotisme* and will be pursued in the writing of *Vie de Henry Brulard.*

Stendhal had no intention of making *Vie de Henry Brulard* correspond to a given technique of writing, or even, for that matter, to a given genre. The book is both an effort to recall the past and a struggle, as the sentences are being consigned to paper, to be sincere and truthful. Whenever he digresses from the narrative, he indulges in that kind of meditation and revery for which he has a marked predilection: *Je vois que la rêverie a été ce que j'ai préféré à tout, même à passer pour homme d'esprit.* In recomposing his memories, Stendhal tends to alter the accuracy of facts in order to write a story that will appear logical and likely. It is paradoxical that the writer's sincerity in both Rousseau and Stendhal tended to deform accuracy. The tone of sincerity is reached at the expense of historical truth.

On turning fifty, Stendhal seems suddenly aware that most of his life is behind him. The past is a treasure house, out of which he can call up the memory of his loves and try to pass judgment on them. As he writes, the past comes back and he ceases worrying about whether he will forget essential episodes. The scenes are fragments from a life rather than a continuous narrative of a childhood. Their power comes from the imperious sense of truthfulness with which Stendhal endows them (even if factual accuracy is sometimes sacrificed). A close reader seldom has the impression that such and such an episode is invented. Stendhal convinces us of his veracity, to such a degree that we recognize the bareness and the cruelty of certain childhood experiences.

What is Stendhal's method of writing in the *Vie de Henry Brulard?* He says that by writing about an event, he sees it more clearly. His childhood memories, as memories in his mind, are amorphous and covered over by a strange light whose source seems to be the acuteness of the original sensations that accompanied the experiences. In writing of them he instinctively employs a scientific method by which he will see friends and members of his family and other acquaintances as *genres.* He tends to classify human beings as a botanist classifies plants. His mind still holds the pictures of the physical traits of these characters thirty or forty years later, but he begins to understand the traits only when he begins writing about them. Some of the characters whom he observed as a child have disappeared from his memory. The fresco of his past is incomplete.

Stendhal's method is a mental investigation of the past. An image comes to his mind and he begins describing it, and thereupon many details rush into his mind and he realizes he understands and sees the past thanks to this exercise of writing it down. As the writing of a given scene continues everything comes to life: furniture in a room, the design of the room, human features, gestures and activities. They are scenes that have been preserved in his memory because of some deeply felt emotion: anger, for example, or sorrow. When his emotion returns clear to him, he is then able to ana-

lyze it and to understand it more fully than he had when it was originally experienced. Stendhal is very much bent on exploring the significance of a given scene. The intensity of the emotion that accompanied the scene is a clue and guide for this research. Within the scenes where Stendhal is describing members of his family, the sense of an autobiography gives way to the sense of a novel, as Henry Brulard takes on the proportions of a protagonist. (pp. 144-49)

Emotionally Stendhal separated himself from his family, and intellectually he separated himself from the bourgeoisie. But he confessed that he could not have lived with the proletariat. He was a new kind of aristocrat, always out of place socially and intellectually, and that is why he founded, in his mind, a tiny community of the "happy few." What Baudelaire was to call *dandysme* corresponded quite closely to Stendhal's attitude. It was a form of isolation, on many levels: artistic, social, intellectual. *Vie de Henry Brulard* is a lengthy explanation and rationalization of this position. It is the demonstration of how a man's life turned into the enactment of a drama of excessive solitude. He himself became the characters in his life. His abundant use of pseudonyms is a proof of the need he felt to multiply his personality. It is significant that throughout *Henry Brulard,* Henri Beyle never tries to solve the dilemma of his life and of his character. He is quite content with reasoning about it and elucidating it. He learned to live with the drama of the many selves, and in his fiction, always depicted the same situation of the hero unable to fit into whatever society and whatever situation were his. (p. 155)

Wallace Fowlie, in his Stendhal, *The Macmillan Company, 1969, 240 p.*

MICHAEL WOOD   (essay date 1971)

[*Wood discusses the dual themes of the social and personal worlds in* The Charterhouse of Parma.]

There is a temptation towards the fairy-tale, towards a vision of *La Chartreuse de Parme* as a late, magical blessing on an awkward, haphazard career. It is Stendhal's own book in a way in which very few books are quite their author's own. Only Proust affords some kind of comparison. Not Balzac, not Dickens, not Flaubert. Not Tolstoy. *La Chartreuse de Parme* is both more limited and more luminous than that, a work remembered rather than imagined. It is less a set of occasions and characters represented with talent, with genius even, than it is Stendhal's life set to Mozartian music, the opera of his lively, well-stocked mind; personal but never private, a confession fully realized in fiction. My images here are not original, they are common currency in Stendhal criticism, what the book calls for, simply. One can't say less. (p. 157)

There is no better measure of the mood of *La Chartreuse de Parme* than Balzac's remark at the end of his famous and generous review: M. Beyle used to be a liberal, but the 'profound meaning' of his new novel is 'certainly not opposed to monarchy'. Balzac is right. Stendhal was cagey all his life, never stuck his neck out extravagantly. Writers are the hussars of liberty, he once said, but he was a fairly cautious hussar. Yet he was not dishonest or scared, and Balzac would not have been able to make this remark about *Le Rouge et le Noir* which, significantly, he disliked, or about *Lucien Leuwen,* had it been possible for him to read it. The stern Jacobin child of *Vie de Henry Brulard,* the man who called kings the vermin of the human species, has now written a novel that a monarchist can feel happy with. Of course Balzac, from another extreme position, disliked the July régime as much as Stendhal did, and there would be nothing strange in a royalist and a republican agreeing there. But that is not what happens in *La Chartreuse de Parme.*

What attracted Balzac was a certain kind of lucid conservatism, and if the book was not about Metternich, as he thought, it was about Metternich's world and Metternich's philosophy, based, as Namier wrote, like all conservatisms, on a 'proper recognition of human limitations'. A character in the story *L'Abbesse de Castro,* part of which was written immediately after *La Chartreuse de Parme,* prefaces the launching of an elaborate piece of simony by these words, which might well have been Stendhal's motto for his novel:

> 'Eminence,' she said, 'we are both very old; there is no reason for us to try to deceive ourselves by giving beautiful names to things which are not beautiful . . .'.

The ironies of *La Chartreuse* regularly run this weary way. Mosca, jealous of Fabrice's effect on Gina, sees that Fabrice might well be killed in a light adventure he is conducting but nevertheless arranges for his life to be saved. 'If the reader is very young,' Stendhal comments, he won't see what is so virtuous in this action. A new prince, towards the end of the book, has 'among other infantile ideas', the hope of having a '*moral* ministry', and Stendhal gets a lot of good comedy out of this dream of innocence. It is impossible, for example, to explain to the prince how crooked most of his administrators are, he would believe you were crooked yourself—how else would you have perceived such things.

But the conservatism of *La Chartreuse de Parme* is not primarily a view, it is a premise, a climate, an assumption enclosing the book. The image of the game hangs over the novel: whist, chess, figures for the play of politics and power. Who complains about the rules of such games? What this means, in the light of Stendhal's known passions and opinions, is not that he has come round but that he has given up—temporarily, as he thinks. Where Julien Sorel goaded himself on through his sticky paths by thoughts of Napoleon's rising star, of the young general who couldn't lose, *La Chartreuse de Parme* is set in the shadow of Waterloo, emblem of the death of a huge vision.

Stendhal is careful to portray the exact quality of this decline. It is a slip from politics to personalities, from unities to pieces, and when Balzac suggests that not even a republican could be stirred to regicide by Gina's having the prince of Parma assassinated, he is, again, right: 'It is a play of private passions, that is all'. It is all, and it is a far cry from the meeting of politics and the individual in Julien. Napoleon's Italy, at the beginning of the novel, is a society; what happens to one man happens to many: 'Lieutenant Robert's story was more or less that of all Frenchmen . . .'. But Waterloo is a breaking, a chipping into fragments, marvellously reflected in Fabrice's piecemeal perceptions of the battle, scattered sensations merely, stills from an early newsreel, a dead man's dirty feet, an open eye, smoke rising beyond a patch of willows, trees clipped by gunfire, a ploughed field plucked by bullets. Other things die at Waterloo too, and it is worth noting that the lyricism of *La Chartreuse de Parme* is released largely by the hopelessness of the case it represents. If Stendhal is able to become his own Tasso or Ariosto—'tales of love, forests (woods and their vast silence), generosity'—it is because the

original is discredited, because chivalry has gone from the world. Fabrice's horse is stolen by the comrades in arms he was romantically warming to, and he weeps.. . . . The failure . . . [of] *Lucien Leuwen,* a novelist's incapacity to render the movement of social forces, is here presented as the failure of history: time has slithered back, it is the eighteenth century again, the old régime, an age of rule by the mistress and the confessor. There are new, post-Napoleonic fantasies, of course: the prince of Parma, a confirmed despot if ever there was one, a man who is imitating Joseph II when he is not imitating Louis XIV, sees himself as the constitutional king of all Lombardy. But the old repression is really in control. There is a revolt towards the end of *La Chartreuse,* put down gallantly but foolishly by Mosca at the head of a couple of battalions—foolishly because he believes as little in what he is defending as in the ideology of the attackers. What would have happened? Two months of a republic, perhaps, before neighbouring powers stepped in. Or a fortnight of looting, before the foreign troops arrived. In any case, nothing durable. People who keep talking about a republic, Mosca says ironically, prevent us from enjoying the best of monarchies, and the novel's republican leader says what amounts to the same thing, sets the seal on all hopeful radical thoughts: 'Anyway, how can you make a republic without republicans?' All Lucien Leuwen's nagging doubts are endorsed, enthroned.

These are sad ideas for some people, Stendhal among them, and my use of the word romance perhaps calls for an explanation. I am not thinking of the shape of *La Chartreuse* or of the characters in it, but rather of what I may call its weather, its flight from the 'tangled, exposed state' which Henry James sees as the proper preoccupation of novelists. James, in fact, in his preface to *The American,* offers the perfect definition:

> The only *general* attribute of projected romance that I can see, the only one that fits all its cases, is the fact of the kind of experience with which it deals—experience liberated, so to speak; experience disengaged, disembroiled, disencumbered, exempt from the conditions that we usually know to attach to it and, if we wish so to put the matter, drag upon it, and operating in a medium which relieves it, in a particular interest, of the inconvenience of a *related,* a measurable state, a state subject to all our vulgar communities . . .

Not true for the private experiences represented in *La Chartreuse de Parme*—old age, for example, drags sadly on Gina and Mosca—and personal relations in the novel are as complex as they are anywhere in fiction. But it is true for the political and social conditions of the book, the *medium,* as James says. *La Chartreuse de Parme,* alone among Stendhal's works, asks no questions of the world.

Two heroes. Ferrante Palla, the doctor-poet-revolutionary who assassinates the prince and is momentarily loved by Gina, a character for whom Stendhal himself plainly feels a good deal of misplaced affection, is perhaps the least successfully drawn of all Stendhal's figures. The climate of the book will not allow him to appear as anything other than a stiff, gesturing buffoon. And then Fabrice. Fabrice is charming and delicate and intelligent but he is also offhand and arrogant, and incurably selfish and irresponsible. He kills an actor, admittedly in self-defence, but nobody in the novel seems to worry much about what actually happened—the cheerful assumption is that Fabrice has a right to bump off a member of the lower classes if he feels like it. Similarly, he wants to stay in prison when his friends are trying desperately to get him out; he doesn't think of his aunt's anguish, he thinks only of staying where Clélia is. He never quite forfeits our sympathy for any of this, and the reason, I think, is that Stendhal sees him as embodying everything that was fine about the *ancien régime*. Stendhal's Jacobinism never blinded him to the good times that were had in the old days, and we occasionally even find him wishing he lived before 1789. Fabrice is the perfect aristocrat, unconscious of the extent of his privilege and therefore able to bask in it with authentic, untroubled grace. Along with his regret at the collapse of comedy, because the new public is too coarse for fine feeling and wit, Fabrice is one of Stendhal's few reservations about the Revolution. (pp. 167-70)

But surely *La Chartreuse de Parme* is a contemporary political novel: Stendhal took the trouble to modernize his old chronicle. How then can it be a romance, in any sense? In fact, the mere possibility of a modernization simply continues and strengthens the argument. Julien Sorel was not able to translate over a period of less than twenty years, the Napoleonic model ran him into all kinds of difficulties in the Restoration. Here Stendhal shifts a whole story, with pope, cardinals and a dazzling courtesan, two hundred years at a blow, and without any effort. For Rome read Parma, for pope read prince, for cardinal read minister. Only Gina is a sparkling anachronism, a restless, brilliant woman from another age. There are changes to be made, of course. The violent vendettas of the Renaissance have given way to the small politics of the Congress of Vienna. The prince of Parma, far from assassinating his enemies wholesale, has once had two liberals hanged, and now goes in mortal fear for his life—Mosca's chief credit with his sovereign being his ability to make the prince's panic look less emasculating than it is. It is Mosca who suggests they look under the bed at night and even in the cases of the bass fiddles. But the general result of the switch from the sixteenth century is not to bring things up to date but to suggest that nothing has changed. Fabrice on his way back from Waterloo is insulted, he thinks, in a café, and promptly forgets all the modern etiquette he has learned. He doesn't consider a duel, he draws his dagger and leaps on his enemy—'Fabrice's first movement was right out of the sixteenth century'.

Italy has progressed only towards pettiness. Otherwise it is the same backward, quarrelling, ungovernable place it always was. Stendhal's portrait is affectionate, but not complimentary.

His novel becomes timeless, then, as ultimately all historical novels are. It is released from contemporary contingencies, a romance. But it is tired romance, an ironic idyll, the world it offers is not better or brighter than the real one, it is simply safer, a world with familiar pitfalls and antagonists, a shelter from the new and unexpected. The retreat is not into fantasy but into chess or mathematics, into a place where the rules of the game are known and if you can keep your scruples quiet—for why should you air them, if they can have no possible effect—the game can be fun. (pp. 171-72)

There is one grim, dizzying sense, though, in which *La Chartreuse de Parme* does speak to its age. Suppose its pictures are literally faithful to a present reality, suppose that small states in Italy in the early nineteenth century are just like the fictional Parma—and we have no reason to believe many of them were very different—then the whole of Europe, by extension, a place of divided and oppressed countries, some

A sketch of Stendhal dancing, by Alfred de Musset.

more progressive than others but all of them reactionary by Stendhal's standards, would itself be trapped in the sad romance, in the absurd, insulated story, the archaic daydream, the fond thought that the French Revolution, and with it Napoleon, could be put away and forgotten. Romance as fiction and romance as a ludicrous but inescapable contemporary truth are distinctly different things. Even as he turns from France and his own day, Stendhal is able to let loose a handful of polemical shot over his shoulder. Metternich, Namier wrote, 'annotated the margins of the great book of human insufficiency and inertia'. Fabrice's Parma, for all its slightly febrile charm, could well have given him a page or two.

One of the indications in Stendhal's source [for the novel] was magic. 'The author', he notes, meaning his Neapolitan chronicler, 'explains a lot of facts by magic . . .'.(p. 172)

The novel is full of minor predictions, most of them registered by Fabrice, but some left for the alert reader to gloat over. They are there to surround a major prophecy, a theme sounded literally more than a dozen times: Fabrice's irrational fear of prison, perfectly justified, although justified with surprisingly pleasant results.

Fabrice's visible enthusiasm on the way to Waterloo, along with his Italian accent and his unmilitary appearance, causes him to be arrested as a spy as soon as he sets out for the front.

Prison, then, instead of glory. He bribes his way out, is given the clothes and the documents of a dead miscreant, which worries him no end. 'I have inherited his being, as it were . . . The presage is clear, I shall suffer much from a prison . . .'. He even thinks that his own imprisonment will bear a relation to his dead benefactor's crime: stealing some silver and a cow, and beating up a peasant. There is a rather ugly joke on Stendhal's part here: Fabrice is later gaoled for killing an actor and running off with the actor's girl.

The theme now shifts key. Various prisons threaten Fabrice on his return from Waterloo, or rather the same prison, the renowned Austrian Spielberg, threatens him for various reasons—for having been to Waterloo at all, for returning to the territory of Milan when he should be in cautious exile, and finally for killing Giletti, the actor. He had to cross into the Austrian states to escape pursuit—what's more, he is once again carrying a dead man's papers, the unfortunate Giletti's passport.

But the Spielberg is not his destined prison. Prison awaits him in Parma, where he ought to be safe, because he has powerful friends in his aunt and her lover Mosca, the prince's minister. In fact, it is their power that lands him in prison, since his crime, committed in self-defence and generally allowed to be insignificant anyway, as only a mountebank was involved, is played up by the political opposition to Mosca, and a severe sentence is delivered against Fabrice as a result of intrigues at court. However, by another too-tidy reversal, Fabrice is not distressed by the much-feared prison, for love and happiness await him there, indeed when he escapes he can't wait to go back, and when he is released again drags out his life in mournful splendour, with one interlude of bliss which Stendhal refuses to describe for us. 'Here, we beg permission to pass, without a single word, over a space of three years'. From there he retreats towards death in his charterhouse. . . . But then the force of the title surely becomes all the clearer. Prison is where Fabrice finds himself, writes religious sonnets, and scribbles in the margins of St Jerome. Secular studies, a means of paying court to Clélia, but then that suits Stendhal's theology well enough. The charterhouse of Parma, the one securely closed, contemplative place in a city of pride and ambition and rancour, is the prison on a high tower where Fabrice is kept.

What are we to make of this rather rickety machinery? Stendhal had used similar devices in *Le Rouge et le Noir*, with a remarkable lack of success. There we were faced with two elementary choices. Julien Sorel, in the church at Verrières, finds an oblique prophecy on a scrap of paper, news of the execution of a man whose name is an anagram of his own. We can assume Stendhal is serious about this, that such meaningful coincidences are a part of the picture of life he is offering—but then not much else in the novel confirms this view. Stendhal certainly thought life was capable of tricks just as fantastic, but he also saw life as more elegant and discreet than that in its echoes and bad jokes. Alternatively, we can assume that the anagram and its accompaniments—spilt holy water, crimson curtains—are simply heavy-handed juggling by a beginning novelist, attempts to ensure the visibility of a theme, to lay tracks for its return later in the book. I find this more likely.

Perhaps Fabrice's fulfilled superstitions represent the same thing, done with slightly more art. Stendhal attributes his own compositional needs to his character's education and temperament, and thereby acquires the freedom to set up his themes as he likes. No. That sounds right, but it wouldn't really be much of an improvement on the lame technique rejected in *Le Rouge et le Noir,* and in any case that isn't how the theme reads in *La Chartreuse de Parme.* Fabrice's prison doesn't suggest bad or even competent orchestration of a motif, it suggests mystery, creates a sense of fate for a sceptical author and his no doubt even more sceptical public.

First, Stendhal himself mocks Fabrice's credulity, tells us that his superstition is in fact his religion, a shaky science converted into a dreamer's happiness. But then, changing hats, becoming creator as well as narrator, he makes Fabrice absolutely right, since everything prophesied for him comes true. Not only for him. The abbé Blanès predicted a prison for Fabrice, but he also predicted a great crime to be connected with his imprisonment: Gina's having the prince assassinated, her revenge, her supreme and impossible gift to the unfeeling Fabrice. The movement created by these denials and endorsements is close to that set up in *Tom Jones,* where Fielding explicitly rules out the happy end as any kind of realistic prospect in life and then winds up his book in a grand, improbable way, the just rewarded, the evil punished and sent to the North. He thereby asserts the genre of his work in a flamboyant way: comedy, a universe of happy ends where life is imitated in various ways but not in its outcomes. Similarly Stendhal proclaims his intentions, announces his world of romance, a place where fantastic prophecies come true.

Do they? Stendhal, like a good rationalist, sketches in a doubt, suggests that Fabrice's sense of things is partial, that he only counts presages that work and forgets the failures of his omens. All right. But then the novel itself forgets the failures too, supports Fabrice, since his anxious readings of his destiny all turn out to be correct, we never see him wrong. In fact, what happens here is what happens later in works like James' "Turn of the Screw" or *The Sacred Fount.* Stories are suspended between rival impossibilities, between two sets of explanations for a puzzling event, neither of which will do. We can't and Stendhal can't, accept Fabrice's view of the future as minutely predictable. But we can't see all his prisons as merely coincidences either. As in James, the fiction tips the scale towards the more orderly but more fantastic of the options: true prophecy here, ghosts in "Turn of the Screw", a magical theory of the transferability of youth and wit in *The Sacred Fount.* In every case the story escapes towards mystery, into a dimension all of its own.

Still, there is something strained about Stendhal's insistence on Fabrice's prison. It comes not from the handling of the theme or from its more far-reaching implications but from its moral meaning, or lack of moral meaning, within the immediate context of the book's action. Prison is at the heart of all the paradoxes of *La Chartreuse* and it is not, finally, the prison's fault if the paradoxes are hollow. It is the fault of paradox as a structural principle, of the weakness of paradox in a world where logic itself, or at least Stendhal's logic, looks helpless, stranded, superannuated. (pp. 173-76)

Conflicting errors stare at each other, the perfection of the discord makes a new harmony, a balanced dance of contraries. It happens again and again in the book. Gina, in her early days at the court of Parma, pleads for the pardon of a prisoner she has met in the citadel. Her plea is granted, evidence of her extreme favour with the prince. But the man she has freed is a squealer, whose confession brought about the death sentence of the poet-revolutionary Ferrante Palla. Fabrice's gaoler, Clélia's father, reports that his client is alone and in despair when his client's affair with Clélia, conducted by signs, is at its height. After Fabrice's escape Gina, irritated by his gloom, sarcastically suggests he ought to write to Clélia's father and apologize for breaking gaol. Fabrice in fact has done just that. These are small forms, echoes, splinters of the main irony built on the prison, which has several faces, or epochs. Fabrice fears his prison but finds happiness there. The boy who is unable to love when he is at liberty, finds a destined love waiting for him in gaol. He wants passionately to stay in prison while his friends want passionately to get him out. Having escaped from prison, he goes back of his own accord.

There is no way of knowing where Stendhal's idea started, but one of his sources offers what is clearly the logical core of his paradox: a prison with a view. When Fabrice's fine view is blocked out, it is replaced by Clélia. The trouble with all this apart from its considerable heaviness, is that it is empty; neat but meaningless, a natty but slender joke, and one cannot sling a large novel on such things.

Except that Stendhal can. It is an extraordinary gamble, and one that just comes off. (pp. 176-77)

Fabrice is . . . shown to be a hypocrite when he is being as sincere as he can; and his prison in one sense saves him, leaves him with no distractions from his love. But the logic of the narrative of *La Chartreuse,* whenever it appears, appears as an intrusion, a visitor from another, stiffer country. Stendhal's logic, as Jean Prévost points out, is design, not sequence, geometry not arithmetic; and the subject of *La Chartreuse,* and to some extent *Lucien Leuwen,* is sequence itself, growing up, growing old, the slow death of hearts and affections. There is no proposition to encompass such realities, no closed form for them except our ultimate mortality.

Paradox will not do then, and yet paradox is Stendhal's oldest habit, the most familiar mode of his mind. Effectively, *La Chartreuse de Parme* rests on a false frame, on a set of ironies which look solid but are in truth extremely fragile. This, perhaps, is the key to a riddle which reading the novel often presents. Why does one go on, what keeps one wanting to know what happens next in this scattered work? It is really little more than six or seven unforgettable *bravura* scenes sustained by a functional narrative, lonely peaks in loosely connected valleys: the French in Italy; Fabrice at Waterloo; Gina at the court of Parma; her duel with the prince; her distress; her revenge; her isolation. One answer is the sheer charm and verve and intelligence of the writing, and it is a good answer. That, above all, is why one keeps reading *Vie de Henry Brulard,* for example, which is even more scattered. But one reads *La Chartreuse* rather more eagerly than that all the same, one is held more firmly. The reason, I think, is that Stendhal's repeating symmetries, the constant suggestion of paradox and tidy irony, make up a mirage of control, of a central, presiding meaning, of a direction which the novel simply doesn't have. But then it has it while we read it. We are shuffled from one expectation to another, waiting for the ironies to meet or unfold into a major action or emotion, and by the time we have realized, if we realize, that they won't, it is too late, the book is over. This is Stendhal's best magic, a culminating piece of sorcery: the place of an absent structure is supplied by an illusion of structure.

It wouldn't work, of course, if the book were not about something else too. *La Chartreuse de Parme,* as Balzac saw [see excerpt dated 1840], is not really about Fabrice at all, and

therefore still less about his prison. Much as the interest of *Ulysses* shifts from Stephen to Bloom, the interest of *La Chartreuse,* beginning with Fabrice, moves towards age, to his aunt, who comes to dominate the book, in terms both of her effect on its actions and of her impact on us. The force of her presence is such that it is often hard even to see Fabrice and harder to believe he deserves such splendid expenses of energy and devotion. The structure and the passion of *La Chartreuse de Parme,* the false structure of paradox and the authentic passion of Gina, are blurred by Stendhal's sleight of hand; we think, briefly, that the two elements are one, as they were in *Le Rouge et le Noir.* Then the haze lifts, and we see how separate they are. Two books, one fairly thin and the other superb. One lends shape to the other's feeling.

Balzac compared *La Chartreuse de Parme* to Racine's *Phèdre,* and he knew what he was doing. Gina's love for Fabrice rejoins the famous forbidden loves of legend, adds to their stock, borrows from their colour. Fabrice, faced with his recognition of his aunt's feelings for him, thinks of Joseph and Potiphar's wife. He knows Gina is not fully conscious of the extent of her love, she would be horrified, would see it as an incest. Stendhal himself, later, adds another loaded allusion: a crown prince who 'unlike Hippolytus son of Theseus, had not rejected the advances of a young step-mother'. And yet there is nothing incestuous or ungrateful about Gina's love for Fabrice. She is probably not related to him, and if she is, she is his aunt. She is not married to Mosca, she knew Fabrice before she met him, and indeed began her affair with Mosca during Fabrice's flight to Waterloo—almost as if to protect herself against the possibility of his not returning. Mosca is, or becomes, Fabrice's benefactor, so there is a comparison with Potiphar there, and perhaps, in a metaphorical sense, with Theseus. (pp. 177-78)

The echoes of Hippolytus and Potiphar, of a young man pursued by the warm attentions of someone too closely connected to him, are in effect an accompaniment, not the main subject. They are there to fire certain associations, to make us think of terse triangles, for example. Mosca, Gina, Fabrice. The names flicker in a series of strange little jokes, as if to indicate both the relationships and the complexities and confusions among them. Fabrice and Gina are briefly mistaken for General Fabio Conti and his daughter Clélia. This would make Fabrice Gina's father, as Gina is quick to point out. Everyone laughs. Then she straightens out the matter by explaining that Fabrice is in fact her son. Later the Paris newspapers get hold of a story about Fabrice's probable succession to the archbishopric of Parma, only they get the names wrong: Gina's nephew Count Mosca is to be the new prelate. By a last irony, when Gina has escaped from Parma with Fabrice, her servant Ludovic tells inquisitive observers that Fabrice is Mosca's son.

There are two triangles. Mosca loves Gina who loves Fabrice. Gina loves Fabrice who loves Clélia. Mosca's love is timid, passionate, silly, beautifully drawn, and the love between Fabrice and Clélia is nicely rendered. They are the basic young lovers of the sentimental imagination, the love-interest. But ultimately only the link between the triangle matters much to us. Gina loves Fabrice who doesn't love her. Which is a way of saying that only Gina matters.

The stages of Gina's passion are very clear, make a progression which looks oddly, deeply inevitable in a novel caught between Fabrice's superstitions and Stendhal's dogged reliance on the idea of chance. She loves Fabrice as a child, watches him grow up. As Balzac says, she has no children of her own—although the Gina which emerges in Balzac's lyrical review of *La Chartreuse de Parme* is in fact rather too maternal, too grand and noble and lofty, one of Balzac's own slightly overblown women. There is, of course, something motherly in Gina's feelings for Fabrice, but she doesn't make a motherly impression, she is too clearly competitive, too young for that. Then Fabrice returns from Waterloo and she falls thoroughly in love with him. The love has a later, reinforcing moment when he comes back, solemn and manly, from the theological college in Naples where he was supposed to be preparing his bright clerical future.

There are rumours of her affair with Fabrice everywhere in Parma. Clélia has heard of it, the prince makes a malicious reference. At one stage almost everyone except Gina herself knows about it. Mosca sees it in her eyes when she is talking to Fabrice, and falls cruelly into envy and a sense of his age. 'Ah! however careful I am, the look in my eyes must be old! Isn't my gaiety always close to irony? . . . I'll say more, I must be sincere here, doesn't my gaiety give a glimpse, as of something very near, of absolute power . . . and meanness?' Fabrice knows. An old rival knows. In a softer novel these rumours and inferences would be wrong, a fine purity would be left to Gina and Fabrice. But for Stendhal, and for Gina, the purity of the affair is an unhappy accident, an absence of physical consequences for a passion that can swell and proliferate without them. When the intrigues of the court have finally thrown Fabrice in prison for his murder of Giletti, she dismisses Mosca, tells him it is all over, and makes an eloquent confession, a declaration of love for an absent hero comparable to Cathy Earnshaw's speech to Nelly in *Wuthering Heights*:

> 'I swear to you before God and on the life of Fabrice that there has not passed between him and me the smallest thing that a third person couldn't have witnessed. But I shall not tell you that I love him as if I were his sister; I love him by instinct, as it were. I love in him his perfect and simple courage . . . In short, if he is not happy I can't be happy. There, that's a phrase which well describes the state of my heart; if it's not the truth, it is at least as much of it as I can see'.

She is in fact saying almost as much as she knows about her love. But she is saying it in the large shadow of all she doesn't know. She doesn't know how jealous she can be, she can't know that she will later hasten Clélia's marriage with a kind of eager rancour, in the faintest of hopes of getting Fabrice back. Her remark about his happiness is perhaps true but it is pathetically partial. If Fabrice is happy without her, she will be in despair.

The heart of the matter, the fissure in Gina's life through which all her distresses will come flooding in, is her own doubt, a shyness, a failure of nerve. Her anxiety about a possible sense of incest is trivial compared with her terror at the thought of being too old for Fabrice—she is fifteen years older than he is. . . . [She] was right to be afraid. Faced with Clélia, Fabrice thought of Gina as fifty. Fabrice *is* her threatened youth, if he could love her she would still be young. His imprisonment thus means a form of death for Gina, fully displayed in the narrative—to her maids, seeing her virtually unconscious on her bed in sorrow, fully clothed, in her diamonds, pale, her eyes closed, she seems to be lying in state. To Mosca she seems to have aged overnight: '. . . and yester-

day so brilliant, so young!' Prison is a place where time passes. Fabrice has plenty of time, Gina hasn't.

But her despair at Fabrice's capture has other components too. She is an active woman, in love with movement. She is attracted to Parma partly by the thought of Mosca's power—'The memory of the count became mingled with the idea of his great power'—and embraces Ferrante Palla when she sees him ready to assassinate the prince. 'There is the only man who has understood me', she murmurs. Her heart returns to Mosca when she has heard of his suppressing the revolt in Parma. Her love for Fabrice itself is connected with Fabrice's expedition to Waterloo, his 'perfect and simple', if mercilessly thwarted courage, and there is a moving echo, or rather a moving absence of echo, late in the book, when he has escaped from prison in best swash-buckling manner and has nothing to tell her, no story. There is no going back to the endless, charming discussions after Waterloo when they weren't sure whether Fabrice had been at a battle at all and if he had, whether it was the right battle. Those childish days, by now, are gone for Fabrice too. He can think only of Parma and getting back to Clélia.

With Fabrice's imprisonment, therefore, there rises in Gina a fierce, suffocating, debilitating rage, because there is nothing she can do. When a sentence was given against Fabrice with him safely out of the country she marched in to see the prince and simply threatened to leave Parma, to withdraw all the light and joy she was shedding. She was happy to be active—as all Stendhal's women are, they are invariably superior to his men in this. Mathilde de la Mole, Mme de Rênal, Gina, Clélia, they are all enlivened by danger, quickened into extraordinary acts of intelligence and courage. The men are brave enough but in a willed, strained and usually comic way, their imaginations exalt their perils, paint dragons on every wall. But now, with Fabrice in the prince's hands, ready and waiting for the first poisoner who is sent along to deal with him, Gina can't leave and she can't do much if she stays. She has been betrayed by the prince, who had promised not to sign Fabrice's sentence and significantly, the order of her fury runs from that to Fabrice, from her sense of humiliation and outrage to a concern for his life. His life is more important to her, but it surfaces second in her anger. And here, in the pit of her impotence, she vows vengeance on the prince. 'You can kill me this way, so be it, you have the power to do it; but afterwards I shall have your life'.

Her vengeance is the moral climax of the novel, as Julien's crime was for *Le Rouge et le Noir,* but with a difference which could hardly be greater. Julien's shooting of Mme de Rênal was his redemption, what he had to do. In spite of all appearances, it was *right*. Gina's crime, equally clearly, and yet for reasons just as hard to bring to the surface and to formulate, is wrong. It doesn't save her, it stains the rest of her life. (pp. 180-83)

The setting is wrong for Gina's vengeance . . . , it belongs in another, older age. But even there, perhaps, it would have seemed excessive. It is too late, Fabrice is free when she orders the signal to be made to Ferrante Palla, who is to poison the prince. Water from a reservoir in her palace is to flood the streets of Parma, and Ferrante will know the time has come. She will give wine, she says, to the inhabitants of her country village, and water to the citizens of Parma, because they would have loved to see Fabrice die. She is hiding her uncertainty about the killing here, perhaps, rejoicing in the sign as if the sign had a meaning of its own. There is something too small for vengeance in her scheme, it is not much better than a resentment, and it is her own half-awareness of this which weakens Gina. In the Renaissance world to which she belongs people were killed for adultery or for having killed others, and even in Stendhal's France the crimes that attracted him were committed for love. Gina has the prince assassinated out of hatred, worse, out of the festering memory of her helplessness on the day Fabrice was put in gaol. It is a crime of the head, the work of slighted self-regard; it is a harsh act without dignity.

But all this could have been overcome if Fabrice had loved Gina. She intended the prince's death as her welcoming gift to him, they were to have exulted over it together. As it is, she can't even tell him. 'I did that for him,' she thinks darkly. She didn't. But without him it has no meaning. Julien was sustained by an intuitively held morality of his own, which was strong enough to batter back all assaults from conventional views of what he had done. Without Fabrice, Gina has no inner mine of energy and defiance, she cannot set up her values against the world's because they have been revealed as barren, as the mere waving of a small fist not, ultimately, at the prince or at Parma, although they were to suffer, but at middle age and death, at the lines on her face, the fading of her pulse and the thought that Fabrice may never love her. The way is open, then, for the world's values to come seeping in, she has no defences. A half-remorse sets up house in her mind, and when Mosca suggests killing an enemy in order to get Fabrice out of prison for a second time, she says no. She doesn't want him to have black ideas in the evenings. The enemy concerned, she adds, owes his life to the fact that she now loves Mosca better than she loves Fabrice. If the tone of the book were different we might see a gentle resolution out of classical comedy here: the old folks together, leaving the young folks alone. But this is Gina's defeat, gracefully acknowledged, for she hardly knows how not to be graceful, but ghastly for a woman whose glory it was never to repent, never to look back, never to think again about something once decided on. What saves the enemy's life and leaves her quietly married to Mosca in the end is not only age but the worst kind of scar brought with her from her youth: shame for a senseless, violent and irrevocable gesture of malice. Stendhal's remarks about the unsullied joys of vengeance in Italy are a smoke-screen, a materialization of Gina's discomfort in the narrative; a way of holding us off from what she herself would rather not know. (pp. 183-85)

Michael Wood, in his Stendhal, *Cornell University Press,* 1971, 208 p.

GITA MAY (essay date 1977)

[*May evaluates* Lamiel, *finding the novel an expression of Stendhal's feminist sympathies.*]

What makes *Lamiel* such a remarkable yet logical work in the slow and roundabout evolution of Stendhal as a writer and as a novelist is the fact that its main protagonist is a young woman.

Of all the major French men of letters Stendhal can unhesitatingly be viewed as one of those most truly sympathetic to the difficult lot of women in society in general, and particularly to the tragic fate that awaits those women of superior intellect and forceful character who do not hesitate to play an aggressive part in a society which is ruled and dominated by men. (pp. 271-72)

This liberal, sympathetic outlook is . . . forcefully demonstrated by Stendhal's unforgettable gallery of women, so finely individualized, so different from Balzac's stereotyped heroines. For Stendhal's female protagonists have the capacity, traditionally reserved for heroes only, to seek and define their own identity and to assert their will and freedom of choice as individuals. And here again, the eighteenth century, more than his own, was Stendhal's frame of reference, for in the novels of Marivaux, Prévost, Diderot, Rousseau, Laclos, and others, women had been the focus of attention, and it had been through their adventures and misadventures that the deceptions, shams, cruelties, and absurdities of contemporary society had been held up for ridicule or eloquently denounced. (pp. 272-73)

If Stendhal's novels, especially *The Red and the Black,* illustrate the idea that the exceptional man, in order to survive in a world where hypocrisy is at the basis of all values, where conformism, uniformity, observance of rules, and religious orthodoxy are prerequisites for social acceptance, *Lamiel* in turn focuses on the even more ambiguous and precarious position of the superior woman. Stendhal's strong feminist sympathies manifest themselves most clearly in this compelling but unfortunately incomplete novel. His lifelong empathy and admiration for women who, like Métilde Dembowski, proudly defied social conventions and with exemplary courage devoted themselves to hazardous political causes found its most forceful expression in *Lamiel.*

Yet Stendhal was determined to couch his ideas and feelings on the subject not in philosophical terms which would mar the narrative, but within a novelistic framework. *Lamiel* was to be the logical culmination of Stendhal's evolution and accumulated experience as a writer and social critic. And of all his fictional heroes and heroines, Lamiel would be the most radical exponent of his philosophy of individualism and enlightened, self-avowed egoism. The fact that he selected a woman as the main protagonist in order to illustrate his thesis has troubled many a reader and even puzzled some of the most penetrating Stendhalians, who cannot help but feel disturbed by a work that tells the story of a country girl who, early in life, achieves an unexpected, startling emancipation from conventional, and especially sexual, taboos.

That it is a young woman, rather than a young man, who sets out to undermine the foundations of society and to subvert its moral fabric is of course rather disturbing for readers conditioned by a novelistic tradition in which the heroine is presented, from the outset, as a noble and touching victim. Lamiel is a more complex and intriguing character, and in many ways she is a forerunner of the twentieth-century liberated woman. (pp. 273-74)

Like Julien Sorel, Lamiel escapes a mediocre fate through her impressive intellectual promise. She becomes the protégée of the local chatelaine, the Duchess of Miossens. Lamiel, however, continues to be dissatisfied with her lot, and her contact with provincial aristocracy only confirms her in her desire to escape from this constricting environment. She falls ill, mainly as a result of her mental depression, and at last a curious figure of a doctor is summoned to treat her, Dr. Sansfin. He is a hunchback, an object of local ridicule, yet a man with a penetrating, corrosive intelligence and a completely cynical outlook on life. He soon becomes Lamiel's adviser and guide, and the philosophy he teaches her is essentially one of subversion and subterfuge.

Fortified with these principles, Lamiel sets out, as her first endeavor, to rid herself of her virginity with a local rustic, whose approach to this business is entirely matter-of-fact, an experience that confirms her in her determination to seek happiness in her own way and to avoid being deceived by the illusion of love. She had read so much about this great passion in books that she had expected something extraordinary. Her disappointment was, of course, quite understandable under the circumstances.

In the course of her lengthy "educational" sessions with Dr. Sansfin, Lamiel had moreover become highly aware of the inferior social status of women and of their legal subservience to their husbands. She was told about the innumerable inequities between the sexes, about the double moral standard that prevailed, especially where a married woman's conduct is concerned. And Dr. Sansfin, an unbeliever in the eighteenth-century tradition, took delight in pointing out to his young pupil the important role the Catholic Church played in reinforcing these codes through religious doctrine and education. Thus, while a man notorious for his infidelities could derive glory from his reputation as a seducer and Don Juan, his unfortunate spouse, if found to be adulterous, was looked upon with loathing by her peers and, her reputation as well as her position irreparably damaged, she had to end her days in isolation and poverty with nothing to look forward to, save an eternity in hell for her misdeed. Hypocrisy and duplicity were the only weapons available to an intelligent young woman aspiring to realize fully her potential as a human being in a society that denied her this fundamental right. Like the superiorly crafty and cunning Marquise de Merteuil of the *Liaisons dangereuses,* Lamiel soon learned that her primary duty in life was to do exactly as she pleased, to have lovers and to pursue sexual and other gratifications while maintaining an irreproachable exterior.

Such a strategy required, of course, boldness and force of character, a strong intellect and a sure knowledge of society and contemporary mores, and sufficient personal charm as well as psychological acumen to manipulate the emotions and feelings of others. But if Lamiel endeavors to be as scheming and ruthless as a Marquise de Merteuil, if she sets out to emulate this notorious eighteenth-century fictional model, she ends up acting in a way that is more congruent with Stendhal's other heroines. Despite Dr. Sansfin's training, despite her self-avowed "principles," Lamiel is too free, impulsive, and quixotic a spirit to practice methodically a system requiring perpetual duplicity and deceit.

If Lamiel succeeds in enticing the aristocratic Duc de Miossens, a rather sympathetic and appealing character in the Stendhalian tradition of the liberal-minded but somewhat weak-willed young nobleman reminiscent in particular of the heroes of **Armance** and **The Pink and the Green,** she soon tires of him and his effete ways and leaves him. Running away to the French capital, she leads an existence that openly flouts the traditional social conventions concerning women. Believing love, as depicted in poetry and fiction, is but a creation of the feverish imagination of writers, Lamiel at last experiences, to her own surprise, dismay, and delight, real love. The object of her affections happens to be a criminal. But this does not unduly disturb her, since one of her favorite books had been a popularization of the daring exploits of Cartouche, a notorious eighteenth-century malefactor. Lamiel's lover,

moreover, is no ordinary criminal; he is well-educated and well-read, and he proudly professes his own brand of social philosophy in the name of which he has declared war upon a society he considers unjust and unfair to the individual, especially the individual who, like himself, is over-qualified for a menial type of job: "I wage war against a society which wages war against me. I read Corneille and Molière. I have too much schooling to work with my hands and earn three francs a day for ten hours of work." Such reasoning is reminiscent of the arguments invoked by the cynical, volatile, and eloquent self-proclaimed social parasite and immoralist in Diderot's brilliant satirical dialogue, *Rameau's Nephew.*

Lamiel is not only impressed by her lover's radical ideology; she is completely won over by his dash, his audacity, and his willingness to take chances with the police for her sake. Thus when he flouts the authorities openly by taking her to the theater, her passion for him knows no bounds. All major Stendhalian protagonists exhibit such boldness and impetuosity of spirit. It is this readiness, even eagerness, to defy death or to risk personal disgrace by challenging the powers that be that makes Stendhal's heroes and heroines such compelling creations. And this capacity to commit impulsive, rash acts, to *"faire des folies,"* as Stendhal liked to put it, was, of course, the novelistic expression of his *espagnolisme,* of his fundamentally individualistic, quixotic outlook on life, of his life-long cult of those human qualities that transcend mere intellectual brilliance or conventional morality. Even in the novels that were left in an unfinished or even fragmentary state, these characteristics stand out very clearly.

There is another eighteenth-century work of fiction that **Lamiel** brings to mind, and which Stendhal himself mentions as a major source of inspiration of his novel. It is Lesage's *Gil Blas,* a work Stendhal had long admired. A lively and deliberately rambling story in the picaresque manner, *Gil Blas* recounts the adventures of a young Spaniard who, during his journey from Oviedo to Salamanca, where he is to pursue his studies, is captured by brigands, escapes, is employed by many masters and, after a number of setbacks and mishaps, eventually makes good and becomes a respectable member of society. What Stendhal doubtless appreciated in *Gil Blas* was its broadly satirical panorama of a wide assortment of social types, classes, and professions.

Lesage's principal purpose, in writing *Gil Blas* and his other works, was to point up the basic human vices: foolishness, greed, envy. As a novelistic hero, Gil Blas was a highly original creation for the period, since he is far from "morally" admirable. He can be hypocritical, cowardly, mendacious, and cynical. But his basic instincts are decent, and he is capable of acts of generosity. Above all, he is unpretentious, good-natured, adaptable, and willing to learn from his experiences; and he has a sense of humor and irony, which he exercises at his own expense with the kind of self-knowledge that Stendhal could not fail to value.

Lamiel would be a modern, female reincarnation of Lesage's hero, a carefree and none too scrupulous adventuress who nevertheless remains loyal to her own integrity as an individual. She may lie to the world and dissemble in order to further her own interests; but she is truthful with herself, and in the final analysis it is this fundamental honesty that alienates her irrevocably from a society she had set out to deceive. In this respect, of course, Lamiel, who ends up, according to Stendhal's sketchy draft, as a radical revolutionist and urban guerrilla and who, in order to avenge the death of her lover at the hands of French justice, sets fire to the Paris court-house and is herself burned to death in the process, acquires a tragic dimension entirely lacking in the more pliable and opportunistic Gil Blas. (pp. 274-78)

> *Gita May, in her* Stendhal and the Age of Napo-leon, *Columbia University Press, 1977, 332 p.*

ROBERT ALTER WITH **CAROL COSMAN** (essay date 1979)

[*In the following excerpt from his critical biography of Sten-dhal,* Alter *considers* The Red and the Black *the pinnacle of Stendhal's artistic achievement, investigating the novel's narra-tive technique, characterization, and themes.*]

[What] is most astonishing about *Le Rouge et le Noir,* espe-cially if one has been following the hesitant and circuitous progress of Stendhal's literary efforts over nearly three dec-ades, is how, suddenly, in the work of a few months, every-thing comes together perfectly; how he is able to use artisti-cally everything he has experienced and observed; how time after time in his management of style and in his insight into character, in his invention of scene, action, and gesture, he exhibits a perfect rightness of touch. The result is not only a splendid piece of fiction but also a novel in certain ways quite unlike any novel that had been written before. As with most imaginative works, an originality of vision that has its roots in the distinctive experience, psychology, and sensibility of the author is intricately intertwined with an originality of technique. Perhaps the two chief aspects of the novel in which both orders of linked originality can be seen most clearly are: Stendhal's imaginative relation to his protago-nists, most especially to Julien, which is inseparable from a consideration of the kind of narrator or dramatized persona he invents to serve as his intermediary; and his less obtrusive manipulation of narrative point of view and related strategies of fictional exposition, which is inseparable from his under-standing of human nature and society, from his perception of what is central and what is peripheral in experience. The issue of point of view and fictional exposition, being suscepti-ble of concrete illustration, may profitably be considered first. In other words, in order to understand Henri Beyle's sudden leap to artistic maturity, we shall have to attend to certain in-novative technical details of his craft as a novelist.

Before *Le Rouge et le Noir,* there had been a split in the han-dling of perspective in the novel between first-person narra-tives (including epistolary novels), on the one hand, and third-person narratives, on the other. The first-person narra-tion attached us to the fictional narrator's single perspective, in some instances—especially in the epistolary novel—bringing us to the very cutting edge of one person's experi-ence as he or she underwent it in all its emotional plenitude. By contrast, third-person narrators tended to take a magiste-rial overview of their personages, keeping at a distance from the subtle movements of the characters' inner life, in some cases treating the characters' consciousness and their materi-al surroundings or their physical manifestations on more or less the same level. Jane Austen (whom Stendhal gives no evi-dence of having read) may have effected a partial compromise between these two traditions of narration, but it was *Le Rouge et le Noir* that signally bridged the gap between them and by so doing laid the technical groundwork for the subse-quent achievements of Flaubert, Tolstoy, Henry James, and many others. For Stendhal, by virtue of all his social and am-atory experience a relentlessly attentive observer and an in-

veterate speculator as to what others were thinking about him as he thought about them, the important thing in any scene was not how it looked but how it looked through one charac-ter's eyes or another's. This led him to build up his narrative through a shifting series of related techniques in which the narrator silently follows the train of sensory perceptions of one character, then switches to another, or, while maintain-ing the third person, closely mimics the interior speech of a character in *style indirect libre,* or summarizes a character's line of unspoken reasoning, or presents actual interior mono-logues, sometimes resembling dramatic soliloquies.

Here, for example, is the very beginning of the first encounter between the young bourgeois mother, Mme de Rênal, and the future tutor of her children, Julien Sorel:

> With the vivaciousness and grace that were natural to her when she was far from the eyes of men, Mme de Rênal was going out through the French doors of the living room which opened onto the garden, when she noticed by the gate the figure of a young peasant, still almost a child, extremely pale, who had just been crying. He was in a very white shirt, and under one arm had a quite decent jacket of vio-let frieze.
>
> The complexion of this young peasant was so white, his eyes so gentle, that to Mme de Rênal's somewhat extravagant imagination it first occurred that this might be a young girl in disguise, who had come to lay some entreaty before His Honor the Mayor. She pitied this poor creature, halted at the gate, who evidently had not dared to raise his hand as far as the bell.

The naturalness and transparency of Stendhal's manner are so evident that one does not immediately realize how much essential information—dramatic, psychological, social, and thematic—is conveyed in a few seemingly casual strokes of narration. True to his strictures against the methods of Wal-ter Scott, Stendhal makes no attempt to provide a detailed physical description of the scene or the characters or to intro-duce his personages formally. Mme de Rênal is characterized only in an introductory prepositional phrase, which is at-tached to the action she is performing at this particular mo-ment but which nevertheless sets up an important view of her as a woman of hidden liveliness and feminine charm shyly subjected to the male-dominated bourgeois order, and in her natural unreflective grace the antithesis of the self-conscious Julien as well as of the histrionic Mathilde de la Mole. (The interweaving of expositional materials with the narrative present is itself an important technical innovation of Sten-dhal's.) This succinct characterization of what Mme de Rênal is like when she is by herself is of course the perception of the omniscient narrator, who then slides deftly into her point of view, emerging only momentarily in the first sentence of the second paragraph to inform us that Mme de Rênal had a "somewhat extravagant imagination" (*l'esprit un peu roman-esque*).

What her eye first picks out when she catches sight of Julien is, with fidelity to the facts of visual perception from a middle distance, the whiteness of his skin. His clothing, which she then notices (after observing his youth and his tearful pallor), identifies him as a peasant, a fact seemingly contradicted by the fairness of his complexion, and this leads her to the fanci-ful conjecture about the young woman in disguise. The sheer efficiency with which Stendhal defines scene, character, incip-ient relationship, and social background is astonishing. We know that Julien, fresh from his father's sawmill, has exerted a great effort to make himself presentable; his shirt is carefully laundered, he has brought with him a very decent, or clean (*propre* can mean both) jacket, though it is, after all, only of coarse wool. We even know that it is a warm day, for he is carrying his jacket under his arm, and the rapid adverbial indications of French doors, garden, and gate are enough to let us visualize the scene as much as we need to for Stendhal's immediate dramatic purposes.

But the reader cannot fully realize until he has continued on into the novel how much more than this he is being told in these few lines. In a moment, the narrative will slip into Julien's point of view as he notices the kind expression in Mme de Rênal's eyes, her beauty, her fine clothing—he is about to step near enough to smell its "fragrance" (*parfum*)—and above all, *her* white complexion, which with his peasant's eyes he finds "dazzling." We have the first discreet hint, then, of the skin-to-skin closeness to which they will attain, but with it a nice suggestion of the class differences that separate them. We also have an appropriate intimation of the maternal aspect that this first and last love of Julien's shows him: she sees him as "almost a child," and her first words to him will be, "What do you want, my child?"

The other expositional elements in the passage are, in the light of what follows, mainly ironic. Here Julien stands below at the gate and Mme de Rênal observes him from above, in a spatial emblem of their social relationship. But as a determined climber, he is repeatedly associated with elevations: we first see him straddling the roofbeam of his father's shed, reading the *Mémorial de Sainte Hélène* (book and boy are then violently knocked off this perch by Papa Sorel); two of his most important experiences of inner assessment take place on a hilltop, watching the flight of a lonely sparrow hawk, and in a mountain cavern; Julien will ultimately realize himself in a prison one hundred eighty steps high—quite like the tower with one hundred twenty steps Henri Beyle had sketched in his journal in 1810—with a view looking out and down. Julien aspires to the boldness, the indomitable strength, the self-protective impenetrability of a Napoleon, but Mme de Rênal's first glance catches him in the full weakness of his weeping and, what is more, almost takes him for a girl. But that, too, foreshadows the course of their relationship, for it will be his spontaneous revelations of weakness, even tears, not his elaborate battle plans of seduction, that will win her for him. Finally, when we recall that the novel, after all, does set into play a whole set of associations of red—imperial military glory, violence, revolution, ritual pomp, passion, incest, *Liebestod*—against black—priesthood, hypocrisy, turpitude, Bourbon reaction, bleak death—the emphasis on white in this initial scene begins to assume the function of a thematic focusing device, visually isolating two frail and lovely human faces caught in this tangled field of historical, social, and political forces. In sum, it is hard to imagine that any novelist could have managed to tell us more than all this in just a few ostensibly casual sentences. When he could write with such easy perfection, Stendhal's long literary apprenticeship was clearly over.

Le Rouge et le Noir, as even this single instance from a whole spectrum of narrative strategies may suggest, is equally impressive in the rendering of individual scenes and in sustaining through them larger architectonic designs. Stendhal, to be sure, was by no means a painstaking architect of fictional structures like Mann or Joyce: a few of the recurring patterns

in the novel may have been carefully planned in advance, others probably occurred to him as he went over his draft and proofs, and a good many of these must have been intuitively woven into the individual passages in the rapid course of his composition by improvisation. As for the "rightness" of the individual scenes themselves, the suddenly accomplished technique he exhibits is finally a function of his shrewd understanding of the characters he has imagined, and that in turn is the ripe fruit of his lifelong cultivation of self-understanding and of the disciplined observation of human nature. The suppleness of the management of narrative point of view, in other words, is a consequence of the writer's experienced subtlety of perception about people.

When, for example, Julien steels himself for the second time to seize Mme de Rênal's hand in the dark of the garden, while her husband is seated four feet away inveighing against the evils of the rabble classes, we are told: "The hand that was yielded to him Julien covered with passionate kisses, or at least that is how they seemed to Mme de Rênal." The corrective second clause, clearly from a very lucid omniscient narrator, pulls us up short, simultaneously reminds us that the perception of "passionate kisses" belongs to Mme de Rênal, that it is a worn literary cliché which has often shabbily covered more ambiguous realities, and that poor Julien at the moment is too desperately preoccupied with what he conceives to be his "duty" as a seducer to allow himself to feel any passion. These few words of narrator's comment swivel our attention around toward three different objects at once: what is going on in Mme de Rênal's mind, what is going on in Julien's mind, and the background of linguistic or literary stereotypes they both draw on to order and interpret their experience. It is a small but characteristic example of how Stendhal's narrative constantly requires little acts of critical intelligence on the part of the reader and for that very reason constantly bypasses, suppresses, or reshapes what would be the climactic actions of a more conventional piece of fiction in order to demonstrate to us that the true interest, the true human facts of the matter, lie elsewhere.

The consistent elision of the moments of sought-after sexual consummation in the novel memorably illustrates this bypassing of the conventional in the interests of intelligent perception. (Respectable novelists in this period, of course, could not permit themselves undue explicitness in sexual scenes, but Stendhal's deliberate short-circuiting of any suggestiveness in such matters remains notable.) When the virtuous Mme de Rênal finally yields to Julien's unpremeditated tears, all we are told of the fateful act itself is the following: "Several hours later, when Julien left Mme de Rênal's bedroom, one could have said, in the style of a novel, that he had nothing more to desire." Life, as most great novels tend to remind us, is not like a novel, and the phrase here turns ironically back on itself because Julien's story is to a large extent a study of the problematic nature of desire, and it is only at the end, in prison, that he discovers the meaning of desire fulfilled. A large measure of Stendhal's modernity as a novelist can be attributed to his grasp of how a protagonist can cease to know what he desires, can be alienated from his own experience by the unrelenting self-consciousness, the constant role playing, that his location in society and history seems to require of him (Beyle's own anguish of self-consciousness in the pursuit of Mélanie, Angela, Alexandrine, and Métilde had not been forgotten). Julien knows that what Mme de Rênal has just accorded him is designated "being happy" in the novels he has read, but he is far too intent on proving his worth as a superior creature to feel anything of the sort.

This elusiveness of experience at the moment of consummation is compounded in the second part of the novel when Julien encounters in Mathilde de la Mole a quixotic role player even more extravagant than himself. His first midnight scene in her bedroom, to which he has been induced to climb on a ladder in the light of the full moon, is surely one of the high points of knowing comedy in the history of the novel. Suspecting that "these people," the haughty aristocrats, have prepared an ambush for him, he climbs up to the window armed with pistol and dagger. Both Julien and Mathilde are performing solemn duties to themselves in becoming lovers, and they approach this first moment of intimacy in the moonlit room with about the same sensation of inward clenching and apprehension with which one might approach a dentist's chair. Mathilde concentrates all her attention on the supreme effort of addressing Julien as *tu,* and he, once he is assured that there are no hidden hirelings about to spring out at him, is too astounded by the sheer usage of the *tu* to notice that the tone with which she invokes this language of intimacy is manic rather than tender. Throughout the scene, they scarcely pay any attention to each other, so intent is each on following all the prescribed steps of a proper lover, so anesthetized are their real feelings by the chill suffusion of self-consciousness. "Passionate love," Stendhal observes with dry precision after the two have finally been in bed together, "was still rather a model to be imitated than a reality." For Julien, in grim pursuit of the exaltation his books have promised him, "this night . . . seemed singular rather than happy."

The British novelist Elizabeth Bowen once aptly observed that the revelation of character in the novel should be unforeseeable before the fact but must seem inevitable after. That rule of thumb is preeminently applicable to *Le Rouge et le Noir,* where the three principal characters, in rather different ways, zigzag sharply in action and feeling, yet seem more fully themselves with each sudden turn they take. Mme de Rênal, the demure Christian wife and mother, becomes a passionate mistress, then a guilt-stricken penitent, then a devotee of love supremely indifferent to the world's censure. The proud Mathilde forces herself to yield to this mere secretary of her father's, then immediately resents the power she has let him obtain over her, then delightedly wallows in the sensation of becoming Julien's "slave" when he seems to threaten her with a sword he has seized from the wall, then resents him again, and finally, through Julien's strategy of arousing her jealousy, resolves on a noble course of devotion unto death, consummating at the end her secret theatrical dream when she is privileged, like the mistress of her Renaissance ancestor, to carry off her lover's severed head.

In the case of Julien, whose consciousness dominates much of the narrative, we are allowed to follow small zigzags as well as large. At one point, for example, he feels a sudden impulse of solidarity with M. de Rênal, the man he has been cuckolding, and anger against Mme de Rênal because she has shown herself able to use feminine wiles to deceive her husband for the sake of her lover; a few hours later, he rebukes himself for the foolishness of this sentiment. The cumulative indication of such quicksilver fluctuations of consciousness in Julien, unpredictable before the fact yet convincing in their revelation, prepares us for the great reversal of the denouement: Julien's somnambulistic journey from Paris to Verrières (conveyed in a few staccato sentences) to fire the pistol at Mme de Rênal, the flood of renewed affection for her when he learns she will survive, his renunciation of the world in the unexpected happiness of his prison retreat.

There is no easy way to explain how Stendhal suddenly acquired the ability to know his fictional personages with such magisterial sureness, though his success as a psychologist of character has at least something to do with the fact that the characters, the women included, are at once splendidly heightened, gratifying fantasy-projections of himself and aspects of himself that had long been held under scrutiny in the cold light of self-analysis. One way *not* to explain the persuasiveness of the characters is to seek, as so many critics have done, especially in the case of the heroines, "real-life" models in the history of Henri Beyle. Stendhal's characters pulsate with the inward movements of his own experience, and he does sometimes lend them actual anecdotal fragments of his past, but the vivid individuality with which he endows them is hardly the result of a scissors-and-paste assemblage from persons remembered and acts performed.

Stendhal's complicated relation to Julien offers the best illustration of the double activity of fantasy and severe scrutiny that generates a sense of psychological depth in the characters. In certain respects, Julien is obviously what his author would have dreamed of being: a perfectly beautiful young man with a natural ability to charm women, especially when he is not trying to do so; a devotee of the Napoleonic ideal of heroism who is prepared to follow his assertion of superiority over the common herd to the utmost limits, even to his own death. Julien, like Henri Beyle, has a detested father with whom he feels no connection, but unlike Beyle, he is given sufficient hints to indulge at length in the supposition that he is really the son of some nobleman and thus to play out the appealing central role in a Freudian Family Romance, even in the end being granted undisputed possession of the mother after having acted out his aggression toward her. The resonance between the lovely, maternal Mme de Rênal and the ardently desired mother, snatched away by death so early, in *Henry Brulard,* has often been noted, and the pointing of the pistol at Mme de Rênal might well be an unconscious transformation of guilt felt by the seven-year-old Henri over his mother's death in childbirth or, better, of guilt fused with anger over having been "abandoned" by the mother.

With all this, Julien remains in important ways his author's inferior. He is a peasant, not a bourgeois, which means that his ignorance about the complexities of social life is even greater than was that of the nineteen-year-old Beyle and that his constant misperceptions of people are partly determined by a feeling Beyle did not share—deep class resentment. He has committed to memory *La Nouvelle Héloïse* as well as the Vulgate, but he uses Rousseau's work only as a source book for the language of seduction, believing that all novels are written by scoundrels in order to get ahead, never having glimpsed the imaginative horizons that literature can open. Julien, in short, has a decidedly limited inner world, and it is not surprising that the narrator should often condescend to him, call him "my poor little Julien," or flatly state that he is a mediocre creature. To be more precise, his notions of human nature, love, happiness, and culture are mediocre, but his innate sensibility, which he goes to such lengths to pervert, is a fine one, and the energy of his desires, however misdirected, is extraordinary, impelling him through the tragicomic twists of the entire plot and making him fit for his hero-ically tragic ending.

Technically, Stendhal is able to keep in focus this figure who embodies his intimate fantasies and is yet inferior to himself by presenting Julien through the mediation of an engagingly urbane Parisian narrator—a more ideal self of the author—who is often chattily sympathetic toward the protagonist but always above him, seeing his limitations and self-deceptions. Thus, when Julien sits on his lofty rock, surveying the world below him, the narrator, perched still higher, observes of his hero: "Placed as though on a high promontory, he could judge, and he dominated as it were extreme poverty and the condition of being well-off which he still called wealth." Julien, it is clear, has much to learn about society as well as about himself. His ignorance is not so much a recollection of the young Beyle's ignorance of the world as an extrapolation, an emphatic comic heightening, of it. Beyond the characterization of the hero, this worldly, conversational narrator gives Stendhal certain distinct advantages in anchoring the action in time, place, class, and politics. Though, as we have seen, the narrator may often choose to disappear into the characters, he also can exercise the option of talking all around them, eliciting the nuances of their motives and values through commentary, moving outward from the characters proper to brief or extended observations on nineteenth-century society, the role of woman, life in the provinces and life in Paris, the nature of the novel itself.

Stendhal had of course been practicing this fluently discursive voice for fifteen years in his art, music, and travel books, but there was probably one model among novelists he had specifically in mind. At the end of an 1832 letter to a Florentine friend, Count Salvagnoli, which he hoped to "plant" as a pseudonymous Italian article on his own book, he describes *Le Rouge et le Noir* as a novel that deserved a place on the bookshelf alongside "the immortal *Tom Jones.*" To mention *Tom Jones* as a touchstone of excellence need not imply that his own novel was necessarily similar in kind to Fielding's, but the one formal device that most clearly connects these two novels so different in mood and theme is the presence in both of a genial expatiating narrator who casts a finely woven net of cultural, social, and political commentary over the narrated events; enriches our perception of the characters through a shifting play of ironies; and by all this subtly enlarges the significance of the novel's action. . . . The informing sensibility of *Le Rouge et le Noir* is ambivalently Romantic, the sense of history and how it impinges on private lives is eminently post-Napoleonic, but the qualities frequently exhibited by the mediating narrator hark back to the poised satiric achievements of the eighteenth century in England and France and are the very attributes of "daring, resourcefulness, liveliness, *sang-froid,* amusing wit" ascribed to Don Juan at the end of *De l'Amour.*

In this connection, it is noteworthy that the famous definition of the novel as a mirror on the road, which Stendhal introduces into the text of *Le Rouge et le Noir,* is perfectly appropriate for Fielding's novel and for the antecedent picaresque tradition, but not, at least at first glance, for his own novel, which moves mostly between salons and bedrooms and attends so often not to a traveling panorama but to the interior vision of the characters. Some critics have read this passage as a naively "reflective" theory of the relation between the novel and the world; others have argued that in context the whole statement is nonsense and so is intended to be ironical-

ly self-subverting, or that it occurs in a long parenthesis, which must somehow complicate any meaning it might have. A simpler justification for the choice of this "Fieldingesque" emblem of the mirror carried along the highway for the novel is that it enabled Stendhal to introduce a set of neatly opposed images that could suggest *symbolically,* though not literally, the very special vision of life which he was translating artistically into the form of the novel. . . . Here is the crucial passage from *Le Rouge et le Noir:*

> Ah, sir, a novel is a mirror carried along a highway. Sometimes it reflects back to you the azure of the sky, sometimes the muck of the quagmires on the road. And the man who carries the mirror in the basket on his back is to be accused by you of immorality! His mirror shows the muck, and you accuse the mirror! Accuse instead the highway where the quagmire is, and still more the road inspector who allows the water to stagnate and the quagmire to form.

The narrator has just been talking about Mathilde's extravagant nature and, by contrast, about the more conventional young women of the day whose social habits, as he acidly puts it, "among all ages will assure such a distinguished rank to the civilization of the 19th century." The link, then, between the imagery of the highway and his Parisian subject is metaphoric but scarcely metonymic. The passive and humble idea, moreover, of the novelist as someone carrying a mirror in a back-basket is surely in some degree ironic, part of the narrator's rhetorical strategy in his argument with the imagined reader. What is important is that, because the emblematic mirror is located on a highway, it can reflect the two opposed elements which since 1811-12 Henri Beyle had used to indicate the opposed spheres of the odious commonality of mankind and the Happy Few—on the one hand, mud, quagmire, excremental filth, and on the other, the fine air of mountaintops, the clear blue of the sky. One recalls that, in his horror of what he saw in the Moscow campaign, Beyle had projected in his private writing a claustrophobic image of the base, venal, brutish mass of men as a contaminating, engulfing bog, and against that he had set a dream of the hills of Lombardy where the lucid air rung with the harmonious clarities of Cimarosa. The transition from the former realm to the latter is in essence the plot of *Le Rouge et le Noir.*

But there is this crucial difference between the twenty-nine-year-old diarist of 1812 and the masterly novelist of 1830: after seven years in Milan, after a decade in the salons of Paris, his response to the quagmire of contemporary French society is not revulsion but dispassionate curiosity, minutely attentive observation. Julien's story is also a brilliant "Chronicle of 1830," as the subtitle of the novel announces, because the novelist, instead of contenting himself with reiterating the denigrating symbol of muck, shrewdly follows the nuanced ways in which personality, family relations, passion itself are distorted by the relentless self-serving, the materialism, the pretence, the pale prudential cast of mind encouraged by the constellation of crown, church, and class in France under the restored Bourbons.

In this regard, the relatively short central section describing Julien's months at the Besançon seminary is the thematic keystone of the novel: set in between the Rênal household and the Hôtel de la Mole, the seminary is the place where the pervasive hypocrisy of society can be seen writ large, where the reactionary Catholicism that flourished under Charles X can be observed as a concentrated presence. After Besançon, Ju-

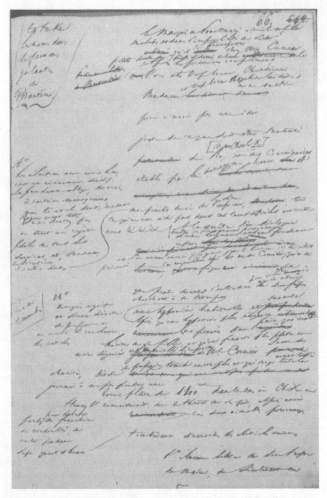

A manuscript page of Lucien Leuwen.

lien's social ascent will be rapid, and step by step with it, his alienation from himself will be more pronounced.

At one point, Stendhal literally plunges his hero into the mire when he subjects Julien to the ordeal of equitation he recalled from his own youth: riding in the Bois de Boulogne with the young Count Norbert de la Mole, Julien tries to avoid a cabriolet, is tossed to the ground, and is covered with mud. Elsewhere, Julien wallows in the moral mire of nineteenth-century society without an explicit invocation of the metaphor. Stendhal keenly perceives that as Julien attains greater accomplishment in the way of the world, finally succeeding beyond expectation with the unpredictable Mathilde, he is inwardly floundering, like a man in a bog, either not knowing who he is or hating what he has become. "Yes, to cover with ridicule this utterly odious creature I call *myself* would amuse me," he reflects as he mechanically carries out the strategy of deception that will win him back Mathilde; or still more bluntly, at the end of the next chapter, he exclaims to himself, "Good God! Why am I me?" Julien, frail by disposition, has exerted an enormous energy of will—hence his appeal for later readers like Nietzsche—but, finally, the relentless hypocrisy to which he has committed himself has the effect of *enervating* him: "His efforts at role playing had ended up draining all strength from his soul." The quagmire contaminates, inexorably drags one down, and the only way Stendhal

can save his hero is by extricating him violently through Mme de Rênal's letter of denunciation, Julien's attempted murder of her, his imprisonment, his elevation, literally and figuratively, above society in his condemned cell.

After Julien fires the two fatal shots, he stands in a daze, seeing nothing, then slowly "comes back to himself"—not only from the trance that has seized him ever since the revelation of the denunciatory letter but also from the self-estrangement into which he has allowed himself to be drawn from the start. In his high cell, Julien ceases to care about what others will think, is at last, in his tender hours with Mme de Rênal, entirely without affectation. "Never have I been so happy," he tells her, and when she questions this surprising assertion, he affirms, "Never, and I speak to you as I would speak to myself."

It is, certainly from our post-Romantic perspective, an odd, even perverse resolution for Stendhal to suggest that in society as it is constituted the only ultimate sincerity, and therefore the only genuine happiness, must be attained in complete isolation from the world, at the door of death. This is the most thoroughly Romantic feature of *Le Rouge et le Noir,* but it is intimated in these concluding chapters of the novel with delicate restraint. The music of Julien's final idyll is more Mozartian than Cimarosan, elegantly controlled, quietly plangent. As throughout the novel, indications of physical setting are minimal but tactically efficient: after his long struggle through the mud below, Julien has his tower, his view of the sky, and Stendhal wants to make us feel that it is enough.

Other French Romantic writers, beginning with Chateaubriand, had made fiction out of the impelling dream of some luminous *ailleurs,* an elsewhere of rapturous fulfillment beckoning to the hero caught in the toils of earthly existence. This dream, however, was characteristically expressed in a vague and lofty style that blurred or distorted the outlines of the real world. Stendhal, by contrast, is able to combine a steady clarity of perception with a chastely understated version of the Romantic dream. One important measure of his originality as a novelist is his ability to articulate in the formal structure of his fiction a bioptic vision that can take in both the varied scene of contemporary society with its characteristic vices and absurdities—the vast quagmire in which the hero is caught—and the glimpse of a beatitude quite beyond the social world. Henri Beyle, lifelong aspirant to literary greatness, had finally discovered how to realize his dream in a finely poised art distinctively his own. (pp. 191-203)

Robert Alter with Carol Cosman, in his A Lion for Love: A Critical Biography of Stendhal, *Basic Books, Inc., Publishers, 1979, 285 p.*

NICOLA CHIAROMONTE   (essay date 1985)

[*Chiaromonte examines the conflict Stendhal's characters experience between external reality and inward beliefs, focusing on Fabrizio del Dongo's perception of the battle of Waterloo.*]

On 8 March 1815, having just learned of Napoleon's return from Elba, the seventeen-year-old hero of *La Chartreuse de Parme,* Fabrizio Valserra, Marquis del Dongo, leaves home to follow Napoleon to Paris, join the emperor's glorious forces, and fight against his enemies for the freedom of Europe and Italy—in short, to become an actor in the Napoleonic pageant.

Leaving the shores of Lake Como, Fabrizio crosses Switzerland and reaches Paris. There, Stendhal writes, "he went every morning to the courtyard of the Tuileries to watch the reviews held by Napoleon." "Our hero," Stendhal continues, "imagined that all the French were as deeply disturbed as he himself by the extreme peril to which the country was exposed." Thus he passes his days in restless expectation, spending his evenings in the company of "young men who were very pleasant and kind, still more enthusiastic than himself and who in a very few days succeeded in robbing him of all the money he possessed." So Fabrizio decides to leave Paris and join the army.

But as soon as the young enthusiast reaches a battalion encampment on the Belgian border, he is arrested as a spy. He remains in prison for thirty-three days and gets out through the courtesy of the jailer's wife, who, for the sum of one hundred francs, provides him with the uniform of a dead hussar. Thus attired, Fabrizio continues his search for military glory.

"It was the eve of the battle of Waterloo," Stendhal announces. For the first time Fabrizio hears the thunder of distant cannon. The next morning, he meets a *cantinière* who takes him to the front lines. There, lying across the road, is a dead body. "A bullet entering one side of the nose had come out by the opposite temple, and disfigured the corpse in a hideous fashion, leaving it with one eye still open . . . Fabrizio was on the point of going off into a dead faint." As the roar of the cannon comes closer, Fabrizio, still accompanied by the tender *cantinière,* manages to buy a real battle horse and climbs into the saddle. "Just at that moment a round shot landed amongst the row of willows, striking them slantwise; and Fabrizio enjoyed the curious sight of seeing all the little branches flying to left and right as if they had been sliced off by a scythe . . . Fabrizio was still under the spell of this strange spectacle when a group of generals followed by a score of hussars, came galloping across one corner of the huge field on the edge of which he had halted."

Giving his horse free rein Fabrizio finds himself trailing after the group. "A quarter of an hour later, from a few words said by one hussar to his neighbor he gathered that one of the generals was the famous Marshal Ney. His happiness was at its height; he could not, however, make out which one of the generals was the famous Marshal Ney." The din of the cannons becomes deafening. "We must admit," says Stendhal, "that our hero was very little of a hero at this juncture. However, fear came to him only as a secondary emotion, he was principally shocked by the noise which hurt his ears." A little later, however, he succeeds in discovering which one of the generals is Marshal Ney. "Lost in childish admiration, he gazed at this famous Prince de la Moskowa, the 'bravest of the brave.'"

> Suddenly they all moved off at a full gallop. A few minutes later Fabrizio saw twenty paces ahead of him a piece of tilled land that was being ploughed up in a singular fashion. The bottoms of the furrows were full of water, and the very damp soil that formed the ridges of these furrows was flying about in little black lumps flung three or four feet into the air. Fabrizio noted this curious effect as he was passing; then his mind turned to dreaming of the Marshal and his glory. He heard a sharp cry close by him; it was two hussars falling, struck by

shot; . . . "Ah, so I am under fire at last," he said to himself. "I have seen the firing!" he repeated with a sense of satisfaction. "Now I am a real soldier" . . . Our hero realized it was shot from the guns that was making the earth fly up all around him. He looked in vain in the direction from which the shots were coming. He saw the white smoke of the battery an enormous distance away and, in the midst of the steady and continuous rumble produced by the firing of the guns, he seemed to hear volleys of shot much closer at hand. He could not make head or tail of what was happening . . .

Fabrizio turns to a sergeant who is standing beside him: "Sir, this is the first time I am present at a battle . . . But is this one a real battle?"

It is indeed a real battle and it takes place on a real battlefield. Finally the Lord of Battles, Napoleon himself, appears, galloping with his escort of generals and cuirassiers. But Fabrizio, his vision and mind befogged by the brandy he has drunk to overcome his horror at the sight of the amputation of a wounded soldier's leg, cannot tell which of the horsemen is the emperor. Disappointment rouses the young man: "Fabrizio felt a strong desire to gallop after the emperor's escort and attach himself to it. What happiness it would be to take part in a war in the train of this hero. It was for this that he had come to France." But by now he feels he is so intimately bound to the soldiers he has met a few hours earlier that he remains, only to have his horse seized from under him to provide a mount for a horseless general. This indignity, together with the jeers of the soldiers, brings him to the brink of despair: "So war was no longer that noble and universal impulse of souls devoted to glory that he had imagined it to be from Napoleon's proclamations!"

To the pain of disillusionment are added hunger and fatigue. After eating a crust of bread thrown to him by a soldier, Fabrizio happens upon the amiable *cantinière* who helped him at the beginning of his adventure. He climbs into her cart and falls fast asleep. "Nothing could wake him, neither the musket shots fired close by the little cart, nor the trotting of the horse which the *cantinière* was belaboring with all her might. The regiment, attacked unexpectedly by swarms of Prussian cavalry, after imagining all day that victory would be theirs, was now beating a retreat, or rather fleeing, in the direction of France."

It was Blücher not Grouchy who "arrived first." When Fabrizio awakes, the battle of Waterloo has already taken place. The Napoleonic drama has ended before he has even understood what it was all about. "I absolutely have to fight . . . At last I'm really going to fight and kill one of the enemy," Fabrizio resolves. He manages to fire a shot, and a cavalryman in blue falls from his horse. Perhaps he has killed one of the enemy. What is actually taking place around him is the total rout of the glorious Napoleonic army. "It's like a flock of sheep running away," Fabrizio says naïvely. Mutiny follows collapse and retreat. The only battle in which Fabrizio takes part is a scuffle with seven French hussars who try to cross a bridge guarded by the least martial but most ardent soldier ever created by a novelist's imagination.

This is how Fabrizio del Dongo in the second, third, and fourth chapters of *La Chartreuse de Parme* sees the battle of Waterloo, the event that brought down the curtain on Napoleon's stupendous performance on the stage of history.

This picture of Waterloo has nothing to do with a view of battle as one great whole animated by a single spirit. Fabrizio's Waterloo is a battle that does not exist; it dissolves altogether naturally, not only into a host of apparently incoherent, yet perhaps Providentially controled, episodes, but also into the completely disconnected encounters, impulses, and impressions of the hero. Fabrizio, wrapped in the spell of dreams of personal glory and historical grandeur, incessantly tries to give epic dimensions to every episode of his adventure, however prosaic, incongruous, or senseless it may be. But in the end he is forced to admit defeat. "He understood for the first time that he was wrong about everything that had happened to him in the last two months," Stendhal dryly remarks.

Napoleon, the Napoleon of those Grande Armée communiqués that nourished Fabrizio and Julien Sorel in *Le Rouge et le Noir,* does not exist; the great saga does not exist; even history does not exist. All that exists are single incidents, single individuals, the fleeting impressions of the mind, and—what is very important—the youthful dream of the Napoleonic saga. And then there is the swarming mass of so-called objective facts.

Stendhal makes us feel all this in the most direct way possible through Fabrizio's innocence, which is, at bottom, the innocence of Candide, Tom Jones, Nicholas Rostov, and Mozart's Cherubino. With pungent irony this innocence is continually contrasted with the stark reality of men, things, and circumstances. The story's grace lies in the fact that although the author shows us that the impulses of Fabrizio's soul are nothing but dreams, illusions, and errors, and that the fragmentary and random incidents which make up a battle are the only incontrovertible reality, he irresistibly engages our sympathies for the dreams, the illusions, and the absurdity of his hero. We cannot help believing that the vicissitudes of one adolescent soul constitute the truth of truths. In fact, it is in these illusions and delusions, it is in our hero's invincible and ridiculous innocence that the story's fundamental meaning is to be found.

Of course the battle of Waterloo, viewed from a distance in all its magnitude, as in a painting by David or Gros, is undeniably real, but Stendhal makes us feel that despite its grandeur it is utterly insignificant.

That does not, however, make Fabrizio's illusions any the less illusory. It is in the captivating "arias" of our hero's soul that the reader hears the voice of truth. For it is in these "arias" that the meaning of Fabrizio's experience is expressed, not in the incidents of the grandiose event, and certainly not in any supposedly total significance of the event, which cannot be experienced by any one individual, because everyone from Napoleon down to the lowest soldier is part of that event and overwhelmed by it.

For Stendhal the ground of truth and meaning is in the encounter and clash of the individual soul with an event, a confrontation that always takes a more or less absurd form. The sudden appearance of a corpse lying across the road, clods of earth scattered in all directions by an invisible force, a cavalryman in blue unhorsed by a wild shot—these are all symbols of the intrinsic absurdity of the event as it actually appears to the person involved. Stendhal's steady, piercing, almost cruel eye discovers in this absurdity the only reality that genuinely interests him: "the uncomfortable gift, father of so many ridiculous actions, called 'the soul'." And this is what he focuses on, bringing it out in sharp relief against the background of so-called real life, which is but the substance of daily existence—always indifferent, if not hostile.

The chasm between the impulses of the soul and common "reality" is just as deep in ordinary life as in a battle. For "real life," filled as it is with the deadly dregs of personal profit, utilitarian calculation (as exemplified by the clearheaded Count Mosca and the Marquis de La Mole), and tinselled philistinism, is the enemy of spontaneous action. Yet the world would be an insubstantial fairy tale without them. Stendhal's double-edged irony is engendered by a vivid, vigilant, and unromantic awareness of this fact. He spares neither youthful impulsiveness nor worldly wisdom. The former is doomed to destruction at its first collision with "real life"; the latter can only be achieved at the expense of natural feeling and free action, that is by selling one's soul. In fact, the illusion of being able to play a double game with life can only be dignified by a tragic end, as in the case of Julien Sorel. (pp. 1-6)

Stendhal's irony annihilates at one stroke the "grandeur" of an historical event and the "solemnity" of a ceremony. When he depicts Fabrizio in ecstasy before the clods of earth being scattered in all directions by an invisible power during the battle of Waterloo, or when in *Le Rouge et le Noir* he shows us Julien coming upon the Bishop Besançon rehearsing benedictions in the mirror, his impassive candor makes nonsense of the notion that human actions have any meaning beyond appearance. "This is the way it is," Stendhal seems to say, "and behind appearance there is nothing but another fiction or another accident." What underlies this reduction of every occurrence to the immediate and the immediately felt is not the rejection (for Stendhal does not debate, he ridicules) but the simple deflation of the idea that events have any rational (i.e., causal) relation to each other. Rationality is present only when events are reduced to a web of concepts in an abstract construction designed to give them a single meaning. But to do this, one must completely disregard the specificity of the event whose "true" meaning one claims to be seeking. Only in the elusive and shifting sphere of emotions does Stendhal perceive some kind of pattern or ordered sequence, but this surely cannot be described as rationality.

The fact is that the author of *La Chartreuse de Parme* does not believe in the story he is telling any more than he believes in the story of history; for his novel is a patently extravagant tale precariously balanced between the realistic and the improbable. Now this can be said of many novelists (perhaps of all great novelists from Fielding to Dickens, from Balzac to Tolstoy), but what distinguishes Stendhal is that he is conscious of this fact, aware that he is "imagining" and desirous of losing himself in the labyrinths of his fancy. His object in creating his fable is not to "mirror" reality (in the sense of the questionable metaphor of the "mirror moving on a high road" which Stendhal proposed in *Le Rouge et le Noir* as the definition of the novel) but to expose the discrepancy between so-called real facts and the daydreams of the innocent and pure individual.

For Stendhal, only feelings are true. Youth, the distinguishing attribute of his characters, is simply the capacity to surrender completely to emotions and be deceived by them. Count Mosca, for example, although not young in years, has this capacity. Feelings are the source of truth and of what little happiness life can give. The realm of "reality," in which Stendhal's characters try to make their way, is nothing but a web of social lies. These have reality because the hypocrites and schemers who know how to play the game of worldly success make it difficult to see through these lies and win the game. They have reality because Fabrizio del Dongo, Julien Sorel, and Lucien Leuwen, the hero of the novel of that name, feel obliged to believe in them in order to exploit them as the schemers do. Curiously enough, the picture of Napoleon these heroes carry in their hearts is two-faced. He is the young genius who unfailingly upsets the intrigues, stratagems, and complacency of the old plotters, but he is also a master of cunning and deceit, symbol of the elected individual who conquers the world by exploiting its arts without being corrupted by its values. At this point Napoleon becomes a mythical creation, a fabulous being who embodies and represents modern man's chief ambition, to shape the material world according to an idea.

That Stendhal himself gives credence to this myth is more than doubtful. But he certainly thinks his characters should accept the fictions of society and, if they really want to achieve worldly success, hide with Napoleonic force of will that "uncomfortable gift known as 'the soul'." Yet we must not forget that Julien Sorel, the most intensely "Napoleonic" of Stendhal's characters, is presented as the victim of outmoded ambition, that is, as a fundamentally naïve young man.

If Stendhal's young heroes really believed in the fictions they pretend to accept and actually became crafty schemers, they too would be plunged into the inferno of the "dreary," "cold," and "vulgar," as Stendhal's terminology goes. But this does not prevent Stendhal from treating them as "simple-minded," "timid," "foolish," "ridiculous," and "weak." If he did not, he would be confessing to the same delusions, the same confusion of dream and imagined reality that makes them so "powerless" in war, in the affairs of the world, and in love. But that does not mean that the creator of Julien Sorel assumes that the world of the astute and the dreary is the only real one, or that the movements of the human spirit are in preordained harmony with the laws of the world. If he did, the ambiguity that distinguishes his heroes would not be so undisguised, so conspicuous, and so engaging.

Stendhal's special magic lies in his ability to balance gaily on the paradox that denies reality not only to events and people in the external world of society but to the feelings and fantasies of the private world of the individual as well. What is "real" for him is the collision of the two worlds and the comedy of errors that ensues. For that is the moment when we see the youthful soul, in all its freshness, trying to come to terms with life and its frustrations. Reality for Stendhal is that which eludes and deludes the impulses of the soul, that which does not fulfill expectations or does so at the wrong time and in the wrong circumstances. Reality is the unresolvable disharmony between the individual and the world.

Completely absorbed as he is in the immediate, Stendhal not only cannot believe that there is a rationality in events, he cannot even conceive of its existence except in the lucubrations of the *esprit de sérieux,* be it political, ecclesiastical, bourgeois, or whatever.

Certainly the battle of Waterloo that Napoleon saw and directed (or thought he directed) is not the same event Fabrizio wanders into. Nor is the explosion of incidents in which Fabrizio finds himself the same event as the mortal engagement of the soldiers who jeer at him. And this engagement bears no resemblance to the battle fought by Marshal Ney or to the

one witnessed by Fabrizio's helpful *cantinière.* The battle of Waterloo was all of these, separately and together, plus countless other happenings. It was also the fateful event that brought down Napoleon's empire. Stendhal, who followed the Grande Armée to Moscow and saw battles at much closer range than Fabrizio saw the fighting at Waterloo, was deeply aware of this inexhaustible multiplicity and final unity.

Yet what are this multiplicity and unity but a dizzying play of mirrors, a labyrinth of infinite perspectives that pursue and contain each other? To recognize this fact is, in the last analysis, to recognize that we exist in other people as they do in us. Impervious to dreams, this is the foundation of "reality." Stendhal's irony derives from his almost febrile awareness that to live means to venture among the reflected images and mirages with which life teems. In fact, his heroes and he himself (as his autobiographical writings show) are haunted by an almost panic awareness of other people.

Stendhal has been described as a *maître d'énergie.* It is true that he and his heroes have dreams of seeing through the illusions engendered by emotions, of acquiring worldly wisdom by an act of will and of living heroically in a world ruled by mediocrities. But the dream is not only continually interrupted by disillusionment and failure, it is checked by irony. For Stendhal no more believes in it than in his heroes' fantasies of glory, cherish them as he may. If there is a lesson to be learned from Stendhal it is certainly not how to master one's feelings, become expert in the ways of the world, and make one's way with self-assurance. The wisdom of Stendhal lies elsewhere—in the ability to sustain with spirit and detachment the situation in which life places one and to play a game in which one knows that the dice are loaded, as Nietzsche put it.

What Stendhal teaches us, after all, is not *égotisme,* ostensibly his guiding principle, but frank awareness of the delusions created by feelings ("Fabrizio understood he had been wrong about everything") as well as of the emptiness of the fictions the world offers as substitutes. The final lesson is a lesson in disbelief. (pp. 7-10)

Nicola Chiaromonte, "Fabrizio at Waterloo," in his The Paradox of History: Stendhal, Tolstoy, Pasternak, and Others, *revised edition, University of Pennsylvania Press, 1985, pp. 1-16.*

ADDITIONAL BIBLIOGRAPHY

Bersani, Leo. "Stendhalian Prisons and *Salons.*" In his *Balzac to Beckett: Center and Circumference in French Fiction,* pp. 91-139. New York: Oxford University Press, 1970.

    Analyzes the interplay and antagonism between the social and private worlds in *The Charterhouse of Parma,* noting the implications of this for the happiness of the individual.

Berthoff, Warner. " 'What Do Other Men Matter to the Passionate Man?': *The Charterhouse of Parma.*" In his *Literature and the Continuances of Virtue,* pp. 124-57. Princeton: Princeton University Press, 1986.

    Examines aspects of virtue in *The Charterhouse of Parma.*

Brombert, Victor, ed. *Stendhal: A Collection of Critical Essays.* Englewood Cliffs, N.J.: Prentice-Hall, 1962, 171 p.

A collection of eleven studies by highly regarded Stendhal critics, including Jean Starobinski's "Truth in Masquerade," a psycholiterary analysis of Stendhal's penchant for self-transformation, and Jean Prévost's critical discussion of the composition and revision of *Lucien Leuwen.*

Brookner, Anita. "Stendhal." In her *The Genius of the Future: Studies in French Art Criticism,* pp. 31-56. London: Phaidon, 1971.

Explicates Stendhal's art and literary criticism, frequently relating it to his life and the concerns of his fiction.

Brooks, Peter. "The Novel and the Guillotine; or, Fathers and Sons in *Le rouge et le noir.*" In his *Reading for the Plot: Design and Intention in Narrative,* pp. 62-89. New York: Alfred A. Knopf, 1984.

Relates narrative technique to the themes of paternity and authority in *The Red and the Black.*

Chaitin, Gilbert D. *The Unhappy Few: A Psychological Study of the Novels of Stendhal.* Indiana University Humanities Series, no. 69. Bloomington: Indiana University Press, 1972, 244 p.

A psychoanalytic study of Stendhal and his fiction.

Colum, Padraic. "Stendhal." *The Dial* LXXXII (January-June 1927): 470-75.

Assesses *The Red and the Black* and *The Charterhouse of Parma,* favoring the latter as Stendhal's best.

Day, James T. *Stendhal's Paper Mirror: Patterns of Self-Consciousness in His Novels.* American University Studies, Series II: Romance Languages and Literature, vol. 20. New York: Peter Lang, 1987, 236 p.

An analysis of "self-reflexive or self-conscious" narrative discourse in Stendhal's novels.

Denommé, Robert T. "Julien Sorel and the Modern Conscience." *Western Humanities Review* XXI, No. 3 (Summer 1967): 227-36.

Analyzes Julien Sorel as the "prototype of the modern hero."

Ehrenburg, Ilya. "Lessons of Stendhal." In his *Chekhov, Stendhal, and Other Essays,* pp. 145-85. New York: Alfred A. Knopf, 1963.

A general discussion of Stendhal as man and writer, concentrating on the autobiographical nature of his work.

Gide, André. "Preface to *Armance,*" translated by Blanche A. Price. In his *Pretexts: Reflections on Literature and Morality,* edited by Justin O'Brien, pp. 260-74. New York: Meridian Books, 1959.

Uses *Armance* as a springboard for a discussion of love and sexuality and the connection between the two.

Giraud, Raymond. "Stendhal: The Bridge and the Gap between Two Centuries." In his *The Unheroic Hero in the Novels of Stendhal, Balzac and Flaubert,* pp. 53-92. New Brunswick, N.J.: Rutgers University Press, 1957.

Studies Stendhal's heroes—particularly Lucien Leuwen—as they relate to their author's conception of contemporary society.

Goldberger, Avriel H., ed. *The Stendhal Bicentennial Papers.* Contributions to the Study of World Literature, no. 19. New York: Greenwood Press, 1987, 111 p.

A collection of eleven essays on Stendhal.

Goodin, George. "The Flawed Victim: *An American Tragedy, L'assommoir, Native Son, The Red and the Black.*" In his *The Poetics of Protest: Literary Form and Political Implication in the Victim-of-Society Novel,* pp. 87-132. Carbondale: Southern Illinois University Press, 1985.

Interprets the conclusion of *The Red and the Black* in terms of Julien's moral status.

Green, F. C. *Stendhal.* Cambridge: Cambridge University Press, 1939, 336 p.

A respected early biography.

Hazard, Paul. *Stendhal (Henri Beyle).* Translated by Eleanor Hard. New York: Coward-McCann, 1929, 315 p.

A translation of a French biography of Stendhal.

Howe, Irving. "Stendhal: The Politics of Survival." In his *Politics and the Novel,* pp. 25-50. New York: Horizon Press, 1957.

Explores the political implications of Stendhal's work.

Huneker, James. "A Sentimental Education: Henry Beyle-Stendhal." In his *Egoists: A Book of Supermen,* pp. 1-65. New York: Charles Scribner's Sons, 1909.

Surveys the writings of Stendhal, the "seductive spiller of souls."

Josephson, Matthew. *Stendhal; or, The Pursuit of Happiness.* Garden City, N.Y.: Doubleday & Co., 1946, 489 p.

A biography containing chapters on Stendhal's major works.

Kayser, Rudolf. *Stendhal: The Life of an Egoist.* New York: Henry Holt and Co., 1930, 278 p.

A noncritical biography described by its author as "almost a novel, which attempts to give living shape to the facts of [Stendhal's] life and intellect."

Kazin, Alfred. "The Plant, Man, Is More Robust and Large in Rome than Elsewhere." In his *Contemporaries,* pp. 265-71. Boston: Little, Brown and Co., 1962.

Describes *A Roman Journal.*

Levin, Harry. "Stendhal." In his *The Gates of Horn: A Study of Five French Realists,* pp. 84-149. New York: Oxford University Press, 1963.

A frequently cited analysis of Stendhal, published in an earlier form as *Toward Stendhal* (1945).

Levowitz, Herbert J., and Levowitz-Treu, Micheline. "Henry Beyle/Stendhal: A Psychodynamic Exploration of the Man and the Writer." In *Psychoanalytic Approaches to Literature and Film,* edited by Maurice Charney and Joseph Reppen, pp. 59-68. Rutherford, N.J.: Fairleigh Dickinson University Press, 1987.

A psychiatric case study of Stendhal.

Lukács, Georg. "Balzac and Stendhal." In his *Studies in European Realism,* pp. 65-84. New York: Grosset & Dunlap, 1964.

Analyzes Balzac's review of *The Charterhouse of Parma* and Stendhal's reply (see excerpts dated 1840) to determine in what ways the authors' theories of the novel agreed and diverged.

Maugham, W. Somerset. "Stendhal and *The Red and the Black.*" In his *Great Novelists and Their Novels: Essays on the Ten Greatest Novels of the World, and the Men and Women Who Wrote Them,* pp. 95-112. Philadelphia: John C. Winston Co., 1948.

Argues that Julien's character is inconsistent but nonetheless proclaims the greatness of *The Red and the Black.*

Maurois, André. "Passionate Love—Heroines of Stendhal." In his *Seven Faces of Love,* translated by Haakon M. Chevalier, pp. 111-48. New York: Didier, 1944.

Examines Stendhal's treatment of women and love in his novels, depicting his heroines as either "the woman Stendhal would have liked to love" or "the woman Stendhal would have been."

May, Gita. "Stendhal and the Age of Ideas." In *Literature and History in the Age of Ideas: Essays on the French Enlightenment Presented to George R. Havens,* edited by Charles G. S. Williams, pp. 343-57. Columbus: Ohio State University Press, 1975.

Traces the influence of eighteenth-century thought and literature on Stendhal.

Miller, D. A. "Narrative 'Uncontrol' in Stendhal." In his *Narrative and Its Discontents: Problems of Closure in the Traditional Novel,* pp. 195-264. Princeton: Princeton University Press, 1981.

Examines patterns of narrative closure in Stendhal's novels.

Mitchell, John. *Stendhal: "Le Rouge et le Noir."* London: Edward Arnold, 1973, 64 p.
    An in-depth analysis of *The Red and the Black.*

Muir, Kenneth. "Stendhal, Racine, and Shakespeare." In *Shakespeare Studies: An Annual Gathering of Research, Criticism, and Reviews,* Vol. XVI, edited by J. Leeds Barroll III, pp. 1-12. New York: Burt Franklin & Co., 1983.
    Describes and evaluates Stendhal's criticism of William Shakespeare's plays.

O'Connor, Frank. "Stendhal: The Flight from Reality." In his *The Mirror in the Roadway: A Study of the Modern Novel,* pp. 42-57. New York: Alfred A. Knopf, 1964.
    Finds the realism of Stendhal's novels compromised by his imagination.

Paton, Andrew Archibald. *Henry Beyle (Otherwise De Stendhal): A Critical and Biographical Study.* London: Trubner & Co., 1874, 328 p.
    The first full-length biography of Stendhal in any language.

Proust, Marcel. "Notes on Stendhal." In his *Marcel Proust on Art and Literature: 1896-1919,* translated by Sylvia Townsend Warner, pp. 373-75. New York: Carroll & Graf Publishers, 1954.
    Miscellaneous thoughts on *The Red and the Black* and *The Charterhouse of Parma.*

Richardson, Joanna. *Stendhal.* New York: Coward, McCann & Geoghegan, 1974, 344 p.
    A life of Stendhal that includes a section detailing the history of his critical reputation and his current significance.

Saintsbury, George. "Beyle and Balzac." In his *A History of the French Novel (To the Close of the 19th Century).* Vol. II, *From 1800 to 1900,* pp. 133-75. London: Macmillan and Co., 1919.
    An analysis of Stendhal's novels, which Saintsbury finds frequently "disagreeable," though always "interesting."

Saldívar, Ramón. "The Rhetoric of Desire: Stendhal's *Le Rouge et le Noir.*" In his *Figural Language in the Novel: The Flowers of Speech from Cervantes to Joyce,* pp. 72-109. Princeton: Princeton University Press, 1984.
    Examines aspects of language in *The Red and the Black.*

Samuel, Horace B. "Stendhal: The Compleat Intellectual." *The Fortnightly Review* C, No. DLIX (1 July 1913): 69-81.
    Evaluates Stendhal's novels, praising their acute psychological characterization.

Searles, Colbert. "Stendhal and French Classicism." *PMLA* XXX, No. 3 (September 1915): 433-50.
    Examines Stendhal's correspondence for clues to a resolution of the author's conflicting tendencies toward classicism and Romanticism.

Sonnenfeld, Albert. "Ruminations on Stendhal's Epigraphs." In *Pre-Text, Text, Context: Essays on Nineteenth-Century French Literature,* edited by Robert L. Mitchell, pp. 99-110. Columbus: Ohio State University Press, 1980.
    Analyzes the implications of Stendhal's choice of epigraphs to embellish *Armance* and *The Red and the Black.*

Strickland, Geoffrey. *Stendhal: The Education of a Novelist.* Cambridge: Cambridge University Press, 1974, 302 p.
    Details Stendhal's intellectual development throughout his life.

Talbot, Emile J. *Stendhal and Romantic Esthetics.* French Forum Monographs, edited by R. C. La Charite and V. A. La Charite, vol. 61. Lexington, Ky.: French Forum, Publishers, 1985, 181 p.
    A study of French Romanticism as it is exemplified by Stendhal's works.

Tenenbaum, Elizabeth Brody. "Stendhal." In her *The Problematic Self: Approaches to Identity in Stendhal, D. H. Lawrence, and Malraux,* pp. 27-64. Cambridge: Harvard University Press, 1977.
    Discusses Stendhal's attempts to unravel the mysteries of the self in both his autobiographical writings and his fiction, focusing on the conflict between the self-assertive will and the submission of the will to impulse.

Tillet, Margaret. *Stendhal: The Background to the Novels.* London: Oxford University Press, 1971, 157 p.
    Considers Stendhal's nonfiction works in an effort to isolate his conception of the ideal human being: the *"âme généreuse."*

Turnell, Martin. "Stendhal's First Novel." In his *The Art of French Fiction: Prévost, Stendhal, Zola, Maupassant, Gide, Mauriac, Proust,* pp. 61-90. London: Hamish Hamilton, 1959.
    A comprehensive examination of *Armance,* surveying the novel's genesis, characterization, themes, and style.

Wahl, Pauline. "Stendhal's *Lamiel:* Observations on Pygmalionism." In *Pre-Text, Text, Context: Essays on Nineteenth-Century French Literature,* edited by Robert L. Mitchell, pp. 113-19. Columbus: Ohio State University Press, 1980.
    Explores Stendhal's treatment of the teacher-student relationship in *Lamiel.*

Ward, Nicole. "The Prisonhouse of Language: *The Heart of Midlothian* and *La Chartreuse de Parme.*" In *Comparative Criticism: A Yearbook,* Vol. 2, edited by Elinor Shaffer, pp. 93-107. Cambridge: Cambridge University Press, 1980.
    Compares the prison motifs in *The Charterhouse of Parma* and Sir Walter Scott's *The Heart of Midlothian* (1818).

Nineteenth-Century Literature Criticism

Cumulative Indexes
Volumes 1-23

This Index Includes References to Entries in These Gale Series

Contemporary Literary Criticism

Presents excerpts of criticism on the works of novelists, poets, dramatists, short story writers, scriptwriters, and other creative writers who are now living or who have died since 1960. Cumulative indexes to authors and nationalities are included, as well as an index to titles discussed in the individual volume. Volumes 1-55 are in print.

Twentieth-Century Literary Criticism

Contains critical excerpts by the most significant commentators on poets, novelists, short story writers, dramatists, and philosophers who died between 1900 and 1960. Cumulative indexes to authors, nationalities, and titles discussed are included in each new volume. Volumes 1-33 are in print.

Nineteenth-Century Literature Criticism

Offers significant passages from criticism on authors who died between 1800 and 1899. Cumulative indexes to authors, nationalities, and titles discussed are included in each new volume. Volumes 1-23 are in print.

Literature Criticism from 1400 to 1800

Compiles significant passages from the most noteworthy criticism on authors of the fifteenth through eighteenth centuries. Cumulative indexes to authors, nationalities, and titles discussed are included in each new volume. Volumes 1-11 are in print.

Classical and Medieval Literature Criticism

Offers excerpts of criticism on the works of world authors from classical antiquity through the fourteenth century. Cumulative indexes to authors, titles, and critics are included in each volume. Volumes 1-3 are in print.

Short Story Criticism

Compiles excerpts of criticism on short fiction by writers of all eras and nationalities. Cumulative indexes to authors, nationalities, and titles discussed are included in each new volume. Volumes 1-3 are in print.

Children's Literature Review

Includes excerpts from reviews, criticism, and commentary on works of authors and illustrators who create books for children. Cumulative indexes to authors, nationalities, and titles discussed are included in each new volume. Volumes 1-18 are in print.

Contemporary Authors Series

Encompasses five related series. *Contemporary Authors* provides biographical and bibliographical information on more than 92,000 writers of fiction, nonfiction, poetry, journalism, drama, motion pictures, and other fields. Each new volume contains sketches on authors not previously covered in the series. Volumes 1-127 are in print. *Contemporary Authors New Revision Series* provides completely updated information on active authors covered in previously published volumes of *CA*. Only entries requiring significant change are revised for *CA New Revision Series*. Volumes 1-26 are in print. *Contemporary Authors Permanent Series* consists of updated listings for deceased and inactive authors removed from the original volumes 9-36 when these volumes were revised. Volumes 1-2 are in print. *Contemporary Authors Autobiography Series* presents specially commissioned autobiographies by leading contemporary writers. Volumes 1-9 are in print. *Contemporary Authors Bibliographical Series* contains primary and secondary bibliographies as well as analytical bibliographical essays by authorities on major modern authors. Volumes 1-2 are in print.

Dictionary of Literary Biography

Encompasses three related series. *Dictionary of Literary Biography* furnishes illustrated overviews of authors' lives and works and places them in the larger perspective of literary history. Volumes 1-78 are in print. *Dictionary of Literary Biography Documentary Series* illuminates the careers of major figures through a selection of literary documents, including letters, notebook and diary entries, interviews, book reviews, and photographs. Volumes 1-6 are in print. *Dictionary of Literary Biography Yearbook* summarizes the past year's literary activity with articles on genres, major prizes, conferences, and other timely subjects and includes updated and new entries on individual authors. Yearbooks for 1980-1988 are in print. A cumulative index to authors and articles is included in each new volume.

Concise Dictionary of American Literary Biography

A six-volume series that collects revised and updated sketches on major American authors that were originally presented in *Dictionary of Literary Biography*. Volumes 1-3 are in print.

Something about the Author Series

Encompasses two related series. *Something about the Author* contains heavily illustrated biographical sketches on juvenile and young adult authors and illustrators from all eras. Volumes 1-54 are in print. *Something about the Author Autobiography Series* presents specially commissioned autobiographies by prominent authors and illustrators of books for children and young adults. Volumes 1-8 are in print.

Yesterday's Authors of Books for Children

Contains heavily illustrated entries on children's writers who died before 1961. Complete in two volumes. Volumes 1-2 are in print.

Literary Criticism Series
Cumulative Author Index

This index lists all author entries in the Gale Literary Criticism Series and includes cross-references to other Gale sources. References in the index are identified as follows:

Author Index

Eliade, Mircea 1907-1986 . . . . CLC 19
   See also CA 65-68; obituary CA 119

Eliot, George 1819-1880. . . . NCLC 4, 13, 23
   See also DLB 21, 35, 55

Eliot, John 1604-1690 . . . . LC 5
   See also DLB 24

Eliot, T(homas) S(tearns)
   1888-1965 . . . . CLC 1, 2, 3, 6, 9, 10, 13,
                          15, 24, 34, 41, 55
   See also CA 5-8R; obituary CA 25-28R;
   DLB 7, 10, 45, 63; DLB-Y 88

Elkin, Stanley (Lawrence)
   1930- . . . . CLC 4, 6, 9, 14, 27, 51
   See also CANR 8; CA 9-12R; DLB 2, 28;
   DLB-Y 80

Elledge, Scott 19??- . . . . CLC 34

Elliott, George P(aul) 1918-1980. . . . . CLC 2
   See also CANR 2; CA 1-4R;
   obituary CA 97-100

Elliott, Janice 1931- . . . . CLC 47
   See also CANR 8; CA 13-16R; DLB 14

Elliott, Sumner Locke 1917- . . . . CLC 38
   See also CANR 2, 21; CA 5-8R

Ellis, A. E. 19??- . . . . CLC 7

Ellis, Alice Thomas 19??- . . . . CLC 40

Ellis, Bret Easton 1964- . . . . CLC 39
   See also CA 118

Ellis, (Henry) Havelock
   1859-1939 . . . . TCLC 14
   See also CA 109

Ellis, Trey 1964- CLC   55

Ellison, Harlan (Jay) 1934- . . . CLC 1, 13, 42
   See also CANR 5; CA 5-8R; DLB 8

Ellison, Ralph (Waldo)
   1914- . . . . CLC 1, 3, 11, 54
   See also CANR 24; CA 9-12R; DLB 2;
   CDALB 1941-1968

Ellmann, Richard (David)
   1918-1987 . . . . CLC 50
   See also CANR 2; CA 1-4R;
   obituary CA 122

Elman, Richard 1934- . . . . CLC 19
   See also CAAS 3; CA 17-20R

Eluard, Paul 1895-1952 . . . . TCLC 7
   See also Grindel, Eugene

Elvin, Anne Katharine Stevenson 1933-
   See Stevenson, Anne (Katharine)
   See also CA 17-20R

Elyot, (Sir) Thomas 1490?-1546 . . . . . LC 11

Elytis, Odysseus 1911- . . . . CLC 15, 49
   See also CA 102

Emecheta, (Florence Onye) Buchi
   1944- . . . . CLC 14, 48
   See also CA 81-84

Emerson, Ralph Waldo
   1803-1882 . . . . NCLC 1
   See also DLB 1; CDALB 1640-1865

Empson, William
   1906-1984 . . . . CLC 3, 8, 19, 33, 34
   See also CA 17-20R; obituary CA 112;
   DLB 20

Enchi, Fumiko (Veda) 1905-1986 . . . CLC 31
   See also obituary CA 121

Ende, Michael 1930- . . . . CLC 31
   See also CLR 14; CA 118; SATA 42

Endo, Shusaku 1923- . . . . . CLC 7, 14, 19, 54
   See also CANR 21; CA 29-32R

Engel, Marian 1933-1985 . . . . CLC 36
   See also CANR 12; CA 25-28R; DLB 53

Engelhardt, Frederick 1911-1986
   See Hubbard, L(afayette) Ron(ald)

Enright, D(ennis) J(oseph)
   1920- . . . . CLC 4, 8, 31
   See also CANR 1; CA 1-4R; SATA 25;
   DLB 27

Enzensberger, Hans Magnus
   1929- . . . . CLC 43
   See also CA 116, 119

Ephron, Nora 1941- . . . . CLC 17, 31
   See also CANR 12; CA 65-68

Epstein, Daniel Mark 1948- . . . . CLC 7
   See also CANR 2; CA 49-52

Epstein, Jacob 1956- . . . . CLC 19
   See also CA 114

Epstein, Joseph 1937- . . . . CLC 39
   See also CA 112, 119

Epstein, Leslie 1938- . . . . CLC 27
   See also CA 73-76

Erdman, Paul E(mil) 1932- . . . . CLC 25
   See also CANR 13; CA 61-64

Erdrich, Louise 1954- . . . . CLC 39, 54
   See also CA 114

Erenburg, Ilya (Grigoryevich) 1891-1967
   See Ehrenburg, Ilya (Grigoryevich)

Eseki, Bruno 1919-
   See Mphahlele, Ezekiel

Esenin, Sergei (Aleksandrovich)
   1895-1925 . . . . TCLC 4
   See also CA 104

Eshleman, Clayton 1935- . . . . CLC 7
   See also CAAS 6; CA 33-36R; DLB 5

Espriu, Salvador 1913-1985 . . . . CLC 9
   See also obituary CA 115

Estleman, Loren D. 1952- . . . . CLC 48
   See also CA 85-88

Evans, Marian 1819-1880
   See Eliot, George

Evans, Mary Ann 1819-1880
   See Eliot, George

Evarts, Esther 1900-1972
   See Benson, Sally

Everson, Ronald G(ilmour) 1903- . . . CLC 27
   See also CA 17-20R

Everson, William (Oliver)
   1912- . . . . CLC 1, 5, 14
   See also CANR 20; CA 9-12R; DLB 5, 16

Evtushenko, Evgenii (Aleksandrovich) 1933-
   See Yevtushenko, Yevgeny

Ewart, Gavin (Buchanan)
   1916- . . . . CLC 13, 46
   See also CANR 17; CA 89-92; DLB 40

Ewers, Hanns Heinz 1871-1943 . . . TCLC 12
   See also CA 109

Ewing, Frederick R. 1918-
   See Sturgeon, Theodore (Hamilton)

Exley, Frederick (Earl) 1929- . . . CLC 6, 11
   See also CA 81-84; DLB-Y 81

Ezekiel, Tish O'Dowd 1943- . . . . CLC 34

Fagen, Donald 1948-
   See Becker, Walter and Fagen, Donald

Fagen, Donald 1948- and Becker, Walter
   1950-
   See Becker, Walter and Fagen, Donald

Fair, Ronald L. 1932- . . . . CLC 18
   See also CA 69-72; DLB 33

Fairbairns, Zoe (Ann) 1948- . . . . CLC 32
   See also CANR 21; CA 103

Fairfield, Cicily Isabel 1892-1983
   See West, Rebecca

Fallaci, Oriana 1930- . . . . CLC 11
   See also CANR 15; CA 77-80

Faludy, George 1913- . . . . CLC 42
   See also CA 21-24R

Fanshawe, Lady Ann 1625-1706 . . . . . LC 11

Fargue, Leon-Paul 1876-1947 . . . . . TCLC 11
   See also CA 109

Farigoule, Louis 1885-1972
   See Romains, Jules

Farina, Richard 1937?-1966. . . . . CLC 9
   See also CA 81-84; obituary CA 25-28R

Farley, Walter 1920- . . . . CLC 17
   See also CANR 8; CA 17-20R; SATA 2, 43;
   DLB 22

Farmer, Philip Jose 1918- . . . . CLC 1, 19
   See also CANR 4; CA 1-4R; DLB 8

Farrell, James T(homas)
   1904-1979 . . . . CLC 1, 4, 8, 11
   See also CANR 9; CA 5-8R;
   obituary CA 89-92; DLB 4, 9; DLB-DS 2

Farrell, J(ames) G(ordon)
   1935-1979 . . . . CLC 6
   See also CA 73-76; obituary CA 89-92;
   DLB 14

Farrell, M. J. 1904-
   See Keane, Molly

Fassbinder, Rainer Werner
   1946-1982 . . . . CLC 20
   See also CA 93-96; obituary CA 106

Fast, Howard (Melvin) 1914- . . . . . . CLC 23
   See also CANR 1; CA 1-4R; SATA 7;
   DLB 9

Faulkner, William (Cuthbert)
   1897-1962 . . . . CLC 1, 3, 6, 8, 9, 11, 14,
                       18, 28; SSC 1
   See also CA 81-84; DLB 9, 11, 44;
   DLB-Y 86; DLB-DS 2

Fauset, Jessie Redmon
   1884?-1961. . . . . CLC 19, 54
   See also CA 109; DLB 51

Faust, Irvin 1924- . . . . CLC 8
   See also CA 33-36R; DLB 2, 28; DLB-Y 80

Fearing, Kenneth (Flexner)
   1902-1961 . . . . CLC 51
   See also CA 93-96; DLB 9

Federman, Raymond 1928- . . . . . . CLC 6, 47
   See also CANR 10; CA 17-20R; DLB-Y 80

Federspiel, J(urg) F. 1931- . . . . CLC 42

Feiffer, Jules 1929- . . . . CLC 2, 8
   See also CA 17-20R; SATA 8; DLB 7, 44

Feinstein, Elaine 1930-........... **CLC 36**
See also CAAS 1; CA 69-72; DLB 14, 40

Feldman, Irving (Mordecai) 1928-.... **CLC 7**
See also CANR 1; CA 1-4R

Fellini, Federico 1920-........... **CLC 16**
See also CA 65-68

Felsen, Gregor 1916-
See Felsen, Henry Gregor

Felsen, Henry Gregor 1916-....... **CLC 17**
See also CANR 1; CA 1-4R; SAAS 2;
SATA 1

Fenton, James (Martin) 1949-...... **CLC 32**
See also CA 102; DLB 40

Ferber, Edna 1887-1968........... **CLC 18**
See also CA 5-8R; obituary CA 25-28R;
SATA 7; DLB 9, 28

Ferlinghetti, Lawrence (Monsanto)
1919?-............... **CLC 2, 6, 10, 27**
See also CANR 3; CA 5-8R; DLB 5, 16;
CDALB 1941-1968

Ferrier, Susan (Edmonstone)
1782-1854 .... **NCLC 8**

Feuchtwanger, Lion 1884-1958..... **TCLC 3**
See also CA 104

Feydeau, Georges 1862-1921...... **TCLC 22**
See also CA 113

Fiedler, Leslie A(aron)
1917-................. **CLC 4, 13, 24**
See also CANR 7; CA 9-12R; DLB 28

Field, Andrew 1938-.............. **CLC 44**
See also CA 97-100

Field, Eugene 1850-1895 .... **NCLC 3**
See also SATA 16; DLB 21, 23, 42

Fielding, Henry 1707-1754 .... **LC 1**
See also DLB 39

Fielding, Sarah 1710-1768 .... **LC 1**
See also DLB 39

Fierstein, Harvey 1954-........... **CLC 33**

Figes, Eva 1932-................. **CLC 31**
See also CANR 4; CA 53-56; DLB 14

Finch, Robert (Duer Claydon)
1900-..................... **CLC 18**
See also CANR 9; CA 57-60

Findley, Timothy 1930-........... **CLC 27**
See also CANR 12; CA 25-28R; DLB 53

Fink, Janis 1951-
See Ian, Janis

Firbank, Louis 1944-
See Reed, Lou

Firbank, (Arthur Annesley) Ronald
1886-1926 .... **TCLC 1**
See also CA 104; DLB 36

Fisher, Roy 1930-................ **CLC 25**
See also CANR 16; CA 81-84; DLB 40

Fisher, Rudolph 1897-1934 .... **TCLC 11**
See also CA 107; DLB 51

Fisher, Vardis (Alvero) 1895-1968.... **CLC 7**
See also CA 5-8R; obituary CA 25-28R;
DLB 9

FitzGerald, Edward 1809-1883 .... **NCLC 9**
See also DLB 32

Fitzgerald, F(rancis) Scott (Key)
1896-1940 .... **TCLC 1, 6, 14, 28**
See also CA 110; DLB 4, 9; DLB-Y 81;
DLB-DS 1

Fitzgerald, Penelope 1916-...... **CLC 19, 51**
See also CA 85-88; DLB 14

Fitzgerald, Robert (Stuart)
1910-1985 .... **CLC 39**
See also CANR 1; CA 2R;
obituary CA 114; DLB-Y 80

FitzGerald, Robert D(avid) 1902-... **CLC 19**
See also CA 17-20R

Flanagan, Thomas (James Bonner)
1923-...................... **CLC 25**
See also CA 108; DLB-Y 80

Flaubert, Gustave
1821-1880 .... **NCLC 2, 10, 19**

Fleming, Ian (Lancaster)
1908-1964 .... **CLC 3, 30**
See also CA 5-8R; SATA 9

Fleming, Thomas J(ames) 1927- .... **CLC 37**
See also CANR 10; CA 5-8R; SATA 8

Flieg, Hellmuth
See Heym, Stefan

Flying Officer X 1905-1974
See Bates, H(erbert) E(rnest)

Fo, Dario 1929-................. **CLC 32**
See also CA 116

Follett, Ken(neth Martin) 1949- .... **CLC 18**
See also CANR 13; CA 81-84; DLB-Y 81

Foote, Horton 1916-............. **CLC 51**
See also CA 73-76; DLB 26

Forbes, Esther 1891-1967........ **CLC 12**
See also CAP 1; CA 13-14;
obituary CA 25-28R; SATA 2; DLB 22

Forche, Carolyn 1950- .... **CLC 25**
See also CA 109, 117; DLB 5

Ford, Ford Madox 1873-1939 ... **TCLC 1, 15**
See also CA 104; DLB 34

Ford, John 1895-1973............ **CLC 16**
See also obituary CA 45-48

Ford, Richard 1944-............. **CLC 46**
See also CANR 11; CA 69-72

Foreman, Richard 1937-.......... **CLC 50**
See also CA 65-68

Forester, C(ecil) S(cott)
1899-1966 .... **CLC 35**
See also CA 73-76; obituary CA 25-28R;
SATA 13

Forman, James D(ouglas) 1932- .... **CLC 21**
See also CANR 4, 19; CA 9-12R; SATA 8,
21

Fornes, Maria Irene 1930-........ **CLC 39**
See also CA 25-28R; DLB 7

Forrest, Leon 1937- .... **CLC 4**
See also CAAS 7; CA 89-92; DLB 33

Forster, E(dward) M(organ)
1879-1970 .... **CLC 1, 2, 3, 4, 9, 10, 13,
15, 22, 45**
See also CAP 1; CA 13-14;
obituary CA 25-28R; DLB 34

Forster, John 1812-1876 .... **NCLC 11**

Forsyth, Frederick 1938-.... **CLC 2, 5, 36**
See also CA 85-88

Forten (Grimke), Charlotte L(ottie)
1837-1914 .... **TCLC 16**
See also Grimke, Charlotte L(ottie) Forten
See also DLB 50

Foscolo, Ugo 1778-1827.......... **NCLC 8**

Fosse, Bob 1925-................ **CLC 20**
See also Fosse, Robert Louis

Fosse, Robert Louis 1925-
See Bob Fosse
See also CA 110

Foucault, Michel 1926-1984 .... **CLC 31, 34**
See also CA 105; obituary CA 113

Fouque, Friedrich (Heinrich Karl) de La
Motte 1777-1843 .... **NCLC 2**

Fournier, Henri Alban 1886-1914
See Alain-Fournier
See also CA 104

Fournier, Pierre 1916-
See Gascar, Pierre
See also CANR 16; CA 89-92

Fowles, John (Robert)
1926-.... **CLC 1, 2, 3, 4, 6, 9, 10, 15, 33**
See also CA 5-8R; SATA 22; DLB 14

Fox, Paula 1923-................. **CLC 2, 8**
See also CLR 1; CANR 20; CA 73-76;
SATA 17; DLB 52

Fox, William Price (Jr.) 1926- ..... **CLC 22**
See also CANR 11; CA 17-20R; DLB 2;
DLB-Y 81

Frame (Clutha), Janet (Paterson)
1924-................. **CLC 2, 3, 6, 22**
See also Clutha, Janet Paterson Frame

France, Anatole 1844-1924 .... **TCLC 9**
See also Thibault, Jacques Anatole Francois

Francis, Claude 19??-............. **CLC 50**

Francis, Dick 1920- .... **CLC 2, 22, 42**
See also CANR 9; CA 5-8R

Francis, Robert (Churchill) 1901-... **CLC 15**
See also CANR 1; CA 1-4R

Frank, Anne 1929-1945 .... **TCLC 17**
See also CA 113; SATA 42

Frank, Elizabeth 1945-........... **CLC 39**
See also CA 121

Franklin, (Stella Maria Sarah) Miles
1879-1954 .... **TCLC 7**
See also CA 104

Fraser, Antonia (Pakenham)
1932-..................... **CLC 32**
See also CA 85-88; SATA 32

Fraser, George MacDonald 1925-.... **CLC 7**
See also CANR 2; CA 45-48

Frayn, Michael 1933-...... **CLC 3, 7, 31, 47**
See also CA 5-8R; DLB 13, 14

Fraze, Candida 19??- .... **CLC 50**

Frazier, Ian 1951-................ **CLC 46**

Frederic, Harold 1856-1898...... **NCLC 10**
See also DLB 12, 23

Fredro, Aleksander 1793-1876..... **NCLC 8**

Freeling, Nicolas 1927-.......... **CLC 38**
See also CANR 1, 17; CA 49-52

Freeman, Douglas Southall
1886-1953 .... **TCLC 11**
See also CA 109; DLB 17

Gide, Andre (Paul Guillaume)
    1869-1951 .... TCLC **5, 12**
    See also CA 104

Gifford, Barry (Colby) 1946- ...... CLC **34**
    See also CANR 9; CA 65-68

Gilbert, (Sir) W(illiam) S(chwenck)
    1836-1911 .... TCLC **3**
    See also CA 104; SATA 36

Gilbreth, Ernestine 1908-
    See Carey, Ernestine Gilbreth

Gilbreth, Frank B(unker), Jr. 1911- and
    Carey, Ernestine Gilbreth
    1908- .... CLC **17**

Gilbreth, Frank B(unker), Jr. 1911-
    See Gilbreth, Frank B(unker), Jr. and
    Carey, Ernestine Gilbreth
    See also CA 9-12R; SATA 2

Gilchrist, Ellen 1935- .... CLC **34, 48**
    See also CA 113, 116

Giles, Molly 1942- .... CLC **39**

Gilliam, Terry (Vance) 1940-
    See Monty Python
    See also CA 108, 113

Gilliatt, Penelope (Ann Douglass)
    1932- .... CLC **2, 10, 13**
    See also CA 13-16R; DLB 14

Gilman, Charlotte (Anna) Perkins (Stetson)
    1860-1935 .... TCLC **9**
    See also CA 106

Gilmour, David 1944-
    See Pink Floyd

Gilroy, Frank D(aniel) 1925- .... CLC **2**
    See also CA 81-84; DLB 7

Ginsberg, Allen
    1926- .... CLC **1, 2, 3, 4, 6, 13, 36**
    See also CANR 2; CA 1-4R; DLB 5, 16;
    CDALB 1941-1968

Ginzburg, Natalia 1916- ...... CLC **5, 11, 54**
    See also CA 85-88

Giono, Jean 1895-1970 .... CLC **4, 11**
    See also CANR 2; CA 45-48;
    obituary CA 29-32R; DLB 72

Giovanni, Nikki 1943- .... CLC **2, 4, 19**
    See also CLR 6; CAAS 6; CANR 18;
    CA 29-32R; SATA 24; DLB 5, 41

Giovene, Andrea 1904- .... CLC **7**
    See also CA 85-88

Gippius, Zinaida (Nikolayevna) 1869-1945
    See Hippius, Zinaida
    See also CA 106

Giraudoux, (Hippolyte) Jean
    1882-1944 .... TCLC **2, 7**
    See also CA 104

Gironella, Jose Maria 1917- .... CLC **11**
    See also CA 101

Gissing, George (Robert)
    1857-1903 .... TCLC **3, 24**
    See also CA 105; DLB 18

Gladkov, Fyodor (Vasilyevich)
    1883-1958 .... TCLC **27**

Glanville, Brian (Lester) 1931- ...... CLC **6**
    See also CANR 3; CA 5-8R; SATA 42;
    DLB 15

Glasgow, Ellen (Anderson Gholson)
    1873?-1945 .... TCLC **2, 7**
    See also CA 104; DLB 9, 12

Glassco, John 1909-1981 .... CLC **9**
    See also CANR 15; CA 13-16R;
    obituary CA 102

Glasser, Ronald J. 1940?- .... CLC **37**

Glendinning, Victoria 1937- .... CLC **50**
    See also CA 120

Glissant, Edouard 1928- .... CLC **10**

Gloag, Julian 1930- .... CLC **40**
    See also CANR 10; CA 65-68

Gluck, Louise (Elisabeth)
    1943- .... CLC **7, 22, 44**
    See also CA 33-36R; DLB 5

Gobineau, Joseph Arthur (Comte) de
    1816-1882 .... NCLC **17**

Godard, Jean-Luc 1930- .... CLC **20**
    See also CA 93-96

Godwin, Gail 1937- .... CLC **5, 8, 22, 31**
    See also CANR 15; CA 29-32R; DLB 6

Godwin, William 1756-1836 ...... NCLC **14**
    See also DLB 39

Goethe, Johann Wolfgang von
    1749-1832 .... NCLC **4**

Gogarty, Oliver St. John
    1878-1957 .... TCLC **15**
    See also CA 109; DLB 15, 19

Gogol, Nikolai (Vasilyevich)
    1809-1852 .... NCLC **5, 15**
    See also CAAS 1, 4

Gokceli, Yasar Kemal 1923-
    See Kemal, Yashar

Gold, Herbert 1924- ...... CLC **4, 7, 14, 42**
    See also CANR 17; CA 9-12R; DLB 2;
    DLB-Y 81

Goldbarth, Albert 1948- .... CLC **5, 38**
    See also CANR 6; CA 53-56

Goldberg, Anatol 1910-1982 ...... CLC **34**
    See also obituary CA 117

Golding, William (Gerald)
    1911- .... CLC **1, 2, 3, 8, 10, 17, 27**
    See also CANR 13; CA 5-8R; DLB 15

Goldman, Emma 1869-1940 ...... TCLC **13**
    See also CA 110

Goldman, William (W.) 1931- .... CLC **1, 48**
    See also CA 9-12R; DLB 44

Goldmann, Lucien 1913-1970 ...... CLC **24**
    See also CAP 2; CA 25-28

Goldoni, Carlo 1707-1793 .... LC **4**

Goldsberry, Steven 1949- .... CLC **34**

Goldsmith, Oliver 1728?-1774 .... LC **2**
    See also SATA 26; DLB 39

Gombrowicz, Witold
    1904-1969 .... CLC **4, 7, 11, 49**
    See also CAP 2; CA 19-20;
    obituary CA 25-28R

Gomez de la Serna, Ramon
    1888-1963 .... CLC **9**
    See also obituary CA 116

Goncharov, Ivan Alexandrovich
    1812-1891 .... NCLC **1**

Goncourt, Edmond (Louis Antoine Huot) de
    1822-1896 and **Goncourt, Jules (Alfred
    Huot) de** 1830-1870 .... NCLC **7**

Goncourt, Edmond (Louis Antoine Huot) de
    1822-1896
    See Goncourt, Edmond (Louis Antoine
    Huot) de and Goncourt, Jules (Alfred
    Huot) de

Goncourt, Jules (Alfred Huot) de 1830-1870
    See Goncourt, Edmond (Louis Antoine
    Huot) de and Goncourt, Jules (Alfred
    Huot) de

Goncourt, Jules (Alfred Huot) de 1830-1870
    and **Goncourt, Edmond (Louis Antoine
    Huot) de** 1822-1896
    See Goncourt, Edmond (Louis Antoine
    Huot) de and Goncourt, Jules (Alfred
    Huot) de

Gontier, Fernande 19??- .... CLC **50**

Goodman, Paul 1911-1972 .... CLC **1, 2, 4, 7**
    See also CAP 2; CA 19-20;
    obituary CA 37-40R

Gorden, Charles William 1860-1937
    See Conner, Ralph

Gordimer, Nadine
    1923- ...... CLC **3, 5, 7, 10, 18, 33, 51**
    See also CANR 3; CA 5-8R

Gordon, Caroline
    1895-1981 .... CLC **6, 13, 29**
    See also CAP 1; CA 11-12;
    obituary CA 103; DLB 4, 9; DLB-Y 81

Gordon, Mary (Catherine)
    1949- .... CLC **13, 22**
    See also CA 102; DLB 6; DLB-Y 81

Gordon, Sol 1923- .... CLC **26**
    See also CANR 4; CA 53-56; SATA 11

Gordone, Charles 1925- .... CLC **1, 4**
    See also CA 93-96; DLB 7

Gorenko, Anna Andreyevna 1889?-1966
    See Akhmatova, Anna

Gorky, Maxim 1868-1936 .... TCLC **8**
    See also Peshkov, Alexei Maximovich

Goryan, Sirak 1908-1981
    See Saroyan, William

Gosse, Edmund (William)
    1849-1928 .... TCLC **28**
    See also CA 117; DLB 57

Gotlieb, Phyllis (Fay Bloom)
    1926- .... CLC **18**
    See also CANR 7; CA 13-16R

Gould, Lois 1938?- .... CLC **4, 10**
    See also CA 77-80

Gourmont, Remy de 1858-1915 .... TCLC **17**
    See also CA 109

Govier, Katherine 1948- .... CLC **51**
    See also CANR 18; CA 101

Goyen, (Charles) William
    1915-1983 .... CLC **5, 8, 14, 40**
    See also CANR 6; CA 5-8R;
    obituary CA 110; DLB 2; DLB-Y 83

Goytisolo, Juan 1931- .... CLC **5, 10, 23**
    See also CA 85-88

Gozzi, (Conte) Carlo 1720-1806 .. NCLC **23**

Grabbe, Christian Dietrich
    1801-1836 .... NCLC **2**

Gracq, Julien   1910- .... CLC 11, 48
See also Poirier, Louis

Grade, Chaim   1910-1982 .... CLC 10
See also CA 93-96; obituary CA 107

Graham, Jorie   1951- .... CLC 48
See also CA 111

Graham, R(obert) B(ontine) Cunninghame
1852-1936 .... TCLC 19

Graham, Winston (Mawdsley)
1910- .... CLC 23
See also CANR 2; CA 49-52;
obituary CA 118

Graham, W(illiam) S(ydney)
1918-1986 .... CLC 29
See also CA 73-76; obituary CA 118;
DLB 20

Granville-Barker, Harley
1877-1946 .... TCLC 2
See also CA 104

Grass, Gunter (Wilhelm)
1927- .. CLC 1, 2, 4, 6, 11, 15, 22, 32, 49
See also CANR 20; CA 13-16R

Grau, Shirley Ann   1929- .... CLC 4, 9
See also CANR 22; CA 89-92; DLB 2

Graves, Richard Perceval   1945- .... CLC 44
See also CANR 9; CA 65-68

Graves, Robert (von Ranke)
1895-1985 ... CLC 1, 2, 6, 11, 39, 44, 45
See also CANR 5; CA 5-8R;
obituary CA 117; SATA 45; DLB 20;
DLB-Y 85

Gray, Alasdair   1934- .... CLC 41

Gray, Amlin   1946- .... CLC 29

Gray, Francine du Plessix   1930- .... CLC 22
See also CAAS 2; CANR 11; CA 61-64

Gray, John (Henry)   1866-1934 .... TCLC 19
See also CA 119

Gray, Simon (James Holliday)
1936- .... CLC 9, 14, 36
See also CAAS 3; CA 21-24R; DLB 13

Gray, Spalding   1941- .... CLC 49

Gray, Thomas   1716-1771 .... LC 4

Grayson, Richard (A.)   1951- .... CLC 38
See also CANR 14; CA 85-88

Greeley, Andrew M(oran)   1928- .... CLC 28
See also CAAS 7; CANR 7; CA 5-8R

Green, Hannah   1932- .... CLC 3, 7, 30
See also Greenberg, Joanne
See also CA 73-76

Green, Henry   1905-1974 .... CLC 2, 13
See also Yorke, Henry Vincent
See also DLB 15

Green, Julien (Hartridge)   1900- .. CLC 3, 11
See also CA 21-24R; DLB 4, 72

Green, Paul (Eliot)   1894-1981 ...... CLC 25
See also CANR 3; CA 5-8R;
obituary CA 103; DLB 7, 9; DLB-Y 81

Greenberg, Ivan   1908-1973
See Rahv, Philip
See also CA 85-88

Greenberg, Joanne (Goldenberg)
1932- .... CLC 3, 7, 30
See also Green, Hannah
See also CANR 14; CA 5-8R; SATA 25

Greene, Bette   1934- .... CLC 30
See also CLR 2; CANR 4; CA 53-56;
SATA 8

Greene, Gael   19??- .... CLC 8
See also CANR 10; CA 13-16R

Greene, Graham (Henry)
1904- ..... CLC 1, 3, 6, 9, 14, 18, 27, 37
See also CA 13-16R; SATA 20; DLB 13, 15;
DLB-Y 85

Gregor, Arthur   1923- .... CLC 9
See also CANR 11; CA 25-28R; SATA 36

Gregory, Lady (Isabella Augusta Persse)
1852-1932 .... TCLC 1
See also CA 104; DLB 10

Grendon, Stephen   1909-1971
See Derleth, August (William)

Greve, Felix Paul Berthold Friedrich
1879-1948
See Grove, Frederick Philip
See also CA 104

Grey, (Pearl) Zane   1872?-1939 ..... TCLC 6
See also CA 104; DLB 9

Grieg, (Johan) Nordahl (Brun)
1902-1943 .... TCLC 10
See also CA 107

Grieve, C(hristopher) M(urray)   1892-1978
See MacDiarmid, Hugh
See also CA 5-8R; obituary CA 85-88

Griffin, Gerald   1803-1840 .... NCLC 7

Griffin, Peter   1942- .... CLC 39

Griffiths, Trevor   1935- .... CLC 13
See also CA 97-100; DLB 13

Grigson, Geoffrey (Edward Harvey)
1905-1985 .... CLC 7, 39
See also CANR 20; CA 25-28R;
obituary CA 118; DLB 27

Grillparzer, Franz   1791-1872 ...... NCLC 1

Grimke, Charlotte L(ottie) Forten   1837-1914
See Forten (Grimke), Charlotte L(ottie)
See also CA 117

Grimm, Jakob (Ludwig) Karl   1785-1863 and
Grimm, Wilhelm Karl
1786-1859 .... NCLC 3
See also SATA 22

Grimm, Jakob (Ludwig) Karl   1785-1863
See Grimm, Jakob (Ludwig) Karl and
Grimm, Wilhelm Karl

Grimm, Wilhelm Karl   1786-1859
See Grimm, Jakob (Ludwig) Karl and
Grimm, Wilhelm Karl

Grimm, Wilhelm Karl   1786-1859 and Grimm,
Jakob (Ludwig) Karl   1785-1863
See Grimm, Jakob (Ludwig) Karl and
Grimm, Wilhelm Karl

Grimmelshausen, Johann Jakob Christoffel
von   1621-1676 .... LC 6

Grindel, Eugene   1895-1952
See also CA 104

Grossman, Vasily (Semenovich)
1905-1964 .... CLC 41

Grove, Frederick Philip
1879-1948 .... TCLC 4
See also Greve, Felix Paul Berthold
Friedrich

Grumbach, Doris (Isaac)
1918- .... CLC 13, 22
See also CAAS 2; CANR 9; CA 5-8R

Grundtvig, Nicolai Frederik Severin
1783-1872 .... NCLC 1

Grunwald, Lisa   1959- .... CLC 44
See also CA 120

Guare, John   1938- .... CLC 8, 14, 29
See also CANR 21; CA 73-76; DLB 7

Gudjonsson, Halldor Kiljan   1902-
See Laxness, Halldor (Kiljan)
See also CA 103

Guest, Barbara   1920- .... CLC 34
See also CANR 11; CA 25-28R; DLB 5

Guest, Judith (Ann)   1936- .... CLC 8, 30
See also CANR 15; CA 77-80

Guild, Nicholas M.   1944- .... CLC 33
See also CA 93-96

Guillen, Jorge   1893-1984 .... CLC 11
See also CA 89-92; obituary CA 112

Guillen, Nicolas   1902- .... CLC 48
See also CA 116

Guillevic, (Eugene)   1907- .... CLC 33
See also CA 93-96

Gunn, Bill   1934- .... CLC 5
See also Gunn, William Harrison
See also DLB 38

Gunn, Thom(son William)
1929- .... CLC 3, 6, 18, 32
See also CANR 9; CA 17-20R; DLB 27

Gunn, William Harrison   1934-
See Gunn, Bill
See also CANR 12; CA 13-16R

Gurney, A(lbert) R(amsdell), Jr.
1930- .... CLC 32, 50, 54
See also CA 77-80

Gurney, Ivor (Bertie)   1890-1937 ... TCLC 33

Gustafson, Ralph (Barker)   1909- .... CLC 36
See also CANR 8; CA 21-24R

Guthrie, A(lfred) B(ertram), Jr.
1901- .... CLC 23
See also CA 57-60; DLB 6

Guthrie, Woodrow Wilson   1912-1967
See Guthrie, Woody
See also CA 113; obituary CA 93-96

Guthrie, Woody   1912-1967 .... CLC 35
See also Guthrie, Woodrow Wilson

Guy, Rosa (Cuthbert)   1928- .... CLC 26
See also CANR 14; CA 17-20R; SATA 14;
DLB 33

Haavikko, Paavo (Juhani)
1931- .... CLC 18, 34
See also CA 106

Hacker, Marilyn   1942- .... CLC 5, 9, 23
See also CA 77-80

Haggard, (Sir) H(enry) Rider
1856-1925 .... TCLC 11
See also CA 108; SATA 16; DLB 70

Haig-Brown, Roderick L(angmere)
1908-1976 .... CLC 21
See also CANR 4; CA 5-8R;
obituary CA 69-72; SATA 12

Hailey, Arthur   1920- .... CLC 5
See also CANR 2; CA 1-4R; DLB-Y 82

Hedayat, Sadeq 1903-1951 . . . . **TCLC 21**
See also CA 120

Heidegger, Martin 1889-1976 . . . . . . **CLC 24**
See also CA 81-84; obituary CA 65-68

Heidenstam, (Karl Gustaf) Verner von
1859-1940 . . . . **TCLC 5**
See also CA 104

Heifner, Jack 1946- . . . . **CLC 11**
See also CA 105

Heijermans, Herman 1864-1924 . . . **TCLC 24**

Heilbrun, Carolyn G(old) 1926- . . . . . **CLC 25**
See also CANR 1; CA 45-48

Heine, Harry 1797-1856
See Heine, Heinrich

Heine, Heinrich 1797-1856 . . . . **NCLC 4**

Heinemann, Larry C(urtiss) 1944- . . **CLC 50**
See also CA 110

Heiney, Donald (William) 1921-
See Harris, MacDonald
See also CANR 3; CA 1-4R

Heinlein, Robert A(nson)
1907-1988 . . . . . . **CLC 1, 3, 8, 14, 26, 55**
See also CANR 1, 20; CA 1-4R;
obituary CA 125; SATA 9; DLB 8

Heller, Joseph
1923- . . . . **CLC 1, 3, 5, 8, 11, 36**
See also CANR 8; CA 5-8R; CABS 1;
DLB 2, 28; DLB-Y 80

Hellman, Lillian (Florence)
1905?-1984 . . . **CLC 2, 4, 8, 14, 18, 34, 44**
See also CA 13-16R; obituary CA 112;
DLB 7; DLB-Y 84

Helprin, Mark 1947- . . . . . **CLC 7, 10, 22, 32**
See also CA 81-84; DLB-Y 85

Hemingway, Ernest (Miller)
1899-1961 . . . **CLC 1, 3, 6, 8, 10, 13, 19,**
30, 34, 39, 41, 44, 50; SSC 1
See also CA 77-80; DLB 4, 9; DLB-Y 81;
DLB-DS 1

Hempel, Amy 1951- . . . . **CLC 39**
See also CA 118

Henley, Beth 1952- . . . . **CLC 23**
See also Henley, Elizabeth Becker
See also DLB-Y 86

Henley, Elizabeth Becker 1952-
See Henley, Beth
See also CA 107

Henley, William Ernest
1849-1903 . . . . **TCLC 8**
See also CA 105; DLB 19

Hennissart, Martha
See Lathen, Emma
See also CA 85-88

Henry 1491-1547 . . . . **LC 10**

Henry, O. 1862-1910 . . . . **TCLC 1, 19**
See also Porter, William Sydney

Hentoff, Nat(han Irving) 1925- . . . . . **CLC 26**
See also CLR 1; CAAS 6; CANR 5;
CA 1-4R; SATA 27, 42

Heppenstall, (John) Rayner
1911-1981 . . . . **CLC 10**
See also CA 1-4R; obituary CA 103

Herbert, Frank (Patrick)
1920-1986 . . . . **CLC 12, 23, 35, 44**
See also CANR 5; CA 53-56;
obituary CA 118; SATA 9, 37, 47; DLB 8

Herbert, Zbigniew 1924- . . . . **CLC 9, 43**
See also CA 89-92

Herbst, Josephine 1897-1969 . . . . . . **CLC 34**
See also CA 5-8R; obituary CA 25-28R;
DLB 9

Herder, Johann Gottfried von
1744-1803 . . . . **NCLC 8**

Hergesheimer, Joseph
1880-1954 . . . . **TCLC 11**
See also CA 109; DLB 9

Herlagnez, Pablo de 1844-1896
See Verlaine, Paul (Marie)

Herlihy, James Leo 1927- . . . . **CLC 6**
See also CANR 2; CA 1-4R

Hernandez, Jose 1834-1886 . . . . . . **NCLC 17**

Herriot, James 1916- . . . . **CLC 12**
See also Wight, James Alfred

Herrmann, Dorothy 1941- . . . . **CLC 44**
See also CA 107

Hersey, John (Richard)
1914- . . . . **CLC 1, 2, 7, 9, 40**
See also CA 17-20R; SATA 25; DLB 6

Herzen, Aleksandr Ivanovich
1812-1870 . . . . **NCLC 10**

Herzog, Werner 1942- . . . . **CLC 16**
See also CA 89-92

Hesse, Hermann
1877-1962 . . . . **CLC 1, 2, 3, 6, 11, 17, 25**
See also CAP 2; CA 17-18

Heyen, William 1940- . . . . **CLC 13, 18**
See also CA 33-36R; DLB 5

Heyerdahl, Thor 1914- . . . . **CLC 26**
See also CANR 5, 22; CA 5-8R; SATA 2,
52

Heym, Georg (Theodor Franz Arthur)
1887-1912 . . . . **TCLC 9**
See also CA 106

Heym, Stefan 1913- . . . . **CLC 41**
See also CANR 4; CA 9-12R; DLB 69

Heyse, Paul (Johann Ludwig von)
1830-1914 . . . . **TCLC 8**
See also CA 104

Hibbert, Eleanor (Burford) 1906- . . . . **CLC 7**
See also CANR 9; CA 17-20R; SATA 2

Higgins, George V(incent)
1939- . . . . **CLC 4, 7, 10, 18**
See also CAAS 5; CANR 17; CA 77-80;
DLB 2; DLB-Y 81

Highsmith, (Mary) Patricia
1921- . . . . **CLC 2, 4, 14, 42**
See also CANR 1, 20; CA 1-4R

Highwater, Jamake 1942- . . . . **CLC 12**
See also CAAS 7; CANR 10; CA 65-68;
SATA 30, 32; DLB 52; DLB-Y 85

Hikmet (Ran), Nazim 1902-1963 . . . . **CLC 40**
See also obituary CA 93-96

Hildesheimer, Wolfgang 1916- . . . . . **CLC 49**
See also CA 101; DLB 69

Hill, Geoffrey (William)
1932- . . . . **CLC 5, 8, 18, 45**
See also CANR 21; CA 81-84; DLB 40

Hill, George Roy 1922- . . . . **CLC 26**
See also CA 110

Hill, Susan B. 1942- . . . . **CLC 4**
See also CA 33-36R; DLB 14

Hilliard, Noel (Harvey) 1929- . . . . . . **CLC 15**
See also CANR 7; CA 9-12R

Hilton, James 1900-1954 . . . . **TCLC 21**
See also CA 108; SATA 34; DLB 34

Himes, Chester (Bomar)
1909-1984 . . . . **CLC 2, 4, 7, 18**
See also CANR 22; CA 25-28R;
obituary CA 114; DLB 2

Hinde, Thomas 1926- . . . . **CLC 6, 11**
See also Chitty, (Sir) Thomas Willes

Hine, (William) Daryl 1936- . . . . **CLC 15**
See also CANR 1, 20; CA 1-4R; DLB 60

Hinton, S(usan) E(loise) 1950- . . . . . **CLC 30**
See also CLR 3; CA 81-84; SATA 19

Hippius (Merezhkovsky), Zinaida
(Nikolayevna) 1869-1945 . . . . . . **TCLC 9**
See also Gippius, Zinaida (Nikolayevna)

Hiraoka, Kimitake 1925-1970
See Mishima, Yukio
See also CA 97-100; obituary CA 29-32R

Hirsch, Edward (Mark) 1950- . . . **CLC 31, 50**
See also CANR 20; CA 104

Hitchcock, (Sir) Alfred (Joseph)
1899-1980 . . . . **CLC 16**
See also obituary CA 97-100; SATA 27;
obituary SATA 24

Hoagland, Edward 1932- . . . . **CLC 28**
See also CANR 2; CA 1-4R; SATA 51;
DLB 6

Hoban, Russell C(onwell) 1925- . . **CLC 7, 25**
See also CLR 3; CA 5-8R; SATA 1, 40;
DLB 52

Hobson, Laura Z(ametkin)
1900-1986 . . . . **CLC 7, 25**
See also CA 17-20R; obituary CA 118;
SATA 52; DLB 28

Hochhuth, Rolf 1931- . . . . **CLC 4, 11, 18**
See also CA 5-8R

Hochman, Sandra 1936- . . . . **CLC 3, 8**
See also CA 5-8R; DLB 5

Hochwalder, Fritz 1911-1986 . . . . . . **CLC 36**
See also CA 29-32R; obituary CA 120

Hocking, Mary (Eunice) 1921- . . . . . **CLC 13**
See also CANR 18; CA 101

Hodgins, Jack 1938- . . . . **CLC 23**
See also CA 93-96; DLB 60

Hodgson, William Hope
1877-1918 . . . . **TCLC 13**
See also CA 111; DLB 70

Hoffman, Alice 1952- . . . . **CLC 51**
See also CA 77-80

Hoffman, Daniel (Gerard)
1923- . . . . **CLC 6, 13, 23**
See also CANR 4; CA 1-4R; DLB 5

Hoffman, Stanley 1944- . . . . **CLC 5**
See also CA 77-80

Ibarguengoitia, Jorge 1928-1983 .... **CLC 37**
See also obituary CA 113

Ibsen, Henrik (Johan)
    1828-1906 .... **TCLC 2, 8, 16**
See also CA 104

Ibuse, Masuji 1898- .... **CLC 22**

Ichikawa, Kon 1915- .... **CLC 20**
See also CA 121

Idle, Eric 1943-
See Monty Python
See also CA 116

Ignatow, David 1914- ...... **CLC 4, 7, 14, 40**
See also CAAS 3; CA 9-12R; DLB 5

Ihimaera, Witi (Tame) 1944- .... **CLC 46**
See also CA 77-80

Ilf, Ilya 1897-1937 and **Petrov, Evgeny**
    1902-1942 .... **TCLC 21**

Immermann, Karl (Lebrecht)
    1796-1840 .... **NCLC 4**

Ingalls, Rachel 19??- .... **CLC 42**

Inge, William (Motter)
    1913-1973 .... **CLC 1, 8, 19**
See also CA 9-12R; DLB 7;
    CDALB 1941-1968

Innaurato, Albert 1948- .... **CLC 21**
See also CA 115, 122

Innes, Michael 1906-
See Stewart, J(ohn) I(nnes) M(ackintosh)

Ionesco, Eugene
    1912- .... **CLC 1, 4, 6, 9, 11, 15, 41**
See also CA 9-12R; SATA 7

Iqbal, Muhammad 1877-1938 ..... **TCLC 28**

Irving, John (Winslow)
    1942- .... **CLC 13, 23, 38**
See also CA 25-28R; DLB 6; DLB-Y 82

Irving, Washington
    1783-1859 .... **NCLC 2, 19; SSC 2**
See also YABC 2; DLB 3, 11, 30;
    CDALB 1640-1865

Isaacs, Susan 1943- .... **CLC 32**
See also CANR 20; CA 89-92

Isherwood, Christopher (William Bradshaw)
    1904-1986 .... **CLC 1, 9, 11, 14, 44**
See also CA 13-16R; obituary CA 117;
    DLB 15; DLB-Y 86

Ishiguro, Kazuo 1954?- .... **CLC 27**
See also CA 120

Ishikawa Takuboku 1885-1912 .... **TCLC 15**
See also CA 113

Iskander, Fazil (Abdulovich)
    1929- .... **CLC 47**
See also CA 102

Ivanov, Vyacheslav (Ivanovich)
    1866-1949 .... **TCLC 33**
See also CA 122

Ivask, Ivar (Vidrik) 1927- .... **CLC 14**
See also CA 37-40R

Jackson, Jesse 1908-1983 .... **CLC 12**
See also CA 25-28R; obituary CA 109;
    SATA 2, 29, 48

Jackson, Laura (Riding) 1901-
See Riding, Laura
See also CA 65-68; DLB 48

Jackson, Shirley 1919-1965 .... **CLC 11**
See also CANR 4; CA 1-4R;
    obituary CA 25-28R; SATA 2; DLB 6;
    CDALB 1941-1968

Jacob, (Cyprien) Max 1876-1944 ... **TCLC 6**
See also CA 104

Jacob, Piers A(nthony) D(illingham) 1934-
See Anthony (Jacob), Piers
See also CA 21-24R

Jacobs, Jim 1942- and **Casey, Warren**
    1935- .... **CLC 12**

Jacobs, Jim 1942-
See Jacobs, Jim and Casey, Warren
See also CA 97-100

Jacobs, W(illiam) W(ymark)
    1863-1943 .... **TCLC 22**
See also CA 121

Jacobsen, Josephine 1908- .... **CLC 48**
See also CA 33-36R

Jacobson, Dan 1929- .... **CLC 4, 14**
See also CANR 2; CA 1-4R; DLB 14

Jagger, Mick 1944- and **Richard, Keith**
    1943- .... **CLC 17**

Jagger, Mick 1944-
See Jagger, Mick and Richard, Keith

Jakes, John (William) 1932- .... **CLC 29**
See also CANR 10; CA 57-60; DLB-Y 83

James, C(yril) L(ionel) R(obert)
    1901- .... **CLC 33**
See also CA 117

James, Daniel 1911-
See Santiago, Danny

James, Henry (Jr.)
    1843-1916 .... **TCLC 2, 11, 24**
See also CA 104; DLB 12, 71;
    CDALB 1865-1917

James, M(ontague) R(hodes)
    1862-1936 .... **TCLC 6**
See also CA 104

James, P(hyllis) D(orothy)
    1920- .... **CLC 18, 46**
See also CANR 17; CA 21-24R

James, William 1842-1910 .... **TCLC 15**
See also CA 109

Jami, Nur al-Din 'Abd al-Rahman
    1414-1492 .... **LC 9**

Jandl, Ernst 1925- .... **CLC 34**

Janowitz, Tama 1957- .... **CLC 43**
See also CA 106

Jarrell, Randall
    1914-1965 .... **CLC 1, 2, 6, 9, 13, 49**
See also CLR 6; CANR 6; CA 5-8R;
    obituary CA 25-28R; CABS 2; SATA 7;
    DLB 48, 52; CDALB 1941-1968

Jarry, Alfred 1873-1907 .... **TCLC 2, 14**
See also CA 104

Jean Paul 1763-1825 .... **NCLC 7**

Jeffers, (John) Robinson
    1887-1962 .... **CLC 2, 3, 11, 15, 54**
See also CA 85-88; DLB 45

Jefferson, Thomas 1743-1826 .... **NCLC 11**
See also DLB 31; CDALB 1640-1865

Jellicoe, (Patricia) Ann 1927- ...... **CLC 27**
See also CA 85-88; DLB 13

Jennings, Elizabeth (Joan)
    1926- .... **CLC 5, 14**
See also CAAS 5; CANR 8; CA 61-64;
    DLB 27

Jennings, Waylon 1937- .... **CLC 21**

Jensen, Laura (Linnea) 1948- ...... **CLC 37**
See also CA 103

Jerome, Jerome K. 1859-1927 ..... **TCLC 23**
See also CA 119; DLB 10, 34

Jerrold, Douglas William
    1803-1857 .... **NCLC 2**

Jewett, (Theodora) Sarah Orne
    1849-1909 .... **TCLC 1, 22**
See also CA 108; SATA 15; DLB 12

Jhabvala, Ruth Prawer
    1927- .... **CLC 4, 8, 29**
See also CANR 2; CA 1-4R

Jiles, Paulette 1943- .... **CLC 13**
See also CA 101

Jimenez (Mantecon), Juan Ramon
    1881-1958 .... **TCLC 4**
See also CA 104

Joel, Billy 1949- .... **CLC 26**
See also Joel, William Martin

Joel, William Martin 1949-
See Joel, Billy
See also CA 108

Johnson, B(ryan) S(tanley William)
    1933-1973 .... **CLC 6, 9**
See also CANR 9; CA 9-12R;
    obituary CA 53-56; DLB 14, 40

Johnson, Charles (Richard)
    1948- .... **CLC 7, 51**
See also CA 116; DLB 33

Johnson, Diane 1934- .... **CLC 5, 13, 48**
See also CANR 17; CA 41-44R; DLB-Y 80

Johnson, Eyvind (Olof Verner)
    1900-1976 .... **CLC 14**
See also CA 73-76; obituary CA 69-72

Johnson, James Weldon
    1871-1938 .... **TCLC 3, 19**
See also Johnson, James William
See also CA 104; DLB 51

Johnson, James William 1871-1938
See Johnson, James Weldon
See also SATA 31

Johnson, Lionel (Pigot)
    1867-1902 .... **TCLC 19**
See also CA 117; DLB 19

Johnson, Marguerita 1928-
See Angelou, Maya

Johnson, Pamela Hansford
    1912-1981 .... **CLC 1, 7, 27**
See also CANR 2; CA 1-4R;
    obituary CA 104; DLB 15

Johnson, Uwe
    1934-1984 .... **CLC 5, 10, 15, 40**
See also CANR 1; CA 1-4R;
    obituary CA 112

Johnston, George (Benson) 1913- ... **CLC 51**
See also CANR 5, 20; CA 1-4R

Johnston, Jennifer 1930- .... **CLC 7**
See also CA 85-88; DLB 14

Jolley, Elizabeth 1923- .... **CLC 46**

Jones, David
1895-1974 . . . . CLC 2, 4, 7, 13, 42
See also CA 9-12R; obituary CA 53-56;
DLB 20

Jones, David Robert 1947-
See Bowie, David
See also CA 103

Jones, D(ouglas) G(ordon) 1929- . . . . CLC 10
See also CANR 13; CA 113; DLB 53

Jones, Diana Wynne 1934- . . . . CLC 26
See also CANR 4; CA 49-52; SATA 9

Jones, Gayl 1949- . . . . CLC 6, 9
See also CA 77-80; DLB 33

Jones, James 1921-1977 . . . . CLC 1, 3, 10, 39
See also CANR 6; CA 1-4R;
obituary CA 69-72; DLB 2

Jones, (Everett) LeRoi
1934- . . . . CLC 1, 2, 3, 5, 10, 14, 33
See also Baraka, Amiri
See also Baraka, Imamu Amiri; CA 21-24R

Jones, Madison (Percy, Jr.) 1925- . . . CLC 4
See also CANR 7; CA 13-16R

Jones, Mervyn 1922- . . . . CLC 10
See also CAAS 5; CANR 1; CA 45-48

Jones, Mick 1956?-
See The Clash

Jones, Nettie 19??- . . . . CLC 34

Jones, Preston 1936-1979 . . . . CLC 10
See also CA 73-76; obituary CA 89-92;
DLB 7

Jones, Robert F(rancis) 1934- . . . . CLC 7
See also CANR 2; CA 49-52

Jones, Rod 1953- . . . . CLC 50

Jones, Terry 1942?-
See Monty Python
See also CA 112, 116; SATA 51

Jong, Erica 1942- . . . . CLC 4, 6, 8, 18
See also CA 73-76; DLB 2, 5, 28

Jonson, Ben(jamin) 1572-1637 . . . . LC 6
See also DLB 62

Jordan, June 1936- . . . . CLC 5, 11, 23
See also CLR 10; CA 33-36R; SATA 4;
DLB 38

Jordan, Pat(rick M.) 1941- . . . . CLC 37
See also CA 33-36R

Josipovici, Gabriel (David)
1940- . . . . CLC 6, 43
See also CA 37-40R; DLB 14

Joubert, Joseph 1754-1824 . . . . NCLC 9

Jouve, Pierre Jean 1887-1976 . . . . . . CLC 47
See also obituary CA 65-68

Joyce, James (Augustine Aloysius)
1882-1941 . . . . TCLC 3, 8, 16, 26; SSC 3
See also CA 104, 126; DLB 10, 19, 36

Jozsef, Attila 1905-1937 . . . . TCLC 22
See also CA 116

Juana Ines de la Cruz 1651?-1695 . . . . LC 5

Julian of Norwich 1342?-1416? . . . . . . LC 6

Just, Ward S(wift) 1935- . . . . CLC 4, 27
See also CA 25-28R

Justice, Donald (Rodney) 1925- . . CLC 6, 19
See also CA 5-8R; DLB-Y 83

Kacew, Romain 1914-1980
See Gary, Romain
See also CA 108; obituary CA 102

Kacewgary, Romain 1914-1980
See Gary, Romain

Kafka, Franz
1883-1924 . . . . TCLC 2, 6, 13, 29
See also CA 105

Kahn, Roger 1927- . . . . CLC 30
See also CA 25-28R; SATA 37

Kaiser, (Friedrich Karl) Georg
1878-1945 . . . . TCLC 9
See also CA 106

Kaletski, Alexander 1946- . . . . CLC 39
See also CA 118

Kallman, Chester (Simon)
1921-1975 . . . . CLC 2
See also CANR 3; CA 45-48;
obituary CA 53-56

Kaminsky, Melvin 1926-
See Brooks, Mel
See also CANR 16

Kane, Paul 1941-
See Simon, Paul

Kanin, Garson 1912- . . . . CLC 22
See also CANR 7; CA 5-8R; DLB 7

Kaniuk, Yoram 1930- . . . . CLC 19

Kantor, MacKinlay 1904-1977 . . . . . . CLC 7
See also CA 61-64; obituary CA 73-76;
DLB 9

Kaplan, David Michael 1946- . . . . . . CLC 50

Karamzin, Nikolai Mikhailovich
1766-1826 . . . . NCLC 3

Karapanou, Margarita 1946- . . . . CLC 13
See also CA 101

Karl, Frederick R(obert) 1927- . . . . . CLC 34
See also CANR 3; CA 5-8R

Kassef, Romain 1914-1980
See Gary, Romain

Katz, Steve 1935- . . . . CLC 47
See also CANR 12; CA 25-28R; DLB-Y 83

Kauffman, Janet 1945- . . . . CLC 42
See also CA 117; DLB-Y 86

Kaufman, Bob (Garnell)
1925-1986 . . . . CLC 49
See also CANR 22; CA 41-44R;
obituary CA 118; DLB 16, 41

Kaufman, George S(imon)
1889-1961 . . . . CLC 38
See also CA 108; obituary CA 93-96; DLB 7

Kaufman, Sue 1926-1977 . . . . CLC 3, 8
See also Barondess, Sue K(aufman)

Kavan, Anna 1904-1968 . . . . CLC 5, 13
See also Edmonds, Helen (Woods)
See also CANR 6; CA 5-8R

Kavanagh, Patrick (Joseph Gregory)
1905-1967 . . . . CLC 22
See also obituary CA 25-28R; DLB 15, 20

Kawabata, Yasunari
1899-1972 . . . . CLC 2, 5, 9, 18
See also CA 93-96; obituary CA 33-36R

Kaye, M(ary) M(argaret) 1909?- . . . . CLC 28
See also CA 89-92

Kaye, Mollie 1909?-
See Kaye, M(ary) M(argaret)

Kaye-Smith, Sheila 1887-1956 . . . . . TCLC 20
See also CA 118; DLB 36

Kazan, Elia 1909- . . . . CLC 6, 16
See also CA 21-24R

Kazantzakis, Nikos
1885?-1957 . . . . TCLC 2, 5, 33
See also CA 105

Kazin, Alfred 1915- . . . . CLC 34, 38
See also CAAS 7; CANR 1; CA 1-4R

Keane, Mary Nesta (Skrine) 1904-
See Keane, Molly
See also CA 108, 114

Keane, Molly 1904- . . . . CLC 31
See also Keane, Mary Nesta (Skrine)

Keates, Jonathan 19??- . . . . CLC 34

Keaton, Buster 1895-1966 . . . . CLC 20

Keaton, Joseph Francis 1895-1966
See Keaton, Buster

Keats, John 1795-1821 . . . . NCLC 8

Keene, Donald 1922- . . . . CLC 34
See also CANR 5; CA 1-4R

Keillor, Garrison 1942- . . . . CLC 40
See also Keillor, Gary (Edward)
See also CA 111

Keillor, Gary (Edward)
See Keillor, Garrison
See also CA 117

Kell, Joseph 1917-
See Burgess (Wilson, John) Anthony

Keller, Gottfried 1819-1890 . . . . NCLC 2

Kellerman, Jonathan (S.) 1949- . . . . . CLC 44
See also CA 106

Kelley, William Melvin 1937- . . . . . . CLC 22
See also CA 77-80; DLB 33

Kellogg, Marjorie 1922- . . . . CLC 2
See also CA 81-84

Kelly, M. T. 1947- . . . . CLC 55
See also CANR 19, 19; CA 97-100, 97-100

Kemal, Yashar 1922- . . . . CLC 14, 29
See also CA 89-92

Kemble, Fanny 1809-1893 . . . . NCLC 18
See also DLB 32

Kemelman, Harry 1908- . . . . CLC 2
See also CANR 6; CA 9-12R; DLB 28

Kempe, Margery 1373?-1440? . . . . LC 6

Kempis, Thomas á 1380-1471 . . . . . . LC 11

Kendall, Henry 1839-1882 . . . . NCLC 12

Keneally, Thomas (Michael)
1935- . . . . . . CLC 5, 8, 10, 14, 19, 27, 43
See also CANR 10; CA 85-88

Kennedy, John Pendleton
1795-1870 . . . . NCLC 2
See also DLB 3

Kennedy, Joseph Charles 1929-
See Kennedy, X. J.
See also CANR 4; CA 1-4R; SATA 14

Kennedy, William 1928- . . . . . . CLC 6, 28, 34
See also CANR 14; CA 85-88; DLB-Y 85

Leffland, Ella 1931- .... **CLC 19**
  See also CA 29-32R; DLB-Y 84

Leger, (Marie-Rene) Alexis Saint-Leger
    1887-1975
  See Perse, St.-John
  See also CA 13-16R; obituary CA 61-64

Le Guin, Ursula K(roeber)
    1929- .... **CLC 8, 13, 22, 45**
  See also CLR 3; CANR 9; CA 21-24R;
    SATA 4, 52; DLB 8, 52

Lehmann, Rosamond (Nina) 1901- ... **CLC 5**
  See also CANR 8; CA 77-80; DLB 15

Leiber, Fritz (Reuter, Jr.) 1910- .... **CLC 25**
  See also CANR 2; CA 45-48; SATA 45;
    DLB 8

Leino, Eino 1878-1926 .... **TCLC 24**

Leithauser, Brad 1953- .... **CLC 27**
  See also CA 107

Lelchuk, Alan 1938- .... **CLC 5**
  See also CANR 1; CA 45-48

Lem, Stanislaw 1921- .... **CLC 8, 15, 40**
  See also CAAS 1; CA 105

Lemann, Nancy 1956- .... **CLC 39**
  See also CA 118

Lemonnier, (Antoine Louis) Camille
    1844-1913 .... **TCLC 22**

Lenau, Nikolaus 1802-1850 ...... **NCLC 16**

L'Engle, Madeleine 1918- .... **CLC 12**
  See also CLR 1, 14; CANR 3, 21; CA 1-4R;
    SATA 1, 27; DLB 52

Lengyel, Jozsef 1896-1975 .... **CLC 7**
  See also CA 85-88; obituary CA 57-60

Lennon, John (Ono) 1940-1980 and
    McCartney, Paul 1942- .... **CLC 12**

Lennon, John (Ono) 1940-1980 ..... **CLC 35**
  See also Lennon, John (Ono) and
    McCartney, Paul
  See also CA 102

Lennon, John Winston 1940-1980
  See Lennon, John (Ono)

Lennox, Charlotte Ramsay 1729 or
    1730-1804 .... **NCLC 23**
  See also DLB 39, 39

Lentricchia, Frank (Jr.) 1940- ...... **CLC 34**
  See also CA 25-28R

Lenz, Siegfried 1926- .... **CLC 27**
  See also CA 89-92

Leonard, Elmore 1925- .... **CLC 28, 34**
  See also CANR 12; CA 81-84

Leonard, Hugh 1926- .... **CLC 19**
  See also Byrne, John Keyes
  See also DLB 13

Lerman, Eleanor 1952- .... **CLC 9**
  See also CA 85-88

Lermontov, Mikhail Yuryevich
    1814-1841 .... **NCLC 5**

Leroux, Gaston 1868-1927 .... **TCLC 25**
  See also CA 108

Lesage, Alain-Rene 1668-1747 .... **LC 2**

Lessing, Doris (May)
    1919- ..... **CLC 1, 2, 3, 6, 10, 15, 22, 40**
  See also CA 9-12R; DLB 15; DLB-Y 85

Lessing, Gotthold Ephraim
    1729-1781 .... **LC 8**

Lester, Richard 1932- .... **CLC 20**

Lever, Charles James 1806-1872 .. **NCLC 23**
  See also DLB 21

Leverson, Ada 1865-1936 .... **TCLC 18**
  See also CA 117

Levertov, Denise
    1923- .... **CLC 1, 2, 3, 5, 8, 15, 28**
  See also CANR 3; CA 1-4R; DLB 5

Levi, Peter (Chad Tiger) 1931- ..... **CLC 41**
  See also CA 5-8R; DLB 40

Levi, Primo 1919-1987 .... **CLC 37, 50**
  See also CANR 12; CA 13-16R;
    obituary CA 122

Levin, Ira 1929- .... **CLC 3, 6**
  See also CANR 17; CA 21-24R

Levin, Meyer 1905-1981 .... **CLC 7**
  See also CANR 15; CA 9-12R;
    obituary CA 104; SATA 21;
    obituary SATA 27; DLB 9, 28; DLB-Y 81

Levine, Norman 1924- .... **CLC 54**
  See also CANR 14; CA 73-76

Levine, Philip 1928- .. **CLC 2, 4, 5, 9, 14, 33**
  See also CANR 9; CA 9-12R; DLB 5

Levinson, Deirdre 1931- .... **CLC 49**
  See also CA 73-76

Levi-Strauss, Claude 1908- .... **CLC 38**
  See also CANR 6; CA 1-4R

Levitin, Sonia 1934- .... **CLC 17**
  See also CANR 14; CA 29-32R; SAAS 2;
    SATA 4

Lewis, Alun 1915-1944 .... **TCLC 3**
  See also CA 104; DLB 20

Lewis, C(ecil) Day 1904-1972
  See Day Lewis, C(ecil)

Lewis, C(live) S(taples)
    1898-1963 .... **CLC 1, 3, 6, 14, 27**
  See also CLR 3; CA 81-84; SATA 13;
    DLB 15

Lewis (Winters), Janet 1899- .... **CLC 41**
  See also Winters, Janet Lewis

Lewis, Matthew Gregory
    1775-1818 .... **NCLC 11**
  See also DLB 39

Lewis, (Harry) Sinclair
    1885-1951 .... **TCLC 4, 13, 23**
  See also CA 104; DLB 9; DLB-DS 1

Lewis, (Percy) Wyndham
    1882?-1957 .... **TCLC 2, 9**
  See also CA 104; DLB 15

Lewisohn, Ludwig 1883-1955 ..... **TCLC 19**
  See also CA 73-76; obituary CA 29-32R

Lieber, Stanley Martin 1922-
  See Lee, Stan

Lieberman, Laurence (James)
    1935- .... **CLC 4, 36**
  See also CANR 8; CA 17-20R

Li Fei-kan 1904-
  See Pa Chin
  See also CA 105

Lightfoot, Gordon (Meredith)
    1938- .... **CLC 26**
  See also CA 109

Ligotti, Thomas 1953- .... **CLC 44**

Liliencron, Detlev von
    1844-1909 .... **TCLC 18**
  See also CA 117

Lima, Jose Lezama 1910-1976
  See Lezama Lima, Jose

Lima Barreto, (Alfonso Henriques de)
    1881-1922 .... **TCLC 23**
  See also CA 117

Lincoln, Abraham 1809-1865 ..... **NCLC 18**

Lind, Jakov 1927- .... **CLC 1, 2, 4, 27**
  See also Landwirth, Heinz
  See also CAAS 4; CA 9-12R

Lindsay, David 1876-1945 .... **TCLC 15**
  See also CA 113

Lindsay, (Nicholas) Vachel
    1879-1931 .... **TCLC 17**
  See also CA 114; SATA 40; DLB 54;
    CDALB 1865-1917

Linney, Romulus 1930- .... **CLC 51**
  See also CA 1-4R

Li Po 701-763 .... **CMLC 2**

Lipsyte, Robert (Michael) 1938- .... **CLC 21**
  See also CANR 8; CA 17-20R; SATA 5

Lish, Gordon (Jay) 1934- .... **CLC 45**
  See also CA 113, 117

Lispector, Clarice 1925-1977 ...... **CLC 43**
  See also obituary CA 116

Littell, Robert 1935?- .... **CLC 42**
  See also CA 109, 112

Liu E 1857-1909 .... **TCLC 15**
  See also CA 115

Lively, Penelope 1933- .... **CLC 32, 50**
  See also CLR 7; CA 41-44R; SATA 7;
    DLB 14

Livesay, Dorothy 1909- .... **CLC 4, 15**
  See also CA 25-28R

Llewellyn, Richard 1906-1983 ...... **CLC 7**
  See also Llewellyn Lloyd, Richard (Dafydd
    Vyvyan)
  See also DLB 15

Llewellyn Lloyd, Richard (Dafydd Vyvyan)
    1906-1983
  See Llewellyn, Richard
  See also CANR 7; CA 53-56;
    obituary CA 111; SATA 11, 37

Llosa, Mario Vargas 1936-
  See Vargas Llosa, Mario

Lloyd, Richard Llewellyn 1906-
  See Llewellyn, Richard

Locke, John 1632-1704 .... **LC 7**
  See also DLB 31

Lockhart, John Gibson
    1794-1854 .... **NCLC 6**

Lodge, David (John) 1935- .... **CLC 36**
  See also CANR 19; CA 17-20R; DLB 14

Logan, John 1923- .... **CLC 5**
  See also CA 77-80; DLB 5

Lombino, S. A. 1926-
  See Hunter, Evan

London, Jack   1876-1916 . . . . **TCLC 9, 15**
  See also London, John Griffith
  See also SATA 18; DLB 8, 12;
    CDALB 1865-1917

London, John Griffith   1876-1916
  See London, Jack
  See also CA 110, 119

Long, Emmett   1925-
  See Leonard, Elmore

Longbaugh, Harry   1931-
  See Goldman, William (W.)

Longfellow, Henry Wadsworth
    1807-1882 . . . . **NCLC 2**
  See also SATA 19; DLB 1;
    CDALB 1640-1865

Longley, Michael   1939- . . . . **CLC 29**
  See also CA 102; DLB 40

Lopate, Phillip   1943- . . . . **CLC 29**
  See also CA 97-100; DLB-Y 80

Lopez Portillo (y Pacheco), Jose
    1920- . . . . **CLC 46**

Lopez y Fuentes, Gregorio
    1897-1966 . . . . **CLC 32**

Lord, Bette Bao   1938- . . . . **CLC 23**
  See also CA 107

Lorde, Audre (Geraldine)   1934- . . . . . **CLC 18**
  See also CANR 16; CA 25-28R; DLB 41

Loti, Pierre   1850-1923 . . . . **TCLC 11**
  See also Viaud, (Louis Marie) Julien

Lovecraft, H(oward) P(hillips)
    1890-1937 . . . . **TCLC 4, 22; SSC 3**
  See also CA 104

Lovelace, Earl   1935- . . . . **CLC 51**
  See also CA 77-80

Lowell, Amy   1874-1925 . . . . **TCLC 1, 8**
  See also CA 104; DLB 54

Lowell, James Russell   1819-1891 . . **NCLC 2**
  See also DLB 1, 11, 64; CDALB 1640-1865

Lowell, Robert (Traill Spence, Jr.)
    1917-1977 . . . **CLC 1, 2, 3, 4, 5, 8, 9, 11,**
                       15, 37
  See also CA 9-12R; obituary CA 73-76;
    CABS 2; DLB 5

Lowndes, Marie (Adelaide) Belloc
    1868-1947 . . . . **TCLC 12**
  See also CA 107; DLB 70

Lowry, (Clarence) Malcolm
    1909-1957 . . . . **TCLC 6**
  See also CA 105; DLB 15

Loy, Mina   1882-1966 . . . . **CLC 28**
  See also CA 113; DLB 4, 54

Lucas, George   1944- . . . . **CLC 16**
  See also CA 77-80

Lucas, Victoria   1932-1963
  See Plath, Sylvia

Ludlam, Charles   1943-1987 . . . . . **CLC 46, 50**
  See also CA 85-88; obituary CA 122

Ludlum, Robert   1927- . . . . **CLC 22, 43**
  See also CA 33-36R; DLB-Y 82

Ludwig, Otto   1813-1865 . . . . **NCLC 4**

Lugones, Leopoldo   1874-1938 . . . . . **TCLC 15**
  See also CA 116

Lu Hsun   1881-1936 . . . . **TCLC 3**

Lukacs, Georg   1885-1971 . . . . **CLC 24**
  See also Lukacs, Gyorgy

Lukacs, Gyorgy   1885-1971
  See Lukacs, Georg
  See also CA 101; obituary CA 29-32R

Luke, Peter (Ambrose Cyprian)
    1919- . . . . **CLC 38**
  See also CA 81-84; DLB 13

Lurie (Bishop), Alison
    1926- . . . . **CLC 4, 5, 18, 39**
  See also CANR 2, 17; CA 1-4R; SATA 46;
    DLB 2

Luther, Martin   1483-1546 . . . . **LC 9**

Luzi, Mario   1914- . . . . **CLC 13**
  See also CANR 9; CA 61-64

Lynn, Kenneth S(chuyler)   1923- . . . . **CLC 50**
  See also CANR 3; CA 1-4R

Lytle, Andrew (Nelson)   1902- . . . . . . **CLC 22**
  See also CA 9-12R; DLB 6

Lyttelton, George   1709-1773 . . . . **LC 10**

Lytton, Edward Bulwer   1803-1873
  See Bulwer-Lytton, (Lord) Edward (George
    Earle Lytton)
  See also SATA 23

Maas, Peter   1929- . . . . **CLC 29**
  See also CA 93-96

Macaulay, (Dame Emile) Rose
    1881-1958 . . . . **TCLC 7**
  See also CA 104; DLB 36

MacBeth, George (Mann)
    1932- . . . . **CLC 2, 5, 9**
  See also CA 25-28R; SATA 4; DLB 40

MacCaig, Norman (Alexander)
    1910- . . . . **CLC 36**
  See also CANR 3; CA 9-12R; DLB 27

MacDermot, Thomas H.   1870-1933
  See Redcam, Tom

MacDiarmid, Hugh
    1892-1978 . . . . **CLC 2, 4, 11, 19**
  See also Grieve, C(hristopher) M(urray)
  See also DLB 20

Macdonald, Cynthia   1928- . . . . . . **CLC 13, 19**
  See also CANR 4; CA 49-52

MacDonald, George   1824-1905 . . . . . **TCLC 9**
  See also CA 106; SATA 33; DLB 18

MacDonald, John D(ann)
    1916-1986 . . . . **CLC 3, 27, 44**
  See also CANR 1, 19; CA 1-4R;
    obituary CA 121; DLB 8; DLB-Y 86

Macdonald, (John) Ross
    1915-1983 . . . . . . **CLC 1, 2, 3, 14, 34, 41**
  See also Millar, Kenneth

MacEwen, Gwendolyn (Margaret)
    1941-1987 . . . . **CLC 13, 55**
  See also CANR 7, 22; CA 9-12R;
    obituary CA 124; SATA 50; DLB 53

Machado (y Ruiz), Antonio
    1875-1939 . . . . **TCLC 3**
  See also CA 104

Machado de Assis, (Joaquim Maria)
    1839-1908 . . . . **TCLC 10**
  See also CA 107

Machen, Arthur (Llewellyn Jones)
    1863-1947 . . . . **TCLC 4**
  See also CA 104; DLB 36

Machiavelli, Niccolo   1469-1527 . . . . . . **LC 8**

MacInnes, Colin   1914-1976 . . . . . . **CLC 4, 23**
  See also CA 69-72; obituary CA 65-68;
    DLB 14

MacInnes, Helen (Clark)
    1907-1985 . . . . **CLC 27, 39**
  See also CANR 1; CA 1-4R;
    obituary CA 65-68, 117; SATA 22, 44

Macintosh, Elizabeth   1897-1952
  See Tey, Josephine
  See also CA 110

Mackenzie, (Edward Montague) Compton
    1883-1972 . . . . **CLC 18**
  See also CAP 2; CA 21-22;
    obituary CA 37-40R; DLB 34

Mac Laverty, Bernard   1942- . . . . **CLC 31**
  See also CA 116, 118

MacLean, Alistair (Stuart)
    1922-1987 . . . . **CLC 3, 13, 50**
  See also CA 57-60; obituary CA 121;
    SATA 23

MacLeish, Archibald
    1892-1982 . . . . **CLC 3, 8, 14**
  See also CA 9-12R; obituary CA 106;
    DLB 4, 7, 45; DLB-Y 82

MacLennan, (John) Hugh
    1907- . . . . **CLC 2, 14**
  See also CA 5-8R

MacNeice, (Frederick) Louis
    1907-1963 . . . . **CLC 1, 4, 10**
  See also CA 85-88; DLB 10, 20

Macpherson, (Jean) Jay   1931- . . . . . . **CLC 14**
  See also CA 5-8R; DLB 53

MacShane, Frank   1927- . . . . **CLC 39**
  See also CANR 3; CA 11-12R

Macumber, Mari   1896-1966
  See Sandoz, Mari (Susette)

Madach, Imre   1823-1864 . . . . **NCLC 19**

Madden, (Jerry) David   1933- . . . . **CLC 5, 15**
  See also CAAS 3; CANR 4; CA 1-4R;
    DLB 6

Madhubuti, Haki R.   1942- . . . . **CLC 6**
  See Lee, Don L.
  See also DLB 5, 41

Maeterlinck, Maurice   1862-1949 . . . **TCLC 3**
  See also CA 104

Mafouz, Naguib   1912- . . . . **CLC   55**
  See also DLB-Y 88, 1988

Maginn, William   1794-1842 . . . . . . **NCLC 8**

Mahapatra, Jayanta   1928- . . . . **CLC 33**
  See also CANR 15; CA 73-76

Mahon, Derek   1941- . . . . **CLC 27**
  See also CA 113; DLB 40

Mailer, Norman
    1923- . . . . . . **CLC 1, 2, 3, 4, 5, 8, 11, 14,**
                       28, 39
  See also CA 9-12R; CABS 1; DLB 2, 16,
    28; DLB-Y 80, 83; DLB-DS 3

Maillet, Antonine   1929- . . . . **CLC 54**
  See also CA 115, 120; DLB 60

Mais, Roger   1905-1955 . . . . **TCLC 8**
  See also CA 105

Maitland, Sara (Louise)   1950- . . . . . . **CLC 49**
  See also CANR 13; CA 69-72

Major, Clarence 1936-....... **CLC 3, 19, 48**
See also CAAS 6; CANR 13; CA 21-24R;
DLB 33

Major, Kevin 1949- .... **CLC 26**
See also CLR 11; CANR 21; CA 97-100;
SATA 32; DLB 60

Malamud, Bernard
1914-1986 ..... **CLC 1, 2, 3, 5, 8, 9, 11,
18, 27, 44**
See also CA 5-8R; obituary CA 118;
CABS 1; DLB 2, 28; DLB-Y 80, 86;
CDALB 1941-1968

Malherbe, Francois de 1555-1628 ..... **LC 5**

Mallarme, Stephane 1842-1898 .... **NCLC 4**

Mallet-Joris, Francoise 1930- ...... **CLC 11**
See also CANR 17; CA 65-68

Maloff, Saul 1922- .... **CLC 5**
See also CA 33-36R

Malone, Michael (Christopher)
1942- .... **CLC 43**
See also CANR 14; CA 77-80

Malory, (Sir) Thomas ?-1471........ **LC 11**
See also SATA 33

Malouf, David 1934- .... **CLC 28**

Malraux, (Georges-) Andre
1901-1976 .... **CLC 1, 4, 9, 13, 15**
See also CAP 2; CA 21-24;
obituary CA 69-72; DLB 72

Malzberg, Barry N. 1939- .... **CLC 7**
See also CAAS 4; CANR 16; CA 61-64;
DLB 8

Mamet, David (Alan)
1947- .... **CLC 9, 15, 34, 46**
See also CANR 15; CA 81-84; DLB 7

Mamoulian, Rouben 1898- .... **CLC 16**
See also CA 25-28R

Mandelstam, Osip (Emilievich)
1891?-1938?............... **TCLC 2, 6**
See also CA 104

Mander, Jane 1877-1949 .... **TCLC 31**

Mandiargues, Andre Pieyre de
1909- .... **CLC 41**
See also CA 103

Manley, (Mary) Delariviere
1672?-1724.................... **LC 1**
See also DLB 39

Mann, (Luiz) Heinrich 1871-1950... **TCLC 9**
See also CA 106

Mann, Thomas
1875-1955 .... **TCLC 2, 8, 14, 21**
See also CA 104

Manning, Frederic 1882-1935 ..... **TCLC 25**

Manning, Olivia 1915-1980 ...... **CLC 5, 19**
See also CA 5-8R; obituary CA 101

Mano, D. Keith 1942- .... **CLC 2, 10**
See also CAAS 6; CA 25-28R; DLB 6

Mansfield, Katherine
1888-1923 .... **TCLC 2, 8**
See also CA 104

Manso, Peter 1940- .... **CLC 39**
See also CA 29-32R

Mapu, Abraham (ben Jekutiel)
1808-1867 .... **NCLC 18**

Marat, Jean Paul 1743-1793....... **LC 10**

Marcel, Gabriel (Honore)
1889-1973 .... **CLC 15**
See also CA 102; obituary CA 45-48

Marchbanks, Samuel 1913-
See Davies, (William) Robertson

Marie de l'Incarnation 1599-1672.... **LC 10**

Marinetti, F(ilippo) T(ommaso)
1876-1944 .... **TCLC 10**
See also CA 107

Marivaux, Pierre Carlet de Chamblain de
(1688-1763) .... **LC 4**

Markandaya, Kamala 1924-...... **CLC 8, 38**
See also Taylor, Kamala (Purnaiya)

Markfield, Wallace (Arthur) 1926-... **CLC 8**
See also CAAS 3; CA 69-72; DLB 2, 28

Markham, Robert 1922-
See Amis, Kingsley (William)

Marks, J. 1942-
See Highwater, Jamake

Marley, Bob 1945-1981 .... **CLC 17**
See also Marley, Robert Nesta

Marley, Robert Nesta 1945-1981
See Marley, Bob
See also CA 107; obituary CA 103

Marmontel, Jean-Francois
1723-1799 .... **LC 2**

Marquand, John P(hillips)
1893-1960 .... **CLC 2, 10**
See also CA 85-88; DLB 9

Marquez, Gabriel Garcia 1928-
See Garcia Marquez, Gabriel

Marquis, Don(ald Robert Perry)
1878-1937 .... **TCLC 7**
See also CA 104; DLB 11, 25

Marryat, Frederick 1792-1848 .... **NCLC 3**
See also DLB 21

Marsh, (Edith) Ngaio 1899-1982..... **CLC 7**
See also CANR 6; CA 9-12R

Marshall, Garry 1935?- .... **CLC 17**
See also CA 111

Marshall, Paule 1929- ..... **CLC 27; SSC 3**
See also CANR 25; CA 77-80; DLB 33

Marsten, Richard 1926-
See Hunter, Evan

Martin, Steve 1945?- .... **CLC 30**
See also CA 97-100

Martin du Gard, Roger
1881-1958 .... **TCLC 24**
See also CA 118

Martinez Ruiz, Jose 1874-1967
See Azorin
See also CA 93-96

Martinez Sierra, Gregorio 1881-1947 and
**Martinez Sierra, Maria (de la
O'LeJarraga)** 1880?-197 ...... **TCLC 6**

Martinez Sierra, Gregorio 1881-1947
See Martinez Sierra, Gregorio and Martinez
Sierra, Maria (de la O'LeJarraga)
See also CA 104, 115

Martinez Sierra, Maria (de la O'LeJarraga)
1880?-1974
See Martinez Sierra, Gregorio and Martinez
Sierra, Maria (de la O'LeJarraga)
See also obituary CA 115

Martinez Sierra, Maria (de la O'LeJarraga)
1880?-1974 and **Martinez Sierra,
Gregorio** 1881-194
See Martinez Sierra, Gregorio and Martinez
Sierra, Maria (de la O'LeJarraga)

Martinson, Harry (Edmund)
1904-1978 .... **CLC 14**
See also CA 77-80

Marvell, Andrew 1621-1678......... **LC 4**

Marx, Karl (Heinrich)
1818-1883 .... **NCLC 17**

Masaoka Shiki 1867-1902 .... **TCLC 18**

Masefield, John (Edward)
1878-1967 .... **CLC 11, 47**
See also CAP 2; CA 19-20;
obituary CA 25-28R; SATA 19; DLB 10,
19

Maso, Carole 19??-............... **CLC 44**

Mason, Bobbie Ann 1940-...... **CLC 28, 43**
See also CANR 11; CA 53-56; SAAS 1

Mason, Nick 1945-
See Pink Floyd

Mason, Tally 1909-1971
See Derleth, August (William)

Masters, Edgar Lee
1868?-1950............... **TCLC 2, 25**
See also CA 104; DLB 54;
CDALB 1865-1917

Masters, Hilary 1928- .... **CLC 48**
See also CANR 13; CA 25-28R

Mastrosimone, William 19??- ...... **CLC 36**

Matheson, Richard (Burton)
1926- .... **CLC 37**
See also CA 97-100; DLB 8, 44

Mathews, Harry 1930-............. **CLC 6**
See also CAAS 6; CANR 18; CA 21-24R

Mathias, Roland (Glyn) 1915-...... **CLC 45**
See also CANR 19; CA 97-100; DLB 27

Matthews, Greg 1949- .... **CLC 45**

Matthews, William 1942-.......... **CLC 40**
See also CANR 12; CA 29-32R; DLB 5

Matthias, John (Edward) 1941-...... **CLC 9**
See also CA 33-36R

Matthiessen, Peter 1927-... **CLC 5, 7, 11, 32**
See also CANR 21; CA 9-12R; SATA 27;
DLB 6

Maturin, Charles Robert
1780?-1824.................. **NCLC 6**

Matute, Ana Maria 1925- .... **CLC 11**
See also CA 89-92

Maugham, W(illiam) Somerset
1874-1965 .... **CLC 1, 11, 15**
See also CA 5-8R; obituary CA 25-28R;
DLB 10, 36

Maupassant, (Henri Rene Albert) Guy de
1850-1893 .... **NCLC 1; SSC 1**

Mauriac, Claude 1914-............. **CLC 9**
See also CA 89-92

Mauriac, Francois (Charles)
1885-1970 .... **CLC 4, 9**
See also CAP 2; CA 25-28

Mavor, Osborne Henry 1888-1951
See Bridie, James
See also CA 104

Meynell, Alice (Christiana Gertrude
    Thompson) 1847-1922 .... TCLC 6
    See also CA 104; DLB 19

Meyrink, Gustav 1868-1932 ...... TCLC 21
    See also Meyer-Meyrink, Gustav

Michaels, Leonard 1933- .... CLC 6, 25
    See also CANR 21; CA 61-64

Michaux, Henri 1899-1984 ...... CLC 8, 19
    See also CA 85-88; obituary CA 114

Michener, James A(lbert)
    1907- .... CLC 1, 5, 11, 29
    See also CANR 21; CA 5-8R; DLB 6

Mickiewicz, Adam 1798-1855 ..... NCLC 3

Middleton, Christopher 1926- ...... CLC 13
    See also CA 13-16R; DLB 40

Middleton, Stanley 1919- .... CLC 7, 38
    See also CANR 21; CA 25-28R; DLB 14

Migueis, Jose Rodrigues 1901- ..... CLC 10

Mikszath, Kalman 1847-1910 ..... TCLC 31

Miles, Josephine (Louise)
    1911-1985 ...... CLC 1, 2, 14, 34, 39
    See also CANR 2; CA 1-4R;
    obituary CA 116; DLB 48

Mill, John Stuart 1806-1873 ..... NCLC 11

Millar, Kenneth 1915-1983
    See Macdonald, Ross
    See also CANR 16; CA 9-12R;
    obituary CA 110; DLB 2; DLB-Y 83

Millay, Edna St. Vincent
    1892-1950 .... TCLC 4
    See also CA 104; DLB 45

Miller, Arthur
    1915- .... CLC 1, 2, 6, 10, 15, 26, 47
    See also CANR 2; CA 1-4R; DLB 7;
    CDALB 1941-1968

Miller, Henry (Valentine)
    1891-1980 .... CLC 1, 2, 4, 9, 14, 43
    See also CA 9-12R; obituary CA 97-100;
    DLB 4, 9; DLB-Y 80

Miller, Jason 1939?- .... CLC 2
    See also CA 73-76; DLB 7

Miller, Sue 19??- .... CLC 44

Miller, Walter M(ichael), Jr.
    1923- .... CLC 4, 30
    See also CA 85-88; DLB 8

Millhauser, Steven 1943- .... CLC 21, 54
    See also CA 108, 110, 111; DLB 2

Millin, Sarah Gertrude 1889-1968 .. CLC 49
    See also CA 102; obituary CA 93-96

Milne, A(lan) A(lexander)
    1882-1956 .... TCLC 6
    See also CLR 1; YABC 1; CA 104; DLB 10

Milosz, Czeslaw 1911- .... CLC 5, 11, 22, 31
    See also CA 81-84

Milton, John 1608-1674 .... LC 9

Miner, Valerie (Jane) 1947- .... CLC 40
    See also CA 97-100

Minot, Susan 1956- .... CLC 44

Minus, Ed 1938- .... CLC 39

Miro (Ferrer), Gabriel (Francisco Victor)
    1879-1930 .... TCLC 5
    See also CA 104

Mishima, Yukio
    1925-1970 .... CLC 2, 4, 6, 9, 27
    See also Hiraoka, Kimitake

Mistral, Gabriela 1889-1957 ...... TCLC 2
    See also CA 104

Mitchell, James Leslie 1901-1935
    See Gibbon, Lewis Grassic
    See also CA 104; DLB 15

Mitchell, Joni 1943- .... CLC 12
    See also CA 112

Mitchell (Marsh), Margaret (Munnerlyn)
    1900-1949 .... TCLC 11
    See also CA 109; DLB 9

Mitchell, W(illiam) O(rmond)
    1914- .... CLC 25
    See also CANR 15; CA 77-80

Mitford, Mary Russell 1787-1855 .. NCLC 4

Mitford, Nancy 1904-1973 .... CLC 44
    See also CA 9-12R

Mo, Timothy 1950- .... CLC 46
    See also CA 117

Modarressi, Taghi 1931- .... CLC 44
    See also CA 121

Modiano, Patrick (Jean) 1945- ..... CLC 18
    See also CANR 17; CA 85-88

Mofolo, Thomas (Mokopu)
    1876-1948 .... TCLC 22
    See also CA 121

Mohr, Nicholasa 1935- .... CLC 12
    See also CANR 1; CA 49-52; SATA 8

Mojtabai, A(nn) G(race)
    1938- .... CLC 5, 9, 15, 29
    See also CA 85-88

Moliere 1622-1673 .... LC 10

Molnar, Ferenc 1878-1952 .... TCLC 20
    See also CA 109

Momaday, N(avarre) Scott
    1934- .... CLC 2, 19
    See also CANR 14; CA 25-28R; SATA 30,
    48

Monroe, Harriet 1860-1936 ...... TCLC 12
    See also CA 109; DLB 54

Montagu, Elizabeth 1720-1800 .... NCLC 7

Montagu, Lady Mary (Pierrepont) Wortley
    1689-1762 .... LC 9

Montague, John (Patrick)
    1929- .... CLC 13, 46
    See also CANR 9; CA 9-12R; DLB 40

Montaigne, Michel (Eyquem) de
    1533-1592 .... LC 8

Montale, Eugenio 1896-1981 ... CLC 7, 9, 18
    See also CA 17-20R; obituary CA 104

Montgomery, Marion (H., Jr.)
    1925- .... CLC 7
    See also CANR 3; CA 1-4R; DLB 6

Montgomery, Robert Bruce 1921-1978
    See Crispin, Edmund
    See also CA 104

Montherlant, Henri (Milon) de
    1896-1972 .... CLC 8, 19
    See also CA 85-88; obituary CA 37-40R;
    DLB 72

Montisquieu, Charles-Louis de Secondat
    1689-1755 .... LC 7

Monty Python .... CLC 21
    See also Cleese, John
    See also Gilliam, Terry (Vance); Idle, Eric;
    Jones, Terry; Palin, Michael

Moodie, Susanna (Strickland)
    1803-1885 .... NCLC 14

Mooney, Ted 1951- .... CLC 25

Moorcock, Michael (John)
    1939- .... CLC 5, 27
    See also CAAS 5; CANR 2, 17; CA 45-48;
    DLB 14

Moore, Brian
    1921- .... CLC 1, 3, 5, 7, 8, 19, 32
    See also CANR 1; CA 1-4R

Moore, George (Augustus)
    1852-1933 .... TCLC 7
    See also CA 104; DLB 10, 18, 57

Moore, Lorrie 1957- .... CLC 39, 45
    See also Moore, Marie Lorena

Moore, Marianne (Craig)
    1887-1972 ... CLC 1, 2, 4, 8, 10, 13, 19,
                                              47
    See also CANR 3; CA 1-4R;
    obituary CA 33-36R; SATA 20; DLB 45

Moore, Marie Lorena 1957-
    See Moore, Lorrie
    See also CA 116

Moore, Thomas 1779-1852 .... NCLC 6

Morand, Paul 1888-1976 .... CLC 41
    See also obituary CA 69-72

Morante, Elsa 1918-1985 .... CLC 8, 47
    See also CA 85-88; obituary CA 117

Moravia, Alberto
    1907- .... CLC 2, 7, 11, 18, 27, 46
    See also Pincherle, Alberto

More, Henry 1614-1687 .... LC 9

More, Thomas 1478-1573 .... LC 10

Moreas, Jean 1856-1910 .... TCLC 18

Morgan, Berry 1919- .... CLC 6
    See also CA 49-52; DLB 6

Morgan, Edwin (George) 1920- ..... CLC 31
    See also CANR 3; CA 7-8R; DLB 27

Morgan, (George) Frederick
    1922- .... CLC 23
    See also CANR 21; CA 17-20R

Morgan, Janet 1945- .... CLC 39
    See also CA 65-68

Morgan, Robin 1941- .... CLC 2
    See also CA 69-72

Morgenstern, Christian (Otto Josef Wolfgang)
    1871-1914 .... TCLC 8
    See also CA 105

Moricz, Zsigmond 1879-1942 ..... TCLC 33

Morike, Eduard (Friedrich)
    1804-1875 .... NCLC 10

Mori Ogai 1862-1922 .... TCLC 14
    See also Mori Rintaro

Mori Rintaro 1862-1922
    See Mori Ogai
    See also CA 110

Moritz, Karl Philipp 1756-1793 ..... LC 2

Morris, Julian 1916-
    See West, Morris L.

Orton, John Kingsley 1933?-1967
  See Orton, Joe
  See also CA 85-88

Orwell, George
  1903-1950 .... TCLC 2, 6, 15, 31
  See also Blair, Eric Arthur
  See also DLB 15

Osborne, John (James)
  1929- .... CLC 1, 2, 5, 11, 45
  See also CANR 21; CA 13-16R; DLB 13

Osborne, Lawrence 1958- .... CLC 50

Osceola 1885-1962
  See Dinesen, Isak
  See also Blixen, Karen (Christentze
  Dinesen)

Oshima, Nagisa 1932- .... CLC 20
  See also CA 116

Ossoli, Sarah Margaret (Fuller marchesa d')
  1810-1850
  See Fuller, (Sarah) Margaret
  See also SATA 25

Otero, Blas de 1916- .... CLC 11
  See also CA 89-92

Owen, Wilfred (Edward Salter)
  1893-1918 .... TCLC 5, 27
  See also CA 104; DLB 20

Owens, Rochelle 1936-............ CLC 8
  See also CAAS 2; CA 17-20R

Owl, Sebastian 1939-
  See Thompson, Hunter S(tockton)

Oz, Amos 1939- ... CLC 5, 8, 11, 27, 33, 54
  See also CA 53-56

Ozick, Cynthia 1928-......... CLC 3, 7, 28
  See also CA 17-20R; DLB 28; DLB-Y 82

Ozu, Yasujiro 1903-1963 .... CLC 16
  See also CA 112

Pa Chin 1904-.................... CLC 18
  See also Li Fei-kan

Pack, Robert 1929-.............. CLC 13
  See also CANR 3; CA 1-4R; DLB 5

Padgett, Lewis 1915-1958
  See Kuttner, Henry

Padilla, Heberto 1932-............ CLC 38

Page, Jimmy 1944- and Plant, Robert
  1948- .... CLC 12

Page, Jimmy 1944-
  See Page, Jimmy and Plant, Robert

Page, Louise 1955-.............. CLC 40

Page, P(atricia) K(athleen)
  1916- .... CLC 7, 18
  See also CANR 4; CA 53-56

Paget, Violet 1856-1935
  See Lee, Vernon
  See also CA 104

Palamas, Kostes 1859-1943 .... TCLC 5
  See also CA 105

Palazzeschi, Aldo 1885-1974 .... CLC 11
  See also CA 89-92; obituary CA 53-56

Paley, Grace 1922-.......... CLC 4, 6, 37
  See also CANR 13; CA 25-28R; DLB 28

Palin, Michael 1943-
  See Monty Python
  See also CA 107

Palma, Ricardo 1833-1919....... TCLC 29

Pancake, Breece Dexter 1952-1979
  See Pancake, Breece D'J

Pancake, Breece D'J 1952-1979 .... CLC 29
  See also obituary CA 109

Papadiamantis, Alexandros
  1851-1911 .... TCLC 29

Papini, Giovanni 1881-1956...... TCLC 22
  See also CA 121

Parini, Jay (Lee) 1948- .... CLC 54
  See also CA 97-100

Parker, Dorothy (Rothschild)
  1893-1967 .... CLC 15; SSC 2
  See also CAP 2; CA 19-20;
   obituary CA 25-28R; DLB 11, 45

Parker, Robert B(rown) 1932-...... CLC 27
  See also CANR 1; CA 49-52

Parkin, Frank 1940-.............. CLC 43

Parkman, Francis 1823-1893 ..... NCLC 12
  See also DLB 1, 30

Parks, Gordon (Alexander Buchanan)
  1912- .... CLC 1, 16
  See also CA 41-44R; SATA 8; DLB 33

Parnell, Thomas 1679-1718......... LC 3

Parra, Nicanor 1914-............. CLC 2
  See also CA 85-88

Pasolini, Pier Paolo
  1922-1975 .... CLC 20, 37
  See also CA 93-96; obituary CA 61-64

Pastan, Linda (Olenik) 1932- ...... CLC 27
  See also CANR 18; CA 61-64; DLB 5

Pasternak, Boris 1890-1960... CLC 7, 10, 18
  See also obituary CA 116

Patchen, Kenneth 1911-1972... CLC 1, 2, 18
  See also CANR 3; CA 1-4R;
   obituary CA 33-36R; DLB 16, 48

Pater, Walter (Horatio)
  1839-1894 .... NCLC 7
  See also DLB 57

Paterson, Katherine (Womeldorf)
  1932- .... CLC 12, 30
  See also CLR 7; CA 21-24R; SATA 13, 53;
  DLB 52

Patmore, Coventry Kersey Dighton
  1823-1896 .... NCLC 9
  See also DLB 35

Paton, Alan (Stewart)
  1903-1988 .... CLC 4, 10, 25, 55
  See also CANR 22; CAP 1; CA 15-16;
   obituary CA 125; SATA 11

Paulding, James Kirke 1778-1860.. NCLC 2
  See also DLB 3

Paulin, Tom 1949- .... CLC 37
  See also DLB 40

Paustovsky, Konstantin (Georgievich)
  1892-1968 .... CLC 40
  See also CA 93-96; obituary CA 25-28R

Paustowsky, Konstantin (Georgievich)
  1892-1968
  See Paustovsky, Konstantin (Georgievich)

Pavese, Cesare 1908-1950 .... TCLC 3
  See also CA 104

Payne, Alan 1932-
  See Jakes, John (William)

Paz, Octavio 1914-.. CLC 3, 4, 6, 10, 19, 51
  See also CA 73-76

Peake, Mervyn 1911-1968....... CLC 7, 54
  See also CANR 3; CA 5-8R;
   obituary CA 25-28R; SATA 23; DLB 15

Pearce, (Ann) Philippa 1920-....... CLC 21
  See also Christie, (Ann) Philippa
  See also CA 5-8R; SATA 1

Pearl, Eric 1934-
  See Elman, Richard

Pearson, T(homas) R(eid) 1956- .... CLC 39
  See also CA 120

Peck, John 1941-................. CLC 3
  See also CANR 3; CA 49-52

Peck, Richard 1934-.............. CLC 21
  See also CLR 15; CANR 19; CA 85-88;
  SAAS 2; SATA 18

Peck, Robert Newton 1928-........ CLC 17
  See also CA 81-84; SAAS 1; SATA 21

Peckinpah, (David) Sam(uel)
  1925-1984 .... CLC 20
  See also CA 109; obituary CA 114

Pedersen, Knut 1859-1952
  See Hamsun, Knut
  See also CA 104

Peguy, Charles (Pierre)
  1873-1914 .... TCLC 10
  See also CA 107

Pepys, Samuel 1633-1703........... LC 11

Percy, Walker
  1916- .... CLC 2, 3, 6, 8, 14, 18, 47
  See also CANR 1; CA 1-4R; DLB 2;
  DLB-Y 80

Pereda, Jose Maria de
  1833-1906 .... TCLC 16

Perelman, S(idney) J(oseph)
  1904-1979 ... CLC 3, 5, 9, 15, 23, 44, 49
  See also CANR 18; CA 73-76;
   obituary CA 89-92; DLB 11, 44

Peret, Benjamin 1899-1959 .... TCLC 20
  See also CA 117

Peretz, Isaac Leib 1852?-1915..... TCLC 16
  See also CA 109

Perez, Galdos Benito 1853-1920 ... TCLC 27

Perrault, Charles 1628-1703 .... LC 2
  See also SATA 25

Perse, St.-John 1887-1975.... CLC 4, 11, 46
  See also Leger, (Marie-Rene) Alexis
  Saint-Leger

Pesetsky, Bette 1932-............. CLC 28

Peshkov, Alexei Maximovich 1868-1936
  See Gorky, Maxim
  See also CA 105

Pessoa, Fernando (Antonio Nogueira)
  1888-1935 .... TCLC 27

Peterkin, Julia (Mood) 1880-1961... CLC 31
  See also CA 102; DLB 9

Peters, Joan K. 1945-............. CLC 39

Peters, Robert L(ouis) 1924-........ CLC 7
  See also CA 13-16R

Petrakis, Harry Mark 1923-........ CLC 3
  See also CANR 4; CA 9-12R

Puig, Manuel 1932- .... CLC **3, 5, 10, 28**
See also CANR 2; CA 45-48

Purdy, A(lfred) W(ellington)
1918- ....CLC **3, 6, 14, 50**
See also CA 81-84

Purdy, James (Amos)
1923- .... CLC **2, 4, 10, 28**
See also CAAS 1; CANR 19; CA 33-36R;
DLB 2

Pushkin, Alexander (Sergeyevich)
1799-1837 .... NCLC **3**

P'u Sung-ling 1640-1715 .... LC **3**

Puzo, Mario 1920- .... CLC **1, 2, 6, 36**
See also CANR 4; CA 65-68; DLB 6

Pym, Barbara (Mary Crampton)
1913-1980 .... CLC **13, 19, 37**
See also CANR 13; CAP 1; CA 13-14;
obituary CA 97-100; DLB 14

Pynchon, Thomas (Ruggles, Jr.)
1937- .... CLC **2, 3, 6, 9, 11, 18, 33**
See also CANR 22; CA 17-20R; DLB 2

Quasimodo, Salvatore 1901-1968 ... CLC **10**
See also CAP 1; CA 15-16;
obituary CA 25-28R

Queen, Ellery 1905-1982 .... CLC **3, 11**
See also Dannay, Frederic
See also Lee, Manfred B(ennington)

Queneau, Raymond
1903-1976 .... CLC **2, 5, 10, 42**
See also CA 77-80; obituary CA 69-72;
DLB 72

Quin, Ann (Marie) 1936-1973 .... CLC **6**
See also CA 9-12R; obituary CA 45-48;
DLB 14

Quinn, Simon 1942-
See Smith, Martin Cruz

Quiroga, Horacio (Sylvestre)
1878-1937 .... TCLC **20**
See also CA 117

Quoirez, Francoise 1935-
See Sagan, Francoise
See also CANR 6; CA 49-52

Rabe, David (William) 1940-... CLC **4, 8, 33**
See also CA 85-88; DLB 7

Rabelais, Francois 1494?-1553........ LC **5**

Rabinovitch, Sholem 1859-1916
See Aleichem, Sholom
See also CA 104

Rachen, Kurt von 1911-1986
See Hubbard, L(afayette) Ron(ald)

Radcliffe, Ann (Ward) 1764-1823 .. NCLC **6**
See also DLB 39

Radiguet, Raymond 1903-1923 .... TCLC **29**

Radnoti, Miklos 1909-1944 ...... TCLC **16**
See also CA 118

Rado, James 1939-
See Ragni, Gerome andRado, James
See also CA 105

Radomski, James 1932-
See Rado, James

Radvanyi, Netty Reiling 1900-1983
See Seghers, Anna
See also CA 85-88; obituary CA 110

Raeburn, John 1941- .... CLC **34**
See also CA 57-60

Ragni, Gerome 1942- and **Rado, James**
1939- .... CLC **17**

Ragni, Gerome 1942-
See Ragni, Gerome and Rado, James
See also CA 105

Rahv, Philip 1908-1973 .... CLC **24**
See also Greenberg, Ivan

Raine, Craig 1944- .... CLC **32**
See also CA 108; DLB 40

Raine, Kathleen (Jessie) 1908- ... CLC **7, 45**
See also CA 85-88; DLB 20

Rainis, Janis 1865-1929 .... TCLC **29**

Rakosi, Carl 1903- .... CLC **47**
See also Rawley, Callman
See also CAAS 5

Rampersad, Arnold 19??- .... CLC **44**

Ramuz, Charles-Ferdinand
1878-1947 .... TCLC **33**

Rand, Ayn 1905-1982 .... CLC **3, 30, 44**
See also CA 13-16R; obituary CA 105

Randall, Dudley (Felker) 1914-...... CLC **1**
See also CA 25-28R; DLB 41

Ransom, John Crowe
1888-1974 .... CLC **2, 4, 5, 11, 24**
See also CANR 6; CA 5-8R;
obituary CA 49-52; DLB 45, 63

Rao, Raja 1909- .... CLC **25**
See also CA 73-76

Raphael, Frederic (Michael)
1931- .... CLC **2, 14**
See also CANR 1; CA 1-4R; DLB 14

Rathbone, Julian 1935- .... CLC **41**
See also CA 101

Rattigan, Terence (Mervyn)
1911-1977 .... CLC **7**
See also CA 85-88; obituary CA 73-76;
DLB 13

Ratushinskaya, Irina 1954- .... CLC **54**

Raven, Simon (Arthur Noel)
1927- .... CLC **14**
See also CA 81-84

Rawley, Callman 1903-
See Rakosi, Carl
See also CANR 12; CA 21-24R

Rawlings, Marjorie Kinnan
1896-1953 .... TCLC **4**
See also YABC 1; CA 104; DLB 9, 22

Ray, Satyajit 1921-............... CLC **16**
See also CA 114

Read, Herbert (Edward) 1893-1968 .. CLC **4**
See also CA 85-88; obituary CA 25-28R;
DLB 20

Read, Piers Paul 1941- ...... CLC **4, 10, 25**
See also CA 21-24R; SATA 21; DLB 14

Reade, Charles 1814-1884 .... NCLC **2**
See also DLB 21

Reade, Hamish 1936-
See Gray, Simon (James Holliday)

Reading, Peter 1946- .... CLC **47**
See also CA 103; DLB 40

Reaney, James 1926-............. CLC **13**
See also CA 41-44R; SATA 43

Rebreanu, Liviu 1885-1944 .... TCLC **28**

Rechy, John (Francisco)
1934-................CLC **1, 7, 14, 18**
See also CAAS 4; CANR 6; CA 5-8R;
DLB-Y 82

Redcam, Tom 1870-1933 .... TCLC **25**

Redgrove, Peter (William)
1932- .... CLC **6, 41**
See also CANR 3; CA 1-4R; DLB 40

Redmon (Nightingale), Anne
1943- .... CLC **22**
See also Nightingale, Anne Redmon
See also DLB-Y 86

Reed, Ishmael 1938-.. CLC **2, 3, 5, 6, 13, 32**
See also CA 21-24R; DLB 2, 5, 33

Reed, John (Silas) 1887-1920 ...... TCLC **9**
See also CA 106

Reed, Lou 1944-................. CLC **21**

Reeve, Clara 1729-1807 .... NCLC **19**
See also DLB 39

Reid, Christopher 1949-........... CLC **33**
See also DLB 40

Reid Banks, Lynne 1929-
See Banks, Lynne Reid
See also CANR 6, 22; CA 1-4R; SATA 22

Reiner, Max 1900-
See Caldwell, (Janet Miriam) Taylor
(Holland)

Reizenstein, Elmer Leopold 1892-1967
See Rice, Elmer

Remark, Erich Paul 1898-1970
See Remarque, Erich Maria

Remarque, Erich Maria
1898-1970 .... CLC **21**
See also CA 77-80; obituary CA 29-32R

Remizov, Alexey (Mikhailovich)
1877-1957 .... TCLC **27**

Renard, Jules 1864-1910 .... TCLC **17**
See also CA 117

Renault, Mary 1905-1983 .... CLC **3, 11, 17**
See also Challans, Mary
See also DLB-Y 83

Rendell, Ruth 1930-........... CLC **28, 48**
See also Vine, Barbara
See also CA 109

Renoir, Jean 1894-1979 .... CLC **20**
See also obituary CA 85-88

Resnais, Alain 1922-.............. CLC **16**

Rexroth, Kenneth
1905-1982 ...... CLC **1, 2, 6, 11, 22, 49**
See also CANR 14; CA 5-8R;
obituary CA 107; DLB 16, 48; DLB-Y 82;
CDALB 1941-1968

Reyes, Alfonso 1889-1959 .... TCLC **33**

Reyes y Basoalto, Ricardo Eliecer Neftali
1904-1973
See Neruda, Pablo

Reymont, Wladyslaw Stanislaw
1867-1925 .... TCLC **5**
See also CA 104

Reynolds, Jonathan 1942?- ...... CLC **6, 38**
See also CA 65-68

Reynolds, Michael (Shane)   1937-... **CLC 44**
See also CANR 9; CA 65-68

Reznikoff, Charles   1894-1976 .... **CLC 9**
See also CAP 2; CA 33-36;
   obituary CA 61-64; DLB 28, 45

Rezzori, Gregor von   1914-........ **CLC 25**

Rhys, Jean
   1890-1979 ...... **CLC 2, 4, 6, 14, 19, 51**
See also CA 25-28R; obituary CA 85-88;
   DLB 36

Ribeiro, Darcy   1922-............. **CLC 34**
See also CA 33-36R

Ribeiro, Joao Ubaldo (Osorio Pimentel)
   1941-...................... **CLC 10**
See also CA 81-84

Ribman, Ronald (Burt)   1932- .... **CLC 7**
See also CA 21-24R

Rice, Anne   1941- .... **CLC 41**
See also CANR 12; CA 65-68

Rice, Elmer   1892-1967......... **CLC 7, 49**
See also CAP 2; CA 21-22;
   obituary CA 25-28R; DLB 4, 7

Rice, Tim   1944- and Webber, Andrew Lloyd
   1948-...................... **CLC 21**

Rice, Tim   1944-
See Rice, Tim and Webber, Andrew Lloyd
See also CA 103

Rich, Adrienne (Cecile)
   1929-......... **CLC 3, 6, 7, 11, 18, 36**
See also CANR 20; CA 9-12R; DLB 5

Richard, Keith   1943-
See Jagger, Mick and Richard, Keith

Richards, I(vor) A(rmstrong)
   1893-1979 .... **CLC 14, 24**
See also CA 41-44R; obituary CA 89-92;
   DLB 27

Richards, Keith   1943-
See Richard, Keith
See also CA 107

Richardson, Dorothy (Miller)
   1873-1957 .... **TCLC 3**
See also CA 104; DLB 36

Richardson, Ethel   1870-1946
See Richardson, Henry Handel
See also CA 105

Richardson, Henry Handel
   1870-1946 .... **TCLC 4**
See also Richardson, Ethel

Richardson, Samuel   1689-1761 .... **LC 1**
See also DLB 39

Richler, Mordecai
   1931-......... **CLC 3, 5, 9, 13, 18, 46**
See also CA 65-68; SATA 27, 44; DLB 53

Richter, Conrad (Michael)
   1890-1968 .... **CLC 30**
See also CA 5-8R; obituary CA 25-28R;
   SATA 3; DLB 9

Richter, Johann Paul Friedrich   1763-1825
See Jean Paul

Riding, Laura   1901-............. **CLC 3, 7**
See also Jackson, Laura (Riding)

Riefenstahl, Berta Helene Amalia   1902-
See Riefenstahl, Leni
See also CA 108

Riefenstahl, Leni   1902- .... **CLC 16**
See also Riefenstahl, Berta Helene Amalia

Rilke, Rainer Maria
   1875-1926 .... **TCLC 1, 6, 19**
See also CA 104

Rimbaud, (Jean Nicolas) Arthur
   1854-1891 .... **NCLC 4**

Ringwood, Gwen(dolyn Margaret) Pharis
   1910-1984 .... **CLC 48**
See also obituary CA 112

Rio, Michel   19??-................ **CLC 43**

Ritsos, Yannis   1909-........ **CLC 6, 13, 31**
See also CA 77-80

Rivers, Conrad Kent   1933-1968...... **CLC 1**
See also CA 85-88; DLB 41

Roa Bastos, Augusto   1917- .... **CLC 45**

Robbe-Grillet, Alain
   1922-...... **CLC 1, 2, 4, 6, 8, 10, 14, 43**
See also CA 9-12R

Robbins, Harold   1916-............. **CLC 5**
See also CA 73-76

Robbins, Thomas Eugene   1936-
See Robbins, Tom
See also CA 81-84

Robbins, Tom   1936-............ **CLC 9, 32**
See also Robbins, Thomas Eugene
See also DLB-Y 80

Robbins, Trina   1938-............. **CLC 21**

Roberts, (Sir) Charles G(eorge) D(ouglas)
   1860-1943 .... **TCLC 8**
See also CA 105; SATA 29

Roberts, Kate   1891-1985 .... **CLC 15**
See also CA 107; obituary CA 116

Roberts, Keith (John Kingston)
   1935-.................... **CLC 14**
See also CA 25-28R

Roberts, Kenneth   1885-1957 ...... **TCLC 23**
See also CA 109; DLB 9

Roberts, Michele (B.)   1949-........ **CLC 48**
See also CA 115

Robinson, Edwin Arlington
   1869-1935 .... **TCLC 5**
See also CA 104; DLB 54;
   CDALB 1865-1917

Robinson, Henry Crabb
   1775-1867 .... **NCLC 15**

Robinson, Jill   1936-............. **CLC 10**
See also CA 102

Robinson, Kim Stanley   19??-....... **CLC 34**

Robinson, Marilynne   1944-........ **CLC 25**
See also CA 116

Robinson, Smokey   1940-.......... **CLC 21**

Robinson, William   1940-
See Robinson, Smokey
See also CA 116

Robison, Mary   1949-............. **CLC 42**
See also CA 113, 116

Roddenberry, Gene   1921-.......... **CLC 17**

Rodgers, Mary   1931-............. **CLC 12**
See also CANR 8; CA 49-52; SATA 8

Rodgers, W(illiam) R(obert)
   1909-1969 .... **CLC 7**
See also CA 85-88; DLB 20

Rodriguez, Claudio   1934-......... **CLC 10**

Roethke, Theodore (Huebner)
   1908-1963 ...... **CLC 1, 3, 8, 11, 19, 46**
See also CA 81-84; CABS 2; SAAS 1;
   DLB 5; CDALB 1941-1968

Rogers, Sam   1943-
See Shepard, Sam

Rogers, Will(iam Penn Adair)
   1879-1935 .... **TCLC 8**
See also CA 105; DLB 11

Rogin, Gilbert   1929-............. **CLC 18**
See also CANR 15; CA 65-68

Rohan, Koda   1867-1947.......... **TCLC 22**

Rohmer, Eric   1920- .... **CLC 16**
See also Scherer, Jean-Marie Maurice

Rohmer, Sax   1883-1959 .... **TCLC 28**
See also Ward, Arthur Henry Sarsfield
See also DLB 70

Roiphe, Anne (Richardson)
   1935-.................... **CLC 3, 9**
See also CA 89-92; DLB-Y 80

Rolfe, Frederick (William Serafino Austin
   Lewis Mary)   1860-1913...... **TCLC 12**
See also CA 107; DLB 34

Rolland, Romain   1866-1944....... **TCLC 23**
See also CA 118

Rolvaag, O(le) E(dvart)
   1876-1931 .... **TCLC 17**
See also CA 117; DLB 9

Romains, Jules   1885-1972 .... **CLC 7**
See also CA 85-88

Romero, Jose Ruben   1890-1952 ... **TCLC 14**
See also CA 114

Ronsard, Pierre de   1524-1585........ **LC 6**

Rooke, Leon   1934-............ **CLC 25, 34**
See also CA 25-28R

Roper, William   1498-1578.......... **LC 10**

Rosa, Joao Guimaraes   1908-1967... **CLC 23**
See also obituary CA 89-92

Rosen, Richard (Dean)   1949-....... **CLC 39**
See also CA 77-80

Rosenberg, Isaac   1890-1918....... **TCLC 12**
See also CA 107; DLB 20

Rosenblatt, Joe   1933-............. **CLC 15**
See also Rosenblatt, Joseph

Rosenblatt, Joseph   1933-
See Rosenblatt, Joe
See also CA 89-92

Rosenfeld, Samuel   1896-1963
See Tzara, Tristan
See also obituary CA 89-92

Rosenthal, M(acha) L(ouis)   1917-... **CLC 28**
See also CAAS 6; CANR 4; CA 1-4R;
   DLB 5

Ross, (James) Sinclair   1908-....... **CLC 13**
See also CA 73-76

Rossetti, Christina Georgina
   1830-1894 .... **NCLC 2**
See also SATA 20; DLB 35

Rossetti, Dante Gabriel
   1828-1882 .... **NCLC 4**
See also DLB 35

Rossetti, Gabriel Charles Dante 1828-1882
  See Rossetti, Dante Gabriel

Rossner, Judith (Perelman)
    1935- .... **CLC 6, 9, 29**
  See also CANR 18; CA 17-20R; DLB 6

Rostand, Edmond (Eugene Alexis)
    1868-1918 .... **TCLC 6**
  See also CA 104

Roth, Henry 1906- .... **CLC 2, 6, 11**
  See also CAP 1; CA 11-12; DLB 28

Roth, Joseph 1894-1939......... **TCLC 33**

Roth, Philip (Milton)
    1933- ...... **CLC 1, 2, 3, 4, 6, 9, 15, 22,
                                   31, 47**
  See also CANR 1, 22; CA 1-4R; DLB 2, 28;
    DLB-Y 82

Rothenberg, Jerome 1931-......... **CLC 6**
  See also CANR 1; CA 45-48; DLB 5

Roumain, Jacques 1907-1944...... **TCLC 19**
  See also CA 117

Rourke, Constance (Mayfield)
    1885-1941 .... **TCLC 12**
  See also YABC 1; CA 107

Rousseau, Jean-Baptiste 1671-1741 ... **LC 9**

Roussel, Raymond 1877-1933 ..... **TCLC 20**
  See also CA 117

Rovit, Earl (Herbert) 1927-......... **CLC 7**
  See also CANR 12; CA 5-8R

Rowe, Nicholas 1674-1718........... **LC 8**

Rowson, Susanna Haswell
    1762-1824 .... **NCLC 5**
  See also DLB 37

Roy, Gabrielle 1909-1983....... **CLC 10, 14**
  See also CANR 5; CA 53-56;
    obituary CA 110

Rozewicz, Tadeusz 1921-........ **CLC 9, 23**
  See also CA 108

Ruark, Gibbons 1941- .... **CLC 3**
  See also CANR 14; CA 33-36R

Rubens, Bernice 192?- .... **CLC 19, 31**
  See also CA 25-28R; DLB 14

Rudkin, (James) David 1936- ...... **CLC 14**
  See also CA 89-92; DLB 13

Rudnik, Raphael 1933-............. **CLC 7**
  See also CA 29-32R

Ruiz, Jose Martinez 1874-1967
  See Azorin

Rukeyser, Muriel
    1913-1980 .... **CLC 6, 10, 15, 27**
  See also CA 5-8R; obituary CA 93-96;
    obituary SATA 22; DLB 48

Rule, Jane (Vance) 1931-......... **CLC 27**
  See also CANR 12; CA 25-28R; DLB 60

Rulfo, Juan 1918-1986............. **CLC 8**
  See also CA 85-88; obituary CA 118

Runyon, (Alfred) Damon
    1880-1946 .... **TCLC 10**
  See also CA 107; DLB 11

Rush, Norman 1933-............. **CLC 44**
  See also CA 121

Rushdie, (Ahmed) Salman
    1947- .... **CLC 23, 31, 55**
  See also CA 108, 111

Rushforth, Peter (Scott) 1945- ..... **CLC 19**
  See also CA 101

Ruskin, John 1819-1900......... **TCLC 20**
  See also CA 114; SATA 24; DLB 55

Russ, Joanna 1937-.............. **CLC 15**
  See also CANR 11; CA 25-28R; DLB 8

Russell, George William 1867-1935
  See A. E.
  See also CA 104

Russell, (Henry) Ken(neth Alfred)
    1927- .... **CLC 16**
  See also CA 105

Rutherford, Mark 1831-1913...... **TCLC 25**
  See also DLB 18

Ruyslinck, Ward 1929-........... **CLC 14**

Ryan, Cornelius (John) 1920-1974 ... **CLC 7**
  See also CA 69-72; obituary CA 53-56

Rybakov, Anatoli 1911?- .... **CLC 23**

Ryder, Jonathan 1927-
  See Ludlum, Robert

Ryga, George 1932- .... **CLC 14**
  See also CA 101; DLB 60

**Séviné, Marquise de Marie de
    Rabutin-Chantal** 1626-1696..... **LC 11**

Saba, Umberto 1883-1957 .... **TCLC 33**

Sabato, Ernesto 1911- .... **CLC 10, 23**
  See also CA 97-100

Sachs, Marilyn (Stickle) 1927- ..... **CLC 35**
  See also CLR 2; CANR 13; CA 17-20R;
    SAAS 2; SATA 3, 52

Sachs, Nelly 1891-1970 .... **CLC 14**
  See also CAP 2; CA 17-18;
    obituary CA 25-28R

Sackler, Howard (Oliver)
    1929-1982 .... **CLC 14**
  See also CA 61-64; obituary CA 108; DLB 7

Sade, Donatien Alphonse Francois, Comte de
    1740-1814 .... **NCLC 3**

Sadoff, Ira 1945-................. **CLC 9**
  See also CANR 5, 21; CA 53-56

Safire, William 1929-............. **CLC 10**
  See also CA 17-20R

Sagan, Carl (Edward) 1934-....... **CLC 30**
  See also CANR 11; CA 25-28R

Sagan, Francoise
    1935- .... **CLC 3, 6, 9, 17, 36**
  See also Quoirez, Francoise

Sahgal, Nayantara (Pandit) 1927-... **CLC 41**
  See also CANR 11; CA 9-12R

Saint, H(arry) F. 1941- .... **CLC 50**

Sainte-Beuve, Charles Augustin
    1804-1869 .... **NCLC 5**

Sainte-Marie, Beverly 1941-
  See Sainte-Marie, Buffy
  See also CA 107

Sainte-Marie, Buffy 1941-......... **CLC 17**
  See also Sainte-Marie, Beverly

**Saint-Exupery, Antoine (Jean Baptiste Marie
    Roger) de** 1900-1944 .... **TCLC 2**
  See also CLR 10; CA 108; SATA 20;
    DLB 72

Saintsbury, George 1845-1933..... **TCLC 31**

Sait Faik (Abasiyanik)
    1906-1954 .... **TCLC 23**

Saki 1870-1916............... **TCLC 3**
  See also Munro, H(ector) H(ugh)

Salama, Hannu 1936-............. **CLC 18**

Salamanca, J(ack) R(ichard)
    1922- .... **CLC 4, 15**
  See also CA 25-28R

Salinas, Pedro 1891-1951........ **TCLC 17**
  See also CA 117

Salinger, J(erome) D(avid)
    1919- .... **CLC 1, 3, 8, 12; SSC 2**
  See also CA 5-8R; DLB 2;
    CDALB 1941-1968

Salter, James 1925- .... **CLC 7**
  See also CA 73-76

Saltus, Edgar (Everston)
    1855-1921 .... **TCLC 8**
  See also CA 105

Saltykov, Mikhail Evgrafovich
    1826-1889 .... **NCLC 16**

Samarakis, Antonis 1919- .... **CLC 5**
  See also CA 25-28R

Sanchez, Luis Rafael 1936-........ **CLC 23**

Sanchez, Sonia 1934-.............. **CLC 5**
  See also CA 33-36R; SATA 22; DLB 41

Sand, George 1804-1876......... **NCLC 2**

Sandburg, Carl (August)
    1878-1967 ...... **CLC 1, 4, 10, 15, 35**
  See also CA 5-8R; obituary CA 25-28R;
    SATA 8; DLB 17, 54; CDALB 1865-1917

Sandburg, Charles August 1878-1967
  See Sandburg, Carl (August)

Sanders, Lawrence 1920-.......... **CLC 41**
  See also CA 81-84

Sandoz, Mari (Susette) 1896-1966 .. **CLC 28**
  See also CANR 17; CA 1-4R;
    obituary CA 25-28R; SATA 5; DLB 9

Saner, Reg(inald Anthony) 1931- .... **CLC 9**
  See also CA 65-68

Sannazaro, Jacopo 1456?-1530 .... **LC 8**

Sansom, William 1912-1976....... **CLC 2, 6**
  See also CA 5-8R; obituary CA 65-68

Santiago, Danny 1911-............ **CLC 33**

Santmyer, Helen Hooven
    1895-1986 .... **CLC 33**
  See also CANR 15; CA 1-4R;
    obituary CA 118; DLB-Y 84

Santos, Bienvenido N(uqui) 1911-... **CLC 22**
  See also CANR 19; CA 101

Sappho c. 6th-century B.C. .... **CMLC 3**

Sarduy, Severo 1937-............. **CLC 6**
  See also CA 89-92

Sargeson, Frank 1903-1982........ **CLC 31**
  See also CA 106

Sarmiento, Felix Ruben Garcia 1867-1916
  See also CA 104

Saroyan, William
    1908-1981 .... **CLC 1, 8, 10, 29, 34**
  See also CA 5-8R; obituary CA 103;
    SATA 23; obituary SATA 24; DLB 7, 9;
    DLB-Y 81

Shackleton, C. C. 1925-
See Aldiss, Brian W(ilson)

Shacochis, Bob 1951-............. **CLC 39**
See also CA 119

Shaffer, Anthony 1926-............ **CLC 19**
See also CA 116; DLB 13

Shaffer, Peter (Levin)
1926-.............. **CLC 5, 14, 18, 37**
See also CA 25-28R; DLB 13

Shalamov, Varlam (Tikhonovich)
1907?-1982.................. **CLC 18**
See also obituary CA 105

Shamlu, Ahmad 1925- .... **CLC 10**

Shammas, Anton 1951-........ **CLC 55**

Shange, Ntozake 1948-....... **CLC 8, 25, 38**
See also CA 85-88; DLB 38

Shapcott, Thomas W(illiam) 1935- .. **CLC 38**
See also CA 69-72

Shapiro, Karl (Jay) 1913- ..... **CLC 4, 8, 15**
See also CAAS 6; CANR 1; CA 1-4R;
DLB 48

Sharpe, Tom 1928-.............. **CLC 36**
See also CA 114; DLB 14

Shaw, (George) Bernard
1856-1950 .... **TCLC 3, 9, 21**
See also CA 104, 109; DLB 10, 57

Shaw, Henry Wheeler
1818-1885 .... **NCLC 15**
See also DLB 11

Shaw, Irwin 1913-1984....... **CLC 7, 23, 34**
See also CANR 21; CA 13-16R;
obituary CA 112; DLB 6; DLB-Y 84;
CDALB 1941-1968

Shaw, Robert 1927-1978 .... **CLC 5**
See also CANR 4; CA 1-4R;
obituary CA 81-84; DLB 13, 14

Shawn, Wallace 1943- .... **CLC 41**
See also CA 112

Sheed, Wilfrid (John Joseph)
1930-.................... **CLC 2, 4, 10**
See also CA 65-68; DLB 6

Sheffey, Asa 1913-1980
See Hayden, Robert (Earl)

Sheldon, Alice (Hastings) B(radley)
1915-1987
See Tiptree, James, Jr.
See also CA 108; obituary CA 122

Shelley, Mary Wollstonecraft Godwin
1797-1851 .... **NCLC 14**
See also SATA 29

Shelley, Percy Bysshe
1792-1822 .... **NCLC 18**

Shepard, Jim 19??-.............. **CLC 36**

Shepard, Lucius 19??-............ **CLC 34**

Shepard, Sam
1943- .... **CLC 4, 6, 17, 34, 41, 44**
See also CANR 22; CA 69-72; DLB 7

Shepherd, Michael 1927-
See Ludlum, Robert

Sherburne, Zoa (Morin) 1912-...... **CLC 30**
See also CANR 3; CA 1-4R; SATA 3

Sheridan, Frances 1724-1766........ **LC 7**
See also DLB 39

Sheridan, Richard Brinsley
1751-1816 .... **NCLC 5**

Sherman, Jonathan Marc
1970?- .... **CLC 55**

Sherman, Martin 19??-............ **CLC 19**
See also CA 116

Sherwin, Judith Johnson 1936-... **CLC 7, 15**
See also CA 25-28R

Sherwood, Robert E(mmet)
1896-1955 .... **TCLC 3**
See also CA 104; DLB 7, 26

Shiel, M(atthew) P(hipps)
1865-1947 .... **TCLC 8**
See also CA 106

Shiga, Naoya 1883-1971.......... **CLC 33**
See also CA 101; obituary CA 33-36R

Shimazaki, Haruki 1872-1943
See Shimazaki, Toson
See also CA 105

Shimazaki, Toson 1872-1943 ...... **TCLC 5**
See also Shimazaki, Haruki

Sholokhov, Mikhail (Aleksandrovich)
1905-1984 .... **CLC 7, 15**
See also CA 101; obituary CA 112;
SATA 36

Shreve, Susan Richards 1939-...... **CLC 23**
See also CAAS 5; CANR 5; CA 49-52;
SATA 41, 46

Shulman, Alix Kates 1932- ...... **CLC 2, 10**
See also CA 29-32R; SATA 7

Shuster, Joe 1914-
See Siegel, Jerome and Shuster, Joe

Shute (Norway), Nevil 1899-1960... **CLC 30**
See also Norway, Nevil Shute

Shuttle, Penelope (Diane) 1947- ..... **CLC 7**
See also CA 93-96; DLB 14, 40

Siegel, Jerome 1914- and **Shuster, Joe**
1914- .... **CLC 21**

Siegel, Jerome 1914-
See Siegel, Jerome and Shuster, Joe
See also CA 116

Sienkiewicz, Henryk (Adam Aleksander Pius)
1846-1916 .... **TCLC 3**
See also CA 104

Sigal, Clancy 1926-............... **CLC 7**
See also CA 1-4R

Siguenza y Gongora, Carlos de
1645-1700 .... **LC 8**

Sigurjonsson, Johann 1880-1919... **TCLC 27**

Silkin, Jon 1930- .... **CLC 2, 6, 43**
See also CAAS 5; CA 5-8R; DLB 27

Silko, Leslie Marmon 1948- .... **CLC 23**
See also CA 115, 122

Sillanpaa, Franz Eemil 1888-1964... **CLC 19**
See also obituary CA 93-96

Sillitoe, Alan 1928-..... **CLC 1, 3, 6, 10, 19**
See also CAAS 2; CANR 8; CA 9-12R;
DLB 14

Silone, Ignazio 1900-1978 .... **CLC 4**
See also CAP 2; CA 25-28;
obituary CA 81-84

Silver, Joan Micklin 1935- .... **CLC 20**
See also CA 114

Silverberg, Robert 1935-............ **CLC 7**
See also CAAS 3; CANR 1, 20; CA 1-4R;
SATA 13; DLB 8

Silverstein, Alvin 1933- and **Silverstein,
Virginia B(arbara Opshelor)**
1937-..................... **CLC 17**

Silverstein, Alvin 1933-
See Silverstein, Alvinand Silverstein,
Virginia B(arbara Opshelor)
See also CANR 2; CA 49-52; SATA 8

Silverstein, Virginia B(arbara Opshelor)
1937-
See Silverstein, Alvin and Silverstein,
Virginia B(arbara Opshelor)
See also CANR 2; CA 49-52; SATA 8

Simak, Clifford D(onald)
1904-1988 .... **CLC 1, 55**
See also CANR 1; CA 1-4R;
obituary CA 125; DLB 8

Simenon, Georges (Jacques Christian)
1903-........... **CLC 1, 2, 3, 8, 18, 47**
See also CA 85-88; DLB 72

Simenon, Paul 1956?-
See The Clash

Simic, Charles 1938-....... **CLC 6, 9, 22, 49**
See also CAAS 4; CANR 12; CA 29-32R

Simmons, Dan 1948-.............. **CLC 44**

Simmons, James (Stewart Alexander)
1933-.................... **CLC 43**
See also CA 105; DLB 40

Simms, William Gilmore
1806-1870 .... **NCLC 3**
See also DLB 3, 30

Simon, Carly 1945-.............. **CLC 26**
See also CA 105

Simon, Claude (Henri Eugene)
1913-................**CLC 4, 9, 15, 39**
See also CA 89-92

Simon, (Marvin) Neil
1927-.............. **CLC 6, 11, 31, 39**
See also CA 21-24R; DLB 7

Simon, Paul 1941- .... **CLC 17**
See also CA 116

Simonon, Paul 1956?-
See The Clash

Simpson, Louis (Aston Marantz)
1923-.................. **CLC 4, 7, 9, 32**
See also CAAS 4; CANR 1; CA 1-4R;
DLB 5

Simpson, Mona (Elizabeth) 1957-... **CLC 44**

Simpson, N(orman) F(rederick)
1919-.................... **CLC 29**
See also CA 11-14R; DLB 13

Sinclair, Andrew (Annandale)
1935-.................... **CLC 2, 14**
See also CAAS 5; CANR 14; CA 9-12R;
DLB 14

Sinclair, Mary Amelia St. Clair 1865?-1946
See Sinclair, May
See also CA 104

Sinclair, May 1865?-1946 ...... **TCLC 3, 11**
See also Sinclair, Mary Amelia St. Clair
See also DLB 36

Spinrad, Norman (Richard)   1940-...   **CLC 46**
See also CANR 20; CA 37-40R; DLB 8

Spitteler, Carl (Friedrich Georg)
1845-1924 .... **TCLC 12**
See also CA 109

Spivack, Kathleen (Romola Drucker)
1938- .... **CLC 6**
See also CA 49-52

Spoto, Donald   1941-............. **CLC 39**
See also CANR 11; CA 65-68

Springsteen, Bruce   1949-.......... **CLC 17**
See also CA 111

Spurling, Hilary   1940-............ **CLC 34**
See also CA 104

Squires, (James) Radcliffe   1917-.... **CLC 51**
See also CANR 6, 21; CA 1-4R

Stael-Holstein, Anne Louise Germaine Necker,
Baronne de   1766-1817....... **NCLC 3**

Stafford, Jean   1915-1979...... **CLC 4, 7, 19**
See also CANR 3; CA 1-4R;
obituary CA 85-88; obituary SATA 22;
DLB 2

Stafford, William (Edgar)
1914- .... **CLC 4, 7, 29**
See also CAAS 3; CANR 5, 22; CA 5-8R;
DLB 5

Stannard, Martin   1947-.......... **CLC 44**

Stanton, Maura   1946- .... **CLC 9**
See also CANR 15; CA 89-92

Stapledon, (William) Olaf
1886-1950 .... **TCLC 22**
See also CA 111; DLB 15

Stark, Richard   1933-
See Westlake, Donald E(dwin)

Stead, Christina (Ellen)
1902-1983 .... **CLC 2, 5, 8, 32**
See also CA 13-16R; obituary CA 109

Steele, Timothy (Reid)   1948-....... **CLC 45**
See also CANR 16; CA 93-96

Steffens, (Joseph) Lincoln
1866-1936 .... **TCLC 20**
See also CA 117; SAAS 1

Stegner, Wallace (Earle)   1909-... **CLC 9, 49**
See also CANR 1, 21; CA 1-4R; DLB 9

Stein, Gertrude   1874-1946... **TCLC 1, 6, 28**
See also CA 104; DLB 4, 54

Steinbeck, John (Ernst)
1902-1968 ... **CLC 1, 5, 9, 13, 21, 34, 45**
See also CANR 1; CA 1-4R;
obituary CA 25-28R; SATA 9; DLB 7, 9;
DLB-DS 2

Steiner, George   1929-............. **CLC 24**
See also CA 73-76

Steiner, Rudolf(us Josephus Laurentius)
1861-1925 .... **TCLC 13**
See also CA 107

Stendhal   1783-1842........... **NCLC 23**

Stephen, Leslie   1832-1904....... **TCLC 23**
See also CANR 9; CA 21-24R; DLB 57

Stephens, James   1882?-1950 .... **TCLC 4**
See also CA 104; DLB 19

Stephens, Reed
See Donaldson, Stephen R.

Steptoe, Lydia   1892-1982
See Barnes, Djuna

Sterling, George   1869-1926 .... **TCLC 20**
See also CA 117; DLB 54

Stern, Gerald   1925- .... **CLC 40**
See also CA 81-84

Stern, Richard G(ustave)   1928-... **CLC 4, 39**
See also CANR 1; CA 1-4R

Sternberg, Jonas   1894-1969
See Sternberg, Josef von

Sternberg, Josef von   1894-1969..... **CLC 20**
See also CA 81-84

Sterne, Laurence   1713-1768......... **LC 2**
See also DLB 39

Sternheim, (William Adolf) Carl
1878-1942 .... **TCLC 8**
See also CA 105

Stevens, Mark   19??-.............. **CLC 34**

Stevens, Wallace   1879-1955..... **TCLC 3, 12**
See also CA 104; DLB 54

Stevenson, Anne (Katharine)
1933- .... **CLC 7, 33**
See also Elvin, Anne Katharine Stevenson
See also CANR 9; CA 17-18R; DLB 40

Stevenson, Robert Louis
1850-1894 .... **NCLC 5, 14**
See also CLR 10, 11; YABC 2; DLB 18, 57

Stewart, J(ohn) I(nnes) M(ackintosh)
1906- .... **CLC 7, 14, 32**
See also CAAS 3; CA 85-88

Stewart, Mary (Florence Elinor)
1916- .... **CLC 7, 35**
See also CANR 1; CA 1-4R; SATA 12

Stewart, Will   1908-
See Williamson, Jack

Still, James   1906-................. **CLC 49**
See also CANR 10; CA 65-68; SATA 29;
DLB 9

Sting   1951-
See The Police

Stitt, Milan   1941-................ **CLC 29**
See also CA 69-72

Stoker, Abraham
See Stoker, Bram
See also CA 105

Stoker, Bram   1847-1912 .... **TCLC 8**
See also Stoker, Abraham
See also SATA 29; DLB 36, 70

Stolz, Mary (Slattery)   1920-....... **CLC 12**
See also CANR 13; CA 5-8R; SAAS 3;
SATA 10

Stone, Irving   1903-................ **CLC 7**
See also CAAS 3; CANR 1; CA 1-4R;
SATA 3

Stone, Robert (Anthony)
1937?- .... **CLC 5, 23, 42**
See also CA 85-88

Stoppard, Tom
1937- ...... **CLC 1, 3, 4, 5, 8, 15, 29, 34**
See also CA 81-84; DLB 13; DLB-Y 85

Storey, David (Malcolm)
1933- .... **CLC 2, 4, 5, 8**
See also CA 81-84; DLB 13, 14

Storm, Hyemeyohsts   1935-......... **CLC 3**
See also CA 81-84

Storm, (Hans) Theodor (Woldsen)
1817-1888 .... **NCLC 1**

Storni, Alfonsina   1892-1938 .... **TCLC 5**
See also CA 104

Stout, Rex (Todhunter)   1886-1975 ... **CLC 3**
See also CA 61-64

Stow, (Julian) Randolph   1935-.. **CLC 23, 48**
See also CA 13-16R

Stowe, Harriet (Elizabeth) Beecher
1811-1896 .... **NCLC 3**
See also YABC 1; DLB 1, 12, 42;
CDALB 1865-1917

Strachey, (Giles) Lytton
1880-1932 .... **TCLC 12**
See also CA 110

Strand, Mark   1934-......... **CLC 6, 18, 41**
See also CA 21-24R; SATA 41; DLB 5

Straub, Peter (Francis)   1943- ...... **CLC 28**
See also CA 85-88; DLB-Y 84

Strauss, Botho   1944- .... **CLC 22**

Straussler, Tomas   1937-
See Stoppard, Tom

Streatfeild, (Mary) Noel   1897-..... **CLC 21**
See also CA 81-84; obituary CA 120;
SATA 20, 48

Stribling, T(homas) S(igismund)
1881-1965 .... **CLC 23**
See also obituary CA 107; DLB 9

Strindberg, (Johan) August
1849-1912 .... **TCLC 1, 8, 21**
See also CA 104

Strugatskii, Arkadii (Natanovich)   1925- and
Strugatskii, Boris(Natanovich)
1933- .... **CLC 27**

Strugatskii, Arkadii (Natanovich)   1925-
See Strugatskii, Arkadii (Natanovich) and
Strugatskii, Boris (Natanovich)
See also CA 106

Strugatskii, Boris (Natanovich)   1933-
See Strugatskii, Arkadii (Natanovich) and
Strugatskii, Boris (Natanovich)
See also CA 106

Strugatskii, Boris (Natanovich)   1933- and
Strugatskii, Arkadii (Natanovich)   1925-
See Strugatskii, Arkadii (Natanovich) and
Strugatskii, Boris (Natanovich)

Strummer, Joe   1953?-
See The Clash

Stuart, (Hilton) Jesse
1906-1984 .... **CLC 1, 8, 11, 14, 34**
See also CA 5-8R; obituary CA 112;
SATA 2; obituary SATA 36; DLB 9, 48;
DLB-Y 84

Sturgeon, Theodore (Hamilton)
1918-1985 .... **CLC 22, 39**
See also CA 81-84; obituary CA 116;
DLB 8; DLB-Y 85

Styron, William   1925-.. **CLC 1, 3, 5, 11, 15**
See also CANR 6; CA 5-8R; DLB 2;
DLB-Y 80

Sudermann, Hermann   1857-1928 .. **TCLC 15**
See also CA 107

Sue, Eugene   1804-1857 .... **NCLC 1**

Author Index

Walser, Robert 1878-1956 . . . . **TCLC 18**
See also CA 118

Walsh, Gillian Paton 1939-
See Walsh, Jill Paton
See also CA 37-40R; SATA 4

Walsh, Jill Paton 1939- . . . . **CLC 35**
See also CLR 2; SAAS 3

Wambaugh, Joseph (Aloysius, Jr.)
1937- . . . . **CLC 3, 18**
See also CA 33-36R; DLB 6; DLB-Y 83

Ward, Arthur Henry Sarsfield 1883-1959
See Rohmer, Sax
See also CA 108

Ward, Douglas Turner 1930- . . . . **CLC 19**
See also CA 81-84; DLB 7, 38

Warhol, Andy 1928-1987 . . . . **CLC 20**
See also CA 89-92; obituary CA 121

Warner, Francis (Robert le Plastrier)
1937- . . . . **CLC 14**
See also CANR 11; CA 53-56

Warner, Rex (Ernest) 1905-1986 . . . . **CLC 45**
See also CA 89-92; obituary CA 119;
DLB 15

Warner, Sylvia Townsend
1893-1978 . . . . **CLC 7, 19**
See also CANR 16; CA 61-64;
obituary CA 77-80; DLB 34

Warren, Mercy Otis 1728-1814 . . . **NCLC 13**
See also DLB 31

Warren, Robert Penn
1905- . . . . . **CLC 1, 4, 6, 8, 10, 13, 18, 39**
See also CANR 10; CA 13-16R; SATA 46;
DLB 2, 48; DLB-Y 80

Washington, Booker T(aliaferro)
1856-1915 . . . . **CLC 34**
See also CA 114; SATA 28

Wassermann, Jakob 1873-1934 . . . . . **TCLC 6**
See also CA 104

Wasserstein, Wendy 1950- . . . . **CLC 32**
See also CA 121

Waterhouse, Keith (Spencer)
1929- . . . . **CLC 47**
See also CA 5-8R; DLB 13, 15

Waters, Roger 1944-
See Pink Floyd

Wa Thiong'o, Ngugi
1938- . . . . **CLC 3, 7, 13, 36**
See also Ngugi, James (Thiong'o)
See also Ngugi wa Thiong'o

Watkins, Paul 1964?- . . . . **CLC   55**

Watkins, Vernon (Phillips)
1906-1967 . . . . **CLC 43**
See also CAP 1; CA 9-10;
obituary CA 25-28R; DLB 20

Waugh, Auberon (Alexander) 1939- . . **CLC 7**
See also CANR 6, 22; CA 45-48; DLB 14

Waugh, Evelyn (Arthur St. John)
1903-1966 . . . **CLC 1, 3, 8, 13, 19, 27, 44**
See also CANR 22; CA 85-88;
obituary CA 25-28R; DLB 15

Waugh, Harriet 1944- . . . . **CLC 6**
See also CANR 22; CA 85-88

Webb, Beatrice (Potter) 1858-1943 and
Webb, Sidney (James)
1859-1947 . . . . **TCLC 22**

Webb, Beatrice (Potter) 1858-1943
See Webb, Beatrice (Potter) and Webb,
Sidney (James)
See also CA 117

Webb, Charles (Richard) 1939- . . . . . . **CLC 7**
See also CA 25-28R

Webb, James H(enry), Jr. 1946- . . . . **CLC 22**
See also CA 81-84

Webb, Mary (Gladys Meredith)
1881-1927 . . . . **TCLC 24**
See also DLB 34

Webb, Phyllis 1927- . . . . **CLC 18**
See also CA 104; DLB 53

Webb, Sidney (James) 1859-1947
See Webb, Beatrice (Potter) and Webb,
Sidney (James)
See also CA 117

Webb, Sidney (James) 1859-1947 and **Webb,**
Beatrice (Potter) 1858-1943
See Webb, Beatrice (Potter) and Webb,
Sidney (James)

Webber, Andrew Lloyd 1948-
See Rice, Tim and Webber, Andrew Lloyd

Weber, Lenora Mattingly
1895-1971 . . . . **CLC 12**
See also CAP 1; CA 19-20;
obituary CA 29-32R; SATA 2;
obituary SATA 26

Wedekind, (Benjamin) Frank(lin)
1864-1918 . . . . **TCLC 7**
See also CA 104

Weidman, Jerome 1913- . . . . **CLC 7**
See also CANR 1; CA 1-4R; DLB 28

Weil, Simone 1909-1943 . . . . **TCLC 23**
See also CA 117

Weinstein, Nathan Wallenstein 1903?-1940
See West, Nathanael
See also CA 104

Weir, Peter 1944- . . . . **CLC 20**
See also CA 113

Weiss, Peter (Ulrich)
1916-1982 . . . . **CLC 3, 15, 51**
See also CANR 3; CA 45-48;
obituary CA 106; DLB 69

Weiss, Theodore (Russell)
1916- . . . . **CLC 3, 8, 14**
See also CAAS 2; CA 9-12R; DLB 5

Welch, (Maurice) Denton
1915-1948 . . . . **TCLC 22**
See also CA 121

Welch, James 1940- . . . . **CLC 6, 14**
See also CA 85-88

Weldon, Fay 1933- . . . . **CLC 6, 9, 11, 19, 36**
See also CANR 16; CA 21-24R; DLB 14

Wellek, Rene 1903- . . . . **CLC 28**
See also CAAS 7; CANR 8; CA 5-8R;
DLB 63

Weller, Michael 1942- . . . . **CLC 10**
See also CA 85-88

Weller, Paul 1958- . . . . **CLC 26**

Wellershoff, Dieter 1925- . . . . **CLC 46**
See also CANR 16; CA 89-92

Welles, (George) Orson
1915-1985 . . . . **CLC 20**
See also CA 93-96; obituary CA 117

Wellman, Manly Wade 1903-1986 . . **CLC 49**
See also CANR 6, 16; CA 1-4R;
obituary CA 118; SATA 6, 47

Wells, H(erbert) G(eorge)
1866-1946 . . . . **TCLC 6, 12, 19**
See also CA 110; SATA 20; DLB 34, 70

Wells, Rosemary 1943- . . . . **CLC 12**
See also CLR 16; CA 85-88; SAAS 1;
SATA 18

Welty, Eudora (Alice)
1909- . . . . **CLC 1, 2, 5, 14, 22, 33; SSC 1**
See also CA 9-12R; CABS 1; DLB 2;
CDALB 1941-1968

Wen I-to 1899-1946 . . . . **TCLC 28**

Werfel, Franz (V.) 1890-1945 . . . . . . **TCLC 8**
See also CA 104

Wergeland, Henrik Arnold
1808-1845 . . . . **NCLC 5**

Wersba, Barbara 1932- . . . . **CLC 30**
See also CLR 3; CANR 16; CA 29-32R;
SAAS 2; SATA 1; DLB 52

Wertmuller, Lina 1928- . . . . **CLC 16**
See also CA 97-100

Wescott, Glenway 1901-1987 . . . . **CLC 13**
See also CA 13-16R; obituary CA 121;
DLB 4, 9

Wesker, Arnold 1932- . . . . **CLC 3, 5, 42**
See also CAAS 7; CANR 1; CA 1-4R;
DLB 13

Wesley, Richard (Errol) 1945- . . . . **CLC 7**
See also CA 57-60; DLB 38

Wessel, Johan Herman 1742-1785 . . . . **LC 7**

West, Anthony (Panther)
1914-1987 . . . . **CLC 50**
See also CANR 3, 19; CA 45-48; DLB 15

West, Jessamyn 1907-1984 . . . . . . **CLC 7, 17**
See also CA 9-12R; obituary CA 112;
obituary SATA 37; DLB 6; DLB-Y 84

West, Morris L(anglo) 1916- . . . . . **CLC 6, 33**
See also CA 5-8R

West, Nathanael 1903?-1940 . . . . **TCLC 1, 14**
See also Weinstein, Nathan Wallenstein
See also DLB 4, 9, 28

West, Paul 1930- . . . . **CLC 7, 14**
See also CAAS 7; CANR 22; CA 13-16R;
DLB 14

West, Rebecca 1892-1983 . . **CLC 7, 9, 31, 50**
See also CA 5-8R; obituary CA 109;
DLB 36; DLB-Y 83

Westall, Robert (Atkinson) 1929- . . . **CLC 17**
See also CANR 18; CA 69-72; SAAS 2;
SATA 23

Westlake, Donald E(dwin)
1933- . . . . **CLC 7, 33**
See also CANR 16; CA 17-20R

Westmacott, Mary 1890-1976
See Christie, (Dame) Agatha (Mary
Clarissa)

Whalen, Philip 1923- . . . . **CLC 6, 29**
See also CANR 5; CA 9-12R; DLB 16

Wharton, Edith (Newbold Jones)
1862-1937 . . . . **TCLC 3, 9, 27**
See also CA 104; DLB 4, 9, 12;
CDALB 1865-1917

Wharton, William 1925-........ **CLC 18, 37**
See also CA 93-96; DLB-Y 80

Wheatley (Peters), Phillis
1753?-1784.................... **LC 3**
See also DLB 31, 50; CDALB 1640-1865

Wheelock, John Hall 1886-1978 .... **CLC 14**
See also CANR 14; CA 13-16R;
obituary CA 77-80; DLB 45

Whelan, John 1900-
See O'Faolain, Sean

Whitaker, Rodney 1925-
See Trevanian

White, E(lwyn) B(rooks)
1899-1985 .... **CLC 10, 34, 39**
See also CLR 1; CANR 16; CA 13-16R;
obituary CA 116; SATA 2, 29;
obituary SATA 44; DLB 11, 22

White, Edmund III 1940-......... **CLC 27**
See also CANR 3, 19; CA 45-48

White, Patrick (Victor Martindale)
1912- .... **CLC 3, 4, 5, 7, 9, 18**
See also CA 81-84

White, Terence de Vere 1912-...... **CLC 49**
See also CANR 3; CA 49-52

White, T(erence) H(anbury)
1906-1964 .... **CLC 30**
See also CA 73-76; SATA 12

White, Walter (Francis)
1893-1955 .... **TCLC 15**
See also CA 115; DLB 51

White, William Hale 1831-1913
See Rutherford, Mark

Whitehead, E(dward) A(nthony)
1933- .... **CLC 5**
See also CA 65-68

Whitemore, Hugh 1936-.......... **CLC 37**

Whitman, Sarah Helen
1803-1878 .... **NCLC 19**
See also DLB 1

Whitman, Walt 1819-1892 .... **NCLC 4**
See also SATA 20; DLB 3, 64;
CDALB 1640-1865

Whitney, Phyllis A(yame) 1903-.... **CLC 42**
See also CANR 3; CA 1-4R; SATA 1, 30

Whittemore, (Edward) Reed (Jr.)
1919- .... **CLC 4**
See also CANR 4; CA 9-12R; DLB 5

Whittier, John Greenleaf
1807-1892 .... **NCLC 8**
See also DLB 1; CDALB 1640-1865

Wicker, Thomas Grey 1926-
See Wicker, Tom
See also CANR 21; CA 65-68

Wicker, Tom 1926-............... **CLC 7**
See also Wicker, Thomas Grey

Wideman, John Edgar
1941-.............. **CLC 5, 34, 36**
See also CANR 14; CA 85-88; DLB 33

Wiebe, Rudy (H.) 1934-...... **CLC 6, 11, 14**
See also CA 37-40R; DLB 60

Wieland, Christoph Martin
1733-1813 .... **NCLC 17**

Wieners, John 1934-.............. **CLC 7**
See also CA 13-16R; DLB 16

Wiesel, Elie(zer) 1928-..... **CLC 3, 5, 11, 37**
See also CAAS 4; CANR 8; CA 5-8R;
DLB-Y 1986

Wight, James Alfred 1916-
See Herriot, James
See also CA 77-80; SATA 44

Wilbur, Richard (Purdy)
1921-.................. **CLC 3, 6, 9, 14**
See also CANR 2; CA 1-4R; CABS 2;
SATA 9; DLB 5

Wild, Peter 1940-................. **CLC 14**
See also CA 37-40R; DLB 5

Wilde, Oscar (Fingal O'Flahertie Wills)
1854-1900 .... **TCLC 1, 8, 23**
See also CA 104; SATA 24; DLB 10, 19,
34, 57

Wilder, Billy 1906-............... **CLC 20**
See also Wilder, Samuel
See also DLB 26

Wilder, Samuel 1906-
See Wilder, Billy
See also CA 89-92

Wilder, Thornton (Niven)
1897-1975 ...... **CLC 1, 5, 6, 10, 15, 35**
See also CA 13-16R; obituary CA 61-64;
DLB 4, 7, 9

Wiley, Richard 1944-............. **CLC 44**
See also CA 121

Wilhelm, Kate 1928-.............. **CLC 7**
See also CAAS 5; CANR 17; CA 37-40R;
DLB 8

Willard, Nancy 1936-........... **CLC 7, 37**
See also CLR 5; CANR 10; CA 89-92;
SATA 30, 37; DLB 5, 52

Williams, Charles (Walter Stansby)
1886-1945 .... **TCLC 1, 11**
See also CA 104

Williams, C(harles) K(enneth)
1936- .... **CLC 33**
See also CA 37-40R; DLB 5

Williams, Ella Gwendolen Rees 1890-1979
See Rhys, Jean

Williams, (George) Emlyn 1905-.... **CLC 15**
See also CA 104; DLB 10

Williams, Hugo 1942-............. **CLC 42**
See also CA 17-20R; DLB 40

Williams, John A(lfred) 1925-.... **CLC 5, 13**
See also CAAS 3; CANR 6; CA 53-56;
DLB 2, 33

Williams, Jonathan (Chamberlain)
1929- .... **CLC 13**
See also CANR 8; CA 9-12R; DLB 5

Williams, Joy 1944-.............. **CLC 31**
See also CANR 22; CA 41-44R

Williams, Norman 1952- .... **CLC 39**
See also CA 118

Williams, Paulette 1948-
See Shange, Ntozake

Williams, Tennessee
1911-1983 .... **CLC 1, 2, 5, 7, 8, 11, 15,
19, 30, 39, 45**
See also CA 5-8R; obituary CA 108; DLB 7;
DLB-Y 83; DLB-DS 4;
CDALB 1941-1968

Williams, Thomas (Alonzo) 1926-... **CLC 14**
See also CANR 2; CA 1-4R

Williams, Thomas Lanier 1911-1983
See Williams, Tennessee

Williams, William Carlos
1883-1963 .... **CLC 1, 2, 5, 9, 13, 22, 42**
See also CA 89-92; DLB 4, 16, 54

Williamson, Jack 1908-........... **CLC 29**
See also Williamson, John Stewart
See also DLB 8

Williamson, John Stewart 1908-
See Williamson, Jack
See also CA 17-20R

Willingham, Calder (Baynard, Jr.)
1922- .... **CLC 5, 51**
See also CANR 3; CA 5-8R; DLB 2, 44

Wilson, A(ndrew) N(orman) 1950- .. **CLC 33**
See also CA 112; DLB 14

Wilson, Andrew 1948-
See Wilson, Snoo

Wilson, Angus (Frank Johnstone)
1913- .... **CLC 2, 3, 5, 25, 34**
See also CA 5-8R; DLB 15

Wilson, August 1945-.......... **CLC 39, 50**
See also CA 115, 122

Wilson, Brian 1942-.............. **CLC 12**

Wilson, Colin 1931-............. **CLC 3, 14**
See also CAAS 5; CANR 1; CA 1-4R;
DLB 14

Wilson, Edmund
1895-1972 .... **CLC 1, 2, 3, 8, 24**
See also CANR 1; CA 1-4R;
obituary CA 37-40R; DLB 63

Wilson, Ethel Davis (Bryant)
1888-1980 .... **CLC 13**
See also CA 102

Wilson, John 1785-1854......... **NCLC 5**

Wilson, John (Anthony) Burgess 1917-
See Burgess, Anthony
See also CANR 2; CA 1-4R

Wilson, Lanford 1937-....... **CLC 7, 14, 36**
See also CA 17-20R; DLB 7

Wilson, Robert (M.) 1944-........ **CLC 7, 9**
See also CANR 2; CA 49-52

Wilson, Sloan 1920-............. **CLC 32**
See also CANR 1; CA 1-4R

Wilson, Snoo 1948-............. **CLC 33**
See also CA 69-72

Wilson, William S(mith) 1932- ..... **CLC 49**
See also CA 81-84

**Winchilsea, Anne (Kingsmill) Finch, Countess
of** 1661-1720.................. **LC 3**

Winters, Janet Lewis 1899-
See Lewis (Winters), Janet
See also CAP 1; CA 9-10

Winters, (Arthur) Yvor
1900-1968 .... **CLC 4, 8, 32**
See also CAP 1; CA 11-12;
obituary CA 25-28R; DLB 48

Wiseman, Frederick 1930-......... **CLC 20**

Wister, Owen 1860-1938 .... **TCLC 21**
See also CA 108; DLB 9

NCLC Cumulative Nationality Index

NCLC Cumulative Title Index

Title Index

Title Index

Title Index

Title Index

Title Index

Title Index

Title Index

Title Index

See *Les frères Zemganno*

Zemsta (*Vengeance*) (Fredro)   **8**:285-87, 289-90, 292-93

The Zenana, and Minor Poems of L. E. L. (Landon)   **15**:161

Der Zerbrochene Krug (*The Broken Jug*) (Kleist)   **2**:439-41, 443-45, 454, 457, 461, 463

Zerstreute Blätter (Herder)   **8**:313

"Die Zigeunerin" (Ludwig)   **4**:353

Zigzags
    See *Caprices et zigzags*

The Zincali; or, An Account of the Gypsies of Spain (Borrow)   **9**:36-40, 42, 66

Zinzendorff, and Other Poems (Sigourney)   **21**:292, 307

Zizine (Kock)   **16**:248

Złota czaszka (*The Golden Skull*) (Słowacki)   **15**:352, 354, 371

La Zobeide (Gozzi)   **23**:108, 119, 123, 126

"Zona modna" ("The Fashionable Wife") (Krasicki)   **8**:403, 407

Zrzędnosc i przecora (*Grumbling and Contradiction*) (Fredro)   **8**:284-85

"Zu der Edlen Jagd" (Gordon)   **21**:159

"The Zucca" (Shelley)   **18**:370

"Zum neven Jahr" (Mörike)   **10**:455

Zur Chronik von Grieshuus (Storm)   **1**:540-41, 546

"Zur Geschichte der Religion und Philosophie in Deutschland" ("Religion and Philosophy in Germany") (Heine)   **4**:255, 263, 264, 266

Zur kritik der politischen Ökonomie (*A Contribution to the Critique of Political Economy*) (Marx)   **17**:289, 302, 304, 318, 321-22, 335

Die Zürcher Novellen (Keller)   **2**:412, 414, 416, 422

"Zürchersee" (Klopstock)   **11**:234, 237-38

"Zwei Johannes würmchen" (Klopstock)   **11**:238

"Zwei Polen" (Lenau)   **16**:286

"Die Zweifler" (Lenau)   **16**:272, 275, 287

Der Zweikampf (Kleist)   **2**:456, 458

Die Zwillinge (Klinger)   **1**:429

Zwischen Himmel und Erde (*Between Heaven and Earth*) (Ludwig)   **4**:346-50, 354-55, 357-58, 360-61, 363-64, 367-68

Zwölf moralische Briefe (Wieland)   **17**:417-18

Zwolon (Norwid)   **17**:367, 371, 379